W9-BMQ-101

Fodor's

AUSTRALIA

20th edition

Fodor's Travel Publications   New York, Toronto, London, Sydney, Auckland

www.fodors.com

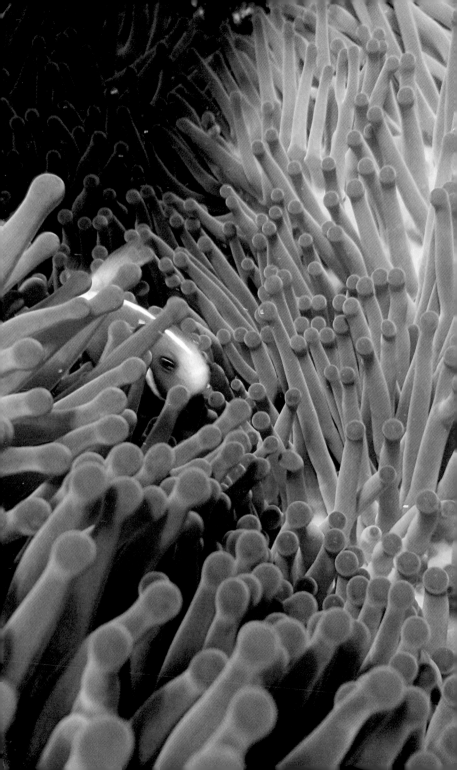

Be a Fodor's Correspondent

Our latest guidebook to Australia—now in full color—owes its success to travelers like you. Throughout, you'll find photographs submitted by members of Fodors.com to our "Show Us Your... Australia" photo contest. Facing this page is a photograph of the underwater world of the Great Barrier Reef diving spot Pixie Gardens as captured by Ronnie Koppel, a runner-up winner. David Menkes, whose grand prize winning photo appears on page 441, described his GBR liveaboard adventure as the best diving experience of his life. We gratefully acknowledge the participation of Tourism Australia and Swain Tours, whose sponsorship of the contest made the inclusion of these photos possible.

We are especially proud of this color edition. No other guide to Australia is as up to date or has as much practical planning information, along with hundreds of color photographs and illustrated maps. We've also included "Word of Mouth" quotes from travelers who shared their experiences with others on our forums. If you're inspired and can plan a better trip because of this guide, we've done our job.

We invite you to join the travel conversation: Your opinion matters to us and to your fellow travelers. Come to Fodors.com to plan your trip, share an experience, ask a question, submit a photograph, post a review, or write a trip report. Tell our editors about your trip. They want to know what went well and how we can make this guide even better. Share your opinions at our feedback center at fodors.com/feedback, or email us at editors@fodors.com with the subject line "Australia Editor." You might find your comments published in a future Fodor's guide. We look forward to hearing from you.

Happy Traveling!

Tim Jarrell, Publisher

FODOR'S AUSTRALIA

Editors: Margaret Kelly, Kelly Kealy

Editorial Contributors: Astrid deRidder, Katie Hamlin, Nicholas McGowan, Josh McIlvain, Eric Wechter.
Writers: Melanie Ball, Caroline Gladstone, Sarah Gold, Graham Hodgson, Helena Iveson, Merran White.

Production Editor: Astrid deRidder
Maps & Illustrations: David Lindroth and Mark Stroud, *cartographers;* Bob Blake, Rebecca Baer, *map editors;* William Wu, *information graphics*
Design: Fabrizio La Rocca, *creative director;* Guido Caroti, Siobhan O'Hare, *art directors;* Tina Malaney, Chie Ushio, Ann McBride, Jessica Walsh, *designers;* Melanie Marin, *senior picture editor*
Cover Photo: (Pinnacles desert, Nambung National Park): Frank Krahmer/Masterfile
Production Manager: Amanda Bullock

COPYRIGHT

Copyright © 2010 by Fodor's Travel, a division of Random House, Inc.

Fodor's is a registered trademark of Random House, Inc.

All rights reserved. Published in the United States by Fodor's Travel, a division of Random House, Inc., and simultaneously in Canada by Random House of Canada, Limited, Toronto. Distributed by Random House, Inc., New York.

No maps, illustrations, or other portions of this book may be reproduced in any form without written permission from the publisher.

20th edition

ISBN 978–1–4000–0857–5

ISSN 1095–2675

SPECIAL SALES

This book is available at special discounts for bulk purchases for sales promotions or premiums. Special editions, including personalized covers, excerpts of existing books, and corporate imprints, can be created in large quantities for special needs. For more information, write to Special Markets/Premium Sales, 1745 Broadway, MD 6-2, New York, New York 10019, or e-mail specialmarkets@randomhouse.com.

AN IMPORTANT TIP & AN INVITATION

Although all prices, opening times, and other details in this book are based on information supplied to us at press time, changes occur all the time in the travel world, and Fodor's cannot accept responsibility for facts that become outdated or for inadvertent errors or omissions. So **always confirm information when it matters,** especially if you're making a detour to visit a specific place. Your experiences—positive and negative—matter to us. If we have missed or misstated something, **please write to us.** We follow up on all suggestions. Contact the Australia editor at editors@fodors.com or c/o Fodor's at 1745 Broadway, New York, NY 10019.

PRINTED IN SINGAPORE

10 9 8 7 6 5 4 3 2 1

CONTENTS

Fodor's Features

ABOUT THIS BOOK

Our Ratings

Sometimes you find terrific travel experiences and sometimes they just find you. But usually the burden is on you to select the right combination of experiences. That's where our ratings come in.

As travelers we've all discovered a place so wonderful that its worthiness is obvious. And sometimes that place is so experiential that superlatives don't do it justice: you just have to be there to know. These sights, properties, and experiences get our highest rating, **Fodor's Choice,** indicated by orange stars throughout this book.

Black stars highlight sights and properties we deem **Highly Recommended,** places that our writers, editors, and readers praise again and again for consistency and excellence.

By default, there's another category: any place we include in this book is by definition worth your time, unless we say otherwise. And we will.

Disagree with any of our choices? Care to nominate a place or suggest that we rate one more highly? Visit our feedback center at www.fodors.com/feedback.

Budget Well

Hotel and restaurant price categories from ¢ to $$$$ are defined in the opening pages of each chapter. For attractions, we always give standard adult admission fees; reductions are usually available for children, students, and senior citizens. Want to pay with plastic? **AE, D, DC, MC, V** following restaurant and hotel listings indicate if American Express, Discover, Diners Club, MasterCard, and Visa are accepted.

Restaurants

Unless we state otherwise, restaurants are open for lunch and dinner daily. We mention dress only when there's a specific requirement and reservations only when they're essential or not accepted—it's always best to book ahead.

Hotels

Hotels have private bath, phone, TV, and air-conditioning and operate on the European Plan (aka EP, meaning without meals), unless we specify that they use the Continental Plan (CP, with a Continental breakfast), Breakfast Plan (BP, with a full breakfast), or Modified American Plan (MAP, with breakfast and dinner), or are all-inclusive (AI, including all meals and most activities).

We always list facilities, but not whether you'll be charged an extra fee to use them, so when pricing accommodations, find out what's included.

Listings
- ★ Fodor's Choice
- ★ Highly recommended
- ⊠ Physical address
- ✛ Directions or Map coordinates
- ⌂ Mailing address
- ☎ Telephone
- 🖷 Fax
- ⊕ On the Web
- ✉ E-mail
- ✒ Admission fee
- ⊙ Open/closed times
- Ⓜ Metro stations
- ⊟ Credit cards

Hotels & Restaurants
- ⊞ Hotel
- ⬏ Number of rooms
- ⟁ Facilities
- ⅏ Meal plans
- ✕ Restaurant
- ⌦ Reservations
- ⋔ Dress code
- ⬎ Smoking
- ⅋ BYOB

Outdoors
- 🏌 Golf
- ⚠ Camping

Other
- ☾ Family-friendly
- ⇨ See also
- ⊠ Branch address
- ☞ Take note

Experience
Australia

WHAT'S WHERE

Numbers refer to chapters.

2 Sydney. One of the most naturally beautiful cities in the world, Sydney blends beachside cool with corporate capitalism and Victorian-era colonial architecture. Arts, tourism, and business interests thrive around spectacular Sydney Harbour.

3 New South Wales including Canberra and A.C.T. Southeastern Australia displays most of the continent's rural and coastal variations: historic towns, mountains, dramatic beaches, and world-class vineyards. The nation's spacious and immaculately landscaped capital showcases myriad Australian national monuments.

4 Melbourne and Victoria. Melbourne is Australia's most European city and a cultural melting pot. Rugged coastline, fairy penguins, wineries, historic towns, and national parks are reason enough to explore the Victorian countryside.

5 Tasmania. From Freycinet Peninsula to wild South West National Park, Tasmania's intoxicating natural beauty testifies to Australia's topographic diversity. Don't miss the numerous relics of the island's volatile days as a penal colony.

6 Brisbane and It's Beaches. Name your pleasure (or poison) and you'll find it in Queensland: mini-Miamis, nearly deserted beaches, and lush rain forests, great restaurants, and easy access to family-friendly adventure parks.

7 The Great Barrier Reef. Queensland's crown jewel is the 2,600-km-long (1,616-mi-long) Great Barrier Reef. More than 3,000 individual reefs and 900 islands make up this vast aquatic universe. There are countless ways to experience this quickly disappearing natural wonder.

8 Adelaide and South Australia. Well-planned and picturesque Adelaide has many charms, including its famous biennial festival of the arts. Be sure to take a tour of the renowned wine country, and then unwind on a Murray River cruise.

9 Outback Adventures. Outback Australia stuns with its diversity. In the country's vast, central desert region are Uluru and Kata Tjuta, monoliths of deep significance to the local Aboriginal people. Closer to Asia than to any other Australian city, Darwin is the gateway to World-Heritage wetlands, monster cattle ranches, and rock art.

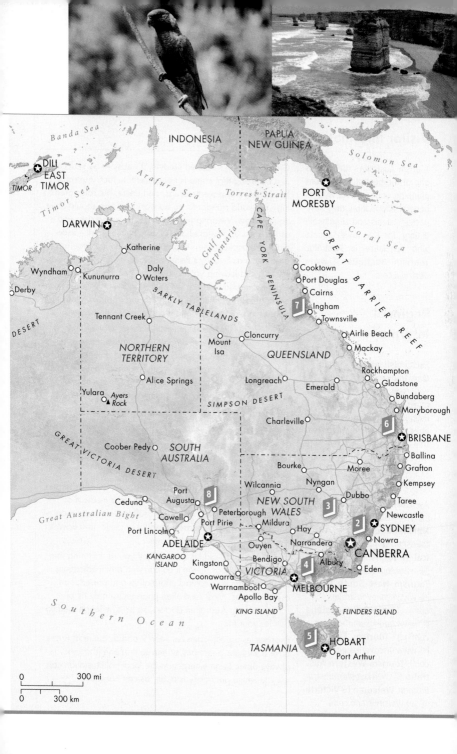

Banda Sea

INDONESIA

PAPUA NEW GUINEA

Solomon Sea

DILI EAST TIMOR
TIMOR

Arafura Sea

Torres Strait

PORT MORESBY

Timor Sea

DARWIN

Great Barrier Reef

Coral Sea

Katherine

Gulf of Carpentaria

Wyndham
Kununurra

Daly Waters

Derby

BARKLY TABLELANDS

CAPE YORK PENINSULA

Cooktown
Port Douglas
Cairns
7 Ingham
Townsville

DESERT

Tennant Creek

NORTHERN TERRITORY

Mount Isa

Cloncurry

QUEENSLAND

Airlie Beach
Mackay

Rockhampton

Alice Springs

Longreach

Emerald

Gladstone

Yulara Ayers Rock

SIMPSON DESERT

Bundaberg

Maryborough

Charleville

6 BRISBANE

GREAT VICTORIA DESERT

Coober Pedy

SOUTH AUSTRALIA

Bourke

Moree

Ballina

Grafton

Kempsey

Wilcannia

Nyngan

Dubbo

Taree

Ceduna

Port Augusta

8

Peterborough

NEW SOUTH WALES

3

Newcastle

2 SYDNEY

Cowell

Port Pirie

Mildura

Hay

Narrandera

Nowra

CANBERRA

Port Lincoln

ADELAIDE

Ouyen

Bendigo

Albury

Eden

KANGAROO ISLAND

Kingston

VICTORIA

4

Coonawarra

Warrnambool

Apollo Bay

MELBOURNE

Great Australian Bight

Southern Ocean

KING ISLAND

FLINDERS ISLAND

5 HOBART

TASMANIA

Port Arthur

0 300 mi

0 300 km

EXPERIENCE AUSTRALIA PLANNER

Visitor Information

Tourism Australia's Web site is one of the best places to start planning your trip. As well as general information, they have package deals and searchable listings for U.S. travel agents who specialize in Australia. **Tourism Australia** ⊕ *www.australia.com.*

Regional Information

Each Australian state has its own tourism Web site where you can find state-specific maps, thematically organized listings, travel information, and links to accommodation and transport. Some have free state travel guides that they'll send to you. In general, they handle queries online.

Australian Capital Tourism (⊕ *www.visitcanberra.com.au).* **Northern Territory** (⊕ *www.tourismnt.com.au).* **South Australian Tourism Commission** (⊕ *www.southaustralia.com).* **Tourism New South Wales** (⊕ *www.sydneyaustralia.com).* **Tourism Queensland** (⊕ *www.queenslandholidays.com.au).* **Tourism Tasmania** (⊕ *www.discovertasmania.com).* **Tourism Western Australia** (⊕ *www.westernaustralia.com).* **Welcome to Victoria** (⊕ *www.visitvictoria.com).*

Safety

Given Australia's relaxed lifestyle, it's easy to be seduced into believing that crime is nonexistent. In fact, Australia has its share of poverty, drugs, and crime, but rates aren't high by world standards, so be wary and you should have no problems. Wearing jewelry in public isn't a risk, and using ATMs in daylight hours is usually fine. Theft—especially pickpocketing—is a problem only in major tourist areas such as Sydney's Bondi or Queensland's Gold Coast. Try to avoid leaving valuables on the beach when you go for a swim or in your car when you park. Australia has had enough cases of children going missing in public places for parents to want to be vigilant on beaches and in malls.

Traveling in Australia is generally safe for women, provided you take a few commonsense precautions. Avoid isolated areas such as empty beaches and quiet streets at night. Single women usually receive attention entering pubs or clubs alone, but a few firm, polite words are normally enough to put a stop to it, if it's unwanted.

Emergencies

Australian emergency services are extremely efficient. Local people usually help each other unquestioningly, too. For theft, wallet loss, small road accidents, and minor emergencies, contact the nearest police station. In a medical or dental emergency, ask your hotel staff for information on and directions to the nearest hospital or clinic; taxi drivers should also know how to find one.

Pack a basic first-aid kit, especially if you're venturing into more remote areas. If you'll be carrying any medication, bring your doctor's contact information and prescription authorizations. Most Australian pharmacies only fill prescriptions from Australian doctors, so bring enough medication for your trip.

Pharmacies usually open between 9 and 5, but most towns have a 24-hour pharmacy system so that one pharmacy is always open. In an emergency, the local police station can tell you which pharmacy is open, as can hospitals.

Eating Out

These days, fusion food is what's putting Australia on the foodie map—indeed, many claim that the very term was invented Down Under. The huge Asian communities in cities like Sydney and Melbourne have brought their traditional condiments and cooking styles to bear on local staples: the resulting combinations are what many of the country's most famous eateries specialize in.

Bush tucker, or indigenous Australian food, was once something you only came across on bushwalking expeditions in the Outback. Suddenly it's become fashionable, and uniquely Australian ingredients like lemon myrtle, wattle seed, and rosella (not to mention kangaroo meat) are appearing on fancy restaurant menus all over the country. Food is an international language, but your English may fail you in Australian restaurants. "Entrée" means appetizer, and "main courses" are what American entrées go by. The term "silver service" indicates upscale dining. French fries are called "chips," chickens are "chooks," sausages are known as "snags," and if you want ketchup, ask for "tomato sauce."

Wines, Beer, and Spirits

Beer and wine are an important part of Australian life. Australia is the world's 10th-largest wine producer, and Australian wine is gaining considerable respect worldwide. Australia's most famous wine-producing areas are the Hunter Valley in New South Wales, the Barossa Valley in South Australia, and Western Australia's Margaret River region. Although there are no native grape varietals in Australia, Shiraz (also known as Syrah) is a local specialty. Cabernet Sauvignon and Pinot Noir are common reds; popular whites include Chardonnay, Sauvignon Blanc, and Pinot Grigio. Australia produces a wide range of beers. As well as big national brands like Fosters, each state has its own brew: Victoria Bitter in Victoria or XXXX (called fourex) in Queensland, for example.

If you're invited to an Australian's home, it's common—indeed, expected—practice to take a bottle of wine at dinnertime or a case of beer for a barbecue. When drinking at pubs, Australians always drink in rounds, British-style.

Accommodations

Australia's state capitals run the gamut of lodging options. But that doesn't mean ALL the interesting accommodation is in town. Family-run bed-and-breakfasts, farmstays, country hotels, and even small-town pubs are some of the alternatives Australia has to offer. Sleeping Down Under is generally cheaper than in North America, and moneysaving accommodation is particularly varied—be it a serviced apartment, a well-appointed caravan, or a bed at a backpackers' dorm.

⇨ *For more detailed information on accommodations, see the Travel Smart chapter at the end of the Guide.*

Tipping

Australians don't tip nearly as much as North Americans. Waitstaff are the exception: hotels and restaurants don't usually add service charges, so a 10%–15% tip for good service is normal. Room service and housemaids are only tipped for special services. Taxi drivers don't expect a tip, but leaving small change will win you a smile. Guides, tour-bus drivers, and chauffeurs don't expect tips either, though they're grateful if someone in the group takes up a collection for them. No tipping is necessary—indeed, it would cause confusion—in hair salons or for theater ushers.

AUSTRALIA
WORLD HERITAGE SITES

Sydney Opera House

(C) Australia's most recent World Heritage property is the country's most recognizable building. A realization of visionary design and 20th-century technological innovation, the Sydney Opera House was listed in 2007 as a masterpiece of human creative genius. It is also a structure of extraordinary beauty. Danish architect Jorn Utzon's interlocking vaulted "shells" appear to hover like wind-filled sails on their Sydney Harbour promontory. Flood lighting at night increases the sense of movement.

Awarded the project in 1957 by an international jury, Jorn Utzon never saw his creation finished. Utzon resigned and left Australia in 1966, amid funding controversies and political change, and his architectural sculpture was completed by others. Familiar to people around the world, the Sydney Opera House is a world-class performing arts venue.

Fraser Island

(B) Remnant rain forest, shifting sand dunes, and half of the world's perched lakes (lakes that are isolated above the ground-water table by rock or organic material) contributed to Fraser Island's World Heritage listing in 1992. The largest sand island on Earth, Fraser lies just off Queensland's coast, about 200 km (124 mi) north of Brisbane. This exquisite island is both ecologically precious and extremely popular for soft-adventure holidays—a sometimes problematic combination. Fraser's dingo population is one of Australia's purest, but be aware that visitors have had fatal interactions with these wild dogs. Humpback whales frequent Fraser's west-coast waters June to November, and the spring tailor fish run lures anglers to the island's wilder ocean shore. Four-wheel-drives barrel along the 76-mi ocean beach, which is Fraser Island's unofficial main highway.

Tasmanian Wilderness

(A) Harsh glacial action over millions of years has put the wild in the Tasmanian Wilderness. Remote and subject to extreme weather, this vast World Heritage area—it covers a fifth of Australia's island state—protects one of the few expanses of temperate rain forest on Earth. Here, too, are stunning landforms fashioned by complex geology, diverse habitats for flora and fauna found nowhere else, and evidence of tens of thousands of years of Aboriginal occupation. Angling, whitewater rafting, and national park walking trails, most of which are suited only to experienced hikers, are some favorite activities in the Tasmanian Wilderness World Heritage Area.

Greater Blue Mountains Area

(D) Sunlight refracting off a mist of eucalyptus oil gives the Blue Mountains, west of Sydney, their distinctive hue. The variety of eucalypts (commonly called gum trees) across this mountain range's varied habitats was integral to its World Heritage listing. The 1.03 million hectares of sandstone country encompasses the Blue Mountains National Park. Ninety-one varieties of eucalypts grow here. So, too, do significant numbers of rare species and "living fossils" such as the Wollemi pine, which was discovered in 1994.

Great Barrier Reef

(E) While its name suggests otherwise, Australia's most famous World Heritage site is not a single reef. The 2,600-km-long (1,616-mi-long) Great Barrier Reef is actually the world's largest collection of reefs. This fragile natural wonder contains 400 types of coral and 1,500 fish species of every size and almost every conceivable color combination. The giant clam, with its voluptuous purple, green, or blue mantle (algae dictate the color) is one of the 4,000 mollusks the reef supports.

Uluru-Kata Tjuta National Park

(F) What you see projecting from the sandy plains of Australia's Red Centre is just the tip, but this majestic monolith still packs a physical and spiritual punch well above its weight. Uluru (also called Ayers Rock) and Kata Tjuta, the seemingly sculpted rock domes clustered 55 km (34 mi) to the west, are deeply significant to the park's traditional owners, the Anangu Aboriginal people.

The Anangu ask visitors not to climb Uluru. Some controversy continues, however, about whether this is because the climb is the traditional route of the ancestral Mala men or because the Anangu think the ascent is just too dangerous. At least 35 people have died on the steep, exposed climb. Independent walks, ranger-guided walks, and Anangu-guided walks (fees apply) offer fascinating cultural perspectives of Uluru and Kata Tjuta from the ground.

Wet Tropics of Queensland

(G) Verdant and ancient, the Wet Tropics of Queensland are the hothouse of Australian flora and fauna. Three thousand plant species, hundreds of mammal types, and over half the country's recorded birds inhabit the tangled rain forests north, south, and west of Cairns, on Australia's far north-eastern coast. The remarkable tree kangaroo and the green possum are found only in this World Heritage area. Reptile residents of the Wet Tropics vary in size from inches-long geckos to 7-meter-long (23-foot-long) amethystine pythons. A shorter but considerably meaner local is the estuarine crocodile, or saltie as it is commonly called.

Purnululu National Park

(H) Geological history is written large across this World Heritage site in Australia's northwest Kimberley region. Twenty million years of erosion and weathering have deeply dissected the Bungle Bungle Range into banded, beehive-shaped sandstone towers. Other examples of cone karst in sandstone, as this remarkable phenomenon is called, are found around the world. None of these sites rival Purnululu for the diversity, size, and grandeur of formations.

Purnululu means sandstone in the Kija aboriginal language, and spectacularly sculpted sandstone is the highlight of the park. Hard-edged gorges softened by fan palms separate the orange-and-black striped towers, however. Wild budgerigars are among the 100-plus bird species in the park. Wallabies, too, are sometimes spotted among the rocks.

Kakadu National Park

(I) X-ray paintings of barramundi, long-necked turtles, and other animals festoon the main gallery at Ubirr Rock in Kakadu National Park. This menu-in-ocher is one of more than 5,000 art sites in the park that collectively date back 20,000 years. Archaeologists have put human habitation at twice that long. Ongoing and uninterrupted connection with Top End Aboriginal peoples was a key factor in Kakadu's World Heritage listing. So were the park's diverse habitats. Estuarine crocodiles prowl the Alligator River. Red-billed jabiru, Australia's only stork, stroll the flood plains. Waterfalls cannon off the Arnhem Land escarpment. Nowhere else in Australia are cultural and ecological significance so richly intertwined.

IF YOU LIKE

Beautiful Beaches

Whether you want to bake in the sun, see and be seen, or try body- or board-surfing in the white-capped waves, Australia has an abundance of beautiful beaches. Miles and miles of pristine sand line the coastline, so you can choose to join the crowd or sunbathe in blissful solitude.

■ **Bondi Beach.** On the edge of the Tasman Sea, Bondi Beach is the most famous perhaps in all of Australia. You can take a surfing lesson here or just immerse yourself in the delights of suburban sand and water. Don't miss the Coast Walk from Bondi to Bronte Beach—it's a breathtaking 2.5-km (1.5-mi) path that will take you along dramatic coastal cliffs to a string of eastern beaches. The walking track continues beyond Bronte Beach to Waverley Cemetery, where many famous Australians are buried in cliff-top splendor.

■ **Queensland's Gold Coast and Islands.** Warm, moderate surf washes the 70-km (43-mi) stretch of Gold Coast beaches, which are perfect for board riding, swimming, or just collecting shells at sunset. Beach bums, however, know to head north to the Great Barrier Reef islands for less-crowded, tropical stretches of sand.

■ **Whitehaven.** The Whitsunday Islands are home to arguably Australia's most beautiful beach. The near-deserted arc of Whitehaven Beach has some of the whitest and most powdery sand on earth.

■ West Coast Fringing the Indian Ocean between Perth and South Fremantle are 19 wide beaches with good breaks, but head down to the south coast for a dip in the crystal-clear waters of the deserted, sandy white beaches around Margaret River.

Wine

Australian wines are among the best in the world, a judgment that international wine shows consistently reinforce. Australians are very proud of their wine. You'll be hard-pressed to find anything but Australian wines on the menus at most places, so take this opportunity to expand your palate beyond the export brands you may have tried at home, like Rosemount, Jacob's Creek, and Penfolds.

■ **Hunter Valley.** The largest grape-growing area in New South Wales, Hunter Valley has more than 120 wineries and a reputation for producing excellent wines. Expect some amazing Semillons and Cabernets.

■ **South Australia.** The Barossa Valley, about an hour's drive northeast of Adelaide, produces some of Australia's most famous Syrah (or Shiraz, as they call it Down Under). You might recognize the Penfolds label, as makers of the renowned Grange Shiraz blend. In the nearby Clare Valley, German immigrants planted Riesling many decades ago and the grape has met with great success there.

■ **Margaret River.** In Western Australia the Margaret River region produces just 1% of the country's total wine output. Yet 25% of Australia's premium and ultrapremium wines come from this small area. Margaret River's Bordeaux-like climate helps producers grow excellent Cabernet-Merlot blends, since these grapes originally came from that region.

■ **Yarra Valley.** More than 70 wineries fill the floor of the Yarra Valley, where Pinot Noir thrives.

Incredible Wildlife

Australia's diverse habitats are home to countless strange and amazing creatures.

■ **Koalas and Kangaroos.** No trip to Australia would be complete without an encounter with Australia's iconic animals: kangaroos and koalas. The Lone Pine Koala Sanctuary in Brisbane is one of many wildlife parks around Australia that let you take a picture with a cuddly koala or hand-feed a mob of kangaroos.

■ **Birds.** Australia has many wild and wonderful creatures of the non-marsupial variety. The waterholes at Kakadu National Park in the Northern Territory attract more than 280 species of birds, including the stately ja biru, Australia's only stork, and the fluroescent rainbow bee-eater, as well as crocodiles, the ubiquitous creatures of Australia's Top End. The much friendlier and cuter fairy penguins draw nighttime crowds at **Philip Island** in Victoria.

■ **Camels.** Don't be surprised if you catch the eye of a camel wandering the desert of the Red Centre. These are descendants of dromedaries shipped in during the 19th century for use on exploratory expeditions and Outback construction projects and for desert transport.

■ **Creatures of the Deep.** The Great Barrier Reef gets plenty of attention for underwater wildlife, but Western Australia has two phenomenal spots of its own. The dolphins at Shark Bay in Monkey Mia, Western Australia, can be hand-fed. Ningaloo Reef, off the Exmouth Peninsula, is home to humpback whales and whale sharks.

Water Sports

With 36,735 km (22,776 mi) of coast bordering two oceans and four seas, Australians spend a good deal of their time in and on the water. Opportunities abound for scuba diving, snorkeling, surfing, waterskiing, windsurfing, sailing, and just mucking about in the waves. Prime diving seasons are September–December and mid-March–May.

■ **Diving.** Avid divers will want to visit the resort islands of the Great Barrier Reef, which provide upscale accommodation and access to some of the country's top diving spots. Cod Hole, off the Lizard Island reef, in far north Queensland, ranks highly among them. You can do a one-day introductory or resort dive, and four-day open water dive certification courses, or if fins and oxygen tanks aren't your speed, opt for snorkeling off the island beaches. Diving expeditions are a specialty of the Cairns area, with carriers like Quicksilver and Tusa Dive running day trips to the reef for diving and snorkeling.

■ **Sailing.** Sailors love the Whitsunday Islands off the mid-north Queensland coast. Almost all the 74 islands in this group are national parks, and only seven have resorts on them, making this an ideal spot to drop anchor and moor for a few days, or to try a vacation on a live-aboard boat or yacht. You can also experience the swashbuckling romance of olden-day sailing on multi-day tall ship cruises.

QUINTESSENTIAL AUSTRALIA

Go Bush

When Aussies refer to the bush, they can mean either a scrubby patch of ground a few kilometers outside the city or the vast, sprawling desert Outback. In most cases it's a way to describe getting out of the daily routine of the city and getting in touch with the natural landscape of this incredibly diverse country.

With 80% of its population living on eastern shores, and with all of its major cities (except Canberra) situated on or near the coast, most of Australia's wild, wonderful interior is virtually empty. Whether you find yourself watching the sun rise (or set) over Uluru, taking a camel trek through the Kimberley, or sleeping under the stars in a swag (traditional Australian camping kit), there are countless ways to go bush and see Australia's most natural, rural, and stunning sights.

Aussie! Aussie! Aussie! Oy! Oy! Oy!

From world-class sporting events like the Australian Open tennis to national obsessions like the Australian Football League Grand Final, Aussies love their sports. The calendar is chock-full of sporting events that give Aussies good reason to drink a cold beer and gather with mates to barrack for (cheer on) their favorite team.

Aussie Rules Football (or footy) is a popular, fast-paced, and rough-and-tumble sport that's played without padding and uses what looks like an American football through four 25-minute quarters. Rugby League Football is a 13-a-side game that is played internationally. Cricket test matches are the sport of summer, though much less happens during these games than in footy matches. Spectators get to soak up the sun and drink a lot of beer while watching the Australians duel international teams in matches that can go for one to five days.

Aussies refer to authentic or genuine things as *fair dinkum*. The folks down under are a fun loving bunch, so don't be shy. Here are a few ways to experience Australia like the locals do.

Swimming Between the Flags

Australians love their beaches as much as they love their barbies, so put on your bathers or your cossie (slang for bathing costume) and slather on good sunblock—the damage to the ozone layer above Australia is very, very severe.

Many Australian beaches are patrolled by volunteer members of the Surf Lifesaving Association (SLSA), who post red and yellow flags to demarcate the safest areas to swim on any beach. The SLSA was formed in 1907, and its tan, buff lifesavers make the *Baywatch* team look like amateurs—it's rumored that no one has ever drowned while swimming in the areas that they patrol. Of course, these hunky heroes can't be everywhere all the time, so use caution when swimming on those picturesque deserted beaches you're bound to come across in your travels. The undertow or rip can be strong and dangerous.

The Barbie

Paul Hogan, aka Crocodile Dundee, showed the world laid-back Australian hospitality by inviting visitors to say "G'day," then throw another shrimp on the barbie, or barbecue. But it's unlikely you'll find shrimp on a barbie in Australia. What you will find is Aussies cooking up steak, sausages (often called snags), beef, chicken, and lamb on gas grills all over the country.

Barbies are so ubiquitous in Australia that almost every public park or beach will have a barbecue area set up for people to come and grill at will. The tools required for "having a barbie" the traditional Aussie way are newspaper and butter. The newspaper helps wipe the barbie clean from the previous grilling, and butter greases it back up again before putting the meat on. Sometimes an onion instead of a newspaper is used to clean off the grill—a slightly more hygienic system.

AUSTRALIA TODAY

Government
Australia is a constitutional monarchy, and the Queen of England is still officially Australia's Queen as well. Her only role under the constitution, however, is to appoint her representative in Australia, the Governor General, which she does on advice from Australia's Prime Minister. In 1975 the then Governor General caused a political crisis when he sacked the Prime Minister and his government and installed the Opposition minority as caretaker until new elections could be held. Today the Governor General still retains that power, but his or her duties are primarily ceremonial. Australia's government is elected for 3-year terms, with no limit on how many terms a Prime Minister can serve. Voting is compulsory for all citizens 18 years and older, and failure to vote can result in a fine.

Economy
Australia is a major exporter of wheat and wool, iron-ore and gold, liquefied natural gas and coal. The major industries are mining, industrial and transport equipment, food processing, chemicals, and steel manufacturing. The services sector dominates the domestic economy. Abundant natural assets and massive government spending have softened the short-term impact of the recent global financial crisis as compared with many other countries.

Tourism
On- and off-shore wonders, unique wildlife, beach culture, indigenous history, and multicultural cuisines help maintain Australia's multibillion-dollar tourism industry. The major challenges are keeping Australia on travelers' radars as other countries gain popularity, and protecting the most fragile attractions.

Climate change has already affected the Great Barrier Reef, a World Heritage site on most visitors' must-see lists, and programs are in place to try to minimize the impact of rising sea temperatures. Contentious logging of old-growth forests for pulp, particularly in Tasmania, continues, and the opening of new mines rarely fits comfortably with conservation and cultural issues.

Religion
Australia's first settlers were predominantly English, Irish, and Scottish Christians. Two centuries later, almost two thirds of Australians call themselves Christians, with Buddhism a distant second (2%), and Islam third (1.7%), however nearly a fifth of the population ticked "no religion" on the last census. Active church worship has declined over recent decades, and many religious orders struggle to attract members.

Literature
Life Down Under has bred contemporary writers who speak with distinctly Australian voices. Tim Winton's book *Breath* brilliantly evokes the power of surfing and the angst of adolescence. Look out for Kate Grenville, Richard Flanagan, Peter Carey, Alex Miller, and Peter Corris, among others. Morris Gleitzman and Paul Jennings write (mostly) laugh-out-loud books for children and the young at heart.

MANAGING THE WATER CRISIS

If you were to suggest that World War III will be fought over water, not oil, many Australians might agree. The country's major river system is in trouble, many urban water storages are below 30% capacity (some rural ones are empty), and rainfall has been below average for years in many places. The subject of water—its supply, collection, and use—is on almost everyone's lips.

The Impact

Australians are learning to live with the water restrictions that are in force across much of the country; limits on watering gardens and lawns, washing vehicles, and hosing paved areas are mandatory, and fines are levied for breaking them. Everyone in Australia is affected by the water crisis, but rural communities dependent of irrigation are feeling the brunt of it. The Murray and its main tributary, the Darling, are Australia's longest river system and the lifeblood of its crop farms. In the past two years the volume of water flowing into the Murray from the rivers that feed it in NSW and Queensland was the lowest since records began in 1892. Officials now say there is a 75 percent chance of even less water in the Murray system by next year. The farms and towns taking water from the Murray-Darling river system have become a huge threat to its survival. In 2009 a heat wave and wildfires in southeast Australia wreaked devastation on wine harvests. Faced with another year of drought, or a potentially new, dryer climate, some farmers are walking away. Australia's native flora and fauna also face dwindling water supplies. Wetlands (and the wildlife they support) are most at risk.

Taking Action

Australia's federal and state governments are implementing measures to reduce the impact of climate change and improve and supplement existing water sources, but critics complain that it's too little, too late. South Australia and Victoria are, controversially, following Western Australia's example and building desalination plants. Authorities are also treading warily around the idea of recycling wastewater for consumption. The grand schemes for piping Top End floodwaters to the thirsty south pop up every few years, despite expert opinion that this is financially unviable—it would, apparently, be cheaper to ship the water south in bulk carriers. More practically, a revamped water trading and buy-out system based on water access entitlements promises to reallocate precious Murray-Darling water, and the voluntary "155" campaign has seen Melbournians reduce their water usage to less than 155 liters per day. Businesses, schools, and private homes are installing tanks to harvest rainwater, installing water-saving shower heads, and landscaping with heartier indigenous plants.

What You Can Do

■ Limit showers to 3 minutes and turn off taps while soaping up in the shower or brushing teeth.

■ Use a sink plug when rinsing food or dishes, and when washing hands.

■ Ask hotel staff to not change your towels and bed linen until you leave.

■ Bring or buy a reusable drinking bottle and fill it from the tap—tap water around Australia is safe, and the production of bottled water uses huge amounts of water and energy.

GREAT TRAIN JOURNEYS

THE INDIAN PACIFIC RAIL ROAD

Australia's longest rail journey snakes 4,352 km (2,720 mi) across mountains, plains, and deserts between Sydney and Perth. Named after the oceans on either side of the country, the Indian Pacific dates back to the late 19th century, when Australia was pushing toward Federation. The independent British colonies of Queensland, New South Wales, Victoria, Tasmania, and South Australia enticed the isolated colony of Western Australia into federation with the promise of an east-west rail link. Construction of the final 1,996-km (1,248-mi) link in the transcontinental line, between Kalgoorlie in the west, and Port Augusta in South Australia, was completed in 1917. Even though passenger services started that year, the Indian Pacific only made its first unbroken journey in 1970. Before then, travelers had to change trains several times to ride narrow-, standard-, and broad-gauge track, and the line was standardized only in 1969.

The Route
The Indian Pacific traverses dramatically diverse Australian landscapes on its 65-hour journey. You have the option of making the whole trip in one sitting or breaking it—for A$200 you can stop off in Adelaide.

The Eastern Leg (from Sydney to Adelaide)
East–west passengers leave Sydney in midafternoon and kick off the journey by traveling over the sandstone escarpments and through the villages of the Blue Mountains as the train scales the Great Dividing Range. Dinner is served as the Western Plains unfurl. After a good

night's rest, tuck into breakfast as the train rolls through Outback New South Wales toward Broken Hill. Morning and afternoon light on the gnarled hills, mulga scrub, and red-soil plains out here inspires artists, many of whom have galleries in Broken Hill. Look out for emus and kangaroos.

The Western Leg (from Adelaide to Perth)
Your second Indian Pacific dinner is served as the train backtracks through Adelaide's northern suburbs to the railway junction at Crystal Brook. Darkness covers the run up Spencer Gulf and into salt-lake country, and dawn finds you on the Nullarbor Plain. Nullarbor is a Latin-based name meaning no trees. There is little to see for mile after mile, and that's the appeal. This is prime hunting ground for the wedge-tailed eagle, symbol of the Indian Pacific, and train drivers sometimes slow down so passengers can see eagle chicks in a nest beside the train.

Whistle Stop Tours—Broken Hill
All Whistle Stop tours can be arranged through the bar staff or the Onboard Hospitality Attendant in each carriage. Three tours are are offered during your 70- to 90-minute stop in Broken Hill. We like the Silver City tour (A$24), which explores the town's rich mining history.

Whistle Stop Tours—Adelaide
If you want to stay on the train, then you've only 3½ hours to explore the city. The one-hour Adelaide–Festival City tour (A$23) shows you Adelaide Oval (arguably Australia's prettiest cricket ground), splendid sandstone buildings, and Rundle Street's famous café scene. If you decide to break up your journey, then your time depends on which Indian Pacific service you rejoin. A three-day itinerary allows

for one day in Adelaide, and the next day can be spent exploring the villages and wineries in the Adelaide Hills. On Day 3 head north to Barossa or south to McLaren Vale for some serious wine appreciation. The trains depart at 6:40 PM on Saturdays and Wednesdays.

Whistle Stop Tours — Kalgoorlie

Around breakfast time the following day, the Indian Pacific starts its run on the world's longest straight stretch of railway. After ninety minutes along this 478-km (300-mi) stretch of track, in the middle of nowhere, the train stops in Cook to take on water and change drivers. Step off and wander around this virtual ghost town. Around nightfall you'll roll into Kalgoorlie for a 3½-hour stop. This is Australia's largest Outback city, and it sits on the world's highest concentration of gold. Join the 75-minute Gold Capital Tour (A$28) and learn about the hardships of early mining and the unique cast of characters that came here to strike it rich. Weather permitting, you also see the 1,090-foot-deep, 3-km-long (2-mi-long) flood-lit Super Pit. From Kalgoorlie, the Indian Pacific continues west through the night, and the journey ends in Perth around 9 AM. Take the Best of Perth & Kings Park tour (A$34) and get a feel

NUTS AND BOLTS

■ Red Service: Daynighter seat A$716, sleeper cabin A$1,362 per person.

■ Gold Service: Twin or single sleeper cabin A$2,008 per person.

■ Chairman's Carriage (private, sleeps eight) A$17,120; Sir John Forest Carriage (private, accommodates six), A$15,340; Prince of Wales Carriage (private, sleeps eight) A$15,300 (The Prince of Wales operates only between Adelaide and Perth).

■ You can book your motor vehicle (up to 5.5 meters long) on the Indian Pacific for A$899.

■ Train Amenities: Restaurant and dining cars, bar service, lounge cars, tour bookings.

■ Duration of Trip: 65 hours.

■ Distance Traveled: 2,720 mi.

for Western Australia's riverside capital before checking into your hotel.

GREAT TRAIN JOURNEYS

THE GHAN RAILROAD

The *Ghan* is one of the world's great train journeys. Named after the Afghan cameleers whose animals were crucial to central Australia's exploration, settlement, and development, this train rides 2,979 km (1862 mi) of track between Adelaide, in South Australia, and Darwin, on the country's north coast. Roughly halfway between these two cities the *Ghan* pulls into Alice Springs, the desert city in Australia's aptly named Red Centre. A north–south transcontinental Australian railway was mooted as early as 1858, but it took 20 more years for track to start creeping northward. Alice Springs consisted of just a hundred people and one hotel when a steam engine hauled the first *Ghan* train into town in 1929. Unfortunately, extreme desert conditions and termites wreaked havoc on the track and train services for years to come. Finally, the rerouted *New Ghan* was launched in 1980, but stories about the old service live on: one tells of a woman who complained to the conductor about the delays because she was due to give birth. When the conductor rebuked her for making a rail journey while pregnant she replied, "I wasn't when I got on!" In contrast to the long, stop-start construction of the Adelaide-Alice line, the northern extension to Darwin was completed in just four years, and the inaugural Darwin-bound *Ghan* service left Adelaide on February 1, 2004.

The Route

On its 53-hour journey, the *Ghan* traverses some of Australia's most unforgiving and surprisingly beautiful country. Book the whole trip, or break it into northern and southern legs—you pay a negligible premium to split the fare—and explore Alice Springs and the ancient landscape surrounding it.

The Southern Leg (from Adelaide to Alice)

South–north passengers leave Adelaide at lunchtime. Watch South Australia roll by as the *Ghan* motors up Spencer Gulf to Port Augusta. From there the train turns inland, passing through ephemeral salt-lake country into darkness. Dawn finds the *Ghan* deep in desert, with red earth flat to the horizon or occasionally gathered into ancient ranges. Enjoy the play of pastel colors on the plains from your cabin's picture window.

The Northern Leg (from Alice to Darwin)

The train leaves Alice for Darwin just in time for dinner. The next morning, after a brief whistle stop in Katherine, you'll spend your final day rolling through the desert and lonely scrubland of the Top End toward the lush tropical city of Darwin. Once in Darwin, celebrate your journey's end with Thai-style barramundi at Hanuman Darwin, one of the Top End's best restaurants.

Whistle Stop Tours—Alice Springs

The *Ghan* rolls into Alice Springs around lunchtime on Day 2 for a four-hour stop. If you're up for a little adventure, a helicopter flight (A$175 per person) over the ancient MacDonnell Ranges might be to your liking. We especially like the Aboriginal Sacred Sites and Cultural Tour (A$79) for it's fascinating insights into the Central Arrernte Aboriginal culture, the explanation of the Yeperenye (caterpillar) stories, and the guided tour of an Aboriginal art gallery. Passengers breaking their train journey in Alice Springs have three or four days, depending on which of the twice-weekly services you rejoin. With

three days, explore Alice's museums, wildlife parks, and Aboriginal art galleries, then do a self-drive or group tour of the gorges, waterholes, and Aboriginal sites in the MacDonnell Ranges. If you have four days, experience the geological and spiritual wonder of Uluru (Ayers Rock) and Kata Tjuta, which are 457 km (285 mi) southeast of Alice Springs by road or an hour by commercial flight.

Whistle Stop Tours—Katherine

You're spoiled for choice with the selection of Whistle Stop Tours during your four-hour stay in Katherine. A passenger favorite—and one of Katherine's main attractions—is the Katherine Gorge boat cruise (A$84) in Nitmiluk National Park. Passengers can cruise between the gorge's soaring sandstone walls or hire a canoe and paddle on this Northern Territory landmark (careful of the crocs!). Double canoes are A$27 per person, single canoes A$32 per person.

NUTS AND BOLTS

■ Red Service: Daynighter seat A$716, sleeper cabin A$1,312.

■ Gold Service: Twin or single sleeper cabin A$1,973; superior cabin A$2,768.

■ Platinum Service: Sleeper cabin A$2,987 per person.

■ Train Amenities: Restaurant and dining car, bar service, lounge car, tour bookings.

■ Duration of Trip: 53 hours.

■ Distance Traveled: 1,862 mi.

GREAT ROAD TRIPS

FROM SYDNEY TO BRISBANE

Drive along one of the most glorious and seductive streches of land in northern New South Wales. It's a big trip—1,100 km (687.5 mi)—so allow a minimum of seven days if you decide to drive the entire route.

Day One—175 km (109 mi):

Frame the Harbour Bridge in your rear-vision mirror and head north out of Sydney. Take the Sydney–Newcastle (F3) Freeway about 75 km (47 mi) north to the Peats Ridge Road exit, and wind through the forested hills to Wollombi, a delightful town founded in 1820. Browse the antiques shops, sandstone courthouse, and museum. Next, head northeast to Cessnock and Pokolbin, the hub of the Lower Hunter, and spend the day tasting—and buying—fine wines and artisanal cheeses. Know that Australia has a zero tolerance policy for driving and drinking. Be sure to choose a designated driver or, better yet, take one of our recommended wine-tasting tours.

Day Two—271 km (168 mi):

Get up with the birds and drive east via Cessnock to the Pacific Highway. Turn north for the long drive to Port Macquarie, Australia's third-oldest settlement. Have a well-earned lunch break in the café at Sea Acres Rainforest Centre and then stroll the elevated boardwalk—or take a guided tour—through centuries-old cabbage tree palms. Now it's into Port Macquarie for a lazy afternoon on a beach, but which of the 13 regional beaches do you laze on?

Day Three—260 km (162.5 mi):

Visit Port Macquarie's Koala Hospital for feeding time (8 AM). Then resume driving up the Pacific Highway. Leave the highway 140 km (87.5 mi) north at the exit to Bellingen, one of the prettiest towns on the New South Wales north coast. It's a nice place to stop for lunch and a quick peek into a few galleries. Continue inland up onto the Dorrigo Plateau. Dorrigo National Park is one of about 50 reserves and parks within the World Heritage–listed Gondwana Rainforests of Australia. Stopping into the Dorrigo Rainforest Centre to learn about the area is gratifying, as is the forest canopy Skywalk. Back in your car, drive on to Dorrigo town and turn right onto the winding, partly unsealed, but scenic road to Corumba and Coffs Harbour. Now you've earned a two-night stay in Coffs.

Day Four—no driving

Scuba-dive on the Solitary Isles? White-water raft the Nymboida River? Or kick back on a beach? However you spend your day, don't miss an evening stroll to Muttonbird Island from Coffs Harbour marina. From September to April you can watch muttonbirds (or shearwaters) returning to their burrows. When the whales are about, it's also a good hump-back viewing spot.

Day Five—247 km (154 mi)

North again, past Coffs Harbour's landmark Big Banana and up the coast to Byron Bay.

There is just too much to do in Byron: kayak with dolphins; dive with grey nurse sharks; go beachcombing and swimming; tread the Cape Byron Walking Track; or tour the lighthouse atop Cape Byron, which is mainland Australia's easternmost point. It's best to decide over lunch at open-air Byron Bay Beach Café, a local legend. When the sun sets, wash off the salt and head out for some great seafood and then overnight in Byron Bay—there's everything from hostels to high-end villas.

Brisbane

QUEENSLAND
GOLD COAST

Mt. Warning ◆   ○ Murwillumbah

Byron Bay ○

SOLITARY ISLANDS

Dorrigo ○
Dorrigo National Park ◆ ○   **Coffs Harbour**
Bellingen

Port Macquarie ○
◆ Sea Acres Rainforest Centre

NEW SOUTH
WALES

Pokolbin ○
Wollombi ○ ○ **Cessnock**

Sydney ○

Day Six—53 km (33 mi)

Catch up on the Byron Bay you missed yesterday before driving north to Murwillumbah and its remarkable natural landmark. Mt Warning is the 3,800-foot magma chamber of an extinct shield volcano. From the top, on a clear day, there is a 360-degree view of one of the world's largest calderas, with mountainous rims on three sides and the Tweed River running through its eroded east rim. Climb this mountain (four hours return), then reward yourself with a night at Crystal Creek Rainforest Retreat (bookings essential).

Day Seven—50 km (31 mi)

Relaxed and reinvigorated, it's over the New South Wales border to Queensland and Australia's most developed stretch of coastline. With Brisbane just 90 minutes' drive farther north, you can spend as much or as little time as you want on the Gold Coast. Visit theme parks; toss dice at the casino; ride waves in gorgeous sunshine. Don't miss feeding the lorikeets at Currumbin Wildlife Sanctuary before Brisbane beckons.

TIPS AND LOGISTICS

■ Unleaded petrol, diesel, and LPG are available at gas stations along most of this route.

■ Motel rooms are easy to find, except during school holidays and long weekends. To avoid driving around after a day at the wheel, book ahead. The staff at your previous night's accommodation should be able to help you arrange the next night.

■ If hiring a car for the trip, check that it contains a street directory. Pick up a good road map or touring atlas heading out of Sydney.

■ Mobile speed radars are used throughout Australia, and fines are high. Stick to the speed limits.

GREAT ROAD TRIPS

THE GREAT OCEAN ROAD

Arguably one of the country's most spectacular drives, the iconic Great Ocean Road hugs the windswept, rugged coastline just west of Melbourne. Allow six days for this 900-km (562-mi) road trip and be prepared to enjoy some of Victoria's best.

Day One — 187 km (117 mi)

Having escaped Melbourne, drive down the Princes Freeway for about 75 km (47 mi) to the Torquay/Great Ocean Road turnoff. A quarter hour more at the wheel brings you to Torquay, Australia's premier surfing and windsurfing resort town. On your way out of town, detour to Bell's Beach, the setting for Australia's premier surfing competition each Easter. The renowned Great Ocean Road officially starts 30 km (19 mi) beyond Bell's Beach, but the dramatic splendor of Victoria's southwest coast reveals itself sooner. Stop in Lorne, at the foot of the lush Otway Ranges, for lunch. Once you're back on the road, slow down and enjoy it. The winding Great Ocean Road is narrow; don't pass unless you can see far ahead, and don't pull onto the shoulder to admire the view! There are designated pull-over areas where you can safely enjoy the vista.

Drive the 45 km (28 mi) to Apollo Bay for dinner and the night.

Day Two — 234 km (146 mi)

The 91-km (57-mi) Great Ocean Walk starts just west of Apollo Bay in Marengo. Here the Great Ocean Road heads inland. Stay on the main road to Lavers Hill; then detour about 17 km (11 mi) east to the Otway Fly. This 1,969-foot-long elevated treetop walk takes you up into the rain-forest canopy for a bird's-eye view of giant myrtle beech, blackwood, and mighty mountain ash. Backtrack to Lavers Hill and the Great Ocean Road. The road's most famous landmarks lie along a 32-km (20-mi) stretch of coast within Port Campbell National Park. First stop is the Twelve Apostles—there are now only eight of these offshore limestone stacks, but who's counting? Take a helicopter flight for a jaw-dropping view of the eroded and indented coast. Next stop is Loch Ard Gorge, named after the iron-hulled clipper that hit a reef and sank here in 1878. Loch Ard is a natural gallery of sea sculpture, where you could wander for hours on a sunny day. Don't stay in your car if the sun doesn't show, though. Only when a howling wind is roughing up the Southern Ocean will you fully appreciate why this is called the Shipwreck Coast. Leaving the Great Ocean Road now, drive to the maritime village of Port Fairy for the night. In whale season (June–November), divert to Logan's Beach, in Warrnambool, where southern right cows and calves often loll just off the beach.

Day Three — 146 km (91 mi)

Take a leisurely post-breakfast promenade around Port Fairy, Victoria's second-oldest town and widely considered to be its prettiest. Then backtrack 7 km (4.4 mi) to the Penshurst/Dunkeld Road and drive 74 km (46 mi) north to Dunkeld, on the edge of the Grampians National Park. Stop for lunch before undertaking the 60-km (37-mi) drive to Halls Gap, the main accommodation base. Be sure to slow down and enjoy one of the most picturesque drives in the Grampians; pull in at the Brambuk Cultural Centre, just before Halls Gap, and learn about the park's rich Aboriginal history.

1

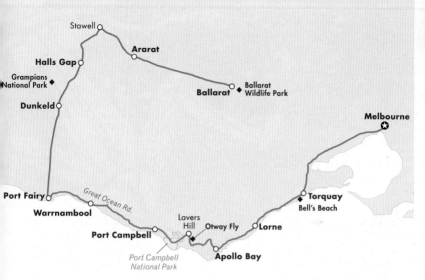

Check into your Halls Gap accommodation for two nights.

Day Four—no driving

Spend a day exploring on foot. Walks of varied grades showcase the Grampians' extraordinary geology; don't miss the Pinnacle Walk, just out of Halls Gap, the valley and ranges view from Chatauqua Peak, and Hollow Mountain in the park's north.

Day Five—140 km (87.5 mi)

Drive out of Halls Gap to Ararat, on the Western Highway, and follow the highway east to the famous gold town of Ballarat. Spend the rest of the morning among the gold-rush-era Victorian architecture on Sturt and Lydiard streets. Visit the Ballarat Fine Art Gallery, if only to see the tattered remains of the Southern Cross flag that the rebels flew during the 1854 Eureka uprising over mine license fees. Spend the afternoon at Sovereign Hill, where you can pan for gold, ride a horse-drawn stage coach through dusty streets, and stick your teeth together with old-fashioned candy.

TIPS AND LOGISTICS

■ Unleaded petrol, diesel, and LPG are available at gas stations in major centers; however, LPG is rare in small country towns.

■ There is a petrol price cycle in Victoria, which authorities can't—or won't—explain; try to fill up on Tuesdays and Wednesdays, and avoid buying fuel on Fridays.

■ Choosing accommodation as you go gives you flexibility in when and where you stop. For peace of mind, though, you might prefer to pre-book.

Day Six—111 km (69 mi)

Have close and not-so-close encounters with saltwater crocodiles, snakes, wombats, kangaroos, and other Australian fauna at Ballarat Wildlife Park. After that, continue your journey or head back to Melbourne.

ABORIGIN
PAST

Today's Australian Aboriginals are guardians of the world's oldest living culture. Most experts agree that it was about 50,000 years ago (possibly as many as 80,000) when the continent's first inhabitants migrated south across a landmass that once connected Australia to Indonesia and Malaysia. These first Australians brought with them a wealth of stories, songs, tribal customs, and ceremonies—many of which are still practiced today.

By Sarah Gold

AL ART,
AND PRESENT

All Aboriginal ideology is based upon the creation period known as The Dreaming. During this primordial time, totemic ancestors (who were associated with particular animals, plants, and natural phenomena) lived on and journeyed across the earth. The legends of these ancestors—what they did, where they traveled, who they fought and loved—are considered sacred, and have been passed down among Aboriginal tribes for thousands of years. Though these stories are largely shared in secret rituals, they have also been documented through the creation of unique, highly symbolic artworks.

This is why Aboriginal art, despite humble beginnings as simple rock carvings and ochre paintings on bark, now hang in some of the world's finest museums. These works aren't just beautiful; they're also profound cultural artifacts—and a window onto humanity's oldest surviving civilizaion.

(top right) Nourlangie Rock, Kakadu;
(top left) Art by Emily Kame Kngwarreye;
(bottom left) Work from Papunya Tula;
(bottom right) Maningrida Art and Culture, Darwin

EARLY ABORIGINAL ART

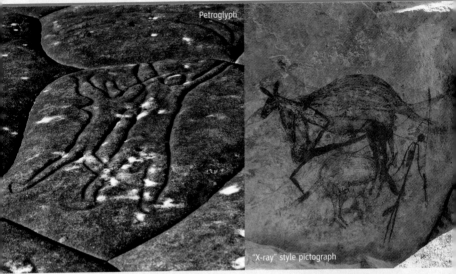

Petroglyph

"X-ray" style pictograph

While dot paintings are the most widely recognized Aboriginal artworks today, they're only the latest incarnation of a creative output that stretches back thousands of years. The achievements of Australia's earliest artists can still be seen—etched right onto the sacred landscapes that inspired them.

PETROGLYPHS
The earliest Aboriginal artworks were petroglyphs—engravings carved into flat rock surfaces or faces of cliffs (most likely using pointed stones or shards of shell). Some surviving etchings show lines and circles similar to those in modern-day paintings; others depict animals, fish, birds, and human or spirit figures. The oldest known engravings on the continent, at Pilbara in Western Australia and Olary in South Australia, are estimated to be 40,000 years old. Perhaps the most visited, though, are those in Ku-rin-gai Chase National Park, less than an hour's drive north of Sydney.

PROTECTING ROCK-ART SITES

Given the centuries of weathering they've endured, it's remarkable that so many ancient rock art sites remain intact. In many places, the longevity of the artworks can be attributed to local Aboriginal tribes, who consider it a sacred responsibility to preserve and repaint fading images. Help preservation efforts by staying on marked paths, not touching the artwork, and taking a tour of the site with an indigenous guide.

Freehand pictograph

Stencil painting

PICTOGRAPHS

Other early Aboriginal artists chose to paint images rather than etch them. Using ochres and mineral pigments, and employing sticks, feathers, and their own fingers as brushes, these ancient painters chose sheltered spots—like the insides of caves and canyons—for their mural-like images. Protection from the elements allowed many of these ancient rock paintings to survive; today they're still found all over Australia.

REGIONAL STYLES

The styles of painting varied by region. In the Northern Territory, in Arnhem Land and what is now Kakadu National Park, early Aboriginals painted "X-ray" portraits of humans and animals with their skeletons and internal organs clearly displayed. The Kimberley and Burrup Peninsula in Western Australia are rich repositories of elegant freehand paintings portraying human, animal, and ancestral Dreaming figures. And Queensland, especially the area that is now Carnarvon National Park, is known for its stencil paintings, in which the artists sprayed paint from their mouths.

EARTH TONES (LITERALLY)

Early Aboriginal artists used the earth to make pigments. Red, yellow, and brown were made from mineral-rich clays. Black was created with charcoal or charred tree bark; white from crushed gypsum rock; and grey from ashes left over from cooking fires. Modern artists may mix their pigments with oil or acrylic, but the traditional palette remains the same.

DECIPHERING "DOT PAINTINGS"

An artist uses a small, straight stick dipped in paint to create a dot painting. Ancient symbols and intricate dot motifs combine to create powerful works of art.

To a visitor wandering through a gallery, Aboriginal artwork can seem deceptively simple. Many traditional paintings feature basic designs—wavy lines, concentric circles—comprised of myriad tiny dots. They look as though they were created with the end of a paint-covered stick (and indeed, most were).

But the swirling motifs in these "dot paintings" aren't just abstractions—they're visual representations of ancestral legends.

According to Aboriginal beliefs, as the ancestors lived their lives during the Dreaming, they also gave shape to the landscape. In each spot where the ancestor shot an arrow, danced, or gave birth, an enduring mark was left on the topography: a hill, a ravine, a rock spire. As they conjured these geographical features, they sang out their names—composing singing maps of the territory they covered. Each is known as a "songline," and they criss-cross the entire continent.

Now thousands of years old, these songs are still memorized and sung by today's Aboriginals. Songlines are the basis of all indigenous traditions and tribal laws; learning and teaching the songs are considered sacred—and very secret—duties. Over many centuries, however, artists have revealed parts of the songlines through the symbology of dot paintings.

The symbols may seem cryptic, but many are recurring and give clues to the ancestral stories they depict. Shapes punctuating dot paintings usually correspond to landmarks: bodies of water, rock formations, campsites, or resting places. The lines that surround the shapes and connect them represent the tracks of the ancestors as they moved from place to place. Each dot painting is, in effect, a sacred walking map that plots an ancestor's journey.

COMMON SYMBOLS
IN ABORIGINAL ART

woman

emu tracks

four women
sitting around
a campfire

ants, fruits,
flowers, or eggs

well or
main campsite

water, fire,
smoke, lightning,
or bushfire

holes, clouds,
or nests

Honey ant

Coolamon
(wooden dish)

kangaroo
tracks

star

meeting place

traveling paths
or heavy rain

running water
connecting
two waterholes

man

Witchetty grub

possum tracks

boomerang

snake

spear

cloud, rainbow,
sandhill, or cliff

people sitting

THE DAWNING OF ABORIGINAL ART APPRECIATION

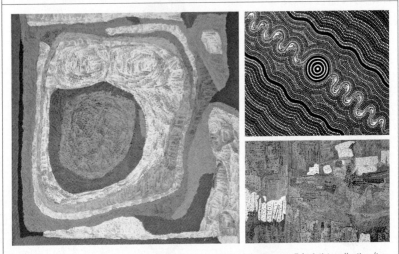

(left) Contemporary painting done in earth tones by a member of the Papunya Tula Artists collective; (top right) artwork from the Warlukurlangu Artists Aboriginal Corporation; (bottom right) Papunya Tula artwork.

IN THE BEGINNING...

It took a long time for Aboriginal art to gain the recognition it enjoys today. Australia's first European colonists, who began arriving in the late 18th century, saw the complex indigenous cultures it encountered as primitive, and believed that, as "nomads," Aboriginals had no claim to the land. Consequently, expansion into tribal lands went unchecked; during the 19th and early 20th centuries, most Aboriginals were forced onto white-owned cattle stations and missionary outposts.

Aboriginal land rights weren't formally acknowledged until 1976, when the first legislation was passed granting claim of title to natives with "traditional association" to the land. This watershed decision (called the Aboriginal Land Rights Act) allowed for the establishment of tribal land councils, which—in partnership with the Australian government—today manage many of the country's national parks and sacred ancient sites.

BREAKING GROUND

The growing awareness of Aboriginal heritage brought with it an increased interest in indigenous art. Before the 1970s, there had been only one celebrated Aboriginal artist in Australia—Albert Namatjira, who grew up on a Lutheran mission in Hermannsburg (in what is now the Northern Territory). In the 1930s, Namatjira studied under a white Australian artist and learned to paint sophisticated watercolor landscapes. Though these had almost nothing in common with traditional indigenous artworks, they won Namatjira enormous fame (by the 1950s, he was listed in *Who's Who*)

Curators often provide relevant historical context.

which reinforced an idea that was already burgeoning in the country: that Aboriginal creativity should receive the same attention and scholarship as non-Aboriginal forms of art.

ABORIGINAL ART CENTERS

Perhaps the single most significant event in modern Aboriginal art history occurred in 1973, with the formation of the Aboriginal Arts Board. The advent of this agency, as part of the government-funded Australia Council for the Arts, heralded a new level of respect for indigenous art. Its aim was to establish a standardized support system for Aboriginal artists through grant money.

But early board members (who came from both white and Aboriginal backgrounds) found this to be another challenge. Aboriginal artists were scattered all over the continent, many of them in isolated, far-flung camps surrounded by vast desert or impenetrable rainforests. How was the organization to find these artists, decide which of them deserved funds, and then dispense those funds in an organized way?

The solution was to set up art centers at specific Aboriginal settlements around

Renouned artist David Malangi, Central Arnhem Land

the country—helmed by art-industry specialists who could both cultivate connections with local artists and manage their nuts-and-bolts requirements (like arranging for deliveries of art supplies, and for transport of finished artworks to exhibitors and buyers).

The plan worked, and is still working. There are some 50 Aboriginal art centers in Australia today (most in the Northern Territory and Western Australia), and they collectively represent more than a thousand artists. These centers are the conduit by which most modern Aboriginal works get to art dealers—and then on to galleries, museums, auction houses, and private collectors.

PAPUNYA TULA

Brenda Nungarrayi Lynch, well-known Western Desert artist

The founding members of the Aboriginal Arts Board were inspired by the example of a particular Northern Territory desert settlement, Papunya Tula. Here, with the help of a white Australian art teacher, residents had begun to create and then sell "Dreaming paintings" (what are known today as dot paintings) to nearby galleries. By 1972, the community had established its own thriving and successful art collective, Papunya Tula Artists.

Today Papunya Tula Artists (which has never been government-subsidized) is the most famous Aboriginal art center in the country. The highly acclaimed dot paintings of its artists have hung in New York's Metropolitan Museum of Art and Paris's Musée du Quai Branly; their annual dollar sales are in the millions.

ABORIGINAL ART TODAY

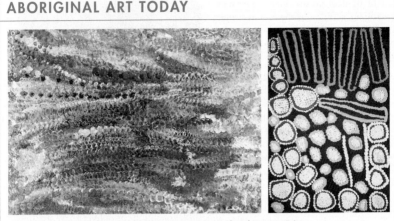

(left) Art by Emily Kame Kngwarreye, Utopia Central Australia; (right) Papunya Tula

Over the past 30 years, the art world's regard for Aboriginal works has sky-rocketed—not just in Australia, but all over the world. Ancient etchings and modern dot paintings now hang in museums from London's British to the Chicago Art Institute; gallerists and art dealers vie to represent rising Aboriginal art stars; and many artists who got their start at art centers in the 1980s (such as Dorothy Napangardi, Michael Nelson Tjakamarra, and Paddy Stewart Tjapaljarri) are near-celebrities today. A few of these pioneers of the modern Aboriginal art movement (like Rover Thomas and David Malangi) were in their seventies and eighties by the time their canvases began decorating exhibit halls and commanding six-figure auction bids.

Some of Australia's most celebrated Aboriginal artists, though, never got to see just how popular their work became. Clifford "Possum" Tjapaltjarri, for example, whose painting *Warlugulong* sold at a Sotheby's auction in 2007 for $2.4 million—the highest price ever paid for a piece of Aboriginal art—died five years beforehand. And Emily Kame Kngwarreye died in 1996, a dozen years before the National Museum of Australia mounted a huge solo exhibition of her work.

The new generation of Aboriginal artists faces its own set of obstacles. The appetite among art dealers for a steady supply of works to sell has led some of them to cut exploitative deals directly with artists (rather than working through the relative safety net of art centers). Other opportunists have mass-produced paintings and then sold them as "authentic"—thus tainting the integrity of the real Aboriginal art market.

But even these problems, unsavory though they are, can be seen from a certain angle as signs of positive change. It was only decades ago, after all, that the phrase "Aboriginal artist" seemed oxymoronic for many Australians. Today, those "primitive" assemblages of lines, circles, and dots account for almost 75 percent of the country's art sales. They have, in effect, helped put Australia on the map.

Today, symbols might be just half the story: colors can range from calm and subdued to bright and vibrant.

TIPS FOR WHERE AND HOW TO BUY ART

The most easily accessible sources for buying Aboriginal art are galleries. When considering a purchase, ascertain the art's authenticity and ethicality. The Australian Indigenous Art Trade Association recommends asking:

■ Is the artwork documented with a certificate of authenticity from a reputable source, or by photos of the artist with the art?

■ How did the artwork get to the gallery? Is the artist represented by a recognized art center, cooperative, or respected dealer?

■ Is it clear that the artist was treated fairly and paid a fair price for putting the artwork on the market?

MUSEUM AND GALLERY COLLECTIONS

Australia has hundreds of galleries and museums at least partially devoted to Aboriginal artworks. Here are some of the best:

PERMANENT COLLECTIONS

The Australian Museum, Sydney
australianmuseum.net.au

The National Gallery of Australia, Canberra
nga.gov.au

Queensland Art Gallery, Brisbane
qag.qld.gov.au

National Gallery of Victoria, Melbourne
www.ngv.vic.gov.au

ROTATING EXHIBITIONS

Gallery Gondwana, Alice Springs
www.gallerygondwana.com.au

Aboriginal Fine Arts Gallery, Darwin
www.aaia.com.au

Gallery Gabrielle Pizzi, Melbourne
www.gabriellepizzi.com.au

WHEN TO GO

Australia is in the southern hemisphere, so the seasons are reversed. It's winter Down Under during the American and European summer.

The ideal time to visit the north, particularly the Northern Territory's Kakadu National Park, is early in the dry season (around May). Birdlife remains profuse on the drying floodplains, and waterfalls are still spectacular and accessible. The Dry (April–October) is also a good time to visit northern Queensland's beaches and rain forests. You can swim off the coast without fear of dangerous stinging box jellyfish, which infest ocean waters between November and March. In rain forests, heat and humidity are lower than later in the year, and crocodile viewing is at its prime, as the creatures tend to bask on riverbanks rather than submerge in the colder water.

During school holidays, Australians take to the roads in droves. The busiest period is mid-December to the end of January, which is the equivalent of the U.S. and British summer break.

Climate

Australia's climate is temperate in southern states, such as Victoria and Tasmania, particularly in coastal areas, and tropical in Australia's far north. The Australian summer north of the Tropic of Capricorn is a steam bath. From September through November (the Australian spring), or from February through April (late summer–autumn), southern regions are generally sunny and warm, with only occasional rain in Sydney, Melbourne, and Adelaide. Perth and the south of Western Australia are at their finest in springtime, when wildflowers blanket the land.

Here are the average daily maximum and minimum temperatures for some major Australian cities.

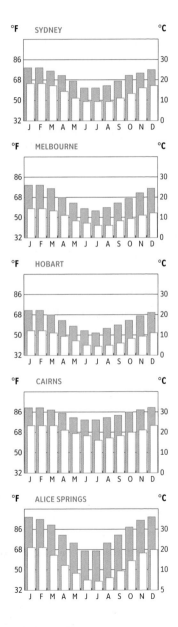

Sydney

WORD OF MOUTH

"You'll find there is no shortage of things to do and see in Sydney. It is a beautiful city, and in November, the weather is typically quite warm or hot so you'll be able to enjoy a few of the great beaches. There are also great places to see outside the city, like the Blue Mountains, the Southern Highlands, and the South Coast."

—RalphR

SYDNEY PLANNER

Tram and Train Information

Sydney Monorail links the city center, Darling Harbour, and Chinatown. The fare is A$4.80 one-way; the A$9.50 Day Pass is better value if you intend to use the monorail to explore. It runs every five minutes from 7 AM to 10 PM—and from 8 AM on Sunday. The Sydney Light Rail is an efficient link between Central Station, Darling Harbour, the Star City casino/entertainment complex, Sydney fish markets, and two inner western suburbs. The modern trams operate at 10- to 30-minute intervals 24 hours a day. One-way tickets are A$3.20; the A$9 Day Pass is good value. The main terminal for long-distance, intercity, and Sydney suburban trains is Central Station. There are a number of good-value train passes including the Backtracker Pass, which at A$232 (for 14 days) allows unlimited travel between Sydney and Melbourne (and back to Brisbane), a trip to the Blue Mountains, and one day's unlimited travel on Sydney buses, trains, and ferries. Sydney's suburban train network, City Rail, links the city with dozens of suburbs as well as Blue Mountains and South Coast towns. Tickets start from A$3.20 one-way and are sold at all City Rail stations.

Airport Information

Sydney's main airport is Kingsford–Smith International, 8 km (5 mi) south of the city. Kingsford–Smith's international (T1) and domestic terminals (T2 and T3) are 3 km (2 mi) apart. To get from one to the other, take a taxi for about A$12, use the Airport Shuttle Bus (called the TBus) for A$5.50, or take the Airport Link train, A$5. Tourism New South Wales has two information counters in the arrival level of the international terminal. One provides free maps and brochures and handles general inquiries. The other books accommodations and tours, and sells travel insurance. Both counters are open daily from approximately 6 AM to 11 PM. You can convert your money to Australian currency at the Travelex offices in both the arrival and departure areas.

Transfers

Airport Link rail travels to the city center in 15 minutes. A one-way fare is A$15.20. Taxis are available outside the terminal buildings. Fares are about A$35 to city and Kings Cross hotels. There are a couple of shuttle-bus services from the airport that drop passenger at hotels in the city center, Kings Cross, and Darling Harbour for around A$13 one-way and A$22 return.

When to Visit

The best times to visit Sydney are in late spring and early fall (autumn). The spring months of October and November are pleasantly warm, although the ocean is slightly cool for swimming. The summer months of December through February are typically hot and humid, February being the most humid. In the early-autumn months of March and April weather is typically stable and comfortable, outdoor city life is still in full swing, and the ocean is at its warmest. Even the coolest winter months of July and August typically stay mild and sunny, with average daily maximum temperatures in the low 60s.

Sydney By Boat

There is no finer introduction to the city than a trip aboard one of the commuter ferries that ply Sydney Harbour. The hub of the ferry system is Circular Quay, and ferries dock at the almost 30 wharves around the harbor between about 6 AM and 11:30 PM. One of the most popular sightseeing trips is the **Manly Ferry** (☎ 13–1500 ⊕ www.sydneyferries.info), a 30-minute journey from Circular Quay that provides glimpses of harborside mansions and the sandstone cliffs and bushland along the north shore. The one-way Manly Ferry fare is A$6.40, and the Manly Fast Ferry costs A$8.20.

A fun, fast, but somewhat expensive way to get around is by water taxi. (Circular Quay to Manly, for example, costs A$150 for four people.) One company, **Darling Harbour Water Taxis** (☎ 02/9211–7730 ⊕ www.watertaxis.net.au), runs a taxi shuttle between Darling Harbour and the Opera House for A$15 one-way, A$25 return. Mini-tours of the harbor in these little yellow taxi boats begin at A$15 per person for 30 minutes. **Captain Cook Cruises** (☎ 02/9206–1111 ⊕ www.captaincook.com.au/sydney) runs a number of good tours, but the best introduction to Sydney Harbour is Captain Cook's two-hour Coffee Cruise, which follows the southern shore to Watsons Bay, crosses to the north shore to explore Middle Harbour, and returns to Circular Quay.

Visitor Information

There are information kiosks at locations throughout the city, including Circular Quay (corner of Alfred and Pitt streets), Martin Place (at the corner of Elizabeth Street), and Town Hall (corner of George and Bathurst streets). The Sydney Harbour Foreshore Authority, which manages The Rocks, Darling Harbour, and other harbor precincts, also has an informative Web site.

The Sydney Visitor Centre is the major source of information for Sydney and New South Wales. There are two locations: The Rocks and Darling Harbour.

Contacts Sydney Harbour Foreshore Authority (☎ 02/9240–8500 ⊕ www.shfa.nsw.gov.au and ⊕ www.therocks.com). **Sydney Visitor Centre** (✉ Level 2, The Rocks Centre, Argyle and Playfair Sts., The Rocks ✉ 33 Wheat Rd., near IMAX Theatre, Darling Harbour ☎ 02/9240–8788 or 1800/067676 ⊕ www.sydneyvisitorcentre.com).

Bus, Car, and Taxi Information

Bus travel in Sydney is slow due to congested streets and the undulating terrain. Fares are calculated in sections; the minimum section fare (A$1.90) applies to trips in the inner-city area, such as between Circular Quay and Kings Cross, or from Bondi Junction railway station to Bondi Beach. Bus information can be found at ⊕ www.sydneybuses.info.

With the assistance of a good road map you shouldn't have too many problems driving in and out of Sydney, thanks to the decent freeway system. However, driving a car around Sydney is not recommended because of congestion and lack of parking space. If you decide to drive a rental car, it will cost between A$75 and A$85 per day. Local operator Bayswater Car Rental has cars from as little as A$27 per day (on a one-year-old vehicle. Campervans that sleep two people can be hired from new operator Jucy Rentals for A$55 a day and A$119 in the January peak season

Taxis charge A$1.80 per kilometer, plus a flag fall (hiring charge) of A$3.20. Extra charges apply to baggage weighing more than 55 pounds, telephone bookings, and Harbour Bridge and tunnel tolls. Fares are 20% higher between 10 PM and 6 AM, when the numeral "2" will be displayed in the tariff indicator on the meter.

Sightseeing Tours

Special-Interest Tours

The Sydney Explorer bus (☎ 13–1500 ⊕ www.sydney-buses.info), which makes a 35-km (22-mi) circuit of all the major attractions, is a great way to see the city. Ticket holders can hop on and off at any of the 27 stops. The bright red buses run every 20 minutes, beginning at 8:40 AM daily. The last bus departs from Circular Quay at 5:20 PM. If you choose to stay on board for the entire circuit trip, it takes two hours.

Harbour Jet (☎ 02/9698–2110 or 1300/887373 ⊕ www.harbourjet.com) runs high-speed jet-boat tours of the harbor, racing around at 75 KPH (47 MPH) and performing 270-degree spins. Trips range from 35 minutes to 1½ hours, and start at A$65 per person.

Mount'n Beach Safaris (☎ 02/9439–3010 ⊕ www.mountnbeachsafaris.com.au) is a four-wheel-drive tour operator offering soft adventures to the beautiful areas around Sydney. The Blue Mountains 4WD Wildlife Discovery tour provides an opportunity to see koalas and kangaroos, have morning tea in the bush, see the highlights of the Blue Mountains, have lunch at a historic pub, and return to Sydney for a performance at the Opera House.

A flight on **Sydney Seaplanes** (☎ 9388–1978 or 1300/732752 ⊕ www.seaplanes.com.au) is a wonderful way to see Sydney's sights and soar over beaches. Short flights taking in the harbor, Bondi Beach, and Manly cost from A$160 per person. The seaplanes take off from Rose Bay.

BridgeClimb (☎ 02/8274–7777 ⊕ www.bridgeclimb.com) is a unique tour that affords the ultimate view of the harbor and city center from Sydney Harbour Bridge. The hugely popular tours take 3½ hours and cost from A$198 per person. Another option is the Discovery Climb, which takes climbers within the bridge's structure on their way to the top. Tours depart from 5 Cumberland Street, The Rocks.

Easyrider Motorbike Tours (☎ 02/9247–2477 or 1300/882065 ⊕ www.easyrider.com.au) conducts exciting chauffeur-driven (you ride as a passenger) Harley-Davidson tours to the city's landmarks, and to the Blue Mountains and rural areas. A two-hour tour is A$190 per person; full-day excursions start at about A$400.

Bonza Bikes (☎ 02/9247–8800 ⊕ www.bonzabiketours.com) lets you see the best Sydney sights without having to worry about heavy traffic. The half-day Classic Sydney Tour cruises past the Opera House, winds around the harbor, and cycles through the Royal Botanic Gardens. Trips start from A$89 for a half day (bike and helmet included).

The **Aboriginal Heritage Tour** (☎ 02/9231–8134 ⊕ www.rbgsyd.nsw.gov.au) (A$25) is a tour of the Royal Botanic Gardens' display of plants that were growing before Europeans arrived on Sydney's shores in 1788. An Aboriginal guide explains the plants and their uses, and introduces visitors to Aboriginal bush foods.

You can go whale-watching from Sydney Harbour with **Bass and Flinders Cruises** (☎ 02/9583–1199 ⊕ www.whalewatchingsydney.net) and **Captain Cook Cruises**. Boats leave from mid-May to early December, venturing a few miles outside Sydney Heads.

Discounts and Deals

For the price of admission to two or three main attractions, the **SmartVisit Card** (☎ 1300/661711 ⊕ www.seesydney-card.com) gets you into 40 Sydney sights and attractions—including the Opera House, Sydney Aquarium, and Koala Park Sanctuary. Several different cards are available, including single-day and weekly versions. Some cards can even include public transportation. Prices start at A$75 for a single-day adult card without transportation. Cards are available from the Sydney Visitor Centre at The Rocks.

A **SydneyPass** (☎ 13–1500 ⊕ www.sydneypass.info) is a good value if you have limited time and the will to travel on public transportation. The pass allows unlimited travel on public buses, harbor ferries, and most suburban train services. It also includes the AirportLink rail service, the Sydney Explorer and Bondi Explorer buses, and any of the three sightseeing cruises operated by the State Transit Authority. A three-day pass is A$115; five-day, A$150; seven-day, A$170. Purchase passes from the Tourism New South Wales counter on the ground floor of the international airport terminal or from the driver of any Explorer bus.

A **TravelPass** (☎ 13–1500 ⊕ www.131500.com.au) allows unlimited travel aboard buses, ferries, and trains (but not the light-rail or monorail systems) within designated areas of the city for a week or more. Another option is the weeklong Red TravelPass (A$38), which covers the city and eastern suburbs and inner-harbor ferries. (Ferries to Manly and Sydney Olympic Park cost extra.) TravelPasses are available from railway and bus stations and from most newsagents (newsstands) on bus routes. Contact the **Transport Info Line** (☎ 13–1500 ⊕ www.sydneybuses.info).

Hotel and Restaurant Costs

DINING AND LODGING PRICE CATEGORIES (IN AUSTRALIAN DOLLARS)

	¢	$	$$	$$$	$$$$
Restaurants	under A$25	A$25–A$35	A$36–A$45	A$46–A$65	over A$65
Hotels	under A$150	A$150–A$200	A$201–A$300	A$301–A$450	over A$450

Restaurant prices are based on the median main-course price at dinner. Hotel prices are for two people in a standard double room in high season, excluding service and tax (Goods and service tax [GST] is 10 percent).

Walking Tours

The **Rocks Walking Tours** (⊠ 23 Playfair St., The Rocks ☎ 02/9247-6678 ⊕ www.rockswalkingtours.com.au) introduce you to Sydney's first European settlement, with an emphasis on the buildings and personalities of the convict period. The 1½-hour tour costs A$30. Tours leave weekdays at 10:30, 12:30, and 2:30 (in January 10:30 and 2:30 only), and weekends at 11:30 and 2.

The Rocks' dark alleyways can be scary, and The Rocks **Ghost Tours** (☎ 1300/731971 ⊕ www.ghosttours.com.au) make sure people are suitably spooked, as the guides, dressed in long black cloaks and carrying lanterns, regale them with stories of the murders and other nasty goings-on in the early days of the colony. Tours depart nightly at 6.45 (April–September) and 7:45 (October–March) from Cadman's Cottage; A$36.

You can literally drink in Sydney's history during The **Rocks Pub Tour** (☎ 02/9240-8788 or 1800/067676 ⊕ www.therockspubtour.com), where you wander the narrow streets with a guide and stop in for drinks at three pubs. The 1¾-hour tours depart from Cadman's Cottage on George Street (near the Museum of Contemporary Art) at 5 PM daily (except public holidays, New Year's Eve, and St. Patrick's Day); A$36.50.

TOP SYDNEY SIGHTS

Ringed with world-class beaches and some of the most spectacular nature on the continent, Sydney is a the continent's cosmopolitan hub, and home to two renowned architectural icons —the Opera House and the Harbour Bridge.

No one ever tires of Sydney's magnificent nature and its two landmark structures. The Sydney Opera House is both awe-inspiring and utterly welcoming. Its stunning "sail" design was the brainchild of Danish architect Joern Utzon, who won an international design competition from 233 submissions. Sydney Harbour Bridge is equally loved especially when the city comes out to see the fireworks explode over it for New Year's Eve celebrations. Opened in 1932, it can experienced by car or train, but we recommend taking it slower and walking across it. Adventure seekers can even climb up and over the arch to the top. Sydney Harbour's shoreline is dotted with large swaths of national park perfect for hiking and picnics. On the north side of the harbor is the ultimate zoo with a view, Taronga Park.

NEED A BREAK

The historic Harbour View Hotel is THE place to sit with a drink and watch the folks in their special jumpsuits begin their climb up the Sydney Harbour Bridge. The pub is so close to the bridge that you feel you could reach out and touch it! The bar menu includes snacks of salt-and-pepper calamari and chicken schnitzel sandwiches (¢); the more upscale restaurant menu features sizzling steaks, slow-cooked lamb shanks, and decadent desserts ($). It's near the south pylon of the bridge, at 18 Lower Fort Street and Cumberland Street (☎ 02/9254–4111 ⊕ www.harbourview. com.au).

FODOR'S CHOICE SIGHTS

2

SYDNEY OPERA HOUSE
Sydney's most famous landmark, listed as a World Heritage site in 2007, had such a long and troubled construction phase that it's almost a miracle it was ever completed. Architect Joern Utzon's concepts were dazzling, and so far ahead of their time that the soaring "sails" that formed the walls and roof could not be built by existing technology.

SYDNEY HARBOUR BRIDGE
Despite its nickname "the coat hanger," the bridge has a fond place in all Sydneysiders' hearts. It's opening on March 19, 1932 (during the height of the Great Depression), lifted the spirits of citizens and provided some very unexpected theatre. As NSW Premier Jack Lang waited to cut the ribbon, Captain Francis de Groot, a member of the paramilitary New Guard, galloped up on his horse, drew his sword, and slashed the ribbon first.

SYDNEY HARBOUR NATIONAL PARK
This national park is a collection of separate areas of native bush land flanking both sides of the harbor and dotted with walking tracks. Miles of paths wind through the bush and up and down rocky outcrops and headlands. One of the best walks is the 9.5-km (6-mi) Manly Scenic Walkway, which travels from Manly Beach to the Spit Bridge via pockets of rainforest, several little beaches, ancient Aboriginal sites, and the historic Grotto Point Lighthouse.

TARONGA ZOO
Sydney's major wildlife sanctuary occupies one of the most prized positions on the north shore of Sydney Harbour. Daily shows, such as the seal and the birds of prey show, are included in the admission price of A$41. A Zoo Pass, using Sydney Ferries, is an excellent deal at A$48.

TIMING

THE OPERA HOUSE AND BRIDGE
A guided Opera House tour takes one hour, while the backstage tour, complete with a full breakfast, takes two hours. If you're exploring sans guided tour, allot about 30 minutes to walk around the outside of the building and into some of the interior areas. The two sites are about 1 km (½ mi) apart, which is a leisurely 30- to 45-minute stroll. It takes three hours to do the BridgeClimb tour and around 30 minutes if you do your own walk across the Harbour Bridge from the south to the north side.

THE HARBOR
Sydney Harbor and its many sites are best visited in spring (September–November) and autumn (March–May). Summers can be hot and sticky and crowded with kids on school break. Winters (June–August) can be mild, and you may even find some lunch bargains at nice restaurants. Midweek visits are always recommended.

DINING ALFRESCO

Grab an outdoor table by the harbor or beach—in an elegant restaurant or beachside burger shack—and savor all that Sydney has to offer; dining alfresco is the Aussie version of heaven!

Two Sydney Center areas are chock-full of outstanding outdoor dining spots: the Overseas Passenger Terminal where cruise ships dock, and East Circular Quay on the concourse leading from the ferry terminal to the Opera House. They're situated almost smack opposite each other and are packed with indoor-outdoor upscale eateries. For a cheap snack and an amazing view, stop by the Boathouse Café and Restaurant in Nielsen Park.

Another favorite option is one of the many casual cafés around Bondi and Manly Beach. The Woolloomooloo Finger Wharf has several alfresco restaurants, the most popular—and a celebrity haunt—being Otto.

The Middle Harbor beach of Balmoral has some lovely cafés and restaurants with great views out to the Sydney Heads.

DRINKING ALFRESCO

Everyone loves The Rocks on a sunny Sunday afternoon. Check out the sensational harbor views from the rooftop bar of the **Glenmore Hotel** (✉ *96 Cumberland St.* ☎ *02/9247-4794*).

Manly Wharf Hotel (✉ *Manly Wharf, East Esplanade* ☎ *02/9977-1266*) has four bars with the Jetty Bar is perched right on the water. Outside heaters make it perfect even for winter drinks.

Watsons Bay Hotel (✉ *1 Military Rd.* ☎ *02/9337-5444*)has a huge outdoor drinking area with brilliant views.

2

TOP SPOTS

✕ **Aquarium Bistro & Bar.** The view and the price are just right at this popular casual weekend bistro and bar at Coogee Beach. Housed in the heritage-listed Beach Palace Hotel, the bistro draws a younger crowd with the sensational views of Coogee beach, as well as the burgers, king prawn chili spaghetti, and an array of sharing plates, known as boards. ✉ *169 Dolphin St., Coogee* ☎ *02/9664–2900* ⊕ *www.beach-palacehotel.com.au* ⊟ *MC, V* ⊘ *Closed Mon.–Thurs.*

✕ **Pellegrini's Seafood Restaurant.** Location, location, location are the draw at this quaint Italian restaurant. Perched right on the harbor at west Balmain you'll have a unique view of Cockatoo Island and all the comings and goings of water traffic. Its laid back café style and million dollar views. Barramundi fillets are a popular choice, as is the Atlantic salmon and the soft-shell crab. ✉ *107 Elliot St., Balmain* ☎ *02/9810–4551* ⊕ *No Web* ⊟ *Credit cards* ⊘ *Closed Mon.–Tues., no dinner Sun.*

✕ **Nielsen Park Restaurant and Café.** A favorite local hangout, this is a great place to laze, picnic in the park, or swim year round in the roped-off harbor pool. The café and restaurant are housed in a heritage 1914 sandstone building. The crab cakes with sweet ginger glaze are a great starter, followed nicely by pan-fried snapper or ocean trout fillet with zucchini flower. ✉ *Nielsen Park, Greycliffe Ave., Vaucluse* ☎ *02/9337–7333* ⊕ *www.nielsenpark.com.au* ⊟ *DC, MC, V* ⊘ *No dinner in the café; restaurant closed Mon.–Thurs.*

✕ **Pilu at Freshwater.** If you love traditional Italian food, and enjoy dining right on the beach, then this is the place. Chef Giovanni Pilu's specialty is Sardinian fare and his signature dish is a feast that takes several hours to slow-cook—oven-roasted roasted suckling pig, served on the bone with traditional farm house suckling pig sausages and condiments. ✉ *On The Beach, Moore Rd., Harbord* ☎ *02/9938–3331* ⊕ *www.piluatfreshwater.com.au* ⊟ *AE, DC, MC, V.*

DINING BY CUISINE

CHINESE
BBQ King ¢
Billy Kwong $
Golden Century ¢–$

FRENCH
Bécasse $$
Bistro Moncur $–$$
Forty One $$$$
Mere Catherine $$
Marque $$–$$$

ITALIAN
Buon Ricordo $$$
Icebergs Dining Room and Bar $$
North Bondi Italian Food ¢–$

JAPANESE
Galileo $$$$

MALAYSIAN
The Malaya ¢–$

MODERN AUSTRALIAN
Altitude $$
The Deck $
Quay $$$
Tetsuya's $$$$
Rockpool $$$$
Swell $
Wharf Restaurant $

SEAFOOD
Fishface ¢–$
Nick's Bondi Beach
Pavilion ¢–$
Pier $$$

Updated
by Caroline
Gladstone

Sydney belongs to the exclusive club of cities that generate excitement. At the end of a marathon flight there's renewed vitality in the cabin as the plane circles the city, where thousands of yachts are suspended on the dark water and the sails of the Opera House glisten in the distance. Blessed with dazzling beaches and a sunny climate, Sydney is among the most beautiful cities on the planet.

With 4 million people, Sydney is the biggest and most cosmopolitan city in Australia. A wave of immigration in the 1950s has seen the Anglo-Irish immigrants who made up the city's original population joined by Italians, Greeks, Turks, Lebanese, Chinese, Vietnamese, Thais, and Indonesians. This intermingling has created a cultural vibrancy and energy—and a culinary repertoire—that was missing only a generation ago.

Sydneysiders embrace their harbor with a passion. Indented with numerous bays and beaches, Sydney Harbour is the presiding icon for the city, and urban Australia. Captain Arthur Phillip, commander of the 11-ship First Fleet, wrote in his diary when he first set eyes on the harbor on January 26, 1788: "We had the satisfaction of finding the finest harbor in the world."

Although a visit to Sydney is an essential part of an Australian experience, the city is no more representative of Australia than Los Angeles is of the United States. Sydney has joined the ranks of the great cities whose characters are essentially international. What Sydney offers is style, sophistication, and great looks; an exhilarating prelude to the continent at its back door.

EXPLORING SYDNEY

Sydney is a giant, stretching nearly 80 km (50 mi) from top to bottom and about 70 km (43 mi) across. The harbor divides the city into northern and southern halves, with most of the headline attractions on the south shore. Most travelers spend their time on the harbor's south side, within an area bounded by Chinatown in the south, Harbour Bridge in the north, Darling Harbour to the west, and the beaches and coastline to the east. North of Harbour Bridge lie the important commercial center of North Sydney and leafy but somewhat bland suburbs. Ocean beaches, Taronga Zoo, Ku-ring-gai Chase National Park,

WORD OF MOUTH

"Five days in Sydney will give you a good opportunity to explore the city, its surrounds and perhaps even a day or so somewhere a little further afield. You could rent a car, see the Blue Mountains, some lovely country towns, and wine country."   —Bokhara2

and great shopping in the village of Mosman are the most likely reasons to venture north of the harbor. Within a few hours drive of Sydney are the World Heritage–listed Blue Mountains and the renowned Hunter Valley vineyards. Although both these spots are worthy of an overnight stay, they're also close enough to visit on day trips from the city.

SYDNEY HARBOUR

Numbers in the text correspond to numbers in the margin and on the Sydney Harbour map.

On a bright sunny day there's no more magical sight than glistening Sydney Harbour. The white sails of the Opera House are matched by the dozens of sailing boats skimming across the blue expanse. It's both a hive of activity and blissfully peaceful: It's easy to get away from the bustle in one of this area's many remote little corners. Explore by taking a ferry, walking across the bridge, or hiking around its native bushland edges. But whatever you do, get up close and enjoy the view.

GETTING HERE AND AROUND

Sydney is well served by public transport. Buses travel from a base in Circular Quay through the city center to the inner surburbs of Kings Cross, Darlinghurst, and Surry Hills and to the eastern suburb beaches. Trains travel from Central Station through the city on a circle line (calling at Circular Quay and Town Hall), out to Bondi Junction, over the bridge to the north shore and out to the west. Ferries leave the Quay for Manly, Balmain, Darling Harbor, and other suburbs, while the new free 555 shuttle bus does a circuit through the city, calling at the main sites.

TOP ATTRACTIONS

❷ Farm Cove. The original convict-settlers established their first gardens on this bay's shores, now home to the **Royal Botanic Gardens.** The enterprise was not a success: the soil was too sandy for agriculture, and most of the crops fell victim to pests, marauding animals, and hungry convicts. The long seawall was constructed from the 1840s onward to enclose the previously swampy foreshore. ✛ *You can enter the Botanic Gardens through gates near the Opera House and in Macquarie Street. From the Opera House, turn right and walk along the harbor foreshore (the seawall will be on your left, the Botanic Gardens on your right). To enter the Macquarie Street gates, take a train to Martin Place railway*

GREAT ITINERARIES

You really need three days in Sydney to see the essential city center, while six days would give you time to explore the beaches and inner suburbs. A stay of 10 days would allow trips outside the city and give you time to explore a few of Sydney's lesser-known delights.

IF YOU HAVE 3 DAYS
Start with an afternoon Harbour Express Cruise for some of the best views of the city. Follow with a tour of The Rocks, the nation's birthplace, and take a sunset walk up onto the **Sydney Harbour Bridge**. The following day, take a Sydney Explorer tour to the famous **Sydney Opera House** and relax in the afternoon in the **Royal Botanic Gardens and Domain park**. On the third day, explore the city center, with another spectacular panorama from the **Sydney Tower**. Include a walk around Macquarie Street, a living reminder of Sydney's colonial history, and the contrasting experience of futuristic Darling Harbour, with its museums, aquarium, and cafés.

IF YOU HAVE 6 DAYS
Follow the three-day itinerary above, then visit Kings Cross, Darlinghurst, and Paddington on the fourth day. You could continue to **Bondi**, Australia's most famous beach. The next day, catch the ferry to **Manly** to visit its beach and the historic Quarantine Station. From here, take an afternoon bus tour to the northern beaches, or return to the city to shop or visit museums and galleries. Options for the last day include a trip to a wildlife or national park, **Taronga Zoo**, or the **Sydney Olympic Park** west of the city.

IF YOU HAVE 10 DAYS
Follow the six-day itinerary above, and then travel beyond the city by rental car or with an organized tour. Take day trips to the Blue Mountains, Hunter Valley, **Ku-ring-gai Chase National Park**, the Hawkesbury River, or the historic city of Parramatta to Sydney's west. Or travel on the Bondi Explorer bus to **Vaucluse** or the charming harborside village of **Watsons Bay**. You could take a boat tour to the historic harbor island of **Fort Denison**, play a round of golf, or just shop or relax on the beach.

station, exit the station, turn left, and walk a few hundred yards down Macquarie Street.

🔟2 **Fort Denison.** For a brief time in the early days of the colony, convicts who committed petty offenses were kept on this harbor island, where they existed on such a meager diet that the island was named Pinchgut. Fortification of the island began in 1841, but was abandoned when cash ran out. It was finally completed in 1857, when fears of Russian expansion in the Pacific spurred the government on. Today the firing of the fort's cannon doesn't signal imminent invasion, but merely the hour—one o'clock. The National Parks and Wildlife Service runs half-hour tours at Fort Denison. You must purchase tickets from Cadman's Cottage and make your own way by ferry to the fort. ⊠ *110 George St., the Rocks, Sydney Harbour* ☎ *02/9247–5033* 💲 *A$27* ⊘ *Tours run daily at 12:15 and 2:30, additional tours Wed.–Sun. at 10:45.*

"Hands down, these giraffes have the best view." —photo by Carly Miller Fodors.com member.

7 Quarantine Station. From the 1830s onward, ship passengers who arrived with contagious diseases were isolated on this outpost in the shadow of North Head until pronounced free of illness. You can access the station as part of a guided tour, and now stay overnight in the newly opened B&B and cottage accommodation known as Q Station (2). There are day tours and three different evening ghost tours (the station reputedly has its fair share of specters) that depart from the visitors center at the Quarantine Station. Tours are led by rangers from the National Parks and Wildlife Service, and involve a fair bit of walking, so good shoes are a must. Reservations are essential. ⊠ *North Head, Manly* ✢ *Take the ferry to Manly from Circular Quay, then bus 135 to the site. Or catch Q Station's complimentary shuttle (Wed.–Sun. only) near Manly Wharf. Call Q Station for shuttle details* ☎ *02/9976–6220* ⊕ *www.q-station. com.au* ✉ *Day tour A\$35, ghost tours A\$34–A\$44* ☉ *General tours are given Fri.–Sun. Call ahead for times. Adult ghost tours Wed., Thurs., and weekends 8 PM; family ghost tour Fri. and Sat. at 6:30 PM.*

8 Sydney Harbour National Park. This massive park is made up of 958 acres of separate foreshores and islands, most of them on the north side of the harbor. To see the best areas, put on your walking shoes and head out on the many well-marked trails. The Hermitage Foreshore Walk skirts through bushland around Vaucluse's Nielsen Park. On the north side of the harbor, Bradleys Head and Chowder Head Walk is a 5-km (3-mi) stroll that starts from Taronga Zoo Wharf. The most inspiring trail is the 9½-km (6-mi) Manly Scenic Walkway, which joins the Spit Bridge with Manly by meandering along sandstone headlands, small beaches, and pockets of rain forest, and past Aboriginal sites and the historic

Fodor's Choice
★

Grotto Point Lighthouse. From Cadman's Cottage, at The Rocks, you can take day tours of Fort Denison and Goat Island, which have interesting colonial buildings. From Circular Quay you can board a cruise to Shark Island on weekends. The other two islands in the harbor park—Rodd and Clark—are recreational reserves that can be visited with permission from the New South Wales National Parks and Wildlife Service. Visitors are allowed in small groups only, between 9 AM and sunset or until 8 PM in summer. There is no public transport. Access is via private vessel, a couple of water taxi operators, and licensed operators including Majestic Cruises and OZ Jet Boating Australia. Water taxi fares are around A$90 to A$120 for two people. A landing fee of A$7 is levied on each person, and this is paid to the NSW National Parks and Wildlife Service. Call ☎02/9246–5033 for more information.

> **WORD OF MOUTH**
>
> "I love Taronga zoo, it's in a beautiful location right on the Harbour and the ferry ride across is great. I particularly like the nocturnal house as well as the platypus and echidna viewing areas and the bird house. Just one cautionary note, avoid the zoo during the summer school holidays when the crowds make the experience fairly unpleasant." —Susan7

⑪ ★ ☾ Taronga Zoo. Sydney's zoo, in a natural bush area on the harbor's north shore, houses an extensive collection of Australian fauna, including everybody's favorite marsupial, the koala. The zoo has taken great care to create spacious enclosures that simulate natural habitats. The hillside setting is steep in parts, and a complete tour can be tiring, but you can use the map distributed free at the entrance gate to plan a leisurely route. The views of the harbor are stunning. Use of children's strollers (the basic model) is free. The best way to get here from the city is by ferry from Circular Quay or Darling Harbour. From Taronga Wharf a bus or the cable car will take you up the hill to the main entrance. The ZooPass, a combined ferry-zoo ticket (A$48) is available at Circular Quay. You can also stay overnight at the zoo in what's billed as the "wildest slumber party in town." The newly relaunched "Roar and Snore" program includes a night tour, two behind-the-scenes tours, drinks, dinner, breakfast, and luxury tent accommodation from A$216 per person. ⊠ *Bradleys Head Rd., Mosman* ☎ *02/9969–2777* ⊕ *www. zoo.nsw.gov.au* ⌖ *A$44* ☾ *Daily 9–5.*

▌ **NEED A BREAK?**

Boathouse Café and Restaurant, Nielsen Park (⊠ *Greycliffe Ave., Vaucluse* ☎ *02/9337-7333* ⊕ *www.nielsenpark.com.au*). Hikers completing the Hermitage Foreshore Walk can pull up a chair at the newly-refurbished Beach House Café and Restaurant at beautiful Nielsen Park, soak in fabulous harbor views, and watch the sailing boats. The casual café is open daily 8-6, serving coffees, breakfast, including treats such as blueberry pancakes, and light lunches such as BLTs and fish-and-chips. The upscale restaurant is open for weekend breakfast and lunch and Saturday dinner. Take the 325 bus from Circular Quay (which will be signposted to Watsons Bay) and tell the driver where you want to get off.

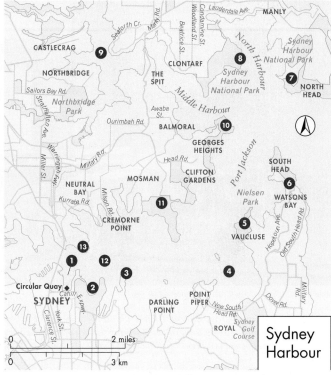

Sydney Harbour

❺ **Vaucluse.** The palatial homes in this glamorous harbor suburb provide a glimpse of Sydney's high society. The small beaches at Nielsen Park and Parsley Bay are safe for swimming and provide wonderful views. Both beaches are packed with families in summer. The suburb takes its name from the 1803 **Vaucluse House,** one of Sydney's most illustrious remaining historic mansions. The 15-room Gothic Revival house and its lush gardens, managed by the Historic Houses Trust, are open to the public. The tearooms, built in the style of an Edwardian conservatory, are popular spots for lunch and afternoon tea on weekends. The house is one of the stops on the Bondi Explorer bus. ⊠ *Wentworth Rd., Vaucluse* ⚓ *Take bus 325 from Circular Quay bus stand* ☎ *02/9388–7922* ⊕ *www.hht.nsw.gov.au* ✉ *A$8* ☾ *Fri.–Sun. 9:30–4; daily in Jan.*

WORTH NOTING

❸ **Garden Island.** Although it's still known as an "island," this promontory was connected with the mainland in 1942. During the 1941–45 War of the Pacific (WWII and a number of preceding conflicts), Australia's largest naval base and dockyard was a frontline port for Allied ships. Part of the naval base is now open to the public. Access to the site is via ferry from Circular Quay. ⚓ *You can take the ferry from Circular Quay to Watsons Bay and get off at Garden Island. No buses go directly to Garden Island. To walk, catch the train from Central or Town Hall*

The boardwalk around Sydney Cove on a typical sunny day.

to Kings Cross station, then walk all the way down either Macleay or Victoria streets toward the harbour (or north). At the very end of Victoria Street is a flight of stone steps that leads down to Woolloomooloo, near Garden Island.

⑬ Kirribilli. Residences in this attractive suburb opposite the city and Opera House have million-dollar views—and prices to match. Two of Sydney's most important mansions stand here. The more modest of the two is **Kirribilli House,** the official Sydney home of the prime minister and not open to the public. Next door and far more prominent is **Admiralty House**—the Sydney residence of the governor-general, the Queen's representative in Australia. This impressive residence is occasionally open for inspection. Both houses can be viewed during harbor cruises. ⊕ *Both Kirribilli and Admiralty House are at the harbor end of Kirribilli Avenue; to get there you can take a ferry from Circular Quay to either Kirribilli Wharf or Milson's Point Wharf, or take the train from Town Hall to Milson's Point Station. The No. 267 bus does a loop from McMahon's Point to North Sydney via Kirribilli. There is no public access to either of these grand houses.*

⑨ Middle Harbour. Except for the yachts moored in the sandy coves, the upper reaches of Middle Harbour are almost exactly as they were when the first Europeans set eyes on Port Jackson more than 200 years ago. Tucked away in idyllic bushland are tranquil suburbs just a short drive from the city. ⊕ *The focal point of Middle Harbour is Spit Bridge. To get there, take a train from either the Central or Town Hall station to Milson's Point then take Bus 229 to Spit Bridge. From Spit Bridge you can walk to Manly and view most of beautiful Middle Harbour.*

Middle Head. Despite its benign appearance today, Sydney Harbour once bristled with armaments. In the mid-19th century, faced with expansionist European powers hungry for new colonies, the authorities erected artillery positions on the headlands to guard harbor approaches. One of Sydney's newest open spaces, Headland Park, has opened on a former military base. A walking track winds past fortifications, tunnels, and heritage buildings, several of which are now used as cafés, including the Tea Room Gunners' Barracks. ✛ *Several buses travel from central Sydney to Mosman, Balmoral, and Chowder Bay, which are all suburbs within the Middle Head area and close to Headland Park. They include buses 244, 245, 246, and 247.*

NEED A
BREAK?

Housed in a beautiful sandstone building that served a number of military purposes for over 130 years, the **Tea Room Gunners Barracks** (✉ *202 Suakin Dr., Sydney Harbour* ☎ *02/8962–5900* ⊕ *www.thetearoom.com.au*) offers breathtaking views of the harbor and the surrounding gardens and bushland. Their high tea (A$35) is a great way to relax after scrambling around the armaments of Middle Head.

④ **Rose Bay.** This large bay was once a base for the Qantas flying boats that provided the only passenger air service between Australia and America and Europe. The last flying boat departed from Rose Bay in the 1960s, but the "airstrip" is still used by floatplanes on scenic flights connecting Sydney with the Hawkesbury River and the central coast. It's a popular place for joggers, who pound the pavement of New South Head Road, which runs along the bay. ✛ *Take Bus 325 from Circular Quay, or take the ferry to Watsons Bay (it stops at Rose Bay).*

① **Sydney Cove.** Bennelong Point and the Sydney Opera House to the east and Circular Quay West and The Rocks to the west enclose this cove, which was named after Lord Sydney, the British home secretary at the time the colony was founded. The settlement itself was to be known as New Albion, but the name never caught on. Instead, the city took its name from this tiny bay. ✛ *Take the train from Central or Town Hall to Circular Quay railway station; or take any number of buses to Circular Quay from all over Sydney. Ferries travel to Circular Quay from many different parts of Sydney, including the north side of the harbor, Rose Bay, Balmain, and Parramatta. Circular Quay is right in the middle of Sydney Cove.*

⑦ **Watsons Bay.** Established as a military base and fishing settlement in the colony's early years, Watsons Bay is a charming suburb, with a popular waterfront pub, that has held on to its village ambience despite the exorbitant prices paid for tiny cottages here. Unlike Watsons Bay's tranquil harbor side, the side that faces the ocean is dramatic and tortured, with the raging sea dashing against the sheer, 200-foot sandstone cliffs of The Gap. When the sun shines, the 15-minute cliff-top stroll along South Head Walkway between The Gap and the **Macquarie Lighthouse** affords some of Sydney's most inspiring views. Convict-architect Francis Greenway (jailed for forgery) designed the original lighthouse here, Australia's first, in 1818. ✉ *Old South Head Rd., Vaucluse* ✛ *To reach Watsons Bay either take the ferry or buses 324 or 325 from Circular Quay. Bus 324 goes past the lighthouse.*

THE ROCKS AND SYDNEY HARBOUR BRIDGE

Numbers in the text correspond to numbers in the margin and on the Rocks and Sydney Harbour Bridge map.

The Rocks is the birthplace not just of Sydney, but of modern Australia. Here the 11 ships of the First Fleet, the first of England's 800-plus ships carrying convicts to the penal colony, dropped anchor in 1788. This stubby peninsula enclosing the western side of Sydney Cove became known simply as the Rocks.

Most of the architecture here dates from the Victorian era, by which time Sydney had become a thriving port. Warehouses lining the waterfront were backed by a row of tradesmen's shops, banks, and taverns, and above them, ascending Observatory Hill, rose a tangled mass of alleyways lined with the cottages of seamen and wharf laborers. By the late 1800s The Rocks was a rough and squalid area. Conditions were so bad that as late as 1900 the black plague swept through The Rocks, prompting the government to offer a bounty for dead rats in an effort to exterminate their disease-carrying fleas.

Today The Rocks is hardly the ghetto it once was. Since the 1970s it's been transformed into a hot spot of cafes, restaurants, and quaint boutiques, and it's one of the city's most popular destinations. And because it's Sydney's most historic area, the old architecture has been beautifully maintained.

GETTING HERE AND AROUND

You can take the train or any number of buses to Circular Quay and then walk to The Rocks. From Bondi and Paddington, take the 380, 382, or 333 bus to Circular Quay via Elizabeth Street. From Clovelly take the 339 bus all the way to The Rocks, via Central Station. The 431, 432, and 433 buses travel the inner western suburbs and terminate in The Rocks. Once there, the best way to get around is on foot—there are quite a few sandstone steps and narrow alleyways to navigate, and your feet are your best friends.

TOP ATTRACTIONS

❿ Argyle Cut. Argyle Street, which links Argyle Place and George Street, is dominated by the Argyle Cut and its massive walls. In the days before the Cut (tunnel) was made, the sandstone ridge here was a major barrier to traffic crossing between Circular Quay and Millers Point. In 1843 convict work gangs hacked at the sandstone with hand tools

MOVIES UNDER THE STARS

The best place for outdoor movies is at Mrs. Macquarie's Point (⊕ www.stgeorgeopenair.com.au). Films are screened at the Royal Botanic Gardens from mid-January to mid-February. Every now and then a flying fox whizzes past the huge screen that hangs over Sydney Harbour. Centennial Park (⊕ www.moonlight.com.au) is where film buffs relax on rugs or rented beanbags. It's the only time you're allowed in the park after sunset. Movies run from early January to mid-March. Bondi Beach (⊕ www.bondiopenair.com.au) screens movies at the 1928 Pavilion in summer.

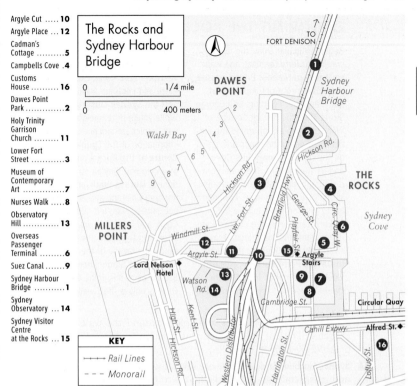

for 2½ years before the project was abandoned due to lack of progress. Work restarted in 1857, when drills, explosives, and paid labor completed the job. On the lower side of the Cut an archway leads to the **Argyle Stairs,** which begin the climb from Argyle Street up to the Sydney Harbour Bridge walkway. There's a spectacular view from the South East Pylon.

4 **Campbell's Cove.** Robert Campbell was a Scottish merchant who is sometimes referred to as the "father of Australian commerce." Campbell broke the stranglehold that the British East India Company exercised over seal and whale products, which were New South Wales's only exports in those early days. The cove's atmospheric sandstone **Campbell's Storehouse** (⊠ *Campbell's Storehouse, 7–27 Circular Quay W, The Rocks* ☎ *No phone*),built from 1838 onward, now houses waterside restaurants. The pulleys that were used to hoist cargoes still hang on the upper level of the warehouses. The cove is also the mooring for Sydney's fully operational tall ships—including the HMAV *Bounty,* an authentic replica of the original 18th-century vessel—which conducts theme cruises around the harbor.

11 **Holy Trinity Garrison Church.** Every morning, redcoats would march to this 1840 Argyle Place church from Dawes Point Battery (now Dawes Point Park), and it became commonly known as the Garrison Church.

EXPLORING THE ROCKS ON FOOT

Begin at Circular Quay, the lively waterfront ferry terminal, and walk west toward Harbour Bridge, passing the Museum of Contemporary Art, and climb the few stairs into George Street. Pass the historic Fortune of War pub, then as you round the corner head down the sandstone stairs on the right to **Campbells Cove** and its warehouses. The waterfront restaurants and cafés are pleasant spots for a drink or meal. Continue along Hickson Road toward the Sydney Harbour Bridge until you are directly beneath the bridge's massive girders. Walk under the bridge to **Dawes Point Park** for excellent views of the harbor, including the Opera House and the small island of Fort Denison. Now turn your back on the bridge and walk south and west, via Lower Fort Street. Explore Argyle Place and continue walking south, past the **Sydney Observatory.** While you're in the neighborhood, be sure to pick up brochures and city information at the **Sydney Visitor Centre at the Rocks**, on the corner of Argyle and Playfair streets. Turn right at **Nurses Walk**, another of the area's historic and atmospheric backstreets, then left into Surgeons Court, and left again onto George Street. On the left is the handsome sandstone facade of the former Rocks Police Station, now a crafts gallery. From this point, Circular Quay is only a short walk away.

As the regimental plaques and colors around the walls testify, the church still retains a close military association. ⊠ *Argyle Pl., The Rocks* ☎ *02/9247–1268* ⊙ *Daily 9–5.*

1   **Sydney Harbour Bridge.** There are several ways to experience the bridge

Fodor's Choice   and its spectacular views. The first is to follow the walkway from its
★   access point near the Argyle Stairs to the **South East Pylon** (☎ *02/9240–1100*). This structure houses a display on the bridge's construction, and you can climb the 200 steps to the lookout and its unbeatable harbor panorama. The fee is A$9.50 and the display is open daily 10–5. Another (more expensive) option—not for those afraid of heights—is the **BridgeClimb tour** (☎ *02/8274–7777* ⊕ *www.pylonlookout.com.au*), which takes you on a guided walking tour to the very top of Harbour Bridge, 439 feet above sea level. The cost is A$198 per person. The third option is to walk to the midpoint of the bridge to take in the views free of charge, but be sure to take the eastern footpath, which overlooks the Sydney Opera House. Access is via the stairs on Cumberland Street, close to the Shangri-La Hotel.

NEED A
BREAK?   While in the west end of Argyle Place, consider the liquid temptations of the **Lord Nelson** (⊠ *19 Kent St., at Argyle St., Millers Point, the Rocks* ☎ *02/9251–4044* ⊕ *www.lordnelson.com.au*), which with at least one other contender claims to be Sydney's oldest hotel. (It has been licensed to serve alcohol since 1841). The sandstone pub has its own brewery on the premises. One of its specialties is Quayle Ale, named after the former U.S. vice president, who "sank a schooner" (drank a beer) here during his 1989 visit to Australia.

WORTH NOTING

⑫ **Argyle Place.** With all the traditional requirements of an English green—a pub at one end, a church at the other, and grass in between—this charming enclave in the suburb of Millers Point is unusual for Sydney. Argyle Place is lined with 19th-century houses and cottages on its northern side and overlooked by Observatory Hill to the south.

WORD OF MOUTH

"Sydney is special and worth your time. If you are adventurous, take the BridgeClimb on Sydney Harbour Bridge. Try to take a side trip to either the Hunter Valley wine area or the Blue Mountains." —lcls

⑤ **Cadman's Cottage.** Sydney's oldest building, completed in 1816, has a history that outweighs its modest dimensions. John Cadman was a convict who was sentenced for life to New South Wales for stealing a horse. He later became superintendent of government boats, a position that entitled him to live in the upper story of this house. The water once practically lapped at Cadman's doorstep, and the original seawall still stands at the front of the house. The small extension on the side of the cottage was built to lock up the oars of Cadman's boats, since oars would have been a necessity for any convict attempting to escape by sea. The upper floor of Cadman's Cottage is now a National Parks and Wildlife Service bookshop and information center for Sydney Harbour National Park. ⊠ *110 George St., The Rocks* ☎ *02/9247–8861* ⊕ *www.cityofsydney.nsw.gov.au* ☉ *Weekdays 9:30–4:30, weekends 10–4:30.*

㊳ **Customs House.** The last surviving example of the elegant sandstone buildings that once ringed Circular Quay, this former customs house now features an amazing model of Sydney under a glass floor. You can walk over the city's skyscrapers, all of which are illuminated by meters of fiber-optic lights. There's an excellent two-level library and plenty of art galleries. The rooftop Café Sydney, the standout in the clutch of restaurants and cafés in this late-19th-century structure, overlooks Sydney Cove. The building stands close to the site where the British flag was first raised on the shores of Sydney Cove in 1788. ⊠ *Customs House Sq., 31 Alfred St., Circular Quay* ☎ *02/9242–8592.*

② **Dawes Point Park.** The wonderful views of the harbor (and since the 1930s, the Harbour Bridge) have made this park and its location noteworthy for centuries. Named for William Dawes, a First Fleet marine officer and astronomer who established the colony's first basic observatory nearby in 1788, this park was also once the site of a fortification known as Dawes Battery. The cannons on the hillside pointing toward the Opera House came from the ships of the First Fleet.

③ **Lower Fort Street.** At one time the handsome Georgian houses along this street, originally a rough track leading from the Dawes Point Battery to Observatory Hill, were among the best addresses in Sydney. Elaborate wrought-iron lacework still graces many of the facades.

⑦ **Museum of Contemporary Art.** This ponderous art deco building houses one of Australia's most important collections of modern art, as well as two significant collections of Aboriginal art and continually changing temporary exhibits. ⊠ *140 George St., The Rocks* ☎ *02/9245–2400* ⊕ *www.mca.com.au* ⊠ *Free* ☉ *Daily 10–5.*

DID YOU KNOW?

Listed in the Guinness Book
of Records as the widest long
span bridge in the world, the
Sydney Harbour Bridge was
the tallest structure in the
city until 1967. It's the fourth
longest single-span steel arch
bridge in the world, behind
Bayonne Bridge in New York
and the New River Gorge
Bridge in West Virginia. The
very longest is the Lupu
Bridge in Shanghai.

8 Nurses Walk. Cutting across the site of the colony's first hospital, Nurses Walk acquired its name at a time when "Sydney" and "sickness" were synonymous. Many of the 736 convicts who survived the voyage from Portsmouth, England, aboard the First Fleet's 11 ships arrived suffering from dysentery, smallpox, scurvy, and typhoid. A few days after he landed at Sydney Cove, Governor Phillip established a tent hospital to care for the worst cases.

> **NEED A BREAK?**
>
> The Gumnut Café (⊠ *28 Harrington St., The Rocks* ☎ *02/9247–9591*), in the 1830 sandstone residence of blacksmith William Reynolds, serves delicious salads, pasta dishes, sandwiches, rolls, and cakes. The best tables are in the shady back garden. Reservations are necessary at lunch, and dinner is served only Wednesday–Friday.

> **HISTORIC WATERING HOLES**
>
> You're sure to get involved in a sing-along when bands take to the stage at the historic **Hero of Waterloo** (⊠ *81 Lower Fort St.2000* ☎ *02/9252–4553*). The pub has a maze of cellars and tunnels said to have been used by smugglers in Sydney's early days. You can get a close-up view of climbers on the Harbour Bridge from a bar stool at the aptly named **Harbour View Hotel** (⊠ *19 Lower Fort St., at Cumberland St.2000* ☎ *02/9252–4111*). The view from the roof of the **Glenmore** (⊠ *96 Cumberland St.2000* ☎ *02/9247–4794*) is inspirational.

13 Observatory Hill. The city's highest point, at 145 feet, was known originally as Windmill Hill, since the colony's first windmill occupied this breezy spot. Its purpose was to grind grain for flour, but soon after it was built the canvas sails were stolen, the machinery was damaged in a storm, and the foundations cracked. The signal station at the top of the hill was built in 1848. This later became an astronomical observatory. This is a great place for a picnic with a view.

6 Overseas Passenger Terminal. Busy **Circular Quay West** is dominated by this multilevel steel-and-glass port terminal, which is often used by visiting cruise ships. There are several excellent waterfront restaurants in the terminal, all with magnificent harbor views. Even if you're not dining in the terminal, it's worth taking the escalator to the upper deck for a good view of the harbor and Opera House.

9 Suez Canal. So narrow that two people can't walk abreast, this alley acquired its name before drains were installed, when rainwater would pour down its funnel-like passageway and gush across George Street. Lanes such as this were once the haunt of the notorious late-19th-century Rocks gangs, when robbery was rife in the area.

14 Sydney Observatory. Originally a signaling station for communicating with ships anchored in the harbor, this handsome building on top of Observatory Hill is now an astronomy museum. During evening observatory shows you can tour the building, watch videos, and get a close-up view of the universe through a 16-inch mirror telescope. Reservations are required for the evening show. ⊠ *Watson Rd., Millers*

CLOSE UP

Building Sydney

Descended from Scottish clan chieftains, Governor Lachlan Macquarie was an accomplished soldier and a man of vision. Macquarie, who was in office from 1810 to 1821, was the first governor to foresee a role for New South Wales as a free society rather than an open prison. He laid the foundations for that society by establishing a plan for the city, constructing significant public buildings, and advocating that reformed convicts be readmitted to society.

Macquarie's policies of equality may seem perfectly reasonable today, but in the early 19th century they marked him as a radical. When his vision of a free society threatened to blur distinctions between soldiers, settlers, and convicts, Macquarie was forced to resign. He was later buried on his Scottish estate, his gravestone inscribed with the words "the Father of Australia."

Macquarie's grand plans for the construction of Sydney might have come to nothing had it not been for Francis Greenway. Trained as an architect in England, where he was convicted of forgery and sentenced to 14 years in New South Wales, Greenway received a ticket of prison leave from Macquarie in 1814 and set to work transforming Sydney. Over the next few years he designed lighthouses, hospitals, convict barracks, and many other government buildings, several of which remain to bear witness to his simple but elegant eye. Greenway was eventually even depicted on one side of the old A$10 notes, which went out of circulation early in the 1990s. Only in Australia, perhaps, would a convicted forger occupy pride of place on the currency.

Point ☎ *02/9921–3485* ⊕ *www.sydneyobservatory.com.au* 🖃 *Museum free, daytime show A$8, evening show A$16* ⊙ *Daily 10–5.*

🅑 **Sydney Visitor Centre at the Rocks.** Known as The Rocks Centre, this ultramodern space is packed with free maps and brochures, and the friendly staff sells SydneyPasses and books tours, hotel rooms, and bus travel. It's near the popular Löwenbräu Keller, where many tourists gather for a beer. ⊠ *The Rocks Centre, Argyle and Playfair Sts., The Rocks* ☎ *02/9240–8788* ⊕ *www.sydneyvisitorcentre.com* ⊙ *Daily 9:30–5:30.*

Upper George Street. The restored warehouses and Victorian terrace houses that line this part of George Street make this a charming section of the Rocks. The covered **Rocks Market** takes place here on weekends.

DOMAIN AND MACQUARIE STREET

Numbers in the text correspond to numbers in the margin and on the Domain and Macquarie map.

Some of Sydney's most notable Victorian-era public buildings, as well as one of its finest parks, can be found in this area. In contrast to the simple, utilitarian stone convict cottages of the Rocks, these buildings

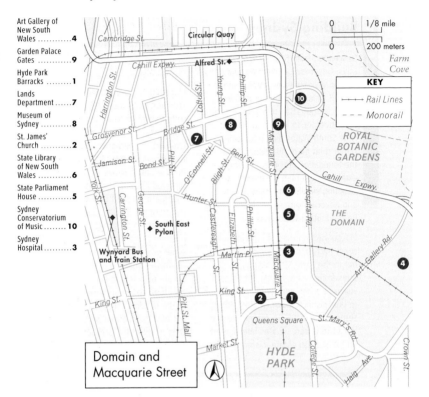

KEY

├───┤ Rail Lines

- - - Monorail

Domain and
Macquarie Street

were constructed at a time when Sydney was experiencing a long period
of prosperity thanks to the gold rushes of the mid-19th century and
an agricultural boom. The sandstone just below the surface of many
coastal areas proved an ideal building material—easily honed into the
ornamentation so fashionable during the Victorian era. Macquarie
Street is Sydney's most elegant boulevard. It was shaped by Governor
Macquarie, who planned the transformation of the cart track leading to
Sydney Cove into a stylish street of dwellings and government buildings.
An occasional modern high-rise breaks up the streetscape, but many of
the 19th-century architectural delights here escaped demolition.

GETTING HERE AND AROUND

The area is served by two train stations—Martin Place and St. James—
but they are not on the same line. You can catch train trains to both
stations from Central and Town Hall. St. James is right next to Hyde
Park, and Martin Place has an exit on Macquarie Street. From Macquarie Street it's a short walk to the Domain via the passageway
that cuts through Sydney Hospital. A number of buses (including the
380/382 and 333 from Bondi Beach and 555 free shuttle) travel along
Elizabeth Street.

TOP ATTRACTIONS

❹ Art Gallery of New South Wales.
Apart from Canberra's National Gallery, this is the best place to explore the evolution of European-influenced Australian art, as well as the distinctly different concepts that underlie Aboriginal art. All the major Australian artists of the last two centuries are represented in this impressive collection. The entrance level, where large windows frame spectacular views of the harbor, exhibits 20th-century art. Below, in the gallery's major extensions, the Yiribana Gallery

> ### ART AND ANGST
>
> If you like a bit of controversy with your culture, head to the Art Gallery of New South Wales to view the finalists in the annual **Archibald Prize** (⊕ www.thearchibaldprize.com.au). Each year since 1921, the competition has attracted plenty of drama as everyone debates the merits of the winners. Prizes are announced in early March, and the exhibition hangs until mid-May.

displays one of the nation's most comprehensive collections of Aboriginal and Torres Strait Islander art. ⊠ *Art Gallery Rd., The Domain, Sydney* ☎ *02/9225–1700* ⊕ *www.artgallery.nsw.gov.au* ☜ *Free; fee for special exhibits* ⊘ *Daily 10–5.*

❽ Museum of Sydney. This museum built on the site of the original Govern-
★ ment House documents Sydney's early period of European colonization. Aboriginal culture, convict society, and the gradual transformation of the settlement at Sydney Cove are woven into an evocative portrayal of life in the country's early days. A glass floor in the lobby reveals the foundations of the original structure. One of the most intriguing exhibits, however, is outside: the striking Edge of the Trees sculpture, the first collaborative public artwork in Sydney between an Aboriginal and a European artist. ⊠ *Bridge and Phillip Sts., Macquarie Street* ☎ *02/9251–5988* ⊕ *www.hht.nsw.gov.au* ☜ *A$10* ⊘ *Daily 9:30–5.*

❶ Hyde Park Barracks. Before Governor Macquarie arrived, convicts were left to roam freely at night. Macquarie was determined to establish law and order, and in 1819 he commissioned convict-architect Francis Greenway to design this restrained, classically Georgian-style building. Today the Barracks houses compelling exhibits that explore behind the scenes of the prison. For example, a surprising number of relics from this period were preserved by rats, which carried away scraps of clothing and other artifacts for their nests beneath the floorboards. A room on the top floor is strung with hammocks, exactly as it was when the building housed convicts. ⊠ *Queens Sq., Macquarie St., Macquarie Street* ☎ *02/8239–2311* ⊕ *www.hht.nsw.gov.au* ☜ *A$10* ⊘ *Daily 9:30–5.*

WORTH NOTING

❾ Garden Palace Gates. These gates are all that remain of the Garden Palace, a massive glass pavilion that was erected for the Sydney International Exhibition of 1879 and destroyed by fire three years later. On the arch above the gates is a depiction of the Garden Palace's dome. Stone pillars on either side of the gates are engraved with Australian wildflowers. ⊠ *Macquarie St. between Bridge and Bent Sts., Macquarie Street.*

NEED A
BREAK?

On a sunny day the courtyard tables of the **Hyde Park Barracks Café**
(✉ *Queens Sq., Macquarie St., Macquarie Street* ☎ *02/9222–1815*) provide
one of the city's finest places to enjoy an outdoor lunch. The café serves
light, moderately priced meals, salads, and open sandwiches, with an
extensive Australian wine list.

❼ Lands Department. The figures occupying the niches at the corners of this
1890 sandstone building are early Australian explorers and politicians.
James Barnet's building stands among other fine Victorian structures
in the neighborhood. ✉ *Bridge St. near intersection of Macquarie Pl.,
Macquarie Street.*

❷ St. James' Church. Begun in 1822, the colonial Georgian–style St. James'
is Sydney's oldest surviving church, and another fine Francis Greenway
design. Now lost among the skyscrapers, the church's tall spire once
served as a landmark for ships entering the harbor. Plaques commemorating Australian explorers and administrators cover the interior walls.
Free guided tours are given weekdays at 2:30 PM. Lunchtime concerts
are presented every Wednesday from late February to late December.
✉ *Queens Sq., 173 King St., Hyde Park* ☎ *02/9232–3022* ⊕ *www.sjks.
org.au* ⊙ *Weekdays 9–5, Sat. 9–3.*

❻ State Library of New South Wales. This large complex is based around
the Mitchell and Dixson libraries, which make up the world's largest
collection of Australiana. Enter the foyer through the classical portico
to see one of the earliest maps of Australia, a copy in marble mosaic
of a map made by Abel Tasman, the Dutch navigator, in the mid-17th
century. Through the glass doors lies the vast Mitchell Library reading
room, but you need a reader's ticket (establishing that you are pursuing
legitimate research) to enter. You can, however, take a free escorted tour
Tuesday at 11 and Thursday at 2. The library continuously runs free
exhibitions, and the Shakespeare Room is open to the public Tuesday 10
AM–4 PM. Inquire at the reception desk of the general reference library
on Macquarie Street. ✉ *Macquarie St. off Bent St., Macquarie Street*
☎ *02/9273–1414 or 02/9273–1768* ⊕ *www.sl.nsw.gov.au* ⊙ *Mon.–
Thurs. 9–8, Fri. 9–5, weekends 10–5 (Mitchell Library closed Sun.).*

❺ State Parliament House. The simple facade and shady verandas of this
Greenway-designed 1816 building, formerly the Rum Hospital, typify
Australian colonial architecture. From 1829, two rooms of the old hospital were used for meetings of the executive and legislative councils,
which had been set up to advise the governor. These advisory bodies
grew in power until New South Wales became self-governing in the
1840s, at which time Parliament occupied the entire building. The Legislative Council Chamber—the upper house of the parliament, identifiable by its red color scheme—is a prefabricated cast-iron structure that
was originally intended to be a church on the goldfields of Victoria.

State Parliament generally sits between mid-February and late May,
and again between mid-September and late November. You can visit
the public gallery and watch the local version of the Westminster system
of democracy in action. When parliament is not sitting, you can take
a free escorted tour or walk around at your leisure and view the large

Sydney has a enough of museums and art galleries to appeal to just about every taste.

collection of portraits and paintings. You must reserve ahead for tours and to sit in the public gallery. ✉ *Macquarie St. across from Martin Pl.,* ☎ *02/9230–2111* ⊕ *www.parliament.nsw.gov.au* ⊘ *Weekdays 9–5; hrs. vary when Parliament is in session—call ahead.*

🔟 Sydney Conservatorium of Music. Providing artistic development for talented young musicians, this institution hosts free lunchtime concerts on Wednesday, jazz on Sunday, and other musical events. The conservatory's turreted building was originally the stables for nearby Government House. The construction cost caused a storm among Governor Macquarie's superiors in London, and eventually helped bring about the downfall of both Macquarie and the building's architect, Francis Greenway. ✉ *Conservatorium Rd. off Macquarie St., Macquarie Street* ☎ *02/9351–1222.*

❸ Sydney Hospital. Completed in 1894 to replace the main Rum Hospital building, this institution offered an infinitely better medical option. By all accounts, admission to the Rum Hospital was only slightly preferable to death itself. Convict nurses stole patients' food, and abler patients stole from the weaker. The kitchen sometimes doubled as a mortuary, and the table was occasionally used for operations.

In front of the hospital is a bronze figure of a boar. This is *Il Porcellino,* a copy of a statue that stands in Florence, Italy. According to the inscription, if you make a donation in the coin box and rub the boar's nose, "you will be endowed with good luck." Sydney citizens seem to be a superstitious bunch, because the boar's nose is very shiny indeed. ✉ *Macquarie St. at Martin Pl.* ☎ *02/9382–7111.*

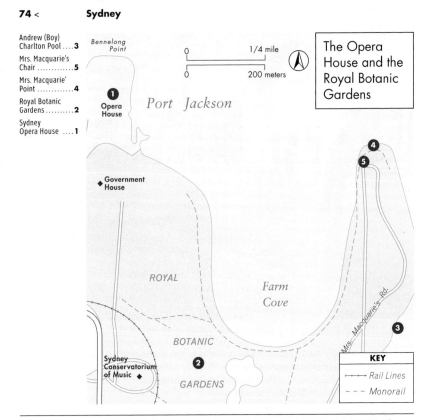

THE OPERA HOUSE AND THE ROYAL BOTANIC GARDENS

Numbers in the text correspond to numbers in the margin and on the The Opera House and the Royal Botanic Gardens map.

Bordering Sydney Cove, Farm Cove, and Woolloomooloo Bay, this section of Sydney includes the iconic Sydney Opera House, as well as extensive and delightful harborside gardens and parks.

The colony's first farm was established here in 1788, and the botanical gardens were laid out in 1816. The most dramatic change to the area occurred in 1959, however, when ground was broken on the site for the Sydney Opera House at Bennelong Point. This promontory was originally a small island, then the site of 1819 Fort Macquarie, later a tram depot, and finally the Opera House, one of the world's most striking modern buildings. The area's evolution is an eloquent metaphor for Sydney's own transformation.

GETTING HERE AND AROUND

The best way to get to the Opera House is to take one of the many ferries, buses, or trains that go to Circular Quay and then walk the pedestrian concourse. Some buses travel down Macquarie Street to the Opera House, which involves a slightly shorter walk. To get to the Royal Botanic Gardens, take the CityRail suburban train from the Town

Hall, Central, or Bondi Junction stations to Martin Place station, exit on the Macquarie Street side, and walk a few hundred yards.

TOP ATTRACTIONS

② **Royal Botanic Gardens.** More than 80 acres of sweeping green lawns,
★ groves of indigenous and exotic trees, duck ponds, greenhouses, and some 45,124 types of plants—many of them in bloom—grace these gardens. The elegant property, which attracts strollers and botany enthusiasts from all over the country, is a far cry today from what it once was: a failed attempt by convicts of the First Fleet to establish a farm. Though their early attempts at agriculture were disastrous, the efforts of these first settlers are acknowledged in the Pioneer Garden, a sunken garden built in their memory.

Among the many other feature gardens on the property are the Palm Grove—home to some of the oldest trees in Sydney, the Begonia Garden, and the Rare and Threatened Plants Garden. Not to be missed is a cutting from the famous Wollemi Pine, a plant thought to be extinct until it was discovered in a secluded gully in the Wollemi National Park in the Blue Mountains in 1994. Plants throughout the gardens have various blooming cycles, so no matter what time of year you visit, there are sure to be plenty of flowers. The gardens include striking sculptures and hundreds of species of birds (along with a large colony of flying foxes, also known as fruit bats). There are spectacular views over the harbor and the Opera House from the two lovely restaurants.

Government House. Completed in 1843, this Gothic Revival building in the Royal Botanic Gardens served as the residence of the Governor of New South Wales—who represents the British crown in local matters—until the government handed it back to the public in 1996. Prominent English architect Edward Blore designed the two-story building without ever having set foot in Australia. The sandstone house's restored stenciled ceilings are its most impressive feature. Paintings hanging on the walls bear the signatures of some of Australia's best-known artists. You are free to wander on your own around Government House's gardens, which lie within the Royal Botanic Gardens, but you must join a guided tour to see the house's interior. Tours leave from the visitor center, near the Art Gallery of New South Wales. There are also maps available for a variety of themed, self-guided walks.

✉ *Domain North, The Domain* ☎ *02/9231–8111 weekends* ⊕ *www. rbgsyd.nsw.gov.au* ✍ *Free* ☉ *Royal Botanic Gardens daily 7–dusk; tours at 10:30* AM.

① **Sydney Opera House.** Sydney's most famous landmark (listed as a World
Fodor's Choice Heritage site in 2007) had such a long and troubled construction phase
★ that it's almost a miracle that the building was ever completed. In 1954 the state premier appointed a committee to advise the government on the building of an opera house. The site chosen was Bennelong Point (named after an early Aboriginal inhabitant), which was, until that time, occupied by a tram depot. The premier's committee launched a competition to find a suitable plan, and a total of 233 submissions came in from architects the world over. One of them was a young Dane named Joern Utzon.

"The Opera House as seen from The Rocks side of Circular Quay." —photo by Gary Ott, Fodors.com member

His plan was brilliant, but it had all the markings of a monumental disaster. The structure was so narrow that stages would have minuscule wings, and the soaring "sails" that formed the walls and roof could not be built by existing technology.

Nonetheless, Utzon's dazzling, dramatic concept caught the judges' imagination, and construction of the giant podium began in 1959. From the start, the contractors faced a cost blowout; the building that was projected to cost A\$7 million and take 4 years to erect would eventually require A\$102 million and 15 years. Construction was financed by an intriguing scheme. Realizing that citizens might be hostile to the use of public funds for the controversial project, the state government raised the money through the Opera House Lottery. For almost a decade, Australians lined up to buy tickets, and the Opera House was built without depriving the state's hospitals or schools of a single cent.

Initially it was thought that the concrete exterior of the building would have to be cast in place, which would have meant building an enormous birdcage of scaffolding at even greater expense. Then, as he was peeling an orange one day, Utzon had a flash of inspiration. Why not construct the shells from segments of a single sphere? The concrete ribs forming the skeleton of the building could be prefabricated in just a few molds, hoisted into position, and joined together. These ribs are clearly visible inside the Opera House, especially in the foyers and staircases of the Concert Hall.

In 1966 Utzon resigned as Opera House architect and left Australia, reportedly embittered by his dealings with unions and the government. He never returned to see his masterpiece, although he had been invited on several occasions.

A team of young Australian architects carried on, completing the exterior one year later. Until that time, however, nobody had given much thought to the *interior.* The shells created awkward interior spaces, and conventional performance areas were simply not feasible. It's a tribute to the architectural team's ingenuity that the exterior of the building is matched by the aesthetically pleasing and acoustically sound theaters inside. Joern Utzon died in Denmark on November 29, 2008, aged 90. Prime Minister Kevin Rudd paid tribute to Utzon's genius in speeches, while the lights of the Opera House sails were dimmed and flags on the Harbor Bridge were flown at half-mast as a mark of respect. Guided tours include the one-hour Essential Tour, departing daily from the lower forecourt level between 9 and 5, and a two-hour backstage tour departing daily at 7 AM. Call in advance. ⊠ *Bennelong Point, Circular Quay* ☎ *02/9250–7111* ⊕ *www.soh.nsw.gov.au* ✉ *General tour A$35, backstage tour A$150.*

WORTH NOTING

❸ **Andrew (Boy) Charlton Pool.** This heated saltwater swimming pool overlooking the navy ships tied up at Garden Island has become a local favorite. Complementing its stunning location is a radical design in glass and steel. The pool also has a chic terrace café above Woolloomooloo Bay. ⊠ *Mrs. Macquarie's Rd., Domain North, The Domain* ☎ *02/9358–6686* ⊕ *www.abcpool.org* ✉ *A$5.50* ⊘ *Daily* 6 AM–7 PM *(until 8 pm in summer).*

❺ **Mrs. Macquarie's Chair.** During the early 1800s, Elizabeth Macquarie often sat on the point in the Domain at the east side of Farm Cove, at the rock where a seat has been hewn in her name.

NEED A BREAK?

Botanic Gardens Restaurant (⊠ *Royal Botanic Gardens, Mrs Macquarie's Rd., Royal Botanic Gardens* ☎ *02/9241–2419* ⊕ *www.rbgsyd.nsw.gov.au* **)** is a lovely place to have lunch during the week or brunch on the weekend. Wide verandas provide tranquil views over the gardens, and the sound of birdsong fills the air. Choices range from goat's cheese tart to crisp-skinned baked snapper and a decadent eggs Benedict for Sunday brunch. The downstairs café serves lighter, more casual fare. Both the café and the restaurant are open Monday to Friday for lunch from noon, while the restaurant brunch starts at 9.30 AM.

❹ **Mrs. Macquarie's Point.** The inspiring views from this point combine with the shady lawns to make this a popular place for picnics. The views are best at dusk, when the setting sun silhouettes the Opera House and the Harbour Bridge.

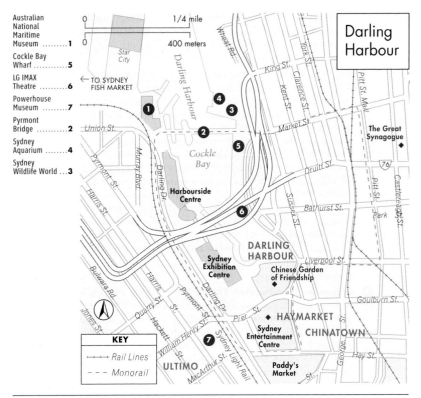

DARLING HARBOUR

Numbers in the text correspond to numbers in the margin and on the Darling Harbour map.

Until the mid-1980s this horseshoe-shaped bay on the city center's western edge was a wasteland of disused docks and railway yards. Then, in an explosive burst of activity the whole area was redeveloped and opened in time for Australia's bicentenary in 1988. Now there's plenty to take in at the Darling Harbour complex: the National Maritime Museum, Sydney Aquarium, Sydney Wildlife World, and the gleaming Exhibition Centre, whose masts and spars recall the square-riggers that once berthed here. At the harbor's center is a large park shaded by palm trees. Waterways and fountains lace the complex together.

The Powerhouse Museum is within easy walking distance of the harbor, and to the south are Chinatown and the Sydney Entertainment Centre. The Star City entertainment complex, based around the Star City Casino, lies just to the west of Darling Harbour.

GETTING HERE AND AROUND

Take the train to either Town Hall or Central Station. From Town Hall it's a short walk down Druitt Street; from Central you walk through Haymarket and Chinatown, passing by the Sydney Entertainment

Centre. The monorail (A$4.80 one-way; A$9.50 day pass) travels in a loop from the city center to Darling Harbour, stopping on both sides of Cockle Bay. The Light Rail tram (A$3.20 one-way; day pass A$9) connects Central Station with Darling Harbour and the Star City Casino a little farther to the west.

TOP ATTRACTIONS

4 ★ ☾ **Sydney Aquarium.** The larger and more modern of Sydney's public aquariums presents a fascinating view of the underwater world, with saltwater crocodiles, giant sea turtles, and delicate, multicolor fish. Excellent displays highlight Great Barrier Reef marine life and Australia's largest river system, the Murray-Darling. The marine mammal sanctuary and touch pool are favorites with children. Two show-stealing transparent tunnels give a fish's-eye view of the sea, while sharks and stingrays glide overhead. Although the adult admission price is high, family tickets are a good value, as is the combined pass with Sydney Wildlife World (A$49.95). Prices are lower if you buy online. ✉ *Aquarium pier, 1–5 Wheat Rd., Darling Harbour* ☎ *02/8251–7800* ⊕ *www.sydneyaquarium.com.au* 🖭 *A$31.95* ☾ *Daily 9* AM*–10* PM.

1 ★ ☾ **Australian National Maritime Museum.** The six galleries of this soaring, futuristic building tell the story of Australia and the sea. In addition to figureheads, model ships, and brassy nautical hardware, there are antique racing yachts and the jet-powered *Spirit of Australia,* current holder of the world water speed record, set in 1978. The USA Gallery displays objects from such major U.S. collections as the Smithsonian Institution, and was dedicated by President George Bush Sr. on New Year's Day 1992. An outdoor section showcases numerous vessels moored at the museum's wharves, including the HMAS *Vampire,* a World War II destroyer. ✉ *Wharf 7, Maritime Heritage Centre, 2 Murray St., Darling Harbour* ☎ *02/9298–3777* ⊕ *www.anmm.gov.au* 🖭 *Free* ☾ *Daily 9:30–5 (until 6 in Jan.).*

WORTH NOTING

VISIT CHINA

Bounded by the Entertainment Centre, George Street, Goulburn Street, and Paddy's Market, Chinatown takes your senses on a galloping tour of the Orient. Within this compact grid are aromatic restaurants, traditional apothecaries, Chinese grocers, clothing boutiques, and shops selling Asian-made electronics. The best way to get a sense of the area is to take a stroll along Dixon Street, now a pedestrian mall with a Chinese Lion Gate at either end. Sydney's Chinese community was first established here in the 1800s, in the aftermath of the gold rush that originally drew many Chinese immigrants

VILLAGE VIBE

If you're seeking a taste of village life, take a ferry to Balmain. The left-of-center community spirit makes it one of Sydney's special places. On the western side of the harbor, Balmain is home to narrow streets, sandstone cottages, and good pubs, including one that welcomes dogs at the **London Hotel** (✉ *234 Darling St.* ☎ *02/9555–1377*). To get here, take the ferry from Circular Quay to Balmain Wharf and connect with buses that climb up Darling Street hill.

to Australia. These days most of Sydney comes here regularly to dine, especially on weekends for dim sum lunches (called *yum cha*).

5 Cockle Bay Wharf. Fueling Sydney's addiction to fine food, most of this sprawling waterfront complex is dedicated to gastronomy. This is also the site of Sydney's biggest nightclub, Home. If you have a boat you can dock at the marina—and avoid the hassle of parking a car in one of the city's most congested centers. ⊠ *201 Sussex St., Darling Harbour* ☎ *02/9269–9800* ⊕ *www.cocklebaywharf.com.*

NEED A BREAK?

Blackbird Café (⊠ *Balcony level, Cockle Bay Wharf, 201 Sussex St., Darling Harbour* ☎ *02/9283-7385* ⊕ *www.blackbirdcafe.com.au*) is an affordable place for lunch or dinner, and has great views across Cockle Bar if you nab a balcony table. There are A$12 meal deals every day (Thursday offers a A$12 curry) and A$10 cocktails. The menu includes burgers, pizza, soups, and Asian dishes.

WELCOME REFUGE

Chinese prospectors came to the Australian goldfields as far back as the 1850s, and the nation's long and enduring links with China are symbolized by the Chinese Garden of Friendship, the largest garden of its kind outside China. Designed by Chinese landscape architects, the garden includes bridges, lakes, waterfalls, sculptures, and Cantonese-style pavilions. The perfect place for a refreshing cup of tea from the café. ⊠ *Darling Harbour* ☎ *02/9281-6863* ☜ A$6 ☉ *Daily 9:30–5.*

6 LG IMAX Theatre. Both in size and impact, this eight-story-tall movie screen is overwhelming. One-hour presentations take you on astonishing, wide-angle voyages of discovery under the oceans and to the summit of the world's highest mountains. ⊠ *Southern Promenade, 31 Wheat Rd., Darling Harbour* ☎ *02/9281–3300* ⊕ *www.imax.com.au* ☜ A$19–A$25 ☉ *Daily 10–10.*

7 Powerhouse Museum. Learning the principles of science is a painless process with this museum's stimulating, interactive displays ideal for all ages. Exhibits in the former 1890s electricity station that once powered Sydney's trams include a whole floor of working steam engines, space modules, airplanes suspended from the ceiling, state-of-the-art computer gadgetry, and a 1930s art deco–style movie-theater auditorium. ⊠ *500 Harris St., Ultimo* ☎ *02/9217–0111* ⊕ *www.powerhousemuseum.com* ☜ A$10 ☉ *Daily 10–5.*

2 Pyrmont Bridge. Dating from 1902, this is the world's oldest electrically operated swing-span bridge. The structure once carried motor traffic, but it's now a walkway that links Darling Harbour's western side with Cockle Bay. The monorail runs above the bridge, but the center span still swings open to allow tall-masted ships into Cockle Bay, which sits at the bottom of the horseshoe-shaped shore.

The Maritime Museum at Darling Harbour.

OFF THE
BEATEN
PATH

Sydney Fish Market. Second in size only to Tokyo's giant Tsukiji fish market, Sydney's is a showcase for the riches of Australia's seas. An easy 10-minute walk from Darling Harbour (and with its own stop on the Metro Light Rail network), the market is a great place to sample sushi, oysters, octopus, spicy Thai and Chinese fish dishes, and fish-and-chips at the waterfront cafés overlooking the fishing fleet. There are cooking demonstratios and classes. It's open daily from 7 AM to about 5. ⊠ *Pyrmont Bridge Rd. at Bank St., Pyrmont West* ☎ *02/9004–1100* ⊕ *www.sydneyfishmarket.com.au.*

❸ **Sydney Wildlife World.** This new Sydney attraction brings 6,000 native Australian animals right to the heart of Sydney. Kangaroos, koalas, and dozens of other species come together under the one huge roof—in nine separate habitats—next door to the Sydney Aquarium. A huge wire-mesh dome covers Flight Canyon, an aviary where dozens of birds fly freely overhead as you stroll the 1-km (½-mi) walkway. You'll find koalas in Gum Tree Gully, and endangered bilbies, together with other nocturnal creatures, in the After Dark habitat. The Lush Canopy rainforest habitat is home to the cassowary and red-legged pademelons (a type of kangaroo), while giant cockroaches and other creepy crawlies can be found in Spineless Wonders. Each day you can watch a different animal being fed (including the snakes). A combined ticket with Sydney Aquarium costs A$49.95. ⊠ *Aquarium Pier, Wheat Rd., Darling Harbour* ☎ *02/9333–9288* ⊕ *www.sydneywildlifeworld.com.au* ⊠ *A$31.95* ⊘ *Daily 9 AM–5:30 PM.*

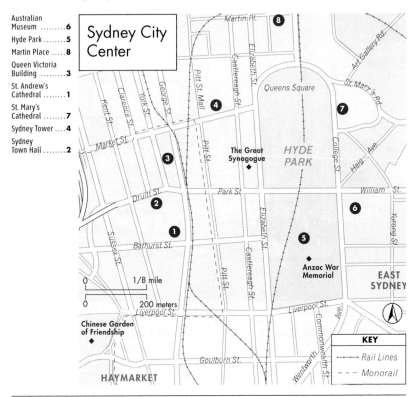

SYDNEY CITY CENTER

Numbers in the text correspond to numbers in the margin and on the Sydney City Center map.

Shopping is the main reason to visit Sydney's city center, but there are several buildings and other places of interest among the office blocks, department stores, and shopping centers.

GETTING HERE AND AROUND

Buses from the eastern suburbs run along Elizabeth Street on the western side of Hyde Park; buses from the inner western suburbs such as Balmain travel to and from the Queen Victoria Building. The main train stations are Town Hall and Martin Place, while Hyde Park is served by both St. James and Museum Station on the City Circle rail line. The monorail has two stops in the city center. The new free shuttle bus (No. 555) completes a circuit around the city center, stopping at the main attractions.

TOP ATTRACTIONS

6 **Australian Museum.** The strength of this natural-history museum, a
★ well-respected academic institution, is its collection of plants, ani-
☉ mals, geological specimens, and cultural artifacts from the Asia-Pacific region. Particularly notable are the collections of artifacts from Papua

New Guinea and from Australia's Aboriginal peoples. The museum also has an ever-changing array of fascinating temporary exhibitions, such as the popular "Eaten Alive: The World of Predators." There's an excellent shop and a lively café. ⊠ *6 College St., near William St., Hyde Park* ☎ *02/9320–6000* ⊕ *www.amonline.net.au* ⊠ *A$12* ⊙ *Daily 9:30–5.*

❺ **Hyde Park.** Declared public land by Governor Phillip in 1792 and used for the colony's earliest cricket matches and horse races, this area was turned into a park in 1810. The gardens are formal, with fountains, statuary, and tree-lined walks, and its tranquil lawns are popular with office workers at lunchtime. In the southern section of Hyde Park (near Liverpool Street) stands the 1934 art deco **Anzac Memorial** (☎ *02/9267–7668*), a tribute to the Australians who died in military service during World War I, when the acronym ANZAC (Australian and New Zealand Army Corps) was coined. The 120,000 gold stars inside the dome represent each man and woman of New South Wales who served. The lower level exhibits war-related photographs. It's open daily 9–5. ⊠ *Elizabeth, College, and Park Sts., Hyde Park.*

> **BOATING BLISS**
>
> A great way to pamper your body and soul simultaneously is to take a Massage and Beauty Cruise on Sydney Harbour. Choose between an hour-long massage or facial aboard the luxury catamaran *Olympic Spirit* (⊕ *www.massageandbeautycruise.com.au*). The pampering starts with a welcome glass of champagne, followed by brunch or afternoon tea. While women love these weekend-only jaunts, couples come as well.

WORTH NOTING

NEED A BREAK?

Stop in at the Marble Bar (⊠ *Hilton Sydney, 259 Pitt St., City Center* ☎ *02/9265–6026* ⊕ *www.marblebarsydney.com.au* ⊙ *Closed Sun.*) to experience a masterpiece of Victorian extravagance. The 1890 bar was formerly in another building that was constructed on the profits of the horse-racing track, thus establishing the link between gambling and majestic public architecture that has its modern-day parallel in the Sydney Opera House. Threatened with demolition in the 1970s, the whole bar was moved—marble arches, color-glass ceiling, elaborately carved woodwork, paintings of voluptuous nudes, and all—to its present site. By night the basement bar serves as a backdrop for live music.

❽ **Martin Place.** Sydney's largest pedestrian precinct, flanked by banks, offices, and shopping centers, is the hub of the central business district. There are some grand buildings here—including the beautifully refurbished Commonwealth Bank and the 1870s Venetian Renaissance–style General Post Office building with its 230-foot clock tower (now a Westin hotel). Toward the George Street end of the plaza the simple 1929 cenotaph war memorial commemorates Australians who died in World War I. ⊠ *Between Macquarie and George Sts., City Center.*

❸ **Queen Victoria Building (QVB).** Originally the city's produce market, this huge 1898 sandstone structure was handsomely restored with sweeping staircases, enormous stained-glass windows, and the 1-ton Royal Clock, which hangs from the glass roof. The clock chimes the hour from 9 AM to 9 PM with four tableaux: the second shows Queen Elizabeth I knighting Sir Frances Drake; the last ends with an executioner chopping off King Charles I's head. The complex includes more than 200 boutiques; those on the upper floors are generally more upscale and exclusive. ⊠ *George, York, Market, and Druitt Sts., City Center* ☎ *02/9264–9209* ⊕ *www.qvb.com.au* ⊙ *Daily 8 AM–10 PM.*

❶ **St. Andrew's Cathedral.** The foundation stone for Sydney's Gothic Revival Anglican cathedral—the country's oldest—was laid in 1819, although the original architect, Francis Greenway, fell from grace soon after work began. Edmund Blacket, Sydney's most illustrious church architect, was responsible for its final design and completion—a whopping 50 years later in 1868. Notable features of the sandstone construction include ornamental windows depicting Jesus's life and a great east window with images relating to St. Andrew. ⊠ *Sydney Sq., George and Bathurst Sts., next to Town Hall, City Center* ☎ *02/9265–1661* ⊙ *Mon.–Sat. 10–4, Sun. for services only 8:30 AM, 10:30 AM, 6:30 PM; tours by arrangement.*

❼ **St. Mary's Cathedral.** The first St. Mary's was built here in 1821, but fire destroyed the chapel. Work on the present cathedral began in 1868. The spires weren't added until 2000, however. St. Mary's has some particularly fine stained-glass windows and a terrazzo floor in the crypt, where exhibitions are often held. The cathedral's large rose window was imported from England.

At the front of the cathedral stand statues of Cardinal Moran and Archbishop Kelly, two Irishmen who were prominent in Australia's Roman Catholic Church. Due to the high proportion of Irish men and women in the convict population, the Roman Catholic Church was often the voice of the oppressed in 19th-century Sydney, where anti-Catholic feeling ran high among the Protestant rulers. ⊠ *College and Cathedral Sts., Hyde Park, City Center* ☎ *02/9220–0400* ✉ *Tour free* ⊙ *Weekdays 6:30 AM–6:30 PM, Sat. 8–7:30, Sun. 6:30 AM–7:30 PM; tour Sun. at noon.*

❹ **Sydney Tower.** Short of taking a scenic flight, a visit to the top of this 1,000-foot golden-turret-topped spike is the best way to see Sydney's spectacular layout. This is the city's tallest building, and the views from its indoor observation deck encompass the entire Sydney metropolitan area. You can often see as far as the Blue Mountains, more than 80 km (50 mi) away. The tower is home to OzTrek, a simulated ride which takes you "high above" Australia's major attractions. However, the real adrenaline rush comes from SkyWalk, a guided walk around the outside of the golden turret some 880 feet above the city. Walkers are attached to the tower's superstructure by harness lines and wear special all-weather suits. For those who work up an appetite, the building houses two restaurants in the turret. ⊠ *100 Market St., between Pitt and Castlereagh Sts., City Center* ☎ *02/9333–9222* ⊕ *www.sydneytower. com.au* ✉ *Observation tower and OzTrek A\$25, with SkyWalk A\$65*

The fountain in Hyde Park with the Australian Museum in the background.

🕙 *Tower Sun.–Fri. 9 AM–10:30 PM, Sat. 9 AM–11:30 PM. Skywalk daily 9:30 AM–8:45 PM.*

❷ **Sydney Town Hall.** Sydney's most ornate Victorian building—an elaborate sandstone structure—underwent a A$60 millon upgrade in 2009 to spruce up its grand interior spaces, especially the vestibule and large Centennial Hall. A centerpiece of the building is the massive 8,000-pipe Grand Organ, one of the world's most powerful, which is used for lunchtime concerts. Mingle with locals on the marble steps of the front entrance. ⊠ *George and Druitt Sts., City Center* ☎ *02/9265–9333 general inquiries* ⊕ *www.cityofsydney.nsw.gov.au* ✉ *Free* 🕙 *Weekdays 8:30–6.*

THE EASTERN SUBURBS

Numbers in the text correspond to numbers in the margin and on the Eastern Suburbs map.

Sydney's eastern suburbs are truly the people's domain. They stretch from the mansions of the colonial aristocracy and the humble laborers' cottages of the same period to the modernized terrace houses of Paddington, one of Sydney's most charming and most desirable suburbs. A good way to explore the area is to take the Bondi Explorer bus that stops at 19 sites including beaches, harbour bays, the exclusive shopping precinct of Double Bay, and the acclaimed Sydney Jewish Museum.

GETTING HERE AND AROUND

The eastern suburbs are well served by buses, although the journey can be quite long in peak hour. Most depart from Circular Quay (Alfred St.). Travel to Paddington and Bondi is on Nos. 380, 33, and 382; and to Watsons Bay and Vaucluse (via Double Bay and Rose Bay) on Nos. 323, 324, and 325). It is quicker to take the train to Edgecliff or Bondi Junction stations to connect with buses traveling to all suburbs including Coogee and Clovelly. A ferry operates between Circular Quay and Watsons Bay, calling at Garden Island, Darling Point, Double Bay, and Rose Bay.

TOP ATTRACTIONS

❶ Elizabeth Bay. Much of this densely populated but still-charming harbor-side suburb was originally part of the extensive Elizabeth Bay House grounds. Wrought-iron balconies and French doors on some of the older apartment blocks give the area a Mediterranean flavor. During the 1920s and 1930s this was a fashionably bohemian quarter, and it remains a favorite among artists and writers. The **Elizabeth Bay House** was regarded in its heyday as the "finest house in the colony." This 1835–39 mansion retains little of its original furniture, although the rooms have been restored in Georgian style. The most striking feature is an oval-shaped salon with a winding staircase, naturally lighted by glass panels in the domed roof. The view from the front-facing windows across Elizabeth Bay is stunning. ⊠ *7 Onslow Ave., Elizabeth Bay* ☏ *02/9356–3022* ⊕ *www.hht.net.au* ✉ *A$8* ☉ *Fri.–Sun. 9:30–4.*

❷ Sydney Jewish Museum. Artifacts, interactive displays, and audiovisual ★ displays chronicle the history of Australian Jews and commemorate the 6 million killed in the Holocaust. Exhibits are brilliantly arranged on eight levels, which lead upward in chronological order, from the handful of Jews who arrived with the First Fleet in 1788 to the 30,000 concentration-camp survivors who came after World War II—one of the largest populations of Holocaust survivors to be found anywhere. A 40-minute guided tour starts every day at noon. ⊠ *148 Darlinghurst Rd., Darlinghurst* ☏ *02/9360–7999* ⊕ *www.sydneyjewishmuseum.com. au* ✉ *A$10* ☉ *Sun.–Thurs. 10–4, Fri. 10–2.*

WORTH NOTING

❺ Centennial Park. More than 500 acres of palm-lined avenues, groves of Moreton Bay figs, paperbark tree–fringed lakes, and cycling and horse-riding tracks make this a popular park and Sydney's favorite workout circuit. In the early 1800s the marshy land at the lower end provided Sydney with its fresh water. The park was proclaimed in 1888, the centenary of Australia's founding as a colony. The Centennial Park Café is often crowded on weekends, but a mobile canteen between the lakes in the middle of the park serves snacks and espresso. Bikes and blades can be rented from the nearby Clovelly Road outlets, on the eastern side of the park. The Moonlight Cinema screens movies during the summer months. ⊠ *Oxford St. at Centennial Ave., Centennial Park* ⊕ *www. cp.nsw.gov.au* ☉ *Daily dawn–dusk.*

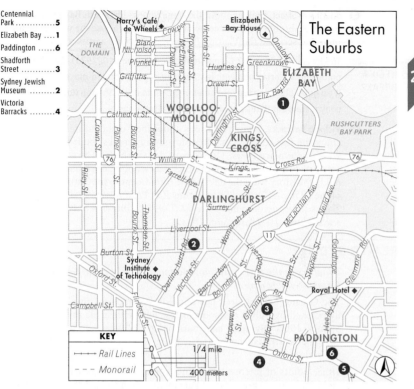

The Eastern Suburbs

2

KEY

⊢⊢⊢⊢ *Rail Lines*

– – – *Monorail*

1/4 mile

400 meters

OFF THE BEATEN PATH

Harry's Café de Wheels. The attraction of this all-day dockyard food stall is not so much the delectable meat pies and coffee served as the clientele. Famous opera singers, actors, and international rock stars have been spotted here rubbing shoulders with shift workers and taxi drivers. This "pie cart" has been a Sydney institution since 1945, when the late Harry "Tiger" Edwards set up his van to serve sailors from the nearby Garden Island base. Drop in any time from 7 AM to the wee hours for a Tiger Pie, made with mushy peas, mashed potatoes, and gravy. ⊠ *1 Cowper Wharf Rd., Woolloomooloo* ☎ *02/9357–3074* ⊕ *www.harryscafedewheels.com.au.*

6 Paddington. Most of this suburb's elegant two-story terrace houses were built during the 1880s, when the colony experienced a long period of economic growth following the gold rushes that began in the 1860s. The balconies are trimmed with decorative wrought iron, sometimes known as Paddington lace, which initially came from England and later from Australian foundries. Rebuilt and repainted, the now-stylish Paddington terrace houses give the area its characteristic village-like charm. The Oxford Street shopping strip is full of upscale and funky boutiques, cafés, and several good pubs.

❸ **Shadforth Street.** Built at about the same time as Elizabeth Bay House, the tiny stone houses in this street were assembled to house the workers who built and serviced the Victoria Barracks, which are across the street.

NEED A BREAK?

The Royal Hotel (✉ *237 Glenmore Rd., Paddington* ☎ *02/9331-2604*) is an enjoyable Victorian pub with leather couches and stained-glass windows. It's a good place to stop for something cool to drink. The top floor has a balcony restaurant that's popular on sunny afternoons.

❹ **Victoria Barracks.** If you're curious about the Australian military, you'll enjoy the free tours of this Regency-style barracks (built from 1841), which take place every Thursday at 10 AM sharp. The tour includes entry to the Army Museum, which has exhibits covering Australia's military history from the days of the Rum Corps to the Malayan conflict of the 1950s. ✉ *Oxford St. at Oatley Rd., Paddington* ☎ *02/9339-3303* ⊕ *www.awm.gov.au/units/place* ✉ *Tours free, museum only A$2* ☉ *Museum Thurs. 10–12:30, Sun. 10–3.*

GREATER SYDNEY

Numbers in the text correspond to numbers in the margin and on the Greater Sydney map.

The Greater Sydney area has numerous attractions that can be easily reached by public transport. These include historic townships, the Sydney 2000 Olympics site, national parks where you can experience the Australian bush, and wildlife and theme parks that appeal to children.

Other points of interest are Sydney's most popular beaches at Bondi and Manly; the historic city of Parramatta, founded in 1788, 26 km (16 mi) to the west; and the magnificent Hawkesbury River, which winds its way around the city's western and northern borders. The waterside suburb of Balmain has pubs and restaurants, an atmospheric Saturday flea market, and backstreets full of character.

GETTING HERE AND AROUND

Trains travel from Central Station to Parramatta daily, and directly to Sydney Olympic Park on weekdays. On weekends you take the train to Lidcombe and then change trains for the short ride to Olympic Park station. The RiverCat travels from Circular Quay to Parramatta, calling at Sydney Olympic Park on the way. Trains depart from Central for the Hawkesbury River (alight at Hawkesbury River station in the town of Brooklyn). They also travel to the Royal National Park (alight at Engadine or Heathcote stations, or Loftus, where a tram travels from the station to the park on Sundays only).

TIMING

Each of the sights below could easily fill the better part of a day. If you're short on time, try a tour company that combines visits within a particular area—for example, a day trip west to the Olympic Games site, Australian Wildlife Park, and the Blue Mountains.

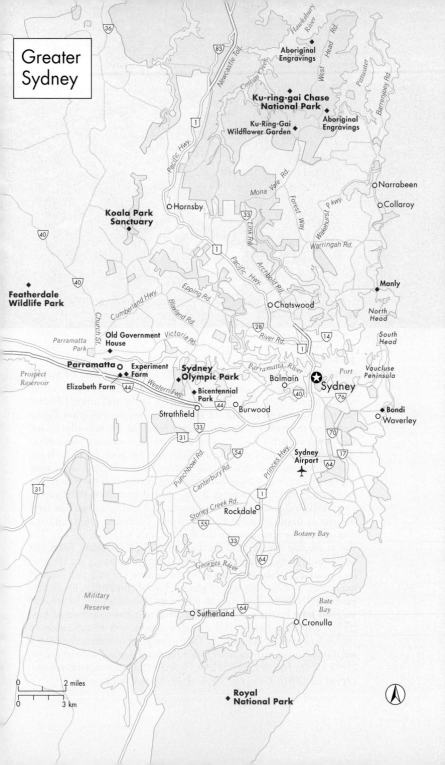

Greater Sydney

36

83

Newcastle Toll

Contan Creek

Hawkesbury River

Aboriginal Engravings

West Head Rd.

Pittwater

Barrenjoey Rd.

Ku-ring-gai Chase National Park

1

Pacific Hwy.

Ku-Ring-Gai Wildflower Garden

Aboriginal Engravings

Mona Vale Rd.

○ Narrabeen

○ Collaroy

Forest Way

Wakehurst P.kwy.

○ Hornsby

33

Link Rd.

Pacific Hwy.

Warringah Rd.

Koala Park Sanctuary

40

1

Archbold Rd.

40

Epping Rd.

Blaxland Rd.

♦ **Featherdale Wildlife Park**

Cumberland Hwy.

28

○ Chatswood

River Rd.

Church St.

Victoria Rd.

1

14

Manly

North Head

Parramatta Park

Old Government House

Parramatta River

South Head

Parramatta ○

Experiment Farm

Sydney Olympic Park

Balmain ○

Port

Vaucluse Peninsula

Prospect Reservoir

Elizabeth Farm

44

Western Fwy.

Bicentennial Park

44

○ Burwood

★ **Sydney**

40

76

♦ **Bondi**

○ Waverley

Strathfield ○

33

31

70

54

Sydney Airport

17

Punchbowl Rd.

Canterbury Rd.

Princes Hwy.

64

31

Stoney Creek Rd.

1

○ Rockdale

55

Botany Bay

33

64

Georges River

Bate Bay

Military Reserve

○ Sutherland

64

○ Cronulla

0 ___ 2 miles
0 ___ 3 km

♦ **Royal National Park**

A bird's eye view of the boats in Parramatta River.

TOP ATTRACTIONS

★ **Parramatta.** This bustling satellite city 26 km (16 mi) west of Sydney is one of Australia's most historic precincts. Its origins as a European settlement are purely agrarian. The sandy, rocky soil around Sydney Cove was too poor to feed the fledgling colony, so Governor Phillip looked to the banks of the Parramatta River for the rich alluvial soil they needed. In 1789, just a year after the first convicts-cum-settlers arrived, Phillip established Rosehill, an area set aside for agriculture. The community developed as its agricultural successes grew, and several important buildings survive as outstanding examples of the period. The two-hour Harris Park Heritage Walk, which departs from the RiverCat Ferry Terminal, connects the key historic sites and buildings. The ferry departs at frequent intervals from Sydney's Circular Quay, and is a relaxing, scenic alternative to the drive or train ride from the city. The site of the first private land grant in Australia, **Experiment Farm** was settled in 1789 by James Ruse, a former convict who was given 1½ acres by Governor Phillip on condition that he become self-sufficient—a vital experiment if the colony was to survive. Luckily for Phillip, his gamble paid off. The bungalow, with its wide verandas, was built by colonial surgeon John Harris in the 1830s; it contains a fine collection of Australian colonial furniture, and the cellar now houses an exhibition on the life and work of James Ruse. The surrounding ornamental garden is most beautiful in early summer, when the floral perfumes are strongest. ⊠ *9 Ruse St., Harris Park* ☎ *02/9635–5655* ⊕ *www.nsw.nationaltrust. org.au* ✉ *A$6* ⊘ *Tues.–Fri. 10:30–3:30, weekends 11–3:30.*

2

On the bank of the Parramatta River, **Old Government House** is Australia's oldest surviving public building, and a notable work from the Georgian period. Built by governors John Hunter and Lachlan Macquarie, the building has been faithfully restored in keeping with its origins, and contains the nation's most significant collection of early Australian furniture. In the 260-acre parkland surrounding the house are Governor Brisbane's bathhouse and observatory and the Government House Dairy. ⊠ *Parramatta Park, Parramatta* ☎ *02/9635–8149* ⊕ *www.nsw. nationaltrust.org.au* ✉ *A$8; A$10 combined ticket with Experiment Farm* ☒ *Weekdays 10–4, weekends 10:30–4.*

The oldest European building in Australia, **Elizabeth Farm** was built by John and Elizabeth Macarthur in 1793. With its simple but elegant lines and long, shady verandas, the house became a template for Australian farmhouses that survives to the present day. It was here, too, that the merino sheep industry began, since the Macarthurs were the first to introduce the tough Spanish breed to Australia. Although John Macarthur has traditionally been credited as the father of Australia's wool industry, it was Elizabeth who largely ran the farm while her husband pursued his official and more-lucrative unofficial duties as an officer in the colony's Rum Corps. Inside are personal objects of the Macarthur family, as well as a re-creation of their furnishings. ⊠ *70 Alice St., Rosehill* ☎ *02/9635–9488* ⊕ *www.hht.net.au/museums* ✉ *A$8* ☒ *Fri.–Sun. 9:30–4 or by group appointment weekdays.*

★ **Royal National Park.** Established in 1879 on the coast south of Sydney, the Royal has the distinction of being the first national park in Australia and the second in the world, after Yellowstone National Park in the United States. Several walking tracks traverse the grounds, most of them requiring little or no hiking experience. The Lady Carrington Walk, a 10-km (6-mi) trek, is a self-guided tour that crosses 15 creeks and passes several historic sites. Other tracks take you along the coast past beautiful wildflower displays and through patches of rain forest. You can canoe the Port Hacking River upstream from the Audley Causeway; rentals are available at the Audley boat shed on the river. The Illawarra train line stops at Loftus, Engadine, Heathcote, Waterfall, and Otford stations, where most of the park's walking tracks begin. There are three campsites in the park. ⊠ *Royal National Park Visitor Centre, 35 km (22 mi) south of Sydney via Princes Hwy. to Farnell Ave., south of Loftus, or McKell Ave. at Waterfall* ☎ *Box 44, Sutherland 1499* ☎ *02/9542–0648, 02/9542–0666 National Parks and Wildlife Service district office* ⊕ *www.nationalparks.nsw.gov.au* ✉ *A$11 per vehicle per day, overnight camping A$5–A$14; booking required* ☒ *Daily 7 AM–8:30 PM.*

WORTH NOTING

☾ **Featherdale Wildlife Park.** This is the place to see kangaroos, dingoes, wallabies, and echidnas (and even feed some of them) in native bush settings 40 km (25 mi) west of Sydney. You can have your picture taken with a koala for free. The daily crocodile feeding sessions are very popular. Take the train to Blacktown station and then board the 725 bus for the park. ⊠ *217 Kildare Rd., Doonside* ☎ *02/9622–1644* ⊕ *www.featherdale.com.au* ✉ *A$22* ☒ *Daily 9–5.*

☺ **Koala Park Sanctuary.** At this private park in Sydney's northern outskirts you can feed a kangaroo or cuddle a koala. (Koala presentations are daily at 10:20, 11:45, 2, and 3.) The sanctuary also has dingoes, wombats, emus, and wallaroos. There are sheep-shearing and boomerang-throwing demonstrations. ⊠ *84 Castle Hill Rd., West Pennant Hills* ☎ *02/9484–3141* ⊕ *www.koalaparksanctuary.com.au* 🎫 *A$19* ☉ *Daily 9–5.*

Ku-ring-gai Chase National Park. Nature hikes here lead past rock engravings and paintings by the Guringai Aboriginal tribe, the area's original inhabitants for whom the park is named. Created in the 1890s, the park mixes large stands of eucalyptus trees with moist, rain-forest-filled gullies where swamp wallabies, possums, goannas, and other creatures roam. The delightful trails are mostly easy or moderate, including the compelling 3-km (2-mi) Garigal Aboriginal Heritage Walk at West Head, which takes in ancient rock-art sites. From Mt. Ku-ring-gai train station you can walk the 3-km (2-mi) Ku-ring-gai Track to Appletree Bay, while the 30-minute, wheelchair-accessible Discovery Trail is an excellent introduction to the region's flora and fauna. Leaflets on all of the walks are available at the park's entry stations and from the Wildlife Shop at Bobbin Head.

The park is 24 km (15 mi) north of Sydney. Railway stations at Mt. Ku-ring-gai, Berowra, and Cowan, close to the park's western border, provide access to walking trails. On Sunday, for example, you can walk from Mt. Ku-ring-gai station to Appletree Bay and then to Bobbin Head, where a bus can take you to the Turramurra rail station. By car, take the Pacific Highway to Pymble. Then turn into Bobbin Head Road or continue on the highway to Mt. Colah and turn off into the park on Ku-ring-gai Chase Road. You can also follow the Pacific Highway to Pymble and then drive along the Mona Vale Road to Terry Hills and take the West Head turnoff.

Camping in the park is permitted only at the **Basin** (☎ *02/9974–1011*) on Pittwater (near Palm Beach). Sites with access to barbecues and picnic tables must be booked in advance. The rate is A$14 per adult per night. Supplies can be purchased in Palm Beach. For more information on the park, contact Ku-ring-gai Chase National Park Visitors Centre. 🖄 *Box 834, Hornsby 2077* ☎ *02/9472–8949* ⊕ *www.basin-campground.com.au.*

NEED A BREAK?   **Parramatta Park Cafe** (⊠ *Parramatta Park, Cnr Mill and Macquarie Sts., Parramatta* ☎ *02/9630-0144*). After visiting Old Government House, amble down to the bank of the river and pull up a seat in this shady spot. It's open for brunch and lunch daily with a menu of gourmet burgers, soup, pastas, and sweet treats.

Sydney Olympic Park. The center of the 2000 Olympic and Paralympic Games lies 14 km (8½ mi) west of the city center. Sprawling across 1,900 acres on the shores of Homebush Bay, the site is a series of majestic stadiums, arenas, and accommodation complexes. Among the park's sports facilities are an aquatic center, archery range, tennis center, and the centerpiece: the 85,000-seat Telstra Olympic Stadium. Since the conclusion of the 2000 Games it has been used for major sporting events like the 2003 Rugby World Cup. The Explore interactive stadium tour, costing A$27.50 per person, takes you behind the scenes to sit in the media room and have your photo taken on the winners' dais. The Games Trail walking tour, A$20 per person, includes a stop at the Cauldron where the Olympic flame burned.

Don't miss the adjacent **Bicentennial Park,** made up of 247 acres of swamps, lakes, and parks dotted with picnic grounds and bike trials. The area, a former quarry, was developed to commemorate Australia's Bicentennial celebrations in 1988. There's a visitor center outlining the history of the park, as well as an upscale restaurant (Bel Parco) and café (Lillies on the Park). The most scenic and relaxing way to get to Sydney Olympic Park is to take the RiverCat from Circular Quay to Homebush Bay. You can also take a train from Central Station, Sydney, to Olympic Park. ⊠ *1 Herb Elliot Ave., Homebush Bay* ☎ *02/9714–7888* ⊕ *www.sydneyolympicpark.com.au* ⊙ *Daily during daylight hrs.*

> ## RUN FOR YOUR LIFE
>
> Pack your jogging shoes for the biggest footrace in the country. **City to Surf** (⊕ *city2surf.sunherald.com.au*) attracts more than 50,000 people each August— some taking it very seriously, others donning a gorilla suit or fairy outfit. The race starts at Hyde Park and winds through the eastern suburbs 14 km (9 mi) to Bondi Beach, via the notorious "Heartbreak Hill" at Rose Bay. For some reason, it never rains on the second Sunday in August.

BEACHES

Sydney is paradise for beach lovers. Within the metropolitan area there are more than 30 ocean beaches, all with golden sand and rolling surf, as well as several more around the harbor with calmer water for safe swimming. If your hotel is on the harbor's south side, the logical choice for a day at the beach is one of the southern ocean beaches between Bondi and Coogee. On the north side of the harbor, Manly is easily accessible by ferry, but beaches farther north involve a longer trip by car or public transportation.

Lifeguards are on duty at most of Sydney's ocean beaches during summer months, and flags indicate whether a beach is being patrolled. "Swim between the flags" is an adage that is drummed into every Australian child, with very good reason: the undertow can be very dangerous. If you get into difficulty, don't fight the current. Breathe evenly, stay calm, and raise one arm above your head to signal the lifeguards.

Although there's no shortage of sharks inside and outside the harbor, the risk of attack is very low. These species are not typically aggressive toward humans, and shark nets protect many Sydney beaches. A more common hazard is jellyfish, known locally as bluebottles, which inflict a painful sting—with a remote risk of more serious complications (including severe allergic reactions). The staff at most beaches will supply a spray-on remedy to help relieve the pain, which generally lasts about 24 hours. Many beaches will post warning signs when bluebottles are present, but you can also determine the situation yourself by looking for the telltale bright-blue, bubblelike jellies washed up along the waterline.

Topless sunbathing is common at all Sydney beaches, but full nudity is permitted only at a couple of locations, including Lady Jane Beach, close to Watsons Bay on the south side of the harbor.

Details of how to reach the beaches by bus, train, or ferry are provided below, but some of the city's harbor and southern beaches are also on the Bondi Explorer bus route. These are Nielsen Park, Camp Cove, Lady Jane, Bondi, Bronte, Clovelly, and Coogee.

Numbers in the margin correspond to beaches on the Sydney Beaches map.

INSIDE THE HARBOR

❹ Balmoral. This 800-yard-long, rarely crowded beach—among the best of
★ the inner-harbor beaches—is in one of Sydney's most exclusive northern suburbs. There's no surf, but it's a great place to learn to windsurf (sailboard rentals are available). The Esplanade, which runs along the back of the beach, has a handful of upscale restaurants, as well as several snack bars and cafés that serve award-winning fish-and-chips. In summer you can catch performances of Shakespeare on the Beach. You could easily combine a trip to Balmoral with a visit to Taronga Zoo. To reach Balmoral, take the ferry from Circular Quay to Taronga Zoo and then board Bus 238. ⊠ *Raglan St., Balmoral.*

❻ Camp Cove. Just inside South Head, this crescent beach is where Sydney's fashionable people come to see and be seen. The gentle slope and calm water make it a safe playground for children. A shop at the northern end of the beach sells salad rolls and fresh fruit juices. The grassy hill at the southern end of the beach has a plaque to commemorate the spot where Captain Arthur Phillip, the commander of the First Fleet, first set foot inside Port Jackson. Parking is limited; arrive by car after 10 on weekends, and keep in mind it's a long walk to the beach. Take Bus 324 or 325 from Circular Quay. ⊠ *Cliff St., Watsons Bay.*

❺ Lady Jane. Lady Jane—officially called Lady Bay—is the most accessible of the nude beaches around Sydney. It's also a popular part of Sydney's gay scene. Only a couple of hundred yards long and backed by a stone wall, the beach has safe swimming with no surf. From Camp Cove, follow the path north and then descend the short, steep ladder leading down the cliff face to the beach.

❼ Nielsen Park. By Sydney standards, this beach at the end of the Vaucluse Peninsula is small, but behind the sand is a large, shady park that's ideal for picnics. The headlands at either end of the beach are especially popular for their magnificent views across the harbor. The beach is protected by a semicircular net, so don't be deterred by the beach's correct name, Shark Bay. The Beachhouse Café behind the beach sells drinks, snacks, and meals; there is also a more upscale restaurant. Parking is often difficult on weekends. Historic Greycliffe House—built in 1840 and now used as National Park offices—is in the park, while the more elaborate and stately Vaucluse House is a 10-minute walk away.

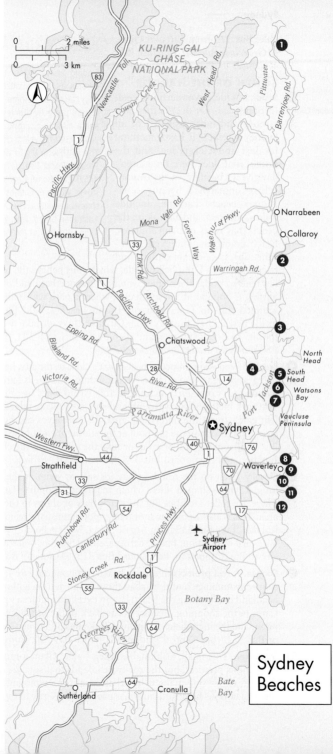

Sydney
Beaches

Take Bus 325 from Circular Quay. ⊠ *Greycliffe Ave. off Vaucluse Rd., Vaucluse.*

SOUTH OF THE HARBOR

8 Fodor'sChoice ★ **Bondi.** Wide, wonderful Bondi (pronounced *bon*-dye) is the most famous and most crowded of all Sydney beaches. It has something for just about everyone, and the droves that flock here on a sunny day give it a bustling, carnival atmosphere unmatched by any other Sydney beach. Facilities include toilets, showers, and a kiosk on the beach that rents out sun lounges, beach umbrellas, and even swimsuits. Cafés, ice-cream outlets, and restaurants line Campbell Parade, which runs behind the beach. Families tend to prefer the calmer waters of the northern end of the beach. Surfing is popular at the south end, where a path winds along the sea-sculpted cliffs to Tamarama and Bronte beaches. Take Bus 380, 382, or the new 333 all the way from Circular Quay, or take the train from the city to Bondi Junction and then board Bus 380, 381, 382, or 333. ⊠ *Campbell Parade, Bondi Beach.*

> ### CUTE COSSIES
>
> Finding great bathing suits (or cossies, as they're called in Sydney) can be a dilemma. If you want a perfectly fitting cossie—and a matching sarong—that you'll wear for years, check out **The Big Swim** (⊠ *74 Campbell Parade, Bondi Beach* ☏ *02/9365-4457*). This Bondi Beach favorite stocks women's cossies for all shapes and sizes. Check out the Australian brand, Jets, which has a huge selection of terrific designs.

9 ★ **Bronte.** If you want an ocean beach that's close to the city, has both sand and grassy areas, and offers a terrific setting, this one is hard to beat. A wooded park of palm trees and Norfolk Island pines surrounds Bronte. The park includes a playground and sheltered picnic tables, and excellent cafés are in the immediate area. The breakers can be fierce, but swimming is safe in the sea pool at the southern end of the beach. Take Bus 378 from Central Station, or take the train from the city to Bondi Junction and then board Bus 378. ⊠ *Bronte Rd., Bronte.*

11 ★ **Clovelly.** Even on the roughest day it's safe to swim at the end of this long, keyhole-shaped inlet, which makes it a popular family beach. There are toilet facilities but no snack bars or shops in the immediate area. This is also a popular snorkeling spot that usually teems with tropical fish. Take Bus 339 from Argyle Street, Millers Point (the Rocks), or Wynyard bus station; Bus 341 from Central Station; or a train from the city to Bondi Junction, then board Bus 329. ⊠ *Clovelly Rd., Clovelly.*

12 **Coogee.** A reef protects this lively beach (pronounced *kuh*-jee), creating calmer swimming conditions than those found at its neighbors. A grassy headland overlooking the beach has an excellent children's playground. Cafés in the shopping precinct at the back of the beach sell ice cream, pizza, and the ingredients for picnics. Take Bus 373 from Circular Quay or Bus 372 from Central Station. ⊠ *Coogee Bay Rd., Coogee.*

10 ★ **Tamarama.** This small, fashionable beach—aka "Glam-a-rama"—is one of Sydney's prettiest, but the rocky headlands that squeeze close to the sand on either side make it less than ideal for swimming. The sea is often hazardous here, and surfing is prohibited. A café in the small park

Besides Bondi, Sydneysiders have more than 30 beaches to choose from.

behind the beach sells sandwiches, fresh juices, and fruit whips. Take the train from the city to Bondi Junction and then board Bus 391, or walk for 10 minutes along the cliffs from the south end of Bondi Beach. ✉ *Tamarama Marine Dr., Tamarama.*

NORTH OF THE HARBOR

2 **Dee Why–Long Reef.** Separated from Dee Why by a narrow channel, Long Reef Beach is remoter and much quieter than its southern neighbor. However, Dee Why has better surfing conditions, a big sea pool, and several good restaurants. To get here, take Bus 136 from Manly. ✉ *The Strand, Dee Why.*

3 **Manly.** The Bondi Beach of the north shore, Manly caters to everyone

Fodor's Choice ★ except those who want to get away from it all. On sunny days Sydneysiders, school groups, and travelers from around the world crowd the 2-km-long (1.25-mi-long) sweep of white sand and take to the waves to swim and ride boards. The beach is well equipped with changing and toilet facilities and lockers. The promenade that runs between the Norfolk Island pines is great for people-watching and rollerblading. Cafés, souvenir shops, and ice-cream parlors line the nearby shopping area, the Corso. Manly also has several non-beach attractions, including Oceanworld, an aquarium about 200 yards from the ferry wharf. The ferry ride from the city makes a day at Manly feel more like a holiday than just an excursion to the beach. Take a ferry or Manly Fast Ferry from Circular Quay. From the dock at Manly the beach is a 10-minute walk. ✉ *Steyne St., Manly.*

1 **Palm Beach.** The golden sands of Palm Beach glitter as much as the bejeweled residents of the stylish nearby village. The beach is on one

Surf Lifesaving Clubs

In 2007 the Australian Surf Lifesaving Association celebrated its 100-year anniversary. The world's first Surf Lifesaving club was formed at Bondi Beach on February 21, 1907. Other clubs formed in quick secession, and today there are more than 300 clubs in Australia, with 36 in Sydney and 129 in New South Wales.

In the last century more than 500,000 swimmers have been rescued from patrolled beaches around the country, and more than 1 million swimmers have received first aid.

Lifesavers are Australian icons; volunteers undertake their five-hour beach patrols on a rostered basis during the summer season from September to April. In addition to the thousands of volunteers across Australia, there are also permanent, paid lifeguards who are employed by the local councils and are on duty year-round.

Lifesavers arrive at the beach bright and early, check the beach conditions, erect the red and yellow flags to indicate the safe swimming areas, and keep an eye on swimmers throughout their patrol. It's easy to spot a surf lifesaver—he or she wears the bright red-and-yellow cap and matching red-and-yellow uniform.

Bondi Beach lifesavers are the busiest in Australia. Each year about 2.5 million people come for a swim: some 2,500 rescues took place in an average year. The worst day in Bondi's history was February 6, 1938, known as Black Sunday. Lifesavers plucked 300 people from the huge surf. Five lives were lost.

It's not all work for Surf Lifesaving clubs. They hold competitions and surf carnivals throughout the summer months at numerous beaches. Events include surf swims, crew boat races (man-powered by oarsmen), surf ski races, and the macho-named "iron man" races where men (and women in separate events) perform all manner of endurance tests. Surf Lifesaving clubs opened their doors to women and children several decades ago.

side of the peninsula separating the large inlet of Pittwater from the Pacific Ocean. Bathers can easily cross from the ocean side to Pittwater's calm waters. You can take a circular ferry trip around this waterway from the wharf on the Pittwater side. The view from the lighthouse at the northern end of the beach is well worth the walk. Shops and cafés sell light snacks and meals. Take Bus 190 from Wynyard bus station. ⊠ *Ocean Rd., Palm Beach.*

WHERE TO EAT

Sydney's dining scene is as sunny and cosmopolitan as the city itself, and there are diverse and exotic culinary adventures to suit every appetite. Mod-Oz (modern-Australian) cooking flourishes, fueled by local produce and guided by Mediterranean and Asian techniques. Look for such innovations as tuna tartare with flying-fish roe and wasabi; emu prosciutto; five-spice duck; shiitake mushroom pie; and sweet turmeric barramundi curry. A meal at Tetsuya's, Bécasse, or Rockpool constitutes

2

a crash course in this dazzling culinary language. A visit to the city's fish markets at Pyrmont, just five minutes from the city center, will also tell you much about Sydney's diet. Look for rudderfish, barramundi, blue-eye, kingfish, John Dory, ocean perch, and parrot fish, as well as Yamba prawns, Balmain and Moreton Bay bugs (shovel-nose lobsters), sweet Sydney rock oysters, mud crab, spanner crab, yabbies (small freshwater crayfish), and marrons (freshwater lobsters).

There are many expensive and indulgent restaurants in the city center, but the real dining scene is in the inner city, eastern suburbs, and inner-western suburbs of Leichhardt and Balmain. Neighborhoods like Surry Hills, Darlinghurst, Paddington, and beachside suburb Bondi are dining destinations in themselves. Plus, you're more likely to find a restaurant that will serve on a Sunday night in one of these places than in the central business district (the city center)—which can become a bit of a ghost town after offices close during the week. Circular Quay and The Rocks are always lively, and the Overseas Passenger Terminal (on the opposite side of the harbor from the Opera House) has several top-notch restaurants with stellar views.

Use the coordinate (✛ 1:B2) at the end of each listing to locate a site on the corresponding map.

SYDNEY HARBOUR

$ ✗ **Bathers' Pavilion Cafe.** Balmoral Beach is blessed. Not only does it have
AUSTRALIAN an inviting sandy beach and great water views, but it also has one of the best eating strips north of Harbour Bridge. Queen of the strip is Bathers' Pavilion, which includes a restaurant, café, and lavish private dining room. Serge Dansereau cooks with one hand on the seasons and the other on the best local ingredients at the acclaimed restaurant, but for a casual breakfast, lunch, or dinner it's hard to beat the café (¢). There's a choice of light meals such as the shellfish soup with potato, leek, and tomato, or larger meals like pan-fried boneless salmon cutlet with muddle cucumber relish, which are around A$32. ⊠ *4 the Esplanade, Balmoral* ☎ *02/9969–5050* ⊕ *www.batherspavilion.com.au* ♺ *Reservations essential* ⊟ *AE, DC, MC, V* ✛ *2:C1.*

$ ✗ **The Deck.** If you've wanted to know just what's inside that giant face
MODERN on the north side of the harbour under the bridge, well this is your
AUSTRALIAN chance. The Deck is located in a swanky refurbished space just as you step through the giant mouth of Luna Park, Sydney's long-estabished fun park. The stunning view, however, across the harbour with the Opera House right in your sights, is the real draw. The restaurant and cocktail bar are above a live venue that cranks up on the weekend, so expect a fun night out rather than a quiet tête-à-tête. There's a selection of seafood and non-seafood tasting plates to share, while wonderful classics such as paella and bouillabaisse are on the menu. Sweet treats include rich Belgian chocolate terrine and pistachio filo wafers with fresh strawberries, honey cream, and berry coulis. ⊠ *1 Olympic Dr., Sydney Harbor* ☎ *02/9033–7670* ⊕ *www.thedecksydney.com.au* ⊟ *AE, MC, V* ✛ *2:A2.*

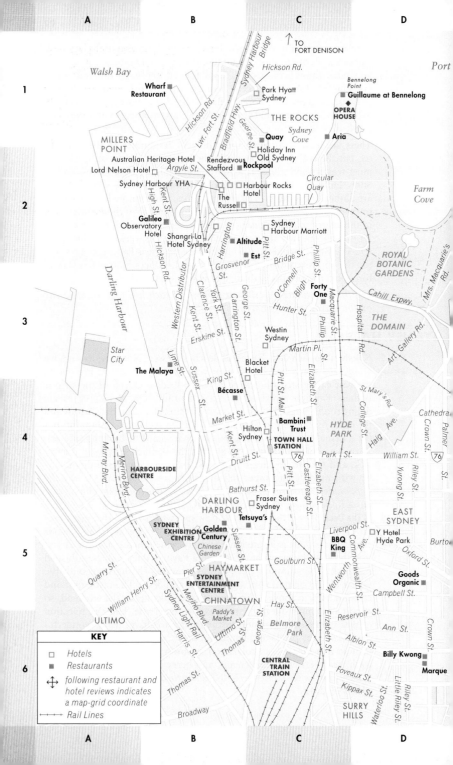

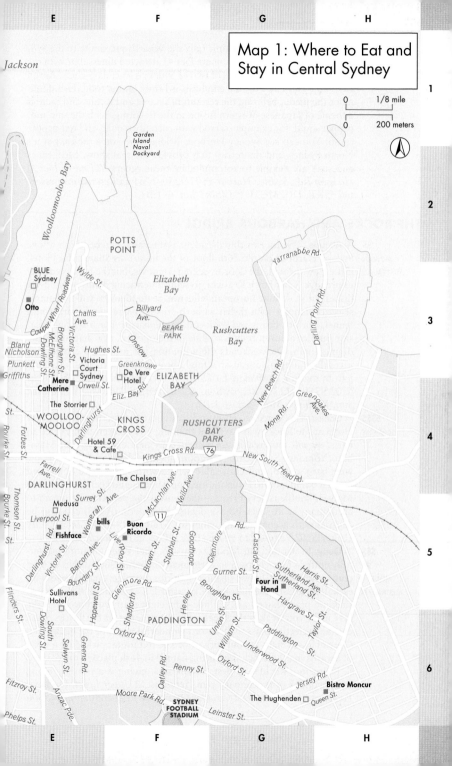

E   F   G   H

Jackson

Map 1: Where to Eat and Stay in Central Sydney

0   1/8 mile
0   200 meters

1

Woolloomooloo Bay

Garden
Island
Naval
Dockyard

POTTS
POINT

2

Yarranabbe Rd.

BLUE
Sydney

Wylde St.

*Elizabeth
Bay*

3

Otto

*Challis
Ave.*

*Billyard
Ave.*

BEARE
PARK

*Rushcutters
Bay*

Darling Point Rd.

Cowper Wharf Roadway
Brougham St.
Victoria St.
McElhone St.
Dowling St.

Hughes St.

Onslow

*Greenknowe
Ave.*

New Beach Rd.

*Greenoaks
Ave.*

*Bland
Nicholson*

Victoria
Court
Sydney

De Vere
Hotel

ELIZABETH
BAY

Mona Rd.

Plunkett
Griffiths

**Mere
Catherine**

Orwell St.

Eliz. Bay Rd.

ELIZABETH
BAY

The Storrier

Forbes St.

WOOLLOO-
MOOLOO

Darlinghurst

KINGS
CROSS

RUSHCUTTERS
BAY
PARK

4

Bourke St.

Hotel 59
& Cafe

Kings Cross Rd.

76

New South Head Rd.

*Farrell
Ave.*

DARLINGHURST

The Chelsea

McLachlan Ave.

Neild Ave.

Thomson St.
Bourke St.

Medusa

Surrey St.
Womerah Ave.

11

Liverpool St.

bills

Buon
Ricordo

Stephen St.

Goodhope

Rd.

Cascade St.

Sutherland Ave.
Sutherland St.

Harris St.

5

Fishface

Darlinghurst Rd.
Victoria St.
Barcom Ave.

Liverpool St.
Brown St.

Gurner St.

Broughton St.

**Four in
Hand**

Hargrave St.
Taylor St.

Flinders St.
Bourke St.

Sullivans
Hotel

Boundary St.
Hopewell St.
Glenmore Rd.
Shadforth

Heeley

Union St.

William St.

Paddington St.

PADDINGTON

Oxford St.

Underwood St.

6

Flinders St.
South Dowling St.
Selwyn St.
Greens Rd.
Anzac Pde.

Renny St.

Oxford St.

Jersey Rd.

Bistro Moncur

Fitzroy St.

Moore Park Rd.

SYDNEY
FOOTBALL
STADIUM

Leinster St.

The Hughenden

Queen St.

Phelps St.

E   F   G   H

$ ✕**Wharf Restaurant.** At one time only the Wharf's proximity to the Syd-
MODERN ney Theatre Company (they share Pier 4) attracted diners, but with the
AUSTRALIAN restaurant now in the hands of two of Sydney's legendary chefs, Aaron
Ross and Tim Pak Poy, the emphasis is firmly on the food. Fish dominates the menu, befitting the restaurant's name and locale, and there is
a theme of Japanese-Western fusion in the flavoring, with the salt-and-
pepper squid, for example, served with cucumber, mint, and red-pepper
relish. You can see Sydney Harbour Bridge from some tables, but it's
North Sydney and the ferries that provide the real show. Meal times
and sizes are flexible to accommodate theatergoers. ✉ *End of Pier 4,
Hickson Rd., Sydney Harbor* ☎ *02/9250–1761* ⚲ *Reservations essential* ▭ *AE, DC, MC, V* ✆ *Closed Sun.* ✛ *1:B1.*

THE ROCKS AND HARBOUR BRIDGE

$$ ✕**Altitude.** The lure of this decadent restaurant, perched high above
MODERN Sydney Harbour on the 36th floor of the luxurious Shangri-La Hotel,
AUSTRALIAN is the view through the floor-to-ceiling windows, but the food is equally
impressive. Chef Steve Krasicki presents an enticing menu of Mod-Oz
dishes with a definite European influence. Seafood lovers will find ample
selection among such dishes as herb-crusted barramundi with confit
fennel, borlotti bean, and rock-cod bouillabaisse. For a special occa-
sion, gather a dozen friends to dine in the opulent, egg-shaped private
dining room. On weekends the adjoining bar attracts a crowd that
loves the thumping music, so it might be a good idea to beat it early or
join in the fun. ✉ *Shangri-La Hotel, 176 Cumberland St., The Rocks*
☎ *02/9250–6123* ⚲ *Reservations essential* ▭ *AE, DC, MC, V* ✆ *Closed
Sun. No lunch Mon.–Sat.* ✛ *1:B2.*

$$$$ ✕**Galileo.** This gracious, salon-style restaurant within the Observatory
JAPANESE Hotel at the Rocks will have you thinking you've been transported to
Paris, as will the French menu created by new executive chef Masa-
hiko Yomonda. À la carte selections include duck and foie gras pie
with baby onion, and corn salad served with sauce aigre doux; and
braised oxtail, potato Dauphinoise, apple puree, and beef jus. The Gran
Marnier soufflé is very French—the twist is the pistachio ice cream to
accompany it. A seven-course degustation menu (A$98) can also be
enjoyed with accompanying wines for $180. ✉ *89–113 Kent St., City
Center* ☎ *02/9256–2215* ▭ *AE, DC, MC, V* ✆ *No lunch* ✛ *1:B2.*

$$$ ✕**Quay.** In his take on Mod-Oz cuisine, chef Peter Gilmore master-
★ fully crafts a four-course à-la-carte menu including such dishes as mud
MODERN crab congee with Chinese-inspired split rice porridge; quail breasts with
AUSTRALIAN eschallots and truffle-infused milk custard; and 24-hour slow-cooked
suckling pig. Desserts are sublime—the eight-textured chocolate cake
may make you weak at the knees—and the wine list fits the flavors of the
cuisine perfectly. Glass walls afford wonderful views of the bridge and
Opera House, right at your fork's tip. The restaurant picked up a swag
of awards in 2009, including being named in 46th place in the coveted
S. Pellegrino World's 50 Best Restaurants, giving it a position along
with Sydney's other culinary gem, Tetusyas. ✉ *Upper Level, Overseas
Passenger Terminal, West Circular Quay, The Rocks* ☎ *02/9251–5600*

⊕ *www.quay.com.au* ♨ *Reservations essential* ⊟ *AE, DC, MC, V* ⊙ *No lunch Sat.–Mon.* ✣ *1:C1.*

$$$$ ✕ **Rockpool.** A meal at Rockpool is a crash course in what Mod-Oz

MODERN cooking is all about, conducted in a glamorous, long dining room with

AUSTRALIAN a catwalk-like ramp. The iconic Rocks restaurant celebrated 20 years

Fodor'sChoice in 2009. Chefs Neil Perry and Michael McEnearney weave Thai, Chi-

★ nese, Mediterranean, and Middle Eastern influences into their repertoire with effortless flair and originality. Prepare to be amazed by the
lobster, abalone mushroom, tea-smoked duck prosciutto, and Asian
pear with pepper caramel dressing as a starter, and the Moroccan-style
lamb, which is slow cooked with almonds, olives, and stuffed dates.
Don't miss the date tart for dessert, which has graced the menu for 20
years. ✉ *107 George St., The Rocks* ☎ *02/9252–1888* ♨ *Reservations
essential* ⊟ *AE, DC, MC, V* ⊙ *Closed Sun. and Mon. No lunch Sat.*
✣ *1:B2.*

OPERA HOUSE AND DOMAIN

$$$ ✕ **Aria.** With windows overlooking the Opera House and Harbour

★ Bridge, Aria could easily rest on the laurels of its location. Instead,

AUSTRALIAN chef Matthew Moran creates a menu of extraordinary dishes that may
be your best meal in the antipodes. (Be warned: the bill will have you
reeling!) Make a reservation before you even get on the plane, and let
your mouth begin to water for the double-cooked sweet pork belly
and the aged beef fillet in béarnaise sauce. There is a 20-minute wait
for the passionfruit soufflé, but the exquisite view makes the time fly.
✉ *1 Macquarie St., East Circular Quay* ☎ *02/9252–2555* ⊟ *AE, DC,
MC, V* ⊙ *No lunch weekends* ✣ *1:C1.*

$$$ ✕ **Guillaume at Bennelong.** Chef Guillaume Brahimi rattles the pans at

AUSTRALIAN possibly the most superbly situated dining room in town. Tucked into
the side of the Opera House, the restaurant affords views of Sydney
Harbour Bridge and the city lights. Brahimi's creations soar: try the
yellowfin tuna infused with soy and mustard-seed vinaigrette, or the
Barossa chicken on Chinese cabbage with ravioli of duck foie gras and a
veal jus. Better yet, work your way through the eight-course degustation
menu (A$200). ✉ *Bennelong Point, Circular Quay* ☎ *02/9241–1999*
♨ *Reservations essential* ⊟ *AE, DC, MC, V* ⊙ *Closed Sun. No lunch
Sat.–Wed.* ✣ *1:C1.*

DARLING HARBOUR

¢ ✕ **BBQ King.** You can find better basic Chinese food elsewhere in town,

CHINESE but for duck and pork, barbecue-loving Sydneysiders know that this
is the place to come. The poultry hanging in the window are the only
decor at this small Chinatown staple, where the food is so fresh you can
almost hear it clucking. Barbecued pork is the other featured dish, and
the suckling pig is especially delicious. It's open until late at night, when
the average customers are large groups of mates sprawled at the Formica
tables feeding their drunken munchies, or Chinatown chefs kicking back
after a day in the kitchen. The service is brusque (some say downright

Continued on page 112

MOD OZ
Australia's Modern
Cuisine

By Erica Watson

It may be referred to as the land down under, but the culinary movement that's sweeping Australia means this country has come out on top. Modern Australian cuisine has transformed the land of Vegemite sandwiches and shrimp-on-the-barbie into a culinary Promised Land with unique flavors, organic produce, and bountiful seafood, fashioned by chefs who remain unburdened by restrictive traditions.

Australia is fast proving to be one of the most exciting destinations in the world for food lovers. With its stunning natural bounty, multicultural inspirations, and young culinary innovators, it ticks off all the requisite foodie boxes.

In Sydney, chefs are dishing up new twists on various traditions, creating a Modern Australian (Mod Oz) cuisine with its own compelling style. Traditional bush tucker, for example, has been transformed from a means of survival into a gourmet experience. Spicy Asian flavors have been borrowed from the country's neighbors to the east, and homage has been paid to the precision and customs brought by Australia's early European settlers.

The diversity of the modern Australian culinary movement also means that it is more than just flavors: it's an experience. And one that can be obtained from the award-winning luxury restaurant down to the small Thai-style canteens, pubs, and outdoor cafés.

While purists might argue that Mod Oz cuisine is little more than a plagiarism of flavors and cultures, others will acknowledge it as unadulterated fare with a fascinating history of its very own. Either way, it still offers a dining experience that's unique from anywhere else in the world.

MENU DECODER

Barbie: barbeque | Snags: sausages | Chook: chicken | Vegemite: salty yeast spread | Lamington: small chocolate sponge cake with coconut | Pavlova: meringue dessert filled with cream and fruit | Floater: meat pie with mushy peas and gravy | Damper: simple bread cooked on a campfire | Sanga: sandwich | Cuppa: cup of tea | Tucker: food | Chips: French fries | Tomato sauce: ketchup | Muddy: mud crab | Prawn: shrimp

Seared tuna with avocado, cilantro, and black sesame seeds, topped with caviar

BUSH TUCKER

Bush Tucker food; Tropical rainforest fruits on paper bark

BACK THEN

Native Australian plants and animals have played a vital role in the diets of the aboriginal people for more than 50,000 years. Generally referred to as bush tucker, these native fruits, nuts, seeds, vegetables, meats, and fish are harvested around the country—from arid deserts to coastal areas and tropical rainforests.

Once little more than a means of survival, today they're touted as gourmet ingredients. And you certainly don't need to go "walkabout" to find them.

RIGHT NOW

Bush tucker has undergone much transformation over the decades, experiencing a renaissance in recent years. Heavily influenced by multicultural cooking techniques, game meats such as emu and wallaby have been elevated from bush-stew ingredients to perfectly seared cuts of meat garnished with seasonal herbs and vegetables. Kangaroo is making its way into stir-fries and curries,

while crocodile—once cooked over coals on the campfire—is now served as carpaccio, tempura, or curry, among the many preparations. Seafood, like rock lobster and barramundi can be found in humble fish-and-chips shops and top-notch eateries.

Of course, bush tucker isn't just about the protein. Native spices, wild fruits, and indigenous nuts have found favor in countless culinary applications. Lemon myrtle leaves lend a lemony flavor to baked goods and savory dishes. Alpine pepper, a crushed herb, gives foods a fiery zing. Quandong is a wild plum-like fruit with subtle apricot flavor. It once was dried as a portable energy source but now is made into jams and pie fillings. Kakadu plums are made into "super" juices with enormous vitamin C content. Bush tomatoes also have become popular in jams and sauces, and are available in supermarkets. Native nuts include bunya bunya, which is chestnut-like with pine notes, the shells of which are used for smoking meat.

Witchitty grub

2

IN FOCUS MOD OZ

Tandoori kangaroo

INDIGENOUS MEATS

CAMEL: With some one million camels in Australia, camel is fast being served up on many menus. The meat is often compared to mutton and has a similar taste and texture to beef.

CROCODILE: The meat may be fish-like in texture and appearance, but it tastes similar to chicken. The most popular cut is the tail, however legs and meat from the body are also consumed. Crocodile is growing in popularity because of its delicate flavor and versatility. It is often fried and grilled, but may be served raw in carpaccio or sushi rolls.

EMU: Although it's fowl, emu meat is similar in texture and flavor to beef with a light flavor and slight gamey tones on the palate. The meat is high in iron and very low in fat and cholesterol. Typical cuts include rump, strip loin, and oyster filet. It may be served pan-seared or lightly grilled.

KANGAROO: A dark red meat, it is extremely lean with only about 2% fat. The filet or rump is best eaten rare to medium rare, and is typically seared, barbecured, or stir-fried. Young kangaroo meat tastes like beef, while aged cuts take on a gamier flavor.

WALLABY: A cousin to the kangaroo, this meat has a somewhat milder flavor. It is a rich burgundy color and is best prepared with simple, delicate cooking styles, such as barbecuing or pan frying.

WITCHETTY GRUB: The larvae of ghost moths, these grubs are eaten raw or barbecued. People describe the taste as similar to egg, with the texture of a prawn.

Macadamia nuts, meanwhile, are among the country's biggest exports.

Despite the presence of numerous bush ingredients in Sydney restaurants, the modern bush tucker dining experience is more prominent in the northern parts of the country with Queensland and Northern Territory being leaders in the culinary movement.

But there are a handful of restaurants specializing in native fare in Sydney. Coogee Beach's Deep Blue Bistro (⊕ www. deepbluebistro.com.au) is among them, with its six-course outback degustation menu, featuring dishes like seared emu with illawarra plum puree and kangaroo three ways—tartare, steak, and croquette—with bunya nut puree. The Sydney Tower Restaurant (⊕ www.sydneytowerrestaurant.com.au), atop the iconic tourist attraction, as well as some five-star hotels also dish up a range of native meats, including emu, crocodile, and kangaroo.

Simple meal of grilled camel with vegetables

UPDATED EUROPEAN FARE

Cuisine at Sean's Panaroma

BACK THEN

Although the foundation of Mod Oz cuisine stems from the arrival of early British settlers, the food scene has certainly steamed ahead since the days of boiled beef and damper.

The real progression of modern Australian food came after World War II when European immigrants brought a new wave of cooking to the country. It was the French and Italians who really opened the eyes of Australians with their distinguished flavors, commitment to freshness, and masterful culinary techniques. They also laid the foundations for some of the finest vineyards and cheese makers in the country.

RIGHT NOW

Though small, there are still degrees of British influence in modern Australian cooking, albeit slightly updated. The quintessential English meat pie is now filled with ingredients such as Murray cod, lamb, bush tomato, and kangaroo. Traditional Sunday roasts and

fish-and-chips spring up in pubs and cafes, but often with a twist. And tea is still a staple on the breakfast table with a true Aussie favorite, Vegemite on toast.

Poaching, roasting, and braising are now popular methods to cook everything from reef fish and yabbies to lamb, suckling pig, and rabbit. Omelettes, cassoulets, and soufflés as well as pasta, risotto, and gnocchi are very well suited to the country's prize-winning meats, vegetables, and seafood. And the rigorous use of garlic, saffron, basil, and tarragon is common in many kitchens.

Greeks, Germans, and Spaniards have also greatly influenced dining, especially in Sydney with tapas bars, tavernas, and schnitzel houses well represented throughout the country. Middle Eastern and North African flavors are also beginning to leave their marks.

Even casual pubs are updating dishes to reflect ethnic influences and local products. It's not unusual to see menu items like Moroccan lamb pizza and

Aussie meat pie

AUSTRALIA'S NATURAL BOUNTY

CHEESE FRUIT: Grown in tropical areas, it's high in vitamin C and has long been used for medicinal purposes. The fruit is eaten while still green since it has a distinct rotting cheese smell when ripe. Leaves can also be eaten raw or cooked.

ILLAWARRA PLUMS: Usually used in jams and chutneys or as a rich sauce to accompany kangaroo, venison, or emu. High in antioxidants, they have a subtle plum flavor with a hint of pine.

LEMON MYRTLE: A native tree with a citrus fragrance and flavor. Leaves can be used fresh or dried and ground in sweet and savory styles of cooking.

MACADAMIA NUTS: known as Kindal Kindal by native Australians, the macadamia a round white nut with a hard brown shell and creamy flavor.

MUNTRIES: Small berry-like fruit that have a distinct apple flavor. Also known as emu apples, they can be eaten fresh in salads or added to desserts.

PAPER BARK: Papery leaves from the Mellaluca tree, used to cook meat and seafood.

QUANDONG: A bright red fruit similar to a native peach. It's commonly used to make jams and sauces.

WARRIGAL GREENS: A herb-like vegetable with a flavor similar to spinach. They must be well cooked to eliminate their toxic oxalate content.

WATTLESEED: Also known as acacia seeds. They have a nutty to coffee-like flavor and are very high in protein. Often ground down and used in baking.

barramundi shepherds pie featured at The Australian (⊕ www.australianheritagehotel.com), a popular pub in the Rocks area.

Another hallmark of Mod Oz cuisine—and one that parallels America's current culinary trends—is its fascination with seasonal vegetables and organic meats. Specialist farms raising free-range poultry and livestock have become extremely popular with many restaurants throughout Sydney. Menus often cite an ingredient's producer, i.e. "Blackmore's wagyu bresaola," and also note whether ingredients are "pasture-raised" or "locally grown."

Taking the trend one step further is Bondi Beach establishment Sean's Panaroma (⊕ www.seanspanorama.com.au). There, owner Sean Moran grows produce for the restaurant on his Blue Mountains farm, which is harvested, prepared, and served to guests the same day. In terms of freshness, it really doesn't get much better than that.

Meringue topped with fresh fruit

ASIAN FUSION

Thai-style kangaroo curry

BACK THEN

Much has changed in the way of Asian food in Australia. Sixty years ago sushi didn't exist in the vocabulary, now there are Japanese restaurants on almost every street.

The Gold Rush of the mid-19th century brought an influx of Chinese immigrants to Australia, prompting Asian cuisine's humble beginnings here. Thai, Vietnamese, Indian, Malaysian, and Japanese migrants quickly followed. Before long, a cuisine that had started out in family-run restaurants in the outer suburbs of Sydney had become a burgeoning new trend. And by the late 1990s the children of the first wave of immigrants had formed the new guard.

RIGHT NOW

Traditional Chinese, Thai, and Japanese restaurants are very popular in Australia. But Asian fusion restaurants are leading the charge in creating Australia-specific taste innovations. Asian fusion cuisine combines the traditional flavors of Thai, Chinese, Japanese, and Vietnamese cooking, using local Australian ingredients and western culinary techniques. Chic contemporary interiors, often with long communal tables and shared dishes are the latest trend. Robust herbs such as mint and coriander, fiery chili, zesty black vinegar, ginger, and pickled vegetables are core ingredients, often wok-fried with fresh Australian ingredients such as Barossa Valley chicken, Thirlmere duck, or Bangalow pork.

Leading the charge is world-renowned chef Tetsuya Wakuda of Tetsuya's Restaurat, in Sydney. His signature dish, a confit of Petuna Tasmanian Ocean Trout with konbu, apple, daikon, and wasabi is a prime example of Asian fusion, uniquely blending French techniques with his Japanese heritage and excellent Australian products.

Yet, smaller modern canteen-style eateries are also serving up contemporary Asian fare that provides excellent quality at a fraction of

Red chile peppers

Chef Simon
of Chinta Ria

LOCAL FISH AND SEAFOOD

ABALONE: A large sea snail with an edible muscular foot. It has a firm, rubbery texture with a very delicate flavor and can retail for about $100 per kilogram. Abalone are often seared or fried.

BALMAIN OR MORETON BAY BUGS: A smaller relative of the rock lobster with a short tail, flat head, and bug-like eyes. They have a sweet taste and a medium texture. A favorite served cold in salads and seafood platters, or split down the middle and grilled.

BARRAMUNDI: A member of the perch family, it's a highly versatile fish with a medium to firm flesh and white to light pink tones. Native to Australia, it lives in both fresh and salt waters and is farmed as well as caught in the wild.

ROCK LOBSTERS: A spiny lobster with long antennae and no claws. The four main types—eastern, southern, western, and tropical—each offer slightly different flavours and textures. The tropical are excellent as sashimi, while the eastern, southern and western lend themselves to baking and barbecue.

SYDNEY ROCK OYSTERS: Despite their name, these bivalves are commonly found throughout the east coast. They're prized for their distinct rich and creamy flavor, and are smaller in size than Pacific oysters. Try eating them raw with a squirt of lemon.

YABBIES: A fresh-water crayfish with firm white flesh and a sweeter taste than rock lobster. Small in size, they can be tricky to eat but are worth the effort. They're often cooked simply in a pot of salted, boiling water.

the price. Some of Sydney's best Asian fusion restaurants include Spice Temple (⊕ www.rockpool.com.au), led by top Australian chef Neil Perry, and the Thai-meets-Southern China concept Longrain Restaurant & Bar (⊕ www.longrain.com. au). The inventive Vietnamese canteen Red Lantern (⊕ www.redlantern.com.au) and inspired Sailors Thai (⊕ www.sail-orsthai.com.au) are also among Sydney's best. It's in these bustling restaurants that flavors and dishes such as shucked oyster with chili and galangal vinaigrette, roasted duck in coconut curry, wagyu-beef hotpot, soft-shell crab with chili jam, and green curry of barramundi bounce off their plates.

While the majority of Asian fusion food in Australia relies heavily on light cooking styles and fresh ingredients, clay pot cooking as well as and heavier-style Malaysian and Indian curries, such as rendang and vindaloo made with local lamb and beef, are also becoming popular.

Neil Perry's salad of yabby tails

rude), but it's all part of the low-budget charm. ✉ *18–20 Goulburn St., Haymarket* ☎ *02/9267–2586* ⊟ *AE, DC, MC, V* ✛ *1:C5.*

¢–$ ✕ **Golden Century.** For two hours—or as long as it takes for you to con-
★ sume delicately steamed prawns, luscious mud crab with ginger and
CHINESE shallots, and *pipis* (triangular clams) with black-bean sauce—you might
as well be in Hong Kong. This place is heaven for seafood lovers, with
wall-to-wall fish tanks filled with crab, lobster, abalone, and schools
of barramundi, parrot fish, and coral trout. You won't have to ask if
the food is fresh: most of it is swimming around you as you eat. The
atmosphere is no-frills, and the noise level can be deafening, but the
food is worth it. Supper is served late evenings from 10 PM until 4 AM.
✉ *393–399 Sussex St., Haymarket* ☎ *02/9212–3901* ⊕ *www.golden-century.com.au* ⊟ *AE, DC, MC, V* ✛ *1:B5.*

¢–$ ✕ **The Malaya.** The cocktails (all A$15) are lethal, the view is captivating,
★ and the food is extraordinary at this modern Asian restaurant on King
MALAYSIAN Street Wharf, a short walk from Darling Harbour. After 40 years in the
business, in different venues around Sydney, this restaurant still does
a roaring trade. Signature dishes include beef Rendang (Indonesian-
style beef curry), and marinated, sticky-sweet, and crunchy Szechuan
eggplant that's so good it may just be the food of the gods. Try one
of the four set menus (for a minimum of three people and A$45 per
person) for a true feast on the extensive menu's flavor combinations.
✉ *39 Lime St., King Street Wharf, Darling Harbour* ☎ *02/9279–1170*
⊟ *AE, DC, MC, V* ✛ *1:B3.*

$ ✕ **Bambini Trust.** It's hidden behind huge black doors in one of the city's
AUSTRALIAN historic sandstone buildings, but once you're inside you'd swear you
were in Paris. Dark-wood paneling, black-and-white photographs, and
mirrors bearing the day's specials in flowing script lend a bistro feel.
The fare is a little French, a little more Italian, and a fair sprinkling of
Mod-Oz. Owners Angela and Michael Potts, who have run cafés for
years, love their truffles; you'll find them mixed with the duck liver pâté
and swirled with the potato mash that makes a tempting extra side dish
to the barramundi fillets. The Italian ice cream or the chocolate and
espresso tart are a lovely way to round off a meal. A pre- or post-meal
drink in the marble-lined, chandelier-adorned Bambini Wine Room is
a must. ✉ *185 Elizabeth St., City Center* ☎ *02/9283–7098* ⊟ *AE, DC, MC, V* ☾ *Closed Sun.* ✛ *1:C4.*

$$ ✕ **Bécasse.** Foodies followed this award-winning French restaurant when
FRENCH it moved to more sophisticated digs in the city center. Justin North, who
Fodor's Choice is currently Sydney's darling chef, has retained its tradition of an open
★ kitchen, which was popular with diners. Inventive, flavorful cuisine
with excellent service accompanies the clink of silverware against din-
ner plates here. The night always starts with an *amuse bouche,* which
may be smoked haddock with red cabbage, followed by mains such as
roast loin of venison or smoked goat's-curd tortellino with figs. What-
ever your choice, you'll want to join the fan club. ✉ *204 Clarence St., City Center* ☎ *02/9283–3440* ✍ *Reservations essential* ⊟ *AE, MC, V* ☾ *Closed Sun. No lunch Sat.* ✛ *1:B4.*

$$ ✕ **Est.** This elegant, pillared dining room is the perfect setting for show-
AUSTRALIAN ing off chef Peter Doyle's modern, light touch with Mod-Oz cuisine.
★

Anything Doyle cooks with scallops is divine; the crisp-skin John Dory fillet is also a sure bet, as is the lamb with sautéed spinach and eggplant caviar. The warm caramelized peach tart with peach-pistachio-nougat ice cream will test any dieter's resolve. The five-course tasting menu (A$155) is a heavenly experience. ✉ *Establishment Hotel, 252 George St., City Center* ☎ *02/9240–3010* ⌕ *Reservations essential* ▭ *AE, DC, MC, V* ☻ *Closed Sun. No lunch Sat.* ✛ *1:C2.*

$$$$ ✕ **Forty One.** The view east over the harbor is glorious, the private din-
FRENCH   ing rooms are plush, and Dietmar Sawyer's Asian-influenced classi-
★   cal food is top-notch. The set-price six-course dinner menu (A$150) might include steamed Western Australian yabby tails with asparagus and bread sauce, and espresso parfait with dark chocolate and Grand Marnier sauce for dessert. The vegetarian menu, with the likes of Ossau Iraty sheep's-milk cheese on a salad of apples, dates, celeriac, and wal-nuts, is sublime. There are two- (A$65) and three-course (A$80) menus for lunch, which is arguably the best time to savour the amazing views. ✉ *Level 42, Chifley Tower, 2 Chifley Sq., City Center* ☎ *02/9221–2500* ⊕ *www.forty-one.com.au* ⌕ *Reservations essential* ▭ *AE, DC, MC, V* ☻ *Closed Sun. No lunch Mon. and Sat.* ✛ *1:C3.*

$$$$ ✕ **Tetsuya's.** It's worth getting on the waiting list—there's *always* a wait-
MODERN   ing list—to sample the unique blend of Western and Japanese-French
AUSTRALIAN   flavors crafted by Sydney's most applauded chef, Tetsuya Wakuda. The
Fodor's Choice   serene, expansive dining room's unobtrusive Japanese aesthetic leaves
★   the food as the true highlight. Confit of ocean trout served with unpas-teurized ocean-trout roe and double-cooked, deboned spatchcock with braised daikon and bread sauce are signature items from the pricey set menu (A$200 for 10 courses) that changes often and never fails to dazzle. Views of a Japanese garden—complete with bonsai and a waterfall—make this place feel miles from the city center. ✉ *529 Kent St., City Center* ☎ *02/9267–2900* ⌕ *Reservations essential* ▭ *AE, DC, MC, V* ☻ *Closed Sun. and Mon. No lunch Tues.–Fri.* ✛ *1:B5.*

DARLINGHURST, KINGS CROSS/POTTS POINT, AND WOOLLOOMOOLOO

DARLINGHURST

¢–$ ✕ **bills.** Named after celebrity chef and cookbook author Bill Granger,
CAFE   this sunny corner café is so addictive it should come with a health
Fodor's Choice   warning. It's a favorite hangout of everyone from local nurses to semi-
★   disguised rock stars, and you never know who you might be sitting next to at the newspaper-strewn communal table. If you're not interested in the creaminess of what must be Sydney's best scrambled eggs, try the ricotta hotcakes with honeycomb butter or the corn fritters. Dinner selections, at the Surry Hills location, are similarly gourmet comfort food. ✉ *433 Liverpool St., Darlinghurst* ☎ *02/9360–9631* ▭ *AE, MC, V* ☻ *No dinner* ✉ *352 Crown St., Surry Hills* ☎ *02/9360–4762* ▭ *AE, MC, V* ✉ *118 Queen St., Woollahra* ☎ *02/9328–7997* ▭ *AE, MC, V* ✛ *1:E2.*

¢–$ ✕ **Fishface.** Get here early, score one of the tiny tables, and you'll be
SEAFOOD   able to dig into some of the most scrumptious seafood in Australia. The
★   best sashimi-grade fish in the country—which is as good as it comes—is

One of the mouthwatering dishes at Bécasse.

served up here to discerning locals. Menu highlights include the salmon pastrami (thinly sliced, cured salmon) with lemon on toast, and the tuna, always served rare and moist. The fish-and-chips redefine the nation's favorite take-out order. Reservations aren't accepted after 7 PM. ⊠ *132 Darlinghurst Rd., Darlinghurst* ☎ *02/9332–4803* ▭ *AE, MC, V* ⌾ *BYO, corkage fee A$8.50* ⊘ *No lunch* ✛ *1:E2.*

¢   ✕ **Goods Organic.** This friendly organic café and food store is the perfect
CAFE   place to stop for a wholesome salad, chicken pie, or ragout of organic goat and brown rice, while shopping in nearby trendy Darlinghurst. All of the produce on the shelves, ingredients used in the meals, and tea and coffee were grown on organic or biodynamic farms. Even the spring water is flavored with organic mint leaves. Here's a place you can happily (and healthily!) browse for an hour or two. ⊠ *253 Crown St., Darlinghurst* ☎ *02/9357–6690* ▭ *MC, V* ⊘ *No dinner* ✛ *1:D2.*

KINGS CROSS AND POTTS POINT

$$ ✕ **Mere Catherine.** You won't find the number of this little hole-in-the-
FRENCH   wall restaurant in any trendy young thing's speed dial, but it is beloved by legions of fans who rejoiced when it reopened a couple of years ago. The decor is retro 1970s, and the dishes are classic French—onion soup, pâté, escargots, duck a l'orange, tarragon chicken, chateaubriand, and crème caramel for dessert. It only seats 14 in a tiny space that is akin to dining in some French family's home. The windows have lace curtains, the tables are candlelit, so come with someone you love and soak in the romantic atmosphere to the strains of Edith Piaf in the background. ⊠ *166 Victoria St., Potts Point* ☎ *02/9358–2000* ▭ *No credit cards* ⊘ *No lunch* ✛ *1:E4.*

WOOLLOOMOOLOO

$$ ✕**Otto.** Few restaurants have the magnetic pull of Otto, a place where
ITALIAN radio shock jocks sit side by side with fashion-magazine editors and
foodies. Yes, it's a scene. But fortunately it's a scene with good Italian
food and waiters who have just enough attitude to make them a chal-
lenge worth conquering. The homemade pastas are very good, and
the selection of Italian wines expensive but rarely matched this far
from Milan. Next door is a sister restaurant, Nove Cucina, offering
pizzas and dishes from Otto's menu at lower prices. ⊠ *Wharf at Wool-
loomooloo, 8 Cowper Wharf Rd., Woolloomooloo* ☎ *02/9368–7488*
⚴ *Reservations essential* ▭ *AE, DC, MC, V* ✛ *1:E3.*

PADDINGTON AND WOOLLAHRA

PADDINGTON

$$$ ✕**Buon Ricordo.** Walking into this happy, bubbly place is like turning
ITALIAN up at a private party in the backstreets of Naples. Host, chef, and sur-
Fodor'sChoice rogate uncle Armando Percuoco invests classic Neapolitan and Tuscan
★ techniques with inventive personal touches to produce such dishes as
warmed figs with Gorgonzola and prosciutto, truffled egg pasta, and
scampi with saffron sauce and black-ink risotto. The fettuccine *al tartu-
fovo,* with eggs, cream, and Reggiano cheese, is legendary. Everything
comes with Italian-style touches that you can see, feel, smell, and taste.
Leaving the restaurant feels like leaving home, especially if you've par-
taken of the wonderful six-course degustation menu (A$115). ⊠ *108
Boundary St., Paddington* ☎ *02/9360–6729* ⚴ *Reservations essential*
▭ *AE, DC, MC, V* ☽ *Closed Sun. and Mon. No lunch Tues.–Thurs.*
✛ *1:F5.*

$ ✕**Four in Hand.** At this cute, popular little pub in Paddington, chef Colin
AUSTRALIAN Fassnidge makes a splash with dishes such as roast chicken with arti-
chokes, grapes, and roast garlic. You too can try these dishes back home
after you've attended one of his new cooking classes held on the first
Monday of the month. ⊠ *105 Sutherland St., Paddington* ☎ *02/9362–
1999* ▭ *AE, DC, MC, V* ☽ *No lunch Mon.–Thurs.* ✛ *1:G5.*

WOOLLAHRA

$–$$ ✕**Bistro Moncur.** Archetypically loud and proud, this bistro in the Wool-
FRENCH lahra Hotel spills over with happy-go-lucky patrons—mostly locals
from around the leafy suburb of Woollahra—who don't mind waiting
a half-hour for a table. The best dishes are inspired takes on Parisian
fare, like the grilled Sirloin Café de Paris and the Bistro Moncur pure
pork sausages with potato puree and Lyonnaise onions. There is a focus
on fresh, high-quality ingredients. A new casual café and bar, Moncur
Terrace, opened last year. Mains include Wagu beef burgers ($23.90)
and Wiener schnitzel with anchovy and wild herbs (A$27). ⊠ *Woollahra
Hotel, 116 Queen St., Woollahra* ☎ *02/9327–9713* ▭ *AE, DC, MC, V*
☽ *No lunch Mon.* ✛ *1:H6.*

SURRY HILLS

$
CHINESE
★
✕**Billy Kwong.** Locals rub shoulders while eating no-fuss Chinese food at TV chef Kylie Kwong's trendy drop-in restaurant. Kwong prepares the kind of food her family cooks, with Grandma providing not just the inspiration but also the recipes. Even the dumplings are made by specialty chefs from Shanghai. If you have a big appetite, indulge in a variety of dishes with Kylie's banquet (A$95). Although the table you're occupying is probably being eyed by the next set of adoring fans, staffers never rush you. But you could always play nice and ask for the bill through your last mouthful of mussels with XO sauce or steamed scallop wontons. ⊠ 3/355 Crown St., Surry Hills ☎ 02/9332–3300 ⊟ AE, MC, V ⬚ BYO, corkage fee A$10 ⊗ No lunch ✛ 1:D6.

$$–$$$
FRENCH
✕**Marque.** Chef Mark Best insists on exemplary service and great food at this elegant Surry Hills restaurant. Few chefs approach French flavors with such passion and dedication (and stints alongside three-star demigods Alain Passard in Paris and Raymond Blanc in England haven't done any harm either). Best's creative fare includes blue swimmer crab with almond jelly, almond gazpacho, sweet corn, and herring roe, and roast suckling pork with milk skin, confit shallots, coffee, and caramelized yogurt. The eight-course tasting menu (A$145) will transport you to foodie heaven. ⊠ 355 Crown St., Surry Hills ☎ 02/9332–2225 ⬚ Reservations essential ⊟ AE, DC, MC, V ⊗ Closed Sun. No lunch Sat.–Thurs. ✛ 1:D6.

EASTERN SUBURBS

$$
ITALIAN
Fodor'sChoice
★
✕**Icebergs Dining Room and Bar.** The fashionable and famous (including celebrities like Mick Jagger) just adore perching like seagulls over the swimming pool at the south end of Australia's most famous beach. After seven years it is still one of the must-visit restaurants in Sydney for both the sensational view and the exquisite food. Take a seat on a low-back suede chair, check your reflection in the frosted glass, and prepare to indulge in sophisticated Mediterranean creations like Livornese-style fish stew, grilled quail with grape salad, or, for a hearty party of eight, whole roasted suckling pig on bay leaves with grilled peppers (with 48 hours notice). ⊠ 1 Notts Ave., Bondi Beach ☎ 02/9365–9000 ⬚ Reservations essential ⊟ AE, DC, MC, V ⊗ Closed Mon. ✛ 2:D3.

¢–$
SEAFOOD
✕**Nick's Bondi Beach Pavilion.** Sydney restaurateur Nick Manettas likes to grab the waterfront locations; his latest venture is a glass-encased modern space attached to the vintage-1928 pavilion on the beach's pedestrian promenade. Although it is a bit touristy for some diners, no one can dismiss the great location, and the classic seafood staples—including the three-tiered platter (designed for two diners) bulging with oysters, shellfish, and crayfish—are sure to please. ⊠ Queen Elizabeth Dr., Bondi Beach ☎ 02/9365–4122 ⊟ DC, MC, V ✛ 2:D3.

¢–$
ITALIAN
✕**North Bondi Italian Food.** This popular spot is more casual and less expensive than Icebergs (both are owned by stylish restaurateur Maurice Terzini), yet the trendy interior and great balcony overlooking the beach are sure to dazzle. The broad menu has more than 60 dishes (appetizers, entrées, and desserts), and is best described as home-style

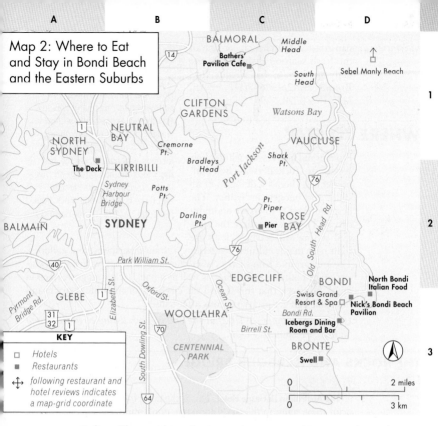

Map 2: Where to Eat and Stay in Bondi Beach and the Eastern Suburbs

KEY

□ Hotels
■ Restaurants
✛ following restaurant and hotel reviews indicates a map-grid coordinate

Italian. The restaurant does not accept reservations, so arrive early to snag a table. ⊠ *118–120 Ramsgate Ave., Bondi Beach* ☎ *02/9300–4400* ▭ *AE, DC, MC, V* ⊗ *No lunch Sun.–Thurs. in winter, Mon. and Tues. in summer* ✛ *2:D3.*

$$$
SEAFOOD
Fodor'sChoice
★

✕ **Pier.** With its wraparound harbor views and shipshape good looks, this wharf restaurant is a great place to enjoy Australia's finest seafood. (Some well-known foodies even say it's the best in the country.) Chef Greg Doyle knows his fish, and manages to reach beyond the predictable char-grills and fish-and-chips without being gimmicky. The all-white Pier Tasting Room is reserved for those who want to sample several dishes. The menu has raw and cooked morsels, oysters, and sashimi. Start with the chilled gazpacho with yabbies. Entrées include the delectable pot-roasted lobster with seasonal garnishings. ⊠ *594 New South Head Rd., Rose Bay* ☎ *02/9327–6561* ▭ *AE, DC, MC, V* ✛ *2:C2.*

$
MODERN
AUSTRALIAN

✕ **Swell.** When you finish the famous Bondi-to-Bronte coastal cliff walk, this is a great place for a meal. By day it's a casual café, but at night it becomes more formal, thanks to white linen tablecloths and tea lights. The salt-and-pepper squid with tamari and chili makes a great light lunch (or appetizer at dinner). When the sun goes down, listen to the surf lapping and order a cocktail while you decide between the crisp-skinned salmon with crab-stuffed zucchini blossoms, the pan-roasted spatchcock, or one of the fresh seafood dishes from the daily specials. ⊠ *465 Bronte Rd., Bronte* ☎ *02/9386–5001* ⊟ *AE, MC, V* ✛ *2:D3.*

WORD OF MOUTH

"I stayed at the Harbour Rocks Hotel and really enjoyed it. The staff was really helpful (it was my first time in Sydney) and within walking distance of many things to see and good restaurants. The location was perfect. On the first day I took the hop on-hop off bus to get acquainted with the city and there is a stop one block from the hotel."   —Lizzie_17

WHERE TO STAY

From grand hotels with white-glove service to tucked-away bed-and-breakfasts, there's lodging to fit all styles and budgets in Sydney. The best addresses in town are undoubtedly in The Rocks, where the tranquil setting and harbor views are right near major cultural attractions, restaurants, shops, and galleries. The area around Kings Cross is another hotel district, with a good collection of boutique properties as well as a backpacker magnet. Keep in mind, however, that this is also the city's major nightlife district, and the scene can get pretty raucous after sunset.

Use the coordinate (✛ 1:B2) at the end of each listing to locate a site on the corresponding map.

THE ROCKS AND HARBOUR BRIDGE

THE ROCKS

$ 🛏 **The Australian Heritage Hotel.** This is the hotel for bargain hunters who want to be right on the city's doorstep, don't mind sharing bathrooms, and like the busy pub scene. The 1913-built pub is located across the road from the BridgeClimb starting point, about a five-minute walk from the harbour. The bar and bistro (meals under $25) gets crowded on a summer's night and on weekends, but can be blissfully peaceful in the off-season mid-week. The rooms are basic, but it's the location you are paying for. There are two guest lounges with TV and coffee and tea stations, a guests-only rooftop terrace with views of the Harbour Bridge and complimentary Continental breakfast. Deals, such as a free Captain Cook coffee cruise or a Rocks Ghost Tour, are included with two-night stays. Rates drop as low as A$115 a night for stays of five nights or longer. **Pros:** great location, excellent price. **Cons:** basic rooms, few amenities. ⊠ *100 Cumberland St., The Rocks* ☎ *02/9261–1111* ⊕ *www.australianheritagehotel.com* 🛏 *9 rooms sharing 4 bathrooms* ⌂ *In-room: no a/c, no phone, Wi-Fi. In-hotel: restaurant, bar, no-smoking rooms* ⊟ *MC, V* �“◗ *CP* ✛ *1:B2.*

$$–$$$ 🛏 **Harbour Rocks Hotel.** Formerly a wool-storage facility, this four-story hotel provides good value for its location, although its historic character is confined to the exterior of the 150-year-old building. Tidy rooms are furnished with flat-screen TVs; DVD players; down quilts; a color scheme in whites, browns, and creams; and overstuffed armchairs and settees. Top-floor rooms on the east side afford glimpses of Circular Quay and the Opera House, while the penthouse suite is a secluded little

gem with fantastic views. The restaurant is called Lanes—so named because the terrace has a view over the intriguing back lanes of The Rocks. **Pros:** excellent in-room entertainment systems, suave modern decor, great location. **Cons:** rooms could be larger. ⊠ *34 Harrington St., The Rocks* ☎ *02/8220–9999* ⊕ *www.harbourrocks.com* ↘ *55 rooms* ⌂ *In-room: safe, DVD, Internet. In-hotel: restaurant, room service, bar, laundry service, no-smoking rooms* ⊟ *AE, DC, MC, V* ♙⏐ *BP* ✢ *1:B2.*

$$ ⊞ **Holiday Inn Old Sydney.** Even though it's been around for a few decades, this hotel with its low-key facade is still a bit of a secret. It's in a great location (right in The Rocks and about a two-minute walk from Circular Quay), and the rooftop pool and terrace offer spectacular views of the Opera House, bridge, and harbor. The eight-story hotel has a dramatic central atrium topped with a glass roof; the guest rooms open out onto passageways that overlook the reception desk, lobby bar, and restaurant several stories below. Rooms have a contemporary design, and many have harbor views. **Pros:** great location, good value. **Cons:** rooms need a facelift. ⊠ *55 George St., The Rocks* ☎ *800/899–960* ⊕ *www.holidayinn.com* ↘ *174 rooms* ⌂ *In-room: safe, Internet. In-hotel: restaurant, room service, bar, pool, laundry facilities, laundry service, Internet terminal, Wi-Fi, parking (paid), no-smoking rooms* ⊟ *AE, D, DC, MC, V* ♙⏐ *EP* ✢ *1:C2.*

$ ⊞ **Lord Nelson Hotel.** If your idea of heaven is sleeping above a pub that brews its own boutique beers (or ales, as they're rightly called) then this is the place. The hotel, hewn from Sydney sandstone, has been a popular watering hole with Sydneysiders and visitors for decades. Built in the early 1840s, the building has recently been restored to its former grandeur. While the nine guest rooms and the first-floor Lord Nelson Brasserie restaurant have exposed sandstone walls, their fittings and decor are very contemporary. Seven of the rooms have en-suite bathrooms and cost A$190 a night with Continental breakfast; the other two double bedrooms share a bathroom and are competitively priced at $130 a night, including breakfast. The hotel is a short walk from the Harbour Bridge, and the bar is always busy on Friday nights and most weekends. **Pros:** great location, fun pub, cheap rates. **Cons:** may be noisy. ⊠ *19 Kent St., The Rocks* ☎ *02/9251–4044* ⊕ *www.lordnelson-brewery.com* ↘ *9 rooms* ⌂ *In-room: phone, no TV. In-hotel: restaurant, room service, bar, Internet terminal, Wi-Fi, parking (paid), no-smoking rooms* ⊟ *AE, D, DC, MC, V* ♙⏐ *CP* ✢ *1:B2.*

$$$$ ⊞ **Observatory Hotel.** More English country manor than inner-city hotel,
Fodor's Choice this gorgeous property feels like a decadent, luxurious sanctuary. The
★ spacious rooms, with their Venetian- and Asian-inspired decor, have mahogany furnishings, antique reproductions, and plush fabrics. The spectacular indoor pool is surrounded by marble and potted palms, with a fresco of a starry night on the ceiling. You can have a drink and check your e-mail with the Wi-Fi in the Globe Bar, Galileo Restaurant, lounge, and lobby. The hotel's single weakness is its lack of views, but that's like saying the Mona Lisa's single weakness is her crooked smile. **Pros:** a location as flashy as its appointments, excellent in-house restaurant. **Cons:** lack of views. ⊠ *89–113 Kent St., The Rocks* ☎ *02/9256–2222* ⊕ *www.observatoryhotel.com.au* ↘ *79 rooms, 21 suites* ⌂ *In-room:*

safe, DVD, Internet. In-hotel: restaurant, room service, bar, pool, gym, concierge, laundry service, public Wi-Fi, parking (fee), no-smoking rooms ▭ AE, DC, MC, V ⊚ BP ✛ 1:A2.

$$$$ 🏨 **Park Hyatt Sydney.** Moored in the shadow of Harbour Bridge, the Park
Fodor'sChoice Hyatt is the first choice for visiting celebrities (a minor irony, consider-
★ ing that the thousands who cross the bridge each day get a bird's-eye view of the guests lazing about the hotel's rooftop pool). Rooms here are decorated with reproductions of classical statuary, contemporary bronzes, and Australian artwork. Nearly all the spacious, elegant rooms have balconies and views of the Opera House. This is also the only hotel in Australia with full-time personal butler service in all rooms. Excellent Australian cuisine awaits at the restaurant. **Pros:** fantastic location and views. **Cons:** slightly corporate feel. ⊠ 7 Hickson Rd., The Rocks ☎ 02/9241–1234 ⊕ www.sydney.park.hyatt.com ➘ 122 rooms, 36 suites ♿ In-room: safe, Internet, DVD. In-hotel: restaurant, room service, bars, pool, gym, spa, concierge, laundry service, public Wi-Fi, parking (fee), no-smoking rooms ▭ AE, DC, MC, V ✛ 1:C1.

$$$ 🏨 **Rendezvous Stafford Hotel Sydney.** Situated in the heart of the historic Rocks precinct, the lodging has a boutique-hotel style. The accommo-dations are a stone's throw from the attractions around Circular Quay, and several rooms have large picture windows with spectacular views of the Opera House. (The terrace restaurant has a similar view.) If you hanker for something a little different—and more charming—seven his-toric two-story houses are available. Each has a bedroom and bathroom upstairs, and lounge (with sofa bed) and kitchen downstairs. The houses are ideal for families or extended-stay vacationers. **Pros:** boutique feel, great location, in-house movies. **Cons:** simply appointed rooms. ⊠ 75 Harrington St., The Rocks ☎ 02/9251–6711 ⊕ www.rendezvousho-tels.com/sydney ➘ 61 apartments, 7 terrace houses ♿ In-room: safe, kitchen, Internet. In-hotel: pool, gym, spa, laundry facilities, laundry service, public Wi-Fi, parking (fee) ▭ AE, DC, MC, V ✛ 1:B2.

$$ 🏨 **The Russell.** For charm, character, and central location, it's hard to beat this ornate Victorian hotel. No two rooms are the same, but all have fresh flowers, down pillows, and Gilchrist & Soames toiletries. The spacious double rooms at the front have views of Circular Quay. There are also somewhat quieter standard-size double rooms overlook-ing Nurses Walk or opening onto an inner courtyard. Ceiling fans and windows allow for a breeze in all rooms, and the rooftop garden is a delight, especially in the evening. This historic building has four floors but no elevator; winding corridors and the steep, narrow staircase to the reception desk can be challenging for those with impaired mobility. **Pros:** personal service, warm decor, included breakfast. **Cons:** lack of amenities, near a pub, so can be noisy. ⊠ 143A George St., The Rocks ☎ 02/9241–3543 ⊕ www.therussell.com.au ➘ 26 rooms, 16 with bath; 1 suite; 1 apartment ♿ In-room: no a/c. In-hotel: restaurant, no elevator ▭ AE, DC, MC, V ⊚ CP ✛ 1:B2.

$$$$ 🏨 **Shangri-La Hotel Sydney.** Towering above Walsh Bay from its prime
★ position alongside the Sydney Harbour Bridge, this sleek hotel is *the* place for a room with a view. North-facing rooms overlooking the water are the best; views on the other sides—Darling Harbour, the city, or the

2

eastern suburbs—are less impressive. Rooms are large, modestly opulent, and decorated in pleasing autumnal colors. All rooms now offer complimentary broadband Internet. With a private bar and lounge, the Horizon Club floor offers impeccable service, with a purser to look after your needs. Altitude restaurant and the adjacent Blu Horizon bar on the 36th floor provide terrific views of Sydney Harbour, especially in the evening. Look for deals on one-night stays over weekends. **Pros:** breathtaking views, soothing decor, great in-house restaurant. **Cons:** impersonal and busy feel at times. ⊠ *176 Cumberland St., The Rocks* ☏ *02/9250–6000* ⊕ *www.shangri-la.com* ⇨ *523 rooms, 40 suites* ⚒ *In-room: safe, Internet. In-hotel: 3 restaurants, room service, bars, pool, gym, spa, concierge, laundry service, public Internet, public Wi-Fi, parking (fee), no-smoking rooms* ⊟ *AE, DC, MC, V* ✛ *1:B2.*

$ ⛺ **Sydney Harbour YHA.** Sydney's newest hostel occupies a brand-new building on the Big Dig, an an active late-18th- and early-19th-century archaeological site. It was first discovered in 1994, and so far 750,000 artifacts from Sydney's early settlement have been unearthed. The hostel is nested on steel pylons and suspended over the Big Dig. Note the innovative Big Dig Educational Centre, a facility open to students and visitors with an interest in history. As part of the Youth Hostel Australia chain (YHA), the accommodation is aimed at budget travelers, but has the added attraction of million-dollar harbor views from many rooms. There's is a mixture of four and six-bed multi-share rooms, twin/double rooms, and family rooms (all with en-suite bathrooms). The family rooms have TVs, and twin/double rooms have hair dryers and towels. The dorms have lockable cupboards for each occupant, complete with power points to charge cell phones. The hostel has a self-catering kitchen, dining area, lounge areas with TV, tour desk, and a grocery store. Dorm beds are A$42, and double or twin rooms with a harbour view are $170 per night in the peak season that runs from Christmas to Easter. **Pros:** great location, budget prices for harbour views, history at your fingertips. **Cons:** few room amenities, little privacy. ⊠ *110 Cumberland St., The Rocks* ☏ *02/9261–1111* ⊕ *www.sydneyharbouryha. com.au* ⇨ *106 rooms* ⚒ *In-room: a/c (some), no phone, TV (some), Wi-Fi (fee). In-hotel: laundry facilities, Internet terminal, no-smoking rooms* ⊟ *AE, D, DC, MC, V* ✛ *1:B2.*

CIRCULAR QUAY

$$$ ⛺ **Sydney Harbour Marriott.** This modern high-rise hotel is a minute's walk from Circular Quay, a two-minute stroll from The Rocks, and a short distance from Pitt Street's best shopping. Many rooms have harbor views, with the best vistas from the executive rooms on the top five floors and the executive lounge on the 30th floor. A drink in the historic Customs Bar is always a lively affair, while Icon's restaurant is popular not only for its seafood buffet (A$39 lunch, A$89 dinner) but its wine buffet, which means a bottomless glass of wine costs A$21 at lunch and A$25 a dinner. **Pros:** hip bar, good location and views. **Cons:** impersonal, could-be-anywhere feel. ⊠ *30 Pitt St., City Center* ☏ *02/9259–7000* ⊕ *www.Marriott.com.* ⇨ *550 rooms, 42 suites* ⚒ *In-room: VCR, Internet. In-hotel: 2 restaurants, room service, bar, pool, gym, laundry service, parking (fee), no-smoking rooms* ⊟ *DC, MC, V* ✛ *1:C2.*

There's no shortage of luxurious accommodations in Sydney.

CITY CENTER

$$ 🏨 **Blacket Hotel.** A study in minimalist chic, this small hotel in a former bank building has been on Sydney's hot list since its debut in 2001. From the moment you step into the fashionably dim, charcoal-and-off-white reception area, the setting delivers the requisite degree of cool. Its great location, at the corner of busy George Street, ensures a steady stream of repeat corporate clientele. Rates are low, as is the price of the Continental breakfast (A$9). The one- and two-bedroom apartments and loft suites all have kitchenettes, whirlpool tubs, and washing machines. Those wanting to sample the city's nightlife need only take the elevator down to the Privilege Bar, deep within the old bank vault. **Pros:** hip decor, great-value breakfast, self-contained option. **Cons:** corporate feel. ⊠ *70 King St., City Center* ☎ *02/9279–3030* ⊕ *www.the-blacket.com* ⤢ *26 rooms, 5 suites, 9 apartments* ⌂ *In-room: kitchen (some). In-hotel: restaurant, bar, public Wi-Fi, parking (fee)* ⊟ *AE, DC, MC, V* ✣ *1:C4.*

$$ 🏨 **Fraser Suites Sydney.** This brand-new serviced-apartment hotel is one of Sydney's swankiest places to stay. Suites are contained in a gleaming 42-story tower (with just seven suites per floor) in central Sydney, just a few minutes' walk from Town Hall. Two amazing penthouses offer fantastic views over Darling Harbour just to the west. The design is ultra hip, from the 18-foot rainfall chandelier that dangles above you in the lobby to the 20-meter lap pool cantilevered over the Regent Place shopping precinct below. Daily breakfast in served in the The Mezzanine, but there is no on-site restaurant for other meals. Each suite has a kitchenette or fully equipped kitchen, and several eateries are located in Regent Square, Sydney's newest shopping precinct, just a short elevator ride away on the ground floor. **Pros:** cutting-edge design, well priced for longer stays. **Cons:** minimalist design may not be everyone's taste. ⊠ *488 Kent St., Sydney Center* ☎ *02/8823–8888* ⊕ *www. sydney.frasershospitality.com* ↝ *201 rooms* ↥ *In-room: safe, kitchen, refrigerator, DVD (some), Internet. In-hotel: room service, pool, gym, laundry facilities, laundry service, Internet terminal, parking (paid), no-smoking rooms* ⊟ *AE, D, DC, MC, V* ¦◎¦ *EP* ✢ *1:C5.*

$$$ 🏨 **Hilton Sydney.** At this landmark hotel in downtown Sydney you enter a spacious, light-filled lobby displaying a stunning four-story sculpture. Among the five different room types are 31 relaxation rooms divided into three zones: relaxation space, spa bathroom, and work zone. Whirlpool baths, body-jet showers, and the latest electronic wizardry are just some of the features. The glass brassiere, run by well-known Sydney chef Luke Mangan, and trendy bar Zeta, designed by New Yorker Tony Chi, are hip places to eat and meet. The circa-1890 Marble Bar also attracts a crowd. The hotel is home to LivingWell, the largest hotel-based health club in Australia, offering group fitness, yoga, and Pilates classes, as well as a plethora of pampering treatments. **Pros:** excellent service, lavishly appointed rooms, hip bar. **Cons:** impersonal, at-times busy feel. ⊠ *488 George St., City Center* ☎ *02/9266–2000* ⊕ *www. hiltonsydney.com.au* ↝ *550 rooms, 27 suites* ↥ *In-room: DVD, Wi-Fi. In-hotel: restaurant, pool, gym, spa* ⊟ *AE, DC, MC, V* ✢ *1:C4.*

$$$$ 🏨 **Westin Sydney.** The Westin hotel chain is renowned for its heavenly ★ beds—in Sydney it offers heavenly service, too. The staff here is cool, efficient, capable, and stylish as at a boutique hotel, but without the hipper-than-thou attitude. Located on stately Martin Place in the center of Sydney's central business district, the hotel's 31-story building incorporates the ornate, Victorian-era shell of Sydney's former General Post Office. Heritage Rooms, in the original building, have soaring ceilings, tall windows, and opulent decor. High-design Tower Rooms have stainless steel, aquamarine glass, and floor-to-ceiling windows for panoramic city views. **Pros:** in-room entertainment systems, great service. **Cons:** slightly corporate feel. ⊠ *1 Martin Pl., City Center* ☎ *02/8223–1111* ⊕ *www.westin.com.au* ↝ *400 rooms, 16 suites* ↥ *In-room: safe, DVD, Internet. In-hotel: 2 restaurants, room service, bar, pool, gym, concierge, laundry service, public Internet, public Wi-Fi, parking (fee), no-smoking rooms* ⊟ *AE, DC, MC, V* ✢ *1:C3.*

¢ 🏨 **Y Hotel Hyde Park.** Comfortable, affordable lodgings in a prime city ★ location mean that rooms here are often booked months in advance. Dorms with shared bathrooms sleep four, while the family, deluxe, and corporate rooms include a fruit platter, daily newspaper, French-press coffeemaker, and toiletries. Studios have a kitchenette, in-room safe, and Internet connection. **Pros:** great value, lots of unexpected extras. **Cons:** have to book far ahead of time. ⊠ *5–11 Wentworth Ave., near corner of Hyde Park and Oxford St., City Center* ☎ *02/9264–4251* ⊕ *www.yhotel.com.au* ↝ *11 dorm rooms with shared baths, 6 studios, 104 rooms* ↥ *In-room: no phone (some), refrigerator (some), no TV (some), Wi-Fi (some). In-hotel: restaurant, no-smoking rooms* ⊟ *AE, DC, MC, V* ¦◎¦ *CP* ✢ *1:D5.*

THE EASTERN SUBURBS

PADDINGTON

$ ★ **Sullivans Hotel.** Set on a quiet stretch in the trendy shopping precinct of Paddington, this small, friendly, family-run hotel has simple accommodations at an outstanding price. Garden rooms overlook an Italianate central courtyard and pool; the corner rooms, Numbers 116, 216, and 316, are the largest and quietest. Triple-glazed windows mean rooms overlooking bustling Oxford Street aren't bombarded by traffic noise. Those on the third floor have harbor views. Extras include free in-house movies. The location, close to shops, restaurants, and nightlife, is a 15-minute walk from the city center. **Pros:** great value, personal service, warm feel. **Cons:** simply appointed rooms. ⊠ *21 Oxford St., Paddington* ☎ *02/9361–0211* ⊕ *www.sullivans.com.au* ⤶ *64 rooms* ♿ *In-room: refrigerator, dial-up. In-hotel: restaurant, pool, bicycles, public Wi-Fi, parking (no fee)* ⊟ *AE, DC, MC, V* ♱ *1:E6.*

WOOLLAHRA

The Hughenden. This cozy, friendly converted Victorian mansion is ideal for travelers who steer clear of big-city hotels. Built by a pioneering doctor in the late 19th century (and now owned by an artist-writer couple), the property has loads of character. Writers' groups meet here regularly, there's high tea on winter weekends, and special events (like Australia Day and Melbourne Cup) are always celebrated. Rooms are decorated in a modern-country style. After enjoying the made-to-order breakfast you can relax on the porch or stroll across the well-manicured lawns of this Anglophile's dream estate. The prestigious eastern suburbs address is close to the great shops of Oxford Street, Centennial Park, and trendy Paddington, while the city and the eastern beaches are just 10–15 minutes away by public transportation. **Pros:** intimate heritage feel, relaxed and friendly vibe. **Cons:** removed from the city center. ⊠ *14 Queen St., Woollahra* ☎ *02/9363–4863* ⊕ *www.hughendenhotel.com.au* ⤶ *36 rooms* ♿ *In-room: Wi-Fi. In-hotel: restaurant, bar, parking (no fee), public Wi-Fi, no-smoking rooms, some pets allowed (fee)* ⊟ *AE, DC, MC, V* ⍄│ *BP* ♱ *1:G6.*

EAST OF THE CITY

DARLINGHURST

¢–$ **The Chelsea.** The motto of this beautiful guesthouse is "Come home to
Fodor's Choice   the Chelsea"—and it won't be long before you're wishing it were *your*
★   home. Occupying adjoining Victorian houses on a quiet, leafy street between Darlinghurst and Rushcutters Bay, this B&B is luxurious and warmly inviting. Rooms are either deluxe, done in a French provincial style with fireplaces and frosted-glass bathrooms, or smaller and more contemporary, with shared facilities. Room 13 has a private courtyard with a fancy fountain, and the two front rooms have balconies overlooking the street. The four rooms without private facilities are a great value (A$94 a night), and are only steps away from two shared bathrooms. Continental breakfast is included and served in the dining room adjoining a lovely Tuscan style courtyard. **Pros:** warm, homey feel, elegantly appointed rooms, self-catering option. **Cons:** contemporary-style rooms

could be bigger. ✉ *49 Womerah Ave., Darlinghurst* ☎ *02/9380–5994* ⟿ *13 rooms, 9 with bath* ⚅ *In-hotel: no a/c, no elevator, public Internet, no-smoking rooms* ▭ *MC, V* ⑂*CP* ⊹ *1:F4.*

$$$ ▪ **Medusa.** If you're tired of the standard travelers' rooms, this reno-
★ vated Victorian terrace house may be just the tonic. Having undergone a massive conversion into 21st-century cool, it sports a decorating scheme of brash colors—blues, yellows, and creams splashed against reds—and furnishings (platform beds and chaise longues) that might have come direct from a Milan design gallery. Every room is slightly different, and each has a kitchenette. Behind the glamour is a comfortable, well-run hotel with friendly, attentive staff. This is one of the few city hotels that welcome guests' dogs. **Pros:** flashy decor, warm service, kichenettes in every room. **Cons:** few amenities. ✉ *267 Darlinghurst Rd., Darlinghurst* ☎ *02/9331–1000* ⊕ *www.medusa.com.au* ⟿ *17 rooms* ⚅ *In-room: safe, kitchen. In-hotel: no elevator, public Wi-Fi, some pets allowed* ▭ *AE, DC, MC, V* ⊹ *1:E5.*

KINGS CROSS

¢ ▪ **Hotel 59 & Cafe.** In its character as well as its dimensions, this friendly B&B on a quiet part of a bar- and club-lined street is reminiscent of a European *pensione*. Simple, tastefully outfitted rooms come with high-quality beds and linens, as well as wooden blinds over the windows. Access to the four floors of rooms is via a small staircase, and there is no elevator. Despite its proximity to the heart of Kings Cross, the hotel has a relaxed, serene atmosphere. There's a two-night minimum stay; book online for cheaper rates. **Pros:** comfortable rooms, included breakfast. **Cons:** removed from the city. ✉ *59 Bayswater Rd., Kings Cross* ☎ *02/9360–5900* ⊕ *www.hotel59.com.au* ⟿ *9 rooms* ⚅ *In-room: refrigerator. In-hotel: restaurant, no elevator* ▭ *MC, V* ⑂*BP* ⊹ *1:F4.*

POTTS POINT

¢ ▪ **De Vere Hotel.** "Simply comfortable and affordable" is the slogan at this 1920s-style hotel at the leafy end of Potts Point, and it's hard to disagree on either count. Location and price are also major draws at this friendly hotel that has a mini-face-lift every year to keep it looking neat. Rooms are spacious; some standard accommodations have balconies, while the studio apartments include kitchenettes. Good standby rates are available through the Internet. **Pros:** good value, spacious rooms. **Cons:** removed from city center. ✉ *44–46 Macleay St., Potts Point* ☎ *02/9358–1211* ⊕ *www.devere.com.au* ⟿ *102 rooms* ⚅ *In-room: kitchen (some). In-hotel: restaurant, laundry facilities, laundry service, parking (fee)* ▭ *AE, DC, MC, V* ⑂*EP, BP* ⊹ *1:F3.*

$$ ▪ **The Storrier.** This gorgeous new boutique hotel is named after Aussie artist Tim Storrier, whose art is hung in the lobby and hallways. Each of the sleek black-and-white rooms is furnished differently, but all have shag bedspreads and plenty of mirrors that will make guests feel a tad risqué. The location in hip Potts Point, on the eastern fringe of the city, is an ideal base for exploring both the city and the eastern suburbs. Several rooms have private balconies, and there's a rooftop where guests can sit and have breakfast if they choose. **Pros:** funky rooms, some with amazing views, and hip staff who can get guests passes to the local gym. **Cons:** neighboring Kings Road can be seedy, and the hotel's lobby and

restaurant often blast loud music. ⊠ *15 Springfield Ave., Potts Point-NSW* ☎ *61–2/8988–6999* ⊕ *www.thestorrier.com.au* ⚲ *In-room: safe, kitchen, minibar, DVD, TV, Wi-Fi. In-hotel: restaurant, room service, laundry facilities, public Wi-Fi, no-smoking rooms (all)* ⊟ *AE, D, DC, MC, V* ✛ *1:E4.*

¢ ⌕ **Victoria Court Sydney.** A small, smart hotel on a Potts Point street lined with budget accommodations, the Victoria Court is appealing for more than just its reasonable rates. Hand-painted tiles and etched-glass doors recall the hotel's Victorian ancestry, yet the rooms come with the modern blessings of en-suite bathrooms and comfortable beds. Most rooms have marble fireplaces, some have four-poster beds, and a few have balconies overlooking Victoria Street. The leafy courtyard is the perfect place to have breakfast (which is included) and read the morning paper. **Pros:** heritage feel, comfortable rooms. **Cons:** simple amenities. ⊠ *122 Victoria St., Potts Point* ☎ *02/9357–3200* ⊕ *www.victoriacourt. com.au* ⤳ *25 rooms* ⊟ *AE, DC, MC, V* ⌹ *CP* ✛ *1:E3.*

WOOLLOOMOOLOO

$$$$ ⌕ **BLUE Sydney.** This ultra hip hotel, part of the prestigious Taj Hotel
★ group of India, occupies a former warehouse. Guests love the authentic structures of the former wharf (pulleys, giant trusses, and brontosaurus-like machinery) and its location (a stone's throw from the Opera House). The lobby is dominated by the hip Water Bar, one of Sydney's places to see and be seen. Guest rooms, which have a light, bright, cappuccino color scheme, are arranged like the cabins on a luxury liner, rising in tiers on the outside of the central cavity. There are five restaurants in the adjoining wharf complex. **Pros:** trendy bar, chic decor, close to good restaurants. **Cons:** busy feel. ⊠ *Wharf at Woolloomooloo, 6 Cowper Wharf Rd., Woolloomooloo* ☎ *02/9331–9000* ⊕ *www.tajhotels.com/sydney* ⤳ *100 rooms, 36 suites* ⚲ *In-room: safe, DVD, Internet. In-hotel: restaurant, bar, pool, gym, concierge, laundry service, public Internet, parking (fee), no-smoking rooms* ⊟ *AE, DC, MC, V* ✛ *1:E3.*

BONDI BEACH AND MANLY

BONDI BEACH

$$$ ⌕ **Swiss Grand Resort & Spa.** With the beach just across the road, a rooftop pool, and a relaxing day spa, a stay at the Swiss Grand makes it easy to forget that you're just 15 minutes away from the action of Sydney. Ask for one of the 62 beachfront rooms, as the rest face the sometimes noisy side streets of this crowded beachside suburb. The hotel, which resembles a huge wedding cake, is often buzzing with wedding parties on weekends, so look out for the good selection of inexpensive package deals for families and couples at other times. **Pros:** good spa, great beachside location. **Cons:** sometimes busy, public feel, street-facing rooms are noisy. ⊠ *Campbell Parade at Beach Rd., Bondi Beach* ☎ *02/9365–5666* ⊕ *www.swissgrand.com.au* ⤳ *203 suites* ⚲ *In-hotel: 2 restaurants, bars, pools, gym, spa, public Internet, parking (fee)* ⊟ *AE, DC, MC, V* ✛ *2:D3.*

2

MANLY

$$ [image] **Sebel Manly Beach.** On a secluded corner of the main beachside drag at Manly, this boutique hotel is one of the best places to stay at this busy tourist mecca. The hotel is a mixture of studios and one- and two-bedroom suites, all with private balconies; the more-spacious accommodations have hot tubs, kitchenettes, and high-tech goodies. Jamil's, the new restaurant and bar, serves until midnight. **Pros:** beachside locale, well-appointed rooms. **Cons:** touristy location. ⊠ *8–13 South Steyne, Manly* ☎ *02/9977-8866* ⊕ *www.mirvachotels.com.au* 🛏 *83 rooms* ⟁ *In-room: kitchen (some), Internet. In-hotel: restaurant, room service, bar, pools, laundry facilities, parking (fee)* ⊟ *AE, DC, MC, V* ⦿ *CP.*

A SEA OF TALENT

A steel whale's tail sticking out of the ocean and retro kettles cunningly disguised as penguins strapped to a huge rock being lashed by waves are some of the imaginative artworks that have wowed visitors to the annual show called **Sculpture by the Sea** (⊕ *www.sculpturebythesea. com*). Since 1996, artists from 15 countries have positioned their sculptures on and under rocky outcrops and on hilltops along the much-trodden Bondi-to-Bronte Coastal Walk. This free exhibition, which runs for two weeks beginning in late October or early November, attracts thousands of visitors.

NIGHTLIFE AND THE ARTS

THE ARTS

While Sydney's contemporary theater pays tribute to the giants of drama, it's also driven by distinctly Australian themes: multiculturalism, relating to the troubled relations between Aboriginal and white Australia, and the search for national identity, characterized by the famous Australian irreverence. Dance, music, and the visual arts are celebrated with equal enthusiasm. At their best, Sydney's artists and performers bring a new slant to the arts, one that reflects the unique qualities of their homeland and the city itself. Standouts on the Sydney arts scene include the Sydney Dance Company, the Museum of Contemporary Arts, the Sydney Opera House, and Belvoir Street Theatre. The most comprehensive listing of upcoming events is in the "Metro" section of the *Sydney Morning Herald,* published on Friday. On other days, browse through the entertainment section of the paper.

Ticketek Phone Box Office (☎ *13–2849* ⊕ *www.premier.ticketek.com. au*) is the major ticket reservations agency, covering most shows and performances.

BALLET, OPERA, AND CLASSICAL MUSIC

Fodor's Choice **Sydney Opera House** (⊠ *Bennelong Point, Circular Quay* ☎ *02/9250-7777* ⊕ *www.soh.nsw.gov.au*) showcases all the performing arts in its ★ five theaters, one of which is devoted to opera. The Australian Ballet, the Sydney Dance Company, and the Australian Opera Company also call the Opera House home. The complex includes two stages for theater and the 2,700-seat Concert Hall, where the Sydney Symphony Orchestra and the Australian Chamber Orchestra perform. The box office is open Monday to Saturday 9–8:30.

DANCE

Bangarra Dance Theatre (⌧ *Pier 4, 5 Hickson Rd., The Rocks* ☎ *02/9251– 5333* ⊕ *www.bangarra.com.au*), the acclaimed Aboriginal dance company, celebrated its 20th anniversary in 2009. It stages dramatic productions based on contemporary Aboriginal social themes.

★ **Sydney Dance Company** (⌧ *The Wharf, Pier 4, Hickson Rd., The Rocks* ☎ *02/9221–4811* ⊕ *www.sydneydance.com.au*) is an innovative contemporary dance troupe with an international reputation from its many years under acclaimed director Graeme Murphy. The company generally performs at the Opera House when it's in town.

THEATER

Belvoir Street Theatre (⌧ *25 Belvoir St., Surry Hills* ☎ *02/9699–3444* ⊕ *www.belvoir.com.au*) has two stages that host innovative and challenging political and social drama. The smaller downstairs space is the home of "B Sharp," Company B's lineup of brave new Australian works. The theater is a 10-minute walk from Central Station. **Capitol Theatre** (⌧ *13 Campbell St., Haymarket* ☎ *02/9320–5000* ⊕ *www.capitoltheatre.com.au*), a century-old city landmark, was refurbished with such modern refinements as fiber-optic ceiling lights that twinkle in time to the music. The 2,000-seat theater specializes in Broadway blockbusters. **Lyric Theatre** (⌧ *20–80 Pyrmont St., Pyrmont, Darling Harbour* ☎ *02/9777–9000* ⊕ *www.starcity.com.au*), at the Star City Casino complex, is one of Sydney's most spectacular performing-arts venues. Despite its size, there's no better place to watch big-budget musicals. Every seat in the lavishly spacious, 2,000-seat theater is a good one.

★ **State Theatre** (⌧ *49 Market St., City Center* ☎ *02/9373–6655* ⊕ *www.statetheatre.com.au*) is the grande dame of Sydney theaters. It operates as a cinema in June each year, when it hosts the two-week-long Sydney Film Festival; at other times this beautiful space hosts local and international performers. Built in 1929 and restored to its full-blown opulence, the theater has a vaulted ceiling, mosaic floors, marble columns and statues, and brass and bronze doors. A highlight of the magnificent theater is the 20,000-piece chandelier that is supposedly the world's second largest, which actor Robin Williams once likened to "one of Imelda Marcos's earrings." **SWB Stables Theatre** (⌧ *10 Nimrod St., Kings Cross* ☎ *02/9361–3817 or 1300/406776* ⊕ *www.griffintheatre.com.au*) is a small 120-seat venue and home of the Griffin Theatre Company, which specializes in new Australian writing. **Wharf Theatre** (⌧ *Pier 4, Hickson Rd., The Rocks* ☎ *02/9250–1777* ⊕ *sydneytheatre.com.au*), on a redeveloped wharf in the shadow of Harbour Bridge, hosts the Sydney Theatre Company, one of Australia's most original and highly regarded performing groups. Contemporary British and American plays and the latest offerings from leading Australian playwrights such as David Williamson and Nick Enright are the main attractions.

Inside Sydney's renowned Opera House

NIGHTLIFE

The *Sydney Morning Herald*'s daily entertainment section is the most informative guide to the city's pubs and clubs. For club-scene coverage—who's been seen where and what they were wearing—pick up a free copy of Drum Media, available at just about any Oxford Street café or pub or via the Internet (⊕ *www.drummedia.com.au*). The CitySearch (⊕ *www.sydney.citysearch.com.au*) and Sydney Gig Guide (⊕ *www. yourgigs.com.au/Sydney*) are other good online sources of entertainment information.

All bars and clubs listed here are open daily unless noted. Entry is free unless we list a cover charge.

BARS AND DANCE CLUBS

A former School of the Arts building, **Arthouse** (⊠ *275 Pitt St., City Center* ☎ *02/9284–1200*) has been renovated into a modern, Belle Époque–style hot spot, with four bars and a restaurant spread over three cavernous floors. Art is the focus here, whether it's visual—life-drawing classes are given on Monday, a burlesque drawing class biweekly on Tuesday—aural, or comestible, and there is a full-time curator dedicated to programming events and installing exhibitions.

★ **Bambini Wine Room** (⊠ *185 Elizabeth St., City Center* ☎ *02/928–7098*) is a sparkling little jewel box encased in marble-clad walls and topped with lovely chandeliers. You can sip cocktails and any number of fine wines late into the night and feast on affordable bar snacks. The **Beach Road Hotel** (⊠ *71 Beach Rd., Bondi Beach* ☎ *02/9130–7247*), a Bondi institution, is famous for its Sunday Sessions, when locals come to drink and dance all day in one of several pub rooms. You can snack on a sausage grilled right out front or dine on inexpensive Italian food on the back patio. **Blu Horizon Bar** (✉ *176 Cumberland St., The Rocks* ☎ *02/9250–6013*) has the stellar view! Situated on the 36th floor of the Shangri-La Hotel, this is a sophisticated place to relax after work or enjoy a late-night drink while taking in the sweeping views of Sydney Harbour and the Opera House. Get here early for a ringside seat.

★ With its primo waterside location at the northern end of King Street Wharf, and famous mussels from its open kitchen, **Bungalow 8** (✉ *8 The Promenade, King Street Wharf* ☎ *02/9299–4660* ⊕ *www.bungalow8sydney.com*) invites a night of posing and partying. This is the place to be seen bobbing your head to the spinning of several ultra-cool resident DJs. Tuesday is especially packed for the all-you-can-eat mussel extravaganza.

★ **Hemmesphere** (✉ *Level 4, 252 George St., City Center* ☎ *02/9240–3040*) is one of a string of swanky venues on the same site. Named for Justin Hemmes, son of iconic 1970s fashion designers Jon and Merivale Hemmes, this is where Sydney's hippest pay homage to cocktail culture from low, leather divans. The mood is elegant and sleek, and so are the well-dressed guests, who often include whichever glitterati happen to be in town. Club members, who pay A$1,500 a year, get priority. Closed Sunday. **Home** (✉ *101 Cockle Bay Wharf, Darling Harbour* ☎ *02/9266–0600* ⊕ *www.homesydney.com*), Sydney's largest nightclub, is a three-story colossus that holds up to 2,000 party animals. The main dance floor has an awesome sound system, and the top-level terrace bar is the place to go when the action becomes too frantic. Outdoor balconies provide the essential oxygen boost. Arrive early or prepare for a long wait. It's open Friday and Saturday 10 PM–4 AM, with a cover charge of up to A$55 for international DJs.

Hugo's Lounge (✉ *Level 1, 33 Bayswater Rd., Kings Cross* ☎ *02/9357–4411*) is the place that transformed Kings Cross from a seedy crossroads of sex shops and smut to a must-be-seen-here destination for Sydney's beautiful people. Red lamps are a nod to the neighborhood's skin trade, but the deep couches, opulent ottomans, and decadent cocktail menu are purely upmarket. The downstairs pizza bar is part of the Hugo's stable of eateries. Closed Monday–Wednesday. **Ivy** (✉ *330 George St. , City Center* ☎ *02/8354–1400*) is the latest must-be-seen-in offering by Sydney's party prince Justin Hemmes (owner of Establishment and Hemmesphere). It's located in the same multi-level venue as the Ivy Lounge, the Den, and the Royal George. Add to all these watering-hole options the A$5 Friday drinks and Wednesday jazz nights, and the crowd never needs to leave. **Jimmy Liks** (✉ *186–188 Victoria St., Potts Point* ☎ *02/8354–1400*), a small, sexy Asian street-food restaurant, serves up drink concoctions with exotic flavors—like lemongrass martinis and "twisted and tasty" iced teas accented with basil—which you can sip under a honeycomb-like lantern that flatters with its golden light.

Mars Lounge (✉ *16 Wentworth Ave., Surry Hills* ☎ *02/9267–6440*) takes its music as seriously as its list of lethal cocktails, including the Desperate Housewife—a mandarin-infused vodka shaken with fresh passion-fruit pulp and cranberry juice. DJs spin everything from funk to fusion, and each night has a different theme, like Thursday's combination of good food and soulful music. It's closed Monday and Tuesday. For a northern Sydney landmark, **The Oaks** (⊠ *118 Military Rd., Neutral Bay* ☎ *02/9953–5515*) encapsulates the very best of the modern pub. The immensely popular watering hole is big and boisterous, with a beer garden, a restaurant, and several bars offering varying levels of sophistication. It's packed on Friday and Saturday nights. **Orbit Bar and Lounge** (⊠ *Australia Square, Level 47, 264 George St., City Center* ☎ *02/9247–7777* ⊕ *www.summitrestaurant.com.au*). The bar sits on level 47 of the Australia Square building, a Sydney icon for more than 40 years. It has floor-to-ceiling windows and, like Sydney Tower, it revolves. The design, to match the name, is Space Age, inspired by the Stanly Kubrick movie *2001: A Space Odyssey*, with white retro furniture and plush red carpet. This is a dressed-up bar perfect for a pre- or post-dinner drink. It's open Monday to Friday for lunch, and from 5 PM until late every night for tapas and cocktails.Perched beneath the concourse of the Opera House and at eye level with Sydney Harbour, **Opera Bar** (⊠ *Sydney Opera House, Circular Quay* ☎ *02/9247–1666*) has the best location in all of Sydney. Cozy up for a drink in the enclosed bar area or grab a waterside umbrella table and take in the glimmering skyline. Live music plays under the stars nightly. The bar has a full menu, though the attraction here is the scenery, not the cuisine. A cross between a swinging '60s London nightspot and the back lot of a James Bond film, the small, groovy **Peppermint Lounge** (⊠ *281 Victoria St., Potts Point* ☎ *02/9356–6634*) has a mod mood, and, naturally, martinis. Tuck into an octagonal red-lighted booth surrounded by frosted glass and try one of the more than 70 libations on offer. It's open Wednesday to Sunday until late. The inner-city **Soho Bar** (⊠ *Piccadilly Hotel, 171 Victoria St., Kings Cross* ☎ *02/9358–6511*) has been transformed into a supper club with four bars over two levels. There's live music on Saturday nights and a fair sprinkling of celebrities.

Tank (⊠ *3 Bridge La., City Center* ☎ *02/9240–3094*) is the grooviest and best looking of all Sydney's nightclubs, with a polar-cool clientele and a slick dress code rigidly enforced at the door. Finding the door can be tricky (painted in shades of blue), but you'll know you're there when you're standing in a grungy lane off Bridge Street, near the George Street corner. The cover charge is A$20, and you'll continue to shell out as much for drinks all evening. The interior is plush and relaxed, and the music a selection of R&B and techno. It's open until 6 AM on Friday and Saturday. **Trademark Hotel** (⊠ *1 Bayswater Rd., Kings Cross* ☎ *02/935–75533* ✉ *A$10–A$30 for events*), the latest Sydney nightspot, gets its name from its unique position under the neon lights of the Southern Hemisphere's biggest billboard—the iconic Coca-Cola sign at the "top of the Cross," the highest point in Kings Cross. There's no chance of getting lost, as everyone knows the billboard, which is heritage listed, and has beamed out its message since 1974. Trademark consists of two stylish bars; the Lounge (an elegant venue for after work) and the Piano Room (jazz nights and late-night dancing). Cover charges apply to special DJ party events.

COMEDY CLUBS

Sydney's Comedy Store (✉ *Fox Studios Entertainment Quarter, Bent St. off Driver Ave., Centennial Park* ☎ *02/9357–1419* ⊕ *www.comedystore.com.au*), the city's oldest comedy club, is found in this plush 300-seat theater in a huge movie-production facility. The difficult-to-find theater is at the rear of the complex, close to the parking lot. Shows are Tuesday–Saturday at 8:30 PM, and admission runs A$15 to A$30. There's a second venue at 302 Church Street in Parramatta.

GAY AND LESBIAN BARS AND CLUBS

Most of the city's gay and lesbian venues are along Oxford Street, in Darlinghurst. The free *Sydney Star Observer,* available along Oxford Street, has a roundup of Sydney's gay and lesbian goings-on, or check the magazine's Web site (⊕ *www.ssonet.com.au*). A monthly free magazine, *Lesbians on the Loose* (⊕ *www.lotl.com*), lists events for women, and the free *SX* (⊕ *www.sxnews.com.au*) lists bars and events.

★ **ARQ** (✉ *16 Flinders St., Darlinghurst* ☎ *02/9380–8700* ⊕ *www.arqsydney.com.au*), Sydney's biggest, best-looking, and funkiest gay nightclub, attracts a clean-cut crowd who like to whip off their shirts as soon as they hear the beat. (Some women head here, too.) There are multiple dance floors, a bar, and plenty of chrome and sparkly lighting. It's open from 9 PM until whenever Thursday through Sunday, with a cover charge of A$25 and upwards. **The Midnight Shift** (✉ *85 Oxford St., Darlinghurst* ☎ *02/9360–4463*) is Sydney's hard-core party zone, a living legend on the gay scene for its longevity and its take-no-prisoners approach. If anything, the upstairs nightclub, with drag acts on "Fake Fridays" and DJs every other night, is a little quieter than the ground-floor bars, where most of the leather-loving men go to shoot pool. Opening hours are Sunday to Thursday from about midday to 2 AM and Friday and Saturday from 2 PM to 6 AM.

JAZZ CLUBS

★ **The Basement** (✉ *29 Reiby Pl., Circular Quay* ☎ *02/9251–2797*) is a Sydney legend, the city's premier venue for top local and international jazz, rock, and blues musicians. Lunch is available weekdays, dinner Monday–Saturday. Expect a cover charge starting at A$10. **The Vanguard** (✉ *42 King St. , Newtown* ☎ *02/9557–7992*) is Sydney's answer to a New Orleans jazz joint, and purposely built by its music-loving owners to mimic the U.S. model. Australian and international jazz, blues, and roots performers love this intimate venue with its 1920s decor and friendly vibe. Ticket prices range from around A$30 (some performances are free); it's advised to book a dinner and show package to get the best seats in the house.

HAVE A GAY OLD TIME

If you're in Sydney in late February and early March, you'll think the whole city has gone gay. The Sydney Gay and Lesbian Mardi Gras parade, which celebrated its 31st anniversary in 2009, is one of Australia's major events. Dozens of floats covered with buff dancers make their way from College Street, near St. Mary's Cathedral, up Oxford Street to Taylor's Square. Thousands of spectators watch this amazing party parade.

PUBS WITH MUSIC

Harold Park Hotel (⌧ *70A Ross St. 2037* ☎ *02/9660–4745*) is a great comedy venue that also serves up great jazz, pop, rock, and blues performances, often featuring artists playing in Australia's top world music and blues festivals when they are in town. Often the performances are free. **Mercantile Hotel** (⌧ *25 George St., The Rocks* ☎ *02/9247–3570*), in the shadow of Harbour Bridge, is Irish and very proud of it. Fiddles, drums, and pipes rise above the clamor in the bar, and lilting accents rejoice in song seven nights a week.

SPORTS AND THE OUTDOORS

Given its climate and its taste for the great outdoors, it's no surprise that Sydney is addicted to sports. In the cooler months rugby league dominates the sporting scene, although these days the Sydney Swans, the city's flag bearer in the national Australian Rules Football (AFL) competition, attract far bigger crowds. In summer cricket is the major spectator sport, and nothing arouses more passion than international test cricket games—especially when Australia plays against England, the traditional enemy. Sydney is well equipped with athletic facilities, from golf courses to tennis courts, and water sports come naturally on one of the world's greatest harbors. **Ticketek Phone Box Office** (☎ *13–2849* ⊕ *www.premier.ticketek.com.au*) is the place to buy tickets for major sports events.

AUSTRALIAN RULES FOOTBALL

A fast, demanding game in which the ball can be kicked or punched between teams of 22 players, Australian Rules Football has won a major audience in Sydney, even though the city has only one professional team—the Sydney Swans—compared to the dozen that play in Melbourne—the home of the sport. **Sydney Cricket Ground** (⌧ *Moore Park Rd., Centennial Park, Paddington* ☎ *02/9360–6601* ⊕ *www.sydneycricketground.com.au*) hosts games April to September.

BICYCLING

Sydney's favorite cycling track is Centennial Park's Grand Parade, a 3¾-km (2¼-mi) cycle circuit around the perimeter of this grand, gracious eastern suburbs park.

Centennial Park Cycles (⌧ *50 Clovelly Rd.Randwick 2031* ☎ *02/9398–5027* ⌧ *Grand Dr., Centennial Park*) rents bicycles for around A$15 per hour, A$50 per day. **Clarence Street Cyclery** (⌧ *104 Clarence St., City Center* ☎ *02/9299–4962* ⊕ *www.cyclery.com.au*) is a major store for all cycling needs. They rent bikes for A$40 for four hours.

BOATING AND SAILING

EastSail (⌧ *D'Albora Marine, New Beach Rd., Rushcutters Bay, Darling Point* ☎ *02/9327–1166* ⊕ *www.eastsail.com.au*) rents bareboat sailing and motored yachts from about A$625 per half day; a skippered yacht costs around A$885 for the same period. **Northside Sailing School** (⌧ *Spit Rd., the Spit, Mosman* ☎ *02/9969–3972* ⊕ *www.northsidesailing.com. au*) at Middle Harbour teaches dinghy sailing to individuals and children's groups. You can learn the ropes on a three-hour, one-on-one

Surf school at Bondi Beach.

private lesson from A$130. **Sydney Harbour Kayaks** (⊠ *81 Parriwi Rd., Mosman* ☎ *02/9969–4590* ⊕ *www.sydneyharbourkayaks.com.au*) rents one- and two-person kayaks. The location beside Spit Bridge offers calm water for novices, as well as several beaches and idyllic coves. Prices per hour start from A$20 for a one-person kayak and A$40 for a double.

CRICKET

Cricket is Sydney's summer sport, and it's often played in parks throughout the nation. For Australians the pinnacle of excitement is the Ashes, when the national cricket team takes the field against England. It happens every other summer, and the two nations take turns hosting the event. Cricket season runs from October through March. International test series games are played at the **Sydney Cricket Ground** (⊠ *Moore Park Rd., Centennial Park, Paddington* ☎ *02/9360–6601* ⊕ *www.sydney-cricketground.com.au*).

HIKING

Fine walking trails can be found in the national parks in and around Sydney, especially in **Royal National Park, Ku-ring-gai Chase National Park,** and **Sydney Harbour National Park,** all of which are close to the city. The **Bondi-to-Bronte Coast Walk** is a lovely 3½-km (2-mi) cliff walk, popular with just about everyone in the eastern suburbs. Signage explains the flora and Aboriginal history, and the area is the venue for the hugely popular Sculpture by the Sea outdoor art display (held every October and November). The **Federation Cliff Walk** from Dover Heights (north of Bondi Beach) to Vaucluse, and on to Watsons Bay, winds past some of Sydney's most exclusive suburbs. At Diamond Bay you can soak in great views of the 20-million-year-old sandstone cliffs from the steps and boardwalks.

RUGBY LEAGUE

Known locally as football (or footy), rugby league is Sydney's winter addiction. This is a fast, gutsy, physical game that bears some similarities to North American football, although the action is more constant and the ball cannot be passed forward. The season falls between March and September. **Sydney Football Stadium** (⊠ *Moore Park Rd., Centennial Park, Paddington* ☎ *02/9360–6601* ⊕ *www.scgt.nsw.gov.au*) is the home stadium of the Sydney Roosters. Other games are played at Telstra Stadium (Sydney Olympic Park) and stadiums throughout the suburbs.

SCUBA DIVING

Dive Centre Manly (⊠ *10 Belgrave St., Manly* ☎ *02/9977–4355* ⊕ *www. divesydney.com*), at the popular North Sydney beach, runs all-inclusive shore dives each day, which let you see weedy sea dragons and other sea creatures. PADI certification courses are also available. The cost for two shore dives starts at A$95. **Pro Dive** (⊠ *27 Alfreda St., Coogee* ☎ *1800/820820* ⊕ *www.prodive.com.au*) is a PADI operator conducting courses and shore- or boat-diving excursions around the harbor and city beaches. Some of the best dive spots—with coral, rock walls, and lots of colorful fish, including "Bazza" the grouper—are close to the eastern suburb beaches of Clovelly and Coogee. The company also has a center in Manly. A four-hour boat dive with a guide costs around A$189, including rental equipment; a four-dive learn-to-dive course is A$447.

SURFING

All Sydney surfers have their favorite breaks, but you can usually count on good waves on at least one of the city's ocean beaches. **Surfcam** (⊕ *www.surfcam.com.au*) has surf reports and weather details. **Lets go Surfing** (⊠ *128 Ramsgate Ave., North Bondi* ☎ *02/9365–1800* ⊕ *www. letsgosurfing.com.au*) is a complete surfing resource for anyone who wants to hang five with confidence. Lessons are available for all ages, and you can rent or buy boards and wet suits. The basic three-class package of two-hour Surf Easy lessons costs A$195. **Manly Surf School** (⊠ *North Steyne Surf Club, Manly Beach, Manly* ☎ *02/9977–6977* ⊕ *www.manlysurfschool.com*) conducts courses for adults and children, and provides all equipment, including wet suits. Adults can join a two-hour group lesson (four per day) for A$55. Private instruction costs A$80 per hour. **Rip Curl** (⊠ *82 Campbell Parade, Bondi Beach* ☎ *02/9130–2660* ⊕ *www.ripcurl.com.au*) has a huge variety of boards and surfing supplies. It's right at Bondi Beach.

SWIMMING

Sydney has many heated Olympic-size swimming pools, some of which go beyond the basic requirements of a workout. Many Aussies, however, prefer to do their "laps" in ocean pools at Bondi and Manly.

Andrew (Boy) Charlton Pool (⊠ *Mrs. Macquarie's Rd., The Domain* ☎ *02/ 9358–6686* ⊕ *www.abcpool.org*) isn't just any heated Olympic-size saltwater pool. Its stunning outdoor location overlooking the ships at Garden Island, its radical glass-and-steel design, and its chic terrace café above Woolloomooloo Bay make it an attraction in itself. Admission is A$5.70, and it's open September–April, daily 6 AM–7 PM.

Cook and Phillip Park Aquatic and Fitness Centre (⊠ *College St., City Center* ☎ *02/9326–0444* ⊕ *www.cookandphillip.org.au*) includes wave, hydrotherapy, children's, and Olympic-size pools in a stunning high-tech complex on the eastern edge of the city center near St. Mary's Cathedral. There's also a complete fitness center and classes. Admission is A$6.20 to swim and A$16.60 for the gym. Open weekdays 6 AM–10 PM, weekends 7 AM–8 PM.

TENNIS

Cooper Park Tennis Centre (⊠ *Off Suttie Rd., Cooper Park, Woollahra* ☎ *02/9389–3100* ⊕ *www.cptennis.com.au*) is a complex of eight synthetic-grass courts and a café in a park surrounded by native bushland, about 5 km (3 mi) east of the city. Court fees are A$24 per hour from 6 AM to 5 PM and A$29 per hour from 5 PM to 10 PM (weekends) and A$29 all day on Saturday 6–7, and Sunday 6–8. **Parklands Sports Centre** (⊠ *Lang Rd. at Anzac Parade, Moore Park, Centennial Park* ☎ *02/9662–7033* ⊕ *www.cp.nsw.gov.au/aboutus/sports.htm*) has 11 courts in a shady park approximately 2½ km (1½ mi) from the city center. The weekday cost is A$16.50 per hour 9–5 and A$25 per hour 5 PM–10:30 PM; it's A$25 per hour 8 AM–6 PM on weekends.

WINDSURFING

Balmoral Windsurfing, Sailing, and Kayak School (⊠ *The Esplanade, Balmoral Beach* ☎ *02/9960–5344* ⊕ *www.sailboard.net.au*) runs classes from its base at this north-side harbor beach. Windsurfing lessons start from A$110 per hour, sailing from A$265 for four hours of lessons over a two-day period. **Rose Bay Aquatic Hire** (⊠ *1 Vickery Ave., Rose Bay* ☎ *02/9371–7036*) rents motorboats, kayaks, and catamarans. The cost is from A$50 per hour for a catamaran; some sailing experience is required to rent these boats. Kayaks are also available for rent from A$10 for the first hour; motorboat rentals cost A$60 per hour for the first hour, other prices apply thereafter.

SHOPPING

Sydney's shops vary from those with international cachet (Tiffany's, Louis Vuitton) to Aboriginal art galleries, opal shops, craft bazaars, and weekend flea markets. If you're interested in buying genuine Australian products, look carefully at the labels. Stuffed koalas and didgeridoos made anywhere but in Australia is a standing joke.

Business hours are usually 9 or 10 to 5.30 on weekdays; on Thursday stores stay open until 9. Shops are open Saturday 9–5 and Sunday 11–5. Prices include the 10 percent Goods and Services Tax (GST).

FLEA MARKETS

Balmain Market (⊠ *St. Andrew's Church, Darling St., Balmain*), in a leafy churchyard less than 5 km (3 mi) from the city, has a rustic quality that makes it a refreshing change from city-center shopping. Crafts, handmade furniture, plants, bread, toys, tarot readings, and massages are among the offerings at the 140-odd stalls. Inside the church hall you can buy international snacks. Every Saturday 8:30–4.

Fodor's Choice
★ **Paddington Markets** (sometimes called Paddington Bazaar) (✉ *St. John's Uniting Church, 395 Oxford St., Paddington*) is a busy churchyard market with more than 100 stalls crammed with clothing, plants, crafts, jewelry, and souvenirs. Distinctly New Age and highly fashion conscious, the market is an outlet for a handful of avant-garde clothing designers. Every Saturday from 10–4. **Paddy's Market** (✉ *9–13 Hay St., Haymarket*) is a huge fresh produce and flea market held under the Market City complex near the Sydney Entertainment Centre in the Chinatown precinct. There has been a market on this site since 1834, and much of the historic exterior remains. The Metro Light Rail, Explorer bus, and Monorail stop at the door. Open Thursday to Sunday 9 to 5. **The Rocks Market** (✉ *Upper George St. near Argyle St., The Rocks*), a sprawling covered bazaar, transforms the upper end of George Street into a multicultural collage of music, food, arts, crafts, and entertainment. Open weekends 10–5.

> **BEACH READS**
>
> Need something to read on Bondi Beach? Take a stroll to **Gertrude & Alice Café Bookshop** (✉ *46 Hall St.* ☎ *02/9130–5155*), named in honor of lovers Gertrude Stein and Alice B. Toklas. Always buzzing with people, it's a great place to sip coffee or have lunch while perusing the mostly secondhand books. Open daily 7:30–9:30.

SHOPPING CENTERS AND ARCADES

Birkenhead Point (✉ *Roseby St. near the Iron Cove Bridge, Drummoyne* ☎ *02/9182–8800*) is a factory outlet with more than 100 clothing, shoe, and housewares stores. Situated on the western shores of Iron Cove about 7 km [4 mi] west of Sydney, it's a great place to shop for discounted labels including Alannah Hill, Witchery, Bendon (Elle Macpherson's lingerie range), and Table Eight. Take Bus 506 or Bus 507 from Circular Quay or Town Hall, or a ferry from Circular Quay. **Oxford Street,** Paddington's main artery (from South Dowling Street east to Queen Street, Woollahra), is dressed to thrill. Lined with boutiques, home-furnishings stores, and cafés, it's a perfect venue for watching the never-ending fashion parade. **Pitt Street Mall** (✉ *Between King and Market Sts., City Center*), at the heart of Sydney's shopping area, includes the Mid-City Center, Westfield Centrepoint Arcade, Imperial Arcade, Skygarden, Myer, and the charming and historic Strand Arcade—six multilevel shopping plazas crammed with more than 450 shops, from mainstream clothing stores to designer boutiques. **Queen Victoria Building** (✉ *George, York, Market, and Druitt Sts., City Center* ☎ *02/9264–9209* ⊕ *www.qvb.com.au*) is a splendid Victorian-era building with more than 200 boutiques, cafés, and antiques shops. The building is open 24 hours, so you can window-shop even after the stores have closed.

SPECIALTY STORES

ABORIGINAL ART

Aboriginal art includes historically functional items, such as boomerangs, wooden bowls, and spears, as well as paintings and ceremonial implements that testify to a rich culture of legends and dreams. Although much of this artwork remains strongly traditional in essence, the tools and colors used in Western art have fired the imaginations of many Aboriginal artists. Works on canvas are now more common than works on bark. Much of the best works of Arnhem Land and the Central Desert Region (close to Darwin and Alice Springs, respectively), finds its way into Sydney galleries.

Cooee Aboriginal Art (✉ *31 Lamrock Ave., Bondi Beach* ☎ *02/9300–9233* ⊕ *www.cooeeart.com.au*), open Tuesday–Saturday 10–5, exhibits and sells high-end Aboriginal paintings, sculptures, and limited-edition prints. **Gavala** (✉ *Shop 131, Harbourside Centre, Darling Harbour* ☎ *02/9213–7232* ⊕ *www.gavala.com.au*) brings you art and artifacts directly from Aboriginal artists. There's a large selection of paintings, boomerangs, didgeridoos, books, music, and clothing. **Hogarth Galleries** (✉ *7 Walker La., Paddington* ☎ *02/9360–6839* ⊕ *www.aboriginal-artcentres.com*) showcases quality contemporary Aboriginal artworks from around the country.

BOOKS

Ariel Booksellers (✉ *42 Oxford St., Paddington* ☎ *02/9332–4581* ✉ *103 George St., The Rocks* ☎ *02/9241–5622* ⊕ *www.arielbooks.com.au*) is a large, bright browser's delight, and the place to go for literature, pop culture, avant garde, and art books. Both branches are open daily 9 AM–midnight. **Dymocks** (✉ *424 George St., City Center* ☎ *02/9235–0155* ⊕ *www.dymocks.com.au*), a big, bustling bookstore packed to its gallery-level coffee shop, is the place to go for all literary needs. It's open Monday to Wednesday and Friday 9 to 6, Thursday 9 to 8, Saturday 9:30 to 5:30, and Sunday 10:30 to 5.

BUSH APPAREL AND OUTDOOR GEAR

Mountain Designs (✉ *499 Kent St., City Center* ☎ *02/9267–3822* ⊕ *www.mountaindesigns.com.au*), in the middle of Sydney's "Rugged Row" of outdoor specialists, sells camping and climbing gear and dispenses the advice necessary to keep you alive and well in the wilderness. **Paddy Pallin** (✉ *507 Kent St., City Center* ☎ *02/9264–2685* ⊕ *www.paddypallin.com.au*) is the first stop for serious bush adventurers heading for wild Australia and beyond. Maps, books, and mounds of gear are tailored especially for the Australian outdoors.

★ **R. M. Williams** (✉ *389 George St., City Center* ☎ *02/9262–2228* ⊕ *www.rmwilliams.com.au*) is the place to go for riding boots, Akubra hats, Drizabone riding coats, and moleskin trousers, the type of clothes worn by Hugh Jackman and Nicole Kidman in the movie *Australia*.

CLOTHING

Belinda (✉ *8 and 14 Transvaal Ave., Double Bay* ☎ *02/9328–6288 or 02/9327–8199* ⊕ *www.belinda.com.au*) is where Sydney's female fashionistas go when there's a dress-up occasion looming. From her namesake store that scores high marks for innovation and imagination, former model Belinda Seper sells nothing but the very latest designs off the catwalks. **Collette Dinnigan** (✉ *33 William St., Paddington* ☎ *02/9360–6691* ⊕ *www.collettedinnigan.com.au*), one of the hottest names on Australia's fashion scene, has dressed Nicole Kidman, Cate

Aboriginal paintings are visual representations of ancestral stories from The Dreaming.

Blanchett, and Sandra Bullock. Her Paddington boutique is packed with sensual, floating, negligee-inspired fashions crafted from silks, chiffons, and lace in soft pastel colors accented with hand-beading and embroidery. Her clothes are also available at the David Jones women's store in the city center. **Country Road** (✉ *142–144 Pitt St., City Center* ☎ *02/9394–1818* ⊕ *www.countryroad.com.au*) stands somewhere between Ralph Lauren and Timberland, with an all-Australian assembly of classic, countrified his 'n' hers, plus an ever-expanding variety of soft furnishings in cotton and linen for the rustic retreat.

Marcs (✉ *Shop 1, QVB, 455 George St., City Center* ☎ *02/9267–0823* ⊕ *www.marcs.com.au*) is located somewhere close to Diesel-land in the fashion spectrum, with a variety of clothing, footwear, and accessories for the fashion-conscious. Serious shoppers should look for the Marcs Made in Italy sub-label for that extra touch of class. **Orson & Blake** (✉ *83–85 Queen St., Woollahra* ☎ *02/9326–1155* ⊕ *www.orsonandblake.com.au*) is a virtual gallery dedicated to great modern design, with eclectic housewares, fashions, handbags, and accessories. **Scanlan & Theodore** (✉ *122 Oxford St., Paddington* ☎ *02/9380–9388* ⊕ *www.scanontheodore.com.au*) is the Sydney outlet for one of Melbourne's most distinguished fashion houses. Designs take their cues from Europe, with superbly tailored women's knitwear, suits, and stylishly glamorous evening wear.

CRAFTS

Collect (✉ *417 Bourke St., Surry Hills* ☎ *02/9361–4511* ⊕ *www.object.com.au*) sells beautiful glass, wood, and ceramic creations. **Object**, its next-door gallery, displays a larger selection of Australian-made crafts.

MUSIC

Birdland Records (⊠ *9th Level, 45 Market St., City Center* ☎ *02/9267–6881* ⊕ *www.birdland.com.au*) has an especially strong selection of jazz, blues, African, and Latin American music, as well as an authoritative staff ready to lend some assistance. It's open Monday to Wednesday and Friday 10–5:30, Thursday 10–8, and Saturday 9–4:30. **Folkways** (⊠ *282 Oxford St., Paddington* ☎ *02/9361–3980*) sells Australian bush, folk, and Aboriginal recordings. The store is open Monday to Wednesday and Saturday 10–6, Thursday 9–8, Friday 9–6, and Sunday 11–6.

OPALS AND JEWELRY

Australia has a virtual monopoly on the world's supply of opals. The least expensive of these fiery gemstones are triplets, which consist of a thin shaving of opal mounted on a plastic base and covered by a plastic, glass, or quartz crown. Doublets are a slice of mounted opal without the capping. The most expensive stones are solid opals, which cost anywhere from a few hundred dollars to a few thousand. You can pick up opals at souvenir shops all over the city, but if you want a valuable stone you should visit a specialist. Sydney is also a good hunting ground for other jewelry, from the quirky to the gloriously expensive.

Dinosaur Designs (⊠ *Shop 77, Strand Arcade, George St., City Center* ☎ *02/9223–2953 or 02/9698–3500* ⊠ *339 Oxford St., Paddington* ☎ *02/9361–3776* ⊕ *www.dinosaurdesigns.com.au*) sells luminous bowls, plates, and vases, as well as fanciful jewelry crafted from resin and Perspex in eye-popping colors. **Hathi Jewellery** (⊠ *19 Playfair St., The Rocks* ☎ *02/9252–4328* ⊕ *www.hathijewellery.com.au*) has a beautiful collection of handmade jewelry including earrings, necklaces, and bracelets. Most pieces are one of a kind.

★ **Makers Mark** (⊠ *72 Castlereagh St., City Center* ☎ *02/9231–6800* ⊕ *www.makersmark.com.au*) has a gorgeous collection of handmade designer jewelry and objects by some of Australia's finest artisans. **The National Opal Collection** (⊠ *60 Pitt St., City Center* ☎ *02/9233–8844* ⊕ *www.gemtec.com.au*) is the only Sydney opal retailer with total ownership of its entire production process—mines, workshops, and showroom—making prices very competitive. In the Pitt Street showroom you can prearrange to see artisans at work cutting and polishing the stones. Hours are weekdays 9 to 6 and weekends 10 to 4.

★ **Paspaley Pearls** (⊠ *2 Martin Pl., City Center* ☎ *02/9232–7633* ⊕ *www.paspaleypearls.com*) derives its exquisite jewelry from pearl farms near the remote Western Australia town of Broome. Prices start high and head for the stratosphere, but if you're serious about a high-quality pearl, this gallery requires a visit. **Percy Marks Fine Gems** (⊠ *62–70 Elizabeth St., City Center* ☎ *02/9233–1355* ⊕ *www.percymarks.com.au*) has an outstanding collection of high-quality Australian gemstones, including dazzling black opals, pink diamonds, and pearls from Broome. **Rox Gems and Jewellery** (⊠ *Shop 31, Strand Arcade, George St., City Center* ☎ *02/9232–7828* ⊕ *www.rox.com.au*) sells serious one-off designs at the cutting edge of lapidary chic that can be spotted on some exceedingly well-dressed wrists.

New South Wales

WITH CANBERRA AND THE A.C.T.

WORD OF MOUTH

"If you like museums, you've got the Australian War Memorial (a must), the National Gallery of Australia, Questacon. The Parliament House and Old Parliament House are both worth a visit as well. If you like the outdoors, there's great hiking/scenery/wildlife at Tidbinbilla Nature Reserve and Namadgi National Park."

—longhorn55

WELCOME TO
NEW SOUTH WALES

TOP REASONS TO GO

★ **Getting in touch with nature:** Exotic birds are prolific in the Blue Mountains and North Coast regions, and Canberra isn't known as the "Bush Capital" for nothing.

★ **The Great Australian Bite:** Fine restaurants have taken root in the Hunter Valley, as well as in the North Coast towns of Coffs Harbour and Byron Bay. Seafood can be excellent, and don't miss fish-and-chips on the beach.

★ **Outdoor Adventure:** The region's mountains and national parks offer opportunities for walks and hikes, horseback riding, rappelling, canyoning, and rock climbing. Outdoorsy folks will enjoy Canberra's wide-open spaces and cycling or walking around the city's Lake Burley Griffin.

★ **World-Class Wineries:** The Hunter Valley has an international reputation for producing excellent Chardonnay, Shiraz, and a dry Semillon.

1 The Blue Mountains. Sydneysiders flock to this UNESCO protected wilderness region with its majestic mountain peaks and deep green valleys sprinkled with charming country guesthouses. The famous sandstone rock formations known as the Three Sisters are the area's best-known attraction.

2 Hunter Valley Wine Region. This is one of the oldest and best-known wine regions in Australia, with vineyards dating back to the 1830s. Oenophiles shouldn't miss a trip to this thriving and perennially busy destination. We also like the food, historic towns, and tranquil countryside.

3 The North Coast. This region has some of the most glorious and seductive stretches of beach in Australia—and that's saying something when you consider the competition. The almost continuous line of beaches is interspersed with lively towns and harbors, with the Great Dividing Range rising to the west.

3

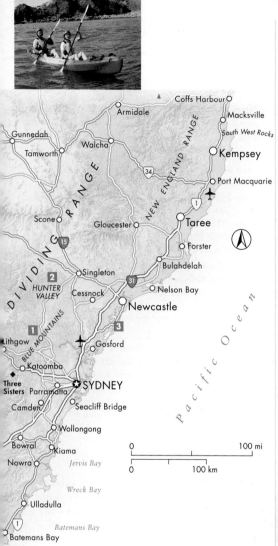

Armidale
Coffs Harbour
Macksville
South West Rocks
Gunnedah
Walcha
Kempsey
Tamworth
34
Port Macquarie
Scone
Gloucester
Taree
15
Forster
Singleton
Bulahdelah
2
HUNTER VALLEY
Cessnock
31
Nelson Bay
1
Newcastle
Lithgow
3
Gosford
Katoomba
Three Sisters
SYDNEY
Parramatta
Camden
Seacliff Bridge
Wollongong
Bowral
Kiama
Nowra
Jervis Bay
Wreck Bay
Ulladulla
Batemans Bay
1

0   100 mi
0   100 km

Pacific Ocean

GETTING ORIENTED

New South Wales, with the country's capital city Canberra and the A.C.T. carved out in an area half the size of Rhode Island, covers the southeast corner of the country. Despite this being Australia's most populous state, the rich variety of landscapes is its biggest selling point. The Blue Mountains, a World Heritage site, lie to the west of Sydney, while the Southern Highlands and South Coast stretch to the south. The Hunter Valley is north of Canberra. The North Coast is exactly where its name suggests, while Lord Howe Island is 700 km (435 mi) northeast of Sydney, a distant offshore environment of its own.

4 Canberra and the A.C.T.
The nation's capital and its environs may be quiet and a little too well-mannered for some, but its museums and galleries are the best in the country, and its diverse range of parks and gardens is a major draw.

NEW SOUTH WALES PLANNER

When to Visit

For visitors from the northern hemisphere the Australian summer (approximately December–February) has great pull. The best times to visit the Hunter Valley are during the February–March grape harvest season and the September Hunter Food and Wine Festival. Spring and autumn are also ideal times to visit Canberra; from February to April autumn leaves paint the city with amber hues. The spring flower celebration, Floriade, lasts from mid-September to mid-October. The North Coast resort region is often booked solid between Christmas and the first half of January, but autumn and spring are good times to visit.

Health and Safety

In an emergency, dial 000 to reach an ambulance, the police, or the fire department. If you decide to hike off the beaten track in the Blue Mountains, tell someone where you're headed. There is an emergency rescue service which can be reached at ☎ 13/2500.

In summer, bush fires are a perennial worry—always obey the no-fire zones and make sure you have enough water to avoid dehydration.

Getting Here and Around

Air Travel

New South Wales is peppered with airports, so flying is the easiest way to get around if you're traveling long distances. Prices are generally low, thanks to the budget airlines. From Sydney, REX (Regional Express) Airlines services Ballina and Lismore (both about ½ hour from Byron Bay). Qantas flies into Canberra, Port Macquarie, and Coffs Harbour, while Virgin Blue flies into Canberra, Port Macquarie, Ballina, and Coffs Harbour.

Information Qantas Airways (☎ 13–1313 ⊕ www.qantas.com.au). **REX Airlines** (☎ 13–1713 ⊕ www.regionalexpress.com.au). **Virgin Blue** (☎ 13–6789 ⊕ www.virginblue.com.au).

Car Rental

Hiring your own car is the most convenient way of getting around the region. The scenic Blue Mountains and Hunter Valley routes and attractions are outside the towns, so having you're own set of wheels is helpful. When visititing the wine country, be aware that Australia has a zero tolerance for drunk drivers. Most towns have major car-rental companies. You can pick up a car at one point and drop off at another for an extra fee.

Train Travel

As in the States, most people drive here, so train services aren't brilliant and can often cost more than other options. It is possible to travel by train to the Blue Mountains with Sydney's Cityrail commuter trains. CountryLink trains link Sydney to towns in the Hunter Valley and towns along the North Coast. Canberra is not a convenient destination to get to by train, so unless you're a rail enthusiast, it's quicker to drive or catch a bus.

Information Cityrail (☎ 13–1500 ⊕ www.cityrail.info). **CountryLink** (☎ 13–2232 ⊕ www.countrylink.info).

Restaurants

Dining varies dramatically throughout New South Wales, from superb city-standard restaurants to average country-town fare. As popular weekend retreats for well-heeled Sydneysiders, the Blue Mountains and Southern Highlands have a number of fine restaurants and cozy tea rooms that are perfect for light lunches or afternoon teas. In the Hunter Valley several excellent restaurants show off the region's fine wines. Unsurprisingly seafood dominates on the North Coast, and again, thanks to weekending Sydneysiders with high standards, you should be able to tuck into some excellent meals. The eclectic selection of eateries in Canberra reflects the city's cosmopolitan residents, so despite the city's size, Canberra's dining spots hold their own against the restaurants of Sydney and Melbourne, although the feeling is generally more casual.

Hotels

Accommodations include everything from run-of-the-mill motels and remote wilderness lodges to historic, cliff-perched properties and expansive seaside resorts. Rates are often much lower on weekdays, particularly in the Blue Mountains and the Hunter Valley, as traffic from Sydney is heavier on weekends. The North Coast is very popular during school holidays so book as far ahead as possible. Hotels in Canberra, with one or two notable exceptions, don't have the character that other places do. But there are plenty of four-star chain hotel options and self-catering apartments. Smoking is banned in all public places in NSW and the A.C.T.

WHAT IT COSTS IN AUSTRALIAN DOLLARS

	¢	$	$$	$$$	$$$$
Restaurants	under A$10	A$10– A$20	A$21– A$35	A$36– A$50	over A$50
Hotels	under A$100	A$100– A$150	A$151– A$200	A$201– A$300	over A$300

Meal prices are per person for a main course at dinner. Hotel prices are for two people in a standard double room in high season, including tax and service, based on the European Plan (with no meals) unless otherwise noted.

Experiencing Aboriginal Culture

The Ngunnawal people were the first inhabitants of the area now known as Canberra and the A.C.T., and the name Canberra comes from the Ngunnawal word "Kambera." In NSW the Cammeraygal, Eora, Kamilaroi, Tharawal, Wiradjuri, and Wonnarua peoples were some of the original inhabitants, each grouping speaking a different language and practicing a culture that stretched back thousands of years.

Jamanee Gunya at Burrill Lake, a 3-hour drive east from Canberra, operates cultural awareness tours for groups. The three-day Indigenous Health Weekend Workshop includes a trip to Meroo National Park, where you can canoe through a pristine coastal lagoon, learn about rare wildlife and bush foods and how to throw a boomerang. (✉ *501 Wheelbarrow Rd., Burrill Lake, NSW* ☎ *02/ 4455–2290* ⊕ *www.jamanee gunya.com.au*).

Muru Mittigar Aboriginal Cultural Centre near Penrith, an hour's drive from Sydney, tells the story of the Dharug people. You can try bush tucker and boomerang throwing, or learn about the native plants used for medicine and food. (✉ *89–151 Old Castlereagh Rd., Castlereagh, NSW* ☎ *02/4729– 2377* ⊕ *www.murumittigar.com. au*).

Updated by
Helena Iveson

For many travelers Sydney is New South Wales, and they look to the other, less-populous states for Australia's famous wilderness experiences. However, New South Wales has many of Australia's natural wonders within its borders. High on the list are the subtropical rain forests of the North Coast, lush river valleys, warm seas, golden beaches, the World Heritage areas of Lord Howe Island, and some of Australia's finest vineyards. Many travelers overlook Canberra, but history buffs and art aficionados will love its selection of galleries and museums that are ranked as the nation's finest.

Today, with approximately 6.7 million people, New South Wales is Australia's most populous state. Although this is crowded by Australian standards, it's worth remembering that New South Wales is larger than every U.S. state except Alaska. In the state's east, a coastal plain reaching north to Queensland varies in width from less than a mile to almost 160 km (100 mi). This plain is bordered on the west by a chain of low mountains known as the Great Dividing Range, which tops off at about 7,300 feet in the Snowy Mountains in the state's far south. On this range's western slopes is a belt of pasture and farmland. Beyond that are the western plains and Outback, an arid, sparsely populated region that takes up two-thirds of the state.

THE BLUE MOUNTAINS

Sydneysiders have been doubly blessed by nature. Not only do they have a magnificent coastline right at their front door, but a 90-minute drive west puts them in the midst of one of the most spectacular wilderness areas in Australia—World Heritage Blue Mountains National Park. This rippling sea of hills is covered by tall eucalyptus trees and

GREAT ITINERARIES

It's wise to decide in advance whether you'd like to cover a lot of ground quickly or choose one or two places to linger a while. If you have less than four days, stick close to Sydney. The most compelling choice would be the Blue Mountains, followed by the Hunter Valley or Southern Highlands. In a very busy week you could visit the Blue Mountains plus either the Hunter Valley or Southern Highlands. Two weeks would allow a Blue Mountains–North Coast–Lord Howe circuit, or brief stops in most of the region's top destinations.

IF YOU HAVE 4 DAYS

Start with a visit to the **Blue Mountains**. You could arrange a round-trip itinerary from Sydney in a fairly hectic day or, preferably, spend a night in **Katoomba, Blackheath**, or **Leura** and make it a two-day excursion. Return to Sydney, and then head north to the **Hunter Valley**. A two-day/one-night driving visit here would allow you enough time to

see the main sights and spend time touring the wineries before traveling back to Sydney on the second day. An alternative would be a quick visit to the Blue Mountains, then two days in Canberra to see the city's excellent museums and galleries.

IF YOU HAVE 7 DAYS

Go to the Blue Mountains and Hunter Valley as described above, then if beach life is appealing continue to the North Coast. In three days of driving you wouldn't get much farther than **Coffs Harbour** (with overnights there and in **Port Macquarie**), and this would be rushing it, but it's possible to fly back to Sydney from Coffs. Alternatively, or if you're looking for something more cerebral, travel northwest to sedate Canberra and have a leisurely few days exploring gems like the National Portrait Gallery, Parliament House, and the Australian War Memorial, while stretching your legs walking or biking around Lake Burley Griffin.

dissected by deep river valleys—the area is perfect terrain for hiking and adventure activities. Standing 3,500-plus feet high, these "mountains" were once the bed of an ancient sea. Gradually the sedimentary rock was uplifted until it formed a high plateau, which was etched by aeons of wind and water into the wonderland of cliffs, caves, and canyons that exists today. Now the richly forested hills, crisp mountain air, cool-climate gardens, vast sandstone chasms, and little towns of timber and stone are supreme examples of Australia's diversity. The mountains' distinctive blue coloring is caused by the evaporation of oil from the dense eucalyptus forests. This disperses light in the blue colors of the spectrum, a phenomenon known as Rayleigh Scattering.

The Blue Mountains Visitor Information Centre is at the foot of the mountains on the Great Western Highway at Glenbrook, the town you'll encounter when driving from Sydney. There is another information office in Katoomba.

Information Blue Mountains Visitor Information Centre (✉ *Great Western Hwy., Glenbrook* ☎ *1300/653408* ☺ *Daily 9–5*).

Numbers in the margin correspond to points of interest on the Blue Mountains map.

WENTWORTH FALLS

95 km (59 mi) west of Sydney.

This attractive township is home to the Blue Mountains' most stunning natural waterfalls and bush walking trails. The Falls themselves straddle the highway, but most points of interest and views of the Jamison Valley and Blue Mountains National Park are south of the road.

ARTIST HAVEN

The Blue Mountains harbor a wealth of talent. You'll find artists, writers, composers, and performers living in this vibrant cultural community. Check out the galleries, browse in the bookshops, or pop into a café or pub to catch some good music. The **Blue Mountains Music Festival** (⊕ www.bmff.org.au), held every March in Katoomba, showcases folk, blues, and roots music.

GETTING HERE AND AROUND

If you are driving from Sydney, head west onto Parramatta Road, then take the M4, following signs to the Blue Mountains. There is a toll to pay at the end of the motorway. Wentworth Falls is clearly signposted and is 95 km (59 mi) from Central Sydney. It's also easy to catch a train to Wentworth Falls, and the journey from Sydney Central Station takes 1¾ hours, with trains leaving roughly every hour. The Blue Mountains Bus Company (☎ 02/4751–1077 ⊕ www.bmbc.com.au) connects towns within the region with routes 685 and 695, connecting Wentworth Falls to Leura and Katoomba.

EN ROUTE

If driving from Sydney, be sure to stop at the National Trust–listed **Norman Lindsay Gallery and Museum,** dedicated to the Australian artist and writer. Considered one of the cultural highlights of the Blue Mountains, Lindsay lived in this house during the latter part of his life until he died in 1969. Lindsay is best known for his paintings, etchings, and drawings, but he also built model boats, sculpted, and wrote poetry and children's books, among which *The Magic Pudding* has become an Australian classic. The delightful landscaped gardens contain several of Lindsay's sculptures, and you can also take a short but scenic bushwalk beyond the garden. ⊠ *14 Norman Lindsay Crescent, Faulconbridge* ☎ *02/4751–1067* ⊕ *www.normanlindsay.com.au* ⊠*A$9* ⊙ *Daily 10–4.*

OUTDOOR ACTIVITIES

HIKING
★
From a lookout in **Falls Reserve,** south of the town of Wentworth Falls, you can take in magnificent views both out across the Jamison Valley to the Kings Tableland and of the 935-foot-high **Wentworth Falls** themselves. To find the best view of the falls, follow the trail that crosses the stream and zigzags down the sheer cliff face, signposted NATIONAL PASS. If you continue, the trail cuts back across the base of the falls and along a narrow ledge to the delightful Valley of the Waters, where it ascends to the top of the cliffs, emerging at the Conservation Hut. The complete circuit takes at least three hours and is a moderately difficult walk. ⊠ *End of Falls Rd.*

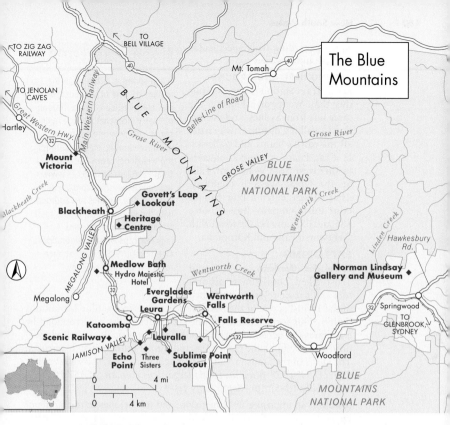

The Blue Mountains

TO ZIG ZAG RAILWAY

TO BELL VILLAGE

TO JENOLAN CAVES

Mt. Tomah

Great Western Hwy.

Hartley

BLUE MOUNTAINS

Grose River

Grose River

Main Western Railway

Bells Line of Road

Mount Victoria

Blackheath Creek

Grose River

GROSE VALLEY

BLUE MOUNTAINS NATIONAL PARK

Govett's Leap Lookout

Blackheath

Heritage Centre

MEGALONG VALLEY

Medlow Bath
Hydro Majestic Hotel

Megalong

Wentworth Creek

Wentworth Creek

Linden Creek

Hawkesbury Rd.

Norman Lindsay Gallery and Museum

Springwood

Everglades Gardens

Leura

Wentworth Falls

Falls Reserve

TO GLENBROOK, SYDNEY

Katoomba

Scenic Railway

Leuralla

JAMISON VALLEY

Echo Point

Three Sisters

Sublime Point Lookout

Woodford

BLUE MOUNTAINS NATIONAL PARK

0   4 mi
0   4 km

WHERE TO EAT

$$
AUSTRALIAN

✕ **Conservation Hut.** From its prime spot in Blue Mountains National Park, on a cliff overlooking the Jamison Valley, this spacious, mud-brick bistro serves simple, savory fare. Lovely breakfast dishes include herbed mushrooms with a poached egg and roast tomatoes on toast. For lunch and dinner, dig into hearty soups, beef pies, or perch fillets with baked fennel and sorrel sauce. Be sure to save room for the dessert cakes. An open balcony is a delight on warm days, and a fire blazes in the cooler months. A hiking trail from the bistro leads down into the Valley of the Waters, one of the splendors of the mountains. It's a wonderful pre- or post-meal walk. ⌂ 88 Fletcher St. ☎ 02/4757–3827 ▭ AE, MC, V ⌟⟪ BYOB ⊙ No dinner Mon.–Thurs. in summer months.

LEURA

5 km (3 mi) west of Wentworth Falls.

Leura, the prettiest and chicest of the mountain towns, is bordered by bush and lined with excellent cafés, restaurants, and gift shops. From the south end of the main street (The Mall), the road continues past superb local gardens as it winds down to the massive cliffs overlooking the Jamison Valley. The dazzling 19-km (12-mi) journey along Cliff Drive skirts the rim of the valley—often only yards from the cliff edge—providing truly spectacular Blue Mountains views.

GETTING HERE AND AROUND

Leura Train Station is one stop further than Wentworth Falls on the same line from Sydney, and the station is walking distance away from all the town's shops and galleries. In a car, Leura is a few kilometers further west from Wentworth Falls on the Great Western Highway. Alternatively, catch a Blue Mountains Bus Company Bus—Routes 685 and 695 connect the town with Wentworth Falls and Katoomba.

EXPLORING

Everglades Gardens, a National Trust–listed, cool-climate arboretum and nature reserve established

BLOOMIN' BEAUTIFUL

When spring is in the air in the mountains, one of the most beautiful places to be is Leura. Dozens of cherry blossoms line the main street, and private gardens are open for viewing. Make a date for the weeklong **Leura Garden Festival** (☎ 02/4757-2359 ⊕ www.leuragardensfestival.com.au) in October. The gardens are adorned with the work of local artists keen to win the annual art prize. A village fair caps off the celebrations. One ticket (A$18) buys entrance to all the gardens on show.

in the 1930s, is one of the best public gardens in the Blue Mountains region. This former home of a Belgian industrialist is surrounded by 5 hectares (13 acres) of native bushland and exotic flora, a rhododendron garden, an alpine plant area, and formal European-style terraces. The views of the Jamison Valley are magnificent. ⊠ *37 Everglades Ave.* ☎ *02/4784–1938* ⊕ *www.evergladesgardens.com.au* ⊠ *A$7* ☉ *Oct.– Mar., daily 10–5; Apr.–Sept., daily 10–4.*

Leuralla is an imposing 1911 mansion, and still belongs to the family of Dr. H. V. ("Doc") Evatt (1894–1965), the first president of the General Assembly of the United Nations and later the leader of the Australian Labor Party. A 19th-century Australian art collection and a small museum dedicated to Dr. Evatt are inside the home. Also on the grounds is the **New South Wales Toy and Railway Museum,** with its extensive collection of railway memorabilia, antique curios from yesteryear, and exhibitions on iconic dolls like Barbie. Directly across the street are the Leuralla Public Gardens, with spectacular views of the Jamison Valley. ⊠ *36 Olympian Parade* ☎ *02/4784–1169* ⊕ *www.toyandrailwaymuseum.com.au* ⊠ *A$12, A$8 for gardens only* ☉ *Daily 10–5.*

★ **Sublime Point Lookout,** just outside Leura, lives up to its name with a great view of the Jamison Valley and the generally spectacular Blue Mountains scenery. It's a quiet vantage point that provides a different perspective from that of the famous **Three Sisters** lookout at nearby Katoomba. ⊠ *Sublime Point Rd.*

WHERE TO EAT AND STAY

$$–$$$ ✕ **Silk's Brasserie.** Thanks to its Sydney-standard food, wine, and ser-
AUSTRALIAN vice, Silk's rates as one of the finest Blue Mountains restaurants. The
Fodor'sChoice menu here changes seasonally, but might include confit of duck with a
★ pumpkin, roast macadamia, and watercress salad with a ruby grapefruit and pomegranate dressing, as well as more casual dishes for lunch. The locals' favorite dessert is the caramelized warm banana tart with coconut

Continued on page 159

HIKING THE BLUE MOUNTAINS

Kanangra Falls

Head west of Sydney along the M4, or simply hop a bus or train, and within an hour you'll be on a gradual climb along a traditional Aboriginal pathway into the heart of the Blue Mountains—a sandstone plateau formed 150 million years ago that tops out at 3,600 feet. Dramatic valleys, canyons, and cliff faces to the north and south of the main road have been carved by wind and water over millennia. And the blue? That's light refracting off the fine oil mist from the world's most ecologically diverse tract of eucalypt forest.

(top) Looking out over the Jamison Valley.

A WORLD HERITAGE WONDERLAND

Part of the Greater Blue Mountains World Heritage Area, Blue Mountains National Park encompasses 2,678 sq km (1,034 sq ft) of prime hiking country. Most tracks skirt the cliff edges or run along the bottom of the canyons; paths that connect the two levels are often at points along the cliff that offer breathtaking panoramas of the Jamison, Megalong, or Grose Valleys.

While the geological landscape is worth the trip alone, the flora and fauna are some of the country's most unique. Within just a few square miles, the world's widest variety of eucalypts in one contiguous forest have evolved to thrive in everything from open scrub plains to dense valley rainforests. The Wollami pine, a tree that grew alongside dinosaurs, can only be found in a few small areas here. Then there are the rare or threatened creatures like the Blue Mountains water skink, the yellow-bellied glider, and the long-nosed potoroo. It seems only fitting that both Charles Darwin and John Muir visited here. In 1932 it became one of the first formally protected tracts of land in Australia.

Towns dot the main highway through the Blue Mountains, but Katoomba is the unofficial capital, fully outfitted with resources for visitors and the starting point for some of the most iconic walks. Less-bustling Blackheath, minutes up the road from Katoomba, has our favorite eco-lodges and is closest to the best walks of the Grose Valley. You can get a feel for the region on a day trip from Sydney, but if your schedule permits, stay a night (or three) to fit in a few different hikes.

HIKING LITE: THREE WAYS TO SEE THE JAMISON VALLEY WITHOUT BREAKING A SWEAT

Scenic Skyway

SCENIC CABLEWAY
Less crowded than the Scenic Railway, the world's steepest cable car feels gentle in comparison. The enclosed gondola glides between the valley floor and the cliff rim with views of the Three Sisters.

SCENIC SKYWAY
This Swiss-style, glass-bottom cable car takes you on a 720 m (1/2 mi) long journey 270 m (886 ft) above the gorge for great 360 degree views across the Jamison Valley, the Katoomba Falls, and the famous Three Sisters.

KATOOMBA SCENIC RAILWAY
An incline of 52 degrees makes this former coal-haul railway the world's steepest. Grab a seat in the front. Be prepared for lines at peak visiting times. The railway runs every 10 minutes until 4:50 PM.

Claustral Canyon

154 <

BLUE MOUNTAIN TRAIL OVERVIEW

Lookout at Echo Point

KATOOMBA-ECHO POINT	TRAIL TIPS	HIGHLIGHTS
ECHO POINT TO SCENIC RAILWAY: This may not be a long walk, but thanks to the 861 steps of the Giant Staircase, don't underestimate it.	This route is very popular, especially on weekends, so set off early. Be aware that the last railway and cable car up leave at 4:50 PM. If you miss them, you'll have to walk.	• Expansive views across the Jamison Valley and beautiful forest vistas. • Brings you right up against the Three Sisters. • Scenic Railway boarding area is at the end of the trail, so you don't have to walk back up.
PRINCE HENRY CLIFF WALK: Start at the Leura Cascades picnic area and head up the mountain to Echo Point. This is a tough hike and not for the faint of heart.	Olympian Rock and Elysian Rock are perfect spots to picnic.	• Thanks to the level of difficulty, you'll be able to escape the crowds at Katoomba. • Spot lyre birds, kookaburras, and glossy black cockatoos.
BLACKHEATH	TRAIL TIPS	HIGHLIGHTS
GRAND CANYON WALK: Possible for anyone who's reasonably fit (though there are some steps) and well worth the effort.	A great choice for hot days: the canyon's cool temperatures will come as welcome relief.	• A winding path through lush vegetation and around plummeting waterfalls. • Spectacular views of gorges, forest, and cliff lines at Evans lookout.
PERRY'S LOOKDOWN TO BLUE GUM FOREST: This track starts at Perry's Lookdown parking lot, 9 km (5.5 mi) northeast of Blackheath, and takes you down a steep track into the lovely Blue Gum Forest.	Stop by the Heritage Centre in nearby Blackheath for excellent information on historic sites and hiking trips.	• Experience for yourself why the ecologically unique Blue Gum Forest attracted conservationists' attention in Australia. • You might spot possums, gliders, bandicoots, brown antechinuses, and swamp wallabies.
GLENBROOK	TRAIL TIPS	HIGHLIGHTS
RED HANDS CAVE TRACK: This moderately difficult circuit walk goes up the Red Hands Creek Valley along a creek and through the rainforest.	It's best to park at the Visitors Centre on Bruce Road and then walk for 10 minutes following the signs to the Glenbrook causeway, as there is no easy parking at the causeway itself.	• Bring your binoculars, because there are many birdwatching opportunities. • See the Blue Mountains' most sacred Aboriginal site, Red Hands Cave. The cave is named after the displays of Aboriginal hand stencils on its walls.

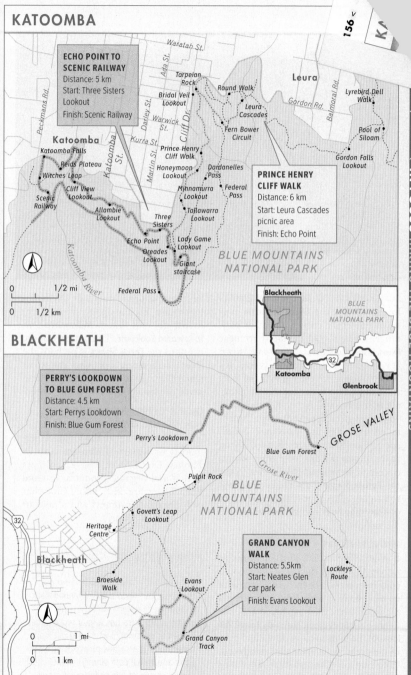

KATOOMBA

Waratah St.

ECHO POINT TO SCENIC RAILWAY
Distance: 5 km
Start: Three Sisters Lookout
Finish: Scenic Railway

Tarpeian Rock

Round Walk

Leura

Lyrebird Dell Walk

Ada St.

Bridal Veil Lookout

Leura Cascades

Gordon Rd.

Balmoral Rd.

Peckmans Rd.

Datley St.

Warwick St.

Cliff Dr.

Fern Bower Circuit

Pool of Siloam

Katoomba

Kurra St.

Prince Henry Cliff Walk

Dardanelles Pass

Gordon Falls Lookout

Katoomba Falls

Martin St.

Honeymoon Lookout

Federal Pass

PRINCE HENRY CLIFF WALK
Distance: 6 km
Start: Leura Cascades picnic area
Finish: Echo Point

Reids Plateau

Katoomba St.

Witches Leap

Minnamurra Lookout

Cliff View Lookout

Scenic Railway

Allambie Lookout

Tallawarra Lookout

Three Sisters

Echo Point

Lady Game Lookout

Oreades Lookout

BLUE MOUNTAINS NATIONAL PARK

Katoomba River

Giant staircase

0   1/2 mi

0   1/2 km

Federal Pass

Blackheath

BLUE MOUNTAINS NATIONAL PARK

Katoomba

32

Glenbrook

BLACKHEATH

PERRY'S LOOKDOWN TO BLUE GUM FOREST
Distance: 4.5 km
Start: Perrys Lookdown
Finish: Blue Gum Forest

Perry's Lookdown

Blue Gum Forest

GROSE VALLEY

Grose River

Pulpit Rock

BLUE MOUNTAINS NATIONAL PARK

32

Govett's Leap Lookout

Heritage Centre

GRAND CANYON WALK
Distance: 5.5km
Start: Neates Glen car park
Finish: Evans Lookout

Lockleys Route

Blackheath

Braeside Walk

Evans Lookout

0   1 mi

0   1 km

Grand Canyon Track

View of Three Sisters from Echo Point lookout

ECHO POINT TO SCENIC RAILWAY

In the 1930s, the **Giant Staircase** was hewn out of the cliff by teams of park rangers. The top of the steps are near **Three Sisters Lookout** and the walk down is very steep and narrow in places. It's difficult going but the views make it all worthwhile. Look out for the encouraging half way sign. At the bottom, keep your eyes peeled for echidnas, brush-tailed and ring-tail possums, bandicoots, quolls, and grey-headed flying foxes. If you're keen for more exertion once you've reached the Railway, take the **Furber Steps**. It's a challenging but rewarding track that offers great views of **Katoomba Falls** and **Mt. Solitary** across the valley.

PRINCE HENRY CLIFF WALK

If you prefer to hike in the mountains rather than along the forest floor, you'll enjoy this section of the Cliff Walk with its superb vistas across the valley. From the picnic area, the trail descends beside Leura Cascades creek towards **Bridal Veil lookout**. Be sure to slow down and take in the great views over the **Leura Forest**. Continue on Prince Henry Drive; at **Tarpeian Rock** you can see Mt. Solitary.

Keep going uphill towards Olympian Rock and Elysian Rock. From here, follow the cliff line to **Millamurra** and **Tallawarra Lookouts**. The last part of the climb to the **Three Sisters** is perhaps the most challenging but also the most rewarding. Take a few minutes and savor the sweeping views of the valley.

QUICK BITES/SUPERMARKETS FOR PICNIC GOODIES

You can stock up at the Coles Supermarket or Kmart at Katoomba or at Thomas Dux Grocer, which specializes in deli and organic products, in **Leura Mall**. There are also two (somewhat over-priced) restaurants and a takeout kiosk at Scenic World.

STAY HERE IF:

On weekends tour buses descend on the town, but once they've headed back to Sydney, the place isn't over-run with visitors. Katoomba has a very relaxed feel helped in no small part by a small hippy community. It also has plenty of nice old pubs and cafés, cute vintage shops, and rural versions of big department stores.

BLACKHEATH

Mount Hay, Grose Valley

GRAND CANYON WALK

From the parking lot, 4.5 km (2.8 mi) from Blackheath, follow the Grand Canyon track signs as the path zig-zags down the hillside and the vegetation becomes more like a rainforest. The trail takes you down into the canyon and over a creek. It winds past a few overhanging rocks, then starts a steep decline towards a sandy overhang called the **Rotunda**. After a break here, follow the signs to **Evans Lookout**, which will lead you through a tunnel and past two waterfalls. You eventually reach the 10-meter-tall (33 ft) **Beauchamp Falls** in the center of the creek. From here head up through a gap in the cliffs, weaving through boulders, again following signs to Evans Lookout. From Evans Lookout, you can do a 6.5 km (4 mi) Cliffside walk to **Pulpit Rock** along the Cliff Top Track.

PERRYS LOOKDOWN
TO BLUE GUM FOREST

From the parking lot, follow the signs pointing out the trail down the hill to **Perrys Lookdown**. You'll have fine views over the **Grose Valley** with its sheer sandstone cliffs with the Blue Gum Forest below. Next, head down the hill and do

a quick detour to **Docker's Lookout** with its view of Mt. Banks to the north. Head back following the Perrys Lookdown–Blue Gum Forest walk signs. The descent to **Blue Gum Forest** will take about 90 minutes. Once you've explored the forest floor and it's dense canopy, head back up the steep track to Perrys Lookdown.

QUICK BITES/SUPERMARKETS
FOR PICNIC GOODIES

Blackheath has something of a gourmet reputation. For a quick pre-walk bite, we recommend **Denise's Pies** at the New Ivanhoe Hotel (corner of Great Western Hwy and Govetts Leap Rd, 02/4787–6156). It's considered by some connoisseurs as Australia's finest pie place. There's also a small IGA supermarket.

STAY HERE IF:

Blackheath is smaller and less-visited than Katoomba, but the old weatherboard houses give it a similar feel. There's also enough quirky shops and quaint cafes and restaurants to keep it entertaining. Several Sydney restaurateurs relocated here, so there's a breadth of excellent dining venues.

GLENBROOK

Glenbrook Gorge

An echidna

Kookaburras

RED HANDS CAVE TRACK

Red Hands Cave has some well preserved Aboriginal hand stencillings. The stencils are behind Plexiglas (called Perspex here) to protect them from graffiti. There are a few good placards explaining the history and describing the artifacts found in the area. The walk starts on the southern side of the causeway, and after about 2 km (1.2 mi) of gentle steps down the gully, the well-defined track forks: take the right-hand path just after a large rocky outcrop near the edge of a gully. ■TIP→ Take care near the edge, there's a significant dropoff. Up the hill near **Camp Fire Creek,** keep an eye out for axe grinding grooves (oval-shaped indentations in sandstone outcrops that Aboriginals used to shape and sharpen stone axes). The trail passes through several types of forest, including dry eucalypt forest, so there's a good variety of birds in the area. Watch for echidnas in the open forest and chestnut-rumped heathwrens and rock warblers in the sandstone area near the Red Hands Cave.

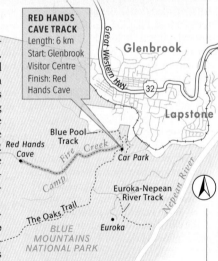

RED HANDS CAVE TRACK
Length: 6 km
Start: Glenbrook Visitor Centre
Finish: Red Hands Cave

QUICK BITES/SUPERMARKETS FOR PICNIC GOODIES

Glenbrook doesn't have the same variety of food and lodging options as Katoomba and Blackheath, but there's a small IGA supermarket on Park Street. Ross Street has a few nice cafes; check out **Mash café's** delicious breakfasts.

ice cream. The restaurant is housed in a Federation-era building, and in colder months a log fire warms the century-old shop's simple but elegant interior, where yellow ocher walls reach from a black-and-white checkerboard floor to high ceilings. ⊠ *128 The Mall* ☎ *02/4784–2534* ⊕ *www.silksleura.com* ▤ *AE, DC, MC, V.*

$$$–$$$$ 🛏 **Bygone Beautys Cottages.** These eight country cottages, scattered around Wentworth Falls and in nearby villages, provide self-contained accommodations for couples, families, and small groups. Some of these are set among leafy gardens; all have wood-burning fireplaces. Fresh flowers, fruit, chocolates, and all the ingredients for a country-size breakfast are included in each unit. There's a two-night minimum stay. **Pros:** antiques collectors will love the decor and the connected antiques store, very romantic surrounds. **Cons:** if olde worlde leaves you cold, this isn't the place for you, bathrooms are chilly in winter. ⊠ *Main office: Grose and Megalong Sts.* ☎ *02/4784–3117* ⊕ *www.bygonebeautys.com.au* ⇖ *8 cottages* ⚘ *In-room: no a/c, kitchen, refrigerator, DVD (some), VCR. In-hotel: laundry facilities, no elevator* ▤ *AE, MC, V.*

$$–$$$ 🛏 **Leura House.** This guesthouse which dates back to 1890 may look grand, but the atmosphere is cozy and welcoming thanks to the family that runs the place. Just five minutes' walk from the main shopping street, this is an ideal place to base yourselves. Rooms are spacious and well furnished, and all have verandas or balconies with views over the lovely gardens. **Pros:** free Wi-Fi access, delicious freshly cooked breakfasts. **Cons:** bathrooms in regular doubles could do with an update, sometimes groups book the B&B out. ⊠ *7 Britain St., Leura* ☎ *02/4784–2035* ⊕ *www.leurahouse.com.au* ⇖ *11 rooms* ⚘ *In-room: refrigerator, Wi-Fi. In-hotel: restaurant, laundry service, Wi-Fi, parking (free), some pets allowed, no-smoking rooms* ▤ *AE, D, DC, MC, V* 🍽 *CP.*

> ## THE SWEET LIFE
>
> If you have a sweet tooth, you'll love the **Blue Mountains Chocolate Company** (⊠ *176 Lurline St., Katoomba* ☎ *02/4782–7071*). Here you can watch chocolate being made (demonstrations at 11:30 AM and 3:30 PM) and taste it for free. There are 60 different varieties of handmade chocolates, as well as hot chocolate (perfect for chilly mountain days) and homemade ice cream (chocolate, of course) for those sultry summer days. It's just the sugar hit you need before you set off bushwalking.

KATOOMBA

2 km (1 mi) west of Leura.

The largest and busiest town in the Blue Mountains, Katoomba developed in the early 1840s as a coal-mining settlement, turning its attention to tourism later in the 19th century. The town center on Katoomba Street has shops, restaurants, and cafés, but most travelers are keen to see the marvels at the lower end of town and don't linger here.

GETTING HERE AND AROUND

The 110-km (68-mi) journey to Katoomba takes between 90 minutes and two hours from Sydney via Parramatta Road and the M4 Motorway, which leads to Lapstone at the base of the Blue Mountains. From there, continue on the Great Western Highway and follow the signs to Katoomba. The town has its own train station, and is also connected to the rest of the Blue Mountains by the Blue Mountains Bus Company.

There is a Blue Mountains Visitor Information Centre at Echo Point in Katoomba. Sydney Visitor Centre has information on Blue Mountains hotels, tours, and sights.

TOURS

The well-established **Blue Mountains Adventure Company** (⊠ *84A Bathurst Rd., Katoomba* ☎ *02/4782–1271* ⊕ *www.bmac.com.au*) runs abseiling, rock-climbing, canyoning, bushwalking, rock climbing, and mountain-biking trips. Most outings (from about A$135) last one day, and include equipment, lunch, and transportation from Katoomba.

High n Wild (⊠ *3/5 Katoomba St., Katoomba* ☎ *02/4782–6224* ⊕ *www.high-n-wild.com.au*) conducts rappelling, canyoning, rock-climbing, and mountain-biking tours throughout the year. One-day rappelling trips cost A$145; combination rappelling and canyoning tours cost A$160.

ESSENTIALS

Hospital Blue Mountains District Anzac Memorial Hospital (⊠ *Great Western Hwy., 1 km [½ mi] east of town center, Katoomba* ☎ *02/4784–6500* ⊙ *Daily 9–5*).

Visitor Information Blue Mountains Visitor Information Centre (⊠ *Echo Point Rd., Echo Point* ☎ *1300/653408* ⊕ *www.visitbluemountains.com.au*).

EXPLORING

Fodor'sChoice ★ **Echo Point,** which overlooks the densely forested Jamison Valley and three soaring sandstone pillars, has the best views around Katoomba. The formations—called the **Three Sisters**—take their name from an Aboriginal legend that relates how a trio of siblings was turned to stone by their witch-doctor father to save them from the clutches of a mythical monster. The area was once a seabed that rose over a long period and subsequently eroded, leaving behind tall formations of sedimentary rock. From Echo Point—where the visitor center is located—you can clearly see the horizontal sandstone bedding in the landscape. There is a wide viewing area as well as the start of walks that take you closer to the Sisters. At night the Sisters are illuminated by floodlights. ⊠ *Follow Katoomba St. south out of Katoomba to Echo Point Rd., or take Cliff Dr. from Leura.*

If you'd like to check out the scenery but don't want to break a sweat, be sure to take one of the three rides at **Scenic World**: the Scenic Railway, the Cableway, or the Scenic Skyway. If you're going to pick one, the railway is more spectacular. ⊠ *Cliff Dr. at Violet St.* ☎ *02/4780–0200* ⊕ *www.scenicworld.com.au* ⊠ *Scenic Pass round-trip Railway, Cableway, or Skyway A$28* ⊙ *Daily 9–5.*

The screen at the **Edge Maxvision Cinema** is the height of a six-story building. Specially filmed for this giant format, *The Edge,* shown six times daily starting at 10:20 (the last show is at 5:30), is an exciting 40-minute celebration of the region's valleys, gorges, cliffs, waterfalls, dramatic scenery, and the mysterious Wollemi Pine (thought to be extinct until it was discovered in the region in the early 1990s). The complex includes a café and gift shop, and regular feature films are also screened here. ⊠ *225 Great Western Hwy.* ☎ *02/4782–8928* ☞ *A$15.*

OUTDOOR ACTIVITIES

A good hiking brochure can be picked up at Echo Point Tourist Information Centre, which lists walks varying in length from ½ hour to 3 days.

HORSEBACK RIDING   At the foot of the Blue Mountains, 10 km (6 mi) south of Blackheath, **Werriberri Trail Rides** (⊠ *Megalong Rd., Megalong Valley* ☎ *02/4787–9171* ⊕ *www.australianbluehorserides.com.au*) conducts reasonably priced (A$190) full-day horseback rides through the beautiful Megalong Valley, as well as the Hartley Historic Ride (A$230). These guided rides are good for adults and children.

HIKING   Experience the Blue Mountains from an Aboriginal perspective with the **Blue Mountains Walkabout** (⊠ *Box 519, Springwood* ☎ *0408/433822* ⊕ *www.bluemountainswalkabout.com* ☞ *A$95*). These challenging one-day walks follow a traditional walkabout song line. Indigenous guides take you on a 7-km (4.5 mi) off-track walk through rain forests while giving some background on Aboriginal culture. The walk involves some scrambling, so you need to be fit.

Seven-day odysseys and easier walks are offered by **Blue Mountains Guides** (⊠ *2/187 Katoomba St., Katoomba* ☎ *02/4782–6109* ⊕ *www.bluemountainsguides.com.au*). The Grand Canyon Walk (A$125) is a great way to experience the rain forest if time is short.

FOUR-WHEEL DRIVES   **Tread Lightly Eco Tours** (⊠ *100 Great Western Hwy., Medlow Bath* ☎ *02/4788–1229 or 0414/976752* ⊕ *www.treadlightly.com.au*) operates small-group tours of the Blue Mountains National Park and guided day and night walks. Four-wheel-drive vehicles take you to lookouts, caves, and waterfalls. A full-day Wilderness Experience for two costs around A$265, depending on destination and food (gourmet picnic or restaurant).

FISHING   **Riverlands Fly and Sportsfishing.** Professional guide Jeff Brown takes beginners and expert anglers to the area's quiet streams and lakes. He offers half-day and multi-day packages that include accommodation. ⊠ *3 Dewdney Rd, Emu Plains* ☎ *0418/435–410* ⊕ *www.riverlandsfly.sweetwaterfishing.com.au .*

WHERE TO EAT

$–$$ ╳ **Paragon Cafe.** With its chandeliers, gleaming cappuccino machine, and wood-paneled 1916 art-deco café recalls the Blue Mountains in their heyday. These days it's more of a tourist eatery, but still worth piling through the crowds to sample its Devonshire teas, waffles, and 52 varieties of homemade chocolates. ⊠ *65 Katoomba St.* ☎ *02/4782–2928* ☐ *MC, V* ☺ *No dinner Sun.–Thurs.*

CAFÉ

WHERE TO STAY

$$$-$$$$ 🖼 **The Carrington.** Established in 1880, this is one of the grandes dames of the Blue Mountains, a Victorian-era relic that, in its heyday, was considered one of the four great hotels of the British Empire. Its public areas are a reminder of its glorious past—the bar contains a mezzanine balcony where the Duke and Duchess of York (later King George VI and Queen Elizabeth, the Queen Mother)—visited in 1927. A permanent conservation order stipulates that 10 of the 59 rooms be kept in their original 1880 style, so they do not have private bathrooms, but at A$145 a night they're a good deal. The other rooms (added in 1927) are a mix of colonial-style rooms, and the deluxe rooms have access to the terrific balcony on the first floor where you can take in the great valley views. The enormous, chandelier-lighted dining room ($$$-$$$$) serves modern Australian and traditional dishes. **Pros:** drinks on their veranda are a pleasant way to end the day, the day spa is excellent. **Cons:** the newer rooms lack character, staff generally lacks hospitality skills. ⊠ *15–47 Katoomba St.* ☎ *02/4782–1111* ⊕ *www.thecarrington. com.au* 🛏 *59 rooms, 49 with bath; 6 suites; 1 apartment* ⚒ *In-room: no a/c (some), kitchen (some), refrigerator, Wi-Fi (some). In-hotel: 2 restaurants, bars, laundry service, public Wi-Fi, no-smoking rooms, no elevator* ⊟ *AE, DC, MC, V* ⊙ *BP.*

$$$$ 🖼 **Echoes Boutique Hotel & Restaurant.** Perched on the edge of the Jamison Valley, this stylish boutique hotel has some of the best views in the Blue Mountains. The marble lobby is impressive, and the glass-enclosed terrace is a great place to take advantage of the spectacular views. A day spa with plenty of indulgent treatments is also on the premises. Rooms are stylish and include the latest TVs, as well as wireless Internet access. The Mod-Oz–Asian fusion menu ($$$$) in the excellent restaurant includes dishes such as salt-crusted kingfish fillet spiced with chili and kaffir lime leaves. The hotel actually runs into the national park. **Pros:** spectacular views from the terrace, slick and funky accommodation. **Cons:** a little overpriced, not for fans of tradition and chintz. ⊠ *3 Lilianfels Ave.* ☎ *02/4782–1966* ⊕ *www.echoeshotel.com.au* 🛏 *14 suites* ⚒ *In-room: refrigerator, Wi-Fi. In-hotel: restaurant, bar, spa, public Internet, public Wi-Fi, no-smoking rooms* ⊟ *AE, DC, MC, V* ⊙ *BP.*

$$$$ 🖼 **Lilianfels Blue Mountains Resort & Spa.** Teetering close to the brink of ★ Echo Point, this glamorous boutique hotel adds a keen sense of manor-house style to the standard Blue Mountains guesthouse experience. This hotel has a lush European feel, and all the luxury you'd expect of a member of the prestigious Orient Express hotel group. Rooms are spacious and luxuriously furnished, with lush fabrics, silk curtains, and elegant marble bathrooms with deep baths. The upscale Darley's restaurant ($$$$), in the Heritage-listed original 1889 homestead, serves a cutting-edge menu; a highlight is the roasted duck breast with red lentils and figs. The first-class spa is the ultimate place to relax after exploring the Jamison Valley. There is a two-night minimum stay on weekends, and good packages are available midweek. **Pros:** luxurious and restful bathrooms, staff give friendly five-star service **Cons:** if 19th-century style doesn't appeal, this isn't the place for you, bar and restaurant are expensive, even considering room rates. ⊠ *Lilianfels Ave. at Panorama*

Dr. ☎ 02/4780–1200 ⊕ www.lilianfels.com.au ⚓ Reservations essential ⟿ 81 rooms, 4 suites ᕼ In-room: safe, refrigerator, VCR, Internet. In-hotel: 2 restaurants, room service, bar, tennis court, pools, gym, spa, bicycles, concierge, laundry service, public Internet, no-smoking rooms ▭ AE, DC, MC, V ℗ BP.

$–$$
Fodor's Choice
★
🏨 **Lurline House.** This historic little B&B is considered the town's best. The Federation-style house dates back to 1910, and its seven rooms, two of which have their own private courtyard, have been carefully restored. The owner used to manage five-star hotels, and it shows in the attention to details, from the full English breakfasts to the complimentary Wi-Fi and immaculate gardens. **Pros:** all rooms have four-poster beds, guests are welcomed with complimentary cakes and port. **Cons:** not really suitable for children, younger trendsetters might find the place not too their tastes. ✉ 122 Lurline St., Katoomba ☎ 02/ 4782–4609 ⊕ www.lurlinehouse.com.au ⟿ 7 rooms ᕼ In-room: DVD, Wi-Fi. In-hotel: restaurant, laundry service, Wi-Fi, parking (free), no-smoking rooms ▭ AE, D, DC, MC, V ℗ CP.

$$$
★
🏨 **Melba House.** The Blaxland, Wentworth, and Lawson suites in this 19th-century house are named after the explorers who toiled across the Blue Mountains in 1813 and opened up the western plains to settlers—and they offer a welcome retreat to visitors today. Two of the suites have king-size beds, hot tubs, and marble-framed wood fireplaces; all have decorative plaster ceilings and windows looking out at a garden full of birds. You'll find a bowl of fruit and port in your room, and afternoon tea is served when you arrive. In the morning you can awake to a sumptuous breakfast brought to your room. There's a two-night minimum stay on weekends in winter. **Pros:** genial hosts, located minutes away from great walking trails. **Cons:** no separate dining area (breakfast is served in rooms). ✉ 98 Waratah St. ☎ 02/4782–4141 ⊕ www.melbahouse.com ⟿ 3 suites ᕼ In-room: refrigerator, DVD, Wi-Fi. In-hotel: room service, no elevator, no-smoking rooms ▭ AE, DC, MC, V ℗ BP.

$$$–$$$$
🏨 **Mountain Heritage Hotel & Spa.** This hotel overlooking the Jamison Valley is steeped in history: it served as a "coffee palace" during the temperance movement, a rest-and-relaxation establishment for the British navy during World War II, and a religious retreat in the 1970s. Check out the collection of rare photographs depicting the Blue Mountains and Sydney in the 1880s. Spacious rooms here are filled with welcoming country-house furnishings; several have hot tubs. If you're looking to splurge, try the round Tower Suite, or one of the two Valley View suites—each has its own veranda, kitchen, living room with fireplace, and hot tub. **Pros:** beautiful gardens, public areas are charming. **Cons:** furniture in suites is dated, piped music in reception areas is irritating. ✉ Apex and Lovel Sts. ☎ 02/4782–2155 ⊕ www. mountainheritage.com.au ⟿ 37 rooms, 4 suites ᕼ In-room: kitchen (some), refrigerator, DVD, dial-up. In-hotel: restaurant, bar, pool, gym, spa, laundry facilities, laundry service, no elevator, no-smoking rooms ▭ AE, DC, MC, V.

BLACKHEATH

12 km (7½ mi) north of Katoomba.

Magnificent easterly views over the Grose Valley—which has outstanding hiking trails—and delightful gardens and antiques shops head the list of reasons to visit the village of Blackheath, at the 3,495-foot summit of the Blue Mountains.

GETTING HERE AND AROUND

Blackheath is an east drive north from Katoomba, travelling on the Great Western Highway, passing Medlow Bath on the way. There's also a train station on the Blue Mountains line and it's also serviced by Blue Mountains Bus Company on Route 698 between Katoomba and Mount Victoria.

ESSENTIALS

Tourist information Heritage Centre (⌷ *End of Govett's Leap Rd., Blackheath* ☎ *02/4787–8877* ⊕ *www.nationalparks.nsw.gov.au* ⊙ *Daily 9–4:30*).

EXPLORING

★ Blackheath's most famous view is from the **Govetts Leap Lookout,** with its striking panorama of the Grose Valley and Bridal Veil Falls. Govett was a surveyor who mapped this region extensively in the 1830s. This lookout is the start or finish of several excellent bushwalks. Brochures are available at the Heritage Centre. ⌷ *End of Govett's Leap Rd.*

OUTDOOR ACTIVITIES

HIKING **Auswalk.** This environmentally conscious company, which also offers walks in other parts of Australia, has self-guided or guided hiking tours through the region, staying at historic inns along the way. They ask that you be in reasonable shape before you start. ⊕ *www.auswalk.com.au* ⌷ *From A$1,000.*

HORSEBACK The **Megalong Australian Heritage Centre,** in a deep mountain valley off
RIDING the Great Western Highway, is the place to saddle up and explore a
ⓒ country property. Both adults and children can go horseback riding around the farm's 2,000 acres, and bigger adults might get to ride a Clydesdale. There's a farm with a baby-animal nursery where children can get close to chickens, ducks, and pigs. ⌷ *Megalong Rd., Megalong Valley ⊹ 15 km (9 mi) south of Blackheath* ☎ *02/4787–8188* ⊕ *www. bluemts.com.au/megalong* ⌷ *Free for heritage center, farm A$8, horse riding for day A$195* ⊙ *Daily 9–5.*

WHERE TO EAT AND STAY

$$ ✕ **Vulcan's.** Some people travel to the Blue Mountains just to dine here,
CAFÉ so make sure you book ahead at this cozy café that revolutionized din-
Fodor'sChoice ing in rural New South Wales. Operated by Phillip Searle (formerly
★ one of the leading lights of Sydney's dining scene) and Barry Ross, Vulcan's specializes in slow-roasted dishes, cooked in a century-old baker's oven and flavored with Asian or Middle Eastern spices. The restaurant's checkerboard ice cream—with star anise, pineapple, licorice, and vanilla flavors—is a favorite that tastes as good as it looks. Dinner is served at two sittings, so diners at the 6 PM sitting have little time to linger before they must vacate their tables for the 8 PM sitting.

✉ *33 Govetts Leap Rd.* ☎ *02/4787–6899* ▭ *AE, DC, MC, V* ⛟ *BYO* ⊘ *Closed Mon.–Thurs. and Feb.*

$$$ ⛺ **Jemby Rinjah Eco Lodge.** Designed for urbanites seeking a wilderness
★ experience, these rustic, self-contained wooden cabins and lodges are set deep in the bush. All have natural-wood furnishings and picture windows opening onto a small deck. One- and two-bedroom cabins have kitchenettes and lounge and dining areas, while the four-bedroom lodges can sleep up to 20 people. Lodges don't have kitchens, but breakfast can be arranged. Dinner is available in the restaurant for A$35 for two courses and A$45 for three courses. Activities include self-guided walks of the Grose Valley, feeding wild parrots, and spotlighting possums at night. The stunning Evans Lookout is 500 yards away. **Pros:** cabins and lodges are private and tranquil, hearty and healthy mountain fare is served at the restaurant. **Cons:** some might find the eco-toilet disconcerting, the lodges can be booked out by groups. ✉ *336 Evans Lookout Rd.* ☎ *02/4787–7622* ⊕ *www.jembyrinjahlodge.com.au* ⤶ *11 cabins, 3 lodges* ⛴ *In-room: no a/c, no phone, kitchen (some), refrigerator. In-hotel: restaurant, no elevator, laundry facilities, no-smoking rooms* ▭ *AE, DC, MC, V.*

MOUNT VICTORIA

7 km (4½ mi) northwest of Blackheath.

The settlement of Mount Victoria is the highest point in the Blue Mountains, and has a Rip Van Winkle air about it—drowsy and only just awake in an unfamiliar world. A walk around the village reveals many atmospheric houses, stores, and a couple of stately old hotels with the patina of time spelled out in their fading paint. Mount Victoria is at the far side of the mountains at the western limit of this region, and the village serves as a good jumping-off point for a couple of out-of-the-way attractions.

GETTING HERE AND AROUND

Mount Victoria is an easy drive north of Blackheath on the Great Western Highway, and it's also on the main Blue Mountains line linking Sydney with Lithgow. The 698 bus route connects the village with Katoomba.

EXPLORING

The pink circa-1888 **Hotel Imperial** (✉ *1 Station St.* ☎ *02/4787–1878* ⊕ *www.hotelimperial.com.au*) was one of several historic Blue Mountains inns built a few years after the railway line was opened from Sydney. It's worth popping your head around the door to have a look, but its accommodations gets mixed reviews at best.

Children and adults will enjoy a browse around **Trains, Planes and Automobiles** (✉ *88 Great Western Hwy.* ☎ *02/4787–1590* ⊕ *www.antique-toys.com.au* ⊘ *Daily 10:30–4:30*) which bills itself as the best antique toyshop in the world.

Stalactites, stalagmites, columns, and lacelike rock on multiple levels fill the fascinating **Jenolan Caves**, a labyrinth of vast limestone caverns sculpted by underground rivers. There are as many as 320 caves in the

One of the hundreds of vineyards that dot the Hunter Valley.

Jenolan area. Three caves near the surface can be explored on your own, but a guide is required to reach the most intriguing formations. Standard tours lead through the most popular caves—many say that Orient Cave is the most spectacular—while more rigorous adventure tours last up to seven hours. The one- to two-hour walks depart every 15 to 30 minutes, on weekends less frequently. Prices range from A$27 for standard tours to A$130 for adventure tours. To get here, follow the Great Western Highway north out of Mount Victoria, then after Hartley turn southwest toward Hampton. ⊠ *59 km (37 mi) from Mount Victoria, Jenolan* ☎ *1300/763311* ⊕ *www.jenolancaves.org.au* ☉ *Daily 9:30–5:30.*

Fodor's Choice
★
☺

You'll be wiping the soot from your face after a ride on the huff-and-puff vintage steam engine, but that's part of the fun of this cliff-hugging 16-km (10-mi) round-trip experience on the **Zig Zag Railway.** Built in 1869, this was the main line across the Blue Mountains until 1910. The track is laid on the cliffs in a giant "Z," and the train climbs the steep incline by chugging back and forth along switchback sections of the track—hence its name. The steam engine operates on weekends, public holidays, and Wednesday, and weekdays during school holidays. A vintage self-propelled diesel-powered railcar is used at other times. ⊠ *Bells Line of Rd., 19 km (12 mi) northwest of Mount Victoria, Clarence* ☎ *02/6355–2955* ⊕ *www.zigzagrailway.com.au* ⊠ *A$25 return, A$17 one-way* ☉ *Departures from Clarence Station daily at 11, 1, and 3.*

WHERE TO EAT

$
CAFÉ
$\times$ **Bay Tree Tea Shop.** A chilly afternoon, when a fire is burning in the grate and scones are piping hot from the kitchen, is the best time to dine at this cozy café. The menu includes hearty soups, salads, pasta dishes, and quiches. Everything is made on the premises—bread, cakes, and even the jam that comes with afternoon tea. At night the café reopens as the Bay Tree Thai restaurant. ⊠ *26 Station St.* ☎ *02/4787–1275, 02/4787–1220 Bay Tree Thai* ▤ *V* ☉ *Closed Mon.–Wed.*

OFF THE BEATEN PATH
Mount Tomah Botanic Garden. This is the cool-climate branch of Sydney's Royal Botanic Gardens (30 km [19 mi] northeast of Mount Victoria). The garden is 3,280 feet above sea level, and is a spectacular setting for native and imported plants. You'll find beautiful rhododendrons and European deciduous trees, as well as plants that evolved in isolation for millions of years in the Gondwana Forest. The famous Wollemi Pine (once thought to be extinct) is also here. There are picnic grounds and a café with views of the ranges. ⊠ *Bells Line of Rd.* ☎ *02/4567–2154* ⊕ *www.rbgsyd.nsw.gov.au* ✉ *A\$5.50* ☉ *Daily 10–4, until 5 Oct.–Mar.*

THE HUNTER VALLEY WINE REGION

To almost everyone in Sydney, the Hunter Valley conjures up visions of one thing: wine. The Hunter is the largest grape-growing area in the state, with more than 120 wineries producing excellent varieties. The Hunter is divided into seven subregions, each with its own unique character. The hub is the Pokolbin/Rothbury region, where many of the large operations are found, along with several boutique wineries.

The Hunter Valley covers an area of almost 25,103 square km (9,692 square mi), stretching from the town of Gosford north of Sydney to 177 km (110 mi) farther north along the coast, and almost 300 km (186 mi) inland. The meandering waterway that gives this valley its name is also one of the most extensive river systems in the state.

OFF THE BEATEN PATH
Wollombi. Nothing seems to have changed in the atmospheric town of Wollombi, 24 km (15 mi) southwest of Cessnock, since the days when the Cobb & Co. stagecoaches rumbled through town. Founded in 1820, Wollombi was the overnight stop for the coaches on the second day of the journey from Sydney along the convict-built Great Northern Road—at that time the only route north. The town is full of delightful old sandstone buildings and antiques shops, and there's also a museum in the old courthouse with 19th-century clothing and bushranger memorabilia. The local pub, the **Wollombi Tavern** (☎ *02/4998–3261* ⊕ *www.wollombitavern.com.au*), serves its own exotic brew, which goes by the name of Dr. Jurd's Jungle Juice. The pub also scores high marks for its friendliness and local color. The century-old **Avoca House** (☎ *02/4998–3233* ⊕ *www.avocahouse.com.au*) is the perfect place to chill out.

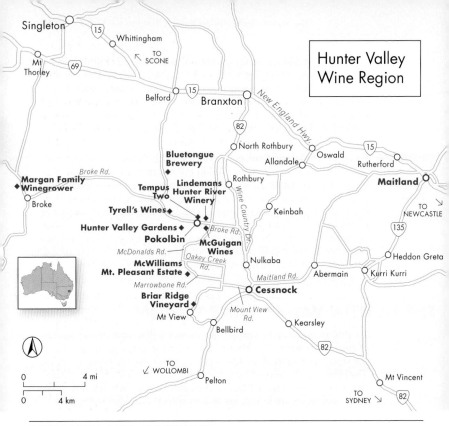

POKOLBIN AND ENVIRONS

163 km (100 mi) north of Sydney.

The Lower Hunter wine-growing region is centered around the village of Pokolbin, where there are antiques shops, good cafés, and dozens of wineries. In peak season, wineries are very busy with tour groups, so if you can visit mid-week or off-season, all the better.

GETTING HERE AND AROUND

A car is the best way to visit the wineries and off-the-beaten-path attractions unless you are on a guided tour. Leave Sydney via the Harbour Bridge or Harbour Tunnel and get onto the Pacific Highway (keep following the signs for Newcastle). Just before Hornsby the road joins the Sydney–Newcastle Freeway. Take the exit from the freeway signposted HUNTER VALLEY VINEYARDS VIA CESSNOCK. From Cessnock, the route to the vineyards is clearly marked. Allow 2½ hours for the journey.

TOURS

Any tour of the area's vineyards should begin at Pokolbin's **Hunter Valley Wine Country Visitors Information Centre**, which has free maps of the vineyards, brochures, and a handy visitor's guide.

From Sydney, AAT Kings operates a daylong wine-tasting bus tour of the Hunter Valley and another to Hunter Valley Gardens. Buses collect passengers from hotels, then make a final pickup from the Star City (Sydney Casino) bus terminal, departing at 8:30 AM. The tour returns to the casino at 6:15 PM. Tours cost from A$154, including lunch and wine tasting.

To avoid driving after sampling too many wines, hop aboard one of the Wine Rover buses which will pick you up from Pokolbin. Minibuses travel between restaurants and about a dozen wineries, and allow you to hop on and off during the day. A day pass with unlimited stops is A$40 during the week and A$50 on weekends.

Locally based Shadows Hunter Wine Country Tours operates a local transfer service between wineries, restaurants, and your accommodation.

ESSENTIALS

Bus Contacts AAT Kings (☎ 02/9700--0133 ⊕ www.aatkings.com) . **Rover Coaches** (☎ 02/4990-1699 ⊕ www.rovercoaches.com.au). **Shadows Hunter Wine Country Tours** (☎ 02/4990-7002 ⊕ shadows@hunterlink.net.au).

Hospital Cessnock District Hospital (⊠ View St., Cessnock ☎ 02/4991-0555).

Visitor Information Hunter River Country Visitor Information Centre (⊠ New England Hwy. at High St., Maitland ☎ 02/4931-2800 ⊕ www.hunter-rivercountry.com.au ⊗ Daily 9–5). **Hunter Valley Wine Country Visitors Information Centre** ⊠ 455 Wine Country Drive, Pokolbin ☎ 02/4990-0900 ⊕ www.winecountry.com.au ⊗ Mon.–Thurs. 9–5, Fri. and Sat. 9–6, Sun. 9–4).

EXPLORING

Drop into **Binnorie Dairy** (at Tuscany Wine Estate) to sample and buy—few can resist—Simon Gough's handcrafted soft cow and goat cheeses made from locally sourced milk. You'd be hard-pressed to find a tastier marinated feta outside Greece—or even in it. ⊠ Hermitage Rd. at Mistletoe La. ☎ 02/4998–6660 ⊕ www.binnorie.com.au ⊗ Tues.–Sat. 10–5, Sun. 10–4.

The low stone-and-timber buildings of the **Hunter Valley Gardens** are the heart of the Pokolbin wine-growing district. This large complex includes a hotel and convention center, gift shops, restaurants, a pub, the underground **Hunter Cellars**, and 12 stunning gardens covering 50 acres. Here you'll find a classic European formal garden, rose garden, Chinese moongate garden, and the delightful children's storybook garden featuring characters such as the Mad Hatter and Jack and Jill. Wonderful chocolate and fudge are to be had in the center's confectionery shop. ⊠ Broke and McDonalds Rds. ☎ 02/4998–4000 ⊕ www.hvg.com.au ✍ A$19.90 for gardens ⊗ Daily 9–5.

EXPLORING THE WINERIES

DID YOU KNOW

Eighteen Hunter Valley wineries are part of the Cellar Door Pass Scheme, which is a bargain if you are looking to stock up while visiting. A pass costs A$99 and gives you a host of benefits, including VIP premium tastings, guided tours to some of the region's best wineries, and six free bottles up to the value of A$120 from big name wineries like Tempus Two. Other famous names like Wyndham Estate, Binnorie Dairy, and Hunter Valley Gardens are also part of the scheme. See ⊕ www.cellardoorpass.com.au for more details.

In a delightful rural corner of the Mount View region, **Briar Ridge Vineyard** is one of the Hunter Valley's outstanding small wineries. It produces a limited selection of sought-after reds, whites, and sparkling wines. The Semillon (especially the 2007 Hunter Gold), Chardonnay, Shiraz, and intense Cabernet Sauvignon are highly recommended. The vineyard is on the southern periphery of the Lower Hunter vineyards, about a five-minute drive from Pokolbin, and their cellar door provides individual and group tastings. If you want to extend your stay, they have B&B accommodation suitable for up to six people. ⊠ *593 Mt. View Rd., Mount View* ☎ *02/4990–3670* ⊕ *www.briarridge.com.au* ☉ *Daily 10–5.*

★ The **Lindemans Hunter River Winery** has been one of the largest and most prestigious winemakers in the country since the early 1900s. In addition to its Hunter Valley vineyards, the company owns property in South Australia and Victoria, and numerous outstanding wines from these vineyards can be sampled in the tasting room. Try the burgundy, Semillon, or Chardonnay. The winery has its own museum, displaying vintage winemaking equipment, as well as two picnic areas, one near the parking lot and the other next to the willow trees around the dam. ⊠ *McDonalds Rd. just south of DeBeyers Rd.* ☎ *02/4998–7684* ⊕ *www.lindemans.com.au* ☉ *Daily 10–5.*

★ At **McWilliams Mount Pleasant Estate,** part of Australia's biggest family-owned wine company, chief winemaker Phil Ryan, the third since the winery was founded in 1921, continues the tradition of producing classic Hunter wines. Flagship Maurice O'Shea Shiraz and Chardonnay, and celebrated Elizabeth Semillon, are among the wines that can be sampled in the huge cellar door, which was recently judged the region's best by the local tourist board. You can also sit down on the terrace to a tasting plate in Elizabeth's Café; this matches three vintages of Elizabeth Semillon and one of premium Lovedale Semillon with four different foods. Guided winery tours run daily at 11 AM. ⊠ *Marrowbone Rd.* ☎ *02/4998–7505* ⊕ *www.mcwilliams.com.au* ☜ *Tours A$5, tastings free* ☉ *Daily 10–4:30.*

A leading light in the new wave of Hunter winemakers, **Margan Family Winegrowers** produces some of the valley's best small-volume wines. Try their full-bodied Verdelho, rosé-style Saignée Shiraz, and House of Certain Views Cabernet Sauvignon. A riper-than-most semillon is the flagship, and the 2004 Decanter World Wine Awards rated Margan's botrytis Semillon the world's best sweet wine under A$10—it's delicious. They recently opened a new, beautifully designed cellar door in the tiny village of Broke, 20 km (12 mi) from Pokolbin. For a fabulous lunch or dinner, try the fine-dining Margan restaurant— their platters of roast lamb or pancetta-wrapped quail are superb. ⊠ *1238 Milbrodale Rd.* ☎☎ *02/ 6579–1372* ⊕ *www.margan.com.au* ☉ *Daily 10–5.*

Founded in 1858, **Tyrrell's Wines** is the Hunter Valley's oldest family-owned vineyard. This venerable establishment crafts a wide selection of wines, and was the first to produce Chardonnay commercially in Australia. Its famous Vat 47 Chardonnay is still a winner. Enjoy the experience of sampling fine wines in the rustic tasting room, or take a picnic lunch to a site overlooking the valley. Guided tours (A$5) are given Monday to Saturday at 1:30. ⊠ *Broke Rd., 2½ km (1½ mi) west of McDonalds Rd.* ☎ *02/4993–7000* ⊕ *www.tyrrells.com.au* ⊙ *Mon.–Sat. 9–5, Sun. 10–4.*

Adjoining the Hunter Valley Gardens is the cellar-door complex of **McGuigan Wines.** Here you can taste wines and the **Hunter Valley Cheese Company**'s superb cheeses—look out for the washed-rind Hunter Valley Gold and the marinated soft, cows'-milk cheese. You can also see the cheeses being made by hand. There is a cheese talk daily at 11, and winery tours are given on weekdays at noon, weekends at 11 and noon. ⊠ *Broke and McDonalds Rds.* ☎ *02/4998–7402* ⊕ *www.mcguigan-wines.com.au.*

You can't miss the ultramodern **Tempus Two** in the heart of Pokolbin. This futuristic winery is a joint venture between two leading Hunter Valley families: the Roches (owners of Hunter Valley Gardens) and the McGuigans, who have made wine for four generations. The winery is best known for its Pinot Gris; however, you can sample a wide variety, including Semillon, Sauvignon Blanc, Chardonnay, and Shiraz in the stylish tasting room. There's also a Belisima Espresso Lounge and Oishii, a fine-dining Japanese-Thai restaurant. In the summer the winery hosts major concerts—past performers include Elton John, Rod Stewart, and the Beach Boys. ⊠ *Broke and McDonalds Rds.* ☎ *02/4993–3999* ⊕ *www.tempustwo.com.au* ⊙ *Daily 9–5.*

OUTDOOR ACTIVITIES

While most people's idea of activity in the Hunter is raising a glass, it is possible to expend more energy and still enjoy a glass or two.

BICYCLING **Hunter Valley Cycling.** You supply the peddle power, and for A$215 Hunter Valley Cycling will supply you with all the all the support (bikes, helmet, maps, luggage transfer, a three-course dinner, and accommodation) for a two-day, 50-km (31-mi) self-guided tour. If that's sounds too hardcore, the company also rents bikes by the hour. ☎ *0418/281480* ⊕ *www.huntervalleycycling.com.au.*

HORSEBACK RIDING **Hunter Valley Horse Riding and Adventures.** These friendly folks welcome equestrians of all levels and ages, and have a nice selection of guided rides around the valley. A favorite is the the sunset ride, when your most likely to see wildlife. ⊠ *288 Talga Rd., Rothbury* ☎ *02/4930–7111* ⊕ *www.huntervalleyhorseriding.com.au .*

HELICOPTER TOURS **Hunter Wine Helicopters.** This small family-run company gives short scenic flights from A$80 around Pokolbin and the Lower Hunter. A more leisurely option would include a private winery tour and lunch (from A$515 per couple). ⊠ *Cessnock Airport Terminal, Wine Country Dr., Cessnock* ☎ *02/4991–7352* ⊕ *www.hunterwinehelicopters.com.au.*

HOT-AIR BALLOONS **Balloon Aloft Hunter Valley.** Drifting above the valley while the vines are still wet with dew is an unforgettable way to see the Hunter Valley. The award-winning Balloon Aloft has been operating for over 25 years, and runs hour-long, sunrise flights for A$295–A$320. ☎ *02/4991–5321 or 1800/028568* ⊕ *www.balloonaloft.com.*

WHERE TO EAT

$$ ╳❙❙ **Cacciatore.** Serving up a vast
ITALIAN selection of northern Italian spe-
cialties, the outdoor terrace at Il
Cacciatore is the perfect place for
a leisurely weekend lunch. The
exterior is classic Australian, with
a veranda overlooking the vine-
yards. Once you step inside, your
senses will be overwhelmed by the
wonderful aromas wafting from the
kitchen. Italian favorites crowd this
menu: try the hearty Aged Hunter
beef fillet served on Gorgonzola
potato rösti with baby spinach
and Nebbiolo jus, or one of their

FOR BEER LOVERS

Here's the dilemma: one of you
likes wine, while the other prefers
beer. Pop into **Bluetongue Brew-
ery** (✉ *Hermitage Rd., Pokolbin*
☎ *02/4998–7777* ⊕ *www.hunter-
valley.com.au*), Hunter Valley's only
brewery. Named after a lizard with
a bright blue tongue, the brewery
makes premium lager, pilsner,
and a very spicy ginger beer. You
can watch it all happening, and
sample the goods, too.

innovative pizzas. Make sure you leave plenty of room for the long
list of *dolci* (desserts), too. An extensive list of local and imported
wines complements the menu. ✉ *609 McDonalds Rd., at Gillard Rds.*
☎ *02/4998–7639* ▭ *AE, MC, V* ⊗ *No lunch weekdays.*

$$–$$$ ╳**Leaves & Fishes.** A rustic boathouse-style café with a deck that proj-
AUSTRALIAN ects over a fish-stocked dam and a lovely garden, this is the place to
dip into a bucket of prawns, down freshly shucked oysters, and graze
antipasto plates any time of day. Fish comes straight from farm to plate,
and wines from local vineyards. Desserts from the specials board might
include Sicilian apple cake with fresh vanilla cream. Lunch is à la carte,
while the dinner menu is a set price for two courses. Reservations are
recommended, especially on weekends. ✉ *737 Lovedale Rd., Lovedale*
☎ *02/4930–7400* ▭ *MC, V* ⊗ *Closed Mon. and Tues. No dinner Wed.,
and Thurs.*

$$$ ╳**Molines Bistro.** Local French-born celebrity chef Robert Molines used
FRENCH to run Roberts Restaurant, but he decamped to open this more tradi-
Fodor's Choice tional bistro in the quiet valley village of Mount View. Try to nab a
★ table out on the veranda for some of the best views in the valley. Food
isn't overly complicated or styled, which fits nicely with the relaxed (but
professional) service. The rack of veal with roasted Jerusalem artichoke
and porcini cream is delicious. At lunch there's a set menu that includes
a glass of local wine. ✉ *Tallavera Grove, 749 Mount View Rd., Mount
View* ☎ *02/4990–9553* ⊕ *www.bistromolines.com.au* ▭ *AE, DC, MC,
V* ⊗ *Closed Tues., Wed., no lunch Mon., Thurs.*

$$$ ╳**Roberts Restaurant.** Incorporating the 1876 Pepper Tree Cottage and
AUSTRALIAN encircled by grapevines, this charming restaurant matches its Old World
surroundings with creative fare. The seasonal modern Australian menu
draws inspiration from the recipes of regional France and Italy, applied
to local game, seafood, beef, and lamb. In the airy, country-style din-
ing room—with antique furniture, bare timber floors, and a big stone
fireplace—you might try grilled quail as a first course, and then follow
with Gorgonzola-stuffed potato gnocchi. The cozy fireside lounge is
perfect for enjoying after-dinner liqueurs. The restaurant is part of the
Tower Estate complex. ✉ *Halls Rd., Pokolbin* ☎ *02/4998–7330* ▭ *AE,
DC, MC, V.*

Many of the wineries also have excellent restaurants.

WHERE TO STAY

$$–$$$ ▥ **Carriages Country House.** On 36 acres at the end of a quiet country lane, this rustic-looking but winsome guesthouse is all about privacy. Each of the suites has antique country pine furniture and a large sitting area with comfy sofas. The two more expensive suites in the Gatehouse also have hot tubs and share a lounge with full kitchen facilities. A Continental breakfast basket is delivered each morning to your door. There's a two-night minimum stay on weekends. **Pros:** romantic in winter with roaring fireplaces in rooms, lovely verandas overlooking the grounds **Cons:** no children allowed, wedding groups sometimes book out most of the place. ✉ *Halls Rd.* ☎ *02/4998–7591* ⊕ *www.thecarriages.com. au* ⊅ *10 suites* ⚄ *In-room: kitchen, DVD (some), dial-up (some). In-hotel: tennis court, pool, no elevator, laundry service, public Internet, no kids* ▭ *AE, MC, V* ⑽ *CP.*

$$$–$$$$ ▥ **Cedars Mount View.** This property, nestled in the hills above the valley, ★ might tempt you to forget about wine tasting for a few days. The peaceful sounds of birds and wind in the eucalyptus leaves are that soothing. Each of the four wooden cottages here is different: the Ridge—a honeymoon cottage—has an open plan with a king-size bed and leather sofas; there's a two-person daybed beneath a picture window in the Gums; the Creek has a mezzanine main bedroom; the Terrace is the most private. All are comfortably luxurious, with fine bed linens, in-room hot tubs, stereos, and magazines to read beside the wood-burning fireplaces. You can pick up your helicopter flight (to whisk you to a nearby winery for lunch) near the front door. A generous breakfast hamper with free-range eggs, bacon, orange juice, breads, and a selection of teas and coffees is provided on arrival. **Pros:** private and luxurious, the bathrooms have decadent sunken baths. **Cons:** strikingly modern decor might not suit everyone, there's nothing to do but relax. ⊠ *60 Mitchells Rd., Mount View* ☎ *0414/533070 or 02/4959–3072* ⊕ *www.cedars.com.au* ⚲ *4 cottages* ⚲ *In-room: kitchen, refrigerator, DVD. In-hotel: no elevator, no-smoking rooms* ⊟ *AE, MC, V* ⦿ *BP.*

$$$ ⬚ **The Cooperage Bed and Breakfast.** This lovely B&B is in the heart of Kelman Vineyards Estate, a working vineyard with a cellar door just a stones throw from the rooms. There are three guest-rooms option: the peaceful rooms in the main house are best described as rustic chic, all with north-facing windows overlooking the vineyards. For more privacy, there's a small Scandinavian-style studio apartment tucked out back. Finally, the Lumberjack Cabin is a fantastic timber structure with a Romeo and Juliet balcony and a magnificent cathedral ceiling. The cabin's interior has been lovingly polished to bring out the rich warmth of the Australian hardwood. Owners Gay and Warren Cooper are the perfect hosts and fantastic cooks—ask for their famous ricotta pancakes with honeycomb butter at breakfast. The B&B has a small private home cinema if you want relax with a movie. **Pros:** big comfy beds, hammocks overlooking the vines, guesthouse rooms have private decks. **Cons:** not particularly family-friendly, can be booked out months ahead. ⊠ 41 Kelman Vineyards, Oakey Creek Rd., Pokolbin ☎ 02/4990–1232 ⊕ *www.huntervalleycooperage.com* ⚲ *5 rooms* ⚲ *In-room: refrigerator, DVD, kitchen (some), Wi-Fi. In-hotel: laundry service, parking (free), no-smoking rooms* ⊟ *AE, D, DC, MC, V* ⦿ *CP.*

$$$$ ⬚ **Peppers Convent.** This former convent, the most romantic property in
Fodor's Choice the Hunter Valley, was transported 605 km (375 mi) from its original
★ home in western New South Wales. Rooms, decorated in a "shabby chic" style with cream and brown tones, have French doors that open onto a wide veranda. All rooms have LCD televisions with movies. The on-site Endota Spa has a huge menu of treatments, from body wraps to massage and facials. The house is surrounded by Pepper Tree Winery's vines and is adjacent to the renowned Robert's Restaurant. Rates include a full country breakfast plus afternoon drinks and canapés. There's a minimum two-night stay on weekends, and rates drop during the week. **Pros:** romantic and secluded, balconies are a superb place to watch the sun set. **Cons:** standard rooms are on the small side, some noise audible from rooms. ⊠ *Halls Rd.* ☎ *02/4993–8999* ⊕ *www.peppers.com.au* ⚲ *17 rooms* ⚲ *In-room: refrigerator, dial-up. In-hotel: tennis court, pool, spa, bicycles, no elevator, no-smoking rooms, public Wi-Fi* ⊟ *AE, DC, MC, V* ⦿ *BP.*

$$ ⬚ **Vineyard Hill.** Smart and modern, these one- and two-bedroom apart-
★ ments are a good value, offering attractive packages both during the week and on weekends. The apartments are close together, but they are set on 32 acres of bushland with views of Brokenback Range. Each pastel-color suite has its own high-ceilinged lounge area, a private deck, and a kitchenette. Full cooked breakfasts are available, as are barbecues in the evening. The new Pamper House offers a range of spa treatments. There's a minimum stay of two nights on weekends. **Pros:** good-value accommodation that is perfect for groups and families. **Cons:** doesn't have the charm of other local properties. ⊠ *Lovedale and Lodge Rds.,*

Pokolbin ☎ *02/4990–4166* ⊕ *www.vineyardhill.com.au* ⤴ *8 apartments* ⌂ *In-room: kitchen, refrigerator, VCR, DVD. In-hotel: pool, no elevator, laundry service, public Internet, no-smoking rooms* ▭ *AE, MC, V.*

THE NORTH COAST

The North Coast is one of the most glorious and seductive stretches of terrain in Australia, stretching almost 600 km (373 mi) up to the Queensland border. An almost continuous line of beaches defines the coast, with the Great Dividing Range rising to the west. These natural borders frame a succession of rolling green pasturelands, mossy rain forests, towns dotted by red-roof houses, and waterfalls that tumble in glistening arcs from the escarpment.

A journey along the coast leads through several rich agricultural districts, beginning with grazing country in the south and moving into plantations of bananas, sugarcane, mangoes, avocados, and macadamia nuts. Dorrigo National Park, outside Bellingen, and Muttonbird Island, in Coffs Harbour, are two parks good for getting your feet on some native soil and for seeing unusual birdlife.

The tie that binds the North Coast is the Pacific Highway, but despite its name, this highway rarely affords glimpses of the Pacific Ocean. You can drive the entire length of the North Coast in a single day, but allow at least three—or, better still, a week—to properly sample some of its attractions.

Numbers in the margin correspond to points of interest on the North Coast map.

PORT MACQUARIE

390 km (243 mi) northeast of Sydney.

Port Macquarie was founded as a convict settlement in 1821, and is the third-oldest settlement in Australia. Set at the mouth of the Hastings River, the town was chosen for its isolation to serve as an open jail for prisoners convicted of second offenses in New South Wales. By the 1830s the pace of settlement was so brisk that the town was no longer isolated, and its usefulness as a jail had ended. Today's Port Macquarie has few reminders of its convict past, and is flourishing as a vacation area. With its pristine rivers and lakes and 13 regional beaches, including beautiful Town Beach and Shelley Beach, which both have sheltered swimming, it's a great place to get into water sports, catch a fish for dinner, and watch migrating humpback whales in season, usually May to July and September to November.

GETTING HERE AND AROUND

It's a 4½-hour drive from Sydney heading north on the Pacific Highway. Greyhound and Premier Motor Service run coaches from Sydney Central Station. CountryLink trains operate three services daily between Sydney and the North Coast, though there is no direct train to Port Macquarie. Passengers have to catch a coach from Wauchope station to

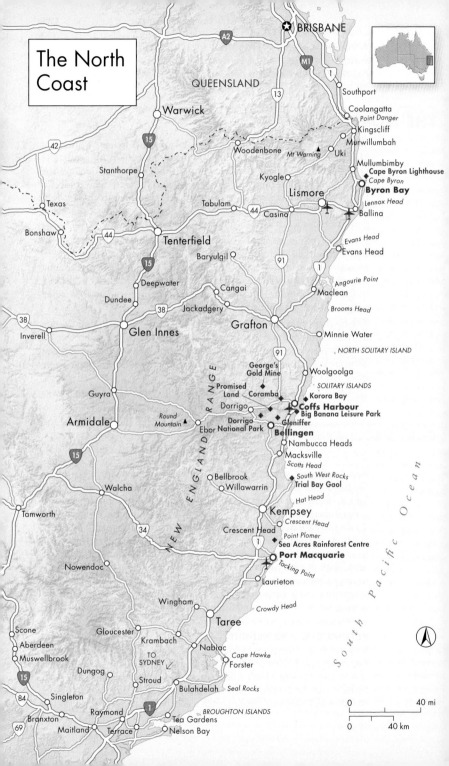

The North Coast

BRISBANE

QUEENSLAND

Warwick

Woodenbone
Mt Warning
Uki

Southport

Coolangatta
Point Danger
Kingscliff
Murwillumbah
Mullumbimby
Cape Byron Lighthouse
Cape Byron
Byron Bay

Stanthorpe

Texas

Bonshaw

Kyogle

Lismore

Lennox Head
Ballina

Tabulam

Casina

Evans Head
Evans Head

Tenterfield

Baryulgil

Cangai

Angourie Point
Maclean

Brooms Head

Deepwater

Dundee

Jackadgery

Grafton

Minnie Water

Inverell

Glen Innes

NORTH SOLITARY ISLAND

George's
Gold Mine

Woolgoolga

SOLITARY ISLANDS

Promised
Land
Coramba
Korora Bay
Coffs Harbour
Big Banana Leisure Park

Guyra

Round
Mountain

Dorrigo

Dorrigo
Ebor National Park

Gleniffer
Bellingen

Armidale

Nambucca Heads
Macksville
Scotts Head

Bellbrook

Willawarrin

South West Rocks
Trial Bay Gaol

Walcha

Hat Head

Tamworth

Kempsey

Crescent Head

Crescent Head
Point Plomer
Sea Acres Rainforest Centre
Port Macquarie

Nowendoc

Tacking Point

Laurieton

Wingham

Crowdy Head

Taree

Scone

Aberdeen

Muswellbrook

Gloucester

Krambach

TO
SYDNEY

Nabiac

Cape Hawke
Forster

Dungog

Stroud

Bulahdelah
Seal Rocks

Singleton

Raymond

Maitland

Terrace

Tea Gardens

Nelson Bay

BROUGHTON ISLANDS

NEW ENGLAND RANGE

South Pacific Ocean

0   40 mi

0   40 km

the coast, which makes the journey 7 hours long. Busway Buses travel to most towns and areas around the region. Timetables are available at the Greater Port Macquarie Visitor Centre or online. Qantas and Virgin Blue have flights from Sydney, and Brindabella Airlines connects Port Macquarie with Brisbane and Coffs Harbour.

ESSENTIALS

Tourist information Visitor Information Centre (✉ *Cnr. Clarence and Hay Sts., Port Macquarie* ☎ *1300/303155* ⊕ *www.portmacquarieinfo.com.au*).

> **THAR SHE BLOWS!**
>
> Whales travel up and down the New South Wales coast by the hundreds, so book a whale-watching cruise to catch all the action at close range. Southern right whales and humpbacks travel up from Antarctica from May to August and down again from September to November. Dolphins can be seen almost any time of the year—you never know when an agile pair will shoot through a wave or bob up near your boat.

EXPLORING

Operated by the Koala Preservation Society of New South Wales, the town's **Koala Hospital** is both a worthy cause and a popular attraction. The Port Macquarie region supports many of these extremely appealing marsupials, and the hospital cares for 150 to 250 sick and injured koalas each year. The staff is passionate about their furry patients, and will happily tell you about the care the animals receive. You can walk around the grounds to view the recuperating animals. Try to visit during feeding times—8 in the morning or 3 in the afternoon. There are guided tours daily at 3. ✉ *Macquarie Nature Reserve, Lord St.* ☎ *02/6584–1522* ⊕ *www.koalahospital.org.au* ✉ *Donation requested* ☉ *Daily 8–4:30.*

Fodor'sChoice ★ The **Sea Acres Rainforest Centre** comprises 178 pristine acres of coastal rain forest on the southern side of Port Macquarie. There are more than 170 plant species here, including 300-year-old cabbage-tree palms, as well as native mammals, reptiles, and prolific birdlife. An elevated boardwalk allows you to stroll through the lush environment without disturbing the vegetation. The center has informative guided tours, as well as a gift shop and a pleasant rain-forest café. ✉ *Pacific Dr. near Shelley Beach Rd.* ☎ *02/6582–3355* ⊕ *www.environment.nsw.gov.au* ✉ *A$8.50* ☉ *Daily 9–4:30.*

Housed in a two-story shop dating from 1836, the eclectic **Port Macquarie Historical Museum** displays period costumes, memorabilia from World Wars I and II, farm implements, antique clocks and watches, and relics from the town's convict days. ✉ *22 Clarence St.* ☎ *02/6583–1108* ⊕ *www.port-macquarie-historical-museum.org.au* ✉ *A$5* ☉ *Mon.–Sat. 9:30–4:30, Sun. 1–4:30.*

The 1828 **St. Thomas Church,** the country's third-oldest house of worship, was built by convicts using local cedar and stone blocks cemented together with powdered seashells. ✉ *Hay and William Sts.* ☎ *02/6584–1033* ☉ *Weekdays 9.30–noon and 2–4.*

OUTDOOR ACTIVITIES

Unsurprisingly, most of the outdoor activities in this area revolve around the town's crystal-clear waters.

Orange fungi growing on the Rainforest Tree at Dorrigo National Park.

HORSBACK RIDING

Bellrowan Valley Horseriding. Thirty minutes outside of Port Macquarie, Bellrowan welcomes experts and beginners, and offers short trail rides and overnight treks. The two-day Great Aussie Pub Ride ends the day's ride in some of the region's most interesting pubs. ✉ *Crows Rd., Beechwood* ☎ *02/6587–5227* ⊕ *www.bellrowanvalley.com.au.*

SURFING

Port Macquarie Surf School. Head back to school and learn to ride the waves from some very competent coaches, all of whom are fully accredited, licensed, and insured with Surfing Australia. There are daily group lessons at 9 AM, 11 AM, and 2 PM, or you can opt for one-on-one tutoring. Surf boards, wet suits, rashvests, and sunscreen are provided. ✉ *35 Flynn St., Port Macquarie* ☎ *02/6585–5453* ⊕ *www.portmacquarie-surfschool.com.au.*

FISHING

Ocean Star. Deep-sea anglers will enjoy the day-long trips on this 40-foot custom Randel charting boat. Typical catches include snapper, pearl perch, dolphin fish, and Jew fish. If you have cooking facilities, the crew is happy to clean, ice, and pack your catch. ✉ *Town Wharf, Port Macquarie* ☎ *0416/240–877* ⊕ *www.oceanstarfishing.com.*

WHALE WATCHING

Port Macquarie Cruise Adventures. Majestic humpback whales migrate past Port Macquarie non-stop from May to the end of November and Cruise Adventures offers great-value cruises on 12-seater boats (A$35). The company also has both long and short cruises to see local bottlenose dolphins that can be spotted year-round. ✉ *Short Street Wharf, Port Macquarie* ☎ *1300/555890* ⊕ *www.cruiseadventures.com.au.*

WHERE TO EAT AND STAY

$$ ✕ **Ça Marche.** This terrific Mod-Oz lunch spot is part of the lovely
AUSTRALIAN   Cassegrain Winery, 20 minutes south of Port Macquarie, just off the
★   Pacific Highway. Entrées such as blue swimmer crab and mascarpone
tortellini, or tempura of Tasmanian salmon with sesame noodles, sweet
chili-tamarind dressing, and toffee lime complement the fine wines.
The dining room has views of the vineyards and formal gardens, and
the cellar door is open 9–5 for daily tastings. ⊠ *764 Fernbank Creek
Rd.* ☎ *02/6582–8320* ⊕ *www.camarche.com.au* ▤ *MC, V* ⊘ *No din-
ner Sat.–Thurs.*

$$ ✕ **The Corner.** This stylish café has been packed with happy diners since
AUSTRALIAN   it opened in early 2007. The reason is clear—they serve fabulously tasty
and inexpensive meals, though you have to be patient, as service can be
sloooow. Try the Spanish omelet with arugula and tomato confit for
breakfast, then return for dinner to sample the char-grilled pork cutlet
with cinnamon apple, shaved fennel salad, and balsamic glaze. As the
name suggests, it sits on a corner, part of the Macquarie Waters Hotel
& Apartments complex. ⊠ *Clarence and Munster Sts.* ☎ *02/6583–3300*
⊕ *www.mwaters.com.au* ▤ *AE, MC, V.*

$–$$$ ▦ **HW Boutique Motel.** Although the building dates from the late
1960s—when its sawtooth shape was considered very stylish—it's filled
with up-to-the-minute amenities: designer furnishings, luxurious linens,
marble bathrooms, and private balconies with ocean and river views.
Molton Brown bath products are supplied and, in some rooms, there
are hot tubs in which to enjoy them. It's a five-minute walk to the Hast-
ings River and into town. Town Beach is opposite the property. **Pros:**
a very good Continental breakfast is brought to your room, toasters in
rooms, viewing lounge on the top floor. **Cons:** some street noise, a few
rooms overlook car park. ⊠ *1 Stewart St.* ☎ *02/6583–1200* ⊕ *www.
hwmotel.com.au* ⇆ *45 rooms* ♿ *In-room: kitchen, refrigerator, Eth-
ernet. In-hotel: room service, pool, laundry facilities, public Internet,
no-smoking rooms* ▤ *AE, DC, MC, V.*

$ ▦ **Beachcomber Resort.** Spacious family-friendly accommodation can
be tough to find in Port Macquarie, which is why this self-catering
resort opposite Town Beach garners high praise for its service and price.
Almost all the apartments spread over three floors have super ocean
views from their private balconies, and inside the light and airy rooms
are very pleasant. Travelers wishing to save a few bucks should request
one of the 17 two-bed apartments that come with washers, dryers and
dishwashers. **Pros:** well-maintained BBQ area and spotless accommo-
dation. **Cons:** no lifts can be a pain if you're lugging children up stairs,
if you don't have kids, you might feel outnumbered. ⊠ *54 William St.,
Port Macquarie* ☎ *02/6584–1881* ⊕ *www.beachcomberresort.com.au*
⇆ *22 apartments* ♿ *In-room: kitchen, refrigerator, DVD, Wi-Fi. In-
hotel: pool, spa, laundry service, Wi-Fi, parking (free), no-smoking
rooms, no lift* ▤ *AE, D, DC, MC, V* ❍⍾ *EP.*

EN
ROUTE   **Trial Bay Gaol,** a jail dating from the 1870s, occupies a dramatic posi-
tion on the cliffs overlooking the seaside village of South West Rocks,
100 km (62 mi) north of Port Macquarie. The building, now partly in
ruins, was used to teach useful skills to the prisoners who constructed

it, but the project proved too expensive and was abandoned in 1903. During World War I the building served as an internment camp for some 500 Germans. The A$8 admission includes entry to a small museum. A moonlight tour (A$12) takes place on the first Saturday of every month at 6 PM. Make sure you climb the tower for a stunning view of the coast. To get there, travel north through Kempsey and turn off to South West Rocks and follow the signs. ☎ *02/6566–6168.*

BELLINGEN

210 km (130 mi) north of Port Macquarie, 520 km (323 mi) from Sydney.

In a river valley a few miles off the Pacific Highway, artsy Bellingen is one of the prettiest towns along the coast. Many of Bellingen's buildings have been classified by the National Trust, and the museum, cafés, galleries, and crafts outlets are favorite hangouts for artists, craft workers, and writers. You'll find food, entertainment, and 250 stalls at the community markets that take place on the third Sunday of every month.

GETTING HERE AND AROUND

It's a six-hour drive from Sydney along the Pacific Highway, but the town is just 30 minutes from Coffs Harbour and its airport. CountryLink trains run from Sydney three times a day and from Brisbane twice daily, stopping at Urunga, which is 10 km (6 mi) away. Both Greyhound and Premier Motor Service also run buses between Sydney and Urunga. From Urunga, either catch a taxi or a local Busways bus to Bellingen—though the bus is quite infrequent. The local tourist office is open 9–4.

ESSENTIALS

Tourist information Waterfall Way Visitor Centre (⊠ *29–31 Hyde St, Bellingen* ☎ *02/6655–1522* ⊕ *www.bellingermagic.com*).

EXPLORING

From Bellingen a meandering and spectacular road leads inland to Dorrigo before reaching the Pacific Highway, close to Coffs Harbour. This circular scenic route, beginning along the Bellinger River, climbs more than 1,000 feet up the heavily wooded escarpment to the **Dorrigo Plateau.**

★ At the top of the plateau is **Dorrigo National Park** (☎ *02/6657–2309*), a small but outstanding subtropical rain forest that is included on the World Heritage list. Signposts along the main road indicate walking trails. The Satinbird Stroll is a short rain-forest walk, and the 6-km (4-mi) Cedar Falls Walk leads to the most spectacular of the park's many waterfalls. The excellent **Dorrigo Rainforest Centre** (☎ *02/6657–2309,* ⊕ *www.dorrigo.com*), open daily 9–4.30, has information, educational displays, and a shop, and from here you can walk out high over the forest canopy along the Skywalk boardwalk. The national park is approximately 31 km (19 mi) from Bellingen.

OUTDOOR ACTIVITIES

HIKING **Hinderland Tour.** Based out of Bellingen, this husband-and-wife team runs tours to the many national parks along the east coast. The company offers multi-day treks which encompass Dorrigo National Park, the New England wilderness, and the white beaches of Bongil Bongil National Park. Accommodation in national-park cabins is included in the price of the package. ☎ *02/6655–2957* ⊕ *www.hinterlandtour. com.au.*

Gambaarri Tours. If you are interested in local Aboriginal culture, join one of these half-day tours led by local elder Wiruunngga. You'll learn about local history and look for bush tucker as you visit the Promised Land and the Never Never River. Morning or afternoon tea is provided. Wiruunngga also offers tours out of Coffs (A$45). ☎ *02/6655–5195* ⊕ *www.heartlanddidgeridoos.com.au.*

HORSEBACK **Valery Trails.** This large horse-riding center is 10 km (6 mi) from Bellin-
RIDING gen on the edge of Bongil Bongil National Park. They have 60 horses, and offer a variety of treks through the local rain forests. Choose from one-hour treks (A$40) to two-day rides that include accommodation (A$300). ✉ *758 Valery Rd., Valery* ☎ *02/6653–4301* ⊕ *www.valery-trails.com.au.*

CANOEING **Bellingen Canoe Adventures.** Hire a canoe or join an organized expedition on the Bellinger River, which meanders its way through some of the most spectacular and picturesque areas in the area. This company, which emphasises safety above everything else, offers a wide range of options including full-moon tours. ☎ *02/6655–9955* ⊕ *www.canoe-adventures.com.au.*

WHERE TO STAY

$ 🏠 **Koompartoo Retreat.** These self-contained hardwood cottages on a hillside overlooking Bellingen are superb examples of local craftsmanship, particularly in their use of timbers from surrounding forests. Each has a complete kitchen, a family room, and a shower (no tub). Breakfast is available by arrangement. **Pros:** from the chalet verandas you can see kookaburras and black cockatoos, each cottage has small library. **Cons:** no wheelchair access, and heating is noisy. ✉ *Rawson and Dudley Sts.* ☎🖨 *02/6655–2326* ⊕ *www.koompartoo.com.au* ⤴ *4 cottages* ⚐ *In-room: no phone, kitchen, VCR. In-hotel: laundry facilities, no elevator, no-smoking rooms* ▭ *MC, V.*

COFFS HARBOUR

35 km (22 mi) northeast of Bellingen via the Pacific Hwy., 103 km (64 mi) from Bellingen via the inland scenic route along the Dorrigo Plateau, 534 km (320 mi) from Sydney.

The area surrounding Coffs Harbour is the state's "banana belt," where long, neat rows of banana palms cover the hillsides. Set at the foot of steep green hills, the town has great beaches and a mild climate. This idyllic combination has made it one of the most popular vacation spots along the coast. Coffs is also a convenient halfway point on the 1,000-km (620-mi) journey between Sydney and Brisbane.

GETTING HERE AND AROUND

Coffs Harbour is about a 6½-hour drive from Sydney and a five-hour drive from Brisbane. Regular Greyhound and Premier buses connect the town to Sydney. There is a train station with daily CountryLink services to and from Sydney and Brisbane. And the local airport, 6 km (4 mi) from the central Ocean Parade, is served by Qantas, Virgin Blue, and Brindabella Airlines. For more information, contact the visitor center, which is open 9–5 daily.

TOURS

Mountain Trails Four-Wheel-Drive Tours (☎ 02/6658–3333) conducts half- and full-day tours of the rain forests and waterfalls of the Great Dividing Range to the west of Coffs Harbour in style—a seven-seat Toyota Safari or a 14-seat, Australian-designed four-wheel-drive vehicle. The half-day tour costs A$65, and the full-day tour is A$95, including lunch and snacks.

ESSENTIALS

Airport Coffs Harbour Airport (✉ Hogbin Dr., Coffs Harbour ☎ 02/6648–4837).

Hospital Coffs Harbour Base Hospital (✉ 345 Pacific Hwy., Coffs Harbour ☎ 02/6656–7000).

Visitor Information Coffs Coast Visitors Information Centre (✉ Pacific Hwy. at McLean St., Coffs Harbour ☎ 02/6648–4990 or 1300/369070 ⊕ www.coffscoast.com.au).

EXPLORING

The town has a lively and attractive harbor in the shelter of **Muttonbird Island,** and a stroll out to this nature reserve is delightful in the evening. To get here, follow the signs to the Coffs Harbour Jetty, then park near the marina. A wide path leads out along the breakwater and up the slope of the island. The trail is steep, but the views from the top are worth the effort. The island is named after the muttonbirds (also known as shearwaters) that nest here between September and April. Between June and September Muttonbird Island is also a good spot for viewing migrating humpback whales.

☼ Near the port in Coffs Harbour the **Pet Porpoise Pool** aquarium includes sharks, colorful reef fish, turtles, seals, and dolphins. A 90-minute interactive sea-circus show takes place daily between 9:30 and 1:45. Children may help feed and "shake hands" with dolphins, as well as interact with kisses from seals. Swimming sessions with dolphins can be arranged if you book in advance. ✉ *Orlando St. beside Coffs Creek* ☎ *02/6659–1900* ⊕ *www.petporpoisepool.com* ☜ *A$28* ☼ *Daily 9–4.*

☼ Just north of the city, impossible to miss, is the Big Banana—the symbol of Coffs Harbour. This monumental piece of kitsch has stood at the site since 1964. It welcomes visitors to the **Big Banana Leisure Park** complex, which takes a fascinating look at the past, present, and future of horticulture. There's a multimedia display called "World of Bananas" and a walkway that meanders through the banana plantations. A lookout high on the plantation hill provides great views to the coast, and is a good whale-watching vantage point July–November. The park also includes toboggan rides (A$5), a waterslide (A$16), and an ice-skating rink (A$12). There's a café on the premises, as well as the Banana Barn, which sells the park's own jams, pickles, and fresh tropical fruit. ⊠ *351 Pacific Hwy.* ☎ *02/6652–4355* ⊕ *www.bigbanana.com* 🖬 *A$12* ⊗ *Daily 9–4:30.*

OUTDOOR ACTIVITIES

SCUBA DIVING   The warm seas around Coffs Harbour make this particular part of the coast, with its moray eels, manta rays, turtles, and gray nurse sharks, a scuba diver's favorite. Best are the Solitary Islands, 7–21 km (4½–13 mi) offshore. **Jetty Dive Centre** (☎ *02/6651–1611* ⊕ *www.jettydive.com. au*) also rents gear, schedules scuba and snorkeling trips, and hosts certification classes.

WHITE-WATER   The highly regarded **Wildwater Rafting** (⊠ *754 Pacific Hwy., Boambee* RAFTING   ☎ *02/6653–2067* ⊕ *www.coffscentral.com/wildwater*) conducts one-, two-, and four-day rafting trips down the Nymboida River. Trips begin from Bonville, 14 km (9 mi) south of Coffs Harbour on the Pacific Highway, but pickups from the Coffs Harbour and Bellingen region can be arranged. One-day trips start at A$160, including meals.

WHERE TO EAT AND STAY

$$ ✕ **Shearwater Restaurant.** This waterfront restaurant with views of Coffs ECLECTIC   Creek (which is spotlighted at night—look for stingrays swimming by) is open for breakfast, lunch, and dinner, and leaves no culinary stone unturned in its search for novel flavors. The menu in the open-air dining room includes dishes such as local barramundi fillet with potato rösti. If you want a table on the deck, book ahead. Service is friendly and attentive. ⊠ *321 Harbour Dr.* ☎ *02/6651–6053* ☐ *AE, MC, V* 🍽 *BYOB.*

$$–$$$ 🏨 **BreakFree Aanuka Beach Resort.** Teak furniture and antiques collected ★   from Indonesia and the South Pacific fill the one-bedroom suites at this resort, which sits amid palms, frangipani, and hibiscus. Each suite has a kitchenette, lounge, laundry, and glass-ceiling bathroom with a two-person whirlpool tub. There are also hotel-room studios and two-bedroom suites and three- and four-bedroom split-level villas. Outside, the landscaping is highly imaginative; the pool is immersed in a miniature rain forest with a waterfall and hot tub. The resort borders a secluded white-sand beach on the blue waters of the Pacific. There is a three-night minimum stay during the high season (December 23–January 20, and during Easter). **Pros:** brilliant setting in a private beachfront cove, great value for families. **Cons:** some guests have complained about room cleanliness, kid-phobes might not appreciate all the families. ⊠ *11 Firman Dr.* ☎ *02/6652–7555* ⊕ *www.breakfreeaanukabeachresort.com.au* 🛏 *32 studio rooms, 38 suites* ⚿ *In-room: kitchen (some), refrigerator, DVD (some). In-hotel: 2 restaurants, room service, bar, tennis courts, pools, gym, spa, no elevator, laundry facilities, children's programs (ages 2–12), public Internet, no-smoking rooms* ☐ *AE, DC, MC, V* 🍽 *BP.*

$$$ 🏨 **Smugglers on the Beach.** Five minutes' drive north of Coffs Harbour's busy city center is this small resort with just 16 self-contained 1- to 3-bedroom apartments spread out among tropical gardens. While the decor may be slightly dated, the location, price, and family-friendly facilities make this place worth recommending, especially to families and groups. **Pros:** resort has fishing equipment and a BBQ, so you can

catch your dinner, beautiful beachside location. **Cons:** minimum stay of two nights, check-out is at 9:30 AM. ⌧ *36 Sandy Beach Rd., Coffs Harbour* ☎ *02/6653–6166* ⊕ *www.smugglers.com.au* ⤳ *16 apartments* ⌂ *In-room: kitchen, DVD, Wi-Fi. In-hotel: pool, tennis, beachfront, diving, water sports, bicycles, laundry facilities, parking (free), no-smoking rooms* ▭ *AE, D, DC, MC, V* ⫼ *EP.*

EN
ROUTE
An hour or so north of Coffs Harbour is the historic town of Grafton, set on the banks of the Clarence River. The town is famous for the **Jacaranda Festival,** which has taken place the last week of October since 1935. A parade is held in the streets—lined with the beautiful purple flowering trees—and a new Jacaranda Queen is crowned each year. Between Grafton and the far North Coast, the Pacific Highway enters sugarcane country, where tiny sugarcane trains and thick, drifting smoke from burning cane fields are ever-present. The highway passes the fishing and resort town of **Ballina,** where beaches are the prime feature.

BYRON BAY

247 km (154 mi) north of Coffs Harbour, 772 km (480 mi) north of Sydney.

Byron Bay is the easternmost point on the Australian mainland, and perhaps earns Australia its nickname the "Lucky Country." Fabulous beaches, storms that spin rainbows across the mountains behind the town, and a sunny, relaxed style cast a spell over practically everyone who visits. For many years Byron Bay lured surfers with abundant sunshine, perfect waves on Watego's Beach, and tolerant locals who allowed them to sleep on the sand. These days a more upscale crowd frequents Byron Bay.

Byron Bay is also one of the must-sees on the backpacker circuit, and the town has a youthful energy that fuels late-night partying. There are many art galleries and crafts shops, a great food scene, and numerous adventure tours. The town is at its liveliest on the first Sunday of each month, when Butler Street becomes a bustling market.

GETTING HERE AND AROUND

Bryon is the North Coast's most popular destination, and is well served by buses and trains from Sydney and Coffs Harbour. If driving, the journey takes 10 hours from Sydney and 3½ hours from Coffs Harbour. The closest airports are at Ballina and Lismore, both 30 minutes drive away. Virgin Blue and Jetstar both fly to Ballina, while REX flies from Sydney to Lismore. All the usual car companies are there, or you could get a taxi into Byron or take a Ballina-Byron shuttle for A$15. For tourist information, the Byron Visitor Centre is open daily 9–5.

ESSENTIALS

Airport shuttle Ballina Byron Shuttle (☎ *0414/660–031* ⊕ *www.ballinabyron-shuttle.com.au*).

Hospital Byron Bay District Hospital (⌧ *Shirley St., Byron Bay* ☎ *02/6685–6200*).

Visitor Information Byron Visitor Centre (⌧ *80 Jonson St., Byron Bay* ☎ *02/6680–8558* ⊕ *www.visitbyronbay.com*).

There's no shortage of activities in Byron Bay.

EXPLORING

Cape Byron Lighthouse, the most powerful beacon on the Australian coastline, dominates the southern end of the beach at Byron Bay and attracts huge numbers of visitors. You can tour the lighthouse (no children under 5) on Tuesday and Thursday year-round, and weekends during the summer and school holidays. Whale-watching is popular between June and September, when migrating humpback whales come close to shore. Dolphins swim in these waters year-round, and you can often see pods of them from the cape. You can stay overnight in the lighthouse, but you must make a reservation at least six months in advance. ⊠ *Lighthouse Rd.* ☎ *02/6685–5955* ⊕ *www.environment. nsw.gov.au* ✉ *Free, lighthouse tours A$8* ⊗ *Lighthouse grounds daily 8–5:30. Lighthouse tours Tues. and Thurs. at 11, 12:30, and 2; weekends at 10, 11, 12:30, 2, and 3:30 during school holidays.*

Cape Byron Walking Track circumnavigates a 150-acre reserve, passes through grasslands and rain forest, and offers sensational seas views as you circle the peninsula and the lighthouse. From several vantage points along the track you may spot dolphins in the waters below. The track begins east of the town on Lighthouse Road.

OFF THE
BEATEN
PATH

★ **Byron Bay Hinterland.** Inland from Byron Bay is some of the most picturesque country in Australia. Undulating green hills that once boasted a thriving dairy industry are dotted with villages with a New Age vibe. There are small organic farms growing avocados, coffee, fruits, and macadamia nuts. The best way to discover this gorgeous part of the world—nicknamed the Rainbow Region—is to grab a map and drive. From Byron, take the road toward the regional town of Lismore for about 15 km (9 mi) to the pretty village of **Bangalow.** Walk along the lovely main street lined with 19th-century storefronts and native Bangalow palms. Carefully follow your map and wind your way northwest for about 20 km (13 mi) to **Federal** for lunch at **Pogel's Wood Café** (☎ *02/6688–4121*). Meander, via the cute towns of **Rosebank** and **Dunoon,** to **The Channon,** where on the second Sunday of every month you'll find a wonderful market with dozens of stalls and entertainment. You may want to relax

HIPPY DAYS

You'll think you've traveled back in time when you arrive in Nimbin, northwest of Byron Bay. There are psychedelic storefronts, a hemp museum, and stores such as Hippy High Herbs and Nimbin Apothecary. The annual "Mardi Grass" Fiesta, which advocates the legalization of cannabis, is held on the first weekend of May, and is a sight to behold.

for a few days at the town's **Eternity Springs Art Farm** (⊠ *483 Tuntable Creek Rd.* ☎ *02/6688–6385* ⊕ *www.eternitysprings.com*), a groovy B&B that also offers art classes and yoga.

BEACHES
Several superb beaches lie in the vicinity of Byron Bay. In front of the town, Main Beach provides safe swimming, and Clarks Beach, closer to the cape, has better surf. The most famous surfing beach, however, is Watego's, the only entirely north-facing beach in the state. To the south of the lighthouse Tallow Beach extends for 6 km (4 mi) to a rocky stretch of coastline around Broken Head, which has a number of small sandy coves. Beyond Broken Head is lonely Seven Mile Beach. Topless sunbathing is popular on many Byron Bay beaches.

OUTDOORS ACTIVITIES
KAYAKING   **Dolphin Kayaking** (☎ *02/6685–8044* ⊕ *www.dolphinkayaking.com.au*) has half-day trips (from 8:30 to noon for A$60 and weather permitting) that take paddlers out to meet the local bottlenose dolphins and surf the waves.

KITE   **Byron Bay Kiteboarding** (☎ *0402/008926 or 0400/103003* ⊕ *www.*
BOARDING   *byronbaykiteboarding.com*) is an International Kiteboarding Organization–accredited school with beginner lessons and clinics. Two-day, two-student courses take place on a choice of local waterways.

SCUBA DIVING   The best local diving is at Julian Rocks Marine Reserve, some 3 km (2 mi) offshore, where the confluence of warm and cold currents supports a profusion of marine life. **Byron Bay Dive Centre** (⊠ *9 Marvel St.* ☎ *02/6685–8333 or 1800/243483* ⊕ *www.byronbaydivecentre.com.au*) has snorkeling and scuba-diving trips for all levels of experience, plus gear rental and instruction. **Sundive** (⊠ *8 Middleton St.* ☎ *02/6685–7755 or 1800/008755* ⊕ *www.sundive.com.au*) is a PADI dive center with courses for all levels of divers, as well as boat dives and snorkel trips.

WHERE TO EAT
$$ ✕ **Byron Bay Beach Café.** A Byron Bay legend, this open-air café is a
CAFÉ   perfect place to sit in the morning sun and watch the waves. Breakfast runs the gamut from wholesome (home made Bircher muesli with berry compote) to total calorific decadence (monstrous omelets with bacon,

mushrooms, and more). For lunch you might try roast pumpkin, feta, beetroot, and pine-nut salad. The fresh juices and tropical fruits alone are worth the 15-minute stroll along the beach from town. Reservations are recommended during the summer. ⊠ *Clarks Beach off parking lot at end of Lawson St.* ☎ *02/6685–8400* ⊕ *www.byronbeachcafe.com.au* ▤ *MC, V* ⊗ *No dinner.*

$$$

AUSTRALIAN

★

✕ **Fig Tree Country Restaurant.** In this century-old farmhouse with distant views of Byron Bay the draw is upmarket Mod-Oz cuisine blending Asian and Mediterranean flavors. Produce fresh from the owners' farm is featured on the menu. There are always lots of seafood dishes as well as an inexpensive set menu option. If it's in season, try the blue-eyed cod with smoked salmon, saffron sauce, and coriander pesto. Ask for a table on the veranda amid the extravagant foliage. The restaurant is 5 km (3 mi) inland from Byron Bay, but if you want to stay, the owners have rooms for rent in the farmhouse next door. ⊠ *4 Sunrise La., Ewingsdale* ☎ *02/6684–7273* ⊕ *www.figtreerestaurant.com.au* ▤ *MC, V* ⌖ *BYO (A$5 corkage fee)* ⊗ *Closed Mon.–Wed. No dinner Sun.*

WHERE TO STAY

$$$$

🛏 **Bryon Bay Beach Bure.** Three luxury bures—the Fijian word for cabin— may be only 200 meters from the city center, but the lush, peaceful setting makes it feel like a private oasis. Double bedrooms are outfitted in calming blues and whites, and bathrooms are stocked with high-end toiletries. Georgi, the host, has gone to great lengths to create a quiet atmosphere, and children are not allowed. Breakfast vouchers for the town's cafés are included in the price. **Pros:** walking distance from everything Bryon has to offer, perfect accommodation for a romantic getaway. **Cons:** despite location, no sea views. ⊠ *36 Lawson St., Bryon Bay* ☎ *02/6288–8483* ⊕ *www.byronbaybeachbure.com.au* ⇥ *3 bures* ⌂ *In-room: refrigerator, Wi-Fi. In-hotel: beachfront, laundry service, Wi-Fi, parking (free), no kids under 16, no-smoking rooms* ▤ *AE, D, DC, MC, V* ⍾ *CP.*

$$

🛏 **Julian's Apartments.** These studio apartments opposite Clarks Beach are neat, spacious, and well equipped. All have a kitchen, a laundry, and either a balcony or a courtyard with rooms opening onto a generous private patio. Furnishings are simple, done in refreshing blond timbers, blue fabrics, and white walls. The beach is so close that the sound of the waves can rock you to sleep. **Pros:** perfect for families, cots and baby supplies can be hired, very helpful owners. **Cons:** don't expect luxury or added extras here. ⊠ *124 Lighthouse Rd.* ☎ *02/6680–9697* ⊕ *www.juliansbyronbay.com* ⇥ *11 apartments* ⌂ *In-room: kitchen, Internet. In-hotel: laundry facilities, no elevator, no-smoking rooms* ▤ *AE, DC, MC, V.*

$$$$

Fodor'sChoice

★

🛏 **Rae's on Watego's.** If a high-design boutique hotel is your cup of tea, you'd be hard-pressed to do better than this luxurious Mediterranean-style villa surrounded by a tropical garden. Each suite is individually decorated with an exotic collection of antiques, Indonesian art, Moroccan tables, and fine furnishings. The secluded rooms have gorgeous four-poster beds, tile floors, huge windows, in-room fireplaces, and private terraces; the service is top-notch, and the alfresco in-house restaurant ($$$) serves creative Australian-Thai dishes like steamed wild barramundi with cherry tomatoes and mushrooms. There's a minimum two-night stay on weekends. **Pros:** perfect for a romantic break, superb international-class spa. **Cons:** breakfast prices too high, you need your own transport or you'll have to catch a taxi into town. ⊠ *Watego's Beach, 8 Marina Parade* ☎ *02/6685–5366* ⊕ *www. raes.com.au* ⟳ *7 suites* ⌂ *In-room: refrigerator, kitchen (some), VCR, Wi-Fi (some). In-hotel: restaurant, room service, pool, spa, no elevator, public Internet, no kids under 13* ⊟ *AE, DC, MC, V.*

NO BULL

If there's one place that has milked its name for all its worth, it's Mooball, a blink-and-you-miss it village about 20 minutes north of Byron Bay. Follow the black-and-white cow prints painted on telegraph poles to the Moo Moo Café, which serves Moo Moo Burgers, Moo Moo shakes, and lots of kitschy souvenirs. If you find cow puns udderly annoying, then it's best to graze in other pastures.

NIGHTLIFE

For a small town, Byron rocks by night. Fire dancing—where bare-chested men dance with flaming torches—is a local specialty. Bars and clubs are generally open until about 2 AM on weekends and midnight on weekdays.

Head to the legendary **Arts Factory Village** (⊠ *Skinners Shoot Rd.* ☎ *02/6685–7709*) —also known as the Piggery—to catch a movie, grab a bite, or see a band. The **Beach Bar** (⊠ *Bay La. and Jonson Sts.* ☎ *02/6685–6402*) in the Beach Hotel often hosts live bands. Lively bar-restaurant-nightclub **Cocomangas** (⊠ *32 Jonson St.* ☎ *02/6685–8493* ⊕ *www.cocomangas. com.au*) is a favorite of carousing backpackers. Bands perform most evenings at the old-school **Great Northern Hotel** (⊠ *Jonson and Byron Sts.* ☎ *02/6685–6454*). Live music rocks the **Railway Friendly Bar** (⊠ *Jonson St. Railway Station* ☎ *02/6685–7662*) every night.

SHOPPING

Byron Bay is one of the state's arts-and-crafts centers, with many innovative and high-quality articles for sale, such as leather goods, offbeat designer clothing, essential oils, natural cosmetics, and ironware. The community market, held on the first Sunday of every month, fills the Butler Street reserve with more than 300 stalls selling art, crafts, and local produce.

Colin Heaney Hot Glass Studio (⊠ *6 Acacia St., Industrial Estate* ☎ *02/ 6685–7044*) sells exquisite hand-blown glass goblets, wineglasses, paperweights, and sculpture. Glassblowers work here on weekdays. The shop is open weekdays 9–5 and weekends 10–4. **In Depth Creations** (⊠ *3/2 Tasman Way, Byron Bay Arts & Industrial Estate* ☎ *02/6628–8333*) sells custom-made surfboards decorated with hand-painted art. It's open sporadic hours, so call ahead before visiting. The **Byron Bay Hat Co.** (⊠ *4 Jonson St.* ☎ *02/6685–8357*) is an institution with great hats and bags perfect for the beach.

Fifty-three km (33 mi) northwest of Byron Bay is the towering, conical **Mt. Warning,** a 3,800-foot extinct volcano that dominates the pleasant town of Murwillumbah. Its radical shape can be seen from miles away, including the beaches at Byron.

A well-marked **walking track** winds up Mt. Warning, which is a World Heritage national park, from the Breakfast Creek parking area at its base. The 4½-km (2½-mi) track climbs steadily through fern forest and buttressed trees where you can often see native brush turkeys and pademelons (small wallaby-like marsupials). The last 650 feet of the ascent is a strenuous scramble up a steep rock face using chain-link handrails. The local Aboriginal name for the mountain is Wollumbin, which means "cloud catcher," and the metal walkways on the summit are sometimes shrouded in clouds. On a clear day, however, there are fabulous 360-degree views of the massive caldera, one of the largest in the world: national parks crown the southern, western, and northern rims, and the Tweed River flows seaward through the eroded eastern wall. Many people undertake the Mt. Warning ascent before dawn, so they can catch the first rays of light falling on mainland Australia.

For information about the walk and Mt. Warning National Park, visit the **World Heritage Rainforest Visitors Information Centre** (⊠ *Corner of Tweed Valley Way and Alma St.* ☎ *02/6672–1340* ⊕ *www.tweedcool-angatta.com.au*) in Murwillumbah. From here it is a 16½-km (10-mi) drive to the start of the walking track. Fill your water bottles in Murwillumbah; there is no drinking water in the park or on the mountain. Allow at least four hours up and back, and don't start the walk after 2 PM in winter.

CANBERRA AND THE A.C.T.

As the nation's capital, Canberra is often maligned by outsiders, who see the city as lacking the coolness of Melbourne or the glamour of Sydney. But Canberra has charms of its own, with its world-class museums, leafy open spaces, and the huge Lake Burley Griffin.

When Australia federated in 1901, both Sydney and Melbourne vied to be the nation's capital. But in the spirit of compromise, it was decided that a new city would be built, and Canberra and the Australian Capital Territory (A.C.T) was created when New South Wales ceded land to build a federal zone, based on the model of America's District of Columbia.

From the very beginning this was to be a totally planned city. Walter Burley Griffin, a Chicago architect and associate of Frank Lloyd Wright, won an international design competition. Griffin arrived in Canberra in 1913 to supervise construction, but progress was slowed by two world wars and the Great Depression. By 1947 Canberra, with only 15,000 inhabitants, was little more than a country town.

Development increased during the 1950s, and the current population of more than 320,000 makes Canberra by far the largest inland city in Australia. The wide, tree-lined avenues and spacious parklands of present-day Canberra have largely fulfilled Griffin's original plan. The

CLOSE UP

Lord Howe Island

A tiny crescent of land in the Pacific Ocean 600 km (373 mi) northeast of Sydney, Lord Howe Island is the most remote and arguably the most beautiful part of New South Wales. With the sheer peaks of Mt. Gower (2,870 feet) and Mt. Lidgbird (2,548 feet) richly clad in palms, ferns, and grasses; golden sandy beaches; and the clear turquoise waters of the lagoon, this is a remarkably lovely place. Apart from the barren spire of Ball's Pyramid, a stark volcanic outcrop 16 km (10 mi) across the water to the southeast, the UNESCO World Heritage listed island stands alone in the South Pacific.

Not only is the island beautiful, but its history is fascinating. The first recorded sighting was not until 1788, by a passing ship en route to the penal settlement on Norfolk Island, which lies to the east. And evidence, or lack of it, suggests that Lord Howe was uninhabited by humans until three Europeans and their Maori wives and children settled it in the 1830s. By the 1870s the small population included a curious mixture of people from America (including whalers and former slaves), England, Ireland, Australia, South Africa, and the Gilbert Islands. Many of the descendants of these early settlers still live on Lord Howe.

Lord Howe is a remarkably safe and relaxed place for its 280 inhabitants, where cyclists and walkers far outnumber the few cars. No one locks their doors, the speed limit is a mere 25 KPH (15 MPH), and there's no cell-phone service. There are plenty of walking trails, both flat and rather precipitous, and fine beaches. Among the many bird species is the endangered Lord Howe wood hen (*Tricholimnas sylvestris*).

In the sea below the island's fringing reef is the world's southernmost coral reef, with more than 50 species of hard corals and more than 500 fish species. For its size, the island has enough to keep you alternately occupied and unoccupied for at least five days. Even the dining scene is of an unexpectedly high quality.

Visitor numbers are limited to 400 at any given time to protect the island's unique natural habitat, and if you want to experience the place, book well ahead. Getting there is part of the fun on Qantaslink's 32-seat Bombardier Dash 8 aircraft. The journey takes 2 hours from Sydney and 90 minutes from Brisbane, and a strict 14-kg (31-lb) luggage limit per person applies on all flights. Fares are expensive, costing from A$380 each way.

Also be aware that it's an expensive destination once you arrive, with most accommodation options more upmarket boutique than bucket and spades. Many of the lodges, restaurants, and tour operators close in winter—generally from June through August—and accommodation prices in the open establishments are reduced considerably during that period. Five- or seven-night flight-and-accommodation packages are the most economic way to visit Lord Howe. To plan your trip, your first port of call should be the Lord Howe Island's visitor center Web site (⊕ *www.lordhoweisland.info*).

major public buildings are arranged on low knolls on either side of Lake Burley Griffin, the focus of the city. Satellite communities—using the same radial design of crescents and cul-de-sacs employed in Canberra—house the city's growing population.

GETTING HERE AND AROUND

Canberra International Airport is 7 km (4½ mi) east of the city center. Flights are about one-half hour to Sydney, an hour to Melbourne, and two hours to Brisbane—Qantas, Tiger Airways, and Virgin Blue fly to and from the capital, but there are no direct international flights. A taxi into the city is about A$23. A shuttle bus operated by Deane's Buslines runs every half hour between the airport and the city for A$9 per person, A$15 return.

Canberra is served by two major bus lines, Greyhound Australia and Murrays Australia. One-way fares to Sydney start from A$35, and the trip takes just over 3 hours.

The ACTION bus network operates weekdays 6:30 AM–11:30 PM, Saturday 7 AM–11:30 PM, and Sunday 8–7. There's a flat fare of A$3 per ride. A one-day ticket costs A$6.60, which allows unlimited travel, while an off-peak daily ticket costs A$4.10.

Canberra is difficult to negotiate by car, given its radial roads, erratic signage, and often large distances between suburbs. Still, because sights are scattered about and not easily connected on foot or by public transportation, a car is a good way to see the city itself, as well as the sights in the Australian Capital Territory. If you're not a good map reader, think about getting a rental car with GPS.

The Canberra Railway Station is about 6 km (4 mi) southeast of the city center. CountryLink trains make the four-hour trip between Canberra and Sydney twice daily. A daily bus-rail service by CountryLink makes the 9-hour run between Canberra and Melbourne.

TOURS

A convenient (and fun!) way to see the major sights of Canberra is with the Red Bus, operated by Canberra Day Tours, which makes a regular circuit around the major attractions. Tickets are A$35, and you can hop on and off all day. Go Bush Tours runs half- and full-day tours of Canberra and the surrounding countryside.

The impressive Canberra and Region Visitor Centre, open weekdays 9–5 and weekends 9–4, is a convenient stop for those entering Canberra by road from Sydney or the north. The staff makes accommodation bookings for Canberra and the Snowy Mountains.

ESSENTIALS

Bus Contacts Bus Information Centre (✉ *East Row, near London Circuit, Canberra City* ☎ *13–1710* ⊕ *www.action.act.gov.au).* **Greyhound Australia** (☎ *1300/4739–4699).* **Murrays Australia** (☎ *13–2251).*

Hospitals Canberra Hospital (✉ *Yamba Dr., Garran* ☎ *02/6244–2222* ⊕ *www. canberrahospital.act.gov.au).*

Pharmacies Capital Chemist (✉ *O'Connor Shopping Centre, Sargood St., O'Connor* ☎ *02/6248–7050).*

DID YOU KNOW?

Masked boobies, brown noddies, providence petrels, red-tailed topic birds, and sooty terns will be more than just the cute names of feathered friends after a few days on LHI (as the locals call Lord Howe Island). The skies are full of birds gliding and swooping on the warm currents, while at ground level Lord Howe wood hens will be picking at your feet. It's a birdlovers' paradise.

Taxis and Shuttles Canberra Cabs
(☎ 13–2227). **Deane's Buslines**
(☎ 02/6299–3722 ⊕ www.deanesbus
lines.com.au).

**Train Contacts Canberra Railway
Station** (☎ 02/6208–9700). **CountryLink** (☎ 13–2232 ⊕ www.coun-
trylink.info).

WORD OF MOUTH

"Canberra is the nation's capital
and there are loads of great
museums and galleries. It's not
the greatest capital city in the
world—but still worth a look."
—fuzzylogic

3

**Tour Information Canberra Day
Tours** (☎ 0418/455099 ⊕ www.canberradaytours.com.au). **Go Bush Tours**
(☎ 02/6231–3023 ⊕ www.gobushtours.com.au). **Destiny Tours** (☎ 02/9943–
0167 ⊕ www.destinytours.com.au).

Visitor Information Canberra and Region Visitor Centre (✉ 330 North-
bourne Ave., Dickson ☎ 02/6205–0044 ⊕ www.visitcanberra.com.au).

EXPLORING CANBERRA

Canberra's most important public buildings stand within the Parliamentary Triangle. Lake Burley Griffin wraps around its northeast
edge, while Commonwealth and Kings avenues radiate from Capital
Hill, the city's political and geographical epicenter, to form the west
and south boundaries. The triangle can be explored comfortably on
foot, but a vehicle is required to see the rest of this area. The monuments and other attractions within the Parliamentary Triangle and
around Lake Burley Griffin are not identified by street numbers but
all are clearly signposted.

*Numbers in the text correspond to numbers in the margin and on the
Canberra map.*

CENTRAL CANBERRA

You can visit virtually all of central Canberra's major attractions by
car, but in some places parking and walking may be more convenient.
Around town you can use the local ACTION buses, which stop at
most of the other sights, or join the hop-on, hop-off Canberra Day
Tours bus.

TOP ATTRACTIONS

①
Fodor'sChoice
★

Australian War Memorial. Both as a moving memorial to Australians
who served their country in wartime and as a military museum, this is
a shrine of great national importance and the most popular attraction
in the capital. The museum explores Australian military involvement
from the late 19th century through the 1970s and Vietnam up to Iraq
and Afghanistan today. Displays include a Lancaster bomber, a Spitfire,
tanks, landing barges, and sections of two of the Japanese midget sub-
marines that infiltrated Sydney Harbour during World War II, as well as
more interactive displays in the new Anzac Hall. You can best appreciate the impressive facade of the War Memorial from the broad avenue of
Anzac Parade. Anzac is an acronym for the Australian and New Zealand
Army Corps, formed during World War I. The avenue is flanked by several memorials commemorating the Army, Navy, Air Force, and Nursing

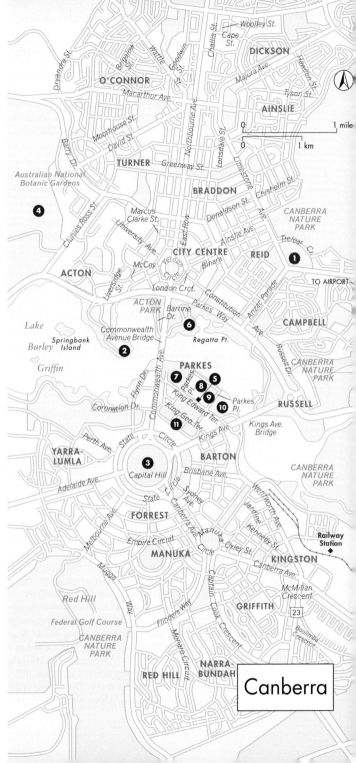

Canberra

Corps, as well as some of the campaigns in which Australian troops have fought, including the Vietnam War. ⊠ *Treloar Crescent., Campbell* ☎ *02/6243–4211* ⊕ *www.awm.gov. au* ⊠ *Free* ⊙ *Daily 10–5.*

⓾ National Gallery of Australia. The most comprehensive collection of Australian art in the country is on exhibit in the nation's premier art gallery, including superlative works of Aboriginal art and paintings by such famous native sons as Arthur Streeton, Sidney Nolan, and Arthur Boyd. The gallery also contains a sprinkling of works by European and American masters, including Rodin, Picasso, Pollock, and Warhol, as well as art and artifacts from closer to home, Southeast Asia. Free guided tours on a variety of topics with excellent guides begin in the foyer each day—check the Web site for details. In 2010 a new wing dedicated to indigenous art will open. ⊠ *Parkes Pl., Parkes* ☎ *02/6240– 6502* ⊕ *www.nga.gov.au* ⊠ *Free* ⊙ *Daily 10–5.*

> **LAKE BURLEY**
>
> Many of the main sights of Canberra are on the edge of Lake Burley Griffin. The Central Basin between Commonwealth and Kings Avenue bridges is a great place to begin a stroll, as it's close to such attractions as the National Library, the National Gallery of Australia, and the National Capital Exhibition. A bike ride or a boat cruise are other great ways to see the lake.

NEED A BREAK?

A good spot to catch your breath amid the Parliamentary Triangle's mix of history, culture, and science is Bookplate (⊠ *Parkes Pl., Parkes* ☎ *02/6262–1154*), in the foyer of the National Library; it extends out onto a patio overlooking the lake. Sandwiches, salads, cakes, and tea and coffee are served weekdays 8:30–6 and weekends 11–3.

❼ National Library of Australia. The library, constructed loosely on the design of the Parthenon in Athens, houses more than 5 million books and 500,000 photographs, maps, drawings, and recordings of oral history. Don't miss the state-of-the-art Treasures Gallery, scheduled to open in 2010, which will feature 80 of the Library's prized pieces, such as Captain James Cook's journal of the *Endeavour* and Australia's only complete original convict uniform. One-hour behind-the-scenes tours take place Tuesday at 12:30. ⊠ *Parkes Pl., Parkes* ☎ *02/6262–1111* ⊕ *www.nla.gov.au* ⊠ *Free* ⊙ *Daily 9–5.*

❷ National Museum of Australia. This unstuffy museum is spectacularly set
Fodor'sChoice on Acton Peninsula, thrust out over the calm waters of Lake Burley
★ Griffin. The museum highlights the stories of Australia and Australians by exploring the key people, events, and issues that shaped and influenced the nation. Memorabilia include a carcass of the extinct Tasmanian tiger, the old Bentley beloved by former Prime Minister Robert Menzies, and the black baby garments worn by dingo victim Azaria Chamberlain (whose story was made famous in the Meryl Streep film *A Cry in the Dark*). ⊠ *Lennox Crossing, Acton Peninsula* ☎ *02/6208– 5000* ⊕ *www.nma.gov.au* ⊠ *Free* ⊙ *Daily 9–5.*

❺ National Portrait Gallery. This terrific space opened in 2009 is dedicated to portraits of people who have shaped Australia and who in some way reflect the national identity. Look out for famous faces like pop star Kylie Minogue and Olympic champion Cathy Freeman, as well as priceless portraits of Captain James Cook. The building on the south shore of Lake Burley Griffin caused some controversy, but most architecture fans like its simple, clean design. The gallery also has a good arts program offering talks and film screenings, and the café's outdoor terrace has lovely views. ⊠ *King Edward Terrace, Parkes* ☎ *02/6270–8236* ⊕ *www. portrait.gov.au* 🔳 *Free* ⊙ *Daily 10* AM–5 PM.

⓫ Museum of Australian Democracy. This new museum is inside of the Old Parliament House. In 1988 politicians moved to their more modern digs, and in 2009 the building was transformed into this highly interactive museum. Curators use stories of real people and events to trace the history of democracy both in Australia and abroad. The museum was three years in the making, and features five exhibits, as well as the opportunity to see the original chambers and prime minister's office. While you're in the area, take a stroll through the delightful **Rose Gardens** on both sides of the Old Parliament House building. Across the road from the entrance, visit the controversial **Aboriginal Tent Embassy,** established in 1972 to proclaim the Aboriginals as Australia's "first people" and to promote recognition of their fight for land rights. ⊠ *King George Terrace, Parkes* ☎ *02/6270–8222* ⊕ *www.moadoph.gov.au* 🔳 *A$2* ⊙ *Daily 9–5.*

❸ Parliament House. Much of this vast futuristic structure is submerged,
Fodor's Choice   covered by a domed glass roof that follows the contours of Capital Hill.
★   You approach the building across a vast courtyard with a central mosaic titled *Meeting Place,* designed by Aboriginal artist Nelson Tjakamarra. Native timber has been used almost exclusively throughout the building, and the work of some of Australia's finest contemporary artists hangs on the walls.

Parliament generally sits Monday to Thursday mid-February to late June and mid-August to mid-December. Both chambers have public galleries, but the debates in the House of Representatives, where the prime minister sits, are livelier and more newsworthy than those in the Senate. The best time to observe the House of Representatives is during **Question Time** (☎ *02/6277–4889 sergeant-at-arms' office*), starting at 2, when the government and the opposition are most likely to be at each other's throats. To secure a ticket for Question Time, contact the sergeant-at-arms' office. Guided tours take place every half hour from 9 to 4. ⊠ *Capital Hill* ☎ *02/6277–5399* ⊕ *www.aph.gov.au* 🔳 *Free* ⊙ *Daily 9–5, later when Parliament is sitting.*

WORTH NOTING

❹ Australian National Botanic Gardens. Australian plants and trees have evolved in isolation from the rest of the world, and these delightful gardens on the lower slopes of Black Mountain display the continent's best collection of this unique flora. The rain forest, rock gardens, Tasmanian alpine garden, and eucalyptus lawn—with more than 600 species of eucalyptus—number among the 125-acre site's highlights. Two self-guided nature trails start from the rain-forest gully, and free guided tours depart from the visitor center daily at 11 and 2. Prebooked and

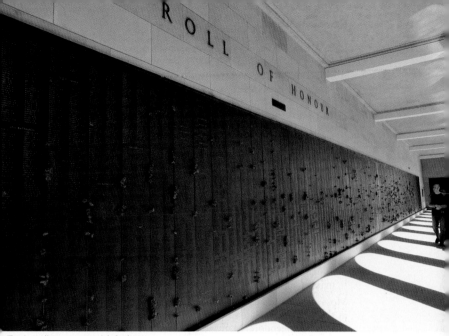

The Australian war memorial, Canberra.

more individualized guided tours cost A$4 per person. In January and February there is also a tour at 9:30 AM. ⊠ *Clunies Ross St., Black Mountain* ☎ *02/6250-9540* ⊕ *www.anbg.gov.au* ☒ *Free* ☉ *Jan., weekends 8:30-8; Feb.–Dec., weekdays 8:30-6, weekends 8:30-5. Visitor center daily 9–4:30.*

⑨ High Court of Australia. As its name implies, this gleaming concrete-and-glass structure is the ultimate court of law in the nation's judicial system. The court of seven justices convenes only to determine constitutional matters or major principles of law. Inside the main entrance, the public hall contains a number of murals depicting constitutional and geographic themes. Each of the three courtrooms over which the justices preside has a public gallery, and you can observe the proceedings when the court is in session. ⊠ *Parkes Pl. off King Edward Terrace, Parkes* ☎ *02/6270-6811 or 02/6270-6850* ⊕ *www.hcourt.gov.au* ☒ *Free* ☉ *Mon.–Fri. 9:45-4:30.*

⑥ National Capital Exhibition. Photographs, plans, audiovisual displays, and a laser model inside this lakeside pavilion illustrate the past, present, and future development of Canberra. Exhibits cover the time of the early settlers, Walter Burley Griffin's winning design for the city, and plans for the coming decades. From the pavilion's terrace there are sweeping views of the Parliamentary Triangle across the lake. The restaurant and kiosk on the terrace serve full meals and light snacks. ⊠ *Regatta Point, Barrine Dr., Commonwealth Park* ☎ *02/6257-1068* ⊕ *www.national-capital.gov.au* ☒ *Free* ☉ *Weekdays 9–5, weekends 10–4.*

⑧ Questacon—The National Science and Technology Centre. This interactive ☼ science facility is the city's most entertaining museum, especially for kids. About 200 hands-on exhibits in seven galleries including spaces on sport and music use high-tech computer gadgetry and anything from pendulums to feathers to illustrate principles of mathematics, physics, and human perception. Staff members explain the scientific principles behind the exhibits, and science shows take place regularly. ⊠ *King Edward Terrace, corner of Mall Rd. W, Parkes* ☎ *02/6270–2800* ⊕ *www.questacon.edu.au* ⬚ *A$18* ⊙ *Daily 9–5.*

WINE TOURING AROUND CANBERRA

Wineries began popping up everywhere around Canberra in the late 1990s, once it was discovered that the cool climate was optimal for producing Chardonnays, Rieslings, Cabernets, Shirazes, Merlots, and Pinots. There are now about 140 vineyards, 30 of which have cellar doors, set in the peaceful rural countryside surrounding the city—mostly small operations, where visiting the cellar door usually involves sampling the wines in the tasting room. There is no charge for tastings, although the vintners hope you'll be impressed enough with the wine to make some purchases.

Most are a maximum of 30 minutes from the city and are concentrated in the villages of Hall and Murrumbateman and in the Lake George area and Bungendore. Many are open to visits on weekends only. If you want to explore the wineries on your own, pick up a copy of *The Canberra District Wineries Guide* from the Canberra and Region Visitor Centre. If you want to leave the driving to someone else, **Wine Wisdom Winery Tours** (☎ *02/6260–7773* ⊕ *www.winewisdom.com.au*) specializes in personally tailored wine-tour itineraries in the region.

WINERIES ALONG THE BARTON HIGHWAY

From Canberra take the Barton Highway (25) in the direction of Yass. After 20 km (12 mi) you'll reach a trio of wineries.

Brindabella Hills Winery. It's worth heading to their cellar door (weekends only) to taste the much-praised 2006 Shiraz, one of the varieties that this family-run operation specializes in. There are picnic and BBQ facilities available, and the nearby mountains make a lovely backdrop to an outdoor feast. ⊠ *156 Woodgrove Close, Via Hall* ☎ *02/6230–2583* ⊕ *www.brindabellahills.com.au* ⊙ *Cellar door weekends only 10–5, weekdays for purchases only 10–5.*

Surveyors Hill Winery. Stop here to taste the Riesling, Chardonnay, and Sauvignon Blanc blends, and, new for 2010, the winery is branching out into Italian varieties like Tempranillo. As well as the simple cellar door, the owners offer light meals to go with their wines. They make ample use of olives from their trees and other produce sourced from the property's gardens. Guests can also stay overnight at their B&B, which can accommodate up to 12 people in both the original family homestead and the new more modern units. ⊠ *215 Brooklands Rd., Wallaroo* ☎ *02/6230–2046* ⊕ *www.survhill.com.au* ⊙ *Cellar door Sat.–Sun. 10–5.*

Wily Trout Winery. This favorite among gourmands is just 25 minutes from Canberra. Here you'll find a tasting room offering good examples

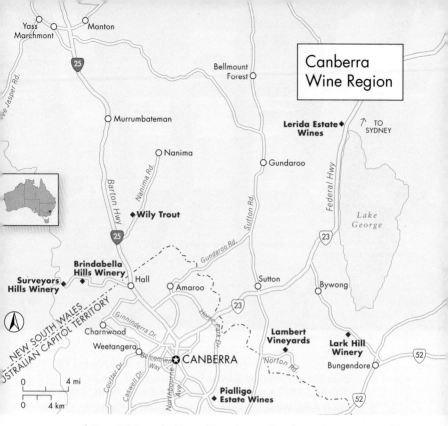

Canberra
Wine Region

of Pinot Noir and Shiraz. The winery also shares its property with **Poachers Pantry** and the award-winning **Smokehouse Cafe.** Stock up on picnic-style smoked meats, poultry, and vegetables at the Pantry, or visit the Cafe for a memorable countryside dining experience. ✉ *431 Nanima Rd., Hall* ☎ *02/6230–2487* ⊕ *www.wilytrout.com.au* ✆ *Daily 10–5.*

WINERIES ALONG THE FEDERAL HIGHWAY

From Canberra take the Federal Highway (23) for about 30 km (19 mi) north toward Sydney until you reach the Lake George area.

Lark Hill Winery. This family-run enterprise overlooking (the usually bone-dry) Lake George specializes in biodynamic Riesling, Chardonnay, and Pinot Noir varieties. After your tasting, be sure to try the renowned fine-dining restaurant (weekends only) and sit out on the deck that looks out over the vines. ✉ *Cnr. Bungendore Rd. and Joe Rocks Rd., Bungendore* ☎ *02/6238–1393* ⊕ *www.larkhillwine.com.au* ✆ *Wed.–Mon. 10–5, restaurant Sat.–Sun. lunch only.*

Lambert Vineyards. You either like the style of this modern complex with cellar door and café or you don't —it provokes strong opinions on the Canberra wine trail. Its wines are generally popular, however. As it is more than 800 m above sea level, it produces mostly red cool-climate varieties. After your tasting, don't miss the barrel room, which holds

The Australian Federal Parliament, Canberra.

approximately 250 barrels of maturing wine. ⊠ *810 Norton Rd., Wamboin* ☎ *02/6238–3866* ⊕ *www.lambertvineyards.com.au* ⊘ *Cellar door Fri.–Sun. 10–5, café Fri.–Sun. lunch and dinner, Thurs. dinner only.*

Lerida Estate Wines. Forty-five km (28 mi) out of Canberra, this award-winning winery is as famous for its design by Pritzker Prize–winning architect Glenn Murcutt as it is for its mid-price bottles. Try the Proprietor's Selection if its available at the cellar door—the 2006 Chardonnay is excellent. The tasting room and adjoining café, which offers light seasonal meals, enjoy lovely views over the often dry Lake George. Visitors who make an appointment in advance can take a tour of the winery followed by tutored wine tasting. ⊠ *Federal Hwy., Lake George* ☎ *02/6295–6640* ⊕ *www.leridaestate.com* ⊘ *Cellar door daily 10–5, café weekends 10–5.*

Pialligo Estate Wines. The closest winery to Canberra is this lovely estate set on the banks of the Molonglo River, close to the airport. The beautiful rose gardens make a perfect backdrop while enjoying a glass of their 2008 Rosé. After your tasting session, the café offers antipasto platters and heartier fare, with much of the produce from their garden. In summer, sit outside and watch the sun set behind Parliament House in the distance. ⊠ *8 Kallaroo Rd., Pialligo* ☎ *02/6262–6692* ⊕ *www. pialligoestate.com.au* ⊘ *Cellar door daily 10–5, café Wed.–Sun. 10–5.*

WHERE TO EAT

CENTRAL CANBERRA AND NORTHERN SUBURBS

\$\$\$ ✕ **Boat House by the Lake.** There's nothing more relaxing than looking out over the water of Lake Burley Griffin as you dine on the superb food in an exc. High ceilings give the restaurant a spacious, open feel, and tall windows provide lovely views of the lake. Unusual and innovative choices, all priced at A\$38, include Snowy Mountains venison loin with porcini pithivier and wilted silverbeet. Several excellent Australian wines are on hand to complement your meal. Leave room for scrumptious desserts like Black Forest brûlée with kirsch cream. ✉ *Menindie Dr., Grevillea Park, Barton* ☎ *02/6273–5500* ⊕ *www.boathousebythelake. com.au* ▭ *AE, DC, MC, V* ⊗ *Closed Sun. No lunch Sat.* ✛ *D4.*

\$\$ ✕ **The Chairman and Yip.** The menu at this longtime fusion favorite gar-
Fodor'sChoice ners universal praise for its innovative mix of Asian and Western flavors
★ against a backdrop of artifacts from Maoist China. Menu standouts include the duck pancakes and the steamed barramundi with kumquats, ginger, and shallots. Finish with a delicious dessert, such as cinnamon-and-star-anise crème brûlée. The service and wine list are outstanding, but you can still bring your own bottle of wine if you like. ✉ *108 Bunda St., Canberra City* ☎ *02/6248–7109* ⊕ *www.thechairmanandyip.com* ⌂ *Reservations essential* ▭ *AE, DC, MC, V* 🍴 *BYO* ⊗ *Closed Sun. No lunch Sat.* ✛ *C2.*

\$\$–\$\$\$ ✕ **Courgette.** Creative food served in spacious, sedate surroundings is
AUSTRALIAN the specialty of this popular restaurant on the city's outer edge. The seasonal menu has such dreamy dishes as thyme-and-sage roast pheasant with smoked bacon or the crispy-skin snapper with salt cod and scallop hash browns. Leave room for the decadent white-chocolate parfait with toasted vanilla marshmallow, fresh raspberries, and raspberry sorbet. The wine cellar here is impressive, and you can sample vintages of Australian and overseas wines by the bottle or glass. ✉ *54 Marcus Clarke St., Canberra City* ☎ *02/6247–4042* ⊕ *www.courgette.com.au* ▭ *AE, DC, MC, V* ⊗ *Closed Sun. No lunch Sat.* ✛ *B2.*

\$\$\$\$ ✕ **The Ginger Room.** A regular haunt of politicians and journalists, the
AUSTRALIAN sensitively restored private members' dining room of old Parliament
Fodor'sChoice House is comfortable and elegant, and offers fine dining at afford-
★ able prices. The contemporary menu offers Asian-influenced dishes like grilled Atlantic salmon with dates, pickled cucumber, and lemon chili vinaigrette. The high quality makes two courses for \$49 is an absolute steal. The wine list is judged to be Canberra's best. ✉ *Old Parliament House, King George Terrace, Parkes* ☎ *02/6270–8262* ⊕ *www. gingercatering.com.au* ⌂ *Reservations essential* ▭ *AE, DC, MC, V* ⊗ *No lunch Tues., Wed., and Sat. Closed Sun. and Mon.* ✛ *B4.*

\$\$ ✕ **Tosolini's.** A long-standing favorite with Canberra's café society, this
ITALIAN Italian-accented brasserie offers a choice of indoor or sidewalk tables to watch the world go by from. As well as excellent coffee and cakes, heartier dishes like homemade pasta, risotto, focaccia, and square-cut pizza are also available—but plan around the lunch crush. You can bring your own bottle of wine to dinner if you like. ✉ *East Row at London Circuit, Canberra City* ☎ *02/6247–4317* ⊕ *www.tosolinis.com.au* ▭ *AE, DC, MC, V* 🍴 *BYOB* ✛ *B2.*

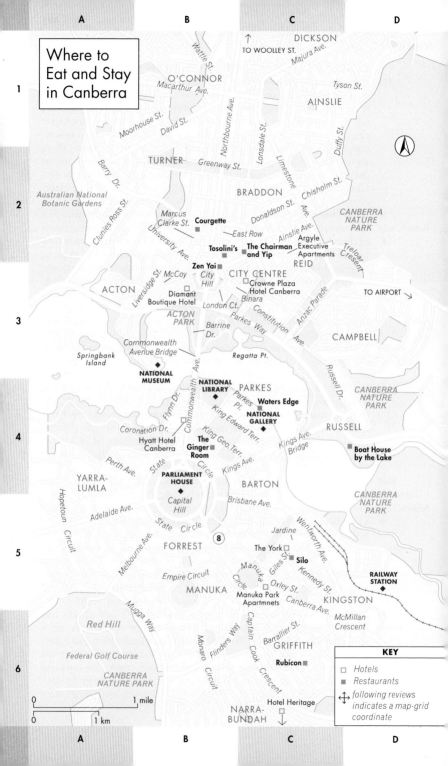

Where to Eat and Stay in Canberra

Key

- □ Hotels
- ■ Restaurants
- ↔ following reviews indicates a map-grid coordinate

0 — 1 mile

0 — 1 km

$ ✕**Zen Yai.** From the deliciously light, tangy stir-fried noodles with king
THAI prawns in tamarind sauce to the roast duck in red curry with lychees,
★ the menu of this casual Thai restaurant is an inventive blend of traditional and contemporary flavors. The spacious dining room is a relaxing
space to share new tastes, and the dedicated staff is on hand to help
you choose dishes that suit your spice tolerance. ✉ *111–117 London
Circuit, Canberra City* ☎ *02/6262–7594* ⊕ *www.zenyai.com* ⊟ *AE,
DC, MC, V* ✛ *B3.*

SOUTHERN SUBURBS

$$ ✕**Rubicon.** Everything about this cozy romantic restaurant speaks of
attention to detail. For instance, savor the melded flavors of pan-roasted
lamb rump served with crisp parsnip, grilled pears, brandied kumquats,
and mint jus. Later you can linger over such delicious desserts as ginger-
and lime-infused crème brûlée. For a lighter meal, sample the cheese
board and a few choice picks from the extensive collection of wines.
✉ *6A Barker St., Griffith* ☎ *02/6295–9919* ⊟ *DC, MC, V* ☾ *Closed
Sun. No lunch Mon., no dinner Sat.* ✛ *C6.*

$ ✕**Silo.** It's not unusual to find a queue of hungry Canberrians waiting
CAFÉ to take away some of the delectable homemade pastries (try the black-
currant and Cabernet tart) and breads. It's also possible to sit down
for a meal at one of the few tables. The brunch menu is full of baked
treats, but we love the grilled chorizo with flat white bread. The staff
is famously rude, but the food is so good this is easy enough to ignore.
✉ *36 Giles St., Kingston* ☎ *02/6260–6060* ⊕ *www.silobakery.com.au*
⊟ *DC, MC, V* ☾ *Closed Sun. and Mon., no dinner* ✛ *C5.*

$$ ✕**Waters Edge.** At this swanky spot tables are set with fine linens and
ECLECTIC crystal, and huge windows look out over the sparkling waters of Lake
Burley Griffin. The menu cleverly blends French and Mod-Oz influences
with dishes such as roast venison loin with roasted beets and garlic
potato puree; or a luscious dessert of bitter-chocolate fondant with
star-anise and white-chocolate ice cream. For a special night out, try the
tasting menu. An impressive wine list has many by-the-glass vintages.
✉ *Commonwealth Pl. off Parkes Pl., Parkes* ☎ *02/6273–5066* ⊟ *AE,
DC, MC, V* ☾ *No lunch Mon.–Tues.* ✛ *C4.*

WHERE TO STAY

CENTRAL CANBERRA AND NORTHERN SUBURBS

$$–$$$ ▦**Crowne Plaza Hotel Canberra.** In a prime location between the city cen-
ter and the National Convention Centre, this atrium-style hotel has a
touch of luxury. Decorated in cream and honey tones, guest rooms are
large, comfortable, and well equipped. Public areas have a cool, contemporary style, with plenty of chrome and glass, giant potted plants, and
fresh flowers. **Pros:** excellent gym and pool, gambling fans will enjoy
being next door to the casino. **Cons:** hotel bars can be noisy, expensive
Internet and parking. ✉ *1 Binara St., Canberra City* ☎ *02/6247–8999
or 1300/662218* ⊕ *www.crowneplaza.com.au* ⇲ *287 rooms, 6 suites*
⛱ *In-room: refrigerator, Internet. In-hotel: 2 restaurants, bars, pool,
gym, concierge, laundry service, public Wi-Fi, parking (fee)* ⊟ *AE, DC,
MC, V* ✛ *C3.*

$$ 🏨 **Diamant Boutique Hotel.** In a city

Fodor's Choice definitely lacking in the funk factor,

★ the Diamant stands out, thanks to its groovy blend of Art Deco chic exterior and quirky interior. The contemporary art on the walls and customized furniture in the lobby make a great first impression, and bedrooms have innovative white-granite desks and Bang & Olufsen plasma TVs. The location is also superb, overlooking Lake Burley Griffen. **Pros:** great array of restaurants for a hotel of this size, beautifully landscaped modern gardens. **Cons:** bars and restaurants close very early, cheaper rooms are on the small side. ⊠ *15 Edinburgh Ave., City Center* ☎ *02/6175–2222* ⊕ *www. diamant.com.au* ⇨ *80 rooms* ⚐ *In-room: safe, DVD, Wi-Fi. In-hotel: 3 restaurants, room service, bar, gym (off-site), spa, bicycles, Wi-Fi, parking (paid), no-smoking rooms* ☐ *AE, D, DC, MC, V* ✛ *B3.*

> **RESTAURANT ROW**
>
> The main restaurant precincts are around the city center and in the trendy suburbs of Manuka and Kingston. However, many fine eateries are tucked away in such suburban centers as Griffith, Ainslie, Belconnen, and Woden. In Dickson, Canberra's Chinatown, a line of inexpensive, casual eateries along Woolley Street includes many little spots serving Vietnamese, Malaysian, Chinese, Turkish, and Italian cuisine.

SOUTHERN SUBURBS

$$–$$$ 🏨 **Hotel Heritage.** Although it's in a quiet leafy area, this budget hotel is only minutes from many of Canberra's attractions. Huddled around a large courtyard and pool, the Plain-Jane rooms are done in neutrals and have patios or balconies. With varying sizes and configurations, they can accommodate couples and family groups. The adjacent Capital Golf Course is open to guests. **Pros:** family-friendly, good-value accommodation in a pleasant area. **Cons:** breakfast buffet is overpriced, rooms look dated. ⊠ *203 Goyder St., Narrabundah* ☎ *02/6295–2944 or 1800/026346* ⊕ *www.hotelheritage.com.au* ⇨ *208 rooms* ⚐ *In-room: Wi-Fi, refrigerator. In-hotel: restaurant, room service, bar, pool, laundry facilities, business center, parking (no fee)* ☐ *AE, DC, MC, V* ✛ *C6.*

$$$$ 🏨 **Hyatt Hotel Canberra.** Occupying a National Heritage building dating

Fodor's Choice from 1924, this elegant hotel has been restored to its original Art Deco

★ splendor. Warm peach and earth tones decorate the large, luxurious rooms and spacious suites. Enormous marble bathrooms will appeal to anyone who enjoys a good soak in the tub. The hotel has extensive gardens and is within easy walking distance of the Parliamentary Triangle. Afternoon tea, served daily between 2:30 and 5 in the gracious Tea Lounge, is one of Canberra's most popular traditions. **Pros:** friendly and unobtrusive service, superb location. **Cons:** rooms that have not yet been refurbished look tired, air-con is noisy. ⊠ *Commonwealth Ave., Yarralumla* ☎ *13–1234 or 02/6270–1234* ⊕ *www.canberra.hyatt.com* ⇨ *231 rooms, 18 suites* ⚐ *In-room: safe, refrigerator, Wi-Fi. In-hotel: 2 restaurants, room service, bars, tennis court, pool, gym, spa, concierge, laundry service, public Wi-Fi, parking (no fee)* ☐ *AE, DC, MC, V* ✛ *B4.*

$$ 🏨 **Manuka Park Apartments.** The comfortable one- and two-bedroom apartments and suites in this low-rise building all have kitchens, living rooms, and laundry areas. The open floor plans give them a clean, contemporary feel. In a leafy suburb, the units are within easy walking distance of the restaurants, boutiques, and antiques stores of the Manuka shopping district. Landscaped gardens surround the apartments, all of which have a private balcony or courtyard. The more expensive two-bed units have beautifully appointed bathrooms. **Pros:** accommodating staff will stock your fridge prior to your arrival, family-friendly with strollers, cots, and baby baths available. **Cons:** heating isn't up to par in winter, some two-bed units are cramped. ⊠ *Manuka Circle at Oxley St., Manuka* ☎ *02/6239–0000 or 1800/688227* ⊕ *www.manukapark.com. au* ⏎ *40 apartments* ⚇ *In-room: kitchen, laundry facilities, refrigerator, Wi-Fi. In-hotel: pool, parking (no fee)* ⊟ *AE, DC, MC, V* ⚟ *C5.*

$$$–$$$$ **The York.** This family-owned boutique hotel in the heart of the
★ trendy Kingston café area provides a blend of comfort and convenience. Choose from roomy one- and two-bedroom suites or attractive studios with fully equipped kitchens and separate dining and living areas. All have balconies, some overlooking a quiet garden courtyard. The chic Artespresso restaurant is also an art gallery presenting quality contemporary exhibitions. **Pros:** flat-screen TVs and DVDs help to pass the time, modern decor. **Cons:** inconvenient location if you don't have your own transport, rooms overlooking the road can be noisy, no reception after 7 PM. ⊠ *31 Giles and Tench Sts., Kingston* ☎ *02/6295–2333* ⊕ *www.yorkcanberra.com.au* ⏎ *9 studios, 16 suites* ⚇ *In-room: kitchen, Internet. In-hotel: restaurant, laundry service, no elevator, parking (no fee)* ⊟ *AE, DC, MC, V* ⚟ *C5.*

NIGHTLIFE AND THE ARTS

Canberra after dark has a reputation for being dull. Actually, the city isn't quite as boring as the rest of Australia thinks, nor as lively as the citizens of Canberra would like to believe. Most venues are clustered in the city center and the fashionable southern suburbs of Manuka and Kingston. Except on weekends, few places showcase live music.

The Thursday edition of the *Canberra Times* has a "What's On" section (in the *Times Out* supplement) listing performances around the city. The Saturday edition's Arts pages also list weekend happenings.

THE ARTS

The **Canberra Theatre Centre** (⊠ *Civic Sq., Canberra City*) is the city's main live performance space. The center has two different theaters, which host productions by the Australian Ballet Company, touring theater companies, and overseas artists. The theater's ticketing agency, **Canberra Ticketing** (⊠ *Civic Sq., Canberra City* ☎ *02/6275–2700 or 1800/802025* ⊕ *www.canberraticketing.com.au*), is in the space joining the two theaters.

Smaller stage and musical companies perform at neighborhood venues like the **Erindale Theatre** (⊠ *McBryde Crescent, Wanniassa* ☎ *02/6207–2703* ⊕ *www.erindale.act.edu.au*). The Australian National University's School of Music has classical recitals and modern-style concerts on-campus at **Llewellyn Hall** (⊠ *Childers St., Acton* ☎ *02/6125–2527* ⊕ *www.anu.edu.au*).

Interior of the National Museum of Australia, Canberra.

The **Street Theatre** (✉ *Childers St. at University Ave., Canberra City* ☎ *02/6247-1223* ⊕ *www.thestreet.com.au*), near the Australian National University campus, showcases the best in local talent with excellent productions ranging from musicals to avant-garde plays.

ART GALLERIES

Apart from the major galleries listed above in the Exploring section, Canberra has a wealth of smaller private art galleries showcasing and selling the works of Australian artists. You can find paintings, sculpture, woodworking, glassware, and jewelry at these spots. Entry to most galleries is free, and it is always advisable to call ahead for business hours.

Beaver Galleries (✉ *81 Denison St., Deakin* ☎ *02/6282-5294* ⊕ *www.beavergalleries.com.au*) has four exhibition galleries and a sculpture garden, where works by contemporary Australian artists are showcased. There is also a café.

Chapman Gallery (✉ *Crescent, Manuka* ☎ *02/6295-2550* ⊕ *www.chapmangallery.com.au* ⊙ *Closed Mon. and Tues.*) has rotating exhibits by leading Australian artists, with a special emphasis on Aboriginal art.

Solander Gallery (✉ *10 Schlich St., Yarralumla* ☎ *02/6285-2218* ⊕ *www.solander.com.au* ⊙ *Closed Mon.–Wed.*) displays a range of paintings and sculpture by leading Australian artists.

NIGHTLIFE

They might not be cutting-edge, but nightspots in the city center offer everything from thumping house music to dance and comedy clubs. Many waive cover charges except for special events.

Academy Club and Candy Bar. Canberra's liveliest nightspot draws the hip crowd to its stylish, glitzy premises. The main room, which hosts DJs and live bands, attracts a young crowd. Upstairs, Candy Bar serves innovative cocktails in a chic lounge setting. ✉ *Centre Cinema Bldg., Bunda St., Canberra City* ☎ *02/6257–3355* ⊕ *www.academyclub.com.au* ✉ *A$5–A$40* ☺ *Academy Thurs.–Sat. 10 PM–late; Candy Bar Wed.–Sat. 5 PM–late.*

Casino Canberra. The European-style gaming room forgoes slot machines in favor of more sociable games like roulette, blackjack, poker, and keno. There are 40 gaming tables here, and the complex includes a restaurant and two bars. ✉ *21 Binara St., Canberra City* ☎ *02/6257–7074* ⊕ *www.casinocanberra.com.au* ✉ *Free* ☺ *Daily noon–6 AM.*

Tilley's Devine Café Gallery. This 1940s-style club was once just for women, but now anyone can sit at the wooden booths and enjoy a relaxing meeting with friends or a meal at this arty café that does a great breakfast. There's a full range of cultural events held here from poetry readings to live music—check the Web site for details. ✉ *Wattle and Brigalow Sts., Lyneham* ☎ *02/6247–7753* ⊕ *tilleys.com.au* ☺ *Mon.–Sat. 9 AM–10 PM, Sun. 9–5.*

OUTDOOR ACTIVITIES

BICYCLING Canberra has almost 160 km (100 mi) of cycle paths, and the city's relatively flat terrain and dry, mild climate make it a perfect place to explore on two wheels. One of the most popular cycle paths is the 40-km (25-mi) circuit around Lake Burley Griffin.

Mr. Spokes Bike Hire rents several different kinds of bikes, as well as tandems and baby seats. Bikes cost A$15 for the first hour, including helmet rental, A$25 for 3 hours, and A$38 for a full day. ✉ *Acton Ferry Terminal, Barrine Dr., Acton Park* ☎ *02/6257–1188* ⊕ *www.mrspokes. com.au* ☺ *Summer, daily 9–5; winter, Mon.–Fri. 10–4, weekends 9–5.*

BOATING You can rent paddleboats, kayaks, and canoes daily (except May–August) for use on Lake Burley Griffin from **Burley Griffin Boat Hire.** Rates start at A$15 for 30 minutes. ✉ *Acton Ferry Terminal, Barrine Dr., Acton Park* ☎ *02/6249–6861* ⊕ *www.actboathire.com.*

Southern Cross Cruises has daily one-hour sailings (A$15) around Lake Burley Griffin on the MV *Southern Cross* at 10 and 3. ✉ *Lotus Bay, Mariner Pl. off Alexandrina Dr., Acton Park* ☎ *02/6273–1784.*

HIKING **Namadgi National Park.** Covering almost half the total area of the Australian Capital Territory's southwest, this national park has a well-maintained network of walking trails across mountain ranges, trout streams, and some of the most accessible subalpine forests in the country. Some parts of the park were severely burned in the January 2003 bushfires, but the recovery powers of the native bush have been truly remarkable. The park's boundaries are within 35 km (22 mi) of Canberra, and its former pastures, now empty of sheep and cattle, are grazed by hundreds of eastern gray kangaroos in the early morning and late afternoon. Snow covers the higher altitudes June–September. ✉ *Visitor center: Naas–Boboyan Rd., 3 km (2 mi) south of Tharwa* ☎ *02/6207–2900 or*

13–2281 ⊕ *www.tams.act.gov.au* ▭ *Free* ☉ *Park daily 24 hrs; visitor center weekdays 9–4, weekends 9–4:30.*

Tidbinbilla Nature Reserve. The walking trails, wetlands, and animal exhibits within this reserve, many of which were badly damaged in the bushfires of 2003, have recovered beautifully since then. The park is 40 km (25 mi) southwest of Canberra. ⊠ *Paddy's River Rd., Tidbinbilla* ☎ *02/6205–1233 or 13–2281* ⊕ *www.tams.act.gov.au* ▭ *Free* ☉ *Visitor center weekdays 9–4:30, weekends 9–5. Reserve Grounds standard time 9–6, daylight saving time 9–8.*

SHOPPING

Canberra is not known for its shopping, but there are a number of high-quality arts-and-crafts outlets where you are likely to come across some unusual gifts and souvenirs. The city's markets are excellent, and the galleries and museums sell interesting and often innovative items designed and made in Australia.

Gold Creek Village. The charming streets of this shopping complex on the city's northern outskirts are lined with all sorts of fun little places to explore. Peek into art galleries and pottery shops, browse through clothing boutiques and gift stores, and nosh at several eateries. ⊠ *O'Hanlon Pl., Nicholls* ☎ *02/6230–2273* ⊕ *www.goldcreekvillage. com* ☉ *Daily 10–5.*

Old Bus Depot Markets. South of Lake Burley Griffin, a lively Sunday market is in the former Kingston bus depot. Handmade crafts are the staples here, and buskers and exotic inexpensive food enliven the shopping experience. ⊠ *Wentworth Ave., Kingston Foreshore, Kingston* ☎ *02/6292–8391* ⊕ *www.obdm.com.au* ☉ *Sun. 10–4.*

Melbourne and Victoria

WORD OF MOUTH

"I highly recommend the Great Ocean Road, staying overnight in Port Campbell—it's breathtakingly beautiful—then driving back via the Otway Ranges. There seemed to be plenty of accommodation at Port Campbell. I also found Sovereign Hill fascinating."

—emerald125

WELCOME TO MELBOURNE AND VICTORIA

TOP REASONS TO GO

★ **International Cuisine:** Melbourne's dining scene is a vast smorgasbord of cuisines: Chinese restaurants on Little Bourke Street are the equal of anything in Hong Kong. Richmond's Victoria Street convincingly reincarnates Vietnam, while a stroll through groovy Fitzroy or St. Kilda will have your mouth watering for some Mod Oz.

★ **The Amazing Outdoors:** Victoria has outstanding national parks. Bushwalking, canoeing, fishing, rafting, and horse riding are all on the menu. If you're pushed for time, there are organized day trips to to Port Campbell and the outcrops of the Grampians National Park.

★ **Wonderful Wineries:** Throughout the state you'll find hundreds of wineries, particularly in the Yarra Valley, Rutherglen, and on the Mornington Peninsula. Winery tours, departing from Melbourne, are a relaxing way to see four to five wineries in one day.

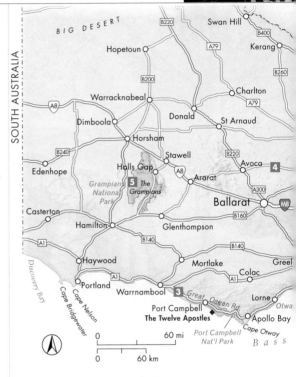

1 **Melbourne.** It's fair to stay that Melbourne revels in its great indoors—it's an elegant city with amazing restaurants, fabulous bars, first-rate entertainment, and funky lanes.

2 **Side Trips from Melbourne.** It's a breeze to visit the Yarra Valley, Morning Peninsula, or Dandenong Ranges on day trips or to rent a car and zip off to stay in grand hotels and cute cottages.

3 **Great Ocean Road.** This is the ultimate road trip along the wave lashed Southern Ocean. From Melbourne it's a 380-km (236-mi) journey that hugs the coast, with occasional detours into wooded hills.

4 **The Gold Country.** You can still pan for gold in rivers about an hour northwest of Melbourne, but today's attractions are the beautiful 19th-century towns constructed from the riches

NEW SOUTH
WALES

Murray River

6
Echuca
Shepparton
B75
Nagambie
Bendigo
Seymour
Kyneton   Yea
M79
Sunbury
YARRA VALLEY
Verribee M1
MELBOURNE
Mornington
Peninsula
Queenscliff
Torquay   Sorrento
at'l Park   PHILLIP
ISLAND   Cowes

S t r a i t

A39
B400
Albury
Wodonga
Wangaratta
B500
M31
Bright
B300
Mansfield
Eildon
GREAT DIVIDING RANGE
Healesville   Alpine
Nat'l Park
DANDENONG RANGE
M1
A1
Traralgon   Sale
Gippsland Lakes
Coastal Park
Leongatha   Yarram
A440
Corner Inlet
Cape Liptrap   Wilsons Promontory
South Point   Wilson's Promontory
National Park

GETTING ORIENTED

4

Melbourne, the capital of Victoria, is situated in the south of the state on Port Phillip Bay. With a population of almost 4 million people, it is the fastest-growing major city in Australia. The Yarra Valley wineries and the Dandenongs Ranges are an hour's drive to the east, while the beaches and vineyards of the Mornington Peninsula are a 90-minute drive south of Melbourne. The Great Ocean Road begins at Torquay, southwest of Melbourne, and continues along the Southern Ocean coast to Portland. The goldfield, spa country, and Grampians are between one and two hours northwest of Melbourne; the Murray River Region and its wineries are about a three-hour drive north to northeast of Melbourne.

of the goldfields. Walking trails outline the stories of lucky strikes and miners' fights for justice, while natural spas and wineries are all within a two-hour drive.

5 The Grampians. A series of rugged sandstone ranges covered with native bushland, the Grampians National Park is a wilderness area just three hours from Melbourne.

6 Murray River Region. The mighty Murray River forms the border between Victoria and New South Wales, and is a natural playground. Houseboats, speedboats, and old paddlewheelers share the river, and golf courses and parks flank the riverbanks.

MELBOURNE PLANNER

Visitor Information

The Melbourne Visitor Centre at Federation Square provides touring details in six languages. Large-screen videos and touch screens add to the experience, and permanent displays follow the city's history. Daily newspapers are available, and there's access to the Melbourne Web site, ⊕ *www.visitmelbourne.com*. The center is open daily 9–6. The Best of Victoria Booking Service here can help if you're looking for accommodations. It also has cheap Internet access.

City Ambassadors—usually mature men and women easily spotted by their red uniforms—are volunteers for the City of Melbourne, and rove the central retail area providing directions and information for people needing their assistance (Monday–Saturday 10–5).

A free bus route map is available from the Melbourne Visitor Centre.

Information Best of Victoria Booking Service (☎ *03/9642–1055 or 1300/780045*). **City of Melbourne Ambassadors Program** (☎ *03/9658–9658*). **Melbourne Visitor Centre** (✉ *Federation Sq., Flinders and Swanston Sts., City Center* ☎ *03/9658-9658* ⊕ *www. melbourne.vic.gov.au or www. thatsmelbourne.com.au*).

Getting Here and Around

By Plane

Melbourne is most easily reached by plane, as it's hours by car from the nearest big city. International airlines flying into Melbourne include Air New Zealand, British Airways, United, Singapore Airlines, Emirates, Thai Airways, Malaysia Airlines, V Australia, and Qantas.

By Train

Southern Cross Railway Station is at Spencer and Little Collins streets. From here the countrywide V-Line has 11-hour trips to Sydney, as well as services to many regional centers in Victoria. V-Line buses connect with the trains to provide transport to coastal towns; take the train to Marshall (one stop beyond Geelong) to connect with a bus to Lorne, Apollo Bay, and Port Campbell, or travel by train to Warrnambool and take a bus to Port Fairy.

By Car

Melbourne's regimented layout makes it easy to negotiate by car, but two unusual rules apply because of the tram traffic. Trams should be passed on the *left*, and when a tram stops to allow passengers to disembark, the cars behind it also must stop. Motorists using various tollways have 72 hours to pay the toll after using the highway. To pay by credit card, call ☎ *13–2629*. Alternatively, you can buy passes at the airport before using the tollways. A weekend pass is around A$10.

By Bus and tram

Melbourne into three zones. Zone 1 is the urban core, where most travelers spend their time. The basic ticket (the Metcard) is the one-zone ticket, which can be purchased on board the bus or tram (or purchased at 7-11 stores, Melbourne Town Hall, and the Melbourne Visitors Centre at Federation Square) for A$3.70. It's valid for travel within a specific zone on any bus, tram or train for two hours after purchase. For travelers, the most useful ticket is probably the Zone 1 day ticket, which costs A$6.80. Trams run until midnight, and can be hailed wherever you see a green-and-gold tram-stop sign.

About the Restaurants

Melbourne teems with top-quality restaurants, particularly in St. Kilda, South Yarra, and the Waterfront City precinct including Docklands. Lygon Street is still a favorite with those who love great coffee and Italian bakeries, while the city center also has many back alleys (known as laneways) with popular cafés. Reservations are generally advised, and although most places are licensed to sell alcohol, the few that aren't usually allow you to bring your own. Lunch is served noon–2:30, and dinner is usually 7–10:30. A 10% tip is customary for exemplary service, and there may be a corkage fee in BYO restaurants. Chefs in Victoria take pride in their trendsetting preparations of fresh local produce. International flavors are found in both casual and upscale spots, while winery restaurants are excellent choices for leisurely lunches. On Sunday be sure to join in the Victorian tradition of an all-day "brekky."

About the Hotels

Staying in the heart of Melbourne, on Collins or Flinders Streets and their nearby laneways, or at Southbank, is ideal for those who like dining and shopping. Another trendy area, a little out of town, is South Yarra, which also has excellent shopping. Wherever you stay, make sure you're near a tram, bus, or train line. Accommodations in Victoria include grand country hotels, roadside motels, secluded bushland or seaside cabins, friendly bed-and-breakfasts, and backpacker hostels.

DINING AND LODGING PRICE CATEGORIES (IN AUSTRALIAN DOLLARS)

	¢	$	$$	$$$	$$$$
Restaurants	under A$10	A$10–A$20	A$21–A$35	A$36–A$50	over A$50
Hotels	under A$100	A$100–A$150	A$151–A$200	A$201–A$300	over A$300

Restaurant prices are based on the median main-course price at dinner. Hotel prices include taxes, and are for two people in a standard double room in high season, excluding service.

When to Go

Melbourne and Victoria are at their most beautiful in autumn, from March to May. Days are crisp, and the foliage in parks and gardens is glorious. Melbourne winters can be gloomy, although the wild seas and leaden skies from June to August provide a suitable backdrop for the dramatic coastal scenery of the Great Ocean Road. By September the weather begins to clear, and the football finals are on. Book early to visit Melbourne during the Spring Racing Carnival and the Melbourne International Festival (late October/early November) and during mid-January when the Australian Open Tennis is staged.

Health and Safety

There are medical centers around the city, but for medical emergencies contact the city hospitals. Melbourne is generally a safe city, although people should avoid deserted dark areas at night and be aware that the nightlife areas around King Street and St. Kilda can get unruly and drugs can be prevalent. There are 23 CCTV surveillance areas in the city, and safe weekend taxi ranks are located at 55 King Street, Flinders Street Station, and at 50 Bourke Street.

OUTDOOR ADVENTURES

Victoria is blessed with amazing natural sculptures. Sandstone ridges and spires tower above country plains, and the ocean is littered with bizarrely shaped coastal sea stacks and cliff faces.

Two of the best places to experience Victoria's spectacular nature is Port Campbell National Park and The Grampian National Park. The first encompasses the "best of the best" of Victoria's dramatic Great Ocean Road coastline. Stretching for about 20 km (12 mi) between the towns of Princetown and Peterborough, the park contains the iconic Twelve Apostles—huge limestone rock stacks, measuring up to 45 meters (148 feet). The Grampian is a striking series of sandstone mountain ranges. They rise dramatically above plains below and harbor several waterfalls. More than 30 walking tracks (from easy to strenuous) wind through gullies, native bushland strewn with wildflowers, and up and over hills. It's possible to drive to the most popular lookout points. There are a dozen wineries within an easy drive of the park.

WHEN TO GO

The Great Ocean Road is a popular summer road-trip, so it's best to visit Port Campbell National Park in winter, spring, or fall. Crowds thin out by the end of February, but holidaymakers return in force during Easter. Winter is suitably cold and windswept, giving an idea of the ferocious sea conditions that claimed hundreds of ships during the 19th century. Grampians National Park is very hot and uncomfortable in summer. Bushwalking and visiting cozy wineries is ideal in spring and winter; fall can still be quite warm. Campsites and hotels in Halls Gap fill up during Easter, and prices rise accordingly.

BEST WAYS TO EXPLORE

PORT CAMPBELL NATIONAL PARK

The Great Ocean Road is ideal for walking, so ideal that a Great Ocean Walk was opened a few years ago. The Great Ocean Walk begins at Marengo, just west of Apollo Bay. It stretches 91 km (57 mi) to Glenample Homestead (which is now closed), adjacent to the Twelve Apostles, passing through national parks and rugged coastline. You can set out on the walk on your own, do a few sections of it, or join an organized walking tour that has overnight stays in B&Bs and other comfortable accommodations. The Parks Victoria dedicated Great Ocean Walk Web site is ⊕ *www.greatoceanwalk.com.au*. It's easy to do something shorter as well. Walking trails and viewing platforms wind past the iconic Twelve Apostles and nearby Loch Ard Gorge, each of which can be viewed just a few hundred yards from the car park. Other major landforms—the Arch, London Bridge, and the Grotto—have boardwalk and platform viewing areas and only about a 10-minute drive (or a longer walk) from each other. Loch Ard Gorge, a bay flanked by towering cliffs and with a narrow opening, is a another spectacular sight.

GRAMPIANS NATIONAL PARK

Bushwalking is by far the most popular activity in the national park. Some of the best walks include Mackenzie Falls, the walk to Mt. Abrupt (or Mt. Murdadjoog in the Aboriginal language), the Hollow Mountain walk, and another to Silverband Falls. Even if you're not a big walker you can still see many of the best-known rock formations. Elephant Hide, the Balconies, the Pinnacle, and the Fortress are only a short walk from a car park. Canoeing is another great way to get away from the crowds and experience the lakes and rivers of the Grampians. And if you'd like a bit education with your nature, we highly recommend a visit to the Brambuk Cultural Centre. Owned and operated by the Koori people (Aboriginal people of southeastern Australia), the centre provides a unique living history of Aboriginal culture in this part of Victoria.

TIMING FOR PORT CAMPBELL

It is possible to visit Port Campbell National Park on an organized day trip from Melbourne, but a better alternative is to stay overnight at one of the nearby towns and explore the region over a half or full day. The 20-km (12-mi) coastal drive is crammed with amazing sea sculptures, and you'll be stopping in the car parks along the way to get out and walk along the boardwalks to viewing platforms and steps that lead down to the coast.

TIMING FOR THE GRAMPIANS

The most popular attractions of the central Grampians region can be visited in one day. However, if you want to visit the fascinating Bambuk Aboriginal Cultural Centre and take in a few wineries, allow yourself another day or two. From the town of Halls Gap it's only a 15-km (9-mi) drive to the spectacular Boroka Lookout (and just a 100-yard walk from the car park).

Updated by Caroline Gladstone

Separated from New South Wales by the Murray River and rimmed by a beautiful coastline, Victoria's terrain is as varied as any in the country. The beauty of visiting Victoria is the diversity of landscapes only a few hours' drive from the Melbourne, Australia's unofficial cultural capital. On Victoria's southwest coast rugged limestone cliffs and amazing off-shore weathered rock formations alternate with thick forests; inland are historic goldfield towns and striking national parks with rugged mountains and waterfalls, while vineyards line the Murray's banks.

Two acclaimed wine-growing regions—Yarra Valley and Mornington Peninsula—are within a 90-minute drive from Melbourne; the walkers' and garden lovers' paradise of the Dandenong Ranges is only an hour away. For years Melbourne's city center was seen as an inferior compared with Sydney's sparkling harbor; however, large-scale developments on both sides of the Yarra River have transformed former eyesores into vibrant entertainment precincts.

MELBOURNE

Consistently rated among the "world's most livable cities" in quality-of-life surveys, Melbourne is built on a coastal plain at the top of the giant horseshoe of Port Phillip Bay. The city center is an orderly grid of streets where the state parliament, banks, multinational corporations, and splendid Victorian buildings that sprang up in the wake of the gold rush now stand. This is Melbourne's heart, which you can explore at a leisurely pace in a couple of days.

In Southbank, one of the new precincts south of the city center, the Southgate development of bars, restaurants, and shops has refocused Melbourne's vision on the Yarra River. Once a blighted stretch of factories and run-down warehouses, the southern bank of the river is now a vibrant, exciting part of the city, and the river itself is finally taking its rightful place in Melbourne's psyche. Just a hop away, Federation Square—with its host of galleries—has become a civic landmark for Melburnians. Stroll along the Esplanade in the suburb of St. Kilda, amble past the elegant houses of East Melbourne, enjoy the shops and cafés in Fitzroy or Carlton, rub shoulders with locals at the Victoria Market, nip into the Windsor for afternoon tea, or rent a canoe at Studley Park to paddle along one of the prettiest stretches of the Yarra—and you may discover Melbourne's soul as well as its heart.

TOURS

A free City Circle tram run by Metropolitan Transit operates every 10 minutes daily 10–6 on the fringe of the Central Business District, with stops on Flinders, Spencer, La Trobe, Victoria, and Spring streets. Look for the burgundy-and-cream trams. A free orange tourist bus (the Melbourne City Tourist Shuttle) does a loop around central and inner Melbourne suburbs daily, every 30 minutes between 9:30 and 4:30, stopping at 13 destinations including Federation Square, Docklands, South Yarra, and the Botanic Gardens. Metropolitan buses operate daily until around 9 PM to all suburbs, while the NightRider bus service runs between 1:30 AM and 5:30 AM on weekends.

Boat Tours. One of the best ways to see Melbourne is from the deck of the Parks Victoria Yarra River Shuttle Service. It travels from Federation Square to Docklands, with eight stops including Southbank, the aquarium, the casino, and Victoria Harbour. Ferries depart daily every 30 minutes. Daily passes allow passengers to jump on and off en route and cost A$14. The ferry operates on weekends and public holidays from 1 AM to 8 PM.

The modern, glass-enclosed boats of the Melbourne River Cruises fleet operate 1- and 2½-hour Yarra River cruises daily (A$23 and A$29, respectively), traversing either west through the commercial heart of the city or east through the parks and gardens, or a combination of the two. Cruises run every half hour from 10 to 4.

Bus Tours. Gray Line has guided tours of Melbourne and environs by bus and boat. The City tour visits the city center's main attractions and some of the surrounding parks. The 3½-hour, A$68 tour departs daily at 8:30.

AAT Kings, Australian Pacific Tours, and Melbourne's Best Day Tours all have similar city highlight tours.

Food Tours. Foodies Dream Tours (A$30) and cooking classes (2½ hours, A$80–A$180) are conducted at Queen Victoria Market.

Chocoholic Tours offers several Saturday tours for chocolate lovers: the Chocoholic Brunch Walk (10–noon) and the Chocoholic Indulgence Walk (12:15–2:15), among others. Each offers a different combination of chocolate-fueled tastings and activities (A$35 each). Bookings are essential and departures points vary.

Vietnam on a Plate runs a guided walking tour of the Asian precincts, visiting traditional Chinese herbalists, food stalls, spice and herb specialists, and the "Little Saigon" shopping districts of Footscray and Springvale. The tour includes lunch and food tasting. Tours are usually given Saturday 9:30–12:30, and cost A$68. Reservations essential.

Walking Tours. The Melbourne Greeters service, a Melbourne Information Centre program, provides free two- to four-hour tours by pairing you with a local volunteer who shares your interests. Melbourne's Golden Mile Heritage Trail runs guided walking tours of the city's architectural and historic sites. Tours, which cost A$20 and take two hours, depart daily at 10 AM from Federation Square and finish at the Melbourne Town Hall weekdays and the Melbourne Museum on weekends.

ESSENTIALS

Tour Operators Melbourne River Cruises (⊠ Vault 11, Banana Alley, 367 Flinders St., City Center ☎ 03/8610–2600 ⊕ www.melbcruises.com.au). **Parks Victoria** (⊠ 535 Bourke St., City Center ☎ 13–1963). **AAT Kings** (⊠ Federation Square E, Flinders and Russell Sts., City Centre ☎ 1300/556100). **Australian Pacific Touring (APT)** (⊠ 475 Hampton St., Hampton ☎ 03/9277–8555 or 1300/656985). **Gray Line** (⊠ Federation Square East, Flinders and Russell Sts., City Center ☎ 1300/858687 ⊕ www.grayline.com.au). **Melbourne's Best Day Tours** (⊠ Federation Square, Flinders and Russell Sts., City Center ☎ 1300/130550 ⊕ www.melbouretours.com.au). **Chocoholic Tours** (⊠ 145/28 Southgate Ave., Southbank ☎ 03/9686–4655 ⊕ www.chocoholictours.com.au). **Foodies Dream Tours** (⊠ Queen Victoria Market, Queen and Elizabeth Sts., City Center ☎ 03/9320–5822 ⊕ www.qvm.com.au). **Vietnam on a Plate** (⊠ Footscray Market, Hopkins and Leeds Sts., Footscray ☎ 03/9687–0908). **Golden Mile Heritage Trail** (☎ 03/9928–0000 ⊕ www.visitvictoria.com). **Melbourne Greeters** (⊠ Federation Sq., Flinders and Swanston Sts., City Center ☎ 03/9658–9658 [weekdays]; 03/9658–9942 [weekends] ✉ greeter@melbourne.vic.gov.au ⊕ www.thatsmelbourne.com.au).

EXPLORING

CITY CENTER

Numbers in margin correspond to numbers on the Melbourne City Center map.

GETTING HERE AND AROUND

Melbourne and its suburbs are well served by trams, trains, and buses. The free loop tram is perfect for sightseeing, but crowded on weekends. Trams run east–west and north–south across the city, and travel to the popular St. Kilda and Docklands. The Connex train network operates a City Loop service with stops at Flinders Street, Parliament, and Southern Cross Station, where you'll find connections with a network of trains to outer areas, including the Dandenong Ranges.

TOP ATTRACTIONS

❽ Block Arcade. Melbourne's most elegant 19th-century shopping arcade dates from the 1880s, when "Marvelous Melbourne" was flush with the prosperity of the gold rushes. A century later, renovations scraped back the grime to reveal a magnificent mosaic floor. Tours (A$9) operate on Tuesday and Thursday at 1 PM and conclude with afternoon tea in the Charles Dickens Tavern. ⊠ 282 Collins St., City Center ☎ 03/9654–5244.

GREAT ITINERARIES

IF YOU HAVE 1 DAY

If you're short on time, the free **City Circle Tram** and the **Yarra River Shuttle Service** (A$14) are both hop-on and hop-off ways to see many of the city's sights without exhausting yourself. The Parliament House tram stop gives access to the Princess Theatre, the grand Windsor Hotel, **Parliament House**, the "Paris End" of Collins Street, and St. Patrick's Cathedral. Get off at Flinders Street to take a peek in **Young and Jackson's** pub at the infamous *Chloe* painting, and then walk over the **Princes Bridge**. There you can stroll along the banks of the Yarra, looking back at Federation Square, and then wander along Southbank while checking out the restaurants and shops and the **Crown Casino**. A trip to the new Eureka Skydeck, the southern hemisphere's highest viewing platform, will put the city into perspective, and you can decide whether or not you want to head northeast to Fitzroy for a meander along groovy **Brunswick Street**, or north towards **Carlton** to immerse yourself in Little Italy.

IF YOU HAVE 3 DAYS

You might squeeze in a bit more exploring on Day 1 with a stroll through Treasury Gardens and over to Fitzroy Gardens for a look at Captain Cook's Cottage, or see the sharks at the **Melbourne Aquarium** opposite Southbank. On your second day, stroll through the **Royal Botanic Gardens** and see the **Shrine of Remembrance**. Then take a tram on St. Kilda Road to the hip **Acland Street area**, in the suburb of **St. Kilda**, for dinner. On Day 3, take a tour of Chapel Street's shops, restaurants, and bars; it's Melbourne's hippest district.

IF YOU HAVE 5 DAYS

Head east to the Yarra Valley on an organized winery tour, or head to the Dandenong Ranges for a ride on the Puffing Billy steam railway from Belgrave through the fern gullies and forests of the Dandenong ranges. On the way back, stop at a teahouse in Belgrave or Olinda and browse the curio stores. Or take an evening excursion to Phillip Island for the endearing sunset **Penguin Parade**. A trip to the **Mornington Peninsula** wineries and **Arthurs Seat**, just 90 minutes south of Melbourne, is another great day trip. There you can rest and recuperate with a soak in the **Peninsula Hot Springs**.

IF YOU HAVE 7 DAYS OR MORE.

Hang out in Melbourne for 2 days, and on Day 3 drive to the Dandenong Ranges and poke around the cute towns and fabulous gardens, or visit one or two wineries in the Yarra Valley.

On Day 4 head south, either to the Mornington Peninsula or Phillip Island; the former promises beaches and wines, the latter beaches and wildlife.

On Day 5 make your way to the Mornington Peninsula town of Sorrento and take the car ferry across to Queenscliff. Check out the old fort in town before heading west to join the Great Ocean. Choose Princetown or Port Campbell for an overnight stop and spend the afternoon exploring the Twelve Apostles. On Day 6 either head north to Ballarat and the goldfields or northwest to the Grampians. Then take the Western Highway back to Melbourne.

4

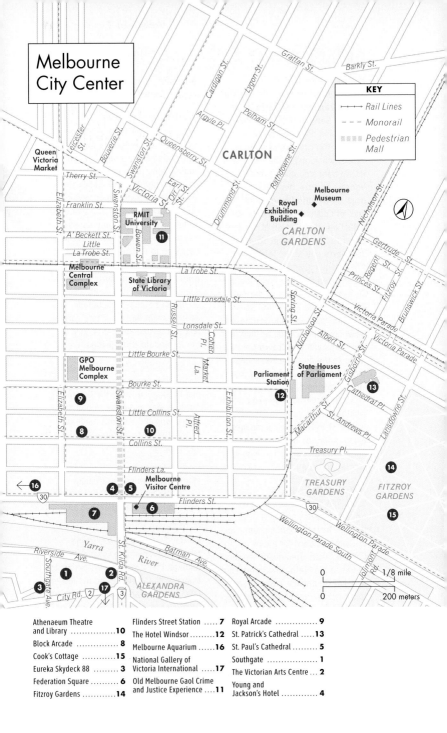

Melbourne City Center

CARLTON

KEY
- Rail Lines
- Monorail
- Pedestrian Mall

Queen Victoria Market

Leicester St.

Bouverie St.

Swanston St.

Queensberry St.

Cardigan St.

Argyle Pl.

Lygon St.

Grattan St.

Pelham St.

Barkly St.

Therry St.

Elizabeth St.

Franklin St.

A' Beckett St.

Little La Trobe St.

RMIT University

Victoria St.

Earl St.

Drummond St.

Rathdowne St.

Melbourne Museum

Royal Exhibition Building

CARLTON GARDENS

Nicholson St.

Gertrude St.

Regent St.

Fitzroy St.

Princes St.

Brunswick St.

11

Melbourne Central Complex

State Library of Victoria

La Trobe St.

Little Lonsdale St.

Spring St.

Victoria Parade

Albert St.

Victoria Parade

Russell St.

Lonsdale St.

Cohen Pl.

Nicholson St.

Princes St.

GPO Melbourne Complex

Little Bourke St.

Market La.

Parliament Station

State Houses of Parliament

Cathedral Pl.

13

Bourke St.

Swanston St.

9

Little Collins St.

Alfred Pl.

Exhibition St.

12

Macarthur St.

St. Andrews Pl.

Lansdowne St.

8

10

Collins St.

Treasury Pl.

Flinders La.

Melbourne Visitor Centre

Flinders St.

TREASURY GARDENS

14

FITZROY GARDENS

Elizabeth St.

16

30

4 **5**

6

7

Flinders St.

Wellington Parade South

Wellington Parade

30

15

Yarra River

Riverside Ave.

Southgate Ave.

St. Kilda Rd.

Batman Ave.

1

2

Jolimont Rd.

3

City Rd. 2

17

3

ALEXANDRA GARDENS

0   1/8 mile

0   200 meters

6 ★ Federation Square. Encompassing a whole city block, the bold, abstract-style landmark was designed to house the second branch of the National Gallery of Victoria, which exhibits only Australian art. The square also incorporates the Centre for the Moving Image; the BMW Edge amphitheater, a contemporary music and theater performance venue; the Victorian Wine Precinct, showcasing the best of local wines; Champions: Australian Racing Museum; the Melbourne Visitor Centre; and restaurants, bars, and gift shops. ✉ *Flinders St. between Swanston and Russell Sts., City Center* ☎ *03/9655–1900* ⊕ *www.fedsquare.com* 🎫 *Free* ⊙ *Daily 10–5; National Gallery of Victoria closed Mon.*

> **EXPLORING THE THEATERS**
>
> Melburnians love their theater, and major shows often open in Melbourne first. If you want to take in Broadway or West End–style theater in grand surroundings, check out what's playing at the Regent and the Princess. Both are owned by Marriner Theatres, which lovingly restored the Regent for its reopening in the mid-1990s. You can tread the boards (i.e., act on stage) with a theater-loving tour guide on the Historic Rambles tour. Contact Wilma Farrow (☎ 03/9820–0239) for details. For performances, check out ⊕ *www.marrinertheatres.com.au.*

14 Fitzroy Gardens. This 65-acre expanse of European trees, manicured lawns, garden beds, statuary, and sweeping walks is Melbourne's most popular central park. Among its highlights is the **Avenue of Elms,** a majestic stand of 130-year-old trees that is one of the few in the world that has not been devastated by Dutch elm disease. ✉ *Lansdowne St. at Wellington Parade, East Melbourne* 🎫 *Free* ⊙ *Daily sunrise–sunset.*

7 Flinders Street Station. Melburnians use the clocks on the front of this grand Edwardian hub of Melbourne's suburban rail network as a favorite meeting place. When it was proposed to replace them with television screens, an uproar ensued. Today there are both clocks and screens. ✉ *Flinders St. at St. Kilda Rd., City Center.*

12 ★ The Hotel Windsor. Not just a grand hotel, the Windsor is home to one of Melbourne's proudest institutions—the ritual of afternoon tea (A$45 mid-week; A$65 weekends), which is served daily from 3–5. The Chocolate Indulgence, available on weekends June–October (from A$65), offers up a vast selection of chocolates, chef-prepared crepes, a chocolate fountain, and other goodies. Although the Grand Ball Room—a Belle Époque extravaganza with a gilded ceiling and seven glass cupolas—is reserved for to private functions, occasionally afternoon tea is served there, so it's best to call first to check. ✉ *111 Spring St., City Center* ☎ *03/9633–6000* ⊕ *www.thewindsor.com.au.*

OFF THE BEATEN PATH **King's Domain Gardens.** This expansive stretch of parkland includes Queen Victoria Gardens, Alexandra Gardens, the Shrine of Remembrance, the Pioneer Women's Garden, the Sidney Myer Music Bowl, and the Royal Botanic Gardens. The temple-style **Shrine of Remembrance** is designed so that a beam of sunlight passes over the Stone of Remembrance in the Inner Shrine at 11 AM on Remembrance Day—the 11th day of the 11th month, when in 1918 the armistice marking the end of World War I was declared. ☒ *Between St. Kilda and Domain Rds., Anderson St., and Yarra River, City Center.*

🔟 **Melbourne Aquarium.** Become part ⚙ of the action as you stroll through transparent tunnels surrounded by water and the denizens of the deep at play. Or take a ride on an electronic simulator. The aquamarine building illuminates a previously dismal section of the Yarra bank, opposite Crown Casino. If you're feeling brave, check out the shark dives—they're held daily, include scuba equipment, and are led by an instructor. ☒ *Flinders and King Sts., City Center* ☎ *03/9620–0999* ⊕ *www.melbourneaquarium.com.au* 💰 *A$31.50, shark dives from A$150* ⊙ *Feb.–Dec., daily 9:30–6; Jan., daily 9:30–9 (last admission at 8).*

WHERE THE WILD THINGS ARE

For most visitors Melbourne is a genteel, highly cultivated experience. However, you can get a taste of the wilds on a Slumber Safari at Werribee Open Range Zoo, a 45-minute drive southwest of Melbourne. Kick off the night with a gourmet barbecue while watching African animals roam freely, then bunk down under canvas with the wild night sounds of Africa only a few hundred yards away. Great fun for city slickers! ⊕ www.zoo.org.au.

🔢 **National Gallery of Victoria International.** This massive, moat-encircled, bluestone-and-concrete edifice houses works from renowned international painters, including Picasso, Renoir, and van Gogh. A second branch of the National Gallery, in Federation Square in the city center, exhibits only Australian art. ☒ *180 St. Kilda Rd., South Melbourne* ☎ *03/8620–0222* ⊕ *www.ngv.vic.gov.au* 💰 *Free* ⊙ *Wed.–Mon. 10–5; closed Tues. except public holidays.*

🟡 **Royal Arcade.** Opened in 1870, this is the country's oldest shopping arcade, and despite alterations it retains an airy, graceful elegance. Walk about 30 feet into the arcade to see the statues of Gog and Magog, the mythical monsters that toll the hour on either side of **Gaunt's Clock.** ☒ *355 Bourke St., City Center* ☎ *03/9670–7777* ⊕ *www.royalarcade. com.au.*

🔢 **St. Patrick's Cathedral.** Ireland supplied Australia with many of its early immigrants, especially during the Irish potato famine in the mid-19th century. A statue of the Irish patriot Daniel O'Connell stands in the courtyard. Construction of the Gothic Revival building began in 1858 and took 82 years to finish. ☒ *Cathedral Pl., East Melbourne* ☎ *03/9662–2233* ⊙ *Weekdays 7–5, Sat. 8–7, Sun. 8–7:30.*

🟡 **St. Paul's Cathedral.** This 1892 headquarters of Melbourne's Anglican faith is one of the most important works of William Butterfield, a leader of the Gothic Revival style in England. In 2006 the cathedral underwent a massive restoration. Outside is a statue of Matthew Flinders, the first seaman to circumnavigate the Australian coastline, between 1801 and 1803. ☒ *Flinders and Swanston Sts., City Center* ☎ *03/9653–4333* ⊙ *Sun.–Fri. 8–6, Sat. 9–4.*

"What a wonderful city! I had fun shopping, visiting museums and eating out." —photo by Carly Miller, Fodors. com member

① ★ **Southgate.** On the river's edge next to the Victorian Arts Center, the development is a prime spot for lingering—designer shops, classy restaurants, bars, and casual eating places help locals and visitors while away the hours. The promenade links with the forecourt of Crown Casino and its hotels. ✉ *Maffra St. at City Rd., Southbank* ☎ *03/9699–4311* ⊕ *www.southgate-melbourne.com.au.*

WORTH NOTING

⑩ Athenaeum Theatre and Library. The first talking picture show in Australia was screened in 1896 at this beautiful theater. Today is houses three venues—a membership library, a theater for live performances, and the Laugh Laugh Comedy *(see separate listing in Nightlife and the Arts).* ✉ *188 Collins St., City Center* ☎ *03/9650–3504* ⊙ *Weekdays 9–5, Sat. 10–3.*

NEED A BREAK?

Journal (✉ *253 Flinders La., City Center* ☎ *03/9650–4399*), next to City Library, has leather couches, bookcases filled with magazines and newspapers, and communal tables where you can enjoy bruschetta, salads, antipasto platters, and selections from an excellent wine list from A$7.50 a glass.

At the **Transport Hotel** (✉ *Federation Sq., City Center* ☎ *03/9654–8808*) there's a choice of a public bar with casual meals, a cocktail lounge, and the upscale Taxi restaurant, with views across the Yarra River.

⑮ Cook's Cottage. Once the residence of the Pacific navigator Captain James Cook, the modest home, built in 1755, was transported stone by stone from Great Ayton in Yorkshire, England, and rebuilt in the lush Fitzroy

Gardens in 1934. It's believed that Cook lived in the cottage between his many voyages. The interior is simple, a suitable domestic realm for a man who spent much of his life in cramped quarters aboard sailing ships. ⊠ *Fitzroy Gardens near Lansdowne St. and Wellington Parade, East Melbourne* ☎ *03/9419–4677* ✉ *A$4.50* ⊙ *Daily 9–5.*

❸ **Eureka Skydeck 88.** Named after the goldfields uprising of 1854, the Eureka Tower (which houses the 88th-level Eureka Skydeck 88) is the tallest residential building in the southern hemisphere. The funky-shaped blue glass building, with an impressive gold cap, opened in May 2007. The Skydeck is the place to get a bird's-eye view of Melbourne and overcome your fear of heights. An enclosed all-glass cube, known as The Edge (A$12 additional charge), projects 3 meters (9.84 feet) out from the viewing platform, where you can stand, seemingly suspended, over the city on a clear glass floor. ⊠ *7 Riverside Quay, Southbank* ☎ *02/9693–8888* ⊕ *www.eurekaskydeck.com.au* ✉ *A$16.50* ⊙ *10–10.*

WORD OF MOUTH

"It was a last minute decision to go to Melbourne, as I was told by many that I shouldn't miss it! I'm glad I went. It's much different than Sydney and I liked it better. Very multicultural city with tons of restaurants and just a great energy overall. Lots to do downtown and lots of shopping!"
—Celine

⓫ **Old Melbourne Gaol Crime and Justice Experience.** A museum run by the Victorian branch of the National Trust is housed in the city's first jail. The building—rumored to be haunted—has three tiers of cells with catwalks around the upper levels. Its most famous inmate was the notorious bushranger Ned Kelly, who was hanged here in 1880. The Hangman's night tours (reservations essential) are a popular, if macabre, facet of Melbourne nightlife. The tour now includes "being arrested" next door at the City Watchhouse, where guides walk visitors through the experience of being incarcerated. ⊠ *Russell between LaTrobe and Victoria Sts., City Center* ☎ *03/9663–7228, 13–2849 (for night tours)* ⊕ *www.oldmelbouregaol.com.au* ✉ *A$20, night tours A$30* ⊙ *Daily 9:30–5. Night tours Sept.–Mar., Mon., Wed., Fri., and Sat. at 7:30; at 8:30 Apr.–Aug.*

❷ **Victorian Arts Centre.** Melbourne's most important cultural landmark is the venue for performances by the Australian Ballet, Australian Opera, and Melbourne Symphony Orchestra. It also encompasses Hamer Hall (formerly the Melbourne Concert Hall), the Arts Complex, the original National Gallery of Victoria, and the outdoor Sidney Myer Music Bowl. One-hour tours begin from the information desk at 11 AM Monday through Saturday. On Sunday a 90-minute backstage tour (no children under 12) begins at 12:15 PM. At night, look for the center's spire, which creates a magical spectacle with brilliant fiber-optic cables. ⊠ *100 St. Kilda Rd., Southbank* ☎ *03/9281–8000* ⊕ *www.theartscentre.net.au* ✉ *Tour A$15, backstage tour A$20* ⊙ *Mon.–Sat. 9 AM–11 PM, Sun. 10–5.*

Young and Jackson's Hotel. Pubs are not generally known for their art-work, but climb the steps to the bar here to see *Chloe,* a painting that has scandalized and titillated Melburnians for many decades. The larger-than-life nude, painted by George Lefebvre in Paris in 1875, has hung on the walls of Young and Jackson's Hotel (now owned by Fosters Brewery) for most of the last century. ⊠ *1 Swanston St. (opposite Flinders Street Station), City Center* ☎ *03/9650–3884.*

RICHMOND

Home of Victoria Street—Melbourne's "little Vietnam"—and the lively discount shopping stretch of Bridge Road, Richmond is 2 km (1 mi) east of the city center (take Tram 48 from Flinders St.). If you're looking for a new wardrobe, a Vietnamese soup kitchen, a Korean barbecue, a Laotian banquet, or a Thai hole-in-the-wall, this is the place to come.

GETTING HERE AND AROUND

Several tram lines connect central Melbourne with Richmond. Take Tram 70 from Flinders Street Station to Swan Street, Richmond; or take No. 109 from Bourke Street to Victoria Street. Tram 48 will take you from Flinders Street to Bridge Road, while Nos. 78 and 9 travel from Chapel Street (in South Yarra) to Richmond. Trains connect Flinders Street Station with Richmond Station. If driving, or even walking, proceed east along Flinders Street, which becomes Wellington Parade, past the Hilton and the Park Hotel to Hoddle Street.

Victoria Street. Fast becoming one of Melbourne's most popular "eat streets," this 2-km (1-mi) stretch has restaurants ranging from simple canteens (eat until you drop for A$10) to dressy, tablecloth-and-candle-light dining spots. The street also features Vietnamese grocers, kitchenware stores, several art galleries, and several chichi drinking spots. Once a year in late September the street comes to life with a Moon Lantern Festival, during which children wander the streets carrying handmade paper lanterns. ⊠ *Victoria St., Richmond.*

Bridge Road. Once a run-down area of Richmond, this street is now a bargain shopper's paradise. It's chockablock with clothing shops, cafés, and factory outlets selling leather goods, shoes, and gourmet foods. Take Tram 48 or 75 from the city. ⊠ *Bridge Rd., Richmond.*

EAST MELBOURNE

The harmonious streetscapes in this historic enclave of Victorian houses, which date from the boom following the gold rushes of the 1850s, make East Melbourne a great neighborhood for a stroll.

GETTING HERE AND AROUND

East Melbourne's attractions are an easy walk from the city center. The Free City Circle tram travels along Spring Street, stopping at Parliament House and the City Museum at Old Treasury Melbourne. The new, free orange-colored Melbourne City Tourist Shuttle bus also does a city loop and stops at the Sports and Entertainment Precinct, which is a short walk from the MCG and Fitzroy Gardens. Trams 48 and 74 travel along Flinders Street and Wellington Parade to East Melbourne sights: Fitzroy Gardens is on the north side of Wellington Parade and the MCG is on the south side.

DID YOU KNOW?

Melbourne is the cultivated sister of brassy Sydney. To the extent that culture is synonymous with sophistication, some call this city the cultural capital of the continent. Melbourne is also known for its rich migrant influences, particularly those expressed through food: the espresso cafés on Lygon Street, Brunswick's Middle Eastern/Indian/Turkish enclave, Richmond's "little Vietnam," or the Chinatown district of the city center.

1 **Melbourne Cricket Ground (MCG).** A tour of this complex is essential for an understanding of Melbourne's sporting obsession. You can get the stories behind it all at the new National Sports Museum. The site is a pleasant 10-minute walk from the city center or a tram ride (Nos. 48 and 75) to Jolimont Station. ⊠ *Jolimont Terrace, Jolimont, East Melbourne* ☎ *03/9657–8888* ⊕ *www.mcg.org.au* ⊠ *A$15* ☯ *Tours daily every half-hr 10–3, except on event days. Museum open 10–5 on non-event days.*

ST. KILDA

It often seems that every Melburnian heads to St. Kilda on Saturday night. The dozens of alfresco restaurants overflow into the streets, and the cafés and bars are buzzing with the young fashionistas. The holiday atmosphere continues on Sunday with open-air markets and people enjoying the beach. The seaside suburb still has a Victorian-era atmosphere—the tree-lined promenade and the classic pier extending out into Port Phillip Bay are perfect for strolling and people-watching. The quaintly named St. Kilda Sea Baths (now a modern swimming pool and spa complex) are housed in a turn-of-the-20th-century building. While no one wanted to live there in the 1970s and '80s, it is now a very smart address, and many visitors choose to stay in St. Kilda and hop on the tram for a short scenic ride into the city.

GETTING HERE AND AROUND
Several trams travel to St. Kilda from central Melbourne. Trams 96 and 112 traverse the city centre from its northern borders and go all the way south to St. Kilda. Tram 79 travels from North Richmond and No. 16 runs from Melbourne University along Swanston Street. A good place to get on a St. Kilda tram is at Flinders Street Station, or in Collins Street. It's a pleasant ride down St. Kilda Road, into Fitzroy Street and on to St. Kilda Beach.

9 **Acland Street.** An alphabet soup of Chinese, French, Italian, and Lebanese eateries—along with a fantastic array of cake shops—lines the sidewalk of St. Kilda's ultrahip restaurant row. The street faces Luna Park. ⊠ *Acland St. between Barkly St. and Shakespeare Grove, St. Kilda.*

8 **Luna Park** is a five-minute stroll southeast of the pier. A Melbourne icon, the park's gates take the shape of an enormous mouth, swallowing visitors whole and delivering them into a world of ghost trains, pirate ships, and carousels. Built in 1912, the **Scenic Railway** is the park's most popular ride. It's said to be the oldest continually operating roller coaster in the world, and was renovated in 2006. The railway

WALTZING MATILDA

Shopping mixes with history and a touch of patriotism at Melbourne Central shopping center. The main attraction, apart from the stores, is the historic brick shot tower, rising 165 feet above the center and encased in a glass cone. Built in 1890, the shot tower was used to make "shot" or bullets. Also suspended from the roof is a hot-air balloon and a huge fob-watch that entertains shoppers on the hour with a musical rendition of Australia's unofficial national anthem, "Waltzing Matilda." You'll find this huge shopping center on the corner of La Trobe and Swanston streets.

4

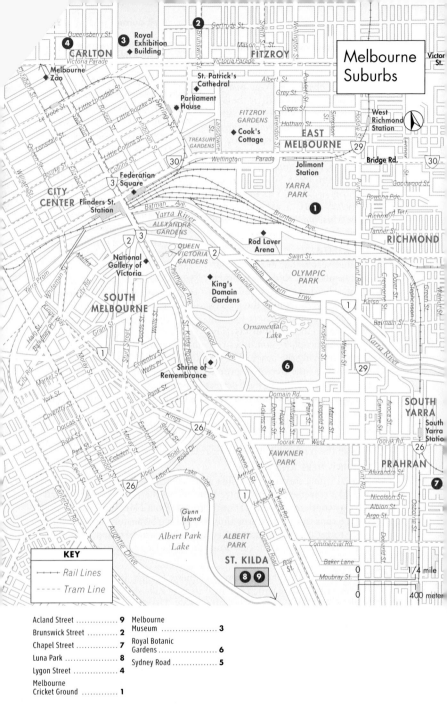

Melbourne Suburbs

Victor St.

Queensberry St.

4 Royal
CARLTON 3 Exhibition
Victoria Parade ◆ Building

2 Gertrude St.

Mason St.

Wellington Parade

FITZROY
Victoria Parade

Melbourne
Zoo

St. Patrick's
Cathedral
Albert St.

Powlett St.

Hoddle St.

Grey St.

Gipps St.

Simpson St.

Lennox St.

West
Richmond
Station

La Trobe St.

Little Lonsdale St.

Russell St.

Swanston St.

Elizabeth St.

Spring St.

Parliament
House

FITZROY
GARDENS

Clarendon St.

Hotham St.

Lonsdale St.

Little Bourke St.

Lansdowne St.

◆ Cook's
Cottage

**EAST
MELBOURNE**

29

Bourke St.

Little Collins St.

TREASURY
GARDENS

Bridge Rd.

30

Goodwood St.

Collins St.

30

Wellington Parade

Jolimont
Station

Rowena Pde.

**CITY
CENTER**

3 Federation
Square

Flinders St.
Station

Batman Ave.

Yarra River

YARRA PARK

Brunton Ave.

Richmond Terr.

Tanner St.

RICHMOND

1

ALEXANDRA
GARDENS

2 3

National
Gallery of
Victoria

QUEEN
VICTORIA
GARDENS

2

Rod Laver
Arena

Swan St.

South Eastern Frwy.

OLYMPIC
PARK

Cremorne St.

Dover St.

Stephenson St.

Green St.

Walnut St.

Kelso St.

Balmain St.

Yarra River

**SOUTH
MELBOURNE**

City Rd.

Grant St.

Sturt St.

Dodds St.

Watts St.

◆ King's
Domain
Gardens

St. Kilda Road

Birdwood Ave.

Alexandra Ave.

Ornamental
Lake

Anderson St.

Walsh St.

1

**SOUTH
YARRA**

Yarra Prom.

Whiteman St.

Kings Way

Haig St.

Balstow Pl.

Moray St.

Coventry St.

Wells St.

◆ Shrine of
Remembrance

6

Domain Rd.

Park St.

Millswyn St.

Domain St.

Marne St.

Caroline St.

Avoca St.

Osborne St.

South
Yarra
Station

26

Market St.

York St.

Coventry St.

Dorcas St.

Bank St.

Park St.

Cecil St.

Clarendon St.

Cobden St.

Moray St.

Kings Way

Glenn Rd.

Eastern Rd.

26

Bank St.

Albert Rd.

Lakeside Dr.

Toorak Rd. West

Arthur St.

Queens Road

St. Kilda Rd.

Leopold St.

FAWKNER
PARK

Toorak Rd.

Alexandra St.

Nicolson St.

Albion St.

Argo St.

PRAHRAN

26

Punt Rd.

Chapel St.

Commercial Rd.

Devonshire St.

7

Canterbury Rd.

Augentine Drive

Gunn Island

Albert Park Lake

**ALBERT
PARK**

1

Queens Road

Roy St.

Baker Lane

Moubray St.

0   1/4 mile

0   400 meter

ST. KILDA

8 9

KEY

←→ *Rail Lines*

--- *Tram Line*

is less roller coaster and more a relaxed loop-the-loop, offering stunning views of Port Phillip Bay between each dip and turn. Numerous music festivals, including Push Over (held each March) are held within the park's grounds each year. ⊠ *Lower Esplanade, St. Kilda* ☎ *03/9525–5033 or 1300/888272* ⊕ *www.lunapark.com.au* ✆ *Free entry, A$8 per ride, A$37.95 for unlimited rides* ⊙ *Summer (late Sept.–Apr. 25), Fri. 7 PM–11, Sat. 11–11, Sun., school holidays, and public holidays 11–6; winter (Apr. 26–Sept. 29), weekends (and public holidays) 11–6.*

A DAY AT THE RACES

The usually serene atmosphere of Albert Park is turned into motorhead heaven every March, when Melbourne stages the Australian Grand Prix. It's the opening event of the Formula One season, with four full-throttle days of excitement on and off the track. Drivers scream around Albert Park Lake to the delight of fans and the horror of some nearby residents. Albert Park is 3 km (2 mi) south of the city center. It's on March 25–28, 2010. ⊕ *www.grandprix.com.au.*

FITZROY

Melbourne's bohemian quarter is 2 km (1 mi) northeast of the city center. If you're looking for an Afghan camel bag or a secondhand paperback, or yearn for a café where you can sit over a plate of tapas and watch Melbourne go by, Fitzroy is the place. Take Tram 11 or 86 from the city.

GETTING HERE AND AROUND

Fitzroy is an easy place to access, both from the city and nearby suburbs. From the city, take the No. 112 from Collins Street (near Parliament House). It will take you all the way up Brunswick Street. In Bourke Street (also near Spring Street), hop on the No. 86 tram for a ride to Gertrude Street. Alternatively, you can take the Epping train line from Flinders Street Station and alight at Clifton Hill. From there you can walk west to Fitzroy or board the No. 86 tram to Gertrude Street.

❷ **Brunswick Street.** Along with Lygon Street in nearby Carlton, Brunswick Street is one of Melbourne's favorite places to dine. You might want to step into a simple lunchtime café serving tasty pizza for less than A$10, or opt for dinner at one of the stylish, highly regarded bar-restaurants. The street also has many galleries, bookstores, and arts-and-crafts shops. ⊠ *Brunswick St. between Alexandra and Victoria Parades, Fitzroy.*

BRUNSWICK

Just 4 km (2 mi) north of the city center, Brunswick is Melbourne's multicultural heart. Here Middle Eastern spice shops sit next to avant-garde galleries, Egyptian supermarkets, Turkish tile shops, Japanese yakitori eateries, Lebanese bakeries, Indian haberdasheries, and secondhand bookstores. Take Tram 19 from the city.

GETTING HERE AND AROUND

Tram 19 travels from Flinders Street Station in the city along Elizabeth Street all the way to Brunswick's main thoroughfare of Sydney Road. You can also catch a train to Brunswick; take the Upfield Railway Line from Flinders Street Station and alight at either Jewell or Brunswick stations—they're both in Brunswick.

❺ **Sydney Road.** There's nowhere in Melbourne quite like Sydney Road. Cultures collide as Arabic mingles with French, Hindi does battle with Bengali, and the muezzin's call to prayer argues with Lebanese pop music. Scents intoxicate and colors beguile. Cafés serving everything from pastries to *tagines* (Moroccan stews) to Turkish delights huddle by the roadside, as do quirky record shops, antiques auction houses, and Bollywood video stores. ⊠ *Sydney Rd. between Brunswick Rd. and Bell St., Brunswick.*

CARLTON

To see the best of Carlton's Victorian-era architecture, walk along Drummond Street, with its rows of gracious terrace houses (notably Rosaville at No. 46, Medley Hall at No. 48, and Lothian Terrace at No. 175), and Canning Street, which has a mix of workers' cottages and grander properties. Take Tram 1 or 8 from the city.

GETTING HERE AND AROUND

Carlton is served by the many of Melbourne's tram routes that run through and terminate at Melbourne University (located in Parkeville, just north of Carlton). Tram routes 1 and 8 ride along Swanston Street in the city, and then turn into Lygon Street. Alternatively, you can take a train to Melbourne Central Station (on the City Loop line) and then walk north to Carlton, or catch a bus (Nos. 200, 201, 203, 207, 253) from that station to Carlton.

Carlton Gardens. Forty acres of tree-lined paths, artificial lakes, and flower beds in this English-style 19th-century park form a backdrop for the outstanding Museum of Victoria, as well as the World Heritage–listed Royal Exhibition Building, erected in 1880. ⊠ *Victoria Parade at Nicholson, Carlton, and Rathdowne Sts., City Center* ☎ *No phone.*

❹ **Lygon Street.** Known as Melbourne's Little Italy, Lygon Street is a perfect
★ example of the city's multiculturalism: where once you'd have seen only Italian restaurants, there are now Thai, Malay, Caribbean, and Greek eateries. The city's famous café culture was also born here, with the arrival of Melbourne's first espresso machine at one of the street's Italian-owned cafés in the 1950s. The Italian-inspired **Lygon Street Festival** in October gathers the neighborhood in music and merriment. ⊠ *Lygon St. between Victoria and Alexandra Parades, Carlton.*

❸ **Melbourne Museum.** A spectacular, postmodern building (in Carlton Gar-
♺ dens) houses displays of the varied cultures around Australia and the Pacific Islands. The Bunjilaka exhibit covers the traditions of the country's Aboriginal groups, while the Australia Gallery focuses on Victoria's heritage (and includes the preserved body of Australia's greatest racing horse, Phar Lap). There's plenty for kids, too, with the wooded Forest Gallery, Children's Museum, Mind and Body Gallery, and Science and Life Gallery. ⊠ *Carlton Gardens, 11 Nicholson St., Carlton* ☎ *13–1102 or 03/8341–7777* ⊕ *www.museumvictoria.com.au/MelbourneMuseum* 🎟 *A$8, children free* ☉ *Daily 10–5.*

The groovy cafés of St. Kilda.

SOUTH YARRA–PRAHRAN

One of the coolest spots to be on any given night is in South Yarra and Prahran. The area is chock full of bars, eateries, and upscale boutiques.

GETTING HERE AND AROUND

Several trams, including Nos. 6, 8, 72, and 78, travel to either South Yarra or Prahran or both. No. 6 comes down St. Kilda Road from Flinders Street Station and turns into High Street, Prahran, while No. 8 turns into Domain Road (just south of the Royal Botanic Gardens) and then travels down Toorak Road. Trams 78 and 79 travel down Chapel Street from North Richmond. You can also catch a train to both South Yarra and Prahran; take the Sandringham Line from Flinders Street Station.

❼ Chapel Street. The heart of the trendy South Yarra–Prahran area, this long road is packed with pubs, bars, notable restaurants, and upscale boutiques—more than 1,000 shops can be found within the precinct. The Toorak Road end of the street (nearest to the city) is the fashion-conscious, upscale section where Australian designers showcase their original designs. Walk south along Chapel Street to Greville Street, a small lane of hip bars, clothing boutiques, and record stores. Past Greville Street, the south end of Chapel Street is grungier, with pawnshops and kitschy collectibles stores. ⊠ *Chapel St. between Toorak and Dandenong Rds., South Yarra–Prahran* ☎ *03/9529–6331* ⊕ *www.chapelstreet.com.au.*

Fodor'sChoice
★

❻ Royal Botanic Gardens. The present design and layout were the brainchild of W.R. Guilfoyle, curator and director of the gardens from 1873 to 1910. Within its 100 acres are 12,000 species of native and imported

CLOSE UP

Australian Rules Football

This fast, vigorous game, played between teams of 18, is one of four kinds of football Down Under. Aussies also play Rugby League, Rugby Union, and soccer, but Australian Rules, widely known as "footy," is the one to which Victoria, South Australia, the Top End, and Western Australia subscribe. It's the country's most popular spectator sport.

Despite its name, novice observers frequently ask the question: "What rules?" The ball can be kicked or punched in any direction, but never thrown. Players make spectacular leaps vying to catch a kicked ball before it touches the ground, for which they earn a free kick. The game is said to be at its finest in Melbourne. Tickets for Australian Rules Football are available through **Ticketmaster7** (☎ 13–6100 ⊕ ticketmaster.com.au) or at the playing fields. The **Melbourne Cricket Ground** (⊠ Brunton Ave., Yarra Park ☎ 03/9657–8867) is the prime venue for AFL games.

plants and trees, sweeping lawns, and ornamental lakes populated with ducks and swans that love to be fed. The Children's Garden is a fun and interactive place for kids to explore. Summer brings alfresco performances of classic plays, usually Shakespeare, children's classics like *Wind in the Willows,* and the popular Moonlight Cinema series. ⊠ *Birdwood Ave., South Yarra* ☎ *03/9252–2300* ⊕ *www.rbg.vic.gov.au* ⊒ *Free* ☉ *Nov.–Mar., daily 7:30–8:30; Apr., Sept., and Oct., daily 7:30–6; May–Aug., daily 7:30–5:30. Children's Garden Wed.–Sun. 10–4.*

OFF THE
BEATEN
PATH

Melbourne Zoo. Flourishing gardens and open-environment animal enclosures are hallmarks of this world-renowned zoo, which sits 4 km (2½ mi) north of the city center. A lion park, reptile house, and butterfly pavilion where more than 1,000 butterflies flutter through the rain-forest setting are also on-site, as is a simulated African rain forest where a group of Western Lowland gorillas resides. The spectacular Trail of the Elephants, home of Asiatic elephants Mek Kapah and Bong Su, has a village, gardens, and a swimming pool. The orangutan sanctuary is one of the highlights. It's possible to stay overnight with the Roar 'n' Snore package (A$185 per adult) and enjoy dinner, supper, breakfast, and an entire day at the zoo. Twilight jazz bands serenade visitors on summer evenings. ⊠ *Elliott Ave., Parkville* ☎ *03/9285–9300* ⊕ *www.zoo.org.au* ⊒ *A$24.40* ☉ *Daily 9–5, select summer evenings to 9 or 9:30.*

OUTDOOR ACTIVITIES

BEACHES

Unlike Sydney, Melbourne is not known for its beaches. Nonetheless, there are several popoular beaches on the shores of Port Phillip Bay. The best known are St. Kilda and Brighton Beach, the latter extremely picturesque, adorned with a colourful row of "bathing boxes" that runs along its shore. These vividly decorated little sheds are basically privately owned changing rooms, but can sell for as much as a house in some parts of the city, with many dating back to the 1940s.

The absence of waves fails to provide the conditions for surfing; however, the brisk winds that whip across Port Phillip Bay make most of these beaches ideal for windsurfing (particularly Elwood Beach) and kitesurfing.

BICYCLING

Melbourne and its environs contain more than 100 km (62 mi) of bike paths, including scenic routes along the Yarra River and Port Phillip Bay. The Beach Road Trail extends 19 km (12 mi) around Port Phillip Bay from Elwood Beach to Sandringham; the new Docklands area of Melbourne can be cycled around—start on the Southbank Promenade, travel west, and then cross over the new Webb Street to Docklands Park and Harbour Esplanade; you can join the Main Yarra Trail bicycle route at the mouth of the Yarra River, just north of the West Gate Bridge or at Southbank. You can then follow the Yarra River for 35 km (22 mi) until it meets up with the Mullum Mullum Creek Trail in Templestowe in Melbourne's eastern suburbs. Bicycle Victoria has all the details on biking trails.

Bicycle Victoria (⊠ *Level 10, 446 Collins St., City Center* ☎ *03/8636–8888* ⊕ *www.bv.com.au*) can provide information about area bike paths. Its excellent Web site has trail maps and descriptions as well as directions. Bikes can be rented for about A\$25 per day from trailers alongside the bike paths. **Melbourne City-Bike Company** (☎ *04/3317–1077* ⊕ *www.city-bike.com.au*) has a fleet of pedal-electric bicycles (emission-free) made out of recycled materials. It's a healthy way—for you and the environment—to see some of the city's best sights. One-hour tours cost A\$55, and operate daily between 10 AM and 4 PM. **Real Melbourne Bike Tours** (⊠ *Vault 14, Federation Square, City Centre* ☎ *0417/339203* ⊕ *www. rentabike.net.au* ✉ *A\$99 per person*) runs daily bike tours that promise to show the very best of Melbourne. The four-hour tours (which depart at 10 AM) include coffee and cakes in Little Italy and lunch. The company also rents bicycles from A\$15 an hour. It's on the edge of the Yarra River just near Princes Bridge and Federation Square.

BOATING

Studley Park Boathouse (⊠ *Boathouse Rd., Kew* ☎ *03/9853–1828* ⊕ *www. studleyparkboathouse.com.au*) rents canoes, kayaks, and rowboats for journeys on a peaceful stretch of the lower Yarra River, about 7 km (4½ mi) east of the city center. Rentals are A\$28 per hour for a two-person canoe or rowboat and A\$36 per hour for a four-person rowboat. The boathouse is open daily 9–5 and has a café and restaurant with lovely river views.

CAR RACING

Australian Formula 1 Grand Prix (⊠ *220 Albert Rd., South Melbourne* ☎ *03/9258–7100* ⊕ *www.grandprix.com.au*) is a popular fixture on Melbourne's calendar of annual events. It's held every March in the suburb of Albert Park, a small neighborhood 4 km (2½ mi) south of the city that encompasses the area surrounding Albert Park Lake.

GOLF

Melbourne has the largest number of championship golf courses in Australia. Four kilometers (2½ mi) south of the city, **Albert Park Golf Course** (⊠ *Queens Rd., Albert Park* ☎ *03/9510–5588*) is an 18-hole, par-72 course that traverses Albert Park Lake, near where the Formula 1 Grand Prix is held in March. Greens fees are A$19.60 (9 holes, weekdays only) and A$26.20–A$27.80 (18 holes). The 18-hole, par-67 **Brighton Public Golf Course** (⊠ *232 Dendy St., Brighton* ☎ *03/9592–1388*) has excellent scenery, but is quite busy on weekends and midweek mornings. Club rental is available. Greens fees are A$19 (9 holes), A$26 (18 holes). **Ivanhoe Public Golf Course** (⊠ *Vasey St., East Ivanhoe* ☎ *03/9499–7001* ⊕ *www.ivanhoegolf.com.au*), an 18-hole, par-68 course, is well suited to the average golfer and is open to the public every day except holidays. Greens fees are A$19 (9 holes), A$25 (18 holes) on weekdays and A$25 for 9 or 18 holes on weekends. Five minutes from the beach, **Sandringham Golf Links** (⊠ *Cheltenham Rd., Sandringham* ☎ *03/9598–3590* ⊕ *www.sandringhamgolfclub.org.au*) is one of the better public courses. The area is known as the "golf links" because there are several excellent courses in the vicinity. Sandringham is an 18-hole, par-72 course. Greens fees are A$28 (18 holes).

HORSE RACING

Melbourne is the only city in the world to declare a public holiday for a horse race—the Melbourne Cup—held on the first Tuesday in November since 1861. The Cup is also a fashion parade, and most of Melbourne society turns out in full regalia. The rest of the country comes to a standstill, with schools, shops, offices, and factories tuning in to the action.

The city has four top-class racetracks. **Caulfield Race Course** (⊠ *Station St., Caulfield* ☎ *03/9257–7200* ⊕ *www.melbourneracingclub.net.au*), 10 km (6 mi) from the city, runs the Blue Diamond in February and the Caulfield Cup in October. **Flemington Race Course** (⊠ *448 Epsom Rd., Flemington* ☎ *03/9371–7171* ⊕ *www.vrc.net.au*), 3 km (2 mi) outside the city, is Australia's premier racecourse and home of the Melbourne Cup. **Moonee Valley Race Course** (⊠ *McPherson St., Moonee Ponds* ☎ *03/9373–2222* ⊕ *www.mvrc.net.au*) is 6 km (4 mi) from town and holds the Cox Plate race in October. **Betfair Park** (formerly Sandown Race Course) (⊠ *Corrigan Rd. and Princes Hwy., Springvale* ☎ *03/9518–1300 www.melbourneracingclub.net.au*), 25 km (16 mi) from the city, hosts the Sandown Cup in November. **Champions–Australian Racing Museum and Hall of Fame** (⊠ *Federation Sq., Flinders St., City Center* ☎ *1300/139407* 🎫 *A$9*) is chock-full of horse-racing information, displays, and a mini-shrine to Australia's most famous race house, Phar Lap.

TENNIS

The **Australian Open** (☎ *03/9286–1175* ⊕ *www.australianopen.com*), held in January at the **Melbourne & Olympic Parks** (⊠ *Batman Ave., City Center* ☎ *03/9286–1244* ⊕ *www.mopt.com.au*), is one of the world's four Grand Slam events. You can buy tickets at the event.

Brought your racket? **Melbourne Park Tennis Centre** (⊠ *Batman Ave., City Center* ☎ *03/9286–1244* ⊕ *www.mopt.com.au*) has 22 outdoor and 4 hard indoor Rebound Ace courts. Play is canceled during the Australian Open in January. **East Melbourne Tennis Centre** (⊠ *Powlett Reserve, Albert St., East Melbourne* ☎ *03/9417–6511* ⊕ *www.melbourne.vic.gov.au*) has five synthetic-grass outdoor courts. **Fawkner Park Tennis Centre** (✉ *Fawkner Park, Toorak Rd. W, South Yarra* ☎ *03/9820–0611* ⊕ *www.fawknerparktenniscentre.com*) has six synthetic-grass outdoor courts.

WHERE TO EAT

Melbourne has fabulous food, and is known in some circles as Australia's food capital. The restaurants themselves are often exceptionally stylish and elegant—or totally edgy and funky in their own individual way. Some are even deliberately grungy. The dining scene is a vast smorgasbord of cuisines and experiences that's constantly evolving. The swankiest (and most expensive) restaurants all have five- to eight-course degustation menus (with the opportunity to wine-match each course), but newer restaurants are opting for tapas-style or grazing plates. Flexibility is the new word in dining—restaurants are also funky bars and vice versa.

CITY CENTER

¢–$ ✗ **Babka.** Food lovers in the know are often found loitering at this
CAFE tiny, bustling café. Try the excellent pastries, fresh-baked breads, or more substantial offerings like the menemen—scrambled eggs with chili, mint, tomoato, and a dash of feta cheese. It's an all-day brunch-style café, and there are often queues, so be prepared to wait for a table. Some complain that the busy staff can be brusque. ✉ *358 Brunswick St., Fitzroy* ☎ *03/9416–0091* ▭ *MC, V (for bills over A$20)* ◷ *Closed Mon. No dinner* ✛ *1:D3.*

$$$ ✗ **Becco.** Every city center needs a place like this, with a drop-in bar
ITALIAN and lively dining room. At lunchtime no-time-to-dawdle business types tuck into papparadelle osso bucco with pangrattato, while those with a sweet tooth will go weak at the knees over the deconstructed Bombe Alaska of strawberry ice cream, yoghurt cake, and Italian meringue. Things get a little moodier at night, when a Campari and soda at the bar is an almost compulsory precursor to dinner. ✉ *11–25 Crossley St., City Center* ☎ *03/9663–3000* ⊕ *www.becco.com.au* ⌣ *Reservations essential* ▭ *AE, DC, MC, V* ◷ *Closed Sun.* ✛ *1:B4.*

¢ ✗ **Bimbo Deluxe.** This eclectic bar, with deep comfy sofas and the feel of a
CAFE local hangout, has the cheapest and possibly the most delicious pizzas in town. On weekdays between noon and 4 PM and Sunday–Thursday from 7 to 11 PM you can order a dinner-plate-size pizza (from 19 choices) for a mere A$4. The queues of students and hungry lunchers start to form outside around 11:55. If you miss the special, fear not: the same great pizzas are only A$6–A$8 at other times. Try the Agnello (tomato, mozzarella, spiced lamb, arugula, pine nuts, and sultanas). If you're hankering for a sugar rush, there are also sweet pizzas such as chocolate with mascarpone. A range of chilled infused vodkas—including watermelon and lychee—is available, and the bar's signature "Blonde Bimbo" beer is a popular choice. ✉ *376 Brunswick St.* ☎ *03/9419–8600* ✉ *179 Chapel St., Windsor* ☎ *03/9525–1288* ▭ *MC, V* ✛ *2:B1.*

$$ ✗ **Brunetti.** This Romanesque bakery is still just as heavenly as when
★ it opened 25 years ago; it's still filled with perfect biscotti and mouth-
CAFE watering cakes. More substantial pastas and risottos have been added

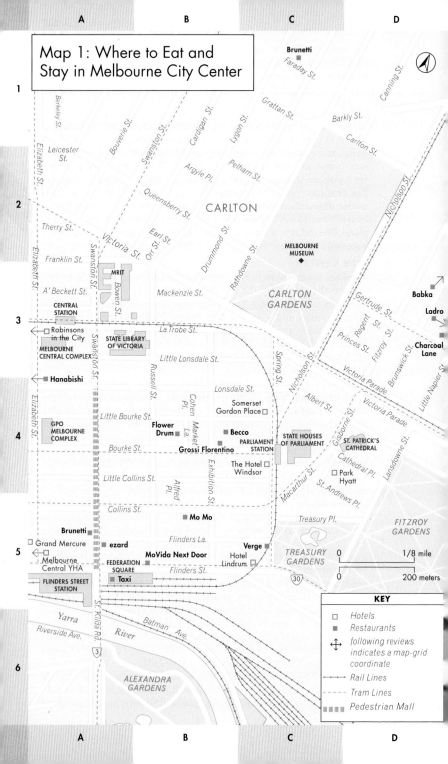

Map 1: Where to Eat and Stay in Melbourne City Center

Grid Coordinates:

A B C D (columns across top and bottom)

1–6 (rows down left side)

Streets and landmarks:

Brunetti — Faraday St.

Berkeley St.

Grattan St.

Canning St.

Barkly St.

Carlton St.

Bouverie St.

Swanston St.

Cardigan St.

Lygon St.

Elizabeth St.

Leicester St.

Argyle Pl.

Pelham St.

Nicholson St.

Queensberry St.

CARLTON

Therry St.

Victoria St.

Earl St.

Orr St.

Drummond St.

Rathdowne St.

MELBOURNE MUSEUM

Franklin St.

A' Beckett St.

MRIT

Bowen St.

Mackenzie St.

CARLTON GARDENS

Gertrude St.

Babka

CENTRAL STATION

Ladro

Regent St.

Princes St.

Fitzroy St.

Charcoal Lane

Robinsons in the City

La Trobe St.

Spring St.

Brunswick St.

STATE LIBRARY OF VICTORIA

Little Lonsdale St.

Nicholson St.

Albert St.

Victoria Parade

Little Napier St.

MELBOURNE CENTRAL COMPLEX

Russell St.

Lonsdale St.

Victoria Parade

Hanabishi

Little Bourke St.

Somerset Gordon Place

Gisborne St.

ST. PATRICK'S CATHEDRAL

Lansdowne St.

GPO MELBOURNE COMPLEX

Cohen Pl.

Market La.

Flower Drum

Becco

PARLIAMENT STATION

STATE HOUSES OF PARLIAMENT

Cathedral Pl.

Elizabeth St.

Bourke St.

Grossi Florentino

The Hotel Windsor

Park Hyatt

St. Andrews Pl.

Little Collins St.

Alfred Pl.

Exhibition St.

Macarthur St.

FITZROY GARDENS

Collins St.

Treasury Pl.

Mo Mo

TREASURY GARDENS

Brunetti

Flinders La.

Verge

0   1/8 mile

Grand Mercure

ezard

MoVida Next Door

Hotel Lindrum

0   200 meters

Melbourne Central YHA

FEDERATION SQUARE

Flinders St.

30

FLINDERS STREET STATION

Taxi

Yarra

Riverside Ave.

St. Kilda Rd.

Batman Ave.

River

3

ALEXANDRA GARDENS

KEY

□ Hotels

■ Restaurants

⊕ following reviews indicates a map-grid coordinate

┼── Rail Lines

- - - Tram Lines

▪▪▪ Pedestrian Mall

to the menu, and you can finish off your lunch with a tremendous espresso and *cornetto con crema* (custard-filled croissant). Dinner and lunch are served in the attached, stylish restaurant every night except Sunday. City workers can now enjoy all these sweet delights with the opening of a branch in Flinders Lane and the suburb of Camberwell a couple of miles east of Richmond. ✉ *194–204 Faraday St., Carlton* ☎ *03/9347–2801* ⊕ *www.brunetti.com.au* ✛ *1:C1.*✉ *214 Flinders La., at Swanston St.* ☎ *03/9663–8085* ✉ *1/3 Prospect Hill Rd., Camberwell* ☎ *03/9882–3100* ▭ *AE, DC, MC, V* ⊗ *No dinner Sun.* ✛ *1:A5.*

$$

AUSTRALIAN

✕ **Charcoal Lane.** This new restaurant could be described as taking a leaf from celebrity chef Jamie Oliver's book, in that disadvantaged people are given an opportunity to transform their lives by gaining a traineeship in the restaurant business. Named after a song by acclaimed Aboriginal singer/songwriter Archie Roach, Charcoal Lane is a joint project between the charity Mission Australia and the Victorian Aboriginal Health Service. It is housed in the former health service community center, dubbed Charcoal Lane by the many Aboriginal people who for decades would drop in and swap stories and wisdom. The menu includes many Australian bushland ingredients, and the dishes have an Aboriginal influence. They include starters of wok-flashed baby abalone with wild ginger and hearty main courses such as slow-cooked lamb saddle with bush herb crust and roasted root vegetables, or native-peppered kangaroo fillet, shallot and bush-tomato tart and rosella jus (rosella is native Australian fruit). ✉ *136 Gertrude St., Fitzroy* ☎ *03/9418–3400* ⊕ *www.charcoallane.com.au* ▭ *MC, V* ⊗ *No dinner Sun; closed Mon.* ✛ *1:D3.*

$$$–$$$$
★

MODERN
AUSTRALIAN

✕ **ezard.** Chef Teage Ezard's adventurous take on fusion pushes the boundaries between Eastern and Western flavors. Some combinations may appear unusual, like the master stock fried pork hock with chili caramel, spicy Thai bean-shoot salad, and fragrant jasmine rice—but everything works deliciously at this spot in the funky Adelphi hotel. And as with all upscale restaurants these days, there's an eight-course tasting menu (A$135 per person) featuring mouth-watering steamed blue swimmer crab wonton dumpling with coconut and lemongrass laksa. ✉ *187 Flinders La., City Center* ☎ *03/9639–6811* ⚱ *Reservations essential* ▭ *AE, DC, MC, V* ⊗ *Closed Sun. No lunch Sat.* ✛ *1:A5.*

$$–$$$
★

CANTONESE

✕ **Flower Drum.** Superb Cantonese cuisine is the hallmark of one of Australia's truly great Chinese restaurants, which is still receiving awards after 34 years in business. The restrained elegance of the decor, deftness of the service, and intelligence of the wine list puts most other restaurants to shame. Those in the know don't order from the menu at all, but simply ask the waiter to bring the day's specials—the crisp-skin Cantonese roast duck is one of the highlights. A gorgeous treat to finish is the double-boiled milk pudding with ginger juice. ✉ *17 Market La., City Center* ☎ *03/9662–3655* ⊕ *www.flower-drum.com* ⚱ *Reservations essential* ▭ *AE, DC, MC, V* ⊗ *No lunch Sun.* ✛ *1:B4.*

$$–$$$$
★

ITALIAN

✕ **Grossi Florentino.** Since 1900, dining at Florentino has meant experiencing the pinnacle of Melbourne hospitality. After taking a seat in the famous mural room, with its wooden panels and Florentine murals, you can sample dishes like braised rabbit with muscatel and *farro* (a speltlike Italian grain), or peppered scallop ravioli. Downstairs, the

Grill Room has more businesslike fare, while the cellar bar is perfect for a glass of wine and pasta of the day. ⊠ *80 Bourke St., City Center* ☎ *03/9662–1811* ⊕ *www.grossiflorentino.com.au* ⌲ *Reservations essential* ⊟ *AE, DC, MC, V* ⊙ *Closed Sun.* ✛ *1:B4.*

$$ ✕ **Hanabishi.** Touted as the city's best Japanese restaurant, Hanabishi sits
★ in slightly seedy King Street, an area known for its bars, club venues,
JAPANESE and occasionally unsavory clientele. With wooden floors, blue walls, and traditional ceramic serving trays, Hanabishi is the playground of Osakan chef Akio Soga, whose menu includes such gems as *hagi kimo* (salty steamed fish liver served with miso). The long list of hot and chilled sake, as well as the expansive wine list, ranges from reasonable to pricey. The bento boxes contain the sought-after Wagyu beef, which is a favorite with the lunchtime crowd. ⊠ *187 King St., City Center* ☎ *03/9670–1167* ⌲ *Reservations essential* ⊟ *AE, DC, MC, V* ⊙ *Closed weekends* ✛ *1:A3.*

$ ✕ **Ladro.** Rita Macalli's stellar Italian bistro emphasizes flavor over
★ starchy linen or stuffy attitude. Here eggplant is molded into gentle
ITALIAN round *polpettes* (meatball-like mounds), lamb rump is scented with garlic and parsley and slow-roasted to impossible tenderness, and the service is as upbeat as the wine list. Delicious wood-fired pizzas are yet another reason to visit this suburban gem (thankfully, it's within walking distance from the city). ⊠ *224 Gertrude St., Fitzroy* ☎ *03/9415–7575* ⌲ *Reservations essential* ⊟ *MC, V* ⊙ *Closed Mon. No lunch* ✛ *2:B1.*

$$-$$$ ✕ **Mo Mo.** This exotic, pillow-filled basement restaurant re-opened in
MIDDLE EASTERN early 2009 in the beautifully redeveloped Grand Hyatt Hotel. With more room to move, chef Greg Malouf has taken his pungent mix of spicy Middle Eastern dishes to a wider audience by adding a casual dining area and bar to accompany his more upscale restaurant. Favorites such as *bastourma* (cured beef) salad with wild arugula and goat cheese, and tagine (Moroccan stew) anchor the menu. Family-style sharing menus (or small banquets from A$100 per table) are available Tuesday–Thursday nights. ⊠ *123 Collins St., City Center* ☎ *03/9650–0660* ⊟ *AE, DC, MC, V* ⊙ *No lunch. Closed Sun., Mon.* ✛ *1:B5.*

$ ✕ **MoVida Next Door.** As the name suggests, this popular Spanish tapas
SPANISH restaurant is next door to something—in this case the grown-up parent restaurant called MoVida. This is the casual little sister (or daughter) for those who don't want to linger too long over their dinner. Dishes range from tapas (from $3.90 to $7.50), like Moorish lamb skewers grilled on charcoal, to the *racion* (bigger plates ranging from $14 to $18.50). Finish the meal off with *churros con chocolate* (Spanish fried dough served with a hot, thick chocolate drink). If you're after a bigger meal, pop into MoVida next door. Both eateries are owned by Frank Camoora, who's made a big splash in the Melbourne dining scene in the last few years. ⊠ *1 Hosier La., City Center* ☎ *03/9663–3038* ⊕ *www.movida.com.au* ⊟ *AE, MC, V* ⊙ *No lunch. Closed Sun. and Mon.* ✛ *1:B5.*

$$$ ✕ **Taxi.** Housed in an innovatively designed steel-and-glass dining
★ room above Federation Square, Taxi boasts both extraordinary food
MODERN and spectacular views over Melbourne. East meets West on a menu
AUSTRALIAN that combines Japanese flavors—tuna tataki chased by udon noodles in a mushroom hot pot—with such European-inspired fare as pork hock with coconut caramel and apple puree. Tempura whiting, salt-

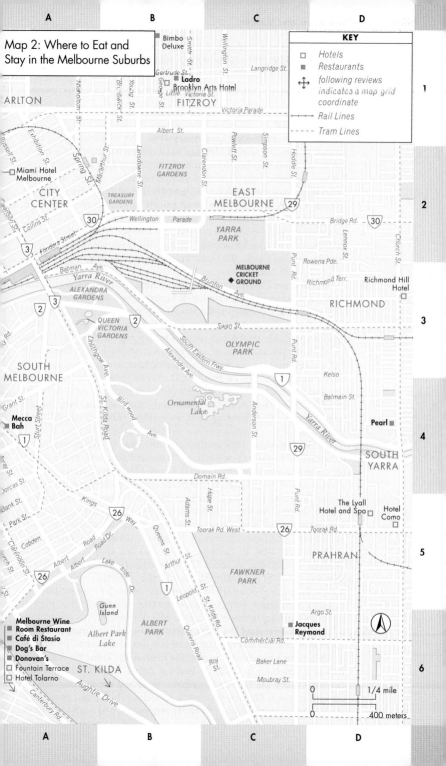

Map 2: Where to Eat and Stay in the Melbourne Suburbs

KEY
□ Hotels
■ Restaurants
⬦ following reviews indicates a map grid coordinate
—⊢ Rail Lines
---- Tram Lines

ARLTON

CARLTON

Bimbo Deluxe

Ladro
Brooklyn Arts Hotel

FITZROY

CITY CENTER

Miami Hotel Melbourne

TREASURY GARDENS

FITZROY GARDENS

EAST MELBOURNE

29

30

YARRA PARK

Bridge Rd. 30

MELBOURNE CRICKET GROUND

Richmond Hill Hotel

RICHMOND

Yarra River

ALEXANDRA GARDENS

QUEEN VICTORIA GARDENS

Swan St.

OLYMPIC PARK

SOUTH MELBOURNE

Ornamental Lake

Pearl

SOUTH YARRA

Mecca Bah

Domain Rd.

The Lyall Hotel and Spa

Hotel Como

Toorak Rd.

PRAHRAN

Gunn Island

FAWKNER PARK

Melbourne Wine Room Restaurant
Café di Stasio
Dog's Bar
Donovan's
Fountain Terrace
Hotel Tolarno

Albert Park Lake

ALBERT PARK

ST. KILDA

Jacques Reymond

Argo St.

Commercial Rd.

Baker Lane

Moubray St.

0   1/4 mile

0   400 meters

Aughtie Drive

Canterbury Rd.

chickpea shoots and marinated feta). ⊠ *631–633 Church St., Richmond* ☏ *03/9421–4599* ⊕ *www.pearlrestaurant.com.au* ▭ *AE, DC, MC, V* ✛ *2:D4.*

WHERE TO STAY

CITY CENTER

$$$ ⊡ **Grand Mercure Flinders Lane Apartments.** The smallest of the city's upscale hotels, the Grand Mercure has a central location and a mix of lovely one- and two-bedroom suites, which sleep four to eight people. Rooms are beautifully furnished and decorated in apricot, burgundy, and pale-green tones. All have kitchenettes with microwaves and refrigerators. Guests have use of a small private terrace on the sixth floor, inspired by the Renaissance gardens of Italy. ⊠ *321 Flinders La., City Center* ☏ *03/9629–4088* ⊕ *www.mercure.com* ⤺ *57 suites* ⌂ *In-room: kitchen, refrigerator, broadband (some), Wi-Fi (some). In-hotel: gym, laundry service, public Wi-Fi, parking (fee), no-smoking rooms* ▭ *AE, DC, MC, V* ✛ *1:A5.*

$$$$ ⊡ **Hotel Lindrum.** Housed in the Heritage-listed Lindrum family billiards
★ center, a short walk from Federation Square, this is one of Melbourne's savviest boutique properties. Rooms are spacious, with high ceilings and timber floors. A smart restaurant, cozy cigar bar, and lounge with an open fireplace are the perfect settings for sipping local wines. Flinders Lane, lined with chic bars and eateries, is a short stroll away. **Pros:** warm feel, exceptional service, full in-room entertainment systems. **Cons:** on busy thoroughfare. ⊠ *26 Flinders St., City Center* ☏ *03/9668–1111* ⊕ *www.hotellindrum.com.au* ⤺ *59 rooms* ⌂ *In-room: safe, refrigerator, DVD, Internet. In-hotel: restaurant, room service, bar, laundry service, public Wi-Fi, parking (fee), no-smoking rooms* ▭ *AE, DC, MC, V* ✛ *1:C5.*

$$$$ ⊡ **The Hotel Windsor.** This century-old aristocrat of Melbourne hotels
★ combines Victorian-era character with modern comforts, and is a must for history lovers. Plush rooms have Laura Ashley–style wall coverings and rosewood furnishings, although the marble bathrooms are modest in size. Standard rooms are a reasonable size; if you need space, book one of the vast Victorian suites or a two-room executive suite. The 111 Spring Street Restaurant serves Continental-style dishes in a formal setting. The hotel commands a position opposite the State Houses of Parliament close to theaters, parks, and fine shops. **Pros:** elegant heritage feel, central location. **Cons:** heritage rooms are fittingly Old World in decor. ⊠ *111 Spring St., City Center* ☏ *03/9633–6000* ⊕ *www. thehotelwindsor.com.au* ⤺ *160 rooms, 20 suites* ⌂ *In-room: Internet. In-hotel: restaurant, bar, gym, room service, laundry service, parking (fee), no-smoking rooms* ▭ *AE, DC, MC, V* ✛ *1:C4.*

$$$$ ⊡ **InterContinental Hotel The Rialto.** After a A$60 million upgrade and an 18-month closure, this five-star hotel was unveiled in late 2008 in one of Melbourne's most historic sites. The impressive Gothic Revival Rialto Building was built in 1889 by William Pitt, a famous architect who designed many Melbourne landmarks, including the Princess Theatre on Spring Street. The new-looking hotel is the only five-star property in the business-heavy precinct of central Melbourne, and is adjacent to the

Rialto Observation Tower, Melbourne's tallest building until a couple of years ago. The renovation has retained the lovely façade; the grand internal atrium (overlooked by five stories of rooms) and the impressive Alluvial Rstaurant are notable as well. Two lobby bars—Bluestone and Market Lane—offer more casual fare, the latter with a 100-martini cocktail list. Rooms are decorated in subdued tones of chocolate, creams, and tan, and equipped with the latest CD and DVD players and coffee machines. The most interesting rooms, with sloping walls and almost "Sleeping Beauty castle" windows are just below the hotel's two turrents at the front of the building. **Pros:** spectacular, historic facade, great bar and club lounge. **Cons:** slightly corporate feel. ⊠ *495 Collins St., City Center* ☎ *03/8627–1400* ⊕ *www.intercontinental.com/melbourne* ⇆ *253 rooms* ⚲ *In-room: safe, refrigerator (some), DVD, Internet. In-hotel: restaurant, room service, 2 bars, pool, gym, spa, laundry, Wi-Fi, parking (free)* ⊟ *AE, D, DC, MC, V* ⍿⊙⎮ *EP* ⊹ *1:A5.*

¢ 🖼 **Melbourne Central YHA.** This budget hostel is run by Youth Hostels Australia (YHA), an organization that likes to occupy heritage buildings or those with plenty of character. This new hostel is no exception; it's located in the former five-story Markillies Hotel, an Edwardian-era structure built in 1915 and once a working man's hotel. Today it has a great rooftop terrace (with barbecue) and the popular Bertha Brown's Bar. It is well situated near Southern Cross Station, the DFO discount shopping center, and Docklands. There are 43 multi-share or dorm rooms, with separate dorms for males and females, and eight double rooms with en-suite bathrooms. Other twin and double rooms share bathroom facilities along with the dorms. While the name implies a younger crowd, the hostel is open to all ages, and guests with a YHA card get a 10 percent discount. It's recommended to book YHA accommodation well in advance. There are several kitchenettes, guest lounges with Internet terminals, and Wi-Fi throughout the building. An outdoor terrace BBQ area, kitchen, TV lounges, and Internet café are on-site. **Pros:** good price, good location. **Cons:** shared bathrooms, student feel may not appeal to all. ⊠ *562 Flinders St., City Center* ☎ *03/9621–2523* ⊕ *www.yha.com.au* ⇆ *74 rooms, including 48 twin or double rooms* ⚲ *In-room: no a/c, no phone, no TV (some), Wi-Fi. In-hotel: bar, laundry facilities, Internet terminal, Wi-Fi* ⊟ *MC, V* ⍿⊙⎮ *EP* ⊹ *1:A5.*

$$$$ 🖼 **Park Hyatt.** Set right next to Fitzroy Gardens and opposite St. Patrick's
Fodor'sChoice Cathedral, this is one of Melbourne's most elegant hotels. It's also a
★ popular choice for celebrities (such as Pink who stayed there in early 2009), though you'd never know: its slightly removed location and three entrances allow the famous to slip through unnoticed. Warm colors, rich wood paneling, and Art Deco–style furnishings adorn the rooms— all of which have walk-in wardrobes, king-size beds, Italian marble bathrooms, and roomy, modern work spaces. Suites are even more luxurious, some with fireplaces, terraces, and hot tubs. The seven-level radii restaurant and bar is artsy and chic; and contemporary artworks by international talents are on exhibit throughout the hotel (some are for sale). The pool is enormous for a city hotel. **Pros:** lavish appointments, new king-size beds, world-class service. **Cons:** slightly removed from the city center. ⊠ *1 Parliament Sq., East Melbourne* ☎ *03/9224–1234*

A delicatessen at Queen Victoria Market

📧 *Melbourne@hyatt.com.au* ⊕ *www.Hyatt.com* ↪ *216 rooms, 24 suites* ☖ *In-room: safe, DVD, Internet. In-hotel: restaurant, room service, bar, pool, gym, spa, concierge, laundry service, public Internet, public Wi-Fi, parking (fee)* ▭ *AE, DC, MC, V* ✚ *1:C4.*

$$ 🏨 **Robinsons in the City.** Melbourne's tiniest and possibly quaintest hotel occupies a converted 1850s bakery. The six beautifully furnished rooms have private bathrooms and are decorated with artworks from around the world. New owners have brightened up the rooms with fresh coats of paint, new air-conditioners, the latest digital TVs, and iPod docking stations, and provide free Wi-Fi. Guests without computers can check their e-mail using the office laptop. Homemade breakfasts—including fruit, smoked trout, sausage, bacon, eggs, and toast—are a real highlight. **Pros:** CBD-fringe location, great breakfast included, close to free circle tram and free shuttle bus. **Cons:** a bit of a walk from the city center. ✉ *405 Spencer St., at Batman St. City Center* ☎ *03/9329–2552* ⊕ *www.ritc.com. au* ↪ *6 rooms* ☖ *In-room: Wi-Fi. In-hotel: bar, laundry facilities, parking (no fee), no elevator* ▭ *AE, DC, MC, V* ❡◉ *BP* ✚ *1:A3.*

$$ 🏨 **Somerset Gordon Place.** This historic 1883 structure is one of the most
★ interesting and comfortable apartment hotels in the city. It's just steps from the Parliament building and the Princess Theatre, and not far from Chinatown's restaurants. The modern, comfortable accommodations contain washing machines, dryers, and dishwashers. The studios and one- and two-bedroom apartments face a courtyard with a 60-foot pool and a century-old palm tree. **Pros:** modern apartment-style furnishings, great location. **Cons:** homey feel. ✉ *24 Little Bourke St., City Center,* ☎ *03/9663–2888* ⊕ *www.somerset.com* ↪ *64 apartments* ☖ *In-room: DVD, kitchen, refrigerator, Internet, Wi-Fi (some). In-hotel: room*

service, pool, gym, laundry facilities, laundry service, public Wi-Fi, no-smoking rooms ☐ *AE, DC, MC, V* ✛ *1:C4.*

THE SUBURBS

$ ⚮ **Brooklyn Arts Hotel.** As the name suggests, the Brooklyn Arts Hotel is filled with art—paintings adorn the walls of the guest rooms and the guest lounge, while the leafy backyard is a blaze of color in spring and summer. Owned by filmmaker and public artist Maggie Fooke, the B&B occupies a lovely turn-of-the-century two-story mansion, and is ideal for travelers who like their boutique surroundings friendly. It's tucked into a quiet street in arty Fitzroy, near parks and cafés and a short tram ride or walk from the city. There are eight guest rooms, two with private bathrooms, while the other six rooms share three bathrooms. The upstairs queen en-suite rooms have enormous bedrooms, and each has a light-filled sitting room; one has a piano. The hotel has a lush courtyard garden, a perfect spot to enjoy the Contintenal breakfast. Bathrobes, hair dryers, and free Wi-Fi make it a perfect home away from home. **Pros:** cosy, arty, lovely garden, free Wi-Fi. **Cons:** some shared bathrooms. ☒ *48–50 George St., Fitzroy* ☏ *03/9419–9328* ⊕ *www.brooklynartshotel.com* ⚲ *8 rooms* △ *In-room: TV (some), Wi-Fi. In-hotel: laundry facilites, Wi-Fi* ☐ *AE, D, DC, MC, V* ⦿ *CP* ✛ *2:B1.*

$–$$ ⚮ **Fountain Terrace.** Set on a tree-lined street in one of Melbourne's picturesque bayside areas, this 1880 property has seven guest suites and two new apartments, all of them immaculate and furnished with opulent antiques. Each suite is named after a prominent Australian figure; the Henry Lawson, for example (named for a famous Aussie poet), is decorated in blue-and-gold brocade and has a hot tub. The Dame Nellie Melba suite is the most spacious, and has French doors opening onto a private balcony. Guests have complimentary access to the nearby St. Kilda Salt Water Sea Baths, a complex with a large pool, hydrotherapy spa, and steam room. **Pros:** breezy bayside locale, warm service. **Cons:** patchy Wi-Fi in two of the rooms. ☒ *28 Mary St., St. Kilda West* ☏ *03/9593–8123* ⊕ *www.fountainterrace.com.au* ⚲ *7 suites, 2 apartments* △ *In-room: no phone, DVD, refrigerator. In-hotel: no elevator, public Wi-Fi* ☐ *AE, DC, MC, V* ⦿ *BP* ✛ *2:A6.*

$$$$ ⚮ **Hotel Como.** With its opulence and funky modern furnishings, this ★ luxury hotel is as popular with business travelers as it is with visiting artists and musicians. Gray marble and chrome are prominent throughout the pop art–meets–Art Deco interior. Suites have king-size beds and bathrobes; several even have Jacuzzis. Some of the third-floor suites have access to private Japanese gardens, while others have fully equipped kitchenettes. Outstanding services (including free limousine rides into the city each day) and a swank clientele make this one of the best picks on the city's fringe. Good restaurants are only a short walk away. While high-season tariffs are high, there are some great package deals at other times. **Pros:** lavishly appointed rooms, great shopping, restaurants nearby. **Cons:** slightly corporate feel. ☒ *630 Chapel St., South Yarra* ☏ *03/9825–2222* ⊕ *www.mirvachotels.com.au* ⚲ *107 suites* △ *In-room: safe, kitchen (some), Internet. In-hotel: room service, bar, pool, gym, laundry service, no-smoking rooms* ☐ *AE, DC, MC, V* ✛ *2:D5.*

$ ⊞ **Hotel Tolarno.** Set in the heart of St. Kilda's café, bar, and club precinct, Hotel Tolarno was once owned by artists who ran a gallery out of the space. Even today the place has an artistic bent; many of the rooms and common spaces are decorated with paintings by students of the Victorian College of the Arts (VCA) and Royal Melbourne Institute of TAFE (RMIT). The color schemes here are a bit garish (red, purple, and orange dominate), and the furnishings are basic, but this is a friendly, funky place to stay (or to have a bite in Tolarno's Mirka restaurant, run by Guy Grossi who runs the Grossi Florentino in Bourke Street). **Pros:** great restaurant, cool vibe, heart-of-breezy-St. Kilda location. **Cons:** area can have a dubious crowd, noisy late at night. ⊠ *42 Fitzroy St., St. Kilda* ☎ *03/9537–0200* ⊕ *www.hoteltolarno.com.au* ↷ *36 rooms* △ *In-room: DVD, kitchen (some), refrigerator, Wi-Fi. In-hotel: restaurant, room service, no elevator, laundry facilities, laundry service, parking (fee)* ⊟ *AE, DC, MC, V* ✛ *2:A6.*

$$$$ ⊞ **The Lyall Hotel and Spa.** The spacious one- and two-bedroom suites at this exclusive hotel come with all the luxuries: CD and DVD players, velour bathrobes and slippers, gourmet minibars, and a pillow "menu." The in-house spa offers a full range of massages, facials, and body treatments (try the lime-and-ginger salt glow); the champagne bar is the perfect place to relax after a day of sightseeing. Mini art galleries adorn each floor of the hotel. **Pros:** an extravagant spa, 24-hour bistro, 24-hour gym. **Cons:** outside city center. ⊠ *14 Murphy St., South Yarra* ☎ *03/9868–8222* ⊕ *www.thelyall.com* ↷ *40 suites* △ *In-room: DVD, Internet, Wi-Fi. In-hotel: restaurant, bar, gym, spa, bicycles, laundry facilities, laundry service, public Wi-Fi, parking (fee), no-smoking rooms* ⊟ *AE, DC, MC, V* ✛ *2:D5.*

¢ ⊞ **Miami Hotel Melbourne.** Like a Motel 6, only fancier, Miami Hotel is an excellent value for the budget- and style-conscious. Located on the city fringe and an 8-minute ride away on the No. 8 tram, the accommodations range from budget rooms with shared bathrooms to newer rooms with TVs (with cable movies) and Wi-Fi. It's suitable for doubles, triples, and families. There are also three TV lounges with cable movies, and breakfast can be provided on request (A$8 Continental and A$14 full). This efficiently run hotel and its friendly staff have picked up top accolades, and it's been short-listed for the Victorian Tourism Awards. **Pros:** excellent service, great value, good location. **Cons:** basic amenities. ⊠ *13 Hawke St., at King St., West Melbourne* ☎ *03/9321–2444 or 1800/132333* ⊕ *www.themiami.com.au* ↷ *81 rooms, 41 with bath* △ *In-room: TV (some), refrigerator (some), Wi-Fi. In-hotel: laundry facilities, public Internet* ⊟ *AE, MC, V* ✛ *2:A2.*

$–$$ ⊞ **Richmond Hill Hotel.** Just a short ride from the city center (on the No. 79 tram), this boutique hotel occupies a regal, garden-skirted mansion. Lodgings here include single and double rooms with shared bathrooms, doubles with in-room bathrooms, and two- and three-bedroom apartments. The basic dorm rooms are used primarily for school groups. There are an Internet room, garden terrace, bar, and guest lounge with newspapers and complimentary tea and coffee. **Pros:** quiet location, friendly service. **Cons:** somewhat Spartan digs. ⊠ *353 Church St., Richmond* ☎ *03/9428–6501* ⊕ *www.richmondhillhotel.com.au* ↷ *60 rooms*

⌂ *In-room: refrigerator (some), Wi-Fi. In-hotel: bar, laundry facilities, parking, Wi-Fi* ⊟ *AE, DC, MC, V* ¶⦿¶ *CP* ✛ *2:D3.*

NIGHTLIFE AND THE ARTS

THE ARTS

Melbourne Events, available from tourist outlets, is a comprehensive monthly guide to what's happening in town. For a complete listing of performing-arts events, galleries, and film, consult the "EG" (Entertainment Guide) supplement in the Friday edition of the *Age* newspaper. The *Age*'s daily "Metro" section has a comprehensive listing of city events such as gallery openings, theater performances, public talks, bands, workshops, and festivals in its "If You Do One Thing Today" pages. Tourism Victoria hosts a fantastic Web site (⊕ *www.visitmelbourne.com*) detailing all of Melbourne's upcoming and current events. The free local music magazine *Beat* is available at cafés, stores, markets, and bars. *Brother Sister* is the local gay paper.

> **TRASHY FILMS**
>
> There's no such thing as a bad movie when it's screened at the Junkyard Cinema in Melbourne's hip, arty, and quirky Fitzroy neighborhood. This outdoor cinema screens "cult" classics every Sunday night in summer. Even if one person's cult classic is another's worst celluloid nightmare, one thing's certain—you won't see any glossy new releases here. ⊕ *www.junkyardcinema.com.au.*

MUSIC AND DANCE
In the 2,000-seat State Theatre at the Arts Centre, the **Australian Ballet** (⊠ *Victorian Arts Centre, 100 St. Kilda Rd., Southbank* ☎ *03/9669–2700 Ballet, 13–6100 Ticketmaster7*) stages five programs annually, and presents visiting celebrity dancers from around the world. The **Hamer Hall** (⊠ *The Arts Centre, 100 St. Kilda Rd., Southbank* ☎ *03/9281–8000*) stages classy concerts. Big-name, crowd-drawing contemporary artists perform at **Melbourne Park** (⊠ *Batman Ave., City Center* ☎ *03/9286–1600*). The **Melbourne Symphony Orchestra** (⊠ *Victorian Arts Centre, 100 St. Kilda Rd., Southbank* ☎ *13–6100 Ticketmaster7*) performs year-round in the 2,600-seat Hamer Hall. Open-air concerts take place December through March at the **Sidney Myer Music Bowl** (⊠ *King's Domain near Swan St. Bridge, South Melbourne* ☎ *13–6100 Ticketmaster7*).

THEATER
The **Half-Tix** (⊠ *Melbourne Town Hall, Swanston and Collins Sts., City Center* ☎ *03/9650–9420*) ticket booth in the Melbourne Town Hall sells tickets to theater attractions at half price on performance days. It's open Monday 10–2, Tuesday–Thursday 11–6, Friday 11–6:30, and Saturday 10–4. Sales are cash only.

The **Melbourne Theatre Company** (⊠ *252 Sturt St., South Melbourne* ☎ *03/9684–4500* ⊕ *www.mtc.com.au*) is Australia's oldest professional theater company. A brand-new theater opened in January 2009 with two performance spaces, the 500-seat Summer Theatre and the 150-seat Lawler Studio. Productions are also staged at the nearby Arts Centre in St. Kilda Road. (⊠ *140 Southbank blvd. [corner Dodds St.], Southbank* ☎ *03/8688–0800* ⊕ *www.mtc.com.au*).

The city's second-largest company, the **Playbox at the CUB Malthouse Company** (✉ *113 Sturt St., Southbank* ☎ *03/9685–5111* ⊕ *www.malthousetheatre.com.au*), stages about 10 new or contemporary productions a year. The CUB Malthouse theater is a flexible space designed for drama, dance, and circus companies.

Revues and plays are staged at the **Comedy Theatre** (✉ *240 Exhibition St., City Center* ☎ *03/9299–9800 or 03/9299–9500*), which along with the Princess, Regent, and Forum theaters is owned by the Marriner's Theatre company and often uses the same telephone number.

The **Regent Theatre** (✉ *191 Collins St., City Center* ☎ *03/9299–9800 or 03/9299–9500* ⊕ *www.marrinertheatres.com.au*), an ornate 1920s building, originally opened to screen movies, but nowadays presents mainstream productions, including the smash hit *Wicked*.

Theatreworks (✉ *14 Acland St., St. Kilda* ☎ *03/9534–3388* ⊕ *www. theatreworks.org.au*) concentrates on contemporary Australian plays.

NIGHTLIFE

BARS AND COCKTAIL LOUNGES

Crown Casino. Melbourne's first gambling center has blackjack, roulette, and poker machines. There are also dozens of restaurants, including branches of the famed Japanese chef Nobu and renowned Sydney chef Neil Perry's Rockpool, shops, bars, and two nightclubs open until late. The casino is on the south bank of the Yarra. ✉ *8 Whiteman St., Southbank* ☎ *03/9292–8888* ⊕ *www.crowncasino.com.au* ☉ *Daily 24 hrs.*

Angelucci's (✉ *500 Chapel St., South Yarra* ☎ *03/9826–3086*) is a sophisticated lounge bar, with an A-list clientele to match. **Atrium** (✉ *25 Collins St., City Center* ☎ *03/9653–0000*), a cocktail bar on the 35th floor of the Hotel Sofitel, has spectacular views. **Cookie** (✉ *252 Swanston St., City Center* ☎ *03/9663–7660*), in a huge warehouse-style space with a balcony, focuses on imported beer and great Thai food. In addition to being a hallowed live music venue, the **Esplanade Hotel** (✉ *11 Upper Esplanade, St. Kilda* ☎ *03/9534–0211*), or "Espy," is home to a historic pub—built in 1878—listed with the National Trust. Reminiscent of Hollywood opulence, **Gin Palace** (✉ *190 Little Collins St., City Center* ☎ *03/9654–0533*) has more than enough types of martinis to satisfy any taste. Enter from Russell Street.

Antique leather sofas and cigars characterize the classy milieu at the **Melbourne Supper Club** (✉ *161 Spring St., City Center* ☎ *03/9654–6300*). Stop by the **Polly** (✉ *401 Brunswick St., Fitzroy* ☎ *03/9417–0880*), which combines antique red-velvet lounges, Art Deco mirrors, one of Melbourne's best wine lists, and a colorful and quirky clientele with a magnificent fish tank, for which it is famous. **Revolver Upstairs** (✉ *229 Chapel St., Prahran* ☎ *03/9521–5985*) caters to the young.

Silk Road (✉ *425 Collins St., City Center* ☎ *03/9693–9444*) is an exotic new bar with lavish decor and a serious collection of chandeliers. It's themed Venetian and Dynasty bars are gorgeous places for a drink. Tony Starr's **Kitten Club** (✉ *267 Little Collins St., City Center* ☎ *03/9650–2448*) has a 1950s feel (Dean Martin songs are popular) and live jazz, and the opulent ladies' powder room is a big hit with the girls.

Melbourne is known for it's top-notch live theater.

The **Undertaker** (✉ *329 Burwood Rd., Hawthorn* ☎ *03/9818–3944*) is the site of what was once an actual undertaker's parlor. Today the building contains a very stylish bar and restaurant. The **Xchange** (✉ *119 Commercial Rd., South Yarra* ☎ *03/9867–5144*) is a popular gay bar in the busy gay district of Prahran.

Most of the central city's dance clubs are along the King Street strip or nestled in Little Collins Street. Clubs usually open at 9 or 10 weekends and some weeknights, and stay open until the early-morning hours. Expect to pay a small cover at most clubs—between A$10 and A$15.

COMEDY CLUBS
The **Comedy Club** (✉ *188 Collins St.* ☎ *03/9650–6668*) is a popular place to see top-class Australian and international acts. Another good place for a laugh is the **Comic's Lounge** (✉ *26 Errol St., North Melbourne* ☎ *03/9348–9488*).

JAZZ CLUBS
Bennetts Lane (✉ *25 Bennetts La., City Center* ☎ *03/9663–2856*) is one of the city center's jazz mainstays. Cutting-edge cabaret acts are featured at **45 Downstairs** (✉ *45 Flinders La., City Center* ☎ *03/9662–9966*). **Manchester Lane** (✉ *36 Manchester La., City Center* ☎ *03/9663–0630*) has late-night jazz and blues. The **Night Cat** (✉ *141 Johnston St., Fitzroy* ☎ *03/9417–0090*) hosts jazzy evening shows most nights of the week, and the Latin big band on Sunday nights is legendary.

POPULAR LIVE MUSIC CLUBS
The **Corner Hotel** (✉ *57 Swan St., Richmond* ☎ *03/9427–7300*) has alternative, reggae, rock, blues, and jazz acts with an emphasis on homegrown bands. At the **Crown Casino** (✉ *Level 3, Crown Entertainment Complex, Riverside Ave., Southbank* ☎ *03/9292–8888* ⊕ *www.crowncasino.com.au*) the Showroom and the Mercury Lounge attract big international and Australian headliners. You can catch headline

rock acts at the **Ding Dong Lounge** (⊠ *Level 1, 18 Market La., City Center* ☎ *03/9662–1020*).

The **Hi-Fi Bar** (⊠ *125 Swanston St., City Center* ☎ *03/9654–0992, 03/9654–7617 show nights*) is a popular venue for live local and lesser-known international rock bands. The **Palais Entertainment Complex** (⊠ *Lower Esplanade, St. Kilda* ☎ *03/9525–3240, 13–6100 Ticketmaster7*) features alternative and hard-rock headline acts, such as Nick Cave and Queens of the Stone Age and U2. A diverse range of Australian and international acts, including rap, rock, reggae, and hip-hop, plays at **Pony** (⊠ *68 Little Collins St., City Center* ☎ *03/9662–1026*). For rock and roll, punk, and grunge, head to the **Prince of Wales** (⊠ *29 Fitzroy St., St. Kilda* ☎ *03/9536–1177*), which attracts a straight and gay crowd.

> ## A FUNNY NIGHT OUT
>
> Melburnians love a laugh, and the annual comedy festival is the funniest place to be to catch top Australian and international performers. The month-long event takes place in the Town Hall and venues across town, and there are free events in open spaces. The festival also seeks out new talent and culminates with the Raw Comedy awards for the best new Australian stand-up performer. If you're in town in April, you won't be laughing if you miss it. ⊕ *www. comedyfestival.com.au.*

SHOPPING

Melbourne has firmly established itself as the nation's fashion capital. Australian designer labels are available on High Street in Armadale, on Toorak Road and Chapel Street in South Yarra, and on Bridge Road in Richmond. High-quality vintage clothing abounds on Greville Street in Prahran. Discount hunters will love the huge DFO (Discount Factory Outlet) right next door to Southern Cross Station on Spencer Street, with its many stores. Most shops are open Monday–Thursday 9–5:30, Friday until 9, and Saturday until 5. Major city stores are open Sunday until 5.

MARKETS

Camberwell Market (⊠ *Station St., Camberwell* ☎ *1300/367712*), open Sunday only, is a popular haunt for seekers of the old and odd. More than 300 stalls display antiques, knickknacks, and food. **Chapel Street Bazaar** (⊠ *217–223 Chapel St., Prahran* ☎ *03/9529–1727*), open daily 10–6, has wooden stalls selling everything from stylish secondhand clothes to curios and knickknacks. **Prahran Market** (⊠ *163 Commercial Rd., South Yarra* ☎ *03/8290–8220* ⊕ *www.prahranmarket.com. au*) sells nothing but food—a fantastic, mouthwatering array imported from all over the world. It's open Tuesday and Saturday dawn–5 PM, Thursday and Friday dawn–6 PM, and Sunday 10–3. **Queen Victoria Market** (⊠ *Elizabeth and Victoria Sts., City Center* ☎ *03/9320–5822* ⊕ *www.qvm.com.au*) is the oldest market in the southern hemisphere. With more than 1,000 stalls, this sprawling, spirited bazaar is the city's prime produce outlet—most of Melbourne comes here to buy its strawberries, fresh flowers, and imported cheeses. On Sunday you can find deals on jeans, T-shirts, and secondhand stuff. It's open Tuesday–Thursday 6–2, Friday 6–6, Saturday 6–3, and Sunday 9–4. Later, it becomes the Suzuki Gaslight Night Market, open nightly from 5:30 to 10 from December to mid-February, and Wednesday nights the rest of the year, it has wandering entertainment and simple food stalls. Market tours take you deep inside the labyrinth, and cooking classes are conducted by well-known chefs.

St. Kilda Esplanade Art and Craft Market (⊠ *Upper Esplanade, St. Kilda* ☎ *03/9209–6777*) has more than 200 stalls selling paintings, crafts, pottery, jewelry, and homemade gifts. It's open Sunday 10–5. **South Melbourne Market** (⊠ *Cecil and Coventry Sts., South Melbourne* ☎ *03/9209–6295*), established in 1867, is Melbourne's second-oldest market. You'll find a huge selection of fresh produce and foodstuffs. It's open Wednesday and weekends 8–4 and Friday 8–6.

SHOPPING CENTERS, MALLS, AND ARCADES

Bourke Street Mall, once the busiest east–west thoroughfare in the city, is now a pedestrian zone (but watch out for those trams!). Two of the city's biggest department stores are here, **Myer** (⊠ *314 Bourke St. between Elizabeth and Swanston Sts.,, City Center* ☎ *03/9661–1111*) and **David Jones** (⊠ *310 Bourke St., City Center* ☎ *03/9643–2222*). An essential part of growing up in Melbourne is being taken to **Myer** at Christmas to see the window displays.

Block Arcade (⊠ *282 Collins St., City Center* ☎ *03/9654–5244*), an elegant 19th-century shopping plaza, contains the venerable Hopetoun Tea Rooms, the French Jewel Box, Orrefors Kosta Boda, Dasel Dolls and Bears, and Australian By Design. **Bridge Road,** in Richmond at the end of Flinders Street, east of the city, is a popular shopping strip for women's retail fashion that caters to all budgets.

★ **Brunswick Street,** northeast of the city in Fitzroy, has hip and grungy restaurants, coffee shops, gift stores, and clothing outlets selling the latest look. **Chapel Street,** in South Yarra between Toorak and Dandenong roads, is where you can find some of the ritziest boutiques in Melbourne, as well as cafés, art galleries, bars, and restaurants. Dotted with chic boutiques, many of them selling merchandise by up-and-coming Australian designers, **Flinders Lane** will make fashionistas happy. Between Swanston and Elizabeth streets, look for shops like Christine and Alice Euphemia, which stock eclectic, sometimes whimsical, clothing designs by young designers. **High Street**, between the suburbs of Prahran and Armadale, to the east of Chapel Street, has the best collection of antiques shops in Australia. The **Jam Factory** (⊠ *500 Chapel St., South Yarra* ☎ *03/9825–4699*) is a group of historic bluestone buildings that house cinemas, fashion, food, and gift shops, as well as a branch of the giant Borders book-and-music store.

★ **Little Collins Street,** a precinct of stores frequented by shoppers with perhaps more money than sense, is still worth a visit. In between frock shops you'll find musty stores selling classic film posters, antique and estate jewelry, and Australian opals. At the eastern end of **Collins Street,** beyond the cream-and-red Romanesque facade of St. Michael's Uniting Church, is **Paris End**, a name coined by Melburnians to identify the elegance of its fashionable shops as well as its general hauteur. The venerable **Le Louvre** salon (No. 74) is favored by Melbourne's high society. **Melbourne Central** (⊠ *300 Lonsdale St., City Center* ☎ *03/9922–1100*) is a dizzying complex huge enough to enclose a 100-year-old shot tower (used to make bullets) in its atrium. **Royal Arcade** (⊠ *355 Bourke St., City Center* ☎ *No phone*), built in 1846, is Melbourne's oldest shopping plaza. It remains a lovely place to browse, and it's home to the splendid Gaunt's Clock, which tolls away the hours.

★ **Southgate** (⊠ *4 Southbank Promenade, Southbank* ☎ *03/9699–4311*) has a spectacular riverside location. The shops and eateries here are a short walk both from the city center across Princes Bridge and from the Victorian Arts Center. There's outdoor seating next to the Southbank promenade.

SIDE TRIPS FROM MELBOURNE

Victoria's relatively compact size makes the state's principal attractions appealingly easy to reach, and the state's excellent road system makes driving the best option. There are a handful of enticing destinations within a 60- to 90-minute drive from Melbourne. Victoria is blessed with 21 distinct wine regions (and a total of 650 cellar doors where you can try and buy the product). The Yarra Valley, 40 km (25 mi) east of Melbourne, is Victoira's oldest wine region and a very pleasant place to spend a day on an organized tour. About 35 km (22 mi) south of the Yarra Valley is Olinda, a cute village at the heart of the Dandenong Ranges. This area of beautifully forested hills and valleys is a favorite weekend escape for Melburnians.The Mornington peninsula is famous for its wineries and beaches. On the western shore of Port Phillip Bay the Bellarine Peninsula is also developing a winery industry, but it's the grand 19th-century hotels of Queenscliff that have been attracting visitors on day trips.

YARRA VALLEY AND HEALESVILLE

★ Healesville is a good base for travel to Yarra Valley wineries and the Dandenongs Region, as it's almost halfway between the two.

On February 7, 2009 (known as Black Saturday), ferocious bushfires ripped through forests and towns to the east and north of Healesville, destroying more than 1,000 homes and claiming the lives of 173 people. Most of the historic town of Marysville (28 km [17 mi] east of Healesville) was destroyed; many of the wooden sculptures from the major attraction, Bruno's Art & Sculpture Garden, were later discovered to be intact, and have been relocated while the garden is being rebuilt. Lake Mountain resort, a winter ski destination and a summer hiking spot, 22 km (14 mi) from Marysville, is still operational. The pretty town of Warburton, 30 km (19 mi) from Healesville was untouched by the fires, but the nearby national parks were burnt and are closed until further notice. The 36-km (22-mi) Acheron Way drive is likely to reopen at the beginning of 2010. The Yarra Valley region and its wineries were not damaged by the fires, and two popular areas within

Side Trips From Melbourne

Marysville

Dixon's Creek

Healesville

Yarra Glen
Coldstream
Lilydale

Maroondah Hwy.

Warburton

✪ MELBOURNE

O Olinda

Kallista

Werribee

Ferntree Gully ♦

Sherbrooke

Belgrave

♦ Dandenong Ranges

Open Range Zoo

Port Phillip Bay

Dandenong

GREAT OCEAN ROAD

Princes Hwy.

Cranbourne

Geelong

Bellarine Hwy.

Frankston

Mount Eliza

Mornington Peninsula

Lang Lang

Bellarine Peninsula

Queens-cliff

Mornington

Nepean Hwy.

Mount Martha

Gippsland Hwy.

Pt. Lonsdale

Portsea

Dromana McRae

Red Hill

Hastings

French Island

Torquay

Point Nepean National Park

Sorrento

Rosebud

Rye

Arthurs Seat State Park

Bittern

Balnarring

Bass Hwy.

Somers

Leongatha

Shoreham

Cowes

Cape Schanck

Flinders

Rhyll

Phillip Island ♦

Penguin Parade

San Remo

0 — 25 miles
0 — 40 km

Bass Strait

the Yarra Ranges National Park—Badger Weir Walk and Maroondah Reservoir—are open and ideal for bushwalking and picnics. ■TIP→ We encourage you to travel to the fire-affected areas, as your business will help rebuild their communities.

🍃 **Healesville Sanctuary** (✉ *Badger Creek Rd.* ☎ *03/5957–2800* ⊕ *www.zoo. org.au* 🎫 *A$24.40* 🕙 *Daily 9–5*)is lovely wildlife sanctuary that was thankfully untouched by the fires and has now become a temporary home for many of the native animals that lost their natural habitats. Many of the injured animals were brought in by nearby residents who found them on roads or wandering in the smoldering bushland. Come face-to-face with wedge-tailed eagles, grumpy wombats, nimble sugar gliders, and shy platypuses. You can also book a behind-the-scenes tour of the animal hospital, where you may see some of the animals still recovering from bushfire injuries.

GETTING HERE AND AROUND
Healesville, on the eastern side of the Yarra Valley, is 65 km (40 mi) from Melbourne. Take the Eastern Freeway from Melbourne to its junction with the Maroondah Highway and follow the signs to Lilydale and on to Healesville. Trains, operated by Connex, travel from central Melbourne to Lilydale, and buses connect Lilydale with Yarra Glen and Healesville It's advisable to have to car to explore the wineries, or take a

half-day or full day tour. Most tours will pick you up at your hotel.

TOURS

There are several companies operating winery tours from either Melbourne or the Yarra Valley itself. Tours generally include visits to four to five wineries and lunch. Victory Winery Tours offers full-day tours departing from Melbourne and visiting four to five wineries, including lunch for A$147 per person. Yarra Valley Winery Tours runs public and private tours with flexible itineraries. For most tours, mini-buses are the most common form of transport, but on weekends from 11 to 3:30 at A$100 per person Swans on Doongalla takes you out to four wineries along St. Huberts Road in a stretched horse-drawn carriage. A light lunch is served at Yering Farm winery. The meeting place is St. Huberts Winery. Rail enthusiasts can still enjoy the tracks even though passenger train services to Healesville stopped in 1980. You can travel along part of the track in open-sided trolley cars operated by the Yarra Valley Tourist Railway. The trolleys travel from Healesville through picturesque country, under bridges and through the historic TarraWarra brick tunnel and back again—a distance of about 8 km (5 mi), taking about 45 minutes. Night Owl tours that include a buffet barbecue meal at the station are offered for groups of 12 or more.

PRECIOUS RESOURCE

You won't be able to escape the "save water" signs as you travel around Victoria. Like much of Australia, parts of Victoria are in the grip of the worst drought in more than a century. Some hotels ask guests to participate in water-saving practices, and may even provide buckets to catch the excess (nonsoapy) shower water and use it on the garden. It's a lot of fun to get involved and help feed those thirsty plants.

ESSENTIALS

Transportation Contacts Connex (☎ 131/636 ⊕ www.metlinkmelbourne. com.au). **McKenzies Tourist Service** (✉ 285 Maroondah Hwy., Healesville ☎ 03/5962–5088 ⊕ www.mckenzies.com.au).

Tour Operators Swans on Doongalla Horse Drawn Carriages (✉ 2A Doongalla Rd., The Basin ☎ 03/9762–1910 ⊕ www.swansondoongalla.com. au). **Victoria Winery Tours** (✉ 9 The Willows , Gisborne ☎ 03/5428–8500 ⊕ www.winetours.com.au). **Yarra Valley Winery Tours** ✉ 299 Maroondah Hwy., Healesville ☎ 03/5966–2372 ⊕ www.yarravalleywinerytours.com.au). **Yarra Valley Speciality Tours & Transport** (✉ 30 Kelly's Rd., Warburton ☎ 03/5966–2372 ⊕ www.yarravalleyspecialtytours.com.au). **Yarra Valley Tourist Railway** (✉ Healesville Station, Healesville Kinglake Rd., Healesville ☎ 03/5962–2490 ⊕ www.yarravalleyrailway.org.au ➔ A$10 trolley rides; A$30 night tours with dinner ⊗ 10–4.

Visitor Information Yarra Valley Visitor Information Centre (✉ Old Courthouse, Harker St., Healesville ☎ 03/5962–2600 ⊕ www.visityarravalleytourism. asn.au).

EXPLORING THE WINERIES

A good time to visit the Yarra Valley is during the **Grape Grazing Festival** (☎ *03/5962–6600* ⊕ *www.grapegrazing.com.au*), which features wine tastings, music, and fine cuisine. While the festival has traditionally been held in February, the date was moved to April in 2009 owing to the bushfires, and the 2010 date has yet to be fixed. Check the Web site for updates. The Yarra Valley is also known for its wonderful produce—fruit, vegetables, herbs, bread, and cheeses—on sale at the monthly regional farmers' markets, including one at Yering Station (*see listing below*).

★ A family winery for three generations, **De Bortoli** (✉ *Pinnacle La., Dixon's Creek* ☎ *03/5965–2271* ⊕ *www.debortoli.com.au* ⊗ *Daily 10–5*) was established in 1928, four years after the founder Vittorio De Bortoli and his wife Giuseppina migrated to Australia from northern Italy. Chardonnays, Pinot Noir, and Rieslings are specialties, and you'll have ample opportunity to sample a few—wine tastings are free, but a $7 charge charge applies for tasting stickies, including Noble One, De Bortoli's most awarded wine since first introduced 25 years ago. The restaurant, which has stunning views of the surrounding vines, landscaped gardens, and mountains, serves delectable dishes using Yarra Valley produce; a four-course chef's lunch is A$55 a head (A$65 on Sundays). You might like to start with a Bellini—a light cocktail of white peach juice and Windy Peak Pinot Chardonnay (a sparkling wine). A popular feature is the new cheese maturation and tasting room in the cellar-door area. Resident cheese maker Richard Thomas creates gourmet cheese tasting plates with matching wines (prices vary depending on produce chosen). A Wine Adventure, which includes a wine tutorial, guided vineyard and winery tours, barrel tastings, hints on food and wine matching, and a three-course lunch is held on the first Saturday of every month at $A125 per head.

★ **Domaine Chandon** (✉ *727–729 Maroondah Hwy., Coldstream* ☎ *03/9738–9200* ⊕ *www.greenpointwines.com.au*) has one of the most spectacular settings in the Yarra Valley. Apart from its sparkling wines, the winery produces Shiraz, Chardonnary, Pinot Gris, and rosé. Its Green Point tasting room has enormous floor-to-ceiling windows providing fantastic views over the vineyards and to the Yarra ranges in the distance. Free guided tours are conducted daily at 11, 1, and 3, and take visitors through the step-by-step production of sparkling wine, including visits to the vines and the bottling area. Lunch is served from 11AM in the Green Room (main courses range from A$19.50 to A$25.50), and each dish has a recommended accompanying wine (from A$8.50 a glass). Selections include venison pie accompanied by the Heathcote Shiraz and pan roasted barramundi accompanied by the Pinot Gris.

Rochford Wines (✉ *Maroondah Hwy. at Hill Rd., Coldstream* ☎ *03/5962–2119* ⊕ *www.rochfordwines.com*) occupies a striking-looking property; a building crafted almost entirely of glass looks over the vineyards and rolling green paddocks. The family-owned winery produces renowned Pinot Noir and Chardonnay, and has in recent years turned the huge property into the most happening place in the Yarra Valley—its huge amphitheatre plays host to international and local performers at the annual Day on the Green festival (recent acts have included Rod Stewart and Lionel Richie); in the summer months it screens movies under the stars. There are a wine-tasting bar and a stylish restaurant (offering two courses for A$55 and three courses for $A65 per person) and casual café, both open seven days a week for lunch and, in the case of the café, all-day light meals. Tastings are daily 10–5.

✕ **Stones of the Yarra Valley** (✉ *14 St. Huberts Rd., Coldstream* ☎ *03/9739–0900* ⊕ *www.stonesoftheyarravalley.com* ⊙ *No lunch Mon.–Thurs.*) is a new addition to the Yarra Valley. Though it's not a winery, it's a fantastic place to sample the region's vino. This restaurant and wine-tasting room are housed in an old weather-beaten barn that has been beautifully restored. Set amid 50 acres of grapevines and surrounded by century-old oak trees, and with views of the Yarra Ranges, it's a great place to partake in wine tasting (A$5), sample light meals, or just have a coffee or a wine at the casual Mezze Wine Bar. The dinner menu could include Atlantic salmon on potato sauté with salsa verde or chicken filled with almonds, goat's cheese, and spinach baked with provincial style French du puy lentils (both A$30). Performances by well-known Australian artists, who have included jazz maestro James Morrison, take place throughout the year, and are excellent value at between A$95 to A$110 for a three-course meal and show. Free Sunday concerts featuring up-and-coming jazz and classical performers are staged at 2 PM in the lovely hand-hewn stone chapel on the site on selected dates.

The **Yering Station Winery** (✉ *38 Melba Hwy., Yarra Glen* ☎ *03/9730–0100* ⊕ *www.yering.com*) shares a property with the historic Yering Chateau boutique hotel. It's Victoria's first vineyard and it and its cellar door still have plenty of rustic charm. The 1859 building is home to the cellar door, a wine and produce store, and the casual Matt's bar, where you can relax all day sipping wine and dining from a tasty menu. The Wine Bar Restaurant is the pièce de résistance, both architecturally and gastronomically. It's a curved, hand-hewn stone building with wonderful floor-to-ceiling windows overlooking spectacular valley scenery. Enjoy a wonderful seasonal menu overseen by chef Colin Swalwell. Main-course dishes (from A$30 to A$33) could include the duck breast and slow-cooked duck leg and walnut and sultana mash with blueberry jus; you may want to finish the meal with the decadent cocoa-dusted Irish-coffee cheesecake with vanilla anglaise. Those who would prefer just to wander and sip wines at the cellar door are free to take the self-guided winery tour through the sculpture gardens. A farmers' market, where local growers sell their region's produce of olives,

WINE AND SONG

Catch a little jazz at lunch or spend the whole day watching great performances from local and international headline acts; Victoria's wineries provide an array of entertainment for music connoisseurs. Vineyards come alive with the summer, so check out the events with local tourist offices. Make sure you book early for the popular Day on the Green concert series held in the Rochford Winery in the Yarra Valley and at All Saints Winery in Rutherglen.

"Just a short drive from Melbourne is the captivating beauty of the Yarra Valley." —photo by lisargold, Fodors. com member

eggs, honey, cheese, coffee, flowers, and jams, takes place on the third Sunday of the month.

OUTDOOR ACTIVITIES

BIKING **Yarra Valley Cycles** (⊠ *108 Main St., Lilydale* ✛ *Across the road from Lilydale Railway Station* ☎ *03/9735–1483* ⊕ *www.yarravalleycycles. com* ✆ *Mon.–Sat. 9–5, Sun. 10–4*) will rent you a bike from A$40 a day and point you in the right direction for the best cycling routes in the valley and nearby scenic regions.

BUSHWALKING Several sections of Yarra Ranges National Park have reopened after the devasting February 2009 bushfires. Stop in the Yarra Valley Visitor Information Centre at Healseville for the best advice on which areas to hike. A Walks and Riding Trails map is available for A$5. You can also check out Parks Victoria's Web site (⊕ *www.parkweb.vic.au*).

BALLOONING **Balloon Sunrise** (⊠ *Bell St., Yarra Glen* ☎ *03/9730–2422* ⊕ *www.hotair-ballooning.com.au*) was founded in 1986, and was the first commerical hot-air ballooning operation in Australia. For A$295–A$320 per person you can take off at dawn and drift peacefully over the vineyards for an hour. A champagne breakfast is served after the flight at the Mercure Balgownie Estate Winery.

GOLFING **Warburton Golf Club** (⊠ *17 Dammans Rd., Warburton* ☎ *03/5966–2306* ⊕ *www.warburtongolf.com.au*) is a hidden gem nestled among the Yarra Ranges. For A$25 for 18 holes you can golf over meandering streams and bushland blooming with wildflowers. Although it's called a semi-private club, visitors are welcome to come and play 9 or 18 holes if they ring and book in advance. Rental clubs are available if you didn't pack your own. Warburton is 30 km (19 mi) southeast of Healesville.

WHERE TO STAY

$$$$ ⚑ **Chateau Yering.** Stockmen William, Donald, and James Ryrie built
Fodor's Choice this homestead in the 1860s, and it was later one of the Yarra Valley's
★ first vineyards. It's now a luxury hotel with opulent suites, beautiful
gardens, and the upscale Eleonore's Restaurant ($$$$). This is a favorite base for sunrise balloon flights over the Yarra Valley, followed by
a champagne breakfast at the on-site Sweetwater Café ($$). Balloon
packages range from A$1,180 to A$1,470 for two, including dinner,
breakfast, and lodging. ⊠ *42 Melba Hwy., Yarra Glen* 🕾 *03/9237–3333
or 1800/237333* ⊕ *www.chateauyering.com.au* 🖙 *32 suites* ⚑ *In-hotel:
2 restaurants, room service, tennis court, pool, no elevator* ⊟ *AE, DC,
MC, V* ❙◎❙ *MAP.*

¢ ⚑ **Healesville Hotel.** Housed in a restored 1910 pub, this famous local
★ lodge has seven bright, modern upstairs rooms (A$130 a night in high
season) with high ceilings, tall windows, and genteel touches such as
handmade soaps. The three bathrooms are shared, so be sure to pack
a suitably funky robe to wear for the short walk along the hallway.
Downstairs you can dine beneath pressed-metal ceilings in a stylish
restaurant that's won many awards for its fine cuisine; try fresh local
catches such as salmon or oil-drizzled yabbies (small crustaceans resem-
bling lobsters). The hotel's front bar has been transformed into a bistro
for casual evening meals, while the adjoining Harvest Café is the place
for breakfast and a light lunch. You can also pick up fresh produce and
gourmet foods at the hotel's Kitchen and Butcher Shop. Guests who
want total serenity can book into either of the two rustic (but luxurious)
cottages at Harvest Farm, located on 18 acres of bushland and gardens
just a few minutes out of town. Cottages can take up to four people, and
breakfast is provided (minimum stay is two nights on weekends and in
January high season—prices A$550 for one couple, A$100 extra if sec-
ond bedroom is used). ⊠ *256 Maroondah Hwy.3777* 🕾 *03/5962–4002*
⊕ *www.healesvillehotel.com.au* 🖙 *7 rooms, 2 cottages* ⚑ *In-hotel: 3
restaurants, bar, no elevator* ⊟ *AE, DC, MC, V* ❙◎❙ *BP.*

$$$$ ⚑ **Mercure Yarra Valley—Balgownie Estate Vineyard Resort and Spa.** A new-
comer to the Yarra Valley scene, this resort has it all—stylish suites
and apartment-style accommodations with balconies overlooking the
vineyards, in addition to a ton of other amenities. But even though it's
one of the bigger offerings in the valley, it still has a boutique feel and
snuggles nicely into the seven acres of vineyard contours. The one and
two-bedroom suites have glass-enclosed whirlpool baths from which
you can look out toward the vines, and all rooms offer free broadband
Internet access for those travelling with laptops. Free wine tastings
showcase the range of Balgownie wines from the Bendigo vineyards,
such as the flagship White Label Bendigo Cabernet Sauvignon and the
White Label Shiraz. The vineyards surrounding the resort, planted with
Pinot Noir and Chardonnay, are just starting to bear usable fruit. The
resort also hosts champagne breakfasts for Sunrise Balloon clients. **Pros:**
excellent facilities, on-site cellar door, great day spa. **Cons:** holds con-
ferences, so may get busy at times. ⊠ *Melba Hwy. and Gulf Rd., Yarra
Glen* 🕾 *03/9730–0700* ⊕ *www.balgownieestate.com.au* 🖙 *65 rooms*
⚑ *In-room: safe (some), kitchen (some), refrigerator (some), DVD,*

Internet (some), Wi-Fi (some). In-hotel: restaurant, room service, bars, tennis court, pool, gym, spa, bicycles, laundry service, Wi-Fi, parking (free) ⊟ *AE, D, DC, MC, V* ⦶⊙⦶ *BP.*

THE DANDENONG RANGES

Melburnians come to the beautiful Dandenong Ranges, also known simply as the Dandenongs, for a breath of fresh air, especially in autumn when the deciduous trees turn golden and in spring when the public gardens explode into color with tulip, daffodil, azalea, and rhododendron blooms. At Mt. Dandenong, the highest point (2,077 feet), a scenic lookout known as SkyHigh Mount Dandenong, affords spectacular views over Melbourne and the bay beyond. Dandenong Ranges National Park, which encompasses five smaller parks, including Sherbrooke Forest and Ferntree Gully National Park, has dozens of walking trails. The many villages (which include Olida, Sassafras, Kalorama, Sherbrooke, and Kallisa) have curio shops, art galleries, food emporiums, cafés, and restaurants, and are dotted with lovely B&Bs. Visitors should be aware that the Dandenong Ranges and the highest point of Mount Dandenong are completely different from Dandenong city (30 km [19 mi] southeast of Melbourne) and on the Pakeham railway line), which is officially designated as an outer suburb of Melbourne.

GETTING HERE AND AROUND

Motorists can either take the Yarra Valley route *(see above)*, and turn off at Lilydale and head south to Montrose and on to Olinda, or take the South Eastern Freeway or M1 (a toll applies) and exit at Ferntree Gully Road. From there, take the Mt. Dandenong Tourist Road and follow it to Olinda, arriving from the south. Trains travel from Flinders Street Station to Belgrave on the Belgrave line. This town is on the southern edge of the Dandenongs and is the home of the steam train called Puffing Billy. Other towns on the same railway line are Ferntree Gully and Upper Ferntree Gully. Bus 694 runs from Belgrave Station to the Mt. Dandenong Lookout, via the villages of Sherbrooke, Sassara, and Olinda. Alternatively, take the train from Flinders Street Station to Croydon (on the Lilydale line), then take the 688 bus to Olinda and the William Ricketts Sanctuary.

TOURS

Half- and full-day trips from Melbourne are run by local tour operators, including Gray Line and Melbourne's Best Day Tours. Tours of the Dandenongs, including afternoon tea and a ride on a steam-operated train known as Puffing Billy, cost A$91 (half day) or A$132–A$162 (full day with one or more winery stops).

ESSENTIALS

Tour Operators Gray Line (⊠ *Federation Square, Flinders and Russell Sts., City Center* ☎ *1300/858687* ⊕ *www.grayline.com.au*) . **Melbourne's Best Day Tours** (⊠ *Federation Square, Flinders and Russell Sts., City Center, Melbourne* ☎ *1300/130550 or 03/9397–4911* ⊕ *www.melbournetours.com.au*).

Visitor Information Dandenong Ranges & Knox Visitor Information Centre
(✉ 1211 Burwood Hwy., Upper Ferntree Gully ☎ 03/9758–7522 ⊕ www.dande-nongrangestourism.com.au) .

EXPLORING

Cloudehill Gardens & Nursery. These glorious gardens were first established in the late 1890s as commercial and cut-flower gardens by the Woolrich family (after whom the next door B&B cottage is named). They are divided into 20 "garden rooms" that include the Rhododendrom Woods, the Azalea Walk, and 80-year-old European beech trees. A central terraced area with manicured hedges and a sculpture of a huge vase is stunning, as is the view across the mountain ranges from the garden café. The café serves breakfast, lunch, and afternoon tea; a popular dish is the "Chatter Platter" for two with a selection of cheeses, dips, prawns, and salad. ✉ 89 Olinda-Monbulk Rd., Olinda ☎ 03/9751–1009 🎫 A$7.50 ⊙ Gardens daily 10–5; café daily 9:30–5.

George Tindale Memorial Garden. This 6-acre garden has azaleas, camellias, and hydrangeas that spill down the hillsides, depending on the season. It's located just 8 km (5 mi) north of Belgrave in the little forest settlement of Sherbrooke, where whipbird calls echo through the trees. ✉ Sherbrooke Rd., Sherbrooke ☎ 13–1963 🎫 A$6 ⊙ Daily 10–4:30.

National Rhododendron Gardens. Try to visit in October, when acres of white, mauve, and pink blooms make for spectacular countryside vistas. A small train provides transportation around the property. The gardens are a short stroll from Olinda village. For a perfect afternoon, combine your visit with tea and scones in one of the many little cafés around town. ✉ Georgian Rd. off Olinda-Monbulk Rd.,Olinda ☎ 13–1963 🎫 A$11 ⊙ Daily 10–5.

☪ ★ **Puffing Billy.** This gleaming narrow-gauge steam engine, housed 40 km (25 mi) from Healesville in the town of Belgrave, was originally built in the early 1900s to assist 20th-century pioneers through the Dandenong ranges. Today the train still runs, and it's a great way to see the foothill landscapes. Daily trips between Belgrave and Emerald Lake pass through picturebook forests and trestle bridges. The 13-km (8-mi) trip takes an hour; it's another hour if you continue to the historic town of Gembrook. There are also lunch and dinner trips. ✉ Old Monbulk Rd., Belgrave ☎ 03/9754–6800 ⊕ www.puffingbilly.com.au 🎫 A$31; A$44 round-trip ⊙ Daily, but hrs vary.

☪ **Skyhigh Mount Dandenong.** This lookout at the top of Mt. Dandenong has breathtaking views from Melbourne to the Morninngton Peninsula and Port Phillip Bay. You can picnic or barbecue on the grounds, eat at the bistro, or stroll along the pleasant Garden Walk while the kids get lost in the garden maze. Other fun attractions include a tree called Percy's Possum House and the Giant's Chair. ✉ 26 Observatory Rd., Mt. Dandenong ☎ 03/ 9751–0443 ⊕ www.skyhighmtdandenong.com. au 🎫 A$5 parking; maze A$6 adults, A$4 children ⊙ Daily from 10 AM; 8 AM on weekends.

★ **William Ricketts Sanctuary.** Fern gardens, Aboriginal sculptures, moss-covered rocks, waterfalls, and mountain ash fill this 4-acre property on Mt. Dandenong. William Rickets, who established the sanctuary in

All aboard the Puffing Billy steam train.

the 1930s, meant it to stand as an embodiment of his philosophy: that people must act as custodians of the natural environment as the Aborigines did. ⊠ *Mt. Dandenong Tourist Rd., Mt. Dandenong* ☎ *13–1963* 🕾 *A$6.90* 🕔 *Daily 10–4:30.*

OUTDOOR ACTIVITIES

HIKING **Danenong Ranges National Park** is made up of several reserves, including the Sherbrooke Forest, which contains Sherbrooke Falls. Trails include the Olinda Forest Trail (from Mt. Dandenong to Kalisa), the western trail from Mt. Dandenong observatory to Ferntree Gully, the Sherbrooke Trail, and the Tourist Track from Sassafras to Emerald. Brochures and a trail map are available from the visitor information center at Upper Ferntree Gully and some cafés in the area. A trail map can be found at ⊕ *www.mtdandenong.net.au*. **Heidelberg School Artists' Trail** (☎ *13–1963* ⊕ *www.artiststrail.com*)is a great way to stay fit and brush up on Australian art. The trail commemorates famous Melbourne artists of the late 19th century, including Arthur Streeton, Tom Roberts, and Frederick McCubbin, who all painted around the Heidelberg area east of Melbourne. The Dandenongs section of this 40-km (25-mi) trail (which begins in Templestow, Melbourne) displays 9 of the route's 57 intepretive signs explaining the artists' work.

GOLFING The **Olinda Golf Course** (⊠ *75 Olinda-Monbulk Rd., Olinda* ☎ *03/9751–1399* ⊕ *www.olindagolfcourse.com.au* 🕾 *A$17–A$20 18 holes; A$13–A$15 9 holes* 🕔 *9–5*)was originally built in 1952 to act as a firebreak. Today this 18-hole course has some pretty steep fairways and fabulous views. Stop by the on-site restaurant for a drink or light meal after a game.

WHERE TO EAT AND STAY

Olinda is the main village in the Dandenong Ranges region and a good base for exploring the area. It's actually two villages (Lower and Upper Olinda, the latter being the prettier) connected by Monash Road, where you'll find a lot of the town's B&Bs and self-catering cottages. Olinda has a handful of good restaurants and cafés, and 26 specialty boutique stores including curio shops and fashion and gift shops. It is a short drive from here

PERFECT PICNICS

The Dandenongs are heaven for fresh-air freaks and food-ies. Pick up some goodies at Olinda's Saturday morning market and work up an appetite taking the 2-km (1½-mi) loop walk to Sherbrooke Falls from Donohue Picnic Grounds. Ask the tourist office about other great walks and picnic spots.

to the National Rhododendrom Gardens, the golf course, Olinda Falls picnic grounds, Cloudehill Gardens, and various hiking trails.

$ ✗ **Wild Oak Restaurant and Bar.** The Dandenongs' often crisp days and
CONTINENTAL cool nights will be warmed up with the soup of butternut pumpkin and blue swimmer crab at this popular restaurant in Olinda village. A hearty winter dish is the garlic herb and almond-stuffed chicken leg, roasted and served on Spanish-style tomato and chorizo ragout. Chef and owner Ben Higgs conducts cooking classes for groups of eight to 10, while jazz performers play on the last Friday night of every month. ✉ *232 Ridge Rd., at Mt. Dandenong Rd. Olinda* ☎ *03/9751–2033* ▭ *AE, DC, MC, V* ⊗ *Closed Mon. and Tues.*

$ ✗ **Ranges.** This café-restaurant right in the heart of Olinda is buzzing
CONTINENTAL all day, and is the perfect place for a snack or meal after browsing the nearby curio shops. It's open daily for breakfast, lunch, and morning and afternoon tea. Lunchtime fare includes homemade beef and mush-room pie and crispy calamari salad; at night you might want to begin with a cocktail while browsing the menu of hearty steaks and Asian-inspired specialties. ✉ *5 Main St., Olinda* ☎ *03/9751–2133* ⊕ *www. ranges.com.au* ▭ *AE, MC, V* ⊗ *No dinner Sun.–Mon.*

$$$ ⌂ **Cottage in the Village.** This cute gingerbread-style cottage is one of four in the Candlelight Cottages collection in the Dandenong Ranges. Cottage in the Village and Candlelight Cottage are both in Olinda, on the same property but several hundred yards—and many trees—away from each other. Although it looks like an historic little house, the vil-lage cottage is only six years old but lovingly designed and furnished by owner Peta Rolls to ensure an Old World feel. Fittings include a brass bed swathed in tulle and a lovely brass wall fitting. An adjacent Jacuzzi is set with a dozen little tea lights to add a romantic glow. The small kitchen has every imaginable appliance, and is stocked with breakfast ingredients such as ham, eggs, fruit, muesli, and a wide selection of teas and coffees. For guests who just want to relax indoors after their journey, Peta stocks the freezer with a selection of gourmet meals (made by a local caterer) and a fully stocked bar, all at extra cost. The most upmarket of the cottage collection is Woolrich, situated right next door to beautiful Cloudehill Gardens, just over a mile from Olinda. Built in 1920 and retaining many original features (like Art Deco stained-glass

windows and doors), it has fantastic views across the ranges from an expansive terrace. Woolrich has two bedrooms, each with its own dressing room, and two bathrooms with oval-shaped hot tubs. There is also a separate room with a four-person Jacuzzi that looks out over the gardens. All the cottages have everything needed for a cozy weekend. A two-night minimum stay applies on weekends—either Friday–Saturday or Saturday–Sunday. ⊠ *7–9 Monash Ave.* ☎ *03/9751–2464 or 1300/553011* 🖷 *02/9751–0552* ⊕ *www.candlelightcottages.com.au* ⌑ *4 cottages* ⌂ *In-hotel: kitchen, Wi-Fi (free), no kids under 11 except infants* ⊟ *AE, DC, MC, V* ⊺⊙⏐ *BP.*

MORNINGTON PENINSULA

The Mornington Peninsula circles the southeastern half of Port Phillip Bay. A much larger piece of land than it first appears, the peninsula is lapped by water on three sides and measures about 65 km (40 mi) by 35 km (22 mi). Along the Port Phillip Bay coast a string of seaside villages stretches from the larger towns of Frankston and Mornington to the summer holiday towns of Mount Martha, Rosebud, Rye, Sorrento, and Portsea (which has one of the most dramatic beaches in the region). On the Western Port Bay side the smaller settlements of Flinders, Somers, and Hastings have prettier and quieter beaches without the crowds.

Together with Main Ridge and Merricks, Red Hill is one of the state's premium producers of cool-climate wines, particularly Pinot Noir and Shiraz. The majority of the peninsula's 60 wineries are clustered around Red Hill and Red Hill South; however, there are another dozen or more dotted around areas farther north, including Moorooduc, Dromana, and Mount Martha. For an afternoon of fine wine, excellent seafood, and spectacular coastal views, plan a route that winds between vineyards. Red Hill has a busy produce and crafts market, which has been operating for 34 years and shows no signs of abating. It's held on the first Saturday morning of each month from September to May. A very good Web site for getting all the low-down on Peninsular wineries is ⊕ *www.visitmorningtonvineyards.com.*

Sorrento is one of the region's prettiest beach towns and one of the most popular day-tripper spots on the peninsula. It's also the peninsula's oldest settlement, and thus is dotted with numerous historic buildings and National Trust sites (among them the Collins Settlement Historical Site, which marks the first settlement site at Sullivan Bay; and the Nepean Historical Society Museum, with its displays of Aboriginal artifacts and settlers' tools). In summer the town transforms from a sleepy seaside village into a hectic holiday gathering place. Sorrento Back Beach, with its rock pools and cliff-side trails, and Point King, with its piers and boathouses, are the two most popular hangouts.

GETTING HERE AND AROUND

Renting a car in Melbourne and driving south along the Nepean Highway is the most practical way of seeing the Mornington Peninsula. At Frankston you can take the Frankston-Moorooduc Highway or stay on the Nepean Highway—eventually they both merge into the Mornington Peninsula Highway, which continues south to the various bayside

Artist sculptor William Ricketts (1898–1993) Mount Dandenong.

towns. A train runs from Flinders Street Station to Frankston. At Frankston, connect with a diesel-train service to towns to the east of the peninsula including Hastings, Bittern, Point Crib, and Stony Point. Buses also run from Frankstown to the bayside towns; the No. 781 bus that goes to Mornington and Mount Martha and the No. 782 bus travel to Flinders and Hastings on the Western Port side.

Inter Island Ferries runs a passenger service from Stony Point (on the eastern side of the peninsula) to Phillip Island, while the Queenscliff–Sorrento car and passenger ferry is the best way to travel between these two towns on opposite side of the bay. The Frankston and Peninsula airport shuttle bus runs from Melbourne Airport's international terminal to Frankstown and several other Mornington Peninsula towns.

TIMING

Set aside at least a day for a drive down the peninsula, planning time for lunch and wine tasting, an afternoon clifftop walk along the bluffs, or even a game of golf at Cape Schanck, one of 30 golf courses in the region. In summer pack a swimsuit and sunscreen for impromptu ocean dips as you make your way around the peninsula's string of attractive beaches. Be careful when driving along the tree-lined roads of the peninsula hinterland (the interior areas where most of the wineries are located). The wineries are often hard to see, as they are tucked away, so slow down, as you may have to make a sudden turn left or right into a driveway.

WINERY TOURS

Wallaces' Mornington Peninsula Winery Tours. These small group tours of four and ten people are run by husband and wife Rob and Cheryl Walace. They'll pick you up from both Melbourne and the Mornington Peninsula accommodation, and visit five to six wineries in a day. Lunch, wine, and coffee are included, and if time allows there is usually a chance to visit Red Hill Brewery, Mornington Peninsula Chocolates, and at least one arts and crafts shop. ☎ *03/9347–5197* ⊕ *www. wmptours.com.au* ✉ *A$125 per person (peninsula pick-up; A$145 Melbourne pick up).*

Victoria Winery Tours. This Melbourne-based company operates private tours of two to ten people using minivans. They visit four to five wineries that may include Box Stallion, Main Ridge, and Red Hill. Lunch with wine and coffee are also on the menu. ✉ *9 The Willows, Gisborne* ☎ *03/5428–8500 or 1300/946386* ⊕ *www.winetours.com. au* ✉ *A$147.*

Amour of the Grape. Set winery tours for groups from two to six passengers and personal tours for those who want to devise their own itinerary are this company's specialty. The day's outing includes tastings at four or five preselected cellar doors, and a gourmet lunch and a glass of wine at a boutique winery café. Passengers coming from Melbourne will be picked up and delivered back to the Frankston railway station. ✉ *Box 529, Mt. Martha* ☎ *03/5974–3286* ⊕ *www.amourofthegrape. com.au* ✉ *A$137 per person Mornington Peninsula pick-up; central Melbourne pick-up A$197 per person (for 2 to 3 people; A$157 per person for 4 to 6 people).*

ESSENTIALS

Visitor Information Mornington Peninsula Visitor Centre (✉ *359B Point Nepean Rd., Dromana* ☎ *03/5987–3078 or 1800/804009* ⊕ *www.visitmorningtonpeninsula.org*). **Mornington Community Information Support Centre** (✉ *320 Main St., Mornington* ☎ *03/5975–1644* ⊕ *www.morninfo.org.au*).

Transportation Frankston and Peninsula Airport Shuttle (☎ *03/9783–1199* ⊕ *www.fapas.com.au*). **Inter Island Ferries** (☎ *03/9585–5730* ⊕ *www.interislandferries.com.au*). **Sorrento-Queenscliff Ferry** (☎ *03/5258–3244* ⊕ *www. searoad.com.au*).

EXPLORING

With sweeping views of the surrounding countryside, Port Phillip Bay, Port Phillip Heads, and—on a clear day—the city skyline, the You Yangs and Mt. Macedon are the attractions at **Arthurs Seat State Park.** Walking tracks meander through stands of eucalyptus, and a marked scenic drive snakes its way up the mountainside. Seawinds, a public garden established by a local gardener in the 1940s, also forms part of the park and is a 10-minute walk or about 500 yards away. The mountain, which gives the park its name, is the highest point on the Mornington Peninsula; it was named after Arthurs Seat in Edinburgh. The road from Mornington is open at all times, so you can enjoy the spectacular mountaintop view even when the park is closed. The once-popular chairlift at the state park is currently closed while authorities debate whether to dismantle it or not. ✉ *Arthurs Seat Rd. at Mornington Peninsula*

Hwy., Arthurs Seat ☎ *03/5987–2565* ⊕ *www.parkweb.vic.gov.au* ✉ *Free* ☉ *Nov.–Mar., daily 8–8; Apr.–Oct., daily 8–5.*

EXPLORING THE WINERIES

A small bus tour that visits four to five wineries is the best way to explore the region. Tours leave from Melbourne and from peninsula towns. Most of the wineries listed here also have excellent restaurants on-site, and many of the restaurants we list are located in wineries, so there's no need to go hungry or thirsty!

WORD OF MOUTH

"I agree if you are going to visit wineries that it might be best to take a tour and then you don't need to watch what you drink. Australian police are very vigilant regarding drink driving, and the legal limit in Victoria is 0.05. Why not take a car for some of the day trips and a bus for the rest? Then you have the best of both worlds."
—lavandula

Box Stallion (✉ *64 Tubbarubba Rd., Merricks North* ☎ *03/5989–7444* ⊕ *www.boxstallioin.com.au* ☉ *Daily 11–5*) winery and restaurant are housed in a huge, rustic barn that was once the home of the Thoroughbred stallions from the illustrious Muranna Park stud. A visit is a reminder of the other important Mornington Peninsula industry—horse breeding. The former horse boxes have been retained as dining areas for small groups. The winery, set on 100 acres, is not only full of country charm, but is said to be the peninsula's leading producer of varietal wine. The Shiraz is the most awarded wine of the stable, while the 2008 Sauvignon Blanc has picked up a few medals as well. All wines are grown and made on the estate by winemaker Alex White. Tours can be arranged for the technically savvy visitor with advanced notice. Meals, served either indoors in the Red Barn Cellar Door or outside under big canvas umbrellas, will not break the bank. A grazing platter of many delicacies such as eggplant rolls filled with ricotta cheese, cheeses, olives, and dips will suit two people (A$30), while the tiger prawn, chorizo, and leek risotto is A$22. The starters (or entrée meals as they're called in Australia) are cheaper and are often quite large. On Sundays there's live music (blues and country folk) from 12.30 PM. Wine tastings are free, but there are no group tastings on Sundays during the busy hours of 11–3.

Crittenden Estate (✉ *25 Harrisons Rd., Dromana* ☎ *03/5981–8322 winery, 03/5981–9555 restaurant* ⊕ *www.crittendenwines.com.au* ☉ *Daily 11–4*) is one of the area's most beautiful wineries, with a lovely lakeside setting. Run by Garry Crittenden and his son Rollo, it produces Chardonnay, Pinot Noir, Pinot Grigio, and recently some Spanish styles under the new Los Hermanos label. The flagship Crittenden Estate Pinot Noir and Chardonnay are made from vines that are among the oldest on the peninsula. The cellar door is open for tastings daily in summer and during public holidays, and on weekends at other times. It doubles as a small area produce store selling olives, olive oil, dakka, and other morsels perfect to have while sipping wine. The tasting room is wonderfully warm in winter, and while you sip away you can admire the artworks that adorn the walls. The restaurant, Stillwater at Crittenden,

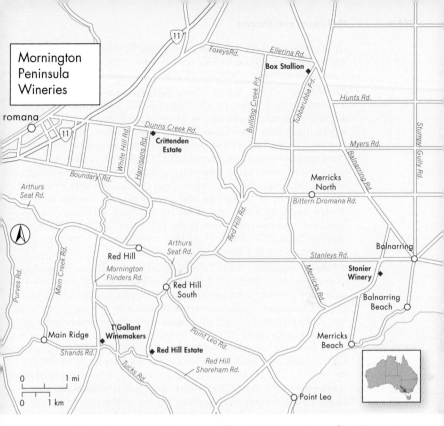

is lovely year-round, but especially when the weather is fine. Diners sit out on a terrace under shady umbrellas while enjoying views over the lake and fine cuisine prepared by Chef Zac Poulier: the braised pork belly with seared scallops is one of his best dishes. It is open daily for lunch and weekends for dinner

Red Hill Estate (⊠ 53 Shoreham Rd., Red Hill South ☎ 03/5989–2838 ⊕ www.redhillestate.com.au ☉ Daily 11–5) has picked up numerous medals for its Chardonnay, Pinot Noir, and Shiraz. And if they were giving out medals for location, Red Hill Estate would claim them all. Not only are there sweeping views of the 30-acre vineyards, but the magnificent waters of Western Port Bay are stretched out in the distance. You see right over to Phillip Island as you wander through the gardens and vines. Be sure to stop at **Max's Restaurant** (☎ 03/5931–0177 ☉ No dinner Sun.–Thurs.). Its award-winning cuisine and fabulous floor-to-ceiling windows make it the perfect place to while away at least half the day. You might start with Max's own antipasto, which includes a mini soup of the day, mini leek, fennel, and sweet-chili pear tart, mini house-cured trout, mini entrée of calamari, and Tassie oyster with wakame and salmon roe. For dessert, don't miss the summer pudding with double cream. Although it may be a little chilly, winter is a good time to visit the winery, as several events are staged, including the Barrel Art Show, the Winter Winery Week in June, and a huge Tuscan feast in July. Visitors are charged a fee of A$5 for wine tastings in the cellar door, which is taken off the price of a bottle of wine if they decide to purchase.

Established in 1978, **Stonier Winery** (⊠ *Frankston–Flinders Rd. and Thompsons La., Merricks* ☎ *03/5989–8300* ⊕ *www.stoniers.com. au*) is considered the preeminent Mornington Peninsula producer of wines, made from the region's oldest vines. Owners Brian Stonier and his wife Noel have concentrated on Chardonnay and Pinot Noir (produced from vines first planted in 1978 and 1982, respectively) and more recently introduced a sparkling—the Stonier Pinot Noir Chardonnay. Although there's no restaurant, cheeses and hors d'oeuvres accompany the daily tastings, and if time permits, visitors may be invited on an informal tour of the fermentation and barrel rooms. Several events take place during the year, such as the Winter Wine Weekend in June, Melbourne Cup Day celebrations in November, and Osyter Shucking and Sparkling in December.

★ **T'Gallant Winemakers** (⊠ *1385 Mornington–Flinders Rd., at Shand Rd., Main Ridge* ☎ *03/5989–6565* ⊕ *www.tgallant.com.au* ⊙ *Daily 10–5*) celebrates just over a decade in business, and its Italian-themed winery and restaurant continue to grow in popularity. Winemaker Kevin McCarthy planted the first Pinto Grigio vines on the peninsula under the Juliet and Grace labels. If you're a stylist as well as an oenophile, you'll also admire the beautiful label artwork. He also produces Pinot Noir, Chardonnay, and Muscat à Petits Grains. La Baracca Trattoria and the Spuntino Bar are always buzzing (just close your eyes and think of Italy)—the food is exceptional, with dishes made from local ingredients (some from the house herb garden). Try the wild Italian herb-ricotta gnocchi with braised duck and wilted spinach for a taste-bud delight; or the chicken pie with T'Gallants Pinot Gris, shallots, bacon, and mushrooms. The cellar door and restaurant/bar are open seven days a week, and there's live music every weekend at lunchtime.

OUTDOOR ACTIVITIES

The Mornington Peninsula is one of the most memorable walking destinations. There are walks for all levels of fitness and interest from clifftop strolls to the ultimate 26-km (16-mi) Two Bays Walking Track. Stop in at the visitor information centers at Dromana or Mornington to see what walking maps they have on hand, or contact Parks Victoria, the government body that manages the national parks in the state.

Here are some walks to get you started:

Arthurs Seat State park: there is a one-hour circuit walk to Kings Falls, and the relaxing Seawinds Gardens walk takes only about half an hour and is less than a mile in length.

Coppin's Track: a pleasant 3-km (2-mi) round-trip walk that stretches from Sorrento ocean beach (or Back Beach as it's known) to Jubliee point along the Bass Strait coastline.

Bushrangers Bay Walk: An exhilarating 6-km (4-mi) walk around West Port. It begins at Fingal Beach and winds past basalt cliffs and Cape Schanck Lighthouse, Bushranger Bay, to finish at Main Creek.

Two Bays Walking track: a hard-core 26-km (16-mi) walking track that links Dromana, on Port Phillip Bay, with Cape Schnank on Western Port Bay.

Parks Victoria (☎ 13/1963 ⊕ www.parkweb.vic.gov.au)is the government agency that manages all of Victoria's national parks. Its informative Web site includes information on bushfire danger and park attractions. **Dunball's Walking Tours** (✉ 29 Hughes Rd. ☎ 03/5984–4484 ⊕ www. mornpenwalks.com.au)has half- and full-day tours, including one along the Millionaires Walk, viewing lovely vistas and expensive mansions in Sorrento and Portsea. A two-day coast-to-coast walk, with accommodaton in Cape Schanck Lighthouse, costs A$80 per person per day, and is cheaper if more people join the walk.

Bayplay Adventure Kayak, Snorkel & Dive Tours (✉ 3755 Port Nepean Rd., Portsea ☎ 03/5984–0888 ⊕ www.bayplay.com.au) is an adventure-tour operator that does it all. Explore colonies of weedy seadragons, swim through an octupus's garden, or play with bottlenose dolphins and seals. Dives start from A$40, while a three- to four-hour dolphin-swim tour costs A$115 per person.

GOLF **Rosebud Park Public Golf Course** (✉ Elizabeth Dr., Rosebud ☎ 03/5981– 2833 ⊕ www.rosebudpark.com.au ✉ Call for greens fee information, bookings, and hours)is situated on the steep slopes of Arthurs Seat overlooking Rosebud and Port Phillip Bay, the course provides spectacular views of the coastline down to Rye, Blairgowrie, and Sorrento, along with views of the hinterland farmlands. The 18-hole course has some extremely challenging holes, a resident teaching professional, plenty of parking, and excellent picnic facilities.

HORSEBACK RIDING In addition to a lot of horses, **Ace-Hi Beach Rides** (✉ 810 Boneo Rd., Cape Schanck ☎ 03/5988–6262 ⊕ www.ace-hi.com.au)runs a 200-acre adventure park complete with a wildlife sanctuary and lots of activities for kids, including pony rides, rockwall climbing, and swinging through the air on a flying fox device. Horse rides start from A$38 for an hour.

WHERE TO EAT AND STAY

$$$$ CONTINENTAL ✗ **Bittern Cottage.** Influenced by their adventures in northern Italy and southern France, chef-owners Jenny and Noel Burrows show off their provincial-style cooking skills using regional Australian produce. The three-course menu (A$64) for Saturday night dinner and Sunday lunch may include Tasmania salmon, duck breast in white wine, and a lovely lemon and apple pudding for dessert. Bittern Cottage now offers a Monday two-course dinner for A$45, and will open for lunch or dinner from Tuesday to Friday when groups of six or more book. Tucked away in the bush, the restaurant has been drawing patrons for 30 years. It's just 1½ km (1 mi) north of tiny Bittern village. ✉ 2385 Frankston–Flinders Rd., Bittern ☎ 03/5983–9506 ⊕ www.bitterncottage.com.au ▭ MC, V.

$$ FRENCH Fodor's Choice ★ ✗ **Montalto Vineyard & Olive Grove.** Overlooking an established vineyard with vistas of rolling green hills, this place serves French-inspired cuisine made with the freshest local ingredients. Chef Barry Davis prepares such creative dishes as Port Phillip Bay snapper fillet on a crushed Montalto Estate Jerusalem artichoke with chervil and tomato beurre

Continued on page 278

In recent decades Australia has emerged as an international wine powerhouse. The country's varied climate has proven favorable for growing high-quality grapes, and winemakers now produce some of the world's best Shiraz (Syrah) wines, as well as acclaimed Pinot Noirs and Rieslings. Wine sales currently contribute about $5.5 billion to the country's economy, and Australia is the third largest supplier to the United States behind France and Italy.

Touring wineries here is easy, as most properties have tasting rooms with regular hours. Whether you're sipping *in situ* at a winery or tasting wines at a shop in Sydney, here's how to get the most from your wine experience.

By Erica Watson

(top) Pinot noir grapes (right) Vineyard in One Tree Hill, South Australia

Wines of
Australia

WINE TRENDS: THEN AND NOW

(top left) Wine bottles await labels, (bottom left) Hunter Valley vista, (right) tasting in Barossa Valley

Although the first grapes in Australia arrived with British settlers in 1787, it really wasn't until the mid 1960s that a more refined tradition of wine making began to take hold. Prior to 1960, Australia's wine repertoire extended little beyond sherry and port, but after WWII, an influx of European immigrants, notably from Germany and Italy, opened the country's eyes to new tastes and production methods.

Australia now produces many classic varietals at prices from A$10 to A$40,000 (for a 1951 Penfolds Grange Hermitage, made by Australian pioneer Max Schubert). There are more than 60 wine regions dotted across the country and many of the smaller producers in lesser-known areas are beginning to flourish.

Although the industry has experienced rapid growth, it hasn't been without its problems. The health of the global economy, international competition, global warming, disease, drought, and bushfire have each presented challenges along the way.

These days, Australian vintners are known for combining old traditions with new ideas and technical innovations. While oak barrels are still widely used, stainless steel and plastic tanks are now recognized as suitable fermentation and storage methods. Screw caps, introduced a decade ago, are becoming more popular with winemakers and consumers.

The industry's lastest trends also include a growing interest in environmental sustainability, with organic and biodynamic wines appearing from numerous producers. The internet has revolutionized business, giving even the smallest vintners access to an international stage.

Like well-cellared wine, the palate of modern Australia is continually maturing. Whether your taste is for robust reds from Coonawarra and Barossa or the delicate and versatile whites of the Hunter Valley and Margaret River, Australia's winemakers are producing beautiful wines perfect to enjoy now or later.

AUSTRALIA'S DOMINANT VARIETALS

REDS

SHIRAZ
Australia's classic varietal. A full-bodied wine that, in hot areas, makes an earthy expression with softer acidity. Cooler regions produce a leaner, peppery style.

CABERNET SAUVIGNON
Dark red with blackcurrant and black cherry flavors, often with firm tannins and more acidity than Shiraz.

MERLOT
Intensely purple colored, full-bodied wine characterized by moderate tannins, aromas of plum, and a velvety mouth-feel.

PINOT NOIR
Lighter-bodied with gentle tannins and fruity aromas of red berries.

WHITES

CHARDONNAY
Full-bodied wine that is often high in alcohol and low in acidity. Most Australian versions are oaked.

RIESLING
Lighter-bodied wines with citrus and honey notes. Most are unoaked and dry or slightly off-dry.

SAUVIGNON BLANC
Makes crisp, dry wines with high acid and aromas of peach and lime.

SEMILLON
Light-bodied wines that have crisp acidity and complex flavors, including herbs, nuts, and honey.

WHITE BLENDS
Chardonnay-Semillon and Sauvignon Blanc-Semillon blends are popular. Semillon adds bright notes.

WINE TOURING TIPS

Large vintners like Rosemount, McGuigan Wines, Jacobs Creek, Yalumba, and Wolf Blass are well equipped for visitors and many offer vineyard tours, as well as restaurants or cafes. Some require appointments.

Many boutique producers also have "cellar doors," a.k.a. tasting rooms, open seven days a week, but it is advisable to check their websites for details. The average tastings cost around A$10 to A$15 for a flight of up to five different styles. Some include cheese, cracker, and fruit plates.

Winery in Clare Valley

AUSSIE WINE REGIONS

SOUTH AUSTRALIA

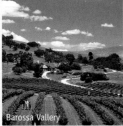

Barossa Valley

❶ BAROSSA VALLEY The country's best-known wine region, Barossa Valley has more than 550 grape growers, including some fifth- and sixth-generation families. Shiraz is highly celebrated, particularly the lauded Penfolds Grange. Cabernet Sauvignon, Grenache, Merlot, Riesling, Semillon, and Chardonnay are all well suited to Barossa's temperate climate, which is slightly cooler on its peaks and in neighboring Eden Valley. Big producers Jacobs Creek and Wolf Blass both have visitors centers with modern tasting rooms and restaurants. For a history lesson, take a tour at Langmeil Winery. An impressive property is Yalumba, with a stone winery and clock tower. So, too, is the well-established Peter Lehmann Estate on the banks of the North Para River.

❷ ADELAIDE HILLS For world-class Chardonnays, Sauvignon Blancs, Rieslings, and sparkling wines, look to the Adelaide Hills. Just 25 minutes from the center of Adelaide, this high-altitude region, amid Mount Lofty and down through the Piccadilly Valley, has nurtured elegantly refined white wines. The cooler climate also means that it's one of South Australia's leading producer of the temperamental Pinot Noir. There are about 25 cellars that offer tastings, including Petaluma Cellar, well known for its sparkling wines, Rieslings, and Chardonnays as well as its modern Bridgewater Mill restaurant. To try Italian varietals, head to Chain of Ponds. For excellent Sauvignon Blanc, stop into Shaw and Smith's 46-hectare estate.

Adelaide Hills

❸ MCLAREN VALE
Situated in the Fleurieu Peninsula region, McLaren Vale is an easy 40-minute trip south of Adelaide. Uniquely located by the coast, it's regarded as one of the more unpretentious regions thanks to laid-back beach lifestyle, passionate vintners, and family-owned wineries. This fusion of ideals, together with its warm climate, has most likely sparked its interest in experimenting with more exotic varieties such as Tempranillo, Zinfandel, and Mourvedre, as well as Viognier and Sangiovese. There are more than 60 cellar tasting rooms, ranging from the large producers such as Rosemount Estate and Tintara Winery to boutique producers such as Wirra Wirra, D'Arenberg, and Gemtree, each offering sales and wine flights that include the chance to sample local foods.

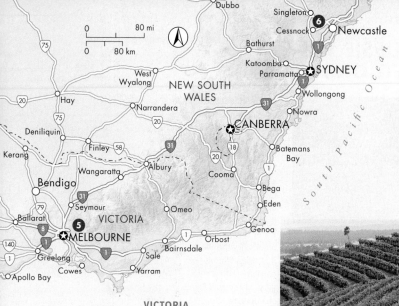

❹ LIMESTONE COAST

Coonawarra's long ripening season coupled with the region's "terra rossa" soil atop rich limestone beds is responsible for some of Australia's most famed wines, most notably full-bodied reds. Often described as the Bordeaux of Australia, Coonawarra is a top spot for Cabernet Sauvignon, Cabernet blends, and spicy Shiraz. And they don't come any better than at places like Penley, Katnook Estate, Hollick, and Wynns Coonawarra Estate. Sixty kilometers to the north is Padthaway. While reds still prevail, the region's slightly warmer climate produces fruity Chardonnay and enjoyable Sauvignon Blanc, Verdelho, and Riesling. Built from limestone in 1882, the historic Padthaway Estate provides the perfect backdrop to sample some of the regions finest. Stonehaven and Henry's Drive are also worth a visit.

VICTORIA

❺ YARRA VALLEY

Close proximity to Melbourne makes the Yarra an easy choice if your touring time is limited. A cool climate and diverse mix of volcanic and clay soils have allowed Chardonnay and Pinot Noir to flourish. Other notable varieties here include Viognier, Gewürztraminer, Pinot Gris, and Sauvignon Blanc, as well as Malbec, Sangiovese, and Nebbiolo. Sparkling wine is also a winner and Domaine Chandon is a magnificent spot to enjoy some perfect bubbly. For a laidback experience, Lillydale is also a good choice. But upping the style stakes is the magnificent Yering Station with its modern Australian restaurant and gallery space. Elsewhere, De Bortoli sells delicious top-end wines.

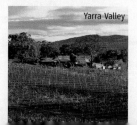

Yarra Valley

NEW SOUTH WALES

❻ HUNTER VALLEY

Despite being a producer of award-winning Chardonnay, Verdelho, and Shiraz, it's the honeyed Semillon, which can mature for up to two decades, that Hunter Valley does best. Split into upper and lower regions, it has more that 150 years of winemaking up its sleeve and 120 cellar doors. It's safe to say the Hunter knows how to entertain. From large-scale music concerts at Bimbadgen Estate and Tempus Two to the annual Jazz in the Vines event and other small food and wine festivals year-round, the region is constantly buzzing. Pokolbin, Broke, Wollombi, Lovedale, Rothbury and Mt View are the main areas to sample the regions best offerings. Autumn is an excellent time to visit.

Hunter Valley

AUSSIE WINE REGIONS

Margaret River

WESTERN AUSTRALIA

7 MARGARET RIVER REGION With the first vines planted in 1967, Margaret River might be one of the country's younger wine areas but that hasn't stopped it from producing exceptionally high quality vintages. Cool breezes from the Indian Ocean and a steady, Mediterranean-style climate offer perfect conditions for developing complex styles of Chardonnay and minty-toned Cabernet Sauvignons. Shiraz, Merlot, Semillon, Sauvignon Blanc, and Chenin Blanc also thrive. Although the area produces about 20% of Australia's premium wines, it only accounts for about 3% of the nation's grapes. Try the West Australian Marron—or crayfish—with a crisp glass of Leeuwin Estate chardonnay. Cape Mentelle and Evans & Tate are also among the region's highlights, with many of their special releases sold only through their cellar doors.

Indian Ocean

Muchea
Sorrento
Scarborough
Fremantle
PERTH
Mundari
ROTTNEST ISLAND
Armadale
GARDEN ISLAND
Rockingham
Mandurah
Pinjarra
Waroona
Harvey
Collie
Bunbury
Geographe Bay
Dunsborough
Yallingup
Busselton
Balingup
Margaret River
Prevelly
Karridale
Nannup
Bridge Town
Kudardup
Augusta
Carlotta
Manjimu
Pemberton
Nortcliffe
Albany Hwy

0   40 mi
0   40 km

READING THE LABEL

Art Series

1 LEEUWIN ESTATE

2 2006
3 MARGARET RIVER
4 RIESLING

5 12.0% vol   **6** WINE OF AUSTRALIA   **7** 750mL

According to Australia's Label Integrity Program, when a wine label states region, grape variety, or vintage, then 85% of the wine contained in the bottle must come from that region, variety, or vintage.

1 The producer of the wine.

2 The vintage year, meaning the year the grapes were picked, crushed, and bottled.

3 Australian GIs, or Geographic Indications, identify the region where the wine grapes were grown.

4 The varietal, or type of grapes used to make the wine.

5 The wine in this bottle contains 12% alcohol content by volume.

6 The wine's country of origin.

7 The volume of wine in the bottle.

MORE TASTING OPPORTUNITIES

Wine tasting at Mitchell Winery, Clare Valley

SIPPING IN SHOPS AND BARS

Even when you're not ensconced in the country's lush vineyards, high-quality wine isn't far away. The capital cities serve as a gateway for many of the wine country's top tastes.

In Sydney, try wine bars like the **Ivy's Ash Street Cellar**, **Glass Brasserie** wine bar at the Hilton Hotel and the **Gazebo Wine Garden** in Elizabeth Bay. **The Australian Wine Centre** in Circular Quay offers private tastings (with prior notice) and the **Ultimo Wine Centre** has free tastings each Saturday.

Heading south, visit **Melbourne's Prince Wine Store** at one of its three locations. Or soak up the atmosphere at **The Melbourne Supper Club** or **Melbourne Wine Room**. The bar of the award-winning **Press Club** restaurant also has an excellent Australian and international selection.

Apothecary 1878 on Adelaide's Hindley Street and **The Wine Underground**, just a few blocks away, both have a cosmopolitan ambience. Smaller vineyards are well represented at the city's **East End Cellars**.

In Perth, wine and dine alfresco at **Must Winebar** in Highgate. And **Amphoras Bar** in West Perth also has a long list of the country's best wines by the glass and bottle. No visit would be complete without heading to **East Fremantle's Wine Shop & Wine Liaisons**, for regular tastings and an extensive range of bottles. It also has an online store.

WINE FESTIVALS

Festivals offer chance to interact with the winemakers as well as sample local produce, especially cheese, fruit, and seafood. **The Barossa Vintage Festival** is one of the largest and longest running wine events in South Australia. Held in April each year it has everything from rare wine auctions to family friendly events. Other notables are **Adelaide's Tasting Australia** (April), **Coonawarra After Dark Wine Festival** (April), and **McLaren Vale Sea and Vines Festival** (June). In Western Australia, the **Margaret River Wine Region Festival** (April) celebrates wine with music and art.

RESEARCH & PLANNING

A little planning will allow you to make the perfect choices when it comes to deciding which regions to visit and where to taste. The websites of Australia's tourism commissions are filled with helpful planning informations. Not only do they offer winery information but also options for tours, accommodation and other sights to see while in the area. These include ⊕ *www.visitvictoria.com*, ⊕ *www.southaustralia.com*, *www.winecountry.com.au*, ⊕ *www.westernaustralia. com*

Once on the ground, visitors centers such as the **Margaret River Wine Centre, Adelaide's National Wine Centre of Australia, and Hunter Valley Wine Country Tourism** can offer sound advice, especially on the best varietals and history of the regions.

For further history, regional information, and primary producers, visit ⊕ *www.wine.org.au* or ⊕ *www.australianwines. com.au*

4

IN FOCUS WINES OF AUSTRALIA

Barossa Vintage Festival

blanc; the dish is best matched with a 2007 Montalto Chardonnary. The menu changes daily, based on the produce available. The wine list borrows from the best of the estate's vintages, as well as classic wines from other regions. If it's a nice day, you can picnic on the grounds from hampers prepared by the restaurant. Take a moment to check out the herb garden and admire the 17 sculptures on permanent display. If you're visiting from mid-February to late April you'll be able to see the entries in the Montalto Sculpture Prize and vote for your favorite. The expansive property also includes a natural wetlands and specially built boardwalks, so visitors have a chance of spotting more than 90 bird species. ⊠ *33 Shoreham Rd., Red Hill South* ☎ *03/5989–8412* ☰ *AE, DC, MC, V* ⊗ *No dinner Sun.–Thurs. (No dinner Sun in Jan.).*

> **BE AMAZED**
>
> Victorians do love their mazes, and you'll find these quaint English-garden features dotted around the Mornington Peninsula. These maze complexes have topiary and sculptured creations, mystery lawn puzzles, and big garden chess sets. Wander through **Arthurs Seat Maze** (⊠ *55 Purves Rd. Arthur's Seat* ☎ *03/5981–8449*), which also has an "amazing" candy shop, or check out the world's first circular rose maze at **Aschombe Maze & Lavender Gardens** (⊠ *15 Shoreham Rd., Shoreham* ☎ *03/5989–8387*), nicely located not far from T'Gallant Winery.

$$ ✕ **Salix at Willow Creek.** Although views of the vineyard through the restaurant's glass walls are spectacular year-round, Willow Creek's gardens break into a flurry of roses come autumn. The restaurant is one of the two dining options at this very popular winery; the more casual Salix bistro is located in the downstairs cellar door. The restaurant, owned by Bernard McCarthy who was once chef at Melbourne's Hairy Canary bar and restaurant, makes much of its own produce on-site. Try the pan-fried potato gnocchi with mushrooms and hazelnuts and a three-cheese crumble. Desserts feature the exotic-sounding Madagascan spiced Belgium chocolate soft-centre pudding with candied-ginger ice cream and biscotti. The downstairs bistro, opened from 12 to 5 daily, serves such classic fare as cassoulet and chicken provençal. The winery, known as Willow Creek Vineyard, opened in 1988, and concentrates on producing excellent Chardonnary and Pinot Noir from 20-year-old vines (which have been tended by the same viticulturist since inception). In more recent times the owners have planted small quantities of Pinot Gris and Sauvignon Blanc. The flagship wines are sold under the Tulum label, while the WCV label offers a less expensive range of Chardonnary, Pinot Noir, and Shiraz. ⊠ *166 Balnarring Rd., Merricks North* ☎ *03/5989–7640* ☰ *AE, DC, MC, V* ⊗ *No dinner Sun.–Thurs.*

AUSTRALIAN
★

$$$ ⊡ **Lakeside Villas at Crittenden Estate.** Wine and dine to your hearts content, then amble home to your apartment overlooking a peaceful lake. Each of the three villas has open-plan living/dining and a full kitchen. A north-facing balcony catches most of the day's sun, and is perched over the lake. There's a whirlpool in the bathroom, and a wood-fire heater. The separate bedroom has a king-size bed, but twin beds are

also available on request. Each unit sleeps up to two persons; however, there is a pull-out sofa that can sleep an additional two persons for A$50 per person. Start the day right with a breakfast hamper of bacon, eggs, jams, and other goodies. **Pros:** fantastic position; stylish and snug. **Cons:** the nearby Stillwater Restaurant is only open on Friday and Saturday nights. ⊠ *25 Harrisons Rd., Dromana* ☎ *03/5987–3275* ⊕ *www.lakesidevillas.com.au* ⤳ *3 rooms* ♿ *In-room: no safe, kitchen, refrigerator, DVD, Wi-Fi (some). In-hotel: restaurant, bar, tennis court, laundry facilities, Internet terminal, Wi-Fi, parking (free), no-smoking rooms* ⊟ *AE, D, DC, MC, V* ⦿| *BP.*

$$$ 🏨 **Hotel Sorrento.** Built in 1871, the Hotel Sorrento still commands a special place in town, and after a recent refurbishment offers some very funky interiors without compromising its historic profile. The heritage rooms, with exposed limestone (from which the original hotel is built) are the best rooms, and have expansive windows with views over Port Phillip Bay. Some have balconies and others have whirlpool baths. Every room and apartment has a new flat-screen TV with cable movies. Park-view rooms and apartments have been built in the adjoining newer buildings. The Limeburners Bar is a popular Sorrento meeting place, and the restaurant serves delicious, well-priced meals, including wild Australian king prawns wok-tossed with coriander, chilli, and palm sugar, and finished with coconut cream (A$21.90). **Pros:** great location, great views from some rooms. **Cons:** limited facilities. ⊠ *5–15 Hotham Rd., Sorrento* ☎ *03/5984–8000* ⊕ *www.hotelsorrento.com. au* ⤳ *60 rooms* ♿ *In-room: safe (some), kitchen (some), refrigerator (some), DVD (some), Internet (some), Wi-Fi (some). In-hotel: restaurant, room service, bar, golf courses, tennis courts, pools, gym, spa, beachfront, diving, water sports, laundry service, Internet terminal, Wi-Fi, parking (paid), no kids, no-smoking rooms* ⊟ *AE, D, DC, MC, V* ⦿| *BP.*

PHILLIP ISLAND

★ A nightly waddling parade of miniature fairy penguins, known as Little Penguins, from the sea to their burrows in nearby dunes is this island's main draw, attracting throngs of onlookers on summer weekends and holidays. But Phillip Island, a pleasant 1½-hour drive from Melbourne, has plenty of other attractions. At low tide you can walk across a basalt causeway to the **Nobbies** (the rugged coastal rocks). A boardwalk takes you around the windswept coastline to a blowhole. Thousands of shearwaters (also known as mutton birds) nest here from September to April, when they return north to the Bering Strait in the Arctic. Farther out, **Seal Rocks** host Australia's largest colony of fur seals; more than 10,000 creatures bask on the rocky platforms and caper about here in midsummer. Boat tours cruise past these playful creatures in the summer months.

There are several ways to view the penguin paragde: general admission, where viewing is from concrete bleachers; a viewing platform that is closer to the action; and an elevated tower where five adults join the ranger who is narrating the action. The Ultimate Penguin Tour, for private groups, includes headphones and night-vision equipment and a spot on the beach. The spectacle begins at around 8 PM each night; booking ahead is essential in summer and during public holidays. Bring warm clothing—even in summer—and rain protection gear. Make sure to arrive an hour before the tour begins. A good deal for visitors staying for a day is the 3 Park Pass, giving admission to the Penguin Parade, the Koala Conservation Centre, and Churchill Island. ⊠ *Summerland Beach, Phillip Island* ☏ *03/5951–2800* ✉ *General admission A$20.50; Penguin Plus viewing platform A$36; skybox A$51.50; Ultimate Penguin Experience A$72; Three Park Pass from A$24.50* ☉ *Daily.*

The **Phillip Island Grand Prix Circuit** continues the island's long involvement with motor sports, dating back to 1928 when the Australian Grand Prix was run on local unpaved roads. The circuit was completely redeveloped in the 1980s, and in 1989 hosted the first Australian Motorcycle Grand Prix. The circuit holds regular races as well as big-ticket events, such as the Grand Prix in October. Speed freaks can travel on the actual circuit on a go-kart (A$28 for 10 minutes) during December and January, or a high-performance sports car (A$210 for 30 minutes) driven by a professional every weekday from 5 PM. You can also drive. There are 45-minute guided tours of the track every day at 11 and 2, and a museum tracing the history of motor sports. ⊠ *Back Beach Rd., Phillip Island 3922* ☏ *03/5952–9400* ⊕ *www.phillipsislandcircuit.com.au* ✉ *A$19* ☉ *Daily 9–7, tours run 11–2.*

GETTING HERE AND AROUND

Phillip Island is 124 km (78 mi) southeast of Melbourne or a 90-minute drive. To reach the island, take the Princes Highway (M1) southeast to the South Gippsland Highway (M420), which eventually becomes the Bass Highway (A420). V/Line runs a combination train and bus service from Southern Cross Station to Cowes (with change at Dandenong railway station), a journey of three hours. You can also take the train from Flinders Street Station to Frankston (on the Mornington Peninsula) and connect with the 2 PM weekday bus to Cowes on Phillip Island, but this is a long trip of about 2½ to 3 hours. If you're on the Mornington Peninsula, there's a regular daily ferry service from Stony Point to Cowes.

TOURS

Day trips from Melbourne are run by local tour operators, including Gray Line. Tours of the Phillip Island Penguin Parade cost A$132 (penguins and koalas only) to A$204 (with an island tour and lunch). **Wildlifecoast Cruises** runs two-hour cruises from Cowes Jetty to the Nobbies and Seal Rocks, spending 20–30 minutes viewing the seal colony. Cruises run from December 27 through to mid-July with varying frequency depending on the season. The company also runs half-day cruises to Fench Island.

ESSENTIALS

Tour Operators Gray Line (⊠ *Melbourne Day Tour Centre, Federation Sq., Flinders and Russell Sts., City Center, Melbourne* ☏ *1300/858687* ⊕ *www.grayline.com*). **Melbourne's Best Day Tours** (⊠ *Melbourne Day Tour Centre, Federation Sq., Flinders and Russell Sts., City Center, Melbourne* ☏ *1300/130550 or*

03/9397–4911 ⊕ *www.melbournetours.com.au*). **Wildlifecoast Cruises** (✉ *The Rotunda, Jetty Carpark, The Esplanade* ☎ *1300/763739* ⊕ *www.wildlifecoast-cruises.com.au* ⌛ *A$68*).

Transportation V/Line (✉ *Southern Cross Railway Station, Spencer St., City Center, Melbourne* ☎ *13–6196* ⊕ *www.vline.com.au*).

Visitor Information Phillip Island Information Centre (✉ *895 Tourist Rd., Newhaven* ☎ *03/5956–7447 or 1300/366422* ⊕ *www.visitphillipisland.com*).

WHERE TO EAT AND STAY

The seaside town of **Cowes** is the hub of Phillip Island; the pier is where you can board sightseeing cruises and the passenger ferry that travels across Western Port Bay to Stony Point on the Mornington Peninsula. It has a lively café scene and several quality gift shops interspersed with the traditionally cheaper tourist fare. Restaurant and hotel bookings are essential in the busy summer months.

$$ ✕ **Harry's on the Esplanade.** Spilling onto an upstairs terrace above
ECLECTIC Cowes's main beach, Harry's is something of a Phillip Island institution. Its menu, which changes regularly, draws heavily on seafood bought fresh from the trawlers and locally raised beef, lamb, and pork. Don't pass up the crayfish if it's on the menu. The wine list has an Australian emphasis and includes local wines. The bread is made on the premises, as are the pastries and ice cream. ✉ *Upper level, 17 The Esplanade, Cowes* ☎ *03/5952–6226* ▭ *AE, DC, MC, V* ⊗ *Closed Mon.*

$$ ⌂ **Glen Isla House.** This luxurious B&B has six individually themed rooms in one lodge. There's also a separate suite as well as a modern two-story cottage that sleeps up to four. Hosts Ian and Madeleine Baker live in an adjoining historic residence that was transported from the United States in the late 1800s and served as one of the island's original homesteads. The property has extensive terraces, lush gardens, and a delightful summerhouse; the beach is right at the doorstep. The gourmet breakfasts include Ian's homemade fruit compote. There is a minimum two-night stay. ✉ *230–232 Church St., Cowes* ☎ *03/5952–1882* ⊕ *www.glenisla.com* ⌲ *1 king suite, 6 house rooms, 1 2-story gate cottage* ♿ *In-room: safe, refrigerator, DVD, free Wi-Fi. In-hotel: restaurant, airport shuttle, no elevator, free public Wi-Fi, parking (no fee), no kids under 12* ▭ *AE, DC, MC, V* ⏸⌂ *BP.*

QUEENSCLIFF

103 km (64 mi) southwest of Melbourne.

In the late 19th century Queenscliff was a favorite weekend destination for well-to-do Melburnians, who traveled on paddle steamers or by train to stay at the area's grand hotels. Some, like the Vue Grand and the Queenscliff Hotel, welcome tourists to this day. Be sure to check out Fort Queenscliff, another landmark from bygone days. Good restaurants and quiet charm are also traits of Queenscliff. The best beach is at Lonsdale Bay, where a long stretch of golden sand and gentle surf makes a great place to wade, walk, or swim in summer. The playground of families during the day and dog walkers come dusk, Queenscliff is a restful alternative to the resort towns of Sorrento and Portsea on the other side of the bay. On the last weekend in November the annual Queenscliff Music Festival (⊕ *www.qmf.net.au*) draws hundreds of visitors to town.

GETTING HERE AND AROUND

The lovely coastal village of Queenscliff and nearby sibling Point Lonsdale make for a worthy—and well-signposted—detour on the drive from Melbourne to the start of the Great Ocean Road.

It's about a 60- to 90-minute drive from Melbourne via the Princes Highway (M1) to Geelong, then via the Bellarine Highway (B110) to Queenscliff. A train runs from Melbourne's Southern Cross Station to Geelong, where buses (Nos. 75, 76, and 80) continue on to Queenscliff. The Queenscliff–Sorrento Ferry departs on the hour (in both directions) from 7 AM to 6 PM and at 7 PM in the summer months. The journey takes 40 minutes and costs A$10 for pedestrians (A$18 round-trip), A$61.50 for cars including two passengers in the high season.

It's easy to walk around Queenscliff's main attractions; ask at the visitor center in Hesse Street for maps. The Bellarine Peninsula Railway, a tourist train, runs between the towns of Queenscliff and Drysdale (a distance of 10 mi) four times a week, while on Saturday nights between August and May the hugely popular Blues Train features dinner and live blues entertainment; tickets are A$80 per person.

ESSENTIALS

Transportation Queenscliff–Sorreto Ferry (✆ *03/5258–3244* ⊕ *www. searoad.com.au*). **Bellarine Peninsula Railway** (and Blues Train) (✉ *Queenscliff Railway Station, 20 Symonds St., Queenscliff* ✆ *03/5258–2068* ⊕ *www.bpr.org. au*). **V/Line** (✉ *Southern Cross Railway Station, Spencer St., City Center, Melbourne* ✆ *13/6196* ⊕ *www.vline.com.au*).

Visitor Information Queenscliff Visitor Information Centre (✉ *55 Hesse St., Queenscliff* ✆ *03/5258–4843* ⊕ *www.queenscliff.org*).

WHERE TO STAY

$$$ 🏠 **Queenscliff Hotel.** Gloriously restored, this 19th-century beauty has soaring, pressed-metal ceilings, stained-glass windows, antique furnishings, and opulent sitting rooms graced with open fires and enormous armchairs. If you're after period charm rather than spacious modernity, this is the place for you. The hotel's suites and the three downstairs sitting rooms are lovely, and instantly transport you to a more genteel era. Fine dining ($$$$) is offered in the beautiful formal restaurant, opened on Friday to Sunday nights, where chef Glenn Waddell has introduced Old Fashioned Fare in keeping with the room's historic decor: you'll find stuffed individual roast sirloin with horseradish sauce and mini Yorkshire pudding on the menu, along with heartwarming bread-and-butter pudding. At other times meals are served in a leafy conservatory, a cozy bar, or in the outdoor courtyard with an ornate fountain. The hotel's location—across from a park and with views to the ocean—is enviable. There are excellent packages in winter months. **Pros:** grandly charming, good location, excellent on-site restaurants. **Cons:** limited room facilities. ✉ *16 Gellibrand St.* ✆ *03/5258–1066* ⊕ *www.queenscliffhotel.com.au* ⤳ *15 rooms* ⚐ *In-room: no a/c, no phone, no TV.*

In-hotel: 2 restaurants, bar, no elevator, laundry facilities ▭ *AE, DC, MC, V* 🍴 *BP.*

$$ ★ **Vue Grand Hotel.** Built in 1881, the Vue Grand blends Old World elegance with modern touchs. The ultra-lavish Turret Suite at the very top of the building has 180-degree views of the bay and all the latest amenitites. It opened in 2008 for the first time since it was gutted by fire 1927. It is the pièce de résistance of the hotel's 30 rooms and suites, and comes with a matching price tag (A$595 per night with breakfast). The hotel's main lobby is a very grand affair with marble columns, an elegant staircase, and Art Deco statues. The Grand Dining Room makes you want to dress to the nines in 1920s elegance before you enter. It has soaring ceilings, antiques, and a grand piano, and tables are set with sparkling stemware and crisp linens. Dinner ($$) may feature fillet of beef with garlic-butter fondant, honey-parsnip puree, and roasted shallots. Don't miss the Vue Grand Chocolate Extravanganza—it's ideal for two. For casual dining, head to the hotel's Café Lure, which has an international menu and a pleasant outdoor setting ($–$$). The hotel's recent multimillion dollar upgrade means that all rooms are nicely equipped. Guests with children should notify the hotel in advance so special arrangements can be made. **Pros:** grand experience, wonderful dining room. **Cons:** not on the seaside. ✉ *46 Hesse St.3225* ☎ *03/5258–1544* 🌐 *www.vuegrand.com.au* *30 rooms, 3 suites* *In-room: Wi-Fi. In-hotel: 2 restaurants, bar, pool, gym, parking (free), Wi-Fi* ▭ *AE, DC, MC, V* 🍴 *BP.*

LIGHT UP YOUR TRIP

If you're into lighthouses, then this coast is a must-see. Here you can find seven historic lighthouses of varying shapes and sizes—from Point Lonsdale in the east to Portland in the west. Don't miss the tall white-black-and-red cap of beautiful **Split Point lighthouse** at Aireys Inlet, while **Cape Otway lighthouse** is the oldest on mainland Australia, and marks the point where the Southern Ocean and Bass Strait collide. Farther west at Portland is majestic **Cape Nelson Lighthouse**, high above ferocious seas. Guided tours are available.

4

EN ROUTE

From Queenscliff, follow signs toward the Great Ocean Road for 45 km (28 mi) to **Torquay**, Australia's premier surfing and windsurfing resort, and Bell's Beach, famous for its Easter surfing contests and its October international windsurfing competitions. Great Ocean Road, a positively magnificent coastal drive, officially begins at Eastern View, 10 km (6 mi) east of Lorne. The seaside towns of Anglesea, Aireys Inlet, and Fairhaven also make good warm-weather swimming stops.

GREAT OCEAN ROAD

Victoria's Great Ocean Road, which travels along rugged, windswept beaches on Victoria's southwestern coast, is arguably the country's most spectacular coastal drive. The road, built during the Great Depression atop majestic cliffs, occasionally dips down to sea level. Here, in championship surfing country, some of the world's finest waves pound mile after mile of uninhabited, golden, sandy beaches.

Although this region is actually on the southeast coast of the Australian mainland, it lies to the west of Melbourne, and so Melburnians refer to it as the "West Coast." From the city, you should allow two or more days for a West Coast sojourn.

Driving is the most convenient way to see the region, and the only way to really enjoy the Great Ocean Road. Although the official Great Ocean Road is deemed to be 243 km (152 mi), between the towns of Torquay in the east and Allansford (near Warnambool) in the west, most people think of it as the much longer route that ventures farther west to Port Fairy and Portland. Its many twists and turns and wonderful sights along the way take many hours to explore.

The going may be slow on the most scenic routes, especially during the summer holiday period. The winding road is notorious for its motor accidents, so take care on the bends and slow down.

TOURS

12 Apostles Helicopter rides are an exciting way to appreciate the awesome force of the Great Southern Ocean and this amazing natural sculpture park. Ten-minute flights take in the Twelve Apostles and Loch Ard George; longer flights travel farther up the coast to the west and inland. Prices start at A$95 per person.

AAT Kings has a six-day tour of the Great Ocean Road to Adelaide from Melbourne that also includes visits to Mount Gambier and Kangaroo Island. The tour is A$1,995.

Absolute Outdoors is a one-stop shop for kayak, bike, and surfing tours around South-West Victoria. There's also a surf school, and all equipment is provided.

Adventure Tours Australia has two three-day tours that include both the Great Ocean Road and the Grampians National Park. Young backpackers are their target market, but anyone can join the tours, and a choice between dorm accommodation and singles or doubles is available. You can choose a round-trip tour from Melbourne or one that continues on to Adelaide. Both tours spend one night in Princeton (just east of the Twelve Apostles) and another night in Halls Gap. It's A$445 for dorm accommodation and A$599 for a double or twin room, with two dinners and two breakfasts.

Auswalk offers a guided and self-guided six-night walk from Torquay to Lorne called the Surf Coast Walk. They also have a guided six-night Great Ocean Walk tour, and a self-guided tour that can take be taken in five-, six-, or nine-night segments. The company picks you up from Melbourne Airport and carries the luggage by car from hotel (or B&B) to hotel. Walkers carry a day pack only. Most meals are provided. Two-night accommodations are in the Cape Otway Lighthouse cottages. Self-guided walks follow the same route and require a minimum of two people. The same accommodations and meals are available and luggage is also transported by a support vehicle. The six-night guided tour ranges from A$2,395 per person (double) depending on the season. Self-guided tours are about A$1,000 less. Daily walks can range from five to seven hours, although the support vehicle can drive those who

Sea kayaking in Apollo Bay.

feel they have had enough walking for one day. ✉ *4 Red Gum Lease Track, Halls Gap* ☎ *03/5356–4971* ⊕ *www.auswalk.com.au.*

Great Ocean Road Helicopters has 10-, 15-, and 25-minute flights that take in the Twelve Apostles and Loch Ard Gorge on the shorter trips, adding London Bridge, the Bay of Martyrs, and the Bay of Islands on longer runs. Prices range from A$95 to A$205 per person.

Great Ocean Road Adventure Tours or G.O.R.A.T.S. as it's called, runs mountain-bike tours from Deans Marsh General Store from 9 AM four days a week (Sunday, Tuesday, Thursday, and Friday). Book at least three days in advance. Tours run to the town of Forrest, considered a mountain-bike mecca, with 15 trails showcasing the natural beauty of the Otway Ranges. Trips can be tailor-made for a group of six or more. Prices run from $85 per person including bike, helmet, map, transport, and guide. Deans Marsh General Store is about 12 km (7½ mi) north-west of Lorne along the Deans Marsh–Lorne Road. Trails are on the Web site. They also operate canoe tours along Aireys Creek.

Lighthouse Tours explore the majestic Split Point Lighthouse at Aireys Inlet, also known as the White Queen. You can see her for miles as you approach this section of the Great Ocean Road west of Anglesea. The 45-minute tours operate year round, but bookings are required on weekdays. Tour cost is $A12. The views are amazing. Just follow the huge white lighthouse with the red cap.

Melbourne's Best Day Tours has a 4WD tour of the Great Ocean Road from Melbourne. Starting at 7.30 AM, it includes breakfast and lunch, a lighthouse tour, rain-forest walks, and sightseeing in Port Campbell

National Park. The 12-hour tour takes a maximum of six people and costs $A348.

Michael J IV Charters runs fishing trips that skim over the famous shipwrecks of the region and seal-watching tours to nearby Lady Julia Island.

Mulloka Cruises give half-hour cruise around the Port Fairy Bay—a quick way to set your sea legs and see Port Fairy from a different angle. Boat owner Jane Grimshaw dispenses interesting information about the area. Cruises cost from A$10.

Port Campbell Boat Charters operates diving tours to the famous wreck sites as well as scenic cruises and fishing trips.

Southern Exposure Adventure Sports runs mountain-bike tours along the coast and in the nearby Otway National Park, kayaking tours, and surfing lessons. Surfing lessons are A$65 for two hours, and combined bike and kayaking tours can be arranged. Bookings are essential.

Spring Creek Horse Rides take you through the beautiful Otway National Park. It's a leisurely way to spend an hour or two. Located at Bellbrae, just a few miles inlands from Torquay, rides are A$35 for one hour and A$55 for two.

ESSENTIALS

Tour Operators 12 Apostles Helicopters (✉ *Twelve Apostles Interpretative Centre, 9400 Great Ocean Rd., Port Campbell* ☎ *03/5598–8283* ⊕ *www.12apostleshelicopters.com.au*). **AAT Kings** (✉ *Melbourne Day Tour Centre, Federation Sq., Flinders and Russell Sts., City Center, Melbourne* ☎ *03/9663–3377 or 1300/556100* ⊕ *www.aatkings.com.au*). **Absolute Outdoors** (✉ *67 Bentinck St., Portland* ☎ *03/5521–7646* ⊕ *www.absoluteoutdoors.com.au*). **Adventure Tours Australia** (✉ *72 The Parade, City Center, Norwood* ☎ *1300/654604 or 0008132–8230* ⊕ *www.advenutretours.com.au*). **Auswalk** (✉ *4 Red Gum Lease Track, Halls Gap* ☎ *03/5356–4971* ⊕ *www.auswalk.com.au*). **Great Ocean Road Adventure Tours** (✉ *200 Bambra Cemetary Rd., Deans Marsh* ☎ *03/5236–3321* ⊕ *www.gorats.com.au*). **Lighthouse Tour** (✉ *Split Point lighthouse, Reserve Rd., Aireys Inlet* ☎ *1800/174045 or 03/5263–1133* ⊕ *www.ecologic.net.au* 🖃 *A$12*). **Melbourne's Best Day Tours** (✉ *Federation Square, Flinders and Russell Sts., City Center* ☎ *1300/130550* ⊕ *www.melbouretours.com.au*). **Michael J IV Charters** (✉ *King George Sq., Port Fairy* ☎ *03/5568–2816*). **Mulloka Cruises** (✉ *Martins Point, end of wharf, Port Fairy* 📱 Mobile: *0408/514382* 🖃 *janegrimshaw@bigpond.com*). **Port Campbell Boat Charters** (✉ *Lord St., Port Campbell* ☎ *03/5598–6411 or mobile 0428/986366*). **Southern Exposure Adventure Sports** (✉ *38 Bell St, Torquay* ☎ *03/5261–9170* ⊕ *www.southernexposure.com.au*). **Spring Creek Horse Rides** (✉ *245 Portreath Rd., Bellbrae* ☎ *03/5266–1541 or mobile 0403/167590* ⊕ *www.springcreekhorserides.com.au*).

Visitor Information The **Geelong Great Ocean Road Visitor Information Centre** (✉ *Stead Park at corner of Princes Hwy. and St. Georges Rd., Corio, Geelong* ☎ *03/5275–5797 or 1800/620888* ⊕ *www.visitgeelong.org*) is open daily 9–5. **Torquay Visitor Information Centre** (✉ *Surf Walk* ☎ *1300/614219* ⊕ *www.visitsurfcoast.com.au*) is open daily 9–5.

LORNE

140 km (87 mi) southwest of Melbourne, 95 km (59 mi) southwest of Queenscliff, 50 km (31 mi) southwest of Torquay.

Located between sweeping Loutit Bay and the Otway Mountain Range, Lorne is one of the main towns on the Great Ocean Road, but one that has a definite surf-and-holiday feel. It's the site of both a wild celebration every New Year's Eve and the popular Pier-to-Pub Swim held on the first weekend in January. Some people make their reservations a year or more in advance. It's also the home of the Great Otway Classic, a footrace held annually on the second weekend in June. The town has a lively café and pub scene, as well as several upscale restaurants, trendy boutiques, and a day spa.

GETTING HERE AND AROUND

You really need a car to get to Lorne and other Great Ocean Road towns; the next best option is to take an organized tour. Public transport is available, but it's a long process: take the V/Line train to Geelong, then transfer to a bus to Apollo Bay, which stops at Lorne (about five hours). If driving, take the the Princes Highway west from Melbourne across the Westgate Bridge to Geelong. From there, follow signs along the Surf Coast Highway to Torquay, where you'll connect with the Great Ocean Road.

ESSENTIALS

Visitor Information Lorne Visitor Information Centre (✉ *15 Muntjoy Parade, Lorne* ☎ *1300/89–1152* ⊕ *www.visitsurfcoast.com*).

Emergencies Lorne Community Hospital (✉ *Albert St., Lorne* ☎ *03/5289–4300* ⊕ *www.swarh.com.au/lorne/index.aspb*). **Lorne Police Station** (✉ *5 Charles St., Lorne* ☎ *03/529–2712* ⊕ *No web*).

OUTDOOR ACTIVITIES

HIKING AND WALKING — The Great Ocean Road and the "Surf Coast" section of it around Torquay, Lorne, and Airleys Inlet have fantastic walks providing great clifftop views, while inland a little way there are waterfalls and picnic grounds to explore.

The 30-km (19-mi) Surf Coast Walk, which begins near Jan Juc carpark (a mile west of Torquay) and ends around Moggs Picnic area at Aireys, can be done in short segments.

Inland from the towns of Fairweather and Eastern View is the vast Otway National Park, which has many picturesque walks, including the 12-km (7.5-mi) walk from Aireys Inlet to Distillery Creek, which can be quite strenuous. There are also shorter and easier walks to Erskine Falls and Sheaoak Falls just inland from Lorne. The Torquay and Lorne visitor centers have trail maps

WHERE TO EAT AND STAY

$ — ✕ **Marks.** Fresh seafood—from fried calamari to grilled flathead—is the

SEAFOOD — draw at this Lorne institution, which has been going strong for 18

★ — years. The decor is "funky seaside," with bright walls, blue chairs, and a smattering of local art and sculpture for sale. The menu changes daily depending what the fishermen have caught and what's growing in

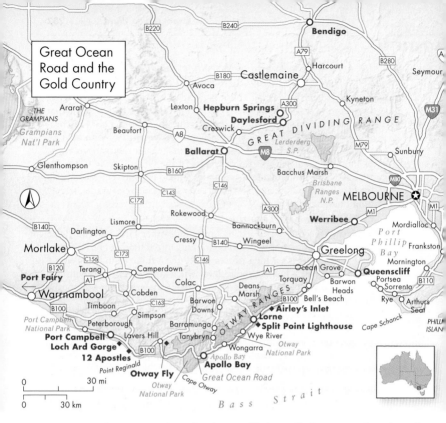

Great Ocean
Road and the
Gold Country

the restaurant's garden, but you'll always find oysters and steak on the menu, along with Atlantic salmon and perhaps fried whitebait with piri piri mayonnaise made from homegrow chilis. It's open for dinner only and located on the main road across from the beach. ⊠ *124 Mountjoy Parade 3232* ☏ *03/5289–2787* ⊟ *AE, MC, V* ⊘ *Closed Wed. and Thurs. from Easter until end July; closed Aug. and Sept. No lunch.*

$ ■ **Mantra Erskine Beach Resort.** This huge complex set on 12 acres near the water's edge reopened in early 2006 following a A$20 million upgrade. All rooms and apartments, including those in the 1868 guesthouse, have been given a face-lift and now have nice touches like hot tubs. A stylish new restaurant, a funky café, and a chic cocktail lounge were also added, along with that must-have resort experience, the day spa. ⊠ *Mountjoy Parade* ☏ *03/5289–1209* ⊕ *www.mantraerskine-beachresort.com.au* ⊃ *157 rooms, 130 apartments* ⊘ *In-room: kitchen (some), DVD, dial-up, refrigerator, VCR, Wi-Fi. In-hotel: 2 restaurants, bar, tennis courts, pool, gym, spa, beachfront, golf course, public Wi-Fi, laundry facilities, parking (no fee)* ⊟ *AE, DC, MC, V* ⫮⚬⎮BP.

EN
ROUTE

About an hour's drive and 70 km (43 mi) from Lorne (follow the Great Ocean Road until it joins Skenes Creek Road, then take Forrest Apollo Bay Road to Beech Forest Road, then Colac Lavers Hill Road until you reach the signed turnoff to Phillips Track) you'll find the entrance to the **Otway Fly** (☎ *03/5235–9200 or 1800/300477* ⊕ *www.otwayfly. com*). The Fly is a 1,969-foot-long elevated treetop walk, where you can meander on a steel walkway structure (one section is springboard-cantilevered, and gently bounces as you pass over Young's Creek) above the rain-forest canopy. You'll see the tops of giant myrtle beech, blackwood, and mountain ash trees, as well as spectacular views of the surrounding region. It's open daily 9–5; tickets are A$17.

APOLLO BAY

GETTING HERE AND AROUND
Apollo Bay is 40 km (25 mi) west of Lorne. Driving is the most convenient way to get here. Otherwise take the combined V/Line train-bus option, which involves taking a train from Melbourne's Southern Cross Station to Geelong and then a bus along the Great Ocean Road to Apollo Bay, via Lorne and other surf coast towns.

OUTDOOR ACTIVITIES

DIVING The Twelve Apostles Marine National Park and the nearby Arches Marine Sanctuary both provide fantastic diving opportunities. Local wrecks that can be explored with experienced guides include the *Napier* at Port Campbell, the famous *Loch Ard* (off Muttonbird Island), the *Schomberg* at Peterborough, and the *Fiji* near Moonlight Head. All wrecks are protected by federal law, and are not to be disturbed in any way. *(See Port Campbell boat charters in Tours, above.)*

HIKING AND The Port Campbell National Park area, which is home to the Twelve
WALKING Apostles, Loch Ard George, and other amazing landforms, has many good walks. Most are along wooden boardwalks; others also include steep stairs down to the beach. The Visitor Centre at Port Campbell has all the details.

Inland from Port Campbell is the Camperdown-Timboon Rail Trail (also known as the Coast to Crater Trail). It passes by lakes and streams and open volcanic plains. It is suitable for walkers and mountain bikers. The 36-km (22-mi) trail has good signage. Ask the tourist offices for details.

WHERE TO STAY

¢–$ 🏠 **Apollo Bay Eco Beach YHA.** More like a hip beach house than a youth
★ hostel, this friendly two-story lodge has earned its name with a low-impact architectural design, solar hot water, and recycling systems. There are dorm rooms as well as single, twin, double, and family rooms, many with balconies with great bay views. Public areas—two lounges with quiet reading nooks, a separate TV room, and an Internet room—have comfy sofas and beanbags. There's plenty of room to create culinary feasts in the two shared kitchens. The hostel is part of the YHA chain and offers discounts for members. **Pros:** good price, good location. **Cons:** shared bathrooms, student feel may not appeal to all. ⊠ *5 Pascoe St.* ☎ *03/5237–7899* ⊕ *www.yha.com.au* ⊅ *30 rooms, 6 dorm rooms (4 beds in each)* ⅅ *In-hotel: bar, bicycles, public Internet, no elevator* ═ *MC, V.*

$$$ ⬚ **Chris's Beacon Point Restaurant and Villas.** Set high in the Otway Ranges
Fodor'sChoice with stunning views over the ocean, this is a wonderful place to dine or
★ bed down for the night. The accommodations have uninterrupted views
from the floor-to-ceiling windows and timber balconies. The studios can
accommodate four people. The restaurant ($$–$$$), opened in 1978
by owner Chris Talihmanidis, draws people from all over the region for
Greek-inspired dishes such as souvlaki (lamb cubes marinated in rose-
mary and honey). To get here, take the Skenes Creek Road turnoff about
3 km (2 mi) from Apollo Bay and wind up a hill to Beacon Point. **Pros:**
sensational views. **Cons:** pricey; steep walk to rooms. ⊠ *280 Skenes
Creek Rd.* ☎ *03/5237–6411* ⊕ *www.chriss.com.au* ⊄ *6 villas, 2 studios*
⚖ *In-room: VCR, no phone, kitchen (some), DVD. In-hotel: restaurant,
room service, parking (no fee), no elevator* ⊟ *AE, DC, MC, V.*

PORT CAMPBELL NATIONAL PARK

Fodor'sChoice *263 km (142 mi) southwest of Melbourne via the Great Ocean Road;*
★ *77 km (48 mi) west of Apollo Bay; 123 km (77 mi) west of Lorne.*

Stretching some 30 km (19 mi) along the southern Victoria coastline,
Port Campbell National Park is the site of some of the most famously beau-
tiful geological formations in Australia. Along this coast the ferocious
Southern Ocean has gnawed at the limestone cliffs for aeons, creating
a sort of badlands-by-the-sea, where strangely shaped formations stand
offshore amid the surf. The most famous of these formations is the
Twelve Apostles, as much a symbol for Victoria as the Sydney Opera
House is for New South Wales. (The name has always been a misnomer,
as there were only nine of these stone columns of sea stacks as they are
correctly termed. Then in July 2005 one of them collapsed into the
sea, leaving behind just eight.) If you happen to be visiting the Twelve
Apostles just after sunset, you're likely to see bands of Little Penguins
returning to their burrows on the beach. There's a population of around
3,000 of the cute creatures in the area.

Loch Ard Gorge, named after the iron-hulled clipper that wrecked on
the shores of nearby Mutton Bird Island in 1878, is another spectacular
place to walk. Four of the *Loch Ard*'s victims are buried in a nearby
cemetery, while a sign by the gorge tells the story of the ship and its
crew. This stretch of coast is often called the Shipwreck Coast for the
hundreds of vessels that have met an untimely end in the treacherous
waters. The Historic Shipwreck Trail, with landmarks describing 25 of
the disasters, stretches from Moonlight Head to Port Fairy.

The best time to visit the park is late September to April, when you
can also witness the boisterous birdlife on nearby Mutton Bird Island.
Toward nightfall, hundreds of hawks and kites circle the island in search
of baby mutton birds emerging from their protective burrows. The
hawks and kites beat a hasty retreat at the sight of thousands of adult
shearwaters approaching with food for their chicks as the last light
fades from the sky. Other amazing sea stacks and stone formations far-
ther west along the Great Ocean Road are also not to be missed. They
include the Grotto, the Arch, London Bridge, and the spectacular Bay
of Islands and Bay of Martyrs.

Loch Ard Gorge in Port Campbell National Park, Great Ocean Road.

The Visitor Centre is open daily 9 to 5. A self-guided, 1½-hour Discovery Walk begins near Port Campbell Beach, where it's safe to swim. The pounding surf and undertow are treacherous at other nearby beaches.

GETTING HERE AND AROUND

The scenic route to Port Campell National Park (which is in fact a few miles east of the town of Port Campbell) is via the Great Ocean Road from Torquay, via Lorne and Apollo Bay. A car is the best way to go. A shorter drive is via the Princes Highway (M1) from Melbourne to Warrnambool, then the Great Ocean Road east to Port Campbell. A V/Line train operates to Warrnambool, and then a bus can be taken to Port Campbell. The journey takes about five hours.

ESSENTIALS

Transportation V/Line (☎ 13–6196 ⊕ www.vline.com.au).

Visitor Information Parks Victoria (✉ Parks office: Tregea St., Port Campbell ☎ 13–1963⊕ www.parkweb.vic.gov.au). The **Port Campbell Visitors Centre** (✉ 26 Morris St., Port Campbell ☎ 03/5598–6089 ⊕ www.visit12apostles.com.au).

WHERE TO EAT AND STAY

$

AUSTRALIAN

✕ **Waves.** You won't see any waves from this relaxed main-street eatery even though it's only yards from the water. You will find enormous breakfasts and fireside seafood dinners, a spacious sundeck, and a friendly staff. The menu may feature such diverse dishes as Asian-spiced Flinders Island wallaby (a dish rarely, if ever, seen on a menu) and sizzling steaks. The menu changes weekly based on locally available ingredients. ✉ 29 Lord St., Port Campbell ☎ 03/5598–6111 ⊕ www.wavesportcampbell.com.au ▭ AE, MC, V.

$–$$ ⌂ **Daysy Hill Country Cottages.** Five sandstone-and-cedar cottages, set alongside manicured gardens, have views over the Newfield Valley. Inside, the spacious rooms have comfortable couches, wooden furnishings, open fireplaces, TVs with cable movies, VCRs, and CD players, and air-conditioning and DVDs in some. Breakfast provisions can be provided for around A$10 per person. Luxury suites with hot tubs and deluxe self-contained cabins are also available. There are three- or four-night stays required in both cabins and cottages over Christmas, Easter, and during long weekends. **Pros:** good price, good location. **Cons:** limited facilities, minimum stay required. ✉ *7353 Timboon/Port Campbell Rd., Port Campbell* ☎ *03/5598–6226* ⊕ *www.greatoceanroad.nu/daysyhill* ↻ *5 cottages, 4 suites, 3 cabins* ⌂ *In-room: air-conditioning (some) kitchen, VCR, DVD (some). In-hotel: laundry facilities, no elevator* ☰ *AE, DC, MC, V.*

$$–$$$ ⌂ **Southern Ocean Villas.** Ideally situated on the edge of Port Campbell National Park, within short walking distance of the town center and beach, these villas are stylishly furnished and fitted with polished wood floors, picture windows, and high ceilings. Each unit has two bedrooms and an upstairs loft. One villa accommodates four to six people. **Pros:** good location near Twelve Apostles. **Cons:** located in sleepy town, difficult to find. ✉ *2 McCue St., Port Campbell* ☎ *03/5598–4200* ⊕ *www.southernoceanvillas.com* ↻ *20 villas* ⌂ *In-room: kitchen, DVD. In-hotel: laundry facilities, no elevator, restaurant, bar* ☰ *AE, DC, MC, V.*

EN ROUTE   About 66 km (41 mi) west of Port Campbell, **Warrnambool** is Victoria's southern right whale nursery. Platforms at Logan's Beach, about 3 km (2 mi) east of the city, provide views of an amazing marine show from June to September. Whales return to this beach every year to calve, with the females and young staying close to the shore and the males playing about 150 yards out to sea. **Warrnambool Visitor Information Centre** (✉ *Flagstaff Hill, Merri St., Warrnambool* ☎ *03/5559–4620 or 1800/637725* ⊕ *www.warrnamboolinfo.com.au*).

PORT FAIRY

377 km (215 mi) southwest of Melbourne via the Great Ocean Road; it is shorter if you take the Princes Highway (M1).

Port Fairy is widely considered to be the state's prettiest village. The second-oldest town in Victoria, it was originally known as Belfast, and there are indeed echoes of Ireland in the landscape and architecture. More than 50 of the cottages and sturdy bluestone buildings that line the banks of the River Moyne have been classified as landmarks by the National Trust, and few towns repay a leisurely stroll so richly. Huge Norfolk Island pines line many of the streets, particularly Gipps Street, and the town is dotted with good cafés, a few pubs, and art galleries.

The town still thrives as the base for a fishing fleet, and as host to the Port Fairy Folk Festival, one of Australia's most famous musical events, held every March. The town has a large colony of short-tailed shearwaters that nest on Griffiths Island. Amazingly, these birds travel here from the Aleutian Islands near Alaska, always arriving within three days of September 22. You can take a 45-minute walk around the island on marked trails to the historic lighthouse.

GETTING HERE AND AROUND

The most convenient form of transport is by car; the 377-km (234 mi) trip alog the Great Ocean Road from Melbourne takes about six and a half hours, and it's advisable to break the journey, as there's so much to see along the way. It's a shorter trip if you take the Princes Highway (M1). V/Line trains travel from Melbourne's Southern Cross Station to Warrnambool (3 hours), and V/Line buses then make the short distance (29-km) to Port Fairy.

ESSENTIALS

Transportation V/Line (☎ 13–6196 ⊕ www.vline.com.au).

Visitor Information Port Fairy Tourist Information Centre (✉ Railway Place, Bank St., Port Fairy ☎ 03/5568–2682 ⊕ www.visitport-fairy.com.au).

EXPLORING

Founded during the whaling heyday in the 19th century, Port Fairy was once a whaling station with one of the largest ports in Victoria. The Port Fairy **Historical Society Museum** contains relics from whaling days and from the many ships that have foundered along this coast. ✉ Old Courthouse, 30 Gipps St. ☎ 03/5568–2263 ⊕ www.historicalsociety.port-fairy.com ✍ A$5 ☉ Sept. 1–mid-July, Wed. and weekends 2–5; mid-July–Aug., Sat. 2–5.

Mott's Cottage is a restored limestone-and-timber cottage built by Sam Mott, a member of the 1830s whaling crew from the cutter *Fairy* who founded the town. ✉ 5 Sackville St. ☎ 03/5568–2682 or 03/5568–2632 ✍ A$2 ☉ Wed. and Sat. 2–4, or by appointment.

OUTDOOR ACTIVITIES

HIKING AND WALKING

There are several walks around Port Fairy that highlight the town's historical aspects and and the area's great beauty. Pick up a Historic Walks map from the visitor center and follow a trail past some 30 beautiful buildings; it takes about an hour. The Maritime and Shipwreck Heritage Walk also takes about an hour. The map will show you where the cannons and gun emplacements are at Battery Hill and pinpoint the position of some of the historic shipwrecks out in the bay.

Griffiths Island is another good place to walk. You can walk around the entire island in about an hour, visting the lighthouse and perhaps spotting a black wallaby along the way.

Just 10 minutes or 14 km (9 mi) east of Port Fairy is Tower Hill Reserve, a national park nested in an extinct volcano. There are several walking trails and plenty of chances to see emus and kangaroos. About 40 minutes northeast is Mount Eccles National Park, another extinct volcano. There are four walks, including a walk to the crater rim and lava caves.

The Port Fairy Maritime & Shipwreck Heritage Walk is a 2-km (1.2-mi) trail that passes the sites of several shipwrecks: the bark *Socrates*, which was battered by huge seas in 1843; the bark *Lydia*, which wrecked off the coast in 1847; the schooner *Thistle*, which went down in 1837;

and the brigantine *Essington,* which sank while moored at Port Fairy in 1852. Other historic attractions en route include the town port, the lifeboat station, riverside warehouses, and Griffiths Island Lighthouse. The walk is well marked.

Parks Victoria, the national park body, manages Tower Hill Reserve together with the Worn Gundidju Co-Operative, an Aboriginal organization that conducts cultural interpretative walks. Take one of their one-hour personalized bush and nature walks on which you'll learn about Aboriginal lifestyles, bush food, and medicine, and hear about the local inhabitants, which include emus, sugar gliders, koalas, kangaroos, various birdlife, and reptiles. There are also evening tours on which you may see nocturnal native animals and view the crater rim under the stars. Tours start from A$18.95. The park's Web site also has a map of the reserve and walking trails. ⊠ *Tower Hill Reserve, Princes Hwy, between Port Fairy and Warrnambool, Tower Hill* ☎ *03/5565–9292; mobile: 0428/318876* ⊕ *www.parkweb.vic.gov.au.*

WHERE TO EAT AND STAY

¢–$
CAFÉ
✕ **time&tide beachfront gallery.** This sensational café and art gallery has made a big impact on this little town. There's a tantalizing array of sandwiches and wraps, and decadent desserts such as Italian trifle with espresso and chocolate liqueur. Dine outside on the sunny deck or drink in the view through the dining room's floor-to-ceiling windows. Browse in the beach-inspired art gallery or take a path down to the water's edge. ⊠ *21 Thistle Pl.* ☎ *03/5568–2134* ▭ *MC, V* ☉ *Closed Tues. and Wed. No dinner.*

¢–$
🔲 **Dublin House Inn.** This solid stone building with a striking pink color scheme dates from 1855. The four suites, however, are contemporary in design and fitted with modern conveniences. The 32-seat restaurant ($$–$$$), open for dinner daily, is where chef Nick Strapp whips up traditional Mediterranean dishes. His zarzuela, a Catalonian stew, features the local seafood catch of the day with sauce and dry bread on the side. **Pros:** good price, good on-site restaurant. **Cons:** town is dead in the off season. ⊠ *57 Bank St.,* ☎ *03/5568–2022* ⊕ *www.myportfairy.com/ dublinhouse* ⋈ *3 suites, 1 cottage* ⟁ *In-room: no phone, kitchen (some), TV. In-hotel: restaurant, laundry facilities, laundry service, parking (no fee), no elevator* ▭ *AE, MC, V* ⦿|*BP.*

$$–$$$
🔲 **Goble's Mill House.** An imaginative refurbishment of an 1865 flour mill on the bank of the Moyne River transformed it into six guest rooms with private bathrooms and spacious sitting areas, all furnished with antiques. The upper-story loft bedroom is especially appealing, with a balcony overlooking the ever-active river. The open fire makes the sitting room cozy, and a separate guest pantry is stocked with juices and freshly baked shortbreads. You can also enjoy fishing off the Mill House's private jetty. **Pros:** great location, charming historic atmosphere. **Cons:** limited facilities. ⊠ *75 Gipps St.* ☎ *03/5568–1118* ⊕ *www.goblesmill. myportfairy.com* ⋈ *6 rooms* ⟁ *In-room: no a/c, no phone, no TV. In-hotel: parking (no fee), no elevator* ▭ *MC, V* ⦿|*BP.*

$$
🔲 **Merrijig Inn.** Overlooking the riverbank from King George Square, this beautifully restored 1841 Georgian-style building is Victoria's oldest inn. In late 2006 the inn was bought by local chef Ryan Sessions

and partner Kirstyn White, who reopened the restaurant for dinner and have gleaned some of Victoria's top "foodie" awards. Some of the signature dishes include polenta soufflé and lamb. Accommodation is a mix of cozy attic bedrooms with storybook atmospheres and ground floor suites with snug sitting rooms. The restaurant is closed Sunday. The roaring fireplaces are perfect for whiling away the hours with a good book. Breakfast is served in the light-filled conservatory with views of the charming cottage garden. **Pros:** cute and cozy; great food. **Cons:** upstairs rooms have character, but they're very small. ⊠ *1 Campbell St., at Gipps St.* ☎ *03/5568–2324 or 1800/682324* ⊕ *www.merrijiginn. com* ➟ *4 rooms, 4 suites* ⚒ *In-room: no TV (some), no phone. In-hotel: restaurant, bar, no elevator* ☰ *AE, MC, V* ⦿ *BP.*

$$$ 🛉 **Oscars Waterfront Boutique Hotel.** Overlooking the waterfront and a
★ marina of yachts, Oscar's takes French provincial style and gives it an Australian edge. There's a grand staircase straight out of *Gone With the Wind* and an inviting downstairs sitting room with open fire. Each room is individually decorated—some in stripes, others in florals—and various communal lounges have open fireplaces, plush armchairs, and regional artwork. Gourmet breakfasts, for which Oscars is renowned, include banana hotcakes and tomato bruschetta with basil butter. If the weather allows, breakfast is served on the lovely veranda overlooking the river. **Pros:** fantastic location, great breakfasts. **Cons:** not all rooms have a bathtub. ⊠ *41B Gipps St.,* ☎ *03/5568–3022* ⊕ *www.oscarswaterfront.com* ➟ *6 rooms, 1 suite* ⚒ *In-room: refrigerator. In-hotel: bar, no elevator* ☰ *MC, V* ⦿ *BP.*

THE GOLD COUNTRY

Victoria was changed forever in the early 1850s by the discovery of gold in the center of the state. Fantastic news of gold deposits caused immigrants from every corner of the world to pour into Victoria to seek their fortunes as "diggers"—a name that has become synonymous with Australians ever since. Few miners became wealthy from their searches, however. The real money was made by those supplying goods and services to the thousands who had succumbed to gold fever.

Gold towns like Ballarat, Castlemaine, Maldon, and Bendigo sprang up like mushrooms to accommodate these fortune seekers, and prospered until the gold rush receded. Afterward, they became ghost towns or turned to agriculture to survive. However, many beautiful buildings were constructed from the spoils, and these gracious old public buildings and grand hotels survive today and make a visit to Bendigo and Ballarat a pleasure for those who love architecture. Victoria's gold is again being mined in limited quantities, while these historic old towns remain interesting relics of Australia's past.

Although Victoria was not the first Australian state to experience a gold rush, when gold was discovered here in 1851 it became a veritable El Dorado. During the boom years of the 19th century, 90% of the gold mined in Australia came from the state. The biggest finds were at Ballarat and then Bendigo, and the Ballarat diggings proved to be among the richest alluvial goldfields in the world.

This region of Victoria is now considered a center for modern-day rejuvenation. Between Ballarat and other historic gold towns to the north are the twin hot spots of Daylesford and Hepburn Springs—which together constitute the spa capital of Australia.

For leisurely exploration of the Gold Country, a car is essential. Public transportation adequately serves the main centers, but access to smaller towns is less assured and even in the bigger towns attractions are spread out.

TOURS

Gray Line, Australian Pacific Tours, and AAT Kings cover the Gold Country; all three depart from the New Day Tour Centre in Federation Square at the corner of Flinders and Russell Sts., Melbourne.

Contacts AAT Kings (☏ 03/9663–3377 or 1300/556100 ⊕ www.aatkings. com.au). **Australian Pacific Tours** (☏ 03/9277–8499 or 1300/656985 ⊕ www. aptouring.com.au). **Gray Line** (✉ Federation Square East, Flinders and Russell Sts., City Center ☏ 1300/858687 ⊕ www.grayline.com.au).

BALLARAT

106 km (66 mi) northwest of Melbourne.

In the local Aboriginal language, the name Ballarat means "resting place." In pre-gold-rush days nearby Lake Wendouree provided the area with a plentiful supply of food. Once the gold boom hit, however, the town became much less restful; in 1854 Ballarat was the scene of the Battle of the Eureka Stockade, a skirmish that took place between miners and authorities over gold license fees that miners were forced to pay. More than 20 men died in the battle. Today their flag—the Southern Cross—is a symbol of Australia's egalitarian spirit.

Despite the harsh times, fortunes made from the mines (and from the miners) resulted in the grand Victorian architecture on Sturt and Lydiard streets—note the post office, the town hall, Craig's Royal Hotel, and Her Majesty's Theater. The Old Colonists' Hall and the Mining Exchange (at 20 and 26 Lydiard Street, respectively) now house shops and cafés. The visitor center has a self-guided heritage walk.

GETTING HERE AND AROUND

It's an easy 80-minute drive to Ballarat along the Western Highway (M8) from Melbourne. The road, however, is the main artery between Melbourne and Adelaide, and many huge trucks are also on the road. Take care and drive within the speed limit. From Ballarat you can easily drive north to the spa-country towns of Daylesford–Hepburn Springs and Bendigo on the Mid-Way Highway. The city itself is well signposted. The city center is built around a well-planned grid and has ample parking. Lock bus services run from Sturt Street, the main thoroughfare, to most of Ballarat's attractions.

V/Line operates trains to Ballarat and Bendigo from Melbourne.

ESSENTIALS

Transportation V/Line (☏ 13–6196 ⊕ www.vline.com.au)

Visitor Information Art Gallery of Ballarat (✉ 40 Lydiard St. N, Ballarat ☎ 1800/446633 ⊕ www.visitballarat. com.au). Ballarat Tourist Information Centre (✉ Eureka Centre, Rodier and Eureka Sts., Ballarat ☎ 1800/446633 ⊕ www.visitballarat.com.au).

EXPLORING

All sorts of native animals, including saltwater crocodiles, snakes, lizards, wombats, echidnas, and kangaroos, can be found at **Ballarat Wildlife Park.** Daily tours of the park are led at 11, with a koala show at 2, a wombat show at 2:30, and a crocodile feeding at 3. The park also has a café and barbecue and picnic areas. ✉ *Fussel and York Sts., East Ballarat* ☎ *03/5333–5933* ⊕ *www.wildlifepark.com.au* ✉ *A$22* ⊗ *Daily 9–5.*

BRUSH STROKES

The riches of Victoria's goldfields are reflected in beautiful Victorian buildings and in the treasures of the art galleries of Ballarat, Bendigo, and Castlemaine. Among Australia's top five regional galleries, they show the works of famous artists such as Arthur Boyd and Sidney Nolan. Take advantage of the opportunity to view the masterpieces away from the big-city crowds.

Ballarat Fine Art Gallery has a large collection of contemporary Australian art. It also has some impressive historical exhibits, the showpiece being the tattered remains of the Eureka Flag (sometimes known as the Southern Cross Flag) that was flown defiantly by the miner rebels at the Eureka Stockade in 1854. ✉ *40 Lydiard St.* ☎ *03/5320–5858* ⊕ *www. balgal.com* ✉ *A$5* ⊗ *Daily 9–5.*

On the shores of Lake Wendouree, Ballarat's **Botanic Gardens** are identifiable by the brilliant blooms and classical statuary. At the rear of the gardens, the Conservatory is the focus of events during the town's Begonia Festival held each March. ✉ *Wendouree Parade* ☎ *No phone* ✉ *Free* ⊗ *Daily sunrise–sunset.*

★ **Sovereign Hill,** built on the site of the Sovereign Hill Quartz Mining Company's mines, this replica town provides an authentic look at life, work, and play in this area during the gold rush. The main street features a hotel, blacksmith's shop, bakery, and post office—all perfectly preserved relics of their time. You can have your photo taken in period costumes, take a mineshaft tour, pan for gold, ride in a stagecoach, or head to the "lolly shop" to sample old-fashioned candy. You can also watch "Blood on the Southern Cross," a 90-minute sound-and-light spectacular that focuses on the Eureka uprising. Your ticket also gets you into the **Gold Museum,** across Bradshaw Street. It displays an extensive collection of nuggets from the Ballarat diggings. ✉ *Bradshaw St.* ☎ *03/5337–1100* ⊕ *www.sovereignhill.com.au* ✉ *A$39.50; A$87 (entry and Blood on the Southern Cross show)* ⊗ *Daily 10–5; two show sessions, times vary.*

WHERE TO EAT AND STAY

$$–$$$ ✕ **Europa Cafe.** The all-day breakfast at this hip yet relaxed dining spot
MEDITERRANEAN is legendary, but the lunches and dinners are also worth a trip. Lunch includes such savory treats as smoked-salmon bruschetta. For dinner, go for the lamb cutlets on polenta or the honey-and-mustard Western

Typical architecture from the gold rush era on a main street in Ballarat.

Plains pork roasted with pear, apple, and onion. *411 Sturt St. 3350* ☎ *03/5331–2486* 🖃 *AE, DC, MC, V* ⊗ *No dinner Mon.–Wed.*

$ ⨯**L'espresso.** Meals at this local institution taste like they're from your
ITALIAN grandmother's kitchen. It's open for breakfast and lunch daily and
★ dinner on Fridays, with specials like salmon fillet with lemon aioli
or bruschetta with mascarpone and figs. This was a popular record
shop back in the 1970s, and after 33 years co-owner Greg Wood is
still selling his blues, jazz, and interesting contemporary music CDs
here. ⊠ *417 Sturt St.* ☎ *03/5333–1789* 🖃 *AE, DC, MC, V* ⊗ *No dinner Sun.–Thurs.*

$$ 🏨 **The Ansonia.** Built in the 1870s as professional offices—and rescued
★ by new owners who refurbished it completely—the Ansonia is now
an excellent boutique hotel. You enter through impressive wrought-
iron gates under a grand portico to a light-filled atrium. There are sev-
eral different styles of accommodation, from studios to two-bedroom
apartments. Hotel guests can dine at several restaurants in Ballarat and
charge their meals back to the hotel. **Pros:** cozy, arty, free parking. **Cons:**
rooms overlooking atrium lack privacy. ⊠ *32 Lydiard St.* ☎ *03/5332–
4678* ⊕ *www.Ansonia.com.au* ⤴ *20 rooms* ♿ *In-room: Wi-Fi. In-hotel:
restaurant, no elevator, laundry service, public Internet, parking (no
fee), non-smoking rooms* 🖃 *AE, DC, MC, V.*

$$$ 🏨 **Ballarat Heritage Homestay.** This group manages a number of historic
★ properties in and around Ballarat, including Ravenswood, Wilton
House, Glen Eira, Kingsley Place, and Tait's Cottage. These range from
self-contained cottages to traditional B&B properties. Tucked behind a
garden brimming with peach trees, pussy willows, fuchsias, and climbing roses, Ravenswood is a three-bedroom timber cottage ideal for

families or small groups. The house, a bit less than 1½ km (1 mi) from the center of Ballarat, has contemporary decor and a full kitchen. Breakfast supplies are provided on the first morning. There's a minimum two-night stay in Dyte Parade, Wilton House, Tait's Cottage, and Kingsley Place on weekends, the two nights ranging from A$400 to A$450 for two people. **Pros:** full kitchen for those who want to eat in **Cons:** minumum stay. ⊠ *185 Victoria St. 3354* ☎ *03/5332–8296* ⊕ *www.heritagehomestay.com* ⤴ *5 properties* ♿ *In-hotel: kitchen, DVD, laundry facilities* ▭ *AE, DC, MC, V* ⭘❙ *CP.*

DAYLESFORD AND HEPBURN SPRINGS

109 km (68 mi) northwest of Melbourne, 45 km (28 mi) northeast of Ballarat.

Nestled in the slopes of the Great Dividing Range, Daylesford and its nearby twin, Hepburn Springs, are a spa lover's paradise. The water table here is naturally aerated with carbon dioxide and rich in soluble mineral salts, making it ideal for indulging in mineral baths and other rejuvenating treatments. The natural springs were first noted during the gold rush, and Swiss-Italian immigrants established a spa at Hepburn Springs in 1875. There are now about 70 natural springs in the area. The best time to visit the area is autumn, when the deciduous trees turn bronze and you can finish up a relaxing day next to an open fire with a glass of local red.

GETTING HERE AND AROUND

The twin towns of Daylesford and Hepburn Springs are easily reached by car from Melbourne. Take the Westestern Highway (M8) to Ballarat, then take the Midland Highway for another 40 km (25 mi) to Daylesford (via Creswick). Hepburn Springs is just a mile or two from Daylesford. V/Line operates trains from Southern Cross Station, Melbourne, to Ballarat or Woodend (near Mount Macedon), and V/Line buses connect with the trains to take passengers to Daylesford.

ESSENTIALS

Transportation V/Line (☎ *13–6196* ⊕ *www.vline.com.au*).

Visitor Information Daylesford Regional Visitor Information Centre (⊠ *98 Vincent St., Daylesford* ☎ *03/5321–6123* ⊕ *www.visitdaylesford.com*).

EXPLORING

Perched on a hillside overlooking Daylesford, the **Convent Gallery** is a former nunnery that has been restored to its lovely Victorian state. At the front of the gallery is Bad Habits, a sunny café that serves light lunches and snacks. Altar Bar is a hip place for a drink. The new second-story penthouse suite is the ultimate in decadence, with its own hydrotherapy bath and a boudoir-style bedroom ($$$). ⊠ *Daly St., Daylesford* ☎ *03/5348–3211* ⊕ *www.theconventy.com.au* ▭ *A$5* ⊗ *Daily 10–5.*

Fodor'sChoice ★ The **Hepburn Bathhouse & Spa** is the new name for the centerpiece of Australia's premier spa destination. The complex reopened on the site of the former Hepburn Spa Mineral Springs Wellness Retreat after a A$13 million, 18-month makeover. The complex retains the original

Edwardian Bathhouse (circa 1895), but now has a stunning contemporary architectural design and has more than 30 wet and dry treatment rooms, making it one of the largest and most spectacular spas in the country. Patrons can buy two-hour passes, which allow them to use either the public bathhouse or the more indulgent sanctuary. The bathhouse includes a relaxation mineral pool and a spa pool (A$15, Tues.–Fri. and A$30 Sat.–Mon.), while the sanctuary has underwater spa couches (for the ultimate in hydrotherapy), an aroma steam room, and a salt therapy pool (A$50 Tues.–Fri. and A$70 Sat.–Mon.). There is also the day spa area, which has a long list of therapies, including body wraps and polishes, facials, and other treatments using the mineral waters. Products used in the spa include La Gaia, Sodashi, and Thalgo, along with a special Hepburn Collection range that has been specifically designed for Hepburn Bathhouse & Spa. ☒ *1 Mineral Springs Crescent, Hepburn Springs* ☎ *03/5321–6000* ⊕ *www.hepburnbathhouse.com.au* ☺ *Bathhouse and Sanctuary daily 9–8; spa daily 10–8.*

> ## LIQUID GOLD
>
> The promise of gold "in them thar hills" drew mobs of prospectors in the 1850s, but today's visitors aren't looking to quench their thirst for riches. The "Great Grape Touring Route" (⊕ *www.greatgraperoute.com.au*) and the "Vine to Vintage Trail" (⊕ *www.bendigotourism.com*) are wonderful itineraries for those who love fine wine and food. Ballarat's climate produces great Pinot Noir and Chardonnay, while the Grampians is the birthplace of Great Western, Australia's first and best-known sparkling wine. The Pyrenees region is known for its classic Shiraz.

Above the Hepburn Bathhouse and Spa a path winds through a series of mineral springs at the **Mineral Springs Reserve.** Each spring has a slightly different chemical composition—and a significantly different taste. You can bring empty bottles, if you like; they can be filled with the mineral water of your choice, for free.

WHERE TO STAY

$$ 🔲 **Dudley House.** Behind a neat hedge and picket gate, this fine example of timber Federation architecture sits on the main street of Hepburn Springs. Each room is decorated in a style that reflects the personality of the four sisters who opened the guesthouse in 1908. In its heyday, when people traveled here to "take the waters," it had 38 rooms. Charming hostess Satish Appleby prepares a full English breakfast and an afternoon tea complete with decadent cakes. The mid-week price for one night, breakfast, and afternoon tea is a good value at A$135. The two-night weekend stay with the same inclusions along with champagne and chocolates is A$395. A nearby cottage, which sleeps six people, is A$430 for two nights on weekends. Spa packages are also available by arrangement. ☒ *101 Main St., Hepburn Springs* ☎ *03/5348–3033* ⊕ *www.dudleyhouse.com.au* ☞ *4 rooms, one cottage* ☺ *In-room: no a/c. In-hotel: restaurant, parking (no fee), no kids under 16, no-smoking rooms, no elevator* ☐ *MC, V* ☺ *BP.*

$$$$
Fodor's Choice
★

🏠 **Lake House & Restaurant.** Consistently rated one of central Victoria's best restaurants, this rambling lakeside pavilion brings glamour to spa country. The seasonal menu ($–$$), which utilizes fresh Australian produce, lists such delicacies as hot gravlax of Atlantic salmon, as well as a selection of imaginative Asian-accented vegetarian dishes. On Saturday the restaurant offers a three-course meal at A$95. Choose the elegant dining room or the deck overlooking the beautiful lake. The accommodations, set in 6 acres of gardens, are standard rooms in the original homestead and waterfront rooms and suites. All have balconies; the suites have private lounges. A day spa offers "treatments with a twist," such as the "aromatherapy sugar shock," along with the more-traditional pampering. A soak in one of the hot tubs housed in its own little cedar "tree house" with views across the lagoon (A$70) is a heavenly treat not to be missed. ✉ *King St., Daylesford* ☎ *03/5348–3329 or 03/5448–3995* ⊕ *www.lakehouse.com.au* ⇌ *21 rooms, 12 suites* △ *In-room: no a/c (some). In-hotel: restaurant, bar, tennis court, pool, bicycles, laundry service, parking (no fee), no elevator* ▭ *AE, DC, MC, V* ⊚ *BP.*

BENDIGO

150 km (93 mi) northwest of Melbourne, 92 km (57 mi) south of Echuca.

Gold was discovered in the Bendigo district in 1851, and the boom lasted well into the 1880s. The city's magnificent public buildings bear witness to the richness of its mines. Today Bendigo is a bustling, enterprising small city, with distinguished buildings lining both sides of Pall Mall in the city center. These include the **Shamrock Hotel, General Post Office,** and **Law Courts,** all majestic examples of late-Victorian architecture. Although these glorious relics of a golden age dominate the landscape, the city is far from a time warp. You'll also find a lively café and restaurant scene, 30 boutique wineries, some of which can be visited on organized winery tours, and one of the best regional art galleries in Australia.

GETTING HERE AND AROUND
To reach Bendigo, take the Calder Highway northwest from Melbourne; the trip takes about 1 hour and 40 minutes. V/Line operates trains to Bendigo from Melbourne's Southern Cross Station, a journey of about two hours.

TOURS
A good introduction to Bendigo is a tour aboard the **Vintage Talking Tram,** which includes a taped commentary on the town's history. The hourly tram runs on its 8-km (5-mi) circuit between the Central Deborah Gold Mine and the Tram Museum, making five stops at historic sites. *03/5442–2821* ⊕ *www.bendigotramways.com* ✉ *A$15* ⊙ *Daily 10–4:20.*

Central Wine Tours. This company, based just a few miles out of town at Golden Square, has full- and half-day tours visiting four to five of the region's best cellar doors. The full highlights tour (A$120 per person) may visit the Chateau Leamon, Marong Vineyard, Sandhurst Ridge, or Connor Park wineries. Lunch is often at Balgownie Estate (also a winery in the Yarra Valley). They also visit the Wine Bank, a wine bar, wine merchant, and café housed in a lovely heritage building in Bendigo. ✉ *21 Magazine Blvd., Golden Square* ☎ *Mobile: 0408/006–603* ⊕ *www.centralwinetours.co.au.*

Bendigo Goldfields Experiece. This company, located in the grounds of Ironbark Riding Centre, runs personalized gold-prospecting tours, as well as do-it-yourself gold-panning. The half- or full-day tours include a guide, transport, food and drinks, and the use of a Minelab metal detector. It's A$170 for a full day (when two people are on the tour) or A$120 for half a day. Gold panning is A$12 per person, including a 15-minute lesson, and you get to keep all the gold you find. If you like the idea of striking it rich, you can also buy your own metal detector at the company's shop. ✉ *Lot 2, Watson St., Bendigo* ☎ *03/5448–4140* ⊕ *www.bendigogold.com.au* ✉ *A$120 half day; A$170 full day* ⊙ *Mon.–Sat. 8.30–5, Sun. by appointment.*

ESSENTIALS

Transportation V/Line (☎ *13–6196* ⊕ *www.vline.com.au*).

Visitor Information Bendigo Tourist Information Centre (✉ *51–67 Pall Mall, Bendigo* ☎ *03/5434–6060 or 1800/813153* ⊕ *www.bendigotourism.com.au*).

EXPLORING

Fodor'sChoice ★ The beautifully refurbished **Bendigo Art Gallery** houses a notable collection of contemporary Australian paintings, including the work of Jeffrey Smart, Lloyd Rees, and Clifton Pugh. (Pugh once owned a remote Outback pub infamous for its walls daubed with his own pornographic cartoons.) The gallery also has some significant 19th-century French realist and impressionist works, bequeathed by a local surgeon. There's a free guided tour every day at 2 PM. ✉ *42 View St.* ☎ *03/5443–6088* ⊕ *www.bendigoartgallery.com.au* ✉ *Free or donation* ⊙ *Daily 10–5.*

Bendigo Pottery, Australia's oldest working pottery shop, turns out the distinctive brown-and-cream style that many Australians have in their kitchens. First established in 1858, the historic workshop offers demonstrations. You can even get your hands dirty with your own clay creation. It's located 6½ km (4 mi) northeast of Bendigo on the way to Echuca. ✉ *146 Midland Hwy., Epsom* ☎ *03/5448–4404* ⊕ *www.bendigopottery.com.au* ✉ *Free, museum A$7* ⊙ *Daily 9–5.*

Central Deborah Gold Mine, with a 1,665-foot mine shaft, yielded almost a ton of gold before it closed in 1954. To experience life underground, take a guided tour of the mine. An elevator descends 200 feet below ground level. ✉ *76 Violet St.* ☎ *03/5443–8322* ⊕ *www.central-deborah.com* ✉ *A$24* ⊙ *Daily 9:30–5 (last tour at 4:05).*

The superb **Golden Dragon Museum** evokes the Chinese community's role in Bendigo life past and present. Its centerpieces are the century-old Loong imperial ceremonial dragon and the Sun Loong dragon, which, at more than 106 yards in length, is said to be the world's longest. When carried in procession, it requires 52 carriers and 52 relievers; the head alone weighs 64 pounds. Also on display are other ceremonial objects, costumes, and historic artifacts, as well as the lovely Yi Yuan Gardens.

✉ *5–11 Bridge St.* ☎ *03/5441–5044* ⊕ *www.goldendragonmuseum.org* 🗺 *A$8* ⊙ *Daily 9:30–5.*

Joss House was built in gold-rush days by Chinese miners on the outskirts of the city. At the height of the boom in the 1850s and 1860s, about a quarter of the miners were Chinese. These men were usually dispatched from villages on the Chinese mainland, and they were expected to work hard and return as quickly as possible with their fortunes. The Chinese were scrupulously law-abiding and hardworking—qualities that did not always endear them to other miners—and anti-Chinese riots were common. ✉ *Finn St., Emu Point 3550* ☎ *03/5442–1685* ⊕ *www.bendigotrust.com.au* 🗺 *A$50* ⊙ *Wed., Sat., and Sun. 11–4.*

WHERE TO EAT AND STAY

4

$$

ECLECTIC

✕ **Whirrakee.** This family-run restaurant and wine bar in one of Bendigo's grand old buildings serves Mediterranean- and Asian-inspired dishes. The twice-cooked lamb shank on roasted pumpkin mash is a great winter choice that literally melts in your mouth. The wine list showcases local wineries. ✉ *17 View Point 3550* ☎ *03/5441–5557* ▤ *AE, DC, MC, V* ⊙ *Closed Mon.*

$

🏨 **Comfort Inn Shamrock.** The lodgings at this landmark Victorian hotel in the city center range from traditional guest rooms to spacious suites. If you're looking for reasonably priced luxury, ask for the Amy Castles or the Dame Nellie Melba suites. Named after famous 19th-century Australian singers, they have hot tubs and overlook beautiful Rosalind Gardens. The hotel's location, its grand public areas, and its beautiful wrought-iron balcony are the big draws. ✉ *Pall Mall at Williamson St.* ☎ *03/5443–0333* ⊕ *www.hotelshamrock.com.au* 🛏 *24 rooms, 4 suites* ᝈ *In-hotel: restaurant, bars, laundry facilities, parking (no fee)* ▤ *AE, DC, MC, V.*

$$
★

🏨 **Langley Hall.** Housed in a circa-1903 Edwardian mansion, Langley Hall was originally built as a residence for the Anglican archbishop of Bendigo. After incarnations as a convalescent home and an orphanage, it was beautifully restored by Allan and Anne Broadhead. Features include a parlor, billiard room, and drawing room—all filled with period details from the town's heyday. Breakfast is served in a grand dining room; you can enjoy drinks from an honor bar in the billiard room. A Continental breakfast is A$15. The house is 4 km (2½ mi) from the center of town. **Pros:** lovely garden, good price **Cons:** few amenities, breakfast is a tad expensive. ✉ *484 Napier St.* ☎ *03/5443–3693* ⊕ *www.innhouse.com.au/langleyhall.html* 🛏 *6 rooms* ᝈ *In-hotel: no elevator* ▤ *AE, DC, MC, V* ⟊*CP.*

THE GRAMPIANS

About 120 km (79 mi) west of the Gold Country are the Grampians, sometimes referred to by their Aboriginal name Gariwerd. This 415,000-acre region combines stunning mountain scenery, abundant native wildlife, and invigorating outdoor activities. The sharp sandstone peaks here were long ago forced up from an ancient seabed, and sculpted by aeons of wind and rain. Today the park has more than

160 km (106 mi) of walking trails, as well as some 900 wildflower species, 200 species of birds, and 35 species of native mammals. The best time to visit is October–December, when wildflowers carpet the landscape, the weather is mild, and summer crowds have yet to arrive. There are several wineries in the region, including the historic Seppelt vineyard and winery at Great Western about 25 km (16 mi) east of Halls Gap, which offers fascinating tours of its underground wine cellars.

SPOIL YOURSELF

If your muscles are stiff from bushwalking, or too much driving has taken its toll, a visit to **Blaze Rock Spa** may be just what you need. The spa serves up a tantalizing choice of pampering treatments that use natural plant ingredients and techniques inspired by traditional Aboriginal methods. Craig, who owns the business with wife Sharon, delivers a massage that will cure your aches and pains. Two new villas ($$$) with claw-foot baths and open fires have opened on the expansive property. ☎ 03/5356–6171 ⊕ www.blazerock.com.au.

THE GRAMPIANS NATIONAL PARK

Fodor's Choice ★ *260 km (162 mi) west of Melbourne, 100 km (62 mi) north of Hamilton.*

Comprising four mountain ranges—Mt. Difficult, Mt. William, Serra, and Victoria—the **Grampians National Park** spills over 412,000 acres. Its rugged peaks, towering trees, web of waterfalls and creeks, and plethora of wildlife make it a haven for bushwalkers, rock climbers, and nature lovers. In spring the region wears a carpet of spectacular wildflowers, while a number of significant Aboriginal rock-art sites make it an ideal place to learn about Victoria's indigenous history. Dawn balloon flights over the park offer visitors the chance to see the park's hidden charms without working up a sweat. The township of Halls Creek (population 300) is in the national park, and with its 10,000 tourist beds becomes quite a busy place in summer and at Easter. If you're staying in a self-catering accommodation, it is very wise to stock up on groceries and wine in the big towns of Ballarat, Arafat, Hamilton, or Horsham, since prices at the Halls Gap general store are inflated. One of the most picturesque drives in the park is the 60-km (37-km) stretch from Halls Gap to Dunkeld.

★ Owned and operated by Aboriginal people, the **Brambuk Cultural Centre** provides a unique living history of Aboriginal culture in this part of Victoria. Displays of artwork, weapons, clothes, and tools here give a glimpse into the life of indigenous Koori people (Aboriginal people of southeastern Australia). In the Dreaming Theatre dancing, music, and educational programs are presented daily, while visitors can learn the significance of paintings at nearby Bunjil's Shelter on rock-art tours conducted on weekdays at 9:30 AM. ✉ *Grampians Tourist Rd., Halls Gap* ☎ *03/5361–4000* ⊕ *www.brambuk.com.au* ✍ *Free; rock-art tours and theater A$35* ☉ *Daily 9–5, show hourly 10–4.*

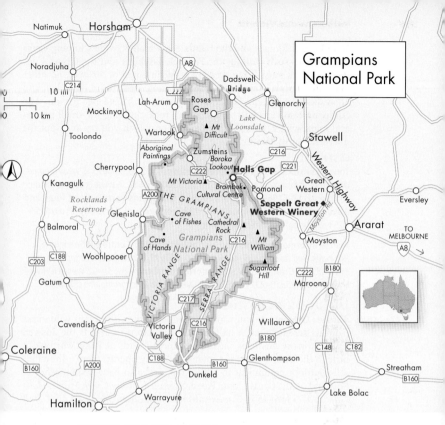

GETTING HERE AND AROUND

Halls Gap (the base town for the Grampians National Park) is reached via Ballarat and Ararat on the Western Highway (Highway 8). The town is 260 km (162 mi) northwest of Melbourne, 97 km (60 mi) northeast of Hamilton, 146 km (91 mi) west of Ballarat. V/Line operates trains to Ballarat or Bendigo from Melbourne. V/Line buses connect with the trains to take passengers to Halls Gap. For timetables and fares, contact V/Line.

TOURS

Gray Line operates a one-day tour of the Grampians (A$144) that departs from Melbourne on Monday and Saturday from October to March.

Grampians Pyrenees Tours has a full-day tour of the Grampians wineries and also runs half- and full-day 4WD tours of the National Park (from A$1,060). A two-night tour from Melbourne includes one night on the Great Ocean Road and another in the Grampians, finishing with a visit to the wineries of the Pyrenees region before returning to Melbourne (A$1,060).

For those who really love the great outdoors and want to camp out, **Grampians Personalised Tours and Adventures** runs half- and full-day treks, as well as three- and four-day treks with accommodation each night in tents at a campsite at Mount Rosea. The walks are through the

Wonderland Ranges and the Bundaleer, which provide stunning views and visits to such icons as the Pinnacle Lookout and the Grand Canyon. Walkers must bring their own sleeping bag or air bed and other items of comfort. Tents, food, and cooking utensils are provided, and all walks are guided. The three-day walk is A$745 per person. The company also runs half- and full-day rock climbing for small groups and night walks (at A$20 per person) on which you try and spot the nocturnal bush creatures.

ESSENTIALS

Tour Operators Grampians Pyrenee tours (☎ 03/5352–5075 ⊕ www.grampianspyreneestours.com.au). **Gray Line** (☎ 1300/858687 ⊕ www.grayline.com.au). **V/Line** (☎ 13–6196 ⊕ www.vline.com.au). **Grampians Personalised Tours and Adventures** (✉ Inside news agency, 143 Grampians Rd., Halls Gap ☎ 03/5356–4654 ⊕ www.grampianstours.com.au).

Visitor Information Halls Gap Visitor Information Centre (✉ Grampians Rd., Halls Gap ☎ 03/5356–4616 or 1800/065599 ⊕ www.visithallsgap.com.au). **Stawell and Grampians Visitor Information Centre** (✉ 50–52 Western Hwy., Stawell ☎ 03/5358–2314 or 1800/330080 ⊕ www.visitgrampians.com.au).

OUTDOOR ACTIVITIES

CANOEING **Absolute Outdoors.** If you want to experience the Grampians wilderness from its serene lakes, a half- or full-day canoeing trip is the answer. This company has trips on Lake Bellfield (south of Lake Wartook, a little to the northwest of the township). They operate from a shop that sells outdoor equipment in Halls Gap, and also have a shop/office in Portland on the Great Ocean Road. ✉ Shop 4, Stony Creek Stores, Halls Gap ☎ 03/5356–4556 ⊕ www.absoluteoutdoors.com.au ⊠ A$60 half day; A$120 full day.

HIKING AND WALKING **Auswalk.** This long-established walking specialist is based at Halls Gap, and its guides know the area like the backs of their hands. It operates guided and self-guided inn-to-inn, five-night hikes with accommodation in B&Bs or motels every night. Trips run throughout the year, with the exception of July, and only two participants are needed for a tour to take place. Auswalk transports the luggage between accommodation stops. The terrain is graded "moderate" for 55 percent of the walk, with about 25 percent considered strenuous. Maps and other information are provided for the self-guided walks. The wildflowers are out from August to November, and wildlife, particularly kangaroos and wallabies, is abundant in many areas. Self-guided walks start at A$1,195 per person, and guided walks range from A$1,995. ✉ 4 Red Gum Lease Track, Halls Gap ☎ 03/5356–4971 ⊕ www.auswalk.com.au.

OFF THE BEATEN PATH

Although many Australians may have never visited **Seppelt Great Western Winery**, it's a good bet that most of them have sampled Great Western "champagne" at one stage of their lives. Today it's referred to as "sparkling," and the winery makes a Salinger and a Fleur de Lys sparkling along with a Sparkling Shiraz and still wines. Beneath the winery is an underground labyrinth of tunnels, known as the Drives, dating back to 1868, originally built by goldminers. This is where the best sparklings are kept. You can take a day tour of these tunnels and the nearby shaft house and taste 20 Seppelt wines, or a candlelight evening tour on the

Sitting on edge of Boroka Lookout in the Grampians National Park.

last weekend of every month, which includes wine tasting and a cheese platter. ⊠ *Moyston Rd., Great Western* 🕾 *03/5361–2239* ⊕ *www.seppelt.com.au* 🗪 *Cellar door free; Tours A$15, night tour A$25* ⊗ *Tastings daily 10–5; tunnel tours Mon.–Sat. at 11 and 2.*

WHERE TO EAT AND STAY

$–$$
AUSTRALIAN

✕ **Kookaburra.** This place is one of the best dining options you'll find in the park area, situated right in the heart of Halls Gap. Venison is popular here; you can try it prepared as steak, sausage, or pie. You can also choose from international dishes such as spinach crepes, veal sçaloppine, bone duckling, or eye fillet steak. Kookaburra's own ice cream, made daily with pure ingredients, is a great way to finish a meal. The restaurant is often closed in winter from late July to early August. ⊠ *125 Grampian Rd., Halls Gap* 🕾 *03/5356–4222* ▤ *AE, DC, MC, V* ⊗ *Closed Mon.*

$$$$
Fodor's Choice
★

▦ **Boroka Downs.** Set on 300 acres of bush, scrub, and grassland, Boroka's five villas are nothing short of spectacular. Studios have soaring ceilings, roof-to-floor windows—which frame the bush-clad ridges of the Grampians—fireplaces, and enormous in-room hot tubs. You can wake to the sound of kookaburras laughing, and sunset finds groups of kangaroos, emus, and wallabies grazing in the paddocks that skirt the villa. New owners Ron and Jo Payne are committed environmentalists. They've continued planting thousands of trees like the original owners did: the resort uses solar and wind energy and recycles just about everything. There's a three-night minimum stay in high season (long weekends, Christmas–New Year's) and a four-night minimum at Easter; however, during non-peak times guests get one free night when they book a two-night package. **Pros:** luxurious and eco-friendly. **Cons:** all of this beauty comes at a steep price. ⊠ *51 Birdswing Rd., Halls Gap* ☎ *03/5356–6243* ⊕ *www.borokadowns.com.au* ⤳ *5 villas* ⊘ *In-room: kitchen, DVD, laundry facilities, VCR. In-hotel: parking (no fee), no kids* ⊟ *AE, DC, MC, V* ⏐◎⏐ *BP.*

¢ ⌂⌂ **Grampians YHA Eco Hostel.** This stylish hostel is one of the new brand of ecofriendly properties in the Youth Hostel Australia (YHA) network. It uses solar energy and water-conservation devices, is open to people of all ages, and has accommodation to suit everyone (dorm rooms, double rooms, and family rooms that can sleep four). The two modern adjoining kitchens are fully equipped, and the three lounges (including an Internet room with two computers) are ideal for socializing. There is an outdoor BBQ and eating area with spectacular mountain views. All bathrooms are shared facilities. **Pros:** great price, eco-friendly. **Cons:** shared bathrooms. ⊠ *Grampians and Buckler Rds., Halls Gap* ☎ *03/5356–4544* ⊕ *www.yha.com.au* ⤳ *8 dorms, 5 double rooms, 5 family rooms* ⊟ *AE, MC, V.*

MURRAY RIVER REGION

From its birthplace on the slopes of the Great Dividing Range in southern New South Wales, the Mighty Murray winds 2,574 km (1,596 mi) on a northwesterly course before it empties into Lake Alexandrina, south of Adelaide. Once prone to flooding and droughts, the river has been laddered with dams that control the floodwaters and form reservoirs for irrigating the regions farms and vineyards.

Today Victoria exports more than A$100 million worth of wine annually, and the muscat and port of many parts of the Murray River Region are legendary. The Rutherglen area, in particular, produces the finest fortified wine (dessert wine or "stickies") in the country.

Steeped in history and natural beauty, the eastern Murray River valley and High Country region has become a gourmet food lovers' heaven known for its fruit, olives, honey, and cheeses, as well as a renowned wine region. The lovely town of Beechworth is an ideal place to stop off on the drive between Sydney and Melbourne.

GETTING HERE AND AROUND

The wide-open spaces of the region surrounding the Murray River make driving the most sensible and feasible means of exploration. Rutherglen is 274 km (170 mi) north of Melbourne, about a 3½- to 4-hour drive along the Hume Highway; Echuca is 204 km (127 mi) northwest of Melbourne, about a 2½-hour drive. These two Murray River towns are 194 km (121 mi) apart. V/Line trains (☎ *13–6196* ⊕ *www.vline.com.au*) run to most of the major towns in the region, including Echuca and Rutherglen, but not Beechworth. This reasonable access is most useful if you do not have a car or want to avoid the long-distance drives. As with most country Victorian areas, direct train access from Melbourne to the main centers is reasonable, but getting between towns isn't as easy.

BEECHWORTH

271 km (168 mi) northeast of Melbourne, 96 km (60 mi) northwest of Alpine National Park, 44 km (26 mi) south of Rutherglen.

One of the prettiest towns in Victoria, Beechworth flourished during the gold rush. When gold ran out, the town of 30,000 was left with all the trappings of prosperity—fine banks, imposing public buildings, breweries, parks, and hotels wrapped in wrought iron—but with scarcely two nuggets to rub together. However, poverty preserved the town from such modern improvements as aluminum window frames, and many historic treasures that might have been destroyed in the name of progress have been brought back to life.

4

GETTING HERE AND AROUND

Beechworth and Rutherglen are on opposite sides of the Hume Freeway, the main Sydney–Melbourne artery. The 44-km (26-mi) Rutherglen-Beechworth Road (C377) connects both towns. Beechworth is about a four-hour drive from Melbourne, twice that from Sydney.

ESSENTIALS

Visitor Information Beechworth Tourist Information Centre (⊠ *Old Town Hall, 103 Ford St., Beechworth* ☎ *03/5728–8065 or 1300/366321* ⊕ *www. Beechworthonline.com.au).*

EXPLORING

A stroll along **Ford Street** is the best way to absorb the character of the town. Among the distinguished buildings are **Tanswell's Commercial Hotel,** the **Town Hall,** and the **Courthouse.** It was in the latter that the committal hearing for the famous bushranger Ned Kelly took place in August 1880. His feisty mother, Ellen Kelly, was also sentenced to three years in jail at this court.

The **Burke Museum** takes its name from Robert O'Hara Burke, who, with William Wills became one of the first white explorers to cross Australia from south to north in 1861. Burke served as superintendent of police in Beechworth from 1856 to 1859. Not surprisingly, the small area and few mementos dedicated to Burke are overshadowed by the Ned Kelly exhibits, including letters, photographs, and memorabilia that give genuine insight into the man and his misdeeds. The museum also displays a reconstructed streetscape of Beechworth in the 1880s. ⊠ *Loch St.* ☎ *03/5728–8067* ⊕ *www.beechworth.com/burke-mus* ⊠ *A\$5* ☉ *Daily 9–5.*

Murray Breweries Beechworth brewed beer in the 1860s, but now concentrates on nonalcoholic cordials produced using old-time recipes. You'll find a display of antique brewing equipment, worldwide beer labels, and rare bottles. Also here is the Carriage Museum, which has a collection of 20 horse-drawn vehicles and Australian Light Horse Infantry memorabilia from World War I. Tastings are free. ⊠ *29 Last St.* ☎ *03/5728–1304* ⊕ *www.murraybreweries.com.au* ⊠ *Free* ☉ *Daily 10–4.*

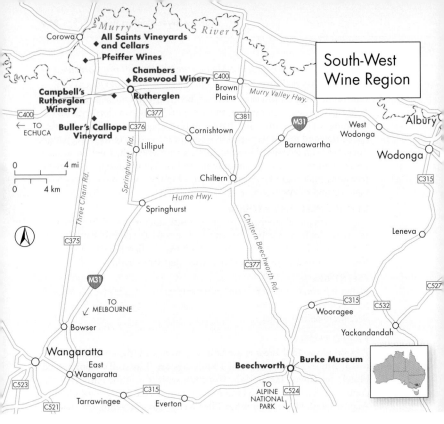

OUTDOOR ACTIVITIES

BICYCLING The area from the Murray River to the mountains of North-East Victoria are ideal for mountain bike enthusiasts. Pick up a bike at **Beechworth Cycle & Saws** (⊠ *17 Camp St., Beechworth* ☎ *03/5728–1402*) on Beechworth's the main street.

Murray to the Mountains Rail Trail (☎ *1800/991–044* ⊕ *www.railtrail.com. au*) is a 98-km (61-mi) paved trail that travels from Wangaratta to Bright. Bicycle hire is available at Wangaratta, Beechworth, Bright, and Myrtleford. A trail map is available from the visitor centers at each of these towns, and can be downloaded from the trail Web site.

HIKING AND WALKING There are several national parks within easy reach of Beechworth: Chiltern-Mt. Pilot National Park, Beechworth Historic Park, Mount Buffalo National Park, Mount Granya State Park, and Warby Range State Park. The Beechworth visitor center and Parks Victoria have information on bushwalks. The town of Beechworth is the perfect place to get out and about and stretch your legs while admiring late 19th-century architecture. You can pick up a copy of "Echoes of History," a self-guided walking tour of the town from the visitor information center.

Parks Victoria (☎ *13–1963* ⊕ *www.parkweb.vic.gov.au*) has information on Victoria's National Parks and walking trails.

CLOSE UP

Ned Kelly

The English have Robin Hood, the Americans Jesse James. Australians have Ned Kelly, a working-class youth whose struggles against police injustice and governmental indifference captured the country's heart. The best way to learn about the local legend is to visit the town of Beechworth, where a Ned Kelly Walking Tour departs from the visitor information center every day at 10:30 AM. You'll see the courthouse where he was tried and the jail where he was imprisoned during his many scrapes with the law. The Burke Museum displays his death mask, made shortly after he was hanged at Melbourne Gaol. If you long to hear more, visit Glenrowan (40 km [25 mi], southwest of Beechworth), the scene of his famous "last stand." It was here that Kelly, dressed in his legendary iron armor, walked alone down the main street fending off police bullets. He was shot in the leg and arrested. A huge statue, and a sound-and-light show that has received rather mixed reviews and is said to be "quite loud" commemorate Australia's most infamous outlaw.

WHERE TO STAY

$$-$$$$ ⊞ **Country Charm Swiss Cottages.** Landscaped gardens overlooking the Beechworth Gorge surround these charming pine and cedar cottages. The units have nice little touches like fireplaces, whirlpool tubs, and fully equipped kitchens. This was the site of the original Beechworth vineyard, established in the 1800s; a 130-year-old drystone wall is all that remains. While walking the grounds, note the views across the Woolshed Valley to Mt. Pilot. There is a two-night minimum stay on weekends. ⊠ *22 Malakoff Rd.* ☎ *03/5728–2435* ⊕ *www.swisscottages. com.au* ➷ *5 cottages* ⚙ *In-room: kitchen, refrigerator, DVD. In-hotel: no elevator* ⊟ *MC, V.*

RUTHERGLEN

274 km (170 mi) northeast of Melbourne, 40 km (25 mi) northwest of Beechworth.

The surrounding red-loam soil signifies the beginning of the Rutherglen wine district, the source of Australia's finest fortified wines. If the term conjures up visions of cloying ports, you're in for a surprise. In his authoritative *Australian Wine Compendium*, James Halliday says, "Like Narcissus drowning in his own reflection, one can lose oneself in the aroma of a great old muscat."

The main event in the region is Tastes of Rutherglen, held over two consecutive weekends in March. The festival is a celebration of food, wine, and music—in particular jazz, folk, and country. Events are held in town and at all surrounding wineries. Another popular day in the vineyards is the Rutherglen Winery Walkabout held in June, when wine, food, and music are again on the menu.

The water of mighty Murray River is at it's lowest level in recorded history.

GETTING HERE AND AROUND
See Beechworth above. Rutherglen is 274 km (170 mi) north of Melbourne, about a 3½- to 4-hour drive along the Hume Highway. A V/Line train and bus service operates daily from Melbourne's Southern Cross Station via Seymour and Wangaratta, a journey of about 3 hours and 15 minutes.

ESSENTIALS
Visitor Information Rutherglen Wine Experience and Visitor Information Centre (⊠ *57 Main St.* ☎ *02/6033-6300 or 1800/622871* ⊕ *www.rutherglenvic.com*).

Transportation V/Line (⊠ *Southern Cross Railway Station, Spencer St., Melbourne* ☎ *13-6196* ⊕ *wwwvline.com.au*).

EXPLORING THE WINERIES
★ **All Saints Vineyards & Cellars** has been in business since 1864. It's housed in an impressive building with an historic castle, built in 1878, which is now used as the wine cellar, an old bottling room now used as a cheese tasting room, and several other 19th-century buildings. A guided tour of the winery takes place on weekends at 11 AM. The winery produces muscat and tokay made from 50-year-old vines and a range of crisp whites and full bodied reds. The Indigo Cheese Co., with its resident cheesemaker Paula Jenkin, produces premium handmade treats, and wine and cheese tasting sessions are available by appointment. The menu at the Terrace restaurant changes daily, but might include starters like prawn-filled zucchini flowers and entrées such as pan-roasted Lake Hume trout filled with ciabatta, tomato, basil, and lemon. Desserts are excellent, especially when combined with a formidable northeast

fortified wine. A degustation menu featuring seven dishes is A$75 per person, or A$95 with paired wines. The cellar door is open daily; the restaurant is open for lunch from Wednesday to Sunday and for dinner on Saturday only ✉ *All Saints Rd., Wahgunyah* ⤷ *9 km (5½ mi) southeast of Rutherglen* ☎ *02/6035–2222* ⊕ *www.allsaintswine.com.au* ✉ *Free* ☉ *Mon.–Sat. 9–5:30, Sun. 10–5:30.*

Established by Reginald Langdon Buller in 1921, **Buller's Calliope Vineyard,** produces delicious fortified wines (muscats and sherries) and gutsy, full-bodied reds, the flagship being the Shiraz. As the old Shiraz vines are not irrigated, the annual yields are low, but the fruit that is produced has intense flavor, which winemaker Andrew Buller crafts into wines of great depth and elegance. There are also small plantings of rarer varieties such as Mondeuse and Cinsaut. There are tastings and sales at the cellar door, but no restaurant. This is a winery for those who like their reds. Also on the winery's grounds is **Buller Bird Park,** an aviary of rare parrots and native Australian birds. ✉ *Three Chain Rd. at Murray Valley Hwy.* ☎ *02/6032–9660* ⊕ *www.buller.com.au* ✉ *Free* ☉ *Weekdays 9–5, Sun. 10–5.*

Campbell's Rutherglen Winery is a family business that dates back more than 130 years. Brothers Colin and Malcolm Campbell, the winemaker and viticulturist, respectively, have been at the helm for the past 30 years, and even despite the challenging severe heat of Februrary 2009 are confident of another great vintage. Famed for its award-winning Bobbie Burns Shiraz and Merchant Prince Muscat, the property spills over a picturesque 160 acres. You can wander freely through the winery on a self-guided tour and taste wines at the cellar door, including rare and aged wines. Campbell Family Vintage Reserve is available only at the cellar door. The winery does not have a restaurant, but takes part in the annual Tastes of Rutherglen wine festival, when food and music are on the agenda. It is 3 km (1 mi) from Rutherglen. ✉ *Murray Valley Hwy.* ☎ *02/6032–9458* ⊕ *www.campbellswines.com.au* ✉ *Free* ☉ *Mon.–Sat. 9–5, Sun. 10–5.*

Chambers Rosewood Winery was established in the 1850s and is one of the heavyweight producers of fortified wines in Australia. Bill Chambers's muscats are legendary, with blending stocks that go back more than a century. His son Stephen has now joined him, and together they run a very relaxed winery, which is rustic in the real sense of the word, being just a combination of a few corrugated iron sheds in an off-the-beaten track laneway. Their cellar door is renowned for offering great value and plenty of tastings; you can take home reasonably priced red and white wines, sherries, ports, muscat, and tokays—from the clean skin variety (no label stock) to big two-liter flagons. There's no restaurant, just a cellar door, which also sells homemade jams, gourmet dressings, pickles, olive oil, and even chocolate-infused wine. ✉ *Barkly St. off Corowa Rd.* ⊕ *www.rutherglenvic.com/wineries* ☎ *02/6032–8641* ✉ *Free* ☉ *Mon.–Sat. 9–5, Sun. 10–5.*

Pfeiffer Wines is another winery with a long history, having been first built on the bend of Sunday Creek, near Wahgunyah, in 1895. The Pfeiffers bought it in the 1980s and have continued the tradition of making exceptional fortified wines and varietal wines, including Chardonnay. It also has one of the few Australian plantings of gamay, the classic French grape used to make Beaujolais. At this small rustic winery you can order spring/summer picnic baskets stuffed with crusty bread, smoke trout, marinated lamb fillets, chicken breast slices, kipler potato salad, cheese, fresh fruit, and a bottle of table wine, or autumn/winter hampers with reats such as soup, curry, and all the other trimmings for A$80 for two including plates and cutlery. Vegetarian baskets are A$72, and children's are A$12.50. Winemaker Christopher Pfeiffer makes an aperitif called Pfeiffer Seriously Pink, along with a Chardonnay-marsanne, Shiraz, Merlot, and fortifieds such as muscadelle and tawnies (which one can no longer call "ports"). Picnic bookings are advised, especially in spring and summer. ⊠ *Distillery Rd., Wahgunyah* ✛ *9 km (5½ mi) southeast of Rutherglen* ☎ *02/6033–2805* ⊕ *www.pfeifferwines.com.au* ⊠ *Free* ☺ *Mon.–Sat. 9–5, Sun. 10–5.*

WHERE TO EAT AND STAY

$$
AUSTRALIAN
✕ **Beaumont's Cafe.** The trio of duck leg, breast, and sausage with pesto and the risotto cake are a highlight at this century-old storefront dining room with exposed brick and distressed walls. On warm nights the rear courtyard with its scented herb garden is the best place to indulge in desserts like hazelnut and sherry cake with raisin ice cream and chocolate sauce. Boutique regional labels dot the wine list. ⊠ *84 Main St.* ☎ *02/6032–7428* ⊟ *AE, DC, MC, V* ☺ *Closed Sun. and Mon.*

$$
★
▥ **Tuileries.** Incorporating a vineyard, olive groves, and a renowned restaurant, Tuileries offers lodging with the feel of an exclusive retreat. Individually decorated suites are spacious, and appointed with romantic touches like hot tubs. There's a reclining lounge on the veranda, with a lovely view of the estate's orchard. The restaurant serves succulent dishes including duck legs with porcini mushrooms or roasted lamb rump with lentils and bok choy covered with olive and feta sauce. Next door are the Rutherglen Estate winery and a boutique brewery. ⊠ *13–35 Drummond St.* ☎ *02/6032–9033* ⊕ *www.tuileriesrutherglen. com.au* ⟿ *16 suites* ⌂ *In-room: DVD, Wi-Fi. In-hotel: restaurant, room service, tennis courts, gymnasium, pool, parking (no fee), no-smoking rooms, no elevator* ⊟ *AE, DC, MC, V* ⎪⎢⎜*BP.*

ALPINE NATIONAL PARK

323 km (200 mi) northeast of Melbourne, 40–50 km (25–31 mi) south to southeast of Mt. Buffalo.

The name **Alpine National Park** actually applies to three loosely connected areas in eastern Victoria that follow the peaks of the Great Dividing Range. One of these areas, formerly called Bogong National Park, contains some of the highest mountains on the continent. As such, it is a wintertime destination for skiers who flock to the resorts at Falls Creek, Mt. Buller, and Mt. Hotham.

The land around here is rich in history. *Bogong* is an Aboriginal word for "big moth," and it was to Mt. Bogong that Aborigines came each year after the winter thaw in search of bogong moths, considered a delicacy. Aboriginals were eventually displaced by cattle ranchers who brought their cattle here to graze. The main townships in the area are Bright, Mount Beauty, and Dinner Plain, all of which have visitor information centers.

GETTING HERE AND AROUND

Bus services to Alpine National Park operate from Albury on the New South Wales border in the north. In ski season Pyles Coaches depart from Mt. Beauty for Falls Creek and Mt. Hotham, and depart from Melbourne for Falls Creek. V/Line's combined train and bus operates from Melbourne's Southern Cross Station to Wangaratta, with a connection on to Bright.

ESSENTIALS

Transportation Pyles Coaches (☎ *03/5754–4024* ⊕ *www.pyles.com.au*). **V/Line** (✉ *Southern Cross Station, Spencer St., City Center, Melbourne* ☎ *13–6196* ⊕ *www.vline.com.au*).

Visitor Information For information on walks and parks in the area, contact the **Parks Victoria Information Centre** (☎ *13–1963* ⊕ *www.parkweb.vic.gov.au*).

OUTDOOR ACTIVITIES

The Alpine National Park really has two seasons—winter (from June to September) and the rest of the year. In winter the main activities are skiing, snowboarding, and tobogganing at Falls Creek, Mt. Buller, Mt. Hotham, and Dinner Plain. In spring, summer, and autumn these areas are perfect for bushwalking, cycling, horseback riding, and kayaking. The visitor centers and Parks Victoria have walking and cycling trail maps. **5 Star Adventure Tours**, a Bright-based operator, can hook you up with bushwalking, horseback riding, kayaking, and camping tours, and half- and full-day ski and snowboarding trips. Kayaking takes place on the Buffalo, Ovens, or Kiewa rivers from spring to autumn, with half-day and all-day trips available. ✉ *Shop 3, 104 Gavan St., Bright* ☎ *03/575505100* ⊕ *www.5staradventure.com.au.*

WHERE TO EAT AND STAY

$$
CONTINENTAL
✗ **Sasha's of Bright.** Crispy-skinned duck is the highlight of Czech-born chef Sasha Cinatl's menu. Hungarian goulash, smoked pork, and spatchcock in a rich port sauce are also dishes to look for, as well as the genuine dumplings, sauerkraut, and all things Czech. The hospitality is as hearty as the food. Round off with apple strudel or crepes with fresh local berries and cream. The well-priced wine list focuses on northeast Victorian vintages, and you can bring your own wine as well (corkage fee of A$7 a bottle). ✉ *2D Anderson St., Bright* ☎ *03/5750–1711* ▭ *AE, DC, MC, V.*

$$$
Fodor's Choice
★
▦ **Villa Gusto.** Colin McLaren is an Australian, but one with a passion for all things Italian. Everything in his Tuscan-inspired lodging has been imported from Italy: cast-iron fountains, marble fittings, 17th-century antiques, and exquisite tapestries—even the retro movie posters above the bar. Each suite is individually designed and has an Italian name: perhaps cioccolato, rosso, or limone will suit your mood. Four-course set meals ($$$$) include dishes that showcase regional ingredients, especially Milawa poultry and cheeses and Ovens Valley veal and lamb. Desserts may include the delicious blue-cheese panna cotta with pear

puree and walnut praline. From Bright, drive toward Porepunkah, then take the Buckland Valley Road turnoff for another 6 km (4 mi). Stays on Friday and Saturday include a set five-course dinner menu at an extra charge of A$70 per person. ⊠ *630 Buckland Valley Rd., Buckland, Bright* ☎ *03/5756–2000* ⊕ *www.villagusto.com.au* ⤵ *9 suites* ⌂ *Inhotel: restaurant, bar, no kids under 10, no elevator* ⊟ *AE, DC, MC, V* ⊗ *No lunch in restaurant* ¶◎¶ *BP.*

ECHUCA

206 km (128 mi) north of Melbourne, 194 km (120 mi) west of Rutherglen, 92 km (57 mi) north of Bendigo.

The name Echuca comes from a local Aboriginal word meaning "meeting of the waters," a reference to the town's location at the confluence of the Murray, Campaspe, and Goulburn rivers. In the second half of the 19th century Echuca was Australia's largest inland port. Many reminders of Echuca's colorful heyday remain in the restored paddle steamers, barges, and historic hotels, and in the Red Gum Works, the town's sawmill, now a working museum.

GETTING HERE AND AROUND

Echuca is a three-hour drive from Melbourne, reached most directly by the Northern Highway (Highway 75). The V/Line train and bus combination takes three hours and 20 minutes from Melbourne's Southern Cross Station to Echuca, via Bendigo. At Bendigo station, a bus connects for the onward bus journey.

TOURS

Gray Line operates a one-day bus tour of Echuca. It departs from Melbourne on Friday and Sunday at 8:45 AM. The cost is A$133.

Adventures Today has a one-day bus tour that visits both Bendigo and Echuca, including a trip on a Murray paddle steamer. It departs Fridays and Sundays in summer, from October to March and costs A$135.

ESSENTIALS

Bus Tours Adventures Today (⊠ *8 Hopman Crt., Oxenford, Gold Coast* ☎ *1300/793759* ⊕ *www.adventurestoday.com.au*). **Gray Line** (⊠ *Melbourne Day Tour Centre, Federation Sq., Flinders and Russell Sts., City Center, Melbourne* ☎ *03/9663–4455 or 1300/858687* ⊕ *www.grayline.com.au*).

Visitor Information Echuca Tourist Information Centre (⊠ *2 Heygarth St., Echuca* ☎ *1800/804446* ⊕ *www.echucamoama.com*).

EXPLORING

A tour of the **Historic River Precinct** begins at the Port of Echuca office on Murray Esplanade, where you can purchase a ticket that gets you into some of the historic buildings. The **Bridge Hotel** was built by Henry Hopwood, ex-convict father of Echuca, who had the foresight to establish a punt, and then to build a bridge at this commercially strategic point on the river. The **Star Hotel,** built in the 1860s, has an underground bar and escape tunnel, which was used by after-hours drinkers in the 19th century to evade the police. The **Historic Wharf** displays the heavy-duty side of the river-trade business, including a warehouse, old

Snow Gum trees on the Bogong High Plains in Alpine National Park.

railroad tracks, and riverboats. Among the vessels docked at the wharf is the *Adelaide*, Australia's oldest operating paddle steamer.

You can hop aboard the historic *Pevensey*, the *Canberra*, and the *Emmylou* for one-hour river excursions, a refreshing treat at the end of a hot summer's day. The paddle wheelers depart regularly from 10 AM to 4 PM; tickets are available from the port office or Bond Store on Murray Esplanade, the PS *Emmylou* costs from A\$20 to A\$28 for a 1- to 1½-hour cruise.

OUTDOOR ACTIVITIES

BOATING **Murray River Houseboats.** It seems that everyone who visits the Murray hires a houseboat and drifts slowly down the river. Today's houseboat is a five-star floating experience with Jacuzzis, state-of-the-art kitchen, and the latest appliances. They can sleep from two to 12 people and can be hired from three days to a week and longer. This operator has four boats for hire. Prices start from A\$1,400 for three nights in the peak late-December/January period for 2 to 7 people. ⊠ *Riverboat Dock, Echuca* ☎ *03/5480–2336* ⊕ *www.murrayriverhouseboats.com.au.*

CANOEING **River Country Adventours.** If you want to canoe up a lazy river—the Goulburn River, which is a tributary of the Murray—then you can for a half or full day with this company run by Rob and Joan Asplin. Tours are from A\$55 per person. ☎ *03/5852–2736 or mobile 0428/585227* ⊕ *www.adventours.com.au.*

HIKING AND BIKING There are many popular hiking and bicycling trails in the area, including the Banyule River Village Forest trail, which travels upstream under the Echuca Moama Bridge for up to 30 km (20 mi); another ventures along the Campaspe River esplanade, while another travels into the Moama bush riverside reserve. The visitor center has all the details and maps.

WHERE TO EAT AND STAY

$$–$$$ ⊡ **PS Emmylou.** Departing from Echuca around sunset, this paddle steamer chugs downriver, fueled by redgum logs, offering passengers either a one-, two-, or three-night cruise with all meals. It's the only wood-fired paddle steamer in the world offering regular overnight trips. It can accommodate 18 passengers in rooms with twin bunks. There's one cabin with a double bed; all have shared bathrooms. Sunrise over the river, as the boat churns past mist-cloaked gum trees and laughing kookaburras, is a truly memorable experience. A one-night trip is A$250 per person with dinner and breakfast; two- and three-night cruises with all meals are A$500 and A$750, respectively. ⊠ *57 Murray Esplanade* ☎ *03/5480–2237* ⊕ *www.emmylou.com.au* ⇆ *9 rooms without bath* ⚲ *In-room: no a/c, no phone, no TV. In-hotel: restaurant, bar, no-smoking rooms, no elevator* ⊟ *AE, DC, MC, V* ⊙ *Closed June–Aug.* ⫶◯⫶ *MAP.*

$$–$$$ ⊡ **River Gallery Inn.** This hotel occupies a 19th-century building just a stone's throw from the port. Each of the rooms is furnished in a different theme, such as French provincial, opulent Victorian, and rustic early Australian. There's even a Tuscan room with sunken bath and private courtyard. Four rooms overlook the street but are still quiet. Six rooms have whirlpool tubs, and all rooms, bar one, have open fireplaces. Rates include breakfast. Saturday night must be booked as part of a two-night stay. ⊠ *578 High St.* ☎ *03/5480–6902* ⊕ *www.rivergalleryinn.com* ⇆ *5 rooms, 3 suites* ⚲ *In-room: no phone, DVD. In-hotel: restaurant, parking (no fee), no kids, no elevator* ⊟ *AE, MC, V* ⫶◯⫶ *EP.*

Tasmania

WORD OF MOUTH

"I spent about 6 days on Tasmania and loved it! Did a 3-day Cradle Mountain hike, went to Hobart weekend markets, toured Cadbury factory, went to Port Arthur penal colony, visited awesome nature preserve with Tasmanian devils and also with lots of kangaroos and wallabies in the open with you! Rented a car for 2 of the 6 days."
—SusanC

WELCOME TO TASMANIA

TOP REASONS TO GO

★ **Tassie Tastes:** While Tasmania's unspoilt surrounds make it hiking heaven, foodies are also well served, thanks to its beautiful produce and excellent wine.

★ **Colonial Homes and Cottages:** Many of the Georgian mansions and charming cottages built during Tasmania's early days as a colony have been turned into unusual and hospitable accommodation options.

★ **Beautiful walks:** Tasmania has some of Australia's best walking terrain. The stunning mountains and coastlines of Mt. Field, South West, and Franklin-Gordon Wild Rivers national parks are a mecca for serious trekkers. Less strenuous but equally stunning walks can be taken around Cradle Mountain or on Freycinet Peninsula.

1 Hobart. Perhaps Australia's most beautiful state capital, the compact city offers history and beautifully preserved colonial architecture in genteel surrounds.

2 Port Arthur and the Tasman Peninsula. The horrors of Tasmania's convict past are there to discover in the notorious penal settlement, which has been sensitively converted into an absorbing museum.

3 Freycinet National Park and East Coast Resorts. Deserted white sand beaches, including the legendary Wineglass Bay, as well as some superb wineries, make the east coast a must-visit.

GETTING ORIENTED

About the size of West Virginia, and with a population of less than a half-million, the island of Tasmania offers geographical diversity in stunning, easily navigable scenery. Surrounded by sea, the climate is of course maritime, with the west coast the wettest thanks to the roaring forties winds. On the other hand, the island's capital of Hobart, a proud port city that is Australia's second oldest settlement, is Australia's second-driest city. The beautiful east coast is nearly always warmer and milder than the rest of the isle. This diversity has contributed to an amazing variety of vegetation, from eucalypt forest, alpine heathlands, and large areas of cool temperate rain forests and moorlands.

4 Launceston. Tasmania's second biggest city is a pleasant place to while away time thanks to its attractive parks and historic colonial mansions.

5 Northwest Cradle Mountains—Lake St. Clair National Park. A nearly deserted rugged coastline and the dramatic landscapes of Cradle Mountain National Park make this area a must-visit for walkers.

TASMANIA PLANNER

Exploring Tasmania

Tasmania is compact—the drive from southern Hobart to northern Launceston takes little more than two hours. The easiest way to see the state is by car, as you can plan a somewhat circular route around the island. Begin in Hobart or Launceston, where car rentals are available from the airport and city agencies, or in Devonport if you arrive on the ferry from Melbourne. Allow plenty of time for stops along the way, as there are some fabulous views to be seen. Bring a sturdy pair of shoes for impromptu mountain and seaside walks; you'll most often have huge patches of forest and long expanses of white beaches all to yourself.

In some cases the street addresses for attractions may not include building numbers (in other words, only the name of the street will be given). Don't worry—this just means either that the street is short and the attractions are clearly visible or that signposts will clearly lead you there.

If you are exploring several National Parks in the space of a few weeks or months it is recommended to buy a Holiday Park Pass that is valid for two months for A$56 in the National Parks of Tasmania.

Getting Here and Around

By Air

Hobart International Airport is 22 km (14 mi) east of Hobart, one hour by air from Melbourne or two hours from Sydney. Although most interstate flights connect through Melbourne, Qantas, Jetstar, Tiger Airways, and Virgin Blue also run direct flights to other mainland cities. Launceston airport is at Western Junction, 16 km (10 mi) south of central Launceston. It's served by Jetstar, Tiger Airways, and Virgin Blue.

On the island, Tasair can get you to the northwest and King Island. Tickets can be booked through the airlines or through the Tasmanian Travel and Information Centre. Tasmanian Redline Coaches has airport shuttle service for A$14.50 per person between the airport and its downtown depot. Metered taxis are available at the stand in front of the terminal. The fare to downtown Hobart is approximately A$40.

By Car

Port Arthur is an easy 90-minute drive from Hobart via the Arthur Highway. A private vehicle is essential if you want to explore parts of the Tasman Peninsula beyond the historic settlement. A vehicle is absolutely essential on the west coast. The road from Hobart travels through the Derwent Valley and past lovely historic towns before rising to the plateau of central Tasmania. Many of the northwest roads are twisty and even unpaved in the more-remote areas, but two-wheel drive is sufficient for most touring. Be prepared for sudden weather changes: snow in the summertime is not uncommon in the highest areas. Lake St. Clair is 173 km (107 mi) northwest of Hobart, and can be reached via the Lyell Highway, or from Launceston via Deloraine or Poatina. Cradle Mountain is 85 km (53 mi) south of Devonport, and can be reached by car via Claude Road from Sheffield or via Wilmot. Both lead 30 km (19 mi) along Route C132 to Cradle Valley.

Discounts and Deals

If you're planning to explore all of the island, the See Tasmania Smartvisit Card (☎ *1300/661771* ⊕ *www.seetasmaniacard.com*) provides unbeatable convenience and value. Three-, 7-, and 10-day cards give you free (or greatly reduced) admission at more than 60 of Tasmania's most popular attractions.

Restaurants

Although there are elegant dining options in the larger towns—especially Hobart—most eateries serve meals in a casual setting. Fiercely proud of their local produce, Tasmania's restaurateurs have packed their menus with home-grown seafood, beef, and cheeses, washed down with their famous cold-climate wines. Tasmanian wine is nearly unknown in the rest of the world, but that's not a comment on its quality; it's because Tasmanians tend to drink the vast majority of it themselves, leaving next to nothing to export.

Hotels

The hospitality industry is thriving in Tasmania, so in popular areas you'll find a wide range of accommodation options, from inexpensive motels to genteel B&Bs, rustic lodges to luxury hotels. Most hotels will have air-conditioning, but bed-and-breakfast lodgings often do not. Apart from a few hotels right in the main city center, most Hobart accommodations have free parking. In many smaller places, especially the colonial-style cottages, no smoking is allowed inside.

When to Visit

Cold weather-phobes beware: Tasmanian winters can draw freezing blasts from the Antarctic, so this is not the season to explore the highlands or wilderness areas. It's better in the colder months to enjoy the cozy interiors of colonial cottages and the open fireplaces of welcoming pubs.

Summer can be surprisingly hot—bushfires are common—but temperatures are generally lower than on the Australian mainland.

The best times to visit are autumn and spring; early autumn is beautiful, with deciduous trees in full color. Spring, with its splashes of pastel wildflowers and mild weather, is equally lovely.

Tasmania is a relaxing island with few crowds, except during the mid-December to mid-February school holiday period and at the end of the annual Sydney-to-Hobart yacht race just after Christmas. Most attractions and sights are open year-round.

DINING AND LODGING PRICE CATEGORIES (IN AUSTRALIAN DOLLARS)

	¢	$	$$	$$$	$$$$
Restaurants	under A$10	A$10–A$20	A$21–A$35	A$36–A$50	over A$50
Hotels	under A$100	A$100–A$150	A$151–A$200	A$201–A$300	over A$300

Meal prices are per person for a main course at dinner. Hotel prices are for two people in a standard double room in high season, including tax and service, based on the European Plan (with no meals) unless otherwise noted.

OUTDOOR ADVENTURES

Tasmania's pristine national parks are a national treasure. Freycinet, with its picture-perfect sandy bays, and the dramatic mountain peaks of Franklin-Gordon Wild Rivers National Park are two of the island's highlights.

Freycinet National Park, with its pristine beaches, eucalypt forests, and jagged granite peaks known as the Hazards is a must for fans of the great outdoors. Set on 169 square km (65 square mi) on the Freycinet Peninsula on the east coast, the park makes for a rewarding visit for a few hours or for a few days. If you visit one beach in Tasmania, make it the iconic Wineglass Bay.

More remote but equally beguiling is Franklin-Gordon Wild Rivers National Park in the west of the island. Stretching from the source of the Franklin River to the sea, it has spectacular mountain scenery. While the park is known to most visitors as the location of the popular Gordon River cruises, hardy walkers can explore the alpine scenery of the Upper Franklin region or attempt the four-day trek up Frenchmans Cap, while daredevil rafters can test their limits on the wild and ferocious river.

WHEN TO GO

Freycinet is very popular with travelers, but remember, this is Tasmania. It's never overcrowded. In summer, the park's peak season, accommodation can be more difficult to come by, so book ahead. Even so, the trails are never congested. Spring is also a good time to visit to see all the wildflowers in bloom.

The best time to visit Franklin-Gordon Wild Rivers National Park is between October and April, but even then visitors should be aware that the weather is temperamental: it rains frequently, and it can snow even in summer. But because of the size of the park, it never feels crowded no matter when you go.

FREYCINET NATIONAL PARK

Magnificent Freycinet National Park draws visitors because of its birdlife, wildflowers, bushwalking, and spectacular coastal scenery. It's probably Tassie's most user-friendly park, with near-endless options for hiking and bushwalking, ranging from 30 minutes in length to multi-day treks. Two of the more popular shorter walks are to the lookouts above Wineglass Bay and the Friendly Beaches, which are usually deserted. The pink granite peaks known as the Hazards are also a major attraction. Most people base themselves in accommodation in Coles Bay, the gateway to the park and the start of many walks. While it is possible to get to Coles Bay by public transport—Tassielink buses run from Hobart or Launceston to Bicheno, where passengers can use the Bicheno Bus Service to Coles Bay—it's much easier to get around if you have your own vehicle.

FRANKLIN-GORDON WILD RIVERS NATIONAL PARK

Untamed and perfect for the adventurous, the Franklin-Gordon Wild Rivers National Park has a rich and remarkable heritage. Best known to most visitors as the location of the popular Gordon River cruises, the park also contains many Aboriginal sites bearing witness to a heritage that extends back more than 36,000 years. Resilient walkers who aren't put off by the initial steep climb to Frenchmans Cap are rewarded by stunning eucalyptus forests before scrambling up the Cap's snow-topped dome at 1,446 meters to enjoy views over the peaks of Cradle Mountain, Barn Bluff, and Ossa. There are basic free campsites at the Collingwood River. If this sounds too adventurous, do as most day visitors do and stay in Strahan and drive along the meandering Lyell Highway, which winds for 56 km (35 mi) through the park.

TIMING FOR FIRST PARK

Freycinet is equally rewarding for quick visits as well as multi-day stays. If time is short, head to Coles Bay and do the short walk to Wineglass Bay, or spot wallabies on Friendly Beaches. However, if you decide you have all the time in the world, you can trek the entire length of the Freycinet Peninsula on a three-day walk.

TIMING FOR SECOND PARK

Much of the Franklin-Gordon Wild Rivers National Park is remote and rugged, and serious walkers would get the most out of a few day's stay (the Frenchmans Cap walk can be extended to 5 days). If time is short, the Franklin River Nature Trail is a quick and easy 20-minute trek, while the Donaghys Lookout walk takes just 40 minutes.

5

Updated by
Helena Iveson

Wild and dramatic landscapes, empty white beaches, heavenly food and wine—Tasmania's charms have been overlooked for too long by international travelers. Hikers have always known about the island's wilderness trails, which lead you through deserted forests and national parks, but now gourmands are discovering Tassie's superb local produce, making it a world-class gourmet destination, too.

Tasmania's attractions encompass the historic, the healthy, and the hedonistic. While Tasmania now is an unspoiled reminder of a simpler, slower lifestyle away from the rat race, its bloody history is never far from the surface. Today, walking through the lovely grounds in Port Arthur, the notorious penal colony, or the unhurried streets of Hobart with its profusion of Georgian buildings, it's difficult to picture Tasmania as a land of turmoil and tragedy. But the destruction of the Aboriginal population, who are thought to have crossed into Tasmania approximately 40,000 years ago, is a dark stain on the island's memory.

In many ways Tasmania is still untamed, making it a hiker's delight. Twenty-eight percent of the land is preserved in national parks, where impenetrable rain forests and deep river gorges cut through the massive mountain valleys. The coastlines are scalloped with endless desolate beaches—some pristine white, fronting serene turquoise bays, and some rugged and rocky, facing churning, choppy seas.

These beautiful surrounds have led to Tasmania's newest claim to fame as a gourmet haven. Thanks to the island's many microclimates, you can grow or harvest virtually anything from superb dairy produce to wonderful meat, and its clear seas abound in wonderful seafood. Oenophiles have also discovered the island's wines, and the island's wine routes are well worth a slow meander.

GREAT ITINERARIES

IF YOU HAVE 3 DAYS

Spend your first morning in **Hobart**, where you can stroll around the docks, Salamanca Place, and Battery Point, and have some caught-that-morning fish-and-chips from the harbor's floating chippies. After lunch, drive to **Richmond** and explore its 19th-century streetscape, then stay in a local B&B. On the second day head for **Port Arthur**, and spend the morning exploring the town's historic park, the site of the island's former penal colony. Take the afternoon to drive through the dramatic scenery of the Tasman Peninsula, noting the tessellated pavement and Tasman Arch blowhole near Eaglehawk Neck. Return to Hobart for the night, then on the third morning take a leisurely drive around the scenic **Huon Valley**. On return to Hobart, finish your tour with a trip to the summit of Mt. Wellington.

IF YOU HAVE 5 DAYS

Explore **Hobart** on foot the first morning, stopping for lunch at one of the waterfront restaurants at Elizabeth Street Pier, and then wander through historic **Richmond**. Spend the night in Hobart, then on the second day drive through the scenic **Huon Valley**. Return to Hobart for the night, and on the Day 3 drive to **Port Arthur**, taking in the beauty of the Tasman Peninsula on the way. Spend the night in Port Arthur, then drive early on the fourth day to

Freycinet National Park. Climb the steep path to the outlook over Wineglass Bay, then descend to the sands for a picnic and swim. Stay the night in the park, then on Day 5 meander back through the east coast wine regions. Return to the capital, topping off the day with city views from Mt. Wellington.

IF YOU HAVE 10 DAYS

Take a walking tour of **Hobart** on the first morning, then take an afternoon drive to **Richmond** before returning for the night. On the second day, drive to the Tasman Peninsula, enjoying the scenic backroads before heading to **Port Arthur** for the night. On the third day, head back southwest through Hobart toward the bucolic orchards of the **Huon Valley** and the Tahune Forest Airwalk. Depart early on the fourth morning for **Strahan**, stopping at Lake St. Clair. Spend the night, take an all-day cruise on the Gordon River, and stay another night. On Day 6 make the long drive north via Zeehan and Marrawah to **Stanley**, a village set beneath the Nut. Have lunch here, then head back east to **Devonport** and stay the night. On Day 7, turn inland via Sheffield or Wilmot to reach **Cradle Mountain National Park**. Stay two nights, using Day 8 to explore the region's natural beauty. On the ninth day, leave early for **Launceston**, spend the night, then head back to Hobart.

HOBART

Straddling the Derwent River at the foot of Mt. Wellington's forested slopes, Hobart was founded as a penal settlement in 1803. It's the second-oldest city in the country after Sydney, and it certainly rivals its mainland counterpart as Australia's most beautiful state capital. Close-set colonial brick-and-sandstone shops and homes line the narrow, quiet

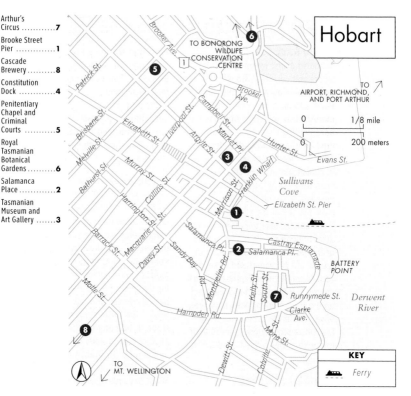

streets, creating a genteel setting for this historic city of 200,000. Life revolves around the broad Derwent River port, one of the deepest harbors in the world. Here warehouses that once stored Hobart's major exports of fruit, wool, and corn and products from the city's former whaling fleet still stand alongside the wharf today.

Hobart sparkles between Christmas and New Year's—summer Down Under—during the annual Sydney-to-Hobart yacht race. The event dominates conversations among Hobart's citizens, who descend on Constitution Dock to welcome the yachts and join in the boisterous festivities of the crews. The New Year also coincides with the Tastes of Tasmania Festival, when the dockside area comes alive with the best of Tasmanian food and wine on offer in numerous cafés, bars, and waterfront stalls. Otherwise, Hobart is a placid city whose nightlife is largely confined to excellent restaurants, jazz clubs, and the action at the Wrest Point Casino in Sandy Bay.

The Hobart Tasmanian Travel and Information Centre hours are weekdays 9–5 and Saturday 9–noon, often longer in summer.

GETTING HERE AND AROUND

Hobart, being teeny-tiny, is eminently walkable; once you're in the city center, no attraction is more than 15 minutes' walk away, apart from the Cascade Brewery. Because of the many one-way streets, it's best to park a car and leave it for the day as you explore. If you prefer two wheels to two legs, you can hire trendy electric bicycles from the Henry Jones Art Hotel on Hunter Street for A$20 an hour.

ESSENTIALS

Visitor Information Tasmanian Travel and Information Centre (✉ *20 Davey St., at Elizabeth St., Hobart City* ☎ *1800/990440 or 03/6230–8233* ⊕ *www.hobarttravelcentre.com.au*).

> **DISAPPEARING DEVILS**
>
> Tasmanian devils are becoming extremely rare because of a deadly cancer that is devastating the devil population—in 2009 they were officially listed on the endangered species list. Experts estimate that 60% of the population has already succumbed, and unless a cure is found the species faces extinction.

EXPLORING HOBART

TOP ATTRACTIONS

8 **Cascade Brewery.** This is Australia's oldest and most picturesque brewery, producing fine beers since 1824. You can see its inner workings only on the two-hour tours, which require lots of walking and climbing, but you're rewarded with three free drinks at the end. Note that appropriate attire (long pants and closed-toe shoes only) is required, and tour reservations are essential. It's a 30-minute walk from the city center, or buses leave from Franklin Square every 35 minutes from 9:15 AM. ✉ *140 Cascade Rd., South Hobart* ☎ *03/6224–1117* ⊕ *www.cascadebrewery.com.au* ⊠ *A$20 Tours weekdays at 11 and 1.*

4 **Constitution Dock.** Yachts competing in the annual Sydney-to-Hobart race moor at this colorful marina dock from the end of December through the first week of January. Buildings fronting the dock are century-old reminders of Hobart's trading history. Nearby Hunter Street is the original spot where British ships anchored. ✉ *Argyle and Davey Sts., Hobart City* ☎ *No phone* ⊠ *Free* ☉ *Daily 24 hrs.*

2 Fodor'sChoice ★ **Salamanca Place.** Old whaling ships used to dock at Salamanca Place. Today many of the warehouses that were once used by whalers along this street have been converted into crafts shops, art galleries, and restaurants. At the boisterous Saturday market, which attracts all elements of Tasmanian society from hippies to the well-heeled, dealers in Tasmanian arts and crafts, antiques, old records, and books—and a fair bit of appalling junk—display their wares between 8:30 and 3. Keep an eye open for items made from beautiful Tasmanian timber, particularly Huon pine. ⊕ *www.salamanca.com.au.*

WORTH NOTING

7 **Arthur's Circus.** Hobart's best-preserved street is a charming collection of tiny houses and cottages in a circle around a village green on Runnymede Street, in the heart of historic Battery Point. Most of these private houses, which were built in the 1840s and 1850s, have been nicely restored.

1 **Brooke Street Pier.** The busy waterfront at Brooke Street Pier is the departure point for harbor cruises. Nearby **Elizabeth Street Pier** has trendy restaurants and bars. ✉ *Franklin Wharf, Hobart City.*

5

OFF THE BEATEN PATH

🐾 **Bonorong Wildlife Conservation Centre.** Situated 25 km (16 mi) north of Hobart on the highway to Launceston, the small park has a wide selection of Australian species, many of which have been rescued, including koalas, wombats, quolls (indigenous cats), and the notorious Tasmanian devil. The excellent and dedicated staff will answer any questions with enthusiasm. Free tours are at 11:30 and 2 every day. ✉ *Briggs Rd., Brighton* ☎ *03/6268–1184* ⊕ *www.bonorong.com.au* 💲 *A$16* ⊙ *Daily 9–5.*

BELLERIVE VILLAGE

Take the ferry across the River Derwent to Bellerive, a lovely little villagelike suburb that will make you feel as if you've stepped back in history. There are great restaurants, and the view back to the city with Mt. Wellington looming in the background is impressive.

❺ **Penitentiary Chapel and Criminal Courts.** Built and used during the early convict days, these buildings vividly portray Tasmania's penal, judicial, and religious heritage in their courtrooms, old cells, and underground tunnels. If you want to get spooked, come for the nighttime ghost tour (reservations recommended). ✉ *Brisbane and Campbell Sts., Hobart City* ☎ *03/6231–0911 or 0417/361392* ⊕ *www.penitentiarychapel.com* 💲 *A$8, ghost tour A$10* ⊙ *Tours weekdays at 10, 11.30, 1, and 2.30; ghost tour daily at 8.30* PM.

❻ **Royal Tasmanian Botanical Gardens.** The largest area of open land in Hobart, these well-tended gardens are rarely crowded and provide a welcome relief from the city. Plants from all over the world are here—more than 6,000 exotic and native species in all. The collection of Tasmania's unique native flora is especially impressive. ✉ *Lower Domain Rd., Queen's Domain* ☎ *03/6236–3076* ⊕ *www.rtbg.tas.gov.au* 💲 *Free* ⊙ *Daily 8–5:30 (Oct.–Mar. until 6:30).*

NEED A BREAK?

Drop into Sugo (✉ **Shop 9, Salamanca Pl., Hobart City** ☎ **03/6224–5690**) if you get hungry while strolling the shops of Salamanca Place. This funky café serves great breakfasts, as well as tasty pizzas, pastas, and coffee. You're welcome to bring your own bottle of wine. It's open 8–4.30 every day.

❸ **Tasmanian Museum and Art Gallery.** This building overlooking Constitution Dock houses is a good starting point for uncovering Tasmania's history. It's the best place in Hobart to learn about the island's Aborigines (the last native Aboriginal inhabitants here died in the late 1800s), and unique wildlife. Kids will love the 7-meter-long giant squid found off the west coast. There are free guided tours every day at 2.30 PM. ✉ *40 Macquarie St., Hobart City* ☎ *03/6211–4177* ⊕ *www.tmag.tas.gov.au* 💲 *Free Daily 10–5.*

OUTDOOR ACTIVITIES

Hobartians are an outdoorsy lot who make the most of the city's waterfront location by fishing, cruising, and sailing or heading inland to Mt. Wellington to explore the many trails that start there.

Continued on page 336

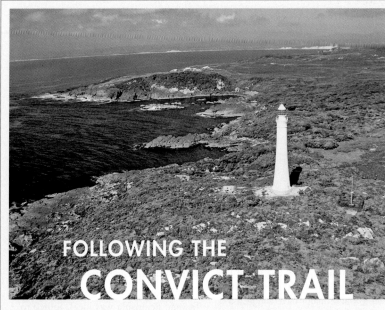

FOLLOWING THE
CONVICT TRAIL

For many, Tasmania conjures up grim images of chain-ganged prisoners: British convicts banished from the motherland to languish on a distant island in a faraway colony.

This humble (and brutal) beginning as a penal colony is a point of pride for many Australians. It's no small feat that a colony comprised of, among others, poor Irish, Scottish, and Welsh convicts— many imprisoned for crimes as petty as stealing a loaf of bread—were able to build what is now Australia. It epitomizes a toughness of character that Australians prize. Many here can accurately trace their lineage back to the incarcerated. Kevin Rudd, the country's Prime Minister, is himself descended from six convicts, including Mary Wade, the youngest female prisoner transported to Australia at the age of 11.

Tasmania has a number of remarkably well-preserved convict sites, most of which are set on the isolated Tasman Peninsula, some 75 km (47 mi) southeast of Hobart. Here, the region's beautifully rugged landscape belies the horrors of the past. Exploring Tasmania's convict heritage and the dramatic beauty of the island are two sides of the same coin. The region's isolation, impenetrable rain forests, and sheer cliffs falling into the sea made it a perfect island prison. By following signs on what's called the Convict Trail, you'll go home with provocative insight into what life was like for the almost 75,000 souls sent to Tasmania between 1803 and 1853.

by Helena Iveson

The rugged and beautiful Tasmanian Coast.

TASMANIA'S CONVICT PAST

Port Arthur Historic Site

"It is impossible to convey, in words, any idea of the hideous phantasmagoria of shifting limbs and faces which moved through the evil-smelling twilight of this terrible prison-house. Callot might have drawn it, Dante might have suggested it, but a minute attempt to describe its horrors would but disgust. There are depths in humanity which one cannot explore, as there are mephitic caverns into which one dare not penetrate."

—Marcus Clarke's description of Port Arthur's Separate Prison in his famous novel *For the Term of his Natural Life.*

They came in chains to this hostile island, where the seasons were all the wrong way around and the sights and smells were unfamiliar. In the 50 years following the establishment of the first settlement in Tasmania (Van Diemen's Land) in 1803, 57,909 male and 13,392 female prisoners were sent to the island. From 1830 on, many ended up at the newly built penal settlement at Port Arthur, where the slightest infraction would be punished by 100 lashes or weeks of solitary confinement on a diet of bread and water. Life was spent in chains, breaking up rocks or doing other menial tasks—all meant to keep criminal tendencies at bay.

The location of the settlement on the Tasman Peninsula was ideal. Joined to the rest of the island by a narrow neck of land with steep cliffs pounded by surging surf, it was easy to isolate and guard with half-starved dogs on the infamous dogline. Even though convicts were sentenced for a specific number of years, conditions were so brutal that even a few years could become a life sentence. With no chance of escape, some prisoners saw suicide as the only way out.

As the number of prisoners increased, more buildings went up. In time, the penal colony became a self-sufficient industrial center where prisoners sawed timber, built ships, laid bricks, cut stone, and made tiles, shoes, iron castings, and clothing.

A sculpture representing the infamous dogline at Eaglehawk Neck, Tasman Peninsula

HOW TO EXPLORE

GETTING HERE

To fully experience the trail, you'll need a car. It's possible to get to Port Arthur via operators such as Tassielink, but you can't access the whole trail by public transportation.

From Hobart head north to the well-preserved village of Richmond before continuing southeast on the Arthur Highway (A9) to the small town of Sorell. Not far from here is the infamous Eaglehawk neck, marking the start of the Tasman Peninsula. The Convict Trail runs in a circle around the peninsula, with signs clearly marking the many sites along the way.

Richmond Bridge and Church

TIMING

Port Arthur is 120 km (75 mi) or an hour and a half away from Hobart, but will take longer if you intend on making stops at Richmond and Sorell (which you should).

This trip can be done in one long day, but if you want to thoroughly explore the Tasman Peninsula, allow for two or three days. The Convict Trail booklet is available from visitor information centers across Tasmania for $2.50 and details the key sites and attractions along the route.

EXPLORING

It's easy to forget that Port Arthur wasn't an isolated settlement. The whole of the Tasman Peninsula was part of a larger penal colony, so, for the full experience, don't overlook the smaller sights. There are plenty of cafés and accommodations along the way, so take your time.

STUNNING VIEWS

Don't miss the vistas at the Tasman National Park Lookout. The walk along dramatic sea cliffs, which are among the highest and most spectacular in Australia, is easy and rewarding. The views of Pirates Bay, Cape Hauy, and the two islands just off the coast called The Lanterns are spectacular.

Isle of the Dead

EN ROUTE

Take a break at the famous Sorell Fruit Farm where from November to May it's pick-you-own-berry season (✉ *174 Pawleena Road, Sorell,* ☎ *03/6265–2744,* ⊕ *www.sorellfruitfarm.com,* ☾ *Oct., Mar., Apr., and May 10–4; Nov., Dec., Jan., and Feb. 8:30–5*). For something more savory, a meal at The Mussel Boys is worth the drive from Hobart alone. Unsurprisingly, this casual restaurant's claim to fame are the mollusks. (*5927 Arthur Highway, Taranna, 03/6250-3088, closed Mon.–Tues.*)

TOURING THE CONVICT TRAIL

It's hard to absorb this disturbing story of human suffering. Around 73,000 convicts were transported here, and about 1 in 5 served time in Port Arthur, on Tasmania's southernmost tip.

Stone bridge at Richmond

① RICHMOND BRIDGE. Australia's oldest bridge was built by convict labor in 1825 and is a lasting symbol of the island's convict heritage. Don't miss the village's gaol, which predates Port Arthur by five years.

② SORELL. This early settlement is where bloody bushranger battles were fought in the colony's formative years. Bushrangers were actually

Sorell Berry Farm

outlaws who lived in the bush. A walk around the town reveals some interesting heritage buildings; there are also plenty of antiques shops and cafes to keep you occupied.

③ THE DOGLINE. Statues of snarling hounds represent the dogs that prevented the convicts from escaping and mark the infamous dogline along the narrow strip of land linking the Tasman Peninsula with the rest of Tasmania.

Old wooden jetty in Norfolk Bay

④ NORFOLK BAY. This is the site of a human-powered tramway. Goods were unloaded from ships at the Convict Station and then transported to Port Arthur by a tram dragged by convicts across the peninsula. This saved the ship a dangerous journey across the peninsula's stormy bays.

⑤ PORT ARTHUR. Walking among the peaceful ruins and quiet gardens, it's difficult to imagine that this place was hell-on-earth for the convicts. When the settlement closed in 1877, the area was renamed Carnarvon in an attempt to disconnect the land from the horrors associated with its former name. However, in 1927 it was reinstated as Port Arthur and opened to a public keen to embrace this aspect of the Australian story.

TRAIL MARKERS

The Convict Trail is marked with a broad arrow symbol that was stamped on convict-made goods. It's framed in yellow to reference the color of convict clothing.

5

Sandstone church at Port Arthur

7 ISLE OF THE DEAD CONVICT CEMETERY. A small island in the harbor near Port Arthur is the final resting place for about a thousand people, most of them convicts and ex-convict paupers who were buried mostly in unmarked graves.

8 NUBEENA was established as an outstation of Port Arthur and for many years was an important convict farming community. It was also the sight of a semaphore station, used to raise the alarm if a convict made a bid for freedom.

9 SALTWATER RIVER. Exploring the abandoned mines reveals the terrible conditions in which the convicts suffered: restored tiny underground cells, totally without light and filled with fetid air give horrifying insight.

10 KOONYA. The probation station here was once an important convict outpost known as the Cascades. It operated between 1843 and 1846 and you'll find a few isolated houses and a well-restored penitentiary that once held 400 men, at least a quarter of them in chains.

6 POINT PUER BOYS PRISON. More than 3,000 boys, some as young as age nine, passed through here from 1834 to 1849. Located just across the harbor from the main Port Arthur settlement, this was the first jail in the British Empire built exclusively for juvenile male convicts. But just because they were young doesn't mean they were spared from hard labor like stone-cutting and construction. The prison was also infamous for its stern discipline—solitary

The Penitentiary Block

confinement, days at a time on a tread wheel, and whipping were standard punishments for even a trivial breach of the rules.

BOAT TOURS   **Hobart Cruises.** Their catamaran zips through the majestic waterways of the Derwent River and the D'Entrecasteaux Channel to Peppermint Bay at Woodbridge. Wildlife is abundant, from sea eagles and falcons soaring above the weathered cliffs to pods of dolphins swimming alongside the boat. Underwater cameras explore kelp forests and salmon in the floating fish farms. ⊠ *Peppermint Bay, 3435 Channel Hwy., Woodbridge* ☎ *03/6267–4088* ⊕ *www.hobartcruises.com.*

Captain Fell's Historic Ferries. Travelers love the old-fashioned ferries that take you on a leisurely cruise around the harbor as friendly tour guides point out the sights. ⊠ *Franklin Wharf Pier, Hobart Waterfront* ☎ *03/6223–5893* ⊕ *www.captainfellshistoricferries.com.au.*

BICYCLING   Although most of Hobart and its surrounding areas are too hilly to make for easy cycling, some old railway lines along the western bank of the Derwent River (which are quite flat) have been transformed into bicycle paths. These offer a relaxing way to explore parts of the city. Electric bikes can be rented from the Henry Jones Art Hotel on Hunter Street, or the more old fashioned versions can be rented from **Derwent Bike Hire** (⊠ *Regatta Grounds, Queens Domain* ☎ *428/899169* ⊕ *www. derwentbikehire.com*). **Island Cycle Tours** (☎ *1800/064726* ⊕ *www.islandcycletours.com*) also rents bikes, as well as providing information on self-guided tours and daily 21-km-long (13-mi-long) guided descents from Mt. Wellington.

FISHING   Tasmania's well-stocked lakes and streams are among the world's best for trout fishing. The season runs from August through May, and licensed trips can be arranged through the Tasmanian Travel and Information Centre.

Several professional fishing guides are based on the island. For information on these guides, as well as related tours, accommodations, and sea charters, check out ⊕ *www.troutguidestasmania.com.au* or inquire at the Tasmanian Travel and Information Centre for a professional guide in the area you are visiting.

Rod & Fly Tasmania. Tasmania offers some world-class fishing, and if you'd like to catch some local trout in the local wonderfully clear rivers, the friendly tour guides here have over thirty years of experience. ☎ *03/6266–4480* ⊕ *www.rodandfly.com.au.*

Mr Flathead. If you'd rather take to the ocean, this company will take you on half- or full-day tours to local fishing hot spots, where you'll find flathead, whiting, and salmon. All rods, reels, and equipment are supplied. ☎ *439/617200* ⊕ *www.mrflathead.com.au.*

HIKING   Pick up a Mt. Wellington Walk Map (A$4) from the tourist office on Elizabeth Street in Hobart to make the most out of the park that towers over Hobart. Although shops around town stock outdoor equipment, you should bring your own gear if you're planning any serious bushwalking. Sneakers are adequate for walking around Mt. Wellington and along beaches. A car is necessary to access several of the trails around the peak. If you prefer to join a tour, try **Adventure Seekers.** They will take care of all the details. Their 9-day South Coast track starts in Hobart and explores the wild south coast, but they do shorter trips, too. See their Web site for dates. ⊕ *www.adventureseekers.com.au.*

WALKING TOURS In Hobart, walks led by the National Trust provide an excellent overview of Battery Point, including visits to mansions and 19th-century houses. Tours, which depart Saturday at 9:30 AM from the Wishing Well (near the Franklin Square post office), include morning tea. The National Trust also conducts daily tours (hourly 10–2) of the courthouse, Campbell Street Chapel, and the old penitentiary (there's also a spooky night tour).

Hobart Historic Tours offers guided walks through old Hobart, around the waterfront and maritime precinct, and a historic pub tour. A minimum of three people is required for all walks.

Battery Point Walking tours (✉ The Wishing Well, Franklin Sq., *Hobart* ☎ 03/6223–7570 ⊕ *www.discovertasmania.com*). **Hobart Historic Tours** (✉ *Elizabeth St., Hobart* ☎ 03/6278–3338 ⊕ *www.hobarthistorictours.com.au*).

WHERE TO EAT

5

Constitution Dock is the perfect place for yacht-watching, as well as for gobbling fresh fish-and-chips from one of the punts (floating fish-and-chips shops) moored on the water. Ask for the daily specials, such as local blue grenadier or trevally, which cost A\$6–A\$8, or go for some freshly shucked oysters. The city's main restaurant areas include the docks and the streets around Salamanca Place.

\$–\$\$
INDIAN
✗ **Annapurna.** In the bustling restaurant strip of North Hobart, this local favorite has maintained an enviable reputation for many years thanks to its consistently good-value food. Tandoori, curries (take care, they can be searingly hot), and a wide selection of other Indian delicacies keep people coming back. Inexpensive lunch boxes are available. ✉ *305 Elizabeth St., North Hobart* ☎ 03/6236–9500 ▤ *AE, DC, MC, V.*

\$\$–\$\$\$
ECLECTIC
✗ **Henry's Harbourside.** Part of the Henry Jones Art Hotel, this small restaurant offers some of Hobart's best fine dining in arty surrounds. The food isn't overshadowed by the contemporary art on the walls thanks to the focus on seasonal produce in hearty dishes like slow cooked pork belly with braised red cabbage, pickled apple, and daikon. The wine list features selections from only the finest Tasmanian, mainland Australian, and overseas wineries. ✉ *25 Hunter St., Hobart City* ☎ 03/6210–7706 ⊕ *www.thehenryjones.com* ▤ *AE, DC, MC, V.*

\$\$
AUSTRALIAN
✗ **Lebrina.** Elegant surroundings in an 1849 brick colonial home inspire classic Tasmanian cooking in Hobart's most formal dining room. The best of the island's fresh produce is well utilized in such dishes as the twice-cooked Gruyère soufflé appetizer, or the seared loin of venison with fresh horseradish, served with red cabbage salad. Leave room for the superb Tasmanian cheese plate. The wine list includes many fine Tasmanian vintages. ✉ *155 New Town Rd., New Town* ☎ 03/6228–7775 ▤ *AE, DC, MC, V* ☉ *Closed Sun. and Mon. No lunch.*

\$\$–\$\$\$\$
★
SEAFOOD
✗ **Mures Fish House Complex.** On the top floor of this complex on the wharf, Mures Upper Deck Restaurant has superb indoor and alfresco views of the harbor. Try the blue-eye trevalla with caponata sauce if it's on the seasonal menu. Downstairs, Mures Lower Deck is a less expensive, cash-only alternative: you order, take a number, pick up your food, and eat it at tables outside. Also in the complex, Mures

The extremely poplular Saturday Salamanca Market

Sushi Bar has Hobart's best and freshest sushi and sashimi. ✉ *Victoria Dock, Hobart City* ☎ *03/6231–1999 Upper Deck, 03/6231–2121 Lower Deck, 03/6231–2009 Sushi Bar* ⊕ *www.muresupperdeck.com. au* ▭ *AE, DC, MC, V.*

$$–$$$
ECLECTIC

✕ **Restaurant 373.** Those who enjoy a little culinary creativity shouldn't miss this casual little bistro in fashionable North Hobart. It's very popular, and you often have to wait for a table, but well worth it for its ambience and modern feel. The salmon smeared in pistou on roasted couscous, asparagus, and wild arugula is delicious, but be sure to leave room for the truly inspired desserts. ✉ *373 Elizabeth St., North Hobart* ☎ *03/6231–9031* ⊕ *www.restaurant373.com.au* ▭ *AE, DC, MC, V* ☽ *Closed Sunday. No lunch.*

$$$
ECLECTIC

✕ **The Quarry Bar and Restaurant.** Set on the waterfront, this buzzy place offers imaginative food alfresco or indoors; it's a lovely place to linger inside in winter thanks to the roaring fire. When it comes to food, local produce is jazzed up—think pickled octopus with orange, fennel, and saffron salad for starters. Happily, there's also an extensive wine list, including more than 30 local drops by the glass. ✉ *27 Salamanca Pl., City Center* ☎ *03/6223–6552* ⊕ *www.thequarry.com.au* ▭ *AE, DC, MC, V.*

WHERE TO STAY

Hobart has some lovely lodgings in old, historic houses and cottages, most of which have been beautifully restored. If you're seeking more modern conveniences, there are plenty of newer hotels, too.

$$$ ⊞ **Corinda's Cottages.** This charming residence was built in the 1880s
★   for Alfred Crisp, a wealthy timber merchant who later became Lord
Mayor of Hobart. Three historic outbuildings—including a gardener's
residence, servants' quarters, and coach house—have been lovingly con
verted into delightful self-contained cottages filled with period antiques.
The B&B is close to the woodland, yet it's only a few minutes from the
city center. **Pros:** wonderfully restored historic accommodation, gen-
erous buffet breakfast. **Cons:** no leisure facilities, expensive Internet.
⊠ *17 Glebe St., Glebe* ☎ *03/6234–1590* ⊕ *www.corindascottages.com.
au* ⤴ *3 cottages* ⚒ *In-room: kitchen. In-hotel: laundry service, parking
(no fee), no elevator* ⊟ *AE, MC, V* ⦿| *BP.*

$$$–$$$$ ⊞ **Henry Jones Art Hotel.** Arguably one of Australia's best hotels, right on
Fodor'sChoice   the Hobart waterfront, this row of historic warehouses and a former
★   jam factory have been transformed into a sensational, art-theme hotel,
where the work of Tasmania's finest visual and performing artists is dis-
played. The friendly full-time curator is on hand to advise and explain,
as is the in-house historian. The spacious guest suites, also artistically
decorated, reflect the influences of a rich colonial trading history with
India and China: all suites have natural wood furnishings and king-
size beds with exotic silk covers. Bathrooms are supermodern, with
stainless-steel and translucent-glass fittings. Some suites have harbor
views; others overlook the stunning glassed-in courtyard atrium. **Pros:**
unstuffy and friendly staff despite the arty surrounds, stunning rooms
worth lingering in. **Cons:** bathrooms could do with more soundproof-
ing, your bill might be higher than you planned if you're tempted to
buy the art on the walls. ⊠ *25 Hunter St., Hobart* ☎ *03/6210–7700
or 1300/665581* ⊕ *www.thehenryjones.com* ⤴ *50 suites* ⚒ *In-room:
dial-up, DVD. In-hotel: restaurant, room service, bar, concierge, pub-
lic Wi-Fi, laundry service, parking (no fee), no-smoking rooms* ⊟ *AE,
DC, MC, V.*

$$–$$$ ⊞ **Hotel Grand Chancellor.** Across the street from the old wharves and
★   steps from some of the best restaurants in Hobart, this imposing glass-
and-stone building seems a bit out of place amid Hobart's colonialism.
What it lacks in period charm, however, it more than makes up for in
luxury. All rooms have large wooden desks and thick, white guest bath-
robes. Some rooms overlook the harbor. **Pros:** steps away from the city's
museums, offers familiar chain comforts. **Cons:** some traffic noise, stark
lobby. ⊠ *1 Davey St., Hobart City* ☎ *03/6235–4535 or 1800/753379*
⊕ *www.ghihotels.com* ⤴ *240 rooms, 12 suites* ⚒ *In-room: dial-up,
Wi-Fi (some). In-hotel: 2 restaurants, bar, pool, gym, laundry service,
airport shuttle, parking (no fee)* ⊟ *AE, DC, MC, V.*

$$$$ ⊞ **Islington Hotel.** Built in 1847, this elegant Regency mansion was con-
Fodor'sChoice   verted to a five-star luxury boutique hotel, and is now considered to
★   be one of the finest in Australia. Set in an acre of landscaped gardens
(complete with a Heritage-listed willow tree over 100 years old) and
with breathtaking views over Mt. Wellington, the property incorporates
six garden suites and the main house. The common areas include a dra-
matic marble conservatory and a library with elegant bookshelves and
flickering fireplaces. All guest suites have been completely refurbished
with a blend of antique and modern styles and an eclectic collection

of art. Full breakfasts and evening cocktails are included in your room rate, and a Rolls-Royce is available to drive you to a local restaurant or for sightseeing. **Pros:** pinchable toiletries in the bathroom, sophisticated service from staff. **Cons:** 30 minutes' walk from the city center, not family-friendly. ✉ *321 Davey St., South Hobart* ☎ *03/6220–2123* ⊕ *www. islingtonhotel.com* ↴ *11 suites* ♿ *In-room: dial-up, Wi-Fi (some). In-hotel: laundry service, parking (no fee), no kids under 16* ▭ *AE, DC, MC, V* ⋈ *BP.*

$$ ⚏ **Lodge on Elizabeth.** This opulent grand manor, convict-built in 1829 and home over the years to many Hobart notables, is within walking distance of the city center, but far enough removed to feel like a sanctuary. The courtyard garden is a fine place to relax, as is the fireside common room, where you can sip a glass of wine before retreating upstairs to your room with its private hot tub. **Pros:** bargain-priced Internet, convenient option for groups or families. **Cons:** a few bedrooms are on the small side, some street noise. ✉ *249 Elizabeth St., Hobart City* ☎ *03/6231–3830* ⊕ *www.thelodge.com.au* ↴ *14 rooms* ♿ *In-room: refrigerator, dial-up. In-hotel: restaurant, laundry facilities, parking (no fee), no elevator* ▭ *MC, V* ⋈ *CP.*

NIGHTLIFE AND THE ARTS

Although Hobart has the only true nightlife scene in Tasmania, it's extremely tame compared to what's in Melbourne and Sydney. There are few dance clubs, but evenings out tend to revolve around a bottle of excellent local wine. Consult the Friday or Saturday editions of the *Mercury* newspaper before heading out. *This Week in Tasmania,* available at most hotels, is a comprehensive guide to current stage performances and contemporary music concerts.

BARS AND DANCE CLUBS

The waterfront area is lined with bars that cater to the local, very thirsty after-work crowds. If you have a chance, be sure to stop by **T42** (✉ *Elizabeth St. Pier, Hobart City* ☎ *03/6224–7742*), a lively waterfront spot popular for both dining and drinking. The food is excellent, too. The **Grand Chancellor** (✉ *1 Davey St., Hobart City* ☎ *03/6235–4535*) has a relaxing piano bar that is popular with local professionals. **Grape** (✉ *55 Salamanca Pl., Battery Point* ☎ *03/6224–0611*) is Tasmania's best wine bar, which has a wonderful shop where you can pick up one of their 300 types of Tasmanian wines and a cheese platter for an impromptu little picnic. It serves all its wines in trendy Reidel O tumblers, and the excellent staff are keen to advise from behind the bar decorated with thousands of corks. There are wine tastings on Tuesday evenings.

The cool kids go for the raucous, art deco **Republic Bar and Cafe** (✉ *299 Elizabeth St., North Hobart* ☎ *03/6234–6954*) which has live music most nights. **Soak Bar** (✉ *237 Elizabeth St., North Hobart* ☎ *03/6231– 5699*) operates as a lounge-style café called Kaos during the day. At night they attract a largely gay clientele. **Round Midnight** (✉ *39 Salamanca Pl., Battery Point* ☎ *03/6223–2491*) is a blues spot and has a mix of youngish live bands and DJs.

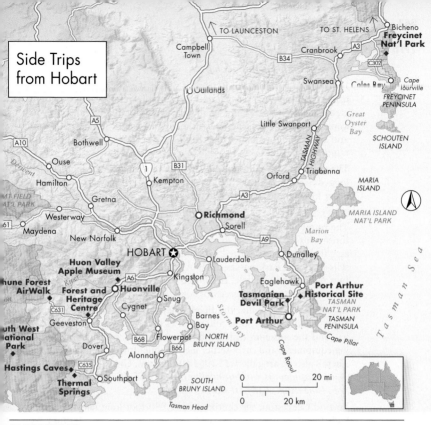

Side Trips
from Hobart

SHOPPING

Tasmanian artisans and craftspeople work with diverse materials to fashion unusual pottery, metalwork, and wool garments. Items made from regional timber, including myrtle, sassafras, and Huon pine, are very popular. The wonderful scenery around the island is an inspiration for numerous artists.

Along the Hobart waterfront at Salamanca Place are a large number of shops that sell arts and crafts. On Saturday (between 8:30 and 3:00) the area turns into a giant market, where still more local artists join produce growers, bric-a-brac sellers, and itinerant musicians to sell their wares.

SIDE TRIPS FROM HOBART

Hobart is a perfect base for short trips to some of Tasmania's most historic and scenic places. Although you can visit them in a day; if you can, stay a night or two and experience their delights at a leisurely pace.

THE HUON VALLEY

★ *40 km (25 mi) south of Hobart.*

En route to the vast wilderness of South West National Park is the tranquil Huon Valley. Sheltered coasts and sandy beaches are pocketed with thick forests and small farms. William Bligh planted the first apple tree here, founding one of the region's major industries. Salmon and trout caught fresh from churning blue rivers are also delicious regional delicacies.

The valley is also famous for the Huon pine, much of which has been logged over the decades. The trees that remain are strictly protected, so other local timbers are used by the region's craftspeople.

EXPLORING

The **Forest and Heritage Centre** has fascinating displays on the history of forestry in the area, as well as some beautiful tables, vases, and cabinetry that have been crafted from the timber. The Heritage Centre also sells National Park passes, daily A\$22 per vehicle, or A\$56 for up to two months per vehicle. ⊠ *Church St., Geeveston* ☎ *03/6297–1836* ⊕ *www.forestandheritagecentre.com.au* ✉ *A\$5* ☉ *Daily 9–5.*

En route to Huonville, the **Huon Valley Apple Museum** is in a former apple-packing shed. Some 500 varieties of apples are grown in the valley, and the museum displays farming artifacts, picking and processing equipment, and early-settler memorabilia from the area's orchards. There's also an art gallery. ⊠ *2064 Huon Hwy., Grove* ☎ *03/6266–4345* ⊕ *www.applemuseum.huonvalley.biz* ✉ *A\$5.50* ☉ *Sept.–May, daily 9–5; June–Aug., daily 10–4.*

Beyond Geeveston, the cantilevered, 1,880-foot-long **Tahune Forest Air-Walk** rises to 150 feet above the forest floor, providing a stunning panorama of the Huon and Picton rivers and the Hartz Mountains. The best views are from the platform at the end of the walkway, and if you have time, follow one of the trails that lead from the center through the surrounding forests. ⊠ *Tahune Forest AirWalk and Visitor Centre, Tahune Forest Reserve, Arve Rd.* ☎ *03/6297–0068* ⊕ *www.forestrytas. com.au* ✉ *A\$22* ☉ *Daily 9–5.*

Spectacular cave formations and thermal pools amid a fern glade await at the **Hastings Caves and Thermal Springs.** The caves are about 125 km (78 mi) south of Hobart, past Huonville and Dover. You can take a tour of the chambers, or just relax at the well-equipped picnic areas and make use of the thermal pool. The route to the site is well marked from the town of Dover. ☎ *03/6298–3209, 1300/135513* ⊕ *www.parks.tas. gov.au* ✉ *A\$24* ☉ *Apr.–Sept., cave tours 11–3, thermal spring 10–4; Sept.–Dec., cave tours 10–4, thermal springs 9–5; Mar. and Apr., cave tours 10–5, thermal springs 9–5.*

WHERE TO EAT AND STAY

\$\$ AUSTRALIAN   ✕ **Home Hill Restaurant.** Large plate-glass windows here open to the Home Hill winery's endless hillside vineyards. The seasonal menu includes such delicacies as grain-fed Longford beef eye fillet on a horseradish-potato gratin with Pinot Noir jus and watercress. The crisp Sylvaner (a light, Alsatian-style white wine) goes beautifully with the quail salad.

After dinner you can head down to the cellar to enjoy a complimentary sampling of more of the winery's excellent cool-climate labels. ⌂ *38 Nairn St., Ranelagh* ☎ *03/6264–1200* ⊕ *homehillwines.com.au* ⊟ *DC, MC, V* ⊘ *No dinner Sun –Thurs.*

$$ ⬚ **Heron's Rise Vineyard.** Mornings in any of the vineyard's three self-contained cottages are bucolic and gorgeous; you'll wake to glorious water views out over the flower gardens, where you might see rabbits nibbling. Both cottages have queen-size beds and wood-burning fireplaces. Dinner is available in your cottage by prior arrangement. **Pros:** peaceful surrounds, owners pride themselves on their eco-friendly accommodation. **Cons:** no leisure facilities, smoke from fireplaces might be a problem for the asthmatic. ⌂ *Saddle Rd., Kettering* ☎ *03/6267–4339* 📠 *03/6267–4245* ⊕ *www.heronsrise.com.au* 🛏 *3 cottages* ⚒ *In-room: kitchen. In-hotel: laundry facilities, parking (no fee), no-smoking rooms* ⊟ *DC, MC, V* ⭑⭑ *CP.*

$$–$$$ ⬚ **Matilda's of Ranelagh.** The official greeters at this delightful, 1850
Fodor'sChoice Heritage-listed B&B are five golden retrievers. Elegant Victorian and
★ Edwardian furnishings provide the ultimate in refinement and comfort. Outside, it's a pleasure to stroll through the 5-acre English-style gardens, which are filled with trees, shrubs, and thousands of flowers that bloom seasonally. A hearty breakfast is served each morning in the pretty blue-and-white dining room. **Pros:** historic place to stay and a great lounge area with books and DVDs. **Cons:** those with dog allergies should beware, no leisure facilities. ⌂ *2 Louisa St., Ranelagh* ☎ *03/6264–3493* 📠 *03/6264–3491* ⊕ *www.matildasofranelagh.com.au* 🛏 *2 rooms* ⚒ *In-hotel: restaurant, laundry facilities, parking (no fee), no-smoking rooms, no kids under 15, no elevator* ⊟ *MC, V* ⭑⭑ *BP.*

RICHMOND

★ *24 km (15 mi) northeast of Hobart.*

Twenty minutes' drive from Hobart and a century behind the big city, this colonial village in the Coal River valley is a major tourist magnet. Visitors stroll and browse through the craft shops, antiques stores, and cafés along the main street. Richmond is also home to a number of vineyards, all of which produce excellent cool-climate wines.

WHERE TO EAT AND STAY

$$$ ✕ **Ashmore on Bridge Street.** Once you've perused all of Richmond's cute
CAFE shops and historic sights, be sure to recharge in this surprisingly trendy café with an open roaring fire and a friendly owner. The creamy scrambled eggs on sourdough toast with Tasmanian cold smoked salmon and house relish is delicious for breakfast, and in the afternoon the huge and delectable Devonshire teas will have you sighing with pleasure. ⌂ *34 Bridge St., Richmond* ☎ *03/6260–2238* ⊕ *www.ashmoreonbridge.com. au* ⊟ *DC, MC, V* ⊘ *No dinner.*

$–$$ ✕ **Coal Valley Vineyard.** This winery restaurant, accessible via the road
AUSTRALIAN from Cambridge, is set amid scenic vineyards with sweeping views over a golf course to the waters of Barilla Bay. It's open daily for lunch from 10 to 4, and the pies at the bakery are delicious for a light(ish) lunch, or try the shoulder of lamb in olive tapenade. Afterward head

to the cellar door (open Thurs.–Sun. 10–4) for a free tasting. ✉ *257 Richmond Rd., Cambridge* ☎ *03/6248–5367* ⊕ *www.colevalley.com. au* ▭ *AE, DC, MC, V* ⊗ *No lunch Mon., no dinner Wed.*

$–$$ ✕ **Meadowbank Estate.** Guided wine tasting and an art gallery comple-
AUSTRALIAN   ment this unpretentious fine-dining restaurant with floor-to-ceiling windows leading out to views over the vineyards of Meadowbank Estate
and the waters of Barilla Bay. The menu of two-course meals emphasizes
food and wine pairings. Try the smoked eel in horseradish sauce, and
make sure to save room for the chocolate pudding and passion-fruit
ice cream. ✉ *699 Richmond Rd., Cambridge* ☎ *03/6248–4484* ⊕ *www.
meadowbankestate.com.au* ▭ *DC, MC, V* ⊗ *No dinner.*

$$ 🏠 **Mrs Currie's House B&B.** This gracious Georgian house, built between
★   1820 and 1860, is set in a peaceful garden with lovely views over the
village of Richmond and the surrounding countryside. Oriental rugs
and wood-burning fireplaces give a cozy feel to both the lounge and
the breakfast room (where a cooked meal is served every morning). The
guest rooms are furnished with antiques and wrought-iron bedsteads;
some have graceful canopy-style nets overhead. **Pros:** quaint accom-
modation and friendly owners. **Cons:** not particularly child-friendly,
showers are on the historic side. ✉ *4 Franklin St.* ☎ *03/6260–2766*
⊕ *www.mrscurrieshouse.com.au* ⤙ *4 rooms* ⌂ *In-hotel: laundry ser-
vice, parking (no fee), no elevator* ▭ *DC, MC, V* ⊚l *BP.*

PORT ARTHUR AND THE TASMAN PENINSULA

102 km (63 mi) southeast of Hobart.

When Governor George Arthur, Lieutenant-Governor of Van Diemen's
Land (now Tasmania), was looking for a site to dump his worst convict
offenders in 1830, the Tasman Peninsula was a natural choice. Joined to
the rest of Tasmania only by the narrow Eaglehawk Neck, the spit was
easy to isolate and guard. Between 1830 and 1877 more than 12,000
convicts served sentences at Port Arthur in Britain's equivalent of Devil's
Island. Dogs patrolled the narrow causeway, and guards spread rumors
that sharks infested the waters. Reminders of those dark days remain
in some of the area names—Dauntless Point, Stinking Point, Isle of
the Dead.

EXPLORING

Fodor'sChoice   **Port Arthur Historic Site.** This property, formerly the grounds of the Port
★   Arthur Penal Settlement, is now a lovely—and quite large—historical
park. Be prepared to do some walking between widely scattered sites.
Begin at the excellent visitor center, which introduces you to the expe-
rience by "sentencing, transporting, and assigning" you before you set
foot in the colony. Most of the original buildings were damaged by
bushfires in 1895 and 1897, shortly after the settlement was abandoned,
but you can still see the beautiful church, round guardhouse, comman-
dant's residence, model prison, hospital, and government cottages.

The old **lunatic asylum** is now an excellent museum, with a scale model
of the Port Arthur settlement, a video history, and a collection of tools,
leg irons, and chains. Along with a walking tour of the grounds and
entrance to the museum, admission includes a harbor cruise, of which

Historic buildings from Tasmania's convict past can be seen in Port Arthor.

there are eight scheduled daily in summer. There's a separate twice-daily cruise to and tour of the **Isle of the Dead,** which sits in the middle of the bay. It's estimated that 1,769 convicts and 180 others are buried here, mostly in communal pits. Ghost tours (reservations are essential) leave the visitor center at dusk and last about 90 minutes. ⊠ *Arthur Hwy.* ☎ *03/6251–2300 or 1800/659101* ⊕ *www.portarthur.org.au* ✉ *1-day entry ticket A$28, Isle of the Dead tour A$12 or included in the 2-day Gold pass A$98, ghost tour A$20 or included in the After Dark pass A$57* ⊙ *Daily 8:30–dusk.*

Tasmanian Devil Park. This is probably the best place in the state to see Tasmanian devils (burrowing carnivorous marsupials about the size of a dog), as well as quolls, boobooks (small, spotted brown owls), masked owls, eagles, and other native fauna. The devils are fed at four times throughout the day; ring the office for times. ⊠ *Arthur Hwy., Taranna* ⟐ *11 km (7 mi) north of Port Arthur* ☎ *03/6250–3230* ⊕ *www.tasmaniandevilpark.com* ✉ *A$19* ⊙ *Daily 9–5.*

WHERE TO EAT AND STAY

$–$$ ✕ **Felons Bistro.** This restaurant at the Port Arthur Historic Site serves
AUSTRALIAN   fresh Tasmanian seafood and game. Appetizers are generally more interesting than the main courses, with fresh local oysters and grilled quail on the menu, though you can't go wrong with the steak of the day. If it's teatime, pop in for one of the exceedingly rich desserts. There is also an inexpensive café in the visitor center. ⊠ *Port Arthur Historic Site, Port Arthur* ☎ *03/6251–2314 or 1800/659101* ▭ *AE, DC, MC, V* ⊙ *No lunch.*

$–$$$ ⊞ **Cascades Colonial Accommodation.** Part of a onetime convict outstation that dates to 1841, the original buildings here have been transformed into luxury accommodations. Each has kitchen facilities with breakfast provisions included. A small museum related to the property is also on-site, and there are some lovely bushwalks on the property— your hosts will welcome you back with some complimentary port. **Pros:** beautifully modernized rustic chic, private beach is stunning. **Cons:** kitchens aren't big enough to whip up a gourmet feast, in peak seasons there is a minimum stay. ⊠ *533 Main Rd., Koonya ✛ 20 km (12 mi) north of Port Arthur* ☎ *03/6250–3873* ⊕ *www.cascadescolonial.com.au* ⥲ *4 cottages* ⌂ *In-room: kitchen. In-hotel: laundry facilities, parking (no fee), no elevator* ⊟ *MC V* ⊺⊙⊦ *CP.*

FREYCINET NATIONAL PARK AND EAST-COAST RESORTS

The east coast enjoy's Tasmania's mildest climate, pristine beaches, and excellent fishing spots. The stretches of white sand here are often so deserted that you can pretend you're Robinson Crusoe. The towns in this region are quiet but historically interesting; in Louisville, for example, you can catch a ferry to the Maria Island National Park, which was a whaling station and penal settlement in the mid-19th century. Farther north, the town of Swansea has numerous stone colonial buildings that have been restored as hotels and restaurants, as well as the unusual Spiky Bridge (so named because of its vertically placed sandstone "spikes") and the convict-built Three Arch Bridge, both of which date from 1845.

The jewel of the eastern coast is Freycinet National Park, renowned among adventure seekers and those who appreciate stunning scenery. The spectacular granite peaks of the Hazards and the idyllic protected beach at Wineglass Bay have been dazzling visitors to this peninsula since it became a park in 1916.

EAST-COAST RESORTS

★ From Hobart the east-coast Tasman Highway travels cross-country to Orford, then passes through beautiful coastal scenery with spectacular white-sand beaches, usually completely deserted, before reaching Swansea. Bicheno, just north of Freycinet National Park, and St. Helens, which is farther north, are both fishing and holiday towns with quiet, sheltered harbors. Taking the four-day guided **Bay of Fires Walk** along the coast north of St. Helens is a wonderful way to enjoy the rugged beauty and tranquility of the coast. The walk, which is about 32 km (20 mi) long, winds along the edge of Mt. William National Park, and allows you to visit stunning beaches, heathlands, Aboriginal sites, and peppermint forests, where a profusion of plant and animal life flourishes. During part of the relatively easy walk you'll stay at an ecologically sound campsite which is as luxurious as it can get, with timber floors and kitchen facilities, and two nights at the dramatic, remote, and ecologically sustainable **Bay of Fires Lodge.** All meals are provided. For details and prices, check out ⊕ *www.bayoffires.com.au.*

OUTDOOR ACTIVITIES

If you're sporty, you'll love Freycinet with its glut of outdoor adventures on land and sea, but even if you're not athletically inclined it's possible to let someone else do the work as you cruise or fly over the bay.

DIVING **Bicheno Dive Centre.** The spectacular coastline and clear, cool-temperate waters make this a great place to go diving. This well-established company offers boat dives twice daily at 9:30 AM and 1:30 PM. They also offer fishing charters targeting flathead, morwong, the elusive Tasmanian striped trumpeter, and tuna when in season. ⊕ *www.bichenodive.com.au.*

HIKING **Wineglass to Wineglass.** This exceptional if expensive tour run by Freycinet Lodge is a 8-km (5-mi) guided walk to Wineglass Bay and then through pristine forests, and it would convert even the most vehement exercise-phobe. The guide is not only informative about the area's history and local animals, he also whips up a mean cup of coffee and brings out morning cakes and biscuits. At the end of the walk you're led to a clearing, where a table beautifully laid out with a white tablecloth is laden with local crayfish and oysters as well as some fine local Pinot Noir and Chardonnay. As if that weren't hedonistic enough, you're then whisked back to the start on a boat, ending the trip in style. ⊕ *www.puretasmania.com.au* ✉ *A$365.*

KAYAKING Freycinet is Tasmania's premier sea-kayaking destination, and it's possible to do guided tours or hire your own kayak and cruise around at your own pace.

Freycinet Adventures. This family-run company offers full-day tours around the peninsula, slowly exploring this spectacular coastline while guides point out local marine life like sea eagles and seals. ⊕ *www.freycinetadventures.com.au* ✉ *Full day tours A$180.*

Trulyaustralia.com. For a longer adventure, this company offers a four-day tour from Hobart, paddling for 3 to 4 hours a day along the pink granite coastline. Check the Web site to see when the tours are running. ⊕ *www.trulyaustralia.com.*

WILDLIFE **Bicheno Penguin Tour.** At Bicheno the nightly hour-long tour to see the WATCHING penguins emerge from the water and clamber up to their nesting area is very popular. ⊕ *www.bichenopenguintours.com.au* ✉ *A$20* ☽ *Dusk.*

WHERE TO STAY

$$–$$$$ ⊡ **Diamond Island Ocean View Apartments.** Located 2½ km (1½ mi) north of Bicheno, this property overlooks the Tasman Sea and has direct beach access. Twelve duplex units, each with two bedrooms, are nestled within 7 acres of landscaped gardens; there are also three smaller one-bedroom units. All have private bathrooms. The resort hosts group tours (for a fee) to see fairy penguins, who come ashore each night after a day of fishing; be sure to reserve a spot when you book your room. **Pros:** minutes from a superb beach, freshly baked bread in kitchen bread maker is a nice touch. **Cons:** rooms are outdated, no daily maid service. ✉ *69 Tasman Hwy., Bicheno* ☎ *03/6375–0100 or 1800/030299*

"We had driven from Friendly Beach further into the Park when we came across this beautiful area." —photo by Gary Ott, Fodors.com member

⊕ *www.diamondisland.com.au* ↝ *26 rooms* ⬧ *In-room: kitchen (some). In-hotel: restaurant, tennis courts, pool, laundry facilities, parking (no fee), no elevator* ▭ *DC, MC, V.*

$–$$ ⊞ **Eastcoaster Resort.** This seaside complex in the town of Louisville is a great jumping-off point for exploring Maria Island National Park; the resort's catamaran, the *Eastcoaster Express*, makes three or four trips a day to the island. There are motel-type rooms here with kitchenettes, and also detached cabins (four of which have hot tubs), as well as a caravan park. The on-site Marlin restaurant specializes in local seafood and Tasmanian wines. **Pros:** family-friendly resort, inexpensive and unpretentious. **Cons:** limited technology and dated decor. ⊠ *Louisville Point Rd., Louisville* ☎ *03/6257–1172* ⊕ *www.eastcoaster.com. au* ↝ *48 rooms, 8 cabins, 30 caravan sites* ⬧ *In-room: kitchen (some). In-hotel: restaurant, tennis court, pools, no elevator* ▭ *DC, MC, V.*

$$ ⊞ **Kabuki by the Sea.** You can look out over Schouten Island and the Hazards from the terraces of the cliff-top inn for some of the most stunning coastal views in the state—then watch the moon rise over Great Oyster Bay while dining at the on-site restaurant offering westernized Japanese food. Cottages are styled as *ryokan* (a traditional Japanese inn), with private sitting and dining rooms and basic kitchen facilities. **Pros:** spectacular views, near Swansea's restaurants. **Cons:** fixtures and fittings are starting to look run-down, staff sometimes absent. ⊠ *Tasman Hwy.* ✛ *8 km (5 mi) south of Swansea* ☎ *03/6257–8588* ⊕ *www. kabukibythesea.com.au* ↝ *5 cottages* ⬧ *In-room: kitchen. In-hotel: restaurant, laundry service, parking (no fee), no elevator* ▭ *AE, MC, V.*

$$-$$$ ⚄ **Meredith House.** Exquisite red-cedar furnishings and antiques decorate
★ this 1853 refurbished residence in the center of Swansea. Comfortable
rooms overlook the tranquil waters of Great Oyster Bay, and are either
in the main house or in adjacent mews-style studio rooms. There are
books and board games to borrow throughout the house, as well as a
computer with free Internet access. **Pros:** excellent service from affable
hosts, superb freshly cooked breakfasts. **Cons:** gets lots of repeat visitors, so you have to book ahead, the mews rooms are not as charming as
the ones in the main house. ⊠ *15 Noyes St., Swansea* ☎ *03/6257–8119*
⊕ *www.meredith-house.com.au* ⇗ *11 rooms* ⬙ *In-room: refrigerator,
kitchen (some). In-hotel: restaurant, parking (no fee), no elevator* ☰ *AE,
MC, V* ⎮◎⎮ *BP.*

FREYCINET NATIONAL PARK

Fodor's Choice *238 km (149 mi) north of Port Arthur, 214 km (133 mi) southwest of*
★ *Launceston, 206 km (128 mi) northeast of Hobart.*

5

The road onto the Freycinet Peninsula ends just past the township of
Coles Bay; from that point the Freycinet National Park begins and
covers 24,700 acres.

EXPLORING

Highlights of the dramatic scenery here include the mountain-size granite formations known as the **Hazards.** On the ocean side of the peninsula there are also sheer cliffs that drop into the deep-blue ocean; views
from the lighthouse at Cape Tourville (reached by a narrow dirt road)
are unforgettable. A series of tiny coves called the Honeymoon Bays
provide a quieter perspective on the Great Oyster Bay side. **Wineglass
Bay,** a perfect crescent of dazzling white sand, is best viewed from the
lookout platform, about a 30-minute walk from the parking lot; if
you're feeling energetic, though, the view from the top of Mt. Amos,
one of the Hazards, is worth the effort. A round-trip walk from the
parking lot to Wineglass Bay takes about 2½ hours. The park's many
trails are well signposted.

Daily entry to the park costs A$11 per person and A$22 per vehicle.

ESSENTIALS

Contact Freycinet National Park (⊠ *Park Office* ☎ *03/6256–7000*).

WHERE TO STAY

$$$ ⚄ **Edge of the Bay.** The views from these modern, minimalist-style beach-
front suites and cottages stretch across Great Oyster Bay to the Hazards.
All have private decks and kitchenettes. The Edge restaurant ($$) uses
Tasmanian produce and serves local wines. Activities like tennis, as well
as bicycles and rowboats for exploring, are all included. **Pros:** animals
wander freely around the resort, idyllic setting. **Cons:** minimum stay
of two nights, restaurant menu is limited and no breakfast is served.
⊠ *2308 Main Rd., Coles Bay* ☎ *03/6257–0102* ⊕ *www.edgeofthebay.
com.au* ⇗ *8 suites, 15 cottages* ⬙ *In-room: kitchen, Wi-Fi. In-hotel:
restaurant, bar, tennis court, beachfront, laundry facilities, parking (no
fee), no elevator* ☰ *AE, MC, V.*

$$$–$$$$ 🖼 **Freycinet Lodge.** These 60 plush cabins are scattered through the
Fodor's Choice densely wooded forest above Great Oyster Bay. They range from rela-
★ tively simple one-bedroom units to "Premier Wineglass cabins," which
have double hot tubs, CD players, and fluffy bathrobes. All have private
balconies, and are outfitted with Tasmanian wood furnishings. The on-
site Bay Restaurant ($$–$$$) has breathtaking sunset views, as well
as an extensive wine list; the more casual Richardson's is the place for
light lunches and coffee, while Hazards Bar and Lounge is a relaxing
place to swap stories or curl up with a book by the open fire. **Pros:**
superb food in fine-dining restaurant, perfect for getting away from it
all; no TVs, phones, or cell reception. **Cons:** utilitarian furniture for
the price, rooms can be on the cold side. ⊠ *Freycinet National Park,
Coles Bay* ☎ *03/6225–7000 or 1800/420155* ⊕ *www.freycinetlodge.
com.au* ⋗ *60 cabins* ⚹ *In-room: no phone, no TV. In-hotel: 2 restau-
rants, bar, tennis court, laundry facilities, parking (no fee), no elevator*
⊟ *AE, DC, MC, V.*

LAUNCESTON

200 km (124 mi) north of Hobart.

Nestled in a fertile agricultural basin where the South Esk and North
Esk rivers join to form the Tamar, the city of Launceston (pronounced
Lon-sess-tun), or Lonie to locals, is the commercial center of Tasma-
nia's northern region. Its abundance of unusual markets and shops is
concentrated downtown (unlike Hobart, which has most of its stores
in the historic center, set apart from the commercial district).

Launceston is far from bustling, and has a notable number of pleasant
parks, late-19th-century homes, historic mansions, and private gardens.
The sumptuous countryside that surrounds the city—rolling farmland
and the rich loam of English-looking landscapes—set off by the South Esk
River meandering through towering gorges, is also very appealing.

EXPLORING

The **Queen Victoria Museum and Art Gallery,** opened in 1891, offers insights
into the city's history including its Aboriginal and colonial past. There's
also a large natural-history collection of stuffed birds and animals
(including the now-extinct thylacine, or Tasmanian, tiger). ⊠ *Welling-
ton St.* ☎ *03/6323–3777* ⊕ *qvmag.tas.gov.au* ⋈ *Free* ☉ *Daily 10–5.*

Almost in the heart of the city, the South Esk River flows through the
exceptionally beautiful **Cataract Gorge** on its way toward the Tamar
River. A 1½-km (1-mi) path leads along the face of the precipices to
the **Cliff Gardens Reserve,** where there are picnic tables, a pool, and a
restaurant. Take the chairlift in the first basin for a thrilling aerial view
of the gorge—at just over 900 feet, it's the longest single chairlift span
in the world. Self-guided nature trails wind through the park, and it's a
great place for a picnic. ⊠ *Paterson St. at Kings Bridge* ☎ *03/6331–5915*
⊕ *www.launcestoncataractgorge.com.au* ⋈ *Gorge free, chairlift A$10*
☉ *Daily 9–4:40.*

Franklin House. Built in 1838 by convicts, this fine Georgian house was
built for a local brewer but is now owned by the National Trust. It's

notable for its beautiful cedar architecture and its collection of period English furniture, clocks, and fine china. Morning and afternoon teas are served in the tearoom. ✉ *413 Hobart Rd., Franklin Village* ☎ *03/6344 7821* 🖂 *A$8* ⊗ *Daily 9 5.*

★ Along both sides of the Tamar River north from Launceston the soil is perfect for grape cultivation. A brochure on the **Wine Route of the Tamar Valley and Pipers Brook Regions**, available from Tasmanian Travel and Information Centre, can help you to plan a visit to St. Matthias, Ninth Island, Delamere, Rosevears, Jansz, Velo, and Pipers Brook wineries. Many establishments serve food during the day, so you can combine your tasting with a relaxing meal.

OUTDOOR ACTIVITIES

There are plenty of opportunities to spot wildlife, fish, or birds in the lovely countryside surrounding Launceston and the Tamar Valley.

BIRD-WATCHING **Tamar Island Wetlands.** This bird sanctuary on the banks of the Tamar River just outside Launceston is the place to see swamp hens and black swans from boardwalks over the wetlands while scanning the sky for white-breasted sea eagles or forest ravens. ✉ *West Tamar Rd., Riverside* ☎ *03/6327–3964* ⊕ *www.parks.tas.gov.au* 🖂 *A$3* ⊗ *Daily dawn to dusk.*

CANOPY TOURS **Hollybank Treetops Adventure.** A new and very popular attraction of particular appeal to kids has visitors gliding along wires on harnesses on this three-hour tour led by guides through the treetops and above the Pipers River. ✉ *66 Hollybank Rd., Launceston* ☎ *03/6395–1390* ⊕ *www.treetopsadventure.com.au* 🖂 *A$99 bookings are essential* ⊗ *Daily 10–5.*

FISHING **Launceston Lakes.** Thirty minutes' drive from the city is picturesque Launceston Lakes, where you'll find five trout-filled lakes set among 900 acres of native bush. Instruction is available for beginners, and prices includes equipment rental. ✉ *1166 Ecclestone Rd., Riverside* ☎ *03/6396–6100* ⊕ *www.launcestonlakes.com.*

RIVER CRUISES **Tamar River Cruises.** This company conducts relaxing trips on the Tamar, past many wineries and into Cataract Gorge. ☎ *03/6334–9900* ⊕ *www. tamarrivercruises.com.au.*

WALKING **Launceston Historic Walks.** This profession outfit conducts a leisurely stroll through the historic heart of the city. Walks leave from the 1842 Gallery. ✉ Corner St. John and Cimitiere Sts., *Launceston* ☎ *03/6331–2213* ⊕ *www.1842.com.au* 🖂 *A$15* ⊗ *Tues.–Sat. at 10, Mon. at 4.*

WILDLIFE-WATCHING **Pepperbush Adventures.** This husband-and-wife team runs tours out of Launceston covering Tasmania's northeast and looking at local wildlife in its natural habitat. The full-day Quoll Patrol takes you to view the "bandit of the Bush," as well as wallabies, platypuses, and, if you're lucky, some devils. ⊕ *www.pepperbush.com.au.*

WHERE TO EAT AND STAY

$$$$ ✕ **Fee and Me.** One of Tasmania's top dining venues, this popular restaurant has won more culinary accolades than you could poke a mixing spoon at. ("Fee" refers to the talented chef, Fiona Hoskin.) Portions are served appetizer size, enabling diners to have a broad spectrum of

Fodor'sChoice
★
AUSTRALIAN

flavors. You might begin your meal here with Tasmanian ocean trout tartare, then choose panfried lambs' brains or twice-cooked pork belly. Three courses are $21 each for course, four courses are $19.50 per course. ✉ *190 Charles St.7250* ☎ *03/6331–3195* ⊕ *www.feeandme. com.au* ⚑ *Reservations essential* ▭ *AE, MC, V* ☾ *Closed Sun. and Mon.* ☾ *No lunch.*

$$ ✕ **Jailhouse Grill.** If you have to go to jail, this is the place to do it, in a
STEAK   130-year-old historic building. Despite being furnished with chains and bars, it was never actually a place for incarceration, so relax and feast on prime beef cuts (or fish and chicken), and an all-you-can-eat salad bar, which is included in the price. The wine list—all Tasmanian—is comprehensive. ✉ *32 Wellington St.7250* ☎ *03/6331–0466* ⊕ *www. jailhousegrill.com.au* ▭ *AE, DC, MC, V* ☾ *No lunch.*

$$$$ ✕ **Stillwater.** Part of Ritchie's Mill (a beautifully restored 1830s flour mill
★   beside the Tamar River), this multi-award-winning restaurant serves
AUSTRALIAN   wonderfully creative seafood dishes, usually with an Asian twist, such as the confit of Petuna salmon loin with miso sauce and ginger-carrot puree. The six-course tasting menu can include wine pairings from the great selection of Tasmanian wines. A produce shop, café, wine bar, and art gallery are part of the same complex. ✉ *2 Paterson St.* ☎ *03/6331–4153* ⊕ *www.stillwater.net.au* ▭ *AE, MC, V.*

$$ ⌂ **Alice's Cottages.** Constructed from the remains of three 1840s build-ings, this delightful B&B is full of whimsical touches. Antique furniture drawers might contain old-fashioned eyeglasses or books; an old turtle shell and a deer's head hang on the wall; and a Victrola and a four-poster canopy bed lend colonial charm. **Pros:** perfect for a romantic getaway, especially the "boudoir"-themed room; spa bathrooms are luxurious and decadent. **Cons:** extra charge for open fires, not child-friendly. ✉ *129 Balfour St.* ☎ *03/6334–2231* ⊕ *www.alicescottages. com.au* ⚑ *9 rooms* ⌂ *In-room: DVD, refrigerator, kitchen. In-hotel: laundry facilities, parking (no fee), no elevator* ▭ *AE, MC, V* ⌂ *BP.*

$ ⌂ **Old Bakery Inn.** History comes alive at this colonial complex made up of a converted stable, the former baker's cottage, and the old bakery. A loft above the stables is also available. All rooms reflect colonial style, with antique furniture and lace curtains. One room in the old bakery was actually the oven. **Pros:** quaint and sensitively restored rooms; great value for money. **Cons:** some noise from busy road; breakfast ends at 9 AM sharp. ✉ *York and Margaret Sts.* ☎ *03/6331–7900 or 1800/641264* ⊕ *www.oldbakeryinn.com.au* ⚑ *24 rooms* ⌂ *In-room: dial up. In-hotel: restaurant, laundry facilities, parking (no fee), no elevator* ▭ *AE, DC, MC, V.*

$$–$$$ ⌂ **TwoFourTwo.** Three contemporary apartments built within a historic Launceston property have all modern conveniences including espresso machines and iPod docks, and feature the wonderful timber design work of Alan Livermore, one of the owners. The city center is but a short stroll away. A small shop on the same site offers an interesting choice of art, souvenirs, and local wines. **Pros:** rooms are stylish and well laid out; plenty of personal touches like fresh flowers and fruit. **Cons:** not particularly child-friendly, no leisure facilities. ✉ *242 Charles St.* ☎ *03/6331–9242* ⊕ *www. twofourtwo.com.au* ⚑ *3 apartments* ⌂ *In-room: kitchen, DVD. In-hotel: laundry facilities, parking (no fee), no elevator* ▭ *AE, DC, MC, V.*

$$$ 🏨 **Waratah on York.** Built in 1862, this grand Italianate mansion has been
★ superbly restored. Spacious modern rooms are tastefully decorated to
reflect the era in which the building was constructed; six rooms have
hot tubs. Many rooms have panoramic views over the Tamar, and the
property is just a quick walk from the city center. Continental breakfast
is served in the elegant dining room. **Pros:** complimentary port in rooms
is a nice touch, helpful staff. **Cons:** a lot of stairs to climb, rooms are on
the dark side. ⊠ *12 York St.* ☎ *03/6331–2081* ⊕ *www.waratahonyork.
com.au* ⌦ *9 rooms* ♨ *In-hotel: restaurant, public Wi-Fi, no kids under
8, no elevator, laundry service, parking (no fee), no-smoking rooms*
▭ *AE, MC, V* ⫶◎⫶ *CP.*

THE NORTHWEST

Tasmania's northwestern region is one of the most beautiful and least
explored areas of the state. For its sheer range of landscapes, from jag-
ged mountain contours to ancient rain forests and alpine heathlands in
the Cradle Mountain area alone, the northwest can't be matched. The
region's beauty saw it designated the Tasmanian Wilderness World Heri-
tage Area, protecting one of the last true wilderness regions on earth.
These regions are a major draw for hikers and sightseers. The western
side of the northwest tip of Tasmania bears the full force of the roaring
forties winds coming across the Indian Ocean, and this part of Tasma-
nia contains some of the island's most dramatic scenery. Mining was a
major industry a century ago, and although some mines still operate,
the townships have a rather forlorn look.

GETTING HERE AND AROUND

This region is not the easiest to get to (the nearest airport is 2 hours
away at Launceston) but the destination is certainly rewarding enough
to make the journey worthwhile. Driving to Cradle Mountain from
Launceston takes 2 hours, and 1½ hours from Devonport. It is possible
to take public transport through coach operator Tassie Link, which
connects the major transportation hubs with Cradle Mountain and
Strahan, but for convenience, nothing beats renting your own car. It
should be noted that the northern part of the Cradle Mountain–Lake
St. Clair National Park (that is, Cradle Mountain itself) is accessed by
roads inland from Devonport and the nearby town of Sheffield. The
southerly Lake St. Clair end of the park, though, is reached by the Lyell
Highway between Hobart and Queenstown at Derwent Bridge.

DEVONPORT AND ENVIRONS

*89 km (55 mi) northwest of Launceston, 289 km (179 mi) northwest
of Hobart.*

In the middle of the North Coast, Devonport is the Tasmanian port
where ferries from Melbourne dock. Visitors often dash off to other
parts of Tasmania without realizing that the town and its surroundings
have many interesting attractions.

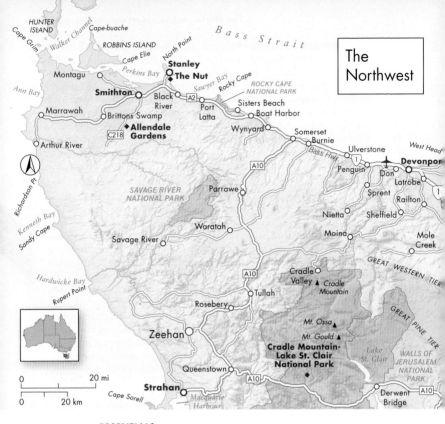

ESSENTIALS

Contact Devonport Visitor Centre (⊠ 92 Formby Rd., Devonport
☎ 03/6424–4466).

WHERE TO EAT AND STAY

$$ ✕ **Pedro's.** Don't expect anything Spanish on the menu despite the name.
SEAFOOD Instead, expect seaside bounty caught fresh and cooked up daily in this
kitchen on the edge of the Leven River. You can relax above the flowing
water while sampling local crayfish, calamari, Tasmanian scallops, floun-
der, or trevally. The take-out fish-and-chips window lets you make a picnic
of your feast in a nearby park. ⊠ *Wharf Rd., Ulverstone* ☎ *03/6425–6663
restaurant, 03/6425–5181 take-out counter* ▭ *MC, V.*

$ ⊞ **Westella House.** This charming 1885 homestead has stunning sea
views. Wood-burning fireplaces in each room, handcrafted banisters
and mantels, and antique furnishings draw you into the cozy setting. A
hearty, home-cooked breakfast starts the day. **Pros:** lovely gazebo in the
garden to sit in and enjoy the views, complimentary sherry goes down
well in winter. **Cons:** on the twee side, far from any restaurants or shops.
⊠ *68 Westella Dr., Ulverstone* ☎ *03/6425–6222* ⊕ *www.westella.com*
↪ *3 rooms* ⚐ *In-hotel: restaurant, laundry facilities, parking (no fee),
no elevator* ▭ *MC, V* ⍟ *BP.*

STANLEY

140 km (87 mi) northwest of Devonport, 430 km (267 mi) northwest of Hobart.

Stanley is one of the prettiest villages in Tasmania, and a must for anyone traveling in the northwest. A gathering of historic cottages at the foot of the Nut, Tasmania's version of Uluru (Ayers Rock), it's filled with friendly tearooms, interesting shops, and old country inns.

EXPLORING

At the atmospheric **Highfield Historic Site** you can explore the town's history at the fully restored Italianate house and grounds where Van Diemen's Land Company, who settled the estate in 1824, once stood. Guides in period costumes are on hand to answer any questions. ✉ *Just outside Stanley, Box 74, Stanley* ☎ *03/6458–1100* ⊕ *www.historic-highfield.com.au* ✉ *A$10* ⊙ *Sept.–May, daily 10–4; June–Aug., weekdays 10–4.*

★ **The Nut,** a sheer volcanic plug some 12.5 million years old, rears up right behind the village. It's almost totally surrounded by the sea. You can ride a chairlift to the top of the 500-foot-high headland, where the views are breathtaking; or, you can make the 20-minute trek on a footpath leading to the summit, where walking trails lead in all directions. ☎ *03/6458–1286 Nut chairlifts* ✉ *Chairlift A$10* ⊙ *Chairlift daily 9:30–5.*

OUTDOOR ACTIVITIES

FISHING **Murray's Day Out.** The exuberant owner will take you on a full day's fishing expedition, providing everything you need including lunch and refreshments. Some of their recommended common fishing spots include Stanley Wharf, Beauty Point, and Garden Island. ☎ *03/6424–5250* ⊕ *www.murraysdayout.com.au.*

WILDLIFE- **Stanley Seal Cruises.** Twice a day, animal lovers can take a 70-minute
WATCHING journey on the motor cruiser Sylvia C. The cruiser takes you offshore to Bull Rock to see Australian fur seals in their natural habitat in Bass Strait. ✉ *Dockside, Stanley* ☎ *03/6458–1295* ⊕ *www.stanleysealcruises.com.au* ✉ *A$40* ⊙ *No tours June–Sept.*

☾ **Wing's Wildlife Park.** This park, 50 minutes' drive from Devonport, has the largest collection of Tasmanian wildlife in Australia, which as well as all the usual suspects includes an aquatic section where you can view albino rainbow trout and Atlantic salmon. Excellent guided tours can be tailored to your interests. ✉ *137 Winduss Rd., Gunn's Plains* ☎ *03/6429–1151* ⊕ *wingswildlife.com.au* ✉ *A$17* ⊙ *Daily 10–4.*

WHERE TO EAT AND STAY

$$ ✕ **Stanley's on the Bay.** Set on the waterfront in the fully restored old
★ Bond Store, this unpretentious restaurant specializes in fine steaks and
AUSTRALIAN seafood. Try the eye fillet of beef—Australian terminology for the top-quality beef cut—topped with prawns, scallops, and fish fillets, served in a creamy white-wine sauce. ✉ *15 Wharf Rd.7331* ☎ *03/6458–1404* ▤ *DC, MC, V* ⊙ *Closed Sun. No lunch July and Aug.*

$$–$$$$ ▥ **Beachside Retreat West Inlet.** These modern, environmentally friendly
★ cabins are set on waterfront sand dunes overlooking the sea. The

180-plus-acre farmland property is also adjacent to protected wetlands, which are perfect for bird-watching (keep an eye out for white-breasted sea eagles) and other wildlife-spotting. Many of the furnishings in the cabins were made by the amenable owners and other local artisans from hand-turned Tasmanian wood. You can relax on your private deck after a morning on the beach and shuck your own oysters for lunch. **Pros:** guests with special needs are well catered to, breathtaking views from cabins. **Cons:** two nights minimum, no food is available on-site. ⊠ *253 Stanley Hwy.* ☎ *03/6458–1350* 🖷 *03/6458–1350* ⊕ *www.beach-sideretreat.com* ⇨ *4 cabins* ♿ *In-room: kitchen, VCR (some), dial-up (some). In-hotel: public Wi-Fi, laundry facilities, parking (no fee), no elevator* ▭ *DC, MC, V* ¶◉¶ *CP.*

$$ **🖪 Touchwood Cottage.** Built in 1840 right near the Nut, this is one of Stanley's oldest homes, and it's furnished with plenty of period pieces. The cottage is known for its doorways of different sizes and its oddly shaped living room. Rooms are cozy, with open fires that add romance. Complimentary afternoon tea is served on arrival. The popular Touchwood crafts shop, where guests receive a discount, and a café are part of the cottage complex. **Pros:** relaxing and romantic play to stay. **Cons:** no baths or leisure facilities. ⊠ *31 Church St.7331* ☎ *03/6458–1348* ⊕ *www.touchwoodstanley.com.au* ⇨ *3 rooms without bath* ♿ *In-hotel: parking (no fee), no elevator* ▭ *MC, V* ¶◉¶ *BP.*

CRADLE MOUNTAIN–LAKE ST. CLAIR NATIONAL PARK

173 km (107 mi) northwest of Hobart to Lake St. Clair at the southern end of the park, 85 km (53 mi) southwest of Devonport, 181 km (113 mi) from Launceston, 155 km (97 mi) northeast from Strahan to Cradle Mountain at the northern end of the park.

Cradle Mountain–Lake St. Clair National Park contains some of the most spectacular alpine scenery and mountain trails in Australia. Popular with hikers of all abilities, the park has several high peaks, including Mt. Ossa, the highest in Tasmania (more than 5,300 feet). The Cradle Mountain section of the park lies in the north. The southern section of the park, centered on Lake St. Clair, is popular for boat trips and hiking. Many walking trails lead from the settlement at the southern end of the lake, which is surrounded by low hills and dense forest. Visitors are advised to park their cars in the free car park and then make use of the shuttle bus that runs from the Cradle Mountain Information Centre and makes stops at all the trails. In summer the bus runs every 15 minutes, in winter every 30 minutes. A vehicle pass costs A$22 per day; if you've traveling without a car the fee is A$11 per person.

One of the most famous trails in Australia, the **Overland Track** traverses 85 km (53 mi) between the park's northern and southern boundaries. The walk usually takes four or five days, depending on the weather, and on clear days the mountain scenery seems to stretch forever. Hikers are charged A$160 to do the Overland during peak walking season (November to April), and Tasmania's Parks and Wildlife Service has provided several basic sleeping huts that are available on a first-come, first-served basis. Because space in the huts is limited, hikers are advised

Looking out across Cradle Mountain–Lake St. Clair National Park.

to bring their own tents. If you prefer to do the walk in comfort, you can use well-equipped, heated private structures managed by Cradle Mountain Huts (☏ 03/6391–9339 ⊕ *www.cradlehuts.com.au*).

ESSENTIALS

Contacts Cradle Mountain Visitor Centre (✉ *4057 Cradle Mountain Rd., Cradle Mountain* ☎ *03/6492–1110*). **Lake St. Clair Visitor Centre** (✉ *Lake St. Clair National Park, Derwent Bridge* ☎ *03/6289–1172*).

OUTDOOR ACTIVITIES

As well as the self-guided day and multi-day walks you can do in Cradle Mountain, there are plenty of opportunities to see the sights from a horse, the air, or even a quad bike.

AIR TOURS **Cradle Mountain Helicopters.** Departing by helicopter from Cradle Mountain village, this flight provides spectacular views over Fury Gorge—Australia's deepest gorge—Cradle Mountain itself, and beautiful Dove Lake. ⊕ *www.adventureflights.com.au* ✉ *A$190.*

FISHING **Venture Fly-fishing Tours.** This Launceston-based company runs fishing tours to Lake St. Clair's fishing lake and St. Clair lagoon, among many other options. ⊕ *www.ventureflyfishing.com.au.*

HIKING **Tiger Wilderness Tours.** This Launceston-based company offers afternoon guided walks to Cradle's glacial lakes and alpine forests with stunning views of Mt. Roland. ⊕ *www.tigerwilderness.com.au* ✉ *A$125.*

HORSEBACK RIDING **Cradle Country Adventures.** There are half-day, full-day, and multi-day rides through stunning natural vistas to choose from that are suitable for both novices and the experienced rider. All equipment, guides, and transfers are included. 🌐 *www.cradlemountainhorseriding.com.au* 🎫 *From A$89 for 2 hours.*

QUAD BIKING **Cradle Mountain Quad Bikes.** All year round you can hire a Suzuki Ozark 250 quake bike and ride it on a special track that winds up through ancient myrtle forest and alpine eucalypt forest. Four-wheel-drives are also available. 🌐 *www.cradlemountainquadbikes.com.au* 🎫 *From A$95 for two hours.*

WILDLIFE-WATCHING **Cradle Mountain Chateau.** Don't miss the dusk Wildlife Spotlight tour run from the Cradle Mountain Chateau. While cruising slowly along for an hour in a 4WD, the fascinating guide will point out the park's nocturnal animals, including wombats, wallabies and—if you're lucky—Tasmanian devils. 🌐 *www.puretasmania.com.au* 🎫 *A$30* ⏲ *Dusk.*

WHERE TO STAY

$$ **Cradle Mountain Chateau.** Five minutes' drive from the entrance to the national park is this corporate-style place—don't be misled by the word chateau—think upmarket lodge. Choose the rustic-style split-level rooms, which face the woods and have perching posts that local birds flock to, though bathrooms are small and could do with an update. There's a great spa that is perfect after a long walk, and an art gallery, too. **Pros:** the excellent dusk safari is unmissable, and the fine-dining restaurant offers delicious meals. **Cons:** only two slow Internet terminals in lobby, can be packed with corporate events, merely adequate breakfast buffet. ✉ *Cradle Mountain Rd., Cradle Mountain* ☎ *1800/420155* 🌐 *www.cradlemountainchateau.com.au* *60 rooms* *In-room: a/c, no phone, refrigerator, DVD. In-hotel: 2 restaurants, bar, gym, spa, laundry service, Internet terminal, parking (free), no-smoking rooms* 💳 *AE, DC, MC, V.*

$$$–$$$$ **Cradle Mountain Lodge.** This wilderness lodge with its collection of cabins is a comfortable place to stay at Cradle Mountain. The high-ceiling guest rooms, two per cabin, are either cheerfully decorated and homey or more contemporary—choose which style you prefer. A couple of walking trails begin at the lodge door. Breakfast is included in your room rate. **Pros:** good range of food options, open fires are a hit in winter. **Cons:** some might rue the lack of home comforts—no room service, TV, or Internet. ✉ *4038 Cradle Mountain Rd., Cradle Mountain* ✢ *60 km (37 mi) from Sheffield* ☎ *03/8296–8010* 🌐 *www.cradlemountainlodge.com.au* *96 rooms* *In-room: CD player (some), no TV, no phone. In-hotel: restaurant, parking (no fee), laundry facilities* 💳 *MC, V* 🍽 *BP.*

Brisbane and its Beaches

WORD OF MOUTH

"The best part about staying [in Mooloolaba] is that is a good base for visiting the Australia Zoo. One day we were there, we made a day trip up to Noosa and explored places en route at a leisurely pace. We also visited the Glass Mountains National Park, with great views of the Hinterlands from its lookout, and hiking trails."

—Diamantina

WELCOME TO BRISBANE AND ITS BEACHES

TOP REASONS TO GO

★ **Experiencing the laid-back vibe:** Queensland's communities have affable, relaxed locals, even at the upmarket hotels and fine-dining restaurants of Brisbane and resort areas.

★ **Enjoying the outdoors:** Choose from rain forests and reefs, unspoiled beaches and islands, rushing rivers, dramatic gorges, distinctive wildlife, hiking, and water sports.

★ **Releasing your inner child:** Queensland's Gold Coast is awash with world-class theme parks—from thrill rides, watery attractions, to Outback-inspired extravaganzas.

★ **Seeing wildlife:** Head out to the southern end of the Reef for millions of fish, rays, turtles, and cetaceans; on the mainland, watch for rare birds and mammals, endangered frogs, dingoes, and koalas.

1 Brisbane. Affectionately dubbed Brisvegas, Queensland's capital city is a breezily cheerful, increasingly sophisticated city with a thriving casino, a riverside cultural complex, and some terrific eateries, nightspots, and markets.

2 The Gold Coast. An hour's drive south of Brisbane, Queensland's first coastal resort has expanded into a busy strip of high-rise hotels, theme parks, casinos, bars, eateries, and nightclubs. If you need a break from the bustle, walk down to the beach and curl your toes in the sand; alternatively, drive west and spend a day (or several) exploring the lush, mountainous hinterland.

3 The Sunshine Coast. This stretch of coastline about an hour north of Brisbane is known for its glorious beaches, fine national parks, and a hinterland dotted with charming townships. In recent years new roads and infrastructure have spurred a boom in accommodations and eateries.

4 Fraser Island. A gigantic sand island off Hervey Bay, Fraser Island has much to offer the active visitor. What it lacks in luxe amenities it makes up for in scenery: miles of white-sand beaches, deep-blue lakes, and bushland bristling with wildlife—including some of the world's most purebred dingoes.

5 Mackay-Capricorn islands. This smattering of coral cays along the southern end of the Great Barrier Reef—including Heron, Wilson, Lady Musgrave, and Lady Elliot islands—shelters significant marine wildlife, including seabirds, turtles, rays, sharks, and millions of tropical fish.

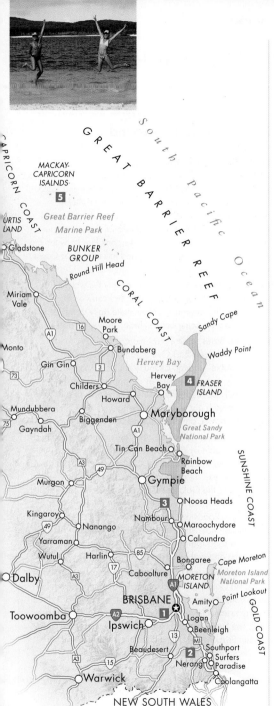

6

GETTING ORIENTED

At 1,727,999 square km (667,180 square mi) and more than four times the size of California, Queensland has enormous geographic variety. Its eastern seaboard stretches 5,200 km (3,224 mi)—about the distance from Rome to Cairo—from the subtropical Gold Coast to the wild and steamy rain forests of the far north. Away from the coastal sugar and banana plantations, west of the Great Dividing Range, Queensland looks as arid and dust-blown as any other part of Australia's interior. Not surprisingly, most of the state's 4 million or so inhabitants reside on the coast; Brisbane and the beach resorts, toward the south of the coast, have experienced dramatic expansion over the past decade. The region's main attractions (apart from the kitschy "Big Things" that dot its highways) are its glorious coastline, the fertile hinterland flanking it, and the reefs and islands that lie offshore.

BRISBANE AND ITS BEACHES PLANNER

When to Go

Temperatures average 15.6°C (60°F) between May and September with chillier nights, and 20 (68°F) to 29°C (80°F) December to February. From December through March, expect heavy rains. Temperatures run slightly cooler inland. Sea- and reef-side Queensland tends to fill up from mid-December through January, and can also be heavily booked in July, September, and Easter. There's no Daylight Saving Time in the state.

Health and Safety

In an emergency, dial 000 to reach an ambulance, the police, or the fire department.

Outdoors, wear a hat and sunscreen whatever the season. Water can be rough; resist anything more than getting your ankles wet without a lifeguard present.

Medical and emergency facilities are basic offshore on the Moreton Bay islands, Fraser Island, and the Mackay-Capricorn Islands. All tour operators recommended here have contingency plans for major medical situations.

Getting Here and Around

Air Travel. Qantas (⊕ www.qantas.com.au), V Australia (⊕ www.vaustralia.com.au), and a number of other carriers fly direct from U.S. cities to Australian capitals and regional tourist hubs. Qantas, Virgin Blue (⊕ www.virginblue.com.au), and Jetstar (⊕ www.jetstar.com.au) link several regional centers throughout Queensland. Budget carrier Tiger Airways (⊕ www.tigerairways.com) flies between the Sunshine Coast and Melbourne, and links the Gold Coast with Melbourne and Adelaide.

Boat Travel. Ferries and charter boats ply the waters between the South-East Queensland mainland and its various islands and offshore resorts. Most make daily or more frequent return trips; some carry vehicles as well as passengers.

Bus Travel. Buses service most major towns and tourist areas around South-East Queensland, and are reliable and affordable—though on many routes it's as cheap, and faster, to fly. In holiday periods on popular routes buses are often heavily booked; buy tickets in advance, and don't expect to stretch out, even on overnight services. Tourist offices can advise on which companies go where.

Car Travel. Traveling outside of cities is often simplest and most comfortable by car. Roads are generally good, but signage varies in clarity; study maps and work out highway exits in advance. Be prepared for heavy traffic between Brisbane and the Gold and Sunshine coasts in peak periods. Expect temporary road closures and detours after heavy rains. Roads are narrow and winding in some parts of the hinterlands. You'll need a 4x4 to get around Fraser Island, the sand islands of Moreton Bay, and some national park roads and outback tracks.

Train travel. Frequent trains service routes between the capital and the Gold and Sunshine coasts. The Queensland Rail network links regional towns and tourist centers, and is a scenic way to travel (though on longer routes it's often cheaper to fly). The Sunlander and high-speed Tilt Train ply the coast between Brisbane and Rockhampton or Cairns, servicing towns that serve as launching pads for island resorts.

Restaurants

The concept of specialized rural cuisines is virtually unknown in Queensland. Steak, seafood, and the occasional Chinese restaurant predominate, apart from tourist hubs. Brisbane, however, has its share of modern Australian, Mediterranean, and Asian-influenced menus capitalizing on fresh regional produce, and the cuisine at many of Queensland's high-end resorts now rivals the standards of big-city fine-dineries. Coastal tourist towns are full of casual open-air restaurants that take advantage of the tropical climate—an increasing number of them helmed by city-class chefs.

Hotels

Accommodations in this state run the gamut from rain-forest lodges, outback pubs, backpacker hostels, and colonial "Queenslander" bed-and-breakfasts—beautiful timber houses built above the ground on stilts, with big wrap-around verandas—to deluxe beachside resorts and big-city hotels. The luxury resorts are clustered around the major tourist areas of the Gold and Sunshine coasts and nearby islands such as Heron and Wilson. In smaller coastal towns accommodation is mostly in motels, apartments, and B&Bs. There are an increasing number of eco-friendly accommodations utilizing green technologies, including waste recycling and water conservation systems, to minimize the impact on their environs: many of Queensland's island resorts fall into this category.

DINING AND LODGING PRICE CATEGORIES (IN AUSTRALIAN DOLLARS)

	¢	$	$$	$$$	$$$$
Restaurants	under A$10	A$10–A$20	A$21–A$35	A$36–A$50	over A$50
Hotels	under A$100	A$100–A$199	A$200–A$299	A$300–A$400	over A$400

Restaurant prices are based on the median main-course price at dinner. Hotel prices are for two people in a standard double room in high season, excluding service and tax (10%).

Bus Tours

Guided day tours are a simple way to see Brisbane if your schedule is tight. View the city's vast sprawl from the comfort of a chauffeured coach, with a driver offering insider information. Buses are also great for covering the relatively short distances between Brisbane and nearly all of the mainland attractions covered in the chapter. Within an hour or two you can be taste-testing your way through the Tambourine or Scenic Rim wineries, or practicing your poker face at a Gold Coast casino.

Most day tours include admission to sights, refreshments, and on full-day tours lunch, as well as commentary en route and time to explore. Australian Day Tours/JPT conducts half- and full-day tours of Brisbane and nearby Moreton Island; one- and two-day trips to and around the Gold Coast, Noosa Heads, and the Sunshine Coast, from A$63–A$379; and a two-day Fraser Island tour for A$429 per person. Greyhound Australia runs daily express coaches to the Gold Coast, as well as day trips that cover southeast Queensland and beyond.

Contacts Australian Day Tours/JPT (☎ 1300–363436 or 07/3489–4666 ⊕ www.australiandaytours.com.au). **Greyhound Australia** (☎ 1300–473946 or 07/5531–6677 ⊕ www.greyhound.com.au).

GOLD COAST TOP AMUSEMENT PARKS

Queensland's Gold Coast is littered with large outdoor theme parks, collectively luring millions of visitors annually with multimillion-dollar thrill rides, waterslides, kids' zones, live shows, and animal attractions.

The Gold Coast's theme parks offer an array of attractions as vast as their acreage. Some, such as WhiteWater World and Wet'n'Wild Water World, draw crowds with massive wave pools, tubes, and waterslides. At others, the attraction is "true-blue Aussie" experiences: Paradise Country has an Outback farm focus with kid-friendly activities, animals, and tours; the Australian Outback Spectacular, a nightly big-budget arena show, highlights jackeroo (Aussie cowboy) skills. Dreamworld excites folk of all ages with high-tech thrill rides and action-packed shows, while Seaworld, a little farther south, has daily dolphin and seal shows and a polar bear park. Some parks double as locations for movies and TV series; Warner Bros. Movie World also has a daily live-action stunt show, wandering cartoon characters, and movie memorabilia. At all six you'll find a glut of merchandising and snack outlets.

BEAT THE CROWDS

The Gold Coast's theme parks are often crowded, especially on weekends and during school holidays. To beat the crowds, arrive early, go midweek, visit on rainy days, or take theme-park excursions in winter, when crowds are thinner but days are often sunny (pools and water-rides are heated).

Pre-buy tickets online (valid for a year), then using the e-ticket express gate. An Early Entry Pass (A$10 extra) lets you enter some parks an hour before opening time (these are limited; book early). Some parks hire out "virtual queueing" devices so you can explore the park while waiting for rides rather than standing in line.

DREAMWORLD

Dreamworld, near the Gold Coast town of Coomera, boasts a vast acreage and the "big six" multimillion dollar, state-of-the-art thrill rides claiming global superiority on various fronts. Here, among the kids' rides, souvenir stalls, and snack-food outlets, you'll find the world's fastest, highest thrill ride, the **Tower of Terror**; the southern hemisphere's tallest high-speed gravity roller coaster; a Guiness-Record-breaking free-fall ride; and what is allegedly the world's largest pendulum, **the Claw**. Dreamworld's latest attraction is a fast and furious race ride involving full-sized replicas of 500cc Moto GP bikes, locked onto a fluid track that lets you tackle tight corners at 70-plus kilometers (40 miles) an hour. Try the **Flowrider**, a mix of surfing and skateboarding, or a surfing lesson in the **Cave of Waves.** The park shelters a group of endangered Bengal and Sumatran tigers, supports one of the largest koala populations in the state, and houses 800-plus native animals in a landscaped sanctuary, viewable up close on the **Sunset Safari.** Don't miss the daily sliming at **Nickolodeon World**.

TIMING

It's tempting to pack both park visits into one day, but unless you're on a super-tight schedule, don't. You'll need a full day to do justice to WhiteWater World's dozens of slides, wave pools, fun zones, and attractions; an equal amount of time to enjoy Dreamworld. Fitting in everyone's activities of choice, queueing, changing, and showering all take time.

6

Virtual queueing with Q4U saves your spot in line for WhiteWater World and Dreamworld's most popular rides, leaving you free to explore (the device gives little reminder beeps). Rides can't be queued for simultaneously, but Q4U still saves you hours. It's A$10 (plus A$5 per person using it) and well worth it.

Pre-book earlybird tickets, Q4U devices, surf lessons, and Flowrider sessions online, as all are limited and sell out fast. A 2-day World Pass, permitting second visits to Dream-world and WhiteWater World within a fortnight, is a smart idea for rainy-day (and cranky-kid) flexibility.

WHITEWATER WORLD

Too hot to traipse around Dreamworld? Pack bathing suits and head to its cooler neighbor, WhiteWater World. The focus of the Gold Coast's latest theme park is aquatic rides and water slides, including **the BRO**, a twisting eight-lane racer slide named after deadly Australian marine critter, the blue ringed octopus, as well as Australia's largest corkscrew-cored whirlpool ride, the A$1.4 million, 26-second **Rip** ride. You can also take a trip on an inner-tube "aquacoaster" known as the **Temple of Huey**; hang five in the **Green Room**, a 65-foot-high "tube" simulating a monster wave's innards; or hone your surfing skills in the **Cave of Waves**, a surfable swell of up to 1.5 meters. Anklebiters will enjoy Nickelodeon's **Pipeline Plunge**, and toddlers can play safely at **Wiggle Bay**. You can even learn to surf here three mornings a week.

SUNSHINE COAST'S TOP BEACHES

Queensland's Sunshine Coast stretches from Caloundra in the south to Noosa Heads in the north. Along it you'll find everything from family-friendly beaches to thundering surf breaks to pretty sheltered coves ideal for snorkeling.

The Sunshine Coast has been developed more slowly and sensitively than its southern counterpart, the Gold Coast. While it has its share of shops, cafés, and resorts, there are still dozens of clean, uncrowded beaches where you can sunbathe, stroll, cast a line, or take the plunge and get in the water to swim, snorkel, and surf.

Some beaches are perfect for water sports such as sailing, windsurfing, kayaking, or wakeboarding. Others are known for their reliable surf breaks. You'll find secluded rocky coves where you can "fossick" (Australian for beachcomb) among rockpools, or don a mask and snorkel and duck beneath the surface to see colorful fish, rays, sea stars, and squid. There are also safe, lifeguard-patrolled swimming beaches with playgrounds, skate parks, kiosks, change rooms, and picnic facilities ideal for families.

WHEN TO GO

The Sunshine Coast is renowned for sunny skies and year-round balmy temperatures, but you can still optimize your experience with some good timing. Beaches can get crowded at peak season, and prices are higher. The most ideal time to visit is early December or March and April (except Easter week and Queensland's week-long fall school break), when crowds are fewer but the weather is still summery. Note that many beaches are only patrolled during peak times. January and February bring the most rain.

SUNSHINE BEACH

Lovely Sunshine Beach, the last easterly-facing beach before Noosa, is patrolled year-round. Beach breaks, reliable swell, a rocky headland sheltering it from winds, and clear, glassy water make Sunshine popular with surfers. When northeast-erlies blow, surf the northern pocket. Fish off the beach year-round for dart, bream, and flathead, or cast a long line into deep water to hook numerous seasonal species. Use covered picnic areas, BBQs, toilets, and parking. From here, hike past nudist-friendly Alexandria Bay to Noosa.

MOOLOOLABA BEACH

This super-safe swimming beach, patrolled year-round, has just enough swell to make it fun. Surfers might want to check out the left-hand break that sometimes forms off the rocks at the northern end. There are shady picnic areas with BBQs, playgrounds, showers, toilets, public phones, exercise areas, and parking—as well as the local meeting point, the Loo with a View. Stroll south along the coastal path to the river mouth and rock wall (off which you can fish, year-round, for bream); north to Alexandra Headland for views of the bay; or along Mooloolaba Esplanade, lined with casual eateries.

COOLUM BEACH

Coolum Beach is family-friendly with a surf club, skate park, playgrounds, change rooms, toilets, kiosk, shorefront parks, and picnic areas. Across David Low Way lie shops, cafés, and restaurants. A long, white-sand beach, Coolum is patrolled year-round, and offers a nice beach break and some decent, uncrowded waves off the headland. Fish from the beach in the evening for jew fish, tailor, bream, and dart; catch bream around the headland, especially in winter. Walk south along the boardwalk to the headland park for magnificent coastal views, or north to quieter Peregian Beach with its patrolled surf, playground, and adjacent Environmental Park.

SAFETY

Most popular Sunshine Coast beaches are patrolled by lifeguards in school holiday and peak periods and on week-ends throughout the warmer months. On some Sunshine Coast beaches sandbanks, strong currents, and riptides make surf conditions challenging. Even on patrolled beaches, swimming unaccompanied is not recommended. Swim between the red-and-yellow flags, and follow lifeguards' direc-tives. Locals are often the best sources of advice on where and when to dive in.

Sharks are rarely a prob-lem; however, lifeguards keep watch and issue warnings if they're sighted. A more constant hazard is the harsh Queensland sun: apply SPF15+ sunscreen at regular intervals. Get infor-mation on local beaches at ⊕ *coastbeaches.com*, and surf reports on Surf Life Saving Queensland's Web site, ⊕ *www.public. lifesaving.com.au.* Con-tact the SLSQ Lifesav-ing Services Manager at ☎ *07/3846–8021.*

6

COASTAL AND WILDERNESS WALKS

Southeast Queensland lays claim to some of the world's most superb wilderness areas, and the best way to explore them is on foot. Behind the Gold and Sunshine coasts are national parks, forests, and nature reserves dense with trails. Several also trace scenic sections of the coastline.

Coastal trails wind along the beachfront, trace rainforest-clad headlands, and meander through waterfront reserves from the Gold Coast to the national parkland north of Noosa.

A string of national parks and wilderness areas connects the Gold and Sunshine coast hinterlands, laced with trails of varying lengths and degrees of difficulty. Walkers are rewarded with memorable sights: dramatic waterfalls and pristine pools, tracts of ancient rain forest, and glowworm caves; wildflowers, wildlife, and exceptional views, some stretching as far as the coast.

SAFETY

For bushwalking you'll need sturdy shoes with grip, a hat, sunscreen, insect repellent, wet- and cold-weather gear, drinking water, food, camping equipment and permits (if overnighting), and a map and compass. Leech-proof yourself by wearing long socks over your pantlegs and carrying a lighter to burn off hitchhikers. Let others know your planned route and timing, even for day hikes.

Over summer's wetter months trails may be muddy or closed. January to March, conditions can be hot. Watch for snakes. The EPA (⊕ *www.epa.qld. gov.au*) provides trail maps, up-to-date information.

QUEENSLAND'S GREAT WALKS

If your schedule allows it, tackle one of Queensland's Great Walks. A A$10 million state government initiative, the Great Walks aim to allow visitors of all ages and of average fitness to explore significant wilderness areas in a safe, eco-sensitive way.

A standout is the 54-km (34-mi) **Gold Coast Hinterland Great Walk,** linking the species-rich, Gondwana Rainforests of Australia World Heritage Area of Lamington and Springbrook plateaus via the glorious Numinbah Valley. En route, you'll traverse ancient volcanic terrain and pristine rain forest, passing torrential streams and waterfalls and 3,000-year-old hoop pines. Allow three days for the full walk, camping at designated sites en route, or trek just one section.

The **Sunshine Coast Hinterland Great Walk,** a 58-km (36-mi) hike traversing the Blackall Range northwest of Brisbane, includes sections of Kondalilla and Mapleton Falls national parks, Maleny Forest Reserve, and Delicia Road Conservation Park. The 4- to 6-day hike takes you past waterfalls and through open eucalypt and lush subtropical rain forest teeming with native birds, reptiles, and frogs.

The **Cooloola Great Walk** meanders through Great Sandy National Park north of Noosa. A 90-km (55-mi) network of graded walking tracks passes the spectacular multi-hued sand dunes of Rainbow Beach, and covers walks of varying distances and difficulty.

Fraser Island Great Walk rewards hikers with exceptional scenery—wide, white-sand beaches, pristine deep-blue lakes, rain-forest tracts, and plenty of birds, reptiles, wallabies, and dingoes.

For downloadable trail maps and detailed information, visit ⊕ *www.epa.qld.gov.au.* For camping information and permits, go to ⊕ *www.qld.gov.au/camping* or phone ☎ *13–1304.*

SHORTER OPTIONS

Coastal Trails. Compact Burleigh Head National Park (☎ *07/5535–3032*), midway between Surfer's Paradise and Coolangatta, includes coastal rain forest and heath that's home to wallabies, koalas, lizards, snakes, and brush turkeys. Trek the 2.8-km (1.75-mi) coastal circuit for excellent views, or the shadier, shorter, 1.2-km (0.75-mi) rain-forest circuit.

Hinterland Trails. Mt. Tamborine, Springwood, Witches Falls-Joalah, and Lamington national parks in the Gold Coast hinterland are all ideal for exploring on foot. Several wilderness retreats in the region offer guided bushwalks as part of the package.

West of the Sunshine Coast, short scenic walking trails in Kondalilla National Park, near Montville, take you past waterfalls, boulder-strewn streams, and lush rain forest teeming with wildlife. Or stroll along easy trails through Mary Cairncross Scenic Reserve, near Montville.

6

Updated by
Merran White

A fusion of Florida, Las Vegas, and the Caribbean, southern Queensland attracts crowd-lovers and escapists alike. Whether you want to surf or soak in the Pacific Ocean, stroll from cabana to casino with your favorite cocktail, hike through subtropical rain forests, or join seabirds and turtles on some pristine coral isle—it's all here.

Local license plates deem Queensland the "Sunshine State," a sort of Australian Florida—a laid-back stretch of beaches and sun where many Australians head for their vacations. The state has actively promoted tourism, and such areas as the Gold Coast, an hour south of Brisbane, and the Sunshine Coast, a roughly equivalent distance north of the capital, have expanded exponentially in recent years, with high-rise buildings, casinos, and beachfront amusements popping up on every block. These thriving coastal strips are the major attraction of southern Queensland for Australians and foreign tourists alike—along with a scattering of islands, notably Fraser Island, off Hervey Bay, and the Mackay-Capricorn islands lying on the southern end of the Great Barrier Reef.

Queensland was thrust into the spotlight when Brisbane hosted the Commonwealth Games in 1982. The World Expo '88 and the 2001 Goodwill Games have ensured that it's remained there. Such big-name competitions exposed Brisbane to the wider world and helped to bring the city, along with other provincial capitals, to social and cultural maturity. Consequently, Queensland is a vibrant place to visit, and Sunshine Staters are far more likely to be city slickers than stereotypical "bushies" who work the land. And, as it is in many regions blessed with abundant sunshine, the lifestyle here is relaxed.

BRISBANE

Founded in 1823 on the banks of the wide, meandering Brisbane River, the former penal colony of Brisbane was for many years regarded as just a big country town. Many beautiful timber Queenslander homes,

GREAT ITINERARIES

IF YOU HAVE 3 DAYS

If you're after a Miami Beach–style holiday, fly into **Brisbane** and head straight for the glitzy **Gold Coast**, overnighting in **Surfers Paradise**. You could end the spree with a final night and day in **Lamington National Park** for its subtropical wilderness and birdlife.

IF YOU HAVE 5 DAYS

Do three days on shore and two days on the reef. Stay a night in **Brisbane**, then head to the **Sunshine Coast** for a hike in the **Glasshouse Mountains** on the way to **Noosa Heads**. Apart from beaches and surf, take in the Sunshine Coast's monument to kitsch, the **Big Pineapple**, and indulge in one of their famous sundaes. Then make your way north to Bundaberg

or Gladstone for a flight to **Lady Elliot, Heron, or Wilson islands to wildlife-watch, dive, and snorkel;** or a ferry to Fraser Island, off Hervey Bay, where you can swim in pristine lakes, 4WD along beaches stretching 50 mi, and see wild dingoes.

IF YOU HAVE 7 OR MORE DAYS

Unless you're keen to see everything, limit yourself to a few areas—**Brisbane**, its surrounding **Sunshine and Gold coasts**, Fraser Island or the coral isles of the Mackay-Capricorn group—taking three to four days to explore each. Extended stays also allow for bushwalking expeditions in national parks, trips to resorts on the reef, traipsing around the wineries of Queensland's **Southern Downs, and enjoying the state's many theme parks**.

built in the 1800s, still dot the riverbanks and suburbs, and in spring the city's numerous parks erupt in a riot of colorful jacaranda, flame tree, and bougainvillea blossoms. Today the Queensland capital is one of Australia's up-and-coming cities: glittering high-rises mark its polished business center, and numerous outdoor attractions beckon. In summer, temperatures here are broilingly hot and days are often humid, a reminder that this city is part of a subtropical region: wear SPF 15+ sunscreen and a broad-brimmed hat outdoors even on overcast days.

Brisbane's inner suburbs, a 5- to 10-minute drive or 15- to 20-minute walk from the city center, have a mix of intriguing eateries and quiet accommodations. Fortitude Valley combines Chinatown with a cosmopolitan influx of clubs, cafés, and boutiques. Spring Hill has several high-quality hotels, and Paddington, New Farm, and the West End in South Brisbane are full of restaurants and bars. Brisbane is also a convenient base for trips to the Sunshine and Gold coasts, the mountainous hinterlands, and the Moreton Bay islands.

GETTING HERE AND AROUND

AIR TRAVEL Brisbane is Queensland's major transit hub. Qantas and Virgin Blue fly to all Australian capital cities and regional hubs around Queensland. Jetstar links Brisbane with the Fraser, Gold, and Sunshine coasts and regional cities farther north.

Brisbane International Airport is 9 km (5½ mi) from the city center. Coachtrans provides a half-hourly bus service to and from Roma Street Station and Brisbane city between 5 AM and 9 PM. Hourly shuttles service Gold Coast hotels, the first leaving the airport at 6 AM; the last at midnight. The one-way fare is A$14 to Brisbane, A$40 to Gold Coast hotels.

Airtrain has rail services to stations throughout Brisbane and the Gold Coast. The one-way fare is A$14 per person, or A$26 round-trip from the airport to City Central. Trains depart up to four times an hour, taking 20 minutes to reach the city center. Taxis to downtown Brisbane cost A$30 to A$50, depending on time of day.

BOAT AND FERRY TRAVEL Speedy CityCat ferries dock at 15 points along the Brisbane River from Apollo Road to the University of Queensland, running half-hourly between 5:30 AM and 11:30 PM. The ferries are terrific for a quick survey of the Brisbane waterfront from the city skyline to luxury homes.

BUS TRAVEL Greyhound Australia, the country's only nationwide bus line, travels to around 1,100 destinations. Bus stops are well signposted, and vehicles usually run on schedule. It's 1,716 km (1,064 mi), a 30-hour journey, between Brisbane and Cairns. Book in person at Greyhound's Roma Street office, by phone, or online. Purchase point-to-point tickets or flexible passes that allow multiple stops.

Crisps Coaches operates a daily service from Brisbane to the Southern Downs and towns to the city's south and west.

TransLink's help line and Web site can help you find bus lines that run to your destination.

RENTAL CAR TRAVEL Most major car-rental companies have offices in Brisbane, including Avis, Thrifty, and Budget. Four-wheel-drive vehicles, motor homes, and camper vans (sleeping two to six people) are available from Britz, Maui Rentals, and KEA Campers. If you're heading north along the coast or northwest into the bush, you can rent in Brisbane and drop off in Cairns or other towns. One-way rental fees usually apply.

Brisbane is 1,002 km (621 mi) from Sydney, a 12-hour drive along the Pacific Highway (Highway 1). Another route follows Highway 1 to Newcastle, then heads inland on the New England Highway (Highway 15). Either drive can be made in a long day, although two days or more are recommended for ample time to sightsee.

TAXI TRAVEL Taxis are metered and relatively inexpensive. They are usually available at designated taxi stands outside hotels, downtown, and at Brisbane Transit and Roma Street stations, although it is often best to phone for one.

TRAIN TRAVEL CountryLink trains make the 14-hour journey between Sydney and Brisbane. Rail services from Brisbane city and airport to the Gold Coast run regularly from 5:30 AM until midnight. The *Sunlander* plies Queensland's coast from Brisbane to Cairns three times weekly, taking 31 hours. Trains departing Sunday and Thursday (returning Tuesday and Saturday) include luxurious *Queenslander*-class carriages with twin-berth sleeping cabins and fine food and wine. Tuesday *Sunlander* services (returning Thursday) don't include *Queenslander* class. The speedy, state-of-the-art *Tilt Train* runs from Brisbane to Rockhampton daily except Saturday; to Bundaberg Monday–Thursday; and to Cairns (a 24-hour trip) Monday and Friday, stopping at Mackay, Proserpine, and Townsville as well as other towns.

Other long-distance passenger trains from Brisbane include the *West-lander,* to and from Charleville (twice weekly); and the *Spirit of the Outback,* to and from Longreach, via Rockhampton (twice weekly). Trains depart from Roma Street Station

TOURS

Australian Day Tours/JPT conducts half- and full-day tours of Brisbane and nearby Moreton Island.CitySights, run by the Brisbane City Council, operates air-conditioned buses that make circuits of city landmarks and other points of interest, including South Bank and Chinatown. They leave from Post Office Square every 45 minutes, starting at 9 AM; last departure is 3:45 PM. You can buy tickets on the bus and get on or off at any of the 19 stops for A$25. At the Brisbane City Council office, pick up a self-guided BrisbaneCityWalk map (also available from tourist information offices and online), as well as brochures and maps detailing other designated Brisbane walking trails.

Kookaburra River Queens are paddle wheelers that run lunch, dinner, tea, and jazz cruises on the Brisbane River. Lunch cruises include scenic and historic commentary; live entertainment and dancing are highlights of dinner cruises. The weekend seafood and carvery buffet dinner cruise is especially popular. Tours run A$20–A$85 per person.

Energetic visitors might want to scale Brisbane's Story Bridge for a 360-degree city overview; a climbing tour with **Story Bridge Adventure Climb** takes 2½ hours and costs A$89–A$99 per person.

ESSENTIALS

Airport Info and Transfers Airtrain (☎ 07/3216–3308 ⊕ www.airtrain.com.au). **Brisbane International Airport** (✉ Airport Dr., Eagle Farm ☎ 07/3406–3191 or 07/3406–3000 ⊕ www.bne.com.au). **Coachtrans** Australia (☎ 07/3358–9700 ⊕ www.coachtrans.com.au).

Boat and Ferry Info CityCat ferries (☎ 13–1230 ⊕ www.translink.com.au).

Bus Info Crisps Coaches (✉ Warwick Transit Centre ☎ 07/4661–8333 ⊕ www.crisps.com.au). **Greyhound Australia** (✉ Brisbane Transit Centre, Roma St., City Center ☎ 1300/473946 ⊕ www.greyhound.com.au). **TransLink** (☎ 13–1230 ⊕ www.transinfo.qld.gov.au).

Currency Exchange Commonwealth Bank of Australia (✉ 240 Queen St., City Center ☎ 13–2221 ⊕ www.commbank.com.au).

Rental Cars Britz Australia Campervan Hire and Car Rentals (✉ 647 Kingsford Smith Dr., Eagle Farm ☎ 07/3868–1248 or 1800/331454 ⊕ www.britz.com. au). **KEA Campers** (✉ 348 Nudgee Rd., Hendra ☎ 1800/252555 or 07/3868–4500 ⊕ www.keacampers.com). **Maui Australia Motorhome Rentals and Car Hire** (✉ 647 Kingsford Smith Dr., Eagle Farm ☎ 1300/363800 or 07/3630–1153 ⊕ www.maui.com.au).

Taxis Black and White Cabs (☎ 13–1008 or 13–3222 ⊕ www.blackandwhite-cabs.com.au). **Yellow Cab Co** (☎ 13–1924 ⊕ www.yellowcab.com.au).

Tour Operators Australian Day Tours/JPT (⊠ *Level 3, Brisbane Transit Centre, Roma St., City Center* ☎ *07/3489–6444 or 1300/363436* ⊕ *www.daytours.com. au*). **Kookaburra River Queens** (⊠ *Eagle Street Pier, 1 Eagle St., City Center* ☎ *07/3221–1300* ⊕ *www.kookaburrariverqueens.com*). **Story Bridge Adventure Climb** (☎ *1300/254627* ⊕ *www.storybridgeadventureclimb.com.au*).

Trains Queensland Rail (QR) Travel Centre Traveltrain Holidays (⊠ *305 Edward St., City Center* ☎ *07/3235–1323 or 1300/131722* ⊕ *www.qr.com.au*).

Visitor Info Brisbane City Council (⊠ *266 George St., City Center* ☎ *07/3403–8888, 13/0013–4199* ⊕ *www.ourbrisbane.com, www.brisbane.qld.gov.au, or www.citysights.com.au*).

EXPLORING

Brisbane's city-center landmarks—a mix of Victorian, Edwardian, and slick high-tech architecture—are best explored on foot. Most lie within the triangle formed by Ann Street and the bends of the Brisbane River. Hint: streets running toward the river are named after female British royalty; those parallel to the river after male royalty. The well-tended South Bank precinct has riverfront parklands and cultural centers, al fresco cafés, and weekend markets. Upriver, the quiet, leafy suburb of Fig Tree Pocket is home to Brisbane's best-known koala sanctuary.

TOP ATTRACTIONS

❷ **Lone Pine Koala Sanctuary.** Queensland's most famous fauna park, founded
Fodor's Choice in 1927, is recognized by the *Guinness Book of World Records* as the
★ world's first and largest koala sanctuary. The attractions for most people
ⓒ are the koalas (more than 130 in all), although emus, wombats, crocs, bats, and lorikeets also reside here. You can hand-feed baby kangaroos in the free-range 'roo and wallaby enclosure, have a snake wrapped around you, or cuddle a koala (and have your photo taken with one for A$15, until 4:30). There's also a thrice-daily sheepdog show and a new birds of prey flight show. The **MV** *Mirimar* (☎ *07/3221–0300 or 0412/749–426*), a historic 1930s ferry, travels daily to Lone Pine Koala Sanctuary from the Cultural Centre pontoon beside Victoria Bridge, departing at 10 sharp (board from 9:30 AM), departing Lone Pine at 1:30 and returning to the city at 2:45 (A$50 round-trip, including entrance to the sanctuary). Bus 430 from Platform B4, Queen Street Bus Station, and Bus 445 from Stop 40 on Adelaide Street also stop at the sanctuary. Taxis cost about A$30 from the city center, from which it's around 11 km (6.5 mi) to the sanctuary. ⊠ *708 Jesmond Rd., Fig Tree Pocket* ☎ *07/3378–1366, 1300/729742 ferry* ⊕ *www.koala.net* ☑ *A$28* ⊙ *Daily 8:30–5.*

❾ **Queensland Cultural Centre.** This is really a collection of centers and facili-
Fodor's Choice ties: the Queensland Museum South Bank and Sciencentre, the State
★ Library of Queensland, and the Queensland Performing Arts Centre
ⓒ (QPAC) are all here, as well as the Queensland Art Gallery and, a short stroll away, the Gallery of Modern Art (GoMA). There's also a host of restaurants, cafés, shops selling quality gifts, art posters, books and cards, a ticketing agent (within QPAC), public-access computer terminals, and various public spaces. The Centre houses significant art,

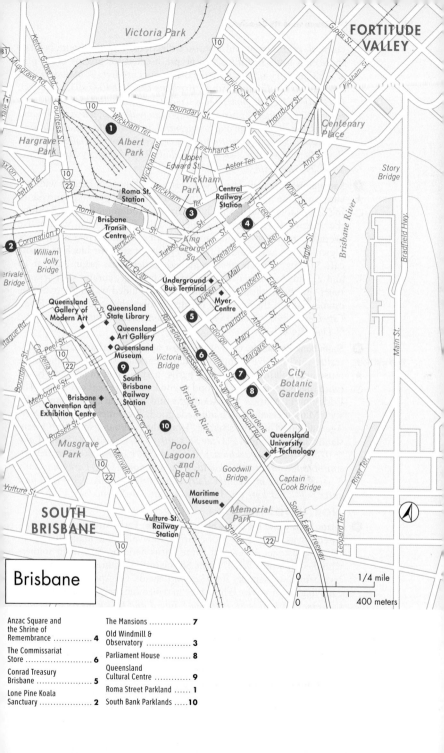

Brisbane

cultural, indigenous, and historic collections. Ninety-minute behind-the-scenes tours of QPAC can be pre-booked for groups of 20-plus at A$8 per person; library and gallery tours are free. ✉ *Melbourne St. at Grey St, Southbank., South Brisbane* ☎ *07/3840–7303 (galleries), 07/3840–7555 (museum), 07/3840–7810 (library), 07/3840–7482 performing arts center* ⊕ *www.qag.qld.gov.au (galleries), www.southbank. qm.qld.gov.au (museum and Sciencentre), www.slq.qld.gov.au (library), www.qpac.com.au (performing arts center)* ⊡ *Free* ☉ *Galleries weekdays 10–5, weekends 9–5; museum daily 9:30–5; library Mon.–Thurs. 10–8, Fri.–Sun. 10–5.*

❶ ★ ☼ **Roma Street Parkland.** The world's largest subtropical garden within a city is a gentle mix of forest paths and structured plantings surrounding a fish-stocked lake. Spot birds, lizards, and unique artworks along the walkways. Highlights include the Lilly Pilly Garden, with native evergreen rain-forest plants; and interesting children's play areas. Pack a picnic, take advantage of the free grills, or stop for lunch at on-site café Melange. Free hour-long guided garden tours begin daily at 10 and 2, and there are also specialist art, heritage, curator's, or sensory tours (pre-book these); brochures for self-guided walks are available online or from the Spectacle Garden Infobooth. ✉ *1 Parkland Blvd., City Center* ☎ *07/3006–4545* ⊕ *www.romastreetparkland.com* ⊡ *Free* ☉ *Daily 24 hrs.*

❿ Fodor'sChoice ★ ☼ **South Bank Parklands.** One of the most appealing urban parks in Australia, this massive complex includes parklands, shops, a maritime museum, walking and cycling paths, a sprawling man-made beach (with lifeguards), a carved-wood pagoda, and excellent city views. The Friday-night Market by Moonlight and weekend South Bank Lifestyle Market bristle with handmade goods, live entertainers, and New Age pundits. The park stretches along the riverbank south of Queensland Cultural Centre. ✉ *Grey St. south of Melbourne St., South Bank* ☎ *07/3867–2051 (parklands), 07/3844–5361 (museum)* ⊕ *www.visit-southbank.com.au* ⊡ *Parklands free, museum A$8* ☉ *Parklands daily 5 AM–midnight, info center daily 9–5, museum daily 9:30–4:30 (last entry 3:30), markets Fri. 5 PM–10 PM, Sat. 10–5, Sun. 9–5.*

WORTH NOTING

❹ **Anzac Square and the Shrine of Remembrance.** Paths stretch across manicured lawns toward the Doric Greek Revival shrine made of Queensland sandstone. An eternal flame burns here for Australian soldiers who died in World War I. In the Shrine of Remembrance, a subsurface crypt stores soil samples from key battlefields. On April 25, Anzac Day, a moving dawn service is held here in remembrance of Australia's fallen soldiers. ✉ *Adelaide St. between Edward and Creek Sts., City Center* ⊡ *Free* ☉ *Shrine weekdays 9–2.*

NEED A BREAK? Duck down Elizabeth Street to the locally owned American Book Store. In the back, **Caffe Libri** serves coffee, cakes, and extravagant sandwiches. The bookstore carries literary fiction, academic, design, and foreign-language titles, and has been run by the same family for more than 50 years.

Lone Pine Koala Sanctuary, Brisbane.

✉ **197 Elizabeth St., City Center** ☎ **07/3229–4677 or 1800/177395** ⊕ **www. americanbookstore.com.au** ▭ **AE, DC, MC, V.**

❻ **The Commissariat Store.** Convict-built in 1829 on the site of the city's original timber wharf, this was Brisbane's first stone building. It has served variously as a customs house, storehouse, and immigrants' shelter, and is currently the headquarters of the Royal Historical Society of Queensland. The RGSQ library and museum, open to visitors, hold exhibitions, historical documents, manuscripts, and artifacts dating back to Brisbane's early colonial days. ✉ *115 William St., City Center* ☎ *07/3221–4198* ⊕ *www.queenslandhistory.org.au* ▱ *A$5* ⊙ *Tues.– Fri. 10–4.*

❺ **Conrad Treasury Brisbane.** This Edwardian baroque edifice overlooking the river stands on the site of military barracks from the original penal settlement, flanked by bronze statuary. Constructed between 1885 and 1889, the former treasury reopened as a **hotel, casino, and entertainment complex.** In addition to three floors of gaming, the casino houses six eateries and five bars. ✉ *Queen St. Mall, at William and Elizabeth Sts., City Center* ☎ *07/3306–8888 or 1800/506888* ⊕ *www.conradtreasury.com.au* ▱ *Free* ⊙ *Daily 24 hrs.*

❼ **The Mansions.** Constructed in 1890, these Victorian terrace homes are a good place to cool off in warm weather. Few buildings like this were build this far north (more of this type of architecture prevailed especially in Melbourne); elegant, wrought-iron lace trim garnishes the exterior. inside are bookshops, a National Trust gift shop, and a restaurant. ✉ *40 George St., City Center* ☎ *07/3221–9365* ⊕ *www.brisbanelivingheritage.org.*

Modern sculpture at the Queensland Cultural Centre, South Bank, Brisbane.

❸ Old Windmill & Observatory. This 1828 construction is the oldest remaining convict-built structure in Brisbane, dubbed the "Tower of Torture" by convicts forced to power a treadmill to crush the colony's grain on windless days. When fire razed part of the city in 1864 the windmill survived, later repurposed as an observatory. Stripped of its blades, the tower now resembles a lighthouse. ⊠ *Wickham Park, Wickham Terr., City Center* ☎ *07/3403–5048.*

❽ Parliament House. Opened in 1868, this splendid, stone-clad, French Renaissance building with a Mount Isa copper roof earned its colonial designer a meager 200-guinea (A$440, or US$370) fee. A legislative annex was added in the late 1970s. The interior is fitted with polished timber, brass, and frosted and engraved glass. There are free half-hour tours weekdays on demand, when Parliament is not in session (when it is, you're welcome to watch from the public gallery). The adjacent, kid-friendly City Botanic Gardens have native and exotic plants and themed areas, including the Bamboo Grove and Weeping Fig Avenue, along with sculptures and ponds. ⊠ *George and Alice Sts., City Center* ☎ *07/3406–7562* ⊕ *www.parliament.qld.gov.au/home.asp* ⌦ *Free* ⊙ *Parliament House weekdays 9–5 (last tour 4 PM), weekends 10–2 (last tour 1:15 PM), gardens daily 24 hrs.*

OUTDOOR ACTIVITIES

ADVENTURE Kangaroo Point cliffs, near the city center, are ideal for climbing and abseiling. You can canoe or kayak on the Brisbane River; and numerous scenic bushwalking, climbing, and abseiling sites lie less than 90 minutes' drive from Brisbane. Government-run Outdoors Queensland

(⊕ *www.qorf.org.au*) gives regional information and lists businesses offering adventure activities from hiking to horse riding.

Adventures Around Brisbane (☎ *1800/689453 or 0421/152147* ⊕ *www. adventuresaroundbrisbane.com.au* ✉ *A$75 (A$25 Wed.) 3-hour rock-climbing session, A$65 2-hour sunset abseil, A$95–A$109 day tours*) runs daily rock-climbing and abseiling sessions off Kangaroo Point cliffs, day and moonlight canoe tours along the Brisbane River, and bushwalks and adventure daytrips to the scenic Glass House Mountains and Mt. Tinbeerwah.

Riverlife Adventure Centre (✉ *Naval Stores, via Lower River Terrace or River Terrace, Kangaroo Point* ☎ *07/3891–5766* ⊕ *www.riverlife.com. au* ✉ *A$45–A$79*) runs guided rock-climbing and abseiling sessions off Kangaroo Point cliffs, cycling tours around Brisbane attractions, day and night kayaking trips on the Brisbane River (followed by prawns and drinks or a barbecue), skate lessons and rollerblade hire, and indigenous culture experiences. A highlight is the Mirrabooka Aboriginal Cultural Experience, which includes a traditional performance by the Yuggera Aboriginal Dancers and hands-on instruction in fire-starting, instrument-playing, boomerang-throwing, and painting, plus food-tasting.

OUTDOOR GEAR OUTFITTERS

Australian-owned**Paddy Pallin** (✉ *108 Wickham St., Fortitude Valley* ☎ *07/3839–3811* ⊕ *www.paddypallin.com.au*) sells quality outdoor and travel gear, including hats, footwear, clothing, backpacks, and equipment. On staff are dedicated bushwalkers, rockclimbers, and travelers. The store is open Monday–Friday 9 AM–5:30 PM, Saturday 9–5, and Sunday 10–4.

WATER SPORTS

A half-hour's drive east of Brisbane city brings you to Moreton Bay, stretching 125 km (78 mi) from the Gold Coast to the Sunshine Coast. A number of operators based in Brisbane's bayside suburbs—Manly, Redcliffe, Sandgate—run sailing, diving, sightseeing, and whale- and dolphin-watching trips around the Bay, and trips to its various islands. Some cruises include tours of St. Helena Island's historic prison ruins; others visit Moreton Island, where you can toboggan down massive sand-dunes.

Moreton Bay Escapes (☎ *1300/559355* ⊕ *www.moretonbayescapes. com.au*) runs tours and charters around Moreton Bay Marine Park and Moreton Island National Park that might include sailing, 4WD-driving, snorkelling, and sand-boarding. They'll also tailor excursions to incorporate hiking, scuba-diving, sea-kayaking, birdwatching, and swimming with dolphins.

BIKING

An extensive network of bicycle paths crisscrosses Brisbane. One of the best paths follows the level Bicentennial Bikeway southeast along the Brisbane River, across the Goodwill Bridge, then along to South Bank Parklands or Kangaroo Point cliffs.

The **Brisbane City Council** (⊕ *www.brisbane.qld.gov.au*) includes downloadable maps and lets you search for bikeways. As of press time, from March 2010 you'll be able to pick up free Council bikes from designated points around the city, dropping them off when you're done. **Gardens Cycle Hire** (☎ *0408/003198* ⊕ *www.cyclebrisbane.com*), on Alice Street, hires out bicycles for A$18 for an hour or A$42 a day, less for longer periods. For A$10 extra they'll deliver a rental bike to your hotel.

GOLF **St. Lucia Golf Links and Golf World** (✉ *Indooroopilly Rd. at Carawa St., St. Lucia* ☎ *07/3870–7084*) is an 18-hole, par-70 course open to visitors; greens fees are A$28 for 18 holes on weekdays, A$33 weekends, and half price on Mondays. Dine on-site at the Clubhouse or 100 Acre Bar (☎ *07/3870–3433*) overlooking the 18th green.

TENNIS Contact **Tennis Queensland** (✉ *190 King Arthur Terrace, Tennyson* ☎ *07/3120–7900* ⊕ *www.tennis.com.au*) for information about court hire, guided tours of the adjacent, ultra-modern **Queensland Tennis Centre,** and details on tournaments.

WHERE TO EAT

In the past decade Brisbane has transformed from a culinary backwater into a city full of inventive dining options. Top chefs have decamped to Brisbane's best eateries, and are busy putting put a fresh sub-tropical spin on Modern Australian, pan-Asian, and Mediterranean cuisine.

Imaginative dishes capitalize on abundant regional produce: fine fresh seafood—notably the local delicacy, Moreton Bay bug (a sweet-fleshed crustacean)—premium steak, Darling Downs lamb, cheeses, macadamia nuts, avocadoes, olives, and fruit, matched with fine regional wines.

Most of the city's hip cafés and smart fine-dineries are clustered in the West End, Fortitude Valley, New Farm, and Petrie Terrace; you'll also find some excellent eateries in the city center and the riverfront South Bank precinct, and a smattering around the suburbs, particularly Rosalie, Paddington, Milton, and Ascot. For terrific fresh seafood, head for Brisbane's bayside suburbs, such as Manly, Redcliffe, and Sandgate, or to South Stradbroke Island.

Typically, dining ambience is relaxed, seating is alfresco, and well-mannered children are welcomed.

Use the coordinate (✛ B2) at the end of each listing to locate a site on the corresponding map.

$$$ ✕**Breakfast Creek Hotel.** A Brisbane institution, this enormous hotel is STEAK perched on the wharf at Breakfast Creek. National Heritage–listed interiors and a lush tropical beer garden are as much of a draw as its superb trademark steaks. Non-steak eaters also have plenty of options, including vegetarian dishes and terrific fresh oysters. ✉ *2 Kingsford Smith Dr., Albion* ☎ *07/3262–5988* ⊕ *www.breakfastcreekhotel.com* ▤ *AE, DC, MC, V* ✛ *C1.*

$ ✕**Caxton Thai.** This unassuming restaurant, where you dine flanked by THAI Thai art and sculpture, is popular with locals and tourists. The most requested dish is the pork chop stir-fried with chili and basil; or try the coral trout fillet with chili-tamarind sauce. Other than these, it's mostly traditional; find curries, soups, plenty of vegetarian options, and many noodle dishes, including a warm Thai salad (a mix of chicken, prawns, glass noodles, and vegetables). ✉ *47B Caxton St., Petrie Terrace* ☎ *07/3367–0300* ⊕ *www.caxtonthai.com.au* ▤ *AE, DC, MC, V* ☾ *No lunch* ✛ *A1.*

$$$

Fodor'sChoice

★

AUSTRALIAN

✕ **e'cco.** Consistently ranked among the best restaurants in town, this petite eatery serves innovative food to a loyal following. The white-columned entry leads into a warm-toned dining room with an open kitchen and bar. Seasonally changing Mediterranean and Asian-inspired dishes incorporate premium local produce. Start with grilled quail or duck terrine, follow it with seared ocean trout or wagyu rump steak. Each seasonal dessert selection is equally delectable: lemon and ricotta torte, passion-fruit panna cotta, chocolate assiette. There's no sommelier, but waiters can suggest accompanying wines. ⊠ *100 Boundary St., City Center* ☎ *07/3831–8344* ⊕ *www.eccobistro.com* ⌕ *Reservations essential* ⊟ *AE, DC, MC, V* ⊘ *Closed Sun. and Mon. No lunch Sat.* ✢ *D1.*

$$

★

✕ **Freestyle Tout.** Tucked away in an inner-city suburb, this gallery-café is famous for its 20 beautiful desserts—including artfully designed sundaes, fruity tarts, sticky tortes, and a memorable white-chocolate raspberry brioche. The all-day dining menu now includes interesting Mod Oz mains as well as café-style fare. The A$30 set lunch menu, for instance, offers a choice of pan-fried barramundi or grain-fed eye fillet, with dessert and a glass of premium wine; the three-course set dinner is A$50. You can also take high tea here. The Australian artwork displayed is often for sale. ⊠ *Shop 50,1000 Ann St., Fortitude Valley* ☎ *07/3252–0214* ⊕ *www.freestyletout.com.au* ⊟ *AE, DC, MC, V* ✢ *A2.*

$$

VIETNAMESE

✕ **Green Papaya.** The small selection of simple dishes here is beautifully prepared from 90% local ingredients (including certified organic meat, poultry, and rice) in modern classic Vietnamese style. Among the most popular choices are grilled lemon-myrtle prawns, seafood stir-fry, turmeric fish, and Emperor pork. Cocktails have an Asian twist (A$14), and set menus (A$55–$85 per head) come with or without matched wines. ⊠ *898 Stanley St., at Potts St., East Brisbane* ☎ *07/3217–3599* ⊕ *www.greenpapaya.com.au* ⊟ *AE, DC, MC, V* ⊘ *Closed Mon. No lunch except Friday (pre-book for Friday lunch and Sundays)* ✢ *D3.*

$$

AUSTRALIAN

✕ **The Gunshop Café.** Named for its previous business, this West End café is the place to go for breakfast on weekends (the potato-feta hash cakes with spinach, house-dried tomato, and herbed sour cream are locally famous). Unfinished brick walls where guns once hung lend a rustic ambience. Dine around wooden tables near the open kitchen or request a seat out on the sidewalk. A select but eclectic Mod-Oz menu fuses Mediterranean and Asian flavors in dishes featuring premium Margaret River lamb, Angus beef, duck, and seafood; they also do vegetarian dishes and exciting salads. Foodies flock here for lunch, dinner, or even just a coffee and dessert; the flourless chocolate cake and passion-fruit-curd tart is particularly memorable. ⊠ *53 Mollison St., West End* ☎ *07/3844–2241* ⊕ *www.thegunshopcafe.com* ⊟ *AE, DC, MC, V* ⊘ *Closed Sun., except breakfast, and Mon.* ✢ *A3.*

$$

AUSTRALIAN

✕ **Luxe.** This casual restaurant-cum-bar serves delicious tapas-style starters and seasonally changing dishes with a Euro-Mediterranean edge. Sample the Lobster "thermidor style," king snapper fillet with confit fennel, bok choy, sesame seeds, and ginger dressing, or beef fillet with wild mushroom gratin. The crème brûlée is delicious, and the wine and

6

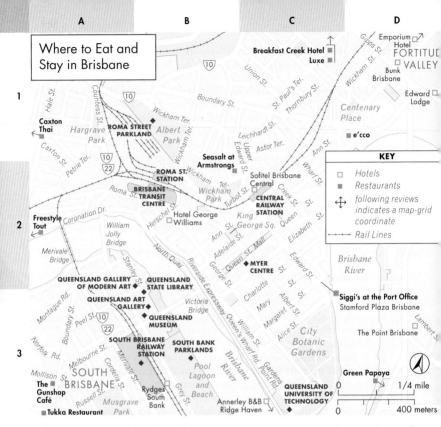

A   B   C   D

Emporium Hotel

FORTITUDE VALLEY

Gloss St.

Wickham St.

Breakfast Creek Hotel ■

Luxe ■

Bunk Brisbane

Edward Lodge

1

Hale St.

Countless St.

10

Boundary St.

Union St.

St. Paul's Ter.

Thornbury St.

Wickham St.

Centenary Place

Caxton Thai

Hargrave Park

Wickham Ter.

ROMA STREET PARKLAND

Albert Park

Leichhardt St.

Astor Ter.

Ann St.

■ e'cco

← Caxton St.

Petrie Ter.

10

Roma St.

Wickham Ter.

Edward St.

Upper Edward St.

Seasalt at Armstrongs ■

Sofitel Brisbane Central ■

Wharf St.

Creek St.

KEY

10 22

ROMA STREET STATION

BRISBANE TRANSIT CENTRE

Wickham Park

Turbot St.

CENTRAL RAILWAY STATION

□   Hotels

■   Restaurants

2

Freestyle Tout ■

Coronation Dr.

William Jolly Bridge

Herschel St.

Hotel George □ Williams

King St.

George Sq.

Queen St.

⊕   following reviews indicates a map-grid coordinate

Merivale Bridge

Stanley St.

North Quay

Ann St.

Adelaide St.

George St.

Queen St. Mall

Elizabeth St.

┅┅┅   Rail Lines

Brisbane River

QUEENSLAND GALLERY OF MODERN ART ◆

QUEENSLAND STATE LIBRARY ◆

QUEENSLAND ART GALLERY ◆

Victoria Bridge

Charlotte St.

Mary St.

Albert St.

Edward St.

♦ **MYER CENTRE**

Siggi's at the Port Office ■
Stamford Plaza Brisbane

QUEENSLAND MUSEUM ◆

Riverside Expressway

Queen's Wharf Rd.

William St.

Margaret St.

Alice St.

Lambert St.

The Point Brisbane

3

Norfolk Rd.

Montague Rd.

Boundary St.

Peel St.

10 22

Melbourne St.

SOUTH BRISBANE RAILWAY STATION

Merivale St.

Cordelia St.

SOUTH BANK PARKLANDS

Brisbane River

City Botanic Gardens

Mollison St.

SOUTH BRISBANE

The ■ Gunshop Café

Russell St.

Rydges South Bank

Grey St.

Pool Lagoon and Beach

Annerley B&B □

Point Rd.

Gardens Point Rd.

Green Papaya ■

0   1/4 mile

■ **Tukka Restaurant**

Musgrave Park

Ridge Haven ◆

QUEENSLAND UNIVERSITY OF TECHNOLOGY

0   400 meters

seasonal cocktail lists are impressive. In nice weather, try for a table on the sidewalk. ⊠ *1/39 James St., Fortitude Valley* ☎ *07/3854–0671* ⊕ *www.luxerestaurant.com.au* ☐ *AE, MC, V* ⊕ *C1.*

$$ ✕ **Seasalt at Armstrongs.** Well-known local chef Russell Armstrong works

AUSTRALIAN   seafood magic at this popular 45-seat restaurant. Choices include "freelance fish"—the day's freshest catch, generally pan-seared and served to suit the chef's mood. You could also have the mixed seafood grill or a tender roast fillet of Lockyer Valley beef. ⊠ *73 Wickham Terrace, City Center* ☎ *07/3832–4566* ☐ *AE, DC, MC, V* ☽ *Closed Sun. except breakfast. No lunch weekends* ⊕ *B2.*

$$$ ✕ **Siggi's at the Port Office.** Socialites rub shoulders with celebrities at this

MODERN   charming restaurant and champagne bar in the Stamford Plaza Bris-

AUSTRALIAN   bane. Service is impeccable; decor capitalizes on the 19th-century Port of Brisbane Office architecture. Monthly five-course degustation menus showcase premium local seafood and seasonal produce, and might feature barramundi, duck, or truffles. Opt for the matched wines. The à la carte menu's ever-changing continental dishes could include ocean trout confit or slow-cooked Wagyu beef cheeks. Dessert might be a lemon tart or Siggi's signature crêpes suzette à deux, prepared at the table. There's a tapas menu for balcony and bar patrons, a tea room open during the day, and an extensive wine list. ⊠ *39 Edward St., City Center*

☎ *07/3221–1999* ⊕ *www.stamford.com.au* ➔ *Reservations essential*
🖙 *AE, DC, MC, V* ☺ *Closed Sun. and Mon. No lunch* ✛ *C3.*

$$ ✕ **Tukka Restaurant.** Earth-tone walls lined with Aboriginal artworks

AUSTRALIAN are a fitting backdrop for chef owner Stéphane Diémont's imaginative
"gourmet Australian" cuisine: seared wallaby, kangaroo, or emu fillet,
croc tail, possum, and mud crab. Leave room for dessert, perhaps the
native spiced poached pear or lemon aspen parfait with cinnamon figs.
The wine list showcases top vintages from boutique wineries around
Australia. You can also buy jams, spices, sauces, and chutneys to take
home. ✉ *145 Boundary St., West End* ☎ *07/3846–6333* 🖙 *AE, DC,*
MC, V ☺ *No dinner Sun.* ✛ *A3.*

WHERE TO STAY

Twenty years ago Brisbane's accommodation options consisted of a
few big hotels and some welcoming but nondescript motels and B&Bs.
These days the inner-city area fairly bristles with luxury hotels and smart
serviced-apartment complexes. There are also a few excellent boutique
hotels, some cut-above B&Bs, and modern backpacker hotels giving
pricier digs a run for their money. Many have good-value packages and
seasonal and last-minute specials: go online for the best deals.

Use the coordinate (✛ B2) at the end of each listing to locate a site on
the corresponding map.

¢–$ 🏨 **Bunk Brisbane.** This terrific backpacker joint is close to the cafés, bars,
★ and attractions of Fortitude Valley. Choose from air-conditioned four-,
six-, and eight-bed dorms; private single, double, and triple rooms;
and loft-style, self-contained studios. All except singles have en-suite
bathrooms; dorms also have lockers, privacy screens, fresh linen and
duvets, and individual bedside lights. Well-maintained on-site facili-
ties include lounge areas with plasma TVs, a lively bar and restaurant
(famous for its Sunday barbecues), a pool area, and an on-site travel
agency–tour desk. There's also a well-equipped guest kitchen and laun-
dry, a pool and hot tub, and a policy against big, noisy groups. **Pros:**
tight security; printing, CD-burning, iTunes and Skype services; cheap
food on-site. **Cons:** can be crowded. ✉ *Ann and Gipps Sts., Fortitude*
Valley ☎ *07/3257–3644 or 1800/682865* ⊕ *www.bunkbrisbane.com.au*
⚐ *In-room: no phone (some), kitchenette (some), refrigerator (some), no*
TV (some), Internet. In-hotel: restaurant, bar, pool, laundry facilities,
Internet terminal, public Wi-Fi (fee), parking (fee), airport shuttle (8
AM*–8* PM*, no fee), no kids under 18 in dorms* 🖙 *MC, V* ✛ *D1.*

$ 🏨 **Edward Lodge.** This affordable inner-suburban sanctuary is set in Asian-
★ style tropical gardens, close to cafés, New Farm Park, and the CityCat
ferry. Each air-conditioned one-bedroom studio has handcrafted Asian
furnishings and is handily appointed with a refrigerator, microwave
oven, and TV; suites have full kitchens. **Pros:** free broadband Internet
access; guest kitchen and laundry; vibrant area. **Cons:** 20 minutes from
the city; no room service. ✉ *75 Sydney St., New Farm* ☎ *07/3358–2680*
⊕ *www.edwardlodge.com.au* ⚑ *9 rooms, 1 suite* ⚐ *In-room: no phone,*
kitchenette, refrigerator, TV, Wi-Fi (free). In-hotel: bicycles, laundry
facilities, Wi-Fi (free) 🖙 *AE, MC, V* ℗⦿ *CP* ✛ *D1.*

6

$$$$
Fodor'sChoice
★
⊞ **Emporium Hotel.** Billing itself as a luxury boutique hotel, this modern establishment is furnished with distinctive pieces sourced from around the world. Customized, individually finished suites have kitchenettes, laundry facilities, and luxe bathrooms with Molton Brown toiletries, as well as workstations, LCD TVs, Bose sound systems, and balconies. Some suites also have separate lounge areas and spa baths. The staff routinely go beyond the call of duty, and thoughtful touches include complimentary newspapers and the loan of GHD hair stylers. All manner of extras are also available, from chocolate-dipped strawberries on arrival to a rose-petal-and-champagne turndown service and in-suite massages. **Pros:** superb decor; terrific facilities; exceptional service. **Cons:** downstairs restaurant not at the same level of excellence; outside the city center. ⊠ *1000 Ann St., Fortitude Valley* ☎ *07/3253–6999 or 1300/883611* ⊕ *www.emporiumhotel.com.au* ☞ *102 suites* ⏚ *In-room: kitchenette, refrigerator, DVD, Wi-Fi (fee). In-hotel: room service, bar, pool, gym, laundry facilities, laundry service, Internet terminal, Wi-Fi (fee), parking (fee)* ▤ *AE, D, DC, MC, V* ⫪◯⫩ *EP* ⊹ *D1.*

$
⊞ **Hotel George Williams.** This modern hotel is right in the heart of the city, 150 yards from Brisbane Transit Center. Rooms and one suite are simply furnished and appointed, though some have private terraces, and all have Wi-Fi access. The on-site restaurant-bar 325 on George serves modern Australian fusion food showcasing local produce, and has two alfresco dining areas. **Pros:** close to Brisbane Transit Centre; fast Internet; ecofriendly. **Cons:** small rooms; fee to use adjoining YMCA gym; access to carpark difficult. ⊠ *317–325 George St., City Center* ☎ *07/3308–0700 or 1800/064858* ⊕ *www.hgw.com.au* ☞ *106 rooms* ⏚ *In-room: refrigerator, Ethernet (fee). In-hotel: restaurant, room service, bar, laundry facilities, laundry service, public Ethernet (fee), parking (fee), no-smoking rooms* ▤ *AE, DC, MC, V* ⫪◯⫩ *BP* ⊹ *B2.*

$$$
★
⊞ **The Point Brisbane.** Across the river from the central business district, this modern hotel on picturesque Kangaroo Point has great city skyline and river views from each balcony. Accommodations include studios, two-bedroom apartments, and executive suites (including customized "women's suites"), all with fast broadband access, free in-house movies, and cable TV. Suites and apartments have fully equipped kitchens and laundries. The gym, refurbished in late 2006, has state-of-the-art equipment. The hotel runs a courtesy shuttle bus to the city on weekday mornings, and there's a ferry stop 100 yards away. **Pros:** terrific on-site facilities; free secure parking; wheelchair- and women-friendly suites. **Cons:** a commute from the city; fee (A$24.95 per day) for in-room Internet access. ⊠ *21 Lambert St., Kangaroo Point* ☎ *07/3240–0888 or 1800/088388* ⊕ *www.thepointbrisbane.com.au* ☞ *106 rooms* ⏚ *In-room: safe, minibar, kitchen (some), Internet, Wi-Fi. In-hotel: restaurant, room service, bar, tennis court, pool, gym, laundry service, public Internet, public Wi-Fi, parking (no fee), no-smoking rooms* ▤ *AE, DC, MC, V* ⊹ *D3.*

$$$
★
⊞ **Rydges South Bank.** Sandwiched between South Bank Parklands and the Brisbane Convention and Exhibition Centre, within walking distance of numerous attractions, this hotel is an excellent choice if location's your focus. There are seven styles of accommodation, from guest

rooms to family suites. Rooms were given a refurbishment in 2007 and now have sleek earth-toned furnishings and computer workstations with fast Internet access. Suites have separate lounge areas; some rooms and suites have balconies. Although there's no pool, the artificial beach at South Bank Parklands is within easy walking distance. **Pros:** friendly, helpful staff; good buffet breakfast. **Cons:** steep fees for Internet and parking. ⊠ *9 Glenelg St., at Grey St., South Brisbane* ☎ *07/3364–0800* ⊕ *www.rydges.com/southbank* 🛏 *240 rooms, 64 suites* ♿ *In-room: kitchen (some), refrigerator, DVD (some), Ethernet (fee). In-hotel: 2 restaurants, room service, bar, gym, spa, laundry facilities, laundry service, public Internet, public Wi-Fi, parking (A$24 daily), no-smoking rooms* ▭ *AE, MC, V* ⊹ *B3.*

$$$
★ 🛏 **Sofitel Brisbane Central.** Despite its position above the city's main rail station, this hotel is a quiet and pleasant place to stay. Completely refurbished in 2005, with a restaurant renovation and a new day spa in 2007, the establishment has a brand-new look that begins with its wood-paneled lobby. The spacious rooms and suites have marble bathrooms (suites have separate baths and showers), and what are advertised as "the world's most comfortable beds." (We think that might not be too far from the trruth.) On floors 26 through 29, the pricier executive floors, the rate includes breakfast, hors d'oeuvres, cocktails, and sweets in a club lounge. The 30th floor—with sweeping views across the city—is an ultrahip lounge with plasma TVs and sleek decor, attracting a commensurate type of clientele. **Pros:** prompt, pleasant service; great bathroom amenities; legendary high teas (A$38). **Cons:** short-staffed front desk, especially in the morning. ⊠ *249 Turbot St., City Center* ☎ *07/3835–4444* ⊕ *www.sofitelbrisbane.com.au* 🛏 *409 rooms, 20 suites* ♿ *In-room: safe, kitchen (some), refrigerator, Internet (fee). In-hotel: restaurant, room service, bars, pool, gym, spa, laundry service, executive floor, public Internet, public Wi-Fi, parking (fee), no-smoking rooms* ▭ *AE, DC, MC, V* ⊹ *C2.*

$$–$$$ 🛏 **Stamford Plaza Brisbane.** This refined riverfront hotel next to the City Botanic Gardens offers a retreat from the city. The soaring lobby, with its floral arrangements, artwork, sweeping timber staircase, and expanses of glass, is inviting and overlooks a leafy courtyard. Guest rooms, decorated in neoclassical style, enjoy clear views over the river and have flat-screen TVs. Four dining spots include the hotel's signature restaurant, Siggi's, and lively Kabuki, considered the city's best teppanyaki restaurant. Arguably the most famous of the many celebrities who've stayed here is HM Queen Elizabeth II, who visited in 2002. **Pros:** upmarket dining options; friendly service; bathroom LCD TVs. **Cons:** plumbing noise from adjacent rooms; expensive parking; pricey breakfasts with slow service. ⊠ *Edward and Margaret Sts., City Center* ☎ *07/3221–1999 or 1800/773700* ⊕ *www.stamford.com.au/spb* 🛏 *232 rooms, 20 suites* ♿ *In-room: safe, kitchen (some), refrigerator, DVD (some), Wi-Fi (fee). In-hotel: 4 restaurants, room service, bars, pool, gym, spa, laundry service, public Internet, public Wi-Fi, parking (fee), no-smoking rooms* ▭ *AE, DC, MC, V* ⊹ *C3.*

6

NIGHTLIFE AND THE ARTS

The Saturday edition of the *Courier–Mail* newspaper lists live gigs and concerts, ballet, opera, theater, jazz, and other events in its *ETC* section. Friday's paper includes a free *Ultimate Weekend Guide,* Brisbane's most comprehensive entertainment guide. Or go to ⊕ *www.news.com.au/couriermail.*

The Heritage-listed **Brisbane Powerhouse** (✉ *119 Lamington St., New Farm P07/3358–8600 box office; 07/3358–8622 reception* ⊕ *www.brisbanepowerhouse.org*), built in a former power plant, hosts live performances in flexible 200- and 400-seat theaters and art exhibits. Cafés, restaurants, bikeways, boardwalks, and picnic areas complement the funky art space. A 2007 renovation added a new café-bar, a roof terrace, and enlarged theater spaces.

> ## EARTH'S FASTEST MOVING ISLAND
>
> Thirty-five km (20 mi) offshore is Moreton Island, the fastest-moving island on Earth. The 38-km-long (23-mi-long) mass is shifting at an estimated 3¼ feet a year toward the Queensland coast. Attractions include tobogganing down sand dunes, bird-watching, water sports, and cetacean- and dugong-watching. You can also hand-feed wild dolphins after dusk at Tangalooma Island Resort (☎ *07/3637–2118* or *1300/652250* ⊕ *www.tangalooma.com*). Camping within Moreton Island National Park is possible (A$4.85 per person permit; info available at ⊕ *www.qld.gov.au/camping*).

Conrad Treasury Casino (✉ *Queen Street Mall at George St., City Center* ☎ *07/3306–8888*) —with a "neat and tidy" dress code geared toward securing an upscale clientele—is a European-style casino. Open 24 hours, the facility has more than 80 gaming tables with 60 games and more than 1,300 machines, as well as six restaurants and six bars.

Cru Bar + Cellar (✉ *James St. Market, 22 James St., Fortitude Valley* ☎ *07/3252–2400* ⊕ *www.crubar.com*) is sleek and sophisticated, with leather ottomans, a long onyx bar, a French chandelier circa 1800, and a fine-wine-loving clientele. Cru's huge cellar houses hundreds of top Australian vintages, to drink on-site or later. Cheese tasting plates all day.

SHOPPING

DEPARTMENT STORES The renowned **David Jones** (✉ *Queens Plaza, 149 Adelaide St., City Center* ☎ *07/3243–9000* ⊕ *www.davidjones.com.au*), downtown in the Queen Street Mall, is open daily until 6 PM (7 PM Thurs., 9 PM Fri.).

Myer (✉ *Myer Centre, 91 Queen St., City Center* ☎ *07/3232–0121* ⊕ *www.myer.com.au*), also in Queen Street Mall, is open daily until 5.30 PM (9 PM Fri.).

Historic **MacArthur Central** (✉ *Edward and Queen Sts., City Center* ☎ *No phone*), the WWII headquarters of General Douglas MacArthur, houses boutiques and specialty shops, a food court, and a museum.

Fun and lively **Queen Street Mall** (✉ *City Center* ☎ *07/3229–5918* ⊕ *www.queenstreetmall.com*), considered the best downtown shopping

State library, Queensland Cultural Centre.

area, attracts numerous buskers and around 26 million visitors a year. Nearly a third of a mile long, the mall incorporates five major shopping centers, including the Myer Centre, Wintergarden, and new Queens-Plaza, as well as two large department stores, Myer and David Jones, and four arcades: historic Tattersall's Arcade and MacArthur Central, Heritage-listed Brisbane Arcade, and Broadway on the Mall, all housing designer boutiques and specialty stores.

For more information on shopping in Brisbane, visit ⊕ *www.ourbrisbane.com/shopping*.

MARKETS The **Brisbane Powerhouse** (⊠ *119 Lamington St., New Farm* ☎ *07/3358–8600* ⊕ *www.brisbanepowerhouse.org*) hosts a farmers' market (all produce) from 6 AM to noon on the second and fourth Saturday of the month. Afterwards, stroll through nearby New Farm Park. At the **Riverside Markets** (⊠ *Riverside Centre, 123 Eagle St., City Center* ☎ *07/3780–2807* ⊕ *www.riversidemarkets.com.au*), an upscale arts-and-crafts bazaar, you can buy everything from pressed flowers to hand-painted didgeridoos and home-made treats. It's open Sunday 8–4.

AUSTRALIAN PRODUCTS The **Woollongabba Art Gallery** (⊠ *613 Stanley St., Woolloongabba* ☎ *07/3891–5551* ⊕ *www.wag.harryscollar.com*) represents indigenous and contemporary artists. Works cost between A$50 and A$10,000, and come with certificates of authenticity. It's open Wednesday–Saturday 11 AM–6 PM.

WINERY TOURS FROM BRISBANE: SOUTHERN DOWNS

From Brisbane, Granite Belt is 225 km (140 mi) west, Mount Tamborine is 62 km (39 mi) southwest, and Scenic Rim wineries are around 135 km (85 mi) southwest.

If the Brisbane cityscape has given you a thirst for pastoral rolling hills—and fabulous wine—you're in luck, because some of Queensland's best viticultural regions lie within a two-hour drive of the city.

Drive two hours west on the Cunningham Highway and you'll reach the Southern Downs, where spring brings the scent of peach and apple blossoms; fall finds the region's 50-plus vineyards, concentrated around Stanthorpe, ripe for harvest; and winter is ideal for wine-country excursions. This area, extending from Cunninghams Gap in the east to Goondiwindi in the west, Allora in the north to Wallangarra in the south, is known as the Granite Belt.

The local Italian community pioneered viticulture here, planting the first Shiraz grapes in 1965. Today the Granite Belt is the state's largest wine region, with nearly 2,000 acres under vines and more than 50 cellar doors, most attached to family-run and boutique wineries. Thanks to its altitude (2,500–4,000 feet above sea level) and decomposed-granite soils, the region enjoys unique growing and ripening conditions, enabling the production of outstanding, full-bodied reds and extra-crisp whites.

Just over an hour's drive southwest of Brisbane, inland from the Gold Coast, you'll find the world's largest caldera and one of the state's most exciting emerging wine regions: the Scenic Rim. The region's rich volcanic soils, first planted with vines in the late 19th century, now produce fine red and white varieties. On the region's easterly edge, you'll find a dozen wineries and a distillery within a compact area around Mount Tamborine.

GETTING HERE AND AROUND

Driving yourself is an option but may not be the best idea if you plan to skip the spit-bucket on your tasting stops. However, for the self-guiders out there, the Granite Belt and Scenic Rim tourism boards provide downloadable maps. Find Granite Belt winery and walking trails at ⊕ *www.granitebeltwinecountry.com.au*, and Scenic Rim winery and trail maps at ⊕ *www.ipswichtourism.com.au*.

Arguably, the safest way to sample the offerings of the region's wineries is via guided tour. More than half a dozen companies run tours of wineries in the Scenic Rim and Mount Tamborine areas, but most require groups of at least six people. Family-run Cork 'n Fork Winery Tours is an exception, running daily and overnight viticultural tours for couples and small groups to Mount Tamborine and the Scenic Rim. Their popular full-day tour (A$130 per person) includes hotel pick-ups from the Gold Coast or Brisbane, lunch, and five winery visits with guided tastings.

Local operators Granite Highlands Maxi Tours runs half-day, full-day, weekend, and customized tours of Granite Belt wineries.

ESSENTIALS

Guided Tours Cork 'n Fork Winery Tours (☎ 07/5543–6584 ⊕ www.corknfork. com.au). **Granite Highlands Maxi Tours** (✉ 19 Amosfield Rd., Stanthorpe, ☎ 07/4681–3969 ⊕ www.maxitours.com.au).

WINERIES

In the tiny town of Glen Aplin, 235 km (146 mi) southwest of Brisbane, is **Felsberg Winery.** Known for red and white wines (including an award-winning Merlot) made from hand-picked grapes grown at 850 meters, and honey mead, this Granite Belt winery has a tasting room inside a German-inspired château, with hilltop views over the Severn River valley and Granite Belt area. Guided tours are available on request. ✉ *116 Townsends Rd., Glen Aplin* ☎ *07/4683–4332* 🖃 *Free* ⊙ *Daily 9:30–4:30.*

Just south of Glen Aplin is the town of Ballandean, home to award-winning **Ballandean Estate Wines**, the oldest family-owned and -operated vineyard and winery in Queensland. The first grapes were grown on the Granite Belt site in 1931, and the tasting room is the original brick shed built in 1950. The Barrel Room Cafe behind it—with massive, 125-year-old wooden barrels lining one wall—serves light lunches and coffee. There are 45-minute tours of the facility daily at 11, 1, and 3. ✉ *354 Sundown Rd., Ballandean* ☎ *07/4684–1226* ⊕ *www.ballandeanestate.com* 🖃 *Free* ⊙ *Daily 9–5.*

Normanby Wines is a friendly, family-run winery-vineyard established a decade ago. All its wines—including many medal winners—are made from grapes grown on the property. There are 16 from which to choose, including Verdelho, Shiraz, Durif, Chaumbourcin, rosé, Veraz, Merlot, Viognier, and traditional fortified varieties. Taste and buy them at the cellar door, then wander through the vineyard and native gardens or enjoy a barbecue under the trees. Guided vineyard tours are available for a small extra charge, if staff are available. ✉ *178 Dunns Ave., Harrisville* ☎ *07/5467–1214* ⊕ *www.normanbywines.com.au* 🖃 *A$3 (tasting fee)* ⊙ *Daily 10–5; 10–7 (Dec.–Feb).*

Sirromet Wines at Mount Cotton. Queensland's largest winery sits midway between Brisbane and the Gold Coast. Sirromet's much-lauded wines—distinctive reds, crisp whites and some terrific blended varieties—can be sampled at their impressive cellar door, along with tasting plates for two. Award-winning on-site restaurant Lurleens, open for breakfast, lunch, morning and afternoon teas, and dinner (Thursday through Saturday), has an alfresco dining area with stupendous views to Moreton Bay. Live jazz livens things up on weekend afternoons. ✉ *850–938 Mount Cotton Rd., Mount Cotton* ☎ *07/3206–2999* ⊕ *www.sirromet. com* 🖃 *Tastings (up to 8 wines) A$5; guided tours from A$20* ⊙ *Cellar door daily 10–4.*

6

EXPLORING

☼ **Girraween National Park.** One of the most popular parks in southeast Queensland, Girraween National Park sits at the end of the New England Tableland, a stepped plateau area with elevations ranging from 1,968 to 4,921 feet. The 17 km (11 mi) of walking tracks, most starting near the information center and picnic area, wind past granite outcrops, giant boulders, eucalyptus forests, and wildflowers in spring. Along the way you might encounter kangaroos, echidnas, brush-tailed possums, and turquoise parrots. To camp, you'll need a permit from the Queensland Parks and Wildlife Service. ⊠ *Ballandean ✢ 11 km (7 mi) north of Wallangarra or 26 km (16 mi) south of Stanthorpe, off the New England Hwy.* ☎ *1300/130372 park info, 13–1304 permits* ⊕ *www.epa.qld.gov.au.*

OUTDOOR ACTIVITIES

GUIDED
GOURMET
BUSHWALKING
Hidden Peaks Walks operates small-group three- and four-day guided hikes through the World Heritage-listed national parks and private nature reserves of the Scenic Rim, camping for one or two nights and staying one night at Peppers Spicers Peak Lodge (complete with 7-course degustation dinner). This is a one-of-a-kind, upmarket, all-inclusive outdoor adventure, geared for eco-friendly appreciation of the Australian bush. ⊠ *10613 Cunningham Hwy. , Maryvale* ☎ *1300/773425* ⊕ *www.hiddenpeaks.com.au* ⌑ *A$1,500 per person (3 days), A$1,800 (4 days)* ☯ *Depart Mon. and Sat., Mar.–Nov.*

WHERE TO STAY

$$$$ ⌖ **Peppers Spicers Peak Lodge.** If you're looking for an exclusive, all-inclusive mountain retreat with an entire mountaintop to itself and the views to match, look no further. Accommodation is in luxuriously appointed suites, three with hot tubs, eight with stone fireplaces, and all with complimentary mini-bars. Warm, muted colours echo the stone, timber, tin, and glass of the architect-designed lodge. Nightly seven-course degustation dinners are a highlight. The focus here is on relaxation, helped along by blazing log fires, extensive lounge areas, a library with a billiard table, a massage room and hot tub, a telescope for stargazing, and an open bar. Guests keen to work off all that food and wine can do so in the heated pool or on the sunken tennis court, mountain-biking trails, and guided walks. **Pros:** meals included in room rates; world-class restaurant with terrific wine list; cordon bleu breakfasts; thoughtful, impeccable service. **Cons:** pricey, albeit worth it; must book months ahead. ⊠ *Wilkinsons Rd., Maryvale* ☎ *1300/773452* ⊕ *www.peppers.com.au* ⌑ *10 suites, 2 lodges* ⌂ *In-room: phone, refrigerator, kitchenette (some), DVD, CD. In-hotel: restaurant, room service, bar, pool, tennis court, no-smoking rooms* ⊟ *AE, DC, MC, V* ⦿ *AI.*

$–$$ ⌖ **Vineyard Cottages and Café.** Built around a turn-of-the-20th-century
Fodor's Choice church that's now the Vineyard Café, this property has four cottages
★ and a row of two-story terrace houses set amid two acres of gardens, two blocks from Ballandean village. The charming lodgings, built in the 1990s in a style that complements the rustic church, are furnished with comfortable sofas, colonial antique furniture, and vases brimming

with roses from the gardens. The one-bedroom cottages (which have in-room hot tubs big enough for two) and terraces can sleep four people; and the two-story, two-bedroom cottage accommodates up to seven. The guests' lounge has an open fireplace, bar, library, and games. Chef Janine Cumming, who co-owns the property with husband Peter, varies her menus seasonally to showcase fresh local produce, and does a great gourmet hamper on request. **Pros:** good food and wine; warm ambience; comfortable. **Cons:** far from city attractions. ⊠ *New England Hwy., near Bents Rd., Ballandean* ☎ *07/4684–1270* ⊕ *www.vineyard-cottages.com.au* ⇴ *4 cottages, 3 terraces* ⚠ *In-room: no a/c (some), no phone, kitchen (some), refrigerator, DVD. In-hotel: restaurant, public Internet, room service, bar, no-smoking rooms* ▭ *AE, DC, MC, V.*

THE GOLD COAST

Three hundred days of sunshine a year and an average temperature of 24°C (75°F) ensure the popularity of the Gold Coast, the most developed tourist destination and one of the fastest-growing regions in Australia, with plenty of amusement complexes and resorts. Easter weekend and December through the last week of January and Australian school holidays are peak seasons. Around 80 km (50 mi)—an hour's drive—south of Brisbane, the Gold Coast stretches some 70 km (43 mi) from Labrador in the north to Coolangatta-Tweed Heads in the south, and has now sprawled as far inland as Nerang. It has around three dozen patrolled beaches and 446 km (277 mi) of canals and tidal rivers, nine times the length of the canals of Venice.

6

GETTING HERE AND AROUND

Gold Coast Airport, also known as Coolangatta Airport, is the region's main transit point.

Access Hope Island via bridges from the west (Oxenford and Coomera) or from the eastern, coastal side (via Paradise Point, Hollywell, and Runaway Bay). Route 4, the Oxenford–Southport Road, begins in Oxenford at the Pacific Motorway's (M1's) Exit 57 and travels through Hope Island on its way to Hope Harbour, on the coast.

Driving distances and times from the Gold Coast via the Pacific Highway are 859 km (533 mi) and 12–13 hours to Sydney, 65 km (40 mi) and less than an hour to Brisbane's outskirts, and 1,815 km (1,125 mi) and 22 hours to Cairns.

The Gold Coast begins 65 km (40 mi) south of Brisbane. The Pacific Motorway, or M1, bypasses Gold Coast towns, but well-marked signs guide you to your destination. If you're coming from Brisbane International Airport by car, take the toll road over Gateway Bridge to avoid traversing Brisbane, then follow the signs to the Gold Coast.

Queensland Rail service connects Brisbane to Coomera, Helensvale, Nerang, and Robina stations on the Gold Coast from 5:30 AM until midnight. Alight at Coomera or Helensvale for the theme parks and northern suburbs; Nerang for Surfer's Paradise; and Robina for Main Beach and all suburbs south of it. From rail stations, cabs and shuttle buses ferry visitors to nearby beaches, tourist centers, theme parks, and the airport. From any of these stations, it's a short (A$15–A$25) cab ride to the nearest Gold Coast town.

Long-distance buses traveling between Sydney and Brisbane stop at Coolangatta and Surfers Paradise. Surfside Buslines' Gold Coast Tourist Shuttle runs around the clock between Gold Coast attractions, theme parks, and the airport, along the strip between Tweed Heads, and Southport. Services run at five-minute intervals during the day and at least half-hourly after dark. Buy single tickets or a 3-, 5-, 7-, or 10-day Gold Pass (A$51–A$113) or Freedom Pass (A$67–A$129), which give you unlimited shuttle travel and theme park transfers; the Freedom Pass also includes a return Gold Coast airport transfer.

Approximate taxi fare from Gold Coast Airport to Currumbin is A$25; to Burleigh Heads, A$33; to Broadbeach, A$50; to Surfers Paradise, A$55; to Main Beach, A$60; and to the northern suburbs, more than A$90. Shuttle buses can be cheaper than cabs at A$5–A$35, depending on your destination: before boarding, confirm that the bus stops near your accommodation.

At Gold Coast Airport the Transport and Information Desk just outside International Arrivals sells tickets for Surfside Buslines, the Gold Coast Shuttle Bus, and Con-x-ion coaches. They'll also direct you to the free Airport Link shuttle that takes you to the Gold Coast Highway, where public transport is readily available. You can also buy tickets for the Gold Coast Shuttle Bus and flexible Go passes (allowing multiple trips and online top-ups) at train stations and 7-11 stores.

Rental cars are a cost-effective option if you plan to tour the area. Most major car-rental agencies have offices in Brisbane, Surfers Paradise, and at Gold Coast Airport. Companies operating on the Gold Coast include Avis, Budget, and Thrifty. Four-wheel-drive vehicles are available. It's strongly recommended that you pre-book.

It's essential to book ahead for private coach or limo transfers; both can be cost-effective options, especially if you're traveling in a group.

Get to South Stradbroke Island via the Couran Cove Island Resort passenger ferry, which makes multiple return trips a day from Hope Harbour Marina, leaving at 10:30, 2, 4, and 6, and returning at 9, noon, 3, 5, and 7, with an extra evening service on weekends (A$47 return). Zane's Water Taxi runs up to six campers plus gear from Runaway Bay Marina to Currigee (A$50, 1-way) and Tipplers (A$90, 1-way); bookings are essential.

From the Gold Coast it's 30 minutes' flying time to Brisbane, 2 hours 10 minutes to Melbourne, and 1 hour 25 minutes to Sydney. Qantas, Virgin Blue, Jetstar, and Tiger Airways operate domestic flights from the Gold Coast to Australian capital cities and some regional centers.

ESSENTIALS

Airport Gold Coast Airport (*Coolangatta Airport* ⊠ *1 Eastern Ave., Bilinga* ☎ *07/5589–1100*).

Public bus and train Translink (☎ *13–1230* ⊕ *www.translink.com.au*). **Queensland Rail** (☎ *13–1617* ⊕ *www.qr.com.au*). **Greyhound Australia** (⊠ *Surfers Paradise Transit Centre, 10 Beach Rd., Surfers Paradise* ☎ *1300/473946 or*

07/5531–6677 ⊕ www.greyhound.com.au). **Surfside Buslines** (✉ *1–10 Mercantile Ct., Ernest* ☎ *07/5539–9388, 13–1230 reservations* ⊕ *www.surfside.com. au or www.translink.com.au).* **Gold Coast Tourist Shuttle** (☎ *07/5574–5111 or 1300/655655* ⊕ *gcshuttle.com.au).* **Con-x-ion** (☎ *07/5556–9888* ⊕ *www.con-x-ion.com).*

Taxi Regent Taxis (☎ *13–1008* ⊕ *www.regenttaxis.com.au).*

Limousine Hughes Chauffeured **Limousines** (☎ *1300/306644* ⊕ *www. hugheslimousines.com.au).*

Car Rental Avis (✉ *Cnr Ferny and Cypress Ave., Surfers Paradise* ☎ *07/5539– 9388, 13–6333 reservations* ⊕ *www.avis.com.au).* **Budget** (✉ *Cnr Palm and Ferny Ave.* ☎ *07/5538–1344, 1300/362848 international reservations* ⊕ *www. budget.com.au).* **Thrifty** (✉ *Cnr Enderly Ave. and Surfers Paradise Blvd., Surfers Paradise* ☎ *07/5570–9999, 1300/139009 reservations* ⊕ *www.rentthrifty.com).*

Ferry Couran Cove Island Resort Ferry (✉ *John Lund Ave., Hope Harbour* ☎ *1800/268726* ⊕ *www.southstradbrokeisland.com.au).* **Zane's Water Taxi** (✉ *Runaway Bay Marina, 247 Bayview St., Runaway Bay* ☎ *0404/905970).*

Visitor Info Gold Coast Tourism Information & Booking Centres (✉ *2 Cavill Ave., Surfers Paradise* ☎ *1300/309400 or 07/5569–3830 international* ✉ *Shop 22, Showcase on the Beach, Griffith Ave., Coolangatta* ☎ *07/5569–3380* ⊕ *www. verygc.com.au).*

COOMERA AND OXENFORD

48–51 km (30–32 mi) south of Brisbane.

The biggest draws of these two northern Gold Coast suburbs are their family-oriented theme parks—Dreamworld, Warner Bros. Movie World, Wet 'n' Wild Water World, Paradise Country, the Australian Outback Spectacular, and WhiteWater World. The sprawling complexes have many attractions: each takes about a day for a leisurely visit.

EXPLORING

The **Australian Outback Spectacular,** one of six Warner Village theme parks in the area, lets visitors experience "the heart and soul of the Australian Outback." The exciting evening show features state-of-the-art visual effects and performances from top local stunt riders, a pig race, and live country music. Guests get a three-course "Aussie barbecue" dinner and complimentary drinks during the 90-minute, A\$23 million extravaganza, plus a souvenir stockman's hat. Doors open at 6:15 PM; showtime is at 7:30 PM. Return transfers from Gold Coast hotels cost A\$15; on-site parking is free. This park (and neighboring theme parks Paradise Country, Warner Bros Movie World, and Wet 'N,' Wild Water World) is a short taxi ride from Helensvale station; if driving, take Exit 60 at Oxenford off the M1 Pacific Motorway. ✉ *Pacific Motorway, Oxenford* ☎ *13–3386 or 07/5519–6200* ⊕ *outbackspectacular.myfun. com.au* A\$99.95.

Fodor'sChoice At Coomera's **Dreamworld** the big draws are the "big six": high-tech ★ thrill rides including the aptly-named Giant Drop, a 120-meter vertical ☺ plummet akin to skydiving; an outsized pendulum, the Claw; a high-

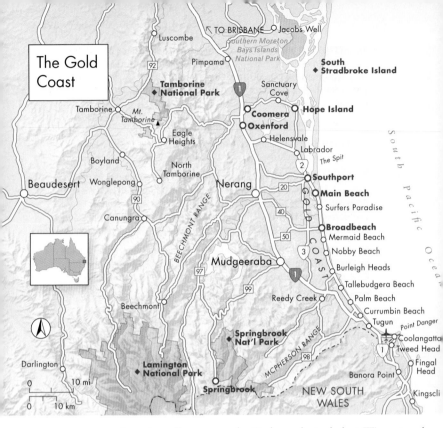

TO BRISBANE Jacobs Well

Luscombe

Southern Moreton
Bays Islands
National Park

Pimpama

92

South
◆ **Stradbroke Island**

Tamborine
◆ **National Park**

Sanctuary
Cove

Tamborine Mt.
Tamborine ▲

Coomera ◆ **Hope Island**

Oxenford

Eagle
Heights

Helensvale

Labrador

Boyland

North
Tamborine

The Spit

Beaudesert Wonglepong

90

Nerang

20

◯ **Southport**

◯ **Main Beach**

◯ Surfers Paradise

Canungra

40

Broadbeach
◯ Mermaid Beach

50

3 ◯ Nobby Beach

Mudgeeraba

97

◯ Burleigh Heads

1

◯ Tallebudgera Beach

Beechmont

99

Reedy Creek ◯ ◯ Palm Beach

◯ Currumbin Beach

◯ Tugun Point Danger

Coolangatta
Tweed Head

Springbrook
Nat'l Park

1

Darlington

0   10 mi

0   10 km

Lamington
◆ **National Park**

98

Fingal
Head

Springbrook

Banora Point

NEW SOUTH
WALES

Kingscli

South Pacific Ocean

GOLD COAST

BEECHMONT RANGE

McPHERSON RANGE

speed gravity roller coaster, the Cyclone; the turbulent Wipeout and screamingly fast, scarily high Tower of Terror; and new Mick Doohan's Motocoaster, a fluid bike-race track with high-speed corners. You can also watch Bengal tigers play and swim with their handlers on Tiger Island, cuddle a koala in Koala Country, see more than 800 native animals at the Wildlife Sanctuary, cool off in an artificial lagoon, or cruise the park's waterways on a paddle wheeler. Bring swimwear, book ahead, and you can also try the Flowrider, an amalgam of surfing and skateboarding. A guided, two-hour Sunset Safari (A$25) promises close-up encounters with tigers and native wildlife from 4:45 PM in season. Beat the queues by buying an Earlybird Pass (A$10 extra) and hiring a Q4U virtual queueing device, preferably well ahead of your visit. The park is 45 minutes outside Brisbane and 25–30 minutes from Surfers Paradise along the M1 Pacific Motorway: take Exit 54 at Coomera. ⊠ *Dreamworld Pkwy., Coomera* ☎ *07/5588–1111 or 1800/073300* ⊕ *dreamworld.myfun.com.au* ⊠ *A$69 single park entry; A$5 per half-hr Flowrider session with Dreamworld entry, or A$20 per hr NightRider pass; A$79 1-day World Pass (entry to Dreamworld and WhiteWater World); A$102 2-day World Pass (2 entries each to Dreamworld and WhiteWater World; 2nd visits within 14 days)* ⊙ *Daily 10–5; Flowrider 10–4:30; NightRider Thurs. and Fri. 5–10.*

☺ **Paradise Country.** Billed as "an authentic Australian farm experience," the park appeals to families with half-day farm tours beginning at 9:30 AM, 11:45 AM, and 1:45 PM (bookings essential). You'll see displays of horsemanship, sheep shearing, boomerang throwing, and whip crack-ing. Kids will enjoy koala cuddling and kangaroo feeding. An optional barbecue lunch is accompanied by bush dancing and Aussie-theme live entertainment. The park is directly behind the Australian Outback Spec-tacular. Car parking spaces are limited. ⊠ *Pacific Motorway, Oxen-ford* ☎ *13–3386 or 07/5519–6200* ⊕ *paradisecountry.myfun.com.au* ⊠ *A$46.50 (tour and lunch)* ☉ *Daily 9:30–4.*

☺ **Warner Bros. Movie World,** one of the few movie theme parks outside the United States, lets you share virtual space with an animated ogre in the eye-popping *Shrek* 4D Adventure, accelerate to 96 km (60 mi) an hour in two seconds on the awesome Superman Escape ride, or get airborne on the Batwing Spaceshot. You can also check out vehicles, props, and costumes from the Batman blockbuster Dark Knight; enter a custom-built "immersive" movie set to watch precision driving and action-film-style stunts in the new *Hollywood Stunt Riders* show; and rocket through the spine-tingling Scooby-Doo Spooky Coaster. Little kids will want to see the daily Main Street Star Parade, visit Bugs Bunny and friends in the WB! Fun Zone and Looney Tunes River Ride, and catch the live show What's Up Rock? (daily at 11:30 AM). You can also indulge yourself at numerous outlets selling Warner Bros. souvenirs. With a large portion of its area now covered by a 4,000-square-meter (43,055-square-foot) roof, this park is a smart choice in inclement weather. It's adjacent to Australian Outback Spectacular. ⊠ *Pacific Motorway, Oxenford* ☎ *07/5573–8495* ⊕ *www.movieworld.com.au* ⊠ *A$69.95; A$104.95 (2 entries, 2nd visit within 14 days)* ☉ *Daily 10–5.*

☺ Oxenford's **Wet 'n' Wild Water World** has magnificent waterslides, includ-ing the aptly named Mammoth Falls, Terror Canyon II, and Super-8 Aqua Racer; a giant whirlpool; a wave pool with 3-foot-high surf; tandem, entwined-tube and family-friendly water slides; and the new Surfrider that simulates the sensation of surfing the world's biggest waves, plummeting you 30 meters (over 100 feet) while you spin on a giant board. In the Extreme H20 zone, you can plunge down pitch-black spirals of water in the Black Hole, hang on through the churning Tornado, or survive the scary Kamikaze, a giant, U-shaped, friction-free slide with a near-vertical 11-meter (36-foot) drop. Enough aquatic thrills? Take it easy on Calypso Beach, a "tropical island" fringed with white-sand beaches and a lazy river; or chill out at a Dive'n'Movie. Keep kids entertained at Buccaneer Bay, a state-of-the-art aquatic playground with multiple levels. All pools and slides are heated May through Sep-tember. The park is ½ km (¼ mi) down the Pacific Highway from War-ner Bros. Movie World. ⊠ *Pacific Hwy., Oxenford* ☎ *07/5573–2255* ⊕ *www.wetnwild.com.au* ⊠ *A$49.95 single entry; A$24.95 afternoon only* ☉ *Feb.–Apr. and Sept.–Dec., daily 10–5; May–Aug., daily 10–4; Jan., daily 10–9.*

6

Fodor's Choice **WhiteWater World.** Next door to Dreamworld, and under the same man-
★ agement, is the Gold Coast's latest thrill-seeker's theme park, White-
☼ Water World. Here you'll find state-of-the-art water rides including the
Blue Ringed Octopus (BRO), a convoluted eight-lane racer slide; The
Rip, Australia's biggest corkscrew-cored whirlpool; the dual-bowl Little
Rippers ride; an inner-tube "aquacoaster" ride known as the Temple of
Huey; and the Green Room, a 65-foot-high "tube" simulating the inside
of a monster wave. Small kids will enjoy Nickelodeon's Pipeline Plunge,
an aquatic activity zone; deposit toddlers at shady, supervised Wiggle Bay,
complete with mini waterslides and water cannons. You can also learn
to surf here: A$115 includes a two-hour lesson in the Cave of Waves
wave pool, a CD of photos, and park entry. Beat the queues with a pre-
booked Q4U device and early-bird entry. The park is close to Coomera
rail station; from there, catch a Surfside bus to the park. ⊠ *Dreamworld
Pkwy., Coomera* ☎ *07/5588–1111 or 1800/073300* ⊕ *www.dreamworld.
com.au* ⊠ *A$43 park entry, A$102 2-day World Pass (2 entries each to
Dreamworld and WhiteWater World; 2nd visits within 14 days)* ☼ *Daily
10–4; surf lessons Mon., Wed., and Sat. 8–10.*

WHERE TO STAY

$$$$ ⊞ **Ruffles Lodge.** The immaculate, architect-designed luxury lodge is 5
★ km (3 mi) from Dreamworld, but its tranquil location makes it seem
worlds away. Set high on a hill in manicured gardens, five private villas, three tree houses, and an executive lodge suite with an expansive
separate living room have views to the Gold Coast beaches and high-
rises as well as the surrounding bushland. The tree houses have their
own plunge pools; the spacious spa villas and executive lodge suite
have wood-burning fireplaces, hot tubs, plasma TVs, and high-speed
Internet connections. Owners John and Jan Nicholls create a warm,
comfortable environment, with a choice of dinner-party-style or private
meals in the main lodge's view-rich, sleekly refurbished dining room.
Pre-dinner drinks, hors d'oeuvres, and a four-course dinner cost A$70
per person. Between meals, get pampered at Ruffles' tranquil day spa.
Pros: architecturally superb; feels luxurious; terrific food. **Cons:** must
book well ahead; off the beaten track; fees for using AmEx. ⊠ *423
Ruffles Rd., Willow Vale* ☎ *07/5546–7411* ⊕ *www.ruffleslodge.com.
au* ⇆ *10 villas (including 3 tree houses and 1 suite)* △ *In-room: no TV,
safe (some), refrigerator, DVD, Wi-Fi (free). In-hotel: restaurant, room
service, bar, pool, spa, public Internet, public Wi-Fi, airport shuttle,
parking (no fee), no kids under 14, no-smoking rooms, no elevator*
⊟ *AE, DC, MC, V* ⏐⭕⏐ *BP.*

SOUTH STRADBROKE ISLAND

1 km (½ mi) east of the Gold Coast.

White-sand beaches, diverse flora and fauna, and a peaceful interior
draw visitors to South Stradbroke Island, which is just 22 km (12 mi)
long and 2 km (1 mi) wide. The island and its northern neighbor, North
Stradbroke Island, were once connected, but in 1896 a fierce storm
separated them at a narrow neck called Jumpinpin. Unlike its northern

namesake, South "Straddie" is less populated, and does not have a public ferry service. It's a good spot for fishing and boating.

GETTING HERE AND AROUND

You can get to the island by taking one of three boat services. Couran Cove Island Resort (☎ *1800/268726*) runs multiple return trips a day from Hope Harbour terminal, leaving at 10:30, 2, 4, and 6, and returning at 9, noon, 3, 5, and 7, with an extra evening service on weekends (A$47 return). Zane's Water Taxi runs up to 6 campers plus gear from Runaway Bay Marina to Currigee (A$50, 1-way) and Tipplers (A$90, 1-way) campgrounds on the island; to book, phone ☎ *0404/905970*.

From Gold Coast Airport, Coolangatta, it's a 50-km (30-mi), 50-minute drive northeast on the Pacific Motorway, then the Oxenford–Southport Road (take Exit 57 at Oxenford) to Hope Harbour.

> ## HOPE ISLAND
>
> This isn't your average island. Like several Gold Coast islands, it is actually a mile or two inland, and is circled by the Coomera River and a series of canals. The resort has a marina full of luxury launches and yachts, two golf courses, a swanky hotel, beautiful condos, and upscale restaurants, nightclubs, and shops. Stop by if you're passing through for window onto jet-set culture, Queensland style.
>
> Hope Island is accessed via bridges from the west or east. Route 4, also known as the Oxenford–Southport Road, passes straight through.

WHERE TO STAY

$$$–$$$$ ☆ **Couran Cove Island Resort.** Just 40 minutes by boat from Gold Coast glitz, this ecotourism resort is a peaceful haven. The vision of Olympic long-distance runner Ron Clarke, the property has an exceptionally wide selection of sports options: biking, swimming, tennis, rock climbing, baseball, basketball, a ropes course, various water sports, guided walks, and more. There's also an Aboriginal culture center, a tour desk, and a general store, as well as music, games, and Internet rooms. The marine resort area includes deluxe rooms, suites, and two- and four-bedroom lodges (all with kitchenettes and cooking facilities). Some are built over the water, so you can fish right off the balcony. The resort's nature cabins were refurbished in 2007. **Pros:** kids under 14 stay for free; broad range of activities (many free); eco-friendly. **Cons:** crowded in peak periods; four-night minimum stay in all but the low season. ✉ *Hope Harbour Marina, John Lund Dr., Hope Harbour, Hope Island* ☎ *07/5509–3000 or 1800/268726* ⊕ *www.couran.com* ⤴ *95 rooms, 92 suites, 22 lodges, 16 villas* ⚄ *In-room: safe, kitchen (some), refrigerator, Internet (some). In-hotel: 3 restaurants, room service (some), bars, tennis courts, pools, gyms, spa, beachfront, water sports, bicycles, children's programs (ages 3–14), laundry facilities, laundry service, public Wi-Fi (free), airport shuttle (fee), parking (fee), no-smoking rooms, no elevator* ▭ *AE, DC, MC, V.*

SOUTHPORT AND MAIN BEACH

16 km (10 mi) southeast of Oxenford.

South of Southport, look for the turnoff to the **Spit**, a natural peninsula that stretches 4 km (2½ mi) north, almost to the tip of South Stradbroke Island. Sea World Drive runs the full length of the Spit, from Mariner's Cove (a popular covered area with affordable restaurants and fast-food outlets) to a nature reserve. This narrow peninsula is bordered by the Pacific Ocean to the east and the calm waters of the Broadwater (a long lagoon) to the west. Two of the Gold Coast's best hotels face each other across Sea World Drive and are connected to Marina Mirage, arguably the most elegant shopping precinct on the Gold Coast. Farther up the road is Sea World itself.

EXPLORING

☺ **Sea World**, Australia's largest marine theme park, has daily shows that highlight the resident dolphins and sea lions, and waterskiing displays. You can also check out the park's polar bears in their state-of-the-art home, fairy penguin and endangered dugong exhibits, and various other marine creatures, including 100-plus eagle, manta, and sting rays at Ray Reef. Don't miss Shark Bay, the world's largest artificial lagoon system for sharks, an innovative dual enclosure with dangerous tiger sharks in one section and harmless reef sharks, rays, and fish in another. Patrons can dive in the latter, and get close-up views of the former through the massive windows that separate the lagoons. Rides include Jet Ski and corkscrew coasters, a monorail, waterslides, the Sky High Skyway cable car, and Sea World Eye, a 95-foot-high observation wheel offering bird's-eye views of the action. ⊠ *Seaworld Dr. (at oceanside end of this long street), The Spit, Main Beach* ☎ *13–3386 or 07/5588–2205* ⊕ *www.seaworld.com.au* 🎟 *A$69.95; A$104.95 2-day pass* ⊗ *Daily 10–5.*

OUTDOOR ACTIVITIES

SURFING   The Gold Coast, renowned for long, sandy beaches and reliable breaks, is a terrific place to surf. Of the patrolled beaches, Main Beach, Surfer's Paradise, Broadbeach, Mermaid, Miami, and Nobby are the most popular; Kirra Beach, in the south, is arguably the area's best surf beach. Though the challenging break at Kirra is perhaps best left to the pros, most Gold Coast beaches are suitable for grommets (beginners). There are plenty of local surf schools happy to teach you, and board and wet-suit hire outlets flank popular beaches. Local surfers and lifeguards are good sources of information about surf conditions and hazards.

Get Wet Surf School ☎ *1800/GETWET or 07/5532–9907 international* ⊕ *www.getwetsurf.com* 🎟 *A$55 (beach); A$95 (private); A$115 (wave pool, includes park entry)* ⊗ *Daily 10 AM and 1 PM (beach); Mon., Wed., Fri. 8 AM (wavepool).*

WHERE TO EAT AND STAY

$$ ✕ **Omeros Bros. Seafood Restaurant.** The Omeros brothers, who arrived
SEAFOOD   from Greece in 1953, have run seafood restaurants in Australia for more than 40 years. This one on the waterfront at the lovely Marina Mirage center offers dishes spanning the seafood spectrum—from bouillabaisse,

Yet another beautiful east coast beach

barbecued prawns, mussels, and barramundi to classic surf-and-turf, lobster, mud crab, and Moreton Bay bugs. There are also meat, vegetarian, and pasta dishes. ✉ *4 Marina Mirage, Seaworld Dr.* ☎ *07/5591–7222* ⊕ *www.omerosbros.com* ▤ *AE, DC, MC, V.*

$$
AUSTRALIAN

✗ **Saks.** Located alongside Broadwater, only a short boardwalk removed from Palazzo Versace, is this hip restaurant and bar with wood floors, floor-to-ceiling windows, and indoor and outdoor areas. Relax on faux-suede lounge seats and ottomans while nibbling tapas, or nab a waterside table. Savor a steak or seafood dish, share a platter or pizza, or go for broke with the Saks Sensation: Moreton Bay bugs, king prawns, scallops, and eye fillet (A$49). There's also a celiac-friendly gluten-free menu. Live music and DJs on Friday and Saturday nights and Sunday afternoons attract a crowd. ✉ *Marina Mirage, 74 Seaworld Dr., Main Beach* ☎ *07/5591–2755* ⊕ *www.saksrestaurantandbar.com* ▤ *AE, DC, MC, V.*

$$$$
Fodor's Choice
★

▥ **Palazzo Versace.** Sink into one of the sofas, armchairs, or circular banquettes in the sensational lobby, refurbished in 2006, and watch the beautiful people walk by. The Italian fashion house lent its flair to this stunning hotel, the first of its kind in the world. The original marble-and-mosaic tiled floor and gigantic chandelier remain, but the ornate marbled columns have been reborn as sleek, cream, black-topped pillars offset by tropical foliage and opulent soft furnishings in turquoise and fuschia. Rooms in low-rise wings surround a lagoon pool edged with palm trees and a sandy artificial beach. Some have balconies with views over the Broadwater; others overlook the pool. Condos have full kitchens and laundries; some come with private plunge pools, barbecues, and marina berths. The signature restaurant, Vanitas, serves fine French-Mediterranean cuisine; Vie's contemporary Australian menu is a relaxed alternative; and Il Barocco does a terrific seafood buffet (A$79). **Pros:** fine dining, five-star service, free Internet. **Cons:** pricey. ✉ *94 Seaworld Dr., adjoining Marina Mirage, Main Beach* ☎ *07/5509–8000* ⊕ *www.palazzoversace.com* ↝ *151 rooms, 54 suites* ⚹ *In-room: safe, refrigerator, dial-up, DVD, Internet. In-hotel: 3 restaurants, room service, bars, pool, gym, spa, laundry service, babysitting, public Internet, public Wi-Fi, airport shuttle, parking (no fee), no-smoking rooms* ▭ *AE, DC, MC, V* ⊙▮ *BP.*

SHOPPING

★ **Marina Mirage Gold Coast** (✉ *74 Seaworld Dr., Main Beach* ☎ *07/5555–6400 or 07/3103–2325 market* ⊕ *www.marinamirage.com.au*) is perhaps the most beautiful shopping and dining complex on the Gold Coast. Among its 60-plus stores are high-end gift and homewares, jewelry and designer fashion boutiques, including Nautica, Louis Vuitton, Hermès, Christiansen Copenhagen, Max&Co, La Perla, MoMA Store, and Calvin Klein, along with famous Australian brands, fine waterfront restaurants, and marina facilities. On the first, third, and fifth Saturday of each month, buy fresh gourmet produce between 7 and noon at the Marina Mirage Farmers' Markets. Surfside buses 750 and 715 stop at the door.

SURFERS PARADISE

Before the Gold Coast existed as a tourism entity, there was Surfers Paradise, a 3-km (2-mi) stretch of beach with great surf, just 5 km (3mi) south of Southport. Now overrun with high-rises, it's still a vibrant beachside town. Nightlife is the main draw; head to Orchid, Elkhorn, and Cavill avenues.

Twice weekly, crowds flock to haggle for handmade crafts and gifts at **Surfers Paradise Beachfront Markets**. ✉ *The Esplanade between Hanlan St. and Elkhorn Ave.,* ☐ *Free* ⊙ *Wed. and Fri. 5:30 PM–10 PM.*

BROADBEACH

8 km (5 mi) south of Southport.

With clean beaches, great cafés, and trendy nightspots, Broadbeach is one of the most popular areas on the Gold Coast, especially with locals. It's home to mega-shopping mall Pacific Fair, and is a good base for visiting the wildlife parks south of town.

EXPLORING

★ **Currumbin Wildlife Sanctuary.** A Gold Coast institution and perhaps the
☺ most ecologically-minded wildlife facility in the region, Currumbin Wildlife Sanctuary is a 70-acre, not-for-profit National Trust Reserve. Established in 1947 as a lorikeet sanctuary, it now shelters many Australian species, including crocodiles, snakes, wombats, dingoes, Tasmanian devils, kangaroos, and endangered frogs. There are more than a dozen daily animal shows, informative talks, Aboriginal dance and didgeridoo sessions, 'roo feedings, and koala cuddling. Come at 8 AM or 4 PM, when the lorikeets are fed. You can also take a treetops ropes course (A$20, weekends and holidays). The nightly guided Wildnight Adventure includes a "Wild Buffet" from 5:30, a tour of the sanctuary's nocturnal inhabitants from 7, and Aboriginal dancing by firelight

afterwards (reservations essential). There's a gourmet produce market in the carpark on Saturday mornings. Return transfers to and from the Gold Coast can be booked with **Surfside Bus Lines** (⊕ *www.surfside-buslines.com*). ⊠ *28 Tomewin St., off Gold Coast Hwy., 14 km (8½ mi) south of Broadbeach, Currumbin* ☎ *07/5534–1266 or 1300/886511* ⊕ *www.cws.org.au* ⊠ *general admission A$44; ropes course A$10; Wildnight Adventure $52* ⊘ *Daily 8–5, grounds close 5:30 for Wildnight Adventure.*

☺ **David Fleay Wildlife Park.** Located in the town of Burleigh Heads and named for an Australian wildlife naturalist, the park features a board-walk trail through pristine wetlands and rain forests. Koalas, kanga-roos, dingoes, platypuses, and crocodiles, grouped together in separate zones according to their natural habitat, are just some of the creatures you might see. A state-of-the-art nocturnal house displays threatened species and the elusive platypus. Daily presentations are free; koala contact sessions, from 2 PM, cost A$8.45. There's also a café and a gift shop. ⊠ *7 km (4½ mi) south of Broadbeach, Tallebudgera Creek Rd. near W. Burleigh Rd., Burleigh Heads* ☎ *07/5576–2411* ⊕ *www.epa. qld.gov.au* ⊠ *A$16.50* ⊘ *Daily 9–5.*

WHERE TO STAY

$$$ 🏨 **Antigua Beach Resort.** Less than a minute's walk from the beach, shop-ping centers, and restaurants, this three-story, Caribbean-style hotel has balconies or patios on all sides. Self-contained, simply-appointed one- and two-bedroom apartments are decorated in bright tropical colors; most have Foxtel cable TV. The pool, hot tub, sauna, and ter-race are encircled by landscaped gardens with a barbecue. **Pros:** quiet but central; comfortable beds; self-contained. **Cons:** minimum 5-night stays in peak periods (e.g., Christmas); short weekend reception hours; slow Internet. ⊠ *6 Queensland Ave.* ☎ *07/5526–2288 or 1800/995068* ⊕ *www.antiguaresort.com.au* ⇗ *23 apartments* ⌂ *In-room: kitchen, refrigerator, dial-up. In-hotel: pool, laundry service, parking (no fee), no elevator, no-smoking rooms* ⊟ *MC, V.*

$$$$ 🏨 **Hotel Conrad and Jupiters Casino.** This massive resort is always bustling. Executive and Superior rooms, the latter refurbished in 2007, have rich, earth-tone furnishings with emerald accents, high-speed Internet access, CD players, and slim-line 32" TVs with iPod interfaces, cable channels, and pay movies; most rooms have either a balcony or a sunny terrace. Front-facing rooms lack balconies, but have great views of the Gold Coast; other rooms look out across the hinterland. Executive room guests get special services and facilities including a guest lounge. Luxury suites are fully self-contained. Restaurants include Andiamo, with a Mod-Oz-meets-Mediterranean menu, and Charters Towers, which specializes in contemporary Queensland cuisine and offers fresh mud crab, lobster, local seafood, and premium steaks. **Pros:** modern furnishings and facilities, great on-site entertainment options; close to shopping centers. **Cons:** expense, no in-room Wi-Fi, fee for park-ing. ⊠ *Broadbeach Island, Casino Dr., off Gold Coast Hwy., Broad-beach* ☎ *07/5592–8100 or 1800/074344* ⊕ *www.conrad.com.au/jupiter* ⇗ *563 rooms, 29 suites, 2 penthouses* ⌂ *In-room: safe, refrigerator, DVD (some), Internet. In-hotel: 7 restaurants, room service, 8 bars,*

6

tennis court, pools, gym, spa, laundry service, public Internet, public Wi-Fi, airport shuttle, tour desk, parking (fee), executive floors, no-smoking rooms ☰*AE, DC, MC, V* ⟦◯⟧ *BP.*

★   ⛰ **The Wave Resort.** This award-winning high-rise apartment resort is one of Broadbeach's newest and most luxurious. Its beachfront location translates into superb ocean or Gold Coast and casino outlooks, but early-morning sun floods east-facing apartments: ensure you book one with blackout drapes if you're a late riser. Spacious, ultra-modern one-, two- and three- bedroom apartments and luxe sub-penthouses (31st floor and above) all have private, furnished balconies designed to maximise the sweeping views. Each is well equipped, with a full gourmet kitchen, quality neutral-toned furnishings, flat-screen TVs (including one in the master bedroom), and firm beds. Though the beach is close by, there's a well-equipped gym, sauna, and steam room in the complex; a large, heated, infinity-edge pool, deckchairs, and an impressive stainless-steel BBQ on level four; and a small pool, Jacuzzi, and second BBQ area on level 29, all accessible only via guest keycard (as is the ultra-secure labyrinth of a carpark). Supermarkets, a post office, and several eateries lie seconds away via a stomach-droppingly-fast elevator. Reservations can pre-book theme-park tickets and park transfers for guests. **Pros:** helpful staff; "granny" babysitting service; well sound-proofed; clean and secure. **Cons:** minimum three-day (or, in peak periods, five-day) stay; limited reception hours 8 or 9 AM to 3 or 5 PM). ⊠ *89–91 Surf Parade, Broadbeach 4218* ☎ *07/5555–9200* ⊕ *www.thewavesresort.com.au* ⤴ *53 rooms* △ *In-room: kitchen, refrigerator, DVD, Internet (fee). In-hotel: pools, gym, beachfront, laundry facilities, parking (no fee)* ☰*AE, D, DC, MC, V* ⟦◯⟧ *EP.*

NIGHTLIFE

Jupiters Casino (⊠ *Casino Dr., off Gold Coast Hwy., Broadbeach* ☎ *07/5592–8100* ⊕ *www.conrad.com.au/jupiters*) provides flamboyant round-the-clock entertainment. There are 70-plus blackjack, baccarat, craps, sic bo, Texas Hold'em poker, and keno tables, and more than 1,300 'round-the-clock slot machines on one level. There's also a member's gaming club. Since the casino's A$53 million expansion over 2006–2008 there are even more dining, drinking, and entertainment options, including seven restaurants and eight bars. The 950-seat showroom hosts glitzy Las Vegas–style productions.

Howl at the Moon (⊠ *Level 1, Neicon Plaza, Victoria Ave., Broadbeach* ☎ *07/5538–9911* ⊕ *www.howlatthemoon.com.au*) is fun if you like sing-alongs and know the words to hits from the '80s, '90s, and today. Every night two pianists with vocal skills belt out a medley of tunes (some requested by patrons) on baby grands to an appreciative crowd of thirty- and fortysomethings. Grab a Cosmopolitan and hit the dance floor (come weekends for the fun crowds).

SHOPPING

Fodor's Choice   **Pacific Fair** (⊠ *Hooker Blvd. at Gold Coast Hwy., opposite Jupiters* ★   *Casino* ☎ *07/5581–5100* ⊕ *www.pacificfair.com.au*), a sprawling outdoor shopping center, is Queensland's largest, featuring a Myer department store, major retailers, and around 300 specialty stores and services (including travel agencies, fashion outlets, and sports and outdoor gear stores). This place should satisfy even die-hard shoppers. There's even the requisite cinema complex. For a breather, head to the landscaped grounds with three small lakes, a children's park, and village green. It's open daily until 5 and until 9 on Thursdays.

GOLD COAST HINTERLAND

No visit to the Gold Coast would be complete without an excursion to the region's verdant Hinterland. The natural grandeur of the area lies in dramatic contrast to the human-made excesses of the coastal strip. The Gold Coast Hinterland's superb national parks and nature reserves protect magnificent waterfalls, natural rock pools, mountain lookouts with expansive views of the surrounding terrain and coast, and an array of wildlife. Walking trails traverse rain forest dense with ancient trees. Among the parks lie boutique wineries and quaint villages where high-rise is anything over one story. The parks form part of a unique, ancient geological region known as the Scenic Rim, a chain of mountains running parallel to the coast through southeast Queensland and northern New South Wales.

Because it rises to 3,000 feet above sea level, some parts of the hinterland are 4°C–6°C (7°F–11°F) cooler than the coast.

GETTING HERE AND AROUND

The Hinterland's main areas—Tamborine Mountain, Lamington National Park, and Springbrook—can be reached from the Pacific Highway or via Beaudesert from Brisbane, and are a 30- to 40-minute drive inland from the Gold Coast. To reach Tamborine, around 80 km (50 mi) south of Brisbane and 36 km (24 mi) from Southport, take Exit 57 off the Pacific Motorway to the Oxenford–Tamborine Road; or take Exit 71 off the Pacific Motorway, the Nerang–Beaudesert Road, to Canungra. From Canungra, follow the signs to Tamborine, 4 km (2½ mi) along Tamborine Mountain Road. The Gold Coast Hinterland is ideal for touring by car: rent a vehicle, arm yourself with local maps, fill the tank, and take to the hills.

TOURS

From the Gold Coast, Mountain Coach Company buses pick passengers up from the major bus depots, most of the major hotels, and from Coolangatta Airport for O'Reilly's Rainforest Retreat in the Gold Coast Hinterland (A$53 round-trip day tour; A$38 one-way transfer).

Australian Day Tours/JPT leaves the Brisbane Transit Centre daily at 8:30, picking up passengers from the Gold Coast at 9 en route to the Hinterland. Day tours stop at O'Reilly's Rainforest Retreat, returning to the Gold Coast at 4:30, Brisbane at 6. The cost—A$84 round-trip—is for a full-day tour, but Retreat guests can use it for transfers. Two-day Hinterland tours, with accommodation, dinner, and breakfast at O'Reilly's included, are A$379. The company also runs a thrice-weekly tour to the Gold Coast and Lamington National Park, including a canal cruise and guided rain-forest walk.

Luke's Bluff Lookout on O'Reilley's Plateau, Lamington National Park.

Hinterland accommodations, including O'Reilly's, Binna Burra Mountain Retreat, and Peppers Spicers Peak, shuttle guests to and from the coast. Various smaller coach tour companies, including winery tour operator Cork 'n Fork *(see Winery Tours)*, also visit Hinterland destinations.

ESSENTIALS

Coach tours and transfers Australian Day Tours/JPT (✉ *Level 3, Brisbane Transit Centre, Roma St.* ☎ *07/3489–6400* ⊕ *www.daytours.com.au*).

Tours Australian Day Tours (✉ *Brisbane Transit Centre, Roma St.* ☎ *07/3003–0700* ⊕ *www.daytours.com.au*). **Mountain Coach Company** (✉ *07/5524–4249* ⊕ *www.mountaincoach.com.au*).

EXPLORING

More than 20 million years ago, volcanic eruptions created rugged landscapes, while fertile volcanic soils produced the luxuriant tracts of rain forest that make up enchanting **Tamborine National Park.** This is the most developed region of the Gold Coast Hinterland, and it's worth spending a day or two here. Apart from the natural environment, there are wineries, lodges, restaurants, and the famed Gallery Walk, a 1-km-long (½-mi-long) street lined with art galleries. Some of the simplest (under two hours) and best trails here are the Cedar Creek Falls Track, with waterfall views; Palm Grove Rainforest Circuit; and Macdonald Rainforest Circuit, a quieter walk popular with bird-watchers. Start your visit with a stop at Tamborine Mountain Visitor Information Centre, open 10 AM to 3 PM daily. ✉ *Doughty Park, Geissman Dr., corner Main Western Rd., North Tamborine* ☎ *1300/130372* ⊕ *www.epa.qld.gov.au.*

Several fragmented parks make up Tamborine National Park. Queensland's first national park, **Witches Falls,** has excellent picnic facilities and a 3-km (2-mi) walk that snakes downhill through open rain forest and past lagoons. To the east of Witches Falls is **Joalah National Park,** where a 1½-km (1-mi) circuit takes you to a rocky pool at the base of Curtis Falls. **MacDonald National Park** has a flat, easy 1½-km (1-mi) walk. ☎ *07/5538–4419 (Gold Coast Tourism) or 1300/130372* ⊕ *www. epa.qld.gov.au* ✉ *Free* ⊙ *Daily dawn–dusk.*

The peaks of **Springbrook National Park** rise to around 3,000 feet, dominating the skyline west of the Gold Coast. The World-Heritage-listed park has four regions: scenic Springbrook plateau, Mt. Cougal, Natural Bridge, and Numinbah. Waterfalls and cascades, Jurassic-Age hoop pines, ancient rain forest, and teeming wildlife are highlights. Thanks to steep, winding roads and longish distances between sections, it takes at least a full day to explore this large park. It's about 30 km (19 mi) from the tiny hamlet of Springbrook to Natural Bridge—a waterfall that cascades through a cavern roof into an icy pool (reach it via a half-mile circuit track, an hour's round-trip). This cavern is home to Australia's largest glowworm colony, which at night illuminates the rock walls to stunning effect. Several waterfalls, including the area's largest, Purling Brook Falls, can be reached via a steepish 4-km (2½-mi) path (allow 15 minutes for each half-mile). The 54-km Gold Coast Hinterland Great Walk extends from the Settlement campground to Green Mountains campsite in Tamborine National Park. For those short on time or energy, the lookout near the parking lot has waterfall views. Camping is permitted only in designated private campgrounds. ☎ 1300/130372 ⊕ *www.epa.qld.gov.au* ✉ *Free* ⊙ *Daily dawn–dusk.*

Lamington National Park is a subtropical-temperate ecological border zone sheltering abundant plant and animal life. Its 50,600-acre expanse comprises two sections: Binna Burra and Green Mountains. Lamington National Park is listed as a World Heritage Area, which protects its varied rain forest, including Antarctic beech trees dating back 3,000 years. Lamington has 160 km (100 mi) of bushwalking tracks ranging from 1.2 km (3/4 mi) to 54 km (34 mi), as well as waterfalls, mountain pools, exceptional views, and some 120 native bird species. The Gold Coast Hinterland Great Walk begins at the Green Mountains campsite. All park camping areas require nightly permits (A$4.85), obtained in advance. ✉ *Binna Burra Rd.* ☎ *07/5543–4501 (Beaudesert Tourism) or 1300/130372; 13–1304 permits and camping* ⊕ *www.epa.qld.gov.au* ✉ *Free* ⊙ *Daily 24 hrs; park offices open limited weekday hours.*

OUTDOOR ACTIVITIES

BUSHWALKING Bushwalking is a popular pastime in the national parks and nature reserves of the Gold Coast Hinterland, where an extensive network of well-maintained scenic trails caters to recreational walkers, serious hikers, campers, and wildlife lovers. The region's many protected wilderness tracts, including World Heritage–listed Gondwana Rainforests of Australia (within Springbook National Park), contain hundreds of well-marked trails that vary from easy half-hour strolls to steep half-day hikes and multi-day treks. Most hinterland walks offer spectacular views and sights.

Conditions can be challenging and changeable, however: before setting out on longer hikes, get suitably equipped. Download local trail maps and detailed park info from the EPA's Web site or regional visitor information offices and follow EPA guidelines.

When walking, wear sturdy shoes, sunscreen, and protective gear, carry maps and a compass, and pack drinking water, emergency food supplies, and a well-charged mobile phone. If possible, walk in a group, especially on long hikes. Check local weather conditions with the Bureau of Meterology and trail conditions on the EPA's Web site before you go.

If exploring the national parks by car, check road conditions with the RACQ's Web site and be sure you have local maps, good tires, sound brakes, water, and a full tank of gas before setting out.

Contacts Environmental Protection Authority (EPA) (☎ 1300/130372; 13–1304 camping permits ⊕ www.epa.qld.gov.au). **RACQ** (☎ 13–1905 ⊕ www. racq.com.au).

WHERE TO STAY

$$–$$$
★
☼
🍴 **Binna Burra Mountain Lodge & Campsite.** Founded in 1933, this group of hilltop cabins has sweeping views across Heritage-listed rain forest and the Hinterland to the Gold Coast. Rustic lodge rooms and log cabins are cozy, secluded, and simply furnished, with a deliberate absence of TVs, radios, telephones, and clocks; heritage lodge guestrooms have shared bathrooms. Two luxury suites were built in 2007. Good-value packages include breakfasts, or all meals, guided nature walks, and other activities, plus evening entertainment. Budget travelers can camp on-site, in tents, powered vans, or furnished safari-style tents with verandas (A$55–$95 for 2–6 people). There's a cozy, well-stocked library and main guest lounge with log fires in winter. The Cliff-Top Dining Room has panoramic views over the Coomera Valley. Rejoove Health Spa offers beauty and massage treatments. Buy local arts and crafts, souvenirs, and essentials from the on-site shop. **Pros:** good facilities and kids' programs; gorgeous setting; abseiling sites nearby. **Cons:** multi-night minimum stays in peak periods. ⊠ *Binna Burra Rd., Lamington National Park, via Beechmont* ☎ *07/5533–3622 or 1300/246622* ⊕ *www.binnaburralodge.com.au* ⇗ *35 cabins (9 with shared bath), 2 suites* ⚏ *In-room: no a/c, no phone, no TV. In-hotel: 2 restaurants, bar, children's programs (ages 5–16), laundry facilities, public Internet, airport shuttle, parking (no fee), no-smoking rooms, no elevator* ⊟ *MC, V* 🍴 *AI, BP.*

$$$–$$$$
☼
★
🍴 **O'Reilly's Rainforest Retreat, Villas & Lost World Spa.** Since 1926, the O'Reilly family has welcomed travelers into their forested world. Accommodations range from original 1930s guesthouse rooms with shared facilities to luxurious lodgings with handcrafted wood furniture, four-poster beds, fireplaces, whirlpool baths, audio systems, and spectacular mountain views. Chic, architect-designed villas have vaulted ceilings and foldback doors; find vast private decks with hot tubs, LCD TVs and Wi-Fi. For a little extra, you can join expert guides on outdoorsy activities such as bird, rain-forest, and glowworm walks; flying fox and giant swing sessions; wine-tasting tours; and four-wheel-drive bus expeditions. The treetop suspension bridge is a must-do. Relax in the

retreat's heated pool, hot tub, sauna, or Lost World day spa. O'Reilly's rate includes country-style morning and afternoon teas, plus some of the available activities—including daily guided bushwalks, stargazing, and audiovisual presentations. Special packages are available. **Pros:** excellent outdoor activities, great facilities, kids under 11 stay and eat free. **Cons:** minimum stays on weekends, Easter, and Christmas; inconsistent mobile phone coverage; fees for many activities; surcharge for credit-card transactions. ⊠ *Lamington National Park Rd., via Canungra* ☎ *07/5502–4911 or 1800/688722* ✍ *reservations@oreillys.com.au* ⊕ *www.oreillys.com.au* ⬪ *67 rooms, 5 suites, 48 villas* ⚘ *In-room: no a/c (some), no phone (some), refrigerator, no TV (some), Wi-Fi (some). In-hotel: 3 restaurants, bar, pools, spa, laundry facilities, public Internet, public Wi-Fi, airport shuttle, no-smoking rooms, no elevator* ▭ *AE, DC, MC, V* ❙❉❙ *AI, BP.*

$$$–$$$$
★
🛏 **Pethers Rainforest Retreat.** On 12 acres of privately owned rain forest, this couples-only resort comprises 10 spacious tree houses with timber floors, French doors opening onto verandas, fireplaces, hot tubs, and open-plan interiors furnished with Asian antiques. Undercover walkways link each house with the main lodge, a stunning building with 16-foot-high glass walls affording rain-forest views. You can while away the hours in the library or hike on the trails, where you might be lucky enough to spot wallabies and koalas. Restaurants are nearby, but a three-course à la carte dinner is available Thursday to Saturday for A$70 (A$60, or A$48 for 2 courses, if you pre-book). **Pros:** luxurious appointments, glorious environs, no kids. **Cons:** no on-site dinner Sunday to Wednesday; limited mobile phone coverage; minimum 2-night stay. ⊠ *28B Geissmann St., North Tamborine* ☎ *07/5545–4577* ✍ *retreat@pethers.com.au* ⊕ *www.pethers.com.au* ⬪ *10 tree houses* ⚘ *In-room: no a/c, no phone, refrigerator, DVD. In-hotel: restaurant, bar, gym, parking (no fee), no-smoking rooms, no kids under 18* ▭ *AE, DC, MC, V* ❙❉❙ *BP.*

SUNSHINE COAST

60 km (37 mi) north of Brisbane.

The Sunshine Coast is a 60-km (37-mi) stretch of white-sand beaches, inlets, lakes, and mountains that begins at the Glass House Mountains, an hour's drive north of Brisbane, and extends to Rainbow Beach in the north. Kenilworth is its inland extreme, 40 km (25 mi) from the ocean. For the most part, the Sunshine Coast has avoided the high-rise glitz of its southern cousin, the Gold Coast. Although there are plenty of stylish restaurants and luxurious hotels, this coast is best loved for its national parks, secluded coves, and relaxed beachside towns.

GETTING HERE AND AROUND

From Brisbane, drive 60 km (35 mi) north on the Bruce Highway, taking the Caloundra Road exit to get to the Sunshine Coast's southernmost beach town, Caloundra. Another five 5 km (3 mi) along the Highway, there's a well-marked exit to the Sunshine Motorway, which funnels you through to Sunshine Coast towns farther north via a series of large roundabouts (stay tuned for the appropriate exit). Follow the motorway north for 9.5 km (6 mi) to get to the Brisbane Road–Mooloolaba exit; 15 km (9 mi) to reach the turn-off to Maroochydore; 29 km (18 mi) to the Yandina-Coolum Rd exit for Coolum Beach; and 34 km (21 mi) to reach the Noosa turnoff.

Sunshine Coast Regional Council, Maroochy Tourist Information Centre has branches at the Sunshine Coast airport, Maroochydore, Mooloolaba, Coolum, and Montville.

AIR TRAVEL   The revamped Sunshine Coast Airport (also known as Maroochy Airport) is the main airport for the Sunshine Coast area, servicing several flights a day by Jetstar, Virgin Blue, and Tiger Airways from Sydney and Melbourne. By air from Maroochydore it's 2 hours 25 minutes to Melbourne, 2 hours 15 minutes to Adelaide, and 1 hour 35 minutes to Sydney. Park at the airport for around A$12 a day, A$65 a week.

BUS TRAVEL   SunAir Bus Service runs daily buses from Brisbane Airport and the Roma Street Transit Centre in Brisbane to all the main Sunshine Coast towns. Distances between towns are short (10 to 30 minutes' drive). SunAir also has several daily services from Brisbane International Airport to Sunshine Coast and Hinterland towns (A$32–$36), meeting every flight into and out of Maroochy Airport and shuttling pre-booked passengers to and from Sunshine Coast towns south of the airport including Maroochydore, Mooloolaba, and Caloundra (A$9–$33 one-way, book between 2 and 5 the previous day).

Henry's Transport Group meets all flights, running buses from Maroochy Airport to the northern Sunshine Coast (A$22 to Noosa) and, on market days, to Eumundi.

CAR TRAVEL   A car is a virtual necessity on the Sunshine Coast. The traditional route to the coast from Brisbane is along the Bruce Highway (Highway 1) to the Glass House Mountains, with a turnoff at Cooroy. Taking the Sunshine Motorway may be faster, however: after 65 km (40 mi), turn off the Bruce Highway at Tanawha (toward Mooloolaba) and follow the signs. On either route, allow 2 hours to get to the central coastal town of Coolum, a further half-hour to reach Noosa, on the northern Sunshine Coast. The most scenic route is to turn off the Bruce Highway at the exit to Caloundra, then follow the coast to Noosa Heads.

TRAIN TRAVEL   Trains leave regularly from Roma Street Transit Centre in Brisbane en route to Nambour, the business hub of the Sunshine Coast. They continue on to Yandina, Eumundi, and other non-coastal towns. Once in Nambour, however, a car is a virtual necessity unless you're a keen cyclist, so it may make more sense to drive from Brisbane.

ESSENTIALS

Airports Sunshine Coast Airport (✉ *Runway Dr. off David Low Way, Marcoola* ☎ *07/5453–1500* ⊕ *www.sunshinecoastairport.com.au*).

Medical services Coolum Beach Medical Centre (✉ *21 Birtwill St., Coolum* ☎ *07/5446–1466*). **Medifirst Noosa 7 Day Medical Centre** (✉ *81 Noosa Dr., Noosa Heads* ☎ *07/5473–5488*).

Bus Contacts Henry's Transport Group (☎ *07/5474–0199* ⊕ *www.henrys.com.au*). **SunAir Bus Service** (☎ *07/5477–0888 or 1800/804340* ⊕ *www.sunair.com.au*).

Train Contacts Queensland Rail (☎ 13–1617 or 1800/627655 ⊕ www.qr.com.au).

Vistor Info Sunshine Coast Regional Council, Maroochy Tourist Informa-tion Centre (✉ 6th Ave., Maroochydore ☎ 07/5459–9050 ⊕ www.maroochy-tourism.com). **Sunshine Coast Tourist Information Centre** (☎ 07/5502–4061 or 1800/330142 ⊕ www.sunshinecoastinformation.com.au). **Tourism Sunshine Coast** (✉ Box 9325, Paradise Palms ☎ 07/5458–8888 ⊕ www.tourismsunshine-coast.com.au). **Tourism Noosa** (✉ 61 Hastings St., near the Surf Club Noosa Heads ✉ Noosa Marina, 2 Parkyn Ct., Tewantin ☎ 1300/066672 ⊕ www.tour-ismnoosa.com.au).

NOOSA HEADS

39 km (24 mi) northeast of Nambour, 17 km (11 mi) north of Coolum, 140 km (87 mi) north of Brisbane.

Set along the calm waters of Laguna Bay at the northern tip of the Sunshine Coast, Noosa Heads is one of Australia's most stylish resort areas. Until the mid-1980s the town consisted of little more than a few shacks: then surfers discovered the spectacular waves that curl around the sheltering headland of Noosa National Park. Today Noosa Heads is a beguiling mix of surf, sand, and sophistication, with a serious reputa-tion for distinctive, evolving cuisine. Views along the trail from Laguna Lookout to the top of the headland north of Main Street take in miles of magnificent beaches, ocean, and dense vegetation.

EXPLORING

About 3 km (2 mi) east of Noosa Heads you'll find the **Teewah Coloured Sands**, an area of multicolored dunes created in the Ice Age by natural chemicals in the soil. Teewah's sands stretch inland from the beach to a distance of about 17 km (11 mi); some of the 72 distinctly hued sands form cliffs rising to 600 feet. A four-wheel-drive vehicle is essential for exploring this area and interesting sites to the north, such as Cooloola National Park, home to 1,300-plus species of plants, 700 native ani-mals, and 44 percent of Australia's bird species; Great Sandy National Park; the wreck of the *Cherry Venture*, near beachside hamlet Fresh-water; and Rainbow Beach. Access is by ferry across the Noosa River at Tewantin.

Tour operators run day trips via cruise boat and four-wheel drive that take in these sights; some include visits to Fraser Island, north of Rain-bow Beach. You can also explore the area on foot: one of Queensland's latest Great Walks winds through Cooloola National Park.

Noosa Everglades Discovery runs day trips that take in these sights, including daily river cruises exploring the Noosa Everglades, and a twice-weekly cruise-and-four-wheel-drive day tour to Cooloola National Park, the Teewah Coloured Sands, and Rainbow Beach. ☎ 07/5449–0393 ⊕ www.noosaeverglades.com.au ✉ A$75, Noosa Everglades afternoon tea cruise; A$155, full-day cruise/tour.

CRUISING **Eco-accredited Noosa Everglades Discovery** runs river cruises around the Noosa Everglades and a combined cruise and four-wheel-drive tour to Cooloola National Park, Teewah Coloured Sands, and Rainbow Beach. ☎ 07/5449–0393 ⊕ www.noosaeverglades.com.au ✉ A$75,

"We were walking along the beach in Noosa at sunset when we came across this guy building the sand castle. He was amazing!" —photo by jenwhitby, Fodors.com member

Everglades Discovery afternoon tea cruise; A$155 full-day Cruise 'n' Coast ⊙ Everglades Discovery: 12–4 daily; Cruise 'n' Coast: 9–4:30, Sun. and Thurs.

WHERE TO EAT

$$ ✕ **Berardo's Bistro on the Beach.** Expatriate New Yorker Jim Berardo came

AUSTRALIAN to Noosa to retire, but he ended up with two restaurants. Berardo's Bistro, the more casual of the pair, has a prime location right on Noosa's beach, and attracts a constant stream of customers. Quirky fish sculptures line the walls; handblown chartreuse carafes are on every table. The weekly menu lists fresh juices, cocktails, extravagant open sandwiches, and light meals with the focus on seafood: have the fish of the day with a garnish of your choice; or linguine with prawns, scallops, mussels, chili, parsley, and garlic. There's also a gourmet deli bar with takeout options. ⊠ *49 Hastings St., beachfront* ☎ *07/5448–0888* ⊕ *www.berardos.com.au* ▭ *AE, MC, V.*

$$ ✕ **Bistro C.** Spectacular views of the bay from the open dining area make

MODERN a stunning backdrop for this restaurant's Mod Oz cuisine. The fresh,

AUSTRALIAN tropical menu highlights seafood, though landlubbers can partake of several meat and vegetarian dishes. Try the signature fresh medley of local seafoods, served in the pan, or seafood antipasto; the barbecued banana prawns on nasi goreng with nam jim jam; or the justly famous egg-fried calamari. Book ahead for Thursday night's "seafood platter": for A$75 you get cold, then hot platters for two, brimming with Moreton Bay bugs, prawns, squid, mussels, barramundi, and more (except in peak season). There's also a kids' menu. ⊠ *On the Beach Complex, 49 Hastings St.* ☎ *07/5447–2855* ⊕ *www.bistroc.com.au* ▭ *AE, DC, MC, V.*

$$$ ✕**Cato's Restaurant and Bar.** This split-level restaurant attached to the
AUSTRALIAN   Sheraton Noosa Resort & Spa has a bar downstairs next to bustling
Hastings Street, and a relaxed dining section above. Seafood dominates
the menu at both; among the favorites are grilled Morton Bay bugs
and beef eye fillets on desiree potato mash and Noosa Valley greens. A
fantastic seafood buffet is available every evening (A$59 Sun.–Thurs.,
A$79 Fri.–Sat.). The extensive wine list includes many wines avail-
able by the glass. ⊠ *16 Hastings St.4567* ☎ *07/5449–4754* ▭ *AE, DC,
MC, V.*

$$ ✕**Ricky's River Bar + Restaurant.** A dining room overlooking the Noosa
CAFE   River makes this restaurant perfect for a relaxed lunch or a romantic
dinner. The menu features "modern Noosa cuisine," in which Mediterranean flavors mingle with Australian ingredients. Sip a mojito or
a mango daiquiri and polish off a plate of tapas before moving on to
a main course of fresh reef fish. There's also a kids' menu. On Thursdays from 5 to 8 PM Ricky's hosts wine tastings (A$5 for 3 wines;
A$5 cheese platters). ⊠ *Noosa Wharf, Quamby Pl.* ☎ *07/5447–2455*
⊕ *www.rickys.com* ▭ *AE, DC, MC, V.*

WHERE TO STAY

¢   🏨 **Halse Lodge.** This National Heritage–listed 1880s guesthouse with
colonial-style furnishings sits in 2 acres of gardens on the edge of Noosa
National Park. Vintage photographs of Noosa decorate the large, functional rooms. Standard rooms and bunk rooms that sleep four or six
people all have shared bathrooms (from A$30 per person, per night).
The restaurant serves daily breakfasts and dinners, and there's a bar
on-site with live music on weekends. Reservations are essential at this
popular backpacker hangout. **Pros:** fantastic setting, good breakfasts,
free use of surfboards. **Cons:** must book ahead, can be noisy on weekends. ⊠ *2 Halse La., at Noosa Dr., near Lions Park* ☎ *07/5447–3377
or 1800/242567* ✍ *backpackers@halselodge.com.au* ⊕ *www.halselo-
dge.com.au* ⇴ *26 rooms without bath* ♿ *In-room: no a/c, no phone,
refrigerator, no TV. In-hotel: safe, restaurant, bar, DVD, beachfront,
diving, laundry facilities, public Internet, airport shuttle (fee), parking
(no fee), no-smoking rooms* ▭ *MC, V.*

$$$$ 🏨 **Sheraton Noosa Resort & Spa.** You can't miss this stepped, six-story,
★   horseshoe-shaped complex as you drive into Noosa Heads. Facing fash-
AUSTRALIAN   ionable Hastings Street on one side, the river on the other, it is playfully
painted apricot with lavender and sea-green trim. The foyer is equally
colorful, though the adjoining River Lounge is stylish and subdued. The
spacious rooms are impeccably appointed, each with a kitchenette (with
coffeemaker), hot tub, and terrace or balcony with river or pool views.
Luxurious spa studios also come with natural products to soothe body
and soul; spa studio packages include free use of selected spa facilities.
Pros: sleek decor; terrific on-site day spa; Cato's Restaurant. **Cons:**
pricey, no in-room Wi-Fi; fees for Internet and parking. ⊠ *14–16 Hastings St.* ☎ *07/5449–4888* ⊕ *www.sheraton.com/noosa* ⇴ *140 rooms,
29 suites, 7 spa studios* ♿ *In-room: safe, kitchen, refrigerator, DVD
(some), Internet (fee). In-hotel: restaurant, room service, bars, pool,
gym, spa, laundry facilities, laundry service, public Internet, public
Wi-Fi (free), parking (fee), no-smoking rooms* ▭ *AE, DC, MC, V.*

6

SUNSHINE BEACH

4 km (2½ mi) south of Noosa Heads.

Ten minutes away from the bustle and crowds of Hastings Street and Noosa Beach, south of the headland and Noosa National Park, is the serene suburb of Sunshine Beach. It's home to a number of good restaurants, a small shopping village, and, as the name suggests, 16 km (10 mi) of beachfront that stretches north to the national park.

COOLUM

17 km (11 mi) south of Noosa Heads, 25 km (16 mi) northeast of Nambour.

At the center of the Sunshine Coast, Coolum makes an ideal base for exploring the countryside. It has one of the finest beaches in the region, a growing reputation for good food and quality accommodation, and all the services you might need: banks with ATMs, medical centers, gas stations, pharmacies, supermarkets, gyms, beauty salons, and day spas—even a beachfront playground, kiosk, and skate park.

OUTDOOR ACTIVITIES

SURFING **Coolum Surf School** is run by an expert surfer and local lifeguard who offers 90-minute group and private lessons as well as board and gear hire. It's the only surf school in the area: find it 50 meters north of Coolum Surf Lifesaving Club, next to the skate park. ⊠ *Coolum Boardriders Clubhouse, Tickle Park, David Low Way , Coolum Beach* ☎ *07/5446–5279* ⊕ *www.coolum.com.au* ✉ *A$80 single; A$50 (4 or more), including gear ⊂Daily, dawn–dusk, by appointment; Sat. 9–11 during school holidays.*

WHERE TO STAY

$$$–$$$$ ⊡ **Coolum Seaside Holiday Apartments.** These spacious one- to four-bedroom apartments and studios, sleekly refurbished in 2007, are just around the corner from Coolum's restaurants, shops, and beach. Each unit has a kitchen, lounge area, entertainment systems, and a large balcony; the ritziest have private rooftop terraces with ocean views, BBQs, and outdoor kitchens. The penthouse's view-laden rooftop comes complete with private Jacuzzi and BBQ; two are fully compliant disabled-friendly apartment. On-site facilities include swimming and lap pools, a well-equipped gym, and an Internet café. The five studio apartments have hot tubs. **Pros:** all modern conveniences, good on-site facilities, close to beach. **Cons:** four- to seven-night minimum stay, except in low season; no Wi-Fi. ⊠ *23 Beach Rd.* ☎ *07/5255–7200* 🖷 *07/5455–7288* ⊕ *www.coolumseaside.com* ⟿ *44 apartments ⊂ In-room: safe, kitchen, refrigerator, DVD, Internet (fee). In-hotel: tennis court, pools, gym, laundry facilities, public Wi-Fi (free), no-smoking rooms* ▭ *AE, MC, V.*

MAROOCHYDORE

18 km (11 mi) south of Coolum, 18 km (11 mi) east of Nambour.

Maroochydore, at the mouth of the Maroochy River, has been a popular beach resort for years, and has its fair share of high-rise towers. Its draw is excellent surfing and swimming beaches.

WHERE TO EAT AND STAY

$
SEAFOOD
✕ **Beach Break Cafe at the Maroochy Surf Club.** Head to this relaxed beachside eatery for lunch or dinner post-surf. The gourmet burgers, steaks, and hearty surf-and-turf—grilled rib fillet with garlic prawns—are hugely popular; the fresh oysters, lemon pepper calamari, almond-pesto-crusted snapper, and grilled mahimahi and barramundi are also excellent. There are also salads, vegetarian dishes, and good-value kids' dishes (all A$7.50). Beachwear is fine by day; smart-casual is the rule after dark. There's a bar, a gaming area, karaoke on Thursday nights, and live bands on weekends. A courtesy bus shuttles patrons to and from local hotels. ✉ *34–36 Alexandra Parade* ☏ *07/5443–1298* ⊕ *www.maroochysurfclub.com.au* ▭ *AE, DC, MC, V.*

$$$
AUSTRALIAN
✕ **ebb Waterfront.** Faux-suede sofas and ottomans in varying shades of cool blue set the mood at this riverside restaurant specializing in top-quality regional produce, particularly sustainably farmed local seafood. Floor-to-ceiling windows line one side of the long, open dining room, and there's a large outdoor dining area. Start with the oysters, perhaps, moving on to duck, lamb, or locally farmed barramundi or Spanner crab; finish with the delectable chocolate fondant. Menus change with the season; there's a kids' menu year-round. Open Wednesday through Sunday for lunch; Wednesday through Saturday for dinner. ✉ *Duporth Riverside, Duporth Ave.* ☏ *07/5452–7771* ⊕ *www.ebbwaterfront.com* ▭ *AE, MC, V.*

$$
🏨 **Novotel Twin Waters Resort.** About 9 km (5½ mi) north of Maroochydore, this hotel was built around a 15-acre saltwater lagoon bordering Maroochy River and Mudjimba Beach. The family-friendly resort lies adjacent to one of Queensland's finest golf courses, where golfers share the greens with kangaroos. There are resident golf, surfing, tennis, and (in peak season) circus pros; catamaran sailing, windsurfing, and canoeing on the lagoon are free for guests. Choose from three accommodation styles: twin Resort rooms, King Spa suites—each with a kitchenette, lounge area, and hot tub—and lavish Lagoon Spa suites, popular with couples. All rooms have high-speed Internet, pay movies, and Sony PlayStation games, and were given fresh soft furnishings in 2007. The overwater day spa incorporates a hair salon and art gallery. **Pros:** great lawns and lagoon; free use of water-sports equipment; terrific kids' programs. **Cons:** housekeeping standards vary; buffet dinners pricey; lackluster spa. ✉ *Ocean Dr., Twin Waters* ☏ *07/5448–8000 or 1800/072277* ⊕ *www.twinwatersresort.com.au* ⇌ *234 rooms, 126 suites* ⚐ *In-room: kitchen (some), refrigerator, Internet, Wi-Fi. In-hotel: 4 restaurants, room service, bars, pool, tennis courts (fee), gym, spa, beachfront, water sports, bicycles (fee), children's programs (ages 2–12; 2 –16 during school holidays), laundry facilities, laundry service, public Internet, public Wi-Fi, parking (no fee), no-smoking rooms, no elevator* ▭ *AE, DC, MC, V* ⏐◎⏐ *BP.*

6

$$$–$$$$ ⊡ **The Sebel Maroochydore.** Each one- or two-bedroom apartment in this stylish hotel has a curved feature wall and a kitchen bristling with European appliances. Most have separate media rooms filled with entertainment wizardry; all have blond-wood furniture, cream-color sofas in sitting areas and bedrooms, and two bathrooms, one with a hot tub. Glass doors lead to spacious, furnished balconies with views over Maroochy River, the beach, or Mt. Coolum and the Hinterland. The rooftop barbecue area (with hot tub) is the perfect place to unwind. A clutch of cafés and restaurants is a short walk away, as is the beach. **Pros:** 25-meter (82-foot) pool and separate kids pool; stylish decor; good service. **Cons:** noise from pool area and traffic at night; beach is across a four-lane road; soft furnishings showing wear. ⊠ *20 Aerodrome Rd., Maroochydore* ☎ *07/5479–8000 or 1800/137106* ⊕ *www. mirvachotels.com* ⟿ *70 apartments, 6 penthouses* ⚫ *In-room: safe, kitchen, refrigerator, laundry facilities, DVD, Internet (fee). In-hotel: room service, pool, laundry service, public Internet (fee), parking (no fee), airport shuttle, no-smoking rooms* ▭ *AE, DC, MC, V.*

MOOLOOLABA

5 km (3 mi) south of Maroochydore.

Mooloolaba stretches along a lovely beach and riverbank, both an easy walk from town. The Esplanade has many casual cafés, upscale restaurants, and fashionable shops. Head to the town outskirts for picnic spots and prime coastal views.

EXPLORING

☾ **Underwater World** has back-to-back marine presentations, including stringray feedings, guided shark tours, and seal and otter shows, all accompanied by informative talks. A clear underwater tunnel lets you get face to face with creatures from the deep. You can also swim with seals for A$90, play with otters for A$150 (including photo), and scuba dive with resident sharks: the cost, including training and 30 minutes underwater, is A$195 for beginners, A$155 for certified divers. The twice-daily behind-scenes tour, taking in the nursery, oceanarium, and marine turtle rehab center, is well worth it at A$15: pre-booking is a must. A souvenir shop and a café are on-site. The aquarium is part of Mooloolaba's Wharf Complex, which also has a marina, restaurants, and a tavern. ⊠ *10 Parkyn Parade, The Wharf* ☎ *07/5458–6280* ⊕ *www.underwaterworld.com.au* ⌨ *A$30* ☾ *Daily 9–5.*

WHERE TO EAT AND STAY

$$
★
ITALIAN
✕ **Bella Venezia Italian Restaurant & Bar.** A large mural of Venice, simple wooden tables, and terra-cotta floor tiles decorate this popular restaurant in an arcade off the Esplanade, You can eat in or take out traditional and modern Italian cuisine, such as the *filetto chianti* (a 250g [8.8 oz], grain-fed eye fillet with field mushrooms, mash, and a Chianti jus); *anatra puccini* (an oven-roasted organic duck with a rich orange–white wine glaze); or pan-fried fish of the day. There's an extensive wine and cocktail list. They'll also deliver to local hotels. ⊠ *Shop 1, Pacific*

Beach Resort, 95 The Esplanade ☎ *07/5444–5844* ⊕ *www.bellav.com. au* ▭ *AE, DC, MC, V.*

$$$$ 🏨 **Mantra Sirocco.** The futuristic curves of this apartment complex loom above Mooloolaba's main drag. Two-, three-, and five-bedroom apartments, just across the road from the beach, have sleek modern furnishings, hot tubs, cable TV, balconies, and magnificent beach views. Several smart restaurants are close by. **Pros:** fantastic views from big balconies; friendly staff. **Cons:** no Wi-Fi; occasional housekeeping lapses; minimum five-night stay late December through January. ⊠ *59–75 The Esplanade* ☎ *07/5444–1400, 1300/553800 reservations* ⊕ *www.siroccoapartments.com.au* ⟿ *41 apartments* ⌂ *In-room: kitchen, refrigerator, laundry facilities, DVD (some), VCR (some), Internet (fee). In-hotel: pool, gym, laundry facilities, laundry service, parking (no fee), no-smoking rooms* ▭ *AE, DC, MC, V.*

CALOUNDRA

29 km (18 mi) south of Maroochydore, 63 km (39 mi) south of Noosa Heads, 91 km (56 mi) north of Brisbane.

This unassuming southern seaside town has nine beaches of its own, which include everything from placid wading beaches (King's Beach and Bulcock Beach are best for families) to bays with thundering surf, such as Dicky, Buddina, and Wurtulla beaches.

WHERE TO EAT AND STAY

$$$ ✕ **mooo char + bar.** Owned by legendary (and now retired) Queensland
SEAFOOD Rugby League footballer Allan "Alfie" Langer, this steak-centric restaurant has an ideal setting right on Bulcock Beach, overlooking the sheltered inlet known as Pumicestone Passage. The decor and design are light and bright, and there's both indoor and outdoor dining. Try the restaurant's deservedly popular steak; wild barramundi; Moreton Bay bug salad; or local king prawns. ⊠ *The Esplanade at Otranto Terr.* ☎ *07/5492–0800* ⊕ *www.alfies.net.au* ▭ *AE, DC, MC, V.*

¢ 🏨 **Caloundra City Backpackers.** This purpose-built modern hostel prides itself on being the best value in town. There are twin rooms (without bathrooms), doubles with en suites, and one triple, plus two eight-bed dorms (from A\$26 per person, per night). All rooms are simple but tasteful, outfitted in blue and white. Guests share two fully equipped kitchens, and when they're not out surfing or sightseeing can watch DVDs or get online in the hostel's sociable common areas. It's a five-minute walk to the beach, two minutes into town. **Pros:** friendly, helpful staff; clean rooms; sociable communal areas. **Cons:** small; few in-room facilities; no a/c. ⊠ *84 Omrah Ave.* ☎ *07/5499–7655* ⊕ *www.caloundracitybackpackers.com.au* ⟿ *20 rooms, 5 with bath; 7 dorms; 1 family room* ⌂ *In-room: no a/c, no phone, no TV(some). In-hotel: refrigerator, laundry facilities, public Internet, parking (no fee), no-smoking rooms* ▭ *MC, V.*

$$–$$$ 🏨 **Rolling Surf Resort.** The white sands of King's Beach front this resort enveloped in tropical gardens. Wooden blinds, cane furniture, and beach prints fill well-equipped one- to three-bedroom beachfront and poolside apartments. All rooms have hot tubs; many also have large,

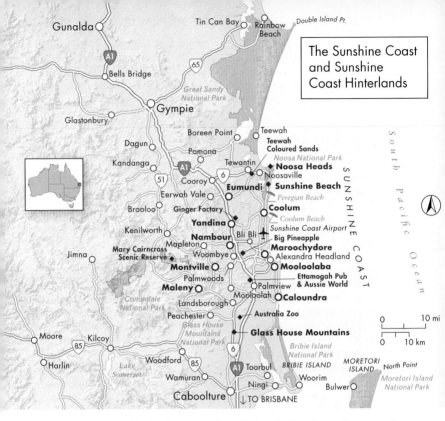

The Sunshine Coast
and Sunshine
Coast Hinterlands

curved balconies overlooking the beach. There's a well-equipped gymnasium, a sauna and steam room, an arcade games room, and a 60-meter (80-yard) heated pool that can be directly accessed from some ground-floor units, or viewed via underwater portholes from the gym and lobby. The resort's own excellent café-restaurant, Tanja's, does big buffet breakfasts on weekends, light and à la carte meals with white-linen service after dark, and Indian feasts on alternate Fridays. The Sun Air Bus Service or A1 Airport Transfers will deliver you to the front door from Brisbane Airport. **Pros:** huge pool, good on-site eatery; right on the beach. **Cons:** no Wi-Fi; 7-night minimum stay in high season. ⊠ *10 Levuka Ave., King's Beach* ☎ *07/5491–9777 or 1800/775559* ⊕ *www. rollingsurfresort.com* ⊅ *74 apartments* ⟆ *In-hotel: restaurant, pool, gym, beachfront, laundry facilities, public Internet, parking (no fee)* ▭ *MC, V.*

SUNSHINE COAST HINTERLAND

The Sunshine Coast Hinterland, extending from the Glass House Mountains just northwest of Brisbane to Eumundi and Yandina, west of the northern Sunshine Coast town of Noosa, is ideal terrain for daytrippers. Tracts of subtropical rain forest and mountainous areas linked by scenic drives and walking trails are interspersed with pretty hillside villages, their main streets lined with cafés, galleries, gift shops, and guesthouses. Here you'll also find thriving markets, renowned restaurants and cooking schools, ginger, nut, and pineapple farms, theme and wildlife parks, and luxury B&Bs.

The Hinterland's southerly extent is the nine distinctive conical outcrops of the Glass House Mountains—the eroded remnants of ancient volcanoes—rising dramatically from a flattish landscape 45 km (27 mi) northwest of Brisbane. Get a great view of the mountains from Glass House Mountains Lookout, also the starting-point for a scenic, 25-minute walk. Several longer trails begin from nearby vantage points, such as Mount Beerburrum and Wild Horse Mountain Lookout. Nearby, you'll find Aussie World amusement park, the Ettamogah Pub, and the late Steve Irwin's Australia Zoo.

Meander north through the mountains to reach the arty village of Maleny, quaint, European-style Montville, and food-friendly Mapleton. Nearby, you'll find tranquil Baroon Lake and easy walking trails in Kondalilla National Park and Mary Cairncross Scenic Reserve.

Continue north to Yandina, where you'll find much-lauded restaurant Spirit House and the Ginger Factory, and Eumundi, known for its thriving twice-weekly markets. Hinterland hub Nambour, east of Mapleton, has shops, banks, and the unmissable Big Pineapple.

6

GETTING HERE AND AROUND

To get to the Sunshine Coast Hinterland from Brisbane, follow the Bruce Highway north for around 35 km (22 mi), taking the Glass House Mountains Road exit. A 10-km (6-mi) drive along Glass House Mountains Road brings you to the quaint Glass House Mountains Village. Access Glass House Mountains Lookout, 10 km (6 mi) from the village, via Glass House Mountains Tourist Route. Drive 10 km (6 mi) north along Glass House Mountains Road from the village to reach Maleny.

From Maleny, take the Landsborough-Maleny Road for 10 km (6 mi), turning right at Maleny–Montville Road, to get to Montville. From Montville it's a 5-minute drive west on Western Avenue to Kondallilla National Park. A further 10-km (6-mi) drive northwest brings you to Mapleton, from which it's a 12-km (7-mi), 15-minute drive east to Nambour, en route to the Sunshine Coast.

From Nambour, 20 minutes' drive east along Petrie Creek Road and David Low Way brings you to the mid-Sunshine Coast town of Maroochydore. Or drive 20 minutes north along the Bruce Highway to reach Eumundi, 20 km (12 mi) away. From here it's a half-hour, 20-km (12-mi) drive east along the Eumundi–Noosa Rd. to Noosa Heads, the northernmost town on the Sunshine Coast.

From Nambour it's an 8-km (5-mi) drive north along the Nambour Connection Road, then Old Bruce Highway, to reach Yandina. From Brisbane, it's an hour's drive north along the Bruce Highway: take the Coolum/Yandina exit.

It's around 60 km (35 mi) to Glass House Mountains Village; just under 100 km (60 mi) to Montville; and nearly 110 km (65 mi) to Maleny from the city. Driving time is 90 minutes to the Glasshouse Mountains; around 2 hours to Maleny and Montville, and a further 15 minutes' drive to Nambour and another 12 minutes' drive to Yandina. From the Sunshine Coast, most parts of the Hinterland are less than an hour's drive inland.

You'll find few banks and money exchanges around the Sunshine Coast Hinterland: ■ TIP➜ get cash in advance from ATMs in larger coastal towns such as Noosa. Alternatively, there is one in Nambour and several are available at Mobil stations along the Bruce Highway.

ESSENTIALS

Banks Bank of Queensland Nambour (⊠ *15 Ann St., Nambour* ☏ *07/5476–2003*).

Visitor Info Hinterland Queensland Information Centre (⊠ *787 Landsborough-Maleny Rd., Maleny* ☏ *07/5499–9033*). **Montville Visitors Information Centre** (⊠ *198 Main St., Montville* ☏ *07/5478–5544*).

GLASS HOUSE MOUNTAINS AREA

35 km (22 mi) north of Brisbane on Bruce Highway to the Glass House Mountains Road exit; 4 km (2.5 mi) south of Beerwah.

More than 20 million years old, the Glass House Mountains consist of nine conical outcrops—the eroded remnants of volcanoes—that rise dramatically from a flattish landscape northwest of Brisbane. Get a great view of the mountains from Glass House Mountains Lookout. Access is 10 km (6 mi) from the village via Glass House Mountains Tourist Route. The lookout is also the starting point for a scenic 25-minute walk. Several longer walks begin from nearby vantage points, such as Mount Beerburrum and Wild Horse Mountain Lookout.

EXPLORING GLASS HOUSE MOUNTAINS AREA

☼ **Australia Zoo,** made famous by the late Steve Irwin, has all manner of Australian animals: koalas, kangaroos, wallabies, dingos, Tasmanian Devils, snakes and lizards—and, naturally, crocodiles. There are also otters, lemurs, tigers, red pandas, and a giant rain-forest aviary. Daily shows feature crocs, birds of prey, and koalas. Don't miss hand-feeding the Asian elephants. A courtesy bus shuttles visitors to and from Beerwah station; get around the park on foot or on free hop-on, hop-off mini-trains. ⊠ *1638 Steve Irwin Way* ⊹ *5 km (3 mi) north of Glass House Mountains, Beerwah* ☏ *07/5436–2000* ⊕ *www.australiazoo. com.au* ☜ *A$54* ⊙ *Daily 9–5 (last entry 4:30).*

The **Ettamogah Pub,** whose name (allegedly, Aboriginal for "place of good drink") and quirky design are based on the fictitious pub made famous by Aussie cartoonist Ken Maynard, looms 18 meters (55 feet) over the Bruce Highway just north of Palmview (21 km [13 mi] north of Glass House Mountains). The much-photographed watering hole, its furniture constructed mainly from wood logged on the site, has an upstairs bistro, a beer garden, and a bar, and is open daily 9

40-minute guided tour of the world's only publically accessible ginger processing plant. A restaurant and shop sell ginger in all forms—incorporated into jams, cookies, chocolates, ice cream, wine, and herbal products. There's a train trip and a boat ride, both with animated puppetry en route, and a new live beehive tour that includes a honey tasting. You can even take cooking classes. ⊠ *50 Pioneer Rd., 1 km (½ mi) east of Bruce Hwy., 9 km (5½ mi) north of Nambour* ☎ *07/5446–7100 or 1800/067686* ⊕ *www.gingerfactory.com.au* ✉ *Free; A$33 (3-hour tour package)* ☉ *Daily 9–5.*

WHERE TO EAT

$$
Fodor'sChoice
★
THAI

✕ **Spirit House.** Mention that you're looking for a place to eat in Yandina, and even Brisbane foodies say "Spirit House." The restaurant's trio of credentialed chefs, who travel annually to Asia to get inspiration and skills, do a remarkable job re-creating contemporary Asian cuisine on Queensland soil. The menu, designed around plates to share, changes seasonally, with most ingredients sourced locally; a worthy signature dish is the whole crispy reef fish with tamarind-chili sauce. Save room for delectable desserts, best sampled in the tasting plate for two. The lush garden setting has a lagoon and Buddhist shrines. A hydroponic farm and cooking school with daily lessons are on-site. ⊠ *20 Ninderry Rd.* ☎ *07/5446–8994* ⊕ *www.spirithouse.com.au* ⚲ *Reservations essential* ▭ *AE, DC, MC, V* ☉ *No dinner Sun.–Tues.*

MACKAY–CAPRICORN ISLANDS

Despite its name, this group of islands lying offshore between Bundaberg and Rockhampton is closer to the southern half of Queensland than it is to the city of Mackay. The Mackay–Capricorn Islands comprise the section of the Great Barrier Reef known as Capricorn Marine Park, which stretches for 140 km (87 mi) and cuts through the Tropic of Capricorn, Heron Island being the closest point. This is a great area for wildlife: turtles use several of the islands as breeding grounds; seabirds nest here; and humpback whales pass through on their migration to Antarctica each spring—generally between July and October.

LADY ELLIOT ISLAND

Fodor'sChoice
★

Lady Elliot Island is a 104-acre coral cay on the southern tip of the Great Barrier Reef, positioned 80 km (50 mi) off the Queensland coast, within easy reach of Bundaberg and Hervey Bay. One of just six island resorts actually on the reef, it's a high-level Marine National Park Zone. Wildlife here easily outnumbers the guests (a maximum of 100 can visit at any one time)—and that reality is underscored by the ammoniacal odor of hundreds of nesting seabirds and, in season, the sounds and sights of them courting, mating, and nesting.

Divers will enjoy the easy access to the reef and the variety of diving sites around Lady Elliot. Fringed on all sides by coral reefs and blessed with a stunning white-sand, coral-strewn shore, this oval isle seems to have been made for diving. There's a busy dive shop and a reef education center with marine-theme exhibits (plus an educational video

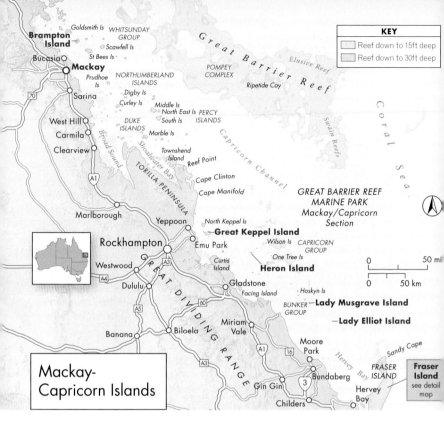

library—great for rainy days). Inclement weather and choppy waves can lead to canceled dives and washed-out underwater visibility. When the waters are calm, you'll see turtles, morays, sharks, rays, and millions of tropical fish. Many divers visit Lady Elliot specifically to encounter the resident population of manta rays that feed off the coral.

From October to April, Lady Elliot becomes a busy breeding ground for crested and bridled terns, silver gulls, lesser frigate birds, and the rare red-tailed tropic bird. Between November and March, green and loggerhead turtles emerge from the water to lay their eggs; hatching takes place after January. During the hatchling season, staff biologists host guided turtle-watching night hikes. From about July through October, pods of humpback whales are visible from the beachfront restaurant.

Lady Elliot is one of the few islands in the area where camping—albeit modified—is part of the resort, and a back-to-basics theme pervades the accommodations.

GETTING HERE AND AROUND

Lady Elliot is the only coral cay with its own airstrip. Small aircraft generally make the flight from Hervey Bay (40 minutes) or Bundaberg (30 minutes), though pickups can be arranged from as far south in Queensland as Coolangatta, on the Gold Coast (2 hours). You can day-trip to Lady Elliot with Seair Pacific, too. The cost includes scenic flight, buffet lunch, reef walking, glass-bottom boat ride, snorkeling, and island tour.

Tours require a minimum of 2 passengers and use planes that can carry up to 12. Strict luggage limits for both hand and checked baggage allow 10 kilograms (22 pounds) per person (for A$20 extra, divers can take an extra 10 kg in dive gear). If you exceed this limit, you can repack at the ticket-counter scale or wave good-bye to the plane.

ESSENTIALS

Airlines Seair Pacific (☎ 07/5599–4509 ⊕ www.seairpacific.com.au).

OUTDOOR ACTIVITIES

At the resort dive shop you can rent equipment and arrange dive courses to more than a dozen excellent sites, including Lighthouse Bommie, home to a 40-strong manta ray colony, and the Blow Hole and Hiro's Cave. Refresher pool dives, a shore snorkeling trip, and guided reef, nature, and historical walks are free for resort guests. Off-boat snorkeling and glass-bottom boat rides are A$20. Shore dives are A$35; boat dives start at A$50; night dives are A$70. Open-water certification courses cost A$525; "Discover Scuba Diving" short courses are A$150; and referral courses, available to those who've completed the classroom and pool portions of a certification course prior to arrival, are A$400. Diving here is weather-dependent, so plan accordingly if you intend doing a dive course over multiple days. Four-night packages, including seven dives, flights (from Hervey Bay, Fraser coast), Bundaberg, the Gold and Sunshine coasts, or Brisbane), guest activities, meals, reef tax, and accommodation, start at A$1,131; all-inclusive seven-night packages, with 15 dives, start at A$1,671. Other special deals are available. There is a onetime A$15 environmental management charge for all nonpackage guests.

WHERE TO STAY

$$$–$$$$ ☷ **Lady Elliot Island Eco Resort.** Here you're more like a marine biologist at an island field camp than a tourist enjoying a luxury resort. Linens are changed every third day, and rooms are simply furnished (though those on the beachfront are air-conditioned). Clearly, the eco-resort's focus is on simplicity, functionality, and conservation. There are four types of rooms: beachfront island suites; reef units with multiple bed configurations and private facilities; shearwater rooms with bunk beds, great for groups of friends; and permanent, powered safari-style tents. The Eco Resort goes to great lengths to protect its pristine environs: there's strictly no fishing; no souveniring coral. A free children's "reef ranger" program runs during Queensland and NSW school holiday periods. Dinner and breakfast, included in the room rates, are served buffet-style in the airy dining room, and may be enjoyed inside or on the covered veranda. It's hearty fare, with limitless tea and coffee. The upbeat staff encourages guests to mingle, with activities such as coconut bowling, pool games, and dress-up theme nights in the bar, daily guided walks, snorkeling trips, and video/information nights. **Pros:** eco-friendly, proximity to nature; friendly, knowledgable staff. **Cons:** few in-room modern conveniences; limited leisure options for rainy, non-diving days. ☞ Box 348, Runaway Bay, QLD 4216 ☎ 07/5536–3644

(head office), 07/4156–4444 (resort) or 1800/072200 ⊕ www.ladyel-liot.com.au ⤵20 reef rooms, 3 shearwater rooms, 5 suites, 12 tents ⚕ In-room: no a/c (some), no phone, refrigerator (some), no TV. In-hotel: restaurant, bar, pool, beachfront, diving, water sports, children's programs (ages 3–12), laundry facilities, public Internet, public Wi-Fi, no-smoking rooms ⊟ AE, DC, MC, V ⍟ MAP.

LADY MUSGRAVE ISLAND

★ Lady Musgrave Island sits at the southern end of the Great Barrier Reef Marine Park, about 40 km (25 nautical mi) north of Lady Elliot Island and 96 km (53 nautical mi) north east of Bundaberg. The cay has a 2,945-acre surrounding reef, about one-third of which is a massive yet calm lagoon, a true coral cay of 39.5 acres. Here day-trippers, yachties, divers, and campers converge, and the island has some of the best diving and snorkeling in Queensland. Campers have a chance to view the myriad sea life surrounding this tiny speck of land in the Pacific.

From October through April the island is a bird and turtle rookery, with black noddies, wedge-tailed shearwaters, bridled terns, more timid black-naped and roseate terns, and green and loggerhead turtles. There's also an abundance of flora, including casuarina and pisonia trees.

GETTING HERE AND AROUND
Lady Musgrave Barrier Reef Cruises is the only carrier servicing Lady Musgrave Island. Boats depart daily at 8 AM from the Town of 1770 marina on Captain Cook Drive, arriving around 90 minutes later (board from 7:30). Baggage is limited to about a cubic foot per person, as space on board is tight. You'll be expected to load most of your gear the evening prior to sailing; on the island, use wheelbarrows to haul it to the campground from the island drop-off point, 250 meters (275 yards) away. The return journey departs at around 10 AM, but doesn't go directly back to the mainland. Before that, you get a day cruise, including a buffet lunch and a 90-minute stopover on the Outer Reef, at a pontoon within a sheltered lagoon where you can snorkel, view coral from a submersible or glass-bottom boat, take a guided island walk, or do a spot of scuba diving or reef fishing before the boat cruises back to the mainland. The day trip, including most extras, is A$165 per person; visitors staying on-island pay A$160 each way—but get to take the cruise twice. If you're carrying a dinghy for getting around the island, it costs an extra A$120 round-trip (hire dinghies from Burnett Boat Hire (☎ 0414/721883); and there's a A$5 per person reef tax. Campers must have an EPA permit at time of boarding (A$4.85 per person, per night). If you're camping, you get substantial discounts on boat transfers April through June.

ESSENTIALS
Cruise Lady Musgrave Barrier Reef Cruises (☎ 07/4974–9077 ⊕ www.lmcruises.com.au).

Coral and Lighthouse, Lady Elliot Island

OUTDOOR ACTIVITIES

SPORT HERE **Lady Musgrave Barrier Reef Cruises** operates a pontoon in the vast deep-water coral lagoon off Lady Musgrave Island, with an underwater observatory, snorkeling deck, changing rooms, and sheltered seating. Their Lady Musgrave day cruises get you out to the reef in 90 minutes, giving you six hours to swim, snorkel, feed the fish, and explore your environs via glass-bottom boat and semisubmersible tours and guided reef walks. Here you can swim with turtles and see 350 varieties of colorful live coral and 1,300 species of tropical fish year-round, and migrating whales in season. Optional extras include reef fishing and scuba diving (for novice and certified divers, with or without gear). There's a per-person reef tax of A$5. Cruises depart daily from the Town of 1770 and include a tropical buffet lunch, morning and afternoon tea, activities on the Reef, and most gear. There's a A$5 per person reef tax. ⊠ *Town of 1770 marina, 535 Captain Cook Drive, Town of 1770* ☎ *07/4974–9077* ⊕ *www.lmcruises.com.au* ⊠ *A$165 day cruise; A$15 reef fishing; A$40 or $55 for 1 or 2 dives, certified diver (A$55 or $80 incl. gear); A$30 or $85, introductory lesson and 1 or 2 dives, with gear* ☺ *Daily, except Wed., 8–5.*

WHERE TO STAY

Camping here can be isolated: take first-aid supplies, food, water, and all gear—including, if possible, an emergency marine radio (mobile phone coverage is limited on the cays). Hurricanes (cyclones) may necessitate emergency evacuation in wet season: marine VHF radios are preferred to mobile phones, which may not get reception on the cays. In an emergency, tune in to VMR477 Round Hill or VMR488 Bundaberg,

7 AM–6 PM on channel 81 marine VHF; or Queensland Police Service, Bundaberg, monitors channel 81 marine VHF day and night. Be aware of local hazards, including large centipedes and bird ticks; and follow EPA guidelines to minimize your impact on island vegetation, nesting seabirds, turtle hatchlings, and the fragile reef. The island is generally closed from after the Australia Day weekend (around January 27) until Easter (March or early April), to minimize impact on emerging turtle hatchlings, breeding seabirds, and sensitive vegetation.

The island, part of the Capricornia Cays National Park, is uninhabited and has only basic facilities (one toilet block and emergency radio equipment) for campers. Commercial tour operators from the Town of 1770 (yes, that's the town's actual name) on the mainland have all camping equipment and necessary provisions available for rent. More information on the national park can be obtained from the Gladstone office of the **Queensland Parks and Wildlife Service** (☎ 07/4971–6500) or the Great Barrier Reef Marine Park Authority (☎ 1800/990177 ⊕ www. gbrmpa.gov.au). The **Environmental Protection Agency** (☎ 1300/130372 ⊕ www.epa.qld.gov.au) is a good source of information on camping in Capricornia Cays National Park. Contact the Queensland Government's 24-hour info line (☎ 13–1304) for camping permits (A$4.85 per person per night). Reservations can be made 11 months in advance. Book early, as school breaks and holidays fill up fast; no more than 40 campers may visit the island at any one time.

HERON ISLAND

Fodor's Choice   Most resort islands lie well inside the shelter of the distant reef, but
★   Heron Island, some 72 km (45 mi) northeast of the mainland port of Gladstone, is actually part of the reef. The waters off this 18-hectare (20-acre) island are spectacular, teeming with fish and coral, and ideal for snorkeling and scuba diving. The water is generally clearest in June and July and cloudiest during the rainy season, January and February. Heron Island operates on "island time"—an hour ahead of Eastern Standard Time—and at its own leisurely pace. You won't find much in the way of nightlife, as the island's single accommodation accepts a cozy maximum of 250 people—and there are no day-trippers. But these might be reasons why you decide to come here.

GETTING HERE AND AROUND

All transfers are booked with your accommodations through Voyages Customer Care Centre. The high-speed launch makes the one-hour and 45-minute run to Heron Island from Gladstone, on the Queensland coast, for A$240 round-trip, departing at 11 AM daily and arriving in time for a late lunch. The return boat departs from Heron Island for the mainland at 2:30 island time (1:30 EST). This can be a rough journey: take ginger or anti-nausea medicine ½ hour before departure. A courtesy shuttle bus transfers guests from Gladstone Airport, leaving at 10 AM daily, and meets all afternoon boats. (Fly to Gladstone from Brisbane, Mackay, Rockhampton, Townsville, and Cairns with Qantas.) You can also arrange transfers to and from Gladstone Station; get here on Queensland Rail's fast Tilt Train or Sunlander from the north or south (⊕ *www.qr.com.au*).

Australian Helicopters makes 30-minute helicopter flights to Heron Island from Gladstone for A$340 one-way, with more services October through April. The baggage restriction is 15 kilograms (33 pounds) per person. Lockup facilities for excess baggage are free (or get it brought over on the daily launch for free). You can charter a helicopter to the island from Gladstone for A$2,191 (max. 5 adults, 1 infant).

ESSENTIALS

Air Travel Australian Helicopters (✉ *Gladstone Airport, Aerodrome Rd., Gladstone* ☎ *07/4978–1177* ⊕ *www.austheli.com*).

EXPLORING

Wilson Island. Only guests of the Heron Island Resort can visit uninhabited Wilson Island, a coral cay 15 km (9 mi) north of (and a 45-minute launch trip from) Heron Island. In January and February Wilson Island becomes the breeding ground for roseate terns and green and loggerhead turtles. The island also has its own exclusive, six-suite, premium tented resort, catering to a maximum of 12 guests (and no children under 13), with all meals included in the rate—for A$446–A$525 per person, per night (more nights mean lower rates). Combination packages allow for nights at both Heron and Wilson islands, including meals. The island closes in February to protect nesting birds. ☎ *1300/134044* ⊕ *www. voyages.com.au/Wilson*.

OUTDOOR ACTIVITIES

Heron Island Marine Center & Dive Shop. You can book snorkeling, scuba diving, and fishing excursions as well as turtle-watching tours and sunset cruises through Heron Island Marine Centre & Dive Shop. Snorkeling lessons and refresher dive courses are free. Snorkeling trips are A$30.

DIVING Various diving options include a resort diving course for beginners, including training and one guided dive, for A$165 (subsequent dives, A$115). For certified divers it's A$65 per dive, and just A$40 per dive upwards of four dives. Referral dive courses cost A$450. A full-day tour of neighboring islands including up to three dives among pristine reefs is A$365 per person (minimum four divers), including lunch and drinks. A half-day, two-dive trip is A$250. Dive charter packages are also available, and you can get a dive package with a 2-day or longer stay, including five dives, for A$275.

For all dives, pre-booking's essential, and gear costs you extra. Children under 7 aren't permitted on snorkeling trips, under-10s can't go diving, and under-14s must be accompanied by an adult (and if diving, must be certified).

SNORKELING AND SEMISUB-MERSIBLE Nondivers wanting to explore their underwater environs can take a half-day snorkeling tour of Heron, Wistari, and Bloomfield reefs, or an hour-long, naturalist-guided semisubmersible tour. Interpretive nature walks, guided reef walks, and visits to the island's Marine Research Station are free.

6

Scuba diving off Heron Island

FISHING Heron Island Marine Centre runs three-hour fishing trips and half- and full-day guided reef-fishing charters for up to four passengers, with gear, tackle, and optional stops for snorkeling. Toast the sunse t on an hour-long wine and cheese cruise; or book a charter cruise for up to eight people. Heron Island resort can pack you a sandwich lunch for A$29; a Mediterranean beach picnic for A$49.

☎ *07/4978–1399* ⊕ *www.marine.uq.edu.au/hirs* ✉ *A$40 semisubmersible tour, A$130 snorkeling tour, A$40–A$450 per person scuba diving, A$80 3-hr fishing, A$800 (half-day, up to 4) to A$1,300 (full-day, up to 4, incl. snorkeling) reef-fishing, A$60 sunset cruise, A$500 (max. 4) or A$700 (max. 8) sunset charter, A$10 stargazing* ☉ *Daily, hours vary, closed Feb.*

WHERE TO STAY

$$$ 🏨 **Voyages Heron Island.** Set among palm trees and connected by sand paths, this secluded, eco-certified resort offers six accommodation types, from the deluxe Beach House with private outdoor shower and beach boardwalk to the comparatively compact, garden-level Turtle Rooms. Large, elegantly modern suites with CD players, well-stocked minibars, separate lounge areas, and furnished private decks or terraces merit the extra expense. Room rates include breakfast, or book a package that includes all meals (A$69 additional per day). There's an Aussie barbecue every Tuesday night. Complimentary activities include non-motorized water sports, guided walks, stargazing, trivia nights, and outdoor movie screenings. Snorkeling and diving excursions cost extra, as does the kids' program, run during Australian school holidays. The delightful Aqua Soul Spa offers treatments with marine-based and

If you prefer your wilderness *sans* dune-buggying, head for the unspoiled interior of the island, where they're not allowed. They're a necessity everywhere else, unless you're a fit walker or cyclist or can ride a motorcycle pretty well.

ESSENTIALS

Airport Fraser Coast (Hervey Bay) Airport (✉ *Don Adams Dr., Urangan* ☎ *07/4194–8100* ⊕ *www.airportshuttleherveybay.com.au*).

Boat and Ferry Contacts Fraser Island Barges (Fraser Dawn, Fraser Venture, Rainbow Venture, and Fraser Explorer) (☎ *07/4194–9300 or 1800/BARGES* ⊕ *www.fraserislandbarges. com.au*). **Kingfisher Bay Ferry & Vehicle Barge** (☎ *1800/072555* ⊕ *www. kingfisherbay.com*). **Manta Ray** (☎ *0418/872599 or 07/5486–8888* ⊕ *www. fraserislandbarge.com.au*).

Car Rental Budget Car Rental (☎ *07/4125–3633* ⊕ *www.budget.com.au*). **Fraser Island Wilderness Co. Tour Desk** (☎ *1800/063933* ⊕ *www.fraserislandco.com.au*). **Kingfisher Bay Resort and Village** (☎ *07/4120–3333 or 1800/072555* ⊕ *www.kingfisherbay.com*).

Shuttle Bundaberg and Wide Bay Shuttle Service (☎ *07/4155–0244 or 1800/333532* ⊕ *www.bundabergshuttleservice.com.au*).

Tours Air Fraser Island/OzHorizons (☎ *07/4125–3600 or 1800/252668* ⊕ *www.ozhorizons.com.au or www.airfraser.com.au*). **Kingfisher Bay Resort** (☎ *1800/072555* ⊕ *www.kingfisherbay.com*).

Vehicle Permits Environmental Protection Agency (EPA) Customer Service Centre (✉ *160 Ann St., Brisbane* ☎ *1300/130372 or 07/3227–8185 info, 13–1304 permits* ⊕ *www.epa.qld.gov.au or www.qld.gov.au/camping*).

Visitor Info Hervey Bay Tourist & Visitors Information Centre (✉ *401 The Esplanade, Hervey Bay* ☎ *07/4124–4050 or 1800/649926* ⊕ *www.herveybaytouristinfo.com.au*).

GETTING HELP

Fraser Island does not have a resident doctor. Emergency medical assistance can be obtained at the ranger stations in Eurong, Waddy Point, and Dundubara, but these have variable hours—if no answer, phone the base station at Nambour on the mainland. Kingfisher Bay Resort has first-aid facilities and resident nursing staff.

6

EXPLORING

Note that swimming in the ocean off the island is not recommended because of the rough conditions and sharks that hunt close to shore. Stick to the inland lakes. For more detail, head to ⊕ *www.epa.qld.gov*.

Highlights of a drive along the east coast, which is known as Seventy-Five Mile Beach for its sheer distance, include **Eli Creek**, a great freshwater swimming hole. North of this popular spot lies the rusting hulk of the *Maheno*, half buried in the sand, a roost for seagulls and a prime hunting ground for anglers when the tailor are running. Once a luxury passenger steamship that operated between Australia and New Zealand (and served as a hospital ship during World War I), it was wrecked during a cyclone in 1935 as it was being towed to Japan to be sold for scrap metal. North of the wreck are the **Pinnacles**—dramatic, deep-red cliff formations. About 20 km (12 mi) south of Eli Creek, and surrounded by massive sand-blow (or dune), is **Lake Wabby**, the deepest of the island's lakes.

Fraser Island, Great Sandy National Park (☎ *07/5449–7792 or 1300/130372* ⊕ *www.epa.qld.gov.au*) covers the top third of the island. Beaches around Indian Head are known for their shell middens—shell heaps that were left behind after Aboriginal feasting. The head's name is another kind of relic: Captain James Cook saw Aborigines standing on the headland as he sailed past, and he therefore named the area after inhabitants he believed to be "Indians." Farther north, past Waddy Point, is one of Fraser Island's most magnificent variations on sand: wind and time have created enormous dunes. Nearby at Orchid Beach are a series of bubbling craters known as the Champagne Pools.

A boardwalk heads south from Central Station to **Wanggoolba Creek**, a favorite spot for photographers. The little stream snakes through a green palm forest, trickling over a bed of white sand between clumps of rare angiopteris fern. The 1-km (½-mi) circuit takes 30 minutes to an hour.

OUTDOOR ACTIVITIES

HIKING The island's excellent network of walking trails converges at **Central Station**, a former logging camp at the center of the island. Services here are limited to a map board, parking lot, and campground. It's a promising place for spotting dingoes, however. Comparative isolation has meant that Fraser Island's dingoes are the most purebred in Australia. They're also wild animals, so remember: don't feed them, watch from a distance, don't walk alone after dark, and keep a close eye on children, especially between late afternoon and early morning. Dingo alerts are in force around Eurong and Happy Valley.

Most of the island's well-marked trails are sandy tracks. Guides advise wearing sturdy shoes, wearing sunscreen, and carrying first-aid supplies and drinking water on all walks.

One trail from Central Station leads through rain forest—growing, incredibly enough, straight out of the sand—to **Pile Valley**, which has a stand of giant satinay trees. Allow two hours to walk this 4½-km (2¼-mi) circuit.

SWIMMING The center of the island is a quiet, natural garden of paperbark swamps, giant satinay and brush box forests, wildflower heaths, and 40 freshwater lakes. The spectacularly clear **Lake McKenzie**, ringed by a beach of incandescent white sand, is the perfect place for a refreshing swim.

FISHING All freshwater fish are protected on Fraser island, so you can't fish in lakes or streams, but just offshore is one of Australia's richest, most diverse fishing areas, with whiting, flathead, trevally, red emperor, snapper, sea perch, coronation trout, cod, and, in summer, mackerel, cobia, amberjack, and more. This is partly due to the diversity of habitat; choose between estuary, surf beach, reef, sport, and game fishing. On reef-fishing trips dolphins are commonly sighted, as are whales in season.

When angling off Fraser Island beaches and jetties, follow EPA guidelines. To discourage dingoes and other undesireable visitors, clean fish away from campsites and dispose of scraps carefully (bury fish scraps at least 30 cm, about a foot, below the tide line). Bag and size limits apply to some species: for details, go to ⊕ *www.dpi.qld.gov.au.*

Contact **Hervey Bay Fishing Charters** (⊠ *15 Tristina Cr., Urangan* ☎ *07/4125-3958* ⊕ *www.herveybayfishingcharters.com.au*)to set up a trip.

WHERE TO STAY

You can pitch a tent anywhere you don't see a NO CAMPING sign; there are four main public campgrounds—Central Station, Dundubara, and two at Waddy Point—that require you to book in advance. These campgrounds have fenced sites (advised if you have kids under 14), toilet blocks, drinking water, hot showers (some coin-operated), gas grills, phones, and other amenities. There are also smaller designated camping areas along Fraser Island's Great Walk, and a number of established beach campsites, all run by Queensland Parks and Wildlife Service. They have toilet blocks, picnic tables, and walking trails. Most lack drinking water, so bring plenty with you. Because the entire island is a World Heritage site, permits for camping (A$5 per person, per night) are required, and there's a maximum stay of 22 nights.

The island's only official private campground, **Frasers at Cathedral Beach** (☎ *07/4127–3933 or 1800/063933* ⊕ *www.fraserislandco.com.au/*), 10 km (6 mi) north of Eurong, costs A$54–A$98 per night. Cabins with two and three bedrooms are A$280–A$440 nightly, depending on the season. Booking well ahead is essential. The University of the Sunshine Coast runs **Dilli Village Campground** (☎ *07/4127–9130* ⊕ *www.dillivillage.com.au*), just south of Eurong, where a 2-bedroom cabin for up to five is A$100, a 4-person bunkhouse is A$40, and camping is A$10 per night. The Queensland Parks and Wildlife Service manages the island, and maintains ranger bases at Dundubara, Eurong, and Waddy Point.

$$ 🏨 **Eurong Beach Resort.** This east-coast resort has the best of Fraser Island at its doorstep. Lake McKenzie and Central Station are 20 minutes away, and the famous Seventy-Five Mile Beach, Eli Creek, and other coastal attractions are within an easy drive. Lodgings range from four-person dorms (mainly for groups) to standard rooms and two-bedroom apartments. Some units overlook the ocean; others, the resort and pool area. Buffet dinners are A$22 per person, and there's a bakery for snacks. The resort store sells everything from food to fuel and fishing gear (also for hire). **Pros:** on-site general store; great location. **Cons:** spotty mobile phone reception; slow Internet. ⊠ *75 Mile Beach* 🏠 *Box 7332, Hervey Bay 4655* ☎ *07/4127–9122 or 1800/111808* ⊕ *www.eurong.com* 🛏 *124 rooms, including 16 apartments* ♿ *In-room: no a/c (some), kitchen (some), refrigerator, DVD (some). In-hotel: restaurant, café, bars, tennis court, pools, beachfront, laundry facilities, shops, public Internet, parking, no elevator* ☰ *MC, V.*

🏨 **Fraser Island Backpackers.** This cluster of wooden beachside cottages has been refurbished to suit backpackers. All cottages now serve as fan-cooled, bunk-free dorms: some small, some large enough for families.

Each cottage is ensuite. Wilderness Bar and Bistro serves three meals daily, and screens live sports matches. The complex nestles in land-scaped gardens on a Happy Valley hillside, midway along the island's eastern coast. It's centrally located, a 15-minute drive from Eli Creek and 20 minutes from the *Maheno* shipwreck and the Pinnacles. **Pros:** on-site store and bottle shop; meals are super-good for the price (A$10–A$30). **Cons:** no in-room facilities; fan-cooled rooms only. ⊠ *Happy Valley* ✆ *Box 5224, Torquay 4655* ☎ *07/4127–9144 or 1800/446655* ⤴ *9 cottages* ⚙ *In-room: no a/c, no phone, no TV. In-hotel: restaurant, bar, pool, beachfront, laundry facilities, public WI-Fi (fee), shops, air-port shuttle* ⊟ *AE, MC, V.*

$$$ ⛺ **Kingfisher Bay Resort and Village.** This stylish, high-tech marriage of
Ⓒ   glass, stainless steel, dark timber, and corrugated iron nestles in tree-
Fodor's Choice   covered dunes on the island's west coast. The impressive lobby, with
★   its cathedral ceiling and polished floorboards, leads out to wraparound decks with outdoor dining areas and one of the resort's four pools. Lodgings include elegantly furnished standard rooms with balconies, lovely villas, and wilderness lodges for groups. Rangers conduct infor-mative 4WD eco tours, free nature walks, spotlighting tours, and cruises (in season) to spot whales, dugongs, and dolphins. Children can join junior ranger or kids' club activities. Free fishing classes and boat rent-als are available: resort chefs will even cook your catch. Hire canoes, catamarans, and snorkeling gear, or get pampered at the spa. There are medical facilities, an ATM, and a general store and post office on-site. Seabelle's excellent menu ($$–$$$) showcases native ingredients and local seafood, with vegetarian options; Maheno restaurant is big on regional produce, and puts on elaborate buffet dinners on Friday and Saturday night. The Wilderness Bar nightclub is a short shuttle-bus ride from reception. Accommodation-meal packages are available. **Pros:** terrific facilities and activities; eco-friendly; food is a cut above. **Cons:** west-coast beaches unsuitable for 4WD vehicles. ⊠ *North White Cliffs, 75 Mile Beach* ✆ *PMB 1, Urangan 4655* ☎ *07/4120–3333 or 1800/072555* ⊕ *www.kingfisherbay.com* ⤴ *152 rooms, 109 villas, 184 beds in lodges (for 18–35s)* ⚙ *In-room: kitchen (some), refrigerator, DVD (some), VCR (some), dial-up. In-hotel: 4 restaurants, bars, tennis courts, pools, spa, beachfront, water sports, children's programs (ages 1–14), laundry facilities, laundry service, public Internet, airport shuttle, 4WD rental, no-smoking rooms, no elevator* ⊟ *AE, DC, MC, V.*

The Great Barrier Reef

INCLUDING CAIRNS AND THE NORTH COAST

WORD OF MOUTH

"If you're into diving and aquatic wildlife exploration and want a taste of the Outback, go to Far North Queensland. You can satisfy a broad array of Australian adventure desires from that area."

—BigRuss

WELCOME TO THE GREAT BARRIER REEF

TOP REASONS TO GO

★ **Reef Explorations:** There are thousands of spectacular dive sites scattered along the coral spine of the Great Barrier Reef. Some draw hundreds of divers and snorkelers a day with clouds of fish and coral formations.

★ **Wildlife Watching:** Flora and fauna on the islands themselves can be fascinating: rain forests, hills and rocky areas, and postcard-perfect beaches might be home to everything from turtles, birds, and lizards to echidnas and bandicoots. On the mainland, Daintree National Park is home to the endangered Southern Cassouary.

★ **Culture Immersion:** The Kuku Yalanji have lived in the area stretching roughly from Port Douglas to Cookdown for thousands of years. A highlight of visiting northern Queensland is experiencing this unique landscape from their perspective. Try to get on a multi-day tour to see some of the region's most spiritual places.

1 Cairns. A laid-back tropical tourist hub built around a busy marina and swimming lagoon, Cairns bristles with hotels, tour agencies, dive-cruise boats, and travelers en route to the rain forest and reef. It has some fine retail precincts and markets, plus a waterfront casino.

2 North of Cairns. The pristine coastline north of Cairns is punctuated by charming villages and tourist towns, including Palm Cove, with its European Riviera ambience, and bustling Port Douglas, with its busy marina, sprawling resorts, and laid-back café scene. North of the Daintree River, World Heritage–listed wilderness extends to Cape Tribulation and beyond; here you'll find few services but some fantastic, eco-friendly rain-forest retreats.

3 Whitsundays/Airlie Beach. The glorious Whitsunday Islands, just off the mid-north-Queensland coast, lure holidaymakers with world-class water sports, sheltered yacht anchorages, and resorts catering to every taste. Airlie Beach, the closest mainland town, buzzes with backpackers, who flock to its manmade lagoon, markets, bars, and budget digs. Well-heeled travelers might prefer the boutique retreats and resorts hugging the hillsides behind the main drag.

4 North Coast islands. The eco-conscious resorts on Hinchinbrook and Orpheus islands, are tailored to nature-loving travelers, while Bedarra Island's upmarket retreat attracts honeymooners and sunbathers. Lizard and Fitzroy Islands, off Cairns, offer ready access to world-class dive and game-fishing sites.

5 Townsville and Magnetic Island. Regional city Townsville has gracious heritage buildings, excellent museums and marine centers, and a revamped waterfront with a manmade swimming lagoon. Offshore, Magnetic Island is a popular holiday spot, with high-end and budget accommodation and an aquatic activities.

GETTING ORIENTED

A map linking all of northern Queensland's coastal ports and offshore resorts from the Whitsundays to as far north as Lizard Island would look like a lace-up boot 1,600 km (1,000 mi) long. However, you'd only see less than half the reef, which extends south as far as Lady Elliot Island and as far north as the roadless wilderness of Cape York and the shores of Papua New Guinea. If you're visiting the reef only briefly, it's easiest and most economical to day-trip from the main towns. Some reef-island resorts are accessible by boat; many others can be reached only by plane, and both airfare and lodging rates can be expensive. Day trips depart from major coastal cities including Cairns, Port Douglas, Townsville, and Airlie Beach. Some island resorts, such as Hinchinbrook and Hamilton, let you visit and use their facilities for the day—then return you to the mainland to continue your travels.

7

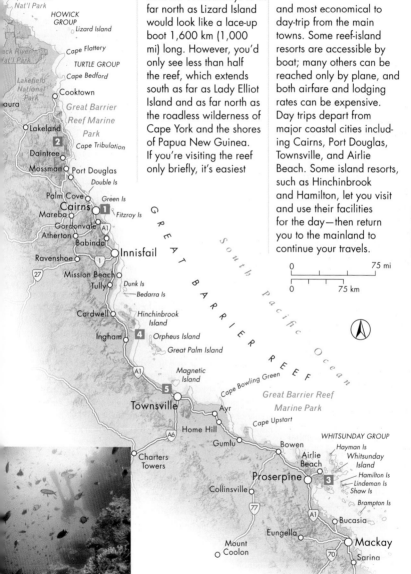

GREAT BARRIER REEF PLANNER

When to Go

The majority of Barrier Reef islands lie north of the tropic of Capricorn and have a distinctly monsoonal climate. In the hot, wet season (roughly December–April), expect tropical downpours that can limit outdoor activities and mar underwater visibility for days.

The warm days, clear skies, and pleasantly cool nights of the Dry season, especially June–August, are ideal for traveling around and above Cairns. Around the Whitsundays, some winter days may be too cool for swimming and nights can be chilly (pack a sweater and long pants).

The islands are warm, even in winter; it's hot during the summer months, reaching 35 degrees Celsius (95 degrees Farenheit) or more: the farther north you go, the hotter it gets. The water temperature is mild to cool, varying only by a few degrees between winter and summer. However, in jellyfish season (November through May or so) you'll need to wear a full-body stinger suit to swim anywhere but patrolled, netted areas.

Getting Here and Around

Air Travel. Jetstar, Virgin Blue, and Qantas have daily direct flights linking capital cities around Australia to Cairns International Airport (which also handles international flights). These airlines also have flights to Townsville, Whitsundays Coast, Hamilton Island, Proserpine, and Mackay airports, linking with east coast capitals and major regional cities throughout Queensland. From these hubs, regular boat and charter air services are available to most of the Great Barrier Reef resorts. Generally, island charter flights are timed to connect with domestic flights, but double-check. *For information about reaching the islands, see Getting Here and Around under each island's heading.*

Boat Travel. Generally, island launches are timed to connect with charter flights from island or mainland airports, but check. Crossings can be choppy; take something for motion sickness ahead of time. If you're based on the mainland or in a hurry, many operators run day trips out to the reef and resort islands. Several operators provide skipper-yourself (bareboat) and crewed charters to explore the Whitsundays. Almost all have five-day minimum charter periods; most offer discounts for multiday hire and optional extras such as catering. Packages start from around A$100 per person, per night, but can be several times that on crewed or luxury vessels.

Car Travel. If you're visiting several North Queensland destinations, it may be simplest to drive. Most popular North Queensland routes are paved, though roads may be flooded in wet season. A 4WD vehicle is advised. Leave plenty of time if you're crossing the Daintree River or going between Port Douglas and Cairns. If you're heading farther north, fill up with gas at or before Wonga Beach, and carry water, tools, and supplies.

Bus travel. Long-distance buses are an economical but often cramped way to travel along the North Queensland coast. Sleeping on them is uncomfortable. Shuttle buses transfer visitors from the airport, Cairns, and beaches and towns to as far north as Cape Tribulation. They link island ferry services departing from Port Hinchinbrook, Mission Beach, Airlie Beach, and Shute Harbour. Hotel pickups are available; call ahead.

Restaurants

Most restaurants on Barrier Reef islands are part of each island's main resort, so many resorts' rates include some or all meals. Some larger resorts have a range of restaurants, with formal dining rooms, outdoor barbecues, and seafood buffets; some have premium dining options for which you pay extra. Dress is generally "island casual." Some upscale restaurants—such as those on Hayman Island—require men to wear jackets for dinner and frown on flip-flop sandals. On the mainland, you'll find plenty of casual, open-air restaurants serving mainly steak and seafood. Cairns is the best bet for upscale dining.

Hotels

Most inhabited islands have just one main resort, usually offering a range of lodging types and prices. Choose island destinations based on your budget and the kind of vacation you want—active, relaxed, or a mix. Offerings range from white-glove service (Bedarra, Lizard, Orpheus, Hayman Islands) to eco-focused island resorts (Hinchinbrook and Long Islands). All but the most rustic and zero-footprint resorts have modern conveniences such as air-conditioning, telephones, televisions, refrigerators, and Internet access—though connections can be slow and mobile phone coverage limited or non-existent.

DINING AND LODGING PRICE CATEGORIES (IN AUSTRALIAN DOLLARS)

	¢	$	$$	$$$	$$$$
Restaurants	under A$15	A$15–A$20	A$21–A$30	A$31–A$45	over A$45
Hotels	under A$100	A$101–A$200	A$201–A$300	A$301–A$450	over A$450

Restaurant prices are based on the median main course price at dinner. Hotel prices are for two people in a standard double room in high season, excluding service and tax (10%).

Health and Safety

You'll find large, well-equipped hospitals in Cairns, Townsville, and Mackay; doctors in Port Douglas and Airlie Beach. Be advised that emergency services are scarce between the Daintree River and Cooktown. Employees at island resort front desks handle emergencies and can summon doctors and aerial ambulance services. Remote islands have "flying doctor" kits; Hamilton Island has its own doctor.

Avoid midday rays, even in winter, and wear a hat and SPF15+ sunscreen to prevent sunburn. Rehydrate often, and take it easy in the heat. Avoid touching coral: it is easily damaged, and can cut and sting. Clean cuts thoroughly, scrubbing with a brush and flushing with saline solution. Toxic and stinging jellyfish frequent waters off the mainland and some Barrier Reef islands over the warmer months. Avoid the ocean without a stinger suit at these times. If in doubt, ask a local.

Mosquitoes, midges, and leeches can be a problem in wet summer months. Wear insect repellent; leeches are best removed by applying a flame or salt. Estuarine crocodiles live in rivers and coastal waters along the north Queensland coast, and on some Barrier Reef islands. Don't swim where crocs live (ask a local), especially in breeding season, September to April. Never dangle your limbs over the sides of boats.

7

SAILING THE WHITSUNDAY ISLANDS

The Whitsundays, 74 islands and dozens of islets scattered off Queensland's central coast off Airlie Beach, are among yachties' and beach-lovers' favorite holiday destinations— and with good reason.

The Whitsunday Islands, protected from Coral Sea swells by sheltering reefs and cooled by trade winds, offer an abundance of yacht anchorages in close proximity, making this ideal cruising territory. The aquamarine waters seem to shimmer and sparkle—a light-scattering effect that results when the fine sediment run-off from mainland river systems is stirred up by the three- to five-meter tides that sweep the coast. Island resorts offer safe moorings for passing yachts and an array of water sports and facilities. Farther out, on the Barrier Reef, you'll find fine snorkeling, diving, and fishing sites. Most Whitsunday islands are unspoiled national parks; just a few—Hayman, Hamilton, Daydream, South Molle, South Long, Lindeman, and Brampton—have resorts.

WHEN TO GO

With a climate moderated by cooling trade winds, the Whitsundays are blessed by balmy temperatures year round, though days can sometimes exceed 100 degrees Fahrenheit in summer. Over winter (June–August) it's generally warm, clear, and sunny by day and cool—even chilly—at night. Steer clear of summer holidays to avoid hordes of local families (who, despite often wet and stormy weather, flock here December to March). Spring and fall weather can be perfect, and these seasons are often the quietest, if you can avoid school and Easter holidays. Southern Right and humpback whales are active between July and September.

WHERE CAN I FIND . . .

Underwater adventure? Most Whitsundays resorts have dedicated dive shops offering scuba and snorkeling lessons and gear hire; all either run or can organize day trips to nearby dive and snorkeling spots. Highlights include Heart Reef and vast Knuckle Reef Lagoon, where a purpose-built pontoon floats in sheltered waters teeming with tropical fish, turtles, and rays. Not keen to get wet? Take a semi-submersible coral-viewing tour, guided reef walk, or scenic heli-flight. Sheltered coves and coral-fringed beaches around many Whitsunday islands also offer good snorkeling.

Luxury? At Qualia, Hamilton Island's most lavish accommodation, sleek suites have infinity pools and alfresco areas, artfully lit after dark, and food and wine are brought in from Hamilton's best restaurants. Secluded Peppers Palm Bay lures luxury lovers with hammocks, architect-designed villas, and bungalows. Bedarra and Lizard island resorts serve up gourmet meals and exclusive accommodations, while Paradise Bay Island Eco Resort pampers its select group of guests with top-quality, all-natural furnishings and fabrics, Molton Brown toiletries, and cruises on the resort's own sailing cat. Hayman Resort, a magnificent sprawl of public areas and opulent suites, is luxurious enough to satisfy the fussiest of visitors, with a 1:1 staff-to-guest ratio and bedside controls.

Family-friendliness? Club Med Lindeman Island's jam-packed sports and activities program offers dozens of aquatic and land-based sports, most included in rates. Daydream Island's got dedicated kids' clubs, playgrounds, and other kid-at-heart features. At Hunt Resort on Fitzroy Island, children's activity programs mean parents can relax or join in the fun, while nature-based activities on Lizard and Hinchinbrook islands are great for older kids.

TOP REASONS TO GO

Aquatic playground. This is a snorkelers' and divers' paradise and one of the world's top sailing and cruising areas. It's also great for kayaking, windsurfing, paragliding, and sailboarding—and most resorts include non-motorized water sports in rates.

Tropical paradise. Enjoy mild climate and warm, clear waters whatever the season, plus some of the most beautiful fine-white-sand beaches in the world.

Gourmet destination. Many Whitsunday island resorts now offer cuisine to rival that of high-end city establishments. Food runs the gamut from traditional four-star gourmet fare to fresh, regional food presented with inventive, site-specific twists.

Resort Variety. This is ideal island-hopping territory: you can easily divide your time between luxurious, leisurely resorts (like one of the South Long Island accommodations) and a gregarious, activity-oriented isle (like Lindeman or Daydream).

7

OUTBACK ADVENTURES

Queensland's Outback region is a vast and exciting place, filled with real Crocodile Dundee types. Everyone lives in extremely isolated townships, so people are used to relying on each other.

Heading west from Townsville on the Flinders Highway (aka Overlanders Highway), stop at once-prosperous gold-mining town **Charters Towers**—a beautiful city with 60 or so historically significant buildings. Farther west is Hughenden, showcasing significant ancient fossils found in the region. Continue via Cloncurry to Mount Isa, a surprisingly multicultural city of around 20,000 people, where you'll find the sprawling Mount Isa Mine, Australia's deepest mine (at 6,234 feet) and one of the world's largest producers of copper, silver, lead, and zinc. The drive takes about 6 days one way.

SAFETY FIRST

When traveling any of these routes by car, take practical precautions. Use a four-wheel-drive vehicle—some roads are unpaved and become slippery after it rains. Always carry spare water, a first-aid kit, a good local map, and sufficient fuel to get to the next town (which may mean carrying spare gas cans). If you're traveling into remote areas, advise local police or another responsible person of your travel plans and report back to them when you return. If you have an on-road emergency, call 000 from the nearest public phone (or 112 from mobile phones) to reach an ambulance or the police.

OVERLANDERS HIGHWAY TOP STOPS

In Hughenden, don't miss meeting "Hughie," a Muttaburrasaurus skeleton on display at **Flinders Discovery Centre** (⌂ 37 *Gray St., Hughenden* ☎ *07/4741–1021* ⊕ *www.hughenden. com* ✉ *A$3.50* ⏱ *Daily 9–5*), alongside natural history, gem and fossil exhibits, a multimedia sheep-shearing installation and a shop with tour brochures, maps, and souvenirs. This is a great place for kids both young and old.

If you're a fan of the movie *Crocodile Dundee*, head south from Cloncurry via Route 66 to McKinlay. This hamlet's claim to fame is **Walkabout Creek Hotel** (⌂ *Middleton St., McKinlay* ☎ *07/4746–8424*), which featured in the movie.

Mount Isa is a good jumping-off point for exploring the spring-fed rivers and gorges of **Boodjamulla (Lawn Hill) National Park** (☎ *07/4722–5224 weekdays 10–4, 13–1304 permits* ⊕ *www.epa.qld.gov.au*), where you can canoe amid freshwater crocodiles and camp in the wilderness for A$5 per person, per night (BYO tents, gear, and water).

The southern hemisphere's biggest rodeo takes place in **Mount Isa** each July or August (☎ *07/4743–2706* ⊕ *www. isarodeo.com.au*). Another must-see is **Outback at Isa**, an interpretative center housing fossil exhibits from the Riversleigh Fossil site, some 300 km (186 mi) away. Here you can take the Hard Times Mine underground tour experience, where you'll dress in a hard hat, white suit, and headlamp, and tour a "mock-up" mine shaft 49½ feet below the surface. ⌂ *19 Marion St., Mount Isa* ☎ *1300/659660 or 07/4749–1555* ⊕ *www.outbackatisa.com.au* ✉ *Mine and all museums A$55, mine only A$45* ⏱ *Daily 8:30–5.*

WHY OVERLANDER?

The Overlander's Highway stretch of the Flinders Highway is a great drive for experiencing a small slice of the Australian Outback, but how did it come to be, exactly? The name gives it away; "overlander" is a term used to refer to someone who helps move cattle from one place to another, and this route used to be used for that purpose. The word has found its way into general usage to describe other distance-traversing feats; a small sampling includes *Overland* magazine which focuses on 4WD vehicles, the town of Overlander in Western Australia, the Overland train that runs between Adelaide and Melbourne, and of course this great drive.

7

OUTDOOR ADVENTURES IN DAINTREE NATIONAL PARK

Cape Tribulation, Daintree National Park is an ecological wonderland. See several of the world's most ancient plants, some of Australia's rarest creatures, and how the Daintree's traditional owners, the Eastern Kuku Yalanji, have been protecting this place for thousands of years.

The park extends over approximately 22,000 acres, although the entire Wet Tropics region—which stretches from Townsville to Cooktown and covers 12,000 square km (4,633 square mi)—was declared a UNESCO World Heritage site in 1988. Within it, experts have identified several species of angiosperms, the most primitive flowering plants in existence, many of which are found nowhere else on the planet.

WHEN TO GO

With clear and sunny days, comfortably cool nights, no stingers in the ocean, and easily negotiated rain forest and mangrove trails, "the Dry" is arguably the best time to visit.

The Wet—roughly December to May—can be wonderful: buds turn into hothouse blooms. Drawbacks include high humidity, flooded roads, slippery tracks, leeches, mosquitoes, and constant sticky heat.

Spring and late fall can be a good compromise: the weather is often fine, but accommodations are less heavily booked than in the dry winter months, when most people choose to come here.

A SACRED SITE

With diverse plant and animal life, abundant fresh water, and tracts of fertile coastal lowland, the Daintree rain forest is rich terrain for the resourceful. Its traditional custodians are the Eastern Kuku Yalanji, a peaceable people who've been coexisting with and subsisting on the forest's abundant flora and fauna for tens of thousands of years Their tribal lands stretch north almost as far as Cooktown, south as far as Mossman and west to the Palmer River, with the Eastern Kuku Yalanji travelling seasonally throughout the region.

Designating five rather than four seasons in a year, the Eastern Kuku Yalanji used changes in weather and growth cycles to guide hunting and foraging expeditions into the rain forest: when the *jun jun* (blue ginger) came into fruit, they'd catch *diwan* (Australian brush-turkey); when *jilngan* (mat grass) flowered, they'd collect *jarruka* (orange-footed scrubfowl) eggs; and year-round, they'd track tree-dwelling *yawa* (possum), *kambi* (flying fox), and *murral* (tree kangaroo). Kuku Yalanji can tell you which local plants can be eaten, used as medicines, and made into utensils, weapons, and shelter.

The Daintree's indigenous inhabitants believe many of the area's natural sites have spiritual significance, attributing particular power to Wundu (Thornton Peak), Manjal Dimbi (Mount Demi), Wurrmbu (The Bluff), and Kulki (Cape Tribulation). Dozens of spots in the rain forest—waterfalls, crags, peaks and creeks—are deemed by the Kuku Yalanji to have spiritual, healing or regenerative powers. Take a walk with one of the area's traditional custodians to get an intimate, intriguing perspective on this extraordinary terrain.

Various indigenous-guided tours and experiences in the Daintree area focus on bush tucker and medicines, wildlife and hunting techniques, culture, history, and ritual. A waterhole just behind Daintree Eco Lodge & Spa is deemed a site of special significance for women: a dip in its healing waters is a female-only ritual.

TOP REASONS TO GO

World Heritage. Tens of thousands of years in the making, this UNESCO World Heritage rain forest (declared in 1988) is one of the world's most ancient.

Animals. Watch for the rare Bennett's tree-kangaroo, believed to have evolved from possums; the endangered, spotted-tailed quoll, a marsupial carnivore; a giant white-tailed rat, prone to raiding campsites; and the Daintree River ringtail possum, found only around Thornton Peak and the upper reaches of the Daintree and Mossman rivers.

Birds. Daintree National Park shelters hundreds of bird species: azure kingfishers swoop on crabs in the creeks, white-rumped swiftlets dart above the canopy. Year-round, you'll see orange-footed scrubfowl, foraging or building gigantic leaf-litter nest-mounds. The six-foot-high, flightless southern cassowary, vital to rain-forest regeneration, is threatened by habitat loss, motorists, and dog attack.

7

Updated by
Merran White

A maze of 3,000 individual reefs and 900 islands stretching for 2,600 km (1,616 mi), the Great Barrier Reef is one of the world's most spectacular natural attractions, and one of which Australia is extremely proud. Known as Australia's "Blue Outback," the reef was established as a marine park in 1975, and is a collective haven for thousands of species of sea life, as well as turtles and birds.

In 1981 the United Nations designated the Great Barrier Reef a World Heritage Site. In 2004 strict legislation was enacted prohibiting fishing along most of the reef—a further attempt to protect the underwater treasures of this vast, yet delicate ecosystem. Any visitor over the age of four must pay an A\$5 (A\$5.50 after April 2010) Environmental Management Charge (also known as the reef tax) to help support the preservation of the reef.

The reef system began to form approximately 6,000–7,000 years ago, according to scientists. It's comprised of individual reefs and islands, which lie to the east of the Coral Sea and extend south into the Pacific Ocean. Most of the reef is about 65 km (40 mi) off the Queensland coast, although some parts extend as far as 300 km (186 mi) offshore. Altogether, it covers an area bigger than Great Britain, forming the largest living feature on earth and the only one visible from space.

Most visitors explore this section of Australia from one of the two-dozen or so resorts along the islands in the southern half of the marine park, most of them lying in or north of the Whitsunday Islands group. Although most Barrier Reef islands are closer to the mainland than to the more spectacular outer reef, all the resorts offer or can organize chartered boats to outer-reef sites. Live-aboard dive boats ply more remote sections of the northern reef and Coral Sea atolls, exploring large cartographic blank spots on maritime charts that simply read, in bold purple lettering, "Area unsurveyed."

GREAT ITINERARIES

Most visits to the Great Barrier Reef combine time on an island with time in Queensland's mainland towns and parks. With a week or more you could stay at two very different resorts, perhaps at an activities-packed Whitsunday resort and a mountainous northern island, allowing a day or two to travel between them. If you want to resort-hop, pick the closely arranged Whitsundays, or Orpheus, Hinchinbrook, and Bedarra islands, all relatively close to one another.

IF YOU HAVE 1 DAY

Take a boat from Cairns or Port Douglas to a pontoon on the outer reef for a day on the water. A helicopter flight back will provide an astounding view of the reef and islands from above. Or catch an early boat from Cairns to **Fitzroy Island**, or from Shute Harbour to **Daydream Island**. Spend a couple of hours snorkeling, take a walk around the island, then settle on a quiet beach for an idyllic afternoon.

IF YOU HAVE 3 DAYS

Pick one island with a variety of aquatic and land-based activities and attractions—flora and fauna, beaches and dive sites, sports and relaxation facilities, resort-style nightlife—and give yourself a taste of everything.

IF YOU HAVE 7 OR MORE DAYS

Planning a full week on an island probably means that you're a serious diver, a serious lounger, or both. Divers should hop on one of the Lizard Island—Port Douglas live-aboards for several days, then recuperate on an island that has fringing coral, such as **Lizard Island**, or stay at any **Whitsundays resort—most have fringing reefs or can arrange dive-boats out to Barrier Reef pontoons.** Live-aboard trips, which can be surprisingly affordable, run from 2 to 10 days. Beach lovers might prefer to skip the live-aboard and concentrate on exploring one or two of the islands with outstanding beaches and hiking terrain, such as **Hinchinbrook, Orpheus, Lizard,** or **Hayman.**

7

CAIRNS

Tourism is the lifeblood of Cairns (pronounced *Caans*). The city makes a perfect base for exploring the wild top half of Queensland, and tens of thousands of international travelers use it as a jumping-off point for activities such as scuba diving and snorkeling trips to the Barrier Reef, as well as boating, parasailing, and rain-forest treks.

It's a tough environment, with intense heat and fierce wildlife. Along with wallabies and grey kangaroos in the savannah and tree kangaroos in the rain forest, you'll find stealthy saltwater crocodiles, poisonous snakes, and jellyfish so deadly they keep the stunning beaches virtually unswimmable for half the year. Yet despite their formidable setting, Cairns and tropical North Queensland are far from intimidating. The people are warm and friendly, the sights spectacular, and the beachside lounging world-class—at the right time of year.

GETTING HERE AND AROUND

AIR TRAVEL Cairns Airport is a major international gateway, and a connection point for flights to other parts of Queensland, including Townsville, Mackay, Rockhampton, Hamilton Island, and the Northern Territory, as well as all Australian capital cities.

Airport Connections runs coaches between the airport and town—an 8-km (5-mi) trip that takes about 10 minutes and costs A$18. The company also services Cairns's northern beaches, Palm Cove, and Silky Oaks Lodge, past Daintree (A$18–A$50). Port Douglas–based Express Chauffeured Coaches & Limousines provides bus services from the airport to Palm Cove and Port Douglas, north of Cairns (A$18–A$33 by coach, A$70–A$160 in a limousine). Private taxis make these trips as well (A$15–A$20 to Cairns).

Airlines based at Cairns Airport include Air New Zealand, Cathay Pacific, Continental, Qantas, Jetstar, and Virgin Blue.

BUS TRAVEL Greyhound Australia operates daily express buses from major southern cities to Cairns. By bus, Cairns to Brisbane takes 30-plus hours, to Sydney it's around 45 hours, and to Melbourne it's a gargantuan trip of nearly 60 hours, best broken into bearable segments.

CAR TRAVEL Between Brisbane and Cairns, the Bruce Highway rarely touches the coast. Unless you're planning to stop off en route or explore the Great Green Way, fly or take the fast Tilt Train to Cairns, renting a vehicle on arrival. Avis, Budget, Hertz, and Thrifty all have rental cars and four-wheel-drive vehicles available. An economical, reliable alternative is Cairns Leisure Wheels, just off Captain Cook Highway; it offers free delivery and pick-up.

TRAIN TRAVEL Trains arrive at the Cairns Railway Station in the city center. The *Sunlander*, with its luxury Queenslander-class sleeping and fine-dining carriages, makes the 32-hour journey between Brisbane and Cairns thrice-weekly in each direction (A$212.30–A$761.20). The fast, modern Tilt Train plies the coast from Brisbane to Cairns twice-weekly in each direction, taking just under 24 hours (A$310.20). The *Savannahlander* links Cairns and Forsyth, traveling four days through rain forest, savanna land, and Outback.

TOURS

BOAT TOURS Ocean Spirit Cruises' streamlined four-hour and full-day tours aboard
Fodor'sChoice the *Ocean Spirit I*, a large catamaran, and the smaller *Ocean Spirit
★ II and III,* cost from A$110 to A$189 per person, snorkeling gear
🕑 included. *Ocean Spirit IV* takes up to 100 guests on a nightly, four-course dinner cruise along Trinity Inlet from 6:45 to 9:30 (A$89). Boats depart from Marlin Jetty, Cairns, and Palm Cove Jetty on demand.

ATM LOGISTICS

Resorts on the following islands have money-changing facilities: Daydream, Fitzroy, Hamilton, Hayman, Lindeman, Lizard, Long, and Orpheus. However, it's better to change money before arriving on any resort island, as rates are generally more favorable elsewhere. Hamilton Island has a National Australia Bank branch with an ATM. Bedarra, Brampton, Dunk, and Hinchinbrook islands have limited currency-exchange facilities and no ATMs.

Transfers from Cairns, Northern Beaches, Palm Cove, and Port Douglas are available (A$15–A$55).

NATURE
TOURS
☾

BTS Tours runs various trips out of Cairns and Port Douglas (and shuttle services between the two). From Port Douglas, the popular full-day Kuranda tour includes the train, cable car, and two hours exploring the township (A$130). You could also take an activity-packed day tour to Cape Tribulation (A$149), a half-day Mossman Gorge tour and Ku Ku Yalanji guided walk (A$55), or a quick trip to the Daintree (A$46) or Mossman Gorge (A$20).

Advanced Eco–certified Wilderness Challenge runs day tours and multiday trips between the Daintree rain forest and the top of the Cape York Peninsula in the Dry, May through November, including off-the-tourist-track "advanced" safaris, and a 3-day rock art and rain-forest safari between Cairns and Cooktown (A$895–A$990 per person). Most tours visit the world-renowned Quinkan Aboriginal rock-art site near Laura and stay in bush cabins or safari tents.

Down Under Tours makes half- and full-day trips and four-wheel-drive excursions to Kuranda, Cape Tribulation, the Daintree, and the southern tablelands (A$72–A$244 per person). The company's luxury arm, Down Under By Appointment, takes small groups on customized journeys, with expert an guide-driver on hand.

Blazing Saddles organizes half-day horse rides (A$105) and all-terrain vehicle tours (A$125) through bushland around Kuranda. A full day's horse-riding and ATV touring is A$215. All riders pay insurance of A$15.

CULTURAL
TOURS
★

The Kuku Yalanji people have called the Daintree area home for tens of thousands of years, and have an intimate understanding of the terrain. Today the Kubirri Warra brothers pass on a little of that boundless ancestral wisdom on a two-hour beach, mudflat, and mangrove walk (daily, 9:30 AM and 1.30 PM, A$75) with Kuku Yalanji Cultural Habitat Tours. Learn techniques for throwing spears, tracking coastal food sources, and much more from your knowledgeable, skilful guides. Multiple trip combinations and themes available, including multiday options. Transfers between the Port Douglas area and Cooya Beach, a 25-minute drive north, are A$30. Pick-ups are from Cairns, Palm Cove, and Port Douglass.

ESSENTIALS

Airport and Transfers Cairns Airport (☎ 07/4080–6703 ⊕ www.cairnsairport. com). **Airport Connections** (☎ 07/4099–5950 ⊕ www.tnqshuttle.com). **Express Chauffeured Coaches & Limousines** (☎ 07/4098–5473 ⊕ www.eccportdoug-las.com).

Boat Info Ocean Spirit Cruises (☎ ⊕ 07/4031–2920 www.oceanspirit.com.au).

Bus Info Greyhound Australia (☎ 07/4051–5899 ⊕ www.greyhound.com.au).

Car Rental Cairns Leisure Wheels (✉ 314 Sheridan St., CBD ☎ 07/4051–8988 ⊕ www.leisurewheels.com.au).

Medical Assistance Cairns Base Hospital (✉ The Esplanade at Florence St., CBD ☎ 07/4050–6333).

7

Tour Operators Blazing Saddles (⊠ *2326 Kennedy Hwy., Kuranda* ☎ *07/4093–9100* ⊕ *www.blazingsaddles.com.au*). **Kuku Yalanji Cultural Habitat Tours** (☎ *07/4098–3437 or 07/4040–7500* ⊕ *www.bamaway.com.au*). **BTS Tours** (⊠ *49 Macrossan St.* ☎ *07/4099–5665* ⊕ *www.btstours.com.au*). **Wilderness Challenge** (☎ *07/4035–4488* ⊕ *www.wilderness-challenge.com.au*). **Down Under Tours** (⊠ *26 Redden St., CBD, Cairns* ☎ *07/4035–5566* ⊕ *www. downundertours.com*).

Train Info Cairns Railway Station (⊠ *Bunda St., CBD* ☎ *07/4036–9250* ⊕ *www.traveltrain.com.au*). **Queensland Rail** (☎ *1300/131722* ⊕ *www.travel-train.com.au*). ***The Savannahlander*** (☎ *1800/793848 or 07/4053–6848* ⊕ *www. savannahlander.com.au*).

Visitor Information The Cairns & Tropical North Visitor Information Centre (TTNQ) (⊠ *51 The Esplanade, between Spence and Shield Sts., CBD* ☎ *07/4051–3588* ⊕ *www.tropicalaustralia.com.au and www.safetraveltnq.com.au*).

EXPLORING

Cosmopolitan Cairns, the unofficial capital of Far North Queensland, is Australia's 16th-largest city, with a burgeoning population pushing 150,000. Once a sleepy tropical town sprawled around Trinity Bay and Inlet, the city has expanded hugely in recent decades, and now extends north to Holloway's Beach, west to the Atherton Tablelands, and south along the Great Green Way as far as Edmonton.

TOP ATTRACTIONS

❶ **The Esplanade.** Fronting Cairns Harbour between Minnie and Spence streets, this is the focal point of life in Cairns. A lagoon-style swimming pool is open well after sunset and is usually busy. A free, convenient place to seek relief rom the sticky air, it's also well situated for viewing the boats lining Marlin Jetty. Some excellent shops, hotels, and restaurants are found along the Esplanade, and backpackers tend to gather here, giving it a lively feel. ⊠ *City Place, Shields and Abbott Sts., CBD* ☎ *07/4046–4800* ⊕ *www.cairnsregionalgallery.com.au* ☞ *A$5 (free, first Sat. of the month and for under-16s)* ⊗ *Mon.–Sat. 10–5, Sun. 1–5.*

❹ **Cairns Regional Gallery.** Occupying the impressive former Public Office building, built in the 1930s, Cairns Regional Gallery houses a hodge-podge of local, national, international, and indigenous artworks, including a fine collection of Australian photography, in its maple-paneled rooms. The shop stocks high-quality Australian ceramics, glassware, jewellery, prints, books, and cards. Pre-book an hour-long guided tour; there are also kids' programs, classes, talks, and workshops. ⊠ *City Place, Shields and Abbott Sts., CBD* ☎ *07/4046–4800* ⊕ *www.cairnsregionalgallery.com.au AA$5 (free, first Sat. of the month and for under-16s)* ⊗ *Mon.–Sat. 10–5, Sun. 1–5.*

❺ **Reef Teach.** At Reef Teach, certified marine biologists present informative, entertaining lectures on the Great Barrier Reef, usually to a packed house. They use slides and samples to teach about the reef's evolution and the inhabitants of this delicate marine ecosystem. Sign up for a seat by midday. ⊠ *2nd floor, Mainstreet Arcade, 85 Lake St., CBD4870*

Fodor's Choice

DID YOU KNOW?

Potato cod (*Epinephelus tukula*), like most other fish in the Epinephelus genus (or in layman's terms: the grouper family), are protogynous hermaphrodites—that is, they're born female and become male later in life.

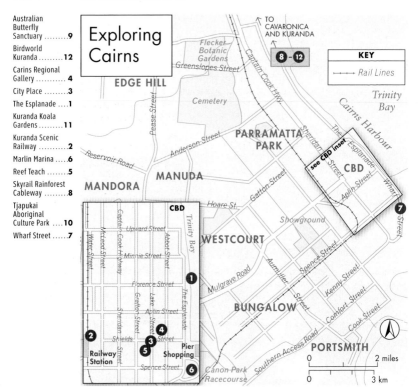

Exploring
Cairns

☎ *07/4031–7794* ⊕ *www.reefteach.wordpress.com* ☑ *A$15* ☉ *Shows Tues.–Sat. 6:30–8:30.*

② **Kuranda Scenic Railway.** The Kuranda Scenic Railway makes a 100-min-
☼ ute ascent through rain forest and 15 hand-hewn tunnels to pretty
★ Kuranda village, gateway to the Atherton Tableland, as excerpts from
Kuranda's WWII history and narration on the railway's construction
are broadcast throughout the historic railway car. Several tours are
available, from full-day rain-forest safaris and visits to local Aboriginal centers and wildlife parks, to simple round-trips combining rail
and cable-car journeys. ⊠ *Cairns Railway Station, Bunda St., CBD*
☎ *07/4036–9333 or 1800/079303* ⊕ *www.ksr.com.au* ☑ *1-way ticket
A$41, round-trip A$61; Dreamtime package A$125.50* ☉ *Departs
from Cairns daily 8:30 AM and 9:30 AM, Kuranda at 2 and 3:30.*

⑧ **Skyrail Rainforest Cableway.** From the remarkable Skyrail Rainforest
☼ Cableway, six-person cable cars carry you on a 7½-km (5-mi) journey
Fodor'sChoice across the rain-forest canopy to the highland village of Kuranda, where
★ you can visit local attractions and shop for Aboriginal art. At two stations along the way you can explore (Skyrail ticket price includes a
short, ranger-guided rain-forest tour at Red Peak, and there's an info
center and lookout at Barron Falls). The cableway base station is 15
km (9 mi) north of Cairns. Many visitors take the Scenic Railway to

SCENIC DRIVE: THE GREAT GREEN WAY

A beautiful drive is along that section of the Bruce Highway locals call the **Great Green Way**. The main road connecting Townsville to Cairns, it travels through sugarcane, papaya, and banana plantations, passing white-sand beaches and an island-dotted ocean. The 349-km (217-mi) drive takes nearly five hours—longer if you get caught behind a tractor or if the sugarcane rail is running—plus stops to explore towns, parks, waterfalls, and rain-forest tracts along the way. Check local weather advisories, especially in the Wet (Dec.–Apr.), as road and trail conditions can get very soggy.

Babinda Boulders is a popular swimming hole—and a sacred Aboriginal site. It's 7 km (5 mi) inland from Babinda, accessible via the Bruce Highway about 60 km (37 mi) south of Cairns. You can also hike to the boulders, taking the 19-km (12-mi) **Goldfield Trail (Wooroonooran National Park)** that starts in Goldsborough Valley, southwest of Cairns. Babinda is kid-friendly yet not kid-overrun. ✉ *Babinda Information Centre, Munro St., Babinda* ☎ *07/4067–1008 info center, 07/4067–6304 park ranger, 13–1304 camping* ⊙ *Information center daily 9 AM–4 PM.*

Paronella Park. A sprawling Spanish-style castle and gardens grace this offbeat National Trust site in the Mena Creek Falls rain forest. Explore the park on a self-guided botanical walk or guided tour, enjoy Devonshire tea on the café's deck, buy local art and craft, and cool off under a 40-foot waterfall. On torch-lit evening tours you might spot eels, water dragons, fireflies, and glowworms. (These are a must-do if

you're travelling with kids.) It's about 1½ hours' drive south of Cairns, via the Bruce Highway. ✉ *Japoonvale Rd., Box 88, Mena Creek* ☎ *07/4065–3225* ⊕ *www.paronellapark.com.au* ✈ *A$32* ⊙ *Daily 9 AM–7:30 PM.*

Tully Gorge. Located in the wettest zone of the Wet Tropics World Heritage area, the mighty Tully River is a magnet for white-water rafters. Access the gorge via Tully, about 140 km (87 mi) or 2 hours south of Cairns, then drive 40 minutes to Kareeya Hydroelectric Station parking lot and viewing platform. Other excellent vantage points are the Flip Wilson and Frank Roberts lookouts. September to February, the short (20-minute) Rainforest Butterfly walk is filled with fluttering creatures. ☎ *07/4068–2288* ⊕ *www.epa.qld.gov.au.*

Wooroonooran National Park. Extending south of Gordonvale to the Palmerston Highway near Innisfail, this is one of the most densely vegetated areas in Australia. Rain forest dominates Wooroonooran—from lowland tropical rain forest to the stunted growth on Mt. Bartle Frere—at 5,287 feet the highest point in Queensland. Tracks range from the easy Tchupala Falls and Josephine Falls circuits (30 minutes) to the hugely challenging Mt. Bartle Frere trail (two days). You may camp throughout the park with permits (A$5 per person, per day), except at Josephine Falls; BYO drinking water and stove). ✉ *Bartle Frere Rd., Box 93, Miriwinni* ☎ *07/4067–6304 or 1300/130372, 13–1304 camping permits* ⊕ *www.epa.qld.gov.au.*

7

Kuranda, the cableway on the return trip. ⊠ *Captain Cook Hwy. at Cairns Western Arterial Rd., Smithfield* ☎ *07/4038–1555* ⊕ *www. skyrail.com.au* ⊠ *1-way A$41, round-trip A$59* ⊙ *Daily 8:15–5:15, last round-trip boards at 2:45; last 1-way trip at 3:30.*

⑨ Australian Butterfly Sanctuary. Thousands of tropical butterflies—including the electric-blue Ulysses—flutter within a rain-forest aviary environment. It's home to Australia's largest butterfly, the Cairns, also known as the birdwing. Free half-hour guided tours are full of fascinating tidbits. ⊠ *8 Rob Veivers Dr., Kuranda* ☎ *07/4093–7575* ⊕ *www.australianbutterflies.com* ⊠ *A$17* ⊙ *Daily 10–4, tours 10:15–3:15.*

⑩ Tjapukai Aboriginal Cultural Park. Located at the base of the Skyrail Rainforest Cableway, this park offers many opportunities to learn about the history and lifestyle of the indigenous Djabugay people. One of Australia's most informative cultural attractions, it's also one of the few that returns profits to the indigenous community. Watch a dance performance, learn traditional songs, throw a spear or boomerang, have a didgeridoo lesson, or learn about bush "tucker" and medicines from friendly, knowledgeable staff. There are also Aboriginal artworks for sale. Ticket options include Tjapukai by Day, A$33 (A$55–A$81 with Cairns, northern beaches, or Port Douglas transfers) and Tjapukai by Night, a nightly buffet dinner and performance package (A$90, A$112–A$143 with transfers). ⊠ *Western Arterial Rd., Cavaronica* ✛ *15 km (9 mi) north of Cairns* ☎ *07/4042–9900* ⊕ *www.tjapukai.com.au* ⊙ *Daily 9–5, show 7:30* PM.

WORTH NOTING

⑥ Marlin Marina. Charter fishing boats moor at Marlin Marina. Big-game fishing is a big business here; fish weighing more than 1,000 pounds have been caught in the waters off the reef. Most of the dive boats and catamarans that ply the Great Barrier Reef dock here or at nearby Trinity Wharf. ⊠ *1 Spence Street, CBD* ⊕ *www.cairnsport.com.au.*

⑦ Wharf Street. Cairns can trace its beginnings to the point where the Esplanade becomes Wharf Street. In 1876 this was a port for gold and tin mined inland. Chinese and Malaysian workers and other immigrants, lured by the gold trade, settled here, and Cairns grew into one of the most multicultural cities in Australia. As the gold rush receded and the sugarcane industry around the Atherton Tableland grew, Cairns turned its attention to fishing. It is still a thriving port. ⊠ *Wharf St., CBD.*

⑧ City Place. Cairns' center is City Place, a pedestrian mall bordered by Lake and Shields streets. Some of the town's few "authentic" pubs, and its major shopping area, flank this square. ⊠ *Lake and Shield Sts., CBD.*

⑪ Kuranda Koala Gardens. All kinds of Australian wildlife are housed here, but the namesake marsupials are star attractions. The compact park is ideal for time-strapped visitors: a half-hour stroll takes you past koalas, wombats, wallabies, freshwater crocs, lizards, and snakes in open, walk-through enclosures. For A$15, have your photo taken with a "teddy," as koalas are known locally. ⊠ *Kuranda Heritage Village, Kuranda* ☎ *07/4093–9953* ⊕ *www.koalagardens.com* ⊠ *A$16* ⊙ *Daily 9–4.*

12 **Birdworld Kuranda.** One of your best chances to see the endangered cassowary, a prehistoric emu-like bird, is at Birdworld Kuranda. It's also home to around 500 or so birds from 25-plus species native to vanishing rain-forest areas—all flying freely in a giant aviary. ✉ *Kuranda Heritage Village, Kuranda* ☎ *07/4093–9188* ⊕ *www.birdworldkuranda.com.au* 🎟 *A$15* ☉ *Daily 9–4.*

> ### KURANDA WILDLIFE PASS
>
> Tropical Kuranda offers several nature-oriented attractions, including the Australian Butterfly Sanctuary, Birdworld Kuranda, and Kuranda Koala Gardens. See these sites individually, visit on a Kuranda Wildlife Entry pass (A$42), which gives entry to all three, or buy a day-tripper's package that includes Skyrail and/or Scenic Railway tickets (A$101–A$131.50).

OFF THE BEATEN PATH **Undara Volcanic National Park.** The lava tubes here are a fascinating geological oddity in the Outback. A volcanic outpouring 190,000 years ago created the hollow basalt, tube-like tunnels, many of which you can wander through on tours led by trained guides. Undara is the Aboriginal word for "long way," and it's apt: the tunnels, 35 km (22 mi) long in total, extend over 19,700 acres. Some are 62 feet high and half a mile long. ☎ *07/4097–1485* ⊕ *www. epa.qld.gov.au* 🎟 *Free* ☉ *Daily dawn–dusk.*

WHERE TO EAT

7

Use the coordinate (✛ B2) at the end of each listing to locate a site on the corresponding map.

$$
SEAFOOD
✗ **Barnacle Bill's Seafood Inn.** Complete with netting and mounted, shellacked fish on the walls, Barnacle Bill's serves fresh, delicious seafood: mud crabs, crayfish, prawns, oysters, and coral trout—cooked various ways. The kitchen also dabbles in Aussie specialties. Try the Taste of Australia plate, with grilled barramundi, kangaroo, and crocodile. The wine list favors quality mid-range Australian vintages. Early diners get a 20% discount. ✉ *103 The Esplanade, near Aplin St., CBD* ☎ *07/4051–2241* ⊕ *www.barnaclebills.com.au* ▭ *AE, DC, MC, V* ☉ *No lunch* ✛ *B2.*

$–$$
INDONESIAN
Fodor's Choice
★
✗ **Bayleaf Balinese Restaurant.** Dining alfresco under the glow of tiki torches, you can enjoy some of the most delicious, innovative cuisine in North Queensland. The expansive menu combines traditional Balinese spices with native Australian ingredients—this may be the only place where you'll have the opportunity to try crocodile satay. The pork in sweet soy sauce sounds simple, but is mouthwatering. The classic rijsttafel course for two—rice with lots of curry and pickle dishes—is the best way to sample the Bali-trained chefs' masterly cooking. ✉ *Bay Village Tropical Retreat, Lake and Gatton Sts., CBD* ☎ *07/4051–4622* ⊕ *www.bayvillage.com.au* ▭ *AE, DC, MC, V* ☉ *No lunch weekends* ✛ *A1.*

¢–$
FAST FOOD
✗ **Cairns Night Markets Food Court.** The food court in these night owl–friendly markets offers something for every palate, from spicy Malaysian *laksa* (coconut-milk soup) to sushi, kebabs, and fried chicken. Officially, it's open daily with the markets, 5 to 11 PM, but many outlets

The Skyrail Rainforest Cableway outside of Cairns.

start serving at 11 AM or earlier. ⊠ *71–75 The Esplanade, between Shield and Spence Sts., CBD* ☎ *07/4051-7666* ⊕ *www.nightmarkets.com.au* ⊟ *No credit cards* ✣ *B3.*

$$$
MODERN FRENCH
★

✕ **M Yogo.** Occupying a prime spot on the pier, M Yogo could be Cairns's best-placed restaurant. Here chef and co-owner Masa puts a deft modern spin on classic French dishes: enjoy his creamy seafood risotto with tiger prawns, squid, and scallops; roasted duck breast in orange or port-wine sauce; grilled barramundi; or grain-fed tenderloin; or tuck into a half-lobster as you take in 180-degree views of the marina, inlet, mountains, and ocean. Waitstaff can help you select the perfect match from a well-chosen Antipodean wine list. If you've room, simple desserts are equally pared back and delectable: espresso or pistachio ice cream, sorbets, cakes, or chocolate soufflé. Give him a day's notice, and Masa will even prepare a degustation dinner. This is refined dining in relaxed environs, perfect for special occasions. ⊠ Shop G9, Pier Shopping, Pierpoint Rd. ☎ *07/4051-0522* ⊕ *www.matureyogo.com* ᗐ *Bookings preferred* ⊟ *AE, DC, MC, V* ✣ *B3.*

$$
AUSTRALIAN
Fodor's Choice
★

✕ **Ochre Restaurant.** Local seafood and native ingredients have top billing at this elegant spot that specializes in bush dining. Try the Australian antipasto platter: seared 'roo with dukka, emu pâté, and crocodile wontons. Most dishes employ native foods and seasonal ingredients: sample wild-caught barramundi or emu fillet with mushroom sauce, or order a vegetarian, Australian game, or seafood platter to share (A$29–A$66). Red Ochre's signature dessert, wattle-seed pavlova with Davidson plum sorbet, makes a fine finish; or settle into a velvet booth and quaff a glass of Australian wine. ⊠ *43 Shields St., CBD* ☎ *07/4051-*

0100 ⊕ www.ochrerestaurant.com.au ⊟ AE, DC, MC, V ⊘ No lunch weekends ✛ A3.

$–$$ AUSTRALIAN ✕ **Perrotta's at the Gallery.** This outdoor café with galvanized-steel tables and chairs at the Cairns Regional Gallery also has a wine bar. Sumptuous breakfasts are served here from 7:30 AM, including French toast with star anise–scented pineapple and lime mascarpone. Lunch fare includes warm chicken salads and a variety of sandwiches. Tuck into modern Italian mains and deserts, such as vanilla-bean panna cotta with seasonal fruits. ⊠ Gallery Deck, Cairns Regional Gallery, Abbott and Shields Sts., CBD ☎ 07/4031–5899 ⊕ www.cairnsregionalgallery.com.au ⊟ AE, DC, MC, V ✛ B3.

WHERE TO STAY

$–$$ ▦ **Bay Village Tropical Retreat.** Resident managers Klaus and Lyn Ullrich have translated years of expertise in high-end Sydney hospitality into this family-friendly accommodation complex. Rooms, ranging from studios to three-bedroom apartments, are clean and comfortable (if a tad bland), and there's a large lagoon pool. The restaurant's imaginative dishes are a highlight. **Pros:** disabled-friendly room and wheelchair-friendly public areas; free airport access 7 AM to 7 PM. **Cons:** bland decor; some rooms lack Internet access, old-fashioned TVs. ⊠ Lake and Gatton Sts., CBD ☎ 07/4051–4622 ⊕ www.bayvillage.com.au ⇗ 62 suites, 28 apartments ⬙ In-room: safe (some), kitchen (some), refrigerator, dial-up (some). In-hotel: restaurant, room service, bar, pool, laundry facilities, laundry service, concierge, public Internet, airport shuttle, parking (no fee), no-smoking rooms ⊟ AE, DC, MC, V ✛ A1.

$–$$ ▦ **Cairns Colonial Club Resort.** Though it's just a few minutes outside the city center, this resort's 11 acres of tropical gardens make you feel a world away from the hubbub of Cairns. The colonial-style compound is built around three lagoonlike swimming pools (including a toddler pool) and a poolside café. A children's playground and babysitting services make it a great spot for families. Rooms, some more chic than others, have simple appointments, ceiling fans, and DVD players; studios also have cooking facilities. There's no spa on-site, but spa-style treatments are available. **Pros:** complimentary hourly city shuttle; free pool towels; good restaurant, Jardines. **Cons:** slow Internet and old TVs in some rooms, pool area can be busy. ⊠ 18–26 Cannon St., Cairns ☎ 07/4053–5111 ⊕ www.cairnscolonialclub.com.au ⇗ 342 rooms, 3 suites ⬙ In-room: safe (some), kitchen (some), refrigerator, dial-up (some). Wi-Fi (some). In-hotel: 2 restaurants, bars, tennis court, pools, gym, bicycles, laundry facilities, laundry service, concierge, executive floor, public Internet, public Wi-Fi, airport shuttle (no fee), parking (no fee), no-smoking rooms, no elevator ⊟ AE, DC, MC, V ✛ B1.

Fodor'sChoice ★ ¢–$ ▦ **Gilligan's Backpackers Hotel & Resort.** If you're headed to Cairns for an active vacation and don't need spa-level silence, this upscale budget property is perfect. Offering clean, modern, hostel-type four-, six-, and eight-bed dorms, deluxe four-bed suites, and private hotel-style twin rooms, all with en-suite facilities. Gilligan's is cheerfully cheap but doesn't feel like a compromise. Suites have fridges, TVs, DVD players, lounges, even balconies. Modern public facilities include a TV lounge,

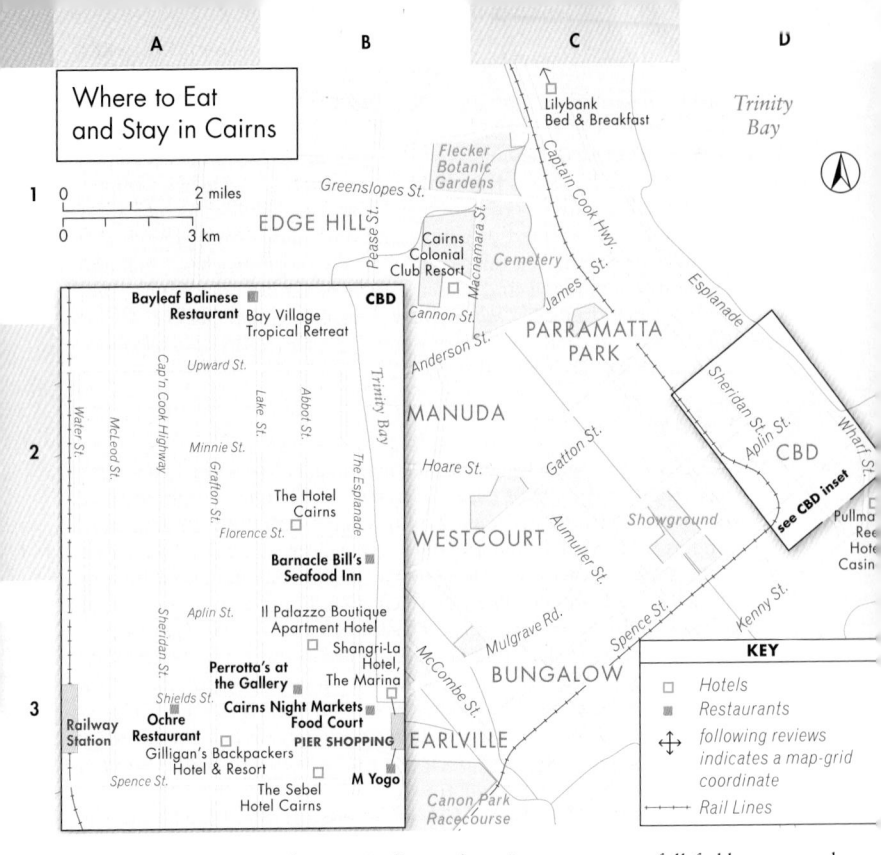

Where to Eat and Stay in Cairns

Scale: 0 — 2 miles / 0 — 3 km

EDGE HILL

Greenslopes St.

Flecker Botanic Gardens

Lilybank Bed & Breakfast

Trinity Bay

Captain Cook Hwy.

Pease St.

Cairns Colonial Club Resort

Cemetery

James St.

Esplanade

CBD

Bayleaf Balinese Restaurant

Bay Village Tropical Retreat

Cannon St.

Anderson St.

PARRAMATTA PARK

Sheridan St.

Aplin St.

CBD

Cap'n Cook Highway

Upward St.

Water St.

McLeod St.

Minnie St.

Lake St.

Abbot St.

Trinity Bay

MANUDA

Hoare St.

Gatton St.

Wharf St.

see CBD inset

Grafton St.

The Esplanade

The Hotel Cairns

Florence St.

WESTCOURT

Aumuller St.

Showground

Pullma Ree Hote Casin

Spence St.

Kenny St.

Barnacle Bill's Seafood Inn

Sheridan St.

Aplin St.

Il Palazzo Boutique Apartment Hotel

Shangri-La Hotel, The Marina

Mulgrave Rd.

McCombe St.

BUNGALOW

Perrotta's at the Gallery

Cairns Night Markets Food Court

Railway Station

Ochre Restaurant

Shields St.

PIER SHOPPING

EARLVILLE

Canon Park Racecourse

Gilligan's Backpackers Hotel & Resort

Spence St.

M Yogo

The Sebel Hotel Cairns

KEY

☐ Hotels
■ Restaurants
⊕ following reviews indicates a map-grid coordinate
⊢⊣ Rail Lines

Internet café-pizzeria, licensed gaming room, waterfall-fed lagoon pool, and on-site nightclub, Pure (open nightly, 10 PM until late). Gilligans is hugely popular with younger travelers, but everyone's welcome—though some might find it a little intense, what with the gigantic beer hall and deck, "dive-in" movies and sportscasts on Cairns's largest outdoor screen, and loud, live entertainment (including big-name bands) Tuesday through Sunday. **Pros:** fun, friendly guests; non-stop on-site entertainment; clean, modern facilities. **Cons:** noisy; nondescript food; fee for Internet use. ⊠ *57–89 Grafton St., CBD* ☎ *07/4041–6566 or 1800/556995* ⊕ *www.gilligansbackpackers.com.au* ⊐ *120 rooms* ⊘ *In-room: no phone, refrigerator (some), no TV (some). In-hotel: restaurant, bar, pool, gym, beachfront, laundry facilities, public Internet, airport shuttle, parking (no fee)* ⊟ *AE, MC, V* ⊕ *A3.*

$$–$$$ 🏨 **The Hotel Cairns.** One of the region's best examples of the Queenslander heritage style, family-run Hotel Cairns retains a genteel ambi-
★ ence despite extensive remodeling and refurbishment. Spacious rooms and suites, most with large, furnished balconies, have plantation shutters, flat-screen TVs with 50-plus complimentary cable channels, DVD and CD players, Molton Brown toiletries, and bathrobes. Rooms are given an elegant spin with soft green cushions and contemporary wood-and-cane furniture. There's a well-equipped gym, and an indoor-outdoor restaurant serving bistro-style dinners and big buffet breakfasts.

It's an easy block from the Esplanade. **Pros:** free cable channels; in-room Wi-Fi; courtesy Smart cars. **Cons:** some rooms lack views (ask); small, chilly pool. ⊠ Abbott St. at Florence St., CBD ☎ 07/4051-6188 ☎ 07/4051-1806 ⊕ www.thehotelcairns.com.au ➟ 89 rooms, 3 suites ⇄ In-room: Wi-Fi (fee). In-hotel: restaurant, room service, pool, gym, bicycles, laundry facilities, public Wi-Fi, public Internet, executive floor, parking (no fee), no-smoking rooms ▭ AE, DC, MC, V ✛ B2.

$–$$ **Il Palazzo Boutique Apartment Hotel.** Cairns is a long way from Europe, but you can imagine yourself on the Riviera at this intimate conti-nental-style hotel. A 6½-foot Italian marble replica of Michelangelo's David greets you in the foyer, and other intriguing objets d'art appear throughout. Spacious suites have a soft-green-and-coral color scheme, forged-iron and glass tables, and cane furniture, plus fully equipped kitchens and laundry facilities. There's a heated pool. **Pros:** free Austar cable channels, Australian produce and wines in mini-bar; clean, well appointed rooms. **Cons:** dated decor; slow in-room Internet. ⊠ 62 Abbott St., CBD ☎ 07/4041-2155 or 1800/813322 ⊕ www.ilpalazzo.com.au ➟ 38 suites ⇄ In-room: safe, kitchen, refrigerator, DVD, VCR, dial-up. In-hotel: pool, laundry facilities, laundry service, parking (no fee), no-smoking rooms, public Wi-Fi ▭ AE, DC, MC, V ✛ B3.

¢–$ **Lilybank Bed & Breakfast.** In the early 1900s this two-story Queen-slander was the home of the mayor of Cairns, and the homestead attached to North Queensland's first tropical-fruit plantation. A wooden veranda surrounds the building, and each pristine, high-ceilinged room has a private balcony area and en-suite bathroom. There's also a guest kitchen, a lounge with books and TV, and a saltwater pool flanked by a brick patio and trees. Hosts Pat and Mike Woolford are happy to book tours and share their extensive local knowledge (and the affections of their pet poodles and galah). They also do a great cooked breakfast, with local specialties such as kangaroo sausage. **Pros:** helpful hosts, warm atmosphere; big breakfasts. **Cons:** a drive from CBD; must love animals. ⊠ 75 Kamerunga Rd., Stratford ☎ 07/4055-1123 ⊕ www.lily-bank.com.au ➟ 5 suites ⇄ In-room: no phone, refrigerator (some), no TV, Internet. In-hotel: pool, laundry facilities, parking (no fee), public Internet, no-smoking rooms, no elevator ▭ AE, MC, V ❘O❙BP ✛ C1.

★ $$$ **Pullman Reef Hotel Casino.** Part of an entertainment complex in the heart of Cairns, this recently rebranded hotel has rooms and suites—as well as gaming tables, bars, a cabaret show, and a nightclub. Spacious accommodations have ceiling fans, plantation shutters, floor-to-ceiling windows, and spa baths, and garden balconies. Pacific Flavours gives a fresh, flavoursome spin on international cuisine, Tamarind serves fine Asian-inspired dishes, and Flinders Bar & Grill is an inexpensive, tasty option. There's even a small zoo on the rooftop. **Pros:** great on-site entertainment and dining options; helpful, high-end service. **Cons:** chilly pool; soft furnishings showing wear. ⊠ 35-41 Wharf St., CBD ☎ 07/4030-8888 ⊕ www.reefcasino.com.au ➟ 128 rooms and suites ⇄ In-room: safe, refrigerator, DVD (some), Internet, Wi-Fi (some). In-hotel: 4 restaurants, room service, bars, pool, gym, concierge, laundry service, public Internet, public Wi-Fi, parking (no fee), no-smoking rooms ▭ AE, DC, MC, V ✛ D2.

$–$$ ☆ **The Sebel Hotel Cairns.** Formerly the Pacific International Hotel, the Sebel faces the waterfront and marina and has an impressive three-story lobby. Guest rooms, smartly refurbished in muted tones, have balconies overlooking Trinity Inlet or the lovely pool area. There's a luxe on-site day spa, a lobby bar with live music on weekends, and all-day dining at Coco's (try the extensive Tastes of Australia buffet). **Pros:** lovely decor and pool area; high-speed Internet access; good on-site bar and dining (including high teas). **Cons:** thin walls; steep fees for use of in-room safe, Internet, and parking; erratic water temperature in showers. ✉ 17 Abbot St., at Spence St., CBD 📞 07/4031–1300 or 1800/079100 ⊕ www.pacifichotelcairns.com ➪ 176 rooms ⬙ In-room: safe (fee), refrigerator, Internet. In-hotel: restaurant, bar, room service, pools, concierge, spa, laundry facilities, laundry service, public Internet, public Wi-Fi, parking (fee), no-smoking rooms ▭ AE, DC, MC, V ✛ B3.

$$$$ ☆ **Shangri-La Hotel, The Marina.** With a minimalist lobby, golden-orb chandeliers, and suede chaise longues, this resort is among Cairns's hippest. Outside areas are suitably sleek, with extensive wooden decking, palm-shaded swimming pools, and a poolside cocktail bar. Spacious rooms have muted decor, flat-screen TVs, and flow-through views of the pool area, gardens, and city, or the mountains, bay, or marina (upgrade, if possible, to a marina-view room). The helpful tour desk can arrange activities off-site, such as reef excursions from the adjacent marina. **Pros:** great views; free Internet; free use of beach towels and umbrellas. **Cons:** service can be offhand; room-to-room plumbing noise; no on-site day spa. ✉ Pierpoint Rd., CBD 📞 07/4031–1411 ⊕ www.shangri-la.com ➪ 230 rooms, 25 suites ⬙ In-room: safe, kitchen (some), refrigerator, DVD (some), VCR (some), Internet, Wi-Fi (no fee) (some). In-hotel: 2 restaurants, room service, bar, pools, gym, concierge, laundry service, executive floor, airport shuttle, parking (no fee), no-smoking rooms ▭ AE, DC, MC, V ✛ B3.

Fodor'sChoice ★

OUTDOOR ACTIVITIES

It's no surprise that lots of tours out of Cairns focus on the Great Barrier Reef. Half-day snorkeling, diving, and fishing trips out of Cairns start from around A$120; full-day trips, from about A$180; scuba dives and gear generally cost extra, and usually you'll pay an additional A$5.50 reef tax.

Ask a few pertinent questions before booking diving tours: dive trips vary in size, and some cater specifically to, say, sightseers, others to experienced divers. If you're a beginner or Open Water diver, ensure that you book a trip that visits suitable dive sites, with certified staff on hand to assist you.

Cairns is also the base for adventure activities and horse riding on the Atherton Tableland, ballooning over the Mareeba Valley, and day tours to the UNESCO World Heritage–listed Daintree rain forest. The offices of adventure-tour companies, tourist offices, and booking agents are concentrated around the Esplanade.

SNORKELING AND DIVING

Deep Sea Divers Den ✉ 319 Draper St., CBD 📞 07/4046–7333 or 1800/612223 ⊕ www.diversden.com.au) has a roaming permit that

"This was taken at Steve's Bommie. This fish struck me as really angry that fate had made him tough-looking, yet pink." —Photo by Rowanne, Fodors.com member

allows guides to visit any part of the reef, including 17 private moorings. Day trips include up to three dives, gear, and lunch. From A$175 for a one-dive day trip; from A$420 for a 2-day, 5-dive live-aboard trip; A$110 for unlimited snorkeling, gear included.

Fodors Choice ★ ☾ Tusa Dive. Among Cairns' best dive boats are the custom-built fast cats run by Tusa Dive, which zoom up to 64 passengers out to sites on the Great Barrier Reef. On board there's space aplenty. Get dive briefs and info en route to the sites, and continual refreshments, including a big lunch. In the water, people of all ages and experience levels can dive (A$180–A$255) or snorkel (A$155) under the watchful gaze of guides. Get your photo taken with marine critters for posterity. ⊠ *Shield St. at The Esplanade, CBD* ☎ *07/4047–9100* ⊕ *www.tusadive.com.*

Fodors Choice ★ Mike Ball Dive Expeditions (⊠ *143 Lake St., CBD* ☎ *07/4053–0500* ⊕ *www.mikeball.com*) has been diving the Great Barrier Reef since 1969, and is credited with many underwater "firsts." Ball, an enthusiastic American, runs multiday, multidive trips along the Queensland coastline on which experienced divers get to set their own bottom times and dive their own plans—or be expertly guided. Custom-built, twin-hulled live-aboard boats loaded with top-end gear, serious divers, and qualified chefs depart twice-weekly to visit renowned dive sites and spot minke whales and sharks. From A$1,480 for a three-night, 12-dive trip; gear (A$40 per day) and courses extra.

Ocean Spirit Cruises (⊠ *140 Mulgrave Rd., CBD* ☎ *07/4031–2920 or 1800/644227* ⊕ *www.oceanspirit.com.au*) offers daily trips that include four hours at the Great Barrier Reef, coral viewing at Upolo Cay, guided snorkeling, optional dives, and a fresh seafood lunch. Introductory diving lessons (A\$115–A\$160) and certified dives (A\$55–A\$90) are available.

BEACHES

ADVENTURE TOURS

Fodor's Choice

★

Raging Thunder (✉ *52–54 Fearnley St., Portsmith* ☎ *07/4030–7990* ⊕ *www.ragingthunder.com.au*) has various adventure packages: dive and snorkel on the Barrier Reef; glide over the Mareeba Valley in one of the world's largest hot-air balloons; horsebackride or whitewater raft through the hinterland's rugged gorges; hike and bungeejump around Atherton Tablelands; or sea kayak around Fitzroy Island. Some tours can be combined with a visit to Tjapukai Aboriginal Cultural Park or wildlife sanctuaries.

Since Cairns lacks city beaches, most people head out to the reef to swim and snorkel. North of the airport, neighboring areas including Machans Beach, Holloways Beach, Yorkey's Knob, Trinity Beach, and Clifton Beach are perfect for swimming from June through September. Avoid the ocean at other times, however, when deadly box jellyfish (marine stingers) and invisible-to-the-eye Irukandji jellyfish float in the waters along the coast.

RnR White Water Rafting (✉ *278 Hartley St., CBD* ☎ *07/4041–9444* ⊕ *www.raft.com.au*) runs white-water expeditions on the North Johnstone and Tully rivers for adults of all skill levels, as well as reef and rain-forest trips, horse rides, ATV tours, balloon rides, and more. From A\$123 for a half-day's Barron River rafting tour.

NIGHTLIFE

Cairns's Esplanade comes alive at night, with most restaurants serving until late, and wine a staple with evening meals. Several rowdy pubs catering to backpackers and younger travelers line the central section of City Place; a few bars and hotel venues manage to be upscale while remaining true to the city's easygoing spirit. Unless noted, bars are open nightly and there's no cover charge.

PJ O'Brien's (✉ *87 Lake St., CBD* ☎ *07/4031–5333*), a traditional Irish pub chain, buzzes with backpackers swapping travel tales over pints and generally enjoying the *craic* (Gaelic for "good time"). It's open until around 3 AM.

Vertigo Bar & Lounge (✉ *Pullman Reef Hotel Casino, 35–41 Wharf St., CBD* ☎ *07/4030–8888 or 1800/808883* ⊕ *www.reefcasino.com.au*) has live bands, including big-name acts, Wednesday through Saturday, and big production shows two or three nights a week, followed by DJs and dancing (Thursdays, it's Latin; Fridays, funk, soul and retro; Saturdays, swing, funk, and disco). From 4 PM until late, Wednesday to Sunday, and all free.

SHOPPING

MALLS

Cairns Central (✉ *McLeod and Spence Sts., CBD* ☎ *07/4041–4111* ⊕ *www.cairnscentral.com.au*), adjacent to Cairns Railway Station, houses 180-plus specialty stores, a Myer department store, a food court, and a six-screen cinema complex. Stroller hire is available.

The Pier at the Marina (✉ *Pier Point Rd., CBD* ☎ *07/4051-7244* ⊕ *www.thepier.com.au*) houses the outlets of top Australian and international designers as well as a newsagent, bookstore, Internet café, salons, fitness facilities, and a visitor information center. Many of its bars and restaurants open onto waterfront verandas and the marina boardwalk.

MARKETS

If you're looking for bargain beachwear, local art and crafts, a massage, a meal, or souvenirs, the **Cairns Night Markets** (✉ *71–75 The Esplanade, at Aplin St., CBD* ☎ *01/4051-7666* ⊕ *www.nightmarkets.com.au*), open 5–11 PM weekdays, are the place to go. Bring cash—many of the 70-plus merchants charge additional fees for credit cards.

Cairns's best street market is **Rusty's** (✉ *Spence and Sheridan Sts., CBD* ☎ *07/4051-5100* ⊕ *www.rustysmarkets.com.au*), with 180-plus stallholders selling homegrown produce, art and crafts, jewelry, clothing, and food on Friday 5 AM–6 PM, Saturday 6–3, and Sunday 6–2.

SPECIALTY STORES

Jungara Gallery (✉ *99 The Esplanade, CBD* ☎ *07/4051-5355* ⊕ *www.jungaraaboriginalart.com.au*) stocks authentic Aboriginal arts and artifacts from artists Australia-wide, plus pieces from Torres Strait Island. They also have a gallery in Palm Cove.

Tusa Dive Shop (✉ *The Esplanade at Shields St., CBD* ☎ *07/4031 –1028* ⊕ *www.tusadive.com* ☉ *Daily 7:30 AM–9 PM*) stocks an impressive range of big-name dive gear as well as wet suits, swimwear, kids' gear, and accessories such as snorkels and sunscreen.

NORTH OF CAIRNS

The Captain Cook Highway runs from Cairns to Mossman, a relatively civilized stretch known mostly for the resort towns of Palm Cove and Port Douglas. Past the Daintree River, wildlife parks and sunny coastal villages fade into sensationally wild terrain. If you came to Australia seeking high-octane sun, pristine coral cays, steamy jungles filled with exotic birdcalls and riotous vegetation, and a languid beachcomber lifestyle, head for the coast between Daintree and Cooktown.

The southern half of this coastline lies within Cape Tribulation, Daintree National Park, part of the Greater Daintree Wilderness Area, a region named to UNESCO's World Heritage list because of its unique ecology. To experience the area's natural splendor, there's no need to go past Cape Tribulation. However, the Bloomfield Track continues on to Cooktown, a frontier destination that tacks two days onto your itinerary. This rugged country breeds some maverick personalities offering fresh perspectives on Far North Queensland.

Prime time for visiting is May through September, when daily maximum temperatures average around 27°C (80°F) and the water is comfortably warm. During the wet season, December through April, expect rain, humidity, and lots of bugs. Highly poisonous box and Irukandji jellyfish make the coastline unsafe for swimming October through May, but "jellies" hardly ever drift out as far as the reefs, so you're safe to get wet there.

Numbers in the margin correspond to points of interest on the North from Cairns map.

PALM COVE

23 km (14 mi) north of Cairns.

Fodor's Choice ★ A 20-minute drive north of Cairns, Palm Cove is one of Queensland's jewels: an idyllic, albeit expensive base from which to explore the far north. It's a quiet place, sought out by those in the know for its magnificent trees, calm waters, exceptionally clean beach, and excellent restaurants.

GETTING HERE AND AROUND
Getting here from Cairns is a cinch: by car, follow the signs from the city center to Captain Cook Highway, then head north, taking the Palm Cove turn-off (a 25- to 30-minute drive). Regular shuttle buses service Palm Cove from the airport and Cairns. Around this compact beach area, though, most people walk or cycle.

ESSENTIALS
Medical Clifton Beach Medical and Surgical (⊠ *Shop 12, Clifton Village, Captain Cook Hwy., Clifton Beach* ☎ *07/4059–1755*).

EXPLORING
A charming beachside village that sprawls back toward the highway, Palm Cove is easily navigated on foot. Many of the best accommodations, bars, and eateries are strung along the oceanfront strip of Williams Esplanade, fronting what has been dubbed Australia's cleanest beach. At its far north end, a five-minute stroll from the "village," there's a jetty and small marina.

TOP ATTRACTIONS
Hartley's Crocodile Adventures. 13.5 km (8 mi) or 15 minutes' drive north of Palm Cove, Hartley's houses crocodiles farmed for meat and skin, as well as koalas, wallabies, snakes, lizards, colorful cassowaries, and other tropical birds in natural environs, accessible via boardwalks and boats. Lagoon boat cruises and crocodile-farm tours guarantee you close-up views of crocs, and there are daily cassowary and koala feedings, croc and snake shows, and more. Lilies Restaurant showcases local delicacies, including crocodile and 'roo. The education center has useful info on how to avoid croc attacks. If you don't feel like driving, **Down Under Tours** (☎ *07/4035–5566*), **Wildlife Discovery Tours** (☎ *07/4099–6612*), and many other operators include Hartley's on their day-tour itineraries. ⊠ *Cook Hwy.* ☎ *07/4055–3576* ⊕ *www.crocodileadventures.com* ⊠ *A$32* ☉ *Daily 8:30–5.*

Palm Cove is one of many pristine beaches along the tropical Queensland coast.

Fodor's Choice
★
Mareeba Tropical Savanna & Wetlands Reserve. Drive 70 km (44 mi) west of Palm Cove along the Kennedy Highway, past Mareeba, and you'll encounter another world: giant termite mounds dot savanna scrub, and vast reclaimed wetlands give refuge to hundreds of bird species, including Australia's only stork, the Jabiru. The reserve runs a raft of nature-based excursions on and around the vast, lily-littered lagoons. A great-value 2½-hour Sunset Reserve Safari combines a bird-watching cruise, a ranger-guided savanna drive on which you'll spot wallabies and kangaroos, a "billy" tea and bird-hide stop, and fine Aussie wine and cheese. Luxury safari-tent accommodation comes with gourmet BBQ and breakfast baskets, wildlife-spotting, and bird-watching walks. You can also paddle canoes or fly-fish for ancient species in the lagoons. All proceeds feed back into the Wetlands' environmental work. ⊠ *142 Pickford Rd., Biboohra 4880* ☎ *07/4093–2514* ⊕ *www.mareebawetlands. org or www.jabirusafarilodge.com.au.*

☺ **Cairns Tropical Zoo.** The 10-acre Cairns Tropical Zoo is home to many species of Australian wildlife, including kangaroos, wombats, echidnas, emus, cassowaries, and reptiles including saltwater crocodiles. Most distinguished among its residents is Sarge, a 17-foot, 660-pound centenarian croc. The park has daily snake, crocodile, and bird shows. You can handle and hand-feed koalas and tame kangaroos, and have your photo taken with a koala, boa, or croc (A$15, 3 pics for A$33). The daily Breakfast at the Zoo (A$52) includes a wildlife presentation on the deck. The sanctuary incorporates Cairns Night Zoo, where, five evenings a week, up to 100 guests get close-up glimpses of Australia's fascinating nocturnal creatures on a guided tour, then tuck in to a big barbecue dinner (reservations essential). ✉ *Captain Cook Hwy.* ☎ *07/4055–3669* ⊕ *www.cairnstropicalzoo.com.au* 🎫 *A$32, A$95 night zoo, A$13–A$40 coach transfers* ☉ *Daily 8:30–5; Night Zoo Mon.–Thurs. and Sat. 6:50–10.*

WORTH NOTING

Outback Opal Mine. At the Outback Opal Mine, see huge specimens of this unique Australian gemstone as well as opalized seashells and fossils. A short documentary shows how an opal is formed, cut, and polished; the walk-through simulated mine has natural opals embedded in its walls. An on-site jewelry store showcases opals, naturally (A$5 to more than A$1,000). The mine is adjacent to Cairns Tropical Zoo. ✉ *Captain Cook Hwy.* ☎ *07/4055–3492* ⊕ *www.outbackopalmine.com.au* 🎫 *Free* ☉ *Daily 8:30–5:30.*

OUTDOOR ACTIVITIES

Palm Cove makes a great base for rain-forest and reef activities—hiking, biking, horseback riding, rafting, ballooning, and ATV adventures on the Atherton Tableland; snorkelling, diving, and sailing around the Low Isles and Barrier Reef; sea kayaking just offshore; and scenic flights over just about anywhere a small plane can get on a tank of gas.

SEA KAYAKING   **Palm Cove Watersports.** Paddling around history-rich Double Island, 100 meters (33 feet) from Palm Cove Jetty, is a tranquil, eco-friendly way to get close to local marine life: you'll often spot dolphins, stingrays, turtles, and colorful fish on this local operator's sunrise sea-kayaking tours and half-day excursions, with stops for refreshments, snorkeling (May–November), and stretching en route. Helpful guides impart labor-saving tips on technique and safety briefings. Not that you're likely to capsize: the single and double kayaks are super-stable. Half-day trips circumnavigate Double Island, stopping off on the fringing reef about 600 meters (½ mi) from shore and on a secluded beach. Transfers from Cairns (A$25) and Port Douglas (A$30) available; bookings essential. Gear provided, but please bring sunglasses, a hat, and sunscreen. ✉ *Palm Cove Jetty, Williams Esplanade (north end)* ☎ *0402/861011* ⊕ *www.palmcovewatersports.com* 🎫 *A$44, sunrise tour; A$80, half-day tour; A$8 reef tax/insurance* ☉ *Daily 6–7:30* AM, *sunrise tour; 8:30–12:30 and 1:30–5, half-day tour.*

WHERE TO EAT

$$ ✕ **Casmar Cafe Bar.** The ocean's bounty is the focus at this innovative water-

AUSTRALIAN   front restaurant. Try the seafood platter for two (A$90), with oysters, prawns, Moreton Bay bugs, chili-salt squid, scallops, reef fish, and various dipping sauces; or the hot-and-cold seafood buffet. Confit of duck, fresh fish-and-chips, and beef sirloin on mash are other crowd-pleasers. The food is a pleasure, as are the creative cocktails. You can also order a chilled seafood take-out feast, perfect for beach picnics. ✉ *73 Williams Esplanade, at Harpa St.* ☎ *07/4059–0013* ☐ *AE, DC, MC, V* ☉ *No lunch.*

$$$ ✕ **Nu Nu Restaurant.** Sexy suede lounges, intimate banquettes, and an

MODERN   uninterrupted view of Palm Cove beach make lingering easy at this top-
AUSTRALIAN   nosh eatery next to the Outrigger Beach Club (vanilla-ginger mojitos
Fodor'sChoice   and lime-coconut daiquiris help). The chef, decamped from Melbourne,
★   prides himself on an ever-changing Asia-meets-Mediterranean-inspired

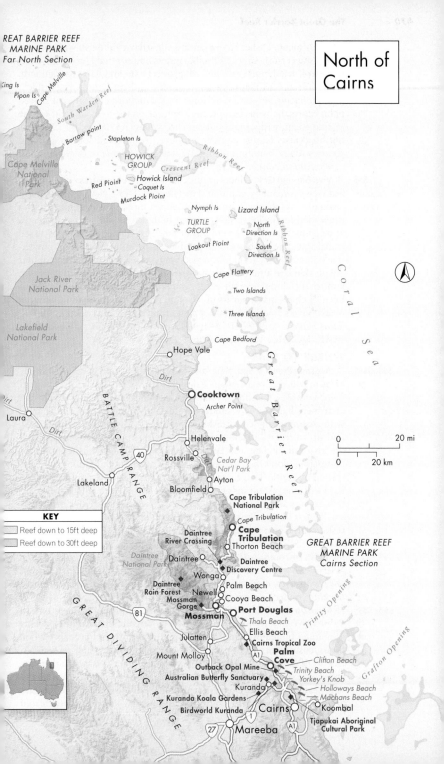

GREAT BARRIER REEF
MARINE PARK
Far North Section

King Is
Pipon Is
Cape Melville

South Warden Reef

Cape Melville
National
Park

Barrow point

Stapleton Is

HOWICK
GROUP

Crescent Reef

Ribbon Reef

Red Pioint
Howick Island
Coquet Is
Murdock Pioint

Nymph Is

Lizard Island

TURTLE
GROUP

North
Direction Is

Ribbon Reef

Lookout Pioint

South
Direction Is

Cape Flattery

Jack River
National Park

Two Islands

Three Islands

Cape Bedford

C o r a l

S e a

Lakefield
National
Park

Dirt

Hope Vale

Dirt

Laura

Cooktown

Archer Point

Dirt

BATTLE CAMP RANGE

40

Helenvale

Rossville

Dirt

*Cedar Bay
Nat'l Park*

Lakeland

Ayton

Bloomfield

G r e a t   B a r r i e r   R e e f

0   20 mi

0   20 km

Cape Tribulation
National Park

◆ *Cape Tribulation*

**Cape
Tribulation**

Thorton Beach

**Daintree
River Crossing**

◆ **Daintree
Discovery Centre**

GREAT BARRIER REEF
MARINE PARK
Cairns Section

*Daintree
National Park*

Daintree

Wonga

KEY

Reef down to 15ft deep

Reef down to 30ft deep

**Daintree
Rain Forest**
◆
**Mossman
Gorge**

Newell

Palm Beach

Cooya Beach

Trinity Opening

Mossman

Port Douglas

GREAT DIVIDING RANGE

81

Julatten

Mount Molloy

Thala Beach

Ellis Beach

Cairns Tropical Zoo
**Palm
Cove**

Outback Opal Mine
◆
Australian Butterfly Sanctuary
◆
Kuranda

A1

Clifton Beach

Grafton Opening

Trinity Beach
Yorkey's Knob

Holloways Beach
Machans Beach

Kuranda Koala Gardens

Birdworld Kuranda

27

Mareeba

1

Cairns

Koombal

A1

**Tjapukai Aboriginal
Cultural Park**

Mod-Oz menu. Dishes have a cutting-edge, flavorful twist, with seafood center stage: fresh-shucked Pacific oysters and roasted Hervey Bay scallops, wok-fried mud crab, line-caught reef fish, and baby barramundi, as well as prime Victorian lamb, honey-and-cardamom roast duck, and interesting vegetarian options: try the millionaires' salad of shaved palm hearts, baby herbs, and chili. Splurge on the four- or eight-course tasting menu, with or without matched wines (A$90–A$200). Nu Nu's big breakfasts feature organic produce, fresh-baked sourdough, and pastries (daily 8–noon). ⊠ *123 Williams Esplanade* ☎ *07/4059–1880* ⊕ *www.nunu.com.au* ⊟ *AE, MC, V.*

$$$
MODERN AUS-
TRALIAN/ITALIAN

✕ **Vivo Bar and Grill.** Diners at this classy eatery enjoy dress-circle Coral Sea views framed by palms and melaleucas. Those views, plus tropical cocktails, vibrant decor, and fresh Mod-Oz-meets-Mediterranean dishes draw food-loving locals and travelers in the know. Panini, pasta, salads, and calamari pack in the crowds at lunch; at dinner, head chef Russell transforms fine fresh seasonal produce, especially seafood, into inventive contemporary food in the gleaming open kitchen. Try his popular crispy-skin barramundi with mango-midori dressing or the king-prawn risotto, then indulge in the wattleseed bombe Alaska with flaming Sambuca. A chic sunken bar forms the hub of this sociable haunt; between meals, Vivo's a popular spot for city-strong coffee and cocktails. ⊠ *Williams Esplanade* ☎ *07/4059–0944* ⊕ *www.vivo.com.au* ⌁ *Book ahead* ⊟ *AE, DC, MC, V* ☉ *Daily from 7* AM.

WHERE TO STAY

$$$–$$$$
★

⛱ **Angsana Resort & Spa.** Fine landscaping, pools, barbecues, and sunny areas in which to relax enhance this classy colonial-style vacation apartment complex fronting a palm-shaded white-sand beach. Each vast apartment has a large veranda, comfortable lounging and dining areas with custom-designed furnishings, Italian espresso-makers, large TVs, and up to three capacious bedrooms with multiple en-suites. There are also full kitchen and laundry facilities. If you're in the mood for pampering, don't miss the Angsana spa's open-air and indoor pavilions staffed by gentle Thai therapists, most trained at Banyan Tree Phuket. Far Horizons restaurant opens onto Palm Cove Beach, and serves cocktails and modern International cuisine. There's a helpful tour desk and a small guest library. **Pros:** helpful staff; terrific location; good on-site bar-restaurant. **Cons:** no elevators; pools on the chilly side. ⊠ *1 Veivers Rd.* ☎ *07/4055–3000 or 1800/ 050019* ⊕ *www.angsana.com* ⌁ *67 apartments* ⌂ *In-room: safe, kitchen, refrigerator, laundry facilities, DVD, Wi-Fi. In-hotel: restaurant, room service, bar, pools, spa, beachfront, laundry service, concierge, public Internet, public Wi-Fi, airport shuttle, parking (no fee), no-smoking rooms, no elevator* ⊟ *AE, DC, MC, V.*

$$$–$$$$
☾
★

⛱ **Kewarra Beach Resort.** This true beachfront property just south of Palm Cove has its priorities right. The sensitively designed, sleekly appointed bungalows and restored pioneer's cottage have silky wood floors, custom furnishings, and high-tech appointments (flat-screen TVs, free VOIP-enabled Wi-Fi). Huge private balconies overlook either rain forest, one of the property's two freeform lagoon pools, or a pristine private beach. Air-conditioning is environmentally sensitive, and all rooms are oriented to maximize seclusion and views—as are the beachfront café/bar and open-sided restaurant. On-site activities include various guided nature walks, spa treatments, sunrise yoga or sea kayaking, beach barbecues, browsing the library or boutique, and serious lounging. If you must venture off-site, the helpful concierge and Adventure Desk can arrange customized excursions and transfers via car or helicopter to Cairns, Palm Cove, and the airport. **Pros:** high-end facilities and service; eco-friendly ethos; spectacular grounds; free Wi-Fi (even on the beach—though please don't be that guy who makes work phone calls from there). **Cons:** a drive from Palm Cove's cafés; no on-site gym. ⊠ Kewarra St., Kewarra Beach ☎ 07/4058–4000 ⊕ *www.kewarra. com* 🛏 *44 rooms* ⚹ *In-room: TVs (some), phone, safe, refrigerator, Wi-Fi. In-hotel: 2 restaurants, room service, bars, golf courses (nearby), pools, spa, beachfront, diving, water sports, bicycles, laundry facilities, laundry service, public Wi-Fi (free), parking (free), no-smoking rooms* ▭ *AE, D, DC, MC, V* ⦿⏐ *AI.*

$$$–$$$$ 🏨 **Peppers Beach Club & Spa.** The open-air reception area of this gorgeous beachfront resort opens onto landscaped grounds and one of the
ℭ Club's three pools, fed by a soothing cascade of water. Chill out with
★ a cocktail at the swim-up bar or a treatment at Sanctum Spa. Rooms and suites have sophisticated, contemporary furnishings, flat-screen TVs, and CD players. With either big balconies, courtyards, or rooftop terraces, an ocean-view penthouse suite is worth the splurge; most have hot tubs. Signature restaurant Lime & Pepper dishes up fresh regional cuisine and tropical buffet breakfasts (6:30 AM–9:30 PM). **Pros:** terrific dining options; laptops for hire; lovely pool. **Cons:** spa standards vary; gym equipment basic; pool area can be noisy. ⊠ *123 Williams Esplanade* ☎ *07/4059–9200 or 1300/987600* ⊕ *www.peppers.com.au* 🛏 *180 rooms and suites* ⚹ *In-room: safe, kitchen, refrigerator, DVD, Internet (fee), room service. In-hotel: 5 restaurants, bars, pools, gym, spa, laundry facilities, laundry service, executive floor, tour desk, public Wi-Fi (fee), airport shuttle (fee), parking (no fee), no elevator* ▭ *AE, DC, MC, V.*

PORT DOUGLAS

61 km (38 mi) northwest of Cairns.

Known simply as "Port" to locals, Port Douglas offers almost as broad a range of outdoor adventures as Cairns, but in a more compact, laid-back setting. In this burgeoning tourist town there's a palpable buzz, despite tropical haze and humidity. Travelers from all over the world base themselves here when making excursions to the north's wild rain forests and Great Barrier Reef. Varied lodgings, restaurants, and bars center on and around Port's main strip, Macrossan Street.

Like much of North Queensland, Port Douglas was settled after gold was discovered nearby. When local ore deposits dwindled in the 1880s it became a port for sugar milled in nearby Mossman until the 1950s. The town's many old "Queenslander" buildings give it the feel of a humble seaside settlement, despite its modern resorts and overbuilt landscape. The rain forests and beaches enveloping the town are, for the most

Have "Breakfast With the Birds" at the Rainforest Habitat Wildlife Sanctuary.

part, World Heritage sites—so while Port's growing in popularity, the landscapes that draw people here should remain undeveloped.

GETTING HERE AND AROUND
By car, it's a scenic, 75-minute drive north to Port Douglas from Cairns: take Sheridan Street to the Captain Cook Highway, following it for 60 km (35 mi) to the Port Douglas turnoff. North of Palm Cove, along the 30-km (19-mi) Marlin Coast, the road plays hide-and-seek with an idyllic stretch of shoreline, ducking inland through tunnels of coconut palm and curving back to the surf to reach Port Douglas.

Around town most people drive, walk, or cycle. It's about 5½ km (3½ mi), or an hour's walk from the highway to the main street. Regular shuttle buses call in at major hotels and resorts, day and night, ferrying travelers to and from Cairns, the airport, and nearby towns and attractions.

ESSENTIALS
Banks Commonwealth Bank of Australia (✉ Shop 1, Pandanus Plaza, Macrossan and Grant Sts., *Port Douglas* ☎ 13/2221 ⊕ www1.commbank.com.au).

Medical Port Douglas Medical Centre (✉ 33 Macrossan St., Port Douglas ☎ 07/4099–5276).

Port Douglas Police (☎ 07/4099–5220).

EXPLORING
Port Douglas is actually an isthmus, bound by Four Mile Beach on one side, Dickson's Inlet on the other, with the town's main retail, café, and restaurant strip, Macrossan Street, running up the center. The town

sprawls as far as the highway, 6 km (4 mi) to the west, along Port Douglas Road, lined with upmarket resorts and holiday apartment complexes. At the far end of Macrossan Street, on Wharf Street, there's a busy marina and shopping complex.

Fodor's Choice ★ ☺ The **Rainforest Habitat Wildlife Sanctuary.** You'll have many creature encounters around Australia, but the Breakfast with the Birds experience here—where the avian residents are so tame they'll perch on your shoulders as you dine—is among the best. The park houses more than 180 species of tropical native wildlife, including cassowaries, parrots, wetland waders, koalas, kangaroos, and crocodiles in world-class "immersion" woodland, wetland, rain-forest, and grassland environs. The sumptuous buffet breakfast, served daily 8–10:30, is A$44, including sanctuary admission and a well-worth-it guided tour. You can also Lunch with the Lorikeets for A$44, noon–2 daily, and attend croc, snake, and koala shows. ⊠ *Port Douglas Rd. at Agincourt St. 4877* ☎ *07/4099–3235* ⊕ *www.rainforesthabitat.com.au* ⊠ *A$30* ☺ *Daily 8–5, last admission at 4.*

OUTDOOR ACTIVITIES

Port Douglas is a great base for activities on the mainland and reef. Several tour companies conduct day trips into the rain forest and beyond in four-wheel-drive buses and vans; most include river cruises for crocodile-spotting and stops at local attractions. Several reef operators either base vessels at or pick up from Port Douglas Marina. You can also horseback ride, bungee jump, raft, go off-roading, hike, mountain-bike, and balloon on and around the Atherton Tablelands, or go Outback for excellent bird-watching west of Mareeba, less than two hour's drive from Port.

REEF TRIPS/ SNORKELING/ DIVING ☺ Fodor's Choice ★ **Poseidon** conducts guided snorkeling and PADI-style diving trips to three separate sites on the Agincourt Ribbon Reef on a small, usually uncrowded boat, and longer cruises to outer Barrier Reef sites, with excellent pre-dive briefings by a marine naturalist, high safety standards, and a wider-than-average choice of dive sites. A day's cruise is A$180; introductory diving, including tuition, cruise, all gear, and up to three underwater forays, is A$240 (with one dive; subsequent dives are A$40 each). For certified divers, a full day in the water, including two or three dives and a buffet lunch, is A$200–A$235. ⊠ *Grant and Macrossan Sts.* ☎ *1800/085674 or 07/4099–4772* ⊕ *www.poseidon-cruises.com.au* ⊠ *A$180–A$240 cruise, A$5–A$25 gear hire, A$5.50 reef tax* ☺ *Daily 8:30–4:30.*

☺ ★ **Quicksilver Connections** runs fast, modern catamarans to a large, commercial activity platform on the outer Barrier Reef, where options include marine-biologist-guided snorkeling tours (A$45–$60), scuba diving (A$97–A$139), 10-minute scenic heli-tours (A$148), and "Ocean Walker" sea-bed tours (A$139). There's also a semisubmersible underwater observatory. A quieter sailing excursion to a Low Isles coral cay includes a biologist-guided glass-bottom-boat trip, and snorkeling or an optional introductory or certified dive (extra A$139/A$97). The staff is patient, efficient, and knowledgeable. All tours depart from Cairns, Palm Cove on request, and Port Douglas. ⊠ *Marina Mirage, Wharf St.* ☎ *07/4087–2100* ⊕ *www.quicksilver-cruises.com.*

FISHING   Long-established **MV Norseman** is one of the best game-fishing boats on the Barrier Reef. Novice and experienced anglers can head out to the reef's edge to trawl for large pelagic fish, including giant black (and occasional) blue marlin, Spanish mackerel, tuna, sailfish, and wahoo. Closer in, find sea perch, sweet lip, red emperor, and coral trout. ☎ *07/4099–6888* ⊕ *www.mvnorseman.com.au.*

DAY TOURS   **Back Country Bliss Adventures** is based in Port Douglas but ranges much farther afield. Its customised, culturally and eco-sensitive small-group day trips take you to nature and adventure hotspots from the Atherton Tablelands to Cape Trib and Cooktown. Go sea kayaking or kite-surfing, rafting and mountain biking, drift-snorkelling in rain-forest streams, or "jungle surfing" over the canopy; or take a guided 4WD trip along the ruggedly scenic Bloomfield Track. Well-chosen wilderness locations, quality equipment, excellent staff including indigenous guides; and World Heritage Tour Operator accreditation give the Bliss team the edge. ☎ *07/4099–3677* ⊕ *www.blissbackcountrytours.com.au.*

Fodor'sChoice ★

SIGHTSEEING TOURS   **Deluxe Safaris** conducts day-long, well-guided trips in top-line 4WD vehicles and custom-built trucks. Visit Mossman Gorge and Cape Tribulation (A$165–A$175); take the rugged track to Bloomfield River Falls (A$175); or sleep in and join a late-departing Trailblazers tour to the Daintree and Cape Trib (A$145). You can also arrange a day-long, private wildlife-spotting charter to the Outback, west of Mareeba. Ample lunch and refreshments, included in all excursions, ensure that you keep your strength up. ⊠ *Shop 3A, 23 Warner St., Port Douglas* ☎ *07/4099–6406* ⊕ *www.deluxesafaris.com.au.*

Reef and Rainforest Connections' day trips out of Port Douglas include visits to Kuranda's key attractions, including the Scenic Railway and Skyrail Rainforest Cableway, with add-ons such as Tjapukai Aboriginal Cultural Park, Hartley's croc farm, and the Rainforest Habitat Centre. The company also runs excursions to Cape Tribulation and Bloomfield Falls, the Daintree River, and Mossman Gorge. ⊠ *40 Macrossan St., Port Douglas* ☎ *1300/780455 or 07/4035–5588* ⊕ *www.reefandrainforest.com.*

BOAT TOURS   **Crocodile Express** (⊠ *5 Stewart St., end of Mossman–Daintree Rd.*), ☎ *07/4098–6120* ⊕ *www.daintreeconnection.com.au*), a flat-bottom boat run by operators who've been plying this waterway since 1979, cruises the Daintree River from three access points on crocodile-spotting excursions. Sixty-minute cruises leave Daintree River crossing half-hourly, 8:30 AM to 5 PM (A$22 per person); 90-minute trips depart from Daintree Village at regular intervals from 10 to 4 (A$27). You can also take sunrise and sunset bird-watching cruises along the Barratt River with renowned birder Ian "Sauce" Worcester.

Fodor'sChoice ★

Tony's Tropical Tours gives entertaining small-group day tours in luxe land cruisers that take in rain-forest sights and attractions as far as Cape Tribulation or, if you're prepared to get up earlier, the renowned and ruggedly beautiful Bloomfield Track. Well-informed, witty commentary from Tony and other local experts, and non-rushed, well-chosen stops and activities—from interpretive rain-forest walks and Daintree River wildlife (croc) cruises, to handmade ice-cream and tropical-fruit tasting—make these trips crowd-pleasers. Refreshments, included in the cost, are a cut above the norm: think plunger (French press) coffee, rain-forest tea, and a satisfying BBQ lunch. ⌂ *Box 206, Port Douglas* ☎ *07/4099–3230* ⊕ *www.tonystropicaltours.com.au*

WHERE TO EAT

$$$

MODERN
AUSTRALIAN

★

✕ **Bistro 3.** This classy, colorful eatery has an unabashedly local focus, showing off the region's best in tasty Mod-Oz dishes. The signature Daintree saltwater whole crispy baby barramundi, served with a red curry sauce, is farmed in Wonga Beach and delivered fresh daily. They also do terrific wok-fried Moreton Bay bugs, handmade pasta, roasted lamb rump, and Black Angus sirloin steak. They mix a mean specialty cocktail and do a lovely Sunday brunch. ⊠ *Wharf and Macrossan Sts.* ☎ *07/4099–6100* ⊕ *www.bistro3.com* ⌂ *Bookings preferred* ▭ *AE, DC, MC, V.*

$$–$$$

SEAFOOD

★

⟳

✕ **On The Inlet.** Choose your own live mud crab from holding tanks at this much-lauded seafood restaurant fronting Dickson Inlet. Watch yachts dock as you sit on the deck and down the sunset special: a generous bucket of prawns and a choice of beer, wine, or bubbly for A$18 (arrive around 5 and you can watch resident giant grouper, George, get fed). Modern Australian dishes—chili-spiked salmon and seafood linguine with sundried tomato; pan-fried fish of the day—put the focus on fine, fresh North Queensland produce and seafood that's delivered direct from local fishing boats to the restaurant's pontoon. Non-pescophiles are well catered for, with eye fillet, tender lamb, chicken, and vegetarian options. There's a good kids' menu, and a terrific wine and cocktail list. ⊠ *3 Inlet St.,* ☎ *07/4099–5255* ⊕ *www.portdouglasseafood.com* ⌂ *Bookings recommended* ▭ *AE, MC, V* ⊙ *Daily from 10 AM.*

$$

MODERN
AUSTRALIAN

★

✕ **Salsa Bar & Grill.** This lively waterside restaurant is a Port Douglas institution. The louver-windowed interior is bright and beachy; the huge wooden deck overlooking Dickson Inlet becomes an intimate dining area after sunset. Seafood, steaks, salads, and light snacks grace the lunch menu; a tropical Modern Australian dinner menu includes kangaroo loin, lamb backstrap, herb-crusted barramundi, yellowfin tuna, a standout seafood linguine, and a Jambalaya loaded with yabbies (local crayfish), tiger prawns, squid, and croc sausage. Happy hour comes daily between 3 and 5, just right for a tropical daiquiri or two. Pre-booking is strongly advised. ⊠ *26 Wharf St.* ☎ *07/4099–4922* ⊕ *www.salsaportdouglas.com.au* ▭ *AE, DC, MC, V.*

WHERE TO STAY

$$$–$$$$

★

☖ **Coconut Grove Port Douglas.** These luxe three-bedroom apartments and penthouses perched above Port's main strip have state-of-the-art furnishings and appliances, spa baths, and huge balconies or decks. Splurge on a first- or top-level apartment and you get a vast entertaining terrace with an impressive barbecue/kitchen, plunge pool, and Jacuzzi. In-house massages are easily arranged, and there are a raft of catering options—from having your fridge stocked on arrival to ordering a late-night supper, beach picnic, or steak and seafood for the barbie (and, if you like, a teppenyaki chef to cook it). There's a public lounge, a tour desk, and a 20-meter (66-foot) lap pool in landscaped grounds. Cafés, bars, boutiques, and the beach are a mere stroll away. **Pros:** smart,

7

user-friendly living areas; central location; gourmet food options. **Cons:** pricey if not sharing; no in-house gym or spa; three-night minimum stay. ⊠ 6 Macrossan St. ☎ 07/4099–0600 ⊕ www.coconutgroveportdouglas. com.au ⌐♪ 31 apartments, 2 penthouses ♿ In-room: safe, kitchen, refrigerator, DVD, Internet, Wi-Fi. In-hotel: room service, pool, beachfront, laundry facilities, Wi-Fi, parking (free), no-smoking rooms ⊟ AE, DC, MC, V ☉ 8 AM–6 PM reception/concierge/tour desk ⦿ EP.

¢   ⊡ **Global Backpackers.** This tidy budget accommodation above Rattle and Hum has modern, air-conditioned dorms, simple yet well-kept doubles with en-suites, and clean, sleek public areas including a lounge with plasma TV. There's Internet access and a tour desk; head downstairs to the bar and grill for free Foxtel cable channels on big screens, pool tables, and nightly entertainment—plus good (albeit not budget-priced) steaks, ribs, and wood-fired pizzas. **Pros:** boutique decor and facilities at budget prices; on-site food and entertainment; clean rooms with better-than-average beds. **Cons:** can be noisy; dorms smallish; no outdoor areas or pool. ⊠ Upstairs, 38 Macrossan St. ☎ 07/4099–5641 ⊕ www.rattleandhumbar.com.au ♿ In-room: no TVs, shared bath (some). In-hotel: restaurant, bar, no-smoking rooms ⊟ AE, D, DC, MC, V ⦿ EP.

$$$–$$$$ ⊡ **Sea Temple Resort & Spa.** A grand marble-columned lobby, flow-through public areas, well-tended grounds, and vast swimming pools flanked by sun-lounges and dramatically torch-lit at night lend a Riviera-meets-Phuket ambience to this exclusive resort. Here there's little to do besides sunbathe, swim, down tropical cocktails, enjoy Mii spa treatments, or stroll along the shore, though energetic guests might play a round of golf on Sea Temple's adjacent 18-hole championship course. Make yourself comfortable in a spacious Spa room or oversize apartment with state-of-the-art appointments: "swimout" apartments have decks opening onto the lagoon pool; penthouses come with private rooftop terraces and Jacuzzis. Most luxe are the lavish "plunge pool" apartments, each with a private deck, pool, and barbecue pavilion. **Pros:** lovely apartments and pools; kids under 12 stay free. **Cons:** pricey food and drinks; sluggish Internet in Spa rooms; service standards vary. ⊠ Mitre St. ☎ 07/4084–3500 or 1800/833762 ⊕ www.mirvachotels.com ⌐♪ 194 spa rooms, apartments, and penthouses ♿ In-room: safe (some), kitchen (some), refrigerator (some), DVD (some), Internet (some), Wi-Fi (some). In-hotel: Restaurant, room service, bars, golf course, pools, gym, spa, beachfront, children's programs (ages 5–14, school holidays only), laundry facilities (some), laundry service, public Wi-Fi, parking (free), no-smoking rooms ⊟ AE, D, DC, MC, V ⦿ EP, BP.

$$–$$$ ⊡ **Thala Beach Resort.** Set on 145 acres of private beach, coconut groves,
★   and forest, this eco-certified nature lodge is about low-key luxury. Guesthouses (linked by meandering, stone-lined paths) are comfy refuges oriented for privacy, with polished-wood floors and restful bush and ocean views. The circular communal lounge and reading room has stupendous vistas that stretch to the Barrier Reef islands and Daintree rain forest; sunset cocktails and buffet breakfasts in the open-sided restaurant are accompanied by a cacophony of birdcalls. There are two

small pools—one split-level, with waterfalls and grottoes, bushwalking trails, a serene wellness center, and areas for secluded sunbathing. Eco-friendly activities include wildlife, indigenous and coconut walks, turtle-spotting from sea kayaks, and star-gazing through Thala's state-of-the-art telescope. There's a tour desk, a small gallery/jewelry outlet, even a helipad for visiting heads of state. **Pros:** interesting activities; beautiful property; eco-friendly ethos. **Cons:** no public Internet terminal; no gym; limited food available between meals; 20-minute drive to Port Douglas. ⊠ *Private Beach Rd., Oak Beach (off Bruce Hwy., 24 mi north of Cairns)* ☎ *07/4098–5700* ⊕ *www.thala.com.au* ⤴ *45 rooms* ⚇ *In-room: safe, refrigerator, CD/DVD (some). In-hotel: restaurant, room service, bars, pools, spa, beachfront, water sports, laundry service, Internet terminal, Wi-Fi, parking (free), no-smoking rooms* ═ *AE, D, DC, MC, V* ⦿ *AI.*

SHOPPING

Marina Mirage (⊠ *65 Macrossan St., at Wharf St.* ☎ *07/4099–5775*) houses fashion, specialty, and souvenir shops; the offices of various cruise, dive, and tour operators; a handful of restaurants; and, at Shop 54, Port Douglas's only late-opening nightclub, Fluid.

At the waterfront Port Douglas Markets (⊠ *Anzac Park, Wharf St. end of Macrossan St.* ☎ *0408/006788* ☉ *Sundays 8* AM*–2* PM), local growers and artisans sell fresh produce and gourmet goodies, original art and crafts, hand-made garments, books, and souvenirs. Street performers of varying quality entertain the browsing crowd.

MOSSMAN

14 km (8½ mi) northwest of Port Douglas, 75 km (47 mi) north of Cairns.

This sleepy sugarcane town of fewer than 2,000 residents attracts few visitors: most merely pass through en route to Mossman Gorge, the Daintree, and rain-forest accommodations.

GETTING HERE AND AROUND

From Port Douglas it's 14 km (8½ mi) or 20 minutes' drive northwest to Mossman. From Cairns it's a 75-km (47-mi) drive along the Captain Cook Highway. There's little here to explore, but it's a good place to stop for supplies or to pick up park info and trail maps from the Queensland Parks & Wildlife Service office.

ESSENTIALS

Medical Mountain View Medical Centre (⊠ *4 Front St.* ☎ *07/4098–1711*).

Visitor Information Daintree Village Tourist Association (☎ *No phone* ⊕ *www.daintreevillage.asn.au*).

EXPLORING

Daintree Village, a 35-minute drive north along the Mossman-Daintree Road, has restaurants, cafés, galleries, and access to croc river cruises. Drive 20 minutes northeast of Mossman toward Daintree to reach Wonga Beach, where you can go horseback riding or go walkabout with indigenous guides.

Shannonvale Tropical Fruit Winery. Call in at the cellar door, open daily 10–4:30, and taste up to a dozen fine single-fruit wines made from organic fruits grown on-site. With mango, pineapple, pawpaw, lychee, grapefruit, kaffir lime, and more, there's a drop to suit every palate, from dry table varieties to dessert wines and ports. Try the medal-winning Black Sapote (chocolate pudding fruit) port; then buy a bottle for the road (or get a case shipped home). Your $5 tasting fee comes off any purchase. ⊠ *Shannonvale Valley* ☏ *07/4098–4000* ⊕ *www.shan-nonvalewine.com.au.*

Fodor's Choice
★

Mossman Gorge. Just 5 km (3 mi) out of town are the spectacular water-falls and river that tumble through sheer-walled Mossman Gorge. Ice-cold water flows here year-round, and there are several boulder-studded, croc-free swimming holes. (Swimming in the river itself is hazardous, crocs or no, due to swift currents, slippery rocks, and flash flooding.) There's a suspension bridge across the Mossman River and a 2½-km (1½-mi) rain-forest walking track. Keep your eyes peeled for tree and musky rat-kangaroos, Boyd's water dragons, scrub fowl, turtles, and big, bright butterflies—and try to avoid stinging vines (plants with serrated-edge, heart-shaped leaves, found at rain-forest edges). If you intend hiking beyond the river and rain-forest circuits, inform park staff and complete a bushwalking registration form. ⊠ *Queensland Parks & Wildlife Service, Level 1, Centenary Bldg., 1 Front St., Mossman* ☏ *07/4098–2188* ⊕ *www.epa.qld.gov.au.*

OUTDOOR ACTIVITIES

ABORIGINAL
TOURS
★

Daintree Eco Lodge & Spa runs a raft of Aboriginal-guided activities. The hour-long Aboriginal Rainforest Culture Walk gives insights into the Kuku Yalanji culture, indigenous bush tucker, medicinal plants, and local wildlife, and takes in a waterfall important for women's healing. A hands-on, sociable Aboriginal art workshop takes place most after-noons on the bar/restaurant's airy deck. You can also dine on cuisine showcasing indigenous local ingredients at the lodge's restaurant, watch a Corroboree performance, take a guided rain-forest night walk with an indigenous guide, browse and buy authentic Aboriginal art (and meet the artists, if requested) at the on-site gallery, watch a didgeridoo demo, and enjoy traditional, all-natural treatments at the on-site spa (daily 10–6). ⊠ *20 Daintree Rd., 3 km (2 mi) past Daintree village, Daintree* ☏ *07/4098–6100* ⊕ *www.daintree-ecolodge.com.au* ⌨ *Prices vary, contact the Lodge* ⊙ *Daily, pre-booking essential.*

♻
★

Kuku Yalanji Dreamtime. On this 1½-hour walk along easy, graded rain-forest tracks you'll visit culturally significant sites and traditional bark settlements with a Kuku Yalanji guide, who'll demonstrate traditional plant use, explain the history of cave paintings, point out bush tucker ingredients, and share Dreamtime legends, conveying the indigenous owners' special relationship with this ancient tropical terrain. After-wards, enjoy billy tea, damper, and a didgeridoo performance. ⊠ *Moss-man Gorge Rd., Mossman* ☏ *07/4098–2595* ⊕ *www.yalanji.com.au* ⌨ *A$32, A$35 with Pt. Douglas transfers* ⊙ *Mon.–Sat. 9, 11, 1, and 3.*

From their watery perch, two visitors survey a swimming hole at Mossman Gorge.

HORSEBACK RIDING

☽
★

This terrain is ideal for exploring on horseback, and one of the area's best guides is **Wonga Beach Horse Rides.** Well-guided two-hour rides take you along Wonga Beach and pristine Daintree rain-forest trails, crossing creeks in wet season. Keep an eye out for rays, dolphins, and jumping cod in the ocean; birds, butterflies, and reptiles in the forest. The cost includes insurance, gear, drinks, and Port Douglas pick-ups. You can also book exclusive guided rides (A$180–A$220, min. 2 persons) and one-hour lessons (A$60). ✉ *Wonga Beach Equestrian Centre, Mossman-Daintree Rd., Wonga Beach* ☏ *07/4098–3900* ⊕ *www.beachhorserides.com.au* 🖃 *A$115* ⊙ *Daily 8:30 AM, 2:30 pm.*

☽ Impressive displays of horsemanship and "jackeroo" (cowboy) skills are the draw at the **Australian Muster Experience.** Daily shows, staged in a 19th-century-inspired "Outback station shed" arena in rain-forest environs, 12.5 km (8 mi) north of Mossman, include whip-cracking, cattle-driving, super-smart cattle dogs, and various Outback animals. It's all delivered with dry Outback humor and followed by a BBQ lunch or dinner. Choose between the Stockman's Lunch Muster (available as a self-drive), the Grand Outback Experience (after which you can test your rodeo skills on a mechanical bull), or the show-and-ATV-riding package. There's a bar and a gallery-giftshop on-site. ✉ *Kingston Rd., Whyanbeel Valley* ☏ *07/4098–1149* ⊕ *www.australianmusterexperience.com.au* 🖃 *A$156 (Grand Outback, with transfers)* ⊙ *Daily 8:30 AM, 2:30 PM.*

Silky Oaks Lodge, near Daintree National Park.

WHERE TO STAY

$$$$
★

Daintree Eco Lodge & Spa. Dozens of stars have taken time out at this 30-acre boutique eco-resort in the ancient Daintree rain forest. Elevated boardwalks protect the fragile environs, linking the spa, heated pool, restaurant-bar-lounge-deck, and 15 freestanding tree houses. Each tree house is equipped with a king-size canopy bed, handcrafted wood furnishings, Aboriginal artworks, and satellite TV, and some with balcony hot tubs. Julaymba restaurant's tropical Australian menu ($$$) incorporates local "bush tucker" ingredients. The Malone family and Aboriginal staff run a terrific activities program that includes bush-tucker walks, wildlife-spotting, indigenous art workshops, and cultural shows. **Pros:** alfresco spa treatments; luxe bathroom amenities; eco-friendly; lower rates with longer stays. **Cons:** some rooms lack seclusion; others can't get Wi-Fi; noise from public areas carries to rooms and spa. ⊠ 20 Daintree Rd. (3 km [2 mi] past Daintree village—110 km [68 mi] north of Cairns), Daintree ☎ 1800/808010 or 07/4098–6100 ⊕ www. daintree-ecolodge.com.au ⤴ 15 rooms ⌂ In-room: refrigerator, dial-up (some), Wi-Fi (some). In-hotel: restaurant, room service, bar, pool, spa, laundry service, airport shuttle, parking (no fee), no kids under 6, no-smoking rooms, no elevator ⊟ AE, DC, MC, V ⦿ BP.

$$$$
Fodor's Choice
★

Silky Oaks Lodge. Surrounded by national parkland, this hotel is reminiscent of high-end African safari lodges. Tropically inspired villas overlook the rain forest, river, or a swimming pool lined with natural rocks; inside, they feature warm timber floors and furnishings, CD players, dimmable lighting, aromatherapy oil burners, hot tubs, day beds, and verandas slung with hammocks. The lodge is the starting point for 4WD, cycling, and canoeing trips into national park rain forest. Or stay put and recharge at the Healing Waters Spa, where treatments incorporate all-natural Australian-made products. Delightful public areas, including the open-sided Tree House restaurant and bar, overlook the Daintree River. Gourmet breakfasts and various activities (river snorkeling, guided walks, bicycles, tennis, board games) are included in the price—which is also reduced for stays longer than two nights. **Pros:** lovely spa; beautiful location. **Cons:** no in-room Internet; à la carte options less inspiring than the environs. ✉ *Finlayvale Rd., Mossman Gorge* ☎ *1300/134044 or 07/4098–1666* ⊕ *www.voyages.com.au/silky* ⇨ *37 rooms, 13 suites* ⚭ *In-room: no TV, refrigerator. In-hotel: safe, restaurant, bar, tennis court, pool, gym, spa, water sports, bicycles, laundry facilities, laundry service, public Internet, concierge, parking (no fee), no kids under 13, no-smoking rooms, no elevator* ▭ *AE, DC, MC, V* ⦿⦿ *BP.*

CAPE TRIBULATION

34 km (21 mi) north of the Daintree River crossing, 139 km (86 mi) north of Cairns.

Set dramatically at the base of Mt. Sorrow, Cape Tribulation was named by Captain James Cook after a nearby reef snagged the HMS *Endeavour,* forcing him to seek refuge at the site of present-day Cooktown. Today the tiny settlement, little more than a general store and a few lodges, is the activities and accommodations base for the surrounding national park.

GETTING HERE AND AROUND

The turnoff for the Daintree River crossing is 29 km (18 mi) north of Mossman on the Daintree–Mossman Road, which winds through sugarcane plantations and towering green hills to the **Daintree River,** a short waterway fed by monsoonal rains that make it a favorite inland haunt for saltwater crocodiles. On the northerly side of the river a sign announces Cape Tribulation National Park. There's just one ferry, carrying a maximum 27 vehicles, so although the crossing takes five minutes, the wait can be 15, especially between 11 AM and 1 PM and in holiday periods. ☎ *07/4098–7536* 🖂 *A$20 per car (round-trip), A$2 walk-on passenger* ⊙ *Daily 6 AM–midnight.*

North of the river the road winds its way to Cape Tribulation, burrowing through dense rain forest and onto open stretches high above the coast, with spectacular views of the mountains and coastline. The 138-km (86-mi) drive from Cairns to Cape Trib takes about three hours. If you're renting a car, do so in Cairns or Port Douglas. This is tough driving territory. Many minor roads are unpaved, and even major thruways around Daintree may be closed in the wet season due to flooding.

Cape Tribulation Shop and Information Centre and PK's Jungle Village, virtually opposite one another on Cape Tribulation Road, are the last stops for food, supplies, and fuel as you head north. At PK's there's an IGA supermarket and a pharmacy.

ATMs are scarce beyond Mossman. Get cash out at the BP or Caltex service stations at Wonga Beach or at PK's. North of Port Douglas

7

mobile phone coverage is limited, except in and around Mossman and Daintree Village.

Public transport is limited throughout the region. Coral Reef Coaches run a daily service between Cairns, Port Douglas, and Mossman (A$35). Sun Palm Express daily services link Cairns, Port Douglas, Daintree, Cow Bay, and Cape Trib: the full journey takes three to four hours, with stops at most resorts on request, and is A$75 ($A45 from Port Douglas; A$50 from Palm Cove).

ESSENTIALS

ATMs Caltex Wonga (⊠ *Daintree Rd., Wonga Beach* ☎ *07/4098–7616*).

Bus Contacts Coral Reef Coaches (☎ *07/4098–2800* ⊕ *www.coralreef-coaches.com.au*). **Sun Palm Express Coaches** (☎ *07/4087–2900* ⊕ *www.sunpalmtransport.com*).

Tours and Visitor Information Cape Tribulation Shop and Information Centre & Mason's Tours (⊠ *CMA 4, Cape Tribulation Rd.* ☎ *07/4098–0070* ⊕ *www.masonstours.com.au*). **PK's Jungle Village** (⊠ *PMB 7, Cape Tribulation Rd.* ☎ *1800/232333 or 07/4098–0040* ⊕ *www. pksjunglevillage.com.au*).

EXPLORING

Cape Tribulation Road winds through rain forest north of Cow Bay, veering east to join the coast at Thornton Beach, then skirting a string of near-deserted beaches en route to Cape Trib. Accommodations, attractions, and access points for beaches, croc cruise boats, and various mangrove and rain-forest boardwalks are well signposted from the main road.

These rugged-looking yet fragile environs, Kuku Yalanji tribal lands, are best explored with experienced, culturally sensitive and eco-conscious guides. Excursions by 4WD and on horseback, bicycle, boat, and foot are all offered by local operators and resorts.

If exploring off-road on your own, arm yourself with detailed local maps, supplies, and good information. Let a reliable person know your intended route and return time, and don't underestimate the wildness of this terrain.

HIKING

Fodor's Choice

★

Cape Tribulation, Daintree National Park, the world's oldest tropical rain forest, is an ecological wonderland: 85 of the 120 rarest species on earth are found here, and new ones are still being discovered. The 22,000-acre park, part of the UNESCO World Heritage–listed Wet Tropics region, stretches along the coast and west into the jungle from Cow Bay, 35 km (22 mi) northwest of Mossman, to Aytor. Traditional owners, the Kuku Yalanji, who live in well-honed harmony with their rain-forest environs, attribute powerful properties to many local sites—so tread carefully. Prime hiking season here is May through September, and many local operators offer guided Daintree rain-forest walks and longer hikes and night wildlife-spotting excursions. Gather information and maps from local rangers or the **Queensland Parks and Wildlife Service** before hiking unguided, and stay on marked trails and boardwalks to avoid damaging your fragile surroundings. Whatever season you go, bring insect repellent. ⊠ *QPWS Office, Level 1, Centenary Bldg., 1 Front St., Mossman* ☎ *07/4098–2188* ⊕ *www.epa.qld.gov.au.*

OUTDOOR ACTIVITIES

HORSEBACK
RIDING

Cape Trib Beach Horse Rides (☎ *1800/ 111124* ⊕ *www.capetribbeach.com. au*) has 3½-hour rides that meander through rain forest, along Myall Beach, and across open paddocks, with opportunities to swim in rain-forest waterholes. The cost includes tea, insurance, and transportation from Cape Tribulation hotels.

TAKE A NIGHT HIKE

Take a guided night hike if you're keen on lots of maamal sightings; most in the Daintree are noctur-nal, though you might see musky rat-kangaroos, the most primitive of Australia's 20-million-year-old kangaroo family, foraging by day.

CANOPY
TOURS

Daintree Discovery Centre. This World Heritage–accredited facility provides detailed information on the rain forest and its ecosystem. There are four audio-guided trails, including a "bush tucker" walk and a cassowary circuit. Take an aerial walkway across part of the bush, and climb the 75-foot-high Canopy Tower. The shop sells books, cards, souvenirs, and clothing. ⊠ *Tulip Oak Rd., off Cape Tribulation Rd. (10 km [6 mi] north of Daintree River ferry station), Cow Bay* ☎ *07/4098–9171* ⊕ *www.daintree-rec.com.au* 🖃 *A$28 (includes 48-page guidebook/ return entry)* ☉ *Daily 8:30–5.*

☺ **Jungle Surfing Canopy Tours.** It's an exhilarating perspective on the rain forest and reef: suspended above the canopy on flying-fox ziplines, your speed controlled by guides, you whiz along (and if you like, flip upside-down), stopping at five tree platforms for killer bird's-eye views. Nightly guided Jungle Nightwalks explore the critter-filled, 45-acre grounds. Transfers from local accommodations are free, or self-drive to the central pick-up point. Thrice-weekly day-tour packages from Port Douglas include lunch at Whet. E*From Cape Tribulation Pharmacy (next to PK's), Cape Tribulation Rd.,* ☎ *07/4098–0043* ⊕ *www.junglesurfing. com.au.*

Rum Runner IX, a fast 40-foot motor-sailer catamaran run by Ocean Spirit Cruises, whisks up to 44 passengers daily from Cape Tribulation beach to the Barrier Reef in just over an hour. This gives you around five hours to snorkel or dive on the magnificent MacKay and/or Undine reefs, teeming with "Nemos" (clown anemone fish), turtles, rays, barracuda, potato cod, giant clams, and nudibranchs, and an array of hard and soft corals. The rate includes wet suits and snorkeling gear, guidance, fruit platters, a tropical buffet lunch, and the EMC (reef tax); introductory and certified dives are extra. Transfers from Cow Bay are A$10; pick-ups from Cape Trib accommodations are free. ⊠ *140 Mulgrave Rd., Cairns* ☎ *07/4098–2920 or 1800/644227* ⊕ *www.rumrunner.com.au* 🖃 *A$140 cruise, A$55–A$75 first dive, A$30–A$45 subsequent dive* ☉ *Daily 8:30–4.*

WILDLIFE
WATCHING
☺

Daintree Rainforest River Trains has what's billed as the world's only float-ing river train, the *Spirit of Daintree*. On the daylong coach tour-cruise (A$169) there are stops for strolls along rain-forest and mangrove boardwalks, tropical-fruit tasting, and lunch (including barramundi salad) at Daintree Village. Keep an eye out for saltwater crocodiles on the river train along the Daintree River, which you can also take as a separate cruise. ⊠ *Daintree River Ferry Crossing, Box 448Mossman*

7

☎ *07/4090–7676 or 1800/808309* ⊕ *www.daintreerivertrain.com*
✉ *A$169 cruise-tour, A$28 1½-hour cruise, $49 2½-hour cruise*
⊙ *Daily, pick-up times vary; 11.30* AM *river train.*

WHERE TO EAT

$$ ✕ **Bundaleer Restaurant & Bar.** At this open-air restaurant in the Daintree
AUSTRALIAN rain forest, wallabies and musky rat kangaroos might join you at the
table as you tuck into fine Tropical Australian food that highlights
local, seasonal, and indigenous ingredients—wild barramundi, Atherton
beef, Cape York duckling, crocodile, and kangaroo. There are vegetar-
ian dishes, desserts like triple-choc assiette, and a wicked macadamia
tartlet, and a well-stocked bar. Bundaleer also does breakfasts and var-
ied, good-value lunches. Arrive early for a dip in the creek, rain-forest
stroll, or spa treatment. ⊠ *Daintree-Cape Tribulation Heritage Lodge
& Spa, Turpentine Rd. (18 km [11 mi] north of Daintree River crossing)*
☎ *07/4098–9138* ▭ *AE, DC, MC, V.*

¢ ✕ **Café on Sea.** Half an hour's drive past the Daintree ferry crossing, on
CAFÉ the rain forest–fringed Coral Sea shore, sits a rustic, beach shack–style
⊙ café. Here you'll find unfussy, family-friendly fare—burgers, calamari,
and fish-and-chips—as well as fresh, healthy, more complex options
like grilled coral trout and a Greek salad topped with garlic prawns.
Alternatively, just order an espresso and a slice of Diana's rich-but-not-
too-sweet Mars Bar cheesecake and contemplate the ocean. ⊠ *90 Cape
Tribulation Rd., Thornton Beach* ☎ *07/4098–9118* ▭ *MC, V.*

$$$ ✕ **Whet Restaurant.** Stylish and hip yet comfortable, Whet's licensed eat-
MODERN ery-bar attracts visitors and locals alike. The outdoor deck is perfect for
AUSTRALIAN cocktails; food, wine, and service would hold their own in the finnicki-
Fodor's Choice est city. Ingredients are seasonal and regional, including lots of local
★ seafood, and are deftly combined in fresh, simple Mod-Oz dishes with
⊙ Asian and Mediterranean influences. Gluten-free and vegetarian meals
are available, as are healthy options for kids. The luxe, licensed 24-seat
cinema upstairs (cleverly named Whet Flicks) runs daily sessions of pre-
DVD-release movies. Relax in air-conditioned comfort on beanbags,
recliners, or leather lounges and enjoy tapas with the film. Meal-movie
deals are available. ⊠ *Lot 1, Cape Tribulation Rd.* ☎ *07/4098–0007*
⚓ *Bookings preferred* ▭ *AE, D, MC, V* ⊙ *Daily 10:30* AM*–late; 2, 4,
and 8* PM *(screenings).*

WHERE TO STAY

Privately run campgrounds and small resorts can be found along Daintree Road at Myall Creek and Cape Tribulation. In Daintree National
Park proper, camping at unpowered, shaded beachside sites is permitted
at **Noah's Beach** (☎ *07/4098–0052 or 07/4098–2188 ranger, 13–1304
permits* ⊕ *www.epa.qld.gov.au*), about 8 km (5 mi) south of Cape Tribulation, for A$5 per person, per night (maximum stay, one week). BYO
tents or small camper vans, fuel stove, and drinking water; buy permits
in advance from Queensland Parks and Wildlife Service. After heavy
storms and during the wet season, rangers sometimes close Noah's;
call ahead.

$ ⌂ **Cape Tribulation Orchard Farmstay.** A handful of simple, solar-powered
cabins sit among rambutan, mangosteen, and breadfruit trees on this

40-hectare exotic fruit farm. Each comfortable cabin has an en-suite bathroom, insect screens, and a veranda with rain forest and mountain views. Three are air-conditioned—though as cooling breezes blow off Mount Sorrow you may not need it. You'll find a guest lounge, kitchen, laundry, and Internet access in the central farmhouse; beach and rain-forest trails adjoin the property. Commune with fellow guests around the nightly campfire, and wake to a chorus of birdsong and a basket of fresh tropical fruit—some of which you've probably never tasted. **Pros:** clean, eco-friendly cabins; fresh fruit; free Internet. **Cons:** few on-site facilities or in-room modern conveniences. ⊠ *Cape Tribulation Rd.* ☎ *07/4098–0042* ⊕ *www.capetribfarmstay.com.au* ⇨ *5 cabins* ⚒ *In-room: no a/c (some), no phone, no TV, Wi-Fi (some). In-hotel: water sports, bicycles, laundry facilities, Internet terminal, Wi-Fi, parking (free), some pets allowed, no-smoking rooms* ⊟ *MC, V* ⓔ⌐ *CP.*

$$–$$$ ⊡ **Cockatoo Hill Retreat.** The simple but elegant treehouses at this impec-
★ cably-run boutique retreat have king-size, handcrafted Balinese-style beds, billowing white mosquito nets, romantic underfloor lighting, and sea-breezy balconies overlooking the infinity-edge pool (with pool bar), a rain forest teeming with wildlife—frogs, birds, and butterflies, and the Coral Sea. At the restaurant and bar, fresh tropical breakfasts and seasonal *table d'hôte* dinners are cooked to suit your preferences (including vegetarian). There's a small library and pool table, and a cheaper, self-contained retreat nearby. **Pros:** helpful, thoughtful hosts; fine food; fab views. **Cons:** few modern conveniences. ⊠ *13 Cape Tribulation Rd., Daintree* ☎ *07/4098–9277* ⊕ *www. cockatoohillretreat.com.au* ⇨ *4 treehouses* ⚒ *In-room: no a/c (some), no TV. In-hotel: restaurant, room service, bar, pool, water sports, Wi-Fi, parking (free)* ⊟ *AE, D, DC, MC, V* ⓔ⌐ *AI.*

$$–$$$ ⊡ **Daintree-Cape Tribulation Heritage Resort & Spa.** Nestled in World
★ Heritage–listed rain forest beside Cooper Creek, this secluded resort
☺ is an antidote to stress. Rain-forest cabins are simply but comfortably appointed, with cool-to-the-touch tile floors, DVD players, screened windows, and ceiling fans. Deluxe villas, geared for romance, have oversized bathrooms, CD and DVD players, minibars, lounges, and balconies. There's a small, pretty pool, but most guests prefer the natural swimming hole, frequented by fish and turtles. Everything you need is right on-site: a restaurant, a well-stocked bar. a spa offering 30- and 60-minute treatments (A$50–A$90), and service-oriented staff who can help you find and book just the right activity or tour. The yoga retreat next door has daily classes, there are lots of walking trails, and guests get free use of kayaks and bikes. Thornton Beach and the Daintree Ice Cream Company are close by, too—that is, if you can tear yourself away from this pace. **Pros:** friendly fauna, good food, great-value spa treatments. **Cons:** limited Internet and cell-phone access; drive or longish trek to beach; critters. ⊠ *Lot 10, Cape Tribulation Rd., 18 km (11 mi) north of the Daintree River* ☎ *07/4098–0033 or 1800/987077* ⊕ *www. heritagelodge.net.au* ⇨ *15 cabins* ⚒ *In-room: no phone, refrigerator, DVD player. In-hotel: restaurant, bar, pool, spa, water sports, bicycles, laundry facilities, airport shuttle, parking (no fee), no-smoking rooms, no elevator* ⊟ *AE, DC, MC, V* ⓔ⌐ *BP.*

7

"Taking a walk of faith across a rope bridge in Daintree Rainforest." —poimuffin, Fodors.com member

¢–$ ⊡ **PK's Jungle Village.** This backpacker's haven attracts active, youthful travelers who often settle in for multiday stays. The lively on-site Jungle Bar, open daily noon–midnight, doubles as the local pub and meeting place, and serves three inexpensive meals (¢–$) daily. Sleeping configurations vary; choose from seven-bed dorms, cabins sleeping up to four, and camping at unpowered sites (A$15 per person, per night). A wide range of tours and activities, including water sports, can be booked on-site. **Pros:** central location; good facilities, food and tours; fun bar. **Cons:** generator power means few modern air-conditioners; can be noisy. ⊠ *Cape Tribulation Rd.* ☎ *07/4098–0040* ⊕ *www.pksjungle-village.com.au* ⇗ *19 cabins, 8 with bath; 14 dorm rooms* ♨ *In-room: no phone, no TV. In-hotel: restaurant, bar, pool, beachfront, water sports, laundry facilities, public Internet, no elevator* ⊟ *AE, DC, MC, V.*

COOKTOWN

96 km (60 mi) north of Cape Tribulation, 235 km (146 mi) north of Cairns.

The last major settlement on the east coast of the continent, Cooktown sits at the edge of a difficult wilderness. Its wide main street consists mainly of two-story pubs with four-wheel-drives parked out front. Despite the frontier air, Cooktown has an impressive history. It was here in 1770 that Captain James Cook beached HMS *Endeavour* to repair her hull. Any tour of Cooktown should begin at the waterfront, where a statue of Cook gazes out to sea, overlooking the spot where he landed.

GETTING HERE AND AROUND

Cooktown is a scenic 40-minute flight from Cairns: Skytrans Airlines has several flights daily. By car from Cairns, take the inland highway, a 327-km (203-mi) stretch of fully paved road that barrels you through Australia's Outback—watch for errant cattle and 'roos on the 4½-hour drive. From Cape Tribulation, head up the 4WD-only Bloomfield Track, just 97 km (60 mi), but challenging and sometimes flooded in the Wet. The scenic journey, which roughly traces a series of indigenous story-line trails known as The Bama Way, takes around 2½ hours, longer in wet weather. Getting around Cooktown, a compact town, is a comparative cinch: walk, cycle, or drive.

ESSENTIALS

Medical Cooktown Hospital (✉ *48 Hope St.* ☎ *07/4069–5433*).

Rental Cars Cooktown Car Hire (☎ *07/4069–5007* ⊕ *www.cooktown-car-hire. com*).

EXPLORING

Cooktown has some lovely old buildings and a cemetery dating from the 1870s Gold Rush. Stroll along Botanic Gardens trails and uncrowded beaches, check out Nature's Powerhouse, cool off in the public swimming pool, and scale Grassy Hill around sunset for stupendous views.

James Cook Historical Museum. Cooktown, in its heyday, was a gold-mining port town, with 64 pubs lining the 3-km-long (2-mi-long) main street. A significant slice of this colorful history is preserved here at the James Cook Historical Museum. The former convent houses relics of the gold-mining era, Aboriginal artifacts, canoes, and a notable collection of seashells, along with mementos of Cook's voyage, including the anchor and cannon jettisoned when the HMS *Endeavour* ran aground. The shop sells books and souvenirs. ✉ *Helen and Furneaux Sts.4895* ☎ *07/4069–5386* ⊕ *www.nationaltrustqld.org* 🎟 *A$7.50* ☽ *Daily 9:30–4, may close Feb.–Mar.*

OUTDOOR ACTIVITIES

There's plenty of outdoorsy fun to be had in and around Cooktown. Book a diving, snorkeling, or game-fishing cruise to the Outer Barrier Reef or Lizard Island; take a guided rock-art or rain-forest walk; go Outback on a multi-day 4WD Cape York excursion; or charter a scenic heli-flight over both World Heritage Areas.

FISHING The closest town on the Queensland coast to the Great Barrier Reef, Cooktown offers fast, easy access to some of the reef's best fishing (and dive) sites. Boats bristling with game-fishing gear depart from the marina daily, bound for famed fishing grounds on the Outer Reef, and at Egret and Boulder, 10 mi offshore. The likely catch: Spanish mackerel, sailfish, coral trout, red and spangled emperor, and black marlin.

Bottom-fish with handlines, troll for giant black marlin, or pop lures over the reef with **Cooktown Fishing Adventures** (☎ *07/4069–5500 or 0409/696775* ⊕ *www.cooktownfishingcharters.com* 🎟 *Prices vary according to charter* ☽ *Daily, pre-booking essential*), an established operator with a 56-foot, 900hp boat and energetic, safety-conscious crew. The company runs guided game-fishing excursions to local sites and specializes in multiday, live-aboard trips to renowned fishing areas off Lizard Island and Cod Hole, with fishing equipment and tackle, snorkeling gear, galley-cooked meals, and more supplied. You can also fish the estuaries or go crabbing in the mangrove flats.

CULTURAL **Guurrbi Tours.** An hour or so's drive inland of Cooktown lie ancient
TOURS Aboriginal rock-art sites of immense significance. Their exact locations
☺ are a closely guarded secret—so who better to guide you than Nugal-
★ warra elder Willie Gordon, a designated storyteller for the sites you'll visit? Willie guides guests around his ancestral rock-art sites, set high in the hills behind Hope Vale, on two scheduled tours: the 5½-hour Rainbow Serpent tour, taking in half-a-dozen sites; and the 3½-hour Emu Dreaming, which stops at three. Both visit the renowned Rainbow Serpent Cave. En route, Willie, an engaging raconteur, shares the Dreamtime stories and traditional lore behind this extraordinary cave art. If driving to the Guurrbi Meeting Point, 45 minutes' drive from town, collect map and directions from **Cooktown Motel Pam's Place** on Boundary St. (☎ 07/4069–6259). ⊠ *Box 417, Cooktown* ☎ *07/4069–6043* ⊕ *www.guurrbitours.com.au.*

WHERE TO STAY

$ ⛺ **Milkwood Lodge Rainforest Retreat.** Six pole cabins oriented for seclusion provide breezy, split-level accommodation overlooking rain forest and bushland at this user-friendly tropical retreat. Cabins that aren't air-conditioned have ceiling fans; all have equipped kitchenettes, comfy beds, and large verandas. The Lodge's lush gardens are atwitter with birdlife and have lovely views of Mount Cook. Chill under the waterfall in the saltwater pool, dine by moonlight at the licensed alfresco bar, and cook the day's catch on the BBQ. There's a helpful tour desk, and you can hire boats, dinghies, and 4WDs on-site. **Pros:** free airport pick-ups; breakfast packs. **Cons:** no restaurant; a bit out of town. ⊠ *Annan Rd.,* ☎ *07/4069–5007* ⊕ *www.milkwoodlodge.com* ⌕ *6 treehouses* ⌂ *In-room: no a/c (some), no phone (some), safe (some), kitchenette, refrigerator), DVD (some), Internet (some), Wi-Fi (some). In-hotel: bar, pool, water sports, laundry facilities, laundry service, Internet terminal, Wi-Fi, parking (free), some pets allowed, no-smoking rooms* ⊟ *AE, D, DC, MC, V* ⦿⧧ *CP.*

$ ⛺ **Seaview Motel.** This older-style seafront establishment has clean, quiet,
☺ recently refurbished rooms with simple appointments and big balconies, some overlooking Cooktown Harbour. Sit out front on lawn furniture for fine views of the harbor and hills—you can buy beer, wine, and soft drinks at reception—or cool off in the pool. It's an easy stroll to the town center. **Pros:** helpful staff, takeout drinks; scenic location. **Cons:** no screens on sliding doors to balconies; small pool; no on-site food. ⊠ *Webber St.* ⌂ *In-room: no phone (some), safe (some), kitchen (some), refrigerator), DVD (some), Internet (some), Wi-Fi (some). In-hotel: pool, beachfront, water sports, bicycles, laundry facilities, laundry service, Internet terminal, Wi-Fi, parking (free), some pets allowed, no-smoking rooms* ⊟ *AE, D, DC, MC, V* ⦿⧧ *CP.*

$–$$ ⊞ **Sovereign Resort Hotel.** This attractive, two-story colonial-style hotel
☕ in the heart of town is the best bet in Cooktown. With a wide front
veranda and horizontal wide-slat shutters, the two-story building has
the air of a plantation house. Guest rooms and apartments are simply
but smartly outfitted with tiled floors, lounge areas, flat-screen TVs,
and furnished balconies overlooking tropical gardens or the Endeav-
our River. The Balcony restaurant ($$), the town's most upscale eatery,
serves classic Aussie dishes, with local seafood always on the menu.
It's open every day for breakfast, served on the veranda. The Café Bar
has Internet access and delivers light lunches, coffee, and local beers;
or chill out in the cocktail bar. **Pros:** good-value apartments (best is
#201); free sport/movie channels; terrific gardens and pool. **Cons:** no
in-room Internet. ⊠ *128 Charlotte St., at Green St.* ☎ *07/4069–5400*
⊕ *www.sovereign-resort.com.au* ⤢ *31 rooms, 7 apartments* ⌂ *In-room:
kitchen (some), refrigerator, laundry facilities (some). In-hotel: 2 restau-
rants, room service, bars, pool, laundry service, public Internet, airport
shuttle, parking (no fee), no-smoking rooms, no elevator* ▭ *AE, DC,
MC, V* ☺ *Café closed Sun. No dinner Sun.*

THE WHITSUNDAY ISLANDS AND AIRLIE BEACH

The Whitsundays are a group of 74 islands situated within 161 km
(100 mi) of each other, 50 km (31 mi) from Shute Harbour, the prin-
cipal mainland departure point, though some boats depart from Airlie
Beach marina nearby. Discovered in 1770 by Captain James Cook of
the HMS *Endeavour*—though in fact not discovered on Whitsunday
itself, thanks to a time-zone change oversight on Cook's part—the Whit-
sundays are a favorite sailing destination and an easy-access base from
which to explore the midsection of the Great Barrier Reef. Some of
the islands' beaches—notably, famous Whitehaven Beach, are picture-
postcard gorgeous, though vegetation on the islands themselves looks
more scrubby than tropical. In fact, the entire region is subtropical,
making for moderate air and water temperatures year-round. Most of
the Whitsunday Islands are national parks, and, although you'll spot
few animals on them, birds are plentiful—more than 150 species make
their homes here. Only a few of the islands have resorts; others serve
as destinations for day trips, beach time, and bushwalks, or simply as
backdrop at scenic moorings.

Camping is popular on the myriad islands of the Whitsunday group.
To pitch a tent on islands lying within national parks, you need a A$5
permit from the Queensland Parks and Wildlife Service. The Whitsun-
day Information Centre, on the Bruce Highway at Proserpine, is open
weekdays 8.30–5, weekends 9–3.

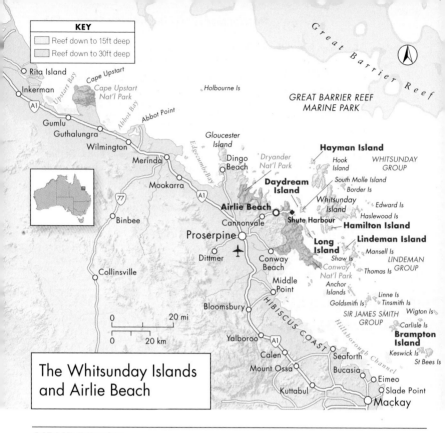

The Whitsunday Islands and Airlie Beach

AIRLIE BEACH

1,130 km (702 mi) north of Brisbane, 635 km (395 mi) south of Cairns.

Airlie Beach's balmy climate and its proximity to the Whitsunday Islands, a resort and water-sports playground, make it hugely popular with partying backpackers and holidaymakers en route to the islands and reef.

GETTING HERE AND AROUND

The Whitsunday Coast Airport near Proserpine, 40 km (25 mi) southeast of Airlie Beach, has direct daily flights to and from Brisbane and less frequent services to Sydney, on Virgin Blue and Jetstar. **Whitsunday Shuttle Service** connects the airport and Proserpine Railway Station to Airlie Beach and Shute Harbour, with services timed to meet all flights and passenger trains (drive time 30–40 minutes). **Greyhound Australia** and **Oz Experience** offer daily services into Airlie Beach from Sydney, Brisbane, and towns between, and from Cairns. **Queensland Rail** operates around six northbound and six southbound trains weekly that stop at Proserpine Railway Station, about 25 km (15 mi) from Airlie Beach.

Koala Adventures is popular with the younger backpacker set, and runs three-day sailing trips around the Whitsundays in a Whitbread round-world maxi racing yacht for A$469, including local charges, all meals, and bedding. Hire snorkeling gear from the marina for A$15. **Whitsunday Sailing Adventures** runs several sailing, scuba, and snorkeling trips around the islands on a dozen-plus owner-operated vessels, including modern sailing cats and tall ships. Choose from dive

BEWARE

From October to May the ocean off beaches north of Rockhampton is rendered virtually unswimmable by toxic-tentacled box jellyfish.

and snorkeling trips, performance sailing, eco-friendly excursions, and two- and three-day sailing cruises with all meals, bedding, and snorkeling gear provided.

ESSENTIALS

Airport Whitsunday Coast Airport (✉ Lascelles Ave., Sir Reginald Ansett Dr., Proserpine ☎ 07/4945–0200).

Airlines Jetstar (☎ 13–1538 ⊕ www.jetstar.com.au). **Virgin Blue** (☎ 13–6789 ⊕ www.virginblue.com.au).

Buses Greyhound Australia (⊕ www.greyhound.com.au). **Oz Experience** (⊕ www.ozexperience.com). **Whitsunday Shuttle Service** (☎ 07/4946–1515 ⊕ www.whitsundayshuttle.com.au).

Trains Proserpine Railway Station (✉ Hinschen St., Proserpine ☎ 13–1617). **Queensland Rail** (☎ 1300/131722 ⊕ www.traveltrain.com.au).

Hospitals Whitsunday Doctors' Service (✉ 257 Shute Harbour Rd., Airlie Beach ☎ 07/4946–6241 ⊕ www.whitsundaydoctors.com.au).

Boat Tour Contacts Cumberland Charter Yachts (✉ Abel Point Marina, Airlie Beach, QLD ☎ 07/4946–7526 or 1800/075101 ⊕ www.ccy.com.au). **Koala Adventures** (✉ Shute Harbour Rd., Airlie Beach ☎ 07/4946–6446 or 1800/466444 ⊕ www.koalaadventures.com). **Queensland Yacht Charters** (✉ Abel Point Marina, Airlie Beach, QLD ☎ 07/4946–7400 or 1800/075013 ⊕ www.yachtcharters.com.au). **Whitsunday Private Yacht Charters** (✉ Office 18, Abel Point Marina, Airlie Beach, QLD ☎ 07/4946–6880 or 1800/075055 ⊕ www.whitsunday-yacht.com.au). **Whitsunday Rent a Yacht** (✉ 6 Bay Terrace, Shute Harbour, Airlie Beach ☎ 07/4946–9232 or 1800/075000 ⊕ www.rentay-acht.com.au). **Whitsunday Sailing Adventures** (✉ Level 2, 293 Shute Harbour Rd., Airlie Beach ☎ 07/4940–2000 or 1300/653100 ⊕ www.whitsundaysailingadventures.com.au).

EXPLORING

Airlie's main street is packed with cafés, bars, tour agencies, and hotels—many catering to the backpacker crowd—with homes and higher-end accommodations extending up the steep hills behind it. The waterfront Esplanade, with its boardwalk, landscaped gardens, and weekend markets, is generally lively.

Airlie Lagoon, a large, stinger-free swimming enclosure on the shorefront, is hugely popular. It's patrolled by lifeguards and has two adjoining children's pools. There's also a playground nearby. ✉ *The Esplanade, at Broadwater Ave.* ☎ *07/4945–0200* ⊕ *www.whitsundayrc.qld.gov.au* 🖾 *Free* ⊗ *Patrolled* 6 AM–9 PM *daily.*

Conway National Park, 10 minutes' drive southeast of Airlie, is a 54,000-acre expanse of mangroves, forest, and tropical lowlands that shelters the endangered Proserpine rock wallaby and other rare species, as well as plenty of sulphur-crested cockatoos, emerald doves, Australian brush-turkeys, and orange-footed scrubfowl. Most walking trails start at the park's picnic area off Shute Harbour Road, 6 km (3½ mi) from Airlie. Mount Rooper Walking Track, a 5.4-km (3-mi) circuit, meanders uphill through bushland to a lookout with breathtaking Whitsundays views. Swamp Bay track follows the creek to a coral-strewn beach with a bush camping area. Campers need permits (A$5 per night), as well as water and all supplies. ⊠ *Shute Harbour Rd. at Mandalay Rd.* ☎ *07/4946–7355 or 1300/130372, 13–1304 permits* ⊕ *www.epa.qld. gov.au or www.qld.gov.au/camping.*

Shute Harbour, 10 km (6 mi) southeast from Airlie Beach, is the main ferry terminal and gateway to the islands and reef. The large, sheltered inlet bristles with boats—it's the second-busiest commuter port in Australia, after Sydney's Circular Quay. Though accommodation is available, the harbor is geared toward transferring visitors. For a great view over Shute Harbor and the Whitsunday Passage, drive to the top of Coral Point.

WHERE TO EAT

$$$
AUSTRALIAN
✕ **Capers at the Beach Bar/Grill.** Tables spill out across terra-cotta tiles at this busy waterside restaurant in the Airlie Beach Hotel, part of a complex that also includes kid-friendly Mangrove Jack's (good for pizzas and steaks) and Tex-Mex-style Cactus Jack's. Capers' mainstream Mod-Oz menu covers all bases, from Wagyu steak to barramundi to Aussie game. If you're game, try the crocodile tail, kangaroo, and emu skewers. A Bloody Mary and the tapas, though, may be your best bet. Plenty of alfresco tables mean you can sit outside on balmy nights, even if you haven't booked. ⊠ *The Esplanade at Coconut Grove 4802* ☎ *07/4964–1777* ⊕ *www.airliebeachhotel.com.au* ▤ *AE, MC, V.*

$$$
MODERN
AUSTRALIAN
Fodor'sChoice
★
☼
✕ **Déjà Vu Restaurant.** Alfresco tables and Balinese-style dining pavilions flank an infinity-edge pool at this classy Airlie eatery. The usual surf'n'turf options are replaced by inventive, seasonally-driven modern Australian dishes. Follow an entrée of lemon-myrtle and chili risotto oysters or Cajun-style crocodile ribs with, say, char-grilled kangaroo in a bush-pepper jus or whole reef fish, crispy-fried and coated in a Thai chili, galangal, and coriander glaze. The Nantua seafood pasta—local fish, crustaceans, and mollusks, tossed with squid-ink linguini—is a worthy favorite. Freshly made desserts (chestnut crepes, chili-chocolate soufflé) are delicious. Vegetarian and children's meals are available, and the wine list is extensive. At lunch, fresh fish-and-chips, interesting salads, and gourmet panini are good value for under A$20—preceded, perhaps, by a swim. Sunday's eight-course epicurean lunches (A$45), with live entertainment, are legendary. *E Water's Edge Resort, 4 Golden Orchid Dr. 4802* ☎ *07/4948–4309* ⊕ *www.dejavurestaurant.com.au* ⩩ *Bookings preferred* ▤ *AE, MC, V* ☉ *Wed.–Sun., lunch noon–2.30, dinner 6–9:30* PM.

WHERE TO STAY

$–$$ 🏨 **Airlie Beach Hotel.** With the beach at its doorstep, three eateries and
☺ bars downstairs, and the main street directly behind it, this hotel makes
a convenient base. Spacious rooms have Wi-Fi access and flat-screen
TVs; most open onto big balconies overlooking the palm-lined waterfront. You can also get cheaper, less salubrious motel-style rooms. **Pros:**
convenient; free parking; on-site food and drink. **Cons:** no room service; small pool; slow Internet in some rooms. ✉ *16 The Esplanade, at
Coconut Grove* ☎ *07/4964–1999 or 1800/466233* ⊕ *www.airliebeach-
hotel.com.au* 🛏 *56 rooms, 4 suites* ⚭ *In-room: refrigerator, dial-up,
Wi-Fi (some). In-hotel: 3 restaurants, bars, pool, beachfront, laundry
facilities, public Wi-Fi, parking (no fee), no-smoking rooms* ▭ *AE, DC,
MC, V.*

¢ 🏨 **Beaches Backpackers.** With a big, lively bar on-site, this central hostel
attracts a party crowd, which makes things noisy (but keeps dorms
near-empty) until around midnight. Eight-bed dorms, doubles, and
twin rooms are air-conditioned and serviced daily; each has an en-
suite bathroom, small TV, fridge, and balcony, and some dorms are
sex-segregated. There's an on-site pool, a clean communal kitchen, and
an Internet–games room. Reception can store your bags and valuables,
and book tours. Beaches Bar & Bistro, downstairs, serves well-priced
lunches, snacks, and dinners. A free shuttle runs between Beaches and
the bus terminal. **Pros:** good in-room and on-site facilities; cheap Internet including CD/DVD burning. **Cons:** noisy; tiny pool. ✉ *356 Shute
Harbour Rd.* ☎ *07/4946–6244 or 1800/636630* ⊕ *www.beaches.com.
au* 🛏 *7 rooms, 24 dorms* ⚭ *In-room: refrigerator. In-hotel: restaurant,
bar, pool, laundry facilities, laundry service, public Internet, parking
(no fee), no elevator, no kids under 18* ▭ *MC, V.*

$$ 🏨 **Peppers Coral Coast.** The expansive one-, two- and three-bedroom
★ apartments at this high-end hillside resort are tailored for comfort,
with spa baths the size of small cars, designer decor, and premium
appliances: flat-screen TVs (with Austar cable channels and pay movies
in the lounge and master bedroom), CD and DVD players, iPod dock-
ing stations. They also have big, furnished balconies with stupendous
views. The price you pay for the panorama is a steep trek or A$7 taxi-
ride from the main strip. In-house dining is rewarding, if a tad pricey.
Smart facilities and services include a deck-chair-flanked wet-edge pool,
a well-equipped gym, and an endota spa offering detox, de-stress, and
anti-ageing treatments using organic Australian ingredients. **Pros:** classy
decor, food, and service; quiet location. **Cons:** up a steep hill; limited
room service; smallish pool area. ✉ *Mt. Whitsunday Dr.* ☎ *07/4962–
5100 or 1300/987600* ⊕ *www.peppers.com.au* 🛏 *102 apartments*
⚭ *In-room: safe, kitchen, laundry facilities, Internet. In-hotel: restau-
rant, room service (11 AM–9 PM), bar, pool, gym, spa, bicycles, laundry
facilities, laundry service, Internet terminal, public Wi-Fi (fee), parking
(free), no-smoking rooms* ▭ *AE, D, DC, MC, V.*

$ 🏨 **Whitsunday Moorings B&B.** Overlooking Abel Point Marina, both
Fodor's Choice self-contained suites here have panoramic views from their patios. The
★ house is surrounded by mango and frangipani trees filled with frolick-
ing lorikeets. Although host Peter Brooks is extraordinarily helpful

7

with regard to local activities, his poolside hammock can sidetrack even energetic guests. Meticulously clean, spacious open-plan rooms include kitchen and lounge areas and have terra-cotta-tiled floors and cedar blinds. Breakfast is a five-star affair with white linen, heavy silverware, beautifully presented tropical fruits and flowers, homemade jams, and freshly squeezed juice. **Pros:** charming, knowledgable hosts; fab breakfasts; free Wi-Fi and cable channels. **Cons:** uphill walk from main street; open room plan best suited to couples; old-style TVs. ⊠ *37 Airlie Crescent* ☏ *07/4946–4692* ⊕ *www.whitsundaymooringsbb.com. au* ⟿ *2 rooms* ♿ *In-room: refrigerator, kitchen, Wi-Fi (free). In-hotel: pool, laundry facilities, Internet terminal, parking (no fee), no-smoking rooms, no elevator* ▭ *AE, DC, MC, V* ⦿| *BP.*

NIGHTLIFE
Shute Harbour Road, the main strip, is where it all happens in Airlie Beach. Most main-street establishments cater to the backpacker crowd, with boisterous, college-style entertainment, live music, and late-opening dance-clubs. Older visitors gravitate to quieter establishments with pleasant outdoor areas, such as the bars attached to some of the hillside resorts.

The crowd's gregarious at **Beaches Bar & Bistro** (⊠ *362 Shute Harbour Rd. 4802* ☏ *07/4946–6244* ⊕ *www.beaches.com.au*), part of the hostel of the same name. Here, you can catch live bands most nights, eat hearty food cheaply, play pool, mingle in the big beer garden, and watch games on big-screen TVs.

When other places close around midnight, Airlie's party kicks on till late at the tribally-themed **Mama Africa** (⊠ *Shute Harbour Rd.* ☏ *07/4948– 0438*). At **Juice Bar** (⊠ *352 Shute Harbour Rd.* ☏ *07/4946–50555*), the decor's arty, the vibe's city-sleek but sociable, and DJs spin the latest club favorites.

BRAMPTON ISLAND

Twelve coral-and-white-sand beaches encircle Brampton Island; kangaroos, rainbow lorikeets, and butterflies populate the rain forests of its hilly interior. This 1,137-acre island at the southern end of the Whitsunday Passage, 32 km (20 mi) northeast of Mackay and 50 km (31 mi) southeast of Hamilton Island, is one of the prettiest in the area. Most of the island is a designated national park, with seven secluded beaches accessible via walking trails and fringing hard and soft coral reefs sheltering countless marine creatures. Though the resort is lively after dark, the biggest attractions are on and under the water: the snorkeling over the reef between Brampton and the adjoining Carlisle islands is world-class.

GETTING HERE AND AROUND
Blue Fin, a high-speed catamaran, leaves Mackay Marina daily at 2, arriving at Brampton at 3:15. Fare is A$65 one-way, including coach transfer from Mackay Airport, departing at 1:30. Return boats leave Brampton marina at 3:45, connecting with the coach at 5 for a 5:15 PM arrival at Mackay Airport. Virgin Blue and Qantas connect all Australian capitals with Mackay daily. Jetstar has flights from Brisbane; Tiger

Beaches at Brampton Island, part of the Whitsunday Islands group, are among the state's best.

Airways from Melbourne. Some Virgin Blue flights tie in with Brampton boat transfers. Australasian Jet flies to Brampton Island from Mackay and Hamilton Island airports, taking 20–30 minutes, a minimum of two passengers, and a maximum 15 kg (33 lbs) of baggage each (plus 5 kg [11 lbs]hand luggage), preferably soft-sided. Fare is A$85 one-way from Mackay via scheduled, twice-daily transfer (departing from the mainland at 11:30 AM and 5 PM, Brampton at 9 AM and 2 PM); upwards of A$175 per person, one-way, from Hamilton Island via charter flight.

ESSENTIALS

Boat transfers Blue Fin (✉ Mulherin Dr., Mackay Harbour *4740* ☎ *1300–134044 or 02/8296–8010* ⊕ *www.brampton-island.com*).

Air transfers Australasian Jet (☎ *07/4953–3261* ⊕ *www.ausjet.com.au or www.bramptonisland.com.au*).

OUTDOOR ACTIVITIES

Most folk are so busy getting on or under the water that they don't explore their island environs. But many Barrier Reef isles include significant tracts of national parkland, with trails often leading to or past spectacular views. Overcast days are perfect for trekking along island trails. Careful walkers may spot possums, goannas (iguanas), blue-tongued lizards, various birds, the odd wallaby, and nesting green and loggerhead turtles on beaches, in season. Carry a map, snacks, and plenty of water; wear a hat and sunscreen regardless of weather, and don't forget your camera.

WATER SPORTS **Brampton Island Activities Desk** schedules an array of aquatic activities and excursions for resort guests. You get free use of paddle-skis, sailboards, catamarans, and snorkeling gear (with a small fee for mouthpieces), and can take complimentary cat and sailboarding lessons. If you have a couple of spare hours, take a guided island tour on a low-noise, low-emission Jet Ski (A$286 per ski) or eco-friendly sea kayak (A$45), a snorkeling safari (A$50), or a fishing excursion (A$60). Other options include scenic flights to pristine Whitehaven Beach (A$375) and 4½-hour "panorama" tours to Whitehaven and the outer Barrier Reef (A$526), with stops to snorkel and dive. The resort can also help you to organize scuba training and dive trips. ☎ *07/4951–4499* ⊕ *www. brampton-island.com.*

WHERE TO STAY

$$$–$$$$ 🏨 **Voyages Brampton Island.** As if in recognition that its greatest assets are outside, this resort has kept its rooms airy and functional, with neutral decor. Beachfront ocean-view rooms have luxe appointments: flat-screen TVs, DVD and CD players, espresso machines, private hammocks, and bathrobes. The Bluewater Restaurant is a plus, serving big buffet breakfasts, smorgasbord lunches, city-quality table d'hôte dinners and a terrific weekly seafood buffet. You can also order balcony meals, beach picnics, and eight-course candlelight dinners on the sand (A$130). After-dark entertainment is low-key but sociable: think karaoke and trivia nights (or in-house movies in your room). Many outdoor activities, from aqua aerobics to volleyball to fish-feeding sessions, are included in the rate, as is the use of non-motorized watersports equipment. For a fee, you can also take archery lessons (A$15); guided walks (A$20–$50); various aquatic tours, and trips to nearby beaches, isles, and golf courses (up to A$526). If it rains, join in an art class, beer tasting, or cocktail-mixing workshop, or have a power-boosting facial at the Sea Spa. The resort has Internet and phone access but no mobile phone reception (though you may get a signal from the opposite end of the island). **Pros:** family-friendly; better-than-average food; picnic hampers (A$40). **Cons:** five-night minimum stay; rooms a tad worn; breakfast ends promptly at 9:30 AM; one small boat to ferry guests around island. ☎ *1300/134044 or 07/4951–4499 (resort)* ⊕ *www.brampton-island.com* ⤳ *108 suites* ⚐ *In-room: refrigerator, DVD (some). In-hotel: restaurant, bar, tennis courts, pools, gym, spa, beachfront, diving, water sports, laundry facilities, laundry service, concierge, public Internet, no kids under 13, no-smoking rooms* ⊟ *AE, DC, MC, V* ⭤ *BP, FAP.*

LINDEMAN ISLAND

More than half of Lindeman Island—which at 2,000 acres is one of the largest in the Whitsunday group—is national park, with 20 km (12 mi) of walking trails that wind through tropical growth and up hills for fantastic views. Bird-watching is excellent here, though the blue tiger butterflies you might spot in Butterfly Valley are, arguably, even more impressive. With its natural and sporting attractions, the island draws lots of families. It lies 40 km (25 mi) northeast of Mackay, near the southern entrance to the Whitsunday Passage.

GETTING HERE AND AROUND
There are four direct 30-minute boat transfers daily to Lindeman Island from Hamilton Island, 17 km (11 mi) away. Transfers are included in Club Med guests' rate (or A$70 each way).

ESSENTIALS
Boat Contact Hamilton Island (☎ 07/4946–9999).

OUTDOOR ACTIVITIES
WATER SPORTS ☺ Not far from Lindeman Island lie Barrier Reef sites ideal for intro-ductory diving and snorkeling. **Club Med Lindeman Island** organizes day cruises to the outer reef, including snorkeling, optional guided dives, and lunch, for resort guests. You can also take refresher scuba-diving courses, go deep-sea fishing, or book shorter boat excursions to snor-keling sites off nearby Whitehaven Beach. Dive trips to the outer reef by air are 30 minutes each way; by boat it's two hours each way, but considerably cheaper. On Lindeman itself, guided snorkeling trips are scheduled only once or twice a week, but if you bring your own gear you can snorkel off the pier for free. ☎ 07/4946–9333 ⊕ www.clubmed. com.au ⊠ Cost varies ⊙ Daily schedule varies, bookings essential.

WHERE TO STAY
$$$$ ☺ ⊞ **Club Med Lindeman Island.** This three-story, palm-tree-filled resort, Australia's only Club Med, sits on 1,750 acres on the southern end of the island. Rooms are sparsely furnished, as is customary at Club Med; poolside rooms and those with hot tubs cost more. All overlook the sea, bordering the beach or pool, and each has a balcony or patio. Various packages—there's no minimum, but the resort recommends that you stay four days or more—include accommodation, buffet-style dining, and an "open bar and snacking service," along with evening entertain-ment of varying quality and a range of outdoor activities: the trademark flying trapeze school, a 9-hole golf course, tennis, basketball, sailing, sea-kayaking, and swimming. You'll pay for motorized water sports and offshore excursions. Kids' clubs operate all day and again after dinner, but older kids may be bored at the afternoon movie sessions. There's a golf course with glorious views (BYO golf balls or pay A$3 apiece) and a day spa, so parents can have fun, too. **Pros:** kids' clubs and babysit-ting; circus school; free inclusions; scenic golf course. **Cons:** inade-quate equipment to meet demand; two over-used computer terminals for public Internet access; repetitive kids' program; slow bar service. ⊠ PMB 1, Mackay Mail Centre, QLD ☎ 1300/855052, 07/4946–9333 resort ⊕ www.clubmed.com.au ⇥ 214 rooms ⌂ In-room: safe, refrig-erator. In-hotel: 2 restaurants, bars, golf course, tennis courts, pools, spa, beachfront, water sports, children's programs (ages 2–17), laundry facilities, public Internet, airport shuttle, no-smoking rooms ☰ AE, DC, MC, V ⎢⎥AI.

7

LONG ISLAND

This aptly named island lies south of Shute Harbour, 12 km (7 mi) west of Hamilton Island. Although it's 9 km (5½ mi) long and no more than 2 km (1.2 mi) wide—around 3,000 acres total—it has several walking trails through tracts of dense rain forest. Most of the island is national parkland, sheltering birds, butterflies, goannas, and wallabies. Some of its beaches are picturesque; others, rocky and windblown. Though its waters are less clear than those off the outer reef islands, there are some excellent snorkeling spots around the island, where you'll share the balmy water with soft and hard corals, tropical fish, and turtles. You may also see dolphins and migrating humpback whales July through September.

GETTING HERE AND AROUND

You can reach Long Island (but not Peppers Palm Bay or Paradise Bay Island Eco Escape) several times a day via air-conditioned catamaran with Cruise Whitsundays from Shute Harbour or Hamilton Island. The 20-minute journey from Hamilton Airport costs A$55 one-way; or pay A$50 from Whitsunday Coast (Proserpine) Airport: reps meet passenger flights at both. From Shute Harbour or Abel Point Marina, the one-way fare is A$30. The transfer, which lands you at Long Island Resort, costs A$90 round-trip. Long Island Resort can transfer you to Palm Bay for A$20 per person. The private Peppers Palm Bay launch runs from Shute Harbour for A$90 per person, round-trip.

Air Whitsunday provides one-way seaplane connections between Hamilton Island's Whitsunday Airport and Peppers Palm Bay for A$120 per person, each way; or charter flights for A$275 (up to 4 passengers) or A$415 (up to 6); and from Whitsunday Coast (Proserpine) for A$170 per person, each way. Flights are timed to coincide with domestic air services. Aviation Tours Australia can fly you by helicopter between Peppers Palm Bay and Hamilton Island (Whitsundays) Airport for A$249 per person, each way, from Whitsunday Coast Airport, Proserpine, for A$410; or from Airlie Beach for A$150, subject to minimum numbers: pre-booking's essential.

Guests of Paradise Beach Island Eco Escape can take a helicopter from Hamilton Island airport to Long Island (or back again) anytime between 7:30 AM and 5 PM; or fly from Airlie Beach on the mainland, a 15-minute trip, between 9 and 5. The scenic flight is included in guests' tariffs. Baggage is limited to 15 kilograms (30 pounds) per person, and should be in soft-sided bags. Excess luggage can be stored at the airport. Virgin, Qantas, and Jetstar fly between Hamilton Island and Sydney, Brisbane, and Cairns daily.

ESSENTIALS

Air Contact Air Whitsunday (☎ 07/4946–9111 ⊕ www.airwhitsunday.com.au). **Aviation Tours Australia** (☎ 07/4946–8249 ⊕ www.avta.com.au).

Boat Contact Cruise Whitsundays (☎ 07/4946–4662 or 1800/426403 ⊕ www.cruisewhitsundays.com).

WHERE TO STAY

$–$$$ ⚏ **Long Island Resort.** A short walk over the hill from Palm Bay, this fam-
☾ ily-focused resort might as well be on a different island. This is not the
place to commune quietly with nature: the resort is big on outdoor activ-
ities, particularly water sports, and group-oriented fun. The free kids'
club is adjourned in periods of low demand (especially in low season),
which means there can be lots of little ones running around. Nighttime
entertainment may include karaoke, live music, beach parties, trivia and
casino nights, or energetic games. Guests in air-conditioned beachfront
and garden-view rooms have extra conveniences (TVs, phones, Inter-
net), balconies, and three daily buffet-style meals included in their rate;
guests in fan-cooled budget lodges fend for themselves. Order a picnic
hamper from the licensed café and escape the crowd. The island and
resort are easily accessed via ferry or launch, making it a good base for
island-hopping. **Pros:** accessible; lots of activities; sociable. **Cons:** noisy;
kids run amok; heavy competition for equipment. ☎ *07/4946–9400
or 1800/075125* ⊕ *www.oceanhotels.com.au* ⊃ *161 rooms, 31 lodges
without bath* ⚐ *In-room: no a/c (some), safe (some, fee), refrigerator
(some), no TV (some), dial-up (some). In-hotel: 2 restaurants, bars, ten-
nis courts, pools, beachfront, diving, water sports, children's programs
(ages 4–14), no-smoking rooms* ⊟ *AE, DC, MC, V* ⦿ *CP, AIP.*

$$$$ ⚏ **Paradise Bay Island Eco Escape.** Talk about secluded—this intimate,
★ eco-friendly lodge on South Long Island's isolated southern tip is acces-
sible only by helicopter. Each bungalow fronts pristine Paradise Bay
beach and is individually appointed, with a king-size bed, reproduction
and antique furnishings, and authentic Aboriginal artworks from the
owner's collection. Crafted from Australian hardwood, airy, cathedral-
ceilinged bungalows have polished wood floors and private verandas
with hammocks, oriented to capture morning sun, glorious sunsets,
and gentle sea breezes. With a maximum 16 guests at a time, a three-
night minimum stay, no kids, no TV, and no mobile phone reception,
it's easy to balance solitude and sociability. The tariff covers all meals,
including a nightly, four-course gourmet dinner with Australian wines;
picnic lunches; afternoon teas; "house" drinks after 6 PM; heli-transfers;
use of snorkeling gear and wet suits; skippered sailing excursions or
fast RIB rides to nearby beaches, islands, and coral gardens every day
but Sunday; plus rain-forest walks; mangrove estuary tours, and sea
kayaking. In addition to its complimentary activities, the lodge offers
half-day helicopter tours over the Whitsunday Islands, including Heart
Reef and Whitehaven Beach for A$600 per person (minimum two).
The tour includes a 40-minute scenic flight each way, snorkeling and
semisubmersible tours at the Hardy Reef pontoon—after the day-visitor
crowds have left—and an optional dive including gear and dive-master
guide for certified divers. The lodge incorporates sustainable technol-
ogy—advanced solar panels; eco-friendly waste management; rainwater
tanks; low-flow showerheads and carbon offset programs—without
compromising on luxury or comfort. Bring essentials and medicines;
leave power-guzzling appliances behind. **Pros:** quality food; no singles
surcharge; eco-friendly. **Cons:** pricey; little variation in food; 15kg (30
lb) baggage limit. ✉ *Box 842, Airlie Beach, QLD4802 07/4946–9777*

7

⊕ *www.paradisebay.com.au* ↝ *8 bungalows* ⌂ *In-room: room service, no a/c, refrigerator, no phone, no TV. In-hotel: restaurant, bar, beachfront, water sports, no kids* ⊟ *AE, MC, V* ⊚| *AI.*

$$$$ ⊡ **Peppers Palm Bay.** This elegant property woos well-heeled travelers
  ★   with a gorgeous setting, discreet service, and gourmet food ($$$). Just 21 simply but stylishly furnished cabins, *bures* (tropical-style bungalows), and A-frame bungalows are strung along a palm-fringed, white-sand shore, their balconies invitingly slung with hammocks. Wallabies, goannas, brush turkeys, and big-eyed curlews wander freely about the grounds; kookaburras cackle from the trees. Spotlessly clean cabins, Palm Bay's equivalent of "standard" rooms, have dark-wood furnishings and sleek tribal decor; *bures* also have lounges; and each bungalow has a daybed in a separate lounge area. Three elevated suites with expansive decks, outdoor dining areas, and whitewashed interiors occupy the hillside behind: each has a chic lounge area with a plasma TV and DVD/CD player. Palm Bay's streamlined tour desk arranges various daytime activities: fly over, snorkel, and dive the reef, go sailing, game fishing, or golfing, cruise to Whitehaven Beach, enjoy a private picnic on a deserted isle, hike or paddle-ski around the island. Or just relax in the large saltwater pool, heated Jacuzzi, library, or endota spa. After-dark entertainment is low-key: sunset cocktails, fine dining, and conversation, a hit of tennis on the floodlit courts, or a film at the resort's mini-cinema. Book just a room, or choose a package that includes meals. **Pros:** new menus daily; organic facials; picnic hampers; on-site library. **Cons:** curlews noisy at night; beds too firm for some; not-so-luxe bathrooms. ⊠ *Long Island, Whitsundays,* ☏ *07/4946–9233 or 1300/987600* ⊕ *www.peppers.com.au* ↝ *7 bungalows, 7 bures, 7 cabins, 3 suites* ⌂ *In-room: no phone, refrigerator, room service, no TV (some), DVD/CD (some). In-hotel: restaurant, bar, tennis court, pool, spa, beachfront, water sports, laundry facilities, concierge, public Wi-Fi, no kids under 14, no-smoking rooms* ⊟ *AE, DC, MC, V* ⊚| *CP.*

HAMILTON ISLAND

Though it's the most heavily populated and developed island in the Whitsunday group, more than 70 percent of Hamilton Island has been preserved in its natural state. The 1,482-acre island abounds in beautiful beaches (such as long, curving, palm-dotted Catseye Beach), bush trails, and spectacular lookouts. Yet for all its natural beauty, Hamilton's is more an action-packed, sociable holiday isle than a place to get away from it all.

Around 30 minutes by ferry from Shute Harbour, Hamilton buzzes with activity. Guests of the resort, and its six types of accommodation, including hotel-style and self-catering establishments, make up most of the itinerant population, but there are private residences here—as well as throngs of day-trippers from the mainland, other islands, and cruising yachts, who wander the island's bustling marina and village each day.

In recent years the island has worked hard to improve the quality of its eateries, and its broad range of dining options includes everything from take-out pizza to upscale restaurants, but most on-island eateries still tend toward the "accessible" end of the culinary scale.

For a family-friendly, one-stop Whitsundays experience, Hamilton Island is a good bet. It's set up as a small city, with its own school, post office, bank branch and ATMs, medical center, pharmacy, supermarket, and video store, plus shops, restaurants, bars, and nightclub, all of which island guests and day-trippers are free to visit. There's also a day spa/relaxation centre (open daily 10–6), offering massage, aromatherapy treatments, and float-tank sessions. But little on Hamilton is free; prices—for food, activities, Internet use, even grocery items—can be steep. The ubiquitous golf carts that visitors hire to zip around the island are A$40 an hour, A$55 for 3 hours, or A$85 for 24 hours from Harbourside Buggy Rentals (7:30 am to 6 PM) or Resort Buggy Hire (8 am to 9 PM). Save a few bucks by using the free Island Shuttle service that runs around the island at regular intervals between 7 AM and 11 PM.

GETTING HERE AND AROUND

Several carriers—Virgin, Qantas, Jetstar—fly directly to Hamilton Island from Sydney, Melbourne, and Brisbane. **Air Whitsunday** provides one-way seaplane connections between Airlie Beach on the mainland and Hamilton Island for A$360 (up to 4 passengers) or A$595 (up to 6); and to other island and mainland destinations and yacht moorings on request. They also operate snorkeling tours and scenic flights over the Great Barrier Reef. **Aviation Tours Australia** transfers visitors from Hamilton Island airport to Long, Daydream, and Hayman and South Molle islands via helicopter, on request. **Fantasea Cruises** makes the 30-minute journey between Shute Harbour and Hamilton Island Marina 10 times daily between 6:30 AM and 5:30 PM for A$43 each way. Fantasea also has five daily services linking Shute Harbour and Hamilton Island airport, via Daydream Island and/or Hamilton Island Marina, between 8 am and 1:40 pm (A$53).

TOURS

Aviation Tourism Australia (Hamilton Island Aviation) (☎ 07/4946–8249 ⊕ www.avta.com.au) has seaplane and helicopter flights over the Whitsunday Islands and Great Barrier Reef, including a Heart Reef and Reefworld tour, a 45-minute scenic flight, and three hours at the well-equipped Reefworld pontoon for A$440 from Hamilton Island; A$499 from other islands and the mainland.

Fantasea Cruises (☎ 07/4967–5455 or 1800/650851 ⊕ www.fantasea. com.au) runs "island discovery" and reef trips daily from Hamilton and Daydream islands and Shute Harbour. From Hamilton Island it's a 55-km (34-mi) trip to Fantasea's Reefworld pontoon inside magnificent **Hardy Reef Lagoon**, where you can swim, snorkel along easy coral trails, scuba dive, ride in a semisubmersible, or simply relax. The cost is A$225, including gear, Reefworld facilities, and a barbecue lunch. While you're there, take a guided snorkel tour for A$40, a dive lesson and introductory dive for A$115, or a certified dive for A$100. A scenic heli-flight over the reef starts from A$129 per person. There's a kid-friendly safe snorkeling area and an on-reef child-minding service, Club Seahorse.

Wind- and motor-powered water sports are popular on many Whitsunday Islands.

Fantasea also runs daily high-speed catamaran cruises to **Whitehaven Beach,** a justifiably famous stretch of pure white silica sand as fine (and as messy) as talcum powder. Find a secluded spot on the 6½-km (4-mi) beach—and apply sunblock: the sand acts as a reflector—or swim in the crystal-clear water. Trips on the air-conditioned vessels, including onboard commentary, barbecue lunch, afternoon tea, beach shelters, and games, costs A$150 from Daydream Island or Shute Harbour (including pick-ups from Airlie Beach); A$110 from Hamilton Island.

Sunsail Australia (✉ *Front St., Hamilton Island* ☎ *07/4948–9509 or 1800/803988* ⊕ *www.sunsail.com.au*) has various boats available for bareboat charter, and runs luxury crewed catamaran cruises, departing Fridays (from A$1,400 per person for a three-night, all-inclusive trip, with snorkeling gear, windsurfers, kayaks, and an onboard hostess).

ESSENTIALS

Medical Hamilton Island Medical Centre (✉ *Resort Dr* ☎ *07/4946–8243*).

Bank National Australia Bank (✉ *Marina Village, Front St.* ☎ *13–2265* ⊕ *www.nab.com.au*).

Buggy Rental Harbourside Buggy Rentals (☎ *07/4946–8095*). **Resort Buggy Hire** (☎ *07/4946–8263*).

Ferry Fantasea Cruises (☎ *07/4967–5455 or 1800/650851* ⊕ *www.fantasea.com.au*).

Seaplane Air Whitsunday (⊕ *www.airwhitsunday.com.au*).

Helicopter Aviation Tourism Australia (⊕ *www.avta.com.au*)..

OUTDOOR ACTIVITIES

Hamilton Island Resort has the widest selection of activities in the Whitsundays: game fishing, snorkeling, scuba diving, waterskiing, parasailing, jet skiing, wakeboarding, sea kayaking, speedboat adventure rides, and fish-feeding tours are all on the agenda, with staff from the resort's **Beach Sports outlet and Watersports Shop** (☎ 07/4946–8286) on hand to give tips. Many non-motorized water sports are free to resort guests. There are also bushwalks, go-karts, a golf driving range, and a brand-new 18-hole golf course (on its own island, a five-minute ferry-ride away), as well as a flying fox, target-shooting range, wildlife sanctuary, and five public-access swimming pools. You can also take a day or twilight 4WD safari and sign up for art classes, portrait sessions, and special events. Reserve ahead through the **Tour Booking Desk** (☎ 07/4946–8305 ⊕ www.hamiltonisland.com.au).

> ## CASTAWAY CUISINE
>
> On Hamilton, the Whitsundays' largest inhabited island, guests can eat and drink at a variety of restaurants and bars. Most are managed by Hamilton Island, whose current owners, the Oatley family, made their millions out of wine. The Oatleys are keen to build on the island's reputation for quality wining and dining—recruiting top chefs, improving supply lines, scheduling epicurean events, and adding to the island's vast central cellar and produce store. Opportunities for young guns to work their way up through Hamilton's hierarchy, training under culinary heavyweights, are bringing fresh talent to the island.

Hamilton Island is so family-friendly it allows kids under age 13 to stay free, provided they stay with parents and use existing beds (no rollaways or cribs). Under-13s also can eat free at some island restaurants when staying at selected resort hotels, choosing from kids' menus, and accompanied by parents. The **Clownfish Club** (☎ 07/4946–8941 ⊕ www.clownfishclub.com.au ☼ Daily 8:30–5:30), for children aged six weeks to 14 years, has simple games and activities: painting, blocks, sand sculpting, dancing, and climbing in three daily sessions for infant–4-year-olds; fishing, snorkeling, beach sports, chocolate-making, and craft in morning and afternoon sessions for 5- to 14-year-olds. Babysitting services (at least A$20 an hour) must be booked before 4 pm. You can also hire strollers and baby backpacks, books, and toys.

GOLF ★ The new, Peter Thomson–designed, par 71 Hamilton Island **Golf Course** (☎ 07/4949–9760 ⊕ www.hamiltonislandgolfclub.com.au) sits on Dent Island, a five-minute ferry-ride from Hammo. The 6,083-meter (19,957-foot) course has sweeping Whitsundays views from all 18 holes. There's also a clubhouse, pro shop, restaurant, and bar. Ferries depart all day from 7:30 AM from Hamilton Island Marina: allow five hours to play 18 holes (A$150); half that to play nine (A$100); prices include ferry transfers.

FISHING Hamilton Island can arrange half- and full-day, share, or private charter sportfishing trips with Renegade Charters for anglers looking to catch coral trout, mackerel, and tuna. You can also hire dinghies here. Charters can be arranged through Hamilton Island's **Tour Booking Desk** (☎ 07/4946–8305 or 0147/151702 boat ⊕ www.renegadecharters.com.au).

SCUBA DIVING Hamilton Island has a free daily pool-based snorkeling lesson and scuba trial (pre-booking is essential). If you sign up for an introductory dive course with **H2O Sportz** (☎ *07/4946–9888* ⊕ *www.h2osportz.com.au*), the island's dive shop, you'll get instruction, equipment, and two guided dives for A$289, gear included. Also available are guided snorkeling safaris (A$85).

WILDLIFE Hamilton Island's **Koala Gallery Wildlife Experience Zoo** (☎ 07/4946–
PARK 8266 ✍A$17.50) houses koalas, kangaroos, wallabies, crocodiles,
Ⓒ wombats, and Tassie devils. There's a daily Breakfast with the Koalas (7:30–9:30), as well as animal talks and feedings. You can also get koala happy snaps.

WHERE TO EAT

Hamilton Island Resort has lots of dining options, including several casual cafés and takeaway outlets, a pub serving counter meals, a dinner cruise boat, and restaurants.

$$$ ✕ The **Denison Star**, a magnificent 107-foot motor cruiser hewn from
DINNER CRUISE Tasmanian Huon pine, glides out of Hamilton Island Marina most evenings for a starlit dinner tour around the neighboring islands. It's all very civilized: canapes and drinks are served to a maximum 40 guests on the sundeck as night falls, then the boat moors in some scenic, secluded spot. You order from a small à la carte selection, and the food duly emerges from the galley. Down a postprandial cocktail and stargaze on the upper deck as you cruise back to base. ⊠ *Hamilton Island Marina* ☎ *07/4946–8613* ▤ *AE, DC, MC, V.*

$$ ✕ **Manta Ray Café**. This could be the island's best all-rounder. Dine
MODERN AUS- right by the marina on Modern Australian dishes—pan-fried reef fish,
TRALIAN, PIZZA lamb with pomegranate sauce—or join the queue for gourmet, wood-
★ fired pizzas (also available as takeout). There's plenty on Manta Ray's
Ⓒ long menu to suit all tastes. The wine list's a winner, too. ⊠ *Front St.* ☎ *07/4946–9999* ▤ *AE, DC, MC, V.*

$$$ ✕ **Mariners Restaurant**. Perched on the marina, this breezy, upscale eatery
SEAFOOD turns the local catch into fresh contemporary dishes: artfully arranged sashimi, mud crab, reef fish, and varied seafood platters. They do duck, eye fillet steak, vegetarian, and gluten-free meals; there's a well-stocked bar. Book a balcony table and watch watercraft dock as you dine. ⊠ *Marina Village* ☎ *07/4946–9999* ▤ *AE, DC, MC, V.*

$$$ ✕ **Romano's Italian Restaurant**. With polished wood floors and a wide bal-
ITALIAN cony overlooking the marina, Romano's is the place to come for casual
★ fine dining. The kitchen produces traditional Italian favorites such as pasta *marina* and Bolognese, but the focus is on fresh produce and local seafood, as in the terrific Boston Bay mussels with fresh tomato sauce, herbs, and chili. ⊠ *Marina Village, Harbourside* ☎ *07/4946–9999* ▤ *AE, DC, MC, V* ⊙ *No lunch*.

$$$ ✕ **Sails Restaurant**. Set right on Catseye Beach, this airy beach shack,
BISTRO recently restyled as a bistro, serves three good-quality meals daily. The
Ⓒ menu is a crowd-pleaser, with pasta, salads, and surf and turf. There's also a good kids' menu and a giant chess set to keep older offspring occupied between courses. After dinner, catch some live jazz or a local band. ⊠ *Main resort complex* ☎ *07/4946–9999* ▤ *AE, DC, MC, V.*

WHERE TO STAY

★ **Hamilton Island Holidays.** Part of the resort, Hamilton Island Hideaways
☾ manages a range of self-catered one- to four-bedroom holiday properties
around the island, including studio, split-level, and two-story designs,
most grouped around a communal pool in landscaped grounds. Each
has a full kitchen, laundry, living-dining area, and a balcony with views;
some are truly luxurious. Rentals include free use of a 4-seater golf
buggy and access to the island's facilities. ✉ *Hamilton Island, Whitsunday Islands, QLD* ☎ *02/9433–0444 or 13/7333* ⊕ *www.hihh.com.au.*

$$$$ ⊞ **Hamilton Island Beach Club.** The upscale amenities and no-kids policy
mean that this hotel swarms with couples. Rooms, given a "designer
beachside" makeover in 2005 but already showing wear, have retro-
look furnishings, flat-screen TVs, entertainment systems, and shuttered
doors leading to private balconies. There's a concierge service, useful for booking activities and making restaurant reservations at the
island's various eateries, plus free motorized buggies to get you there.
Also complimentary are use of the on-site library, infinity pool, and
sports complex facilities, non-motorized water-sports equipment, buffet
breakfasts, and Internet access. Staff are friendly, but don't expect them
to go that extra mile. **Pros:** infinity pool; beachside location; no kids.
Cons: overpriced; service lacks attention to detail; decor a tad worn.
✉ *Hamilton Island, Whitsunday Islands, QLD* ☎ *02/9433–0444 or
13–7333* ⊕ *www.hamiltonisland.com.au* ⟲ *57 rooms* ☾ *In-room: safe,
refrigerator, VCR, dial-up. In-hotel: restaurant, room service, bar, tennis
courts, pool, gym, spa, diving, water sports, laundry service, concierge,
executive floor, public Internet, public Wi-Fi, airport shuttle, no kids
under 18, no-smoking rooms* ⊟ *AE, DC, MC, V* ⊞⧲ *BP.*

$$$ ⊞ **Hamilton Island Palm Bungalows.** These steep-roofed, freestanding bun-
☾ galows resemble Polynesian huts; each has a private furnished balcony,
cool tile or polished-wood floors, a basic kitchenette, king-size and sofa
beds; and ceiling fans (plus air-conditioning). The neighboring Palm
Terraces are closed for refurbishment. Family packages let kids under
13 stay and eat for free in selected resort restaurants with their parents.
Pros: family-friendly; free use of non-motorized water-sports equip-
ment; close to main pool, beach and wildlife park. **Cons:** few on-site
facilities; buggy hire not included; up a steepish hill. ✉ *Hamilton Island,
Whitsunday Islands, QLD* ☎ *02/9433–0444 or 13–7333* ⊕ *www.
hamiltonisland.com.au* ⟲ *49 bungalows* ☾ *In-room: refrigerator, dial-
up. In-hotel: resort children's program (infant–14 years), airport shuttle,
no-smoking rooms* ⊟ *AE, DC, MC, V* ⊞⧲ *BP.*

$$$–$$$$ ⊞ **Hamilton Island Reef View Hotel.** Only rooms on higher floors of this
★ hotel live up to the name—those on the fifth floor and above have spec-
☾ tacular vistas of the Coral Sea, while rooms on lower levels overlook
a landscaped, tropical garden—but all are comfortable, with private
balconies. Smartly refurbished rooms on the higher floors have neu-
tral-toned soft furnishings, flat-screen TVs, and large bathrooms with
dual sinks. Split-level suites on the 17th, 18th, and 19th levels have
sleek blond-wood dining settings and fantastic ocean views; individu-
ally furnished Presidential Suites have private terraces with hot tubs.
Suite guests get complimentary use of Hamilton's sports club facilities

7

including tennis and squash courts; family packages mean under-13s stay and eat for free in selected resort restaurants with their parents. If you must work, there's an on-site business center. **Pros:** good breakfasts; terrific outlook; better-than-usual service. **Cons:** lower-level rooms can be noisy; pricey in-house food and drinks; cockatoos fly in open windows. ⊠ *Hamilton Island, Whitsunday Islands, QLD* ✉ *02/9433–0444 or 13–7333* ⊕ *www.hamiltonisland.com.au* ↻ *382 rooms and suites* 🛆 *In-room: safe, refrigerator. In-hotel: restaurant, bar, room service, tennis courts, pool, gym, spa, children's program (infant–14 years), laundry facilities, laundry service, concierge, airport shuttle, no-smoking rooms* ⊟ *MC, V* ¶⊙¶ *BP.*

$$$–$$$$ 🔝 **Hamilton Island Whitsunday Holiday Apartments.** These twin 13-story towers, overlooking Catseye Beach and the Coral Sea, house one-bedroom serviced apartments with comfy wood-and-cane furniture, large furnished balconies, full kitchens, and dining and sitting areas equipped with cable TV, DVD players, and PlayStation units. Those on the seventh floor and above have contemporary decor and guaranteed ocean views. Kids under 13 stay and eat for free at selected resort restaurants with parents; buffet breakfasts and use of the resort's paddle-skis, cats, Windsurfers, and snorkeling gear are free. **Pros:** self-catering; family-friendly; free water sports. **Cons:** unrenovated lower-floor apartments a tad shabby; fee for daily servicing in lower-floor units; on-island supplies pricey (BYO groceries from the mainland). ⊠ *Hamilton Island, Whitsunday Islands, QLD* ✉ *02/9433–0444 or 13–7333* ⊕ *www.hamiltonisland.com.au* ↻ *165 apartments* 🛆 *In-room: kitchen, refrigerator, DVD, dial-up. In-hotel: water sports, children's program (infant–14 years), airport shuttle, no-smoking rooms* ⊟ *AE, DC, MC, V* ¶⊙¶ *BP.*

$$$$ 🔝 **Qualia.** The latest addition to Hamilton Island's accommodations is
★ easily its most luxurious. Qualia's architect-designed complex of luxe freestanding pavilions has the tranquil, decadent ambience of a high-end Southeast Asian resort. Sited well away from the main resort complex and marina, Qualia caters to a privileged few. Guests enjoy exclusive access to a pair of infinity-edge pools, private beaches, two gourmet restaurants and a private dining room, two bars, and an on-site spa, gym, and library. Gloriously appointed guest pavilions and a lavish beach house, handcrafted from Australian timbers, stone, and glass, harmonize beautifully with their tropical surroundings. Expansive, flow-through lounge areas with designer furnishings and high-end entertainment systems open onto large private decks with stupendous views. Windward Pavilions also have their own plunge pools; the extravagant Beach House has a dining room for 10 and its own guesthouse. Dozens of resort facilities and services—gourmet meals, non-alcoholic drinks, the use of two Hobie cats and a raft of other water-sports equipment, wireless Internet, and buggies to get to the resort complex (if you can drag yourself away)—are included in the rate, as are guided walks, kayaking and snorkeling tours, beach drop-offs, kitchen tours, wine-tasting, and more. Diving, fishing, sailing, scenic flights, golfing tours, private beach picnics, and catered, crewed cruises are available at extra cost. **Pros:** glorious, tranquil location; fine food and wine; high-end everything. **Cons:** pricey. ⊠ *Hamilton Island, Whitsunday Islands, QLD*

☎ 02/9433–3349 or 1300/780959 ⊕ www.qualia.com.au 🛏 60 suites ⚴ In-room: refrigerator, safe, DVD, Wi-Fi (no fee), Internet (no fee), pool (some). In-hotel: 2 restaurants, bars, room service, concierge, public Wi-Fi (free), pools, gym, spa, tennis courts (nearby), water sports, beachfront, diving, airport shuttle, no kids, no-smoking rooms ▭ AE, DC, MC, V ⌾ BP.

NIGHTLIFE

Hamilton Island has several resort bars as well as a handful of independent ones: all except Qualia's are open to visitors. At **Boheme's Bar & Nightclub** (✉ Front St., Marina Village ☎ 07/4946–9999) you can dance to live or DJ-spun music and shoot a round of pool. The bar is open Tuesday–Saturday 9 PM–late, and the nightclub is open 11 PM–late.

SHOPPING

Hamilton Island's Marina Village, along Front Street, houses many shops selling resort wear, children's clothes, souvenirs, and gifts. You'll also find an art gallery, art studio, florist, small supermarket, pharmacy, real-estate agent, bakery, bottle shop, video store, and a hair salon on the island. In general, you'll pay more for goods and services here than for their equivalents on the mainland.

DAYDREAM ISLAND

The resort on this small, 42-acre island is especially welcoming to day-trippers. Just 30 minutes' boat ride from Shute Harbour, it's a perfect place to relax or pursue outdoor activities such as snorkeling and water sports—all of which are comparatively affordable here. The resort's lush gardens blend into a small tract of rain forest, frequented by tame wallabies and mournful Stone curlews. The island is surrounded by clear blue water and coral reefs.

GETTING HERE AND AROUND

Cruise Whitsundays runs several daily services between Daydream Island and Hamilton Island and Whitsunday Coast Airport or Proserpine Rail Station for A$50 each-way, and between the island and Abel Point Marina or Shute Harbour (A$30 each way). Cruise Whitsunday Resort Connections offers direct island transfers from Hamilton Island Airport on modern, air-conditioned catamaran cruisers. Island Escape Day Cruises has half- and full-day cruise options, calling in at Daydream, Hook, and Long islands and Whitehaven Beach (A$79–A$165). Fantasea Cruises runs several daily catamarans between Daydream Island and Shute Harbour (A$29 each way), and several daily services linking Daydream with Hamilton Island Marina (A$43) and Airport (A$53).

Although most people arrive by boat from Hamilton Airport, an alternative is to fly to Proserpine Airport on the mainland, catch a bus to Shute Harbour, and take a boat to the island. Several major airlines operate flights to and from Hamilton Island and Proserpine airports, and capital cities, as well as Townsville and Cairns. Check with each carrier for weight restrictions.

ESSENTIALS

Cruise Whitsundays (☎ 07/4946–4662 ⊕ www.cruisewhitsundays.com). Fantasea Cruises (☎ 07/4967–5455 ⊕ www.fantasea.com.au).

OUTDOOR ACTIVITIES

At Daydream Island Resort & Spa many activities, such as water polo, beach volleyball, and the use of kayaks and catamarans, are included in room rates. Guided fishing, snorkeling, and scuba diving day trips, parasailing, jet skiing, waterskiing, and wakeboarding sessions, guided sea kayak and ocean rafting excursions, glass-bottom boat tours, banana-boat tube rides, croc safaris, wetlands tours, and more can be arranged through the resort's Tour Desk for an additional charge.

Daydream offers day trips to Whitehaven Beach on catamaran *Camira*; snorkel and dive cruises to Knuckle Reef with classy local operator Cruise Whitsundays; sailing excursions on maxi-yacht *Ragamuffin*; and introductory dives through **Whitsunday Dive** (☎ 07/4984–8782 or 07/4984–1239 ⊕ www.daydreamdive.com) for around A$110, as well as dive packages for certified divers from A$200. You can also take a two-day scuba diving course, starting in Daydream's pool, then venturing onto the reef, for A$475, including two open-water dives.

An ocean rafting excursion on fast, semi-rigid inflatable boats takes you to neighboring islands and gorgeous Whitehaven Beach, with stops to snorkel and stroll around. Half- and full-day sportfishing trips around the Whitsundays on *Sea Fever* (☎ 07/4984–2734 or 0427/524975 ⊕ www.seafever.com.au) include bait, tackle, and lines. Or take a helicopter flight to Fantasea's ReefWorld pontoon, where you can snorkel, take semi-submersible tours, and try out the giant waterslide. Nonguests can also book activities through the resort.

WHERE TO STAY

$$$$ 🏨 **Daydream Island Resort & Spa.** Colorfully decorated, with whimsical touches like starfish-and-shell-embedded toilet seats, mermaid and dolphin statues perched on rocks, a giant chess set, and outsize marine mobiles and murals, this family-friendly resort has youthful, cheerful staff, a well-run, albeit pricey kids' club, a terrific pool, and a lovely day spa. Condo-style garden- or ocean-view rooms and suites have cane and blond-wood furniture, cool tiled floors, and beach-theme fabrics, and are equipped with cable TV, pay-per-view movies, Playstation games, and Wi-Fi; suites also have hot tubs. Complimentary activities include aqua aerobics, makeup and beading workshops, spa tours, scavenger hunts, and daily fish-feeding at the ocean-fed aquarium that meanders through the grounds. The tour desk can arrange various offshore excursions and water sports. The million-dollar, Australiana-theme 19-hole miniature-golf course at the island's southern end is bargain-priced hilarity. Breakfast is included in most room packages. For a fee, child care is available: drop the kids off and head out on a day cruise, or to the 16-room Daydream Rejuvenation Spa. **Pros:** family-friendly; classy spa (unfortunately sited above the kids' club); mini-golf and movies; snorkeling off Lovers' Cove. **Cons:** teeming with kids; food lackluster; steep fees for kids' club, babysitting, and PlayStation games. ✉ *Daydream Island, Whitsunday Islands, QLD* ☎ 07/4948–8488 or

1800/075040 ⊕ *www.daydreamisland.com* ↻*280 rooms, 9 suites* ♿ *In-room: safe, refrigerator, Wi-Fi (fee). In-hotel: 4 restaurants, bars, tennis courts, pools, gym, spa, beachfront, diving, water sports, children's program (infant–12 years), laundry facilities, laundry service, public Internet, concierge, airport shuttle, no-smoking rooms* ⊟*AE, DC, MC, V* ⊺◎⊺*BP.*

SHOPPING

A small bakery at the southern end of the island serves sandwiches and cakes during the day. A convenience store in the main resort complex, near Reception, sells essentials, candy, pharmacy goods, resort wear, cards, and gifts, and is open daily until 5.

NIGHTLIFE

As Daydream is primarily a family resort, there's little to do after dinner: live musical ensembles often play in the Lobby Bar, but ambience is low-key—think quiet conversation over a postprandial drink rather than dancing and carousing. Theme nights occasionally take place in the bar at the island's southern end, where you can also watch nightly, new-release movies on a gigantic beachfront screen (deck chairs and blankets provided), then stroll home along the coast-hugging boardwalk. Babysitting's not cheap, here (and escalates with every extra child), so staying in and watching pay-per-view movies may be your best option.

7

HAYMAN ISLAND

Fodor's Choice
★

Hayman Island, in the northern Whitsunday Passage, is the closest of the Whitsundays to the Outer Barrier reef. The island, a 900-acre crescent with a series of hills along its spine, has just one resort, one of the oldest and most opulent in the region and popular with jet-setters who take their leisure seriously. The service—understated yet attentive—merits the price you pay for it; staff members even traverse the resort via tunnels so they're less of a "presence." Reflecting pools, sandstone walkways, manicured tropical gardens, statuary, and waterfalls provide the feel of an exclusive club, while beautiful walking trails crisscross the island, leading to pristine coves and vantage points. The main beach sits right in front of the resort complex, but more secluded sands and fringing coral can be reached by boat.

GETTING HERE AND AROUND

Hayman doesn't have its own airstrip, but you can fly to Hamilton Island and from there transfer onto one of Hayman's luxury motor yachts or charter a seaplane. From Hayman's wharf a shuttle whisks you to the resort about ½ km (¼ mi) away. Australian sparkling wine is served during the 60-minute motor-launch trip to the island. On the return journey you'll get full bar service, platters of food, tea, and espresso coffee. Make sure you're ticketed all the way to Hayman Island, including the motor-yacht leg, as purchasing the round-trip yacht journey from Hamilton Island to Hayman separately costs upward of A$300. Air Whitsunday provides seaplane connections from Whitsunday Airport on Hamilton Island to Hayman for A$490 each way (up to 4 passengers) or A$760 (up to 6) and, on request, from mainland airports including Whitsunday Coast (Proserpine), Mackay, and Cairns. They also run scenic flights around the Whitsundays and over the reef.

TOURS

Hayman Island Guest Services provides information on all guided tours around the island and excursions offshore. All listed costs are per person.

An hour-long scenic seaplane flight over Whitehaven Beach and the Great Barrier Reef, including renowned Heart Reef, is A$340 per person—or get a bird's-eye glimpse of your environs on a 10-minute **Whitsunday Scenic helicopter ride** (A$145).

Various half-day seaplane and helicopter excursions let you explore neighboring islands and the reef from aloft and underwater, and be back to Hayman for lunch. Fly to Whitehaven Beach for a morning's snorkeling, strolling, and sunbathing for A$300 by seaplane; A$399 by helicopter, refreshments and scenery included.

An **Air Whitsunday's** seaplane excursion to Knuckle Reef pontoon, with 90 minutes' snorkeling and a private semi-submersible coral viewing tour, is A$390 for 3 hours, A$530 for 4½ hours.

Pick of the bunch are the three-hour tours to Fantasea ReefWorld, where Hayman guests get exclusive use of the huge pontoon and its facilities, refreshments, scenic overflights, and commentary en route: A$480 by seaplane, A$699 by helicopter.

Golfers can fly to Turtle Point Golf Course on the mainland and play 18 holes: by seaplane, it's A$A375; by helicopter, it's A$999. Anglers can choose from half-day bottom-fishing excursions for coral trout, red emperor, sweetlip, and scarlet sea perch (A$250) or gamefishing trips for black marlin, tuna, and mackerel on White Fishing Charters' 30-foot Kevlacat Sportsfisher 3000 (A$280, min. 2 persons). Various sailing options are offered, and most of Hayman's immaculate fleet is available for private charter.

Cruise Whitsundays runs a daily full-day dive-snorkel cruise on a 121-foot wave-piercer craft from Hayman (and the mainland and neighboring isles) to Knuckle Reef Lagoon pontoon on the outer Reef: the A$205 per person fare includes use of pontoon facilities, snorkeling gear, buffet lunch and refreshments, and priority access to coral-viewing tours. Optional extras include diving (A$99–A$110, second dives A$55), heli scenic flights (A$129–A$199), even massages (A$25–A$90).

ESSENTIALS

Seaplane Air Whitsunday (☎ *07/4946–9111* ⊕ *www.airwhitsunday.com.au*).

Tour Operators Hayman Island Guest Services (☎ *07/4940–1234* ⊕ *www. hayman.com.au*). **Cruise Whitsundays** (☎ *07/4946 –4662* ⊕ *www.cruisewhitsundays.com*).

OUTDOOR ACTIVITIES

All nonmotorized water sports on Hayman Island—well-maintained catamarans, Windsurfers, paddle skis, and kayaks—are included in the room rates, as are use of the well-equipped indoor-outdoor gym, five floodlit tennis courts, two squash courts, badminton, Ping-Pong,

Parasailing off Hayman Island.

and croquet equipment, and a golf driving range and nine-hole putting green. Swim in the vast lagoon pools; take a self-guided art or garden walk or an exercise class. An exhilarating inflatable tube ride is A$38; a half-hour waterskiing or wakeboarding session is A$70. Or order a picnic hamper and set off to one of the island's secluded beaches.

The fully-accredited five-star PADI Hayman Dive and Snorkel Centre has a training tank for diving lessons, and runs various dive courses, trips, and packages, including a signature Hayman Experience night dive aboard the resort's dive vessel, *Sun Aura*, to nearby Castle Rock Wall, on which you'll see crabs, shrimp, crayfish, moray eels, parrot fish, and more, for A$210 (min. 2 persons). It also sells everything from snorkel gear to wet suits and sports clothing.

Here you can book waterskiing, windsurfing, sailing, boating, game- and bottom-fishing, and snorkeling excursions, as well as dive trips *(see Tours, above)*.

You can also arrange scenic flights to nearby beaches, Turtle Point Golf Course, and over the reef through the resort's **Recreation Information Centre** (☎ *07/4940–1882*).

WHERE TO EAT

All restaurants are within the resort complex. Reservations are recommended and can be booked through the resort's concierge, and dress for all evening restaurants is "smart resort wear"—no singlets, shorts, or flip-flops. Restaurant opening times are staggered, so you always have at least two dining options; by day, eat at Azure or the Beach Pavilion, or snack by the Pool Bar.

Hayman schedules various epicurean events, including weekly six-course degustation dinners and behind-scenes tours of its vast kitchens, impressive wine cellar, and chocolate room (A$245 per person); chef and wine-maker events; and Hayman Culinary Academy cooking classes (A$220–A$240 per person, including the resulting three-course meal).

ONE WITH NATURE

At Barrier Reef resorts part of the fun is sharing your vacation with the local wildlife. On Hinchinbrook, lace monitor lizards up to 3 feet long frequently wander into the pool area and open-sided restaurant looking for food. Cute wallabies and big-eyed, mournful Stone curlews roam the grounds of many Whitsunday resorts. Hayman supports a colony of endangered Proserpine rock wallabies; Hamilton has a small wildlife sanctuary at which you can breakfast with koalas. Unsuspecting Hayman and Hamilton Island guests may be subject to fly-by room raids from cheeky white cockatoos.

$$$$ ╳ **Azure.** Right on the island's main
AUSTRALIAN beach, this casually elegant restaurant affords glorious views. Dine
★ indoors or alfresco: seating extends onto the sand. There's a splendid buffet breakfast each morning, with à la carte options, freshly baked breads and pastries, tropical fruits and juices, and brewed coffee. A contemporary Australian menu showcasing seafood, and candlelit, white-linen dining, are the draw cards. A lavish seafood grill is available on selected evenings for A$95 per person. There's also a kids' menu. ▭ *AE, DC, MC, V.*

$$$$ ╳ **La Fontaine.** With Waterford crystal chandeliers, Louis XVI furnish-
ECLECTIC ings, and a central fountain, this elegant restaurant, open seasonally for
★ dinner, is the resort's culinary showpiece. Its fine "modern European" cuisine has a definite French accent. Live music generally accompanies dinner. A private dining room, with the option of designing your own menu in consultation with the resort's executive chef, is available year-round (A$320, min. 4). ▭ *AE, DC, MC, V* ☾ *No lunch.*

$$$ ╳ **La Trattoria.** With its red-and-white-checked tablecloths, hand-beaten
ITALIAN hanging lamps, and rustic furnishings, "Tratt's" is a classic provincial Italian restaurant. Sit inside or outdoors, and choose from an extensive list of pastas and traditional Italian dishes, a spectacular antipasto buffet, and a well-chosen wine list with some excellent reds. A live jazz band adds to the sociable atmosphere. ▭ *AE, DC, MC, V* ☾ *No lunch.*

$$$ ╳ **Oriental Restaurant.** This lovely pan-Asian establishment, a Hayman
ASIAN staff favorite, overlooks a tranquil Japanese garden complete with rock pools and waterfalls, a teahouse, and dining platforms. Menu choices include exotic and classic Thai, Chinese, Japanese, and Indian dishes, and there's a separate vegetarian menu. ▭ *AE, DC, MC, V* ☾ *No lunch.*

WHERE TO STAY

$$$$ ⊞ **Hayman.** This magnificently solid, hurricane-proof resort is the grande dame of the Whitsundays, attracting high-flying guests seeking precious down time. Lavish decor, including the significant Hayman collection, Asian and Australian artifacts, European tapestries, Persian rugs, and exquisite objets d'art set a quietly elegant tone in the lobby, restaurants, walkways, and rooms. Lagoon, pool, garden, penthouse, and beach-front suites are all large and beautifully appointed, with balconies or decks overlooking the areas of the resort they're named for. For luxury, nothing tops the penthouse suites, decorated in distinct French, English, Moroccan, Asian, and Italian themes. Children here are virtually invisible, thanks to a crèche and organized kids' activities from 9 to noon and 2 to 5 daily. Expect to pay handsomely for all this excellence—even small things like drinks cost that little bit more. **Pros:** meticulous, personalized service; terrific food, wine, and activities; lovely public areas; well-stocked boutiques. **Cons:** pricey, albeit top-notch food, drinks, and spa treatments; room-raiding cockatoos; older-style TVs. ✉ *Hayman Island, Great Barrier Reef QLD* ☎ *07/4940–1234 resort, 07/4940–1838 or 1800/075175 reservations* ⊕ *www.hayman.com.au* ↩ *182 rooms, 18 suites, 11 penthouses, 1 villa* ⚒ *In-room: safe, refrigerator, DVD. In-hotel: 4 restaurants, room service, bars, tennis courts, pools, gym, spa, beachfront, diving, water sports, children's programs (ages infant–12), laundry service, concierge, public Wi-Fi (no fee), airport shuttle* ▭ *AE, DC, MC, V.*

SHOPPING

Hayman has its own chi-chi shopping arcade next to the spa. Predictably, prices aren't cheap, but the merchandise is well chosen. There are a couple of lovely boutiques stocked with designer clothes and accessories, swimwear, and resort wear for men, women and kids, including enough stylish pieces to ensure that you meet Hayman's "smart-resort-wear-for-dinner" dress code. There's De Pazzi, a small high-end jeweler, and a gift shop stocked with quality Australian-made merchandise, art, and crafts. If you're lucky, you'll visit during a sale: in the low season you might snare a bargain designer swimsuit, kaftan, or beach bag. Stores are open daily until 5 or 6, depending on the season.

NIGHTLIFE

Hayman's genteel ambience extends to its nighttime entertainment options. After dinner, most folk are so busy digesting fine food and wine that dancing's not an option—which is fortunate, perhaps, as you'll find no loud, live entertainment or obnoxiously intoxicated bar patrons here. Guests gather in the Club Lounge next to reception, where the ambience is warm but low-key, to play billiards or chess, read a book from the library, or converse quietly over a cognac. You could also organize a private moonlight cruise or join Hayman's popular local night dive.

NORTH COAST ISLANDS

ORPHEUS ISLAND

Volcanic in origin, this narrow island—11 km (7 mi) long and 1 km (½ mi) wide, 3,500 acres total—uncoils like a snake in the waters between Halifax Bay and the Barrier Reef. It's part of the Palm Island Group, which consists of 10 islands, 8 of which are Aboriginal reservations.

Continued on page 526

WHAT LIVES ON THE REEF?

Equivalent to the Amazon Rainforest in its biodiversity, the Reef hosts the earth's most abundant collection of sea life. Resident species include (but aren't limited to):

- More than 1,500 species of fish
- 5,000 species of mollusk
- 400 species of hard and soft coral
- 30 whale and dolphin species
- More than 500 species of sea plants and grasses
- 14 sea-snake species
- Six sea-turtle species
- 200 sea-bird species
- More than 150 species of shark

DIVING THE REEF

(left) purple anthias; (above) pink coral

To astronauts who've seen it from space, the Great Barrier Reef resembles a vast, snaking wall—like a moat running parallel to Australia's entire northeastern coast. Almost unimaginably long at 1,430-odd miles, it's one of the few organic structures that can be seen from above the earth's atmosphere without a telescope.

Up close, though, what looks (and from its name, sounds) like a barrier is in fact a labyrinthine complex with millions of points of entry.Mind-boggling in size and scope, encompassing more than 4,000 separate reefs, cays, and islands, the Reef could rightly be called its own subaqueous country.

An undersea enthusiast could spend a lifetime exploring this terrain—which ranges from dizzying chasms to sepulchral coral caves, and from lush underwater "gardens" to sandy sun-dappled shallows—without ever mapping all its resident wonders. Not only is the Reef system home to thousands upon thousands of sea-life species, the populations are changing all the time.

So how is a visitor—especially one with only a week to spend—supposed to plan a trip to this underwater Eden? How to choose among the seemingly endless spots for dropping anchor, donning fins and tanks, and plunging in?

With this many options, figuring out what you want to experience on the Reef is essential. If you've dreamed of floating among sea turtles, you'll likely need to head to a different location than if you want to swim with sharks; if you're an experienced deepwater diver with a taste for shipwrecks, you'll probably need to make separate arrangements from your friends who prefer to hover near the surface. There really is a spot for every kind of diver on the Reef; the trick is knowing where they are.

Luckily, many veteran divers agree about some of the Reef's most reliably excellent sites (and the best ways to access them). The selection compiled here should help you to—ahem—get your feet wet.

by Sarah Gold

BEST DIVING EXPERIENCES

Potato Cod and diver at Cod Hole

BEST WRECK DIVE

The coral formations of the Reef, while dazzling for divers, have proved treacherous to ship captains for centuries. More than 1,500 shipwrecks have been found on the Reef thus far—and there are almost certainly more waiting to be discovered.

S.S. *YONGALA*

The hulk of this 360-foot steamship, which sank during a cyclone in 1911, is easily the most popular wreck dive on the Reef. Part of the appeal is its easy accessibility; the Yongala lies just a half-hour's boat ride off the coast of Townsville, and though some sections are fairly deep (around 90 feet), others are just 45 feet below the surface. The entire wreck is now encrusted with coral, and swarms with a profusion of species including giant grouper, sea snakes, green sea turtles, and spotted eagle rays.

Difficulty level: Intermediate. Divers should have some previous deep-water experience before visiting this site.

How to get there: Yongala Dive (www.yongaladive.com.au), based in Alva Beach (south of Townsville), runs trips to the wreck several times per week.

BEST SITE TO GET YOUR HEART RATE UP

For some thrill-seeking divers, the wonders of the Great Barrier Reef are even better when accompanied by an extra shot of adrenaline—and a few dozen sharks.

OSPREY REEF

More than 200 miles north of Cairns (and only accessible via a live-aboard dive trip), Osprey is peerless for divers hell-bent on a rendezvous with the ocean's most famous predators. The northernmost section of the reef, where two ocean currents converge (it's known as the North Horn) is an especially thronged feeding ground for white-tipped reef, gray reef, hammerhead, and tiger sharks.

Difficulty level: Intermediate. Though the North Horn's best shark-viewing areas are only at about 60 feet, even seasoned divers may feel understandably anxious.

How to get there: Both Taka Dive (www.takadive.com.au) and John Rumney's Marine Encounters (www.marineencounters.com.au) offer multi-day packages to Osprey Reef from Cairns and Port Douglas.

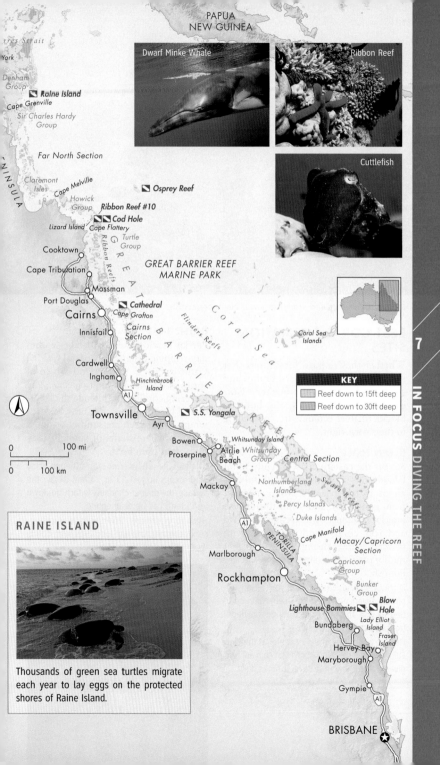

PAPUA
NEW GUINEA

Dwarf Minke Whale

Ribbon Reef

Cuttlefish

Torres Strait

York

Denham
Group

🐚 *Raine Island*

Cape Grenville

Sir Charles Hardy
Group

Far North Section

PENINSULA

Claremont
Isles   Cape Melville

Cape Melville

Howick
Group   🐚 *Osprey Reef*

Ribbon Reef #10

🐚🐚 *Cod Hole*

Lizard Island   Cape Flattery

Cooktown

Turtle
Group

Cape Tribulation

GREAT BARRIER REEF
MARINE PARK

Coral Sea

Mossman

Port Douglas

Cairns

🐚 *Cathedral*

Cape Grafton

Innisfail

Cairns
Section

Flinders Reefs

Coral Sea
Islands

Cardwell

Ingham

A1

Hinchinbrook
Island

KEY

Reef down to 15ft deep
Reef down to 30ft deep

Townsville

Ayr   🐚 *S.S. Yongala*

Bowen

Whitsunday Island

Proserpine   Airlie   Whitsunday
              Beach   Group   Central Section

Mackay

Northumberland
Islands

Percy Islands

Duke Islands

A1

RAINE ISLAND

TORILLA PENINSULA

Cape Manifold

Macay/Capricorn
Section

Marlborough

Rockhampton

Capricorn
Group

Bunker
Group

Lighthouse Bommies 🐚   🐚 *Blow
                          Hole*

Bundaberg

Lady Elliot
Island

Hervey Bay

Fraser
Island

Maryborough

Gympie

A1

BRISBANE ⭐

GREAT BARRIER REEF

0   100 mi
0   100 km

Thousands of green sea turtles migrate
each year to lay eggs on the protected
shores of Raine Island.

Scuba isn't the only option; snorkelers have plenty of opportunities to get up close to coral, too.

BEST CORAL-FORMATION SITES

Whether they're hard formations that mimic the shapes of antlers, brains, and stacked plates, or soft feathery Gorgonians and anemones, the building blocks of Reef ecology are compelling in their own right.

BLOW HOLE

Set off the eastern coast of Lady Elliot Island, this cavern-like coral tube is almost 60 feet in length. Divers can enter from either end, and swim through an interior festooned with Technicolor hard and soft corals—and swarming with banded coral shrimp, crayon-bright nudibranchs (sea slugs), and fluttery lionfish.

Difficulty level: Easy. Unless you're claustrophobic. Divers need only be Open-Water certified to visit this site, which ranges in depth from about 40 to 65 feet.

How to get there: The dive center at the Lady Elliot Island resort (www.ladyelliot.com.au) runs dives to the Blow Hole several times daily.

CATHEDRAL

Part of Thetford Reef, which lies within day-tripping distance of coastal Cairns, Cathedral is a wonderland of coral spires and swim-through chasms. The towering coral heads include thick forests of blue staghorn, sea fans, and sea whips; in between are sandy-bottomed canyons where shafts of sunlight play over giant clam beds.

Difficulty level: Intermediate. Though many coral peaks lie just 15 to 20 feet below the surface, the deeper channels (which go down to 85 feet) can be disorienting.

How to get there: Silverseries (www.silver-series.com.au) runs day-long trips from Cairns that visit several Thetford sites.

Divers explore a swim-through coral formation.

BEST GUARANTEED CLOSE-ENCOUNTER SITES

While just about any dive site on the Reef will bring you face-to-face with fantastic species, a few particular spots maximize your chances.

RIBBON REEF NUMBER 10

The northernmost of the Ribbon Reefs (a group that extends off the Cairns coast all the way to the Torres Strait) is home to some famously curious sea creatures. At Cod Hole, divers have been hand-feeding the enormous, 70-pound resident potato cod for decades. Ribbon Reef Number 10 is also one of the only places on earth where visitors can have breathtakingly close contact with wild dwarf minke whales. These small, playful baleen whales stop here every June and July —and they often approach within a few feet of respectful divers.

Sea turtle and diver

Difficulty level: Easy. Divers need only be Open-Water certified to dive at the 50-foot Cod Hole; dwarf minke encounters are open to snorkelers.

How to get there: Several dive operators run live-aboard trips to the Ribbon Reefs, including Mike Ball Expeditions (www.mikeball. com), ProDive Cairns (www.prodivecairns.com), and John Rumney's Marine Encounters (www. marineencounters.com.au).

LIGHTHOUSE BOMMIES

Part of the southerly Whitsunday group, Lady Elliot Island is surrounded by shallow, pristine waters that teem with life. In particular, the Lighthouse Bommies—freestanding coral formations set off the island's northwest coast—host a large population of manta rays, some of which have a wingspan twelve feet across.

Difficulty level: Easy. Divers need only be Open-Water certified to visit this site; the depth averages about 50 feet.

How to get there: The dive center at the Lady Elliot Island Resort (www.ladyelliot.com. au) runs dives to the Bommies daily.

RAINE ISLAND

Set in the far north reaches of the Coral Sea off Cape York, this coral cay is one of the Reef's greatest—and most inaccessible—treasures. Its beaches comprise the world's largest nesting ground for endangered green sea turtles; during November and December more than 20,000 turtles per week mob the shores to lay their eggs. Because Raine is a strictly protected preserve, seeing this annual phenomenon is an exceedingly rare privilege. In fact, only one dive operator, John Rumney, is currently sanctioned by the Marine Park Authority to visit the site—and only twice a year.

Difficulty level: Intermediate to Expert. Rumney's dive trips involve what he calls "a heavy research component;" participants not only dive among the turtles, but also collect data on them and fit them with satellite tags (some also tag tiger sharks, another rare endemic species).

How to get there: The 18 spots on these ten-day trips are in high demand; learn more at www.marineencounters.com.au.

SCUBA DIVING 101

(left) ProDive is one of several great dive companies on the Reef; (right) snorkelers receive instruction.

Visiting the Reef can be a snap even if you've never dived before; most local dive operators offer Open Water (entry-level) certification courses that can be completed in just three to five days. The course involves both classroom and pool training, followed by a written test and one or more open-water dives on the Reef. Once you're certified, you'll be able to dive to depths of up to 60 feet; you'll also be eligible to rent equipment and book dive trips all over the world.

TIGHT SCHEDULE?

If time is of the essence, ask about doing your Open Water class and in-pool training near home; some Reef operators may allow you to complete your certification (and get right to the good part—the actual ocean dives) once you arrive in Australia.

Though most serious divers insist that certification is necessary for scuba safety, if you're short on time you may find yourself tempted to take advantage of what are generally called "resort courses"—single-day instruction programs that allow you to dive at limited depths under strict supervision. As long as you choose a reputable operator

(like Mike Ball Dive Expeditions, www.mikeball.com) and do exactly as your dive guides say, you'll likely be fine.

FLYING

No matter how you get yourself underwater, you'll need to make sure you don't schedule a flight and a dive in the same day. Flying too soon after diving can lead to "the bends"—an excruciating buildup of nitrogen bubbles in the bloodstream that requires a decompression chamber to alleviate. Since that's not anything you'd want to develop at the beginning of a transatlantic flight, be sure to wait 12 hours before flying after a single dive, 18 hours after multiple dives, and 24 hours if your dive(s) required decompression stops.

Regulators up! Reef visitors learn Scuba basics.

LOGISTICS

CERTIFYING ORGANIZATIONS

You'll find that all reliable dive operators—on the Reef and elsewhere—are affiliated with one of the three major international dive-training organizations: PADI (www.padi.com), NAUI (www.naui.org), or SSI (www.divessi.com). The certification requirements for all three are similar, and most dive shops and outfitters consider them interchangeable (i.e., they'll honor a certification from any of the three).

COSTS

The price for taking a full Open Water certification course (usually over four or five days of training) averages around $400-$500—but in many cases, rental equipment, wetsuits, and instruction manuals cost extra. Some dive shops have relationships with hotels, and offer dive/stay packages. One-day scuba resort courses usually cost around $200-$300, with all gear included.

EMERGENCIES

Before diving on the Reef, it's a good idea to purchase divers' insurance through the Divers Alert Network (DAN), an international organization that provides emergency medical assistance to divers. (Learn more about the different plans at www.diversalertnetwork.org). DAN also has a 24-hour emergency hotline staffed by doctors, emergency medical technicians, and nurses; for help with diving injuries or immediate medical advice, call (001) 919-684-4326 from Australia.

SNORKELING TIPS

Snorkelers explore Fitzroy Reef Lagoon.

■ If you're a beginner, avoid snorkeling in areas where there's chop or strong currents.

■ Every few minutes, look up and check what's floating ahead of you—you'll want to avoid boats, jellyfish, and other surface-swimmers.

■ Give corals, plants, and sea creatures a wide berth—for their protection and yours.

■ Coat every part of your back with high-SPF, waterproof sunscreen; the water's reflection greatly intensifies the sun's rays.

DIVING TIPS

■ Before heading off on a dive trip, have your doctor rule out any possible health complications.

■ Be sure your dive operator is affiliated with an internationally known training organization, such as PADI or NAUI.

■ Stick to dive trips and sites that are within your expertise level—the Reef is not the place to push safety limits.

■ Remember that in Australia, depths and weights use the metric system—so bring a conversion table if you need to.

■ Always dive with a partner, and always keep your partner in sight.

■ Never dive when you're feeling ill—especially if you're experiencing sinus congestion.

■ Never dive after consuming alcohol.

■ If you feel unwell or disoriented while diving, signal to your partner that you need to surface so she or he can accompany you.

DANGERS OF THE REEF

(left) The Irukandji box jellyfish sting causes severe pain; (right) small sharks inhabit areas of the Reef.

Like any other wild natural habitat, the Reef is home to creatures that are capable of causing you harm—and possibly even killing you. But surprisingly, the most lethal Reef inhabitants aren't of the Shark Week variety. In fact, they're just about invisible.

THE DEADLIEST REEF DWELLER

Chironex fleckeri—better known as box jellyfish—are native to the same waters as the Reef. They also just happen to be the most poisonous sea creatures on the planet. Cube-shaped and transparent (which makes them almost impossible to see in the water), these jellies have tentacles whose stinging cells release an enormously potent venom on contact. A box-jelly sting causes excruciating pain, often followed very quickly (within three or four minutes) by death.

The good news about box jellies is that they're only rarely encountered on the outer Reef and islands (they're much more prevalent close to the mainland shore, especially in summer—which is why you may see beautiful North Queensland beaches completely empty on a hot December day). While the only

sure way to prevent a box jellyfish sting is to stay out of the sea altogether, there are measures you can take to lessen the already minimal risks. First, consider wearing a full-length Lycra "sting suit" when you dive. Second, make sure your dive operator carries a supply of Chironex antivenom onboard your dive boat, just in case.

OTHER (LESS DEADLY) DANGERS

Although box jellyfish are by far the most dangerous creatures on the Reef, there are other "biteys" and "nasties" to be aware of. In particular, you should try to stay clear of a smaller box-jelly variety called Irukandji (whose sting causes delayed but often intense pain); Millepora, or stinging coral (which causes irritation and welts when it touches bare skin); sea snakes (who seldom bite humans, but whose poison can cause paralysis); and, yes, sharks (although you'll likely only see small ones on the Reef—the much more hyped Hammerheads, Tiger Sharks, and Great Whites prefer deeper and colder waters).

PROTECTING THE REEF

(left) Even the tiniest coral can serve as protective habitat; (right) divers explore a large coral formation.

Enormous though it may be, the Great Barrier Reef's ecosystem is one that requires a delicate balance. The interdependence of species here means that harming even a single food source—like a particular type of plankton—can have wide-ranging and even devastating effects.

The majority of the Reef is an official marine preserve that's managed and protected by the Great Barrier Reef Marine Park Authority. This government agency has developed a series of long-range programs to help protect the Reef—including population-monitoring of sealife species, water-temperature and salinity studies, and screening of all commercial fishing and tourism/recreational operations.

Since almost 2 million tourists visit the Reef each year, even day-trippers should be mindful of their impact on this fragile environment. Specifically, if you're planning to dive and snorkel here, you should:

- Make sure your dive gear is secure, with no loose straps or dangling hoses that might snag on corals.

- Swim slowly to avoid brushing against corals (and be especially mindful when wearing swim fins).

- Avoid picking up or touching any corals, plants, or creatures (for your protection and theirs). No souvenirs, even empty shells or dead-looking coral.

- Keep clear of all free-swimming sea creatures like sea turtles, dolphins, dugongs, or whales.

VOLUNTEERING ON THE REEF

If you'd like to do more to protect the Reef, the following organizations offer volunteer programs that allow you to help collect study data and monitor the health of reef species:

- The Australian Marine Conservation Society: http://www.amcs.org.au/

- Reef Check Australia: http://www.reefcheckaustralia.org/

- UNESCO (United Nations Educational, Scientific, and Cultural Organization): http://whc.unesco.org

Orpheus is a national park, occupied only by a marine research station and the island's fantastic resort. Although there are patches of rain forest in the island's deeper gullies and around the sheltered bays, Orpheus is a true Barrier Reef island, ringed by seven unspoiled sandy beaches and superb coral. Incredibly, 340 of the known 350 species of coral inhabit these waters, as well as more than 1,100 types of tropical fish, and the biggest giant clams in the southern hemisphere. The marine life is so easily accessed and so extraordinary here, it's no wonder the island is the sole domain of the maximum 42 guests allowed at the resort. You may occasionally see unfamiliar boats offshore, which is their right according to a marine park treaty, but you'll know everyone on Orpheus at any given time, maybe even by name.

GETTING HERE AND AROUND

Orpheus Island lies 24 km (15 mi) offshore of Ingham, about 80 km (50 mi) northeast of Townsville, and 190 km (118 mi) south of Cairns. The 25-minute seaplane flight from Townsville Airport to Orpheus aboard a Nautilus Aviation seaplane costs A\$450 per person round-trip; from Cairns it's A\$850 including a connecting Qantas flight to Townsville; a mixed-port trip is A\$650. Twice-daily scheduled flights depart from Townsville at 11:30 and 2:15, returning at 12:15 and 3. You can also charter flights from other mainland ports and islands. Baggage is limited to a maximum of 15 kilograms (33 pounds) per person. Book flights with Orpheus Island Resort.

ESSENTIALS

Seaplane Nautilus Aviation (☎ *07/4725–6506* or *0412/591732* ⊕ *www. orpheus.com*).

OUTDOOR ACTIVITIES

Orpheus Island Resort is surrounded by walking trails, and there are spectacular snorkeling and diving sites right off the beaches, with manta rays the highlight. Resort guests get complimentary use of snorkeling and light fishing gear, as well as canoes, paddle-skis, catamarans, and motorized dinghies in which to buzz from cove to cove. The coral around Orpheus is some of the best in the area, and cruises to the outer reef can be arranged through the resort for an additional fee. Whereas most of the islands are more than 50 km (31 mi) from the reef, Orpheus is just 15 km (9 mi) away. Dive operators on the island provide scuba courses (without certification) and various boat-diving options.

Picnic & Snorkel Cruise. A dozen guests at a time can join a daily five-hour cruise around the Palm Isles, stopping at a variety of snorkeling sites, some on the outer reef, on the resort's purpose-built catamaran, with a gourmet seafood lunch mid-excursion. The resort also runs hour-long PADI Discover Snorkeling pool training sessions, and 2½-hour marine-naturalist-led tours of snorkeling spots around the Palm Island group. ⊠ *Orpheus Island Resort jetty*☎ *07/4777–7377* ⊕ *www.orpheus.com. au* ☏ *Free for guests* ⊗ *Daily 10–3 picnic cruise.*

Outer Reef Dive & Snorkel Excursion. A true Great Barrier Reef island, Orpheus is surrounded by some of the reef's most diverse coral gardens, sheltering more than 1,100 species of fish. Orpheus Island Resort organizes charter excursions to the Outer Barrier Reef that include two guided dives, the chance to swim and snorkel, and a generous smorgasbord. ✉ *Pick-ups from Orpheus Island Resort jetty* ☎ *07/4777–7377* 🌐 *www.orpheus.com.au* *Price on application* ⏲ *Daily on demand (pre-booking essential, subject to weather conditions).*

WHERE TO STAY

$$$$ Fodor's Choice ★ **Orpheus Island Resort.** Nestled amid lush tropical gardens, this intimate island sanctuary offers two types of beachfront accommodation: Nautilus Suites and Orpheus Retreats. Retreats are immaculate, comfortable, and decorated with tasteful sophistication and an eye to intimacy: each has a hammock-slung private patio, kitchenette, lounge area, CD player, hot tub, aromatherapy oil burner, and bathrobes. Suites have similarly luxurious appointments but are considerably larger. You won't want to spend long inside, though—there are coral gardens under cerulean water and white-sand beaches to explore. With a maximum of 42 guests (and no clocks) on the island, you're not competing for equipment and activities: gourmet beach picnics, snorkeling excursions, hikes to the summit for sunset drinks, dives and cruises to the outer reef are easily scheduled. Extravagant seven-course degustation dinners showcasing exotic delicacies and local seafood are served nightly in the open-sided restaurant, and the kitchen will pack you picnic hampers for a fee. Dining by candlelight on the jetty, feeding local mullet and rays, is an unforgettable experience. **Pros:** attentive staff; cut-above food; good dive and snorkeling sites nearby. **Cons:** pricey; resort's scuba gear a tad worn; occasional lizards and insects in rooms. ☎ *07/4777–7377* 🌐 *www.orpheus.com.au* *17 rooms, 4 suites* *In-room: no phone, safe (some), refrigerator, no TV. In-hotel: restaurant, bars, tennis court, pools, gym, beachfront, diving, water sports, laundry service, public Internet, airport shuttle, no kids under 15, no-smoking rooms* *AE, DC, MC, V* ⏲ *Closed Feb.* *AI.*

7

HINCHINBROOK ISLAND

This 97,000-acre national park is the largest island on the Great Barrier Reef. It's a nature lover's paradise, with dense tropical rain forests, mangroves, mountain peaks, and sandy beaches. When Captain Cook discovered it in 1770, he didn't realize it was an island, and mistakenly named it Mt. Hinchinbrook—likely imagining that 3,746-foot Mt. Bowen, Australia's third-highest mountain, was part of the mainland. Dolphins, dugongs, tiger sharks, and sea turtles inhabit the waters, as well as fish that you're permitted to catch (a rarity, given the strict protection of the reef's marine life). There are also estuarine crocodiles, adders, numerous birds, goannas, and small mammals. The island is virtually untouched, save for a small resort on its northeast corner and a few toilets and campsites.

GETTING HERE AND AROUND

Hinchinbrook is a 50-minute ferry ride from mainland marina Port Hinchinbrook, near Cardwell, 190 km (118 mi) south of Cairns and 161 km (100 mi) north of Townsville. Scheduled ferries depart at 9 AM and return at 5 PM (round-trip fare A$125). Nonscheduled ferry transfers are A$300 per adult, minimum two passengers. Pre-book scheduled coach transfers from Cairns and Townsville to Port Hinchinbrook from A$100 per person return; unscheduled coach transfers are A$100–A$200 per adult, one-way from Port Douglas, Palm Cove, Cairns, Townsville, or Mission Beach.

ESSENTIALS

Tours Port Hinchinbrook Resorts & Cruises (☎ 07/4066–2000 ⊕ www. porthinchinbrook.com.au).

OUTDOOR ACTIVITIES

The focus here is on the island's environment, not the one underwater, though snorkeling and swimming are both good here (do take the regular snorkeling trip, generally offered every second day). Guests get free use of canoes and kayaks, and dive and fishing excursions on *Black Magic* can be arranged through the resort.

> ## THORSBORNE TRAIL
>
> The Thorsborne Trail runs the length of Hinchinbrook Island's east coast. The walk takes three to four days and includes steep climbs. Carry plenty of supplies; it's not for the faint-hearted. Catch a ferry from Lucinda on the mainland to the island's southern end, then follow the marked trail for 32 km (20 mi). Since only 40 walkers are permitted to camp along the Thorsborne Trail at a time (in groups of six, maximum), contact the **Rainforest and Reef Information Centre** (☎ 07/4066–8601 or 13–1304 ⊕ www.epa.qld. gov.au) at least eight weeks in advance for camping permits.

Nature walks through varied and spectacular landscapes are the primary attraction. Conditions can be hot and, on some tracks, demanding: wear sturdy shoes and take drinking water, sunscreen, and a map of the island. The Hinchinbrook Island Wilderness Lodge has morning and afternoon beach and island drop-offs/pick-ups (you walk one way). All bushwalking guests must sign in and out, ensuring their safe return. Experienced walkers (preferably with prior training) can trek the famed but difficult **Thorsborne Trail**.

WHERE TO STAY

$$$–$$$$ 🏨 **Hinchinbrook Island Wilderness Lodge & Resort.** With a limited number of guests, this small, eco-accredited resort specializes in quiet enjoyment and natural attractions. Set amid bushland on the northeast corner of the island, clean, modern, elegantly appointed Treetop Bungalows have expansive windows and polished timber floors, timber balconies, and CD players; some are suitable for groups or families. Refurbished, self-contained Beach Cabins set in bushland below have private balconies screened from insects but with no air-conditioning, and can be hot in summer. A single chef caters from a kitchen with self-generated power: hence meal options are limited, and service can be slow. At lunchtime there are light meals or sandwich lunch packs to go. A well-stocked if pricey bar is open 10 AM–midnight. A barbecue area near the pool is available for guests. Self-catering is an option for those occupying beach cabins; bring your own provisions or have the resort transport them from the mainland with 24 hours' notice. Service here is friendly but low-key: guests are left largely to their own devices. There's a tiny video lounge and library with board games, but if you're not one for simple pleasures, this may not be your place. **Pros:** unspoiled wilderness

Hinchinbrook Island is a hiker's paradise.

environs; terrific bushwalks; eco-friendly. **Cons:** few modern conveniences; lackluster food; basic bathrooms and guest laundry; little to do if it rains. ⊠ *Cape Richards, Hinchinbrook Island* ✆ *Box 3, Cardwell, QLD 4849* ☎ *07/4066–8270 or 1800/777021* ⊕ *www.hinchinbrook-lodge.com.au* ⇆ *15 treetop bungalows, 8 beach cabins* ♿ *In-room: no a/c, kitchen (some), refrigerator, no phone, no TV. In-hotel: restaurant, bar, pool, beachfront, water sports, laundry facilities, public Internet, airport shuttle, no-smoking rooms, no elevator* ▭ *MC, V.*

DUNK ISLAND

A member of the Family Islands, this 2,397-acre island is divided by a hilly spine that runs its entire length. The eastern side consists mostly of national park, with dense rain forest and secluded beaches accessible only by boat. Beautiful paths have been created through the rain forest, where you might be lucky enough to glimpse a Ulysses butterfly—a beautiful blue variety with a wingspan that can reach 6 inches. Dunk is located 4½ km (2 mi) from Mission Beach on the mainland, making it a popular spot for day-trippers.

GETTING HERE AND AROUND

Quick Cat Cruises runs fast, comfortable catamarans to Dunk Island Resort from Clump Point Jetty at Mission Beach four times daily. Departures are at 8:30, 10, 2, and 4, returning at 9:15, 1:30, 3:30, and 4:30. The round-trip fare is A\$56; one way is A\$30. Quick Cat also runs Barrier Reef cruises for A\$165 from Mission Beach or Dunk Island.

Mission Beach–Dunk Island Connections runs coaches from Cairns, Cairns Airport, the northern beaches, Port Douglas, and Silky Oaks

Lodge that connect with most Quick Cat services (A$75–A$118, one-way to Dunk Island) and water taxis (A$62–A$95, one-way to Dunk Island). Despite the very choppy ride, the Mission Beach–Dunk Island Water Taxi is the best option for day-trippers. It's necessary to disembark in shallow waters, but staff is on hand to keep your luggage from getting wet. The round-trip fare is A$35 for day-trippers, A$40 for those not returning the same day.

Dunk Island has its own landing strip. Hinterland Aviation serves the island twice daily from Cairns for A$115 per person, each way (flight time 45 minutes). Private transfers are also available. You can check up to 27 kilograms (60 pounds) of luggage and bring an additional 4 kilograms (9 pounds) on board as hand luggage. Secure baggage storage is available at Cairns Airport.

ESSENTIALS

Transportation Quick Cat Cruises (☎ 07/4068–7289 ⊕ www.quickcatcruises. com.au). **Mission Beach–Dunk Island Connections** (☎ 07/4059–2709 ⊕ www. missionbeachdunkconnections.com.au). **Mission Beach–Dunk Island Water Taxi** (☎ 07/4068–8310 ⊕ www.missionbeachwatertaxi.com). **Hinterland Aviation** (☎ 1300/134044 or 02/8296–8010 ⊕ www.voyages.com.au).

OUTDOOR ACTIVITIES

In addition to reef cruises and fishing charters, the resort has many choices of land and water sports. Rates include a dozen-plus sports and outdoorsy activities, including tennis, squash, and fitness classes, and the use of paddle-skis, catamarans, and snorkeling gear.

You'll pay extra for beach and rain-forest horseback rides, kayak and mountain-bike tours, guided reef and bush walks, golf, and archery, as well as activities requiring fuel—skydiving, waterskiing, tube rides, wake boarding, and beach drop-offs. Prices range from A$5 to A$230. The resort also organizes sportfishing charters, snorkeling, and scuba diving trips through local operators.

The resort provides a bushwalking map of the island's well-maintained trails. Kids will enjoy the farm, Coonanglebah; you can also visit the island's artists' colony.

WHERE TO STAY

$$$–$$$$ 🔲 **Voyages Dunk Island.** Coconut palms, flowering hibiscus, and frangipani surround this informal, family-oriented resort on the island's west side. Spacious beachfront suites and rooms have split-level designs (bedroom upstairs, living area downstairs) and glass doors leading onto big balconies, as well as minibars and bathrobes; suites also have CD players. Airy garden rooms lack beach views, but sit amid tropical gardens a short stroll from the main resort. Beachfront and garden rooms can be configured to suit families and groups. Beachcomber Restaurant, with its polished wood floors and killer views, serves tropical Australian cuisine, with lots of local seafood, has a kids' menu on table d'hôte nights, and does three themed buffet dinners weekly. The Terrace, overlooking the beachfront butterfly pool, serves pasta and pizza; poolside Noodle Café does good-value Asian stir-fries and noodle dishes, and you can get light lunches and fresh seafood at the rustic Jetty Café. Picnic hampers can also be arranged. Although the resort touts itself

as an activity-fueled holiday spot (a broad menu of activities includes social and water sports, fitness and art classes, wine tastings and bush-walks), relaxation is easily found beachside, poolside, or at the resort's aptly-named Spa of Peace and Plenty—probably the best place to escape from noisy kids (who stay and eat here for free). **Pros:** family-friendly; Asian-style options at lunch; discounts for longer stays; kids under 13 stay and eat free. **Cons:** kid and aircraft noise; service and food standards erratic; slow Internet; user-unfriendly activities and kids' club schedules. *Voyages, GPO 3859, Sydney, NSW 2000* *1300/134044 or 02/8296–8010* *www.voyages.com/dunk* *160 rooms* *In-room: safe, refrigerator, dial-up (fee). In-hotel: 4 restaurants, room service, bars, golf course (9 holes), tennis courts, pools, gym, spa, beachfront, water sports, children's programs (limited hours, ages 3–12), laundry facilities, laundry service, concierge, public Internet, no-smoking rooms* *AE, DC, MC, V* *BP, MAP.*

BEDARRA ISLAND

This tiny, 247-acre island 5 km (3 mi) off the coast of Mission Beach has natural springs, dense rain-forest tracts, and eight unspoiled beaches. Bedarra Island is a tranquil getaway, popular with affluent executives and entertainment notables who want complete escape. It's one of a select few Great Barrier Reef resorts with an open bar, and the liquor—especially champagne—flows freely. Bedarra accommodates a maximum of 32 people; you stay in one of 16 freestanding villas, hidden amid thick vegetation but steps from the golden sand.

GETTING HERE AND AROUND

Bedarra Island lies about 20 minutes by boat from Dunk Island. Boat transfers are included in the resort rate. To get to the Barrier Reef from Bedarra, you have to return to Dunk Island, from which all reef excursions depart.

OUTDOOR ACTIVITIES

Bedarra's geared for relaxation (a massage on the beach anyone?), but there's still plenty to engage active guests. Snorkeling is possible around the island, but it's not on the reef and the water can be cloudy during summer rains. You can also play tennis, scuba dive, paddle-ski, sail catamarans, explore local beaches in a motorized dinghy, or fish. Other sporting activities can be organized on nearby Dunk Island, along with transfers, and reef fishing, sailing, and diving charters can be arranged if you're prepared to rise early to do the transits needed to get you there.

WHERE TO STAY

$$$$
Fodor's Choice
★

Voyages Bedarra Island. Elevated on stilts, the open-plan, tropical-style villas at this exclusive resort blend into the island's dense vegetation. With polished wood floors, exposed beams, and expansive use of glass, these sophisticated two-story or split-level accommodations bear little resemblance to standard hotel rooms. Each villa has a balcony with a double hammock, a view of the ocean, a custom-built king-size bed, a bells-and-whistles entertainment system, and a complimentary minibar. Secluded, luxurious pavilions and split-level Points suites, a short walk from the main compound, have ultramodern appointments including

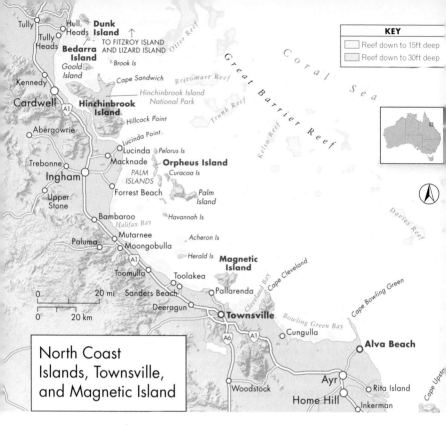

North Coast
Islands, Townsville,
and Magnetic Island

complimentary in-room laptops, oversized bathrooms, and big, private decks with daybeds and oceanfront plunge pools. All meals and drinks, plus various activities and water sports, are included in the rate, and although there's no room service, there's a 24-hour, fully stocked, serve-yourself open bar. The restaurant's modern Australian cuisine showcases local seafood, regional produce, and tropical fruit in a daily-changing à la carte menu (with degustation dinners on weekends); you're also urged to request dishes. With no children under 12 or motorized watercraft buzzing around, you're assured of a tranquil ambience: food, liquor, and lounging are the focus. **Pros:** warm, unobtrusive service; open bar; tranquillity. **Cons:** interiors a tad worn; villas dark (and hot in summer); reef excursions involve a long trek; occasional snakes. ⌂ *Voyages, Box 3589, Sydney, NSW 2000* ☎ *02/8296–8010 or 1300/134044* ⊕ *www.bedarraisland.com* ⌁ *12 villas, 4 bungalows* ⌂ *In-room: refrigerator, DVD, Internet (some). In-hotel: restaurant, bar, tennis court, pool, gym, spa, beachfront, water sports, laundry facilities, laundry service, concierge, public Internet, airport shuttle, no kids under 15, no-smoking rooms* ⊟ *AE, DC, MC, V* ⋈ *FAP.*

FITZROY ISLAND

PACKING TIPS

Even if you plan on diving, pack light for your Barrier Reef vacation—especially if you're flying in on light aircraft. Most resort dive shops have newish, well-maintained gear, so, at most, bring your favorite mask-snorkel set and dive computer.

This ruggedly picturesque, heavily forested island is 94% national park, with vegetation ranging from rain forest to heath, and an extensive fringing coral reef. Only 6 km (4 mi) from Cairns (less than an hour's cruise), the 988-acre island, once connected to the mainland, was a hunting, gathering and ceremonial ground for the Gungandji people, who called it Kobaburra, before Cook re-named it in 1770. Today, it's popular with day-trippers, and houses a newly built resort and a water-sports hut. From June to August, manta rays and humpback whales swim around the island as part of their migratory route.

GETTING HERE AND AROUND

The Fitzroy Ferries, which take 45 minutes to reach the island, depart daily at 8:30 AM from Reef Fleet Terminal in Cairns, leaving the island for the return journey at 4:30 pm. Round-trip fare is A$63.

ESSENTIALS

Ferry Fitzroy Ferries (☎ 07/4030–7907 ⊕ www.ragingthunder.com.au).

OUTDOOR ACTIVITIES

Half a dozen marked walking trails traverse Fitzroy Island National Park, ranging from half-hour rain-forest strolls to steep, challenging three-hour hikes. Take drinking water, wear sturdy closed shoes, insect repellent, sunscreen, and a hat, and watch for snakes (and in estuaries and mangroves, crocs). For maps and detailed information, visit the **Queensland Parks & Wildlife Service** (⊕ www.epa.qld.gov.au).

Day-trippers can rent paddle-skis, diving and snorkeling gear, and stinger suits, or book an ocean trampoline from the Beach Hire Hut at the southern end of Fitzroy Island run by **Raging Thunder Adventures** (☎ 07/4030–7907 ⊕ www.ragingthunder.com.au). The Cairns-based outfit also runs guided rain-forest and snorkeling tours (A$40), half-day sea-kayaking tours (A$109 from Cairns, including levies), and daily half-hour glass-bottom boat tours for A$15. The new resort has a dedicated dive shop.

WHERE TO STAY

Hunt Resort, the island's only accommodation, reopened late in 2009. Day-trippers can still get food and drinks at the bar and café located at the Beach Bar at the southern end of the island, and can hire water-sports gear from the adjacent Beach Hire Hut run by Raging Thunder. The old resort's dorm rooms have given way to a Cairns council-run campground, but it's not always open (⊕ www.cairns.qld.gov.au).

$–$$ 🏨 **Hunt (aka Fitzroy) Island Resort.** The extensively redeveloped reef retreat has brand-new accommodation in five categories and various configurations: sleekly outfitted hotel rooms, one- and two-bedroom apartments, beach suites, and a penthouse. All have a luxurious Balinese feel, with tropical ceiling fans, but are far from rustic, with thoroughly modern bathrooms, luxury appointments, and LCD TVs. They also have balconies from which to admire the ocean or garden views, and in all but the hotel rooms full kitchen and laundry facilities. The new resort complex has two eateries: a signature restaurant, Zephyr, serving buffet breakfasts, lunches, and à la carte dinners, and Hibiscus Café, open 9.30 AM to 4:30 PM. There are indoor and outdoor bars, a tour desk running island activities, and conference facilities upstairs in the impressive main building. A small boutique sells gift items and beach and resort wear, and there's a day spa and a dive shop. **Pros:** sleek new decor; high-end facilities; kids under 12 stay free. **Cons:** possible construction noise; activities may be limited initially. ⌂ *Hunt Island Resort, Box 3058, Cairns, QLD 4870* ☎ *07/4051–9588* ⊕ *www.fitzroyisland. com.au* ⇄ *48 apartments 1 penthouse* ⚒ *In-room: refrigerator, safe, kitchen (some). In-hotel: 2 restaurants, bars, pool, gym, tennis court, spa, diving, water sports, laundry facilities, no-smoking rooms* ⊟ *AE, DC, MC, V.*

LIZARD ISLAND

★ The small, upscale resort on secluded Lizard Island is the farthest north of any Barrier Reef hideaway. At 2,500 acres, it's larger than and quite different from other islands in the region. Composed mostly of granite, Lizard has a remarkable diversity of vegetation and terrain, where grassy hills give way to rocky slabs interspersed with valleys of rain forest.

Ringed by stretches of white-sand beaches, the island is actually a national park with some of the best examples of fringing coral of any of the resort areas. Excellent walking trails lead to key lookouts with spectacular views of the coast. The highest point, Cook's Look (1,180 feet), is the historic spot from which, in August 1770, Captain Cook finally spied a passage through the reef that had held him captive for a thousand miles. Large monitor lizards, for which the island is named, often bask in this area.

GETTING HERE AND AROUND
Lizard Island has its own small airstrip served by Hinterland Aviation. Flights to the island depart up to twice a day from Cairns, at 11 and 2, returning at 12:30 and 3:25; taking an hour and costing A$255 per person each way. Allow two hour's transit time for connecting international flights, one for domestic flight transits: check-in is 30 minutes prior to flight time. You can also arrange charter flights to the island.

ESSENTIALS
Plane Hinterland Aviation (☎ *1300/134044* ⊕ *www.voyages.com.au*).

EXPLORING
Fodor's Choice For divers and snorkelers, the crystal-clear waters off Lizard Island are ★ a dream. **Cod Hole,** 20 km (12 mi) from Lizard Island, ranks among the best dive sites on earth. Massive potato cod swim up to divers like hungry puppies—an awesome experience, considering these fish weigh 300 pounds and are around two meters (6 feet) long. The Island lures

big-game anglers from all over the world from September to December, when black marlin are running.

OUTDOOR ACTIVITIES

The lodge has catamarans, outboard dinghies, paddle-skis (including glass-bottomed ones), snorkeling gear and lessons, and fishing supplies. There is superb snorkeling around the island's fringing coral, or cruise over it on a glass-bottomed paddle-ski tour. Self-guided bushwalking trails and nature slide shows get guests in touch with the local flora and fauna. Arrange a picnic hamper with the kitchen staff, and you can take a rowboat or sailboat out for an afternoon on your own private beach. All these activities are included in your room rate.Contact the **Voyages Lizard Island Activities Desk**(☎ *1300/134044* ⊕ *www.lizardisland. com.au*) for details.

FISHING
★
Lizard Island is one of the big game-fishing centers in Australia, with several world records set here since the mid-1990s. Game fishing is generally best in spring and early summer, and giant black marlin weighing more than 1,000 pounds are no rarity. September through December, the folk from Voyages Lizard Island run full-day game-fishing trips to the outer reef on 51-foot Riviera Platinum Model Flybridge cruiser, *Fascination III*; the cost, including heavy tackle, lunch, and light refreshments for up to four people is A$2,950. January through August, the resort offers half-day bottom-fishing excursions on *Fascination III*, with bait, light tackle, and refreshments for up to four people, for A$1,800, and full-day trips for A$2,750.

SCUBA DIVING
The reefs around Lizard Island have some of the best marine life and coral on earth. The resort arranges supervised scuba-diving and snorkeling trips to the inner and outer reef, as well as local dives.

Half- or full-day dive-snorkel reef trips are A$155/A$210, plus A$80 for an optional dive or on the full-day trip, A$145 for two dives, and A$19/A$30 for dive gear. You can also book a private guided dive for A$250 (half day) or A$400 (full day). If you have a queasy stomach, take ginger or seasickness tablets before heading out to the reef, as crossings between dive sites in the exposed ocean can make for a bumpy ride.

There's good diving, day and night, just offshore: a guided local day dive is A$165; a night dive is A$175; or do both for A$210 (plus A$15 for gear). Guided day and twilight snorkeling tours are A$85. You can even dive right off the beach for A$95 by day, A$105 by night. Need scuba skills? The resort can organize PADI-accredited introductory, referral and refresher scuba diving courses on request.

WHERE TO STAY

$$$$ ▦ **Voyages Lizard Island.** One of Australia's premier resorts, this property has simply but stylishly appointed beachside suites and sumptuous villas with sail-shaded decks and views of the turquoise bay, as well as an elegant pavilion on the point. Simple but comfortable rooms with restful oceanic blue, sand, and white color schemes have polished wood floors and blinds, ceiling fans, CD players, and private verandas as well as fully-stocked minibars and bathrobes. Meals, included in the rate, change daily, with seafood and tropical fruit the focus: dinner here

might be coral trout with passion-fruit sauce. For an extra fee, the chef will design a five-course degustation dinner served on a secluded strip of sand. The food is high-quality, given the remote location, and the wine list is city-standard—though both food and wine could take some time to reach your table (attentive service is not a given: some staff appear to be on island time). Luckily, most folk come for the environs, and it is these—and the diving, snorkeling, or deep-sea fishing excursions you take offshore—that will probably prove the highlights of your stay. **Pros:** world-class location, superb diving and fishing; quality food and wine. **Cons:** service can be slow and offhand; meal portions small; lighting inadequate for reading. ⌨ *Voyages, GPO 5389, Sydney, NSW 2000* ☎ *02/8296–8010 bookings, 07/4043–1999 resort or 1300/134044* ⊕ *www.lizardisland.com.au* ⤳ *39 villas, 1 pavilion* ⌂ *In-room: safe, refrigerator, no TV, dial-up. In-hotel: restaurant, bar, tennis court, pool, gym, spa, beachfront, diving, water sports, laundry facilities, laundry service, public Internet (free), no kids under 15, no-smoking rooms* ☰ *AE, DC, MC, V* ⍭ *FAP.*

TOWNSVILLE AND MAGNETIC ISLAND

Townsville and its adjacent twin city of Thuringowa make up Australia's largest tropical city, with a combined population of around 160,000. It's the commercial capital of the north, and a major center for education, scientific research, and defense. Spread along the banks of Ross Creek and around the pink granite outcrop of Castle Hill, Townsville is a pleasant city of palm-fringed malls, historic colonial buildings, and lots of parkland and gardens. It's also the stepping-off point for Magnetic Island, one of the state's largest islands and a haven for wildlife.

GETTING HERE AND AROUND

Qantas flies frequently from Townsville Airport to Brisbane, Cairns, Cloncurry, Mt Isa, Mackay, and Hervey Bay, as well as to capital cities around Australia and overseas destinations. Jetstar has services to Brisbane, Sydney, and Melbourne; Virgin Blue connects Townsville with Cairns, Brisbane, the Gold Coast, Rockhampton, Sydney, and Canberra. There are no air connections to Magnetic Island; you need to take a ferry from Townsville. Townsville Taxis are available at the airport. The average cost of the ride to a city hotel is A$18, more after 7 PM.

Townsville is a flat, somewhat dull 1,400-km (868-mi) drive from Brisbane. The 370-km (230-mi) journey from Townsville to Cairns, with occasional Hinchinbrook Island views, is more scenic. Greyhound Australia coaches travel regularly to Cairns, Brisbane, and other destinations throughout Australia from the Sunferries Terminal on the Breakwater in Townsville.

Traveling to and from Townsville via rail is a low-stress, and scenic. The *Sunlander* plies the coast between Brisbane and Townsville three times weekly in each direction, taking approximately 24 hours. On the smooth, state-of-the-art *Tilt Train*, business-class passengers can watch individual TV screens, or plug laptops into seat-side sockets during less scenic segments of the journey. From Brisbane to Townsville it's A$269, business class. The *Inlander* connects Townsville with Mount Isa twice weekly (A$123.20 to A$280.28, one-way). Trains are operated by Queensland Rail.

Once in town, you can can flag Townsville Taxis on the street, find one at stands, hotels, and at the island's ferry terminal, or book one online.

TOURS

Coral Princess Cruises has regular three- and seven-night cruises that leave from Townsville, bound for Cairns and Lizard Island. The comfortable 46- and 50-passenger ship stops for snorkeling, diving, fishing, beach BBQs, and rain-forest hikes. Onboard marine biologists give lectures and lead excursions. Get dive gear or lessons on board. Prices start at A$1,496, twin-share (A$1,840, sole use) for a three-night, four-plus-dive live-aboard trip.

The Tropicana Guided Adventure Company runs expertly guided, small-group Magnetic Island expeditions to normally inaccessible bays and beaches in a converted, extra-long jeep. Bush-tucker adventures let you taste native foods; on other trips you get to meet and feed island wildlife. Day trips start from A$66 per person for a three-hour eco-orientation tour, departing daily at 11 from Nelly Bay (catch the 10:30 Sunferry from the mainland). A nine-hour sightseeing tour of Townsville and the island leaves daily at 9:30 AM from Townsville's Breakwater Ferry Terminal (A$235, including meals and admissions).

ESSENTIALS

Taxi Townsville Taxis (☎ 13–1008 ⊕ www.tsvtaxi.com.au).

Tours Coral Princess Cruises (✉ c/o Sunferries Terminal, Townsville ☎ 07/4040–9999 or 1800/079545 ⊕ www.coralprincess.com.au). **Tropicana Guided Adventure Company** (☎ 07/4758–1800 ⊕ www.tropicanatours.com.au).

Transportation Sunferries (☎ 07/4726–0800 ⊕ www.sunferries.com.au). **Queensland Rail** (☎ 07/3235–7322 or 1300–131722 ⊕ www.traveltrain.com.au).

Medical Emergencies Townsville Hospital (✉ 100 Angus Smith Dr., Douglas Townsville ☎ 07/4796–1111).

Police Townsville District Police HQ (✉ 134 Stanley St., Townsville ☎ 07/4579–9777 ⊕ www.townsville.qld.gov.au).

Visitor Information Townsville Enterprise Visitor Information Centres (✉ Flinders Mall, near Stanley St., Townsville ☎ 07/4721–3660 or 1800/801902 ⊕ www.townsvilleonline.com.au)

TOWNSVILLE

The Queensland Parks and Wildlife Service has an office on Magnetic Island, but Townsville Enterprise's Flinders Mall and Museum of Tropical Queensland (MTQ) information kiosks, on the mainland, are the best sources of visitor info about the island. The Mall kiosk is open weekdays 9–5, weekends 9–1.

EXPLORING

The summit of **Castle Hill**, 1 km (½ mi) from the city center, provides great views of the city as well as Magnetic Island. While you're perched on top, think about the proud local resident who, along with several scout troops, spent years in the 1970s piling rubble onto the peak to try to add the 23 feet that would officially make it Castle Mountain. (Technically speaking, a rise has to exceed 1,000 feet to be called a mountain, and this one tops out at just 977 feet.) Most people walk to the top, along a steep walking track that doubles as one of Queensland's most scenic jogging routes.

A stroll along **Flinders Street** will show you some of Townsville's turn-of-the-20th-century colonial architecture. **Magnetic House** and other buildings have been beautifully restored. The old **Queens Hotel** is built in Classical Revival style, as is the 1885 **Perc Tucker Regional Gallery**, originally a bank. The former post office, now **the Brewery**, had an impressive **masonry clock tower** when it was erected in 1889. The tower was dismantled in 1942 so it wouldn't be a target during World War II air raids, but was put up again in 1964. The Exchange, Townsville's oldest pub, was built in 1869, burned down in 1881, and was rebuilt the following year.

Ⓒ The **Museum of Tropical Queensland** displays relics of the HMS *Pandora,* which sank in 1791 carrying 14 crew members of the infamous ship *Bounty.* There's a fun introduction to North Queensland's culture and lifestyle; a shipwreck exhibit, and the fresh, ecology-focused Enchanted Rainforest. Also on display are tropical wildlife, dinosaur fossils, local corals, and deep-sea creatures. ⊠ *70–102 Flinders St. E 4810* ☎ *07/4726–0600* ⊕ *www.mtq.qm.qld.gov.au* ⊠ *A$13.50* ⊙ *Daily 9:30–5.*

Ⓒ **Queen's Gardens** is a lovely place to spend a cool couple of hours. The compact four-hectare (10-acre) park is bordered with frangipani and towering Moreton Bay fig trees, whose unique hanging roots veil the entry to the grounds. Don't miss the aviary, housing peacocks, lorikeets, and sulphur-crested cockatoos. ⊠ *Gregory St. near Warburton St. (enter off Paxton St.)* ☎ *07/4727–8330* ⊠ *Free* ⊙ *Daily dawn–dusk.*

★ **Reef HQ Aquarium,** on the waterfront, a few minutes' walk from the city
Ⓒ center, casino, and ferry terminal, houses the world's largest live coral-reef aquarium, containing more than 100 species of hard coral, 30 soft corals, and hundreds of fish, sea star, urchin, and sponge species: open to the elements, it's a living slice of the Great Barrier Reef (the behind-scenes tour is fascinating). There's a 20-meter (65-foot) Perspex underwater walkway, a predator tank teeming with sharks, rays, turtles, and large pelagic fish, several daily talks and tours, and a theater, café, and shop. ⊠ *2–68 Flinders St. E 4810* ☎ *07/4750–0800* ⊕ *www.reefhq.com. au* ⊠ *A$24.75* ⊙ *Daily 9:30–5.*

★ **Townsville Town Common Conservation Park** (☎ *07/4722–5224* ⊕ *www.epa.*
Ⓒ *qld..gov.au*) is home to a huge variety of birdlife, including spoonbills, jabiru storks, pied geese, herons, and ibis, and occasional wallabies, goannas, echidnas, and dingoes. Most birds leave the wetlands in dry season, May–August, but they're back by October. The park is open

Townsville's main beach features calm surf and jellyfish-free enclosures.

daily 6:30 AM–6:30 PM; entry is free. Take Cape Pallarenda Road north to Pallarenda, 6 km (4 mi) from Townsville. Most walking tracks begin from the Bald Rock carpark, 7 km (4½ mi) from the park entrance.

OUTDOOR ACTIVITIES

BEACHES Townsville is blessed with a golden, 2-km (1-mi) beach that stretches along its northern edge. Four man-made headlands jut into the sea, and a long pier is just the spot for fishing. There is no surf, as the beach is sheltered by the reef and Magnetic Island. The Strand's permanent swimming enclosure, known as the Rock Pool (closed Thursday), is fitted with temporary nets during box-jellyfish season, November–May. Townsville's beaches and waterfront pools are patrolled by lifeguards year-round on weekdays, as well as weekends in summer and Australian school holidays. The surrounding area has picnic facilities, barbecues, toilets, formal gardens, and gazebos. ☎ 07/4727–9000 ⊕ www.townsville.qld.gov.au/recreation.

BOATING **Magnetic Island Sea Kayaks** (✉ Horseshoe Bay Rd., Horseshoe Bay ☎ 07/4778–5424 ⊕ www.seakayak.com.au) organizes kayak trips to the quieter bays of Magnetic Island. The 4½-hour morning tour includes a tropical breakfast and costs A$69 per person in double kayaks, A$125 for single person kayaks; the 2½-hour seasonal sunset tour is A$45 per person.

SCUBA DIVING Surrounded by tropical islands and warm waters, Townsville is a top-notch diving center. Diving courses and excursions tend to be less crowded than those in the hot spots of Cairns or the Whitsunday Islands.

The wreck of the SS *Yongala*, a steamship that sank just south of Townsville in 1911, lies in 99 feet of water about 16 km (10 mi) offshore,

60 km (37 mi) from Townsville. It teems with marine life and is one of Australia's best dive sites. It can be approached as a one- or two-day trip. All local dive operators conduct excursions to the wreck.

Adrenalin Dive (⊠ *252 Walker St.* ☎ *07/4724–0600 or 1300/664600* ⊕ *www.adrenalindive.com.au*) has day trips to a number of popular sites in the region, including the wreck of the *Yongala*. From A$185 for a day trip with two dives, plus A$40 for gear and a A$25 fuel and environmental levy. A three-day, three night liveaboard Eco-dive trip including up to 10 dives (with two night dives) is A$630 for divers, A$595 for snorkelers; gear hire is an extra A$95.

WILDLIFE WATCHING

☾

Billabong Sanctuary. This 22-acre nature park 17 km (11 mi) south of Townsville shelters crocodiles, koalas, wombats, dingoes, wallabies, and birds—including cassowaries, kookaburras, and red-tailed black cockatoos. Educational shows throughout the day give you the chance to learn more about the native fauna. There's a café and a swimming pool on-site. The sanctuary, a 20-minute drive south of Townsville, is well signposted. ⊠ *Bruce Hwy., Nome* ☎ *07/4778–8344* ⊕ *www. billabongsanctuary.com.au* ⊠ *A$28* ☉ *Daily 8–5.*

WHERE TO EAT

$$ AUSTRALIAN

✗ **The Australian Hotel.** This restored 1888 building, with its beautiful bull-nose veranda and original iron lacework, is a classic example of Townsville colonial architecture. Rumor has it that back when it was a hotel actor Errol Flynn once stayed here and paid for his keep by selling autographs. Today the building houses a restaurant serving everything from gourmet pizzas to "reef and beef" specialties with an upmarket spin. ⊠ *11–13 Palmer St. 4810* ☎ *07/4722–6999* ⊕ *www.australian-hotel.com.au* ⊟ *AE, DC, MC, V.*

$$ CONTEMPORARY AUSTRALIAN

☾

★

✗ **Table 51.** This casually chic eatery specializes in fresh contemporary Australian food that makes the most of fine seasonal, regional produce. Your entrée might be a coconut Moreton Bay bug salad, seafood chowder, or kangaroo medallions; follow with a delectable honey duck, Moroccan lamb, Creole-spiced salmon, the day's fresh catch, or tender eye fillet. There are good vegetarian options, a kids' menu, and a varied lunch menu. Desserts are worth the calories: indulge in the macadamia-encrusted pavlova with wattleseed cream, mango coulis, and vanilla-bean ice cream. ⊠ *51 Palmer St.* ☎ *07/4721–0642* ⊕ *www.table51.com. au* ☉ *No lunch weekends, closed Sun.* ⊿ *Reservations preferred* ⊟ *AE, DC, MC, V.*

WHERE TO STAY

¢–$ ★

🛏 **Yongala Lodge by the Strand.** This late-19th-century lodge was originally the home of building magnate Matthew Rooney, whose family was shipwrecked off the Townsville coast on the SS *Yongala* in 1911. Public areas retain much of their 1880s and 1920s decor: original wrought-iron ceiling fittings are complemented by old photographs and antiques. There are also simple, motel-style rooms, some with heritage decor, and modern one- and two-bedroom apartments. Chef-owner Rob Flecker ($–$$) turns fresh regional produce into cut-above modern Mediterranean-inspired dishes: dine in the historic Queenslander dining room, or outside on the wide, colonial-style veranda. **Pros:** historic environs, top-notch food; genteel, welcoming ambience; Austar cable TV. **Cons:** few in-room modern conveniences; slow Internet; Yongala Lodge Restaurant closed Sunday. ⊠ *11 Fryer St.* ☎ *07/4772–4633* ⊕ *www.historicyongala.com.au* ⤳ *10 rooms, 10 apartments* ⚘ *In-room: kitchen (some), refrigerator, VCR, dial-up. In-hotel: restaurant, room service, bar, pool, beachfront, laundry facilities, parking (no fee), no elevator* ▭ *AE, DC, MC, V.*

🖭 **Hotel M Townsville.** This ultramodern, 11-story establishment in Townsville's Palmer Street dining precinct is handy to cafés and restaurants, bars, and Jupiters Casino. Space-agey, somewhat soulless but impressively functional self-contained studio rooms and suites have LCD TVs, free Austar cable, wireless Internet access, and desks. They're long and narrow, but cleverly configured, with laundries and compact kitchens concealed along one wall. All guest rooms have balconies overlooking the action, and there's a small on-site gym and outdoor pool, as well as free on-site parking. The complex includes the historic Metropole Hotel, which houses conference rooms and dining facilities. **Pros:** great Value, everything new, modern facilities. **Cons:** feels a tad clinical, service isn't outstanding. ⊠ *81 Palmer St., Townsville* ☎ *1800/760–144* ⊕ *www.theoaksgroup.com.au* ⤳ *104 rooms* ⚘ *In-room: safe, Internet (some). In-hotel: pool, gym, laundry facilities, laundry service, Internet terminal, Wi-Fi, parking (fee), no kids under 18* ▭ *AE, DC, MC, V.*

NIGHTLIFE

The Brewery (⊠ *Flinders Mall, 252 Flinders St.,* ☎ *07/4724–2999* ⊕ *www.townsvillebrewery.com.au*), once the Townsville Post Office, now houses a bar serving light meals, an award-winning microbrewery, a sports bar and a chill-out lounge, and has DJs on weekends. The owners have done a fine job combining ultramodern finishes with the original design, incorporating old post office fittings, such as the bar—once the stamp counter. **Monsoons Bar & Grill** (⊠ *194 Flinders St. E* ☎ *07/4772–0900* ⊕ *www.monsoons.com.au*), a smart riverfront establishment on Flinders Street's dining and entertainment strip, draws a mixed, convivial crowd. Billiard tables, arcade games, plasma TVs screening sports matches, and live acoustic entertainment on weekends ensure that everyone's entertained. If it's fine, drink and dine on the deck overlooking the Ross River. It's open noon till midnight weekdays, until 2 AM weekends, and is closed Mondays.

MAGNETIC ISLAND

More than half of Magnetic Island's 52 square km (20 square mi) is national parkland, laced with miles of walking trails and rising to a height of 1,640 feet on Mt. Cook. The terrain is punctuated with huge granite boulders and softened by tall hoop pines, eucalyptus forest, and rain-forest gullies. A haven for wildlife, the island shelters rock wallabies, echidnas, frogs, fruit bats, nonvenomous green tree snakes, and Northern Australia's largest population of wild koalas. Its beaches, mangroves, sea-grass beds, and fringing reefs support turtle nesting, fish hatching, and a significant dugong population. You can escape to 23 beaches and dive nine offshore shipwrecks.

Bigeye trevally (*Caranx Sexfasciatus*), a type of jack, can form schools of up to 1500 fish during the day. At night, these schools break up and individuals or small groups hunt sea-borne insects, crustacians, jellyfish, and smaller species of fish.

The 2,500-plus residents, who fondly call their island "Maggie," mostly live on the eastern shore at Picnic Bay, Arcadia, Nelly Bay, and Horse-shoe Bay. Many locals are artists and craftspeople, and there are numerous studios and galleries around the island.

GETTING HERE AND AROUND
The 40-minute Fantasea Cruising Magnetic runs several departures daily, between 5:20 AM and 6:05 PM, from the mainland to Nelly Bay on Magnetic Island, 10 km (6 mi) offshore. Round-trip fares are A$160 for a vehicle with up to six people, or A$25 per person, return trip, for those without a vehicle. Sunferries has 25-minute catamaran service daily between Townsville and Nelly Bay on Magnetic Island. Bus and island transfers meet the ferry during daylight hours. There are up to 18 departures daily between 5:35 AM (6:30 Sun.) and 12:30 AM (1 AM Fri. and Sat.); a round-trip ticket costs A$29. Get an overview of Magnetic Island riding the **Magnetic Island Bus Service.** An unlimited day pass, allowing travel to different points on the island and enabling you to return to places you like, is available from the driver for A$12. A three-hour driver-guided tour, including morning or afternoon tea, is A$40. Reservations are essential; tours depart daily at 9 and 1 from Nelly Bay jetty.

The tiny Mini Moke, a soft-top convertible version of the Minor Mini car, provides an ideal means of exploring Magnetic Island. **Moke Magnetic,** diagonally opposite the Magnetic Island ferry terminal, rents Mini Mokes for A$73 a day, including fuel (60-km [35-mi] worth free); driver's license required.

Motorbikes or scooters are a cheap and easy way to get around. **Road Runner Scooter Hire** rents trail bikes for A$60 per day, scooters from A$35, and new, dual-seat scooters from A$50 (9 AM–5 PM). The cost includes helmets and unlimited mileage; you top up the gas yourself.

ESSENTIALS
Transportation Fantasea Cruising Magnetic (☎ 07/4772–5422 ⊕ www.magneticislandferry.com.au). **Magnetic Island Bus Service**(☎ 07/4778–5130 ⊕ www.magnetic-island.com.au). **Moke Magnetic** (✉ 112 Sooning St., Nelly Bay ☎ 07/4778–5377 ⊕ www.mokemagnetic.com). **Road Runner Scooter Hire** (✉ 3/64 Kelly St., Nelly Bay ☎ 07/4778–5222).

Visitor Information Queensland Parks and Wildlife Service, Magnetic Island (✉ 22 Hurst St., Picnic Bay ☎ 07/4778–5378 ⊕ www.epa.qld.gov.au).

OUTDOOR ACTIVITIES
The island has 24 km (15 mi) of hiking trails, most of which are relatively easy. The popular Forts Walk leads to World War II gun emplacements overlooking Horseshoe and Florence bays. At a leisurely pace it takes 45 minutes each way from the Horseshoe–Radical Bay Road. Look up en route, and you may spot a sleepy koala.

The best views are on the 5-km (3-mi) Nelly Bay to Arcadia Walk. Look out for shell middens created over thousands of years by the island's Aboriginal owners, the Wulgurukaba, or "Canoe People."

Swimming and snorkeling are other popular activities, but from November to May stingers are a hazard: swim at Picnic and Horseshoe bays, which have stinger nets, and wear a protective suit. At other times, Alma Bay and Nelly Bay, as well as Picnic, Florence, Radical, Horseshoe, and Balding bays, are all suitable for swimming. Horseshoe has daily lifeguards; Alma and Picnic bays are patrolled over weekends and school holidays from September to May.

Geoffrey Bay has a well-marked snorkel trail, and free, self-guiding trail cards identifying local corals and sea life are available at the information center adjacent to the Picnic Bay Jetty. Other good snorkeling spots include Nelly Bay, and the northern ends of Florence and Arthur bays. Near the northeastern corner of the island, Radical Bay has a small, idyllic beach surrounded by tree-covered rock outcrops. Horseshoe Bay has the largest beach, with boat rentals.

HORSEBACK RIDING
☼
★
With **Horseshoe Bay Ranch,** you can take a two-hour bush-and-beach ride with the chance to take the horses swimming (A$100), daily at 9 and 3. Half-day rides are also offered (A$130). ⊠ *38 Gifford St., Horseshoe Bay* ☎ *07/4778–5109* ⊕ *www.horseshoebayranch.com.au.*

SNORKELING AND SCUBA DIVING
Pleasure Divers (⊠ *10 Marine Parade, Arcadia* ☎ *07/4778–5788 or 1800/624634* ⊕ *www.pleasuredivers.com.au*) rents snorkeling and diving gear (including marine-stinger-proof suits), and runs trips to various sites off Magnetic Island. The company also runs dive trips to the wreck of the SS *Yongala* and sites on the outer Barrier Reef: a full-day trip to pristine Wheeler Reef is A$170 for snorkelers, A$210 for divers, with optional introductory dive (A$80) and gear (A$40), runs four days a week from Nelly Bay Ferry Terminal and Townsville. You can also do a great-value four-day PADI Open Water dive course package for A$329 per person: the package includes training, dives, four nights' lodging at Magnums on Magnetic, and dinners.

TOAD RACES
One of the more unusual evening activities on Magnetic Island is the weekly toad racing at backpacker resort **Magnums on Magnetic** (⊠ *7 Marine Parade, Arcadia* ☎ *07/4778–5177 or 1800/663666*). Held at 8 PM every Wednesday night for more than two decades, the event raises funds for local charities. The crowd is generally a mix of tourists and locals. After the race, the winner kisses his or her toad and collects the proceeds.

WATER SPORTS
Adrenalin Jet Ski Tours (⊠ *46 Gifford St., Horseshoe Bay* ☎ *07/4778–5533 or 0407/785538*) provides three-hour guided, self-drive tours around Magnetic Island on Jet Skis, as well as a 75-minute "Top End" Jet Ski tour, with up to two people on each ski.

Horseshoe Bay Watersports (⊠ *Boat ramp, Horseshoe Bay* ☎ *07/4758–1336* ⊕ *www.sailonhorseshoe.com.au/activities*) can take you parasailing, tube riding, wakeboarding, waterskiing, and parasailing, and has a variety of water-sports equipment—cats, windsurfers, kayaks, surfskis, and paddleboats—for rent on weekends.

WHERE TO STAY

Magnetic Island began "life" as a holiday-home getaway for Townsville residents, and has only recently attracted the kind of large-scale development that has transformed other islands near the Barrier Reef. Accommodations here are a mix of functional 1970s properties; small budget lodges; and newer, upmarket but relatively small apartment

MIGALOO THE ALBINO WHALE

Migaloo, the world's only documented white humpback whale, was first spotted in 1991 as he made his way up the Queensland coastline. The albino humpback was named on the suggestion of an indigenous elder, who recommended he be dubbed Migaloo, an Aboriginal word for "white fella."

Every year thousands eagerly watch for a glimpse of Migaloo's distinctive pure-white dorsal fin, as the 14-meter (46-foot) humpback makes his annual migration from the Antarctic to tropical waters in June and July. He's been spotted all the way up Australia's east coast as far as Port Douglas, north of Cairns—usually from the decks of dive and cruise boats. Sometimes Migaloo travels alone; on other journeys he's accompanied by dolphins or fellow humpbacks.

Migaloo's not the only albino marine creature you might spot on your visit to Queensland: in early 2006 a tiny white sea turtle was found on Blacks Beach, Mackay, and shipped off to Reef HQ in nearby Townsville for rehab. Today he's doing well and has more than doubled in size.

Keen to know where Migaloo's heading? Go to the Pacific Whale Foundation's dedicated Web site, ⊕ www.migaloo.org, where whale-spotters document the migratory movements of this unique cetacean. To help to protect Migaloo and his mates, make a donation via the PWF's Adopt-A-Whale program.

complexes and resorts. Luxurious Peppers Blue Resort, opened in 2007, is the exception to the rule.

★ **Bungalow Bay Koala Village.** Set in 6.5 hectares (16 acres) of bushland, this eco-accredited YHA hostel has the air of a secluded campground. Freestanding A-frame bungalows, some configured as dorms, are fan-cooled and simply appointed, and there are a few suites in the original 1930s building. A lovely pool has hammocks slung around it; wildlife roams the grounds. Service here is low-key but friendly, and there's a terrific bar and restaurant (¢–$): try the fish curry. The on-site Internet café has Skype, CD burners, fast Internet, and five computer terminals. Movie nights, coconut bowling, fire-twirling, and more keep guests entertained after dark. By day, two-hour wildlife tours, with koala cuddling (A$19), thrice-weekly champagne bush-tucker breakfasts with the local fauna (bring an appetite), walking, cycling, and snorkeling are on the agenda. **Pros:** wildlife; good food and Internet access, 24-hour ATM. **Cons:** can be chilly in winter; rooms basic; deposit for cutlery. ✉ 40 Horseshoe Bay Rd., Horseshoe Bay ☎ 07/4778–5577 or 1800/285577 ⊕ www.bungalowbay.com.au ➹ 30 bungalows and suites ⌂ In-room: refrigerator, no TV, no air-conditioning (some). In-hotel: restaurant, bar, pool, bicycles, car hire, tour desk, laundry facilities, public Ethernet (fee), parking (no fee), no-smoking room, no kids under 18 ☰ MC, V.

$$$–$$$$ **Peppers Blue On Blue Resort.** This five-star waterfront resort adjacent to ℭ Nelly Bay Ferry Terminal overlooks the island's private marina. Ultra-modern dual-key guest rooms and two- and three-bedroom suites have chic decor, fabulous deep baths, high-end entertainment systems, and

7

luxury appointments. Suites have full kitchen and laundry facilities, and all rooms have balconies with water, pool, and marina views. The Boardwalk Restaurant & Bar ($$) has full-frontal bay views and a modern Australian menu: dinners are worthwhile, though the buffet breakfasts (A$30) are disappointing. Tropical landscaping, two free-form lagoon pools, the larger of which bisects the resort, and a marina-front boardwalk encourage guests to get outside. Shops, restaurants, cafés, water-sports outlets, and an IGA supermarket are a pleasant stroll away. **Pros:** well-appointed rooms; lovely Endota day spa; terrific pool. **Cons:** service variable; breakfast buffet lackluster; marina-front rooms can be noisy. ⊠ *123 Sooning St., Nelly Bay* ☎ *07/4758–2400* ⊕ *www. peppers.com.au/Blue-On-Blue* ⤴ *60 dual-key (twin) rooms, 127 suites* ⚲ *In-room: room service, kitchen (some), refrigerator, DVD, dial-up, Wi-Fi. In-hotel: restaurant, bar, pool, spa, gym, beachfront, laundry service, executive floor, public Wi-Fi, concierge, tour desk, parking (fee), no-smoking rooms, no elevator* ⊟ *AE, DC, MC, V.*

$$–$$$ ⛱ **Sails on Horseshoe.** As the name suggests, this modern complex is located at Horseshoe Bay, the biggest of Magnetic Island's 23 beaches. It's also the farthest from the ferry terminal—but on Maggie, that's not far. The one-bedroom beachside studio apartments, two-bedroom villas (one disabled-friendly), and town houses have pastel color schemes and worn-in, tropically-themed soft furnishings, older-style but fully equipped kitchens and laundries, and lounge areas with TVs and DVD/VCR players. The low-rise units are set around a palm-shaded pool with a hot tub and barbecue area. **Pros:** good location; lovely grounds. **Cons:** dated furnishings and TV; housekeeping erratic. ⊠ *13–15 Pacific Dr., Horseshoe Bay* ☎ *07/4778–5117* ⊕ *www.sailsonhorseshoe.com.au* ⤴ *2 studios, 2 villas, 10 apartments* ⚲ *In-room: kitchen, DVD, VCR, dial-up, Wi-Fi. In-hotel: pool, beachfront, laundry facilities, parking (no fee), no-smoking rooms, no elevator* ⊟ *MC, V.*

Adelaide and
South Australia

WORD OF MOUTH

"If you're only allowing one day for Kangaroo Island, do a tour. If you have 2 days or more, rent a car and do it yourself. It's all off the beaten track; few Australians have been."

—margo_oz

WELCOME TO ADELAIDE & SOUTH AUSTRALIA

TOP REASONS TO GO

★ **Arts and Music:** South Australia has fantastic festivals, from the Adelaide Festival of Arts, the internationally acclaimed Come Out festival, and the annual WOMADelaide celebration of world music.

★ **Bush Tucker:** The Australian palate has been re-educated in the pleasures of bush tucker—food that has been used for millennia by the Aboriginal people. Kangaroo, crocodile, emu, and other regional fare are now embraced by all.

★ **Historic Homes:** There are historic properties in both North Adelaide and in the Adelaide Hills, which have the best of both worlds: easy access to the city as well as to countryside vineyards and rustic villages.

★ **Wonderful Wines:** South Australia is considered Australia's premier wine state, and the top-notch wines of the Barossa Region, Clare Valley, McLaren Vale, Adelaide Hills, and Coonawarra are treasured by connoisseurs.

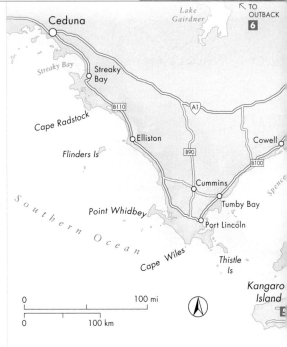

1 **Adelaide.** Heritage buildings line the small but perfectly formed center of South Australia's capital city. A diverse range of attractions, eateries, and bars makes the city a livelier option than its reputation would suggest.

2 **The Barossa Region.** One of the country's best-known wine regions—expect rolling hills, delicious local produce, and some of the best Shiraz in the world.

3 **The Clare Valley.** Less visited than the Barossa. Riesling fans should meander through the valley, tasting as they go while enjoying some spectacular views of the Flinders Ranges.

4 **Fleurieu Peninsula.** Wine buffs on a short time frame shouldn't miss beautiful McLaren Vale and its amenable cellar doors, while beautiful beaches and dramatic cliff walks are only a short drive away.

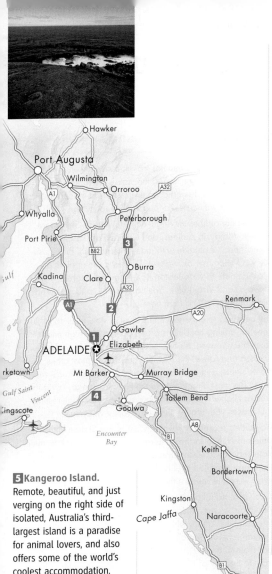

GETTING ORIENTED

South Australia encompasses both the dry hot north of the Outback and the greener, more-temperate south coast. The green belt includes Adelaide and its surrounding hills and orchards, the Barossa and Clare Valley vineyards, the beautiful Fleurieu Peninsula, and the cliffs and lagoons of the mighty Murray, Australia's longest river. Offshore, residents of Kangaroo Island live at a delightfully old-fashioned pace, savoring their domestic nature haven.

8

5 Kangeroo Island. Remote, beautiful, and just verging on the right side of isolated, Australia's third-largest island is a paradise for animal lovers, and also offers some of the world's coolest accommodation.

6 The Outback. Heading south, a trip to South Australia's Outback gives visitors a glimpse into an arid and dramatic landscape that is unmistakably Australian.

ADELAIDE AND SOUTH AUSTRALIA PLANNER

When to Go

Adelaide has the least rainfall of all Australian capital cities, and the midday summer heat is oppressive. The Outback in particular is too hot for comfortable touring during this time, but Outback winters are pleasantly warm. South Australia's national parks are open year-round. The best times to visit are in spring and autumn. In summer extreme fire danger may close walking tracks, and in winter heavy rain can make some roads impassable. Boating on the Murray River and Lake Alexandrina is best from October to March, when the long evenings are bathed in soft light. The ocean is warmest from December to March.

Health and Safety

In an emergency, dial 000 to reach an ambulance, the police, or the fire department. Adelaide has the majority of the state's hospitals, though healthcare throughout the region is excellent. Summer 2009 saw temperatures of 43 degrees in Adelaide and even higher in the Outback, so be wary of sun stroke and dehydration.

Getting Here and Around

Adelaide Airport, 15 minutes from the city center, is a pleasant place to fly into and the state's main hub. The international and domestic terminals share a modern building complete with cafés, a tourist office, and free Wi-Fi.

International airlines serving Adelaide include Singapore Airlines, Malaysia Airlines, and Cathay Pacific. Qantas also connects Adelaide with many international cities (usually via Melbourne or Sydney). Domestic airlines flying into Adelaide include Jetstar, REX/Regional Express, Tiger Airways, and Virgin Blue. You can also fly to Coober Pedy and Kangaroo Island from here.

The best way to experience this diverse state is by road. In general, driving conditions are excellent, although minor lanes are unpaved. It's two hours from Adelaide to the Barossa and Clare, the southern coast, and most other major sights, and less than an hour to McLaren Vale's wineries. The most direct route to the Flinders Ranges is via the Princes Highway and Port Augusta, but a more interesting route takes you through the Clare Valley vineyards.

Adelaide's recently renovated Central Bus Station is the state's main hub for travel across the region as well as interstate services to Melbourne and Sydney. It's difficult and time-consuming to travel by bus to the wine regions, however; we recommend either renting a car or taking a tour.

If you love train travel, you might find yourself stopping in Adelaide, as two classic train journeys also wind through this state: the *Ghan,* which runs north via Alice Springs to Darwin, and the *Indian Pacific,* which crosses the Nullarbor Plain to reach Perth. More prosaically, you can catch a train to Sydney or Melbourne, though often budget airlines are much cheaper.

About the Restaraunts

Foodies are spoiled for choice in south Australia; the region famous throughout the country for its excellent produce. Make sure you try some of Adelaide's Mod-Oz cuisine, with dishes showcasing oysters, crayfish, and King George whiting prepared with Asian and Mediterranean flavors. Bush foods are also available in some eateries; look for kangaroo, emu, and wattle seed.

Many restaurants close for a few days a week, so call ahead to check. Some upscale institutions require booking well in advance, and tables are tight during major city festivals and holidays.

About the Hotels

As well as all the standard chains, South Australia is packed with delightful lodgings in contemporary studios, converted cottages, and grand mansions. Modern resorts sprawl along the coastal suburbs, the Barossa Valley, and other tourist centers, but intimate properties for 10 or fewer guests can easily be found

There is plenty of competition in Adelaide, so shop around for great deals. Outside the city, weekday nights are usually less expensive and two-night minimum bookings often apply.

DINING AND LODGING PRICE CATEGORIES (IN AUSTRALIAN DOLLARS)

	¢	$	$$	$$$	$$$$
Restaurants	under A$10	A$10–A$20	A$21–A$35	A$36–A$50	over A$50
Hotels	under A$100	A$100–A$150	A$151–A$200	A$201–A$300	over A$300

Restaurant prices are based on the median main course price at dinner. Hotel prices are for two people in a standard double room in high season, excluding service and tax.

Winning Wineries

Oenophiles rejoice. in South Australia you've arrived in wine heaven. SA is the country's wine powerhouse, producing most of the nation's wine and boasting some of the oldest vineyards in the world. Thanks to its diverse geography and climate, the region produces a huge range of grape varieties—from cool-climate Rieslings in the Clare Valley to the big, full bodied Shiraz wines of the world-famous Barossa. Less well known, McLaren Vale now punches above its weight with an exceptional variety of grapes, including Merlot, Chardonnay, and Cabernet Sauvignon, while just 20 minutes' drive from Adelaide is Adelaide Hills, where temperatures are lower than the rest of the region, leading to great sparkling wines and Pinot Noir.

While you can drive yourself to any of these regions, strict drunk driving laws mean that the unfortunate designated driver will be restricted to a few sips, if that. We highly recommend that you leave the driving to professionals. The most luxurious option is to go with Mary Anne Kennedy, the owner of A Taste of South Australia, who is one of the most knowledgeable regional food and wine guides. Her private tours of any region you choose (A$398 and up, min. 2 people) are a taste treat.

A Taste of South Australia (☎ 08/8271–7777 📠 0419/861588 ⊕ www.tastesa.com.au).

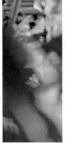

Updated by
Helena Iveson

Renowned for its celebrations of the arts, its multiple cultures, and its bountiful harvests from vines, land, and sea, South Australia is both diverse and divine. Here you can taste some of the country's finest wines, sample its best restaurants, and admire some of the world's most valuable gems. Or skip the state's sophisticated options and unwind on wildlife-rich Kangaroo Island, hike in the Flinders Ranges, or live underground like opal miners in the vast Outback.

Spread across a flat saucer of land between the Mt. Lofty ranges and the sea, the capital city of Adelaide is easy to explore. The wide streets of its 1½-square-km (½-square-mi) city center are organized in a simple grid that's ringed with parklands. The plan was laid out in 1836 by William Light, the colony's first surveyor-general, making Adelaide the only early-Australian capital not built by English convict labor. Today Light's plan is recognized as being far ahead of its time. This city of 1.1 million still moves at a leisurely pace, free of the typical urban menace of traffic jams thanks to Light's insistence that all roads be wide enough to turn a cannon.

Nearly 90% of South Australians live in the fertile south around Adelaide, because the region stands on the very doorstep of the harshest, driest land in the most arid of Earth's populated continents. Jagged hills and stony deserts fill the parched interior, which is virtually unchanged since the first settlers arrived. Desolate terrain and temperatures that top 48°C (118°F) have thwarted all but the most determined efforts to conquer the land. People who survive this region's challenges do so only through drastic measures, such as in the far-northern opal-mining town of Coober Pedy, where residents live underground.

Still, the deserts hold great surprises, and many clues to the country's history before European settlement. The ruggedly beautiful Flinders Ranges north of Adelaide hold Aboriginal cave paintings and fossil remains from when the area was an ancient seabed. Lake Eyre, a great salt lake, filled with water in the year 2000 for only the fourth time in its recorded

GREAT ITINERARIES

Many of the state's attractions are an easy drive from Adelaide. However, for a taste of the real South Australia a trip to a national park or to the Outback is definitely worth the extra travel time. Short flights between destinations make any journey possible within a day or overnight, but the more time you leave yourself to explore the virtues of this underrated state, the better.

IF YOU HAVE 3 DAYS

Spend a leisurely day in **Adelaide** enjoying the museums and historic sights, as well as the bustling Central Market. Take a sunset stroll along the Torrens, then have dinner and drinks at one of the city's vibrant restaurants or wine bars. Spend the night, then on Day 2 tour the **Adelaide Hills,** strolling the streets of 19th-century villages and taking in the panorama from atop **Mt. Lofty.** Stay the night in a charming bed-and-breakfast in one of the region's small towns, or come back down to North Adelaide and rest among the beautiful sandstone homes. Save Day 3 for wine tasting in the **Barossa Region.**

IF YOU HAVE 5 DAYS

After exploring Adelaide for a day, expand your horizons beyond the city and take a tram-car ride to the beach at touristy Glenelg or its posher neighbors Brighton or Henley Beach, where you can laze on the white sands and dine at tasty outposts. Spend the night here or at a B&B on the **Fleurieu Peninsula,** then take Day 3 to explore the vineyards and catch the ferry to **Kangaroo Island.** After a night here, use Day 4 to explore and appreciate the island's wildlife and untamed beauty. Return to Adelaide

in the afternoon on Day 5 and drive up to the **Adelaide Hills** for sunset at **Mt. Lofty.**

IF YOU HAVE 7 DAYS

Spend Day 1 in **Adelaide** nosing through museums and picnicking in a park or on the bank of the River Torrens. After a night in the city, head into the leafy **Adelaide Hills** to meet nocturnal Australian wildlife at Cleland Wildlife Sanctuary. Stay the night in a local B&B, then on Day 3 travel to the **Barossa Region,** where German and English influences are strong and the dozens of wineries offer tempting free tastings. Spend the evening at a country house, then on Day 4 cross to **Kangaroo Island.** Stay two nights, giving you Day 5 to fully explore the island's remote corners and unwind. On Day 6, plunge into the Outback at extraordinary **Coober Pedy** (consider flying to maximize your time). There you can eat, shop, and stay the night underground as the locals do and "noodle" (rummage) for opal gemstones.

If you're a hiker, consider heading for **Flinders Ranges National Park** on Day 7 to explore one of the country's finest Outback parks.

history. The Nullarbor ("treeless") Plain stretches west across state lines in its tirelessly flat, ruthlessly arid march into Western Australia.

Yet South Australia is, perhaps ironically, gifted with the good life. It produces most of the nation's wine, and the sea ensures a plentiful supply of lobster and famed King George whiting. Cottages and guesthouses tucked away in the countryside around Adelaide are among the most charming and relaxing in Australia. Farther afield, unique experiences like watching seal pups cuddle with their mothers on Kangaroo Island would warm any heart. South Australia may not be grand in reputation, but its attractions are extraordinary, and after a visit you'll know you've indulged in one of Australia's best-kept secrets.

ADELAIDE

Australians think of Adelaide as a city of churches, but Adelaide has outgrown its reputation as a sleepy country town dotted with cathedrals and spires. The Adelaide of this millennium is infinitely more complex, with a large, multiethnic population and thriving urban art and music scenes.

Bright and clean, leafy and beautiful Adelaide is a breeze to explore, with a grid pattern of streets encircled by parkland. The heart of the greenbelt is divided by the meandering River Torrens, which passes the Festival Centre in its prettiest stretch.

GETTING HERE AND AROUND

A car gives you the freedom to discover the country lanes and villages in the hills region outside the city, and Adelaide also has excellent road connections with other states. But South Australia is a big place, and we recommend flying if you're looking to save time. Adelaide has an excellent bus system, including the no-cost Adelaide FREE buses which make about 30 downtown stops. Free guides to Adelaide's public bus lines are available from the Adelaide Metro Info Centre. The city's only surviving tram route now runs between City West and the beach at Glenelg. Ticketing is identical to that on city buses; travel between South Terrace and North Terrace is free.

TOURS

Adelaide Sightseeing operates a morning city sights tour for A$59. The company also runs a daily afternoon bus tour of the Adelaide Hills and the German village of Hahndorf for A$59. For A$58, Gray Line Adelaide provides morning city tours that take in all the highlights. They depart from 87 Franklin Street at 9:30 AM.

Tourabout Adelaide has private tours with tailored itineraries. Prices run from around A$35 for an Adelaide walking tour to A$330 for day-long excursions to the Barossa Valley. Jeff Easley, the owner and chief tour guide, can arrange almost anything.

Rundle Mall Information Centre hosts 30-minute free guided walks. The First Steps Tour points out the main attractions, facilities, and transportation in central Adelaide. Call for exact departure times. Bookings are not required.

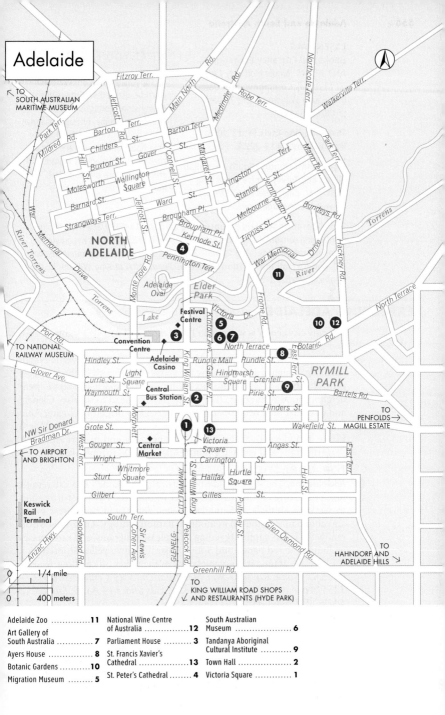

ESSENTIALS

Banks and Currency Exchange
ANZ (✉ 148 Rundle Mall, City Center
☎ 13–1314). **Commonwealth Bank**
(✉ 96 King William St., City Center
☎ 08/8206–4467).

Taxi Suburban Taxis (☎ 13–1008).
Yellow Cabs (☎ 13–2227).

**Visitors Information South Australian
Visitor and Travel Centre** (✉ 18 King
William St., City Center ☎ 1300/655276
⊕ www.southaustralia.com).

Tour Operators Adelaide Sightseeing (☎ 08/8413–6199 ⊕ www.adelaide-sightseeing.com.au). **Gray Line Adelaide** (☎ 1300/858687 ⊕ www.grayline.com). **Tourabout Adelaide** (☎ 08/8333–1111 ⊕ www.touraboutadelaide.com.au). **Rundle Mall Information Centre** (✉ Rundle Mall at King William St., City Center ☎ 08/8203–7611).

WHAT YOU'LL SEE

As soon as you pull into Adelaide you'll be greeted with the sight of tiny stone cottages aglow in morning sunshine, or august sandstone buildings gilded by nighttime floodlights. These are visual cues to the relaxed but vibrant arts and culture that emanate from here.

EXPLORING ADELAIDE

The tiny city center is where you'll find most of Adelaide's sights, shops, and grand stately buildings. Staying here means you're in the heart of what action there is in Adelaide. North of the Torrens River is North Adelaide, which is dominated by the spires of St. Peter's Cathedral. This genteel suburb is where the city's yuppies live, and it has some great neighborhood restaurants. For fun in the sun, head to touristy Glenelg and its cooler near neighbors, Henley Beach and Brighton. Greater Adelaide has attractions encompassing delicious wines at Penfolds Magill Estate and views over the city at Mount Lofty and in Port Adelaide. Seafaring fans will enjoy the South Australian Maritime Museum.

TOP ATTRACTIONS

⓫ Adelaide Zoo. The second-oldest in Australia, Adelaide's zoo still retains much of its original architecture. Enter through the 1883 cast-iron gates to see such animals as Sumatran tigers, Australian rain-forest birds, and chimpanzees housed in modern, natural settings. The zoo is world renowned for its captive breeding and release programs, and rare species including the red panda and South Australia's own yellow-footed rock wallaby are among its successes. Ask at the ticket office about feeding times. ✉ Frome Rd. near War Memorial Dr., City Center ☎ 08/8267–3255 ⊕ www.zoossa.com.au ☑A$26, kids under 14 A$15, families (2 adults, 2–3 kids) A$68 ⊙ Daily 9:30–5.

❼ Art Gallery of South Australia. Many famous Australian painters, including Charles Conder, Margaret Preston, Clifford Possum Tjapaltjarri, Russell Drysdale, and Sidney Nolan, are represented in here. Extensive Renaissance and British artworks are on display, and the atrium houses Aboriginal pieces. There is usually a visiting exhibition, too. A café and bookshop are also on-site. ✉ North Terr. near Pulteney St., City Center ☎ 08/8207–7000 ⊕ www.artgallery.sa.gov.au ☑ Free ⊙ Daily 10–5.

Dusky leaf monkey langurs at the Adelaide Zoo.

🔟 Botanic Gardens. These magnificent formal gardens include an inter-
★ national rose garden, giant water lilies, an avenue of Moreton Bay fig
trees, acres of green lawns, and duck ponds. The Bicentennial Conservatory—the largest single-span glass house in the southern hemisphere—
provides an environment for lowland rain-forest species such as the
cassowary palm and torch ginger. Daily free guided tours leave from the
Schomburgk Pavilion at 10:30. On weekends there's often a wedding
ceremony taking place somewhere on the grounds ⊠ *North Terr., City
Center* ☎ *08/8222–9311* ⊕ *www.botanicgardens.sa.gov.au* ☎ *Gardens
free, conservatory A$4.50* ⊙ *Open 10–4.*

5️⃣ Migration Museum. Chronicled in this converted 19th-century Desti-
tute Asylum, which later in the 19th century served as a school where
Aboriginal children were forced to train as servants to the British, are
the origins, hopes, and fates of some of the millions of immigrants
who settled in Australia during the past two centuries. The museum is
starkly realistic, and the bleak welcome that awaited many migrants is
graphically illustrated. ⊠ *82 Kintore Ave., City Center* ☎ *08/8207–7580*
⊕ *www.history.sa.gov.au* ☎ *Free* ⊙ *Weekdays 10–5, weekends 1–5.*

3️⃣ Parliament House. Ten Corinthian columns are the most striking features
of this classical parliament building. It was completed in two stages 50
years apart: the west wing in 1889 and the east wing in 1939. Alongside
is **Old Parliament House,** which dates from 1843. There's a free guided
tour of both houses weekdays at 10 and 2 during nonsitting weeks, and
on Monday and Friday only when parliament is in session. The viewing
gallery is open to the public when parliament is sitting. ⊠ *North Terr.
at King William St., City Center* ☎ *08/8237–9467* ☎ *Free.*

An exhibition at the Pacific Cultures Gallery, Adelaide.

⑥ South Australian Museum. This museum's Australian Aboriginal Cultures Gallery—the world's largest—houses 3,000 items, including ceremonial dress and paintings from the Pacific Islands. Old black-and-white films show traditional dancing, and touch screens convey desert life. Also in the museum are an exhibit commemorating renowned Antarctic explorer Sir Douglas Mawson, after whom Australia's main Antarctic research station is named; a Fossil Gallery housing the fantastic opalized partial skeleton of a 19-foot-long plesiosaur; and—new for 2010—a biodiversity gallery. There's also a café overlooking a grassy lawn ⊠ *North Terr. near Gawler Pl., City Center* ☎ *08/8207–7500* ⊕ *www.samuseum.sa.gov.au* ✉ *Free* ◷ *Daily 10–5; tours weekdays at 11, weekends at 2 and 3.*

⑨ Tandanya Aboriginal Cultural Institute. A must-see, Tandanya is the first major Aboriginal cultural facility of its kind in Australia. You'll find high-quality changing exhibitions of works by Aboriginal artists and a theater where you can watch didgeridoo performances (Tuesday to Friday at noon) and shows from Pacific Islanders at the same times at the weekend. There's a great gift shop, too, where you can buy CDs of local music. ⊠ *253 Grenfell St., City Center* ☎ *08/8224–3200* ⊕ *www. tandanya.com.au* ✉ *Free* ◷ *Daily 10–5.*

WORTH NOTING

⑧ Ayers House. Between 1855 and 1897 this sprawling colonial structure was the home of Sir Henry Ayers, South Australia's premier and the man for whom Uluru was originally named Ayers Rock. Most rooms—including the unusual Summer Sitting Room, in the cool of the basement—have been restored with period furnishings, and the state's best examples of 19th-century costumes are sometimes displayed in changing exhibitions. Admission includes a one-hour tour. ⊠ *288 North Terrace, City Center* ☏ *08/8223–1234* ⊕ *www.ayershousemuseum.org.au* ⊠ *$8, kids under 16 A$4* ☉ *Tues.–Fri. 10–4, weekends 1–4.*

⑫ **National Wine Centre of Australia.** Timber, steel, and glass evoke the ribs of a huge wine barrel, and a soaring, open-plan concourse make this a spectacular showcase for Australian wines set in the Botanic Gardens. The Wine Discovery Journey takes you from neolithic pottery jars to a stainless-steel tank; you can even make your own virtual wine on a touch-screen computer. Some of the best vintages from more than 20 Australian wine-growing regions are also available for tasting at the Concourse Café from A$5. ⊠ *Hackney and Botanic Rds., City Center* ☏ *08/8303–3355* ⊕ *www.wineaustralia.com.au* ⊠ *Free* ☉ *Weekdays 9–5, weekends 10–5.*

⑬ **St. Francis Xavier's Cathedral.** This church faced a bitter battle over construction after the 1848 decision to build a Catholic cathedral. It's now a prominent, decorative church with a soaring nave, stone arches through to side aisles with dark-wood ceilings, and beautiful stained-glass windows. ⊠ *Wakefield St. at Victoria Sq., City Center* ☏ *08/8231–3551* ⊠ *Free* ☉ *Mass weekdays 8 AM, 12:10, and 5:45 PM; Sat. 8 and 11:30 AM; Sun. 7, 9, 11 AM, and 6 PM.*

④ **St. Peter's Cathedral.** The spires and towers of this cathedral dramatically contrast with the nearby city skyline. St. Peter's is the epitome of Anglican architecture in Australia, and an important example of grand Gothic Revival. Free 45-minute guided tours are available Wednesday at 11 and Sunday at 12:30. ⊠ *1–19 King William St., North Adelaide* ☏ *08/8267–4551* ⊠ *Free* ☉ *Services daily.*

② **Town Hall.** An imposing building constructed in 1863 in Renaissance style, the Town Hall was modeled after buildings in Genoa and Florence. Tours visit the Colonel Light Room, where objects used to map and plan Adelaide are exhibited, and there are frequently traveling art exhibitions. If the guards aren't busy, they will show you around even when there isn't a tour scheduled. ⊠ *128 King William St., City Center* ☏ *08/8203–7203* ⊠ *Free* ☉ *Tours by appointment Mon. at 10, 11, and noon.*

① **Victoria Square.** The fountain in the square, which is floodlighted at night, celebrates the three rivers that supply Adelaide's water: the Torrens, Onkaparinga, and Murray are each represented by a stylized man or woman paired with an Australian native bird. Dominated by the huge Australian and Aboriginal flags overhead (the square is also known by its aboriginal name Tarndanyangga), the park has benches that attract lunching office workers while shoppers and tourists come and go from the Glenelg-City Tram, which stops here. ⊠ *King William, Grote, and Wakefield Sts., City Center.*

GREATER ADELAIDE

☺ **National Railway Museum.** Steam-train buffs will love this collection of locomotives and rolling stock in the former Port Adelaide railway yard. The finest of its kind in Australia, the collection includes enormous "mountain"-class engines and the "Tea and Sugar" train, once the lifeline for camps scattered across the deserts of South and Western Australia. ⊠ *Lipson St. near St. Vincent's St., Port Adelaide* ☎ *08/8341–1690* ⊕ *www.natrailmuseum.org.au* 🖃 *A\$12, kids 5–16 A\$5* ⊙ *Daily 10–5.*

★ **Penfolds Magill Estate.** Founded in 1844 by immigrant English doctor Christopher Rawson Penfold, this is the birthplace of Australia's most famous wine, Penfolds Grange, and one of the world's only city wineries. Introduced in 1951, Grange is the flagship of a huge stable of wines priced from everyday to special-occasion (collectors pay thousands of dollars to complete sets of Grange). Hour-long winery tours (A\$15) leave daily at 11 and 3. The Great Grange Tour is the ultimate Magill Estate experience; over 2½ hours you visit the original Penfold family cottage, tour the winery, and enjoy a tasting of premium wines, including Grange. This tour departs at 1 PM every Sunday and costs A\$150 per person (minimum of four); reservations are essential. ⊠ *78 Penfold Rd., Magill* ☎ *08/8301–5400* ⊕ *www.penfolds.com.au* 🖃 *Free* ⊙ *Daily 10–5.*

☾ **South Australian Maritime Museum.** Inside a restored stone warehouse, this museum brings maritime history vividly to life with ships' figureheads, shipwreck relics, and intricate scale models. In the basement you can lie in a bunk bed aboard an 1840s immigrant ship and hear passengers telling of life and death on their journeys to South Australia. In addition to the warehouse displays, the museum includes a lighthouse (worth climbing the 75 steps up to see the view), restored steam tug, and a WWII tender at the nearby wharf. ⊠ *126 Lipson St., Port Adelaide* ☎ *08/8207–6255* ⊕ *www.history.sa.gov.au/maritime/maritime.htm* 🖃 *A\$8.50 (lighthouse entry included)* ⊙ *Daily 10–5; lighthouse closed Sat.*

WHERE TO EAT

Melbourne, Gouger, O'Connell, and Rundle streets, along with the Norwood Parade and Glenelg neighborhoods, are the main eating strips. In any of these areas it's fun to stroll around until a restaurant or café takes your fancy. Chinatown is also lively, and if you feel like an alfresco picnic, pick some some delicious local produce from Central Market.

Use the coordinate (✛ B2) at the end of each listing to locate a site on the corresponding map.

\$ ✕ **Amalfi Pizzeria Ristorante.** This place is rustic and noisy. If it weren't for
ITALIAN the Australian accents here, you'd swear you were in a regional Italian eatery. The terrazzo-tiled dining room is furnished with bare wooden tables, around which sit professionals and university students in enthusiastic conversation. The paper place-mat menu lists traditional pizza and pasta dishes in two sizes—appetizer and entrée—a must-order is the spaghetti marinara. ⊠ *29 Frome St., City Center* ☎ *08/8223–1948* ▤ *AE, DC, MC, V* ⊙ *Closed Sun. No lunch Sat.* ✛ *C2.*

¢ ✕ **Big Table.** Simply the best breakfast choice in Adelaide, Big Table has
CAFE been at the Central Market for over 15 years, and regulars know to get there early for a chance at one of the few tables. Sitting up at the counter isn't too bad an option, however, especially when you have

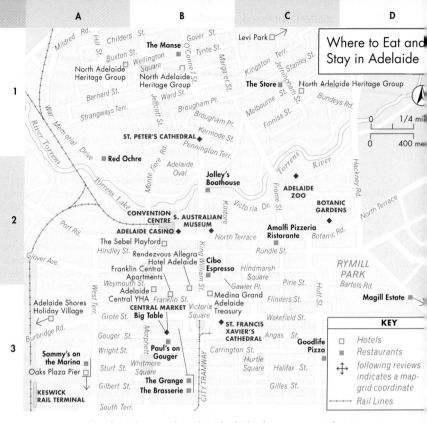

A   **B**   **C**   **D**

Mildred Rd. · Hill St. · Childers St. · Buxton St. · Gover St. · Tynte St. · Levi Park

The Manse · O'Connell St. · Marg-aret St. · Kingston Terr. · Stanley St. · Jerningham St.

North Adelaide Heritage Group · Wellington Square · North Adelaide Heritage Group · The Store · North Adelaide Heritage Group

Barnard St. · Ward St. · Jeffcott St. · Brougham Pl. · Melbourne St. · Finniss St. · Bundeys Rd.

Strangways Terr. · Brougham Pl. · Kermode St. · Finniss St.

ST. PETER'S CATHEDRAL · Pennington Terr.

War Memorial Drive · River Torrens · Montefiore Rd. · Adelaide Oval · Torrens River · Hackney Rd. · North Terrace

Red Ochre · Jolley's Boathouse · ADELAIDE ZOO · BOTANIC GARDENS

Torrens Lake · CONVENTION CENTRE · S. AUSTRALIAN MUSEUM · Victoria Dr. · Frome St. · North Terrace

Port Rd. · ADELAIDE CASINO · North Terrace · Amalfi Pizzeria Ristorante · Botanic Rd. · RYMILL PARK

Glover Ave. · The Sebel Playford · Hindley St. · Rundle St. · Bartels Rd.

Rendezvous Allegra Hotel Adelaide · Cibo Espresso · Hindmarsh Square · Pirie St. · Hutt St. · Magill Estate

Franklin Central Apartments · Gawler Pl. · Flinders St.

Weymouth St. · Adelaide Central YHA · Franklin St. · Medina Grand Adelaide Treasury

West Terr. · Grote St. · CENTRAL MARKET · Big Table · Victoria Square · Wakefield St.

Adelaide Shores Holiday Village · Burbridge Rd. · ST. FRANCIS XAVIER'S CATHEDRAL · Angas St. · Goodlife Pizza

Gouger St. · Wright St. · Paul's on Gouger · Carrington St. · Hurtle Square · Halifax St.

Sammy's on the Marina · Oaks Plaza Pier · Sturt St. · Whitmore Square · Gilbert St. · The Grange · The Brasserie · Gilles St.

KESWICK RAIL TERMINAL · South Terr. · CITY TRAMWAY

0 — 1/4 mi
0 — 400 me

KEY

□	Hotels
■	Restaurants
✛	following reviews indicates a map-grid coordinate
├──┤	Rail Lines

treats like fresh banana bread with rhubarb conserve and ricotta to look forward to. The enormous Big Brekkie lives up to its name, and offers quality as well as quantity with delicious thick-sliced local bacon and field mushrooms cooked with pesto and served on Turkish bread. ⊠ *Stall 39/40, Southern Roadway Adelaide Central Market, City Centre* ☎ *08/8212–3899* ⊜ *No credit cards* ⊙ *Closed Mon. and Sun. and evenings* ✛ *B3.*

$
AUSTRALIAN
✕ **The Brasserie.** While the Grange, the Hilton's other flagship restaurant, offers subdued and serious fine dining, local celebrity chef Simon Bryant runs a more fun and relaxed place. It's livelier and more relaxed, except when it comes to the chef's insistence on top-quality local produce. The menu from the open kitchen changes every season, but always makes use of local specialties from the Fleurieu Peninsula and Kangaroo Island. If Australia's national animal is on the menu, give it a try here. ⊠ *Hilton Hotel, 233 Victoria Sq., City Center* ☎ *08/8237–0697* 🖃 *AE, DC, MC, V* ⊙ *No lunch weekends* ✛ *B3.*

$$$
CAFE
✕ **Cibo Espresso.** Caffeine addicts head here for a little taste of Italy in stylish fun surroundings. The small local chain has branches dotted around the city, and in each one you are guaranteed a fabulous espresso from their Wega machines and irresistible sweet treats. If you're there at lunchtime, the freshly baked panini are good, too. All branches have

free Wi-Fi. ⊠ *Shop 7, 82 King William St., City Center* ☎ *08/8410–4088* ▤ *AE, DC, MC, V above A$10* ☉ *Closed Sat. after 1* PM ✛ *B2.*

¢ ✕**Goodlife Modern Organic Pizzas.** Forget about greasy pepperoni-loaded
PIZZA pizzas—the pies at this local trend-setting favorite are as different from the norm as you can get. It was the country's first pizzeria to be certified as organic, and the innovative toppings like kapunda free-range chicken are as tasty as they sound, especially with a glass of their well-priced local wine. The dessert pizzas are worth a try if you're not carb-ed out. ⊠ *170 Hutt St., City Center* ☎ *08/8223-2618* ▤ *AE, DC, MC, V* ☉ *No lunch weekends* ✛ *C3.*

$$$$ ✕**The Grange.** With a philosophy of pursuing "the flavor of things,"
Fodor'sChoice world-renowned chef Cheong Liew works nightly culinary magic. Liew,
★ who pioneered East-West fusion cuisine in Australia in the early 1970s,
MODERN offers three- to eight-course tasting menus, most of which open with the
AUSTRALIAN famous "Four Dances of the Sea"—snook, raw calamari with black-ink noodles, octopus, and spiced prawn sushi. Each course can be paired with thrilling wines. Be prepared to splurge, though; this is one of South Australia's most expensive, as well as inventive, restaurants—and don't expect there to be crowds of people dining. ⊠ *Hilton Hotel, 233 Victoria Sq., City Center* ☎ *08/8237–0737 or 08/8217–2000* ☖ *Reservations essential* ▤ *AE, DC, MC, V* ☉ *Closed Jan. and July. No lunch* ✛ *B3.*

✕**Jolleys Boathouse.** Blue canvas directors' chairs and white-clothed wooden tables create a relaxed, nautical air here—which perfectly suits the location on the south bank of the River Torrens. Sliding glass doors open onto a full-width front balcony for alfresco dining. The imaginative modern Australian menu changes seasonally, but might include a salad of grilled Kangaroo Island marron, green mango, basil and shallots, or sweet pork belly with red cheeks. Executives make up most lunch crowds, and warm evenings attract couples. There is an unfriendly minimum of A$23 per person, however. ⊠ *King William St. at Victoria, City Center* ☎ *08/8223–2891* ▤ *AE, DC, MC, V* ☉ *No dinner Sun.* ✛ *B2.*

$$$ ✕**Magill Estate.** Do you inhale deeply from your wine glass before drink-
ECLECTIC ing? Do you know your back palate from your front? Then you're ready to join the wine buffs at this pavilion-style vineyard restaurant. The restaurant overlooks vineyards and the distant city skyline and coast. The view alone makes eating here a memorable experience. The seasonal menu might include such European-flavored Oz delights as Grange-marinated venison served with braised red cabbage, Barossa bacon, and game jus. You can enjoy the multicourse degustation menu or dine à la carte. The wine list is a selection of Penfolds' finest. ⊠ *78 Penfold Rd., Magill* ☎ *08/8301–5551* ☖ *Reservations essential* ▤ *AE, MC, V* ☉ *Closed Sun. and Mon. No lunch Tues.–Thurs. and Sat.* ✛ *D3.*

$$ ✕**The Manse.** Tailcoats were de rigueur dinner attire when this Victo-
FRENCH rian church manse was built in the heart of North Adelaide, but the dress code for the modern French gem it houses now is thankfully more relaxed. Continental cuisine, such as duck breast with sunflower, witlof, and buckwheat cake, is prepared with flair, and special effort is made to add local ingredients to classic and contemporary dishes (try the blue-eye trevally with celeriac and pearl barley); there is a degustation

menu in case you can't choose! Wood-burning fireplaces and an outdoor terrace make dining a pleasure any time of year. *The Australian newspaper recently* picked this place as their fine-dining restaurant of the year. The same family also owns the trendy Sparrow Kitchen and Bar at 10 O'Connell Street, North Adelaide. ⊠ *142 Tynte St., North Adelaide* ☎ *08/8267–4636* ⚫ *Reservations essential* ⊟ *AE, DC, MC, V* ☉ *Closed Sun. No lunch Sat. and Mon.–Thurs.* ✚ *B1.*

$ ✕ **Paul's on Gouger.** It may look like your run of the mill chippie, but this
CAFE   Gouger-street veteran of more than 60 years is the place to get hooked on King George whiting. It's been hailed as one of Adelaide's best—and best-priced—seafood restaurants. The salt-and-pepper squid is another local favorite. For a great view of the bustle in the open kitchen, request a table upstairs on the ship's-deck-like mezzanine floor. ⊠ *79 Gouger St., City Center* ☎ *08/8231–9778* ⊟ *AE, DC, MC, V* ✚ *B3.*

$$ ✕ **Red Ochre.** A sweeping view of Adelaide is the backdrop for con-
MODERN   temporary workings of traditional bush meats, herbs, and fruits at
AUSTRALIAN   this riverfront restaurant. The downstairs River Café, the restaurant's sister venue, is more informal, and offers a modern Italian menu for lunch Monday to Friday, while Red Ochre is only open for dinner. For a splurge, head upstairs, where you can tuck into crisp fried barramundi in aniseed myrtle-spiced flour served with wild lime and pawpaw salsa, or order a game platter for two and graze on kangaroo, wallaby, and emu. Don't miss the wattle-seed pavlova, Red Ochre's version of Australia's famous meringue dessert. ⊠ *War Memorial Dr., North Adelaide* ☎ *08/8211–8555* ⊟ *AE, DC, MC, V* ☉ *Closed Sun.* ✚ *A2.*

$$ ✕ **Sammy's on the Marina.** Enormous fishbowl windows frame views of
SEAFOOD   million-dollar yachts at this restaurant—one of Adelaide's top seafood eateries—at the far end of Glenelg's glitzy Holdfast Marina. Watch the setting sun silhouette playing dolphins or a storm rolling across Gulf St. Vincent as you tuck into skewered scallops or crispy-skin Atlantic salmon on roasted chili and garlic pilaf. The menu here charts South Australia's ocean bounty, and the hot seafood platter (for two people) would feed a school of sharks. ⊠ *1–12 Holdfast Promenade, Glenelg* ☎ *08/8376–8211* ⚫ *Reservations essential* ⊟ *AE, DC, MC, V* ✚ *A3.*

¢   ✕ **The Store.** North Adelaide yuppies fuel up on aromatic coffee, fresh-
CAFE   squeezed juices, and some of Adelaide's most fabulous food here before trawling the adjacent delicatessen and upscale supermarket. Grab a table and order at the bar—try the field mushroom, leek, and mozzarella omelet for brunch. More substantial meals are available after 11 AM. Weekend crowds mean slow service, so try to score a sidewalk table, kick back, and watch the comings and goings of couples, families, and dogs (there's a water bowl for thirsty pooches). ⊠ *157 Melbourne St., North Adelaide* ☎ *08/8361–6999* ⊟ *AE, DC, MC, V* ✚ *C1.*

WHERE TO STAY

At first glance, large international, business-style hotels seem to dominate Adelaide—there's a Hilton, a Hyatt, and, new for 2010, a Crowne Plaza—but there's actually a wide choice of places to rest your head. Adelaide's accommodations are a mix of traditional mid-rise hotels, backpacker hostels, self-contained apartments, and charming bed-and-breakfasts, many in century-old sandstone buildings. With a car you'll be within easy reach of a Glenelg beach house or an Adelaide Hills B&B.

Use the coordinate (⊹ 1:B2) at the end of each listing to locate a site on the corresponding map.

¢ ⊡ **Adelaide Central YHA.** Mostly young people buzz around this purpose-built, city-center hostel like bees at a hive. Adelaide's only YHA far exceeds the standards of its affiliation. There's a community feel throughout the property, from the declaration of human rights on the front door to the free big-screen movie nights and seven-day activity program, including quiz nights and Ping-Pong competitions. Bright, airy standard rooms, family rooms, and dorms (eight beds maximum) have metal-frame beds with comfy new mattresses and individual luggage lockers. There's a huge, modern communal kitchen as well as TV rooms. Nightclubs, restaurants, and city attractions are within easy walking distance. Doors lock at 11 PM, but if you pick up the external phone, the night staff will let you in whatever the hour. **Pros:** extremely clean, friendly staff. **Cons:** sometimes impossible to book ahead during peak season, older people will feel outnumbered. ⊠ *135 Waymouth St., City Center* ☎ *08/8414–3010* ⊕ *www.yha.com.au* ⤳ *63 rooms* ♿ *In-room: no phone, no TV, Wi-Fi. In-hotel: laundry facilities, public Internet, public Wi-Fi, parking (fee), no-smoking rooms* ⊟ *AE, DC, MC, V* ⊹ *B3.*

$$ ⊡ **Adelaide Shores Holiday Village.** The breeze is salty, the lawns are green, and white sand is only a few lazy steps from this summery resort on the city's coastal fringe. The seldom-crowded beach beyond the dunes fronts a mix of raised two- and three-bedroom bungalows with private balconies (some have hot tubs), two-bedroom deluxe villas, standard holiday units with combined kitchen/lounge areas, and budget vans. It's a 20-minute drive to the city, but the pools, many sports facilities, and barbecues are reasons enough to stay put. **Pros:** very family-friendly, with plenty of activities for kids and well-planned family rooms. **Cons:** bad choice for a romantic break, in peak season service levels drop. ⊠ *Military Rd., West Beach* ☎ *08/8355–7360* ⊕ *www.adelaideshores. com.au/holidayvillage.htm* ⤳ *22 bungalows, 30 villas, 32 units* ♿ *In-room: no phone, kitchen (some), refrigerator, DVD. In-hotel: tennis court, pools, beachfront, no elevator, laundry facilities, public Internet, parking (no fee), no-smoking rooms* ⊟ *MC, V* ⊹ *A3.*

$$ ⊡ **Franklin Central Apartments.** Check in here and you'll have room to move in one of Adelaide's most crowded quarters. Behind a historic facade within sniffing distance of the Central Market and Gouger Street eateries, the one-, two-, and three-bedroom apartments have everything you need for a short or long stay, including a pantry service; all are decked out in polished timbers and shades of blue. **Pros:** around the corner from foodie heaven, the Central Market, good-sized rooms. **Cons:** not much in the way of soundproofing, furnishings on the simple side. ⊠ *36 Franklin St., City Center* ☎ *08/8221–7050 or 1300/662288* ⊕ *www.franklinapartments.com.au* ⤳ *62 apartments* ♿ *In-room: kitchen, refrigerator, Internet. In-hotel: restaurant, laundry facilities, laundry service, public Wi-Fi, parking (fee), no-smoking rooms* ⊟ *AE, DC, MC, V* ⊹ *B2.*

$ ⚓ **Levi Park.** Port Lincoln parrots and black ducks are regulars at this caravan park overlooking the River Torrens 5 km (3 mi) from central Adelaide. From here it's a scenic walk or cycle along a shared river path to the city, and buses pass the front gate. Grassy tent sites have river frontage, with en-suite cabins and camper vans behind. A fully equipped camp kitchen and separate children's and disabled-access bathrooms are bonuses. In the middle of the park is Adelaide's oldest surviving colonial residence. Built within five years of South Australia's settlement, Heritage-listed Vale House is now a six-suite luxury B&B. **Pros:** very family-friendly, with a host of activities available, inexpensive. **Cons:** cabins can be close together, not the place for a romantic interlude. ✉ *69 Lansdowne Terr., Walkerville* ☎ *08/8344–2209 or 1800/442209* ⊕ *www.levipark.com.au* ♿ *Flush toilets, partial hookups (electric and water), dump station, drinking water, guest laundry, showers, grills, picnic tables, electricity, public telephone, general store, play area* ⬒ *20 unpowered sites, 66 powered sites, 30 cabins* ▭ *MC, V* ✛ *C1.*

$$$ ⊞ **Medina Grand Adelaide Treasury.** Contemporary Italian furnishings in
★   white, slate-gray, and ocher are juxtaposed with 19th-century Adelaide architecture in this stylish Victoria Square hotel. Cast-iron columns, archways, and barrel-vaulted ceilings—original features of the former Treasury building—add texture to clean lines in the studio rooms and serviced apartments. The lobby lounge incorporates an 1839 sandstone wall, one of the oldest remaining colonial structures in South Australia. Great food is as close as the adjoining Treasury Restaurant. **Pros:** beautiful and classic building with light and airy reception rooms. **Cons:** no close parking, reception staff get harassed at peak periods. ✉ *2 Flinders St., City Center* ☎ *08/8112–0000 or 1300/633462* ⊕ *www.medina.com. au* ⬒ *20 studio rooms, 59 apartments* ♿ *In-room: safe, kitchen, refrigerator, Internet. In-hotel: restaurant, bar, pool, gym, laundry facilities, laundry service, public Wi-Fi, parking (fee), no-smoking rooms* ▭ *AE, DC, MC, V* ✛ *B3.*

$$$–$$$$ ⊞ **North Adelaide Heritage Group.** Tucked into the city's leafy, oldest sec-
Fodor's Choice   tion, these 18 lodgings are stunningly unique. Antiques dealers Rodney
★   and Regina Twiss have converted Heritage-listed mews houses, a meeting chapel, an arts-and-crafts manor house, and a fire station (complete with 1942 fire engine) into apartments and suites, and filled them with Australian antiques and contemporary furnishings. Each one- to four-bedroom unit has a bath or hot tub, sitting room, and kitchen, most complete with a milk-shake maker; all are charming. The Bishop's Garden apartment is the most luxurious and secluded spot in Adelaide, with a sophisticated kitchen and lounge opening into a private garden with a rock-adorned fish pool. American, lactose-free, kosher—any breakfast can be arranged. **Pros:** historic properties in Adelaide's most upscale suburb, friendly owners give helpful tips on what to do. **Cons:** some properties can be on the dark side, not child-friendly. ✉ *Office: 109 Glen Osmond Rd., Eastwood* ☎ *08/8272–1355* ⊕ *www.adelaideheritage.com* ⬒ *7 cottages, 3 suites, 8 apartments* ♿ *In-room: kitchen (some), refrigerator, DVD (some), Wi-Fi (some), dial-up. In-hotel: room service, no elevator, laundry facilities (some), laundry service, parking (no fee), no-smoking rooms* ▭ *AE, DC, MC, V* ✛ *A1, B1, C1.*

8

$$–$$$ Oaks Plaza Pier. Sea air wafts through open balcony doors in this all-apartment complex on Adelaide's favorite beach. Floor-to-ceiling windows frame either Glenelg and parkland views or white sand and turquoise sea. The spacious suites have fully equipped kitchens and many high-tech gadgets. After a night spent exploring Glenelg's waterfront restaurants and bars you can fall asleep in your huge, comfortable bed listening to waves washing ashore. **Pros:** steps from the beach, helpful reception staff who are full of advice. **Cons:** corporate feel to the lobby, and the bars can get noisy at peak times, expensive Internet. ⊠ *16 Holdfast Promenade, Glenelg* ☎ *08/8350–6688 or 1300/551111* ⊕ *www.theoaksgroup.com.au* ⇨ *121 1-bedroom apartments, 34 2-bedroom apartments* ♿ *In-room: safe, kitchen, refrigerator, Internet. In-hotel: restaurant, room service, bars, pool, gym, beachfront, concierge, laundry facilities, laundry service, parking (fee), no-smoking rooms* ▭ *AE, DC, MC, V* ✛ *A3.*

$$$$ Rendezvous Allegra Hotel Adelaide. Black-tile-and-timber columns
Fodor's Choice   frame the Hollywood-glamorous marble lobby of this ultrasleek upscale
★   hotel. Beveled-glass elevators with marble floors, designed to resemble the interior of a diamond, whisk you to snazzy, contemporary quarters of glass, marble, and wood. A picture window separates bathroom and bedroom. The first-floor Glasshouse restaurant can deliver treats day and night; you can work them off in the cerulean-blue tile pool, which has underwater portholes for watching the hotel entrance. **Pros:** five-star facilities and an excellent wine list at the restaurant. **Cons:** tiny gym, and more corporate than boutique in feel. ⊠ *55 Waymouth St., City Center* ☎ *08/8115–8888* ⊕ *www.rendezvoushotels.com/adelaide/* ⇨ *166 rooms, 35 suites* ♿ *In-room: refrigerator, Internet. In-hotel: restaurant, room service, bar, pool, gym, concierge, laundry service, public Wi-Fi, no-smoking rooms* ▭ *AE, DC, MC, V* ✛ *B2.*

$$$$ The Sebel Playford. Showy chandeliers illuminate a movie-set-like cel-
★   ebration of art nouveau in the lobby of this luxury hotel. Check your reflection in a huge gilt mirror before relaxing in a club lounge or around the grand piano in the bar, where the tables have statue bases and marble tops. Room decorations are a subtler nod to the art nouveau era. In the unusual loft suites, wrought-iron stairs climb to a king-size bed on the mezzanine floor. The colonnaded indoor hotel pool feels like a Roman bathhouse. **Pros:** excellent breakfast spread, convivial bar. **Cons:** expensive Internet and parking. ⊠ *120 North Terr., City Center* ☎ *08/8213–8888* ⊕ *www.sebelplayford.com.au* ⇨ *110 rooms, 72 suites* ♿ *In-room: safe (some), kitchen (some), refrigerator, Internet. In-hotel: restaurant, room service, bar, pool, gym, concierge, laundry facilities, laundry service, public Wi-Fi, parking (fee), no-smoking rooms* ▭ *AE, DC, MC, V* ✛ *B2.*

NIGHTLIFE AND THE ARTS

THE ARTS

The three-week **Adelaide Festival of Arts** (⊕ *www.adelaidefestival.com. au*), Australia's oldest arts festival, takes place in February and March of even-numbered years. It's a cultural smorgasbord of outdoor opera, classical music, jazz, art exhibitions, comedy, and cabaret presented by some of the world's top artists. Recent highlights include Book of Longing by Phillip Glass and Leonard Cohen. Contact the South Australian Visitor and Travel Centre for more information. The annual three-day **WOMADelaide Festival** (⊕ *www.womadelaide.com.au*) of world music, arts, and dance takes place in early March and raises consciousness on stages in Botanic Park. There's also a fringe festival (⊕ *www.adelaidefringe.com.au*), the southern hemisphere's biggest with hundreds of shows around town.

For a listing of performances and exhibitions, look to the entertainment pages of the *Advertiser,* Adelaide's daily newspaper. *The Adelaide Review,* a free monthly arts paper, reviews exhibitions, galleries, and performances and lists forthcoming events. Tickets for most live performances can be purchased from **BASS Ticket Agency** (⊠ *Adelaide Festival Centre, King William St., City Center* ☎ *13–1246* ⊕ *www.bass. net.au*).

The **Adelaide Festival Centre** (⊠ *King William St. near North Terr., City Center* ☎ *13–1246* ⊕ *www.adelaidefestivalcentre.com.au*) is the city's major venue for the performing arts. The State Opera, the State Theatre Company of South Australia, and the Adelaide Symphony Orchestra perform here regularly. Performances are in the Playhouse, the Festival and Space theaters, the outdoor amphitheater, and Her Majesty's Theatre at 58 Grote Street. The box office is open Monday–Saturday 9–6.

NIGHTLIFE

There's something going on every evening in Adelaide, although clubs are especially packed on weekends. Cover charges vary according to the night and time of entry. Nightlife for the coming week is listed in "*Adelaide (Scene),*" a pullout section of Thursday's edition of *The Advertiser. Rip It Up* is a free Thursday music-and-club publication aimed at the younger market. *Onion,* published fortnightly on Thursday, is Adelaide's top dance music magazine. *dB,* a twice-monthly free independent publication, covers music, arts, film, games, and dance.

Bars along Rundle Street and East Terrace are trendy, while Hindley and Waymouth streets are lined with traditional pubs. North Adelaide's O'Connell Street buzzes every night, and the popular Sunday-evening beer-and-banter sessions really pack in the crowds.

BARS AND CLUBS **Austral Hotel** (⊠ *205 Rundle St., City Center* ☎ *08/8223–4660*), the first bar in South Australia to put Coopers beer on tap, is a local favorite and a great place to drink outdoors. You can down shooters or sip cocktails from a long list while listening to a band play or a DJ spin groovy tunes. It's open daily 11 AM–3 AM.

Botanic Bar (⊠ *310 North Terr., City Center* ☎ *08/8227–0799*), a cool city lounge, has cordovan banquettes encircling the U-shaped, marble-top bar. Muddlers (crushed ice drinks) are the specialty, and they bring in mostly young professionals, including off-duty medics from the hospital opposite. It's open until the wee hours Tuesday to Sunday.

★ **The Gov** (⊠ *59 Port Rd., Hindmarsh* ☎ *08/8340–0744*) is the favorite venue of a mixed crowd. Young homeowners and long-term regulars come for Irish music sessions, all-weekend metal fests, and everything

The Art Gallery of South Australia.

in between. Cabaret, comedy, Latin music—if you can name it, you can probably hear it here. There's good pub grub, too. It's open weekdays 11 AM to late and Saturday noon to late. It's closed Sunday unless there is a show.

Grace Emily (⊠ *232 Waymouth St., City Center* ☎ *08/8231–5500*), a multilevel music-lover's pub, has bartenders spouting the mantra "No pokies, no TAB, no food." (Pokies are the poker machines found in many pubs, and TAB, Australia's version of OTB, lets you place bets on horse races.) Instead, there's live music nightly, and a pool table. The beer garden is one of the city's best, with secluded spots for those wanting a quiet tipple and big round tables for groups to drink en masse and alfresco. It's open daily 4 PM–late.

The cavernous **Supermild** (⊠ *182 Hondley St., City Center* ☎ *08/8212–8077* ⊘ *Closed Mon. and Tues.)* has a retro feel and is as unpretentious as they come, which perfectly fits in with the local nightlife scene. Grab a comfy sofa and chill out with a bunch of friends while listening to the local DJs going their thing—either indie, retro, or funk, depending on the night.

The **Wellington Hotel** (⊠ *36 Wellington Sq., North Adelaide* ☎ *08/8267–1322*), first licensed in 1851, is hops lovers' heaven, with 32 Australian-brewed beers on tap. Line up six "pony" (sample) glasses on a taster tray, then enjoy a schooner (large glass) of your favorite.

CASINO Head to **SkyCity** for big-time casino gaming, including the highly animated Australian Two-up, in which you bet against the house on the fall of two coins. Four bars, including the stylish venue Loco, and four restaurants are also within the complex. It's one of a handful of places in Adelaide that keep pumping until dawn. ⊠ *North Terr., City Center* ☎ *08/8212–2811* ◷ *24 hrs.*

OUTDOOR ACTIVITIES

PARTICIPANT SPORTS

BICYCLING   Adelaide's parks, flat terrain, and uncluttered streets make it a perfect city for two-wheel exploring. **Linear Park Mountain Bike Hire** (⊠ *Elder Park adjacent to Adelaide Festival Centre, City Center* ☎ *0400/596065*) rents 21-speed mountain bikes by the hour or for A\$20 per day and A\$80–A\$100 per week, including a helmet, lock, and maps. They're open daily 9–5 in winter, 9–6 in summer, or by appointment.

Just a 10-minute walk outside of the city, the **City of Adelaide Golf Links** (⊠ *Entrance to par-3 course is off War Memorial Dr.; 18-hole courses are off Strangways Terr., North Adelaide* ☎ *08/8267–2171* ⊕ *www. cityofadelaide.com.au*) runs one short (par-3) and two 18-hole courses. You can rent clubs and carts from the pro shop. Greens fees are from A\$19.20 weekdays and A\$22.50 weekends for the north course, A\$23.00 weekdays and A\$28.00 weekends for the south course. Playing hours are dawn to dusk daily.

WATER   **The Beachhouse** (⊠ *Colley Terrace, Glenelg* ☎ *08/8295–1511* ⊕ *www.*
SPORTS   *thebeachhouse.com.au*) is a kid's dream come true, with an array of attractions like waterslides, fairground rides, and boats steps from the Glenelg beach. Youngsters—and the young at heart—will love a cruise on **The Dolphin Boat** (⊠ *Holdfast Shores Marina, Glenelg* ☎ *04/1281– 1838* ⊕ *www.dolphinboat.com.au* 🗒 *A\$98 to swim, A\$58 to watch*), which allows you to swim with the cute and friendly animals. The dolphins and tour guides have developed a close relationship over the years, so you're guaranteed to get up close.

SPECTATOR SPORTS

Venue*Tix (⊠ *Shop 24, Da Costa Arcade, Grenfell St. at Gawler Pl., City Center* ☎ *08/8225–8888* ⊕ *www.venuetix.com.au*) sells tickets for domestic and international one-day and test (five-day) cricket matches, other major sporting events, and concerts.

CRICKET   Cricket season is October–March, and the main venue for interstate and
★   international competition is the Adelaide Oval. Two-hour tours (A\$10) of the Oval and the **Bradman Collection Museum** (⊠ *Adelaide Oval, War Memorial Dr. and King William St., North Adelaide* ☎ *08/8300–3800*), dedicated to the legendary Sir Donald Bradman, depart weekdays at 10 AM (except on match days and public holidays).

FOOTBALL   Australian Rules Football is the most popular winter sport in South Australia. Games are played at **AAMI Stadium** (⊠ *Turner Dr., West Lakes* ☎ *08/8268–2088*). Teams play in the national AFL competition on Thursday, Friday, Saturday, or Sunday. The season runs March to August. Finals are in September.

SHOPPING

If you are wondering where everyone in Adelaide is, you'll find them at Rundle Mall, the city's main shopping area. Shops in the City Center are generally open Monday–Thursday 9–5:30, Friday 9–9, Saturday 9–5:30, and Sunday 11–5. In the suburbs shops are often open until 9 PM on Thursday night instead of Friday. As the center of the world's opal industry, Adelaide has many opal shops, which are around King William Street. Other good buys are South Australian regional wines, crafts, and Aboriginal artwork. The trendiest area to browse is King William Road in Hyde Park, a 20-minute walk south from Victoria Square.

MALLS

Adelaide's main shopping area is **Rundle Mall** (⊠ *Rundle St. between King William and Pulteney Sts., City Center* ☎ *08/8203–7611*), a pedestrian plaza lined with boutiques, department stores—including Australia's two best known stores, Myers and David Jones—and arcades. Heritage-listed Adelaide Arcade is a Victorian-era jewel, with a decorative tiled floor, skylights, and dozens of shops behind huge timber-framed windows.

MARKETS

★ One of the largest produce markets in the southern hemisphere, and Adelaide's pride and joy, **Central Market** (⊠ *Gouger St., City Center* ☎ *08/8203–7494*) is chock-full of stellar local foods, including glistening-fresh fish, meat, crusty Vietnamese and Continental breads, German baked goods, cheeses of every shape and color, and old-fashioned lollies (candy). You can also buy souvenir T-shirts, CDs, books, cut flowers, and a great cup of coffee. Hours are Tuesday 7–5:30, Thursday 9–5:30, Friday 7 AM–9 PM, and Saturday 7–3. The enthusiastic couple behind Adelaide's Top Food and Wine Tours showcase Adelaide's food-and-wine lifestyle—as in the behind-the-scenes guided tour of the Central Market (A\$35), which lets you meet stall holders, share their knowledge, and taste the wares. Tours are scheduled Tuesday and Thursday–Saturday at 9:30 AM. **Adelaide's Top Food and Wine Tours** (☎ *08/8263–0265* ⊕ *www.topfoodandwinetours.com.au*).

SPECIALTY STORES

CHOCOLATE **Haigh's Chocolates** (⊠ *2 Rundle Mall at King William St., City Cen-*
★ *ter* ☎ *08/8231–2844* ⊠ *Haigh's Visitors Centre, 154 Greenhill Rd., Parkside* ☎ *08/8372–7077*), Australia's oldest chocolate manufacturer, has tempted people with corner shop displays since 1915. The family-owned South Australian company produces exquisite truffles, pralines, and creams—as well as the chocolate bilby (an endangered Australian marsupial), Haigh's answer to the Easter bunny. Shop hours are Monday to Saturday 8.30–6, Sunday 10.30–5. Free chocolate-making tours at the visitor center run Monday–Saturday at 11, 1, and 2; bookings are essential.

HOMEWARES The **Jam Factory** (⊠ *19 Morphett St., City Center* ☎ *08/8231–0005*), a contemporary craft-and-design center at the Lion's Arts Centre, exhibits and sells unique Australian glassware, ceramics, wood, and metal work. For quirky locally made jewelry, pottery, glass, and sculptures, visit **Urban Cow Studio** (⊠ *11 Frome St., City Center* ☎ *08/8232–6126*).

JEWELRY   **Adelaide Exchange** (✉ *10 Stephens Pl., City Center* ☎ *08/8212–2496*), off
AND GEMS   Rundle Mall, sells high-quality antique jewelry. The **Australian Opal and
           Diamond Collection** (✉ *14 King William St., City Center* ☎ *08/8211–9995*)
           sells and manufactures superb handcrafted one-of-a-kind opal jewelry.

SIDE TRIPS TO THE ADELAIDE HILLS

With their secluded green slopes and flowery gardens, the Adelaide Hills are a pastoral vision in this desert state. The patchwork quilt of vast orchards, neat vineyards, and avenues of tall conifers resembles the Bavarian countryside, a likeness fashioned by the many German immigrants who settled here in the 19th century. During the summer months the Hills are consistently cooler than the city, although the

> ### NICE VIEWS
>
> There is no better view of Adelaide—day or night—than the city-and-sea sweep from atop 2,300-foot Mt. Lofty. There's an appropriately named glass-front restaurant here called Summit, though prices at both the café and restaurant are sky-high.

charming towns and wineries are pleasant to visit any time of year. To reach the region from Adelaide, head toward the M1 Princes Highway or drive down Pulteney Street, which becomes Unley Road and then Belair Road. From here signs point to Crafers and the freeway.

MT. LOFTY
16 km (10 mi) southeast of Adelaide.

There are splendid views of Adelaide from the lookout atop 2,300-foot Mt. Lofty, the coldest location in Adelaide, where snow is not uncommon in winter months. The energetic can follow some of the many trails that lead from the summit, or alternatively, have a cup of coffee in the café and enjoy the view in the warmth.

GETTING HERE AND AROUND
By car from Adelaide, take the Crafers exit off the South Eastern Freeway and follow Summit Road or from the eastern suburbs via Greenhill Road. You can get to the summit as well as the Botanic Gardens and Cleland Wildlife Park in about 40 minutes by catching Bus 860F, 864, or 864F from Currie or Grenfell Street in the city center. Alight at bus stop 24A and connect to Bus 823.

A 3½-km (2-mi) round-trip walk from the Waterfall Gully parking lot in Cleland Conservation Park (15 minutes' drive from Adelaide) takes you along Waterfall Creek before climbing steeply to the white surveying tower on the summit; the track is closed on Total Fire Ban days.

ESSENTIALS
Transportation Adelaide Metro Info Centre (✉ *Currie and King William Sts., City Center* ☎ *08/8210–1000* ⊕ *www.adelaidemetro.com.au*).

EXPLORING
Mt. Lofty Botanic Gardens, with its rhododendrons, magnolias, ferns, and exotic trees, is glorious in fall and spring, when free guided walks leave the lower parking lot on Thursday at 10. ✉ *Picadilly entrance*

8

off Lampert Rd. ☎*08/8370–8370* ⊕*www.environment.sa.gov.au/
botanicgardens* 🖻 *Free* ☯ *Weekdays 8:30–4, weekends 10–5.*

☾ A short drive from Mt. Lofty Summit brings you to delightful **Cleland
Wildlife Park**, where many animals roam free in three different forest
habitats. Walking trails crisscross the park and its surroundings, and
you're guaranteed to see emus and kangaroos in the grasslands and pelicans around the swampy billabongs. There are also enclosures for wombats and other less sociable animals. Koala cuddling is a highlight of
koala close-up sessions (daily 10–noon, 2–4). Monthly two-hour night
walks (A$24) let you wander among nocturnal species such as potoroos
and brush-tailed bettongs. Private guided tours can be arranged for
A$74.50 per hour (A$111.50 on Sunday). Reservations are essential
for tours. The park is closed when there's a fire ban (usually between
December and February). ⊠ *Summit Rd.* ☎*08/8339–2444* ⊕*www.cle-
landwildlifepark.sa.gov.au* 🖻 *A$16* ☯ *Daily 9:30–5.*

WHERE TO EAT AND STAY

$$ ✕ **Summit.** If you suffer from vertigo, think twice about dining here; this
★ glass-front building atop Mt. Lofty is all about dining with altitude. The
ECLECTIC menu here is a frequently changing play of flavors; dishes might include
citrus-, cinnamon-, and rosemary-encrusted chicken breast on tabouleh
with Moroccan eggplant relish and goat curd. The wine list similarly
promotes Adelaide Hills vintages. While the food is good, you pay a
premium for the view. ⊠ *Mt. Lofty Lookout* ☎*08/8339–2600* 🖑 *Reser-
vations essential* ▭*AE, DC, MC, V* ☯ *No dinner Mon. and Tues.*

$$$ ⊡ **Mt. Lofty House.** From very English garden terraces below the sum-
mit of Mt. Lofty, this refined country house overlooks a patchwork of
vineyards, farms, and bushland. Relax over dinner in the glass-fronted
restaurant, read the daily paper on a settee in the lounge, then retreat
to a large bedroom sumptuously decorated with silks and brocades in
lush Victorian hues and florals. Heritage rooms have their own wood-
burning fireplaces. It's a very popular spot for weddings. **Pros:** peaceful location in stunning surroundings. **Cons:** dated furniture in rooms,
restaurant is overpriced. ⊠ *74 Summit Rd., Crafers* ☎*08/8339–6777*
🖷*08/8339–5656* ⊕*www.mtloftyhouse.com.au* ⇘*25 rooms, 1 suite*
⚘ *In-room: refrigerator, DVD (some), Wi-Fi. In-hotel: restaurant, bars,
tennis court, pool, no elevator, concierge, public Wi-Fi, laundry service,
no-smoking rooms* ▭*AE, DC, MC, V* ⦿*BP.*

BRIDGEWATER

6 km (4 mi) north of Mylor, 22 km (14 mi) southeast of Adelaide.

Bridgewater came into existence in 1841 as a refreshment stop for bullock
teams fording Cock's Creek. More English than German, with its flowing
creek and flower-filled gardens, this leafy, tranquil village was officially
planned in 1859 by the builder of the first Bridgewater flour mill.

GETTING HERE AND AROUND

From the city center, drive onto the Mount Barker Expressway until
you see the Stirling exit. From there, travel through lush countryside
following the signs to Bridgewater. The town itself is very small and
walkable. By public transport, catch Bus 864 or 864F from Currie Street
in the city to stop 45.

ESSENTIALS

Transportation Adelaide Metro Info Centre (⊠ *Currie and King William Sts., City Center* ☎ *08/8210–1000* ⊕ *www.adelaidemetro.com.au*).

The handsome **stone flour mill**, built in 1860, stands at the western entrance to the town, where its waterwheel still churns away. These days the mill houses the first-class Bridgewater Mill Restaurant, and serves as the shop front for Petaluma Wines, one of Australia's finest labels; try the Chardonnay and Viognier. The prestigious Croser champagne is matured on the building's lower level. ⊠ *Bridgewater and Mt. Barker Rds.* ☎ *08/8339–9222* ⊡ *Free* ⊙ *Daily 10–5.*

WHERE TO EAT AND STAY

$$ ✕ **Aldgate Pump Bistro.** You get a leisurely glimpse of local culture at this
ECLECTIC friendly two-story country pub. There is an extensive, eclectic selection of hearty fare such as Pump platters with mini pies hearty enough for at least two people. Warmed by log fires in winter, the dining room overlooks a shaded beer garden. The place is 2 km (1 mi) from Bridgewater, in the delightful village of Aldgate. ⊠ *Strathalbyn and Mt. Barker Rds., Aldgate* ☎ *08/8339–2015* ⊟ *AE, DC, MC, V.*

$$$$ ✕ **Bridgewater Mill Restaurant.** A stylish and celebrated restaurant in a
AUSTRALIAN converted flour mill, this is one of the state's best dining spots. Using
Fodor's Choice mostly local produce, chef Le Tu Thai creates an imaginative contempo-
★ rary Australian lunch menu; dishes might include beetroot millefeuille with a leek and goats'-cheese tart or or barramundi with spicy tomato sauce and pearl-barley risotto. In summer book ahead to get a table on the deck beside the waterwheel. If you're feeling flush, ask to see the special wine list. ⊠ *Bridgewater and Mt. Barker Rds.* ☎ *08/8339–9200* ⊟ *AE, DC, MC, V* ⊙ *Closed Tues. and Wed. No dinner.*

¢–$ ✕ **Organic Market and Café.** Pram-wheeling parents, hikers resting their
CAFE walking poles, and friends catching up on gossip keep this red-and-blue café and adjoining organic supermarket buzzing all day. Reasons to linger include focaccias, soups, home-baked muffins and cakes, and all kinds of purportedly healthy and unquestionably delicious drinks. It's in Stirling (3 km [2 mi] from Bridgewater). ⊠ *5 Druids Ave., Stirling* ☎ *08/8339–7131 café, 08/8339–4835 market* ⊟ *MC, V* ⊙ *No dinner.*

$$$$ ⛺ **Thorngrove Manor Hotel.** This romantic Gothic folly of turrets and
★ towers is *Lifestyles of the Rich and Famous* writ large. Opulent suites, set amid glorious gardens, have different decorative themes: a four-poster bed carved with heraldic lions is the centerpiece of the tapestry- and brocade-draped Queen's Chambers, and there are 1860 Scottish stained-glass windows and a Hapsburg piano in the King's Chambers. All the suites have entrances that ensure total privacy. Valet Kenneth Lehmann makes your every wish his command. **Pros:** perfect for the archetypal romantic getaway. **Cons:** if you have to ask how expensive it is, you can't afford it. ⊠ *2 Glenside La., Stirling* ☎ *08/8339–6748* ⊕ *www.slh.com/thorngrove* ⤶ *6 suites* ⌂ *In-room: safe, refrigerator, DVD, dial-up. In-hotel: restaurant, room service, no elevator, laundry service, public Internet, airport shuttle, no-smoking rooms* ⊟ *AE, DC, MC, V* ⓘⓞⓘ *BP.*

8

THE BAROSSA WINE REGION

Some of Australia's most famous vineyards are in the Barossa, just over an hour's drive northeast of Adelaide. More than 200 wineries across the two wide, shallow valleys that make up the region produce some of Australia's most celebrated wines, including aromatic Rhine Riesling, Seppelt's unique, century-old Para Port—and Penfolds Grange, which sells for more than A$600

Cultural roots set the Barossa apart. The area was settled by Silesian immigrants who left the German–Polish border region in the 1840s to escape religious persecution. These farmers brought traditions that you can't miss in the solid bluestone architecture, the tall slender spires of the Lutheran churches, and the *kuchen,* a cake as popular as the Devonshire tea introduced by British settlers. Together, these elements give the Barossa a charm that is unique among Australian wine-growing areas.

Most wineries in the Barossa operate sale rooms—called cellar doors—that usually have 6 to 12 varieties of wine available for tasting. You are not expected to sample the entire selection; to do so would overpower your taste buds. It's far better to give the tasting-room staff some idea of your personal preferences and let them suggest wine for you to sample. Some cellar doors charge a A$5 tasting fee, refundable against any purchase.

There is also zero tolerance when it comes to drunk driving—the legal blood-alcohol limit is 0.05 g/100ml—so the best advice is to get someone else to drive you round the wine regions if you're planning on tasting a glass or two.

GETTING HERE AND AROUND

The most direct route from Adelaide to the Barossa is via the town of Gawler. From Adelaide, drive north on King William Street. About 1 km (½ mi) past the Torrens River Bridge, take the right fork onto Main North Road. After 6 km (4 mi) this road forks to the right—follow signs to the Sturt Highway and the town of Gawler. At Gawler leave the highway and follow the signs to Lyndoch on the Barossa's southern border. The 50-km (31-mi) journey should take just over an hour. A more attractive, if circuitous, route to Lyndoch takes you through the Adelaide Hills' Chain of Ponds and Williamstown.

Because the Barossa wineries are relatively far apart, a car is by far the best way to get around. But keep in mind that there are stiff penalties for driving under the influence of alcohol. Police in patrol cars can pull you over for a random breath test anywhere in the state, and roadside mobile breath-testing stations—locally known as "Booze Buses"—are particularly visible during special events, such as the biennial Barossa Vintage Festival, held over the Easter weekend in odd-numbered years. The best advice is to take a tour—**Barossa Epicurean Tours** (⊕ *www. barossatours.com.au*) are highly praised.

The vineyards of the Barossa Valley.

TOURS

Tracey and Tom Teichert have lived in the Barossa for 20 years and make excellent guides to the region's best wineries as well as where to buy some excellent local produce. They will make suggestions or they will take you wherever you fancy. They can pick you up from Adelaide (A$160) or more cheaply, from anywhere in the Barossa. Gray Line Adelaide's full-day tour of the Barossa Region (A$117) leaves from Adelaide Central Bus Station. It includes lunch at a winery. Enjoy Adelaide runs a full-day (A$69) Barossa tour that visits four vineyards and includes lunch. Groovy Grape Getaways offers full-day (A$79) Barossa tours with a visit to the Adelaide Hills and a barbecue lunch.

ESSENTIALS

Tour Operators Barossa EpicureanTours (☎ 0402/989647 ⊕ www.barossa-tours.au). **Enjoy Adelaide** (☎ 08/8332–1401 ⊕ www.enjoyadelaide.com.au). **Gray Line Adelaide** (☎ 1300/858687 ⊕ www.grayline.com.au/adelaide). **Groovy Grape Getaways** (☎ 08/8371–4000 or 1800/661177 ⊕ www.groovygrape.com.au).

Visitor Information Contact Barossa Visitors Centre (✉ 66–68 Murray St., Tanunda ☎ 08/8563–0600 ⊕ www.barossa.com ⊗ Weekdays 9–5, weekends 10–4).

LYNDOCH

58 km (36 mi) northeast of Adelaide.

This pleasant little town surrounded by vineyards was established in 1840 and is the Barossa's oldest settlement site. It owes the spelling of

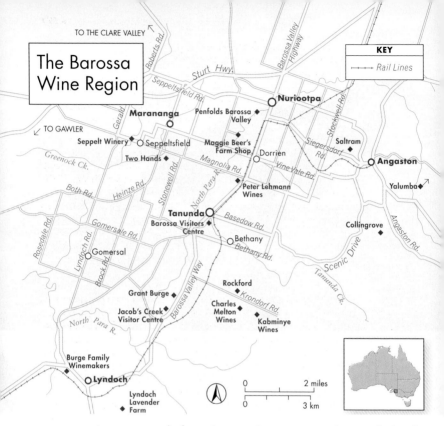

The Barossa Wine Region

KEY
····→ Rail Lines

TO THE CLARE VALLEY

TO GAWLER

its name to a draftsman's error—it was meant to be named after the British soldier Lord Lynedoch.

Burge Family Winemakers. You can drink in a leafy vineyard view while tasting from the wine barrels in this understated cellar door. Winemaker Rick Burge's best include the powerful yet elegant Draycott Shiraz and Olive Hill Shiraz-Grenache-Mourvedre blend. There is also sometimes A Nice Red—read the label! ⊠ *Barossa Valley Way near Hermann Thumm Dr.* ☎ *08/8524–4644* ⊕ *www.burgefamily.com.au* ✉ *Free* ⊙ *Fri., Sat., and Mon. 10–5 (call ahead).*

Lyndoch Lavender Farm, a family-friendly tribute to the purple flower that adorns the hills, grows more than 90 varieties on 6 lush acres high above Lyndoch. Light café meals are available, and the farm shop sells essential oils, creams, and other products, including wine from their adjacent vineyard. ⊠ *Hoffnungsthal and Tweedies Gully Rds.5351* ☎ *08/8524– 4538* ⊕ *www.lyndochlavenderfarm.com.au* ✉ *A$2* ⊙ *Aug.–Jan., daily 10–4:30; Feb.–July, weekends 10–4:30.*

WHERE TO STAY

$$$$

Fodor's Choice

★

🏨 **Abbotsford Country House.** Tranquility reigns at this property on 50 acres of rolling beef farm with Barossa views. Silence and blissfully comfortable beds with superhigh-thread-count Egyptian linens make drifting off easy. Collected antiques decorate the eight rooms, one of which has a jetted tub, another a deep, claw-foot enamel bathtub, and the rest double showers. All have complimentary port and chocolate. Relax in your room (TVs are available on request) or venture out to sit by the fireplace in the main house. The abundant, home-cooked breakfast,

TAKE IT SLOW

Allow yourself only one day in the Barossa and you'll regret it. Slow down and savor the food and wine and warm hospitality.

which uses local and farm-grown ingredients (some from the 600-plant vegetable and rose garden), will fuel you up for a day of exploring the valley. **Pros:** a serene and luxurious place to recover from all the wine tasting you will no doubt do, very welcoming hosts. **Cons:** dining in the restaurant is expensive, health nuts might rue the lack of gym and leisure facilities. ⊠ *Yaldara Dr. at Fuss Rd., Lyndoch* ⬤ *Box 675, Lyndoch, SA, 5351* ☎ *08/8254–4662* ⊕ *www.abbotsfordhouse.com* ⟿ *8 rooms* ⬧ *In-room: no phone, refrigerator, no TV, Wi-Fi. In-hotel: restaurant, laundry service, public Wi-Fi, no-smoking rooms, no kids under 12* ⊟ *MC, V* ⦿ *BP.*

$–$$$ ⚿ **Belle Cottages.** Rose-filled gardens or sweeping rural acres surround these classic Australian accommodations. Wood-burning fireplaces in several invite you to relax with a bottle of red after a day in the Barossa region, and comfy beds tempt you to sleep late. In Christabelle Cottage, an 1849 Heritage-listed former chapel, a spiral staircase winds up to a mezzanine bedroom. The other cottages, houses, and suites have one, two, or three bedrooms and country kitchens. **Pros:** great discounts available for groups, comfortable and homely accommodation. **Cons:** not the place for an anonymous stay, some quirks to the plumbing. ⬤ *Box 481, Lyndoch, SA, 5351* ☎ *08/8524–4825* ⊕ *www.bellescapes.com* ⟿ *8 cottages, 3 suites* ⬧ *In-room: no phone (some), kitchen, refrigerator, VCR (some), DVD (some). In-hotel: no elevator, laundry facilities (some), no-smoking rooms, some pets allowed* ⊟ *AE, MC, V* ⦿ *BP.*

TANUNDA

13 km (8 mi) northeast of Lyndoch, 70 km (43 mi) northeast of Adelaide.

The cultural heart of the Barossa, Tanunda is its most German settlement. The four Lutheran churches in the town testify to its heritage, and dozens of shops selling German pastries, breads, and wursts (sausages)—not to mention wine—line the main street. Many of the valley's best wineries are close by.

At **Charles Melton Wines** tasting is relaxing and casual in a brick-floor, timber-wall cellar door, which is warmed by a log fire in winter. After making sure the resident cats have vacated it first, settle into a director's chair at the long wooden table and let the staff pour. Nine Popes, a huge, decadent red blend, is the flagship wine, and the ruby-red Rose of Virginia is arguably Australia's best rosé. You can enjoy a glass of either with a cheese platter or game pie on the veranda. ⊠ *Krondorf*

8

Rd. near Nitschke Rd. ☎ *08/8563–3606* ⊕ *www.charlesmeltonwines. com.au* 🖾 *Free* ☉ *Daily 11–5.*

Grant Burge is one of the most successful of the Barossa's young, independent wine labels. Wines include impressive Chardonnays, crisp Rieslings, and powerful reds such as Meshach Shiraz. Don't miss the Holy Trinity—a highly acclaimed Rhône blend of Grenache, Shiraz, and Mourvedre. The cellar door is at Jacob's Creek, 5 km (3 mi) south of Tanunda. Don't come hungry, as there isn't any food available here. ⊠ *Barossa Valley Way near Koch Rd.* ☎ *08/8563–7471* ⊕ *www.grant-burgewines.com.au* 🖾 *Free* ☉ *Daily 10–5.*

An impressive block of glass, steel, and recycled timber, **Jacob's Creek Visitor Centre** overlooks the creek whose name is familiar to wine drinkers around the world, as they export to more than 60 countries. The informative staff makes the place well worth a visit. Inside the building, plasma screens and pictorial displays tell the history of the label. Cabernet Sauvignon, Merlot, Chardonnay, and the Shiraz-rosé, served chilled, can be tasted at a 60-foot-long counter. There is a lunch-only restaurant with broad glass doors opening onto a grassy lawn edged with towering eucalyptus trees. ⊠ *Barossa Valley Way near Jacob's Creek* ☎ *08/8521–3000* ⊕ *www.jacobscreek.com* 🖾 *Free* ☉ *Daily 10–5.*

★ Built from local mud brick and corrugated iron, with a winglike roof, the light-filled cellar door at **Kabminye Wines** was a controversial addition to the valley—but there's no argument about the wines and the food. Each wine has its own unique and surprising taste, particularly the excellent Ilona rosé and the full-frontal flagship Hubert Shiraz. The café cooks up traditional Silesian fare such as pork chops with a dried fruit sauce on egg noodles. Changing art exhibitions are often displayed in the upstairs gallery. ⊠ *Krondorf Rd. near Nitschke Rd.* ☎ *08/8563–0889* ⊕ *www.kabminye.com* 🖾 *Free* ☉ *Daily 11–5.*

Peter Lehmann Wines is owned by a larger-than-life Barossa character whose wine consistently wins international awards. Art-hung stonework and a wood-burning fireplace make the tasting room one of the most pleasant in the valley. This is the only place to find Black Queen Sparkling Shiraz. Wooden tables on a shady lawn encourage picnicking on Barossa platters. Served daily, it's full of local produce and big enough for two. They also offer VIP tastings in a private room with food matchings. But you must book in advance. ⊠ *Para Rd. off Stelzer Rd.* ☎ *08/8563–2500* ⊕ *www.peterlehmannwines.com.au* 🖾 *Free* ☉ *Weekdays 9:30–5, weekends 10:30–4:30.*

★ Nestled in a lovely cobbled stable yard, **Rockford** is a small winery with a tasting room in an old stone barn. The specialties are heavy, rich wines made from some of the region's oldest vines. Several notable labels have appeared under the Rockford name—be sure to try the Cabernet Sauvignon and the Basket Press Shiraz (at cellar door from March until sold out), outstanding examples of these most traditional of Australian varieties. The owners pride themselves on their old-school methods. The same equipment (you can see in the yard) has been used for over a century. ⊠ *Krondorf Rd. near Nitschke Rd.* ☎ *08/8563–2720* ⊕ *www. rockfordwines.com.au* 🖾 *Free* ☉ *Daily 11–5.*

WHERE TO EAT AND STAY

$$
AUSTRALIAN
✕ **1918 Bistro & Grill.** This rustic and whimsical restaurant in a restored villa makes exemplary use of the Barossa's distinctive regional produce in a seasonal Oz menu flavored with tastes from Asia and the Middle East. Local olive oil, cold cuts, venison, quail, and seasonal fruits and vegetables influence the dishes like the delicious grilled kangaroo fillet, minted peas, pancetta, and corn bread and pepper jam. Meals are served beside a two-sided fireplace in winter and alfresco in the garden in summer. The mostly Barossa wine list includes rare classics and newcomers. ✉ *94 Murray St.* ☎ *08/8563–0405* ✍ *Reservations essential* ▭ *AE, DC, MC, V.*

> ### PACE YOURSELF
>
> Home-smoked meats, organic farmhouse cheeses, and mouth-filling Shiraz—the Barossa is the ultimate picnic basket. Use this fact as an excuse for a long lunch, which will give you time to recover from all that wine tasting. Remember to pace yourself as you taste, and wherever possible, make use of those spit buckets you see at each winery. You'll be glad you did.

¢–$
GERMAN
✕ **Die Barossa Wurst Haus & Bakery.** For a hearty German lunch at a reasonable price, no place beats this small, friendly café and shop. The wurst is fresh from local butchers, the sauerkraut is direct from Germany, and the potato salad is made on-site from a secret recipe. ✉ *86A Murray St.* ☎ *08/8563–3598* ▭ *No credit cards* ◷ *No dinner.*

$–$$
⊡ **Blickinstal Barossa Valley Retreat.** Its name means "view into the valley," which understates the breathtaking panoramas from this lovely B&B. Amid vineyards in foothills five minutes from the Barossa's heart, the retreat is a tranquil base for exploring. Gardens surround the self-contained lodge apartments and studios, and breakfast is served on the homestead veranda. You can also indulge in afternoon tea. **Pros:** great-value rooms with superb views across the valley, complimentary port in the evening. **Cons:** don't expect corporate-style facilities or an anonymous stay. ⌂ *Box 17, Rifle Range Rd., 5352* ☎ *08/8563–2716* ⊕ *www.users.bigpond.com/blickinstal* ⇆ *4 studios, 2 apartments* ⌂ *In-room: no phone, kitchen, refrigerator, DVD. In-hotel: no elevator, laundry facilities, public Internet, no-smoking rooms* ▭ *AE, MC, V* ⦿ *BP.*

$$–$$$
★
⊡ **Lawley Farm.** Amid 20 acres of grapes, in a courtyard shaded by gnarled peppercorn trees, these delightful stone cottage-style suites were assembled from the remains of barns dating from the Barossa's pioneering days. A wood-burning stove warms the Krondorf Suite in the original 1852 cottage, while in the Para Suite—former stables with ceiling beams from Adelaide shearing sheds—you can soak in a hot tub and then sleep late in a brass bed. The farm is within easy walking distance of six wineries. **Pros:** original buildings have been lovingly preserved, the breakfasts are legendary. **Cons:** no exercise facilities for working off all the local wine and produce. ✉ *Krondorf and Grocke Rds., Box 103* ☎ *08/8563–2141* ⊕ *www.lawleyfarm.com.au* ⇆ *4 suites* ⌂ *In-room: no phone, refrigerator, dial-up (some). In-hotel: room service, no elevator, laundry service, public Internet, no-smoking rooms* ▭ *MC, V* ⦿ *BP.*

8

ANGASTON

16 km (10 mi) northeast of Tanunda via Menglers Hill Rd. Scenic Drive, 86 km (53 mi) northeast of Adelaide.

Named after George Fife Angas, the Englishman who founded the town and sponsored many of the German and British immigrants who came here, Angaston is full of jacaranda trees, and its main street is lined with stately stone buildings and tiny shops. Schulz Butchers has been making and selling wurst (German sausage) since 1939; 17 varieties hang above the counter. You can buy other delicious regional produce every Saturday morning at the Barossa Farmers Market, behind Vintners Bar & Grill.

Collingrove was the ancestral home of the Angas family, the descendants of George Fife Angas, one of South Australia's founders. At the height of its fortunes, the family controlled more than 14 million acres from this house. Today the property is administered by the National Trust, and you can inspect the Angas family portraits and memorabilia, including Dresden china, a hand-painted Louis XV cabinet, and Chippendale chairs, on guided tours. You can also stay overnight at Collingrove in evocative Old World B&B luxury. ⊠ *Eden Valley Rd. near Collingrove Rd.* ☎ *08/8564–2061* ⊕ *www.collingrovehomestead.com.au* ☜ *A$10* ⊙ *Tours everyday 1:30, 2:30, and 3:30; booking advised, as hotel guests get priority.*

Low-beamed ceilings and ivy-covered trellises give **Saltram** an urbanized sort of rustic charm. The vineyard's robust wine list includes the Pepperjack Barossa Grenache Rosé, a delightful vintage available only in summer. It's a delicious accompaniment to the Italian-influenced menu at the adjacent—and excellent—Salter's Kitchen restaurant. ⊠ *Nuriootpa Rd., 1 km (½ mi) west of Angaston* ☎ *08/8561–0200* ⊕ *www.saltramwines. com.au* ☜ *Free* ⊙ *Daily 10–5.*

Australia's oldest family-owned winery, **Yalumba** sits within a hugely impressive compound resembling an Italian monastery. The cellar door is decorated with mission-style furniture, antique wine-making materials, and mementos of the Hill Smith family, who first planted vines in the Barossa in 1849. The Octavius Shirazes are superb, and the "Y Series" Viognier is thoroughly enjoyable. ⊠ *Eden Valley Rd. just south of Valley Rd.* ☎ *08/8561–3200* ⊕ *www.yalumba.com* ☜ *Free* ⊙ *Daily 10–5.*

WHERE TO EAT

$$ ✕ **Vintners Bar & Grill.** The Barossa region is at its best in this sophisti-
★ cated spot, where vivid contemporary artworks adorn the walls and
AUSTRALIAN wide windows look out on rows of vineyards. The short menu blends Australian, Mediterranean, and Asian flavors in such dishes as grainfed chicken, tomato confit, salsa verde, and caper berries, and chargrilled kangaroo loin with lentil and barley toast. Scarlet and charcoal suede chairs and an upbeat jazz sound track make it easy to relax; top winemakers often come here to sample from the cellar's 160 wines. ⊠ *Nuriootpa Rd. near Stockwell Rd.* ☎ *08/8564–2488* ⌲ *Reservations essential* ⊟ *AE, DC, MC, V* ⊙ *No dinner Sun.*

NURIOOTPA

8 km (5 mi) northwest of Angaston, 74 km (46 mi) northeast of Adelaide.

Long before it was the Barossa's commercial center, Nuriootpa was used as a bartering place by local Aboriginal tribes, hence its name: Nuriootpa means "meeting place." Most locals call it Nurie.

SHIPPING WINE

Wouldn't it be wonderful if international airlines showed some empathy for wine fanciers and stopped charging exorbitant excess baggage fees for cases of wine? In the meantime you can appeal to the better nature of the Barossa vignerons who have overseas stockists or can arrange shipping.

★ Renowned cook and food writer Maggie Beer is an icon of Australian cuisine. Burned-fig jam, ice cream, *verjuice* (a golden liquid made from unfermented grape juice and used for flavoring), and her signature Pheasant Farm Pâté are some of the delights you can taste and buy at **Maggie Beer's Farm Shop.** Treat-filled picnic baskets are available all day to take out or dip into on the deck overlooking a tree-fringed pond full of turtles. Don't miss the daily cooking demonstrations at 2 PM. ⊠ *End of Pheasant Farm Rd. off Samuel Rd.* ☎ *08/8562–4477* ⊕ *www.maggiebeer.com.au* ⊠ *Free* ⊙ *Daily 10:30–5.*

Penfolds Barossa Valley. A very big brother to the 19th-century Magill Estate in Adelaide, this massive wine-making outfit in the center of Nuriootpa lets you taste Shiraz, Cabernet, Merlot, Chardonnay, and Riesling blends—but not the celebrated Grange—at the cellar door. To savor the flagship wine and other premium vintages, book a Taste of Grange Tour (A$150 per person, minimum of two). ⊠ *Barossa Valley Hwy. at Railway Terrace* ☎ *08/8568–9408* ⊕ *www.penfolds.com.au* ⊠ *Free* ⊙ *Daily 10–5.*

OFF THE BEATEN PATH

Banrock Station Wine & Wetland Centre. The salt-scrub-patched Murray River floodplain 150 km (94 mi) east of Nuriootpa is an unlikely setting for a winery, but it is worth making the journey to this spot at Kingston-on-Murray. Within the stilted, mud-brick building perched above the vineyard and river lagoons you can select a wine to accompany an all-day grazing platter or lunch on the outdoor deck—try the emu burger with bush tomato, star-anise salsa, and pepperleaf damper. Afterward, you can take an 8-km (5-mi) walk (A$5, bookings essential) to view the surrounding wetlands (which can be "drylands" during a drought), and learn about the ongoing wildlife habitat restoration and conservation work funded by Banrock Station wine sales. ⊠ *Holmes Rd. just off Sturt Hwy., Kingston-on-Murray* ☎ *08/8583–0299* ⊕ *www. banrockstation.com.au* ⊠ *Free* ⊙ *Daily 9–5.*

MARANANGA

6 km (4 mi) west of Nuriootpa, 68 km (42 mi) northeast of Adelaide.

The tiny hamlet of Marananga inhabits one of the prettiest corners of the Barossa. This area's original name was Gnadenfrei, which means "freed by the grace of God"—a reference to the religious persecution

Fish Tales

CLOSE UP

With nearly 4,800 km (3,000 mi) of coastline and hundreds of miles of rivers, South Australia has almost as many opportunities for fishing as it has varieties of fish. You can join local anglers of all ages dangling hand lines from a jetty, casting into the surf from coastal rocks, hopping aboard charter boats, or spending a day sitting on a riverside log.

The Murray River is the place to head for callop (also called yellow belly or golden perch) and elusive Murray cod. In the river's backwaters you can also net a feed of yabbies, a type of freshwater crayfish, which make a wonderful appetizer before you tuck into the one that didn't get away. In the ocean King George whiting reigns supreme, but there is also excellent eating with mulloway, bream, snapper, snook, salmon, and sweep. The

yellowtail kingfish, a great fighter usually found in deep water, prefers the shallower waters of Coffin Bay, off the Eyre Peninsula. **Baird Bay Charters & Ocean Eco Experience** (☎ 08/8626–5017 ⊕ www.bairdbay. com) runs fishing charters to Coffin Bay and other top spots. Another popular destination is the Yorke Peninsula. **S.A. Fishing Adventures** (☎ 08/8854–4098 ⊕ www.safishingadventures.com.au) takes anglers to great spots around the Yorke Peninsula. Last, but certainly not least, is legendary Kangaroo Island. You can spend from a few hours to a few days fishing the waters around Kangaroo Island with **Kangaroo Island Fishing Charters** (☎ 08/8552–7000 ⊕ www. kifishchart.com.au).

—Melanie Ball

the German settlers suffered before they emigrated to Australia. Marananga, the Aboriginal name, was adopted in 1918, when a wave of anti-German sentiment spurred many name changes in the closing days of World War I.

★ Joseph Seppelt was a Silesian farmer who purchased land in the Barossa after arriving in Australia in 1849. Under the control of his son, Benno, the wine-making business flourished, and today **Seppelt Winery** and its splendid grounds are a tribute to the family's industry and enthusiasm. Fortified wine is a Seppelt specialty; this is the only winery in the world that has ports for every year as far back as 1878. Most notable is the 100-year-old Para Liqueur Tawny. The Grenache, Chardonnay, Cabernet, and sparkling Shiraz are also worth tasting. Tours of the 19th-century distillery are run daily; you can also book 24 hours ahead for the Journey into Fortifieds tour (minimum 4 people) and Legend of Seppelt tour (minimum 2, weekends only). There's a small snack bar that offers delicious cakes and afternoon teas. ⊠ *Seppeltsfield Rd., 3 km (2 mi) west of Marananga, Seppeltsfield* ☎ *08/8568–6217* ⊕ *www. seppelt.com* ⊠ *Free; Heritage Tour A$10, Journey into Fortifieds tour A$25, Legend of Seppelt tour A$55* ⊗ *10:30–5. Heritage Tours daily 11:30, 1:30, and 3:30; Journey into Fortifieds daily (by appointment) 2:30; Legend of Seppelt weekends (by appointment) 10:30.*

★ **Two Hands.** The interior of this 19th-century sandstone cottage is every bit as surprising as the wines produced here. Polished wood and glass surround the contemporary counter where the excellent staff leads you through the tasting of several "out of the box" red and white varietals and blends. The main event is Shiraz sourced from six wine regions. Compare and contrast Shiraz from Victoria and Padthaway (South Australia); and try the Barossa-grown Bad Impersonator. From Thursday to Sunday you can join a structured Masterclass Tasting (maximum 8 people, bookings recommended) in the adjoining bake house, which has a glass floor over the original cellar. ⊠ *Neldner Rd. just off Seppeltsfield Rd.* ☎ *08/8562–4566* ⊕ *www.twohandswines.com* ⊠ *General Tastings A$5 (refundable with purchase), Bakehouse Masterclass A$25* ⊙ *Daily 10–5.*

WHERE TO STAY

$$$$ ⊞ **The Lodge Country House.** Rambling and aristocratic, this bluestone
★ homestead 3 km (2 mi) south of Marananga was built in 1903 for one of the 13 children of Joseph Seppelt, founder of the showpiece winery across the road. Barossa vintages fill the wine cellar, crystal and polished timber gleam in the formal dining room, and big, comfortable sofas inspire relaxing in the sitting room, perhaps with a book from the library. The four large guest rooms are furnished in period style; a bay-window seat in each looks out at the gorgeous garden. Set-menu dinners (A$80), available by reservation, make good use of local produce. There's a minimum two-night stay on weekends. **Pros:** beautiful gardens, informative hosts who delight in telling guests about the history of the place. **Cons:** not particularly suitable for kids. ⊠ *Seppeltsfield Rd., 3 km (2 mi) west of Marananga, Seppeltsfield* ☎ *08/8562–8277* ⊕ *www.thelodgecountryhouse.com.au* ⇲ *4 rooms* ⌂ *In-room: no phone, no TV. In-hotel: restaurant, TV lounge, library, tennis court, pool, no elevator, laundry service, public Wi-Fi, no kids under 16, no-smoking rooms* ⊟ *AE, MC, V* ⭕ *BP.*

$$$$ ⊞ **The Louise.** Prepare for pampering and privacy at this country estate on a quiet back road with glorious valley views. Step from your personal Mediterranean-style courtyard into a plush world of charcoal, chocolate, and cappuccino hues. There are wide-screen LCD televisions, wood-burning fireplaces, whirlpool tubs, and double-head rainwater showers in all suites; some also have a walled rear terrace with an outdoor shower. Appellation restaurant (reservations essentials) serves sophisticated, innovative regional cuisine ($$$$) such as thin slices of Barossa corn-fed chicken and Lachsschinken ham with garlic and sage, and rare venison with pickled black cherries. **Pros:** stunning rooms with beautiful private gardens. **Cons:** extras like nternet access are annoyingly expensive, pool and spa could use a facelift. ⊠ *Seppeltsfield and Stonewell Rds.,* ☎ *08/8562–2722, restaurant 08/8562–4144* ⊕ *www.thelouise.com.au, restaurant www.appellation.com.au* ⇲ *15 suites* ⌂ *In-room: safe, refrigerator, DVD, Ethernet, Wi-Fi. In-hotel: restaurant, room service, bar, pool, bicycles, concierge, no elevator, laundry service, public Internet, no-smoking rooms* ⊟ *AE, DC, MC, V* ⭕ *CP.*

8

Stomping the grapes at the Barossa Vintage Festival.

THE CLARE VALLEY

Smaller and less well known than the Barossa, the Clare Valley nonetheless holds its own among Australia's wine-producing regions. Its robust reds and delicate whites are among the country's finest, and the Clare is generally regarded as the best area in Australia for fragrant, flavorsome Rieslings. On the fringe of the vast inland deserts, the Clare is a narrow sliver of fertile soil about 30 km (19 mi) long and 5 km (3 mi) wide, with a microclimate that makes it ideal for premium wine making.

The first vines were planted here as early as 1842, but it took a century and a half for the Clare Valley to take its deserved place on the national stage. The mix of small family wineries and large-scale producers, 150-year-old settlements and grand country houses, snug valleys and dense native forests, has rare charm.

GETTING HERE AND AROUND
The Clare Valley is about a 90-minute drive from Adelaide via Main North Road. From the center of Adelaide, head north on King William Street through the heart of North Adelaide. King William becomes O'Connell Street. After crossing Barton Terrace, look for Main North Road signs on the right. The road passes through the satellite town of Elizabeth, bypasses the center of Gawler, and then runs due north to Auburn, the first town of the Clare Valley when approaching from the capital. Main North Road continues down the middle of the valley to Clare.

As with the Barossa, a car is essential for exploring the Clare Valley in any depth. Taste wine in moderation if you're driving; as well as keeping yourself and others safe, you'll avoid paying the extremely high penalties for driving while intoxicated.

TOURS

Clare Valley Tours combines wine tasting with history and culture on its daylong tour of the region's major towns and sites (A$100 including lunch), departing from Clare. Barossa Epicurean Tours also offer a Clare option.

Contact Clare Valley Tours (☎ *0418/832812 or 08/8843-8066* ⊕ *www. cvtours.com.au*). **Barossa EpicureanTours** (☎ *0402/989647* ⊕ *www.barossa-tours.au*).

ESSENTIALS

Visitor Information Contact Clare Valley Visitor Information Centre (✉ *Main North and Spring Gully Rds.* ⊕ ✛ *6 km (4 mi) south of Clare* ☎ *1800/242131 or 08/8842-2131* ⊕ *www.clarevalley.com.au* ☉ *Weekdays 9–5, Sat. 9:30–4:30, Sun. 10–4.*

SEVENHILL

126 km (78 mi) north of Adelaide.

Sevenhill is the Clare Valley's geographic center, and the location of the region's first winery, established by Jesuit priests in 1851 to produce altar wine. The area had been settled three years earlier by Austrian Jesuits who named their seminary after the seven hills of Rome.

The Riesling Trail, a walking and cycling track that follows an old Clare Valley railway line, runs through Sevenhill. The 25-km (16-mi) trail passes wineries and villages in gently rolling country between Auburn and Clare, and three loop trails take you to vineyards off the main track.

Bikes can be rented from **Clare Valley Cycle Hire** (✉ *32 Victoria Rd., Clare* ☎ *0418/802077*).

Kilikanoon Wines. A rising star of the Clare Valley, Kilikanoon is already renowned for multilayered reds, such as the dense, richly colored Oracle Shiraz (occasionally available for tasting); Prodigal Grenache is another beauty. ✉ *Penna La., Penwortham, 2 km (1 mi) off Main North Rd.* ☎ *08/8843-4206* ⊕ *www.kilikanoon.com.au* ☎ *Free* ☉ *Thurs.–Mon. 11–5.*

Fodors Choice ★ The area's first winery, **Sevenhill Cellars** was created by the Jesuits, and they still run the show, with any profits going to education, mission work, and the needy within Australia. In the 1940s the winery branched out from sacramental wine to commercial production, and today 21 wine varieties, including Riesling (try the St. Aloysius label), Verdelho, Grenache, and fortified wines, account for 75% of its business. Book a guided tour with the charming Brother John May, Jesuit winemaker emeritus, who takes you to the cellars, the cemetery, and the church crypt where Jesuits have been interred since 1865. You can also rent bicycles here to explore the rolling hills and vineyards. ✉ *College Rd. just off Main North Rd.* ☎ *08/8843-4222* ⊕ *www.sevenhillcellars.com. au* ☎ *Free, tours A$6* ☉ *Weekdays 9–5, weekends 10–5; tours Tues. and Thurs. at 2.*

Skillogalee Winery is known for its excellent Riesling, Gewürztraminer, and Shiraz, as well as its wonderful restaurant. Wine tasting takes place in a small room in the 1850s cottage (the restaurant occupies the others). Don't miss the sparkling Riesling. ⊠ *Hughes Park Rd.* ☎ *08/8843–4311* ⊕ *www.skillogalee.com* 🖬 *Free* ☉ *Daily 10–5.*

WHERE TO EAT

$–$$ ✕ **Rising Sun.** People have watched the world go by from the veranda of
AUSTRALIAN   this landmark hotel in Auburn, 16 km (10 mi) south of Sevenhill, since
it was built in 1849. Pull up a chair overlooking the street and partake
of the delicious modern Australian food, perhaps kangaroo fillet with
quandong (a native fruit) and sweet-potato mash, or butterfish in a batter of Coopers Pale Ale (Adelaide's own beer). The wine list shows off
the Clare Valley's best. ⊠ *Main North Rd., Auburn* ☎ *08/8849–2015*
🖬 *AE, DC, MC, V.*

$–$$ ✕ **Skillogalee Winery.** The dining area here spills from a 1850s cottage
★   onto a beautiful veranda overlooking a flower-filled garden and rows
AUSTRALIAN   of grapevines. The menu changes seasonally, but you can't go wrong
with the "vine pruner's lunch," chef Diana Palmer's spin on the British
plowman's meal, a platter of rum-glazed local ham, cheddar cheese,
chutney, and crusty bread. Entrées might include fish tagine with olives,
apricots, and Skillogalee figs with saffron and lemon couscous or dukkah-crusted chicken breast. While most Clare restaurants have limited
hours, Skillogalee is so popular it's open 7 days a week. Gourmet picnic baskets can be ordered, and group dinners are available by prior
arrangement. Skillogalee also has self-contained cottage accommodation. ⊠ *Hughes Park Rd.* ☎ *08/8843–4311* 🍴 *Reservations essential*
🖬 *AE, DC, V* ☉ *No dinner.*

CLARE

10 km (6 mi) north of Sevenhill, 136 km (84 mi) north of Adelaide.

The bustling town of Clare is the Clare Valley's commercial center.
Unusual for ultra-English South Australia, many of its early settlers
were Irish—hence the valley's name, after the Irish county Clare, and
place-names such as Armagh and Donnybrook.

On Clare's fringe is **Leasingham Wines,** among the biggest producers in
the valley. The winery began operation in 1893, which also makes it
one of the oldest. The tasting room is in an old, vine-covered two-story
stone still house complete with copper still. Leasingham's reputation of
late has been forged by its red wines, particularly the peppery Shiraz;
they also have a sparkling version. ⊠ *7 Dominic St.* ☎ *08/8842–2785*
⊕ *www.leasingham-wines.com.au* 🖬 *Free* ☉ *Daily 10–4.*

★   The small, no-frills tasting room means there is nothing to distract
you from discovering why **Tim Adams Wines** has a big reputation. The
standout in an impressive collection of reds and whites, which includes a
celebrated Riesling and delicious Pinot Gris, is the purple-red Aberfeldy
Shiraz, made from hundred-year-old vines. You can buy wine by the
glass and bottle to enjoy with a bring-your-own-picnic on the veranda.
⊠ *Warenda Rd. just off Main North Rd., 5 km (3 mi) south of Clare*
☎ *1800/356326* ⊕ *www.timadamswines.com.au* 🖬 *Free* ☉ *Weekdays
10:30–5, weekends 11–5.*

WHERE TO STAY

$ **Bungaree Station.** Your journey back to colonial Australia begins at check-in at this family-owned farm; the reception area is in the original station store. Outlying cottages and the Heritage-listed stables beside the stone homestead have been converted into family-friendly accommodations, some with shared facilities. The sandstone stallion box is now the honeymoon cottage! Rooms have fans only and can heat up in summer; wood-burning, slow-combustion stoves give winter warmth. Take time exploring the property; down the hill is an unusual sandstone woolshed. Bungaree is popular with groups, and may be booked up for private functions. **Pros:** fascinating insight into a working homestead, accommodation options for all budgets. **Cons:** city types might find it too rustic, food options are limited. ✉ *Main North Rd., 11 km (7 mi) north of Clare* ☎ *08/8842–2677* ⊕ *www.bungareestation.com.au* ⛵ *7 cottages, 3 rooms with shared bathrooms* ⚐ *In-room: no a/c, kitchen (some), refrigerator (some), no TV (some). In-hotel: pool, gym, no-smoking rooms* ▭ *AE, DC, MC, V.*

$$$$ **North Bundaleer.** The spoils of wealthy pastoral life await you at this
Fodor's Choice   century-old sandstone homestead 61 km (38 mi) north of Clare, on the
★   scenic route to the Flinders Ranges. Beyond the jewel-box hall lined with hand-painted wallpaper is a ballroom where you can play the grand piano, and a peppermint-pink drawing room that's perfect for reading. After dining with hosts Marianne and Malcolm Booth at a Georgian table, you can slip into the canopy bed in the Red Room Suite, the most luxurious of four bedrooms. Rural isolation is a great excuse for taking a dinner/bed-and-breakfast package here. **Pros:** relaxed and informal despite the grandeur, perfect for getting away from it all. **Cons:** city types might find it too secluded and intimate. ✉ *Spalding–Jamestown Rd., Jamestown* ✉ *Box 255, Jamestown, 5491* ☎ *08/8665–4024* ⊕ *www.northbundaleer.com.au* ⛵ *3 rooms, 1 suite* ⚐ *In-room: no a/c (some), no phone, no TV. In-hotel: restaurant, bar, pool, no elevator, public Wi-Fi, no-smoking rooms* ▭ *AE, DC, MC, V* ⋈ *BP, MAP.*

FLEURIEU PENINSULA

The Fleurieu has traditionally been seen as Adelaide's backyard. Generations of local families have vacationed in the string of beachside resorts between Victor Harbor and Goolwa, near the mouth of the Murray River. McLaren Vale wineries attract connoisseurs, and the beaches and bays bring in surfers, swimmers, and sunseekers. The countryside, with its rolling hills and dramatic cliff scenery, is a joy to drive through.

Although the region is within easy reach of Adelaide, you should consider spending the night if you want to enjoy all it has to offer. You can also easily combine a visit here with one or more nights on Kangaroo Island. The ferry from Cape Jervis, at the end of the peninsula, takes less than an hour to reach Penneshaw on the island, and there are coach connections from Victor Harbor and Goolwa.

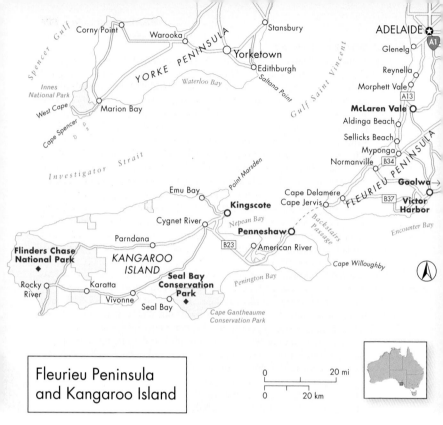

Fleurieu Peninsula and Kangaroo Island

0   20 mi

0   20 km

GETTING HERE AND AROUND

Renting a car in Adelaide and driving south is the best way to visit the Fleurieu Peninsula, especially if you wish to tour the wineries, which aren't served by public transportation.

The Fleurieu is an easy drive south from Adelaide. McLaren Vale itself is less than an hour away. Leave central Adelaide along South Terrace or West Terrace, linking with the Anzac Highway, which heads toward Glenelg. At the intersection with Main South Road, turn left. This road takes you almost to McLaren Vale. After a detour to visit the wineries, watch for signs for Victor Harbor Road. About 20 km (12 mi) south the highway splits. One road heads for Victor Harbor, the other for Goolwa. Those two places are connected by a major road that follows the coastline. Drivers heading to Cape Jervis and the Kangaroo Island ferries should stay on Main South Road.

ESSENTIALS

Visitor Information Contacts McLaren Vale and Fleurieu Visitor Centre (✉ Main St., McLaren Vale ☎ 08/8323–9944 ⊕ www.mclarenvale.info/visitorcentre ◷ Daily 10–5). **Victor Harbor Visitor Information Centre** (✉ The Causeway, Victor Harbor ☎ 08/8552–5738 ⊕ www.tourismvictorharbor.com.au ◷ Daily 9–5).

MCLAREN VALE

39 km (24 mi) south of Adelaide.

The nearest wine region to Adelaide, this area has a distinctly modern, upscale look, even though many of the more than 80 wineries in and around town are as old as their Barossa peers. The first vines were planted in 1838 at northern Reynella by Englishman John Reynell, who had collected them en route from the Cape of Good Hope. The McLaren Vale region has always been known for its big—and softer—reds, including Shiraz, as well as a few white varietals.

The 1860s stone cellar door at **Coriole Vineyards** sits among nasturtiums and hollyhocks on a hill with stunning St. Vincent Gulf views. From the surrounding vines, winemakers Simon White and Mark Lloyd make some of Australia's best Italian varietal wines, such as Sangiovese and Nebbiolo. Coriole grows olives, too, and you can taste olive oils as well as wine. Enjoy a platter of estate-grown and local produce—cheese, smoked kangaroo, roasted vegetables, and chutney—in the flagstone courtyard (Friday to Monday). The hosted tastings led by Rachel Whitrow are excellent and should be booked ahead. ⊠ *Chaffeys Rd. near Kays Rd.* ☎ *08/8323–8305* ⊕ *www.coriole.com* ⊑ *Free* ☉ *Weekdays 10–5, weekends 11–5.*

A fine restaurant complements excellent wine at **d'Arenberg Wines**, family run since 1912. Winemaker Chester d'Arenberg Osborn is known for his quality whites, including the luscious Noble Riesling dessert wine, as well as powerful reds and fortified wines with equally compelling names. Reservations are essential for d'Arry's fine-dining Verandah restaurant, which overlooks the vineyards, the valley, and the sea. The tempting seasonal lunch-only menu uses local produce for its Mod-Oz dishes. ⊠ *Osborn Rd.* ☎ *1800/882335 cellar door; 08/8329–4848 restaurant* ⊕ *www.darenberg.com.au* ⊑ *Free* ☉ *Daily 10–5.*

On a quiet, unpaved back road, boutique winery **Pertaringa** (meaning "belonging to the hills") makes limited quantities of mouth-filling reds and several whites. At the cellar-door, facing the vines, you can sip Two Gentlemen's Grenache and Scarecrow Sauvignon Blanc, a great accompaniment to a bring-your-own picnic. It is worth buying some of the premium Over the Top Shiraz even without tasting—you won't be disappointed. ⊠ *Hunt and Rifle Range Rd.* ☎ *08/8323–8125* ⊕ *www. pertaringa.com.au* ⊑ *Free* ☉ *Weekdays 10–5, weekends 11–5.*

WHERE TO EAT AND STAY

$ ✕ **Blessed Cheese.** It's hard to disappoint when cheese and chocolate are AUSTRALIAN your specialties, particularly when they're adeptly paired with local wines. Cheese maker and co-owner Mark Potter uses his Ph.D. in biochemistry to mix up flavorful combinations of small-vineyard wines and cheese, available in A$15-per-head platters. He also runs daylong home cheese-making courses. The organic coffee is the best in the vale, and the baked cherry cheesecake is its perfect match. ⊠ *150 Main Rd.* ☎ *08/8323–7958* ⊟ *AE, DC, MC, V* ☉ *No dinner.*

$–$$ ✕ **Market 190.** With its worn floorboards and pressed-metal ceilings,
★ this café feels like a country corner store. Bottled olive oil and local
AUSTRALIAN jams line the shelves, and an assortment of cakes, savory baked goods
and cheeses fills the glass-front counter. Come early for a cup of coffee
and the best breakfast outside Adelaide. The menu shows off Fleurieu
Peninsula produce: for a taste of McLaren Vale, order a regional platter,
and for something spicier, tuck into gluten-free salt-and-pepper squid (in
season). To finish, try the lemon-curd tart. Book ahead for weekends.
Afterwards, check out The Almond Train next door, where everything
nut-related can be bought from this converted railway carriage. ⊠ *190
Main Rd.* ☏ *08/8323–8558* ⊟ *AE, DC, MC, V* ☺ *No dinner.*

$$ ✕ **Star of Greece.** More for the linen-slacks-and-deck-shoes set than the
★ board-shorts-and-sunscreen crowd, this extended weatherboard kiosk
AUSTRALIAN on the cliffs at Port Willunga, 10 km (6 mi) southwest of McLaren Vale,
is beach-ball bright and extremely popular. Wooden chairs painted in
mandarin, lime, and sky-blue stripes sit at paper-draped tables, and
windows frame the aqua sea. (The offshore buoy marks where the
three-masted *Star of Greece* foundered in 1888.) Reading the menu
nets mostly seafood. You could order seared scallops wrapped in octo-
pus bacon, or crispy skinned ocean trout on prawn salsa, but every
white-plated dish the hip staff carries past may make you question your
choice. ⊠ *The Esplanade, Port Willunga* ☏ *08/8557–7420* ⌲ *Reserva-
tions essential* ⊟ *AE, DC, MC, V* ☺ *Closed Mon. No dinner Tues. and
Wed. Apr.–Oct.*

$$$ 🛏 **Wine and Roses B&B.** It may look like a regular residential house
from the outside, but this luxury B&B has an interior that's far from
ordinary. Liqueur-filled chocolates and port await you in your suite,
where you can set the mood for romance with music or a movie, and
relax in the double jetted tub or wrapped in a plush bathrobe beside
the wood-burning fire. Choose from the pillow menu for bedtime. The
house is five minutes from the main McLaren Vale road. **Pros:** perfect
for a romantic getaway, the complimentary port is delicious. **Cons:** if
all four suites are booked it's a little cramped, not child-friendly. ⊠ *39
Caffrey St.* ☏ *08/8323–7654* ⊕ *www.wineandroses.com.au* ➦ *4 suites*
⌂ *In-room: safe, kitchen (some), refrigerator, VCR, DVD, Wi-Fi. In-
hotel: restaurant, no elevator, laundry service, no-smoking rooms, no
kids* ⊟ *AE, MC, V* 🍽 *BP.*

GOOLWA

*44 km (27 mi) southeast of McLaren Vale, 83 km (51 mi) south of
Adelaide.*

Beautifully situated near the mouth of the mighty Murray River, which
travels some 2,415 km (1,594 mi) from its source in New South Wales,
Goolwa grew fat on the 19th-century river paddle-steamer trade. Today,
with its enviable position close to the sea and the combined attractions
of Lake Alexandrina and Coorong National Park, tourism has replaced
river trade as the main source of income.

☉ **Goolwa Wharf** is the launching place for daily tour cruises. The *Spirit
of the Coorong*, a fully equipped motorboat, has a six-hour cruise

(A$84) to Coorong National Park that includes three guided walks, lunch, and afternoon tea. ⊠ *Goolwa Wharf* ☎ *08/8555–2203, 1800/442203 tour cruises* ⊕ *www.coorongcruises.com.au.*

Goolwa is also the home port of paddle-steamer **Oscar W**. Built in 1908, it's one of the few remaining wood-fired boiler ships. This boat holds the record for bringing the most bales of wool (2,500) down the Darling River, which flows into the Murray River. When not participating in commemorative cruises and paddleboat races, the boat is open for inspection. ⊠ *Goolwa Wharf* ☎ *1300/466592* 🖙 *Donation to inspect boat, fees charged for cruises.*

> ### LIFE'S A PICNIC
>
> Created by local winemakers after an afternoon of wine apprecia-tion, the McLaren Vale Cheese & Wine Trail is the most civilized way to sample the region's best. Pick up a picnic hamper of four artisan cheeses, crackers, olives, and dried muscatel grapes at **Blessed Cheese** (⊠ *150 Main Rd.* ☎ *08/8323–7958* ⊕ *www. cheeseandwinetrails.com.au* ▤ *AE, DC, MC, V* ⊘ *No dinner*) and spend the next few hours following the trail map from cellar door to cellar door, tasting recommended wines with each cheese course.

VICTOR HARBOR

18 km (11 mi) west of Goolwa, 83 km (51 mi) south of Adelaide.

As famous for its natural beauty and wildlife as for its resorts, Victor Harbor is South Australia's favorite seaside getaway. In 1802 English and French explorers Matthew Flinders and Nicolas Baudin met here at Encounter Bay, and by 1830 the harbor was a major whaling center. Pods of southern right whales came here to breed in winter, and they made for a profitable trade through the mid-1800s. By 1878 the whales were hunted nearly to extinction, but the return of these majestic crea-tures to Victor Harbor in recent decades has established the city as a premiere source of information on whales and whaling history.

The **South Australian Whale Centre** tells the often graphic story of the whaling industry along South Australia's coast, particularly in Encoun-ter Bay. Excellent interpretive displays spread over three floors focus on dolphins, seals, penguins, and whales—all of which can be seen in these waters. In whale-watching season the center has a 24-hour informa-tion hotline on sightings. There's a Discovery Trail and craft area for children. ⊠ *2 Railway Terrace* ☎ *08/8551–0750, 1900/942537 whale information* ⊕ *www.sawhalecentre.com* 🖙 *A8* ⊘ *Daily 9:30–5.*

The **Bluff,** 7 km (4½ mi) west of Victor Harbor, is where whalers once stood lookout for their prey. Today the granite outcrop, also known as Rosetta Head, serves the same purpose in very different circumstances. It's a steep, 1,400-foot climb to the top, on a formed trail, to enjoy the bluff views.

For cycling enthusiasts, there's also **Encounter Bikeway,** a paved track that runs 30 km (19 mi) from the Bluff along a scenic coastal route to

Laffin Point (east of Goolwa). Almost flat, the bikeway is suitable for riders of most ages and experience levels.

☼ **Granite Island** is linked to the mainland by a 650-yard causeway, along which Clydesdales pull a double-decker tram. Within Granite Island Nature Park a self-guided walk leads around the island, and guided walking tours to view the colony of about 500 fairy penguins are run from the penguin interpretive center. There is also an excellent restaurant (lunch only) with deck dining overlooking the harbor entrance. Look out for seals in the shallows. ⊠ *Granite Island* ☎ *08/8552–7555* ⊕ *www. graniteisland.com.au* ⊠ *Round-trip tram A$7, penguin tours A$12.50, penguin interpretive center A$6* ☉ *Daily; penguin tours at dusk*

☼ The **Cockle Train** travels the route of South Australia's first railway line. Originally laid between Goolwa and Port Elliot, and extended to Victor Harbor in 1864, the line traces the lovely Southern Ocean beaches on its 16-km (10-mi), half-hour journey. The train runs by steam power daily during summer school holidays (late December to late January), on Easter weekend, and on the third Sunday of each month from June to November. A diesel locomotive pulls the heritage passenger cars (or a diesel railcar operates) on other Sundays and public holidays, and days of Total Fire Ban. ⊠ *Railway Terrace near Coral St.* ☎ *08/8552–2782 day of train journey, 1300/655991* ⊕ *www.steamranger.org.au* ⊠ *Round-trip A$26.*

OFF THE BEATEN PATH   **Coorong National Park** (⊠ *34 Princes Hwy., Meningie* ☎ *08/8575–1200*), a sliver of land stretching southeast of the Fleurieu Peninsula and completely separate from it, hugs the South Australian coast for more than 150 km (94 mi). Many Australians became aware of the Coorong's beauty from the 1970s film *Storm Boy*, which told the story of a boy's friendship with a pelican. These curious birds are one reason why the Coorong is a wetland area of world standing. There's a A$5 charge per vehicle.

WHERE TO STAY

¢ ⚠ **The Port Elliott Holiday Park.** Six kilometers (4 mi) east of Victor Harbor, this grassy park fronts beautiful tree-lined Horseshoe Bay, one of South Australia's best swimming beaches. Choose from campsites and self-contained cabins, villas, and spacious cottages (basic linens are provided). The park is within a regional reserve and close to cycling tracks and coastal walking paths. In whale-watching season (usually June to October) you can sometimes see southern right whales from the park. **Pros:** great location on the beach, wide range of accommodation options. **Cons:** overcrowded in peak season, not for kid-phobes. ♿ *Flush toilets, partial hookups (electric and water), dump station, drinking water, guest laundry, showers, picnic tables, electricity, public telephone, general store, play area, swimming* ⊷ *7 unpowered and 258 powered campsites, 9 villas, 3 cottages, 4 units, 4 cabins* ⊠ *Off Goolwa Rd. near Hussey St., Port Elliot* ☎ *08/8554–2134* ⊕ *www.portelliotholidaypark.com.au* ⊟ *MC, V.*

$–$$ 🍴 **Whalers Inn Resort.** The vibe is more tropical than maritime at Victor Harbor's upscale resort complex, with palm trees and spectacular surf as the backdrop for spacious, well-equipped rooms of varying configurations. Rooms (here called suites), all decorated in hazy seaside hues,

DID YOU KNOW?

To travel through South Australia is to experience an array of magnificent landscapes: miles of dramatic coastline, expansive beaches, lush hills, and the vast outback. And thanks to the temperate climate, the delicious wines of Barossa can be enjoyed by many. Seventy percent of Australia's wine exports comes from South Australia.

can be joined together to make family quarters. Cook meals in your modern kitchen or head down to the Waterside restaurant and bar for fresh seafood and shoreline views. **Pros:** stunning views of three islands, real "getaway" feel. **Cons:** expensive unless you get a last-minute deal, 15-minute drive from downtown. ⊠ *121 Franklin Parade* ☎ *08/8552– 4400* ⊕ *www.whalersinnresort.com.au* ⇨ *12 rooms, 14 apartments, 12 studios, 1 cottage* ⚐ *In-room: kitchen (some), refrigerator, VCR, dial-up. In-hotel: restaurant, bar, tennis court, pool, bicycles, no elevator, laundry facilities, laundry service, public Internet* ▭ *AE, DC, MC, V.*

KANGAROO ISLAND

Kangaroo Island, Australia's third-largest (after Tasmania and Melville), is barely 16 km (10 mi) from the Australian mainland. Yet the island belongs to another age—a folksy, friendly, less sophisticated time when you'd leave your car unlocked and knew everyone by name.

The island is most beautiful along the coastline, where the land is sculpted into a series of bays and inlets teeming with bird and marine life. The stark interior has its own charm, however, with pockets of red earth between stretches of bush and farmland. Wildlife is probably the island's greatest attraction; in a single day you can stroll along a beach crowded with sea lions and watch kangaroos, koalas, pelicans, and fairy penguins in their native environments.

Its towns and most of its accommodations are on the island's eastern third. The standout sights are on the southern coast, so if you've only one day—you could easily spend a week—it's best to tour the island in a clockwise direction, leaving the north-coast beaches for the afternoon. Before heading out, fill your gas tank and pack a picnic lunch. Shops are few and far between outside the towns, general stores being the main outlets for food and gas.

The Kangaroo Island Pass (A\$59, A\$160.50 families) is available from any National Parks and Wildlife site, or from the **National Parks and Wildlife SA Office** (⊠ *37 Dauncey St., Kingscote* ☎ *08/8553–2381* ⊕ *www. parks.sa.gov.au/parks/visitorinformation/parkpasses*). The pass covers a selection of guided tours and park entry fees and is valid for a year.

GETTING HERE AND AROUND

REX/Regional Express flies three times daily between Adelaide and Kingscote, the island's main airport. Ask about holiday packages in conjunction with SeaLink. Flights to the island take about 30 minutes.

SeaLink ferries allow access for cars through Penneshaw from Cape Jervis, at the tip of the Fleurieu Peninsula, a 90-minute drive from Adelaide. There are three daily sailings each way, with up to eight crossings at peak times. Reservations are advisable during the holidays. SeaLink operates the vehicular passenger ferry Sea Lion 2000 and Spirit of Kangaroo Island, a designated freight boat with passenger facilities. These ferries make 45-minute crossings between Cape Jervis and Penneshaw. There are three daily sailings each way, with up to eight crossings at peak times. Ferries are the favored means of transportation between the island and the mainland, and reservations are advisable during the

"Bryson on top of a Remarkable Rock at Flinders Chase National Park." —photo by Rich_B_Florida, Fodors.com member

holidays. Adelaide Sightseeing operates coach tours of Kangaroo Island out of Adelaide in conjunction with the SeaLink ferry services from A$377 for a (very long) day trip.

Kangaroo Island's main attractions are widely scattered; you can see them best on a guided tour or by car. The main roads form a paved loop, which branches off to such major sites as Seal Bay, and Admirals Arch and Remarkable Rocks in Flinders Chase National Park. Stretches of unpaved road lead to lighthouses at Cape Borda and Cape Willoughby, South Australia's oldest. Roads to the island's northern beaches, bays, and camping areas are also unpaved. These become very rutted in summer, but they can be driven carefully in a conventional vehicle. Be alert for wildlife, especially at dawn, dusk, and after dark. Slow down and dip your lights so you don't blind the animals you see.

TOURS

Exceptional Kangaroo Island has quality four-wheel-drive and bush-walking tours from A$348 per person per day. Tailor-made itineraries, including bird-watching and photography, and flight-accommodation packages can also be arranged. Kangaroo Island Odysseys operates luxury four-wheel-drive nature tours from one to three days priced from A$345 per person. Kangaroo Island Wilderness Tours has five personalized four-wheel-drive wilderness tours from one to four days and starting from A$388 per person (tour only); a range of accommo-dation packages is available.

SeaLink Kangaroo Island operates one-day (A$234) bus tours of the island, departing from Adelaide, in conjunction with the ferry service from Cape Jervis. They also can arrange fishing and self-drive tours and extended packages. Two-day/one-night tours are A$383 and up per person; two-day/one-night self-drive tours start at A$187 per person.

ESSENTIALS

Banks ANZ (✉ *62 Dauncey St., Kingscote* ☎ *13–1314*).

Transportation REX/Regional Express (☎ *13–1713* ⊕ *www.rex.com.au*). **Adelaide Sightseeing** (✉ *85 Franklin St., City Center, Adelaide* ☎ *1300/769762* ⊕ *www.adelaidesightseeing.com.au*). **SeaLink** (☎ *13–1301* ⊕ *www.sealink.com.au*).

> **HOW REMARKABLE**
>
> Balanced precariously on the promontory of Kirkpatrick Point in Flinders Chase National Park, the Remarkable Rocks are aptly named. Sitting with your back against one of these fantastically shaped boulders is the best way to view sunset or sunrise on Kangaroo Island.

Tour Operators Exceptional Kangaroo Island (☎ *08/8553–9119* ☐ *08/8553–9122* ⊕ *www.exceptionalkangarooisland.com*). **Kangaroo Island Odysseys** (☎ *08/8553–0386* ☐ *08/8553–0387* ⊕ *www.kiodysseys.com.au*). **Kangaroo Island Wilderness Tours** (☎ *08/8559–5033* ☐ *08/8559–5088* ⊕ *www.wildernesstours.com.au*). **SeaLink Kangaroo Island** (✉ *440 King William St., Adelaide* ☎ *13–1301* ⊕ *www.sealink.com.au*).

Visitor Information Gateway Visitor Information Centre (✉ *Howard Dr., Penneshaw* ☎ *08/8553–1185* ☐ *08/8553–1255* ⊕ *www.tourkangarooisland.com.au* ☉ *Weekdays 9–5, weekends 10–4*).

KINGSCOTE

121 km (75 mi) southwest of Adelaide.

Kangaroo Island's largest town, Kingscote is a good base for exploring. Reeves Point, at the town's northern end, is where South Australia's colonial history began. Settlers landed here in 1836 and established the first official town in the new colony. Little remains of the original settlement except Hope Cottage, now a small museum; several graves; and a huge, twisted mulberry tree that grew from a cutting the settlers brought from England—locals still use the fruit to make jam. Today American River, about halfway between Kingscote and Penneshaw, the island's second-largest town, is another accommodation and restaurant hub.

☉ ★   Make sure you catch the **Pelican Feeding** "show" at 5 PM daily on the rock wall beside Kingscote Jetty. A guide in fishing waders gives an informative and entertaining talk as he feeds handfuls of seafood to a comic mob of noisy pelicans. This is great fun. ✉ *Kingscote Jetty* ☎ *08/8553–3112* ☐ *A$3* ☉ *Daily 5 PM.*

WHERE TO STAY

$$$ 🏠 **Acacia Apartments.** A huge movie collection in the reception area confirms that the self-contained one- and two-bedroom units at this Reeve's Point complex are family-friendly. All the units have tile floors, brick walls, and enough room for different generations to have their own space. Allergy sufferers can check into apartments cleaned with natural products rather than chemicals. Special units for travelers with disabilities and restricted mobility have easy access and bathroom

doors that open both ways. Four-wheel-drive tours can be arranged. The state's first British colonial settlement, Reeve's Point, is ½ km (¼ mi) down the hill. Book two nights or more for reduced rates. **Pros:** kid-friendly, very amenable owner. **Cons:** slightly overpriced, 10 AM check-out time. ☒ *3–5 Rawson St., Reeve's Point* ☎ *08/8553–0088 or 1800/247007* ⊕ *www.acacia-apartments.com.au* ➚ *10 apartments* ⚷ *In-room: kitchen, refrigerator, DVD, VCR, dial-up. In-hotel: pool, no elevator, laundry facilities, public Internet, no-smoking rooms* ▭ *AE, DC, MC, V* ⫟ *CP.*

$$ ⊞ **Kangaroo Island Lodge.** The island's oldest resort faces beautiful Eastern Cove at American River. Rooms overlook open water or the saltwater pool; the most attractive are the "waterview" rooms, which have mud-brick walls, warm terra-cotta tones, and king-size beds. You can taste some of Kangaroo Island's bounty in the restaurant ($–$$), one of the island's best. Two great choices are panfried scallop risotto and grilled Kangaroo Island whiting. It's 39 km (24 mi) southeast of Kingscote. **Pros:** set in beautiful and peaceful surroundings, nearby trails lead to kangaroos and pelicans. **Cons:** dated rooms, overpriced and distinctly ordinary breakfast. ⌂ *Box 232, American River 5221* ☎ *08/8553–7053 or 1800/355581* ⊕ *www.kilodge.com.au* ➚ *38 rooms* ⚷ *In-room: kitchen (some), refrigerator, DVD. In-hotel: restaurant, room service, bar, pool, beachfront, no elevator, laundry facilities, public Internet, no-smoking rooms* ▭ *AE, DC, MC, V.*

$–$$$ ⊞ **Ozone Seafront Hotel.** The Victorian facade on this two-story 1920s hotel hides surprisingly modern and spacious rooms that overlook Nepean Bay. The choicest accommodations, however, are in the newer adjoining wing. Lots of windows, flat-screen TVs, vibrant modern artworks, and some in-room whirlpool tubs make the new suites and Penthouse Apartments among the island's best. The huge bistro menu stars local seafood, and the wine list runs to 100 vintages, many of them local. There are daily wine tastings in the bar. The airport is a 15-minute drive away. **Pros:** across the street from the penguin colony, friendly staff. **Cons:** older rooms are old-fashioned, as is the breakfast. ☒ *Chapman Terrace at Commercial St.* ☎ *08/8553–2011 or 1800/083133* ✍ *info@ ozoneseafront.com* ⊕ *www.ozonehotel.com* ➚ *63 rooms, 3 apartments* ⚷ *In-room: safe (some), refrigerator, DVD (some). In-hotel: restaurant, bars, pool, gym, beachfront, no elevator, laundry facilities, public Internet, public Wi-Fi, no-smoking rooms* ▭ *AE, DC, MC, V.*

$$ ⊞ **Wanderers Rest.** Delightful local artworks dot the walls in this country inn's stylish units, all of which have king-size beds. The elevated veranda and à la carte restaurant, where breakfast is served, have splendid views across American River to the mainland. **Pros:** simple, high-quality accommodation with stunning views. **Cons:** kids under 10 aren't allowed, tours and extras quickly add up. ☒ *Bayview Rd., Box 34, American River* ☎ *08/8553–7140* ⊕ *www.wanderersrest.com.au* ➚ *9 rooms* ⚷ *In-room: no phone, DVD, refrigerator, Wi-Fi (some). In-hotel: restaurant, bar, pool, no elevator, public Wi-Fi, no kids under 10, no-smoking rooms* ▭ *AE, DC, MC, V* ⫟ *BP.*

8

Lots of Remarkable Rocks, Flinders Chase National Park.

PENNESHAW

62 km (39 mi) east of Kingscote.

This tiny ferry port has a huge population of penguins, which are visible on nocturnal tours. Gorgeous shoreline, views of spectacularly blue water, and rolling green hills are a few lovely surprises here.

Penneshaw Penguin Centre offers two ways to view the delightful fairy penguins indigenous to Kangaroo Island. From the indoor interpretive center, where you can read about bird activity—including mating, nesting, and feeding—a boardwalk leads to a viewing platform above rocks and sand riddled with burrows. Because the penguins spend most of the day fishing at sea or inside their burrows, the best viewing is after sunset. You can take a self-guided walk or an informative guided tour, which starts with a talk and video at the center. You might see penguins waddling ashore, chicks emerging from their burrows to feed, or scruffy adults molting. ⊠ *Middle and Bay Terraces* 🕿🖪 *08/8553–1103* 🖃 *Interpretive center free, guided tours A\$10, self-guided walks A\$8* ⊙ *Tours at 7:30 and 8:30 PM in winter, 8:30 and 9:30 PM in summer.*

Sunset Winery. Sip smooth Chardonnay while overlooking Eastern Cove at this calm, cool, and pristine addition to Kangaroo Island's thriving wine industry. You can sample wines for free at the cellar door, or opt for the Tasting Experience: three wines, three local cheeses, freshly baked bread, and olive oil for A\$7; savory platters for two people, with six wines, cost A\$19. ⊠ *Hog Bay Rd.* 🕿 *08/8553–1378* 🖪 *08/8553–1379* ⊕ *www.sunset-wines.com.au* 🖃 *Free* ⊙ *Daily 11–5.*

OFF THE BEATEN PATH

Australia's oldest lighthouse stands on Kangaroo Island's easternmost point, Cape Willoughby, 27 km (17 mi) from Penneshaw, on a mostly unpaved road. You can explore the property around the towering, white lighthouse, but only guided tours (A$12 or KI Pass) can enter the 1852 building itself. Tours depart from the National Parks office in one of the three 1920s lighthouse keepers' cottages. The other two cottages have been converted into self-contained accommodations that let you experience Kangaroo Island at its most remote and wildest—it's always windy here!

WHERE TO EAT AND STAY

¢-$$
★
SEAFOOD

✕ **Fish.** Belly up to the counter in this tiny shop for cheap local seafood—named by *The Australian* newspaper as some of the best in the country—to take out or enjoy with a glass of wine in the seating area next door. Choose your fish—whiting, John Dory, garfish—from the blackboard menu and have it beer-battered, crumbed, or grilled. Or you might prefer a paper-wrapped parcel of scallops, prawns, lobster, and oysters (in season) shucked to order. The team behind the shop also runs 2 Birds & A Squid, which prepares seafood packs and cooked meals for pickup or delivery to your accommodation anywhere on the island. ⊠ *43 North Terrace* ☎ *08/8553–1177 Fish, 08/8553–7406 2 Birds & A Squid* ⊕ *www.2birds1squid.com* ⊟ *No credit cards* ⊘ *Closed June–Sept. No lunch.*

$-$$

⌂ **Kangaroo Island Seafront Resort.** This hotel has an ideal position near the ferry terminal and overlooking Penneshaw Bay. You can choose an ocean-view room or stay amid tropical gardens in freestanding chalets. There are also two- and three-bedroom self-contained cottages with full kitchens. The sky-blue-and-sand-yellow restaurant, which spills out onto a seafront terrace, serves marron, oysters, whiting, and other fresh local produce. **Pros:** steps away from ferry terminal and penguin viewing, spacious rooms. **Cons:** older parts of the hotel are showing their age, no air-conditioning. ⊠ *49 North Terrace,* ☎ *08/8553–1028* ⊕ *www.seafront.com.au* ⇥ *18 rooms, 6 chalets, 3 cottages* ⌂ *In-room: no phone (some), kitchen (some), refrigerator, VCR (some), Ethernet (some), dial-up (some). In-hotel: restaurant, bar, tennis court, pool, no elevator, laundry facilities, no-smoking rooms* ⊟ *AE, DC, MC, V* ⎟◯⎟ *CP.*

$$-$$$

⌂ **Seaview Lodge.** Host Barara Ewens welcomes you into her 1860s home at this elegant yet relaxing B&B. Roses fill the cottage garden, and the cane chairs on the wide veranda are perfectly positioned for watching the sun set over the sea. Three of the five rooms have original timber floors and wood-burning fireplaces; all are decorated with colonial-style furniture. From the lace-draped four-poster beds in the Rose and Jasmine rooms to the temptingly deep claw-foot bathtub in Tecoma, you're pampered all the way. Barara Ewens also offers self-contained accommodation in Seaview Cottage. **Pros:** beautiful cottage-style gardens, stylishly furnished rooms. **Cons:** if full, the B&B can feel claustrophobic, limited views of the ocean. ⊠ *Willoughby Rd.,* ☎ *08/8553–1132* ⊕ *www.seaviewlodge.com.au* ⇥ *5 rooms, 1 cottage* ⌂ *In-room: no phone, no TV. In-hotel: restaurant, bar, no elevator, no-smoking rooms* ⊟ *MC, V* ⎟◯⎟ *BP.*

8

SEAL BAY CONSERVATION PARK

60 km (37 mi) southwest of Kingscote via South Coast Rd.

This top Kangaroo Island attraction gives you the chance to visit one of the state's largest Australian sea-lion colonies. About 300 animals usually lounge on the beach, except on stormy days, when they shelter in the dunes. You can only visit the beach, and get surprisingly close to females, pups, and bulls, on a tour with an interpretive officer; otherwise, you can follow the self-guided boardwalk to a lookout over the sand. Two-hour sunset tours depart on varied days in December and January; a minimum of four people is required, as is 24-hour advance booking. The park visitor center has fun and educational displays, and a touch table covered in sea-lion skins and bones. There is also a shop. ⊠ *End of Seal Bay Rd., Seal Bay* ☎ *08/8559–4207* ⌨ *Group tour A$14 per person, sunset tour A$32, boardwalk A$10* ⊙ *Tours Dec. and Jan., daily 9–5:15, every 15–45 mins; Feb.–Nov., daily 9–4:15, every 45 mins.*

FLINDERS CHASE NATIONAL PARK

★ *102 km (64 mi) west of Kingscote.*

Some of Australia's most beautiful coastal scenery is in Flinders Chase National Park on Kangaroo Island.

The effects of seas crashing mercilessly onto Australia's southern coast are visible in the oddly shaped rocks on the island's shores. A limestone promontory was carved from beneath at Cape du Couedic on the southwestern coast, producing what is known as **Admiral's Arch.** From the boardwalk you can see the New Zealand fur seals that have colonized the area around the rock formation. About 4 km (2½ mi) farther east are the aptly named **Remarkable Rocks,** huge, fantastically shaped boulders balanced precariously on the promontory of Kirkpatrick Point. This is a great place to watch the sun set or rise.

Much of Kangaroo Island has been cultivated since settlement, but after being declared a national treasure in 1919, a huge area of original vegetation has been protected in Flinders Chase. In December 2007 a bushfire burned a large part of Flinders Chase, and its destructive power and the various stages of regeneration are now on show.

Flinders Chase has several 1½-km to 9-km (1-mi to 5½-mi) loop walking trails, which take one to three hours to complete. The trails meander along the rivers to the coast, passing mallee scrub and sugar gum forests, and explore the rugged shoreline. The 4-km (2½-mi) Snake Lagoon Hike follows Rocky River over and through a series of broad rocky terraces to the remote sandy beach where it meets the sea. The sign warning of freak waves is not just for show.

The park is on the island's western end, bounded by the Playford and West End highways. The state-of-the-art visitor center, open daily 9–5, is the largest National Parks and Wildlife office. Displays and touch screens explore the park's history and the different habitats and wildlife in Flinders Chase. The center provides park entry tickets and camping permits, and books stays at the Heritage cabins. A shop sells souvenirs and provisions, and there is also a café.

"Naptime on the beach at Kangaroo Island." —photo by Istarr, Fodors.com member

WHERE TO STAY

Accommodations within the national park (and in Cape Willoughby Conservation Park at the other end of the island) are controlled by the **Flinders Chase National Park Office** (☎ *08/8559–7235* ⊕ *www.parks.sa.gov. au/parks/sanpr/flinders_chase*). Rustic sofas, chairs, and tables furnish huts, cottages, homesteads, and lighthouse lodgings at Cape Willoughby (at the island's southeastern point), Cape du Couedic (southwest), and Cape Borda (northwest). All accommodations have kitchens or cooking facilities; blankets and pillows are supplied, and you can rent bed linens and towels. Camping is allowed only at designated sites at Rocky River and in bush campgrounds, and permits are essential.

$–$$$$

AUSTRALIAN

🏠 **Kangaroo Island Wilderness Retreat.** With wallabies and possums treating the grounds as their own domain, this eco-friendly retreat is everything a wildlife-loving traveler could want. Rooms in the low-slung log courtyard buildings have recycled Oregon pine furniture; private rear decks in the two corner suites open onto thick banksia scrub. Family-friendly one-bed apartments and motel-style rooms share the barnlike Lodge. Rain is the only water source, and showers are solar heated. The dining room ($$) serves Mod-Oz fare that uses many island products; the kitchen also prepares picnic lunches. The gas pump here is the last one for 35 km (21 mi). **Pros:** wonderful experience for animal lovers, free Internet access and DVD rental. **Cons:** only two time slots for dinner, basic rooms might disappoint city slickers. ⊠ *1 South Coast Rd., Flinders Chase* ☎ *08/8559–7275* ⊕ *www.kiwr.com* ⤳ *18 courtyard rooms, 2 suites, 4 apartments, 7 lodge rooms* ⌂ *In-room: no phone (some), kitchen (some), refrigerator, DVD (some), no TV (some),*

8

Ethernet (some), Wi-Fi (some). In-hotel: restaurant, bar, no elevator, laundry facilities, laundry service, public Internet, public Wi-Fi, no-smoking rooms ⊟ *AE, MC, V.*

$$$$
Fodor's Choice
★
⛺ **Southern Ocean Lodge.** This truly remarkable hotel might be the highlight of your trip—if money is no object. Snaking along the edge of a cliff, this architectural masterpiece was made completely of recycled timbers and glass, and no expense was spared. All the luxury suites have fabulous coastal views, and the floor-to-ceiling windows in the bathrooms will entice guests to spend hours in the deep tubs. While luxury abounds, from the spa to each suite enjoying a private chef, the surroundings and wildlife are also divine. All food, wine, and tours are included in the (sky-high) tariff. **Pros:** superb restaurant, simple but stunning decor exudes luxury and class. **Cons:** if you have to ask the price, you can't afford this place, sophisticated surroundings are not really suitable for children. ⊠ *Hanson Bay, Kingscote* ☎ *08/8559–7347* ⊕ *www.southernoceanlodge.com.au* ↩ *21 suites* ⌂ *In-room: a/c, phone, safe, mini-bar DVD, TV (some), (Wi-Fi (some). In-hotel: restaurant, room service, bar, gym, spa, laundry service, no-smoking rooms* ⊟ *AE, D, DC, MC, V* ⍾◎⍿ *AI.*

OUTDOOR ACTIVITIES

FISHING Fishing is excellent on Kangaroo Island's beaches, bays, and rivers. The island's deep-sea fishing fleet holds several world records for tuna. No permit is required for recreational fishing, but minimum lengths and bag limits apply. You can pick up a fishing guide from the information center in Penneshaw.

Cooinda (☎ *08/8553–1072*) runs fishing, diving, and combined fishing and diving charters from half a day to three days out of American River. You can rent fishing equipment from **Grimshaw's Corner Store & Cafe** (⊠ *3rd St. at North Terr., Penneshaw* ☎ *08/8553–1151*). **Kangaroo Island Fishing Charters** (☎ *08/8242–0352* ⊕ *www.kifishchart.com.au*) has fast, clean boats and a live-aboard mother ship; the company takes groups in a 30-foot cruiser out in the Western River region (the island's north coast). The **Kings** (☎ *08/8553–7003*) offer fishing tours (maximum six passengers) and personalized charters from half a day in American River waters. **Turner Fuel** (⊠ *26 Telegraph Rd., Kingscote* ☎ *08/8553–2725*) sells fishing tackle and bait.

SCUBA DIVING Kangaroo Island waters also offer arguably the best temperate-water diving in Australia. Divers can explore some of the more than 50 shipwrecks around the coast, and swim among corals, sponges, and fish. The beautiful leafy sea dragon is endemic to the island's north-coast waters. **Kangaroo Island Diving Safaris** (☎ *08/8559–3225* ⊕ *www. kidivingsafaris.com*) runs day trips, live-aboard tours, and dive training courses. They promise interactions with seals and dolphins on most trips.

THE OUTBACK

South Australia is the country's driest state, and its Outback is an expanse of desert vegetation. But this land of scrubby salt bush and hardy eucalyptus trees is brightened after rain by wildflowers—including the state's floral emblem, the blood-red Sturt's desert pea, with its black, olive-like heart. The terrain is marked by geological uplifts, abrupt transitions between plateaus broken at the edges of ancient, long-inactive fault lines. Few roads track through this desert wilderness—the main highway is the Stuart, which runs all the way to Alice Springs in the Northern Territory.

PONY EXPRESS

The Coober Pedy–Oodnadatta Mail Run Tour is the most unusual experience you'll have anywhere. Former miner-turned-entrepreneur Peter Rowe and his brother Derek Rowe, a renowned horseman, run the tour, delivering mail and supplies to remote cattle stations and Outback towns. You also get a good look at the Dog Fence, and at the dingoes it was built to keep away.

The people of the Outback are as hardy as their surroundings. They are also often eccentric, colorful characters who happily bend your ear over a drink in the local pub. Remote, isolated communities attract loners, adventurers, fortune-seekers, and people simply on the run. In this unyielding country, you must be tough to survive.

COOBER PEDY

850 km (527 mi) northwest of Adelaide.

Known as much for the way most of its 3,500 inhabitants live—underground in dugouts gouged into the hills to escape the relentless heat—as for its opal riches, Coober Pedy is arguably Australia's most singular place. The town is ringed by mullock heaps, pyramids of rock and sand left over after mine shafts are dug.

Opals are Coober Pedy's reason for existence. Australia has 95% of the world's opal deposits, and Coober Pedy has the bulk of that wealth; this is the world's richest opal field.

Opal was discovered here in 1915, and soldiers returning from World War I excavated the first dugout homes when the searing heat forced them underground. In midsummer temperatures can reach 48°C (118°F), but inside the dugouts the air remains a constant 22°C–24°C (72°F–75°F).

Coober Pedy is a brick-and-corrugated-iron settlement propped unceremoniously on a scarred desert landscape. It's a town built for efficiency, not beauty. However, its ugliness has a kind of bizarre appeal. There's a feeling that you're in the last lawless outpost in the modern world, helped in no small part by the local film lore—*Priscilla Queen of the Desert, Pitch Black, Kangaroo Jack*, and *Mad Max 3* were filmed here. Once you go off the main street, you get an immediate sense of the apocalyptic.

8

GETTING HERE AND AROUND

REX/Regional Express Airlines flies direct to Coober Pedy from Adelaide Sunday–Friday. Because it's the only public carrier flying to Coober Pedy, prices are sometimes steep. However, anyone holding a valid ISIC, YHA, or VIP card is eligible for unlimited air travel throughout Australia on the Backpackers Pass for a flat rate of A$499 for one month, or A$949 for two months. The airport is open only when a flight is arriving or departing. At other times, contact the Desert Cave Hotel.

Greyhound Australia buses leave Adelaide's Central Bus Station for Coober Pedy daily. Tickets for the 12-hour ride cost A$167 each way.

The main road to Coober Pedy is the Sturt Highway from Adelaide, 850 km (527 mi) to the south. Alice Springs is 700 km (434 mi) north of Coober Pedy. The drive from Adelaide to Coober Pedy takes about nine hours. From Alice Springs it's about seven hours.

A rental car enables you to see what lies beyond Hutchison Street, but an organized tour is a much better way to do so. Budget is the only rental-car outlet in Coober Pedy. Although some roads are unpaved—those to the Breakaways and the Dog Fence, for example—surfaces are generally suitable for conventional vehicles. Check on road conditions with the police if there has been substantial rain.

The most interesting route to Flinders Ranges National Park from Adelaide takes you north through the Clare Valley vineyards and Burra's copper-mining villages. For a more direct journey to Wilpena Pound, follow the Princes Highway north to Port Augusta, and then head east toward Quorn and Hawker. A four-wheel-drive vehicle is highly recommended for traveling on the many gravel roads around the national park.

ESSENTIALS

Banks ANZ (✉ 11 Wilpena Rd., Hawker ☎ 13–1314). **Westpac** (✉ Lot 1, Hutchison St., Coober Pedy ☎ 13–2032).

Emergencies Coober Pedy Hospital (✉ Hospital Rd., Coober Pedy ☎ 08/8672–5009). **Hawker Memorial Hospital** (✉ Craddock St., Hawker ☎ 08/8648–4007).

Transportation Coober Pedy Airport (✉ Stuart Hwy., 2 km [1 mi] north of town, Coober Pedy ☎ 08/8672–5688). **REX/Regional Express** (☎ 13–1713 ⊕ www.rex.com.au). **Greyhound Australia** (☎ 1300/473946863 ⊕ www.greyhound.com.au).

Visitor Information Coober Pedy Visitor Information Centre (✉ Coober Pedy District Council Bldg., Hutchison St., Coober Pedy ☎ 1800/637076 ⊕ www.opalcapitaloftheworld.com.au ⊙ Weekdays 8:30–5, weekends 10–1). **Wilpena Pound Visitor Centre** (✉ Wilpena Rd., Wilpena Pound ☎ 08/8648–0048 ⊙ Daily 8–5).

EXPLORING

Fossicking for opal gemstones—locally called noodling—requires no permit at the Jewellers Shop mining area at the edge of town. Take care in unmarked areas, and always watch your step, as the area is littered with abandoned opal mines down which you might fall. (Working mines are off-limits to visitors.)

Although most of Coober Pedy's devotions are decidedly material in nature, the town does have its share of spiritual houses of worship. In keeping with the town's layout, they, too, are underground. **St. Peter and St. Paul's Catholic Church** is a National Heritage–listed building, and the Anglican **Catacomb Church** is notable for its altar fashioned from a windlass (a winch) and lectern made from a log of mulga wood. The **Serbian Orthodox Church** is striking, with its scalloped ceiling, rock-carved icons, and brilliant stained-glass windows. The **Revival Fellowship Underground Church** has lively gospel services.

★ The **Old Timers Mine** is a genuine opal mine turned into a museum. Two underground houses, furnished in 1920s and 1980s styles, are part of the complex, where mining memorabilia is exhibited in an extensive network of hand-dug tunnels and shafts. You can also watch demonstrations of opal-mining machines. Tours are self-guided. ⊠ *Crowders Gully Rd. near Umoona Rd.* 🖼 *08/8672–5555* ⊕ *www.oldtimersmine.com* 🖼*A$10* ⊘ *Daily 9–5.*

Umoona Opal Mine & Museum is an enormous underground complex with an original mine, a noteworthy video on the history of opal mining, an Aboriginal Interpretive Centre, and clean, underground bunk camping and cooking facilities. Guided tours of the mine are available. ⊠ *14 Hutchison St.* 🖼 *08/8672–5288* ⊕ *www.umoonaopalmine.com.au* 🖼*Museum is free, tour A$10* ⊘ *Daily 8–7; tours at 10, 2, and 4.*

AROUND TOWN

Breakaways, a striking series of buttes and jagged hills centered on the Moon Plain, is reminiscent of the American West. There are fossils and patches of petrified forest in this strange landscape, which has appealed to makers of apocalyptic films. *Mad Max 3—Beyond Thunderdome* was filmed here, as was *Ground Zero*. The scenery is especially evocative early in the morning. The Breakaways area is 30 km (19 mi) northeast of Coober Pedy.

Fodor'sChoice The Coober Pedy–Oodnadatta **Mail Run Tour** (⊠ *Post Office Hill Rd.* ★ 🖼 *08/8672–5226 or 1800/069911* ⊕ *www.mailruntour.com*), a 12-hour, 600-km (372-mi) tour through the Outback (A$185), is one of the most unusual experiences anywhere, with stops at outback cattle stations, bush pubs, and the world's longest man-made structure, the Dingo Fence. Tours depart Monday and Thursday at 8:45 AM from Underground Books on Post Office Hill Road.

WHERE TO EAT AND STAY

¢–$
PIZZA
✗ **Stuart Range Caravan Park Pizza Bar.** Locals swear that the pizzas at this popular Caravan Park are among Australia's best. The toppings combinations can be classic, creative, or gourmet, such as the Noon (with tomato, mushrooms, and onions) and the Garlic Prawn (with basil pesto and semi-dried tomatoes). ⊠ *Stuart Hwy. at Hutchison St.* 🖼*08/8672–5179* ▭ *MC, V* ⊘ *No lunch.*

$$
AUSTRALIAN
✗ **Umberto's.** Perched atop the monolithic Desert Cave Hotel, this eatery named after the hotel's founding developer is Coober Pedy's most urbane restaurant. The Mod-Oz menu takes you from the Outback (oven-baked kangaroo loin with grilled figs) to the sea (lemon sole). ⊠ *Hutchison St.* 🖼 *08/8672–5688* ▭ *AE, DC, MC, V* ⊘ *No lunch.*

8

DID YOU KNOW?

The spectacular Wilpena Pound in Flinders Ranges National Park is a natural amphitheatre—a huge crater rim that rises from the plain. Here you can explore the plunging gorges, Aboriginal rock art sights, and trek the Heysen Trail (the longest walking trail in Australia).

$$ 🛏 **Desert Cave Hotel.** What may be the world's only underground hotel presents a contemporary, blocky face to the desert town. In the 19 spacious, subsurface rooms, luxurious white and dark blue duvets complement and contrast the red-striated rock walls that protect sleepers from sound and heat. Aboveground rooms are also available. The hotel offers daily tours of the town and surrounding sights. The owners have another hotel, the Opal Inn (☎ 08/8672–5054 or 1800/088523 ⊕ www.opalinn.com.au), where you can chat with opal buyers. **Pros:** unique place to stay, pool is welcome relief in the heat. **Cons:** not for the claustrophobic, overpriced for what you get. ⊠ Hutchison St. at Post Office Hill Rd. ☎ 08/8672–5688 or 1800/088521 ⊕ www.desertcave.com.au ⌁ 50 rooms ⌂ In-room: no a/c (some), refrigerator, dial-up, Wi-Fi. In-hotel: 2 restaurants, room service, bar, pool, gym, no elevator, laundry facilities, public Internet, no-smoking rooms ☰ AE, DC, MC, V.

¢ 🛏 **The Underground Motel.** The Breakaways sometimes seem close enough to touch at this hilltop motel, where you can lounge on a veranda watching the sun set on the rock formations 30 km (19 mi) across the desert. Each room is uniquely shaped, comfortably furnished, and decorated with Aboriginal designs. Two secluded suites have kitchenette facilities, and main rooms share a communal kitchen. A complimentary light breakfast is provided. **Pros:** lovely patio to sit out on and watch the stars, very helpful owners. **Cons:** slightly out of town, which in the heat is a disadvantage. ⊠ 1185 Catacomb Rd. ☎ 08/8672–5324 or 1800/622979 ⊕ www.theundergroundmotel.com.au ⌁ 6 rooms, 2 suites ⌂ In-room: no a/c, kitchen (some), refrigerator (some), dial-up. In-hotel: no elevator, laundry facilities, no-smoking rooms ☰ AE, DC, MC, V ⍨ CP.

FLINDERS RANGES NATIONAL PARK

690 km (430 mi) southeast of Coober Pedy, 460 km (285 mi) northeast of Adelaide.

Extending north from Spencer Gulf, the Flinders Ranges mountain chain includes one of Australia's most impressive Outback parks. These dry, folded and cracked mountains, once the bed of an ancient sea, have been sculpted by millions of years of rain and sun. Cypress pine and casuarina cover this furrowed landscape of deep valleys, which slope into creeks lined with river red gums. The area is utterly fascinating—both for geologists and for anyone else who revels in wild, raw scenery and exotic plant and animal life.

★ The scenic center of the Flinders Ranges is **Wilpena Pound,** an 80-square-km (31-square-mi) bowl ringed by hills that curve gently upward, only to fall away from the rims of sheer cliffs. The only entrance to the Pound is a narrow cleft through which Wilpena Creek sometimes runs. A mud-brick **visitor center** (⊠ Wilpena Rd. ☎ 08/8648–0048), part of the Wilpena Pound Resort, has information about hiking trails and campsites within the park. The numerous steep trails make the Flinders Ranges ideal for bushwalking, even though the park has few amenities. Water in this region is scarce, and should be carried at all times. The best time for walking is during the relatively cool months between April and October. This is also the wettest time of year, so you should be prepared for rain. Wildflowers, including the spectacular Sturt's desert pea, are abundant between September and late October.

The park's most spectacular walking trail leads to the summit of 3,840-foot **St. Mary's Peak,** the highest point on the Pound's rim and South Australia's second-tallest peak. The more scenic of the two routes to the top is the outside trail (15 km [9 mi] return); give yourself a full day to get up and back. The mid section of the ascent is steep and strenuous, but views from the summit—including the distant white glitter of the salt flats on Lake Frome—make the climb worthwhile. ⊠ *End of Wilpena Rd., 156 km (97 mi) off Princes Hwy., via town of Hawker* ☎ *08/8648–4244* ⊕ *www.flindersoutback.com.*

WHERE TO STAY

$$ 🏨 **Wilpena Pound Resort.** You couldn't ask for a more idyllic and civi-
★ lized nature outpost than this popular resort at the entrance to Wilpena Pound. Here are units (10 with kitchenettes); well-equipped, spacious motel-style rooms; backpacker rooms; and permanent tents (from A$65) and campsites (from A$20) with and without electrical hookups. Kangaroos laze on the lawn by the kidney-shaped pool to a relaxing sound track of birds singing and chirping. A restaurant serves meals throughout the day, and you can stock up on goods at the small supermarket. The resort runs four-wheel-drive tours, guided walks, and scenic flights, and the visitor center is a major attraction. **Pros:** quiet and peaceful rooms, perfect for animal lovers. **Cons:** campsites can be overrun with school groups, permanent tents are overpriced. ⊠ *End of Wilpena Rd., Wilpena Pound* ✛ *156 km (97 mi) off the Princes Hwy. via the town of Hawker* ☎ *08/8648–0004* ⊕ *www.wilpenapound.com. au* ⬎ *34 rooms, 26 units* △ *In-room: no phone, kitchen (some), refrigerator. In-hotel: 2 restaurants, bar, no elevator, pool, laundry facilities, public Internet, public Wi-Fi, no-smoking rooms* ▭ *AE, DC, MC, V.*

Outback Adventures

WORD OF MOUTH

"If you are into hiking/bush walking and would like to see some of the "outback", I would suggest a flight to Darwin, and hire a rental car from there for a few trips around some fantastic national parks (Kakadu, Katherine Gorge, Litchfield). Could be interesting weather up north at that time of year (November)—likely quite warm and humid, but most likely some fantastic thunderstorms!"

—mmemarmalade

WELCOME TO OUTBACK ADVENTURES

TOP REASONS TO GO

★ **Old Culture:** The Red Centre, Top End, and the Kimberley are the best places to experience one of the oldest cultures in the world, that of Australia's Aborigines.

★ **National Parks:** With spectacular terrain and one-of-a-kind plant and animal species, rugged national parks tell the story of Australia's ancient landforms, especially across the Top End and Kimberley regions.

★ **Beach Heaven:** Some of Australia's finest beaches are in Western Australia. Hundreds of kilometers of virtually deserted sandy coves and bays are there inviting you to swim, surf, snorkel, or laze about.

★ **West Coast Cooking:** Innovative chefs blend immigrant Asian, European, and African flavors with local produce to create distinctive plates.

★ **Wine Trails:** Follow the wine trails from Perth to the south coast to enjoy free tastings of internationally renowned wines at the cellar doors.

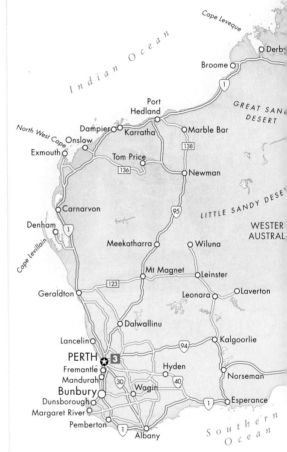

1 Red Centre. Uluru (Ayers Rock) is one of Australia's iconic images, and the main reason people visit the Red Centre. A striking sight, it is one of the world's largest monoliths, the last vestige of an ancient mountain range that looms 1,100 feet above the surrounding plain. But, there is more than just "the Rock" in the Red Centre—traditional Aboriginal "Dreamtime" stories overlie a region rich in geological wonders.

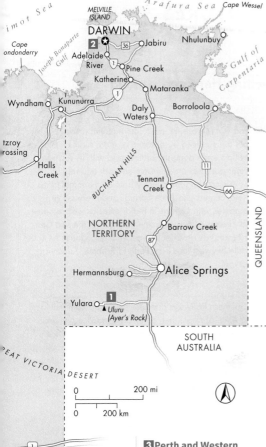

GETTING ORIENTED

Big, vast, expansive, huge—whichever way you cut it, Western Australia and the Northern Territory are daunting. Western Australia sprawls across nearly 1 million square miles—3.6 times the size of Texas—while the Northern Territory adds another 520,000 square mi, together accounting for half of Australia's land-mass, but just about 11 percent of the population. This, in many respects, is the "real Australia" as you imagine it—remote, mostly uninhabited, the landscape ground down over millennia. Getting around by road will absorb days, if not weeks, but fortunately air services can cut the travel times between the gems of this vast area.

3 **Perth and Western Australia.** Most trips to Western Australia begin and end in Perth. Here the major air, road, and rail transport links terminate in a city dubbed the most remote in the world. But, don't expect some backwards Hicksville—Perth is breezy, sophisti-cated, and culturally diverse, with an energetic outdoor lifestyle. Outside the city are untouched natural environ-ments, plus exceptional food and wine.

2 **Darwin and the Kim-berley.** The "Top End" of Australia packs in some of the world's great natural environments—and with few people to crowd the views. Add in modern and ancient Aboriginal art and locals with a definite individualistic attitude, and you have an Australia so very different from Sydney and Melbourne.

9

OUTBACK ADVENTURES PLANNER

Health and Safety

If you are self-driving—especially in remote areas—make sure you have enough fuel, water, and food and carry a first-aid kit. Let others know where you are going and for how long. Going off bushwalking or hiking without adequate supplies, directions, and alone or without letting others know your plan is also risky and perhaps just stupid.

There are "critters" to avoid—snakes, crocodiles, and box jellyfish, for example. Mosquitoes can carry encephalitis, dengue fever, and Ross River fever, so cover up and use a good insect repellent; the worst times for mosquitoes are dawn and dusk.

Respect the Australian sun, especially in the summer months. Sunburn is a real danger if you don't do what the Australians are urged to do: slip, slap, slop, that is, slip on a hat, slap on sunglasses, and slop on sunscreen. On popular beaches around major cities and towns lifesavers (lifeguards) are usually on duty, but generally most beaches are unguarded. Take extra care, especially where there are strong currents.

The emergency contact number for police, fire, and ambulance is *000*. From a GSM mobile (cell) phone the number is *112*.

Getting Here and Around

By Plane

Perth and Darwin are the main international arrival points, and both are serviced by a dozen or more airlines. Qantas is Australia's main domestic airline, and with its subsidiary Jetstar operates an extensive network and regular services crisscrossing the country from all the major cities to regional centers like Alice Springs and Broome. Virgin Blue competes with Qantas in major cities as well as some regional centers such as Broome, though not the Red Centre. Air North has an extensive network throughout the Top End, while Skywest flies from Perth to Broome, Kununurra, and Darwin.

By Train

Great Southern Railways operates the *Ghan* from Adelaide north to Alice Springs, then on to Darwin twice a week; return services from Darwin to Adelaide are also twice a week. The *Indian Pacific,* also operated by Great Southern, links Sydney and Perth via Adelaide with twice-weekly services each way. The trip takes around 60 hours.

From Perth, TransWA operates train services to Bunbury twice daily and to Northam and Kalgoorlie.

Getting around Perth by train is quick and easy, with lines to Armadale, Clarkson, Midland, Fremantle, and Mandurah.

By Car and Bus

Driving around Western Australia and the Northern Territory is relatively easy, with mostly good paved roads and light traffic outside Perth and Darwin. But distances can be daunting. For example, Adelaide to Alice Springs via the Stuart Highway is 1,000 mi, and can take 24 hours. From Darwin to Broome is 1,152 mi, a tiring two-day drive. On the other hand, Perth to Margaret River in the South-West is less than four hours along good roads. Greyhound Australia operates an extensive network of long-distance coaches. From Perth to Broome takes two days, with another day on to Darwin. From Perth to Adelaide, expect to be on the road for 36 hours.

About the Restaurants

Restaurants and cafés in Western Australia and the Northern Territory are largely reflective of their location: in the Red Centre you'll find "bush tucker" menus with crocodile, kangaroo, camel, and native fruits, berries, and plants; in Darwin and Broome locally caught seafood are prepared with flavor influences from Asia; in Perth—and the winery restaurants down south—fusion cuisines are influenced by the continual influx of immigrants from Europe, Asia, and Africa.

Expect to find Western Australian wines on the wine list when dining in most licensed restaurants in Perth and, of course, in the Margaret River wine region, where first-class food is matched with highly-regarded wines.

Many restaurants and cafés offer alfresco dining. Tips aren't expected, but an extra 10% for exceptional service is welcome.

About the Hotels

From five-star to basic, you'll find suitable accommodations throughout the region. The well-known international chains are largely in Perth and Darwin, but there are also sublime boutique accommodations set in wilderness or natural settings outside these centers. Both the Kimberley and Western Australia's South-West are especially noted for these types of properties. You can also experience Outback Australia at homesteads and working cattle stations, while owner-run bed-and-breakfasts provide comfort, charm, and a glimpse of local life. In the cities and the Outback there are plenty of less-than-memorable motels where you can at least get a clean bed for the night. Popular options—especially for families and small groups—are self-contained apartments, villas, and chalets. With two or three bedrooms, living areas, and kitchens, they allow you to save on dining costs by cooking your own meals; these are best if staying more than one night.

DINING AND LODGING PRICE CATEGORIES (IN AUSTRALIAN DOLLARS)

	¢	$	$$	$$$	$$$$
Restaurants	under A$10	A$10–A$20	A$21–A$35	A$36–A$50	over A$50
Hotels	under A$100	A$100–A$150	A$151–A$200	A$201–A$300	over A$300

Prices are for a main course at dinner.

When to Go

May through September (Australia's winter) are the best months to visit the Red Centre and the Top End; nights are crisp and cold and days are pleasantly warm. Summer temperatures in the Centre—which can rise above 43°C (110°F)—are oppressive, while the wet season (December–April) means that Darwin and surroundings are hot, humid, and, well, wet. Perth and the South-West you can visit year-round, though the weather will influence your activities and sightseeing. Summer (December–February) in Perth is *hot* and temperatures can rise to 40°C (100°F) and higher. In the Kimberley May–November is the preferred season, with usually clear skies and balmy days and nights.

In the Top End the year is divided into the wet season (the Wet; December–April) and the dry season (the Dry; May–November). The Dry is a period of idyllic weather with warm days and cool nights, while the Wet brings monsoonal storms that dump an average of 52 inches of rain in a few months. You can also catch spectacular electrical storms, particularly over the ocean. The Kimberley has a similar wet season; however, the rainfall is less and generally comes in short, heavy storms. Cyclones also occur during this period and can disrupt travel arrangements.

9

ABORIGINAL CULTURE

When Europeans arrived to establish a permanent colony in what was to become New South Wales, Aboriginal people had been living across the continent for at least 50,000 years.

Perhaps 600 different "clan groups" or "nations"—each with its own distinctive culture and beliefs—greeted the new settlers in a clash of civilizations that remains largely unresolved today. Despite the efforts of governments of all persuasions and society at large, Aboriginal people by all measures—economic, health, social, education— remain an underprivileged group.

But Aboriginal culture as expressed in oral tradition, art, and lifestyle and by sacred sites such as Uluru is of growing interest to national and international travelers. Tours and experiences that promote Aboriginal culture and lifestyle are available throughout Western Australia and the Northern Territory. Experiences range from organized tours to dance performances, shopping for traditional Aboriginal artifacts and art, and the opportunity to stay on Aboriginal land to experience the daily lives of Aboriginal people. Tourism represents an important source of income ensuring that Aboriginal communities prosper and that their heritage is preserved.

COMMUNITY VALUES

Welcome to Country is the ritual of Australia's Aboriginal people. Protocol dictates that people are welcomed when entering and learning about Country or crossing through another clan or nation's land; for many this is simply good manners and respect. It's likely you will enjoy a Welcome to Country if you join any Aboriginal-guided tour.

In some cultures there were once strict rules about eye contact; you may find that some people follow this practice and won't make eye contact with you. Not making eye contact or lowering the eyes are often a show of respect toward older people.

SACRED SITES

Uluru (Ayers Rock) is probably Australia's best known natural site, but it also has significant cultural meaning for the traditional owners, the Anangu people. They believe they are direct descendants of the beings—which include a python, an emu, a blue-tongue lizard, and a poisonous snake—who formed the land and its physical features during the Tjukurpa (the "Dreamtime," or creation period). Rising more than 1,100 feet from the surrounding plain, Uluru is one of the world's largest monoliths, though such a classification belies the otherworldly, spiritual energy surrounding it.

Kakadu National Park contains some of the best ancient rock art accessible to visitors in Australia. The Anbangbang Gallery has a frieze of Aboriginal rock painting dating back thousands of years, while among the six galleries at Ubirr there is a 49-foot frieze of X-ray paintings depicting animals, birds, and fish. Warradjan Aboriginal Cultural Centre's large display, developed by the local Bininj/Mungguy people, provides detailed information about Aboriginal culture in Kakadu. **Purnululu National Park** (the Bungle Bungles) is an amazing geological wonder and a site for Aboriginal culture. Although the Bungle Bungle Range was extensively used by Aboriginal people during the wet season, when plant and animal life was abundant, few Europeans knew of its existence until the mid-1980s. The area is rich in Aboriginal art, and there are also many burial sites.

Farther west in the **Kimberley Region** the former pearling town of **Broome** is the starting point for many adventure tours into the remote Outback, and visiting Aboriginal communities such as Bardi Creek, Biridu Community, and One Arm Point Community with local Aboriginal guides. Geickie Gorge, Windjana Gorge, and Tunnel Creek combine wilderness scenery with indigenous rock art, lifestyles, and stories from the Dreamtime.

TOP SIGHTS

By far the best way to experience Aboriginal culture is on foot and with an experienced guide, though at some national parks, interpretive centers, signage and—occasionally—self-guided audio equipment mean you can visit on your own. On foot generally requires a level of fitness and surefootedness for trails and pathways; even the best locations are uneven and stony, and can include steep climbs. Boats provide an alternative, such as at Geickie Gorge and Kakadu, where guided tours along the waterways include information about Aboriginal culture. In Margaret River you can canoe to Aboriginal sites and enjoy bush tucker as well. From Broome, four-wheel-drive safaris can get you into remote Aboriginal communities where you can meet the locals and listen to campfire stories. If mobility is an issue, there are easily accessible interpretive centers at places like Uluru and Kakadu national parks that have extensive displays describing Aboriginal life.

9

MARGARET RIVER WINE REGION

From humble beginnings more than 30 years ago, the Margaret River Wine Region now ranks as one of the premium wine-producing regions of the world.

Agronomist Dr. John Gladstones is credited with the birth of the area's wine industry—his 1965 report identified climate, soil, and weather conditions in the South-West as similar to the Bordeaux region of France. A handful of pioneers took his advice, and by the mid-1970s were turning out outstanding wines. Today more than 120 wineries claim Margaret River origins. At 90 or so on-farm cellar-door outlets you can taste and buy wines and often have a delicious meal as well.

While the wine gives the region its cachet and is the prime reason for touring the area, there is more to explore. With gorgeous landscapes and seascapes, world-renowned surf breaks and swimming beaches, arts and crafts outlets, locally-produced foods, and forest and beachside hiking trails, the region attracts some 1.5 million visitors a year.

WHEN TO GO

The region is a year-round destination. Most wineries are open seven days a week, but its popularity with visitors from Perth means that weekends are busiest and public holidays, such as Easter, can be crowded and accommodations booked solid. The summer school holidays in December and January are also popular times for Western Australians to visit, and accommodations can be at a premium. Vintage—when the grapes are picked and crushed—is usually between February and April, while in mid-winter from June through August the vines are bare and you'll see pruning teams in the vineyards.

Margaret River wineries are owned and run by international corporations, midsized companies, and families. This ownership structure influences your experience when visiting a cellar door—often, though not always, the family-run operations offer a friendlier welcome and a more authentic winery experience.

Cullen Wines is one of the region's founding wineries, established by the late industry patriarch Dr. Kevin Cullen in 1971. His daughter Vanya now runs the operation, producing wines using biodynamic practices, one of the few such wineries in Australia. The tasting room is small, but the experience is archetypal Margaret River. Their flagship wines are named after mum and dad—the Kevin John Chardonnay and the Diana Madeline Cabernet.

Happs Winery is the product of another pioneer vigneron, Erl Happ, who hand-built his winery and adjoining pottery with mudbricks, recycled timbers, and stained glass in 1978. The eclectic architecture of the cellar door is also reflected in Happ's passion for trying something new—the biggest choice in wines is found here.

Hayshed Hill has been through the circle of ownership. Established as a family operation—the first vines were planted in 1973—it was bought out in 2000 by a national wine investment company and then bought again by winemaker Michael Kerrigan in 2006, in a move he describes as "winemakers buying back the farm." The white-clapboard building that houses the cellar door and a small café is the perfect setting for tasting the wines and enjoying a light lunch.

Leeuwin Estate is one of the iconic wineries in the area, established by the entrepreneurial Denis Horgan in 1975 with the assistance of legendary American winemaker Robert Mondavi. Before you taste the wines in the stone-and-timber tasting room, head downstairs to view the art gallery of original commissioned works from Robert Juniper, Peter Cole, Sidney Nolan, and Clifton Pugh, among others.

TIMING

There are some 90 wineries with cellar-door outlets in the region, so deciding which ones to visit can be a challenge. We suggest that you don't try to visit more than four or five wineries in a day—this gives you time to appreciate the architecture and ambience of each cellar door, learn about and taste the wines on offer, talk with the staff (maybe even the winemaker), stop for a leisurely lunch at a vineyard restaurant, and avoid getting completely bamboozled. If you're driving, make sure you choose a "skipper," a non-drinking driver.

9

NEED A BREAK

One of the great pleasures of touring the Margaret River wineries is lunch, and there are some excellent winery restaurants to choose from. Vasse Felix's restaurant is set on top of the cellar door, shop, and winery complex with views over landscaped gardens, bushland, and a billabong. Chef Aaron Carr's menus include "share options" such as cooked, cured, and raw seafood plates, as well as fantastic main courses.

Updated
by Graham
Hodgson

A vast mass of the earth's surface—almost half the area of the United States—dating back millions of years, Western Australia and the Northern Territory combine to offer some of Australia's most fascinating and unique natural attractions. Weathered down over the millennia, the region presents no snow-capped mountains. Instead, it offers deeply carved rock canyons, rock formations that leap up from surrounding plains, giant hardwood forests, tropical wetlands, deserts with unending horizons, mile upon mile of untrammeled white-sand beaches, and crystal-clear marine parks.

Indigenous peoples have been here for around 50,000 years, bringing with them legends and myths from their "Dreaming" to describe the land, animals, and plants. European settlement is *much* younger. Perth, in Western Australia, only dates back to inauspicious beginnings in 1829; Darwin, in the Northern Territory, dates to around the same time. Many other towns and villages have a history of less than 100 years. With a population of 2.4 million, and 1.4 million of those in Perth, only a scant human toehold exists here, making it one of the most lightly populated areas on earth.

And remote, too—it's close to a five-hour flight from Sydney to Perth, about the same to Darwin. Western Australians and Territorians bemoan and celebrate their isolation from the rest of Australia. On the one hand, there is what they derisively call SCAM, the Sydney, Canberra, and Melbourne triangle, where the nation's political, financial, and social decisions are made. On the other hand, their isolation engenders strong feelings of independence, and pride in what they regard as "the real Australia."

Residents of Western Australia—once dubbed the "Cinderella State"—now repeatedly point out that they are the nation's economic powerhouse, producing much of its export mineral, energy, and agricultural wealth. From a modest start when gold was discovered in the 1890s to the 1970s, when other massive mineral deposits were discovered—notably iron ore—to today, the state has now become inextricably linked to global markets. That has resulted in a strong inflow of people from around the world. Many have settled in Perth and southward, where the population growth rate is among the fastest in Australia. The Mediterranean climate fosters an easy-going outdoor lifestyle, the attractions of sport, superb local food and wine, beaches and bush married to an energetic, go-getting economic drive.

Territorians, living mainly in Darwin and Alice Springs, in the Red Centre, make the most of their isolation with a strongly independent and individualistic attitude. For thousands of years these areas have been home to Aboriginal communities who have undiminished ties to the land. With an art history dating back at least 20,000 years, Aboriginal artwork has now moved into Australia's mainstream art movement, and some expensive canvasses by Aboriginal artists decorate galleries, homes, and corporate boardrooms around the world. Across the state border in Western Australia, the Kimberley region is a largely untouched wilderness. Four-wheel-drive vehicles are de riguer for this area with many unsealed (unpaved) roads, while between Derby and Wyndham there are some 1,000 km (625 mi) of glorious coastline unreachable except by sea.

TOURS

If you want to avoid the hassles of getting yourself around this vast region, then a tour group is certainly an option. Hundreds of tours and tour operators cover Western Australia and the Northern Territory, and can introduce you to the many experiences on offer here: four-wheel-drive treks, helicopter flights, bush-tucker-gathering expeditions, Aboriginal-guided walks, fishing safaris, and national park tours to name a few.

You can also take a day tour or shorter overnight tours up to, say, five days. Most of these operate from Darwin, Broome, Perth, and Alice Springs. The benefit is that all your transport, accommodation, meals, and sightseeing arrangements are pre-set, and you will get to see and do things you may otherwise miss if you try to organize them yourself.

To see a larger part of the country you can join an extended tour.

Casey Australia Tours (✉ *63 Burwood Cr., Bicton* ☎ *08/9339–4291* ⊕ *www.caseytours.com.au*) has a range of extended tours departing from Perth, including a 16-day fly and coach tour that takes in Broome, Kununurra, Darwin, Kakadu, Alice Springs, and Uluru. Accommodation is in motels and cabins. The price is from A$3,490.

Australian Adventure Travel (✉ *39 Oxleigh Drv., Malaga* ☎ *08/9248–2355* ⊕ *www.australianadventuretravel.com.au*) has comfortable camping safaris for small groups through the Kimberley, using four-wheel-drive vehicles. Highlights of their nine-day Broome to Darwin safari (from A$2,255) include Gibb River Road, Cable Beach, Broome, Derby, Windjana Gorge, Tunnel Creek, Bells Gorge, the King Leopold Ranges, Aboriginal rock art, wildlife, El Questro Station, Kununurra, Bungle Bungles, and Darwin.

North Star Cruises (⊠ *Shop 2, 25 Carnarvon St., Broome* ☎ *08/9192–1829* ⊕ *www.northstarcruises.com.au*) operates the small luxury-expedition cruise ship *True North*, which takes just 36 passengers on 6- and 13-night cruises between Broome and Wyndham along the inaccessible Kimberley coastline. The cruises are adventure oriented, with daily activities including scenic walks, fishing, diving, snorkeling, and on-shore picnics. The ship has six expedition craft and its own helicopter for scenic flights.

Bill Peach Journeys (⊠ *Unit 20, 77 Bourke Rd., Alexandria* ☎ *02/9693–2233* ⊕ *www.billpeachjourneys.com.au*) runs Aircruising Australia, using 34-seat Dash 8 aircraft to fly you to the icon attractions of central Australia, staying overnight in best-available hotels and motels. Their 12-day Great Australian Aircruise departs from and returns to Sydney, and includes stops at Longreach (Queensland), Katherine, Kakadu, and Darwin in the Northern Territory, Kununurra and Broome in Western Australia, and finally Uluru and Alice Springs in the Northern Territory. The inclusive cost starts at A$12,995.

RED CENTRE

The light in the Red Centre—named for the deep color of its desert soils—has a purity and vitality that photographs only begin to approach. For tens of thousands of years this vast desert territory in the south of the Northern Territory has been home to Australia's Aboriginal people. Uluru, also known as Ayers Rock, is a great symbol in Aboriginal traditions, as are many sacred sites among the Centre's mountain ranges, gorges, dry riverbeds, and spinifex plains.

The essence of this ancient land is epitomized in the paintings of the renowned Aboriginal landscape artist Albert Namatjira and his followers. Viewed away from the desert, their images of the MacDonnell Ranges may appear at first to be garish and unreal in their depiction of purple-and-red mountain ranges and stark-white ghost gum trees. Seeing the real thing makes it difficult to imagine executing the paintings in any other way.

Uluru (pronounced *oo-loo-roo*), that magnificent stone monolith rising from the plains, is but one focus in the Red Centre. Kata Tjuta (*ka*-ta *tchoo*-ta), also known as the Olgas, are another. Watarrka National Park and Kings Canyon, Mt. Conner, and the cliffs, gorges, and mountain chains of the MacDonnell Ranges are other worlds to explore.

The primary areas of interest are Alice Springs, which is flanked by the intriguing eastern and western MacDonnell Ranges; Kings Canyon; and Uluru–Kata Tjuta National Park, with neighboring Ayers Rock Resort. Unless you have more than three days, focus on only one of these areas.

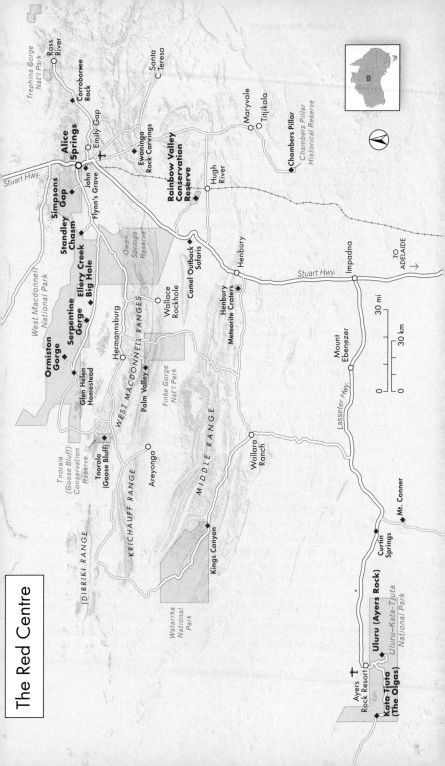

The Red Centre

Ross River
Trephina Gorge Nat'l Park
Corroboree Rock
Emily Gap
Santa Teresa
Alice Springs
Simpsons Gap
John
Flynn's Grave
Standley Chasm
Ewaninga Rock Carvings
Maryvale
Titjikala
Chambers Pillar
Chambers Pillar Historical Reserve
Stuart Hwy.
Ellery Creek Big Hole
Owen Springs Reserve
Rainbow Valley Conservation Reserve
Hugh River
Serpentine Gorge
West Macdonnell National Park
Wallace Rockhole
Camel Outback Safaris
Henbury
Impadna
TO ADELAIDE
Ormiston Gorge
Hermannsburg
Henbury Meteorite Craters
Stuart Hwy.
Glen Helen Homestead
WEST MACDONNELL RANGES
Palm Valley
Finke Gorge Nat'l Park
Mount Ebenezer
Tnorala (Goose Bluff) Conservation Reserve
Tnorala (Goose Bluff)
Areyonga
MIDDLE RANGE
Wallara Ranch
Lasseter Hwy.
IDIRRIKI RANGE
KRICHAUFF RANGE
30 mi
30 km
0
Watarrka National Park
Kings Canyon
Mt. Conner
Curtin Springs
Uluru (Ayers Rock)
Uluru-Kata-Tjuta National Park
Ayers Rock Resort
Kata-Tjuta (The Olgas)

ALICE SPRINGS

2,021 km (1,256 mi) northwest of Sydney, 1,319 km (820 mi) north of Adelaide, 1,976 km (1,228 mi) northeast of Perth.

Once a ramshackle collection of buildings on dusty streets, Alice Springs—known colloquially as "the Alice" or just "Alice"—is today an incongruously suburban tourist center with a population of more than 28,000 in the middle of the desert. Alice derives most of its income from tourism, and more than 300,000 tourists visit annually. The town's ancient sites, a focus for the Arrernte Aboriginal people's ceremonial activities, lie cheek-by-jowl with air-conditioned shops and hotels. The MacDonnell Ranges dominate Alice Springs, changing color according to the time of day from brick red to purple.

GETTING HERE AND AROUND

Alice Springs Airport is 15 km (9 mi) southeast of town. Qantas flies in and out of Alice Springs daily with direct flights from Brisbane, Sydney, Melbourne, Adelaide, Perth, Darwin, and Cairns, as well as Ayers Rock. Tiger Airways flies direct from Melbourne to Alice Springs twice daily on Tuesday, Thursday, and Saturday. It's three hours' flying time from Sydney, Melbourne, and Brisbane; two hours from Adelaide and Darwin; and about 40 minutes from Ayers Rock. Flights run less frequently in the summer months. Alice Springs Airport Shuttle Service meets every flight. The ride to all hotels and residential addresses in town costs A$15 each way. On request, the bus will also pick you up at your hotel and take you back to the airport. From the airport, taxi fare to most parts of town is about A$25.

The *Ghan* train leaves Adelaide at 12:20 PM Sunday and Wednesday, arriving in Alice Springs at 1:45 PM Monday and Thursday. Return trains leave Alice Springs at 12:45 PM Thursday and 3:15 PM Sunday, arriving in Adelaide at 1:10 PM on Friday and Monday. On Monday and Thursday at 6 PM the *Ghan* continues to Darwin via Katherine, arriving at 5:30 PM Tuesday and 6:30 PM Friday. Trains from Darwin depart Wednesday at 10 AM and Saturday at 9 AM. The Alice Springs railway station is 2½ km (1½ mi) west of Todd Mall. **Ghan** (*Great Southern Railway* ☎ *13–2147 bookings, 1300/132147 holiday packages* ⊕ *www.gsr.com.au*).

The Stuart Highway, commonly called the Track, is the only road into Alice Springs. The town center lies east of the highway. The 1,693-km (1,000-mi) drive from Adelaide takes about 24 hours. The drive from Darwin is about 160 km (100 mi) shorter, and takes about 21 hours. Bus tours run between all Red Centre sites, as well as between Alice Springs and Ayers Rock Resort. Traveling by car will give you the most flexible itinerary—although the trade-off is that you'll travel many long, lonely stretches of one-lane highway through the red-dust desert. Vehicles can be rented at Alice Springs and Ayers Rock Resort. The Central Australian Tourism Industry Association in Alice Springs books tours and rental cars, and provides motoring information.

SAFETY AND PRECAUTIONS

Please note that many Aborigines living in or around Alice Springs have been asked to leave their native villages by tribal elders because of their problems with alcohol. Crime and violence stemming from alcohol abuse can make Alice unsafe at night. Sections of the dry Todd river-bed function as makeshift campsites for some Aborigines, so caution is advised when traversing the Todd, particularly after dark.

TIMING

The best time to visit is between May and August, when the weather is mild; the summer months can be blisteringly hot, and some tourism services are less frequent or stop altogether. Alice Springs is pleasant enough, but most of the Red Centre's attractions are outside the town. If visiting Uluru is the main reason for your visit to the Red Centre, you can skip Alice Springs and go directly to Uluru–Kata Tjuta National Park.

TOURS

The *Alice Explorer* bus completes a 70-minute circuit (with narration) of 15 tourist attractions in and around Alice Springs 9–5 daily. You can leave and rejoin the bus whenever you like over two days for a flat rate of A$42. Entry into attractions is extra. It's part of Alice Wanderer Centre Sightseeing, a company that also runs half-day tours of Alice. AAT Kings and Tailormade Tours operate three-hour trips that include visits to the Royal Flying Doctor Service Base, School of the Air, Telegraph Station, and Anzac Hill scenic lookout.

ESSENTIALS

Banks and Currency Exchange ANZ, Commonwealth, National Australia, and **Westpac** all have branches and ATMs in Alice Springs, open 9:30–4 weekdays.

Medical Emergencies Alice Springs Hospital (⊠ *Gap Rd. between Traeger Ave. and Stuart Terrace, Alice Springs* ☎ *08/8951–7777).*

Police Police (☎ *08/8956–2166 Yulara, 08/8951–8822 Alice Springs).*

Taxi Alice Springs Taxis (☎ *08/8952–1877).*

Visitors Information Tourism Central Australia (⊠ *60 Gregory Terrace, Alice Springs* ☎ *08/8952–5800 or 1800/645199* ⊕ *www.centralaustraliantourism.com* ⊙ *Weekdays 8:30–5:30, weekends 9–4)* dispenses information, advice, and maps and will book tours and cars.

Tour Operators AAT Kings (⊠ *74 Todd St., Alice Springs* ☎ *08/8952–1700 or 1300/556100* ⊕ *www.aatkings.com).* **Alice Explorer** (☎ *08/8952–2111 or 1800/722111* ⊕ *www.alicewanderer.com.au).* **Tailormade Tours** (☎ *08/8952–1731 or 1800/806641* ⊕ *www.tailormadetours.com.au).*

EXPLORING ALICE SPRINGS

WHAT TO SEE: CITY CENTER

❶ **Aboriginal Australia Arts & Culture Centre.** You can learn about Arrernte Aboriginal culture and music in this gallery of western desert art and artifacts. Try playing the didgeridoo at the music school, or wander through the Living History Museum. An outstanding place to purchase Aboriginal art, the center also runs half-day cultural tours of the Alice Springs region that allow for a deeper understanding of the

GREAT ITINERARIES

The sheer size of Western Australia and the Northern Territory—together making up half of Australia's landmass—means it is impossible to cover it all on a short visit. You will need to be selective.

For the most part, the major draws are clustered and accessible by air and road: in the Northern Territory Uluru and Kakadu National Park, for both an Aboriginal experience and the natural environment; in Western Australia Purnululu (Bungle Bungle) National Park for an amazing geological formation; Perth and Rottnest Island for a city-based trip and unique wildlife (quokkas); and the South-West for wine-tasting trails, beaches, and forests.

IF YOU HAVE 3 DAYS
Don't even think about trying to do more than one of the major spots or you'll be spending all your time in airports or on the road.

If you choose one of Australia's great icons— Uluru—you could fly directly to Ayers Rock Airport and spend two days there, taking a hike around the rock followed by a look at the **Uluru–Kata Tjuta Cultural Centre** near its base.

The next day take a sight-seeing flight by helicopter or fixed-wing aircraft, then visit **Kata Tjuta** (the Olgas) to explore its extraordinary domes and end the day with sunset at the rock. A flight will get you to Alice Springs, where you can tour out to either the Eastern or Western MacDonnell Ranges to explore the gorges and take a dip in a waterhole.

If you make **Darwin** your starting point, head east early on the Arnhem Highway to Fogg Dam to view the birdlife. Continue into **Kakadu National Park** and picnic at the rock-art site at Ubirr. Take care, a scenic flight in the afternoon, then a trip to the Bowali Visitors Centre, and you can overnight in **Jabiru**.

On the second day, head to Nourlangie Rock; then continue to the Yellow Water cruise at **Cooinda** and stay there for the night. The next day, drive to **Litchfield National Park** and visit Florence, Tjaynera, or Wangi Falls.

The easiest way to see **Purnululu's** amazing "beehive" rock formations is from the air. To do this you'll need to fly to **Kununurra** from Darwin or **Broome**, then take a sight-seeing flight.

If you fly into **Perth**, spend most of the first day knocking around the city center. Take the train to pleasantly restored **Fremantle** and stroll through the streets, stopping for breaks at sidewalk cafés. In the evening in either city, have dinner overlooking the water.

Next day, take a ferry to **Rottnest Island** and cycle around, walk on the beach, fish, or try to spot the small local marsupials called quokkas. A coach tour on the final day will get you to the **Margaret River** wine region.

IF YOU HAVE 5 DAYS
Five days allows you to spend more time at your preferred destination, or, indeed, combine two, though it will still be rushed.

In the Red Centre follow the three-day itinerary, finishing in Alice Springs, then fly to Darwin for a two-day trip to Kakudu National Park. Alternatively, start in Perth with the three-day itinerary then add on a return flight to Ayers Rock Airport to visit Uluru; you'll be there in time for sunset before departing the next morning.

Another option is to fly to Kununurra from Perth, then take a sightseeing flight over Purnululu's rock formations, though this is time-consuming, as the flight time to Kununurra is around three hours.

Yours truly, could also spend a couple of days in Perth and Rottnest, then fly to **Broome, a fascinating onetime pearl town,** for two days.

IF YOU HAVE 7 DAYS
Seven days will allow you to hop, skip, and jump around Western Australia and the Northern Territory. Start in **Perth**, spending half a day in the city, including **King's Park**, then take the bus or train to the heritage city of **Fremantle** for lunch of fish-and-chips by the water and a stroll through the heritage precinct.

The next day, fly to **Ayers Rock** and watch sunset at Uluru and spend the next day driving to Alice Springs, visiting the **Aboriginal Australia Arts and Culture Centre** before a late afternoon camel ride along the dry **Todd River**.

The next morning fly to **Darwin** and head to **Kakudu National Park** for two days before returning to Darwin and flying back to Perth. Alternatively, fly west to **Kununurra** for a night, taking in a sightseeing flight over the **Bungle**

Bungles in Purnululu National Park before flying on to Perth; or, pass over Kununurra and fly on to Broome, where you can laze on the fabulous **Cable Beach** before taking a camel ride or checking out the locally crafted jewelry of pearls and diamonds. You could start this itinerary in the Red Centre, flying in from Sydney or Melbourne before returning there from Perth.

IF YOU HAVE 10 DAYS
If you follow the seven-day itinerary above, you can afford to spend an extra day in Perth, either taking the ferry to **Rottnest Island**, a lunch and wine-tasting cruise on the **Swan River**, or even a winery tour to **Margaret River**. You could also add in a two-day safari trip from **Kununurra** to **Purnululu National Park**, camping out in the bush camps there.

9

art and the stories it represents. ⊠ *125 Todd St.* ☎ *08/8952–3408* ⊕ *www.aboriginalart.com.au* ✉ *Free* ☉ *Daily 9–5.*

② **Alice Springs Reptile Centre.** Thorny
↻ devils, frill-neck lizards, some of the world's deadliest snakes, and "Terry" the saltwater crocodile inhabit this park in the heart of town, opposite the Royal Flying Doctor Service. May to August (winter) the viewing is best from 11 to 3, when the reptiles are most

ART HUNT

If you're looking for Aboriginal art, galleries abound along Todd Mall (the main shopping street); they're filled with canvas and bark paintings, as well as handcrafted didgeridoos and other artifacts. You can also buy art directly from Aborigines on weekends outside Flynn Memorial Church in the mall.

active. You can even feed the snakes by hand and pick up the pythons. There's also a fossil cave. Free talks are conducted daily at 11, 1, and 3:30. ⊠ *9 Stuart Terrace* ☎ *08/8952–8900* ⊕ *www.reptilecentre.com.au* ✉ *A$12* ☉ *Daily 9:30–5.*

③ **Royal Flying Doctor Service (RFDS).** Directed from this RFDS radio base, doctors use aircraft to make house calls at settlements and homes hundreds of miles apart. Like the School of the Air, the RFDS is a vital part of Outback life. The visitor center has historical displays and an audio-visual show. Tours run every half hour throughout the year. ⊠ *8–10 Stuart Terrace* ☎ *08/8952–1129* ⊕ *www.flyingdoctor.net/Alice-Springs.html* ✉ *A$7* ☉ *Mon.–Sat. 9–4, Sun. 1–4.*

WHAT TO SEE AROUND ALICE SPRINGS

④ **Araluen Cultural Precinct.** The most distinctive building in this complex
★ is the Museum of Central Australia, which charts the evolution of the land and its inhabitants—human and animal—around central Australia. Exhibits include a skeleton of the 10½-foot-tall duck relative *Dromornis stirtoni,* the largest bird to walk on earth, which was found northeast of Alice. Also in the precinct are the Aviation Museum, Territory Craft, and Araluen Centre, home to the Araluen Art Galleries and the Namatjira Gallery, a collection of renowned Aboriginal landscapes. The precinct is 2 km (1 mi) southwest of town, and is on the Alice Wanderer tourist bus itinerary. ⊠ *61 Larapinta Dr.* ☎ *08/8951–1120* ✉ *A$10* ☉ *Weekdays 10–4, weekends 11–4.*

⑤ **Alice Springs Desert Park.** Focusing on the desert, which makes up 70% of
↻ the Australian landmass, this 75-acre site contains 320 types of plants
★ and 120 animal species in several Australian ecosystems—including the largest nocturnal-animal house in the southern hemisphere. Local Aboriginal guides share their native stories about the wildlife and the land. Allow about four hours to explore the park; it's 6½ km (4 mi) west of Alice Springs, and is on the Alice Wanderer bus itinerary. ⊠ *Larapinta Dr.* ☎ *08/8951–8788* ⊕ *www.alicespringsdesertpark.com.au* ✉ *A$20* ☉ *Daily 7:30–6.*

OFF THE BEATEN PATH
Spectacular scenery and Aboriginal rock art in the MacDonnell Ranges east of the Alice are well worth a day or more of exploration. Emily Gap (a sacred Aboriginal site), Jessie Gap, and Corroboree Rock, once a setting for important men-only Aboriginal ceremonies, are within the

The outback just outside of Alice Springs

first 44 km (27 mi) east of Alice Springs. Beyond these are Trephina Gorge, John Hayes Rockhole, and N'Dhala Gorge Nature Park (with numerous Aboriginal rock carvings).

Arltunga Historical Reserve, 110 km (69 mi) northeast of Alice, contains the ruins of a 19th-century gold-rush site. If you fancy fossicking (prospecting) for your own semiprecious stones, you can take your pick—and shovel—at Gemtree in the Harts Ranges, 140 km (87 mi) northeast of Alice. Ranger stations (☎ 08/8956–9765) are at Trephina Gorge and John Hayes Rockhole.

OUTDOOR ACTIVITIES

CAMEL RIDING **Pyndan Camel Tracks** (☎ 0416/170164 ⊕ *www.cameltracks.com*) has daily one-hour camel rides at noon, 2:30, and sunset (A$45) that explore a valley of diverse habitat about 15 km (9 mi) from Alice Springs and surrounded by the ancient MacDonnell Ranges. Half-day morning rides at 9 AM (A$95) allow you to spend more time with your camel, discovering the Ilparpa Valley and stopping for morning tea in a sandy river bed.

HIKING/ BUSHWALKING The MacDonnell Ranges, the craggy desert mountains that frame Alice Springs, are rich with desert landscapes and Aboriginal significance. The **Emily and Jessie Gaps Nature Park**, located in the East MacDonnells, just 10 km (6 mi) east of Alice Springs along the Ross Highway, contains registered sacred Aboriginal sites, including rock paintings depicting the caterpillar story of the Dreamtime—the Aboriginal stories of the world's creation.

The **Larapinta Trail** is a 223-km-long (145-mi-long) walking track that runs west from Alice Springs into the West MacDonnell Ranges. It's a spectacular, though challenging, track that takes hikers through

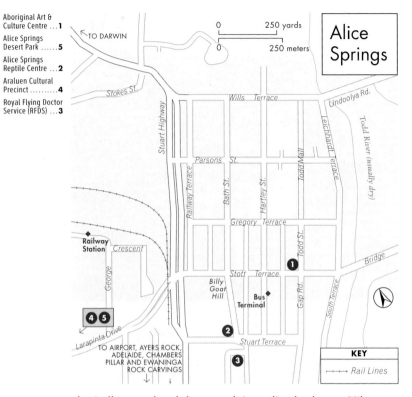

classically rugged and dry central Australian landscape. Hikers are encouraged to participate in the voluntary Overnight Walker Registration Scheme, designed to insure that all trekkers on the trail can be tracked and accounted for in case of emergency. Contact the **Northern Territory Parks & Wildlife Service** (☎ *08/8951–8250*) for more information. **Tourism Central Australia** in Alice Springs (☎ *08/8952–5800*) can also advise you if you're interested in planning bushwalking itineraries.

HOT-AIR BALLOONING
At dawn on most mornings hot-air balloons float in the sky around Alice Springs. **Outback Ballooning** (✉ *Box 2702, Alice Springs* ☎ *1800/809790* ⊕ *www.outbackballooning.com.au*) makes hotel pickups about an hour before dawn and returns between 9 AM and 10 AM. The A$275 fee covers 30 minutes of flying time, insurance, and a champagne breakfast. A 60-minute flight costs A$385.

QUAD-BIKE RIDING
Hop aboard a motorbike with four huge wheels and explore the Northern Territory's oldest working cattle station with **Outback Quad Adventures** (✉ *Undoolya Station, Undoolya Rd.* ☎ *08/8953–0697*). The company collects you from Alice Springs and takes you to the station, 17 km (10 mi) out of town on the edge of the MacDonnell Ranges. No special license is needed, and all tours are escorted by guides with two-way radios. Rides of 2½ hours (A$120) and 3½ hours (A$195) and overnight tours—which include barbecue dinner with wine, sleeping bags, and breakfast (A$345)—operate year-round.

WHERE TO EAT

$$-$$$
★
SEAFOOD

✕ **Barra on Todd.** Northern Territory barramundi prepared three ways—char-grilled, grilled, and battered—is the highlight at this classy restaurant and bar, at Voyages Alice Springs Resort. It's popular with locals, too. Other delicious seafood dishes on offer include South Australian oysters and prawns flambéed in Malibu. Like any good Aussie restaurant, though, it still caters to carnivores with artful beef, chicken, and lamb dishes, which you can eat under thatch-roof ceilings, overlooking the happening pool. ✉ *34 Stott Terr.* ☎ *08/8952–3523* 🗖 *AE, DC, MC, V.*

WORD OF MOUTH

"I suggest two nights in Alice Springs, especially if you are flying in and out from either Sydney, Melbourne, or Adelaide. Most (but not all) flights to Alice Springs arrive and depart around mid-day, and after checking or fetching your baggage and checking into and out of your hotel, you may be left with barely one-half day of any travel day to sightsee."

—AliceSprings

$-$$$
AUSTRALIAN

✕ **Bojangles Saloon and Restaurant.** Cowhide seats, tables made from old *Ghan* railway benches, and a life-size replica of bushranger Ned Kelly give this lively restaurant true Outback flavor. Food is classic Northern Territory tucker: barramundi, kangaroo, camel, emu, thick slabs of ribs, and huge steaks—and the peanuts are free! Bojangles also broadcasts its own live radio show across the Territory via Sun FM radio, and around the world via the Internet, every night from 8.30 PM. Come along and be part of this unique concept, and wave to family and friends on one, or all, of their four webcams which are featured on their Web site. ✉ *80 Todd St.* ☎ *08/8952–2873* ⊕ *www.bossaloon.com.au* 🗖 *AE, DC, MC, V.*

$-$$
ITALIAN

✕ **Casa Nostra.** Red-and-white checkered tablecloths, Chianti bottles, and plastic grapes festoon this family-run Alice old-timer. Locals crowd in for traditional meat dishes, pizza, and pasta, including Al's Special, a dish of chicken parmigiana paired with pasta in a cream-and-black-pepper sauce that the chef took 15 years to perfect. Take a tip from the regulars and preorder a serving of vanilla slice for dessert, or you might miss out on this scrumptious cake of layered papery pastry and custard cream. ✉ *Undoolya Rd. at Sturt Terrace* ☎ *08/8952–6749* ☜ *Reservations essential Fri.–Sat.* 🗖 *MC, V* ⊙ *Closed Sun. and late Dec.–mid-Jan. No lunch.*

$-$$
Fodor'sChoice
★
PAN-ASIAN

✕ **Hanuman Thai.** With its Thai, Nonya (Malaysian), and Tamil-flavored menu, this comfortable spot is the only place in the desert to offer a range of big-city-quality Southeast Asian food. The grilled Hanuman oysters—seasoned with lemongrass and sweet basil—are the main draw. The wild barramundi with a sticky passion-fruit-and-ginger sauce is also popular. Desserts include black-rice brûlée, and banana spring rolls with dates. ✉ *Crown Plaza Alice Springs, 82 Barrett Dr.* ☎ *08/8953–7188* ⊕ *www.hanuman.com.au* 🗖 *AE, DC, MC, V* ⊙ *No lunch weekends.*

WHERE TO STAY

$$
🛏 **Alice Springs Resort.** This lush spot might make you forget that you're surrounded by desert; the thatched ceilings, palm trees, and broad, foliage-fringed lawns would be right at home in the Queensland tropics.

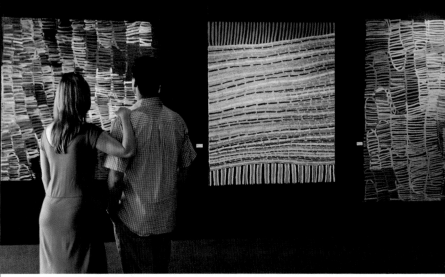

The Mbantua Gallery in Alice Springs.

Many of the comfortable rooms, with their jewel-tone fabrics and blond-wood furniture, open directly onto lawns or gardens where dozens of native birds chatter. A bar in the middle of the tiki-torch lighted, blue-tile pool is a booming nightspot for locals and travelers. Though the relaxed environment may make you want to laze the day away, the center of Alice is just a five-minute walk away. **Pros:** few minutes' walk to shops; tour desk can book variety of tours; lush gardens. **Cons:** convention facilities attract tour groups; no views. ⊠ *34 Stott Terrace* ☎ *08/8951–4545* 🖷 *08/8953–0995* ⊕ *www.alicespringsresort.com.au* 🛏 *139 rooms* ♿ *In-room: refrigerator, Internet. In-hotel: restaurant, room service, bars, pool, laundry facilities, laundry service, public Internet, Wi-Fi, parking (no fee), no-smoking rooms* ═ *AE, DC, MC, V.*

★ 🖳 **Crowne Plaza Resort Alice Springs.** Landscaped lawns with elegant eucalyptus and palm trees greet you at this upscale international chain about a mile outside town. Inside, the rooms are decorated in light, tropical colors like a seaside resort, and have balcony views of the garden and pool or of the Alice Springs Golf Club and the low, barren mountains behind. The on-site Hanuman Thai restaurant is a local favorite; some room rates include breakfast at the more-casual Balloons Bistro. **Pros:** excellent restaurant; many rooms have views of MacDonnell Ranges; winner of environmental awards. **Cons:** in suburban area; no shopping nearby. ⊠ *82 Barrett Dr.* ☎ *08/8950–8000* ⊕ *www.crowneplaza.com.au* 🛏 *229 rooms, 7 suites* ♿ *In-room: safe, refrigerator, Internet. In-hotel: 2 restaurants, room service, bars, tennis courts, pool, gym, laundry facilities, laundry service, public Internet, public Wi-Fi, parking (no fee), no-smoking rooms* ═ *AE, DC, MC, V* ⏋� *BP, EP.*

$ ⊡ **Desert Palms Resort.** Although just a few minutes' walk from the center of Alice Springs, this resort property feels a million miles away from the red desert. Dip your toes in the 24-hour island pool with a waterfall and you might just stay put, lounging and gazing up at the umbrella-like palm trees and red-and-pink bougainvillea. Accommodation, should you choose to get out of the water, is in self-contained, freestanding A-frame units, each with one bedroom and a private balcony. Guests can dine at the adjacent Alice Springs Golf Club. **Pros:** villas are private, screened by foliage; palms trees and bougainvillea create a tropical garden; golf course adjacent. **Cons:** no restaurant; villas are adequate, not fancy. ⊠ *74 Barrett Dr.* ☎ *08/8952–5977* ⊕ *www.desertpalms.com.au* ↘ *80 cabins* ⚸ *In-room: kitchen, refrigerator, Wi-Fi. In-hotel: tennis court, pool, laundry facilities, laundry service, Wi-Fi, airport shuttle, parking (no fee)* ▤ *AE, DC, MC, V.*

$$$ ⊡ **Lasseters Hotel Casino.** There are great views of the MacDonnell Ranges from your balcony or the courtyard. The rooms are spacious and modern, with brightly colored upholstery that echoes the casino's neon lights. You can escape the ringing of the slot machines by lounging by the pool or by borrowing a bike and riding about the expansive property. The adjoining casino is a big part of Alice Springs' nightlife. **Pros:** mountain bikes are complimentary; excellent views of MacDonnell Ranges; casino and nightlife on-site. **Cons:** nights can be noisy with casino open till 3 AM; adjacent convention center attracts big groups. ⊠ *93 Barrett Dr.* ☎ *08/8950–7777* ⊕ *www.hotel.lhc.com.au* ↘ *127 rooms, 13 suites* ⚸ *In-room: safe, refrigerator, DVD (some), Internet. In-hotel: 3 restaurants, room service, bar, tennis court, pool, gym, bicycles, laundry facilities, laundry service, public Internet, public Wi-Fi, parking (no fee), no-smoking rooms* ▤ *AE, DC, MC, V.*

NIGHTLIFE AND THE ARTS

Entry is free at **Lasseters Hotel Casino** (⊠ *93 Barrett Dr.* ☎ *08/8950–7777 or 1800/808975*), where the action goes late into the night. More than 290 slot machines sit here, plus blackjack, roulette, craps, and baccarat tables. The Irish pub has entertainment most nights, as well as karaoke.

Maxim's Bar (⊠ *1 Todd Mall* ☎ *08/8952–1255*), in Todd Tavern, the only traditional Australian pub in town, has something going on every night. The property also includes a restaurant, bottle shop (liquor store), and gambling facilities. You can bet on horse races across the country with TAB (the Australian equivalent of OTB)—but keep some change aside to lose in the slot machines.

Sounds of Starlight (⊠ *40 Todd Mall* ☎ *08/8953–0826*) is the place to enjoy evocative Outback theater performances and didgeridoo music accompanied by a slide show of Red Centre images. Concerts (A$30) are held at 8 PM Tuesday, Friday, and Saturday April–November; call ahead to check schedule. A pre-theater dinner-and-show package (with dinner at the Red Ochre Grill across the street on the mall or at Bojangles Saloon) costs A$75.

9

SHOPPING

Shopping in Alice Springs is all about Aboriginal art and artifacts. Central Australian Aboriginal paintings are characterized by intricate patterns of dots—and are commonly called sand paintings because they were originally drawn on sand as ceremonial devices. The **Aboriginal Desert Art Gallery** (⊠ *87 Todd Mall* ☎ *08/8953–1005*) is one of the best local galleries for Aboriginal art. From bush poetry to traditional bush tucker recipes to anthropological texts on Aborigines and their culture, **Red Kangaroo Books** (⊠ *79 Todd Mall* ☎ *08/8953–2137*) has an outstanding collection of literature pertaining to all things Australian. **Gallery Gondwana** (⊠ *43 Todd Mall* ☎ *08/8953–1577* ⊕ *www.gallerygondwana.com.au*) sells wonderful contemporary and traditional Aboriginal art, and also has a branch in Sydney's suburbs. Colorful and traditional Aboriginal and wildflower-print fabrics for dressmaking and patchwork are available from **SewForU** (⊠ *Reg Harris La. off Todd Mall* ☎ *08/8953–5422*). The **Todd Mall Markets** (⊠ *Todd St.* ☎ *08/8952–9299*) are held on Sunday morning twice monthly from late February to early December (weekly in July). Local arts, crafts, and food are displayed while musicians entertain.

WEST MACDONNELL RANGES

The West MacDonnell Ranges—stretching westward from just a few kilometers outside Alice Springs for around 200 km (125 mi)—are a spectacular series of red-capped mountains interspersed by rocky canyons and narrow gorges. Each of the chasms and gorges has its own unique character, and in many there are waterholes where you can swim. Black-footed rock wallabies are among the wildlife to be spotted. The 223 km (139 mi) Larapinta Trail in the park is the showpiece of Central Australian bushwalking. The trail is broken into 12 sections, each a one- to two-day walk.

GETTING HERE AND AROUND

To reach all the major sights, the Red Centre Way follows Larapinta Drive (the western continuation of Stott Terrace) from Alice Springs and Namatjira Drive westward to Glen Helen, about 130 km (81 mi) from Alice Springs. Roads leading off it access the highlights.

SAFETY AND PRECAUTIONS

Take care when bushwalking or hiking, as paths are usually rocky and uneven. Snakes inhabit most areas, so be cautious when walking through tall grass. You should always carry and drink plenty of water; at least one liter of water for every hour of walking in very warm weather.

TIMING

Most of the best locations are within the West MacDonnell National Park, and can be visited on a half-day or one-day trip from Alice Springs.

TOURS

Trek Larapinta (⊠ *Box 3317, Alice Springs 0871* ☎ *0428/402027* ⊕ *www.treklarapinta.com.au*) has small-group guided bushwalks along the Larapinta Trail. Their six-day tour costs from A$1,290; a longer tour completing the whole trail is 20 days (A$4,400).

Wayoutback Desert Safaris (✉ *30 Kidman St., Alice Springs* ☎ *08/8952–4324* ⊕ *www.wayoutback.com*) has a two-day, four-wheel-drive tour to the West MacDonnells, camping out overnight. The cost is from A$245.

Emu Run Tours (✉ *25 Undoolya Rd., Alice Springs* ☎ *08/8953–7057* ⊕ *www.emurun.com.au*) has a one-day tour by air-conditioned bus to all the major sights in the park, including Simpsons Gap, Standley Chasm, the Ochre Pits, and Ormiston Gorge. The cost is from A$99.

ESSENTIALS

Visitors Information Simpsons Gap Visitor Information Centre (☎ *08/8951–8250*) is 1 km from the turn-off into Simpsons Gap, 18 km from Alice Springs.

EXPLORING

These sights are organized by distance—from closest to farthest—from Alice Springs.

John Flynn's Grave memorializes the Royal Flying Doctor Service founder. It's on a rise with the stark ranges behind, in a memorable setting 6 km (4 mi) west of Alice Springs. ✉ *Larapinta Dr.* ☎ *No phone* 🖃 *Free* ⊙ *Daily 24 hrs.*

Simpsons Gap isn't dramatic, but it's the closest gorge to town. Stark-white ghost gums, red rocks, and the purple-haze mountains provide a taste of the scenery to be seen farther into the ranges. The gap can be crowded in the morning and late afternoon, since these are the best times to see rock wallabies, but unlike Standley Chasm, it's only a short walk from the parking lot. ✉ *Larapinta Dr., 18 km (11 mi) west of Alice Springs, then 6 km (4 mi) on side road* ☎ *08/8951–8250* 🖃 *Free* ⊙ *Daily 5–8.*

★ **Standley Chasm** is one of the most impressive canyons in the MacDonnell Ranges. At midday, when the sun is directly overhead, the 10-yard-wide canyon glows red from the reflected light—this lasts for just 15 minutes. The walk from the parking lot takes about 20 minutes, and is rocky toward the end. There's a kiosk selling snacks and drinks at the park entrance. ✉ *Larapinta Dr.* ✛ *40 km (25 mi) west of Alice Springs, then 9 km (5½ mi) on Standley Chasm Rd.* ☎ *08/8956–7440* 🖃 *A$8* ⊙ *Daily 8–5:30.*

Ellery Creek Big Hole is one of the coldest swimming holes in the Red Centre. It's also the deepest and most permanent water hole in the area, so you may glimpse wild creatures like wallabies or goannas (monitor lizards) quenching their thirst. Take the 3-km (2-mi) Dolomite Walk for a close-up look at this fascinating geological site. ✉ *Namatjira Dr.* ✛ *88 km (55 mi) west of Alice Springs* ☎ *08/8951–8250.*

Serpentine Gorge , is best seen by taking a refreshing swim through the narrow, winding gorge. According to an Aboriginal myth a fierce serpent makes its home in the pool, hence the name. ✉ *Namatjira Dr.* ✛ , 99 km (61 mi) west of Alice Springs ☎ *08/8951–8250.*

Glen Helen Gorge slices through the MacDonnell Ranges, revealing dramatic rock layering and tilting. The gorge was cut by the sporadic Finke River, often described as the oldest river in the world. Here the river

The Heartland

For most Australians the Red Centre is the mystical and legendary core of the continent, and Uluru is its beautiful focal point. Whether they have been there or not, locals believe its image symbolizes a steady pulse that radiates deep through the red earth, through the heartland, and all the way to the coasts.

Little more than a thumbprint within the vast Australian continent, the Red Centre is harsh and isolated. Its hard, relentless topography (and lack of conveniences) makes this one of the most difficult areas of the country to survive in, much less explore. But the early pioneers—some foolish, some hardy—managed to set up bases that thrived. They created cattle stations, introduced electricity, and implemented telegraph services, enabling them to maintain a lifestyle that, if not luxurious, was at least reasonably comfortable.

The people who now sparsely populate the Red Centre are a breed of their own. Many were born and grew up here, but many others were "blow-ins," immigrants from far-flung countries and folk from other Australian states who took up the challenge to make a life in the desert and stayed on as they succeeded. Either way, folks out here have a few common characteristics. They're laconic and down-to-earth, canny and astute, and very likely to try to pull your leg when you least expect it.

No one could survive the isolation without a good sense of humor: where else in the world would you hold a bottomless-boat race in a dry riverbed? The Henley-on-Todd, as it is known, is a sight to behold, with dozens of would-be skippers bumbling along within the bottomless-boat frames.

As the small towns grew and businesses quietly prospered in the mid-1800s, a rail link between Alice Springs and Adelaide was planned. However, the undercurrent of challenge and humor that touches all life here ran through this project as well. Construction began in 1877, but things went wrong from the start. No one had seen rain for ages, and no one expected it; hence, the track was laid right across a floodplain. It wasn't long before locals realized their mistake, when intermittent, heavy floods regularly washed the tracks away. The railway is still in operation today, and all works well, but its history is one of many local jokes here.

For some, the Red Centre is the real Australia, a special place where you will meet people whose generous and sincere hospitality may move you. The land and all its riches offer some of the most spectacular and unique sights on the planet, along with a sense of timelessness that will slow you down and fill your spirit. Take a moment to shade your eyes from the sun and pick up on the subtleties that nature has carefully protected and camouflaged here, and you will soon discover that the Red Centre is not the dead center.

–Bev Malzard

Standley Chasm, West MacDonnell Ranges near Alice Springs.

forms a broad, cold, permanent water hole that's perfect for a bracing swim. ⊠ *Namatjira Dr* ✛ 132 km (82 mi) west of Alice Springs ☎ *08/8951–8250.*

Ormiston Gorge is truly breathtaking. A short climb takes you to Gum Tree Lookout, where you can see the spectacular 820-foot-high red gorge walls rising from the permanent pool below. There is a water hole suitable for swimming. Trails include the 7-km (4½-mi) Ormiston Pound Walk. ⊠ *Namatjira Dr.* ✛ 135 km (84 mi) west of Alice Springs ☎ *08/8951–8250.*

WHERE TO STAY

¢–$$ 🏨 **Glen Helen Resort.** Better described as an Outback lodge, Glen Helen ★ Resort earns its charm from its traditional bush welcome and atmosphere. As guests relax outdoors on the back veranda they enjoy impressive views of the stunning cliffs and riverbed immediately behind the resort. With a huge natural swimming hole at its back door, this accommodation in the West MacDonnell Ranges doesn't need a conventional pool as well—but it has both. You can camp under the stars, sleep in a bunkhouse room with shared facilities, or splurge on a motel room. Guests are often rewarded with wildlife sightings, including many bird species, rock wallabies, dingoes, lizards. Hosts Colin and Shelagh O'Brien help with identifications. There's a restaurant, plus live music five times weekly from March through November. Take a helicopter ride for a fantastic view of the ranges, or a four-wheel-drive safari to surrounding attractions. This outpost is the only place to refuel your vehicle for 100 km (62 mi). **Pros:** traditional Outback Australia atmosphere; easy access to Larapinta Walking Trail; plenty of opportunities to see local fauna. **Cons:** one hour from Alice Springs; limited amenities in motel rooms; need your own transport. ✉ *Namatjira Dr.* ☏ *Box 2207, Alice Springs 0871* ✚ *135 km (84 mi) west of Alice Springs* ☎ *08/8956–7489* ⊕ *www.glenhelen.com.au* ☞ *25 rooms, 10 bunkhouse rooms, 105 unpowered sites, 22 powered sites* ♿ *In-room: no phone, refrigerator, no TV. In-hotel: restaurant, bar, pool, no elevator, laundry facilities* ▭ *MC, V.*

ULURU AND KATA TJUTA

It's easy to see why the Aborigines attach spiritual significance to Uluru (Ayers Rock). It rises magnificently above the plain and dramatically changes color throughout the day. The Anangu people are the traditional owners of the land around Uluru and Kata Tjuta. They believe they are direct descendants of the beings—which include a python, an emu, a blue-tongue lizard, and a poisonous snake—who formed the land and its physical features during the Tjukurpa (the "Dreamtime," or creation period). At more than 1,100 feet, Uluru is one of the world's largest monoliths, though such a classification belies the otherworldly, spiritual energy surrounding it. Historically, it's been a sacred site to the Aborigines, and from that a great controversy has arisen over whether it's appropriate to climb the rock. The Anangu people have politely requested that visitors not scale Uluru, but thousands of tourists wish to do so every year. If you want to make the climb, a well-marked path will help you do it.

Kata Tjuta (the Olgas), 53 km (33 mi) west, is a series of 36 gigantic rock domes hiding a maze of fascinating gorges and crevasses. The names Ayers Rock and the Olgas are used out of familiarity alone; at the sites themselves, the Aboriginal Uluru and Kata Tjuta are the respective names of preference. The entire area is called Yulara, though the airport is still known as Ayers Rock.

Uluru and Kata Tjuta have very different compositions. Monolithic Uluru is a type of sandstone called arkose, while the rock domes at Kata Tjuta are composed of conglomerate. Both of these intriguing sights lie within Uluru–Kata Tjuta National Park, which is protected as a World Heritage Site. The whole experience is a bit like seeing the Grand Canyon turned inside out, and a visit here will be remembered for a lifetime.

GETTING HERE AND AROUND

Qantas operates daily direct flights from Sydney, Perth, and Cairns (and twice weekly flights from Melbourne) to Ayers Rock Airport, which is 5 km (3 mi) north of the resort complex. Passengers from other capital cities fly to Alice Springs to connect with flights to Ayers Rock Airport. Qantas flies daily 40-minute flights from Alice Springs to Ayers Rock.

AAT Kings runs a complimentary shuttle bus between the airport and Yulara, which meets every flight. If you have reservations at the resort, representatives wait outside the baggage-claim area of the airport to whisk you and other guests away on the 10-minute drive.

If you're driving from Alice Springs, it's a five-hour-plus 440-km (273-mi) trip to Ayers Rock Resort. The road is paved, but lacks a shoulder, and is one lane in each direction for the duration. The un-scenic route often induces fatigue.

From the resort it's 19 km (12 mi) to Uluru or 53 km (33 mi) to Kata Tjuta. The road to Kata Tjuta is paved.

If you prefer to explore Uluru and Kata Tjuta on your own schedule, then renting your own car is a very good idea; the only other ways to get to the national park are on group bus tours or chauffeured taxi or coach. Avis, Hertz, and Thrifty–Territory Rent-a-Car all rent cars at Ayers Rock Resort. Arrange for your rental early, since cars are limited. **Automobile Association of N.T.** (☎ 08/8981–3837, 13–1111 emergency road assistance ⊕ www.aant. com.au). **N.T. Road Report** (☎ 1800/246199 ⊕ www.ntlis.nt.gov.au/ roadreport).

Greyhound and AAT Kings coaches (which runs day and extended tours) make daily departures from Alice Springs to Ayers Rock. **AAT Kings** (☎ 08/8952–1700 or 1300/556100 ⊕ www.aatkings.com). **Greyhound Australia** (☎ 08/8952–7888 or 1300/473946 ⊕ www.greyhound. com.au).

> ## WATCH THE SKY
>
> More stars and other astronomical sights, such as the fascinating Magellanic Clouds, are visible in the southern hemisphere than in the northern, and the desert night sky shows off their glory with diamond-like clarity. Look out for the Southern Cross, the constellation that navigators used for many centuries to find their way—most Australians will proudly point it out for you.

SAFETY AND PRECAUTIONS

Water is vital in the Red Centre. It is easy to forget, but the dry atmosphere and the temperatures can make you prone to dehydration. Drinking plenty of water is essential to enjoying your holiday in the Red Centre. If you are walking or climbing, you will need to consume additional water at regular intervals. You should carry at least two liters of water for every hour. Regardless of where you plan to travel, it is essential to carry plenty of water, 20 liters minimum.

TIMING

If seeing Uluru is your reason for visiting the Red Centre, there are tours that fly in and out, stopping just long enough to watch the rock at sunset. However, for a more leisurely visit, allow two days so you can also visit Kata Tjuta (the Olgas) nearby.

TOURS

ABORIGINAL TOURS Owned and operated by local Aboriginal people, Anangu Tours organizes trips through the Uluru and Kata Tjuta region. Tours, which leave from the Ayers Rock Resort, include the Aboriginal Uluru Tour (A$139 with breakfast), led by an Aboriginal guide; the Kuniya Sunset Tour (A$116); and the Uluru–Kata Tjuta Pass, which combines the first two tours and Kata Tjuta over 24 hours (A$229). You can drive to the trailhead of the Liru Walk (A$69). Guides are Aborigines who work with interpreters. Aboriginal art aficionados can attend dot-painting workshops (A$87). **Anangu Tours** (☎ *08/8950–3030* ⊕ *www.anangu-waai.com.au/anangu_tours/*).

AIR TOURS   The best views of Uluru and Kata Tjuta are from the air. Light plane tours, with courtesy hotel pick-up from Ayers Rock Resort hotels, include 40-minute flights over Ayers Rock and the Olgas, and day tours to Kings Canyon. Prices run from A$90 to A$550 per person; for options, contact Ayers Rock Scenic Flights. Helicopter flights are A$120 per person for 15 minutes over Ayers Rock, or $230 for 30 minutes over the Olgas and the rock. **Ayers Rock Helicopters** (☎ *08/8956–2077* 🖷 *08/8956–2060* ⊕ *www.helicoptergroup.com*). **Ayers Rock Scenic Flights** (☎ *08/8956–2345* 🖷 *08/8956–2472* ⊕ *www.ayersrockflights.com*).

CAMEL TOURS   A great way to get out in the open and see the sights is from the back of one of the desert's creatures. Uluru Camel Tours, a subsidiary of Anangu Tours, has sunrise and sunset tours that last for 2½ hours for A$99; tours leave from the Ayers Rock Resort. **Uluru Camel Tours** (☎ *08/8950–3030* 🖷 *08/8950–3034* ⊕ *ulurucameltours.ananguwaai. com.au*). En Route from Alice Springs you'll find **Camels Australia**. Owners Neil and Jayne Waters offer everything from quick jaunts to multi-day safaris. Phone beforehand for all rides; 72 hours' notice for day and longer treks. It's A$40 for a one-hour ride, and A$150 for a day trek with lunch; safaris, including camping gear and meals, cost A$450 for three days and A$750 for five days, and depart three times each month in fall and winter (check the dates). ✉ *Stuarts Well, Stuart Hwy., 90 km (56 mi) south of Alice Springs* ☎ *08/8956–0925* 🖷 *08/8956–0909* ⊕ *www.camels-australia.com.au*.

WALKING   Discovery Ecotours specializes in small-group tours with guides who
TOURS   have extensive local knowledge. The Uluru Walk, a 13-km (8-mi) hike around the base, gives fascinating insights into the area's significance to the Aboriginal people. Book at least a day in advance. **Discovery Ecotours** (☎ *08/8956–2563* ⊕ *www.ecotours.com.au*).

ESSENTIALS

Banks and Currency Exchange ANZ bank has a branch and ATM at Yulara Village at Ayers Rock Resort.

Emergencies The medical center at the **Royal Flying Doctor Base** at Ayers Rock Resort in Yulara is open weekdays 9–noon and 2–5 and (for emergencies only) weekends 10–11 AM. Ayers Rock Medical Centre (✉ *Royal Flying Doctor Base, Yulara Dr. near police station, Ayers Rock Resort* ☎ *08/8956–2286* ⊕ *www.flyingdoctor.net/central/yulara.htm*).

Police Yulara Police (☎ *08/8956–2166*).

Taxi Uluru Express minibuses can whisk you from the lodgings at Ayers Rock Resort to the sights for much less than the cost of a guided bus tour—plus, you can go at your own convenience. Uluru Express (☎ *08/8956–2152* ⊕ *www.uluruexpress.com.au*).

Visitor Information The **Uluru–Kata Tjuta Cultural Centre** is on the park road just before you reach the rock. It also contains the park's ranger station. The Cultural Centre is open daily 7–6. The Ayers Rock Visitor Centre next to the Desert Gardens Hotel on Yulara Drive is open daily 9–5. **Ayers**

Rock Visitor Centre (📞 *08/8957–7377*). **Uluru–Kata Tjuta Cultural Centre** (📞 *08/8956–1128*).

OFF THE BEATEN PATH

The 440-km (273-mi) drive to Uluru from Alice Springs along the Stuart and Lasseter highways takes about five hours—or longer if you veer off the track to see some other impressive geological sites.

Rainbow Valley Conservation Reserve. Amazing formations in the sand-stone cliffs of the James Range take on rainbow colors in the early-morning and late-afternoon light. The colors have been caused by water dissolving the red iron in the sandstone, and further erosion has created dramatic rock faces and squared towers. To reach the reserve, turn left off the Stuart Highway 75 km (46 mi) south of Alice. The next 22 km (13 mi) are on a dirt track, requiring a four-wheel-drive vehicle. ✉ *Stuart Hwy.* 📞 *08/8951–8250* ⊕ *www.nt.gov.au/nreta/parks/find/ rainbowvalley.html* 💲 *Free.*

The **Henbury Meteorite Craters,** 12 depressions between 6 feet and 600 feet across, are believed to have been formed by a meteorite shower about 5,000 years ago. One is 60 feet deep. To get here, you must travel off the highway on an unpaved road. ✉ *Ernest Giles Rd., 114 km (71 mi) south of Alice Springs and 13 km (8 mi) west of Stuart Hwy.* 📞 *08/8951–8250.*

More than 3,000 ancient Aboriginal rock engravings (petroglyphs) are etched into sandstone outcrops in **Ewaninga Rock Carvings Conservation Reserve,** 39 km (24 mi) south of Alice on the road to Chamber's Pillar. Early-morning and late-afternoon light are best for photographing the lines, circles, and animal tracks. A 2-km (1-mi) trail leads to several art sites. The reserve is open all day year-round and is accessible by ordi-nary (rather than four-wheel-drive) cars. ✉ *Old South Rd., 39 km (24 mi) south of Alice Springs* 📞 *08/8951–8250* 💲 *Free.*

Fodor's Choice ★

Kings Canyon, in **Watarrka National Park,** is one of the most spectacular sights in central Australia. Sprawling in scope, the canyon's sheer cliff walls shelter a world of ferns and woodlands, permanent springs, and rock pools. The main path is the 6-km (4-mi) Canyon Walk, which starts with a short but steep climb to the top of the escarpment; the view 886 feet down to the base of the canyon is amazing. The trail then leads through a colony of beehive sandstone domes, known as the Lost City, to a refreshing water hole in the so-called Garden of Eden, half-way through the four-hour walk. All this is visible during the half-hour scenic helicopter flight over the canyon and range from Kings Canyon Resort (A\$220 or A\$115 for 15 minutes). ✉ *Luritja Rd., 167 km (104 mi) from turnoff on Lasseter Hwy.*

9

WHERE TO STAY AND EAT

\$–\$\$\$\$ 🏨 **Kings Canyon Resort.** The only place to stay within Watarrka National Park, this resort is 7 km (4½ mi) from the canyon. Accommodations include two- and four-bed lodge rooms in desert hues, but even the deluxe rooms are sparse and functional. There are casual and upscale dining options, and two swimming pools. **Pros:** deluxe rooms offer floodlit views of adjacent ranges at night; view the ranges from your Jacuzzi in some rooms. **Cons:** room rates are pricey; room amenities are limited; dining options are pricey. ✉ *Box 136, Alice Springs, NT 0871*

☎ *08/8956–7442* ⊕ *www.kingscanyonresort.com.au* ⊷ *128 deluxe rooms, 36 budget rooms, 72 powered caravan sites, unlimited tent sites* ⚐ *In-room, refrigerator. In-hotel: restaurant, bars, tennis court, pools, no elevator, laundry facilities, public Internet, no-smoking rooms* ⊟ *AE, DC, MC, V.*

ULURU

An inevitable sensation of excitement builds as you approach the great monolith. If you drive toward it in a rental car, you may find yourself gasping at the first glimpse of it through the windshield; if you're on a tour bus, you'll likely want to grab the person sitting next to you and point out the window as it looms larger and larger. Rising like an enormous red mountain in the middle of an otherwise completely flat desert, Uluru is a marvel to behold.

Fodor'sChoice
★

The **Uluru–Kata Tjuta Cultural Centre** (⊠ *Off Lasseter Hwy.* ☎ *08/8956– 1128*) is the first thing you'll see after entering the park through a tollgate. The two buildings are built in a serpentine style, reflecting the Kuniya and Liru stories about two ancestral snakes who fought a long-ago battle on the southern side of Uluru. Inside, you can learn about Aboriginal history and the return of the park to Aboriginal ownership in 1983. There's also an excellent park ranger's station where you can get maps and hiking guides, as well as an art shop, and a pottery store with lovely collectibles.

EXPLORING

Uluru is circled by a road and walking trails. Two carparks—Mala and Kuniya—provide access for several of the walks, or you can choose to do the full circle of the Rock on the **Base Walk**.

As you work your way around Uluru, your perspective of the great rock changes significantly. You should allow four hours to walk the 10 km (6 mi) around the rock and explore the several deep crevices along the way. Some places are Aboriginal sacred sites and cannot be entered, nor can they be photographed. These are clearly signposted. Aboriginal art can be found in caves at the rock's base.

If you're looking for an easy walk that takes you just partway around the base, the **Mala Walk** is 2 km (1 mi) in length and almost all on flat land. The walk goes to the Kanju Gorge from the base of the climbing trail; park rangers provide free tours daily at 8 AM from October to April and at 10 AM from May to September.

The Liru Walk starts at the cultural center and takes you to the base of the Rock. Along the way are stands of mulga trees and—after rain—wildflowers. The track is wheelchair accessible, and the walk is an easy 1½ hours.

On the southern side of Uluru, the Kuniya Walk and Mutitjulu Waterhole trail starts of the Kuniya carpark and is an easy 45-minutes walk along a wheelchair-accessible trail to the waterhole, home of Wanampi, an ancestral snake. A rock shelter used by Aborigines houses rock art.

Another popular way to experience Uluru is far less taxing but no less intense: watching the natural light reflect on it from one of the two sunset-viewing areas. As the last rays of daylight strike, the rock positively

The monumental Uluru as seen from the air.

glows as if lighted from within. Just as quickly, the light is extinguished and the color changes to a somber mauve and finally to black.

CLIMBING THE ROCK—OR NOT There's only one trail that leads to the top of the rock. Though many people visit Uluru with the explicit intention of climbing it, there are a few things you should bear in mind before attempting this. First, Aboriginal people consider climbing the rock to be sacrilege—so if you believe in preserving the sanctity of sacred native sites, you may have to be content with admiring it from below. Your entry pass into the park even says, "It is requested that you respect the wishes of the Anangu by not climbing Uluru." The climb is not closed; the Aboriginal people prefer that you choose to respect their law and culture by not climbing because of your education and understanding. Second, if you do decide to make the climb, be aware that it's a very strenuous hike, and not suitable for those who aren't physically fit. The ascent is about 1½ km (1 mi), and the round-trip climb takes about three hours. Sturdy hiking boots, a hat, sunscreen, and drinking water are absolute necessities. The climb is closed when temperatures rise above 36°C (97°F)—which means after 9 AM most mornings in summertime.

SHOPPING

The Uluru–Kata Tjuta **Cultural Centre** (☎ 08/8956–1128) not only has information about the Anangu people and their culture, it also houses the **Ininti Store** (☎ 08/8956–2214), which carries souvenirs. The adjoining **Maruku Arts** (☎ 08/8956–2558) is owned by Aborigines, and sells Aboriginal paintings and handicrafts. There's also a display of traditional huts and shelters. The Cultural Centre is open daily 7–6 (information desk 8–5:30); Ininti Store is open daily 7–5:15; Maruku Arts is open daily 8:30–5:30.

KATA TJUTA

Fodor's Choice
★

Many visitors feel that Kata Tjuta is more satisfying to explore than Uluru. Uluru is one immense block, so you feel as if you're always on the outside looking in. Kata Tjuta, as its Aboriginal name ("many heads") suggests, is a collection of huge rocks hiding numerous gorges and chasms that you can enter and explore.

EXPLORING

There are three main walks, the first from the parking lot into Walpa Gorge (formerly known as **Olga Gorge)**, the deepest valley between the rocks. This is a 2-km (1-mi) walk, and the round-trip journey takes about one hour. The gorge is a desert refuge for plants and animals. The rocky track gently rises along a moisture-rich gully, passing inconspicuous rare plants and ending at a grove of flourishing spearwood.

More rewarding, but also more difficult, is the Valley of the Winds Walk. This 7.4-km (4.6-mi) walk is along a stony track to two spectacular lookouts—Karu and Karingana. Experienced walkers can complete this walk in about three hours. The Valley of the Winds walk is closed when temperatures rise above 36°C (97°F), which is after 11 AM most days in summer.

The **Kata Tjuta Viewing Area,** 25 km (16 mi) along the Kata Tjuta Road, offers a magnificent vista, and is a relaxing place for a break. It's just 600 meters from the carpark and interpretive panels explain the natural life around you.

AYERS ROCK RESORT

Officially is known as the township of Yulara, Ayers Rock Resort is a complex of lodgings, restaurants, and facilities, and is base camp for exploring Uluru and Kata Tjuta. The accommodations and services here are the only ones in the vicinity of the national park. Uluru is about a 20-minute drive from the resort area (there's a sunset-viewing area on the way); driving to Kata Tjuta will take another 30 minutes. The park entrance fee of A$25 is valid for three days.

The resort "village" includes a bank, newsstand, supermarket, several souvenir shops, Aboriginal art gallery, hair salon, and child-care center.

The accommodations at the resort, which range from luxury hotels to a campground, are all run by Voyages Hotels & Resorts and share many of the same facilities. Indoor dining is limited to each hotel's restaurants and the less-expensive Geckos Cafe, all of which can be charged back to your room. All reservations can be made through Voyages Hotel & Resorts on-site, or their central reservations service in Sydney. **Central reservations service** (☎ *02/8296–8010 or 1300/134044* ⊕ *www. ayersrockresort.com.au*).

WHERE TO EAT

$$$$
★
AUSTRALIAN

✕ The most memorable group-dining experience in the region is the unique, but expensive (A$155) **Sounds of Silence,** an elegant (although heavily attended) outdoor dinner served on a june (dune) that provides sunset views of either Uluru or Kata Tjuta (though you can request to attend a dinner being held at the site that allows you to view both). Champagne and Northern Territory specialty dishes—including bush salads and Australian game—are served on tables covered with crisp white linens, right in the desert. An astronomer takes you on a stargazing tour of the southern sky while you dine.

$$ ✕ **Geckos Cafe** in the resort's main shopping center is the most casual
AUSTRALIAN dining option on-site, but it is by no means cheap. The all-day dining options include affordable appetizers, yellowfin tuna kebabs, and several pastas and pizzas. ✉ *Town Sq., Yulara Centre, Yulara* ☏ *08/8957–7722* ▭ *AE, DC, MC, V.*

$$$$ ✕ **Kuniya Restaurant** has the resort's best food. The decor reflects local
AUSTRALIAN legends, with images of Kuniya and Liru burned into two magnificent wooden panels at the entrance, and a Kuniya Dreaming mural covering the rear wall. Appetizers and main courses are named after the Australian states. Specialties include barramundi, duck, and crayfish, prepared with a combination of traditional and Mod-Oz flavors. ✉ *Sails in the Desert hotel, Yulara Dr., Yulara* ☏ *08/8957–7714* ⚓ *Reservations essential* ▭ *AE, DC, MC, V* ⊘ *No lunch.*

$–$$ ✕ You'll see why Australians love cooking and dining outdoors at the
AUSTRALIAN casual open-air **Pioneer BBQ and Bar** eatery at the hostel-style **Outback Pioneer Hotel & Lodge.** You can order steak, prawn skewers, or a kangaroo kebab from the server, and then cook it to your liking on huge barbecues. ✉ *Outback Pioneer Hotel & Lodge, Yulara Dr., Yulara* ☏ *08/8957–7606* ▭ *AE, DC, MC, V* ⊘ *No lunch.*

$$$ ✕ **Rockpool Restaurant** is a casual alfresco eatery at Sails in the Desert
ECLECTIC hotel that closes seasonally during the hottest part of summer and the worst of winter (check with hotel for details). ✉ *Sails in the Desert hotel, Yulara Dr., Yulara* ☏ *08/8957–7417* ⚓ *Reservations essential* ▭ *AE, DC, MC, V* ⊘ *No lunch.*

WHERE TO STAY

$ ☷ **Ayers Rock Resort Campground** has 220 tent sites. Permanent tents (with linen) and air-conditioned cabins come with linens, full kitchens, and TVs—but no bathrooms. It's a 50-yard walk to the nearest amenities block. **Pros:** cheapest accommodations at Yulara; camper's kitchen and guest laundry. **Cons:** no private en suites available; limited shopping; need to catch resort shuttle to reach shops, dining outlets. ✉ *Yulara Dr., Ayers Rock Resort, Yulara* ☏ *08/8957–7001* ⟿ *418 sites, 14 permanent tents, 14 cabins (all without bath)* ♿ *Pool, flush toilets, partial hookups, drinking water, guest laundry, showers, fire grates, grills, picnic tables, electricity, public telephone, general store, play area* ▭ *AE, DC, MC, V.*

$$$$ ☷ **Desert Gardens Hotel.** Extensive native gardens surround the clusters of rooms in this one- and two-story hotel. Modern suede headboards and blond-wood furniture complement desert hues in the small, neat rooms, all of which are named after different Australian flora and have a balcony or courtyard. You're more likely to see wildlife wandering around the gardens here than in any other part of the resort property. **Pros:** central location for resort facilities; shady gardens among gum trees. **Cons:** busy resort entrance road passes hotel; rooms are pricey; no views. ✉ *Yulara Dr., Yulara* ☏ *08/8957–7714* ⟿ *218 rooms* ♿ *In-room: safe (some), refrigerator. In-hotel: 2 restaurants, room service, bar, pool, no elevator, laundry service, public Internet, airport shuttle, parking (no fee), no-smoking rooms* ▭ *AE, DC, MC, V.*

9

"As we drove from Uluru (Ayers Rock), we approached Kata Tjuta. It consists of 36 domes and is as impressive and spiritual as Uluru." –Photo by Gary Ott, Fodors.com member

$$$$ ☷ Self-catering one- and two-bedroom apartments with fully equipped kitchens, separate living rooms, and daily maid service are available at **Emu Walk Apartments.** One-bedrooms can sleep four, and the balconied two-bedrooms can accommodate six. **Pros:** extra beds ideal for families or traveling companions; kitchen allows for self-catering; adjacent to resort dining options and shops. **Cons:** room rates are pricey; rooms need refurbishment; limited amenities in rooms. ✉ *Yulara Dr., Yulara* ☎ *08/8957–7714* ↳ *40 1-bedroom and 20 2-bedroom apartments* ♺ *In-room: kitchen, refrigerator. In-hotel: no elevator, laundry service, airport shuttle* 🖃 *AE, DC, MC, V.*

$$$$ ☷ **Longitude 131°** is set on its own in the desert 3 km (2 mi) from Ayers Rock Resort and accessible only by four-wheel-drive vehicle. This is the be-all and end-all of Outback luxury, and the price is steep. Fifteen "tents" that pop out of the desert like a colony of perfect white mushrooms make up this unique resort, which caters to a maximum of 30 guests at any one time. Each tent has a balcony with floor-to-ceiling sliding-glass doors for a panoramic view of the rock from the king-size bed. The excellent, discreet staff provides a customized turndown service, stocking your minibar according to your specifications. Gourmet meals are served in the Dune House, which also contains a formal lounge with an extensive library and an honor bar of top-shelf liquors. **Pros:** luxury tented accommodation; dinner under the stars; touring included; attentive staff. **Cons:** isolated location; taking all the tours can be tiring. ◈ *Yulara Dr., Yulara* ☎ *08/8957–7131* ⊕ *www.longitude131. com.au* ↳ *15 tents* ♺ *In-room: safe, refrigerator, no TV. In-hotel: restaurant, bar, pool, no elevator, laundry service, public Internet, airport shuttle, no kids under 16* 🖃 *AE, DC, MC, V* ⍥ *FAP.*

$$$$ ⊡ Blocks and splashes of lime, purple, and orange in boxy white rooms make the **Lost Camel Hotel** the funkiest for a thousand miles. The resort's boutique hotel-style property is built around a blue-tile, rivet-and-glass-paneled, reverse infinity pool. Central to each room is the bed, which backs onto an open hand-basin area. The only windows are in the divided bathroom—which is an enclosed balcony with separate rooms for the toilet and shower—so remember to draw the curtains. There's a café, wine bar, and plasma-screen TV with cable channels in the lobby lounge. **Pros:** brightly colored decor; unusual bathroom layout; Aboriginal-themed photographs on walls. **Cons:** Internet costs $25 per day and is slow; rooms in need of refurbishment. ⊠ *Yulara Dr., Yulara* ☎ *08/8957–5650* ⌁ *99 rooms* ⚙ *In-room: safe, refrigerator. In-hotel: restaurant, room service, bar, pool, airport shuttle* ⊟ *AE, DC, MC, V.*

$–$$$ ⊡ **Outback Pioneer Hotel & Lodge** is the most affordable hotel option at the resort and the most popular. The theme here is the 1860s Outback, complete with corrugated iron, timber beams, and camel saddles, but you won't be roughing it here—not with a pool and two restaurants. Guests at the adjoining lodge, a budget accommodation with large and small dorms and a communal kitchen, share the hotel's facilities. A shuttle bus connects the lodge to the other properties every 15 minutes. **Pros:** lodge rooms are cheapest in the resort; swimming-pool area. **Cons:** resort shuttle bus to shops; hotel rooms somewhat dark. ⊠ *Yulara Dr., Yulara* ☎ *08/8957–7606* ⌁ *125 hotel rooms, 42 budget rooms; 168 lodge bunk beds* ⚙ *In-room: no phone (some), kitchen (some), refrigerator (some), no TV (some). In-hotel: 2 restaurants, bar, pool, no elevator, laundry facilities, public Internet, public Wi-Fi, airport shuttle, no-smoking rooms* ⊟ *AE, DC, MC, V.*

$$$$ ⊡ **Sails in the Desert.** Architectural shade sails, ghost-gum-fringed lawns, Aboriginal art, and numerous facilities distinguish this upscale hotel option. Rooms are located in three-tiered blocks that frame the white-tiled pool, which extends out from a busy reception area with a tour desk and Aboriginal art gallery. Step out of your richly colored gold, green, and midnight-blue room onto a private balcony overlooking either the huge, lawn-surrounded pool area or the garden. **Pros:** Aboriginal artworks featured throughout; best restaurant at resort; distinctive architecture. **Cons:** pricey; rooms need refurbishment. ⊠ *Yulara Dr., Yulara* ☎ *08/8957–7417* ⌁ *214 rooms, 18 suites* ⚙ *In-room: refrigerator. In-hotel: 3 restaurants, room service, bar, tennis courts, pool, laundry facilities, laundry service, public Internet, public Wi-Fi, airport shuttle, no-smoking rooms* ⊟ *AE, DC, MC, V.*

9

DARWIN AND THE KIMBERLEY

The Top End is a geographic description—but it's also a state of mind. Isolated from the rest of Australia by thousands of miles of desert and lonely scrubland, Top Enders are different and proud of it. From Arnhem Land in the east—home to remote Aborigines—to the lush tropical city of Darwin and on to Broome in the west, the Top End is a region where individualistic people carve out their lives in what could be considered the real Australia.

The stark isolation of the Top End and Western Australia's Kimberley is reflected in its tiny population. Although the Northern Territory occupies one-sixth of Australia's landmass, its population of 200,000 makes up just more than 1% of the continent's citizenry—an average density of one person per 8 square km (3 square mi). The Kimberley, an area larger than the state of Kansas, is home to only 30,000 people. Traveling by road from Darwin to Broome is the best way to see the Kimberley, but you pass through only nine communities in 2,016 km (1,250 mi).

The region offers some of the most dramatic landscapes in Australia. A land of rugged ranges, tropical wetlands, and desert, of vast cattle stations and wonderful national parks, including the bizarre, beautiful, red-and-black-striped sandstone domes and towers of Purnululu National Park and Kakadu National Park, a wilderness area that is one of Australia's natural jewels and the reason many people come to the Top End.

DARWIN

3,146 km (1,955 mi) northwest of Sydney, 2,609 km (1,621 mi) north of Adelaide.

No other city in Australia defines its history by a single cataclysmic event. For the people of Darwin—including the vast majority who weren't here at the time—everything is dated as before or after 1974's Cyclone Tracy, which hit on Christmas Eve. It wasn't just the death toll (65 people) that left a lasting scar in the area; it was the immensity of the destruction. More than 70% of Darwin's homes were destroyed or suffered severe structural damage; all services—communications, power, and water—were cut off. The resulting food shortage, lack of water, and concerns about disease moved government officials to evacuate the city; some 25,600 were airlifted out and another 7,200 left by road.

It's a tribute to those who stayed and to those who have come to live here after Tracy that the rebuilt city now thrives as an administrative and commercial center for northern Australia. Old Darwin has been replaced by something of an edifice complex—such buildings as Parliament House and the Supreme Court all seem too grand for such a small city, especially one that prides itself on its relaxed, multicultural openness.

The seductiveness of contemporary Darwin lifestyles belies a Top End history of failed attempts dating back to European attempts to establish an enclave in a harsh, unyielding climate in 1824. The original 1869 settlement, called Palmerston, was built on a parcel of mangrove wetlands and scrub forest that had changed little in 15 million years. It was not until 1911, after it had already weathered the disastrous cyclones of 1878, 1882, and 1897, that the town was named after the scientist who had visited Australia's shores aboard the *Beagle* in 1839.

Today Darwin is the best place from which to explore Australia's Top End, with its wonders of Kakadu and the Kimberley region.

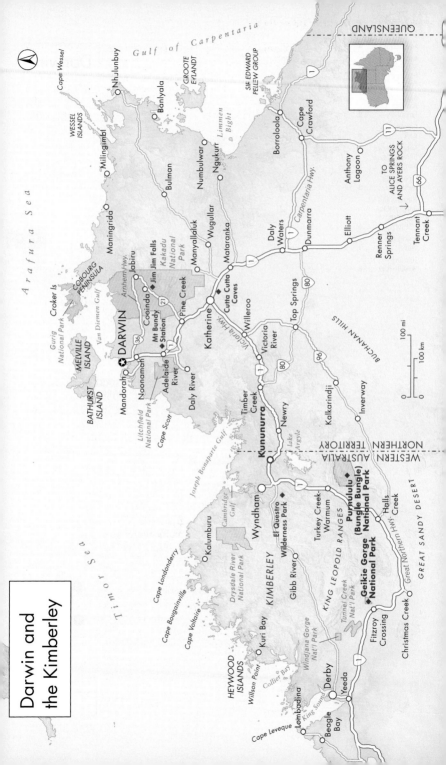

Darwin and the Kimberley

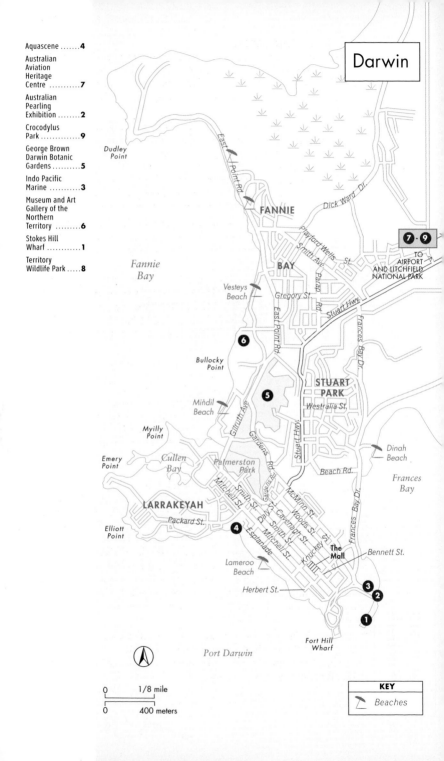

Darwin

Dudley
Point

East Point Rd.

Dick Ward Dr.

FANNIE

Playford Wells

Smith Ave.

Parap Rd.

7 · **9**

TO
AIRPORT
AND LITCHFIELD
NATIONAL PARK

Fannie
Bay

BAY

Vesteys
Beach

Gregory St.

East Point Rd.

Stuart Hwy.

Frances Bay Dr.

6

Bullocky
Point

**STUART
PARK**

Mindil
Beach

5

Westralia St.

Myilly
Point

Gardens Rd.

Goyder Rd.

Stuart Hwy.

Emery
Point

Cullen
Bay

Palmerston
Park

Dinah
Beach

Beach Rd.

Frances
Bay

LARRAKEYAH

Mitchell St.

Smith St.

McMinn St.

Woods St.

Cavenagh St.

Smith St.

Mitchell St.

Knuckey St.

Packard St.

4

Esplanade

Bennett St.

**The
Mall**

Elliott
Point

Lameroo
Beach

Herbert St.

3

2

1

Fort Hill
Wharf

Port Darwin

0   1/8 mile

0   400 meters

KEY
Beaches

GETTING HERE AND AROUND

Darwin's International Airport is serviced from overseas by Qantas, Garuda, Royal Brunei, Jetstar, Tiger Airways, and Air North. Qantas and Garuda fly from Darwin to Bali several times a week, Tiger Airways and Jetstar connect Darwin with Singapore, and Air North flies to East Timor.

Qantas, Air North, Virgin Blue Airlines, Skywest, and Jetstar fly into Darwin regularly from other parts of Australia and operate regional flights within the Top End. Air North flies west to Kununurra and Broome, and east to Gove. The Darwin Airport Shuttle has regular service between the airport and the city's hotels. The cost is A$10 one-way, A$18 round-trip; book a day in advance. Taxis await at the airport's taxi rank. The journey downtown costs about A$25–A$30.

The *Ghan* train connects Darwin with Adelaide via Alice Springs on a two-night 2,979-km (1,861-mi) journey a couple of times a week. **Ghan** (☎ *13–2147 bookings, 1300/132147 holiday packages ⊕ www. gsr.com.au*).

The best way to get around Darwin is by car. The Stuart Highway is Darwin's land connection with the rest of Australia. By road Darwin is 15 hours from Alice Springs (1,491 km [926 mi]), 2½ days from Broome via the Great Northern Highway (1,875 km [1,165 mi]), 4–5 days from Brisbane (3,387 km [2,105 mi]), and 5–6 days from Perth (3,981 km [2,474 mi]).

For drivers headed outside the Northern Territory, one-way drop-off fees for rental vehicles are often twice as much as a weekly rental. If you don't feel like driving, the bus network in Darwin links the city with its far-flung suburbs, and a choice of minibus operators, including the 24-hour Arafura minibuses, run all over town for fixed prices starting at A$4. The main bus terminal (Darwin Bus) is on Harry Chan Avenue, near the Bennett Street end of Smith Street Mall. A minibus stand is also located at the front of Darwin's airport terminal.

SAFETY AND PRECAUTIONS

Swimming in the ocean is not recommended because of the box jellyfish. Salt and freshwater crocodiles are found in most Top End billabongs and rivers, and are occasionally seen on remote beaches. The accessible rivers and billabongs are generally signposted if saltwater crocodiles are known to inhabit the area, but if you are not sure, don't swim. If you are driving, avoid driving outside towns after dark due to the dangers presented by buffalo, cattle, horses, donkeys, and kangaroos on the road. If your vehicle breaks down, stay with it; it is easier to find a missing vehicle than missing people. If you are going for a bushwalk, always tells someone your plan and when you expect to return.

TIMING

While Darwin has some attractions, many people view the city as the entry point to the Top End's national parks, in particular Kakadu and Litchfield. Two days in the city will be enough to see the main attractions, after which you will want to head to Kakadu.

TOURS

Every day but Sunday, Darwin Day Tours conducts afternoon trips for A$64, and for A$104 (April–November) you can take the afternoon tour and finish with a harbor cruise. Tours include historic buildings, the main harbor, the Botanic Gardens, the Northern Territory Museum of Arts and Sciences, East Point Reserve, and Stokes Hill Wharf. Alternatively, for A$35 you can hop on and off the Tour Tub "City Sights" bus. It picks up at Knuckey Street, at the end of Smith Street Mall, and runs daily 9–4. Daytime and sunset cruises explore a harbor five times the size of Sydney's. A 2-hour cruise on the *Spirit of Darwin* begins at A$40. Trips depart daily from Cullen Bay Marina between April and October.**Darwin Day Tours** (☎ *1300/721365* ⊕ *www.aussieadventure. com.au*). **Spirit of Darwin** (☎ *0417/381977* ⊕ *www.spiritofdarwin.net*). **Tour Tub** (☎ *08/8985–6322* ⊕ *www.tourtub.com.au*).

ESSENTIALS

Banks and Currency Exchange The main banks with tourist services are Westpac and Commonwealth on the intersection of Smith and Bennet streets. Banking hours are Monday–Thursday 9:30–4 and Friday 9:30–5. Currency-exchange facilities are available on Smith Street Mall and Mitchell Street.

Medical Emergencies Royal Darwin Hospital (⊠ *Rocklands Dr. at Floreyr Ave., Tiwi* ☎ *08/8922–8888*).

Police Police (☎ *000 emergency, 08/8922–3344 general inquiries*).

Taxi City Radio Taxis (☎ *08/8981–3777*). Darwin Radio Taxis (☎ *13–1008*). Tropical Taxis (☎ *08/8947–3333*). Yellow Cab Co. (☎ *13–1924*).

Visitor Information Top End Tourism (⊠ *6 Bennett St., City Center* ☎ *08/8980–6000 or 1300/138886* ⊕ *www.tourismtopend.com.au*).

EXPLORING: CITY CENTER

TOP ATTRACTIONS

❶ Stokes Hill Wharf. The best views of Darwin Harbour are from this working pier, which receives cargo ships, trawlers, defense vessels, and, occasionally, huge cruise liners. It's also a favorite spot for Darwinites to fish, and when the mackerel are running you can join scores of locals over a few beers. The cluster of cafés and restaurants becomes crowded on weekends and when cruise ships arrive. ⊠ *McMinn St., Darwin Harbour* ☎ *08/8981–4268*.

IF YOU HAVE TIME

❷ Australian Pearling Exhibition. Since the early 19th century, fortune seekers have hunted for pearls in Australia's northern waters. Exhibits at this museum cover everything from pearl farming to pearl jewelry settings. It shows years of pearling history, from the days of the lugger and hard-hat diving to modern farming and pearl culturing techniques. ⊠ *Kitchener Dr., Wharf Precinct* ☎ *08/8999–6573* 🖾 *A$6.60* ☉ *Daily 10–3.*

NEED A BREAK? The balcony of the **Victoria Hotel** (⊠ *27 Smith St. Mall, City Center* ☎ *08/8981–4011* ⊕ *www.thevichotel.com*), overlooking the passing parade on Smith Street Mall, is a good place for a cool drink. A Darwin institution since its construction in 1890, the Vic has been hit by every cyclone and rebuilt afterward.

③ Indo Pacific Marine. This marine interpretative center houses a large open tank with one of the few self-contained coral-reef ecosystems in the southern hemisphere. Other exhibits include a static display of rare, deepwater coral skeletons and an exhibit explaining the effects of global warming on the planet. Night tours, which begin at 7 on Wednesday, Friday, and Sunday, take you by flashlight to view the biodiversity of the fluorescing reef and live venomous animals. The tours include a four-course seafood dinner, followed by a nocturnal coral reef tour of the exhibitions. Bookings are essential. The pearling exhibition tracks the history of this important local industry. ⊠ *Stokes Hill Wharf, Wharf Precinct* ☎ *08/8981–1294* ⊕ *www. indopacificmarine.com.au* ⊠ *A$18, night tours A$104* ۞ *Apr.–Oct., daily 10–5; Nov.–Mar., weekdays 9–1, weekends and public holidays 10–5.*

> ## CROCS BITE!
>
> The crocodile has long been a dominant predator in the wetland regions of Australia. Powerful and stealthy, the saltwater (estuarine) crocodile has little to fear—and that includes humans. More than 70,000 crocodiles are found in the coastal and tidal areas of rivers, as well as floodplains and fresh-water reaches of rivers. In fact, they can be found in the larger rivers, lagoons, and billabongs right across northern Australia. Attacks on people are rare and deaths few (an average of one a year), but you should observe all no swimming and warning signs, and treat crocs with the respect.

EXPLORING: AROUND DARWIN

TOP ATTRACTIONS

⑤ George Brown Darwin Botanic Gardens. First planted in 1886 and largely destroyed by Cyclone Tracy, the 92-acre site today displays rain forest, coastal fore dunes, mangroves, and open woodland environments. There are more than 450 species of palms growing in the gardens. A popular walk takes visitors on a self-guided tour of plants Aborigines used for medicinal purposes. The Children's Evolutionary Playground is an award-winning playground that traces the changes in plant groups through time, while the plant display house has tropical ferns, orchids, and other exotic plants. ⊠ *Gardens Rd. at Geranium St., Mindil Beach* ☎ *08/8981–1958* ⊠ *Free* ۞ *Geranium St. gates daily 7 AM–7 PM, Gardens Rd. gates daily 7 AM–7 PM; information center weekdays 8 AM–4 PM, weekends and public holidays 8:30–4.*

⑥ Museum and Art Gallery of the Northern Territory. Collections at this premier cultural institution encompass Aboriginal and Southeast Asian art and material culture, visual arts, crafts, maritime archaeology, Northern Territory history, and natural sciences. One gallery is devoted to Cyclone Tracy, and you can see "Sweetheart," a 16-foot 10-inch stuffed saltwater crocodile that attacked fishing boats on the Finniss River in the 1970s. The Cornucopia Museum Café overlooks tropical gardens and the Darwin harbor and is open all day for meals. ⊠ *19 Conacher St., Bullocky Point, Fannie Bay* ☎ *08/8999–8264* ⊠ *Free* ۞ *Weekdays 9–5, weekends and public holidays 10–5.*

9

8 **Territory Wildlife Park.** In 1,000 acres of natural bushland, this impressive park is dedicated to the Northern Territory's native fauna and flora. In addition to saltwater crocodiles, water buffalo, dingoes, and waterbirds, it also has an underwater viewing area for observing freshwater fish and a nocturnal house kept dark for late night creatures. The treetop-level walkway through the huge aviary allows you to watch native birds from the swamps and forests at close range. Daily events include feeding at 9:30 and a birds of prey display at 11 AM and 2:30 PM. ⊠ *Cox Peninsula Rd., 47 km (29 mi) south of Darwin, Berry Springs* ☎ *08/8988–7200* ⊕ *www.territorywildlifepark.com. au* ⊠ *A$20* ⊙ *Daily 8:30–4; exit open until 6.*

A TROPICAL SUMMER

Darwin's wet season—when the humidity rises and monsoonal rains dump around 52 inches—runs from December to April. The days offer a predictable mix of sunshine and afternoon showers, along with some spectacular thunder and lightning storms. There are fewer visitors at this time of the year, and Darwin slows to an even more relaxed pace. Across the Top End, waterfalls increase in size, floodplains rejuvenate to a lush green, and flowers bloom. Despite the rains, Darwinites still prefer the outdoors—eating, drinking, and shopping at the markets.

9 **Crocodylus Park.** This world-renowned research facility has an excellent air-conditioned crocodile museum and education center. There are more than 1,000 crocodiles here, from babies to giants up to 5 meters long. The saurian section of the zoo includes the croc-infested Bellairs Lagoon and pens for breeding and raising. The park also has enclosures with lions, tigers, cassowaries, primates, and turtles. Tours and feedings are at 10, noon, 2, and 3:30. ⊠ *815 McMillans Rd., opposite Berrimah Police Centre, Berrimah* ☎ *08/8922–4500* ⊕ *www.crocodyluspark.com* ⊠ *A$27.50* ⊙ *Daily 9–5.*

IF YOU HAVE TIME

4 **Aquascene.** You can hand-feed hundreds of fish at this beach on the northwestern end of the Esplanade. At high tide people wade into the water with buckets of bread to feed the schools of batfish, bream, catfish, milkfish, and mullet that come inshore in a feeding frenzy. ⊠ *28 Doctor's Gully Rd., Doctor's Gully* ☎ *08/8981–7837* ⊕ *www. aquascene.com.au* ⊠ *A$11* ⊙ *Daily at high tide; check local publications or hotels for feeding times.*

7 **Australian Aviation Heritage Centre.** Due to its isolation and sparse population, the Northern Territory played an important role in the expansion of aviation in Australia, and this impressive museum traces the history of flight Down Under. Planes on exhibition include a massive B-52 bomber on permanent loan from the United States as well as a Japanese Zero shot down on the first day of bombing raids in 1942. ⊠ *557 Stuart Hwy., 8 km (5 mi) northeast of city center, Winnellie* ☎ *08/8947–2145* ⊕ *www.darwinsairwar.com.au* ⊠ *A$12* ⊙ *Daily 9–5.*

Enjoying an outdoor festival in Darwin.

OUTDOOR ACTIVITIES

BICYCLING Darwin is fairly flat and has a good network of bike paths, so cycling is a nice way to get around—although you might need something waterproof during the wet season. Rentals are available at some hotels.

FISHING Barramundi, the best-known fish of the Top End, can weigh up to 110 pounds and are excellent fighting fish that taste great on the barbecue afterward. The **Northern Territory Fisheries Division's Recreational Fishing Office** (⌂ *Berrimah Research Farm, Makagon Rd., Berrimah* ☎ *08/8999–2372* ⊕ *www.nt.gov.au/dpifm/Fisheries*) has information on licenses and catch limits.

Equinox Fishing Charters (⌂ *Shop 2, 64 Marina Blvd., Cullen Bay* ☎ *08/8942–2199* ⊕ *www.equinoxcharters.com.au*) has day and extended fishing trips on the *Hammer*, a 33-foot aluminum vessel, and the 38-foot *Tsar*. Both are licensed to carry 12 passengers and two crew. *Equinox II* can carry 23 people on full-day fishing trips. Full-day fishing charters with all meals and tackle provided are from A$240 per person.

SCUBA DIVING **Darwin Dive Centre** (⌂ *Shop 2, 48 Marina Blvd., Cullen Bay* ☎ *08/8981–3049* ⊕ *www.darwindivecentre.com.au*) runs reef trips and dives on wrecks from World War II and Cyclone Tracy, as well as scuttled Vietnamese fishing vessels. Training and classes are available, including PADI and technical diving certification courses. Prices are from A$130 to A$220 for half-day dives.

OFF THE BEATEN PATH **Litchfield National Park.** This beautiful, relatively new park lies just 122 km (76 mi) south of Darwin off the Stuart Highway. The 1,340 square km (515 square mi) are an untouched wilderness of monsoonal rain forests, rivers, and striking rock formations. The highlights are four

separate, spectacular waterfalls—
**Florence, Tjaynera, Wangi, and
Tolmer Falls**—all of which have
secluded plunge pools (there are
crocs here, so observe the NO SWIM-
MING signs). There is also a dramatic group of large, freestanding
sandstone pillars known as the
Lost City; and the **Magnetic Termite Mounds,** which have an eerie
resemblance to eroded grave mark-
ers, dot the black-soiled plains of
the park's northern area. You'll
need to camp if you want to stay
in the park; campgrounds and RV
sites are near several of the major
sights (call the Parks and Wildlife
Service of the Northern Territory

> ### GONE FISHING
>
> Joining a local tour guide is the
> best way to hook a big one. They
> know the best spots and tech-
> niques, and their local knowl-
> edge can make an enjoyable
> experience even better. In the
> estuaries you can catch threadfin
> and blue salmon, cod, queenfish,
> golden snapper, and the Top End's
> most famous fighting fish, the
> barramundi—barra in the local
> parlance. You don't have to go
> far—Darwin's harbor teems with
> fish.

at ☎ *08/8976–0282* for information). There are also a few restaurants
and a modest hotel (the Batchelor Resort [☎ *08/8976–0123*], which
has comfortable hotel rooms, as well as RV and camping facilities) in
the nearby town of Batchelor.

WHERE TO EAT

$–$$ ✕ **Buzz Café.** This is just one of many thriving waterfront eateries on
AUSTRALIAN   the finger peninsula northwest of downtown, where Darwinites come
to socialize. You can mingle at the bar with neighborhood millionaires,
visiting boaties, and locals relaxing by the water, then dine on fresh
seafood presented in a contemporary Australian style. There's air-conditioned comfort in the glass-walled dining room, or you can head out
to the umbrella-shaded decks overlooking yachts and cruisers moored in
the marina. One of the more curious panoramas is from the men's glass-
sheeted urinal, which has one-way views over the restaurant. ✉ *The
Slipway, 48 Marina Blvd., Cullen Bay* ☎ *08/8941–1141* ▭ *AE, DC,
MC, V* ⊘ *Closed Sun. and Christmas Eve–New Year's Day.*

$$–$$$$ ✕ **Crustaceans on the Wharf.** In a corrugated-iron storage shed at the end
SEAFOOD   of a commercial pier, this large restaurant is dominated by a traditional
Macassan fishing prau. Open to sea breezes, it's an ideal place to escape
the city's summer heat. Seafood takes center stage here; standout choices
include the Moreton Bay bugs (which are like small lobsters), calamari,
and chili mud crabs, a specialty of the house. ✉ *Stokes Hill Wharf,
Wharf Precinct* ☎ *08/8981–8658* ▭ *AE, DC, MC, V* ⊘ *Closed Sun.*

$–$$ ✕ **Hanuman Darwin.** Very good food and a wine list that includes the
THAI   best from every grape-growing region in Australia are served against
Fodor'sChoice   a backdrop of furnishings, tableware, and artworks from around the
★   world in Hanuman's indoor and alfresco dining areas. By drawing on
Thai, Nonya (Malaysian), and Indian tandoori culinary traditions,
Hanuman's chefs turn local herbs, vegetables, and seafood into sumptuous and innovative dishes. Of special note are Hanuman oysters,
lightly cooked in a spicy coriander-and-lemongrass sauce; barramundi
baked with ginger flower; and any of the curries. ✉ *93 Mitchell St., City*

Center, Darwin ☎ 08/8941–3500
☐ AE, DC, MC, V ⊘ No lunch
weekends.

$$–$$$ ✕ **Pee Wee's at the Point.** Uninter-
★ rupted views of Darwin Harbour
at East Point Reserve make this restaurant a favorite with locals and
visitors. Dine inside with views
of the harbor through large glass
doors, or out on the tiered timber
decks beneath the stars. The cooking is modern Australian with a
touch of Creole, and the carefully
considered wine list has good val-
ues. Highlights include salt-and-
pepper tempura bug tails with
a hot sour curry emulsion; pan-
roasted wild saltwater barramundi cooked in sea urchin butter; and
marinated lamb rump with candied fennel on roasted butternut squash.
✉ Alec Fong Ling Dr., East Point Reserve, Fannie Bay ☎ 08/8981–
6868 ⊕ www.peewees.com.au ⊜ Reservations essential ☐ AE, DC,
MC, V ⊘ No lunch.

WORD OF MOUTH

"We went on to Wangi Falls [in
Litchfield National Park]. There
were many people there. We ate
our picnic and then went to the
pool below the Falls. It was such
a large pool that there was plenty
of room to swim, and I had a
good swim over to the Falls and
back. We then walked along the
boardwalk and through the mon-
soon forest and up to the Treetop
Platform. It was shady and very
pleasant."   —Suelynne

WHERE TO STAY

$$$$ ⊡ **Holiday Inn Esplanade Darwin.** With its colorful, round exterior, this
five-story hotel is one of the city's most architecturally striking. Rooms,
arranged around a central foyer, are decorated in subtle earthy hues and
accented by natural wood. Most have city or harbor views. **Pros:** city
center location; large swimming pool; good breakfast. **Cons:** convention center attracts tour groups. ✉ The Esplanade, ☎ 08/8980–0800
or 1800/007697 ⊕ www.holiday-inn.com/hidarwin ➠ 163 rooms, 34
suites ⊘ In-room: safe. In-hotel: restaurant, bars, pool, gym, laundry
service, parking (fee), no-smoking rooms ☐ AE, DC, MC, V.

¢–$$$ ⊡ **Mount Bundy Station.** This station near Adelaide River, 115 km (72 mi)
south of Darwin, is handy for visiting Litchfield National Park, then
continuing on to Kakadu National Park, Nitmaluk National Park, the
Douglas Daly region, including the thermal springs, and Katherine.
There's a choice of accommodation including a caravan park, bud-
get rooms with shared facilities, or the Homestead, where rooms have
king-size beds and private baths (some have a balcony). A silver-service
cooked breakfast, afternoon tea, and sunset drinks are included for all
Homestead guests. A self-contained, self-catering cottage is an eco-
nomical option for families (A$165 for four people). Mount Bundy
Station also offers trail rides on Australian Quarter Horses for all
ages and all levels of riding from 30-minute rides to overnight treks.
Pros: Australian cattle station experience; lots of birdlife around the
billabongs; family-run and friendly staff. **Cons:** one-hour drive from
Darwin; own transport essential; limited dining options. ✉ Haynes
Rd., Adelaide River ☎ 08/8976–7009 ⊕ www.mtbundy.com.au
➠ 5 rooms ⊘ In-room: no phone, no TV. In-hotel: pool, laundry facili-
ties, no-smoking rooms ☐ AE, DC, MC, V ⅋ BP.

9

Tiwi islands sculptures at a gallery in Darwin.

$$$ Novotel Atrium. Vying for the title of Darwin's prettiest hotel, the
★ Atrium has five floors served by glass elevators opening onto a central,
vine-hung atrium. The bar and restaurant are set around a tiny artificial
stream amid tropical plants. Guest rooms are attractive and airy, deco-
rated in off-white with touches of deep blue and gold. **Pros:** tropical gar-
den in the atrium; some rooms have views over Darwin Harbor; close
to shopping precinct. **Cons:** atrium can mean rooms are noisy; standard
rooms are small, especially bathrooms. ⊠ *100 Esplanade,* ☎ *08/8941–
0755* ⊕ *www.novotel.com* ⤴ *138 rooms, 2 suites* ♿ *In-room: Internet.
In-hotel: restaurant, bar, pool, laundry service, public Wi-Fi, parking
(no fee), no-smoking rooms (some)* ⊟ *AE, DC, MC, V.*

$$$$ Sky City Darwin. Shaped like pyramids with square tops, this casino
and the smaller adjoining hotel are two of the most distinctive struc-
tures in the city. The three-story hotel has beachfront accommodations
set amid lush lawns and gardens. Dark marble, cherrywood furniture,
and Italian-designer lighting fixtures fill the rooms, some of which
have Jacuzzi tubs. **Pros:** close to Mindil Beach Sunset Markets; excel-
lent lagoon-style swimming pool; watch sunset while dining. **Cons:**
casino operates 24 hours, so nights can be noisy; convention center
attracts big groups. ⊠ *Gilruth Ave., Mindil Beach* ☎ *08/8943–8888 or
1800/891118* 🖷 *08/8943–8999* ⊕ *www.skycitydarwin.com.au* ⤴ *101
rooms, 16 suites* ♿ *In-room: safe, Internet. In-hotel: 3 restaurants, bars,
golf course, tennis court, pools, gym, beachfront, laundry service, Wi-Fi,
parking (no fee), no-smoking rooms* ⊟ *AE, DC, MC, V.*

NIGHTLIFE AND THE ARTS

BARS AND
LOUNGES

The **Blue Heeler Bar** (⊠ *Mitchell and Herbert Sts., City Center* ☎ *08/8941–7945*) is a laid-back watering hole with good dancing and Australian Outback decor. Irish flavor and pub food are found at **Kitty O'Shea's** (⊠ *Mitchell and Herbert Sts., City Center* ☎ *08/8941–7947*). **Monsoons** (⊠ *46 Mitchell St., City Center* ☎ *08/8941–7188*) is in the restored and remodeled original Darwin cinema building. It has an 80-foot-long granite bar with 20 different beers on tap and wines from Australia and New Zealand. The kitchen serves up African- and Eastern-influenced seafood, pastas, and meats. **Shenannigans Irish Pub** (⊠ *69 Mitchell St., City Center* ☎ *08/8981–2100*) has Guinness on tap, along with Kilkenny and Harp. Traditional Irish pub food is served, with meat roasts on Sunday. **Throb** (⊠ *64 Smith St., City Center* ☎ *08/8942–3435*), a wild and wicked nightclub renowned for its floor shows and drag acts, is Darwin's premier gay nightclub. Open Friday and Saturday only, the fun starts around 11 PM and doesn't end until 4 AM. Cover charge is A\$10. For a beer and live music, visit the **Top End Hotel** (⊠ *Daly and Mitchell Sts., Bicentennial Park* ☎ *08/8981–6511*), a Darwin landmark, which has the city's biggest beer garden, a sports bar, a nightclub, and a band room.

CASINO

SkyCity Darwin Casino (⊠ *Gilruth Ave., Mindil Beach* ☎ *08/8943–8888* ⊕ *www.skycitydarwin.com.au*) is one of Darwin's most popular evening spots. The 460 gaming machines are open 24 hours, while gaming tables are open Friday and Saturday 10 AM–6 AM, Sunday to Thursday 10 AM–4 AM.

CINEMA

Deckchair Cinema. At this outdoor, 350-seat movie theater you can catch a flick beneath the stars against a backdrop of harbor lights. On show are Australian and major-release foreign films, screened every night April–November. Gates open at 6:30 for the sunset, and picnic baskets are permitted, although there are a snack kiosk and bar. The first movie screens at 7:30. ⊠ *Jervois Rd. off Kitchener Dr., Wharf Precinct* ☎ *08/8981–0700* ⊕ *www.deckchaircinema.com* 🎟 *A\$13* 🕐 *Apr.–Nov. 6:30 PM.*

THEATERS AND
CONCERTS

The **Darwin Entertainment Centre** (⊠ *93 Mitchell St., City Center* ☎ *08/8980–3333* ⊕ *www.darwinentertainment.com.au*), behind the Carlton Hotel, has a large theater that stages concerts, dance, and drama. It also doubles as booking office for other touring concerts in town—especially those at the Amphitheatre, Australia's best outdoor concert venue (entrance next to Botanic Gardens on Gardens Road). Check their Web site or the *Northern Territory News* or the *Sunday Territorian* for current shows.

THE INDIGENOUS ARTS SCENE

Start at the Museum and Art Gallery of the Northern Territory for a comprehensive understanding of indigenous art and artifacts. Then head to one of many art and craft outlets in and around Darwin to purchase an authentic and unique piece of art. In many indigenous communities throughout the tropical Outback—including Maningrida, Oenpelli, Tiwi islands, and Yirrikala—you can buy direct from the artist.

9

SHOPPING

MARKETS   The **Mindil Beach Sunset Market** (⊠ *Beach Rd., Mindil Beach* ☎ *08/8981–3454* ⊕ *www.mindil.com.au*) is an extravaganza that takes place every Thursday 5 PM–10 PM and every Sunday 4 PM–9 PM from April to October. Come in the late afternoon to snack at a choice of 60 stalls offering food from more than 25 different countries; shop at more than 200 artisans' booths; and enjoy singers, dancers, and musicians. Or join the other Darwinites with a bottle of wine to watch the sun plunge into the harbor.

Nightcliff Market (⊠ *Progress Dr., Nightcliff* ☎ *0414/368773*) takes place Sunday 8 AM–2 PM in Nightcliff Village, with craft and food stalls and entertainers. North of downtown, the **Parap Markets** (⊠ *Parap Sq., Parap* ☎ *0438/882373*) are open Saturday 8 AM–2 PM and have a great selection of ethnic Asian food. The **Rapid Creek Markets** (⊠ *Rapid Creek Shopping Centre, Trower Rd., Rapid Creek* ☎ *08/8930–0441*), open Fridays 3 PM–late and Sundays 6:30 AM–1 PM, has fresh food produce, as well as locally made handicrafts.

KAKADU NATIONAL PARK

Begins 117 km (73 mi) east of Darwin.

Fodor's Choice   Kakadu National Park is a jewel among the many Top End parks,
★   and many come to the region just to experience this tropical wilderness. Beginning east of Darwin, and covering some 19,800 square km (7,645 square mi), the park protects a large system of unspoiled rivers and creeks, as well as a rich Aboriginal heritage that extends back to the earliest days of humankind.

The superb gathering of Aboriginal rock art is one of Kakadu's major highlights. Two main types of Aboriginal artwork can be seen here. The Mimi style, which is the oldest, is believed to be up to 20,000 years old. Aborigines believe that Mimi spirits created the red-ocher stick figures to depict hunting scenes and other pictures of life at the time. The more recent artwork, known as X-ray painting, dates back fewer than 9,000 years and depicts freshwater animals—especially fish, turtles, and geese—living in floodplains created after the last ice age.

Most of the region is virtually inaccessible during the wet season. As the dry season progresses, billabongs (water holes) become increasingly important to the more than 280 species of birds that inhabit the park. Huge flocks often gather at Yellow Water, South Alligator River, and Magela Creek. Scenic flights over the wetlands and Arnhem Land escarpment provide unforgettable moments in any season.

GETTING HERE AND AROUND

From Darwin it's about a two-hour drive along the Arnhem Highway east to the entrance to the park at Bowali Visitor Center. Although four-wheel-drive vehicles are not necessary to travel to the park, they are required for many of the unpaved roads within, including the track to Jim Jim Falls. Entry is free.

SAFETY AND PRECAUTIONS

If you are driving, watch out for road trains—large trucks up to 160 feet in length with up to four trailers behind a prime mover. They are common on Northern Territory roads, and you should give them plenty of room. Avoid driving after dark outside towns because of the high likelihood of straying animals—kangaroos and cattle in particular. It is a good idea to always tell someone of your plans if your intend traveling to remote places; the same applies when bushwalking. Always make sure you have adequate water and food.

TIMING

The best time to visit is between May and August during the Dry. The shortest time you should allow is a three-day, two-night itinerary from Darwin. This will provide opportunities to visit the major sights—a cruise on the East Alligator River; Ubirr, a major Aboriginal rock-art site; a flight-seeing flight from Jabiru airport; Nourlangie Rock, another Aboriginal rock-art site; the Warradjan Aboriginal Cultural Centre, to learn about traditional Aboriginal people; a sunset cruise on Yellow Water Billabong to see birds, crocodiles, and other wildlife. On the return to Darwin, you can visit Mamukala Wetlands for an abundance of birds and wildlife. A five-day itinerary will give you time to visit Jim Jim Falls and Twin Falls, a four-wheel-drive excursion.

TOURS

During the Dry, park rangers conduct free walks and tours at several popular locations. You can pick up a program at the entry station or at either of the visitor centers.

Kakadu Air (☎ *1800/089113 or 08/8941–9611* ⊕ *www.kakaduair.com. au*) makes scenic hour and half-hour flights out of Jabiru. In the Dry the flight encompasses the northern region, including floodplains, East Alligator River, and Jabiru Township. During the Wet only, a one-hour flight takes in the Jim Jim and Twin falls.

The Gagudju Lodge Cooinda (☎*08/8979–0145* ⊕ *www.yellowwater-cruises.com*) arranges boat tours of Yellow Water, the major water hole, where innumerable birds and crocodiles gather. There are six tours throughout the day; the first (6:45 AM) is the coolest. Tours, which run most of the year, cost A$55 for 90 minutes and A$74 for two hours.

Connections Safaris (✉ *Level 3, Harrington St., The RocksSydney* ☎ *02/8252–5300* ⊕ *www.connections.travel*) provides camping and accommodation tours in Kakadu of two to five days. **Far Out Adventures** (✉ *Box 54, Katherine 0850* ☎ *04/2715–2288* ⊕ *www.farout.com. au*) runs customized tours of Kakadu, as well as other regions of the Top End, for small groups. **Odyssey Tours and Safaris** (✉ *38 Graffin Crs., Darwin0800* ☎ *08/8953–7800* ⊕ *www.odysaf.com.au*) offers two- to seven-day deluxe four-wheel-drive safaris into Kakadu, Litchfield, and Nitmiluk national parks, as well as a two-day Arnhem Land Aboriginal Tour to Nipbamjen.

ESSENTIALS

Banks and Currency Exchange Westpac bank (✉ *Town Plaza, Jabiru* ⊙ *9:30–4 Mon.–Thurs.; 9:30–5 Fri.*).

Medical Emergencies The Jabiru Remote Health Center (☎ 08/8979–2018 ⏱ 8:30 am to 4:30 pm, plus 24-hour emergencies). The nearest hospital is **Royal Darwin Hospital** (✉ Rocklands Dr. at Floreyr Ave., Tiwi ☎ 08/8922–8888)

Police Jabiru Police Station (✉ Tasman Crescent, Jabiru ☎ 13–1444).

Visitors Information Kakadu National Park (📮 Box 71, Jabiru 0886 ☎ 08/8938–1120 ⊕ www.environment.gov.au/parks/kakadu/). **Tourism Top End** (✉ 6 Bennett St., Darwin ☎ 08/8980–6000 ⊕ www.tourismtopend.com.au). **Bowali Visitor Centre** has state-of-the-art audiovisual displays and traditional exhibits that give an introduction to the park's ecosystems and its bird population, the world's most diverse. ✉ Arnhem and Kakadu Hwys. ☎ 08/8938–1121 💲 Free ⏱ Daily 8–5. **Warradjan Aboriginal Cultural Centre**, named after the pig-nose turtle unique to the Top End, provides an excellent experience of local Bininj (pronounced *bin*-ing) tribal culture. Displays take you through the Aboriginal Creation period, following the path of the creation ancestor Rainbow Serpent through the ancient landscape of Kakadu. ✉ 5 km (3 mi) off Kakadu Hwy. on road to Gagudju Lodge, Cooinda ☎ 08/8979–0051 💲 Free ⏱ Daily 9–5.

LOCAL LANGUAGE

The name Kakadu comes from an Aboriginal floodplain language called Gagudju, which was one of the languages spoken in the north of the park at the beginning of the 20th century. Although languages such as Gagudju and Limilngan are no longer regularly spoken, descendants of these language groups are still living in Kakadu.

EXPLORING

Like the main Kakadu escarpment, **Nourlangie Rock** is a remnant of an ancient plateau that is slowly eroding, leaving sheer cliffs rising high above the floodplains. The main attraction is the **Anbangbang Gallery,** an excellent frieze of Aboriginal rock paintings. ✉ *19 km (12 mi) from park headquarters on Kakadu Hwy.; turn left toward Nourlangie Rock, then follow paved road, accessible yr-round, 11 km (7 mi) to parking area* 💲 *Free* ⏱ *Daily 7* AM*–sunset.*

Ubirr has an impressive display of Aboriginal paintings scattered through six shelters in the rock. The main gallery contains a 49-foot frieze of X-ray paintings depicting animals, birds, and fish. A 1-km (½-mi) path around the rock leads to all the galleries. It's just a short clamber to the top for wonderful views over the surrounding wetlands, particularly at sunset. ✉ *43 km (27 mi) north of park headquarters along paved road* 💲 *Free* ⏱ *Apr.–Nov., daily 8:30–sunset; Dec.–Mar., daily 2–sunset.*

The best way to gain a true appreciation of the natural beauty of Kakadu is to visit the waterfalls running off the escarpment. Some 39 km (24 mi) south of the park headquarters along the Kakadu Highway, a track leads off to the left toward **Jim Jim Falls,** 60 km (37 mi) away (about a two-hour drive). The track is unpaved, and you'll need a four-wheel-drive vehicle to navigate it. From the parking lot you have to walk 1 km (½ mi) over boulders to reach the falls and the plunge pools they have created at the base of the escarpment. After May, the water flow over the falls may cease, and the unpaved road is closed in the Wet.

Gunlom Falls in the Kakadu National Park

As you approach the **Twin Falls**, the ravine opens up dramatically to reveal a beautiful sandy beach scattered with palm trees, as well as the crystal waters of the falls spilling onto the end of the beach. This spot is a bit difficult to reach, but the trip is rewarding. Take the Jim Jim Falls Road, turn off just before the parking lot, and travel 10 km (6 mi) farther to the Twin Falls parking lot. A regular boat shuttle (A$12.50) operates a return service up the Twin Falls gorge, and then you need to walk over boulders, sand, and a boardwalk to the falls. Saltwater crocodiles may be in the water in the gorge, so visitors are urged not to enter the water. The round-trip, including the boat shuttle, takes around two hours.

WHERE TO STAY

There are several lodges in the park, and campgrounds at Merl, Muirella Park, Mardugal, and Gunlom have toilets, showers, and water. Sites are A$5.40 per night. Alcohol is not available in Jabiru, so stock up in Darwin.

¢–$$ 🏨 **Aurora Kakadu.** This comfortable hotel has doubles and family rooms that sleep up to five. Spread through lush tropical gardens, the rooms, bare cabins, and campgrounds are clean and provide good value for the money. There's plenty of local wildlife such as wallabies, corellas, and magpie geese in and around the resort. Rates are significantly lower during the Wet. Gas and diesel fuel are available. **Pros:** fauna is abundant; tropical garden setting. **Cons:** some distance from park attractions; limited amenities in rooms; own transport essential. ✉ *On Arnhem Hwy., 2½ km (1½ mi) before the highway crosses the South Alligator River* 🏠 *Box 221, Winnellie 0822* ☎ *08/8979–0166 or 1800/818845* 🌐 *www. auroraresorts.com.au* 🛏 *138 rooms, 20 powered sites, 250 tent sites*

⚏ *In-hotel: restaurant, tennis court, pool, laundry facilities, parking (no fee), no-smoking rooms (some)* ⊟*AE, DC, MC, V.*

$$$ ⊞ **Gagudju Crocodile Holiday Inn.** Shaped like a crocodile, this unusual hotel with spacious rooms is the best of the area's accommodation options. The reception area, a de facto art gallery, is through the mouth, and the swimming pool is in the open courtyard in the belly. **Pros:** friendly, helpful staff; Aboriginal artwork on sale; Jabiru village in walking distance. **Cons:** pool area is small; ground-floor rooms can have "critters." ⊠ *1 Flinders St., Jabiru* ☎ *08/8979–9000 or 1300/666747* ☎ *110 rooms* ⚏ *In-hotel: restaurant, bar, pool, parking (no fee), no-smoking rooms, no elevator* ⊟*AE, DC, MC, V.*

ANCIENT ART AND NATURE

Almost the size of West Virginia, Kakadu National Park is an ancient landform, with wetlands, gorges, waterfalls, and rugged escarpments. It also has one of the highest concentrations of accessible Aboriginal rock-art sites in the world. Take a tour with an Aboriginal guide from one of the cultural centers near Jabiru or Cooinda. The art sites date back 20,000 years.

¢–$$$ ⊞ **Gagudju Lodge Cooinda.** Near Yellow Water, this facility has light, airy lodgings looking out over tropical gardens. Budget quarters—with bunks and shared baths but no phone or TV—are also available. The restaurant typically has barramundi on the menu. A general store provides essential groceries and goods. Gagudju Lodge Cooinda is the base for the world renowned Yellow Water Cruises, where crocodiles, birds, fresh-water mangroves, and exotic tropical trees are regular sightings. **Pros:** center for Yellow Water Cruises; close to Aboriginal cultural center. **Cons:** 30 minutes from Jabiru shops; limited amenities in rooms; limited dining options. ⊠ *Kakadu Hwy., 2 km (1 mi) toward Yellow Water Wetlands, Cooinda* ☎ *08/8979–0145 or 1800/500401* ⊕ *www.gagudjulodgecooinda.com.au* ☎ *48 rooms* ⚏ *In-hotel: restaurant, bar, pool, parking (no fee), no-smoking rooms* ⊟*AE, MC, V.*

THE KIMBERLEY

Perched on the northwestern hump of the loneliest Australian state, only half as far from Indonesia as it is from Sydney, the Kimberley remains a frontier of sorts. The first European explorers, dubbed by one of their descendants as "cattle kings in grass castles," ventured into the heart of the region in 1879 to establish cattle stations. They subsequently became embroiled in one of the country's longest-lasting conflicts between white settlers and Aborigines led by Jandamarra of the Bunuba people.

The Kimberley remains sparsely populated, with only 30,000 people living in an area of 351,200 square km (135,600 square mi). That's 12 square km (4½ square mi) per person. The region is dotted with cattle stations and raked with desert ranges, rivers, tropical forests, and towering cliffs. Several of the country's most spectacular national parks are here, including Purnululu (Bungle Bungle) National Park, a vast area of bizarrely shaped and colored rock formations that became widely known to white Australians only in 1983. Facilities in this remote region are few, but if you're looking for a genuine bush experience, the Kimberley represents the opportunity of a lifetime.

This section begins in Kununurra, just over the northwestern border of the Northern Territory, in Western Australia.

KUNUNURRA

516 km (322 mi) west of Katherine, 840 km (525 mi) southwest of Darwin.

Kununurra is the eastern gateway to the Kimberley. With a population of 6,000, it's a modern, planned town developed in the 1960s for the nearby Lake Argyle and Ord River irrigation scheme. It's a convenient base from which to explore local attractions such as Mirima National Park (a mini–Bungle Bungle on the edge of town), Lake Argyle, and the River Ord. The town is also one starting point for adventure tours of the Kimberley; the other option is to start from Broome.

GETTING HERE AND AROUND

Distances in this part of the continent are colossal. Flying is the fastest and easiest way to get to the Kimberley. Air North has an extensive air network throughout the Top End, linking Broome to Kununurra and Darwin.

From Darwin to Kununurra and the eastern extent of the Kimberley it's 827 km (513 mi). The route runs from Darwin to Katherine along the Stuart Highway, and then along the Victoria Highway to Kununurra. The entire road is paved but quite narrow in parts—especially so, it may seem, when a road train (an extremely long truck convoy) is coming the other way. Drive with care. Fuel and supplies can be bought at small settlements along the way, but you should always keep supplies in abundance.

SAFETY AND PRECAUTIONS

Driving long distances through the Kimberley can be an adventure, but also carries risks. For drivers not used to the conditions, and not taking adequate rest breaks, the combination of warm sun through the windscreen, long, straight sections of road, the soothing hum of wheels and lack of traffic, can have a hypnotic effect. Take regular breaks every two hours to walk and have a stretch, and get plenty of sleep the night before. If you are feeling sleepy, stop immediately and take a break. Many vehicle crashes in this area are vehicle versus animal, often a kangaroo or straying cattle. Dusk and dawn are when animals are most active. If you see an animal on the road in front of you, brake firmly in a straight line and sound your horn. Do not swerve: it is safer to stay on the road.

TIMING

You should allow at least five days to see Kununurra and the East Kimberley, including your arrival and departure days. That will allow enough to visit the Ord River and cruise Lake Argyle, take a scenic flight to the Bungle Bungles and hike the area with a guide, and take a

9

four-wheel-drive excursion to El Questro Wilderness Park. Winter—May to November—is the most popular time to visit, as days are warm and there is little rain. November to April is the wet season, and temperatures can be a lot higher—up to 45°C.

TOURS

APT Kimberley Wilderness Adventures (☎ *03/9277–8555 or 1300/656985* ⊕ *www.aptwildernessadventures.com.au*) conducts tours from Broome and Kununurra, which include excursions along Gibb River Road and into Purnululu National Park. A two-day tour from Kununurra includes the Mitchell Plateau and Mitchell Falls, with an overnight in a wilderness camp. **East Kimberley Tours'** (☎ *08/9168–2213* ⊕ *www.eastkimberleytours.com.au*) most popular day tour includes a flight to Purnululu National Park, a four-wheel-drive tour to the famous "beehives," lunch, and scenic flights over the national park. The tour costs A$615. Overnight fly-in, fly-out tours to the park cost from A$1,435.

Alligator Airways (☎ *08/9168–1333* ⊕ *www.alligatorairways.com.au*) operates fixed-wing floatplanes from Lake Kununurra and land-based flights from Kununurra Airport. A 30-minute scenic flight costs A$120. **Slingair** (☎ *08/9169–1300 or 1800/095500* ⊕ *www.slingair.com.au*) conducts both fixed-wing and helicopter flights from Kununurra and Purnululu National Park. A 30-minute helicopter flight costs A$295 from their helipad in the Purnululu National Park. An alternative 2½-hour fixed-wing flight over the Bungle Bungle and Lake Argyle is A$295. A full-day scenic flight and ground tour shows you settings from Australia, the movie, including the fictional Faraway Downs Homestead. The cost is from A$365

Lake Argyle Cruises (✉ *Box 710, Kununurra 6743* ☎ *08/9168–7687* ⊕ *www.lakeargylecruises.com*) operates excellent trips on Australia's largest expanse of freshwater, the man-made Lake Argyle. Tours run daily March to October, and it's A$65 for the two-hour morning cruise, A$145 for the six-hour cruise, and A$85 for the sunset cruise (which starts around 2:45).

ESSENTIALS

Banks and Currency Exchange Bankwest, Commonwealth Bank, Westpac and National Australia banks all have branches in Kununurra.

Medical Emergencies Kununurra District Hospital (✉ *96 Coolibah Dr., Kununurra* ☎ *08/9166–4222*).

Police Kununurra Police Station (✉ *94 Coolibah Dr., Kununurra* ☎ *08/9166–4530*).

TaxiKununurra Yellow Taxi (☎ *08/9168–2356*). **Spud's Taxis** (☎ *08/9168–2553*).

Visitors Information Kununurra Visitor Centre (✉ *75 Coolibah Dr., Kununurra* ☎ *08/9168–1177* ⊕ *www.kununurratourism.com*).

WHERE TO STAY

$$ 🛏 **All Seasons Kununurra.** Set in tropical gardens, the brightly furnished rooms provide a comfortable base from which to explore the eastern Kimberley. The hotel is at the edge of town, just 4 km (2½ mi) from the

airport; its swimming pool, which is surrounded by shady palm trees, is the place to be on a hot day. **Pros:** walking distance to downtown; colorful Aboriginal art theme in rooms; swimming pool in tropical gardens setting. **Cons:** limited amenities in rooms; limited dining options. ⊠ *Victoria Hwy. and Messmate Way* ☎ *08/9168–1455 or 1300/656565* ⊕ *www.accorhotels. com.au* 📞 *60 rooms* ᗑ *In-room: refrigerator, Internet. In-hotel: restaurant, bar, pool, laundry facilities, parking (no fee), no-smoking rooms* ▭ *AE, DC, MC, V.*

$$ 🏨 **Kununurra Country Club Resort.** In the center of town, this hotel is encircled by its own little rain forest of tropical gardens. The hotel has a cocktail bar and several spots for dining, including one beside the pool. The two-story complex has ground-floor and upstairs rooms—all smartly furnished—as well as two 2-bedroom apartments sleeping up to six people. **Pros:** complimentary airport shuttle; poolside dining and bars; easy walk to downtown. **Cons:** tour groups stay here; Internet is dial-up. ⊠ *47 Coolibah Dr.* ☎ *08/9168–1024* ⊕ *www.kununurracountryclub.com.au* 📞 *90 rooms* ᗑ *In-room: Internet. In-hotel: 2 restaurants, bars, pool, laundry facilities, parking (no fee), no elevator* ▭ *AE, DC, MC, V.*

$$ 🏨 **Kununurra Lakeside Resort.** On the shores of Lake Kununurra sits this understated, tranquil resort, where you can see beautiful sunsets over the water (especially toward the end of the Dry), and watch for fruit bats flying overhead. The resort also has a campground, with powered sites from A$26. **Pros:** lakeside location; crocodile spotting at night; abundant fauna. **Cons:** limited amenities in rooms; own transport essential. ⊠ *Casuarina Way off Victoria Hwy.* ✉ *Box 1129, Casuarina Way, Kununurra 6743* ☎ *08/9169–1092 or 1800/786692* ⊕ *www.lakeside. com.au* 📞 *50 rooms* ᗑ *In-hotel: 2 restaurants, bars, pool, laundry facilities* ▭ *AE, DC, MC, V.*

OFF THE BEATEN PATH

With 1 million acres, **El Questro Wilderness Park** is a working ranch in some of the most rugged country in Australia. Besides providing an opportunity to see Outback station life, El Questro has a full complement of such recreational activities as fishing and swimming, and horse, camel, and helicopter rides. Individually tailored walking and four-wheel-drive tours let you bird-watch or examine ancient spirit figures depicted in the unique *wandjina* style of Kimberley Aboriginal rock painting—one of the world's most striking forms of spiritual art. At **Zebedee Springs,** a short walk off the graded road, leads you through dense Livingstonia palms to a series of thermal pools for soaking and relaxing. Five independent accommodation facilities are on-site,

---

DROUGHT DOWN SOUTH

The Top End's wet season drenches the region with more than 50 inches of rain. Just a tiny fraction is captured in Lake Argyle at Kununurra (with nine times the water volume of Sydney Harbour) and later used to irrigate crops. Meanwhile, in Australia's more densely populated and heavily farmed southern states, a severe drought and declining annual rainfall—some say caused by global climate change—has sparked a major debate: How to bring the Top End's water south, or how to convince people to move north.

9

each different in style and budget: the luxury Homestead; the safari-style tented cabins at Emma Gorge Resort; air-conditioned Riverside Bungalows and Riverside Campgrounds at the Station Township; and Mt. Cockburn Lodge, which runs two-day adventure safaris around Cockburn Range. Each has a restaurant, and rates (minimum two nights) at the Homestead include drinks and food, laundry, and activities. Round-trip transportation from Kununurra is available from A$220 per person. ⊠ *100 km (60 mi) west of Kununurra, via Great Northern Hwy.; take Gibb River Rd. for 42 km (14 mi) from the highway exit* ✆ *Box 909, Kununurra 6743* ☎ *08/9169–1777, 08/9161–4388 Emma Gorge Resort* ⊕ *www.elquestro.com.au* ⤳ *6 suites, 60 tented cabins, 12 bungalows, 28 campsites, 6 lodge cabins* ⚐ *In-room: no a/c (some), no phone, no TV. In-hotel: 4 restaurants, bars, tennis court, pools, laundry facilities, parking (no fee)* ⊟ *AE, DC, MC, V* ⊙ *Closed Nov.–Mar.* ⊠ *El Questro Wilderness Park permit (required) A$17 for 1- to 7-day pass with access to gorge walks, thermal springs, fishing holes, rivers, and use of the Emma Gorge Resort swimming pool* ⊙ *Daily Apr.–Oct. Entry to Zebedee Springs closes at noon.*

A FANTASY LANDSCAPE

For millions of years nature has savaged the rocks of Purnululu National Park with water and wind, creating one of the most unusual landscapes in the world. Traveling into the area is a remarkable experience—the timelessness of the ancient rocks draws you back across the millennia. All around, the conically weathered formations cluster together like a meeting of some metamorphic executives.

PURNULULU (BUNGLE BUNGLE) NATIONAL PARK

252 km (156 mi) southwest Kununurra.

Fodor'sChoice
★ Purnululu (Bungle Bungle) National Park covers nearly 3,120 square km (1,200 square mi) in the southeast corner of the Kimberley. Australians of European descent first "discovered" its great beehive-shaped domes—their English name is the Bungle Bungle—in 1983, proving how much about this vast continent remains outside of "white" experience. The local Kidja Aboriginal tribe, who knew about these scenic wonders long ago, called the area Purnululu.

The striking, black-and-orange-stripe mounds seem to bubble up from the landscape. Climbing on them is not permitted, because the sandstone layer beneath their thin crust of lichen and silica is fragile, and would quickly erode without protection. Walking tracks follow rocky, dry creek beds. One popular walk leads hikers along the **Piccaninny Creek** to **Piccaninny Gorge,** passing through gorges with towering 328-foot cliffs to which slender fan palms cling.

GETTING HERE AND AROUND

The Bungle Bungle are 252 km (156 mi) south of Kununurra along the Great Northern Highway. A very rough, 55-km (34-mi) unpaved road, negotiable only in a four-wheel-drive vehicle, is the last stretch of road leading to the park from the turnoff near the Turkey Creek–Warmum

Community. That part of the drive can take about 2–3 hours, depending on the condition of the road. It's further on to one of the three campgrounds, two public and one used exclusively by tour operators. The most-visited section of the park is in the south, where there are rough walking trails to the main sights.

SAFETY AND PRECAUTIONS

The park is usually open from April to December (depending on whether the road is passable after the Wet), however temperatures in April, May, September, October, November, and December can be blisteringly hot. If you travel in these months, make sure you have plenty of water and be sun-smart.

TIMING

Purnululu National Park can be visited in a day from Kununurra, but you need to take a flight and safari package. There are also tours available that include overnight camping, but the road trip from Kununurra takes the best part of a day. Driving yourself to the park is not recommended, as the last section is a very rough track suitable only for four-wheel-drive vehicles; it has been kept deliberately so to limit visitation. If you do decide to drive in yourself, be aware that there are few facilities in the park; you need to take in all your own food and camping equipment.

ESSENTIALS

Visitor Information Kununurra Visitor Centre (☎ 08/9168–1177). Purnululu Visitor Centre (⊠ Park entrance ⊙ Daily 8–12 and 1–4).

EXPLORING

The most popular walking trails are in the south of the park, where the famous "beehives" are located. From Piccaninny Creek carpark you can hike in to **Cathedral Gorge**; the walk takes about an hour. Take a 20-minute detour on the **Domes Walk** to see more of the famous sandstone "beehives." If you have more time, you can follow the **Piccaninny Creek** walk into the **Piccaninny Gorge**, following an eroded riverbed and sandstone ledges. This will take all day, but you can return at any time. In the north of the park there are walks to **Echidna Gorge** (about one hour), where livistonia palms cling to the cliffs and the gorge narrows to about three feet across, and **Mini Palms Gorge**, a rock-strewn gorge again filled with livistonia palms. At the end there is a viewing platform overlooking the valley. Allow an hour for this walk.

WHERE TO STAY

Although there are two designated campsites in the area, neither has facilities. Both the Bellburn Creek and Walardi campgrounds have simple chemical toilets; fresh drinking water is at both campgrounds. Kununurra Visitor Centre has information about the campsites. The nearest accommodations are in Kununurra. Tour operators often fly clients in from Kununurra, Broome, and Halls Creek and drive them around in four-wheel-drive vehicles. April through December, the most popular tours include a night of camping. The mounds are closed from January through March.

DID YOU KNOW?

The stunning Bungle Bungle Range—a series of beehive-shaped, outlandishly striped sandstone mounds surrounding deep gorges. Many lizard species live here, including blue-tongued skinks; so do several species of wallaby (smaller, marsupial cousins to the kangaroo).

GEIKIE GORGE NATIONAL PARK

16 km (10 mi) northeast of Fitzroy Crossing, 400 km (250 mi) east of Broome.

Geikie Gorge is part of a 350-million-year-old reef system formed from fossilized layers of algae—evolutionary precursors of coral reefs—when this area was still part of the Indian Ocean. The limestone walls you see today were cut and shaped by the mighty Fitzroy River; during the Wet, the normally placid waters roar through the region. The walls of the gorge are stained red from iron oxide, except where they have been leached of the mineral and turned white by the floods, which have washed as high as 52 feet from the bottom of the gorge.

WORD OF MOUTH

"Australia is easy to do on your own. However, if you are adventurous and interested in seeing some of the wilder, more isolated parts of the Australian Outback, doing a camping tour is a very good way to go. My wife and I did such a trip several years ago across the vast, empty and ruggedly beautiful Kimberly region in NW Australia - one of best, if not the best, vacations we've taken."   —RalphR

When the Indian Ocean receded, it stranded a number of sea creatures, which managed to adapt to their altered conditions. Geikie is one of the few places in the world where freshwater barramundi, mussels, stingrays, and prawns swim. The park is also home to the freshwater archerfish, which can spit water as far as a yard to knock insects out of the air. Aborigines call this place Kangu, meaning "big fishing hole."

Although there's a 5-km (3-mi) walking trail along the west side of the gorge, the opposite side is off-limits because it's a wildlife sanctuary.

The best way to see the gorge is aboard one of the several daily 90-minute boat tours led by a ranger from the **National Park Ranger Station** (⌂ *Box 37, Fitzroy Crossing, WA 6765* ☎ *08/9191–5121 or 08/9191–5112* ⊕ *www.naturebase.net*). The rangers are extremely knowledgeable, and helpful in pointing out the vegetation, strange limestone formations, and the many freshwater crocodiles along the way. You may also see part of the noisy fruit-bat colony that inhabits the region. The park is open for day visits daily from 6:30 AM to 6:30 PM between April and November. Entry is restricted during the Wet, from December to March when the Fitzroy River floods

BROOME

1,032 km (640 mi) southwest of Kununurra via Halls Creek, 1,544 km (957 mi) southwest of Katherine, 1,859 km (1,152 mi) southwest of Darwin.

Broome is the holiday capital of the Kimberley. It's the only town in the region with sandy beaches, and is the base from which most strike out to see more of the region. In some ways, with its wooden sidewalks and charming Chinatown it still retains the air of its past as a boisterous shantytown. However, with tourism increasing every year it is becoming more upscale.

Long ago Broome depended on pearling for its livelihood. By the early 20th century 300 to 400 sailing boats employing 3,000 men provided most of the world's mother-of-pearl shell. Many of the pearlers were Japanese, Malay, and Filipino, and the town is still a wonderful multicultural center today. Each August during the famous Shinju Matsuri (Festival of the Pearl), Broome commemorates its early pearling years and heritage. The 10-day festival features many traditional Japanese ceremonies. Because of the popularity of the festival, advance bookings for accommodations are highly recommended. Several tour operators have multiday cruises out of Broome along the magnificent Kimberley coast. The myriad deserted islands and beaches, with 35-foot tides that create horizontal waterfalls and whirlpools, make it an adventurer's delight.

Broome marks the end of the Kimberley. From here it's another 2,250 km (1,395 mi) south to Perth, or 1,859 km (1,152 mi) back to Darwin.

GETTING HERE AND AROUND

Distances in this part of the continent are colossal. Flying is the fastest and easiest way to get to the Kimberley.

Qantas and its subsidiaries fly to Broome from Brisbane, Sydney, Melbourne, and Adelaide via Perth. Direct flights from Sydney and Melbourne are twice a week. Air North has an extensive air network throughout the Top End, linking Broome to Kununurra and Darwin. Virgin Blue also services Broome from Perth and Adelaide. Skywest flies to Broome from Perth. Broome's airport is right next to the center of town, on the northern side. Though it's called Broome International Airport, there are no scheduled overseas flights, but charter flights and private flights arrive there. Approvals are in place for international flights in the future.

SAFETY AND PRECAUTIONS

From November to April there is a possibility of cyclones off the Kimberley coast. It is important that visitors are aware of the procedures to follow in the event of a cyclone alert. These procedures are provided in all accommodations and are also at the Broome Visitor Centre or the Shire of Broome office. Call ☎ *1300/659210* for cyclone watch and warning messages, or go online at ⊕ *www.bom.gov.au.*

November to April is also when mosquitoes are at their most prevalent. To avoid the discomfort of mosquito bites and any risk of infection, it is advisable to cover up at dawn and dusk and apply insect repellant. Sandflies become more active in Broome on high tides; use the same prevention methods.

Tropical waters can contain various stingers. The two types of dangerous jellyfish are the chironex box jellyfish (a large but almost transparent jellyfish up to 12 inches across with ribbon-like tentacles from each of the four corners) and Irukandji (a tiny transparent jellyfish less than 1 inch across with four thin tentacles). Both are found during the summer months of November to May. Take care when swimming (wear protective clothing—a wet suit or lycra stinger suit to reduce exposure to potential stings) and obey signs displayed on the beaches at all times. Medical attention (pour vinegar onto the sting and call 000 for an ambulance) should be sought in case someone is stung.

Saltwater crocodiles live in estuaries throughout the Kimberley, and freshwater Johnsons crocodiles hang out in freshwater gorges and lakes. Look for warning signs. Even if not signposted, advice from a reliable local authority should always be sought before swimming in rivers and waterholes.

TIMING

Ideally, you need at least five days in Broome and the West Kimberley, including your arrival and departure days. This will give you time to go swimming and sunbathing on Cable Beach, take a camel ride or go kayaking, then cruise on a restored pearl lugger. A scenic flight will show you the pristine Kimberley coastline and the horizontal waterfalls of Buccaneer Archipeligo. A day tour will get you to Cape Leveque or Windjana Gorge. To go farther afield, join a four-wheel-drive safari; a two-day tour will show you the gorges of the area, including Geikie Gorge.

The most popular time to visit is from May to November, during the dry season.

TOURS

APT Kimberley Wilderness Adventures conducts tours from Broome, which include excursions along Gibb River Road and into Purnululu National Park. Their 13-day Kimberley Complete tour includes the gorges along the Gibb River Road, the Aboriginal culture of the Mitchell Plateau, a scenic flight over the Mitchell Falls, Purnululu National Park, and an Aboriginal-guided tour through Geikie Gorge. The price is from A$5,895.

Broome Top Deck Tours has a two-hour Broome town tour (A$40) in an open-top double-decker bus that includes visits to Cable Beach, Chinatown, Roebuck Bay, and the Japanese cemetery.

Pearl Sea Coastal Cruises has multiday Kimberley adventures along the region's magnificent coastline in their luxury *Kimberley Quest 11* cruiser. All meals and excursions (including fishing trips) are included in the cost of A$8,345 for 7 days to A$12,095 for 13 days. Cruising season runs from March to September.

Astro Tours organizes entertaining, informative night-sky tours of the Broome area. Two-hour shows (offered four nights a week) cost A$75, including transfers from your hotel, folding-stool seating, hot beverages, and cookies. The company also offers four-wheel-drive Outback stargazing adventures farther afield.

ESSENTIALS

Banks and Currency Exchange Banks with branches and ATMs in Broome include ANZ, Bankwest, Commonwealth, National Australia Bank, and Westpac.

Medical Emergencies Broome District Hospital (✉ *Robinson St., Broome* ☎ *08/9194–2222*).

Tour Operators APT Kimberley Wilderness Adventures (☎ *03/9277–8555 or 1300/656985*). **Broome Top Deck Tours** (☎ *08/9193–7276*). **Pearl Sea Coastal Cruises** (✉ *Box 2838, Broome 6725* ☎ *08/9193–6131* ⊕ *www.kimberleyquest. com.au*). **Astro Tours** (✉ *Box 2537, Broome 6725* ☎ *08/9193–5362* ⊕ *www. astrotours.net*).

Broome By Camelback

Though not native to Australia, camels played a big part in exploring and opening up the country's big, dry, and empty interior. In the 1800s around 20,000 camels were imported from the Middle East to use for cross-country travel—along with handlers (many from Afghanistan) who cared for them.

When railways and roads became the prime methods of transport in the early 20th century, many camels were simply set free in the desert. A steady population of wild camels—some 400,000 of them—now roams across the Australian Outback.

Broome has for many years been a place where people enjoy camel rides—especially along the broad, desertlike sands of Cable Beach. Two tour companies in town now offer camel "adventures" on a daily basis; they're a great way to see the coast and get a taste of history.

Red Sun Camels (☎ *08/9193–7423* ⊕ *www.redsuncamels.com.au*) runs both morning and sunset rides every day on Cable Beach. The morning rides last for 40 minutes and cost A$45; the sunset rides take an hour and cost A$60.

Broome Camel Safaris (☎ *0419–916101* ⊕ *www.broomecamelsafaris. com.au*) operates Monday–Saturday, and offers 30-minute afternoon rides (A$25) and one-hour sunset rides (A$60).

Visitors Information Broome Visitor Centre (✉ *Broome Rd. at Short St., Broome* ☎ *08/9192–2222* ⊕ *www.broomevisitorcentre.com.au*).

CITY CENTER

☾ At **Broome Crocodile Park** there are more than 1,500 saltwater (estuarine) crocodiles, as well as many of the less fearsome freshwater variety. The park is also home to a collection of South American caimans and some grinning alligators from the United States. Feeding time is 3 PM during the Dry and 4:30 PM during the Wet. ✉ *Cable Beach Rd.* ☎ *08/9192– 1489* ⊕ *www.malcolmdouglas.com.au* ✉ *A$25* ☾ *Apr.– Nov., weekdays 10–5, weekends 2–5; Dec.–Mar., daily 4-6.*

The life-size bronze statues of the **Cultured Pearling Monument** are near Chinatown. The monument depicts three pioneers of the cultured pearling industry that is so intertwined with the city's development and history. ✉ *Carnarvon St.*

More than 900 pearl divers are buried in the **Japanese Cemetery,** on the road out to Broome's deepwater port. The graves testify to the contribution of the Japanese to the development of the industry in Broome, as well as to the perils of pearl gathering in the industry's early days. ✉ *Port Dr.*

★ The **Pearl Luggers** historical display sheds light on the difficulties and immense skill involved in pearl harvesting. It has two restored luggers along with other such pearling equipment as diving suits. Pearl divers, who spent years living aboard pearling luggers and diving for pearl shells, offer tours (allow 1½ hours). Tours run daily at 9, 11, 1, and 3. This is a must-see for those interested in Broome's history.

9

Camel riding on Cable Beach, Broome.

✉ *31 Dampier Terrace* ☎ *08/9192–2059* 🌐 *www.pearlluggers.com.au* 🎫 *A$18.50* ⏲ *Mon.–Sat. 9–5.*

Opened in 1916, **Sun Pictures** is the world's oldest operating outdoor movie theater. Here silent movies—accompanied by a pianist—were once shown to the public. These days current releases are shown in the very pleasant outdoors. Historical tours of the theater are also available weekdays at 10:30 AM and 1 PM for A$5 per person. ✉ *8 Carnarvon St.* ☎ *08/9192–3738* 🌐 *www.sunpictures.com.au* 🎫 *A$16* ⏲ *Daily 6:30 PM–11 PM.*

AROUND BROOME

The **Broome Bird Observatory,** a nonprofit research and education facility, provides the perfect opportunity to see many of the Kimberley's 310 bird species, some of which migrate annually from Siberia. On the shores of Roebuck Bay, 25 km (15 mi) east of Broome, the observatory has a prolific number of migratory waders. The observatory offers a variety of daily guided tours, costing A$70 per person from the observatory. Pick-up from Broome can also be arranged. A full-day tour costs A$150 from the observatory and A$190 from Broome. Start times depend on the day of the week and the tides and season, but are typically from 7:30 AM to 3 PM. ✉ *Crab Creek Rd., 15 km (9 mi) from Broome Hwy.* ☎ *08/9193–5600* 🌐 *www.broomebirdobservatory.com* 🎫 *A$15 for day visitors* ⏲ *Reservations essential.*

You can watch demonstrations of the cultured pearling process, including the seeding of a live oyster, at **Willie Creek Pearl Farm,** 38 km (23½ mi) north of Broome. Drive out to the farm yourself (you must make reservations first), or join a two-hour tour bus leaving from town. ✉ *Drive*

9 km (5½ mi) east from Broome on Broome Hwy., turn left onto Cape Leveque Rd. for 15 km (9 mi), turn left onto Manari Rd. for 5 km (3 mi), turn left and follow signs for 2½ km (1½ mi). Allow about 1 hr ☎ *08/9192–0000* ⊕ *www.williecreekpearls.com.au* ✍ *Self-drive A$40, coach tour A$80* ☉ *Guided tours daily 9, 10, 11, 1, 2, and 3.*

WHERE TO STAY

$$$$
★
🏨 **Cable Beach Club Resort and Spa.** Just a few minutes out of town opposite the broad, beautiful Cable Beach, this resort is the area's most luxurious accommodation. The Broome-style bungalows—with corrugated-iron walls and timber flooring—are spread through 26 acres of tropical gardens. Villas have private enclosed courtyards, plunge pools, and butler service. The decor is colonial with a hint of Asian influence. The Chahoya Spa has seven treatment rooms, a double vichy shower room, hair salon, and yoga deck, and offers customized skin treatments, as well as a range of traditional and contemporary massage techniques. Some rooms and facilities are closed during the Wet. **Pros:** walk to Cable Beach; peaceful, tropical atmosphere; distinctive architecture; separate swimming pool for adults. **Cons:** no shopping nearby; no ocean views. ⊠ *Cable Beach Rd.* ☎ *08/9192–0400* ⊕ *www. cablebeachclub.com* ⟲ *176 rooms, 45 bungalows, 7 villas, 3 suites* ⚷ *In-room: kitchen (some). In-hotel: restaurants, bars, tennis courts, pools, gym, spa, beachfront, laundry service, parking (no fee)* ▭ *AE, DC, MC, V.*

$$–$$$
🏨 **Mangrove Hotel.** Overlooking Roebuck Bay, this highly regarded hotel has one of the best locations of any accommodation in Broome. All the spacious rooms have private balconies or patios, many with bay views, and several dining and drinking spots are on-site. Plus, it's a five-minute walk to Chinatown. **Pros:** good-value beds for the area; views over Roebuck Bay; few minutes' walk to main shopping areas. **Cons:** limited leisure facilities; limited room amenities. ⊠ *47 Carnarvon St.* ☎ *08/9192–1303 or 1800/094818* ⊕ *www.mangrovehotel.com.au* ⟲ *68 rooms* ⚷ *In-room: refrigerator. In-hotel: restaurant, bars, pools, laundry facilities, parking (no fee)* ▭ *AE, DC, MC, V.*

$$$$
★
🏨 **McAlpine House.** Originally built for a pearling master, this luxury guesthouse in tropical gardens is full of exquisite Javanese teak furniture. With an inviting pool, a library, and personalized service, this is a good place to recover from the rigors of a regional tour, as well as a great place to simply hang out for a day or two. Breakfast can be either light and tropical (with fruits and pastries) or a substantial affair. Alfresco dining is available five nights a week. Closed from November to March. **Pros:** restored pearling master's residence; luxurious suites; intimate, private spaces; complimentary airport transfers. **Cons:** limited leisure facilities; no dining in off-season. ⊠ *84 Herbert St.* ☎ *08/9192– 0510* ✉ *reservations@mcalpinehouse.com* ⊕ *www.mcalpinehouse.com* ⟲ *8 rooms* ⚷ *In-hotel: restaurant, bar, pool, laundry facilities, parking (no fee), no kids under 16, no elevator* ▭ *AE, DC, MC, V* ⦿ *BP.*

$$$
★
🏨 **Moonlight Bay Suites.** Rooms with bay views and a five minute stroll from Chinatown add luxury and convenience to this complex of posh, self-contained apartments. It's a great place to recuperate by the pool after a rugged Kimberley tour. **Pros:** next to a good brewery

9

and restaurant; watch "Stairway to the Moon" (dependent on tides); handy to central shopping area. **Cons:** limited gym; not on beach. ⊠ *51 Carnarvon St.* ⬧ *Box 198, Broome 6725* ☎ *08/9193–7888* ⊕ *www. broomeaccommodation.com.au* ↪ *59 apartments* ⬧ *In-room:, kitchen, DVD, Internet. In-hotel: restaurant, pool, gym, spa, laundry facilities, parking (no fee), no-smoking rooms* ⊟ *AE, DC, MC, V.*

SHOPPING

Broome has an abundance of jewelry stores. **Kailis Australian Pearls** (⊠ *Shop 3, 23 Dampier Terrace* ☎ *08/9192–2061* ⊕ *www.kailis-australianpearls.com.au*) specializes in high-quality, expensive pearls and jewelry.

Linneys (⊠ *25 Dampier Terrace* ☎ *08/9192–2430* ⊕ *www.linneys.com*) sells high-end jewelry. They also have an outlet at Cable Beach Club Resort and Spa.

Family-owned **Paspaley Pearling** (⊠ *2 Short St.* ☎ *08/9192–2203*), in Chinatown, sells pearls and stylish local jewelry.

WESTERN AUSTRALIA

Western Australia—sprawling across more than 1 million square mi, one-third of Australia—is a stunningly diverse place, with rugged interior deserts, endless, untrammeled white-sand beaches, a northern tropical wilderness and a temperate forested south.

It took more than 200 years after Dutch seafarer Dirk Hartog first landed on the coast of "New Holland" in 1616 in today's Shark Bay before British colonists arrived to establish the Swan River Colony (now Perth) in 1829.

Progress was slow for half a century, but the discovery of gold around Kalgoorlie and Coolgardie in the 1890s brought people and wealth, especially to the fledgling city of Perth; much later, in the 1970s, the discovery of massive mineral deposits throughout the state began an economic upswing that still continues.

Today Western Australia produces much of Australia's mineral, energy, and agricultural wealth. Perth, the capital city and home to nearly 75% of the state's 2.2 million residents, is a modern, pleasant metropolis with an easygoing, welcoming attitude. However, at 3,200 km (2,000 mi) from any other major city in the world, it has fondly been dubbed "the most isolated city on earth." The remoteness, though, is part of what makes Western Australia so awe-inspiring. The scenery here is magnificent; whether you travel through the rugged gorges and rock formations of the north; the green pastures, vineyards, and hardwood forests of the south; or the coastline's vast, pristine beaches, you'll be struck by how much space there is here. If the crowds and crush of big-city life aren't your thing, this is the Australia you may never want to leave.

PERTH

Buoyed by mineral wealth and foreign investment, Perth now has high-rise buildings dotting the skyline, and an influx of immigrants gives the city a healthy diversity. Some of Australia's finest sandy beaches, sailing, and fishing are on the city's doorstep, and seaside villages and great beaches lie just north of Fremantle. The main business thoroughfare is St. George's Terrace, an elegant street with a number of the city's most appealing sights. Perth's literal highlight is King's Park, 1,000 acres of greenery atop Mt. Eliza, which affords panoramic city views.

GETTING HERE

The main gateway to Western Australia is Perth's busy airport. It has two separate terminals—the domestic terminal (by far the busiest, especially during the early morning and late afternoon rush hours) is about 11 km (7 mi) from Perth's central business district, while the international terminal is about 16 km (10 mi) away. A shuttle bus (A$8) connects the two terminals if you need to transfer.

Taxis are at the airport 24 hours a day. Trips to the city cost about A$33 and take around a half hour. Airport City Shuttles (☎ 08/9277–7958) operates frequent coach services from both terminals to Perth city hotels, and between the airport terminals. The cost between terminals is A$8, and to downtown Perth is A$15 from the domestic terminal and A$20 from the international terminal (unless prepaid with your air ticket).

Fewer people arrive by road or rail from the east. Crossing the Nullarbor Plain from the eastern states is one of the great rail journeys of the world. Great Southern Railways' *Indian Pacific* makes three-day runs from Sydney on Saturday and Wednesday and two-day runs from Adelaide on Sunday and Thursday. The train arrives at the East Perth Terminal in the central business district.

Greyhound Australia has long-distance coaches to Perth from eastern states capitals, arriving at the Public Transport Center, West Parade, East Perth. From Adelaide, the trip takes about 24 hours. If you are driving, the Eyre Highway crosses the continent from Port Augusta in South Australia to Western Australia's transportation gateway, Norseman. From there, take the Coolgardie–Esperance Highway north to Coolgardie and the Great Eastern Highway on to Perth. Driving to Perth—2,580 km (1,600 mi) and 30 hours from Adelaide, and 4,032 km (2,500 mi) and 56 hours from Sydney—is an arduous journey, which should be undertaken only with a car (and mental faculties) in top condition. Spare tires and drinking water are essential. Service stations and motels are spaced at regular intervals along the route.

GETTING AROUND

Driving in Perth is relatively easy; just remember to stay on the left-hand side of the road, and give way to traffic on your right. Friday afternoons are especially busy, as Perth natives head away from the city to country destinations, mostly in the South-West. Country roads are generally well maintained and have little traffic. All major car-rental companies have branches at the international and domestic airport terminals.

9

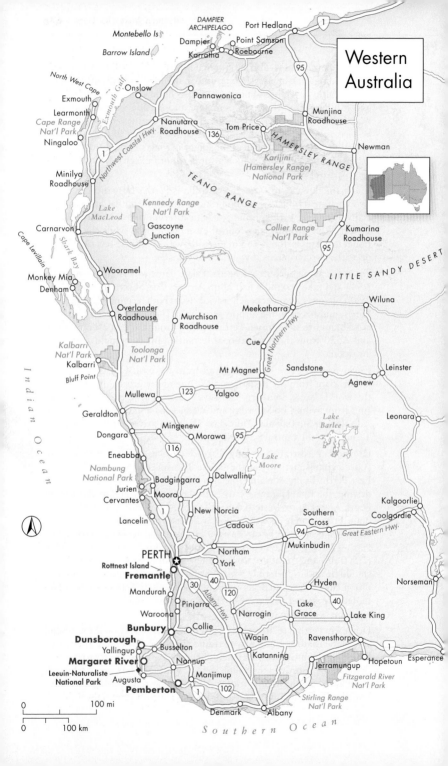

The Perth central business district and suburban areas are well connected by Transperth buses. The main terminals are at Perth Central Bus Station on Mounts Bay Road and at Wellington Street Bus Station. Buses run daily 6 AM–11:30 PM, with reduced service on weekends and holidays. Rides within the city center are free. CAT (Central Area Transit) buses circle the city center, running approximately every 10 minutes weekdays 7–6 and Saturday 9–5. Routes and timetables are available from Transperth.

Transperth tickets are valid for two hours and can be used on Transperth trains and ferries. Transperth ferries make daily runs from 6:50 AM to 7:15 PM between Barrack Street Jetty in Perth to Mends Street, across the Swan River in South Perth. Reduced service runs on weekends and holidays.

Transperth trains also provide a quick way to get around the city. From Perth, lines run east–west to Midland and Fremantle, north to Clarkson, southeast to Armadale, and south to Mandurah. Perth to Fremantle takes about 30 minutes, while Perth to Mandurah takes 50 minutes. Central-city train stations are in Wellington Street and Perth Underground at the corner of Williams and Murray streets. Tickets must be purchased at vending machines before boarding.

TransWA trains cover routes in Western Australia, including the *Prospector* to Kalgoorlie, the *Australind* to Bunbury, and the *Avonlink* to Northam. TransWA also has coach services to towns not serviced by passenger trains.

South West Coachlines (☎ *08/9324-2333* ⊕ *southwestcoachlines.com.au*) has daily coach services from Perth Central Bus Station on Mounts Bay Road to South-West towns.

SAFETY AND PRECAUTIONS

You'll find Perth a safe city to visit; there aren't any "no-go" neighborhoods, though there are some precautions you should take. Pickpocketing isn't a particular risk, but it's best to keep your personal belongings close, especially in busy shopping areas. Don't leave valuables—such as cameras—in the car when parked overnight at hotels or motels, or when visiting attractions. For your personal safety, avoid walking alone, especially late at night. There are instances of assault on Transperth trains and at suburban train stations, despite security guards and closed-circuit television monitors. A strong police presence—both on foot and on horse—usually ensures that late-night hot spots like Northbridge and Fremantle—are safe, though there are long lines for taxis, especially in the early morning hours when the nightclub crowds start to go home. Alcohol and impatience are a troublesome combination.

TIMING

Perth and surroundings can be visited in two or three days, if you're short on time and plan to explore farther afield. Spend the first day in central Perth, visiting Kings Park, the Western Australian Museum, the Hay Street and Murray Street shopping malls and, perhaps, the Swan Bells Tower. On the second day, head to Fremantle, about 30 minutes by train, where you can spend the day exploring this heritage port city or even take a day-trip to Rottnest Island by ferry (30 minutes each way from Fremantle). An upriver cruise to the Swan Valley that includes a visit to a winery and lunch makes for a relaxing day. The third day offers a choice of one-day tours to attractions such as Nambung National Park—with its weird limestone formation—Margaret River, to visit its renowned wineries, or the Treetop Walk deep in the southern forests near Walpole (be aware this is a very long 14½-hour tour).

TOURS

Australian Pinnacle Tours and Feature Tours conduct day tours of Perth and its major attractions. You can also take a day tour of outer sights like Nambung National Park and the Pinnacles, Wave Rock near Hyden, and the Treetop Walk near Walpole. Australian Pacific Touring has six-day tours from Perth to Monkey Mia. The Perth Tram Company has hop-on-hop-off circle trips around central Perth and to Kings Park on either a wooden replica tram or a double-decker, open-top bus. Tickets ($30) are valid all day, and you can get on and off as you choose. If you stay on, the full tour takes 90 minutes by bus and two hours by tram. Outstanding Tours has half-day and full-day personalized coach tours, as well as chauffeured rides aboard Harley-Davidson motorcycles from A$110 for one hour.

Rottnest Express runs excursions to Rottnest Island three times daily from Perth and five times daily from Fremantle.

Captain Cook Cruises has trips on the Swan River, traveling from Perth to the Indian Ocean at Fremantle. Cruises cost A$21–A$139.50 and *may* include meals and wine. Oceanic Cruises runs several boat cruises, including tours of the Swan River with stops at wineries; they also offer trips to Rottnest Island. Golden Sun Cruises also has tours upriver to the vineyards, as well as trips to Fremantle.

West Coast Rail and Coach uses trains and buses in conjunction with local operators to provide tours to Margaret River, Bunbury, Busselton, Esperance, Walpole, Kalbarri, Albany, and Kalgoorlie.

Springtime in Western Australia (September–November) is synonymous with wildflowers, as 8,000 species blanket an area that stretches 645 km (400 mi) north and 403 km (250 mi) south of Perth. Tours of these areas, by companies such as Feature Tours, are popular, and early reservations are essential.

ESSENTIALS

Banks and Currency Exchange Banks with dependable check-cashing and money-changing services include ANZ, Westpac, Commonwealth, and National Australia Bank. ATMs—which accept Cirrus, Plus, Visa, and Master-Card—are ubiquitous.

Medical Emergencies Royal Perth Hospital (⊠ *Victoria Sq., East Perth* ☎ *08/9224–2244*).

Police Police (☎ *13–1444 assistance, 08/9222–1111 general inquiries*).

Taxi Cab fare between 6 AM and 6 PM weekdays is an initial A$3.60 plus A$1.47 every 1 km (½ mi). From 6 PM to 6 AM and on weekends the rate rises to A$5.20 plus A$1.47 per 1 km (½ mi). **Black & White** (☎ *13–1008*). **Swan Taxis** (☎ *13–1330*).

Visitors Information Western Australia Visitor Centre (⊠ *Forrest Pl. at Wellington St., CDD* ☎ *00/9403–1111, 1300/361351, 61/89483–1111 from outside Australia*).

Orientation and Wildflower Tours **Perth Tram Company** (☎ *08/9322–2006* ⊕ *www.perthtram.com.au*). **Australian Pacific Touring** (☎ *1300/655965* ⊕ *www.aptouring.com.au*). **Australian Pinnacle Tours** (☎ *08/9471–5555* ⊕ *www.pinnacletours.com.au*). **Feature Tours** (☎ *08/9475–2900* ⊕ *www.ft.com.au*). **Outstanding Tours** (⬡ *Box 712, South Perth, WA 6951* ☎ *08/9368–4949* ⊕ *www.outstandingtours.com.au*).

THE SWAN RIVER

Perth sits astride the Swan River. Though not a great river by global standards, it is the focus of many of the city's festivities, from weekend sailing and boating to annual fireworks spectaculars. For the visitor, it's best to start exploring the riverside at the cluster of boat sheds, cafés, jetties, and ticket offices at the bottom of Barrack Street. From here you can take trips up or downriver.

Boat Tours **Captain Cook Cruises** (⊠ *Pier 3, Barrack Sq. Jetty, CBD* ☎ *08/9325–3341* ⊕ *www.captaincookcruises.com.au*). **Golden Sun Cruises** (⊠ *Pier 4, Barrack Sq. Jetty, CBD* ☎ *08/9325–9916* ⊕ *www.goldensuncruises.com.au*). **Oceanic Cruises** (⊠ *Pier 5, Barrack Sq. Jetty, CBD* ☎ *08/9325–9916* ⊕ *www.oceaniccruises.com.au*). **Rottnest Express** (⊠ *Barrack St. Jetty, CBD* ☎ *1300/467688* ⊕ *www.rottnestexpress.com.au*).

Bus Tour **West Coast Rail and Coach** (☎ *08/9221–9522* ✉ *wcrc@astro.com.au*).

EXPLORING

Because of its relative colonial youth, Perth has an advantage over most other capital cities in that it was laid out with foresight and elegance. Streets were planned so that pedestrian traffic could flow smoothly from one avenue to the next, and this compact city remains easy to negotiate on foot. Most of the points of interest are in the downtown area close to the banks of the Swan River, while shopping arcades and pedestrian malls are a short stroll away.

The city center (CBD, or Central Business District), a pleasant blend of old and new, runs along Perth's major business thoroughfare, St. George's Terrace, as well as on parallel Hay and Murray streets.

WHAT TO SEE
TOP ATTRACTIONS

❼ **Art Gallery of Western Australia.** More than 1,000 treasures from the state's art collection are on display, including one of the best exhibits of Aboriginal art in Australia. Other works include Australian and international paintings, sculpture, prints, crafts, and decorative arts. Free guided tours run at 11 AM and 1 PM Monday, Wednesday, Thursday, and Sunday, and at 1 PM on Saturday. The 12:30 PM Friday's Focus tour examines one particular painting, and guest speakers are scheduled at 2 PM the first Sunday of every month. ⊠ *Perth Cultural Centre, 47 James St. Mall, at corner of Beaufort and Roe Sts., CBD* ☎ *08/9492–6600* ⊕ *www.artgallery.wa.gov.au* ☞ *Free* ☉ *Wed.–Mon. 10–5.*

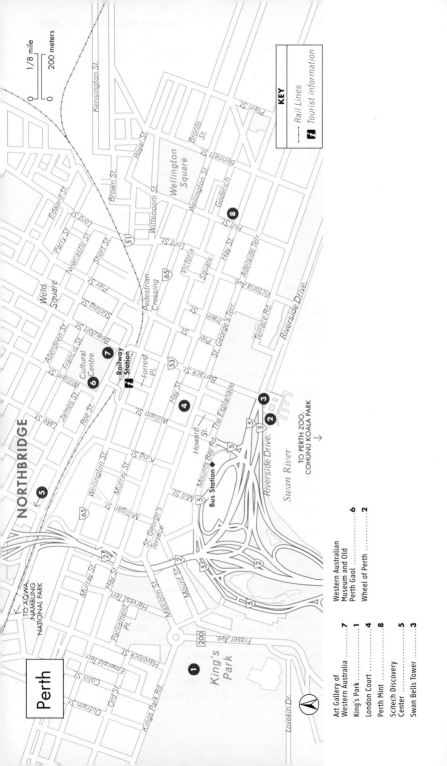

Perth

NORTHBRIDGE

TO AQWA NAMBUNG NATIONAL PARK

King's Park

Swan River

TO PERTH ZOO, COHUNU KOALA PARK

Bus Station

Railway Station

Cultural Centre

Wellington Square

Weld Square

Forrest Pl.

Pedestrian Crossing

KEY

Rail Lines
🛈 Tourist information

1/8 mile
200 meters

Art Gallery of
Western Australia 7
King's Park 1
London Court 4
Perth Mint 8
Scitech Discovery
Center 5
Swan Bells Tower 3

Western Australian
Museum and Old
Perth Gaol 6
Wheel of Perth 2

1 **King's Park.** Once a gathering place
★ for Aboriginal people, and estab-
🕐 lished as a public space in 1890,
this 1,000-acre park overlooking
downtown Perth is one of the city's
most-visited attractions. Both tourists and locals enjoy picnics, parties, and weddings in the gardens,
as well as regular musical and theater presentations and the summer
Moonlight Cinema. In spring the
gardens blaze with orchids, kangaroo paw, banksias, and other wildflowers, making it ideal for a walk
in the bushland. The steel-and-tim-

**THE VIEW FROM
KING'S PARK**

The best spot is the manicured
eastern edge of the park, overlooking Perth's Central Business
District and the Swan River. Picture-perfect lookout points have
the city in the background, as
well as many of the city's most-
treasured memorials, including the
most recent to local victims of the
2002 terrorist bombing in Bali.

ber **Lotterywest Federation Walkway** takes you into the treetops and
the 17-acre botanic garden of Australian flora. The **Synergy Parkland**
details Western Australia's fossil and energy history. The **Lotterywest
Family Area** has a playground for youngsters. Free walking tours take
place daily at 10 AM and 2 PM, and details on seasonal and themed
tours are available from the information kiosk near Fraser's Restaurant.
✉ *Fraser Ave. at King's Park Rd., West Perth* ☎ *08/9480–3634* ⊕ *www.
bgpa.wa.gov.au* 🖃 *Free* ⊗ *Daily 24 hrs.*

6 **Western Australian Museum and Old Perth Gaol.** The state's largest and most
🕐 comprehensive museum includes some of Perth's oldest structures, such
as the Old Perth Gaol. Built of stone in 1856, this was Perth's first and
only prison until 1888. Today it has been reconstructed in the museum
courtyard, and you can go inside the cells for a taste of life in Perth's
criminal past. Exhibitions include "Diamonds to Dinosaurs," which
uses fossils, rocks, and gemstones to take you back 3.5 billion years;
and "Katta Djinoong: First Peoples of Western Australia," which has a
fascinating collection of primitive tools and lifestyle artifacts used thousands of years ago by Australia's Aboriginals. ✉ *Perth Cultural Centre, James and William Sts., CBD* ☎ *08/9212–3700* ⊕ *www.museum.
wa.gov.au* 🖃 *Free* ⊗ *Thurs.–Tues. 9:30–5.*

8 **Perth Mint.** All that glitters is gold at the Perth Mint, one of the oldest
mints in the world still operating from its original premises. Established
in 1899, it first refined gold from Western Australia's newly discovered
goldfields, striking gold sovereigns and half sovereigns for the British
Empire. Today it still produces Australia's legal tender in pure gold,
silver, and platinum bullion and commemorative coins for investors
and collectors. Visitors can have a hands-on experience at the Mint—
watch molten gold being poured in time-honored fashion to form a 6
kilogram solid gold bar; see the world's largest collection of gold investment bars from more than 30 countries; handle more than $400,000
worth of gold bullion; and see Australia's best collection of natural
gold nuggets, including the 369 ounce Golden Beauty, one of the largest
natural nuggets in the world. You can also engrave your own medallion
and discover the value of your weight in gold. ✉ *310 Hay St., CBD*
☎ *08/9421–7222* ⊕ *www.perthmint.com.au* 🖃 *A$15* ⊗ *Weekdays 9–5;*

weekends and public holidays 9–1; guided talk on the half-hour from 9:30; gold pour on the hour from 10.

IF YOU HAVE TIME

⟳ **AQWA: Aquarium of Western Australia.** Huge tanks filled with some 400 different species of local sea creatures from along the 12,000 km of Western Australia's coastline let you view what's beneath the waves. Sharks, stingrays, octopus, cuttlefish, lobsters, turtles, and thousands of fish swim overhead as you take the moving walkway beneath a clear acrylic tunnel. You can even snorkel or scuba dive with the sharks at 1 PM and 3 PM daily. The newest exhibit is "DANGERzone," which puts Western Australia's most dangerous marine creatures on display; the line-up includes creatures that sting, stab, bite, or wrap their prey with suckered arms to immobilize or kill. ⊠ *Hillarys Boat Harbour, 91 Southside Dr., Hillarys ✛ AQWA is a 20-minute drive north of Perth's CBD via the Mitchell Freeway, turn left at Hepburn Ave. and continue to Hilarys Boat Harbour. Or, take the northern Joondalup train line. Alight at Warwick station and take bus No. 423* ☎ *08/9447–7500* ⊕ *www.aqwa.com.au* ✉ *A$26.50; shark experience A$139, plus A$20 snorkel or A$40 scuba equipment rental* ⊙ *Daily 10–5.*

⟳ **Cohunu Koala Park.** The 30-acre Cohunu (pronounced co-*hu*-na) lets you cuddle with a koala. But the other native animals, such as emus, dingoes, wallabies, kangaroos, and wombats are worth visiting, too. The walk-through aviary is the largest in the southern hemisphere, and a restaurant overlooks the city. A miniature steam railway (A$2) operates mostly on weekends and school and public holidays. ⊠ *Lot 103 Nettleton Rd., Byford ✛ Cohuna is a 40-minute drive south of Perth's CBD. Take the South Western Hwy. to Byford, turn left at Nettleton Rd. for 500 meters* ☎ *08/9390–6090* ⊕ *www.cohunu.com.au* ✉ *A$15* ⊙ *Daily 10–5, koala cuddle with photo souvenir A$25, daily 10–4.*

❹ **London Court.** Gold-mining entrepreneur Claude de Bernales built this outdoor shopping arcade in 1937. Today it's a magnet for buskers (street performers) and anyone with a camera. Along its length are statues of Sir Walter Raleigh and Dick Whittington, the legendary lord mayor of London. Above the arcade costumed mechanical knights joust with one another when the clock strikes the quarter hour. ⊠ *Between St. George's Terrace and Hay St., CBD.*

⟳ **Perth Zoo.** Some 1,100 creatures—from 190 different species—are housed in spacious natural habitats. One of the zoo's famous experiences is the Australian Walkabout, featuring an extensive number of native wildlife and flora. You can wander among Australian animals in an environment that replicates the amazing diversity of the Western Australian landscape. The Australian Walkabout includes the Reptile Encounter (home to Australian snakes and other reptiles), the Australian Wetlands, with a huge walk-through aviary and wetlands, the Penguin Plunge, freshwater and estuarine crocodile exhibits, the Rainforest Retreat, and the walk-through Australian Bushwalk. For something a little more exotic, there's the African Savannah, with rhinoceros, giraffe, lions, cheetahs, and baboons, and the Asian Rainforest, with elephants, red pandas, tigers, otters, and a colony of Sumatran orangutans. A

King's park with downtown Perth in the distance.

one-hour guided tour around the zoo on an electric Zebra Car, seating seven passengers and the driver, costs A$3.50. ⊠ *20 Labouchere Rd., South Perth✤ Catch the number 30 or 31 bus at Esplanade Busport or take a ferry ride across the Swan River from the bottom of Barrack St. and then a 10-minute walk following the signs* ☎ *08/9474–0444 or 08/9474–3551* ⊕ *www.perthzoo.wa.gov.au* ✉ *A$20* ☙ *Daily 9–5.*

⑤ Scitech Discovery Centre. Interactive science and technology displays educate and entertain children of all ages. There are more than 100 hands-on exhibits, including a stand where you can freeze your own shadow and another that examines the science and technology used in movies and television. Visitors can star in their own mini-movie, scaling an ice mountain, or jumping from a 14-story building. ⊠ *City West Centre, Sutherland St., West Perth* ☎ *08/9215–0700* ⊕ *www.scitech.org. au* ✉ *A$14* ☙ *Weekends, school holidays, and public holidays 10–5; weekdays 9:30–4.*

❸ Swan Bells Tower. Comprising one of the world's largest musical instruments, the 12 ancient bells installed in the tower are originally from St. Martin-in-the-Fields Church of London, England. The same bells rang to celebrate the destruction of the Spanish Armada in 1588, the homecoming of Captain James Cook in 1771, and the coronation of every British monarch. The tower contains fascinating displays on the history of the bells and bell ringing, and provides stunning views of the Perth skyline. ⊠ *Barrack Sq., Barrack St. at Riverside Dr., CBD* ☎ *08/6210–0444* ⊕ *www.swanbells.com.au* ✉ *A$11* ☙ *Daily from 10; close varies by season; bell-handling demonstrations (single bell) Wed. and Fri. 11:30 AM–12:30 PM; full bell ringing Mon., Tues., Thurs., and*

9

weekends noon–1 PM. *Flat, closed shoes must be worn for access to the observation deck; strollers, large bags, backpacks, and bulky items are not permitted in the tower.*

❷ **Wheel of Perth.** This observation wheel with 36 passenger capsules—taking up to eight people each—rises about 160 feet above the foreshore near the Swan River, providing views over the river, the city, and King's Park. The trip takes about 13 minutes, and the wheel operates throughout the day and into the night, when the city's office towers light up. ✉ *Barrack Sq., Barrack St. at Riverside Dr., CBD* ☎ *08/6101–1676* ⊕ *www.thewheelofperth.com.au* 💰 *A$15* ⊙ *Daily 10–10.*

CITY-DWELLING WATERBIRDS

When a series of lakes was created with construction of the freeways and the Narrows Bridge across the Swan River in 1959, city planners probably didn't realize that these bodies of water would become an oasis for waterbirds. It's a pleasant stroll or bike ride along the riverside, west from the Barrack Street jetties. Laze on the grassy banks, or relax under a tree and check out the different species of waterbirds, including the famous black swan, egret, and red-necked stint, migrating from as far afield as Siberia.

OFF THE BEATEN PATH

Nambung National Park. Set on the Swan coastal plain 245 km (152 mi) north of Perth, Nambung National Park surrounds its most famous attraction: the **Pinnacles Desert.** Over the years, wind and drifting sand have sculpted eerie limestone forms that loom as high as 15 feet. These "pinnacles" are actually the fossilized roots of ancient coastal plants fused with sand, and you can walk among them along a 1,650-foot-long trail that starts at the parking area. There's also a 3-km (2-mi) one-way Pinnacles Desert Loop scenic drive (not suitable for large RVs or buses). August through October the heath blazes with wildflowers. Entrance fees are A$10 per car. Call ☎ *08/9652–7043* for more information.

Batavia Coast. A drive along this part of the coast, which starts at Greenhead, 285 km (178 mi) north of Perth, and runs up to Kalbarri, takes you past white sands and emerald seas, and some lovely small towns. Among them are the fig-shaded, seaside village of **Dongara** and the more northerly **Greenough Historical Hamlet,** whose restored colonial buildings—including a jail with original leg irons—date from 1858. A few miles north is **Geraldton,** whose skyline is dominated by the beautiful Byzantine St. Francis Xavier Cathedral. The huge Batavia Coast Marina has a pedestrian plaza, shopping arcades, and the Western Australian Museum.

BEACHES

Perth's beaches and waterways are among the city's greatest attractions. Traveling north from Fremantle, the first beach you come to is **Leighton,** where windsurfers and astonishing wave-jumpers ride boards against the surf and hurl themselves airborne. **Cottesloe** and **North Cottesloe** attract families. **Trigg,** a top surf site and arguably Perth's best beach, overlooks an emerald-green bay. **Scarborough** is favored by teenagers and young adults. **Swanbourne** (between North Cottesloe and City Beach) is a "clothing optional" beach.

OUTDOOR ACTIVITIES

BICYCLING Perth's climate and its network of excellent trails make cycling a safe and enjoyable way to discover the city. But beware: summer temperatures can exceed 40°C (100°F) in the shade. A bicycle helmet is required by law, and carrying water is prudent. About Bike Hire, which rents bikes for A$36 a day or A$80 a week, is open daily 9–5, 9–6 Dec.–Mar., 11–3 on wet days. Free brochures detailing trails, including stops at historic spots, are available from the Western Australia Visitor Centre. Rentals are available at **About Bike Hire** (✉ *Behind Causeway Car Park, Riverside Dr.* ☎ *08/9221–2665* ⊕ *www.about-bikehire.com.au*).

CATCHING WAVES

Western Australians have a love affair with the beach. During the summer months you'll find thousands of them lazing on sandy beaches, swimming, and surfing. There are popular beaches on Perth's doorstep, but serious board surfers will head south to the rugged coastline from Cape Naturaliste to Cape Leeuwin. Favorite surf breaks are Surfer's Point, Lefthanders, Three Bears, Grunters, the Bommie, Moses Rock, the Guillotine, the Farm, Barnyards, Suicides, and Supertubes. There are some 50 recognized surf breaks along this coast. Check out ⊕ www.oceanoutlook.com.au for up-to-date surf reports.

GOLF Perth has numerous public golf courses, all of which rent out clubs. The **Western Australia Golf Association** (☎ *08/9367–2490* ⊕ *www.wagolf.com.au*) has details on golf courses in the state and a program of events.

SURFING Western Australians take to the surf from a young age—and with world-famous surfing beaches right on the city's doorstep, it's no wonder. The most popular year-round beaches for body and board surfing are Scarborough and Trigg, where swells usually reach 6–9 feet, and occasionally rear up to 12 feet. There are also more than a dozen beaches heading north from Leighton (near Fremantle), including the Cables Artificial Reef (near Leighton) and Watermans (in the northern suburbs of Perth). Cottesloe is favored by novice surfers and children.

If you venture outside the city, Rottnest also has good surf, and if you head south on the coast, you'll find more than 20 surf locations from Cape Naturaliste to Cape Leeuwin. The Main Break at Margaret River is the best known, where waves often roll in at more than 12–15 feet, setting the scene for the annual Margaret River Pro, a world-qualifying series event held in April at Surfers Point. Western Australia's top board surfers head to Scarborough in August for the final round of the state competition. Wet suits are de rigueur for the winter months (May–September), when the surf is usually at its best. **Big Wave Surf School** (☎ *08/9524–7671* ⊕ *www.surfingschool.com.au*) has a range of classes available, starting at A$25 for a one-hour casual class, Saturday only at 11:45

WATER SPORTS Parasailing is available from Mill Point Road on the South Perth shore of the Swan River every day, weather and winds permitting. It's A$80 for a single for 15 minutes and A$140 tandem. Contact **South Perth**

Parasailing (⊠ *Mill Point Rd., South Perth* ☎ *0408/382595*). If you want to enjoy the Swan River at a leisurely pace, rent a catamaran or a sailboard from **Funcats Surfcat Hire** (⊠ *Coode St. Jetty, South Perth* ☎ *08/9387–4336 or 0408/926003*). It costs A$30 per hour; reservations are essential on weekends. Funcats operates from October to April.

WHERE TO EAT

Northbridge, northwest of the railway station, is *the* dining and nightclubbing center of Perth, and reasonably priced restaurants are everywhere. Elsewhere around Perth are seafood and international restaurants, many with stunning views over the Swan River or city, and cantilevered windows that make for a seamless transition between indoor and alfresco dining.

For those on a budget, the noisy fun of a dim sum lunch at one of Perth's many traditional Asian teahouses (especially in Northbridge) is cheap and delicious. Along with a refreshing cup of green tea, you can enjoy steamed pork buns, fried chicken feet, and egg tarts served at your table from the trolley. Food halls in Perth, Northbridge, and Fremantle are other budget options. These one-stop eateries cater to diverse tastes; not all are the same, but you can usually take your pick from stalls selling vegetarian items, roast meats, fresh fruits and juices, Aussie burgers, and fried chicken. Some also serve Southeast Asian, Indian, Japanese, Korean, and Thai cuisine, usually for less than A$10.

Use the coordinate (✛ B2) at the end of each listing to locate a site on the corresponding map.

$$–$$$
AUSTRALIAN
✕ **CBD.** The trendiest place in Perth's West End, this spot has an unusual leaf-shaped bar where both diners and drinkers congregate. The menu changes regularly, but could include pot-roast chicken, red braised pork belly, and lamb shank curry. There's a pizza oven as well, with pizzas from A$23. A big selection of table wine and "stickies" (dessert wines) is available by the glass. Late hours bring in the nightcap crowd after shows at the adjacent His Majesty's Theatre. ⊠ *Hay and King Sts., CBD* ☎ *08/9263–1859* ⊕ *www.ridges.com/perth* ⊟ *AE, DC, MC, V* ✛ *C3.*

$$–$$$
AUSTRALIAN
✕ **Coco's Riverside Bar and Restaurant.** Overlooking the Swan River in South Perth, this restaurant has a menu that changes daily depending on fresh produce. Most dishes are available in both appetizer and main-course portions. Start with a Japanese sake oyster shooter with pickled ginger. Mains include grilled boneless free-range chicken with vegetables and a mango vinagrette; crumbed lamb cutlets with roasted French beans; or double-roasted duckling with grapes and port-wine jus. The extensive wine list includes many of the best labels from the Margaret River region. ⊠ *Southshore Centre, 85 Esplanade, South Perth* ☎ *08/9474–3030* ⊕ *www.westvalley.com.au* ✍ *Reservations essential* ⊟ *AE, DC, MC, V* ✛ *D4.*

$$–$$$
THAI
✕ **Dusit Thai Restaurant.** Come here for authentic Thai food, lovingly prepared and served among traditional sculptures and artwork. Starters include *kra thong tong* (stir-fried diced prawns, minced chicken, and sweet corn on deep-fried tartlets); or *gai hor bai-toey* (marinated breast of chicken wrapped in Padang leaves and deep-fried). Main-course specialties include *gang keo-wan* (green curry chicken) and

gang-pa (hot and spicy red curry without coconut milk, served with green beans, bamboo strips, and basil leaves). ⊠ *249 James St., North-bridge* ☎ *08/9328–7647* ⊕ *www.dusitthai.com.au* ▤ *AE, DC, MC, V* ⊙ *No lunch Sat.–Wed. Closed Mon.* ✛ *A3.*

$$$–$$$$
AUSTRALIAN
✕ **Fraser's Restaurant.** In fair weather the large outdoor area at this King's Park restaurant fills with people enjoying food and views of the city and Swan River. The ever-changing menu highlights daily seafood specials, and the wines include Australian and New Zealand bottles, plus imported champagnes, many available by the glass. Look for panfried goat-cheese gnocchi; baby octopus with chili and ginger paste; cumin-spiced lamb with adzuki beans; and, Waygu beef with Yorkshire pudding. Fraser's has also opened the adjacent **Botanical Cafe** (☎ *08/9482–0122*), serving breakfast, lunch, and dinner daily, with mains from A$15 to A$26. ⊠ *Fraser Ave., King's Park, West Perth* ☎ *08/9481–7100* ⊕ *www.frasersrestaurant.com.au* ⌕ *Reservations essential* ▤ *AE, DC, MC, V* ✛ *D1.*

$$$
AUSTRALIAN
✕ **Jackson's Restaurant.** A long list of awards over the past two decades has established Jackson's Restaurant as one of Perth's top dining establishments. Chef Neal Jackson began his career in London, but it was in the tiny Western Australian town of Donnybrook, in the South-West, that he burst onto the local scene. Over 17 years he impressed South-West diners before establishing Jackson's in Perth, where since 1998 he continues to impress by creating innovative and intensely flavored foods. À la carte choices include pork belly, scallops, broccoli, cashews, and chili; lamb loin and shoulder with Moroccan spices and couscous; and sea bass with piggy bits. There are excellent vegetarian choices as well. The Dego—a nine-course degustation menu—costs A$120. ⊠ *483 Beaufort St., Highgate* ☎ *08/9328–1177* ⊕ *www.jacksonsrestaurant. com.au* ▤ *AE, DC, MC, V* ⊙ *Closed Sun.* ✛ *A5.*

$–$$
AISAN
✕ **Joe's Oriental Diner.** On the street level of the Hyatt Regency Hotel on Adelaide Terrace, Joe's serves a wide range of dishes from China, Indonesia, Thailand, Malaysia, and Singapore. The rattan-and-bamboo interior is reminiscent of the many noodle houses throughout Southeast Asia, and meals are prepared in the spectacular open kitchen. Hearty soups and delicious noodle dishes, like *laksa* (rice noodles in a spicy coconut-milk broth with chicken, bean curd, fish cakes, fish balls, and prawns), are the standouts. Each dish carries a chili coding indicating its relative spiciness—so you won't breathe fire unless you want to. ⊠ *Hyatt Regency, 99 Adelaide Terrace, CBD* ☎ *08/9225–1268* ⊕ *www.joesorientaldiner.com. au* ▤ *AE, DC, MC, V* ⊙ *Closed Sun. No lunch Sat.* ✛ *D6.*

$$$$
FRENCH
Fodor'sChoice
★
✕ **Loose Box.** Perth's finest French restaurant is run by owner-chef Alain Fabregues, who has received France's highest culinary honor, the Meilleur Ouvrier de France, as well as a French knighthood—Chevalier Dans L'Ordre National du Merite—for his contribution to French culture and cuisine. His degustation menu applies classical French culinary principles to Australia's best seasonal bounty: there's *le blinis d'oiseaux au Raifort* (quail, duck and chicken folded with kipfler potato in a blinis of chives and olives) and *le nougat glacé* (French traditional nougat, made with honey, pistachio and hazelnut, served chilled on a strawberry coulis with caramel strands). There is no à la carte option. Each room

9

The Pinnacles of Nambung National Park, Western Australia

(the restaurant used to be a house) is cozy, intimate, and warm. Accommodations are available, if you just can't bring yourself to leave. ⊠ *6825 Great Eastern Hwy., Mundaring, WA* ☎ *08/9295–1787* ⊕ ⌂ *Reservations essential* ▭ *AE, DC, MC, V* ⊙ *Closed Mon., Tues., and last 2 wks July. No lunch Wed.–Sat.* ✛ *D6.*

$–$$ ✕ **Matsuri Japanese Restaurant.** Discerning diners fill every table most
JAPANESE nights at this contemporary glass-and-steel restaurant. At the base of an office tower, Perth's most popular casual Japanese dining spot is famous for its fresh, flavorful, and authentic cuisine. Served with steamed rice, miso soup, salad, and green tea, the sushi and sashimi sets start at A$18.90 and are an excellent value. House specialties include delicately light tempura vegetables and *una don* (grilled eel in teriyaki sauce). ⊠ *Lower level 1, QV1 Bldg., 250 St. George's Terrace, CBD* ☎ *08/9322–7737* ⊕ *www.matsuri.com.au* ▭ *AE, DC, MC, V* ⊙ *No lunch Sat. Closed Sun.* ✛ *B2.*

$$–$$$ ✕ **Perugino.** Chef Giuseppe Pagliaricci takes an imaginative yet simple
ITALIAN approach to the cuisine of his native Umbria. Only the freshest produce
★ is used for such creations as *filetto in crosta* (an eye fillet of beef double crumbed, pan-fried, and served in a bed of porcini mushrooms); or *nodini di vitello con salsa d'asparagi* (loin of veal pan-fried and served in a fresh asparagus sauce). The six-course degustation menu highlights the best of the house. ⊠ *77 Outram St., West Perth* ☎ *08/9321–5420* ⊕ *www.perugino.com.au* ⌂ *Reservations essential* ▭ *AE, DC, MC, V* ⊙ *Closed Sun. and Mon. No lunch Sat.* ✛ *A1.*

$–$$$$ ✕ **Yu.** Some of the best Chinese food in the city is cooked up at this
CHINESE elegant restaurant in the Burswood Entertainment Complex. Cantonese flavors predominate under the guidance of chef de cuisine Pat Cheong,

with signature dishes Peking duck, fillet steak with Szechuan or Cantonese sauce, Portuguese crab, and sea-salt prawns. The setting is that of a Cantonese manor, with woodcarvings and silk tapestries, and an entrance over a "bridge" across marble floors laden with gold coins. Banquet menus start at A$70. ⊠ *InterContinental Perth Burswood, Great Eastern Hwy. at Bolton Ave., Burswood* ☎ *08/9362–7551* ⊕ *www.yurestaurant.com.au* ▭ *AE, DC, MC, V* ✛ *D6.*

WHERE TO STAY

Businesspeople from around the world are flocking to Western Australia, and consequently hotel rooms in Perth are at an unprecedented premium. Few new hotels have been built, so hotels are frequently at capacity, and prices are up. ■ TIP➔ The wise will book early.

Use the coordinate (✛ B2) at the end of each listing to locate a site on the corresponding map.

$ | 🖫 **Comfort Inn Wentworth Plaza Hotel.** This Federation-era inn is one of
Fodor's Choice | Perth's most centrally located hotels; it's a block away from the Perth
★ | Railway Station in one direction and a block from the Hay Street Mall in the other. The rooms here (there are also some two-room apartments) have period decor; downstairs, Bobby Dazzler's is a "true blue" Aussie pub, while Moon and Sixpence serves 30 different international and local beers in the atmosphere of a traditional British pub. **Pros:** few minutes' walk to city-center shopping malls and arcades; Aussie pub scene; heritage-style rooms. **Cons:** no private en-suites with some rooms; no on-site parking; somewhat rundown area of CBD, especially at night. ⊠ *300 Murray St., CBD* ☎ *08/9481–1000 or 1800/355109* ⊕ *www. wentworthplazahotel.com.au* ⇱ *88 rooms* ⚏ *In-room: refrigerator. In-hotel: restaurant, room service, bars, laundry service, no parking, no-smoking rooms* ▭ *AE, DC, MC, V* ✛ *B3.*

$$$$ | 🖫 **Duxton Hotel.** Adjacent to the Perth Concert Hall, this elegant hotel
★ | is within easy walking distance of the city center. Soothing autumn colors, paintings by local artists, and furniture crafted from Australian timber fill the comfortable rooms, some of which have views of the Swan River. The Grill, which opens on to a broad terrace, is open for breakfast, lunch, and dinner, serving international cuisine, with many wines from Western Australia's premium wine regions. **Pros:** few minutes' walk to city-center shopping malls; popular restaurant with alfresco terrace; some rooms have river views. **Cons:** in business district; few evening dining options nearby. ⊠ *1 St. George's Terrace, CBD* ☎ *08/9261–8000 or 1800/681118* ⊕ *www.duxtonhotels.com/ perth* ⇱ *291 rooms, 15 suites* ⚏ *In-room: Wi-Fi. In-hotel: restaurant, room service, bar, pool, gym, public Wi-Fi, laundry service, parking (no fee)* ▭ *AE, DC, MC, V* ✛ *C5.*

$$$$ | 🖫 **Hyatt Regency.** Within walking distance of Perth's central business
★ | district, this hotel overlooking the Swan River is one of Perth's best. Standard rooms are spacious, while the higher-priced Regency Club rooms and suites (on the top two floors) have stunning views, complimentary Continental breakfast, and evening drinks and canapés. The Conservatory, a sitting area with tasteful cane furniture and a fountain under a large domed atrium, is a civilized spot for relaxing. **Pros:** river views from many rooms; evening nibbles and drinks in

9

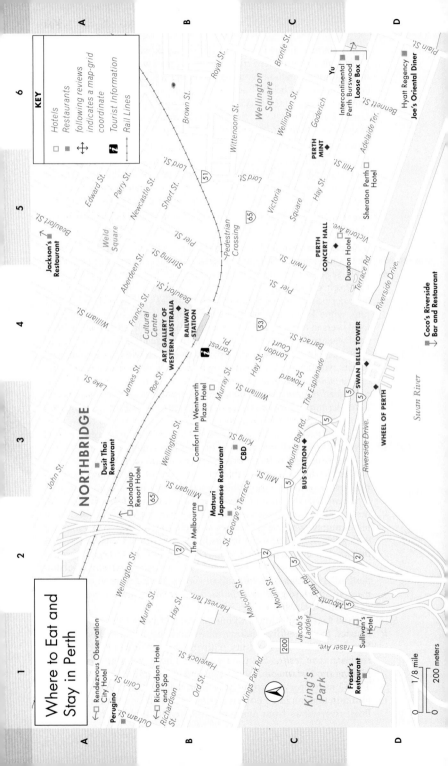

Where to Eat and Stay in Perth

KEY

□ Hotels

■ Restaurants (following reviews indicates a map-grid coordinate)

✛

🛈 Tourist Information

Rail Lines

NORTHBRIDGE

■ Dusit Thai Restaurant

□ Joondalup Resort Hotel

■ Jackson's Restaurant

← □ Rendezvous Observation City Hotel
■ Perugino

← □ Richardson Hotel and Spa

□ The Melbourne

■ Matsuri Japanese Restaurant

□ Comfort Inn Wentworth Plaza Hotel

ART GALLERY OF WESTERN AUSTRALIA ◆

Cultural Centre

RAILWAY STATION

CBD ■

BUS STATION ◆

Mounts Bay Rd. ◆

SWAN BELLS TOWER ◆

WHEEL OF PERTH ◆

□ Sullivan's Hotel

■ Fraser's Restaurant

King's Park

Jacob's Ladder

PERTH CONCERT HALL ◆

□ Duxton Hotel

PERTH MINT ◆

Wellington Square

Yu ■

□ Intercontinental Perth Burswood

■ Loose Box

□ Sheraton Perth Hotel

Hyatt Regency ■

■ Joe's Oriental Diner

Coco's Riverside Bar and Restaurant ■

Swan River

0   1/8 mile

0   200 meters

A   B   C   D

1   2   3   4   5   6

the executive lounge; good choice of on-site dining. **Cons:** rooms have corporate decor; few dining options nearby. ⊠ *99 Adelaide Terrace, CBD* ☎ *08/9225–1234* ⊕ *www.perth.hyatt.com* ⤷ *367 rooms, 32 suites* ⬧ *In-room: safe (some), Internet. In-hotel: 3 restaurants, room service, bars, tennis court, pool, gym, concierge, laundry service, Wi-Fi, parking (paid)* ⊟ *AE, DC, MC, V* ⍾ *CP* ⊹ *D6.*

$$$$
Fodor's Choice
★

Intercontinental Perth Burswood. From the 10-story glass atrium atop its pyramid-shaped exterior to its 18-hole golf course, everything about Burswood conveys luxury. Spacious rooms have Japanese shoji screens between the bedrooms and bathrooms, and views of either the

EATING OUT

While there are plenty of high-end restaurants in Perth, it's also possible to eat on the cheap. Northbridge has a plethora of competitively priced restaurants, especially along James Street, and especially at lunchtime. A dim sum lunch at a traditional Asian teahouse is inexpensive and delicious. Food halls in Perth, Northbridge, and Fremantle are another budget option. These one-stop eateries cater to diverse tastes; not all are the same, but you can usually take your pick from stalls selling all sorts of delicious food, usually for less than A$10.

river or the city. Suites have hot tubs. The adjoining casino is enormous, and open around the clock for roulette, blackjack, baccarat, keno, and video games. Seven restaurants within the complex include upscale and buffet-style dining. **Pros:** impressive lobby rises the full height of the building; extensive, all-you-can-eat buffet for breakfast, lunch and dinner. **Cons:** adjacent casino and nightclub attracts a boisterous crowd; Thursday through Saturday nights notable for party-goers; atrium-style lobby creates noise to some rooms. ⊠ *Great Eastern Hwy. at Bolton Ave., Burswood* ☎ *08/9362–7777 or 1800/999667* ⊕ *www.burswood.com.au* ⤷ *413 rooms, 16 suites* ⬧ *In-room: safe, refrigerator, Internet. In-hotel: 7 restaurants, room service, bars, golf course, tennis courts, pools, gym, spa, laundry service, parking (fee), no-smoking rooms* ⊟ *AE, DC, MC, V* ⊹ *D6.*

$$$
★

Joondalup Resort Hotel. Although it's 30 km (19 mi) from Perth's business district, this palm-shaded building—which resembles a southern plantation owner's mansion—is a comfortable place to relax for a few days, especially if you like golf. Spacious rooms, decorated in subdued pastels and warm tones, all have views over the lagoon or the 27-hole, Robert Trent Jones, Jr.–designed golf course. A free shuttle runs daily to the Joondalup train station and Lakeside Shopping Centre. **Pros:** international-standard golf courses; country-club atmosphere; some rooms have golf-course views. **Cons:** in suburban area; no other attractions nearby; conventions can make venues crowded. ⊠ *Country Club Blvd., Connolly* ☎ *08/9400–8888 or 1800/803488* ⊕ *www.joondalupresort.com.au* ⤷ *66 rooms, 4 suites* ⬧ *In-room: safe, Wi-Fi. In-hotel: 2 restaurants, bars, golf courses, tennis courts, pool, gym, laundry service, parking (no fee), no-smoking rooms* ⊟ *AE, DC, MC, V* ⊹ *A2.*

$$
The Melbourne. A restored 1890s building listed on the National Heritage Register houses this stylish boutique hotel. The Perth landmark

9

retains all the original design elements of the era, including a grand staircase and elevator, along with contemporary accommodations and facilities. The elegant Melbourne Restaurant serves very good Australian cuisine; you can have a drink in the Melbourne Bar, or a snack and coffee at M Café. **Pros:** city-center location; heritage decor throughout; few minutes' walk to shopping malls. **Cons:** leisure facilities off-site; parking is off-site. ⊠ *Hay and Milligan Sts., CBD* ☎ *08/9320–3333 or 1800/685671* ⊕ *www.melbournehotel.com.au* ⟿ *34 rooms* ⚿ *In-room: kitchen (some), Internet. In-hotel: 2 restaurants, room service, bar, tennis courts, gym, laundry service, parking (fee)* ☰ *AE, DC, MC, V* ✛ *B2.*

$$$ ⛱ **Rendezvous Observation City Hotel.** Watch the sun dip into the Indian Ocean from this beachside resort. Elegant blues and golds decorate the stylish rooms, all of which have superb ocean views and many a private balcony. The top three floors offer access to the Club Lounge, with complimentary Continental breakfast and drinks at sunset. You can dine at Savannahs Restaurant or have the buffet for breakfast, lunch, or dinner at Pines Grand Buffet and Carvery. A shuttle-bus service operates to the city center (30 minutes), Fremantle, and shopping centers. **Pros:** great views of the Indian Ocean; walk straight on to Scarborough Beach; lagoon-style pool is heated. **Cons:** few other attractions nearby; limited shopping nearby. ⊠ *Esplanade, Scarborough Beach* ☎ *08/9245–1000 or 1800/067680* ⊕ *www.rendezvoushotels.com* ⟿ *327 rooms, 6 suites* ⚿ *In-room: refrigerator, Internet (some). In-hotel: 2 restaurants, bars, tennis courts, pool, gym, spa, Wi-Fi, parking (no fee)* ☰ *AE, DC, MC, V* ✛ *A1.*

$ ⛱ **The Richardson Hotel and Spa.** Tucked away in a quiet, leafy, tree-lined street in West Perth, The Richardson offers a discrete stay without forgoing any of the amenities of the bigger downtown hotels. Understated elegance means muted tones of gold and brown, with a splash of red in the large rooms and suites. All but the standard rooms have balconies—a rarity in Perth hotels—so you can step outside for some fresh air, though the views of surrounding West Perth aren't that great. For a small hotel, the gym is surprisingly spacious and well-equipped, while the indoor pool is heated to a very comfortable 28C. The spa—a recent Conde Naste readers' award winner—offers four treatment rooms, while the Opus Restaurant with indoor and outdoor spaces is winning praise from locals in the hands of chef Todd Cheavins. **Pros:** large rooms and suites; evening turn-down service in all rooms; convenient meal packs in rooms; modest mini-bar prices; balconies off most rooms. **Cons:** views mostly of surrounding buildings; limited shopping within walking distance. ⊠ *32 Richardson St., West Perth* ☎ *08/9217–8888* ⊕ *www.therichardson.com.au* ⟿ *56 rooms, 18 suites* ⚿ *In-room: safe, kitchen (some), refrigerator, Internet, Wi-Fi (some). In-hotel: restaurant, room service, bar, pool, gym, spa, laundry service, Wi-Fi, parking (paid), no-smoking rooms* ☰ *AE, D, DC, MC, V* ✛ *B1.*

$$$$ ⛱ **Sheraton Perth Hotel.** Sweeping views over the Swan River from many guest rooms are a feature of this 23-story, five-star hotel, a handy 10-minute walk from downtown. Deluxe rooms and suites on the top five floors have the best views, with club floor guests getting access to the Executive

Club Lounge on level 7 for complimentary breakfast, predinner drinks, and canapés. One of the two restaurants, Montereys, has lavish breakfasts, and the Lobby Lounge is popular with locals for predinner and preshow drinks: Perth Concert Hall is just a short walk away. **Pros:** many rooms have river views; gym with steam rooms open 24 hours; Wi-Fi is complimentary. **Cons:** in an office area; limited night-time dining options nearby. ⊠ *207 Adelaide Terrace, CBD* ☎ *08/9224–7777* ⊕ *www.sheraton.com/perth* ⤳ *468 rooms, 18 suites* ⚲ *In-room: safe, refrigerator, Internet. In-hotel: 2 restaurants, room service, bars, pool, gym, Wi-Fi, laundry service, parking (fee)* ⊟ *AE, DC, MC, V* ✛ *D5.*

> ### ROCKIN' IN PERTH
>
> Thanks to pop, rock, and metal bands like Eskimo Joe, the John Butler Trio, the Waifs, Karnivool, Little Birdy, the Panda Band, and the Sleepy Jackson—who all started in Perth—the music scene here is thriving. Despite their isolation from the rest of Australia, Western Australian musos are turning out some top-notch material. Music commentators claim there isn't a "Perth sound" as such, just a talented bunch of artists writing and performing original music. Check out ⊕ *www. xpressmag.com.au* for an up-to-date guide on live shows.

$$ ⛿ **Sullivan's Hotel.** A family-run hotel opposite waterfront parkland at the foot of King's Park, Sullivan's is handy to the center of Perth and King's Park; it's a 10-minute walk to the city center, less to the Barrack Street jetties and the Swan River. The airport shuttle bus stops at the hotel, and the city's free CAT buses—which stop right outside—will get you to inner-city attractions. There are complimentary bicycles for guests. Rooms are brightly decorated, and the deluxe rooms have balconies with city and parkland views. **Pros:** good-value beds for the area; close to King's Park; free public bus service at front. **Cons:** no night service for free public bus service; no dining options nearby; no shopping nearby. ⊠ *166 Mounts Bay Rd., CBD* ☎ *08/9321–8022* ⊕ *www.sullivans.com.au* ⤳ *71 rooms* ⚲ *In-room: kitchen (some), Wi-Fi. In-hotel: restaurant, bar, pool, Wi-Fi, bicycles, laundry facilities, parking (no fee)* ⊟ *AE, DC, MC, V* ✛ *D1.*

NIGHTLIFE AND THE ARTS

Details on cultural events in Perth are published in the comprehensive Saturday edition of the *West Australian.* A free weekly, *X-Press Magazine,* lists music, concerts, movies, entertainment reviews, and who's playing at pubs, clubs, and hotels. *SCOOP* magazine (⊕ *www. scooptraveller.com.au*), published quarterly, is an excellent guide to the essential Western Australian lifestyle.

THE ARTS

BOCS Ticketing (☎ *08/9484–1133* ⊕ *www.bocsticketing.com.au*) is the main booking hotline in Perth for the performing arts.

Local talent dominates the arts scene in Perth, although the acclaimed **Perth International Arts Festival (PIAF)** (☎ *08/6488–5555 for information and bookings* ⊕ *www.perthfestival.com.au*), held February in venues throughout the city, attracts international music, dance, and theater stars. This is Australia's oldest and biggest annual arts festival, and it's been running for more than 50 years. As part of the festival, the Lotterywest Festival Films screens films outdoors December–March.

BALLET The **West Australian Ballet Company** (✉ *825 Hay St., CBD* ☎ *08/9481–0707* ⊕ *www.waballet.com.au*), one of just three ballet companies in Australia, focuses on classical ballet, but also has contemporary ballet and dance in its diverse repertoire. Performances are at His Majesty's Theatre, although you can also see the 20-person troupe at outdoor venues like the Quarry Amphitheatre (at City Beach) and on country tours. The company also tours nationally and internationally, and has performed in China, Japan, and the Philippines.

CONCERTS The **Perth Concert Hall** (✉ *5 St. George's Terr., CBD* ☎ *08/9231–9900* ⊕ *www.perthconcerthall.com.au*), a modern building overlooking the Swan River, stages regular recitals by the excellent West Australian Symphony Orchestra, as well as Australian and international performers. Adding to the appeal of the fine auditorium is the 3,000-pipe organ surrounded by a 160-person choir gallery.

OPERA The **West Australian Opera Company** (✉ *825 Hay St., CBD* ☎ *08/9278–8999* ⊕ *www.waopera.asn.au*) presents three seasons annually—in April, August, and November—at His Majesty's Theatre. They also perform Opera in the Park in Perth's Supreme Court Gardens each February. The company's repertoire includes classic opera, Gilbert and Sullivan operettas, and occasional musicals.

THEATER The **Burswood Theatre** (✉ *Great Eastern Hwy., Burswood* ☎ *13–2849* ⊕ *www.burswood.com.au*) has regular theatrical and musical productions from around Australia. The opulent Edwardian **His Majesty's Theatre** (✉ *825 Hay St., CBD* ☎ *08/9494–1133* ⊕ *www.hismajestystheatre.com.au*), opened in 1904, is loved by all who step inside. Home to the West Australian Opera Company and the West Australian Ballet Company, it hosts most theatrical productions in Perth. The **Playhouse Theatre** (✉ *3 Pier St., CBD* ☎ *08/9323–3400* ⊕ *www.playhousetheatre.com.au*) stages local productions. For outdoor performances, the **Quarry Amphitheatre** (✉ *Waldron Drive [left off Oceanic Dr.], City Beach* ☎ *08/9385–7144* ⊕ *www.quarryamphitheatre.com.au*) is popular, particularly during the Perth International Arts Festival. The **Regal Theatre** (✉ *474 Hay St., at Rokeby Rd., Subiaco* ☎ *1300/795012* ⊕ *www.regaltheatre.com.au*) hosts local and visiting performances.

NIGHTLIFE

Most luxury hotels in Perth have upscale nightclubs that appeal to the over-30 crowd. Apart from these, however, nightlife in the city center is virtually nonexistent. Twentysomethings most often head to Northbridge, Subiaco, or Fremantle. Pubs and bars generally close by 11 PM, which is when the crowds start arriving at the nightclubs; these tend to stay open until around 5 AM.

BARS The **Brass Monkey** (✉ *William and James Sts., Northbridge* ☎ *08/9227–9596* ⊕ *www.thebrassmonkey.com.au*) is in a huge, old, crimson-painted building with potted plants flowing over the antique verandas. There's live stand-up comedy every Wednesday night. On Saturday nights a DJ keeps the music booming. There's no cover charge. **Queen's Tavern** (✉ *520 Beaufort St., Highgate* ☎ *08/9328–7267*) has an excellent

The London Court shopping mall façade at Hay Walking Street, Perth.

outdoor beer garden. The upstairs bar has a relaxed lounge vibe, with DJs on Friday, Saturday, and Sunday. The bar at the **Subiaco Hotel** (⌂ *465 Hay St., Subiaco* ☎ *08/9381–3069*) attracts a lively after-work crowd during the week, with live rock bands on Saturday in Bianca's Bar and live jazz on Wednesday and Saturday in the cocktail bar.

JAZZ AND BLUES On Tuesday nights try the **Charles Hotel** (⌂ *509 Charles St., North Perth* ☎ *08/9444–1051*) for live jazz every Monday night; live blues performances every Tuesday night. The **Hyde Park Hotel** (⌂ *331 Bulwer St., North Perth* ☎ *08/9328–6166*), a no-nonsense Aussie pub, hosts live entertainment every night, including contemporary jazz and rock bands, soloists, and comedy. The **Universal Bar** (⌂ *221 William St., Northbridge* ☎ *08/9227–6771*) has live jazz and blues every night till late.

NIGHTCLUBS The **Hip-e Club** (⌂ *663 Newcastle St., Leederville* ☎ *08/9227–8899*), a Perth legend, capitalizes on its hippie-era image with a neon kaleidoscope, 3-D color explosions, murals, and 1960s paraphernalia decorating the walls. Surf parties and backpacker nights take place weekly. **Eve** (⌂ *Intercontinental Perth Burswood, Great Eastern Hwy. at Bolton Ave., Burswood* ☎ *08/9362–7699*) is a glitzy, two-story venue done up with stainless steel and retro fittings. Wednesday through Sunday, the four bars, cozy lounge areas, stage, and dance floor with sound-and-light show are packed with merrymakers. **Varga Lounge** (⌂ *161 James St., Northbridge* ☎ *08/9328–7200*) mixes it up New York-style, with DJs who spin techno, rap, and hip-hop.

SHOPPING

Shopping in Perth, with its pedestrian-friendly central business district, vehicle-free malls, and many covered arcades, is a delight. Hay Street Mall and Murray Street Mall are the main city shopping areas, linked by numerous arcades with small shops. In the suburbs, top retail strips include Napoleon Street in Cottesloe (for clothing and cooking items), Hampden Road in Nedlands (for crafts), and Beaufort Street in Mount Lawley (for antiques).

MALLS AND ARCADES
Forrest Place, flanked by the post office and the Forrest Chase Shopping Plaza, is the largest mall area in the city. **David Jones** (☎ *08/9210–4000*) department store opens onto the Murray Street pedestrian mall. **Myer** (✉ *Murray St. Mall at Forrest Pl.* ☎ *08/9265–5600*) is a popular department store that carries all manner of goods and sundries. The **Hay Street Mall,** running parallel to Murray Street and linked by numerous arcades, is another extensive shopping area. Make sure you wander through the arcades that connect Hay and Murray streets, such as **Carillion Arcade,** which have many more shops.

AUSTRALIAN
Australian souvenirs and knickknacks are on sale at small shops throughout the city and suburbs. **Purely Australian Clothing Company** (✉ *38–39 London Court, CBD* ☎ *08/9325–4328* ⊕ *www.purelyaustralian.com*) carries the most comprehensive selection of Oz-abilia in Perth. There are also stores at Perth International Airport. **R. M. Williams** (✉ *Shop 38 Carillon City, Hay St. Mall, CBD* ☎ *08/9321–7786* ⊕ *www.rmwilliams. com.au*) sells everything for the Australian bushman, including moleskin pants, hand-tooled leather boots, and Akubra hats.

CRAFTS
You can find authentic Aboriginal artifacts at **Creative Native** (✉ *Shop 58, Forrest Chase, Forrest Pl., CBD* ☎ *08/9221–5800* ⊕ *www.creative-native.com.au*) ; their selection of Aboriginal art is extensive. Each piece of original artwork comes with a certificate of authenticity. **FORM: Contemporary Craft and Design** (✉ *King St. Arts Centre, 357–365 Murray St., CBD* ☎ *08/9226–2161*) carries a large selection of Western Australian crafts and giftware from established and emerging artists, including some Aboriginal art, jewelry, metal, ceramics, glass, textiles, and wood. A former car dealer's workshop has been transformed into the Outback at **Indigenart–The Mossenson Gallery** (✉ *115 Hay St., Subiaco* ☎ *08/9388–2899* ⊕ *www.indigenart.com.au*), an art gallery–cum–Aboriginal culture center where you can view works and talk with the Aboriginal creators. **Maalia Mia** (✉ *10070 W. Swan Rd., Henley Brook* ☎ *08/9296–0704* ⊕ *www.maalimia.com.au*), an Aboriginal-owned and -operated cultural center, art gallery, and gift shop, sells art and artifacts purchased only from Aboriginal artists. Boomerangs, didgeridoos, and clapping sticks are made on-site.

FREMANTLE

About 19 km (12 mi) southwest of Perth.

The port city of Fremantle is a jewel in Western Australia's crown, largely because of its colonial architectural heritage. Freo (as the locals call it) is also a city where locals know each other, and there are plenty of interesting (and sometimes eccentric) residents. Modern Fremantle is a far cry from the barren, sandy plain that greeted the first wave of English settlers back in 1829 at the newly constituted Swan River Colony. Most were city dwellers, and after five months at sea in sailing ships they landed on salt-marsh flats that sorely tested their fortitude. Living in tents with packing cases for chairs, they found no edible crops, and the nearest freshwater was a distant 51 km (32 mi)—and a tortuous trip up the salty waters of the Swan. As a result they soon moved the settlement upriver to the vicinity of present-day Perth.

Fremantle remained the principal port, and many attractive limestone buildings were built to service the port traders. Australia's 1987 defence of the America's Cup—held in waters off Fremantle—triggered a major restoration of the colonial streetscapes. In the leafy suburbs nearly every other house is a restored 19th-century gem.

Like all great port cities, Freo is cosmopolitan, with mariners from all parts of the world strolling the streets—including 20,000 U.S. Navy personnel on rest and recreation throughout the year.

It's also a good jumping-off point for a day trip to Rottnest Island, where lovely beaches, rocky coves, and unique wallaby-like inhabitants called quokkas make their home.

GETTING HERE AND AROUND

Bus information for service from Perth is available from Transperth (☎ *13–6213* ⊕ *www.transperth.wa.gov.au*). Their Central Area Bus Service (CAT) provides free transportation around Fremantle in orange buses. The route begins and ends outside the Fremantle Bus/Train terminus, and stops include the Fremantle Museum and Arts Centre, the cappuccino strip, and the Fremantle Market. CAT buses run every 10 minutes weekdays 7:30–6:30, and 10–6:30 on weekends and public holidays.

Trains bound for Fremantle depart from Perth approximately every 20–30 minutes from the Perth Central Station on Wellington Street. You can travel from Perth to Fremantle (or vice versa) in about 30 minutes. Tickets must be purchased at the ticket vending machines prior to travel. It is illegal to travel without a ticket.

If you are driving from downtown Perth, the most direct route is via Stirling Highway, from the foot of Kings Park; it will take about 40 minutes, depending on traffic.

SAFETY AND PRECAUTIONS

Fremantle is a safe destination, and is popular with families, particularly on weekends and during the school holidays. It also has a lively nightlife, and late-night crowds leaving pubs and clubs can—and do—cause problems. Taxis are in high demand late at night when other public transport stops operating.

TIMING

Fremantle can easily be visited in a day from Perth, though if you want to trip over to Rottnest Island you will have to add an extra day. Most of the sights are clustered in a relatively small area close to the Fishing Boat Harbour, and you can take a walking tour or take a hop-on-hop-off tour bus.

TOURS

Fremantle Tram Tours runs hop-on-hop-off tours (A$22) around the city daily from 9:45 AM to approximately 3:30 PM, with six stops all close to the major sights. A tour around Fremantle is a great way to get to know each area of the port city. A full-day tour is the Triple Tour, which includes a guided tour of Fremantle, a cruise on the Swan River to Perth, and a sightseeing tour in Perth. The tour finishes in Perth, but you can catch a train or bus back to Fremantle. The cost is A$56, not including your return to Fremantle. On Friday nights, "ghostly tours" take in suspected haunted premises, with a dinner of fish-and-chips included. The cost is A$56 per person. (⊡ *Box 1081, Fremantle 6959* ☎ *08/9433–6674* ⊕ *www.fremantletrams.com*).

ESSENTIALS

Banks and Currency Exchange Banks with dependable check-cashing and money-changing services include ANZ, Westpac, Commonwealth, and National Australia Bank. **UAE Australia** (⊠ *62 South Terrace, Fremantle* ☎ *1300/705050* ⊕ *www.xpressmoney.com.au* ⊗ *Mon.–Sat. 9:30–5, Sun. 10–5*).

Medical Emergencies Fremantle Hospital (⊠ *Alma St.* ☎ *08/9431–3333*).

Police Police (☎ *13–1444 assistance, 08/9222–1111 general inquiries*).

Taxi Cab fare between 6 AM and 6 PM weekdays is an initial A$3.60 plus A$1.47 every 1 km (½ mi). From 6 PM to 6 AM and on weekends the rate rises to $5.20 plus A$1.47 per 1 km (½ mi). **Black & White** (☎ *13–1008*). **Swan Taxis** (☎ *13–1330*).

Visitors Information Fremantle Visitor Centre (⊠ *Kings Sq. at High St., Fremantle* ☎ *08/9431–7878* ⊕ *www.fremantlewesternaustralia.com* ⊗ *Weekdays 9–5, Sat. 10–3, Sun. 11:30–3*).

EXPLORING

An ideal place to start a leisurely stroll is South Terrace, known as the Fremantle cappuccino strip. Wander alongside locals through sidewalk cafés or browse in bookstores, art galleries, and souvenir shops. No matter how aimlessly you meander, you'll invariably end up where you began. From South Terrace walk down to the Fishing Boat Harbour where there's always activity—commercial and pleasure craft bob about, and along the timber boardwalk is a cluster of outdoor eateries and a microbrewery.

Between Phillimore Street and Marine Terrace in the West End is a collection of some of the best-preserved heritage buildings in the state. The Fremantle Railway Station on Elder Place is another good spot to start a walk. Maps and details for 11 different are walks available at the Fremantle Visitor Center; a popular heritage walk is the Convict Trail, passing by 18 different sights and locations from Fremantle's convict past.

TOP ATTRACTIONS

The former **Fremantle Prison,** built in 1855, is where 44 inmates met their fate on the prison gallows between 1888 and 1964. Tours include the classic-art cell, where a superb collection of drawings by convict James Walsh decorates his quarters. Reservations are essential for the 90-minute Torchlight Tours (evening tours by flashlight). For the 2½-hour Tunnel Tour, visitors are provided with hard hats, overalls, boots, and headlamps before descending 65 feet into the labyrinthine tunnels that run beneath the prison; some of the tour is by boat in underground waterways. Reservations are essential. ⌧ *1 The Terrace6160* ☎ *08/9336–9200* ⊕ *www.fremantleprison.com* 🖃 *A\$18, including a 75-min tour; Torchlight Tour A\$24, Tunnel Tour A\$59* ☉ *Daily 10–5 with tour every 30 minutes, last tour at 5 PM. Torchlight Tours Wed. and Fri., regularly from 6:30 PM; last tour usually 9 PM. Tunnel Tour at 9, 9:45, 10:40, 12:20, 1:40, 2:40, 3:25.*

The **Fremantle Market**, housed in a classic Victorian building, sells everything from potatoes to paintings, incense to antiques, and sausages to Chinese takeout from around 150 stalls. On weekends and public holidays the market can get crowded, but a small café and bar make it a wonderful place to refresh yourself while street musicians entertain. ⌧ *South Terrace at Henderson St.6160* ☎ *08/9335–2515* ⊕ *www. fremantlemarkets.com.au* ☉ *Fri. 9–9, Sat. 9–5, Sun. and public holidays 10–5.*

Fodor's Choice The **Western Australian Maritime Museum**, which resembles an upside-
★ down boat, sits at the edge of Fremantle Harbour. It houses *Australia*
ⵣ *11*, winner of the 1983 America's Cup, and the hands-on exhibits are great fun for children. You can also take one-hour guided tours of the adjacent submarine *Ovens*, a former Royal Australian Navy World War II submarine. Tours depart from the maritime museum every 30 minutes; bookings are essential during school holidays. The Shipwreck Gallery houses the recovered remains of the Dutch wrecks, including the *Batavia* (wrecked offshore in 1629), and the 1872 SS *Xantho* steamer. ⌧ *Maritime Museum: west end of Victoria Quay; Shipwreck Gallery: Cliff St.* ☎ *08/9431–8444 museum, 08/9431–8444 gallery* ⊕ *www. museum.wa.gov.au/maritime* 🖃 *Museum A\$10 day pass, Ovens A\$8, museum and Ovens A\$15, gallery free* ☉ *Thurs.–Tues. 9:30–5.*

IF YOU HAVE TIME
Like most of Fremantle, the fine, Gothic Revival **Western Australian Museum–Fremantle History** was built by convicts in the 19th century. First used as a lunatic asylum, by 1900 it was overcrowded and nearly shut down. It became a home for elderly women until 1942, when the U.S. Navy turned it into its local headquarters. Artifacts trace the early days of Fremantle's history from pre-settlement times to the 1930s. The complex contains a restaurant and gift shop, and Sunday-afternoon courtyard concerts are a regular feature. ⌧ *Ord and Finnerty Sts.6160* ☎ *08/9430–7966* 🖃 *Donation suggested in museum* ☉ *Museum Thurs.–Tues. 9–5.*

A landmark of early Fremantle atop the limestone cliff known as Arthur's Head, the **Round House** was built in 1831 by convicts to house other convicts. This curious, 12-sided building is the state's oldest surviving structure. From its ramparts great vistas span out from High Street to the Indian Ocean. Underneath, a tunnel was carved through the cliffs in the mid-1800s to give ships lying at anchor offshore easy access from town. Volunteer guides are on duty during opening hours.

✉ *West end of High St.* ☎ *08/9336–6897* 🖃 *Donation suggested* ⏱ *Daily 10:30–3:30.*

Bounded by High, Queen, and William streets, **King's Square** is at the heart of the central business district. Shaded by 100-year-old Moreton Bay fig trees, it's a perfect place for a rest. Medieval-style benches complete the picture of European elegance. Bordering the square are **St. John's Anglican Church** and the **town hall.**

WHERE TO EAT

$–$$ ✕ **Capri Restaurant.** You may need to wait for a table, but the complimen-
ITALIAN tary minestrone and crusty bread will tide you over at this Fremantle institution. You'll get a warm welcome from the Pizzale family, who have owned and run the restaurant for more than 50 years, before you sit down to fried calamari, panfried scaloppini in white wine, rich spaghetti Bolognese, excellent steaks, and fresh salads. Simple white-linen tablecloths, carafes of chilled water, and the sounds of laughter and clinking glasses round out the experience. This is old-style Fremantle at its best. ✉ *21 South Terrace* ☎ *08/9335–1399* ▭ *MC, V.*

$–$$ ✕ **Cicerello's.** No visit to Fremantle is complete without a stop at this
SEAFOOD locally famous and widely beloved fish-and-chips shop. Housed in a boathouse-style building fronting the famous Fishing Boat Harbour, this joint serves the real thing: freshly caught oysters, mussels, crabs, fish, lobsters, and chips, all wrapped up in butcher paper (no cardboard boxes or plastic plates here). While you eat, you can check out the huge aquarium, where more than 50 species of Fremantle marine life swim. Cicerello's also has a restaurant in Mandurah. ✉ *Fisherman's Wharf, 44 Mews Rd.* ☎ *08/9335–1911* ✉ *73 Mandurah Terrace, Mandurah* ☎ *08/9535–9777* ⊕ *www.cicerellos.com.au* ▭ *No credit cards.*

$$–$$$ ✕ **The Essex.** This 1886 cottage is one of the best places for upscale dining
★ in Western Australia. Its elegant dining room has flickering candlelight,
SEAFOOD thick carpets, and antiques, and the fresh local seafood is excellent. Head chef Noel Friend offers an extensive menu, including twice-baked Kervella goat-cheese soufflé, grilled fillet of beef filled with local scallops, served with potato mash and garlic cream, and Tasmanian salmon with spiced Israeli couscous, sun-dried tomato tapenade, and Kaffir lime butter. Adventurous diners can opt for grilled Balmain bugs—not insects but the delicious tails of rock-lobsterlike crustaceans caught in ocean waters around Australia and New Zealand—a specialty of the region. The extensive wine list includes some of Australia's best vintages. ✉ *20 Essex St.* ☎ *08/9335–5725* ⊕ *www.essexrestaurant.com.au* ▭ *AE, DC, MC, V.*

$–$$ ✕ **Gino's Café.** There are 21 different ways to take your coffee at this cap-
ITALIAN puccino-strip property with an alfresco terrace. Among the most popular drinks are the house coffee (Gino's Blend), and the Baby Chino—a froth of milk dusted with chocolate powder that young children love. Gino's opens at 6 AM to serve coffee, then cooks breakfasts from 7:30. For lunch and dinner, more than two dozen different pasta dishes are available, including a superb penne alla vodka with chicken. ✉ *South Terrace at Collie St.* ☎ *08/9336–1464* ⊕ *www.ginoscafe.com.au* ▭ *MC, V.*

$$–$$$
SEAFOOD
✕ **Joe's Fish Shack.** Fremantle's quirkiest restaurant looks like everyone's vision of a run-down, weather-beaten Maine diner. With uninterrupted harbor views, authentic nautical bric-a-brac, and great food, you can't go wrong. Recommendations include the salt-and-pepper squid, stuffed tiger prawns, and chili mussels. An outdoor dining area provides restaurant food at take-out prices. ⊠ *42 Mews Rd.* ☎ *08/9336–7161* ⊕ *www.joesfish-shack.com.au* ⊟ *AE, DC, MC, V.*

WHERE TO STAY

$$$$
🕆 **Esplanade Hotel Fremantle.** Part of a colonial-era hotel, this establishment has provided accommodations (with sea views) for more than a century. The property is geared toward business travelers, and the stylish, bright pastel rooms have desks and in-room broadband. It's just a short walk to the heart of Fremantle's cappuccino strip and markets. Café Panache, right on the Esplanade, draws crowds all day, while the Atrium Garden Restaurant has a lavish buffet. **Pros:** central to Fremantle attractions; garden setting for heated pool; ample dining options nearby. **Cons:** sea views are limited to some rooms; functions can make venues crowded. ⊠ *Marine Terrace at Essex St.* ☎ *08/9432–4000 or 1800/998201* ⊕ *www.esplanadehotelfremantle.com.au* ➷ *293 rooms, 7 suites* ↺ *In-room: safe, refrigerator, Internet. In-hotel: 2 restaurants, pools, gym, laundry service, parking (fee)* ⊟ *AE, DC, MC, V.*

$$–$$$
🕆 **Fothergills of Fremantle.** Antiques and Italian pottery furnish this two-story, 1892 limestone terrace house opposite the old Fremantle prison. Food and service are excellent here, and although the house is some distance from the waterfront, the balconies have harbor and sunset views. Breakfast in the Provençal-style dining room is included. **Pros:** Heritage decor throughout; personalized service. **Cons:** some distance from central Fremantle; limited facilities on-site. ⊠ *20–22 Ord St.* ☎ *08/9335–6784* ⊕ *www.babs.com.au/fothergills* ➷ *7 rooms* ↺ *In-room: safe, refrigerator, DVD. In-hotel: restaurant, laundry facilities, Wi-Fi* ⊟ *AE, DC, MC, V* ⊙ *BP.*

$$$
🕆 **Fremantle Prison Cottages.** These three restored colonial-style cottages are next to the old Fremantle prison, just a few minutes' walk from town. Rooms are cozy, furnished in colonial style with lace curtains at the windows, eiderdown quilts on the antique wrought-iron beds, and Victorian era lamp shades. Each has a kitchen and laundry facilities, with TVs and microwave ovens. Fremantle Colonial Accommodation also has five self-contained apartments and four en-suite rooms in the nearby **Terrace House. Pros:** Australian colonial decor; kitchens well

THE CUP

In 1848, Britain's Queen Victoria authorized the creation of a solid silver cup for a yacht race that would be "open to all nations." In 1851, the New York Yacht Club challenged 16 English yachts and won with the boat *America.* The U.S. continued to win for 132 years straight until the upstart *Australia 11* won 4–3 in sensational style, and the Cup came to Fremantle. Australia was euphoric. Fremantle spruced up for the defense of the Cup in 1987, but the fairy tale ended in a 4–0 loss to the San Diego Yacht Club entrant. Today *Australia 11* is a centerpiece display at the WA Maritime Museum.

Kookaburra 12-metre yachts are tack-training for the Americas Cup.

equipped. **Cons:** no leisure facilities; some distance from central Fremantle. ✉ *215 High St.* ☎ *08/9430–6568* ⊕ *www.fremantlecolonialaccommodation.com.au* ⤵ *3 cottages, 5 apartments, 4 rooms* ⌂ *In-room: kitchen, DVD. In-hotel: laundry facilities, parking (no fee)* ☷ *AE, DC, MC, V.*

$

AUSTRALIAN

🏨 **Rosie O'Grady's Fremantle.** The restored heritage rooms of this Irish-theme, landmark Australian pub offer comfy lodging right in the middle of town. The deluxe rooms are spacious, and furnished with heavy pine furniture and floral print upholstery and bedspreads. Bars and a restaurant ($) are downstairs. **Pros:** large rooms with heritage decor; good-value beds for the area. **Cons:** bar downstairs can be noisy; parking is off-site. ✉ *23 William St.* ☎ *08/9335–1645* ⊕ *Fremantle.rosieogradys. com.au* ⤵ *17 rooms* ⌂ *In-hotel: restaurant, bar, parking (paid), no-smoking rooms (some), no elevator* ☷ *AE, DC, MC, V.*

NIGHTLIFE

There's nothing more pleasant than relaxing in the evening at one of the sidewalk tables on the cappuccino strip. This area, along South Terrace, opens at 6 AM and closes around 3 AM.

Dome Cafe (✉ *13 South Terrace* ☎ *08/9336–3040*) is a big, airy space that gets a little frantic during busy periods. **Little Creatures** (✉ *40 Mews Rd.* ☎ *08/9430–5555* ⊕ *www.littlecreatures.com.au*) is a funky bar and restaurant surrounded by a gleaming state-of-the-art microbrewery. The industrial-style warehouse building, which overlooks Fremantle's busy harbor, cuts into a courtyard. The pale ale is quite good. It's open weekdays 10 AM–midnight; weekends 9 AM–midnight.

Away from the waterfront, **Rosie O'Grady's** (✉ *23 William St.* ☎ *08/9335–1645*) is as Irish as it gets in the heart of Fremantle. Locals come for the numerous draft beers and filling food, as well as nightly live music. Thanks to its selection of home-brewed beers, the **Sail and Anchor Pub–Brewery** (✉ *64 South Terrace* ☎ *08/9431–1666*) is a popular watering hole. A shady courtyard beer garden makes a fair-weather gathering place.

Fremantle's swankiest nightclub, the **Clink** (✉ *14–16 South Terrace* ☎ *08/9336–1919* ⊕ *www.theclink.com.au*), caters to a well-dressed, sophisticated clientele Friday–Sunday. The industrial-style decor reflects the building's heritage—it used to be the police station with prison cells. Many local bands and soloists owe their big breaks to **Fly By Night Musicians Club** (✉ *1 Holdsworth St., at Parry St.* ☎ *08/9430–5976* ⊕ *www. flybynight.org*), a smoke-free venue.

In the heart of Fremantle's cappuccino strip, **Metropolis Concert Club Fremantle** (✉ *58 South Terrace* ☎ *08/9336–1880* ⊕ *www.metropolis-fremantle.com.au*), a nonstop techno and funk dance venue, is a great place to go on a Friday or Saturday night.

SHOPPING

At **Bannister Street Craftworks** (✉ *8–12 Bannister St.* ☎ *08/9336–2035*), a restored 19th-century warehouse, craftspeople have gathered in their own workshops to turn out everything from woodwork to glass engraving, wildlife painting, textile printing, stained glass, and pottery. The artists, working as a cooperative, invite you to come in and watch as they demonstrate their skills, or just to browse among the exhibits. All of the crafts on display are for sale.

Into Camelot (✉ *Shop 9, South Terrace Piazza* ☎☎ *08/9335–4698* ⊕ *www.intocamelot.com.au*), a medieval-style dress shop, sells romantic wedding gowns and cloaks, street and evening wear, and peasant smocks for all occasions. Period boots, classic Saxon and Celtic jewelry, and masks (feathered and plain) are sold at affordable prices.

Kakulas Sisters (✉ *29–31 Market St.* ☎ *08/9430–4445*), a unique produce shop, overflows with fragrances and sacks of goodies from across the globe, including Costa Rican coffee beans, Colorado black-eyed beans, Brazilian quince and guava pastries, and Japanese teas.

☺ A fairy theme pervades the **Pickled Fairy & Other Myths** (✉ *Shop 7B, South Terrace Piazza* ☎ *08/9430–5827* ⊕ *www.pickledfairy.com.au*), making it a delight for children and elves. Celtic jewelry is sold here, along with books on magic and mythology.

ROTTNEST ISLAND

19 km (12 mi) west of Fremantle.

An easy cruise from Fremantle, or down the Swan River from Perth, sunny, quirky Rottnest Island makes an ideal day trip. The island has an interesting past. Though records of human occupation date back 6,500 years, when Aboriginal people inhabited the area, European settlement only dates back to 1829. Since then the island has been used for a variety of purposes, including attempts at agriculture, as a location to reform young boys in trouble with the law, and for military purposes in both the Great War and the Second World War. The Rottnest Museum is a great place to get the history of the place, and you can take a train trip and tour to the Oliver Hill fort to see gun emplacements from the Second World War.

Of course most West Australians go to the island for the beaches, the swimming, and the laid-back atmosphere on Perth's doorstep.

GETTING HERE AND AROUND

Speedy air service to Rottnest Island flies from Perth's Jandakot airport with **Rottnest Air Taxi** (☎ 08/9292–5027 or 1800/500006). Round-trip fare is from A$72 per person, and the service operates daily, weather permitting. Flight time is around 15 minutes. Telephone for flight times. **Oceanic Cruises** (☎ 08/9325–1191 ⊕ www.oceaniccruises.com.au) and **Rottnest Express** (☎ 1300/467688 ⊕ www.rottnestexpress.com.au) run ferries to Rottnest Island from Fremantle, as well as from Perth, and **Rottnest Fast Ferries** (☎ 08/9246–1039 ⊕ rottnestfastferries.com.au) runs boats from Hillarys Boat Harbour. The ferries take approximately 25 minutes from Fremantle, 40 minutes from Hillarys, or an hour-plus from Perth—though the latter trip also includes a scenic cruise on the Swan River. Round-trip prices, including entry to Rottnest, are from A$59.50 per person from Fremantle and from A$74.50 per person from Perth and A$77 from Hillarys.

There are no taxis on Rottnest Island.

SAFETY AND PRECAUTIONS

Be sun-smart especially from October through April. Even on cloudy days people unused to being outdoors for any length of time can suffer severe sunburn. Wear a hat, long-sleeved shirt, and high-strength sunscreen. If you are a weak or novice swimmer, always swim with a friend; there are no lifesavers on Rottnest beaches.

TIMING

Rottnest Island can be visited in a day. An early ferry gets you to the island with plenty of time to tour the main attractions or beaches, returning to Fremantle or Perth in the late afternoon. Staying an extra day or two gives you time to laze at a beach or go surfing or diving.

TOURS

The **Rottnest Island Railway Train** (✉ Thomson Bay ☎ 08/9372–9732), known as the *Captain Hussey*, is an ideal way to see the island. The route from the Main Settlement to Oliver Hill is run daily at 11:30, 1:30, and 2:30, and connects with a guided tour of the historic Oliver Hill gun battery. The fare is A$23 and includes the guided tour. The train fare without the guided tours is A$17.50. Tickets are available at the visitor information center.

The **Bayseeker Bus** (✉ Thomson Bay ☎ 08/9372–9732), which runs a continuous hop-on, hop-off island circuit, picks up and drops off passengers at the most beautiful bays and beaches. Day tickets are A$110 and can be purchased from the Rottnest island Visitor Centre or the driver.

Wadjemup Aboriginal Bus Tour (☎ *08/9372–9749*) has 105-minute coach tours providing an insight into the traditions and spirituality of Aboriginal people who are believed to have occupied Rottnest back to a time when sea levels were so low the island was part of the mainland. The tour costs A$45 and departs from the Main Bus Stop at 11:15 AM and 1:45 PM daily.

The Rottnest Island Authority also runs a daily two-hour coach tour of the island's highlights, including convict-built cottages, World War II gun emplacements, and salt lakes. The Oliver Hill Railway made its debut in the mid-1990s, utilizing 6 km (4 mi) of reconstructed railway line to reach the island's gun batteries. Information is available from the Rottnest Island Visitor Information Centre.

ESSENTIALS

Banks and Currency Exchange Bankwest (☎ *13-1718* ⊕ *www.bankwest. com.au*) has an ATM adjacent to the Rottnest Island Authority office at the Main Settlement.

Medical Emergencies The Rottnest Nursing Post (✉ *Thomson Bay* ☎ *08/9292–5030* ⊙ *Daily 8:30–5*).

Police The police station is in Somerville Drive in the Main Settlement.

Visitors Information Rottnest Island Visitor Information Centre (✉ *Adjacent to Dome Café, Thomson Bay beachfront* ☎ *08/9372–9752* ⊕ *www.rottnestisland. com* ⊙ *Sat.–Thurs. 7:30– 6:15, Fri. 7:30–7:30*).

EXPLORING

The most convenient way to get around Rottnest is by bicycle, as cars are not allowed on the island and bus service is infrequent. A bicycle tour of the island covers 26 km (16 mi) and can take as little as three hours, although you really need an entire day to enjoy the beautiful surroundings

Heading south from Thomson Bay, between Government House and Herschell Lakes, is a quokka colony. Another colony lies down the road to the east, near the amphitheater at the civic center in sparkling Geordie Bay. Here tame quokkas eat right out of your hand.

Past the quokka colony are gun emplacements from World War II. As you continue south to Bickley Bay you can spot the wreckage of ships—the oldest dates from 1842—that came to rest on Rottnest's rocky coastline.

Follow the main road past Porpoise, Salmon, Strickland, and Wilson bays to West End, the westernmost point on the island and another graveyard for unfortunate vessels. Heading back to Thomson Bay, the road passes a dozen rocky inlets and bays. Parakeet Bay, the prettiest, is at the northernmost tip of the island.

You can rent bikes at **Rottnest Bike Hire** (✉ *Thomson Bay* ☎ *08/9292– 5105*) from A$19 per day, with a returnable deposit of A$25 per bike. Tandem bikes and pedal cars can also be rented. It's open daily 8:30–5, though hours vary according to the season.

At the Thomson Bay settlement, visit the **Rottnest Museum** (⊠ *Digby Dr., Thomson Bay* ☎ *08/9372–9732* 📧 *Donation suggested*), which includes mementos of the island's long and turbulent past. Displays show local geology, natural history, and maritime lore; there's also a convict building and an Aboriginal prison. It's open daily 10:45–3:30. The **Wadjemup Lighthouse Tours**—providing 360-degree panoramic views of Rottnest—allow the public into the Heritage-status lighthouse building for the first time in more than a century. Tours depart daily at 9 AM and cost A$30.

MARSUPIALS, NOT RATS

Quokkas were among the first Australian mammals ever seen by Europeans. In 1658, the Dutch Captain Willem De Vlamingh described them as rats, but in fact they are marsupials, carrying their young in a pouch. Once common around Perth, quokkas are now confined to isolated pockets on the mainland, but still thrive on their namesake Rottnest Island, where they are safe from predators (mainly foxes). Their cute, furry faces and small, round bodies make them very photogenic.

BEACHES

There are some 63 beaches on Rottnest Island, suitable for swimming, surfing, snorkeling, and diving. The most popular include Fish Hook Bay, Geordie Bay, Little Armstrong, Little Parakeet, Little Salmon Bay, Parakeet, Parker Point, Ricey Beach, Salmon Bay, Stark Bay, Strickland Bay, The Basin, and West End.

Surfers and bodyboarders will head for Stark Bay, Strickland Bay, and West End, while swimmers will enjoy sandy white beaches at The Basin, Geordie Bay, Parakeet and Little Parakeet, Ricy Beach, and Salmon Bay. Beach spots for snorkeling and diving include Fish Hook Bay, Salmon Bay, Parker Point, and Little Armstrong.

The Basin, West End, Parker Point, Stark Bay, Strickland Bay, and Geordie Bay have public toilets; however, there are no other amenities.

WHERE TO STAY

Accommodation on the island ranges from basic camping sites to self-contained holiday villas and hotels. Space is at a premium during the summer months, Easter, and school holidays, and there is a ballot system, with the closing dates months in advance. November sees the so-called "schoolies week," when high-school students boisterously celebrate the end of five years of high school. Outside these times, accommodation is easier to find. Check ⊕ *www.rottnestisland.com* for details.

$$$ 🏨 **Hotel Rottnest.** Previously known as the Rottnest Hotel, this property was once the official summer residence for the governors of Western Australia. Comfortable rooms, which overlook Thompson Bay or a grassy courtyard area, are motel-style, with cane furniture and neutral decor. As well as a popular beer garden, Hampton's Bar ($–$$) is open every day for lunch and dinner, and features a charcoal grill with buffet salad bar. **Pros:** overlooks pleasure craft at anchor; refurbished in 2008; casual atmosphere. **Cons:** beach not ideal for swimming; popular with day-trippers. ⊠ *Bedford Ave., Thomson Bay* ☎ *08/9292–5011*

Snorkelling at the Basin on Rottnest Island, Western Australia.

⊕ *www.hotelrottnest.com.au* ⤴ *18 rooms* ⚲ *In-hotel: restaurant, bar, pool* ▭ *AE, MC, V.*

$–$$$ 🏨 **Rottnest Lodge.** Rooms at the island's largest hotel range from premium to budget. After a day of walking or biking around the island you can take a dip in the pool or relax at the bar. The Marlin Restaurant ($$) serves up Thai seafood salad, chowder, and bruschetta with prawns and mangoes, and there's a buffet lunch from 11 to 2. **Pros:** close to shops and some attractions; some rooms have lake views; some rooms ideal for families. **Cons:** not on beachfront; limited leisure facilities. ✉ *Kitson St.* ☎ *08/9292–5161* ⊕ *www.rottnestlodge.com.au* ⤴ *78 rooms, 2 suites* ⚲ *In-room: refrigerator. In-hotel: restaurant, bar, pool* ▭ *AE, DC, MC, V.*

THE SOUTH-WEST WINE REGION

The South-West—Western Australia's most popular destination, with more than 1.5 million visitors annually—should not be missed if you are coming to this state, a fact well known by Perth residents who flock here year-round for the wines, beaches, and marine wildlife, forests, locally-produced crafts and artisan products, and the country vistas.

The region stretches from the port city of Bunbury—about two hours south of Perth by freeway and highway—through Busselton, Dunsborough, and on to Margaret River, a further 1½ hours south.

Margaret River is, perhaps, best known for its wines, but the South-West has wineries from well north of Bunbury to the south coast. Busselton, Dunsborough, and Margaret River are all suitable places to

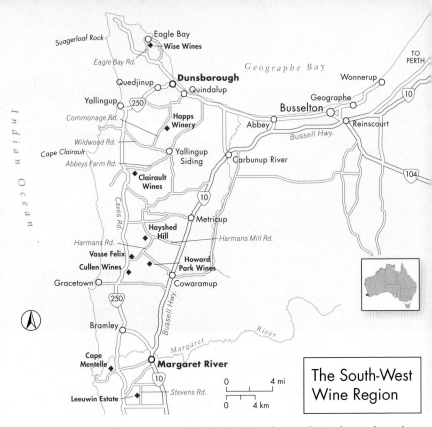

The South-West
Wine Region

stay if you want to visit wineries; Busselton and Dunsborough works for those who prefer calm family beaches (Margaret River is not on the coast).

The best surfing beaches are on the coast between Cape Naturaliste and Cape Leeuwin.

All major South-West towns have visitor centers that can arrange tours, book accommodations, and provide free information.

EN ROUTE Bunbury is a great stop-over point where you can visit the Dolphin Discovery Centre, swim with wild dolphins (in season), or wade in shallow waters with them under the watchful eye of center volunteers and biologists. About 100 bottlenose dolphins make their permanent home in and around the waters of Koombana Bay off Bunbury, making your chances of seeing them in their natural habitat very high. You can also take a dolphin cruise with Naturaliste Charters.

Bunbury Visitor Centre (⌂ Carmody Pl., Bunbury ☎ 08/9792-7205 ⊕ www. visitbunbury.com.au ⊙ Weekdays 9–5; weekends 9:30–4:30).

Dolphin Discovery Centre (EKoombana Dr., Bunbury P08/9791-3088 wdol-phins.mysouthwest.com.au ⊙ June–Sept., daily 9–2; May and Oct., daily 8–3; Nov.–Apr., daily 8–4 ☒ A$8).

Naturaliste Charters (☎ 08/9755-2276 ⊕ www.whalesaustralia.com).

DUNSBOROUGH
252 km (157 mi) south of Perth.

The attractive seaside town of Dunsborough is perfect for a few days of swimming, sunning, and fishing—which is why it's become a popular holiday destination for many Perth families. Onshore attractions include Meelup Beach, a protected cove with calm swimming water, and the nearby wineries of Margaret River. Offshore, you can dive on the wreck of the HMAS *Swan,* the former Royal Australian Navy ship deliberately sunk in Geographe Bay at the end of its useful life, or take a cruise to see migrating humpback and southern right whales September–December.

⚠ November sees so-called "schoolies week," when teenage students boisterously celebrate the end of five years of high school. Dunsborough is a popular destination.

GETTING HERE AND AROUND
Take Highway 1 down the coast from Perth to Bunbury, switch to Route 10 through Busselton, then Caves Road to Dunsborough. If you drive from Perth, it will take around 3 hours. Alternatively, **South West Coachlines** (☎ *08/9324–2333* ⊕ *southwestcoachlines.com.au*) has daily coach services from Perth Central Bus Station on Mounts Bay Road to South-West towns, including Dunsborough. Once here, a hire car is recommended, as there is very limited public transport, and some accommodations are in bushland or beach settings away from the towns.

Dunsborough Car Rentals (✉ *201 Geographe Bay Rd., Quindalup* ☎ *1800/449007* ⊕ *www.dunsboroughcarrentals.com.au*) has late-model vehicles available at reasonable rates for touring the Margaret River region.

SAFETY AND PRECAUTIONS
The calm waters of Geographe Bay are home to a jellyfish with a nasty sting—colloquially named "stingers." They are not deadly but they are painful, and a sting occasionally requires hospitalization. They are hard to spot—the main body of the stinger is translucent and only about 2 inches across, and they trail hard-to-see black tentacles that are the cause for concern. They like very calm water, so still days during the summer months are when you are most likely to encounter them as they drift close to shore. Rubbing a sting is not recommended; try bathing in vinegar.

Mosquitoes carrying Ross River virus are more prevalent in summer, and especially along the South-West coast. Ross River virus is not life-threatening, but can leave victims with weeks of fatigue, aching limbs, and painful joints. The only solution is to avoid being bitten by mosquitoes—cover up and use a repellent, especially around dawn and dusk, when mosquitoes are most active.

TIMING
Dunsborough (and the surrounding area) deserves at least two days, preferably three. Western Australian school holidays, especially the summer break over Christmas and New Year's Day, and Easter, are usually booked solid by Perth holidaymakers with families. One week in November is also crowded for "schoolies week." The summer months

(December–March) are best for swimming and beaches, while the heaviest surfing conditions are often best during the winter months (May–September) when wet suits are required.

TOURS

Cape Dive (⊠ *222 Naturaliste Terrace, Dunsborough* ☎ *08/9756–8778* ⊕ *www.capediveexperience.com* ☯ *Daily 9–5*) has dive tours to the wreck of the HMAS *Swan*, deliberately scuttled in 30 meters of water off Dunsborough to become an artificial reef and dive wreck. They also offer dives around the Busselton Jetty, where an abundance of corals and marine life have made their homes on the pylons.

Cellar d'Or Winery Tours (☎ *0428/179729* ⊕ *www.cellardortours.com.au*) has daily tours of Margaret River region wineries from A$75 per person. The tours include pick-up at your accommodation, wine tastings at five wineries, platter lunch, beer tasting, chocolate sampling, cheese and local produce tasting, and morning and afternoon coffee and tea.

Busselton Jetty and Underwater Observatory (⊠ *Beachfront, Busselton* ☎ *08/9754–0900* ⊕ *www.busseltonjetty.co.au* ☯ *Interpretive Center May–Nov., daily 9–5; Dec.–Apr., daily 8–6. Underwater Observatory May–Nov., daily 9–5; Dec.–Apr., daily 8–5* ⊠ *Jetty and Underwater Observatory Tour A$22.50; jetty only A$2.50; Interpretive Centre free*). At almost two km, the 143-year-old Busselton Jetty is the longest timber jetty in the southern hemisphere. You can visit the Interpretive Center at the start of the jetty, then walk 1.9 km to the Underwater Observatory, where tours for up to 40 people are run every hour. The observatory allows visitors to walk down a spiral staircase to some 12 meters below the water, observing the marine life through large acrylic windows. The warm Leeuwin Current and the sheltering effect of the jetty above has created a unique microclimate rich with colorful tropical and sub-tropical corals, sponges, fish, and invertebrates.

ESSENTIALS

All major credit cards are widely accepted at restaurants, lodgings, and shops. Mastercard and Visa are always taken; American Express and Diners Club are less acceptable and the merchant may add a small surcharge.

Medical Emergencies Busselton Hospital (⊠ *Mill Rd., Busselton* ☎ *08/9754–0333*).

Police Police (☎ *13–1444 assistance, 08/9222–1111 general inquiries*).

Taxi Dunsborough Taxis (☎ *08/9756–8688*).

Visitors Information Dunsborough Visitor Centre (⊠ *Shop 14, Dunsborough Park Shopping Centre., Dunsborough* ☎ *08/9752–1288* ⊕ *www.geographebay. com* ☯ *Mon.–Fri. 9–5; Sat. 9:30–4:30; Sun. 10–2*). **Busselton Visitor Centre** (⊠ *38 Peel Terrace, Busselton* ☎ *08/9752–1288* ⊕ *www.geographebay.com* ☯ *Mon.–Fri. 9–5; Sat. 9–4; Sun. 10–4*).

OUTDOOR ACTIVITIES

The north-facing coastline of Geographe Bay from Busselton to Cape Naturaliste—unique in Western Australia because of its aspect—provides long sandy beaches and coves readily accessible from Dunsborough. From Dunsborough village, simply walk about 500 meters down to the sandy beach, which stretches east and west for miles. Heading toward Cape Naturaliste, the coastline changes into sandy bays and coves bracketed by rocky headlands. Meelup Beach is popular with families; its sister beach, Castle Rock, just around the headland, is a little quieter. Another charming sheltered beach is Eagle Bay, closer to the cape, with multimillion-dollar homes perched along the hillside. The only facilities you will find at these beaches are public toilets.

EXPLORING THE WINERIES

Happs Winery. Hand-made mudbricks, recycled timbers, and stained-glass windows point back to the origins of this family-owned and -built winery that is one of the pioneers in the Margaret River wine region. Just a few kilometers from Dunsborough you'll find a friendly welcome, a huge range of wines to taste (26 at last reckoning) and—unique in this area—a working pottery in the same building. Erl Happ began the winery, planting his first vines in 1978, going against local wisdom by putting in 31 varieties, building the winery himself, and producing pottery for sale. Later, a second vineyard was established near Karridale some 90 km (55 mi.) to the south, its wines produced under the Three Hills label. Free tastings allow you to try some wines only available at the cellar door, such as Sweet Rosie Jane and Muscat a Pink. His daughter-in-law Jacquie now runs the pottery, where you are almost certain to see a potter at work. ⊠ *575 Commonage Rd., Dunsborough* ☎ *08/9755–3300* ⊕ *www.happs.com.au* ☯ *Daily 10–5.*

★ **Clairault Wines.** One of the few family-owned wineries in the region is also one of the region's best, known for its award-winning Cabernet Merlot, Cabernet Sauvignon, and Chardonnay. Set in a natural bushland about 18 km (11 mi) south of Dunsborough, the cellar door is in a modern style with polished timber floors, natural stone, and walls of glass overlooking the bushland. The spacious restaurant (open daily for lunch, noon–3) has glass doors that open on to a large timber deck in warm weather, while two huge stone fireplaces warm the tables in winter. The winery and restaurant are popular for weddings, especially during the spring and fall months. ⊠ *Caves Rd., Wilyabrup* ☎ *08/9755–6225* ⊕ *www.clairault.com.au.*

Wise Wines. The view from the hilltop overlooking Geographe Bay is almost as good as the wines at this northernmost winery in the region, about a 15-minute drive from Dunsborough towards Cape Naturaliste. Their wines have received accolades, especially their Semillon Sauvignon Blanc and Chardonnay. The adjacent Wise Vineyard restaurant is open for lunches, dinner on Friday and Saturday nights, and breakfasts on Saturday and Sunday. Five homey chalets with names such as Teahouse, Potter's Cottage, and Doll House are also available for accommodation. ⊠ *80 Eagle Bay Rd., Dunsborough* ☎ *08/9756–8098* ⊕ *www.wisewine.com.au* ☯ *Daily 10–5.*

NEED A BREAK?

When you have had your fill of wineries, or just need something for your sweet tooth, head on down to Simmo's, about a five-minute drive from Dunsborough. Simmo's Ice Creamery and Fun Park (⊠ *161 Commonage Rd., Dunsborough* ☎ *08/9755–3745* ⊕ *www.simmos.com.au* ☯ *Daily*

9

10:30–5) is an institution for families and sweet tooths whatever the season. Their menu includes up to 39 different flavored ice creams and sorbets, made fresh daily, to have in cones, waffles, and sundaes. There's coffee to go, and—for the kids—a great fun park with games including mini-golf, giant snakes and ladders, Twister, and Tower Blocks. You can have a picnic in the shady grounds and meet Edward, the ice cream–eating emu. Irishmen Gordon and Garth Simpson set up Simmos in 1993, using family recipes.

WORD OF MOUTH

"If you base yourself at Dunsborough or Margaret River you will be able to visit the large number of wineries and other attractions which are close by. However, these places become very popular especially during the Christmas and school holidays." —albaaust

WHERE TO EAT AND STAY

$$–$$$
AUSTRALIAN

✕ **Wise Vineyard Restaurant.** Verdant bushland and a carefully manicured vineyard surround Heath Townsend's restaurant at the Wise winery. Simple, mostly local ingredients are transformed into such culinary delights as twice-cooked duck with porcini mushroom risotto; and lamb rump on a white bean mash. Views of Geographe Bay complete the dining experience. Reservations for the restaurant are essential. ⊠ *80 Eagle Bay Rd.* ☎ *08/9755–3331* ⊕ *www.wisefood.com* ⊟ *AE, DC, MC, V* ⊗ *No dinner Sun.–Thurs.*

$

▦ **Dunsborough Central Motel.** This motel for the dollar-conscious provides comfortable accommodations and proximity to town and the beach. Rooms are equipped with a range of amenities, including electric kettles and coffee and tea, while the property includes a swimming pool and barbecue area. An arrangement with selected local restaurants allows you to charge your dining bill back to your room account. **Pros:** good-value beds for the area; close to shops and dining options. **Cons:** not on the beachfront; no restaurant. ⊠ *50 Dunn Bay Rd.* ☎ *08/9756–7711* ⊕ *www.dunsboroughmotel.com.au* ⟿ *48 rooms* ♿ *In-room: kitchen (some), Internet. In-hotel: pool, parking (no fee)* ⊟ *AE, DC, MC, V.*

$$$

▦ **Quay West Bunker Bay Resort.** Sprawling down the hillside of the Cape Naturaliste Ridge in bushland, Bunker Bay Resort occupies a rare location with north-facing views of the calm blue waters of Geographe Bay. This villa property has one-, two-, and three-bedroom apartments, each with its own private courtyard. Villas are light and bright thanks to cathedral ceilings, and are finished in natural materials like limestone and Western Australia's famous jarrah timber. The property is also home to the award-winning restaurant the Other Side of the Moon and a day spa. **Pros:** large rooms; quiet environment; walk straight onto the beach. **Cons:** limited sea views from rooms; own transport essential; no shopping nearby; limited dining options nearby. ⊠ *Bunker Bay Rd. off Cape Naturaliste Rd.* ☎ *1800/010449 or 08/9756–9100* ⊕ *www. mirvachotels.com.au* ⟿ *150 villas* ♿ *In-room: Internet, kitchen, DVD. In-hotel: restaurant, bar, concierge, tennis courts, pool, gym, spa, laundry service, parking (no fee)* ⊟ *AE, DC, MC, V.*

LEEUWIN–NATURALISTE NATIONAL PARK

The northernmost part of the park is 266 km (165 mi) south of Perth, 25 km (16 mi) northwest of Dunsborough.

Leeuwin-Naturaliste National Park lies along one of Western Australia's most spectacular coastlines, from Cape Naturaliste on Geographe Bay in the north to Augusta, close to Cape Leeuwin in the south. The park is not a composite destination, rather a narrow patchwork of protected areas along the coast, intersected by beach access roads and small beachside villages.

The mostly-unspoiled coastal vistas are as awe-inspiring as any in the world—on a calm day the view northwards from Yallingup past Sugarloaf Rock towards Cape Naturaliste is nature at its best. Farther south, between Cowaramup Bay and Karridale, scenic lookouts allow you to access coastal cliffs and rocky shoreline that bears the brunt of giant ocean swells generated across thousands of miles of the Indian Ocean.

In addition to the scenic attractions of the coast, the park sits over limestone ridges where numerous caves have formed over the millennia, leached out by dripping water; a number of these caves are open to the public, including Lake, Mammoth, Jewel, and Ngilgi. Boranup Karri Forest, near Karridale, is the largest "patch," and creates a contrast to the coast—the distinctive, pale-bark hardwood giants reach 190 feet or more and dominate the hills and valleys of this area. This is the farthest west that karri trees grow in Western Australia, and, interestingly, Boranup is a regrowth forest; it was cut over by loggers more than 100 years ago, and 1961 wildfire destroyed many trees.

GETTING HERE AND AROUND

Take Highway 1 south from Perth to Bunbury, switch to Route 10 through Busselton to Dunsborough. Because of its patchwork boundaries, Leeuwin-Naturaliste National Park can be accessed at many points along the coast. Caves Road, a secondary road from Dunsborough to Augusta, provides the best access—all the side roads to the best coastal spots come off this road. Only on a section through the Boranup Karri Forest does Caves Road actually travel through the park for any distance. Marked trails are available from most of the coastal carparks; they vary from an easy 1-km (½-mi) trail from the carpark at Cape Naturaliste Lighthouse to a challenging 20-km (12-mi) full-day hike between Cosy Corner and Skippy Rock, near Augusta.

SAFETY AND PRECAUTIONS

Although the temptation is to climb all over the rocky outcrops, such as Canal Rocks, Sugarloaf Rock, and Skippy Rock, be aware of "king waves" that rise up with little warning from the ocean. Occasionally people have been swept from the rocks to their deaths. Take note of the warning signs; at a few locations lifebuoys have been stationed for just such incidents.

TIMING

Any time of the year is suitable for visiting the park. You can picnic, go for a scenic drive, explore the caves, and go fishing, surfing, and bushwalking year-round. The summer months are best for swimming and snorkeling, while whale-watching months are usually from June–December.

TOURS

Blue Spirit Surf and Adventure Retreats (⊠ *Box 1876, 6285* ☎ *08/9757–9284* ⊕ *www.bluespiritretreats.com.au*) offers Cape-to-Cape assisted walks to people who would like to walk all (135 km [84 mi], about seven days) or sections of the Cape-to-Cape Walk Trail. Blue Spirit provides a drop-off and pick-up service between your accommodation and the trail, allowing you to walk without having to carry luggage. They will also pre-book your accommodations—your choice, or they will make recommendations—plus provide picnic packs and a guide for the day if you wish.

Bushtucker Tours (☎ *08/9757–9084* ⊕ *www.bushtuckertours.com*) has canoe, cave, and bush-tucker tours daily from Margaret River. The tours give you an opportunity to see inaccessible parts of the Margaret River, Aboriginal sites, and caves while canoeing sections of the Margaret River down to the mouth at Surfers Point. A short walk shows you the rich variety of "bush tucker" Aboriginals would have eaten, while lunch includes a selection of authentic bush-tucker foods. The tours take about four hours.

EXPLORING

At the northern end of the park stands **Cape Naturaliste Lighthouse,** open daily 9–4:30 (last entry at 4); school and public holidays daily 9–5 (last entry at 4:30). Fully guided tours of the lighthouse cost A$11.50. A 1½-km-long (1-mi-long) trail leads from Cape Naturaliste to Canal Rocks, passing rugged cliffs, quiet bays, and curving beaches. This is also the start of the 120-km (75-mi) Cape-to-Cape Walk. Four major cave systems are easily accessible. The **CaveWorks** (☎ *08/9757–7411* ✉ *caveworks@margaretriver.com*) display center at Lake Cave presents a good introduction to the whole cave system. CaveWorks is open daily from 9–5. **Jewel** (☎ *08/9757–7411*), the southernmost of the system, has one of the longest straw stalactites in any tourist cave in the world. It's open daily with tours every hour 9:30 AM–3:30 PM. **Lake** (☎ *08/9757–7411*), centered around a tranquil, eerie-looking underground lake, is also open daily with tours every hour 9:30–3:30. Tour cost at both Jewel and Lake caves is A$19.50. **Mammoth** (☎ *08/9757–7411*), which has ancient fossil remains of extinct animals, is open daily 9–5, with the last entry at 4. Self-guided tours cost A$19.50. **Ngilgi** (☎ *08/9755–2152*), near Yallingup, is a main site for adventure caving. It's open daily 9:30–4:30, staying open to 5 PM during summer school holidays. Semi-guided cave tours cost A$18.50 and run every half hour. Adventure caving tours operate at 9:30 AM Monday to Friday. Pre-booking at least 48 hours in advance is highly recommended. Adventure tours cost from A$42 to A$135, and vary from 2 to 4 hours in length, depending on the tour.

The view from the top of the **Cape Leeuwin Lighthouse** (☎ *08/9758–1920* ⊕ *www.margaretriver.com*), a 10-minute drive south of Augusta and the third-highest working lighthouse in Australia, allows you to witness the meeting of the Southern and the Indian oceans. In some places

Canal Rocks near Yallingup, Leeuwin-Naturaliste National Park, Western Australia.

this alliance results in giant swells that crash against the rocks. In others, small coves are blessed with calm waters ideal for swimming. The lighthouse precinct is open daily 8:45–5, entry is A$5. Guided tours to the top of the lighthouse cost A$14 and run daily every 40 minutes. The last tour is at 4:20 PM.

CAMPING

Campgrounds with toilets and barbecues are at Conto (Conto Road off Caves Road) and Boranup (southern end of Boranup Drive, off Caves Road) and cost A$6.50 per adult per night. For more information on camping in the state, visit ⊕ *www.naturebase.net*.

MARGARET RIVER

★ *181 km (112 mi) south of Perth, 38 km (24 mi) south of Cape Naturaliste.*

The town of Margaret River is considered the center of the South-West's wine region, though vineyards and wineries stretch from well north of Bunbury to the south coast. Nevertheless, close to Margaret River are some 90 wineries offering tastings and sales of some of the world's best wines. The region, often compared to France's Bordeaux for its similar climate and soils, produces only around 1% of Australia's total wine grape crush, but this is spread into around 25% of the country's premium and ultrapremium wines. Both red and white vintages here are exceptional, the most notable labels toting Chardonnay, Sauvignon Blanc, or Sauvignon Blanc–Semillon, and Cabernet-Merlot blends.

GETTING HERE AND AROUND

Take Highway 1 south from Perth to Bunbury, switch to Route 10 through Busselton and on to Margaret River. Once here, you are best advised to rent a car. Public transport is non-existent around the area, and using taxis will soon blow the budget. The best accommodation—farmstays, bushland chalets, and boutique hotels—as well as the wineries, the beaches, and other attractions, are outside the town, and you need your own transportation to reach them.

SAFETY AND PRECAUTIONS

You are unlikely to have any personal safety concerns in the Margaret River area, except, perhaps, on the roads. Many of the roads leading to the wineries, the beaches, and your accommodation are narrow and winding, though traffic is usually light. While the roads are mostly paved, driveways into properties are often gravel roads, which need to be negotiated with care. As a precaution, you should avoid leaving expensive items, such as cameras, in your car when parked at attractions or overnight at accommodation.

TIMING

Margaret River is a year-round destination, with each season bringing its pleasures. Summer is generally busier, especially December and January, as families from Perth arrive during the school holidays. Winter (May–Sept.) brings rain and cooler temperatures, but the paddocks are green and there are not too many days when the rain doesn't ease to showers with lengthy fine breaks in between. If you are traveling from Perth, you can easily spend a week in the region; at the least, try to schedule several days to truly appreciate the area's attractions.

TOURS

Margaret River Visitor Centre is the best starting point if you want to do a tour. They will find the right tour for you, make the booking, and arrange pick-up at your accommodation if necessary. Tour operators in the area offer tours as diverse as wineries and food tasting, horse-back riding, surfing, bushwalks, whale-watching, scenic flights, mountain biking, river cruises, rock climbing, and abseiling.

ESSENTIALS

Banks and Currency Exchange Banks where you can exchange money and cash travelers checks, including ANZ, Westpac, National Australia, Bankwest, and the Commonwealth Bank, are open weekdays, generally 9:30–4. There are ATMs (which accept Cirrus, Plus, Visa, and MasterCard), and all major credit cards are widely accepted at restaurants, lodgings, and shops.

Medical Emergencies Margaret River Hospital (✉ *Farrelly St., Margaret River* ☎ *08/9757–0400*).

Police (☎ 13–1444 assistance, 08/9222–1111 general inquiries).

Taxi Margaret River Taxis (☎ *08/9757–3444*).

Visitors Information Margaret River Visitor Centre (✉ *100 Bussell Hwy., Margaret River* ☎ *08/9780–5911* ⊕ *www.margaretriver.com* ⊙ *Daily 9–5*) has extensive information on the region. The friendly staff will answer all your questions, and can book accommodation, tours, and activities at no additional cost.

EXPLORING THE WINERIES

Cape Mentelle. One of the "founding five" wineries in the area, Cape Mentelle planted their first vines in 1970 on a 16-hectare block just outside Margaret River. Today it's still one of the most notable wineries. The adobe-style rammed-earth building and tasting rooms, so typical of the buildings in the Margaret River district, are as handsome and memorable as the wine. The winery produces Chardonnay, Sauvignon Blanc, Semillon, Cabernet/Merlot, Cabernet Sauvignon, Shiraz, and Zinfandel wines. "Behind-the-scenes" tours (A$25) are available Mondays, Wednesdays, and Saturdays at 11:30 AM, while Tasting Plates (A$39.95 for two) are served daily between noon and 3 PM. In summer, visitors take time out for impromptu games of petanque. ⊠ *Wallcliffe Rd., 3 km (2 mi) west of Margaret River* ☎ *08/9757–0888* ⊕ *www. capementelle.com.au* ⊘ *Daily 10–4:30.*

Cullen Wines. The late industry patriarch Dr. Kevin Cullen established this winery in 1971. Today his daughter Vanya runs the operation. It's one of the few vineyards and wineries in Australia to produce wines using biodynamic practices. Their flagship wines—Sauvignon Blanc Semillon, Chardonnay, Merlot, and Cabernet Sauvignon–Merlot—can be sampled at their charming, small tasting room. The granite and timber building includes a small restaurant, where a wall of glass provides great views across the vineyards. The restaurant serves only organic or biodynamically grown foods. ⊠ *Caves and Harman S Rds., Wilyabrup* ☎ *08/9755–5277* ⊕ *www.cullenwines.com.au* ⊘ *Daily 10–4:30.*

Hayshed Hill. Winemaker Michael Kerrigan—formerly chief winemaker at neighboring Howard Park and Madfish Wines—has taken the reins at Hayshed Hill with the view of producing "modern wines from old vines." The hands-on approach in using the best grapes from the 30-year-old plantings at Hayshed Hill has won show awards and lavish endorsements by wine writers. The tasting room breaks from the usual Margaret River vernacular architecture—no rammed earth, timber, and stone here, rather a lovely white-painted clapboard building, polished concrete floors, and pitched ceiling. As the name suggests, the building is the original hayshed on what was a dairy farm. The adjacent winery has now been turned into a pleasant café, where you can get a casual lunch—pizzas, curries, and cold meat and cheese platters. Also available is a large selection of Australian and imported cheeses from Spain, France, Italy, and the UK. ⊠ *511 Harmans Mill Rd., Wilyabrup* ☎ *08/9755–6046* ⊕ *hayshedhill.com.au* ⊘ *Daily 10–5*

Howard Park Wines. Feng Shui principles were used to design the spacious tastings room at Howard Park's Margaret River winery (they also have another operation at Denmark in the Great Southern Region). The polished timber ceiling soars up 30 feet above a generous bar, capable of handling a couple of coachloads of visitors at once. Floor-to-ceiling windows allow in plenty of light as well as giving views over the property, and even the door has specific measurements to allow good luck to flow through. Wines produced under the Howard Park label include Riesling, Chardonnay, Sauvignon Blanc, and Cabernet Sauvignon. They also have a second range called Madfish (named after a small bay near Denmark on the south coast), which is extremely popular. ⊠ *Miamup Rd.,*

Cowaramup ☎ *08/9756–5200* ⊕ *www.howardparkwines.com.au* ⊙ *Daily 10–5.*

★ **Leeuwin Estate.** Their Art Series wines—especially the Chardonnay and Cabernet Sauvignon—have a deserved reputation as some of the best in the country. Tastings and guided tours (A$12.50) are conducted on the property daily at 11 AM, noon, and 3 PM, and the restaurant has daily lunch and Saturday dinner. In February the estate holds a series of concerts, and many international superstars—including John Farnham, Tom Jones, Diana Ross, Sting, and the late Ray Charles—have performed there against a backdrop of floodlighted karri trees. ⊠ *Stevens Rd. off Gnarawary Rd.* ☎ *08/9757–9000* ⊕ *www.leeuwinestate. com.au* ⊙ *Daily 10–5.*

Vasse Felix. Here you'll find an excellent upstairs restaurant, a basement cellar, landscaped grounds, and an art gallery, which houses regular exhibitions from the celebrated Holmes à Court Collection, featuring works from Arthur Boyd, Sidney Nolan, Lloyd Rees, and other prominent Australian artists. The estate wines—Semillon, Sauvignon Blanc Semillon, Chardonnay, Cabernet Merlot, Shiraz, and Cabernet Sauvignon—come from vines planted as far back as 1967, when pioneer Dr. Tom Cullity established Vasse Felix as the first commercial winery in the area. A small gift shop adjacent to the tasting room features clothing with the Vasse Felix logo—the peregrine falcon. ⊠ *Harmans S and Caves Rds., Cowaramup* ☎ *08/9756–5000* ⊕ *www.vassefelix.com.au* ⊙ *Daily 10–4:30.*

OUTDOOR ACTIVITIES

HIKING Marked trails through the Leeuwin-Naturaliste National Park provide many opportunities for hiking through the natural bushland and on coastal walks, with vistas along untouched rugged cliffs, rocky outcrops, and sandy bays. The **Cape-to-Cape Walk Track** runs 140 km (87 mi) from Cape Naturaliste to Cape Leeuwin, but can be broken into shorter sections. You will find the start points generally at beachside carparks. **Canal Rocks to Wyadup** is a 2-hour return walk from the carpark on Canal Rocks Road; a one-hour walk via beach, rocks, and bushland begins at the Leeuwin Waterwheel, near Cape Leeuwin Lighthouse in Augusta; and, a 4-hour walk with expansive coastal views starts at the Hamelin Bay boat ramp and heads to Cosy Corner.

Away from the coast, a popular short walk is from the historic homestead of **Ellensbrook** (Ellensbrook Road, off Caves Road, 13 km (8 mi) from Margaret River). The walk takes about 40 minutes to the **Meekadarabee Falls**, known to Aboriginal people as the "bathing place of the moon," and is best in winter and spring.

Brochures and maps on all walk trails in the region are available from the Margaret River Visitor Centre.

WHERE TO EAT

$–$$ ✕ **Flutes Restaurant.** The pastoral setting—over the dammed waters of
★   Wilyabrup Brook and encircled by olive groves in the midst of the
AUSTRALIAN Brookland Valley Vineyard—is almost as compelling as the food. The modern Australian cooking by executive chef François Morvan makes use of prime local produce. Try the beef fillet and braised cheek, with

a wild mushroom sauce, or the signature dish of Pemberton marron, Tasmanian salmon, wild Kimberley barramundi with goat's cheese, and macadamia-nut crumble. ☒ *Caves Rd., 5 km (3 mi) south of Metricup Rd.* ☎ *08/9755–6250* ⊕ *www.flutes.com.au* ⌂ *Reservations essential* ⊙ *Daily from noon, dinner reservations for 10 or more* ☰ *AE, DC, MC, V.*

$$–$$$ ✕ **Lamont's Margaret River.** The signature dish at this lovely lakefront res-
AUSTRALIAN taurant is the local marron—served grilled with roasted baby potatoes and a lime-and-chive beurre blanc. Another sure bet is the vine-leaf and prosciutto-wrapped chicken. You can also stop in for wine tasting and sales at their winery (⊙ *Thurs.–Mon. 11–5*) without having to dine at the restaurant. ☒ *Lot 1, Gunyulgup Valley Dr., Yallingup* ☎ *08/9755–2434*⊕ *www.lamonts.com.au* ☰ *AE, DC, MC, V* ⊙ *No lunch Tues., Wed. Dinner Sat.*

WHERE TO STAY

$$$ ⊡ **Basildene Manor.** Each of the rooms in this grand, circa-1912 house has been lovingly refurbished. Rich lilacs, golds, and reds decorate the guest rooms. Breakfast—included in the rates—is served in the conservatory, where you can look out over the property's 14 beautifully landscaped acres. **Pros:** large, heritage decor rooms; lavish breakfast; in quiet location. **Cons:** limited leisure facilities; own transport essential; no dining options nearby. ☒ *100 Wallcliffe Rd.* ☎ *08/9757–3140* ⊕ *www.basildene.com.au* ⇆ *17 rooms* ⌂ *In-room: refrigerator. In-hotel: restaurant, pool, laundry facilities, parking (no fee)* ☰ *AE, DC, MC, V* ⎮⊙⎮ *BP.*

$$$$ ⊡ **Cape Lodge.** The Cape Dutch architecture perfectly suits this elegant
Fodor's Choice lodge in the midst of Margaret River wine country. Since undergo-
★ ing a A$3 million refurbishment in 2004, the property now offers 22 luxury suites, a lakeside restaurant with over-water alfresco dining, and a 14,000-bottle, temperature-controlled wine cellar stocked with premium vintage Margaret River wines. Several of the opulent and spacious suites have their own balconies or terraces overlooking a private lake; others look out over woodlands or gardens. **Pros:** intimate country estate atmosphere; large, luxurious rooms; highly-regarded restaurant. **Cons:** no shopping nearby; limited dining options nearby; own transport essential. ☒ *1344 Caves Rd., Yallingup, WA* ☎ *08/9755–6311* ⊕ *www.capelodge.com.au* ⇆ *22 suites* ⌂ *In-room: DVD. In-hotel: restaurant, room service, tennis court, pool, parking (no fee), no kids under 15* ☰ *AE, DC, MC, V* ⎮⊙⎮ *CP.*

$–$$$ ⊡ **Gilgara Retreat.** This stunning property, a replica of an 1870 station homestead, sits amid 23 gently rolling, bucolic acres. Antiques and lace furnish the romantic rooms in the Main Lodge, so it's no surprise that honeymooners frequently choose to stay here. A rose-covered veranda, open fireplaces, and a cozy lounge add to the charm. Eight suites in a separate wing have self-catering facilities. You might breakfast surrounded by spectacular blue wrens and sacred ibises, or catch a few kangaroos lounging near the front door. Rates include a Mediterranean-style breakfast in the Main Lodge. **Pros:** private lounge with log fire for Lodge guests; lavish breakfast; birdlife abundant. **Cons:** standard rooms are small; no shopping nearby, limited dining options nearby;

9

own transport essential. ✉ *Caves and Carter Rds.* ☎ *08/9757–2705* ⊕ *www.gilgara.com.au* ⮡ *6 rooms, 8 suites* ⚴ *In-room: no phone, no TV (some), kitchen (some). In-hotel: laundry facilities, parking (no fee), no kids under 15* ▭ *AE, DC, MC, V* ⧆ *BP (some).*

$$$ ⛺ **Heritage Trail Lodge.** Nestled among the trees, this luxury retreat is only about ½ km (¼ mi) from Margaret River township. Spacious suites have hot tubs, king-size beds, and private balconies overlooking the forest. Walk the trails early, then enjoy a complimentary Continental breakfast of local produce in the conservatory. **Pros:** walking trails nearby; minutes walk to shops and restaurants; bushland setting. **Cons:** no leisure facilities; children discouraged. ✉ *31 Bussell Hwy.,* ☎ *08/9757–9595* ⊕ *www.heritage-trail-lodge.com.au* ⮡ *10 suites* ⚴ *In-room: DVD. In-hotel: laundry facilities, public Wi-Fi, parking (no fee)* ▭ *AE, DC, MC, V* ⧆ *CP.*

**EN
ROUTE**   Rustic timber cottages and historic buildings characterize the small, lovely town of **Nannup,** 100 km (62 mi) east of Margaret River. Several scenic drives wind through the area, including the Blackwood River Tourist Drive, a 10-km (6-mi) ride along a section of river surrounded by hills with karri and jarrah forests. You can also canoe on the Blackwood River and wander through the Blythe Gardens. If you'd like to spend the night, **Holberry House** (☎ *08/9756–1276* ⊕ *www.holberryhouse.com*), a charming colonial B&B with exposed beams and stone fireplaces, sits amid timbered acres overlooking the Blackwood Valley.

Travel Smart

WORD OF MOUTH

"I recently spent 12 days driving from Sydney up to Cairns (tried to save money by not flying) and found that I didn't have a lot of time to see everything I wanted as a result! The first thing I'd say is not to underestimate how big Australia is!"

—kristieb

GETTING HERE & AROUND

Australia is divided into six states and two territories—Northern Territory (NT) and Australian Capital Territory (ACT)—similar to the District of Columbia. Tasmania, the smallest state, is an island off mainland Australia's southeast point.

■ BY AIR

Sydney is Australia's main international hub, though it is also easy to get international flights to Melbourne, Brisbane, Cairns, and Perth. You can catch nonstop or one-stop flights to Australia from New York (21 hours via Los Angeles); Chicago (19 hours via Los Angeles); Los Angeles (14 hours nonstop); Vancouver (17 hours via Honolulu); Toronto (20 hours via Los Angeles); and London (20–24 hours via Hong Kong, Singapore, or Bangkok).

Since Pacific-route flights from the United States to Australia cross the international dateline, you lose a day, but regain it on the journey home.

Airlines and Airports Airline and Airport Links.com (⊕ www.airlineandairportlinks.com) has links to many of the world's airlines and airports.

Airline Security Issues Transportation Security Administration (⊕ www.tsa.gov) has answers for almost every question that might come up.

AIRPORTS

Sydney Airport (SYD) is Australia's main air hub and the first port of call for more than half of the country's visitors. Terminal 1 is for all international flights, Qantas domestic flights operate out of Terminal 3, and Terminal 2 is for all other domestic flights (including Qantaslink and Jetstar). A rail link connects the terminals underground, and frequent shuttle buses run between them aboveground. There is an excellent range of shops and restaurants in the international terminal.

Brisbane International Airport (BNE) is southern Queensland's main airport and rivals Sydney's in quality and services. There are separate domestic and international terminals—the latter was recently expanded. Cairns International Airport (CNS), in north Queensland, is the hub for northern Queensland and visits to the Great Barrier Reef.

Melbourne Airport (MEL) is sometimes known as "Tullamarine," after a neighboring suburb. International flights leave from Terminal 2; Qantas and Jetstar use Terminal 1 for their domestic operations. Virgin Blue makes up the bulk of the other domestic flights, which go from Terminal 3. Tiger Airways flies from Terminal 4.

South Australia's main airport is Adelaide International (ADL). Domestic flights and a few services to nearby Asian cities land at Darwin International Airport (DRW) in Northern Territory. The hub for the Red Centre is Alice Springs Airport (ASP), which only receives domestic flights. Perth International Airport (PER) is the gateway to Western Australia. International flights operate from Terminal 1; Qantas domestic flights leave from Terminal 2; Terminal 3 is for Alliance Airlines, Ozjet, Skywest Airlines, and Virgin Blue.

Airport Information Adelaide Airport (☎ 08/8308–9211 ⊕ www.aal.com.au). **Alice Springs Airport** (☎ 08/8951–1211 ⊕ www. alicespringsairport.com.au). **Brisbane International Airport** (☎ 07/3406–3000 ⊕ www. brisbaneairport.com.au). **Cairns Airport** (☎ 07/4080–6703 ⊕ www.cairnsairport.com). **Darwin International Airport** (☎ 08/8920–1811 ⊕ www.darwin-airport.com.au). **Sydney Airport** (☎ 02/9667–9111 ⊕ www.sydneyairport.com). **Melbourne Airport** (☎ 03/9297–1600 ⊕ www.melbourneairport.com.au). **Perth Airport** (☎ 08/9478–8888 ⊕ www.perthairport.com).

FLIGHTS

TO AUSTRALIA

Qantas is Australia's flagship carrier. It operates direct flights to Sydney from New York, San Francisco, and Los Angeles, and from Los Angeles to Melbourne and Brisbane. There are connecting Qantas flights to many other North American cities, and direct flights from various Australian airports to many Asian and European destinations. It's part of the oneworld alliance, and has excellent standards of safety and comfort. Qantas flights aren't always the cheapest, but their Aussie Airpass includes three stops within Australia for the same price as your ticket from North America.

Jetstar is a low-cost local airline owned by Qantas, and has flights from Sydney, Melbourne, Brisbane, Cairns, Perth, Adelaide, and Darwin to Bali, Japan, New Zealand, Singapore, Thailand, Vietnam, and Honolulu. Other budget carriers, Pacific Blue and Polynesian Blue (part of Virgin Blue), fly to Tonga, Samoa, Fiji, Vanuatu, New Zealand, Indonesia, and the Cook Islands. Singapore Airlines–owned budget airline Tiger Airways flies from Perth to Singapore.

Airline Contacts Air New Zealand (☎ 800/262–1234 in U.S., 61/2/8248/0030 ⊕ www.airnewzealand.com.au). **British Airways** (☎ 800/AIRWAYS in U.S., 1300/767177 in Australia ⊕ www.britishairways.com). **Cathay Pacific** (☎ 800/233–2742 in U.S., 13–1747 in Australia ⊕ www.cathaypacific.com). **Qantas** (☎ 800/227–4500 in U.S., 13–1313 in Australia ⊕ www.qantas.com). **United** (☎ 800/538–2929 in U.S., 13–1777 in Australia ⊕ www.united. com). **Virgin Blue** (☎ 13–6789 in Australia ⊕ www.virginblue.com.au).

WITHIN AUSTRALIA

Australia's large distances mean that flying is the locals' favorite way of getting from one city to another. In general, safety standards on domestic flights are high, flights are punctual, and there's plenty of timetable choice. On routes between popular destinations like Sydney, Melbourne, and Brisbane there are often several flights each hour.

Airline Contacts Airnorth (☎ 1800/627474 ⊕ www.airnorth.com.au). **Jetstar** (☎ 13–1538 ⊕ www.jetstar.com). **Qantas** (☎ 13–1313 ⊕ www.qantas.com.au). **Regional Express** (☎ 13–1713 ⊕ www.rex.com.au). **Skywest** (☎ 1300/660088 ⊕ www.skywest.com.au). **Tiger Airways** (☎ 03/9335–3033 ⊕ www.tigerairways.com). **Virgin Blue** (☎ 13–6789 ⊕ www.virginblue.com.au).

■ BY BOAT

Organized boat tours from the Queensland mainland are the only way to visit the Great Barrier Reef. Cairns is the number-one point of departure, but boats also leave from Mackay, Airlie Beach, Townsville, and Port Douglas. Boats also run between the Whitsunday Islands. The Great Barrier Reef Marine Park Authority Web site has helpful advice on how to choose a tour operator, and lists which companies are ecotourism-certified.

The daily ferries *Spirit of Tasmania I* and *II* take 10 hours to connect Melbourne with Devonport on Tasmania's north coast. Make reservations as early as possible, particularly during the busy December and January school holidays.

Sealink Ferries transport passengers and vehicles between Cape Jervis on the South Australian coastline south of Adelaide, and Penneshaw on Kangaroo Island.

You can find out about ferry and cruise schedules for these and other scenic rides at most state tourism offices and on their Web sites. All operators accept major credit cards and cash.

Information Great Barrier Reef Marine Park Authority (⊕ www.gbrmpa.gov.au). **Sealink Ferries** (☎ 13–1301 ⊕ www.sealink.com.au). **Spirit of Tasmania** (☎ 1800/634906 ⊕ www.spiritoftasmania.com.au).

▌ BY BUS

Bus travel in Australia is comfortable and well organized. Long-distance buses, also called "coaches," have air-conditioning, on-board toilets, reclining seats, and even attendants and videos on longer routes. By law, all are required to provide seat belts, and you are required to use them. Smoking is prohibited on all buses.

Australia's national bus network is run by Greyhound Australia (no connection to Greyhound in the United States), which serves far more destinations than any plane or train services. However, Australia is a vast continent, and bus travel here requires plenty of time. The journey from Sydney to Melbourne takes 15 hours, Adelaide to Perth takes 39 hours, and Brisbane to Cairns takes 30 hours. If you plan to visit specific regions, it could be worthwhile considering flying to a major hub, then using buses to explore the region when you get there.

Oz Experience is a private bus company aimed at budget travelers. They work in a similar way to Greyhound, and their routes take in both major cities and adventure destinations. They have a great selection of routes—you buy a pass, and then have unlimited stopovers along that route. You book onto each section by telephone as you travel. Oz Experience also has a hostel booking service, and will take you to the door of your hostel for no extra cost. For example, their Bruce Pass takes you along the coast between Melbourne and Cairns and costs A$575.

You can book passes and individual tickets on Greyhound and Oz Experience buses online through their Web sites, over the telephone, or in person at their desks in bus terminals.

Bus Information Greyhound Australia (☎ 1300/473946 ⊕ www.greyhound.com.au). **Oz Experience** (☎ 61/2/9213–1766 ⊕ www. ozexperience.com).

▌ BY CAR

Endless highways, fabulous scenery, bizarre little towns in the middle of nowhere: Australia is road-trip paradise. Even if you don't have time for major exploring, traveling by car can be a great way to explore a particular region at your own pace. Traffic in city centers can be terrible, so keep the car for the open road.

Driving is generally easy in Australia, once you adjust to traveling on the left side of the road. Road conditions on busy coastal highways usually pose few problems, though remote roads (even big highways) and routes through the desert are often a different story. When you're preparing a driving itinerary, it's vital to bear in mind the huge distances involved and calculate travel time and stopovers accordingly.

Most rental companies in Australia accept driving licenses from other countries, including the United States, provided that the information on the license is clear and in English. Otherwise, an International Driver's Permit is required (but they'll still want to see your regular license, too).

GASOLINE

Gas is known in Australia as "petrol." Self-service petrol stations are plentiful near major cities and in rural towns. In remote regions they can be few and far between, so fill up whenever you can. In really out-of-the-way places, carrying a spare petrol can is a good idea. Smaller petrol stations often close at night and on Sunday, though in major cities and on main highways there are plenty of stations open round the clock.

PARKING

On-street parking is usually plentiful in Australian cities, except in the traffic-heavy CBD (downtown area) of the big capitals. Electronic meters are the norm—you pay in advance, and there's usually a maximum stay, which you should respect, as Australian parking inspectors are very vigilant. Paid parking lots are also common, and are usually clearly signposted.

Outside the capitals, on-street parking is usually free, as are the lots outside malls and supermarkets.

RENTING A CAR
Australia's cities have good public transport, so there's not much point in renting a car if you're staying in an urban area, especially one popular with tourists. Step outside city limits, and a car is practically a necessity.

Rates for economy cars (a Hyundai Getz, Excel, or Accent or a Nissan Pulsar, for example) with unlimited mileage start at A$58 a day (plus fees).

Intercity highways are usually in good condition, but remoter roads—even those that look important on maps—are often unpaved or full of potholes. You can manage short distances on these in a car (for example, an access road to an attraction a few miles from the highway). For longer stretches and any outback driving, a 4WD is necessary, as insurance generally doesn't cover damage to other types of cars traveling such roads. Only rent a 4WD if you're competent to drive one on tough surfaces like sand and bogs: rescue vehicles take a long time to get to the middle of nowhere.

Rental companies have varying policies and charges for unusual trips, such as lengthy cross-state expeditions around the Top End and Western Australia. Ask about additional mileage, fuel, and insurance charges if you're planning to cover a lot of ground.

Another popular way to see Australia is to rent a camper van (motor home). Nearly all have a toilet, shower, and cooking facilities; utensils and bed linen are usually included, too. Smaller vans for two can be rented for A$40–A$150 a day with unlimited mileage (there's usually a five-day minimum).

In Australia you must be 21 to rent a car, and rates may be higher if you're under 25. There is no upper age limit for rental so long as you have a valid international driver's license. Most companies charge

BUYING A CAR

For road trips longer than a couple of months, renting costs add up, so buying a car or van (and selling it at the end of your trip) might be more economical. Most camper-van agencies have a sales department; Kings Cross Car Market and Travellers Auto Barn are two reputable agencies that specialize in selling to and rebuying from visitors.

extra for each additional driver. It's compulsory for children to use car seats, so be sure to notify your agency when you book—most charge around A$8 per day for a baby or booster seat.

Your driver's license may not be recognized outside your home country. You may not be able to rent a car without an International Driving Permit (IDP), which can be used only in conjunction with a valid driver's license and which translates your license into 10 languages. Check the AAA Web site for more info as well as for IDPs ($15) themselves.

Car Rental Resources Automobile Associations U.S.: **American Automobile Association** (AAA ☎ 315/797–5000 ⊕ www.aaa.com) ; most contact with the organization is through state and regional members.

National Automobile Club (☎ 650/294–7000 ⊕ www.thenac.com) ; membership is open to California residents only. In Australia: **Australian Automobile Association** (☎ 02/6247–7311 ⊕ www.aaa.asn.au).

Local Rental Agencies Red Spot Rentals (☎ 61/2/8303–2222 ⊕ www.redspotrentals.com.au). **Wicked Campers** (☎ 61/7/ 3634–9000 ⊕ www.wickedcampers.com.au).

Major Agencies Alamo (☎ 877/222-9075 ⊕ www.alamo.com). **Avis** (☎ 800/331–1212 ⊕ www.avis.com). **Budget** (☎ 800/472–3325 ⊕ www.budget.com). **Hertz** (☎ 800/654–3001 ⊕ www.hertz.com). **National Car Rental** (☎ 877/222–9058 ⊕ www.nationalcar.com). **Thrifty** (☎ 800/847–4389 ⊕ www.thrifty.com).

Local Car Purchase Agencies **Kings Cross Car Market** (☏ 1800/808188 in Australia ⊕ *www. carmarket.com.au).* **Travellers Auto Barn** (☏ *61/2/9360–1500* ⊕ *www.travellers-auto-barn.com.au).*

ROAD CONDITIONS

Except for some expressways in and around the major cities, most highways are two-lane roads with frequent passing lanes but no barrier separating the two directions of traffic. Main roads are usually paved and well maintained, though lanes are narrower than in the United States.

Outside big urban areas roundabouts are far more common than traffic lights—some towns have dozens of them. Remember that when driving on the left you go around a roundabout clockwise and give way to traffic entering from the right and already on the roundabout.

Potential road hazards multiply in rural areas. Driving standards, which are generally high in Australia, become more lax. Road surfaces deteriorate, becoming potholed or uneven. Fine sand sometimes fills the holes, making them hard to see. Windshield cracks caused by small stones are practically routine. Flash floods are also common during the summer months in northern Australia: when in doubt, turn back or seek advice from the police before crossing.

Animals—kangaroos and livestock, primarily—are common causes of road accidents, especially at night. If you see an animal near the edge of the road, slow down immediately, as they may just decide to step out in front of you. If they do, hitting the animal is generally preferable to swerving, as you can lose control of your car and roll. However, braking too suddenly into the animal can send it through your windshield. Ideally, you should report any livestock you kill to the nearest ranch, and should check dead kangaroos for joeys (babies carried in their pouches): if you find one, wrap it up and take it to the nearest vet.

"Road trains" are another Outback hazard: they're truck convoys made of several connected trailers, totaling up to 170 feet. They take a LONG time to brake, so keep your distance and overtake them only with extreme caution.

Outback driving can be very exhausting and potentially dangerous. Avoid driving alone, and rest often. Carry plenty of water with you (4–5 liters per person per day)—high temperatures make dehydration a very common problem on the road. Don't count on your cell phone working in the middle of nowhere, and if an emergency occurs never ever leave your vehicle: it's visible, and provides you shelter from the sun and cold. Stick by the side of the road: sooner or later, someone will come along.

ROADSIDE EMERGENCIES

If you have an emergency requiring an ambulance, the fire department, or the police, dial **000**. Many major highways now have telephones for breakdown assistance; you can also use your cell phone if you have one. Otherwise, flag down and ask a passing motorist to call the nearest motoring service organization for you. Most Australian drivers will be happy to assist, particularly in country areas.

Each state has its own motoring organization that provides assistance for vehicle breakdowns. When you rent a vehicle, check that you are entitled to assistance from the relevant motoring organization free of charge. A toll-free nationwide number is available for roadside assistance.

Emergency Services Emergency Services (☏ *000).* **Motoring Organization Hotline** (☏ *13–1111).*

RULES OF THE ROAD

Speed limits vary from state to state. As a rough guide, 50–60 kilometers per hour (KPH) is the maximum in populated areas, reduced to 40 KPH near schools. On open roads limits range from 100 to 130 KPH—the equivalent of 62–80 MPH. Limits are usually signposted clearly and regularly, and are enforced by police speed checks and—in state capitals—by automatic cameras.

Drunk driving, once a big problem in Australia, is controlled obsessively. The legal limit is 0.05% blood-alcohol level, and penalties are so high that many Aussies just don't drink if they're driving. Seat belts are mandatory nationwide. Children must be restrained in a seat appropriate to their size. Car-rental agencies can install these for about A$30 per week, with 24 hours' notice. It is illegal to use a mobile-phone handset when driving.

Traffic circles, called "roundabouts," are widely used at intersections; cars that have already entered the circle have the right-of-way. At designated intersections in Melbourne's central business district you must get into the left lane to make a right-hand turn—this is to facilitate crossing streetcar lines. Watch for the sign RIGHT-HAND TURN FROM LEFT LANE ONLY. Everywhere, watch for sudden changes in speed limits.

The Australian Automobile Association has a branch in each state, known as the National Roads and Motorists Association (NRMA) in New South Wales and Canberra, the Automobile Association in the Northern Territory (AANT), and the Royal Automobile Club (RAC) in all other states. It's affiliated with AAA worldwide, and offers reciprocal services to American members, including emergency road service, road maps, copies of each state and territory's Highway Code, and discounts on car rental and accommodations.

▌ BY TRAIN

Australia has a network of long-distance trains providing first- and economy-class service along the east and south coasts, across the south of the country from Sydney to Perth, and through the middle of the country between Adelaide and Darwin.

Most long-distance trains are operated by various state-government-owned enterprises. The luxurious exceptions to the rule are the *Ghan, Indian Pacific,* and *Overland,* all run by the private company Great Southern Rail. Rail Australia is the umbrella organization for all of these services outside the country.

The state-owned trains are usually punctual and comfortable. Economy class has reclining seats, and on longer routes there are sleeper classes. Second-class sleepers have shared bathrooms and sometimes you share your cabin with strangers, too. In first class you have the cabin to yourself and a small en suite bathroom. Meals are sometimes included. Comfort levels increase in Premium Red Service on the Overland, and Gold and Platinum Service on the *Ghan and Indian Pacific* and in the *Sunlander's* Queenslander class. The high-speed Tilt Train is aimed at business travelers, and has business-class-style reclining seats.

Information Countrylink (☎ *13–2232* ⊕ *www.countrylink.info*). **Great Southern Rail** (☎ *13–2147* ⊕ *www.gsr.com.au*). **Queensland Rail** (☎ *13–1617* ⊕ *www.qr.com.au*). **Rail Australia** (⊕ *www.railaustralia.com.au*).

ESSENTIALS

▌ ACCOMMODATIONS

Australia operates a rating system of one to five stars. Five-star hotels include on-site dining options, concierge and valet services, a business center, and, of course, very luxurious rooms. Four stars denote an exceptional property that probably just doesn't have all the extras they need for five. Three stars means quality fittings and service. We list the best lodgings for each price category. The available facilities are specified, but we don't indicate whether they cost extra. Always ask about additional costs when pricing your hotel room.

▌TIP➜ Assume that hotels operate on the European Plan (**EP**, no meals) unless we specify that they use the Breakfast Plan (**BP**, with full breakfast), Continental Plan (**CP**, Continental breakfast), Full American Plan (**FAP**, all meals), or Modified American Plan (**MAP**, breakfast and dinner), or are **all-inclusive** (**AI**, all meals and most activities).

APARTMENT AND HOUSE RENTALS

Judging from the huge number of short-term rental properties in Australia, locals prefer doing their own thing to being in a hotel. It's easy for you to do likewise. Serviced apartments are the norm in big cities, and you can often rent one for only a night or two. Booking agency Move and Stay has an enormous range of properties, usually aimed at executives. Medina has top-end apartments and apart-hotels in all the big cities. Quest owns apartment complexes all around the country. Furnished Properties focuses on the Sydney area, and have reasonable rates.

In beach areas "units" are the thing: they're usually small detached houses or bungalows, often with a communal area with laundry facilities and a swimming pool. Maid service is usually optional here. In summer, units at popular beach resorts will often be booked months in advance, so make reservations in plenty

of time. To find beach units online, you usually need to search for agencies dealing with a specific area rather than a nationwide company.

Contacts Furnished Properties (🖅 *61/2/9518–8828* ⊕ *www.furnishedprop-erties.com.au*). **Medina Hotel Apartments** (🖅 *61/2/9356–5061* ⊕ *www.medina.com.au*). **Move and Stay** (⊕ *www.moveandstay.com.au*). **Quest Serviced Apartments** (🖅 *61/3/9645–8357 or 1800/334033* ⊕ *www.questapart-ments.com.au*). **Villas & Apartments Abroad** (🖅 *212/213–6435* ⊕ *www.vaanyc.com*). **Villas International** (🖅 *415/499–9490 or 800/221–2260* ⊕ *www.villasintl.com*).

BED AND BREAKFASTS

B&Bs are a big deal in Australia, and are popular in both urban and rural areas. The classic Aussie B&B is a family-run affair: expect clean, homey rooms, private bathrooms, and bountiful breakfasts. A room for two usually ranges from A$80 to A$200 a night. The word "boutique" in conjunction with a B&B implies a higher level of luxury—decorative, gastronomic, or both—and facilities, but all at a higher price.

The Bed & Breakfast Book, Australia lists a number of excellent properties. OzBe-dandBreakfast.com has comprehensive listings that include boutique properties. Australian Bed and Breakfast has listings of B&Bs, farm stays, cottages, and more, all over the country.

Local tourist-information centers throughout Australia also have lists of B&Bs in their area.

Reservation Services Australian Bed and Breakfast (⊕ *www.australianbedandbreakfast. com.au*) has links to Web sites for each state. **Bed & Breakfast Farmstay Association of New South Wales & ACT** (🖅 *1300/888862 or 02/4367–5505* ⊕ *www.bedandbreakfast.org. au*). **Bed & Breakfast.com** (🖅 *512/322–2710 or 800/462–2632* ⊕ *www.bedandbreakfast. com*) also sends out an online newsletter. Bed

& Breakfast Inns Online (📠 *310/280–4363 or 800/215–7365* ⊕ *www.bbonline.com*). Oz Bed and Breakfast (⊕ *www.ozbedandbreak-fast.com*).

The Bed & Breakfast Book (⊕ *www.bbbook.com.au*) publishes a yearly guide to Australian B&Bs and has online listings, too.

HOME AND FARM STAYS
Home and farm stays combine B&B-style accommodation with the chance to join in farm activities or explore the country-side. Some hosts run day trips, as well as horseback riding, hiking, and fishing trips. Accommodations vary from mod-est shearers' cabins to elegant homesteads; some include breakfast in the room price, others an evening meal. Families are usu-ally welcomed. For two people the cost varies from A$100 to A$250 nightly. Many of the B&B sites above also have farm stay listings.

Reservation Services Australian Farm Stay (⊕ *www.australianfarmstay.com.au*) is a private company dealing with luxury farm stays.

HOME EXCHANGES
With a direct home exchange you stay in someone else's home while they stay in yours. Some outfits also deal with vaca-tion homes, so you're not actually staying in someone's full-time residence, just their vacant weekend place.

Although home exchanges aren't a really popular choice in Australia, there are still many options available, particularly on the east coast.

Exchange Clubs Home Exchange.com (📠 *800/877–8723* ⊕ *www.homeexchange.com*) ; $99.95 for a 1-year online listing. **HomeLink International** (📠 *800/638–3841* ⊕ *www.homelink.org*) ; $115 yearly for Web-only membership; $175 includes Web access and two catalogs. **Intervac U.S.** (📠 *800/756–4663* ⊕ *www.intervacus.com*) ; $99.99 for Web-only membership.

HOW WAS YOUR TRIP?
Did the resort look as good in real life as it did in the photos? Did you sleep like a baby, or were the walls paper-thin? Did you get your money's worth? Rate hotels and write your own reviews in Travel Ratings, or start a discussion about your favorite places in Travel Talk on *www.fodors.com*. Your comments might even appear in our books. Yes, you, too, can be a correspondent!

HOSTELS
Australian hostels are among the world's best. Often called "backpackers," hos-tels generally have a mix of dormitory and private accommodation, with well-equipped communal facilities, including a kitchen, laundry, and living area. In-house bars and travel agencies are popular, too. Owners and staff are often veteran Aussie backpackers who know from experi-ence what budget travelers are looking for—they're lots of fun and full of useful advice. Guests are mostly globe trotters in their twenties and thirties, but families and older people are also common.

If you think "hostelling" is synonymous with "roughing it," think again. So-called luxury or boutique hostels and hostel resorts are a growing Australian trend, especially in tourist hot spots like Cairns. These mix high-quality dorms with floors of nicely furnished private rooms with en suite bathrooms. Prices are much lower than at hotels, and you still get the hostel vibe in the communal areas, which usually include a swimming pool.

Information Hostelling International Australia (⊕ *www.yha.com.au*). **Base Back-packing Hostels** (📠 *1800/242–273* within Australia, *61/2/8268–6000* ⊕ *www.stayat-base.com*). **Hostelling International—USA** (📠 *301/495–1240* ⊕ *www.hiusa.org*). **Hostels.com** (⊕ *www.hostels.com*). **Hostel World.com** (⊕ *www.hostelworld.com*). **Travellers' Point** (⊕ *www.travellerspoint.com*). **VIP Backpackers** (📠 *61/7/3395–6111* ⊕ *www.vipbackpackers.com*).

■ COMMUNICATIONS

INTERNET

Internet access is widely available to travelers in Australia. Top-end hotels always have some sort of in-room access for laptop users—Wi-Fi is becoming the norm, otherwise there are data ports. Note that sometimes you are charged a hefty premium for using this service. Hostels are also well connected and charge reasonable rates. Many have free Wi-Fi, others have large on-site cybercafés, or, at worst, some terminals for guests to use.

Australia's main telephone network, Telstra, has wireless hot spots all over the country. McDonalds and Starbucks (iiNet customers only) have free Wi-Fi. Alternatively, you can pay using Telstra Phone-Away calling cards: there's no connection charge and online time costs A$0.20 per minute. Connections can be slow, however. You can buy a card at newsagents, Australia Post, convenience stores, or online. Telstra's Web site also has hot spot listings.

Contacts Cybercafes (⊕ www.cybercafes. com) lists more than 4,000 Internet cafés worldwide. Telstra (⊕ www.telstra.com.au).

PHONES

The country code for Australia is 61. To call Australia from the United States, dial the international access code (011), followed by the country code (61), the area or city code without the initial zero (e.g., 2), and the eight-digit phone number.

CALLING WITHIN AUSTRALIA

Australia's phone system is efficient and reliable. You can make local and long-distance calls from your hotel—usually with a surcharge—or from any public phone. There are public phones in shopping areas, on suburban streets, at train stations, and outside rural post offices—basically, they're everywhere. You can use coins or phone cards in most public phones; credit-card phones are common at airports.

All regular telephone numbers in Australia have eight digits. There are five area codes: 02 (for New South Wales and Australian Capital Territory), 03 (Victoria and Tasmania), 04 (for cell phones), 07 (for Queensland), and 08 (for Western Australia, South Australia, and Northern Territory). Toll-free numbers begin with 1800, and numbers starting with 13 or 1300 are charged at local rates anywhere in the country.

Calls within the same area code are charged as local: A0.50¢ for an unlimited amount of time. Long-distance call rates vary by distance, and are timed. When you're calling long distance within Australia, remember to include the area code, even when you're calling from a number with the same area code. For example, when calling Canberra from Sydney, both of which have an 02 prefix, you still need to include the area code when you dial.

Directory Assistance Local Directory Assistance (☎ 1223).

CALLING OUTSIDE AUSTRALIA

To call overseas from Australia, dial 0011, then the country code and the number. Kiosks and groceries in major cities sell international calling cards. You can also use credit cards on public phones.

The country code for the United States is 1.

You can use AT&T, Sprint, and MCI services from Australian phones, though some pay phones require you to put coins in to make the call. Using a prepaid calling card is generally cheaper.

Useful Numbers International Directory Assistance (☎ 1225). **International Call Cost Information** (☎ 1300/362162).

Access Codes AT&T Direct (☎ 1800/881011 from Telstra phones, 1800/551155 from Optus phones). **MCI WorldPhone** (☎ 1800/881100 from Telstra phones, 1800/551111 from Optus phones) . **Skype** (⊕ www.skype.com). **Sprint International Access** (☎ 1800/881877 from Telstra phones, 1800/551110 from Optus phones).

CALLING CARDS

It's worth buying a phone card in Australia even if you plan to make just a few calls.

Telstra, Australia's main telephone company, has three different calling cards. Their simply named Phonecard is a prepaid card you can use for local, long-distance, or international calls from public pay phones. There are many other calling cards in Australia as well, often with better rates than Telstra's. Gotalk and onesuite.com are two popular examples, but there are many more. The best way to find one is to ask in a convenience store or newsagent's: they usually have a selection on hand, and you can compare rates to the country you're calling to. Note that many companies don't even print their access numbers on cards any more, but instead give you a slip of paper.

Contacts Gotalk (⊕ www.gotalk.com.au). onesuite.com (⊕ www.onesuite.com). Telstra (⊕ www.telstra.com.au).

MOBILE PHONES

If you have a multiband phone (some countries use different frequencies from the ones used in the United States) and your service provider uses the world-standard GSM network (as do T-Mobile, Cingular, and Verizon), you can probably use your phone abroad. Roaming fees can be steep, however: 99¢ a minute is considered reasonable. And overseas you normally pay the toll charges for incoming calls. It's almost always cheaper to send a text message than to make a call, since text messages have a very low set fee (often less than 5¢).

If you just want to make local calls, consider buying a new SIM card (note that your provider may have to unlock your phone for you to use a different SIM card) and a prepaid service plan in the destination. You'll then have a local number and can make local calls at local rates. If your trip is extensive, you could also simply buy a new cell phone in your des-

tination, as the initial cost will be offset over time.

■TIP➡ If you travel internationally frequently, save one of your old mobile phones or buy a cheap one on the Internet; ask your cell-phone company to unlock it for you, and take it with you as a travel phone, buying a new SIM card with pay-as-you-go service in each destination.

Nearly all Australian mobile phones use the GSM network. If you have an unlocked tri-band phone and intend to make calls to Australian numbers, it makes sense to buy a prepaid Australian SIM card on arrival—rates will be much better than using your U.S. network. Alternatively, you can rent a phone or a SIM card from companies like Vodafone. Rates start at A$5 per day for a handset and A$1 a day for a SIM. You can also buy a cheap, pay-as-you-go handset from Telstra, Virgin Mobile, or Optus. Cell-phone stores are abundant, and staff are used to assessing tourists' needs.

Contacts Cellular Abroad (☎ 800/287–5072 ⊕ www.cellularabroad.com) rents and sells GMS phones and sells SIM cards that work in many countries. Mobal (☎ 888/888–9162 ⊕ www.mobalrental.com) rents mobiles and sells GSM phones (starting at $49) that will operate in 140 countries. Per-call rates vary throughout the world. Optus (⊕ www.optus.com.au). Planet Fone (☎ 888/988–4777 ⊕ www.planetfone.com) rents cell phones, but the per-minute rates are expensive. Telstra (⊕ www.telstra.com.au). Virgin Mobile (⊕ www.virginmobile.com.au). Vodafone (⊕ www.vodarent.com.au) rents phones from stands in many airports.

▌ CUSTOMS AND DUTIES

Australian customs regulations are unlike any other. As an island long isolated from the rest of the world, Australia is free from many pests and diseases endemic in other places, and it wants to stay that way. Customs procedures are very thorough, and it can take up to an hour to clear them.

All animals are subject to quarantine. Many foodstuffs and natural products are forbidden, including meat, dairy products, fresh fruit and vegetables, and all food served on aircraft. Most canned or preserved foods may be imported, but you have to declare them on your customs statement and have them inspected, along with wooden artifacts and seeds.

Airport sniffer dogs patrol arrivals areas, and even an innocent dried flower forgotten between the pages of a book could incur a serious fine. If in doubt, declare something—the worst-case scenario is that it will be taken from you, without a fine.

Otherwise, nonresidents over 18 may bring in 250 cigarettes (or 250 grams of cigars or tobacco) and 2¼ liters of alcohol. Adults can bring in other taxable goods (that is, luxury items like perfume) to the value of A$900.

Information Australian Customs Services (⊕ www.customs.gov.au) : for information about duty-free allowances. **Australian Quarantine and Inspection Services** (⊕ www.daffa.gov. au/aqis/travel/entering-australia) tells you exactly what you can and cannot bring into Australia.

U.S. Information U.S. Customs and Border Protection (⊕ www.cbp.gov).

∎ EATING OUT

Fresh ingredients, friendly service, innovative flavor combinations, and great value for your money mean that eating out Down Under is usually a happy experience.

Australia's British heritage is evident in the hearty food served in pubs, roadhouses, and country hotels. It all seems to taste much better than food in Britain, though. Roast meat and potatoes; fish-and-chips; pasties and pies swimming in gravy; flaky sausage rolls; sticky teacakes and fluffy scones—-all these things are cheap and tasty counter staples. They give the big fast-food franchises a serious run for their money.

Some Australian restaurants serve prix-fixe dinners, but most are à la carte. The restaurants we list are the best in each price category. Properties indicated by a ✕🖬 are hotels with restaurants that deserve a special trip.

MEALS AND MEALTIMES

Australians eat relatively early. Breakfast is typically between 7 and 10 AM, and eating it out (usually at a café) is popular. Options range from toast or cereal through fruit and yogurt and muffins, pastries, and hotcakes to a full fry-up—eggs, bacon, sausages, baked beans, hash browns, tomatoes, and mushrooms. Morning coffee and afternoon tea are popular in-between meals.

For most locals lunch is usually lighter than dinner: a salad or a sandwich, say, usually between 11:30 AM and 2:30 PM. Dinner is the main meal and begins around 6:30. In the cities, dining options are available outside these hours, but the choices are far more restricted in the countryside and smaller towns, where even take-aways close at 8:30 PM.

Unless otherwise noted, the restaurants listed in this guide are open daily for lunch and dinner.

PAYING

At most restaurants you ask for the bill at the end of the meal. At sandwich bars, burger joints, and take-aways you pay up front. Visa, MasterCard, and American Express are widely accepted in all but the simplest eateries.

For guidelines on tipping see Tipping below.

RESERVATIONS AND DRESS

Regardless of where you are, it's a good idea to make a reservation if you can. In some places (Sydney, for example) it's expected. We only mention them specifically when reservations are essential (there's no other way you'll ever get a table) or when they are not accepted. For popular restaurants, book as far ahead as you can (often 30 days), and reconfirm as soon as you arrive. (Large parties should always call ahead to check the reservations policy.) We mention dress only when men are required to wear a jacket or a jacket and tie.

ELECTRICITY

The electrical current in Australia is 240 volts, 50 cycles alternating current (AC), so most American appliances can't be used without a transformer. Wall outlets take slanted three-prong plugs and plugs with two flat prongs set in a V.

Consider making a small investment in a universal adapter, which has several types of plugs in one lightweight, compact unit. Most laptops and mobile-phone chargers are dual voltage (i.e., they operate equally well on 110 and 220 volts), so require only an adapter. These days the same is true of small appliances such as hair dryers. Always check labels and manufacturer instructions to be sure. Don't use 110-volt outlets marked FOR SHAVERS ONLY for high-wattage appliances such as hair dryers.

Contacts Steve Kropla's Help for World Traveler's (⊕ www.kropla.com) has information on electrical and telephone plugs around the world. **Walkabout Travel Gear** (⊕ www.walkabouttravelgear.com) has a good coverage of electricity under "adapters."

HEALTH

The most common types of illnesses are caused by contaminated food and water. If you have problems, mild cases of traveler's diarrhea may respond to Imodium (known generically as loperamide) or Pepto-Bismol. Be sure to drink plenty of fluids; if you can't keep fluids down, seek medical help immediately.

Infectious diseases can be airborne or passed via mosquitoes and ticks and through direct or indirect physical contact with animals or people. Some, including Norwalk-like viruses that affect your digestive tract, can be passed along through contaminated food. Condoms can help prevent most sexually transmitted diseases, but they aren't absolutely reliable, and their quality varies from country to country. Speak with your physician and/or check the CDC or World Health Organization Web sites for health alerts, particularly if you're pregnant, traveling with children, or have a chronic illness.

OVER-THE-COUNTER REMEDIES
Familiar brands of nonprescription medications are available in pharmacies. Note that Tylenol is usually called paracetomol in Australia.

SHOTS AND MEDICATIONS
Unless you're arriving from an area that has been infected with yellow fever, typhoid, or cholera, you don't need to get any shots or carry medical certificates to enter Australia.

Australia is relatively free from diseases prevalent in many countries. In the far north there have been occasional localized outbreaks of dengue and Ross River fever—just take the usual precautions against mosquito bites (cover up your arms and legs and use ample repellent), and you should be fine.

SPECIFIC ISSUES IN AUSTRALIA
Australian health care is excellent, with highly trained medical professionals and well-equipped hospitals. Hygiene standards are also high and well monitored, so you can drink tap water and eat fresh produce without worrying. You may take a four weeks' supply of prescribed medication into Australia (more with a doctor's certificate)—if you run out, pharmacies require a prescription from an Australian doctor. The quickest way to find one is to ask your hotel or look under "M" (for Medical Practitioner) in the Yellow Pages.

Sunburn and sunstroke are the greatest health hazards when visiting Australia. Remember that there's a big hole in the ozone layer over Australia, so even on cloudy days the rays of light coming through are harmful. Stay out of the sun at midday and, regardless of whether you normally burn, follow the locals' example and slather on the sun cream. Protect your eyes with good-quality sunglasses, and try to cover up with a long-sleeve shirt, a hat, and pants or a beach wrap whenever possible. Keep in mind that you'll burn more easily at higher altitudes and in the water.

Dehydration is another serious danger, especially in the Outback. It's easy to avoid: carry plenty of water and drink it often.

Australia is free of malaria, but several cases of Ross River and dengue fevers have been reported in recent years. The best way to prevent both is to avoid being bitten: cover up your arms and legs, and use ample repellent, especially during summer months and in the north of the country. No rural scene is complete without bush flies, a major annoyance. These tiny pests, found throughout Australia, are especially attracted to the eyes and mouth in search of the fluids that are secreted there. Some travelers resort to wearing a face net, which can be suspended from a hat with a drawstring device.

Some of the world's deadliest creatures call Australia home. The chances of running into one are low, but wherever you go, pay close heed to any warnings given by hotel staff, tour operators, lifeguards, or locals in general. In the Outback you need to worry about snakes and spiders. On the coast there's everything from sharks through deadly octopi and stonefish to jellyfish to reckon with. In northern Australia, rivers, lakes, billabongs, and even flooded streams are home to estuarine crocodiles, known to attack and kill humans. The best advice we can give you is to always be cautious, and check, check, and double-check the situation at each stop on your visit with the appropriate authority.

As if deadly sea critters weren't enough, Australian coastal waters are also home to seriously strong currents known as "rips." These kill tens of swimmers every year. Pay close attention to the flags raised on beaches, and only swim in areas patrolled by lifeguards. If you get caught in a rip, the standard advice is never to swim against it, as you rapidly become exhausted. Instead, try to relax and float parallel to the shore: eventually the current will subside and you will be able to swim back to the shore, albeit farther down the coast.

▌HOLIDAYS

New Year's Day, January 1; **Australia Day,** January 26; **Good Friday,** April 2, 2010, and April 22, 2011; **Easter Monday,** April 6, 2010, and April 25, 2011; **Anzac Day,** April 25; **Christmas,** December 25; **Boxing Day,** December 26. There are also several state- and territory-specific public holidays.

▌MAIL

All regular mail services are run by the efficient Australia Post, which has offices all over the country. Post offices are usually open only during business hours weekdays, but stamps are available from newsagents at other times. Postboxes for regular mail in Australia are usually bright red; express postboxes are yellow. Postage rates are A0.55¢ for domestic letters, A$2.10 per 50-gram (28.35 grams = 1 ounce) airmail letter, and A$1.40 for airmail postcards to North America—allow a week for letters and postcards to arrive.

Contact Australia Post (⊕ *www.auspost. com.au*).

SHIPPING PACKAGES

Rates for large parcels shipped from Australia depend on their weight, shape, and contents. Printed papers (including books) are cheaper to send than clothes, for example. Sending parcels through Australia Post is usually reliable. It's worth paying the extra for recorded delivery, as you can track the parcel and claim insurance if it gets lost. Many stores—particularly upmarket ones—can ship your purchases for you, for a price.

Sending a 1-kilogram (2-pound) parcel to the United States with Australia Post costs A$18.80 by seamail, and A$27.30 by airmail. If you're shipping items in excess of 50 kilograms (110 pounds), it's often less expensive to send goods by sea via a shipping agent. Shipping time to the United States is 10–12 weeks.

Both DHL and Federal Express operate fast, reliable express courier services from Australia. Rates are around A$120 for a 1-kilogram (2-pound) parcel to the United States, including door-to-door service. Delivery time between Sydney and New York is approximately three days.

Express Services DHL Worldwide Express (☎ 13–1406 ⊕ www.dhl.com.au). **Federal Express** (☎ 13–2610 ⊕ www.fedex.com/au).

∎ MONEY

The most expensive part of your trip to Australia will probably be getting there. Australian hotels are generally cheaper than similar establishments in North America, as is food.

Australians use debit cards wherever possible to pay for things—you can use your credit card, or pay cash, always in Australian dollars. ATMs are ubiquitous; it's very hard to change traveler's checks.

Prices for goods and services can be volatile at times. A 10% Goods and Services Tax (or GST—similar to V.A.T. in other countries) applies to most activities and goods, though some unprocessed foods are exempt.

Prices throughout this guide are given for adults. Substantially reduced fees are almost always available for children, students, and sometimes for senior citizens.

∎ TIP➔ Banks never have every foreign currency on hand, and it may take as long as a week to order. If you're planning to exchange funds before leaving home, don't wait until the last minute.

ATMS AND BANKS

Your own bank will probably charge a fee for using ATMs abroad; the foreign bank you use may also charge a fee. Nevertheless, you'll usually get a better rate of exchange at an ATM than you will at a currency-exchange office or even when changing money in a bank. And extracting funds as you need them is a safer option than carrying around a large amount of cash.

∎ TIP➔ PIN numbers with more than four digits are not recognized at ATMs in many countries. If yours has five or more, remember to change it before you leave.

For most travelers to Australia, ATMs are the easiest—and often cheapest—way to obtain Australia dollars. Australia's biggest banks are Westpac, ANZ, the Commonwealth Bank of Australia, and the National Australia Bank. Their ATMs all accept Cirrus and Plus cards. Smaller state-based banks are also common, but may not accept foreign cards. Major cities often have branches of international banks like Citibank or HSBC.

Before traveling, check if your bank has an agreement with any Australian banks for reduced ATM fees. For example, Bank of America customers can use Westpac ATMs to withdraw cash without incurring a fee.

CREDIT CARDS

Throughout this guide, the following abbreviations are used: **AE**, American Express; **DC**, Diners Club; **MC**, Master-Card; and **V**, Visa.

It's a good idea to inform your credit-card company before you travel, especially if you're going abroad and don't travel internationally very often. Otherwise, the credit-card company might put a hold on your card owing to unusual activity—not a good thing halfway through your trip. Record all your credit-card numbers—as well as the phone numbers to call if your cards are lost or stolen—in a safe place, so you're prepared should something go wrong. Both MasterCard and Visa have general numbers you can call (collect if you're abroad) if your card is lost, but you're better off calling the number of your issuing bank, since Master-Card and Visa usually just transfer you to your bank; your bank's number is usually printed on your card.

If you plan to use your credit card for cash advances, you'll need to apply for a PIN at least two weeks before your trip. Although it's usually cheaper (and safer) to use a credit card abroad for large purchases (so you can cancel payments or be reimbursed if there's a problem), note that some credit-card companies *and* the banks that issue them add substantial percentages to all foreign transactions, whether they're in a foreign currency or not. Check on these fees before leaving home, so there won't be any surprises when you get the bill.

■ TIP→ Before you charge something, ask the merchant whether or not he or she plans to do a dynamic currency conversion (DCC). In such a transaction the credit-card *processor* (shop, restaurant, or hotel, not Visa or MasterCard) converts the currency and charges you in dollars. In most cases you'll pay the merchant a 3% fee for this service in addition to any credit-card company and issuing-bank foreign-transaction surcharges.

Dynamic currency conversion programs are becoming increasingly widespread. Merchants who participate in them are supposed to ask whether you want to be charged in dollars or the local currency, but they don't always do so. And even if they do offer you a choice, they may well avoid mentioning the additional surcharges. The good news is that you *do* have a choice. And if this practice really gets your goat, you can avoid it entirely thanks to American Express; with its cards, DCC simply isn't an option.

Most Australian establishments take credit cards: Visa and MasterCard are the most

widely accepted, American Express and Diners Club aren't always accepted outside the cities. Just in case, bring enough cash to cover your expenses if you're visiting a national park or a remote area.

Reporting Lost Cards American Express (☎ 800/992-3404 in the U.S., 336/393-1111 collect from abroad, 1300/132639 in Australia ⊕ www.americanexpress.com). **Diners Club** (☎ 800/234-6377 in the U.S., 303/799-1504 collect from abroad, 1300/360060 in Australia ⊕ www.dinersclub.com). **MasterCard** (☎ 800/627-8372 in the U.S., 636/722-7111 collect from abroad, 1800/120113 in Australia ⊕ www.mastercard.com). **Visa** (☎ 800/847-2911 in the U.S., 410/581-9994 collect from abroad, 1800/125440 in Australia ⊕ www.visa.com).

CURRENCY AND EXCHANGE

Australia has its own dollar—assume all prices you see in Australia are quoted in Australian dollars. The currency operates on a decimal system, with the dollar (A$) as the basic unit and 100 cents (¢) equaling A$1. Bills, differentiated by color and size, come in A$100, A$50, A$20, A$10, and A$5 denominations, and are made of plastic rather than paper—you can even take them swimming with you. Coins are minted in A$2, A$1, A0.50¢, A0.20¢, A0.10¢, and A0.05¢ denominations.

At this writing, the exchange rate was about A$1.187 to the U.S. dollar.

■ TIP→ Even if a currency-exchange booth has a sign promising no commission, rest assured that there's some kind of huge, hidden fee. (Oh . . . that's right. The sign didn't say no *fee*.) And as for rates, you're almost always better off getting foreign currency at an ATM or exchanging money at a bank.

■ PACKING

If Crocodile Dundee is your idea of an Aussie style icon, think again: Melburnians and Sydneysiders are as fashion-conscious as New Yorkers. In the big cities, slop around in shorts and you might as well wear an "I'm a tourist" badge. Instead, pack nicer jeans, Capri pants, skirts, or dress shorts for urban sightseeing. A jacket and tie or posh dress are only necessary if you plan on some seriously fine dining.

Things are a bit different out of town. No Aussie would be seen dead on the beach without their "thongs," as flip-flops are confusingly called here. Wherever you are, your accessories of choice are high-quality sunglasses and a hat with a brim—the sun is strong AND dangerous. Carry insect repellent and avoid lotions or perfume in the tropics, as they attract mosquitoes and other insects.

A light sweater or jacket will keep you comfy in autumn, but winter in the southern states demands a heavier coat—ideally a raincoat with a zip-out wool lining. You should pack sturdy walking boots if you're planning any bushwalking, otherwise sneakers or flats are fine.

Australian pharmacies stock all the usual hygiene products (including tampons and condoms) and toiletries, plus a whole lot of fabulous local brands often not available overseas. There's also a mind-boggling range of sunscreens and insect repellents, so have no qualms about bringing everything in travel-size bottles and stocking up when you arrive. Oral contraceptive pills are usually prescription-only, though emergency contraceptive pills are available over the counter. Grocery stores and supermarkets frown on your using too many plastic bags—carry a foldable canvas tote and you'll blend in perfectly.

▌ PASSPORTS AND VISAS

To enter Australia for up to 90 days you need a valid passport and a visa (New Zealand nationals are the exception). These days, instead of a visa label or stamp in your passport, citizens of the United States (and many other countries) can get an Electronic Travel Authority (ETA). This is an electronically stored travel permit. It saves you time both when you apply—the process is all online—and when you arrive in Australia.

To obtain an ETA for Australia you must: 1) hold an ETA-eligible passport; 2) be visiting Australia for tourism, family, or business; 3) stay less than three months; 4) be in good health; and 5) have no criminal convictions. The Visitor ETA allows you as many visits of up to 90 days as you like within a 12-month period, but remember that no work in the country is allowed. If you're visiting Australia on business, a Short Validity Business ETA might be more appropriate. Technically, both are free of charge, but you need to pay a A$20 service charge by credit card. Children traveling on a parent's passport also need an ETA. You can apply for the ETA yourself or your travel agent can do it for you.

If you don't meet the ETA requirements or need a different kind of visa, you should contact your nearest Australian diplomatic office well in advance of your trip, as processing other visas takes time. Equally, if you plan to stay longer than three months you must obtain a paper visa (there's a A$105 fee). If you travel to Australia on an under-three-month ETA and later decide to extend your visit, then you must apply for a visa at the nearest Australian Immigration regional office (there's a A$250 fee).

At present, Australia doesn't require a notorized letter of permission if only one parent is traveling with a child, but it's always best to err on the side of caution and take along such a letter if you can.

▌ TAXES

Everyone leaving Australia pays an A$47 departure tax, euphemistically known as a Passenger Movement Charge. It's included in your airline ticket price. There's also a 10% V.A.T. equivalent known as Goods and Services Tax (GST), which is included in displayed prices. There is a G.S.T. refund for visitors on purchases totaling over A$300 made in one store. You need to keep the receipts for these and present them at the Australian Customs Services booths that are after passport control in international airports. The tax is refunded to a credit card, even if you paid cash for the purchases. Allow an extra 30 minutes for this process.

▌ TIME

Without daylight saving time, Sydney is 14 hours ahead of New York and Toronto; 15 hours ahead of Chicago and Dallas; and 17 hours ahead of Los Angeles.

Australia has three major time zones. Eastern Standard Time (EST) applies in Tasmania, Victoria, New South Wales, and Queensland; Central Standard Time applies in South Australia and Northern Territory; and Western Standard Time applies in Western Australia. Central Standard Time is ½ hour behind EST, and Western Standard Time is 2 hours behind EST.

Within the EST zone, each state chooses a slightly different date on which to commence or end daylight saving—except for Queensland, where the powerful farm lobby has prevented the state from introducing daylight saving at all, since it would make the cows wake up an hour earlier. Western Australia and Northern Territory also decline to recognize daylight saving, which means that at certain times of the year Australia can have as many as six different time zones.

Time Zones Timeanddate.com (⊕ *www. timeanddate.com*) can help you figure out the correct time anywhere.

▌ TOURS

SPECIAL-INTEREST TOURS

ABORIGINAL ART
Australian Aboriginal Fine Art Gallery of New York runs collectors' art tours to Australia every year. Pilot and art lover Helen Read flies you and guides you on Didgeri Air Art Tours' small-group tours. Aboriginal Travel has several Aboriginal

art tours, including a five-day collectors tour and shorter rock-art tours. The Wayward Bus Touring Company runs four-day charter tours for small groups visiting artists in different Aboriginal communities in Northern Territory. Kimberley Dreams runs a 12-day Aboriginal art tour through the Kimberley Region in northern Western Australia.

Contacts Aboriginal Travel (☎ *61/8/8234–8324* ⊕ *www.aboriginaltravel.com*). **Didgeri Air Art Tours** (☎ *61/8/8948–5055* ⊕ *www.didgeri. com.au*). **Kimberley Dreams** (☎ *61/8/8942–0971* ⊕ *www.kimberleys.com.au*). **Wayward Bus Touring Company** (☎ *61/8/8132– 8230* ⊕ *www.waywardbus.com.au*).

BIKING
Remote Outback Cycle (ROC) Tours combine biking with 4WD transportation and camping on remote desert tours. Epic Adventures runs a month-long transcontinental bike ride through Australia's red Centre. You get biking, hiking, and water sports on the Great Barrier Reef in Backroads' multisport family Australian tour.

▌TIP→ Most airlines accommodate bikes as luggage, provided they're dismantled and boxed.

Contacts Backroads (☎ *800/462-2848* ⊕ *www.backroads.com*). **Epic Adventures** (☎ *61/1300/948911* ⊕ *www.epicadventures. com.au*). **ROC Tours** (☎ *61/1300/948911* ⊕ *www.cycletours.com.au*).

BIRD-WATCHING
Kirrama Wildlife Tours runs several tours a year in northern and southwestern Australia—they range from 6 to 16 days. There are around five small-group tours run every year by Kimberley Birdwatching: some are camping-based, others involve farmstays. Follow That Bird is a Sydney-based company that runs shorter tours in southeastern Australia.

Contacts Kirrama Wildlife Tours (☎ *61/7/4065–5181* ⊕ *www.kirrama.com.au*). **Kimberley Birdwatching** (☎ *61/8/9192–1246* ⊕ *www.kimberleybirdwatching.com.au*).

Follow That Bird (☎ 61/2/9973–1865 ⊕ www.followthatbird.com.au).

CULTURE

Desert Tracks, owned by the Aboriginal Pitjantjatjara people, operates 3- and 5-day cultural tours in desert Northern Territory and South Australia. Learning is the focus of Smithsonian Journeys' small-group tours, which are led by university professors—their 26-day Great Trains, Wineries & Cultures tour covers a lot of Australia—and New Zealand, too. Local experts also lead National Geographic's Around The World trip, which takes in the Great Barrier Reef, but all that knowledge doesn't come cheap, nor does the private air transport they use.

Contacts Desert Tracks (☎ 0439500419 ⊕ www.deserttracks.com.au). **Smithsonian Journeys** (☎ 877/338–8687 ⊕ www.smithsonianjourneys.org). **National Geographic Expeditions** (☎ 888/966–8687 ⊕ www.nationalgeographicexpeditions.com).

DIVING

Dive Directory and Diversion Dive Travel run multi-day live-aboard diving tours on the Great Barrier Reef. Local flighsteeing company Daintree Air's Ultimate Dive package includes 18 dives in nine days—the Great Barrier Reef, Coral Sea, and a wreck dive are included.

Contacts Daintree Air (☎ 1800/246206 within Australia, 61/7/4034–9300 ⊕ www.daintreeair.com.au). **Dive Directory** (☎ 61/7/4046–7304 ⊕ www.dive-australia.com). **Diversion Dive Travel** (☎ 1800/607913 within Australia, 61/7/4039–0200 ⊕ www.diversionoz.com).

ECO TOURS AND SAFARIS

Oz Tours and Wayoutback are certified eco-tour operators that run camping and accommodated safaris in northern Australia. Sacred Earth Safaris and Odyssey Tours and Safaris specialize in tented 4WD tours around Australia's Top End. Outback Private Tours takes you back to nature without sacrificing creature comforts.

Contacts Odyssey Tours and Safaris (☎ 1800/891190 within Australia, 61/8/8952–6811 ⊕ www.odysaf.com.au). **Outback Private Tours** (☎ 61/04 222 555 00 ⊕ www.outbackprivatetours.com.au). **Oz Tours** (☎ 1800/079006 within Australia, 61/7/4055–9535 ⊕ www.oztours.com.au). **Sacred Earth Safaris** (☎ 61/8/8981–8420 ⊕ www.sacredearthsafaris.com.au). **Wayoutback** (☎ 1300/551510 within Australia, 61/8/8952–4324 ⊕ www.wayoutback.com).

FLIGHTSEEING

Bill Peach Journeys has ten different air-cruising packages in Australia; the longest lasts 12 days and covers over 10,000 km (6,200 mi). Daintree Air is a Queensland-based flightseeing company with several multi-day packages.

Contacts Bill Peach Journeys (☎ 61/2/9693–2233 ⊕ www.billpeachjourneys.com.au). **Daintree Air** (☎ 1800/246206 within Australia, 61/7/4034–9300 ⊕ www.daintreeair.com.au).

FOOD AND WINE

Artisans of Leisure's nine-day Food and Wine Australia tour divides time between vineyards, markets, and seriously luxurious hotels.

Contacts Artisans of Leisure (☎ 800/214–8144 ⊕ www.artisansofleisure.com).

GOLF

Koala Golf Tours organizes short golfing packages—with or without a guide—all over Australia.

Contacts Koala Golf Tours (☎ 61/2/9746–6646 ⊕ www.koalagolf.com).

HIKING

Auswalk has a huge range of hiking expeditions all over Australia. There are group departures and customized self-guided tours. You can mix hiking with other adventure activities with one of Australian Walking Holidays' guided trips.

Contacts Australian Walking Holidays (☎ 61/2/8270–8400 ⊕ www.australianwalkingholidays.com.au). **Auswalk** (☎ 61/3/5356–4971 ⊕ www.auswalk.com.au).

INDEX

A

A.C.T. (Australian Capital Territory). ⇨ *See* Canberra and the A.C.T.
Abbotsford Country House 🛏, *576–577*
Aboriginal art, *32–41*. ⇨ *See also* Museums and art galleries
Adelaide and South Australia, 556–557, 558, 605
Brisbane, 374, 376
Great Barrier Reef, 454, 458, 489
Melbourne and Victoria, 230, 304
New South Wales, 195, 206
Outback, 614–615, 623, 625, 640, 657, 660, 681, 708
Sydney, 71, 82–83, 137–138
Tasmania, 330
Aboriginal Australia Arts & Cultural Centre, *623, 625*
Aboriginal Tent Embassy, *196*
Aboriginal tours, *740*
Great Barrier Reef, 453, 480, 490
New South Wales, *145*
Outback, *637–638*
Acland Street, *227*
Adelaide and South Australia, *10, 274–275, 548–608*
Adelaide Hills, *274, 571–573*
Adelaide Zoo, *556*
Admiral's Arch, *600*
Admiralty House, *60*
Adventure trips and vacations, *10*
Brisbane, *378–379*
Great Barrier Reef, 446, 466
Melbourne and Victoria, *315*
Outback, *610–722*
Air travel and tours, *724–727, 741*
Brisbane, 371–372, 408, 431, 433
Great Barrier Reef, 442, 452, 503, 512
Melbourne and Victoria, 212
New South Wales, 144, 171
Outback, 612, 638
Sydney, 46
Tasmania, 322, 357
Airlie Beach, *491–515*
Airlie Lagoon, *493*
Albert Park, *229*

Alice Springs, *622–623, 626–632*
Alice Springs Desert Park, *626*
Alice Springs Reptile Centre, *626*
All Saints Vineyards & Cellars, *312–313*
Alpine National Park, *314–316*
Anbangbang Gallery, *660*
Andrew (Boy) Charlton Pool, *77*
Angaston, *580*
Angsana Resort & Spa 🛏, *472*
Ansonia, The 🛏, *299*
Anzac Memorial, *83*
Anzac Parade, *193, 195*
Anzac Square and the Shrine of Remembrance, *376*
Apartment and house rentals, *730*
Apollo Bay, *289–290*
Apollo Bay Eco Beach YHA 🛏, *289*
Aquascene, *652*
AQWA: Aquarium of Western Australia, *684*
Araluen Cultural Precinct, *626*
Argyle Cut, *62–63*
Argyle Place, *65*
Argyle Stairs, *63*
Aria ✕, *103*
ARQ (gay and lesbian club), *132*
Art galleries. ⇨ *See* Aboriginal art; Museums and art galleries
Art Gallery of New South Wales, *71*
Art Gallery of South Australia, *556–557*
Art Gallery of Western Australia, *681*
Arthur's Circus, *329*
Arthurs Seat State Park, *265–266*
Arts. ⇨ *See* Nightlife and the arts
Athenaeum Theatre and Library, *223*
ATMs, *737*
Aussie World, *418*
Australia Zoo, *418*
Australian Aviation Heritage Centre, *652*
Australian Butterfly Sanctuary, *458*
Australian Capital Territory. ⇨ *See* Canberra and the A.C.T.

Australian Grand Prix, *229*
Australian Museum, *82–83*
Australian National Botanic Gardens, *196–197*
Australian National Maritime Museum, *79*
Australian Outback Spectacular, *393*
Australian Pearling Exhibition, *650*
Australian Rules Football
Adelaide and South Australia, 569
Melbourne, 232
Sydney, 133
Australian War Memorial, *193, 195*
Avenue of the Elms, *221*
Avoca House 🛏, *167*
Ayers House, *558–559*
Ayers Rock Resort, *642*
Azure ✕, *514*

B

Babinda Boulders, *457*
Back Country Bliss Adventures, *476*
Ballandean Estate Wines, *389*
Ballarat, *296–299*
Ballarat Fine Arts Gallery, *297*
Ballarat Heritage Homestay 🛏, *298–299*
Ballarat Wildlife Park, *297*
Ballina, *184*
Ballooning
New South Wales, 171
Melbourne and Victoria, 257
Outback, 628
Balmoral, *94*
Bambini Trust ✕, *112*
Bambini Wine Room, *129–130*
Bangalow, *186*
Banks, *737*
Banrock Station Wine & Wetland Centre, *581*
Barossa Wine Region, *274, 574–583*
Barra on Todd ✕, *629*
Barton Highway, *198–199*
Base Walk, *640*
Basement, The (jazz club), *132*
Basin, *92*
Bay of Fires Walk, *346–347*
Bayleaf Balinese Restaurant ✕, *459*

PHOTO CREDITS

1, Southern Grampians Shire/Tourism Victoria. 2, Ronald Koppel, Fodors.com member. 5, Pictor/age fotostock. **Chapter 1: Experience Australia:** 8-9, Konrad Wothe/age fotostock. 10, Kelly Kealy. 11 (left), Scott Sherrin, Fodors.com member. 11 (right), Robert Imhoff, Fodors.com member. 14 (left), Garry Moore/Tourism Tasmania . 14 (top right), Annie Doyle, Fodors.com member. 14 (bottom right), Gary Ott, Fodors.com member. 15 (left), Carol Matz, Fodors.com member. 15 (right), tab hauser, Fodors. com member. 16 (left), jonathanvlarocca/Flickr. 16 (right), The Rainforest Habitat Port Douglas. 17 (left), Tourism Australia. 17 (right), Barry Skipsey/Tourism NT. 18, Ashley M. Greig, Fodors.com member. 19 (left), Cindy Wichser, Fodors.com member. 18 (right), ms_go, Fodors.com member. 20, Oliver Strewe/Tourism Australia. 21, Jamie MacFadyen/Tourism Australia. 22, Liz and Wade Davis, Fodors. com member. 23, Marilyn Mayers, Fodors.com member. 32 (top), Peter Eve/Tourism NT. 32 (bottom), Alma Webou/Short St. Gallery. 33 (top), Penny Tweedie/Alamy. 33 (bottom), Peter Eve/Tourism NT. 34 (top left), emmettanderson/Flickr. 34 (top right), safaris/Flickr. 34 (bottom), David B. Simmonds/Tourism Australia. 35 (top left), Thomas Schoch/wikipedia.org. 35 (top right), Jochen Schlenker/age fotostock. 35 (bottom), Paul Blackmore/Tourism Australia. 36, Sheila Smart/Alamy. 38 (top left), Lydia Balbal /Short St. Gallery. 38 (top right), Courtesy of Kara Napangardi Ross and Warlukurlangu Artists Aboriginal Corporation www.warlu.com. 38 (right center), Daniel Walbidi/Short St. Gallery. 38 (right bottom), Barry Skipsey/Tourism NT. 39 (top), Penny Tweedie/Alamy. 39 (bottom), Iconsinternational. Com/Alamy. 40 (left), Penny Tweedie/Alamy. 40 (right), Donald Moko/Short St. Gallery. 41 (top), Steve Strike/Tourism Australia/Tourism NT. 41 (bottom), Weaver Jack/Short St. Gallery. **Chapter 2: Sydney:** 43, ARCO/Schulz, I/age fotostock. 44, wizalt711, Fodors.com member. 45 (top), Mayitaazul, Fodors. com member. 45 (bottom), Kelly Kealy. 50, Robert Wallace/Tourism Australia. 51 (top), Carol Matz, Fodors.com member. 51 (bottom), archana bhartia/Shutterstock. 52, Gary Ott, Fodors.com member. 53 (top), Anson Smart. 53 (bottom), Mark Bean/Pier Restaurant. 54, varkster, Fodors.com member. 57, Carly Miller, Fodors.com member. 60, ImageState/Alamy. 66-67, Jose Fuste Raga/age fotostock. 73, Norman Price/Alamy. 76, Gary Ott, Fodors.com member. 81, Walter Bibikow/age fotostock. 85, David Coleman/Alamy. 90, R1/Alamy. 97, Jose Fuste Raga/age fotostock. 104, Tony Yeates/Tourism Australia. 105, Ming Pao Weekly/Tourism Australia. 106 (top), Oliver Strewe/Tourism Australia. 106 (bottom), Ron Hohenhaus/iStockphoto. 107 (top), Tony Yeates/Tourism Australia. 107 (bottom), CuboImages srl/Alamy. 108 (top), Murray Hilton/Sean's Panaroma. 108 (bottom), Matthew Cole/ iStockphoto. 109 (top), Basquali Skamaachi/Tourism Australia. 109 (bottom), Dallas Events Inc/Shutterstock. 110 (top), Bon Appetit/Alamy. 110 (bottom), Christopher Meder - Photography/Shutterstock. 111 (top), Graham Monro /Tourism Australia. 111 (bottom), Tom Keating/Tourism Australia. 114, Anson Smart. 122, MAISANT Ludovic/age fotostock. 129, Dattatreya/Alamy. 134, Oliver Gerhard/age fotostock. 139, Dominic Harcourt Webs/age fotostock. **Chapter 3: New South Wales:** 141, Don Fuchs/ Tourism NSW. 142, Scott Sherrin, Fodors.com member. 143 (top), Sharyn Cairns/Tourism NSW. 143 (bottom), Mucky, Fodors.com member. 146, Melanie Ball. 151 (top), Susan Wright/Tourism NSW. 151 (bottom), Chris Jones/Tourism NSW. 152 (left), Kitch Bain/Shutterstock. 152 (right), Darren Tieste/ Tourism Australia. 153, Don Fuchs/Tourism NSW. 154, Jeff Davies/Shutterstock. 156, Vivian Zinc/ Tourism Australia. 157, Chris Jones/Tourism NSW. 158 (left), LOOK Die Bildagentur der Fotografen GmbH/Alamy. 158 (top right), Keiichi Hiki/iStockphoto. 158 (bottom right), Inc/Shutterstock. 166, Oliver Strewe/Tourism. 173, Sydney Seaplanes/Tourism NSW. 178, David Wall/Alamy. 185, Grenville Turner/ Tourism NSW. 192, Sally Mayman/Tourism NSW. 197, Chris Howarth/Australia/Alamy. 200, Rob Walls/Alamy. 206, Wiskerke/Alamy. **Chapter 4: Melbourne and Victoria:** 209, Mark Chew/Tourism Victoria. 210, Rachel Levine, Fodors.com member. 211 (top), sheldon Meyers, Fodors.com member. 211 (bottom), lisargold, Fodors.com member. 214 and 215 (top), Melanie Ball. 215 (bottom), Mark Watson/Tourism Victoria. 216, Neale Cousland/Shutterstock. 223, sgusky, Fodors.com member. 226, Jose Fuste Raga/age fotostock. 231, Richard Nebesky/age fotostock. 239, David Wall/Alamy. 244, Andrew Watson/age fotostock. 249, Tim Webster/Tourism Victoria. 257, lisargold, Fodors.com member. 261, David Wall/Alamy. 264, Ern Mainka/Alamy. 270, Nick Osborne/Shutterstock. 271, kwest/ Shutterstock. 272 (top left), iStockphoto. 272 (bottom left), Oliver Strewe/Tourism. 272 (right), Chris Kapa/Tourism Australia. 273 (top), kwest/Shutterstock. 273 (2nd from top), Phillip Minnis/iStockphoto. 273 (3rd from top), kwest/Shutterstock. 273 (4th from top), Vidler Steve/age fotostock. 273 (5th from top), Alison Griffiths/Campbell's Winery, Rutherglen. 273 (6th from top), giovanni rivolta/age fotostock. 273 (7th from top and bottom), Claver Carroll/age fotostock. 274 (top), Tom Keating/Tourism Australia. 274 (bottom), kwest/Shutterstock. 275 (top), Oliver Strewe/Tourism Australia. 275 (bottom), Shoot/age fotostock. 276, Doug Pearson/age fotostock. 277 (top and bottom), Milton Wordley/ Photolibrary. 285, Mark Watson/Tourism Victoria. 291, David Wall/Alamy. 298, Darroch Donald/

Alamy. 307, Bill Bachman/Alamy. 312, CuboImages srl/Alamy. 317, Ern Mainka/Alamy. **Chapter 5: Tasmania:** 319, Mago World Image/age fotostock. 321 (top), logicaldog, Fodors.com member. 321 (bottom left), Gary Ott, Fodors.com member. 321 (bottom right), Masha1, Fodors.com member. 323, Nick Osborne/Tourism Tasmania. 324, Matthew Newton /Tourism Tasmania. 325 (top), Paul Sinclair/ Tourism Tasmania. 325 (bottom), Jochen Schlenker/age fotostock. 326, Joe Shemesh /Tourism Tasmania. 331 (top), Tourism Tasmania. 331 (bottom), Rachael Bowes/Alamy. 332 (top), Tourism Tasmania. 332 (bottom), Lyndon Giffard/Alamy. 333 (top), Tourism Tasmania. 333 (bottom), Alistair Scott/ Alamy. 334 (top), David Moore/Alamy. 334 (center), David Parker/Alamy. 334 (bottom), Nick Osborne/ Tourism Tasmania. 335 (top), Alistair Scott/Alamy. 335 (bottom), David Parker/Alamy. 338, Christian Kober/age fotostock. 345, Chris Bell/Tourism Tasmania. 348, Gary Ott, Fodors.com member. 357, Gabi Mocatta/Tourism Tasmania. **Chapter 6: Brisbane and its Beaches:** 359, Alan Jensen/Tourism Queensland. 360, Scott Sherrin, Fodors.com member. 361, Allison Kleine, Fodors.com member. 364 and 365 (top and bottom), Dreamworld. 366, Alan Jensen/Tourism Queensland. 367 (top), Ezra Patchett/Tourism Queensland. 367 (bottom), Peter Lik/Tourism Queensland. 368, Murray Waite & Assoc./ Tourism Queensland. 369 (top), Alan Jensen/Tourism Queensland. 369 (bottom), Murray Waite & Assoc/Tourism Queensland. 370, ROSS EASON/Tourism Queensland. 377, Michael Schmid/Flickr. 378, Bjanka Kadic/Alamy. 387, Andrew Holt/Alamy. 399, Dattatreya/Alamy. 404, Murray Waite & Associates/Tourism Queensland. 410, jenwhitby, Fodors.com member. 419, ROSS EASON/Tourism Queensland. 422, Ezra Patchett/Tourism Queensland. 427, Darren Jew/Tourism Queensland. 430, Gary Bell/Tourism Queensland. **Chapter 7: The Great Barrier Reef:** 439, Lincoln J. Fowler/Tourism Australia Copyright. 440 (top), carla184, Fodors.com member. 440 (bottom), sgusky, Fodors.com member. 441, David Menkes, Fodors.com member. 444, Tourism Queensland. 445 (top), Daydream Island/Tourism Queensland. 445 (bottom), Murray Waite & Associates/Tourism Queensland. 446, Media Link Pty Ltd/Tourism Queensland. 447 (top and bottom), Peter Lik/Tourism Queensland. 448, Jess Moss. 449 (top and bottom), Daintree Eco Lodge & Spa. 450, Stuart Ireland/Spirit of Freedom. 455, Mark Nissen/ Tourism Queensland. 460, Skyrail Rainforest Cableway, Cairns, Tropical North Queensland, Australia. 465, Rowanne, Fodors.com member. 469, Robert Francis/age fotostock. 474, The Rainforest Habitat Port Douglas. 481, edoardo hahn/age fotostock. 482, Voyages Hotels & Resorts. 488, poimuffin, Fodors.com member. 497, Tourism Queensland. 504, Paul Ewart/ Tourism Queensland. 513, Arco Images GmbH/Alamy. 516, Pictor/age fotostock. 517 (top), Tourism Queensland. 518, Ulla Lohmann/age fotostock. 519 (top left and bottom left), John Rumney/marineencounters.com.au. 519 (top right), Richard Ling/wikipedia.org. 519 (bottom right), JUNIORS BILDARCHIV/ age fotostock. 520 (top), Tourism Queensland. 520 (bottom), Tourism Australia. 521, Reinhard Dirscherl/age fotostock. 522 (top left), Pro Dive Cairns. 522 (top right), Murray Waite & Associates/ Tourism Queensland. 522 (bottom), Pro Dive Cairns. 523, Darren Jew/Tourism Queensland. 524 (left), Visual&Written SL/Alamy. 524 (right), Per-Andre Hoffmann/age fotostock. 525 (left), Gary Bell/age fotostock. 525 (right), JTB Photo/age fotostock. 529, Don Fuchs/age fotostock. 539, Chris McLennan/ Tourism Queensland. 542, Reinhard Dirscherl/age fotostock. **Chapter 8: Adelaide and South Australia:** 547, Wayne Lynch/age fotostock. 548, cyndyq, Fodors.com member. 549 (top left), David Menkes, Fodors.com member. 549 (bottom left), Ira Starr, Fodors.com member. 549 (right), David Menkes, Fodors.com member. 552, Chris Kapa/Tourism Australia. 557, David Moore/Alamy. 558, Paul Kingsley/Alamy. 568, V H/age fotostock. 575, Tom Keating/Tourism Australia. 584, South Australian Tourism Commission. 593, Robert Francis/age fotostock. 595, Rich_B_Florida, Fodors.com member. 598, Matt Netthiem/SATC. 601, Ira Starr, Fodors.com member. 606, Craig Ingram/SATC. **Chapter 9: Outback Adventures:** 609, Steve Strike/Tourism Australia. 610, Jane Horlings, Fodors.com member. 611, reginaca, Fodors.com member. 614, David Silva/Tourism NT. 615 (top), Anson Smart/Tourism Australia. 615 (bottom), Andrew Frolows/Tourism Australia. 616, robertpaulyoung/Flickr. 617 (top), iStockphoto. 617 (bottom), Juergen Hasenkopf/Alamy. 618, Rowanne, Fodors.com member. 627, Chris McLennan/Connections/Tourism Australia. 630, Steve Strike/Tourism Australia/Tourism NT. 635, David Wall/age fotostock. 641, Corey Leopold/wikipedia.org. 644, Gary Ott, Fodors.com member. 653, Peter Eve/Tourism NT. 656, Sylvain Grandadam/age fotostock. 661, Jennifer Fry/age fotostock. 668-69, Gunter Lenz/age fotostock. 674, Darren Tieste/Tourism Australia. 685, Michael Willis/Alamy. 690, Martin Rugner/age fotostock. 697, Ingo Jezierski/age fotostock. 704, Kos Picture Source Ltd/ Alamy. 709, Jon Arnold Images Ltd/Alamy. 717, Jochen Schlenker/age fotostock.

NOTES

NOTES

NOTES

NOTES

NOTES

ABOUT OUR WRITERS

A journalist and travel writer for 20 years, Caroline Gladstone has traveled across Australia, around the world, and on the high seas. Caroline writes for newspapers and magazines in Australia including the Sunday Telegraph, the Sun Herald, The Australian, Luxury Travel, Cruise Passenger magazine, and many more. Cruising is a her speciality and she's sailed on and dined in dozens of ships of all shapes and sizes. She's also an expert on French Polynesia and co-authored the Fodor's inaugural guide to Tahiti and French Polynesia. For this book she updated the Sydney and Melbourne-Victoria chapters.

Despite frequent jokes about whinging poms (people from England), Helena Iveson feels very at home in Australia and heads to Oz whenever she can. She currently lives in Malaysia, and from there writes for newspapers like The Australian, the Guardian, the South China Morning Post, and a number of in flight magazines. She's contributed to many a travel guide on Asia, including the latest Fodor's China.

A fourth-generation Western Australian, Graham Hodgson, has spent most of his life in the state's beautiful South West region. His 40-year career spans stints in newspaper journalism, publishing, government and corporate public communications, regional tourism planning and marketing, and regional economic development. He has travelled to and written about travel in Australia, New Zealand, Indonesia, Malaysia, Singapore, Vietnam, Zimbabwe, Thailand, France, Italy, and Turkey for numerous newspapers, magazines and online publications. He lives on a small, 5-acre holding (an escape from the 21st century), alternating his work commitments with tending to fruit trees, vegetables, pet dogs, a cat, and a colorful brigandry of wildlife.

Merran White, a former National Travel Editor for Australia's CitySearch, has worked with Time Out Guides in London, Conde Nast Traveler's www.concierge.com, Australia's Vacations & Travel, P&O Cruises publications, and Virgin Blue's inflight magazine Voyeur. She's authored two books for solo women travelers, and spends her vacations beachcombing, scuba diving, and communing with the wildlife.